For Reference

Not to be taken from this room

CRITICAL SURVEY

OF

POETRY

CRITICAL SURVEY

OF

POETRY

Second Revised Edition

Volume 1

Dannie Abse - Ernesto Cardenal

Editor, Second Revised Edition

Philip K. Jason

United States Naval Academy

Editor, First Edition, English and Foreign Language Series

Frank N. Magill

SALEM PRESS, INC.

Pasadena, California   Hackensack, New Jersey

Editor in Chief: Dawn P. Dawson
Managing Editor: Christina J. Moose
Developmental Editor: Tracy Irons-Georges
Research Supervisor: Jeffry Jensen
Acquisitions Editor: Mark Rehn
Photograph Editor: Philip Bader
Manuscript Editors: Sarah Hilbert, Leslie Ellen Jones,
Melanie Watkins, Rowena Wildin
Assistant Editor: Andrea E. Miller
Research Assistant: Jeff Stephens
Production Editor: Cynthia Beres
Layout: Eddie Murillo

Library of Congress Cataloging-in-Publication Data

Critical survey of poetry / Philip K. Jason, editor.—2nd rev. ed.

     p. cm.

Combined ed. of: Critical survey of poetry: foreign language series, originally published 1984, Critical survey of poetry: supplement, originally published 1987, and Critical survey of poetry: English language series, rev. ed. published 1992. With new material. Includes bibliographical references and index.

    ISBN 1-58765-071-1 (set : alk. paper) — ISBN 1-58765-072-X (v. 1 : alk. paper) —

    1. Poetry—History and criticism—Dictionaries. 2. Poetry—Bio-bibliography. 3. Poets—Biography—Dictionaries. I. Jason, Philip K., 1941 -   .

PN1021 .C7 2002
809.1′003—dc21

2002008536

PUBLISHER'S NOTE

Critical Survey of Poetry, Second Revised Edition follows in the Magill tradition of *Critical Surveys*: *Long Fiction, Short Fiction, Drama,* and *Poetry.* In these multivolume reference sets, the world's major writers—novelists, short-fiction writers, dramatists, and poets—were treated in depth, in essays ranging from four or five pages to more than a dozen, with full biographical, bibliographical, and analytical coverage. Supplemental volumes and revised editions of the *Critical Surveys* began to appear in the late 1980's. Then, beginning in 2000, the editors of Salem Press, in collaboration with academic genre-experts acting as editors, began to issue the heavily revised and expanded *Second Revised Editions.* To date, three of the four planned new editions have appeared: The *Critical Survey of Long Fiction, Second Revised Edition* (appearing in 2000 at 8 volumes) increased the 401 previously covered novelists to 463 and updated, revised, or expanded the previously published essays, also adding a full volume of "overview essays" on major theories, world and ethnic literatures, and research aids. The *Critical Survey of Short Fiction* (7 volumes) appeared in 2001, increasing the previous coverage of short-story writers from 347 to 480, with 133 new writers and 29 overview essays, more than half new. The third of the *Second Revised Editions* is the current *Critical Survey of Poetry* (8 volumes). With more than 20 percent new material, 20 percent revised material, more than 740 heavily revised or completely new essay-bibliographies, a new format that allows easy access to listings and text discussions, several new research tools and indexes, and, for the first time, photographs of more than 450 poets, the *Critical Survey of Poetry* is the first significant expanded and revised edition of the *Critical Survey* volumes in more than a decade. Similar expansion and updating of the *Critical Survey of Drama* is well under way, scheduled for publication in 2003.

The *Critical Survey of Poetry, Second Revised Edition* combines all previously published essays in the *Critical Survey of Poetry* from the *Foreign Lan-*guage Series (1984), the *Supplement* (1987), and the *English Language Series, Revised Edition* (1992) into one eight-volume edition containing all 580 previously covered poets as well as 117 poets never before covered in any Salem Press publication. These poets are arranged alphabetically, from Dannie Abse through Louis Zukofsky, and range in diversity: They are as ancient as Ovid or Pindar and as recent as Li-Young Lee and Martín Espada; as culturally diverse as Yehuda Amichai and Aimé Césaire; as geographically divided as Australia's Les Murray and Mexico's Octavio Paz. Of the 698 poets covered (in 697 essays—Guillaume de Lorris and Jean de Meung, thirteenth century authors of *The Romance of the Rose,* being paired in one essay), 301 are identified with the United States (the Colonials Anne Bradstreet, Edward Taylor, and Phillis Wheatley are included in this group) and 195 with other English-speaking nations: Australia (2), Canada (7), England (151), Ireland (20), Scotland (11), and Wales (4). Of the remaining poets, 6 are from Africa; 5 are from the Caribbean or West Indies; 7 are from China; 39 are from France; 22 are from German-speaking European nations; 8 are from ancient Greece; 7 are from modern Greece; 4 are from Japan; 7 are from Mexico and Central America; 11 are from the Middle East, Asia Minor, or Persia/Iran; 7 are from Poland; 2 are from Portugal; 11 are from Rome; 15 are from Russia; 4 are from South America; 7 are from South or Southeast Asia; 20 are from Spain; 4 are from Sweden; 4 are from the nations of the former Yugoslavia; and several are multinational. Those poets from the United States represent the full range of the nation's major cultures and ethnic groups, with 30 African Americans, 10 Native Americans, 7 Asian Americans, and 7 Latino poets. More than a dozen gay poets are represented, and 108 women are represented. It was the editors' goal to present the poets most often addressed in North American secondary and university curricula, as well as to present new voices that have received recognition since the previous editions of more than a decade ago: More than 30 poets born in or after 1950 are included in these pages. Finally, the increasingly global and multinational/multiethnic nature of our world has dictated the combination of the previous English Language and Foreign Language editions of the *Critical Survey of Poetry* into this *Second Revised Edition*, in which readers will find listed many more English-language titles-in-publication which have appeared since the 1984 Foreign Language edition for those poets who did not originally write in English.

The "poet essays" found in volumes 1-7 vary in length, with none shorter than 2,000 words and most significantly longer. Each essay provides ready-reference top matter, including full birth and (where applicable) death data; full listings of literary works by genre, including first dates of publication in both languages where English translation was preceded by foreign-language publication; and bibliographical sources for further study. As an aid to students, those foreign-language titles that have not yet appeared in translation are followed by a "literal translation" in roman and lowercase letters when these titles are mentioned in the text. If a title has appeared in English publication, the full English-language title is italicized and followed by its date of publication.

The format of the articles is standardized to allow predictable and easy access to the types of information of interest to a variety of users. Each poet essay is broken into the following sections:

Principal poetry: Lists the author's major collections of poetry through the first half of 2001, including titles and dates of original appearance.

Other literary forms: Describes the author's work in other genres, helping the student to identify those authors known primarily as poets, as opposed to those whose work in other genres garnered equal or greater fame.

Achievements: Lists honors, awards, and other tangible recognitions, as well as a summation of the writer's influence and contributions to poetry and literature, where appropriate.

Biography: A condensed biographical sketch with vital information from birth through (if applicable) death or the author's current activities.

Analysis: An overview of the poet's themes, tech-

niques, style, and development, leading into subsections on major poetry collections, poems, or aspects of the person's work as a poet.

Other major works: Principal works in other genres, by genre and, within each genre-subsection, chronologically listed by year of publication.

Bibliography: Secondary print sources for further study, annotated to assist students and librarians in evaluating focus and usefulness.

Contributor byline(s): The original contributor of the article; if the article appeared previously and has been updated, the names of updaters follow. Fully 117 new articles, acquired for the *Second Revised Edition*, carry only the original author's name (no updating was required); another 117 (coincidentally) were heavily updated because the poets were still living at the time of the previous edition, or other circumstances dictated the need to update the text.

The final volume (8) is devoted to a block of 58 "overview essays" and research aids, divided into three sections: "Criticism and Theory" (7 essays), "Poetry Around the World" (45 essays), and "Research Tools" (6 teaching aids and reference appendices). Of these overview essays and reference aids, 8 are completely new, and 23 have been updated. To each of the overview essays—most of which previously lacked bibliographies for further study—the editors or updaters have added a substantial Bibliography section listing critical and interpretive books and articles, as well as anthologies where appropriate and useful.

The "Research Tools" in the final section of volume 8 offer several features that students and librarians will find particularly useful as study aids: The new "Awards for Poetry and Poets" lists major awards alphabetically and includes not only poetry-specific awards but also general awards where applicable to poetry or poets; the awards listed go all the way back to the inception of the award and run through the year 2001. The section "Explicating Poetry" identifies the basics of versification, from meter to rhyme, in an attempt to demonstrate how sound, rhythm, and image fuse to support meaning. "Language and Linguistics" (not to be confused with the essay "Linguistic Criticism," also included in volume

8) is a look at the origins of language and at linguistics as a discipline. "Poetical Terms" is a lexicon of more than 150 literary terms pertinent to the study of poetry. The new "Chronological List of Poets" lists all 698 poets covered in the set by year of birth, in chronological sections. A new general "Bibliography" joins those appended to the individual articles to identify major general reference works and then works on various categories of poetry.

Indexes to the set are entirely new: A Geographical Index lists all the essays by nation. The Categorized Index lists all essays by topic; included here are identities and ethnicities such as African American Culture and Women Poets; schools and movements, from Acmeist Poets through the Romantics and Surrealists to the Vienna School; periods and eras, such as the Renaissance, the Enlightenment, and the Victorian Age; and genres or styles, from Avant-garde to Symbolist. A Subject Index closes the set, listing poets, poems, collections, and copious cross-references (including alternative names for poets and foreign-language titles for works whose main entry is the more familiar title in English translation). The Subject Index will assist readers in locating topics that are not necessarily the focus of a particular essay. To enable users of these volumes to determine whether the *Critical Survey* does include an entire essay on a particular poet or topic, each volume includes in its front matter a full "Alphabetical List of Contents."

Such an undertaking would not have been possible without the editorial counsel of Philip K. Jason of the United States Naval Academy, along with the many area experts who contributed new articles and updated old ones. Their names and affiliations, along with those of the original contributors, are identified in the "Contributors" list that follows. To all, the editors extend their sincere appreciation.

CONTRIBUTORS

Philip K. Jason
Editor, Second Revised Edition

Claude Abraham
University of California, Davis

Paul Acker
Brown University

Robert Acker
University of Montana

Sidney Alexander
Virginia Commonwealth University

James Lovic Allen
University of Hawaii at Hilo

John Alspaugh
Independent Scholar

Phillip B. Anderson
University of Central Arkansas

Andrew J. Angyal
Elon University

Stanley Archer
Texas A & M University

Rosemary Ascherl
Independent Scholar

James R. Aubrey
United States Air Force Academy

Jane Augustine
Independent Scholar

Linda C. Badley
Middle Tennessee State University

Peter Baker
Southern Connecticut State University

Angela Ball
University of Southern Mississippi

Lowell A. Bangerter
University of Wyoming

James John Baran
*Louisiana State University—
Shreveport*

Stanisław Barańczak
Harvard University

Judith L. Barban
Winthrop University

Theodore Baroody
American Psychological Foundation

David Barratt
Independent Scholar

Jean-Pierre Barricelli
University of California, Riverside

Melissa E. Barth
Appalachian State University

Larry David Barton
Independent Scholar

Enikő Molnár Basa
Library of Congress

Fiora A. Bassanese
University of Massachusetts, Boston

Sharon Bassett
*California State University,
Los Angeles*

Robert Bateman
Concord College

Walton Beacham
Beacham Publishing Corp.

Cynthia S. Becerra
Humphreys College

Kirk H. Beetz
Independent Scholar

Kate Begnal
Utah State University

Elizabeth J. Bellamy
Winthrop College

Todd K. Bender
University of Wisconsin—Madison

Robert Bensen
Hartwick College

Richard P. Benton
Trinity College

Eleanor von Auw Berry
Independent Scholar

Dorothy M. Betz
Georgetown University

Peter Bien
*University of Massachusetts,
Dartmouth*

M. D. Birnbaum
University of California, Los Angeles

Margaret Boe Birns
New York University

Nicholas Birns
New School University

Richard Bizot
University of North Florida

Patrick Bizzaro
East Carolina University

Franz G. Blaha
University of Nebraska—Lincoln

Robert G. Blake
Elon University

Lynn Z. Bloom
University of Connecticut

Patricia J. Boehne
Eastern College

Robert E. Boenig
Texas A & M University

Allyson Booth
United States Naval Academy

András Boros-Kazai
Beloit College

Neal Bowers
Iowa State University

Kevin Boyle
Elon University

Harold Branam
Savannah State University

Gerhard Brand
*California State University,
    Los Angeles*

Marie J. K. Brenner
Bethel College

Anne Kelsch Breznau
Kellogg Community College

Jeanie R. Brink
Arizona State University

J. R. Broadus
University of North Carolina

David Bromige
Sonoma State University

Mary Hanford Bruce
Monmouth College

Joseph Bruchac
Independent Scholar

Mitzi M. Brunsdale
Mayville State College

Edward Butscher
Independent Scholar

Susan Butterworth
Salem State College

Joseph P. Byrne
Belmont University

Richard J. Calhoun
Clemson University

Glauco Cambon
University of Connecticut

Edmund J. Campion
University of Tennessee

David Cappella
Boston University

H. W. Carle
Independent Scholar

David A. Carpenter
Eastern Illinois University

John Carpenter
University of Michigan

Peter Carravetta
*Queens College, City University of
    New York*

Caroline Carvill
Rose-Hulman Institute of Technology

Michael Case
Arizona State University

Leonard R. Casper
Boston College

Francisco J. Cevallos
Independent Scholar

G. A. Cevasco
St. John's University

Carole A. Champagne
*University of Maryland—Eastern
    Shore*

Allan Chavkin
Southwest Texas State University

Chih-Ping Chen
Alma College

Luisetta Elia Chomel
University of Houston

Balance Chow
San Jose State University

Paul Christensen
Texas A & M University

C. L. Chua
California State University, Fresno

John R. Clark
University of South Florida

Kevin Clark
*California Polytechnic State
    University*

Patricia Clark
Grand Valley State University

Peter Cocozzella
*State University of New York at
    Binghamton*

Steven E. Colburn
Independent Scholar

David W. Cole
*University of Wisconsin Center—
    Baraboo*

Richard Collins
Xavier University of Louisiana

Robert Colucci
Independent Scholar

John J. Conlon
University of Massachusetts, Boston

Julian W. Connolly
University of Virginia

Peter Constantine
Independent Scholar

Victor Contoski
University of Kansas

Joseph Coulson
Southwest Texas State University

Carrie Cowherd
Howard University

John W. Crawford
Henderson State University

Galbraith M. Crump
Kenyon College

Diane D'Amico
Allegheny College

Robert Darling
Keuka College

Reed Way Dasenbrock
New Mexico State University

Delmer Davis
Andrews University

J. Madison Davis
Independent Scholar

Todd F. Davis
Goshen College

William V. Davis
Baylor University

Dennis R. Dean
University of Wisconsin—Parkside

Andonis Decavalles
Fairleigh Dickinson University

Paul J. deGrategno
Independent Scholar

Mary De Jong
Pennsylvania State University

Bill Delaney
Independent Scholar

Lloyd N. Dendinger
University of South Alabama

K. Z. Derounian
University of Arkansas—Little Rock

Joseph Dewey
University of Pittsburgh

Robert DiYanni
Pace University

Margaret A. Dodson
Independent Scholar

Lillian Doherty
University of Maryland

David C. Dougherty
Loyola College in Maryland

Lee Hunt Dowling
University of Houston

Paul A. Draghi
Indiana University

John Drury
University of Cincinnati

Doris Earnshaw
University of California, Davis

Robert Eddy
Fayetteville State University

K Edgington
Towson University

Cliff Edwards
Fort Hays State University

Richard A. Eichwald
Independent Scholar

Robert P. Ellis
Independent Scholar

Richard Kenneth Emmerson
Walla Walla College

Ann Willardson Engar
University of Utah

Bernard F. Engel
Michigan State University

David L. Erben
University of South Florida

Thomas L. Erskine
Salisbury University

Clara Estow
University of Massachusetts

Welch D. Everman
University of Maine

Christoph Eykman
Boston College

Robert Faggen
Claremont McKenna College

Rodney Farnsworth
Indiana University

Nettie Farris
University of Louisville

Massud Farzan
Boston University

Howard Faulkner
Washburn University

William L. Felker
Independent Scholar

Sandra K. Fischer
State University of New York at Albany

John Miles Foley
University of Missouri

Thomas C. Foster
University of Michigan—Flint

Margot K. Frank
Randolph-Macon Women's College

Walter B. Freed, Jr.
State University of New York at Geneseo

Kenneth Friedenreich
Independent Scholar

Lawrence S. Friedman
Indiana University

Jean C. Fulton
Landmark College

Kenneth E. Gadomski
Independent Scholar

Ann D. Garbett
Averett College

Elaine Gardiner
Independent Scholar

Daniel H. Garrison
Northwestern University

Katherine Gyékényesi Gatto
Independent Scholar

Edward V. Geist
Independent Scholar

Donna Gerstenberger
University of Washington

Jay A. Gertzman
Mansfield University

Scott Giantvalley
Independent Scholar

Kenneth Gibbs
Independent Scholar

Keiko Matsui Gibson
*Kanda University of International
    Studies*

Morgan Gibson
Independent Scholar

Richard F. Giles
Wilfrid Laurier University

Ronald K. Giles
East Tennessee State University

C. Herbert Gilliland
United States Naval Academy

Dennis Goldsberry
College of Charleston

Vincent F. A. Golphin
The Writing Company

Lois Gordon
Fairleigh Dickinson University

Sidney Gottlieb
Sacred Heart University

Robert Edward Graalman, Jr.
Oklahoma State University

William H. Green
Independent Scholar

John R. Griffin
Independent Scholar

Daniel L. Guillory
Millikin University

Jeff Gundy
Bluffton College

Stephen I. Gurney
Bemidji State University

R. S. Gwynn
Lamar University

Tasha Haas
University of Kansas

Donald P. Haase
Wayne State University

Steven L. Hale
Georgia Perimeter College

Elsie Galbreath Haley
Metropolitan State College of Denver

Shelley P. Haley
Independent Scholar

William T. Hamilton
Metropolitan State College of Denver

Katherine Hanley
St. Bernard's Institute

Todd C. Hanlin
University of Arkansas

Maryhelen Cleverly Harmon
University of South Florida

John Harty III
Independent Scholar

Nelson Hathcock
Saint Xavier University

Robert Hauptman
St. Cloud State University

Robert W. Haynes
Texas A & M University

David M. Heaton
Ohio University

William J. Heim
University of South Florida

Michael Heller
Independent Scholar

Michael Hennessy
Southwest Texas State University

Sarah Hilbert
Independent Scholar

Ann R. Hill
Independent Scholar

Jeffrey D. Hoeper
Arkansas State University

Hilary Holladay
University of Massachusetts, Lowell

Elizabeth A. Holtze
Metropolitan State College of Denver

Donald D. Hook
Trinity College

Gregory D. Horn
*Southwest Virginia Community
    College*

Wm. Dennis Horn
Independent Scholar

David Harrison Horton
Patten College

Kenneth A. Howe
Independent Scholar

Anne Howells
Occidental College

Mary Hurd
East Tennessee State University

Teresa Ishigaki
California State University, Fresno

Miglena I. Ivanova
University of Illinois at Urbana-Champaign

Maura Ives
Texas A & M University

Karen Jaehne
Independent Scholar

Gerald Janecek
University of Kentucky

Helen Jaskoski
California State University, Fullerton

Alfred W. Jensen
Independent Scholar

Jeffry Jensen
Independent Scholar

Ed Jewinski
Wilfrid Laurier University

Juan Fernández Jiménez
Pennsylvania State University

Christopher D. Johnson
Francis Marion University

Joe Johnson
Georgia Southwestern State University

Mark A. Johnson
Central Missouri State University

Sheila Golburgh Johnson
Independent Scholar

Judith L. Johnston
Independent Scholar

William Jolliff
George Fox University

Ginger Jones
Lincoln University—Missouri

Leslie Ellen Jones
Independent Scholar

Robert C. Jones
Independent Scholar

Paul Kane
Vassar College

Leela Kapai
Prince George's Community College

Irma M. Kashuba
Independent Scholar

Theodore L. Kassier
University of Texas—San Antonio

Richard Keenan
Independent scholar

James M. Kempf
United States Air Force Academy

Claire Keyes
Salem State College

Mabel Khawaja
Hampton University

Karen A. Kildahl
South Dakota State University

Sue L. Kimball
Independent Scholar

Arthur Kincaid
Independent Scholar

Frederick Kirchhoff
Independent Scholar

Elaine Laura Kleiner
Indiana State University

B. G. Knepper
Independent Scholar

Jürgen Koppensteiner
University of Northern Iowa

Philip Krummrich
University of Georgia

Katherine C. Kurk
Northern Kentucky University

Vera M. Kutzinski
Yale University

Norris J. Lacy
University of Kansas

Jeanne Larsen
Hollins College

Patricia Ondek Laurence
City College, City University of New York

John Richard Law
Independent Scholar

William T. Lawlor
University of Wisconsin—Stevens Point

Carolina D. Lawson
Independent Scholar

Linda Ledford-Miller
University of Scranton

John M. Lee
Independent Scholar

Raymond LePage
George Mason University

Robert W. Leutner
University of Iowa

Michael M. Levy
University of Wisconsin—Stout

Leon Lewis
Appalachian State University

Marie-Noëlle D. Little
Independent Scholar

James Livingston
Northern Michigan University

Archie K. Loss
Pennsylvania State University, Erie

Rick Lott
Arkansas State University

Dieter P. Lotze
Allegheny College

Michael Loudon
Eastern Illinois University

Bernadette Flynn Low
*Community College of Baltimore
County*

Perry D. Luckett
United States Air Force Academy

Steven R. Luebke
University of Wisconsin—River Falls

R. C. Lutz
University of the Pacific

John D. Lyons
*University of Massachusetts,
Dartmouth*

Sara McAulay
California State University, Hayward

Janet McCann
Texas A & M University

Joanne McCarthy
Tacoma Community College

Dennis McCormick
University of Montana

John F. McDiarmid
New College of Florida

Fred R. McFadden
Independent Scholar

Ron McFarland
University of Idaho

Richard D. McGhee
Arkansas State University

Arthur E. McGuinness
University of California, Davis

S. Thomas Mack
University of South Carolina—Aiken

Joseph McLaren
Hofstra University

Kevin McNeilly
University of British Columbia

Magdalena Mączyńska
The Catholic University of America

Mary E. Mahony
Wayne County Community College

Cherie R. Maiden
Furman University

David Maisel
Independent Scholar

Joseph Maltby
University of Hawaii at Manoa

John Marney
Oakland University

Bruce K. Martin
Drake University

Richard Peter Martin
Princeton University

Linda K. Martinez
Independent Scholar

Richard E. Matlak
College of the Holy Cross

Anne Laura Mattrella
Southeastern University

Richard A. Mazzara
Oakland University

Laurence W. Mazzeno
Alvernia College

Richard E. Meyer
Western Oregon State College

Julia M. Meyers
Duquesne University

Michael R. Meyers
Shaw University

Vasa D. Mihailovich
University of North Carolina

Edmund Miller
Long Island University

Jane Ann Miller
*University of Massachusetts,
Dartmouth*

Jim Wayne Miller
Western Kentucky University

P. Andrew Miller
Northern Kentucky University

Paula M. Miller
Biola University

Mark Minor
Westmar College

Leslie B. Mittleman
*California State University,
Long Beach*

Christian H. Moe
*Southern Illinois University—
Carbondale*

Thomas Moisan
Saint Louis University

Gene M. Moore
Virginia Commonwealth University

Michael D. Moore
Wilfrid Laurier University

Christina J. Moose
Independent Scholar

Ronald Moran
Clemson University

Bernard E. Morris
Independent Scholar

Claire Clements Morton
Independent Scholar

Gerald W. Morton
Auburn University—Montgomery

Carole Moses
Lycoming College

C. L. Mossberg
Independent Scholar

Adriano Moz
Spring Hill College

C. Lynn Munro
Independent Scholar

Russell Elliott Murphy
University of Arkansas at Little Rock

Monique F. Nagem
McNeese State University

Károly Nagy
Middlesex County College

Moses M. Nagy
University of Dallas

Joseph Natoli
Independent Scholar

William Nelles
*University of Massachusetts,
   Dartmouth*

David Nerkle
Independent Scholar

Evelyn S. Newlyn
*Virginia Polytechnic Institute and
   State University*

Cynthia Nichols
North Dakota State University

Edward A. Nickerson
University of Delaware

Emma Coburn Norris
Troy State University

Leslie Norris
Brigham Young University

Michael Paul Novak
Saint Mary College

Hermine J. van Nuis
*Indiana University—Purdue
   University, Fort Wayne*

George O'Brien
Georgetown University

James O'Brien
University of Wisconsin

Mahmoud Omidsalar
University of California, Los Angeles

Elizabeth Spalding Otten
Independent Scholar

Robert M. Otten
Marymount University

Cóilín Owens
George Mason University

Edward F. Palm
Maryville University of St. Louis

Richard J. Panofsky
Independent Scholar

Makarand Paranjape
Indian Institute of Technology

David J. Parent
Independent Scholar

Michael P. Parker
United States Naval Academy

Ward Parks
Independent Scholar

Jay Paul
Christopher Newport University

John P. Pauls
Independent Scholar

La Verne Pauls
Independent Scholar

Craig Payne
Indian Hills Community College

David Peck
*California State University,
   Long Beach*

Margaret T. Peischl
Virginia Commonwealth University

Charles A. Perrone
University of Florida

Peter Petro
University of British Columbia

Alice Hall Petry
Rhode Island School of Design

Chapel Louise Petty
Independent Scholar

Allene Phy-Olsen
Austin Peay State University

Carol Lawson Pippen
Goucher College

Janet Polansky
University of Wisconsin

Susan G. Polansky
Carnegie Mellon University

Francis Poole
University of Delaware

John Povey
University of California, Los Angeles

Verbie Lovorn Prevost
*University of Tennessee at
   Chattanooga*

Rado Pribic
Lafayette College

Norman Prinsky
Augusta State University

Charles H. Pullen
Queen's University

Honora Rankine-Galloway
University of Sourthern Denmark

Jed Rasula
University of California, Santa Cruz

Ralph Reckley, Sr.
Morgan State University

James R. Reece
University of Idaho

Rosemary M. Canfield Reisman
Charleston Southern University

Mark Rich
Independent Scholar

Sylvie L. F. Richards
Northwest Missouri State University

David Rigsbee
Virginia Tech

Helene M. Kastinger Riley
Clemson University

J. Thomas Rimer
University of Pittsburgh

Danny Robinson
Bloomsburg University

Nancy Weigel Rodman
Independent Scholar

Samuel J. Rogal
Illinois State University

Jill Rollins
Trafalgar School

Joseph Rosenblum
*University of North Carolina,
Greensboro*

Diane M. Ross
Lake Forest College

Robert L. Ross
University of Texas—Austin

Sven H. Rossel
University of Vienna

Patrizio Rossi
*University of California, Santa
Barbara*

Norman Roth
University of Wisconsin

Victor Anthony Rudowski
Clemson University

Kathy Rugoff
*University of North Carolina—
Wilmington*

Jay Ruud
Northern State University

Gregory M. Sadlek
University of Nebraska—Omaha

Ruth Salvaggio
Virginia Tech

Mark Sanders
College of the Mainland

Stephanie Sandler
Amherst College

Alexa L. Sandmann
University of Toledo

Minas Savvas
San Diego State University

John F. Schell
University of Arkansas at Little Rock

Paul Schlueter
Independent Scholar

Richard J. Schneider
Independent Scholar

Beverly Schneller
Millersville University

Joachim Scholz
Washington College

Steven P. Schultz
Loyola University of Chicago

Paul J. Schwartz
Independent Scholar

Robert W. Scott
American University

James Scruton
Bethel College

Paul Serralheiro
Dawson College

Roberto Severino
Georgetown University

Mary de Shazer
University of Oregon

Nancy E. Sherrod
Georgia Southern University

John C. Shields
Illinois State University

Anne Shifrer
Utah State University

Jack Shreve
Allegany Community College

R. Baird Shuman
*University of Illinois at Urbana-
Champaign*

Thomas J. Sienkewicz
Monmouth College

Linda Simon
Independent Scholar

Carl Singleton
Fort Hays State University

William Skaff
Independent Scholar

Katherine Snipes
Eastern Washington University

Robert Lance Snyder
Georgia Institute of Technology

Janet L. Solberg
Kalamazoo College

Sherry G. Southard
Oklahoma State University

Madison U. Sowell
Brigham Young University

Charlotte Spivack
University of Massachusetts, Amherst

Richard Spuler
Rice University

Vivien Stableford
Independent Scholar

Kenneth A. Stackhouse
Virginia Commonwealth University

Tuula Stark
Independent Scholar

Virginia Starrett
California State University, Fullerton

Christine Steele
Independent Scholar

Karen F. Stein
University of Rhode Island

Shelby Stephenson
Pembroke State University

L. Robert Stevens
North Texas State University

Eve Walsh Stoddard
St. Lawrence University

Stefan Stoenescu
Independent Scholar

James Stone
Independent Scholar

Laura M. Stone
Independent Scholar

Michael L. Storey
Independent Scholar

Gerald H. Strauss
Bloomsburg University

Ann Struthers
Coe College

Christopher J. Stuart
University of Tennessee at Chattanooga

Ernest Suarez
The Catholic University of America

Alan Sullivan
Independent Scholar

James Sullivan
California State University, Los Angeles

Roy Arthur Swanson
University of Wisconsin—Milwaukee

Judith K. Taylor
Northern Kentucky University

Betty Taylor-Thompson
Texas Southern University

Christopher J. Thaiss
George Mason University

George Thaniel
University of Toronto

John Thomson
United States Air Force Academy

Jonathan L. Thorndike
Belmont University

Shelley Thrasher
Lamar State College—Orange

John H. Timmerman
Calvin College

Rogelio A. de la Torre
Indiana University at South Bend

John Clendenin Townsend
Independent Scholar

Janet G. Tucker
University of Arkansas

Thomas A. Van
University of Louisville

Karen Van Dyck
Columbia University

Paul Varner
Oklahoma Christian University

Martha Modena Vertreace-Doody
Kennedy-King College

Edward E. Waldron
Yankton College

Sue Walker
University of South Alabama

Catharine E. Wall
University of California, Riverside

Gary F. Waller
Wilfrid Laurier University

Marie Michelle Walsh
College of Notre Dame of Maryland

Gordon Walters
DePauw University

John Chapman Ward
Kenyon College

Klaus Weissenberger
Rice University

Craig Werner
University of Wisconsin

David Allen White
United States Naval Academy

Bruce Wiebe
Independent Scholar

Barbara Wiedemann
Auburn University at Montgomery

Thomas Willard
University of Arizona

Edwin W. Williams
East Tennessee State University

Patricia A. R. Williams
Amherst College

Tyrone Williams
Xavier University

Judith Barton Williamson
Sauk Valley Community College

Nance Van Winckel
Lake Forest College

Rosemary Winslow
The Catholic University of America

Donald E. Winters, Jr.
Minneapolis Community College

Michael Witkoski
University of South Carolina

Philip Woodard
National University

Pauline Yu
University of Minnesota

Chester L. Wolford
Penn State Erie, The Behrend College

Eugene P. Wright
North Texas State University

Gary Zacharias
Palomar College

Cynthia Wong
Western Illinois University

Qingyun Wu
California State University, Los Angeles

Harry Zohn
Brandeis University

CONTENTS

COMPLETE LIST OF CONTENTS

VOLUME 1

VOLUME 2

VOLUME 3

VOLUME 4

VOLUME 5

VOLUME 6

VOLUME 7

VOLUME 8

CRITICISM AND THEORY

POETRY AROUND THE WORLD

RESEARCH TOOLS

INDEXES

CRITICAL SURVEY

OF

POETRY

A

DANNIE ABSE

Born: Cardiff, Wales; September 22, 1923

PRINCIPAL POETRY

After Every Green Thing, 1949

Walking Under Water, 1952

Tenants of the House: Poems, 1951-1956, 1957

Poems, Golders Green, 1962

A Small Desperation, 1968

Demo, 1969

Selected Poems, 1970

Funland and Other Poems, 1973

Collected Poems, 1948-1976, 1977

Way Out in the Centre, 1981 (in United States as
    One-Legged on Ice)

Ask the Bloody Horse, 1986

White Coat, Purple Coat: Collected Poems, 1948-
    1988, 1989

Remembrance of Crimes Past: Poems, 1986-1989,
    1990

On the Evening Road, 1994

Selected Poems, 1994

Welsh Retrospective, 1997

Arcadia, One Mile, 1998

Be Seated, Thou: Poems, 1989-1998, 2000

OTHER LITERARY FORMS

Dannie Abse has always been a prolific writer, not only contributing poems to many journals, including *The American Review*, *The Times Literary Supplement*, *Encounter*, and *The Jewish Chronicle Literary Supplement*, but also producing a volume of semiautobiographical prose (sometimes called a novel), *Ash on a Young Man's Sleeve* (1954), and the novels *Some Corner of an English Field* (1956) and *O. Jones, O. Jones* (1970). In 1974 he published his autobiography, *A Poet in the Family*. *A Strong Dose of Myself* (1983), another collection of autobiographical pieces and reflections on the writing of poetry and autobiography, was followed in 1986 by *Journals from the AntHeap*, a set of musings on various public and personal events, and in 2001 by *Goodbye, Twentieth Century: The Autobiography of Dannie Abse*. He has also written several plays, among them *House of Cowards* (pr. 1960), *The Dogs of Pavlov* (pr. 1969), *Pythagoras* (pr. 1976), and *Gone in January* (pr. 1978).

ACHIEVEMENTS

Dannie Abse's literary achievement is all the more remarkable considering that he is a practicing physician. He became head of the chest clinic at the Central Medical Establishment in London in 1954. His literary interests extend naturally into the field of medicine, as may be seen in *Medicine on Trial* (1967).

Abse's literary honors span several decades. He won the Charles Henry Foyle award for *House of Cowards*, the Welsh Arts Council Literature award for *Selected Poems* (in 1970) and for *Pythagoras* (1979), and the *Jewish Chronicle* Book Award for *Selected Poems* (1970). In 1973-1974 he held a Visiting Fellowship of the Humanities at Princeton University. He became a fellow of the Royal Society of Literature in 1983 and received the Cholmondeley Award in 1985 for distinction in poetry.

BIOGRAPHY

Dannie Abse was born in 1923 in South Wales, the youngest of four children. Two of his brothers were influential in his education. Wilfred (the oldest), who became a psychoanalyst, introduced him to Sigmund Freud and guided him toward medicine as a profession. His other brother, Leo, was instrumental in his becoming interested in politics. (Leo Abse has been Member of Parliament for Pontypoll—a Welsh Labour constituency—for many years and is a vocal and dynamic Labour figure.) Both of these interests have remained with Dannie Abse throughout his life and have had a pronounced effect upon his writing.

Abse had become interested in poetry during the Spanish Civil War (1936-1939) and began writing during his last year at school. In the Royal Air Force during World War II, he served in the Mass Radiography Section in London; it was during this period that he became acquainted with art historian Joan Mercer, who would become his wife. His first book of poems was accepted for publication in 1946, and in 1947, as he relates in his essay "My Medical School," he returned to Cardiff, having virtually decided that he no longer wished to be a physician. Strongly urged by his family, however, he returned to London, where he was qualified in 1950. He served in the Royal Air Force from 1951 to 1955 and thereafter continued to pursue simultaneously his medical and artistic careers, with considerable success in both.

Between 1949 and 1954, Abse and some friends edited a poetry magazine called *Poetry and Poverty*, which led to the anthology *Mavericks* (1957), edited by Abse and Howard Sergeant. This collection was intended to rival the fashionable *New Lines* anthology, which featured the work of such poets as Philip Larkin, John Wain, and Kingsley Amis. In his autobiography, Abse explains his editorial policy in producing *Mavericks*, comparing it to A. Alvarez's *The New Poetry* (1962). He concedes that *Mavericks* was not a success, attributing its failure to the fact that not enough of the poems lived up to his editorial ideal "of being written out of the heat of personal predicament and therefore imbued with a strong current of feeling."

He was married to Mercer in 1951, and she and his family became an important stimulus to his writing. In fact, it might be said that Abse is essentially a family man, for parents, brothers, wife, and children, as well as his Jewish heritage—and, since the publication of *A Small Desperation* in 1968, his medical profession as well—have all had their influence on his writing.

ANALYSIS

Poetically, Dannie Abse owes allegiance to no particular school. A humanist, his tendency is to explore complex philosophical themes through things visible and comprehensible in daily existence. At the beginning of his career, he was strongly influenced by the work of Dylan Thomas. Later, however, he moved away from the mode of adjectival and rhetorical excess that was Thomas's hallmark, to a quieter, more questioning style of writing. Drawing on his professional life for incident and metaphor, he acquired his own poetic style, easily recognized by the student of modern poetry. His voice is

Dannie Abse

gentle, never strident; the personality that emerges from the writing is endearing, not irritating. He expresses ideas which occur to all but which not everyone has the ability to voice.

In the "Introductory Note" to *Collected Poems, 1948-1976*, he outlines briefly some of the impulses that motivate his writing and makes it clear that one of his strongest motivations is his desire to share the wealth of his experiences with the reader. There is a strand of humanism in his work reinforced by his obvious belief that in communication lies humankind's hope of salvation. Over and over again, his poetry stresses all people's common humanity and the vulnerability of each person without the support and understanding of his fellows. Paradoxically, however, Abse also states that one of his ambitions is "to write poems which appear translucent but are in fact deceptions. I would have the reader enter them, be deceived he could see through them like seawater, and be puzzled when he cannot quite touch the bottom." Here, he seems to be balancing a wish to communicate with an artist's prerogative to retain some of his work for himself.

EARLY POEMS

In his early work (perhaps surprisingly, considering the fact that many of his most impressionable early years were overshadowed by World War II), neither Abse's Jewishness nor his role as a physician is particularly noticeable—although the scientific (if not always specifically medical) cast of his mind is ever-present in his analytical, questioning style. He is capable of seeing at least two sides to every question. Apparently he believes that nothing is as it seems; all is deception and ambiguity, and when he speaks of attempting to achieve a "translucence" in his writing, what he seems to mean is poetry of infinite possibility, an effect produced by infinite ambiguity.

His ability to see two sides of every question is clearly illustrated in such poems as "Duality" and "Odd." In later works, he writes less fancifully and rhetorically, having taken very much to heart the aphorisms which he quotes at the beginning of his *Collected Poems, 1948-1976:* William Carlos Williams's "No ideas but in things," and Alfred North Whitehead's "Truth adds to interest."

In his early writing, Abse is concerned with religion in an abstract rather than a personal sense, as though his emotions become engaged in the question only after he has first thought the matter through. His feelings of paranoia are much more noticeable in the early work, combined with an uncertainty of identity and expressions of anger and alarm, directed against those impersonal forces that may shape the ultimate destiny of modern man. Questions of faith come to interest him only later in his writing. For example, in "Verses at Night" and "New Babylons," he expresses his anxiety, both about the possibility of the Holocaust and the intolerable social pressures that human beings exert upon one another.

These themes appear repeatedly in Abse's work, sometimes expressed rather enigmatically. For example, in "The Uninvited," Abse reflects on the effect of the unforeseen and unexpected events in his life, those occasional moments when he may feel that one of life's overwhelming questions may be about to be answered. In this poem, the moment of revelation passes, leaving the speaker changed by disappointment and very much aware of his own isolation. There is often an almost mystical strain in Abse's early work that seems to have diminished as he has matured.

A related preoccupation is how people react to the unexpected and to change. In his autobiography, Abse relates that even moving from one street to another nearby in the same city caused him considerable distress as a child, and this awareness of and sensitivity to change has remained with him throughout his life. The related questions of change and humankind's search for identity appear in "Duality," "The Trial," "The Magician," and, in modified form, in "The Second Coming," among other poems.

WALES AND DYLAN THOMAS

Less elusive than some of his other themes, Abse's sense of nationality permeates his writing, especially in such poems as "Leaving Cardiff," "The Game," and "Return to Cardiff," as well as in his more colloquial poems relating to childhood figures and incidents. Especially in these latter poems, which are worlds away from his usual abstract, questioning style, the influence of Dylan Thomas is apparent. It must be pointed out that the influence of Thomas upon most writers of this generation, and especially on Welsh writers, was virtually unavoidable. In Abse's case, it is possible to see an awareness of Thomas's work in "Epithalamion," "The Meeting," "The Mountaineers," and, more appropriately, in "Elegy for Dylan Thomas." He then seems to shake himself free of Thomas's ghost until much later in his poetic career, when his character sketches begin to emerge.

CRISES OF IDENTITY

Abse has gradually shaped his own voice. In his autobiography, he relates the tale of his visit to America under the aegis of John Malcolm Brinnin, where he followed in Thomas's footsteps, watched hopefully but apprehensively by an audience that seemed constantly to be waiting for him to give evidence of being a wild Welsh bard. "I, at once," says Abse, "became nicer than myself, more polite, better behaved." Perhaps this ever-present reminder of a very different artistic persona serves to underline Abse's preoccupation with crises of identity: in his own case, as a Welshman, a Jew, and a physician.

Abse's allegiance seems stronger to his family and to the ties of memory than to Wales. In his poetry, there is no equivalent to Swansea and Cwmdonkin Park to nurture his imagination, however necessary they were to Thomas. The importance of his Jewish heritage and his family can be seen in the 1981 collection *Way Out in the Centre*, in which he also explores his two roles as poet and physician. In fact, until the 1960's, Abse grappled with his difficulty in acknowledging his medical life in his poems. Critic Howard Sergeant noted a turning point in Abse's poetry when, with the publication in 1968 of *A Small Desperation*, Abse began to write "as a whole man" and incorporate the "complexity of his experience" into his work.

"FUNLAND"

The essence of Dannie Abse's poetry is to be found in his longest and perhaps most impressive poem, "Funland," from the collection of the same name. The poem was read on BBC Radio 3 in 1971, and in his introductory remarks, Abse made this observation about the poem's origin: "Many years ago in conversation, the novelist, Elias Canetti, said to me, 'The man suffering from paranoia is correct. Someone *is* standing behind that door pumping invisible gas through the keyhole. For we are dying, right now, a little every minute.'" Abse believes that a kind of paranoia is natural to human beings. (Perhaps this stems from the fact that he is himself a member of three minority groups, two ethnic and one professional.)

Abse's roles as Welshman, Jew, and practicing physician are significant in this work. Speaking of "Funland," he has said that "the earth is no ordinary 'hospital' but a lunatic asylum whose inmates live out suffering lives of black comedy." In "Funland" he combines elements of the surreal with images of deception and illusion, utilizing his knowledge of psychoanalysis as well as a more elementary overview of human motivations to produce what is one of the cornerstones of his poetic achievement. Magicians, illusion, and the difficulties human begins create for themselves in society are major themes in "Funland."

In the poem's introduction, Abse refers to the contrast between the modern white "disguise" of today's medicine and the purple cloak of an old-style charismatic magician, as though recognizing the important part played by faith and illusion in the work of the modern healer, just as faith and illusion were of paramount importance in more primitive times. Here a half-expressed tendency toward mysticism is found, which provides continual tension in Abse's writing. Hand in hand with his apparent belief that humankind as a whole is involved in a collective crisis of identity, Abse also seems to believe that those foolish enough to take life at its face value deserve to be deceived by it. This is all a part of his attempt to imbue his work with "translucence."

ARCADIA, ONE MILE

Arcadia, One Mile appeared as Abse turned seventy-five, and it marks his mature development and the integration of many of his themes. One poem, "O Taste and See," is a celebration of all that is temporary; another, "The Maestro," focuses on the role of music in Abse's poetic; several are grounded in Welsh lore; others, such as "Alzheimer's," reflect Abse's experience as a physician. Even stories of the Bible are retold here. Above all, however, Abse contemplates life and its inevitable definer, death, from the vantage of a cultured, wise, and erudite person well positioned to contemplate both his own mortality and the meaning of life to a secular Jew and scientist who seeks that meaning, that immortality, in ongoing life—whether contemplating a newborn in "New Granddaughter" or contemplating the memory of his deceased wife in "An Interrupted Letter."

There is also a sense of history, dominated not surprisingly by the Holocaust, as Abse looks back at the twentieth century and gratefully, without bitterness, acknowledges both the century's brutality and his fortune in having lived a good life in a world where life justifies itself merely by its own survival.

OTHER MAJOR WORKS

LONG FICTION: *Some Corner of an English Field*, 1956; *O. Jones, O. Jones*, 1970; *There Was a Young Man from Cardiff*, 1991.

PLAYS: *Fire in Heaven*, pr. 1948 (also known as *In the Cage*, pb. 1967); *Hands Around the Wall*, pr. 1950; *House of Cowards*, pr. 1960, pb. 1967; *The Eccentric*, pr. 1961; *The Joker*, pr. 1962; *Gone*, pr. 1962, pb. 1967; *Three Questor Plays*, pb. 1967 (includes *In the Cage*, *House of Cowards*, and *Gone*); *The Dogs of Pavlov*, pr. 1969, pb. 1990; *Pythagoras*, pr. 1976, pb. 1979; *Gone in January*, pr. 1978; *The View from Row G: Three Plays*, pb. 1990 (includes *House of Cowards*, *The Dogs of Pavlov*, and *Pythagoras*).

NONFICTION: "My Medical School," 1947; *Ash on a Young Man's Sleeve*, 1954; *Medicine on Trial*, 1967; *A Poet in the Family*, 1974; *Miscellany One*, 1981; *A Strong Dose of Myself*, 1983; *Journals from the Ant Heap*, 1986; *Intermittent Journals*, 1994; *Goodbye, Twentieth Century: The Autobiography of Dannie Abse*, 2001.

EDITED TEXTS: *Mavericks*, 1957 (with Howard Sergeant); *European Verse*, 1964; *Modern Poets in Focus*, nos. 1, 3, 5, 1971-1973; *Thirteen Poets*, 1972; *My Medical School*, 1978; *Wales in Verse*, 1983; *Doctors and Patients*, 1984; *Voices in the Gallery: Poems and Pictures Chosen by Dannie and Joan Abse*, 1986; *The Music Lover's Literary Companion*, 1988 (with Joan Abse); *The Hutchinson Book of Post-War British Poets*, 1989; *Twentieth Century Anglo-Welsh Poetry*, 1997.

BIBLIOGRAPHY

Abse, Dannie. "Interview: Dannie Abse." Interview by J. P. Ward. *The New Welsh Review* 2 (Autumn, 1989): 8-12. Abse reveals his poetic goal: to illuminate allegory with human experience. He describes how his work as a medical doctor informs his poetry. An interesting article for both undergraduates and advanced students.

Cohen, Joseph, ed. *The Poetry of Dannie Abse: Critical Essays and Reminiscences*. London: Robson Books, 1983. Authors of the appreciations collected here are mostly fellow poets; they include Donald Davie, D. J. Enright, Theodore Weiss, Vernon Scannell, and Daniel Hoffman. John Ormond contributes "An ABC of Dannie Abse," cataloging numerous recurring images in the poetry. Abse's musicality, his treatment of Jewish identity, and other important themes in the poetry and plays are examined as well. Includes an interview with Abse and a selected bibliography. Not indexed.

Curtis, Tony. *Dannie Abse*. Cardiff: University of Wales Press/Welsh Arts Council, 1985. An artfully made book that reviews Abse's life and works chronologi-

cally. Curtis examines influences on the poet; his study is more thematic than technical, calling attention to Abse's views of religion, the practice of medicine, and love. Provides a bibliography.

Davies, Daniel. "Not Mourning, but Waving." Review of *Arcadia, One Mile*. *The Lancet*, October 24, 1998, 70. Surveys this late collection as a reflection of Abse's themes as a whole.

Hoffman, Daniel. "Doctor and Magus in the Work of Dannie Abse." *Literature and Medicine* 3 (1984): 21-31. In our modern culture, scientists have replaced priests in the role of wise men. Dannie Abse is like a sorcerer, or a magus, for he blends his real-life role as a man of science into his poetry, thus melding art and science.

Walters, Michael. Review of *Remembrances of Crimes Past: Poems, 1986-1989*. *The Times Literary Supplement*, November 2-8, 1990, 1184. A rather uncomplimentary review of Abse's 1990 collection. Walters faults "hackneyed writing" that at times is "too comfortably nonchalant," at other times manifests "overexertion." Yet, "two or three poems . . . recall how fine a craftsman Abse can be," says Walters.

Vivien Stableford, revised and updated by Christina J. Moose and Sarah Hilbert

---

LÉONIE ADAMS

Born: Brooklyn, New York; December 9, 1899
Died: New Milford, Connecticut; June 27, 1988

PRINCIPAL POETRY
Those Not Elect, 1925
High Falcon and Other Poems, 1929
This Measure, 1933
Poems: A Selection, 1954

OTHER LITERARY FORMS

Aside from her poetry, Léonie Adams's main contribution to literature was her participation in the translation and editing of François Villon's lyrics. She also translated some of the poems of Yvan Goll.

ACHIEVEMENTS

Although few talented poets with her longevity have left such a small body of work, Léonie Adams enjoyed quite a distinguished career as poet and teacher. After graduating magna cum laude from Barnard College and publishing her first book of poetry, she was awarded a Guggenheim Fellowship in 1928.

In 1948 she became poet laureate of the United States, and in 1949 she became a member of the National Institute of Arts and Letters. After publishing *Poems: A Selection* in 1954, she received the Shelley Memorial Award. In conjunction with Louise Bogan, Adams received the Bollingen Prize in Poetry the next year. Also in 1955, she was appointed as a Fulbright lecturer in France.

In 1959 the Academy of American Poets awarded her a fellowship, and in 1966 the National Commission on Arts gave her a sabbatical grant. In 1969 Adams received the Brandeis University Poetry Medal.

BIOGRAPHY

Léonie Fuller Adams was born on December 9, 1899, in Brooklyn, New York. Because her grandfather had business interests in Cuba, her father, Charles F. Adams, had been born there. His mother was from Venezuela. Adams's father practiced law in New York.

At eighteen, Léonie Adams enrolled at Barnard College, where she was soon writing poetry. In 1921 *The New Republic* published her poem "April Mortality," her first published work. After graduating from Barnard, she held various editorial positions while continuing to write poetry. Thanks to assistance from interested friends, she was able to submit a collection of her poems to a publisher who issued it in 1925 under the title *Those Not Elect*, a phrase taken from English writer John Bunyan. Both Allen Tate and Louis Untermeyer reviewed this volume favorably, putting Adams in a position to apply for the recently established Guggenheim Fellowship program. She received the fellowship in 1928.

As a Guggenheim Fellow, Adams traveled to Europe. In Paris she moved into an apartment which, according to one source, had been lent by Ford Madox Ford to Allen Tate and his wife, Carolyn (later Caroline) Gordon. In this small apartment, Adams slept in a closet, the Tates and their daughter taking up the rest of the living space.

In 1929 Adams's second book, *High Falcon and Other Poems*, appeared. Returning to New York the next year, she took up what was to be a long sequence of teaching appointments, this one at New York University. After two years, she moved to Sarah Lawrence College and, between 1935 and 1948, taught at Bennington College and the New Jersey College for Women. In 1947 she began teaching at Columbia University. She taught there for twenty-one years.

In 1933 Adams married William Troy, to whom she remained wed until he died twenty-eight years later. Adams published *This Measure*, a long poem, as a chapbook in the year of her marriage. Although she was to live until 1988, she would publish relatively little new work in the ensuing five and one-half decades. The main exception is *Poems: A Selection*, which was published in 1954 and which includes only twenty-four "new" poems, along with sixty-one poems from her earlier volumes.

In 1948 Adams was selected to hold the Chair of Poetry at the Library of Congress, and in 1949 she became a member of the National Institute of Arts and Letters. She held a sequence of fellowships and distinguished positions as lecturer from the 1950's to the early 1970's. She received the Brandeis University Poetry Medal in 1969.

Retiring at length to the home she and her husband (who had died in 1961) had established in Connecticut, Adams maintained a private life until 1988, when she died in a nursing home in New Milford.

ANALYSIS

Léonie Adams's poetic works are known for their almost obsessive formality. One frequent consequence of writing rhymed and formally metrical verse in English in the twentieth century was obscurity, and Adams's poems are often difficult. This difficulty, along with her lack of the flamboyance or the controversy which characterized many twentieth century poets, resulted in her being referred to in a 1997 review as "the neglected Léonie Adams." Another disadvantage suffered by the reputation of Adams's poetry has been the tendency of critics to compliment her in terms which are ultimately disparaging, as when Allen Tate pronounced, "the fusion of her qualities brings her closer to [Thomas] Carew than to any other poet." This comment, from Tate's 1926 review of *Those Not Elect*, set an unfortunate example for future commentators on Adams, some of whom also found it easier to dismiss her with problematic comparisons than to read her difficult poems with an eye to understanding them.

Despite the tendency of critics to explain Léonie Adams by alluding to influences upon her or by comparing her to other poets, her work is demonstrably original and often unique in its highly wrought brilliance. Although many of her passages are difficult, she remains one of the finest lyric poets of the twentieth century.

THOSE NOT ELECT

The first poem of this collection is "Those Not Elect," a sixteen-line poem in four quatrains of fairly strict form. It begins:

> NEVER, being damned, see Paradise.
> The heart will sweeten at its look;
> Nor hell was known, till Paradise
> Our senses shook.

This and the three succeeding stanzas follow the same pattern. The first line of each of the stanzas lacks a stated subject, unless the subject of each is, as seems likely, the title phrase, "Those Not Elect." In each stanza, the first and third lines end with the same word, while the other lines rhyme. Each stanza begins with the word "never" and ends with a line having fewer than the four stresses of the first three lines. The title is a phrase contained in John Bunyan's tract *Reprobation Asserted: Or, The Doctrine of Eternal Election and Reprobation Promiscuously Handled* (c. 1674), and the phrase refers to those who are reprobate, or damned.

This poem lists pleasures that should be denied to the damned but that evidently are not denied; thus there is a sense of comic futility in the putative assertion of a grim religious doctrine, and the poem's voice becomes an ironic one. It is also highly musical, particularly the third quatrain:

> Never fall dreaming on celestials,
> Lest, bound in a ruinous place,
> You turn to wander with celestials
> Down holy space.

These resonant and mellifluous lines belie their own warning. Surely "to wander with celestials/ Down holy space" does not sound so terrible. As often in Adams's poetry, the reader must consider the music of the language as an essential component of its meaning. While the poem at first appears to be in accord with a religious doctrine that has seemed to some cruel and unjust, the irony, the playful musicality and ellipticality, and the tone of the poem make it a gentle mockery of such uncompromising attitudes, and the "Never" that begins each stanza is quietly canceled.

Many of the works in this volume share characteristics illustrated by the first poem. Irony, ellipsis, and a strong reliance upon musicality of language are, however, accompanied in several poems by imagery and symbolism which seem calculated to work on a subconscious level. Some poems are personal statements that achieve a certain directness. For example, "Quiet" expresses the predicament of the loss of emotional intensity and sensitivity. It begins:

> SINCE I took quiet to my breast
> My heart lies in me, heavier
> Than stone sunk fast in sluggish sand . . .

Desensitized by the loss of emotion, the speaker grieves,

> How could I know I would forget
> To catch breath at a gull's curved wing,
> Strange quiet, when I made thee guest?

The last line of the poem sums up the paradox, "Thou, quiet, hast no gift of rest." Another lyrical and formal piece, this poem achieves the simplicity of song.

Although Adams wrote the poems of *Those Not Elect* in her early twenties, her voice is that of a mature and reflective poet. Deeply concerned with religious themes and concepts as well as with the elusive nature of beauty and the difficulty of art, these poems show a powerful commitment to the exercise of artistic rigor as manifested in controlled poetic form.

HIGH FALCON AND OTHER POEMS

This volume begins with "Windy Way," a poem of renunciation that is phrased in colloquial speech rhythms, using a rhyme pattern that is notably less strict than that of most of Adams's earlier poems. This poem, in fact, employs quickness of motion as a structural principle, accelerating the departure from remembered love. The narrator declares:

> And somewhere in the running wind
> I cast a thing I had away.
> It was my life, or so I said,
> And I did well, forsaking it,
> To go as quickly as the dead.

Accepting the departure of love and the arrival of an unspecified new guest within her heart, the narrator observes, "The cage is open, he may go./ For since winged love has languished there,/ I'll use no other winged thing so." The effect achieved by altering the brisk, matter-of-fact rhythm of the preceding lines in the concluding two lines is that of hesitation in the word "languishing" and a stumbling or faltering meter in the final line ("winged thing"). This effect undermines the blithe tone of preceding phrases, such as "I did well" and "I did not give a backward look." It suggests instead an intense regret which cannot be entirely concealed by assuming a businesslike manner.

In "Elegy Composed in Late March," Adams represents the beauty that attracts love as "mortal beauty," not something to be represented in inorganic form ("Never hewn in stone") but only in nature. Alluding to Greek myth, she writes:

> To what they loved and destroyed,
> Never had their fill of cherishing and would not save,
> Even the gods fixed no star;
> But more in sign
> The rainbow's meltings and the reed
> And the slight narcissus gave.

The relevant myths are those of Iris (the rainbow), Syrinx (the reed), and the story of Narcissus, and the point seems to be that these are beings who are not constellations in the sphere of the fixed stars but rather part of the realm of the human. In this poem the phrasing is meditative and not strikingly regular, but the sibilants and liquids furnish a music that, as elsewhere, dimensionalizes and unifies the work. Here also the reader can detect the somewhat suppressed erudition of this poet.

"Song from a Country Fair" represents a paradoxical situation that illustrates the infinite variety of human perspective:

> WHEN tunes jigged nimbler than the blood
> And quick and high the bows would prance
> And every fiddle string would burst
> To catch what's lost beyond the string,
> While half afraid their children stood,
> I saw the old come out to dance.
> The heart is not so light at first,
> But heavy like a bough in spring.

Adams notes the reversal of the convention that the old are more burdened than the young, and her suggestion that they are lightened by the divestiture of their prospects is a merry thought in accord with the music of the lines. These eight lines of regular iambic tetrameter avoid monotony first by requiring some phonological dexterity from the reader ("tunes jigged nimbler," "To catch what's lost") and then by shifting gears but not meter in the final line, where the slow word "heavy" follows a sequence of eighteen tripping monosyllables in the preceding lines, and the line itself expresses both the burden of potentiality and the pressure of the plant sap that loads deciduous trees with leaves in the spring of the year.

"ALAS, KIND ELEMENT"

Adams found the sonnet a congenial literary form. Her love of rhyme, parallelism, ellipsis, and complex but efficient syntax enabled her to write some of the finest sonnets of her day. An example is "Alas, Kind Element," in which she explains that she had entered a period of spiritual dormancy during which she had been immune to pain "like the wintering tree." The octave of the sonnet describes this period, closing with the line, "Thus I lived then, till this air breathed on me," and the sestet begins with a repetition and the statement of a change, "Till this kind air breathed kindness everywhere." The "kind air" brings a new awakening of sensibility, but the speaker knows that it also brings renewed vulnerability. Just as the dormant tree generates new leaves in response to the "kind air" of spring, so it yields to a cycle in which the loss of those leaves is a certainty. As the speaker concludes, "My every leaf leans forth upon the day/ Alas, kind element! which comes to go."

The "wishful leaves" mark the rebirth of hope for one who has no long-term faith in hope, yet the bittersweet sensations evoked by the "kind element" may not be avoided. Here again one senses Adams's concealed learning, for the word "kind" in Middle English often means "nature."

"THE REMINDER"

Another poem treating the subject of hope is "The Reminder," a description of a wakeful night "With will that churned alone/ And sight pinned bleak as stone/ To what the heart could bring." The contrast between the lonely individual's bleak hope and the majestic spectacle of the cold night sky changes in the third and final stanza as nature alters with the advent of morning and the bustle of daily life resumes, but still, "A lone, a steadfast eye/ Silently looks in." As in "Alas, Kind Element," hope persists, despite its poor prospects.

OTHER MAJOR WORKS

TRANSLATIONS: *Lyrics*, 1933 (with others; of François Villon); *Jean Sans Terre*, 1958 (with others; of Yvan Goll).

BIBLIOGRAPHY

Tate, Allen. "Distinguished Minor Poetry." *The Nation* 122 (March 3, 1926): 237-238. Tate, poet and critic (and later good friend of Adams), traces sources and influences in a discussion of *Those Not Elect*. Tate states that Adams's poetry draws heavily upon the work of such British Renaissance poets as John Webster and George Herbert.

Tuthill, Stacy Johnson, ed. *Laurels: Eight Woman Poets*. Catonsville, Md.: SCOP Publications, 1998. This work, which showcases the artistic achievements of the major women poets associated with the Library of Congress in the second half of the twentieth century, includes a chapter on Léonie Adams, who held the Chair of Poetry at the library in 1948-1949.

Untermeyer, Louis. "Three Younger Poets." *English Journal* 21 (December, 1932): 796-797. Opposing Yvor Winters's dismissal of Adams as excessively obscure, Untermeyer argues that what seems to be obscure in her poetry is actually originality, and he goes on to argue that her insight actually functions to provide clarity.

Wehr, Wesley. *The Eighth Lively Art: Conversations with Painters, Poets, Musicians, and the Wicked Witch of the West*. Seattle: University of Washington Press, 2000. Vignettes of Adams and others, drawn from the author's journals.

Winters, Yvor. Review of *High Falcon and Other Poems*. *The Hound and Horn* 3 (April-June, 1930): 458-461. Less than enthusiastic about the possibility of there being genuine meaning behind the obscurity of Adams's poetry, Winters grudgingly proposes a suspension of disbelief, which he stipulates "in most cases can be no more than extremely temporary." Unmoved, finally, Winters designates Adams's poems as "momentary luxuries."

Robert W. Haynes

JOSEPH ADDISON

Born: Milston, Wiltshire, England; May 1, 1672
Died: London, England; June 17, 1719

PRINCIPAL POETRY

"To Mr. Dryden," 1693
A Poem to His Majesty, 1695
Praelum Inter Pygmaeos et Grues Commisum, 1699
"A Letter from Italy," 1703
The Campaign, 1705
"To Her Royal Highness," 1716
"To Sir Godfrey Kneller on His Portrait of the King," 1716

OTHER LITERARY FORMS

Joseph Addison wrote in almost every genre frequent in British literature during the reigns of William III and Queen Anne. Besides poetry in Latin and English, Addison composed an opera, a tragedy, a comedy, a travel book, a scholarly account of ancient Roman coins, political pamphlets, and hundreds of essays contributed to *The Tatler* (1709-1711), *The Spectator* (1711-1712, 1714), and other periodicals. The variety of works he attempted is a reflection of the active literary culture of the time, an index of Addison's wide learning, and the story of a writer in search of his proper niche. The numbers show that he found it in periodical journalism.

Because of Addison's varied canon, there has yet to be a satisfactory complete edition. The first collection, edited by Thomas Tickell in 1721, omitted some embarrassing early works and many of the periodical essays. A new collected edition a century later restored some early works and offered a fuller selection of essays. Two good modern critical editions cover most of Addison's corpus: *The Miscellaneous Works* (1914) includes everything but the essays, and Donald Bond's *The Spectator* (1965) covers the most famous periodical to which Addison contributed. The other papers for which he wrote await modern editions. Addison's *Letters*, an unrevealing collection, was published in 1941.

ACHIEVEMENTS

Joseph Addison's literary reputation has risen and fallen periodically, for reasons which have had little to do with his artistic achievement. His contemporaries and the next generation praised Addison highly for expressing not only Whig political principles but also classical qualities which gave English literature a dignity it had previously lacked. Readers and writers in the Romantic Age, however, found Addison unoriginal and conventional. The Victorians restored Addison to the pedestal because he spoke well of virtue and painted the picture of the Christian gentleman. Twentieth century critics often assail his work as only a historical reflection of growing bourgeois society; many personally dislike the man for accommodating himself to the class structure of eighteenth century England.

While such judgments affect how often Addison is reprinted and how much he is read, his place in literary history rests firmly on two achievements: his role in the development of the periodical essay and his prose style. Through his collaboration with Richard Steele on *The Tatler*, *The Spectator*, and *The Guardian* (1713), Addison helped establish the periodical essay as a permanent part of literature. These periodicals made the twin activities of reading and thinking about literary topics part of an educated person's daily life. Although ostensibly essays, Addison's and Steele's works really constitute a fascinating variety of stories, sketches, sermons, and lectures. What won readers to the periodical essay was its resourcefulness and flexibility in both form and content.

Addison's second lasting achievement was his prose style, seemingly informal and natural yet rhetorical and artistic, capable of handling a wide range of topics. Addison was one of several writers (including John Dryden and Jonathan Swift) whose innovations enabled prose to rival poetry as a fit medium for literary expression. For the next two centuries, writers literally went to school with Addison; stylists as diverse as Benjamin Franklin and Thomas Hardy began by imitating Addison. Samuel Johnson defined Addison's achievement in an immortal assessment: "Whoever wishes to attain an English style, familiar but not coarse, and elegant but not ostentatious, must give his days and nights to the volumes of Addison."

BIOGRAPHY

Joseph Addison might easily have followed in his father's footsteps: attending Oxford University, becoming a minister of the Anglican Church, pursuing a series of increasingly important ecclesiastical posts, and supporting the divine right of the Stuart kings. Like many other sons, however, Addison took a different path.

Two revolutionary currents swept up Addison while he was at Oxford. The first was an enthusiasm for the "New Philosophy," the scientific method that was challenging the supremacy of classical learning. The second was the Glorious Revolution of 1688 which brought William III to the throne in place of James II and established the principle that Parliament's choice of a king weighed equally with God's anointing of his earthly representative. Addison followed the traditional classical curriculum at Oxford (so well that he achieved repute for his Latin poetry), but with the idea of supporting a new English culture and political order. Modeled on the Roman concept of an educated citizenry, this new order would be the greatest civilization England had ever known: A literate and cultivated populace would sensibly cooperate in their own governance with an eye toward developing a thriving commercial economy at home and leadership among European nations.

While at Oxford, Addison expressed his enthusiasm for this new concept of civilization in poems that brought him to the attention of leading Whig politicians. In 1699, Lord Somers and Lord Halifax secured for Addison a grant from William III allowing him to travel throughout the Continent and to prepare for government service. Addison remained abroad until late 1703, when the death of William ended his pension. He did little for a year until, at the request of two of Queen Anne's ministers, Halifax and Sidney Godolphin, he wrote "The Campaign" to celebrate the military victories of the Duke of Marlborough against the French. This successful poem won for him a position as a commissioner of appeals.

Addison now moved in a circle of Whig politicians and writers called the Kit-Kat Club. The politicians, when in power, supported the writers by patronage; the writers helped the politicians gain or keep power by writing public relations puffs and pamphlets. Addison's new position and circle of contacts paved the way for a series of increasingly important appointments within the government. His contacts with other writers introduced him to new literary endeavors, some of which were taken up to support the government and some for their own sake.

In the next decade, from 1707 to 1717, Addison worked his way to prestigious positions in both the po-

Joseph Addison (Library of Congress)

litical and the literary worlds. His governmental progress was not even, for ministers came and went rapidly under Queen Anne, and Addison's party was sometimes out of favor. Addison was elected to Parliament in 1708, served as secretary to the council that oversaw the accession of George I in 1714, and became secretary of state in 1717. His literary progress was likewise by fits and starts. His first try at the theater, an opera, *Rosamond* (1707), was a failure. His joint ventures into periodical journalism with Richard Steele (1709-1712) were spectacularly successful. His writing for *The Tatler* and *The Spectator*, along with his dramatic success *Cato* (1713), enabled Addison to create his own literary circle, "The Little Senate," which met at Button's Coffeehouse and continued the traditions of the Kit-Kat Club.

His pen was at his party's call. When George I's accession in 1714 brought a military challenge from the Stuart "Pretender," Addison's literary skills came to the Hanovers' support. In poems such as "To Sir Godfrey Kneller on His Portrait of the King" and in the periodical *The Freeholder: Or, Political Essays* (1715-1716) Addison argued that the nation was better off with a king who supported the reforms of 1688 than one who promised a return to Stuart absolutism.

Political and literary success had substantial rewards. Addison bought the pleasant estate of Bilton Hall, married the widowed Countess of Warwick, and fathered a daughter, Charlotte. In 1718, however, illness forced him to resign the post of secretary of state, and the last months of his life were marred by a public fight with his former partner Steele over the Peerage Bill. On his deathbed, legend holds, Addison summoned his dissolute stepson to witness "how a Christian can die." Addison never lacked confidence in his religious, political, or literary convictions.

ANALYSIS

Joseph Addison wished to incorporate the style and qualities of classical Greek and Roman poetry, with appropriate adjustments, into English. The adaptation met with some success: His poetry brought him literary recognition and political favor, but—unlike his prose—it has not endured. The reasons are clear: His ideas about poetry were limited, his comic talent found better expression in other genres, and popular taste turned away from classicizing when it grew sated. Addison's ideas about poetry were simple ones and commonplace in his time. He defined poetry as ornamented thought, as a truth, which the poet wished to teach, made pleasant to the mind by the images created through elegant language. He judged the most important kind of poetry to be public poetry which treated moral and heroic topics.

These criteria were derived from classical Roman poetry, which Addison praised highly in his youthful essays for its power to raise "in our minds a pleasing variety of scenes and landscapes, whilst it teaches us." Addison especially admired the concept of the poet as a teacher who expressed to his society its highest ideals and principles. He wished England to have its Vergils and Horaces who would be the familiar acquaintances of the nation's leaders and would sing the glory of their country. Finally, Addison found in the classical Roman poets an urbane and cultured tone that stressed simplicity and civility. To a nation that had undergone a political revolution in 1688 and would experience two decades of intense Whig and Tory rivalry for office, such virtues seemed appropriate for the whole society as well as for individuals.

LATIN VERSE AND PRAELUM INTER PYGMAEOS ET GRUES COMMISUM

Addison first published in Latin and first achieved note among his contemporaries for a series of Latin poems written in the 1690's and issued collectively in *Musae Anglicanarum Analecta* (1699). Two are complimentary odes to Oxford professors, two are descriptions (of an altar and a barometer), three are comic verses (on a puppet show, on a bowling match, and on an imaginary war), and one is a celebration of peace with France. They are, for the most part, elegant pieces designed to show off the author's stylistic ability to ornament mundane as well as special topics.

The best of these Latin poems is the *Praelum Inter Pygmaeos et Grues Commisum* (the war between the pygmies and the cranes), a mock-heroic poem whose humor derives from applying the conventions of epic poetry to the strife between foot-and-a-half-tall men and a flock of birds. Filled with descriptions of the combatants, landscapes, and fighting, the poem nevertheless hinges on the reader's appreciation of the incongruity between epic conventions and unheroic matter, and Ad-

dison wisely does not prolong the narration; the tale comprises one hundred and fifty-nine lines.

ENGLISH VERSE

Latin verse, however, could please only an academic audience. If Addison wished to reach a wider audience, he would have to try his hand at English verse. His success in Latin verse won for him a chance to translate passages of Vergil and Ovid for an anthology. While keeping the original stories intact, Addison did not hesitate to add running explanations to his translations or to substitute familiar allusions for unfamiliar ones. In these poems and in subsequent translations, Addison strove to make classical literature accessible to an audience whose knowledge of the originals was often perfunctory and polite.

POETRY OF PERSONAL COMPLIMENT

One classical poetic form that Addison imitated in English was the poem of personal compliment to an important person. Most of his major poems are in this mode: "To Mr. Dryden," "To the King," "A Letter from Italy," "To Her Royal Highness," and "To Sir Godfrey Kneller on His Portrait of the King." Each addresses some personage at a crucial moment in that personage's or the nation's life. Each expresses the writer's admiration for the subject with the implication that the writer speaks on behalf of the larger public. Since the occasion is noteworthy, the writer achieves dignity by finding an appropriate classical parallel.

Holding these works together as dignified statements is the poetic line. Addison's consistent verse form is the iambic (a pair of ten-syllable, rhyming lines), which he writes almost prosaically. His couplets have been called "correct" or "polite" because they are obviously arranged and proceed logically. They are not difficult to follow, either alone or in groups; single couplets seldom invert word order, and pairs or triplets tend to restate central themes or images. Addison's poetry requires little effort from reader or listener; rather, it suggests authoritative and declarative statements that are already within the reader awaiting expression.

"A LETTER FROM ITALY"

Addison's use of ornamental but subdued poetic structures reflects his belief that on important public occasions, "Poetry in higher thoughts is lost." Clear expression of important ideas outweighs virtuoso technique. In each of his compliment poems Addison mixes personal admiration, classical ornament, and public sentiment. The best of them is "A Letter from Italy," which Addison addresses, while on his European tour, to his patron Charles Montagu, who helped secure the pension that allowed him to travel. The poem was highly regarded in the eighteenth century because of its easy mixing of personal experience and political themes.

The first forty lines report the pleasure of the Latin scholar looking for the first time at the actual landscape depicted in the poems he knows so well: "I seem to tread on Classic ground." The poet realizes that the landscape, while attractive, does not possess in reality the greatness which the ancient poets attributed to it in their verse. Their words have worked upon the reader's imagination, revealing an importance or meaning in the landscape undetected by the senses.

The next section applies this insight to Charles Montagu, who himself had written a poem praising King William's victory over James II in the Battle of the Boyne. Montagu's verse brings out the significance of a clash that in numbers appears minor but in meaning is crucial. The battle reminds all Englishmen that they are the maintainers of European liberty against the French and their Stuart lackeys.

The rest of the poem contrasts the warm climate and natural fertility of Italy with the cool climate and rocky soil of England. The former appears more fortunate but suffers under the oppression of French occupation, while the latter is happily free under a brave king and wise statesmen. The most vigorous lines in the poem are those describing the political liberty that Englishmen enjoy. When Addison wrote the poem, his patron had just been removed from the ministry, and the traveler must have wondered whether his tour of the Continent would ever lead to a government position. "A Letter from Italy" offers the consolation that both poet and patron, exiles of different sorts, are suffering for a good cause.

THE CAMPAIGN

Addison tried his hand once at an epic poem, *The Campaign*, written to celebrate the Duke of Marlborough's victories over the French army in the summer of 1704. The poem was popular upon publication, gained Addison a government post, and remained in cir-

culation for most of the century, but a growing sense that it was little more than "a gazette in rhyme," to use Joseph Warton's famous phrase, gradually eliminated it from the ranks of great English poems. It is not, however, a mean performance; it demonstrates how Addison applied classical poetic conventions and values to English material. Of many poems written about Marlborough's victory, only *The Campaign* comes close to being remembered. While modern readers seldom appreciate poems that make warfare seem gallant—especially if that gallantry is expressed in polite couplets—this poem is an accurate and just celebration of one of England's most extraordinary generals, John Churchill.

Addison might have written a great poem because the situation boasted "a theme so new" that it could have revolutionized heroic poetry. Churchill was not a typical epic hero; he was a commoner whose father's loyalty to Charles II and whose own military prowess had brought him into aristocratic rank. Addison intends to praise a man who achieves princely honors more on "the firm basis of desert" than by birth.

Unfortunately, despite this new theme, Addison had difficult material with which to work. Churchill had indeed won two crucial and bloody battles over the French in that summer of 1704, but important to his success was the skillful way he had marched his troops into enemy territory and seized tactical advantages in the field. Marching and maneuvering are not the stuff of great epic poetry, yet Addison could hardly omit them, because his readers knew all the details from newspaper accounts.

Addison is therefore restricted to obvious sequences of march, fight, march, fight, march. Classical conventions help elevate this mundane structure: The marches rise in dramatic intensity by epic similes of the hunt as Marlborough's army stalks the French. The battles are similarly pictured in heroic metaphors that describe them as clashes of elemental powers in nature. Around and in between these sections, Addison recounts the context of the battles of Blenheim and Schellenberg: England's struggle against France for European leadership. As does any epic hero, Marlborough fights (as England does) with divine sanction. In the style of his complimentary poems Addison finds a classical parallel for the new kind of hero: the Roman general Flavius

Stilicho who, although not a patrician, won honor by marching from frontier to frontier to protect the empire against barbarian invasion.

The Campaign may be likened to a series of tableaux which verbally depict the crucial episodes of that summer; to make sure that no observer misses the importance of the occasion, Addison arrays all the mighty personages there, and the hero is dressed resplendently. Such dignified and static description is not to modern taste, but in his time Addison's adaptation of classical trappings to English materials was fresh and novel.

HYMNS

Ironically, Addison's most lasting poems are those least concerned with public statements. In the late summer and early fall of 1712, Addison published, as part of five *Spectator* essays, five original hymns. Each hymn appeared as an illustration of the essay's thesis. For example, the topic of *Spectator* 444 is the vulnerability of human beings to unexpected catastrophes which can only be countered by humankind's reliance upon God's supporting grace. As a model of reliance, Addison offers a rendering of the Twenty-third Psalm, in which David trusts the Lord, his shepherd.

Addison's hymns have none of the drama of the religious poetry of John Milton or John Donne, but they offer common Christian attitudes in beautifully simple language. They were frequently anthologized in hymnals after their publication. The hymn of *Spectator* 465, "The Spacious Firmament on High," expresses what might be called Addison's "classical Christianity," that rational piety which found its motive for faith in the magnificence of the world instead of in the preachings of churchmen:

> The spacious firmament on high
> With all the blue ethereal sky,
> And spangled heavens, a shining frame,
> Their great original proclaim. . . .

Such hymns have neither the insight nor the form to capture the drama of spiritual struggle, but there are many occasions on which a community prefers to celebrate its faith rather than express its doubts or review its struggles. For those occasions Addison's hymns are just right.

OTHER MAJOR WORKS

PLAYS: *Rosamond*, pr., pb. 1707 (libretto; music by Thomas Clayton); *Cato*, pr., pb. 1713; *The Drummer: Or, The Haunted House*, pr., pb. 1716.

NONFICTION: *Remarks upon Italy*, 1705; *The Tatler*, 1709-1711 (with Richard Steele); *The Whig Examiner*, 1710; *The Spectator*, 1711-1712, 1714 (with Steele); *The Guardian*, 1713 (with Steele); *The Lover*, 1714 (as Marmaduke Myrtle, Gent.; with Steele); *The Reader*, 1714; *The Freeholder: Or, Political Essays*, 1715-1716; *The Old Whig*, 1719; *Dialogues upon the Usefulness of Ancient Medals*, 1721; *The Letters of Joseph Addison*, 1941 (Walter Graham, editor); *The Spectator*, 1965 (Donald Bond, editor).

TRANSLATION: *Fourth Georgic*, 1694 (of Vergil's *Georgics*).

MISCELLANEOUS: *The Miscellaneous Works*, 1914 (A. C. Guthkelch, editor).

BIBLIOGRAPHY

Bloom, Edward R., and Lillian D. Bloom. *Joseph Addison's Sociable Animal: In the Market-Place, on the Hustings, in the Pulpit*. Providence, R.I.: Brown University Press, 1971. This study of Addison as a social critic focuses on the range of his intellectual curiosity and on his combination of the study of human nature, in various contexts, with moral judgment.

Bond, Donald Frederic. *The Spectator*. 5 vols. Oxford: Clarendon Press, 1987. This multivolume set contains writings from the original *Spectator* of Joseph Addison and Richard Steele, with an introduction and notes by Donald F. Bond. It includes writings that spanned the length of the publication, which began in March, 1711, and continued intermittently until in December, 1714.

Carritt, E. F. "Addison, Kant, and Wordsworth." *Essays and Studies* 22 (1937): 26-36. This landmark study reveals Addison's anticipation of the succeeding era of poets. Shows how Immanuel Kant, often connected with the first Romantic generation in England, was influenced by Addison and how Samuel Taylor Coleridge was the catalyst between Kant and William Wordsworth.

Damrosch, Leopold, Jr. "The Significance of Addison's Criticism." *Studies in English Literature* 19 (1979):

421-430. Shows Addison's humanistic viewpoint and concentrates on Addison's own view of the critic as aid to the reader for purposes of clarification, rather than the deviser of meaning for a text.

Ellison, Julie. *Cato's Tears and the Making of Anglo-American Emotion*. Chicago: University of Chicago Press, 1999. Taking issue with what Ellison sees as a dominantly Americanist criticism that has studied sentiment as a female, and specifically domestic, possession, Ellison instead theorizes sentiment as a widely circulating and historically contingent discourse in canonical and lesser-known Anglo-American literature of the eighteenth century. Such a critical position produces an intense discursive exploration of the changing literary trope of the sentimental man.

Gay, Peter. "The Spectator as Actor: Addison in Perspective." *Encounter* 29 (1967): 27-32. Although the article is a review of Donald F. Bond's edition of *The Spectator*, it is useful in a broader sense because Gay discusses traditional assessments of Addison. Samuel Johnson saw Addison as a moralist in the classical tradition, while twentieth century critics, led by Bonamy Dobrée, have considered him more like the Victorians.

Smithers, Peter. *The Life of Joseph Addison*. 2d ed. Oxford, England: Clarendon Press, 1968. The standard biography, this comprehensive study covers the private and public life of the visible and influential poet, essayist, and critic. A comprehensive portrait is developed of the statesman and administrator, as well as the man of letters. Smithers explains how Addison patterned his life in the English Augustan Age after the Roman ideal of citizenship.

Robert M. Otten;
bibliography updated by the editors

ENDRE ADY

Born: Érdmindszent, Hungary; November 22, 1877
Died: Budapest, Hungary; January 27, 1919

PRINCIPAL POETRY

Versek, 1899
Még egyszer, 1903
Új versek, 1906 (*New Verses*, 1969)
Vér és arany, 1908 (*Blood and Gold*, 1969)
Az Illés szekerén, 1909 (*On Elijah's Chariot*, 1969)
A minden titkok verseiből, 1910 (*Of All Mysteries*, 1969)
Szeretném, ha szeretnének, 1910 (*Longing for Love*, 1969)
A menekülő élet, 1912 (*This Fugitive Life*, 1969)
A magunk szerelme, 1913 (*Love of Ourselves*, 1969)
Ki látott engem?, 1914 (*Who Sees Me?*, 1969)
A halottak élén, 1918 (*Leading the Dead*, 1969)
Margita élni akar, 1921
Az utolsó hajók, 1923 (*The Last Ships*, 1969)
Rövid dalok egyről és másról, 1923
Poems of Endre Ady, 1969 (includes *New Verses*, *Blood and Gold*, *On Elijah's Chariot*, *Longing for Love*, *Of All Mysteries*, *This Fugitive Life*, *Love of Ourselves*, *Who Sees Me?*, *Leading the Dead*, and *The Last Ships*)

OTHER LITERARY FORMS

Endre Ady was a journalist who wrote numerous articles, reports, reviews, criticisms, essays, and short stories for the press. These were collected after his death under the titles *Az új Hellász* (1920; new Hellas), *Levelek Párizsból* (1924; letters from Paris), *Párizsi noteszkönyve* (1924; Paris notebook), and *Ha hív az aczélhegyű ördög* (1927; if the steel-tipped devil calls). In his lifetime, Ady published *Vallomások és tanúlmányok* (1911; confessions and studies), containing his important prose writings, both political and literary. Some of these writings are available in English translation in *The Explosive Country: A Selection of Articles and Studies, 1898-1916* (1977). His collections of short stories combine subjective, personal confession with a depiction of early twentieth century Hungary. They are *Sápadt emberek és történetek* (1907; pale men and stories), *Így is történhetik* (1910; it can happen thus also), *A tízmilliós Kleopátra és egyébb történetek* (1910; Cleopatra of the ten millions and other stories), *Új csapáson* (1913; on a new track), and *Muskétás tanár úr* (1913; Professor Muskétás). His letters have been published in *Ady Endre válogatott levelei* (1956; selected letters of Endre Ady), with an introduction by Béla György.

ACHIEVEMENTS

Endre Ady is one of Hungary's greatest lyric poets. Inspired by Western European models, primarily French, he created a new lyrical style that both shocked and inspired his contemporaries. At the same time, he revitalized indigenous Hungarian literary traditions, looking back to the seventeenth and eighteenth centuries rather than to the example of his immediate predecessors. His topics, too, were considered revolutionary: physical passion and erotic love, political and social reform. He remained, however, within the tradition of the great nineteenth century Hungarian poets who expressed the spirit of the nation in their works.

BIOGRAPHY

Endre Ady's heritage and birthplace had a profound influence on his poetry. His ancestry was the relatively poor nobility, or gentry, which on his mother's side also boasted a tradition of Calvinist ministers. In the small village of Érdmindszent, he came to know the peasantry intimately, for his own family's life differed little from theirs. His father wished him to enter the civil service, so he was educated with a view to obtaining a legal degree. The area in which Ady grew up (today Sălaj, Romania) is situated in the Partium, a region of eastern Hungary that had stormy ties to Transylvania during the sixteenth and seventeenth centuries, when that principality had been a bulwark of Hungarian autonomy and traditions while the rest of the country was under Turkish or Habsburg rule. The Partium was thus doubly a frontier area in whose Calvinist and *kuruc* (anti-Habsburg) traditions Ady saw justification for his own rebellious, individualistic nature. He was always proud of his ancestry and considered himself much more Magyar than many of his contemporaries with more mixed ethnic backgrounds.

After completing five elementary grades in his village, Ady was sent first to the Piarist school in Nagykároly, then to the Calvinist gymnasium at Zilah, which he regarded as his alma mater; he always fondly remembered his teachers there. Several of his classmates were

later to become prominent among the more radical thinkers and politicians of the early years of the twentieth century. He also read voraciously, both earlier Hungarian literature and European Naturalistic writers, and became acquainted with the works of Arthur Schopenhauer. After a brief period in law school in Debrecen and time spent as a legal clerk in Temesvár (Timisoara, Romania) and Zilah (Zălău), he realized that his true vocation was in journalism. He followed this career until his death.

Ady first worked in Debrecen, and in this period not only did his horizons widen, but his critical theses began to crystallize as well. "Life" and "truth" became important bywords for him, and he continued his readings: Auguste Comte, Herbert Spencer, Nietzsche, Henrik Ibsen, Fyodor Dostoevski, and especially the late eighteenth century poet Mihály Csokonai Vitéz, a native of Debrecen. It was in Nagyvárad (today Oradea, Romania) that Ady became familiar with the life of a large city and the more cosmopolitan society it represented. He wrote for liberal papers, and for a while his political views agreed with the pro-government stance of such journals. In time, however, he became disillusioned with their reluctance to press for universal suffrage and other reforms affecting the poor and the national minorities. It was at this time that he became acquainted with *Huszadik század*, a progressive journal begun in 1900.

The years in Nagyvárad were also important in Ady's personal life and poetic development, for it was during this period that he met Adél Brüll, whom he was to immortalize as the Leda of his poems. This older, married woman (her married name was Diósi)—more experienced, more worldly, more cultured than he—was an important influence on his life. Their passionate and at times tempestuous love affair, which finally ended in 1912, is recorded in poems that were to revolutionize Hungarian love poetry. When Ady went to Paris as the foreign correspondent of his paper, Adél Brüll was there, and his impressions of the French city were acquired under her tutelage. When he returned from the 1904 trip, he burst on the world with a new poetic style.

By 1905, Ady was working in Budapest for the liberal *Budapesti napló*. In numerous articles, he wrote of the need for radical reforms; independence from Austria was also debated. At this time, Ady turned his attention to the social problems that were destroying the country; in both his poetry and his prose writings, he championed the disenfranchised. The important journal *Nyugat* was started in 1908, and Ady soon became associated with it—all the more so as his increasingly radical views did not agree with the middle-of-the-road liberalism of the *Budapesti napló.*

When war broke out in 1914, Ady opposed Hungarian participation in the conflict, increasing his isolation from official political life. His antiwar poems were inspired by humanism and patriotism. The poor and the politically powerless suffered most heavily, Ady argued, and he believed that the war was being fought against Hungarian interests, purely for Austrian goals. During this time, Ady lived mostly in Érdmindszent and at Csucsa, the estate of Berta Boncza, whom he had met in 1914 and married the following year. Berta, the daughter of a well-to-do nobleman and prominent politician, was considerably younger than Ady; she had been attracted to him some time earlier, when she read his *Blood and Gold* while still in school in Switzerland. The poems written to her reflect a different mood from that of the Leda poems: The love is deeper and less intensely erotic. They project the hope that Csinszka (as Berta is called in the poems addressed to her) will preserve the thoughts and ideals of the poet. By this time, Ady was gravely ill with the syphilis that had been progressively destroying him since his Nagyvárad days.

The revolution that Ady had awaited came to Hungary in October of 1918. Ady went to Budapest, where the revolutionary government celebrated him, even though he had reservations about the Socialist system. He also doubted whether the Karolyi government's courting of the Entente powers would bring any positive results. As it turned out, his instincts were right, and the Entente did little for Hungary. Ady died in January of 1919, spared the knowledge that Hungary's territory would be drastically reduced and that his own birthplace and home region would be awarded to Romania.

ANALYSIS

Endre Ady came from the deep center of the nation, and he sought to raise the nation to a new consciousness, just as János Arany and others had done before him. Ady was an innovator because the literary and political establishment had failed to grasp the need for change. Ady's "Hungarianness" is a central part of his work; he was intensely aware of his struggle "with Europe for Europe."

Ady never abandoned his native traditions. He built instead on folklore, the *kuruc* poetry of the eighteenth century, the folk-song-inspired lyrics of Mihály Csokonai Vitéz, and the revolutionary verse of the great national poet of nineteenth century Hungary, Sándor Petőfi. Ady also drew heavily on Hungarian Calvinism and the rich vernacular tradition of Protestant writings to create a highly personal modern style, animated by the tension between Hungarian and Western European influences. His great love poems to Leda and Csinszka, his poems on materialism and on national traditions—all incorporated European philosophies, preoccupations, and styles, reflecting the influence of Friedrich Nietzsche and Henri Bergson as well as of Charles Baudelaire and Paul Verlaine. Today, Ady is recognized as one of the most important of the generation of writers and thinkers who transformed the intellectual life of Hungary in the first decades of the twentieth century.

NEW VERSES

Endre Ady's first two volumes of verse, *Versek* (poems) and *Még egyszer* (once more), did not attract great interest; they were relatively insignificant collections in the traditional vein. In 1906, however, Ady's own style emerged in *New Verses*. Here, he presented new subjects and new themes, new images and a fresh, new style. The emphasis in *New Verses*—an emphasis continued in Ady's next three collections—was on brevity and impact: short, concise lines; short poems packed with meaning; condensed language with multiple levels of reference. Many of the early poems develop a single metaphor. A very conscious innovator, Ady prefaced *New Verses* with a manifesto that identifies the tension that persists throughout his oeuvre: Hungary is a nation caught at the crossroads between East and West. While proudly claiming his descent from the conquering Hungarians of the ninth century, who came through the Eastern gate, he asks if *he* can break in from the *West* with "new songs of new times." Answering in a defiant affirmative, he states that, in spite of opposition by conservatives, these poems are "still victorious, still new and Hungarian."

TRANSFORMATIONS

After the burst of energy that characterized his style in the period from 1906 to 1909, Ady paused in mid-career to adopt a quieter style and grayer moods. His themes and concerns remained much the same, but there was a deepening of thought, and a more pessimistic note entered his poems. His concern for the fate of the country, particularly its ordinary citizens, grew as he saw policies that could only bring ruin being blindly followed by the political elite. His relationship with Adél Brüll also cooled.

After 1914, during the war years, Ady's style underwent another transformation. His sentences became more complex as his verse became increasingly reflective, and he turned from softer, French-inspired tones to the somber and sublime style of the Bible and of sixteenth century Calvinist poetry. In this late poetry, Ady retained two themes from his earlier collection: patriotism, which broadened into humanitarianism, and love—no longer the unfulfilled and unsatisfying erotic encounters of earlier years but the deeper, more fulfilling passion of the Csinszka poems.

LEDA POEMS

Ady's poems can be organized thematically into four large groups, though there is considerable overlapping; also, some important minor themes are eventually subsumed into one or another of the major ones reflecting Ady's intellectual development. One of Ady's most enduring themes was romantic love. The Leda cycles, with their portrayal of destructive yet irresistible passion, reveal the influence of Baudelaire. These poems represented a break with Hungarian tradition in their emphasis on the physical aspects of love. Ady's poems to his wife, on the other hand, are more in the tradition of Petőfi, in which the emotional-spiritual content is on a par with the physical. It would be misleading, however, to dismiss the Leda poems as purely physical: Adél Brüll offered Ady much more than physical excitement, and these poems reflect a world of shared ideas. They are more significant and generally more successful than the poems on fleeting alliances with insignificant partners.

"Félig csókolt csók" ("Half-Kissed Kiss"), from *New Verses*, and "Léda a kertben" ("Leda in the Garden"), from *Blood and Gold*, emphasize the intense desire that cannot be satisfied even in physical union. The "half-kissed kiss" is a metaphor for an erotic relationship that leaves the lovers still restless for fulfillment: "tomorrow, then perhaps tomorrow." Nature sympathizes with them in their eternal hunger, as an image from "Leda in the Garden" suggests: "even the poppy/ pities us, [itself] satisfied." Consummation, Ady suggests in "Héja nász az avaron" ("Kite-Wedding on the Loamy Earth"), can come only in death. In "A mi násznagyunk" ("Our Best Man"), Ady returns to this theme. There are also love poems of great tenderness in the Leda cycles, as "Add nekem a szemeidet" ("Give Me Your Eyes") illustrates. The beloved's eyes "always see him grand . . . always build, have mercy . . . see him in a better light," yet "they kill, burn, and desire." The poem, comprising four stanzas of three lines each, repeats the title line as the first line of each stanza and follows it with two rhymed lines. This *abb* tercet in anapestic meter echoes the lyrical mood and the melody of the words as well as the expansive ideas.

OF ALL MYSTERIES

The 1910 volume *Of All Mysteries*, chronicles the waning of Ady's love for Adél Brüll. This collection offers a virtual outline of Ady's characteristic themes, as is indeed suggested in the poem's motto: "youthful All vanquished, with the spear of Secrecy, Death in my heart: but my heart lives, and God lives." Here, Ady seems determined to hope in spite of disappointments. The decadent pose of earlier poems is shed as the poet develops a real faith in man that culminates in the humanism of the war poems. Each of the six cycles in *Of All Mysteries* is devoted to a "secret": of God, of love, of sorrow, of glory, of life, and of death. In the "Love" cycle, dedicated to Leda, the poem "A türelem bilincse" ("The Fetters of Patience") significantly refers to the "fetters" of their love in the past tense. Their whole life was fetters, yet the "kisses, exhaustions, flames, oaths" were all good fetters. The farewell becomes explicit in "Elbocsátó, szép üzenet" ("Dismissing, Beautiful Message"), where pity wins over the regretful remembrance of love.

LOVE POEMS

The poems of 1912 to 1914 show a man in search of love. In the final volumes, this love is found. "A Kalota partján" ("On the Banks of the Kalota") records the "security, summer, beauty and peace" brought to his life by Berta Boncza. The poem's two long free-verse stanzas depict a summer Sunday in which the peace and joy of the service and of the feast (Pentecost) mingle to overwhelm the poet, and the eyes of his beloved draw him into a magic circle.

DEATH

Ady saw life and death not as opposing forces but as two components of the same force. "Párizsban járt az ősz" ("Autumn Passed Through Paris") is a beautiful evocation, through the breath of autumn on a summer day, of the presence of death. Although death comes for all men, it need not be accepted passively, as Ady suggests in the melodic "A halál lovai" ("Death's Horsemen"). The riderless horse with the unclaimed saddle is always in the troop of death's horses, but "He before whom they stop/ Turns pale and sits into the saddle." The act is presented as voluntary. In "Hulla a búza-földön" ("Corpse on the Wheat-Field"), a corpse, forgotten on the snowy plain, will not have carnations, artemisia, and basil blooming on its grave, but "the victorious wheat-kernel" will win through; life will triumph.

RELIGIOUS POEMS

To some extent, Ady's God-fearing poems continue the life-death theme. They chronicle the same doubts and seek answers to the same questions. In time, Ady found the answers and the refuge, but as with John Donne, the struggle was a fierce one; indeed, Ady's love poems, much as in Donne's case, have a close and direct relationship to his religious verse. While many of Ady's religious poems describe his struggle to achieve union with God, others reflect the peace of childlike faith. Ady seeks rest and forgiveness and creates powerful symbols to concretize these feelings.

In "A Sion-hegy alatt" ("Under Mount Sion"), he creates an image of God as a man in a huge bell coat inscribed with red letters, ringing for the dawn Mass. The figure is kindly yet sad; he cannot answer the poet's plea for simple, unquestioning faith. The poem is a poignant expression of the dilemma of modern man. In "Hiszek hitetlenül Istenben" ("I Believe, Unbelieving, in God"), Ady longs for belief in the great mystery of God, convinced that such faith will bring peace to his tormented soul.

The poems from the cycle "Esaias könyvének margójára" ("To the Margins of the Book of Isaiah"), often prefaced by biblical quotations that emphasize their prophetic intentions, transcend the personal religious quest and become pleas for the nation and for humanity. "Volt egy Jézus" ("There Was a Jesus") not only testifies to a personal acceptance of Jesus Christ but also proclaims the need for all humankind to heed his teachings on peace and brotherhood. "A szétszóródás elött" ("Before the Diaspora"), another poem with a biblical inspiration, scourges the nation for its sins, concluding with the powerful line: "And we were lost, for we lost ourselves."

PATRIOTIC POEMS

Many of Ady's poems can be classified as patriotic. This group, however, unites several different themes that were significant at different points in his career. Two important early threads are the "I" poems and the "money" poems. The I poems are more than personal lyrics; they present the speaker (the poet) as a representative of the nation. As such, they evolve into the patriotic poems in a fairly direct line. The money poems startled readers with their "nonpoetic" theme: Ady went beyond complaints against poverty to question the role of money in society at large.

THE KURUC THEME

An important thread in Ady's patriotic-revolutionary poetry is the use of the *kuruc* theme. *Kuruc* was the name applied to the supporters of Ferenc Rákóczi II, who had led a popular uprising against the Habsburgs in the eighteenth century. In Ady's vocabulary, the *kuruc* is the true but disenfranchised Hungarian, a fighter for national goals betrayed by his self-serving masters to Austrian interests. In the war years, Ady identified the *kuruc* with the common man everywhere, oppressed by political power plays.

"MAN IN INHUMANITY"

Ady's last poem, "Ember az embertelenségben" ("Man in Inhumanity"), was an appeal to humanity addressed to the victors of the war. He appealed, fruitlessly, to the Allies "not to tread too harshly" on Hungarian hearts. The nation sought reform, but suffered instead "War, the Horror." Defeated in a war fought against Hungarian sentiments and interests, Hungary paid for its all-too-recent union with Austria with the loss of much of its territory and millions of its citizens. Foreseeing this tragedy even before the war, Ady offered a poignant comment on its aftermath.

While Ady was a very subjective poet, one of the first purely personal lyric voices in Hungarian poetry, he did not break with the national tradition of committed literature. Deeply influenced by Western European models, he transformed what he took by the force of his genius, exploiting the rich resources of the Hungarian tradition in the service of a powerfully modern vision. Thus, it is not surprising that Ady continues to inspire poets in Hungary today.

OTHER MAJOR WORKS

SHORT FICTION: *Sápadt emberek és történetek,* 1907; *A tízmilliós Kleopátra és egyébb történetek,* 1910; *Így is történhetik,* 1910; *Muskétás tanár úr,* 1913; *Új csapáson,* 1913.

NONFICTION: *Vallomások és tanúlmányok,* 1911; *Az új Hellász,* 1920; *Levelek Párizsból,* 1924; *Párizsi noteszkönyve,* 1924; *Ha hív az aczélhegyű ördög,* 1927; *Ady Endre válogatott levelei,* 1956; *The Explosive Country: A Selection of Articles and Studies, 1898-1916,* 1977.

BIBLIOGRAPHY

Bóka, Lazlo. "Endre Ady the Poet." *The New Hungarian Quarterly* 3, no. 5 (January-March, 1962): 83-108. A biographical and critical study of Ady's life and work.

Cushing, G. F. Introduction to *The Explosive Country: A Selection of Articles and Studies, 1898-1916,* by Endre Ady. Budapest, Hungary: Corvina Press, 1977. Cushing offers some biographical insight into Ady's life.

Frigyesi, Judit. *Béla Bartók and Turn-of-the-Century Budapest.* Berkeley: University of California Press, 1998. A broad perspective on Bartók's art grounded in the social and cultural life of turn-of-the-century Hungary. Includes a discussion of Endre Ady and his influence on Bartók.

Hanák, Péter. *The Start of Endre Ady's Literary Career (1903-1905).* Budapest: Akadémiai Kiadó, 1980. A brief study of Ady's early work, with bibliography.

Nyerges, Anton N. Introduction to *Poems of Endre Ady.* Buffalo, N.Y.: Hungarian Cultural Foundation, 1969. Nyerges gives some biographic details of Ady's life.

Reményi, Joseph. *Hungarian Writers and Literature.* New Brunswick, N.J.: Rutgers University Press, 1964. A history and critical analysis of Hungarian literature including the works of Ady.

Enikő Molnár Basa;
bibliography updated by the editors

—

Æ

George William Russell

Born: Lurgan, County Armagh, Ireland; April 10, 1867

Died: Bournemouth, England; July 17, 1935

PRINCIPAL POETRY

Homeward: Songs by the Way, 1894
The Earth Breath and Other Poems, 1897
The Divine Vision and Other Poems, 1903
The Nuts of Knowledge: Lyrical Poems Old and New, 1903
By Still Waters: Lyrical Poems Old and New, 1906
Collected Poems, 1913, 1919, 1926, 1935
Gods of War with Other Poems, 1915
Voices of the Stones, 1925
Midsummer Eve, 1928
Dark Weeping, 1929
Enchantment and Other Poems, 1930
Vale and Other Poems, 1931
The House of the Titans and Other Poems, 1934
Selected Poems, 1935

OTHER LITERARY FORMS

In addition to his enormous amount of poetry, Æ wrote pungent essays in almost every imaginable field, from literary criticism to politics, economics, and agriculture. These essays are collected in such volumes as *Some Irish Essays* (1906) and *The Living Torch* (1937). His interest in that department of letters would eventually lead him to become editor of *The Irish Homestead,* and later *The Irish Statesman.* He also tried his hand at fiction with *The Mask of Apollo and Other Stories* (1904), ranging from the Orientalism of "The Cave of Lillith" and "The Meditation of Ananda" to the Celticism of "A Dream of Angus Oge," in which Æ characteristically blends East and West.

He also attempted drama with *Deirdre* (1902), the first important play to be performed by the company that was later to become the Irish National Theatre. Æ compiled his own spiritual autobiography, *The Candle of Vision* (1918), and in both it and *Song and Its Fountains* (1932) he attempted to explain his mysticism and poetic theory, which for him were one and the same. In *The National Being* (1916) Æ combines history with prophecy. *The Interpreters* (1922) consists of a dialogue between several characters typifying various positions in the Irish revolutionary movement—the heretic, the poet, the socialist, the historian, the aesthete, and the industrialist. In *The Avatars* (1933) Æ created a "futurist fantasy" in which mythical heroes, avatars, appear and spread joy wherever they go. They are removed by the authorities but their cult grows through legends and artistic records.

In addition to his literary and journalistic work, Æ managed to keep up an extensive correspondence, a part of which has been published in *Some Passages from the Letters of Æ to W. B. Yeats* (1936), *Æ's Letters to Mínán-labáin* (1937), and *Letters from Æ* (1961).

ACHIEVEMENTS

Æ's greatest contribution to Irish literature came from neither his artistic endeavors nor his journalistic and political involvement but rather from his unceasing kindness to younger writers. Frank O'Connor has said that Æ was the father of three generations of Irish poets. Among his discoveries were James Joyce, Padraic Colum, James Stephens, Frank O'Connor, Austin Clarke, and Patrick Kavanagh. As a poet, Æ is less known today for his own work, most of which is now out of print, than for his enormous influence on the younger generation, including William Butler Yeats. Although earlier critics grouped Æ with Yeats and John Millington Synge as one of the three major figures in the Irish literary revival, later criticism, such as Richard Finneran's *Anglo-Irish Literature* (1976), generally considers Æ among the lesser revival figures such as Lady Gregory, Oliver St. John Gogarty, and James Stephens.

The Irish poet Æ, also known as George William Russell.
(©Bettmann/Corbis)

It is difficult to select one artistic achievement for which Æ is remembered today, so much of his work being indirect, involving support of other artists, ideas, revivals, friendship, political expression, agriculture, economics, nationalism, mysticism, the Abbey Theatre, and art in general. Yeats's wife may have best summarized Æ's achievements when she told her husband that he was a better poet but that Æ was a saint.

BIOGRAPHY

The events of Æ's early years are somewhat obscure. He was born George William Russell into the Northern Irish Protestant family of Thomas Elias Russell and Mary Anne (Armstrong) Russell. When he was eleven his family moved to Dublin, and Æ was educated at the Rathmines School. From 1880 to 1900 he attended the Dublin School of Art for a few months each year, where he met Yeats, a fellow student. Their long friendship was a troubled one, since Yeats felt that Æ never fulfilled his artistic potential.

Æ's first employment may have been as a clerk in a Guinness brewery, a job he soon quit. Painting was Æ's natural activity but this was sacrificed because his family could not afford such luxuries, and he turned to literature. From 1890 to 1897 he worked in a warehouse twelve hours a day; in the evenings he served as librarian of the Dublin Lodge of the Theosophical Society, where he lived. In the midst of all this, he still found time to publish his first two volumes of poetry, *Homeward: Songs by the Way* and *The Earth Breath and Other Poems*.

The most important event in Æ's life occurred in 1887 when he discovered Theosophy. He had been a mystic from childhood, and, becoming an ardent adherent, he utilized the principles of Theosophy. It was only after the death of Madame Blavatsky, the founder of the Theosophical Society, that he severed his official connection with Theosophy.

The mystic Æ later evolved into a philosopher and a political sage respected on both sides of the Atlantic. For his entire adult life he was active in the cooperative agricultural movement of Sir Horace Plunkett's Irish Agricultural Organization Society and in the Home Rule movement.

Having achieved a certain security through his position as organizer in the Irish villages for Horace Plunkett, the agrarian reformer, Æ married Violet North. They had two sons, one of whom became an American citizen. Æ was never a domestic man since his variety of interests kept him busy and often away from home. When his health showed signs of deteriorating, Plunkett made him editor of the cooperative journal *The Irish Homestead*. In 1923 it merged with *The Irish Statesman*, with Æ again as editor; in 1930, however, the paper failed because of enormous legal expenses. Æ remained in Ireland until late in his life, when he toured the United States, and after the death of his wife, he spent most of his time abroad.

Æ was nearly six feet tall and became corpulent in old age. He had a russet beard, "mousecolored" hair, and blue-gray eyes covered by spectacles; he wore shabby clothes and was a perpetual pipe smoker. Æ looked like what he was—a thinker somewhere between a farmer and a mystical poet. In accord with Irish tradition, he was a great talker and an inspired speaker. His voice was mellow, with a strong north Irish accent. He painted all

his life but never exhibited or sold his paintings, preferring instead to give them to his friends. Æ was intensely involved in the arts, but he always felt that man was more important, and he worked throughout his life for the welfare of humankind.

His pen name Æ (or A. E.) grew out of this tradition. It was originally Æon but a proofreader let it appear as Æ. Russell accepted the change and used it from that point on. Why Æon? John Eglinton recounted that once Æ made a drawing of the apparition in the Divine Mind of the idea of Heavenly Man. Unable to sleep one night, a voice gave him a title for his work, "Call it the Birth of Aeon." His eye was caught by a passage in Johann Neander's *General History of the Christian Religion* (1858), on the doctrine of the Aeons. In a letter, he described the following elements of the word: *A*, the sound for God; *Æ*, the first divergence from *A; Au* sound continuity for a time; and *N*, change. Thus, Æon represents revolt from God, the soul's passage through its successive incarnations in man homeward to God, and finally God's amplification.

In 1935 Æ died from cancer at Bournemouth, England, his home after the death of his wife. Some years earlier he had written that the dead are happier than the living and that he did not fear death for himself or for others.

ANALYSIS

In his excellent introduction to *The Living Torch*, Monk Gibbon remarks that Æ's poetry began as that of a mystic and remained so to the end. Æ saw the poet not as an artisan of beauty but rather as a seer and prophet who derived a special authority from communion with the esoteric wisdom of the past. As Gibbon points out, Æ's poetry contains a beauty of thought and a sincerity of utterance, but in some poems the form seems inadequate and the imagery vague.

Like other poets in the Irish Renaissance, Æ attempted to define Irishness in terms of the mysticism, reverie, and wavering rhythms of the Celtic Twilight, but his poetic voice remained a faint one. Some of Æ's best poetry is contained in his first two books: *Homeward: Songs by the Way* and *The Earth Breath and Other Poems*. Some of his late work is also very good, but it is marred by a tendency to philosophize.

Æ will continue to have a place in literary history, but his prose and poetry are comparable only to the best imaginative work of the secondary figures of his day. Æ survives not as a painter or poet but as an exemplar of his age.

HOMEWARD: SONGS BY THE WAY

Æ's philosophy includes a pantheistic adoration of nature, and he argues that the important thing about Ireland is the primitiveness of the country and its people. The very title of *Homeward: Songs by the Way* indicates the author's attitude toward life. Ernest Boyd in his *Appreciations and Depreciations: Irish Literary Studies* (1918) has stated that "home" for Æ signifies the return of the soul to the Oversoul, the spirit's absorption into the Universal Spirit—a doctrine which reflects his interest in Ralph Waldo Emerson, Henry David Thoreau, and Walt Whitman.

Homeward: Songs by the Way is a narrative of Æ's spiritual adventures, a record of the soul's search for the Infinite. Æ's poems are songs with sensuous, unearthly notes, records of the inner music of his life. They do not speak of humankind's mundane experiences but rather those moments of divine vision and intuition when humankind's being dissolves into communion with the Eternal. In that moment when the seer has come to his spiritual vision, he is truly at home.

Alone with Nature, Æ beholds in his poetry the beauties of the phenomenal world and through this experience the poet is lifted toward participation in the Eternal. The conditions which usually produce an exalted mood are those associated with morning or evening twilight, the quietude of the hills, and the silent, lonely countryside; such scenes are typical of his paintings as well as of his poetry. On innumerable occasions the poet seeks the soft dusk of the mountains for meditation. Often his verses suggest the coming of daylight and the initial glories of sunlight as the seer pays homage to the light after a night of rapture on the mountainside.

Yet solitude is not the sine qua non for Æ's visions. In "The City" one finds his mood unaltered by the change of setting. The poet's immortal eyes transfigure the mortal things of the city. One is reminded of another Metaphysical poet, T. S. Eliot, as Æ paints the gloom of the metropolis while managing to retain bright glimmers of hope.

Wayne Hall in his *Shadowy Heroes* (1980) has pointed out that, in recording his most intense experiences (his ecstatic visions), Æ produced his most notable work. The most successful poems in *Homeward: Songs by the Way* are "By the Margin of the Great Deep," "The Great Breath," and the sequence "Dusk," "Night," "Dawn," and "Day." "Dusk" begins at sunset, that special moment for poetic visions. At this early point in the volume the vision of the speaker draws him away from domestic life and human contact toward "primeval being." Sunset also introduces "The Great Breath." The fading sky of this poem seems to suggest both a cosmic flower and an awareness that the death of beauty occasions its most complete fulfillment. This unstable insight, Hall points out, as with the paradox of spiritual union through physical separation in "By the Margin of the Great Deep," becomes more nearly resolved in the four-poem sequence. In "By the Margin of the Great Deep," rather than a sunset, chimney fires of the village mingle in the sky, signifying the merging of humanity within the vastness of God.

For Æ, night usually brings despair and the loss of vision, as in "The Dawn of Darkness." In "Waiting" the speaker can only hope that dawn will reawaken humanity to its former joy. In the poem "Night," however, Æ changes directions as night brings on a rebirth of spirit and beauty, a complete union of souls, while "Dawn" initiates a fragmentation of unity. In the light of common day vision is lost but not entirely forgotten.

The sequence of poems from "Dusk" to "Day" succeeds far better than Æ's other attempts to link mortal pain with immortal vision. For Æ, in order for one to have a human spirit one must know sorrow. The path to wisdom is a road paved with the burdens of the world. Too often, however, he fails to integrate one world into the other, beyond the level of unconvincing abstraction.

OTHER MAJOR WORKS

LONG FICTION: *The Avatars*, 1933.

SHORT FICTION: *The Mask of Apollo and Other Stories*, 1904.

PLAY: *Deirdre*, pr. 1902.

NONFICTION: *Some Irish Essays*, 1906; *The National Being*, 1916; *The Candle of Vision*, 1918; *The Interpreters*, 1922; *Song and Its Fountains*, 1932;

Some Passages from the Letters of Æ to W. B. Yeats, 1936; *The Living Torch*, 1937 (Monk Gibbon, editor); *Æ's Letters to Mínánlabáin*, 1937; *Letters from Æ*, 1961.

BIBLIOGRAPHY

Davis, Robert Bernard. *George William Russell ("Æ")*. Boston: Twayne, 1977. The first chapter sketches the external events of Æ. His varied interests are elaborated in six succeeding chapters, with focuses on the mystic, the poet, his drama and fiction, the economist, the statesman, and the critic. A brief conclusion assesses Æ's contributions. Provides a chronology, notes, an index, and an annotated, select bibliography.

Kain, Richard M., and James H. O'Brien. *George Russell (A.E.)*. Lewisburg, Pa.: Bucknell University Press, 1976. The first three chapters, by Kain, present a biography of Æ by examining his personality, his early success, and his decline. The last two chapters, by O'Brien, examine Æ's interests in Theosophy and his work as a poet. Contains a chronology and a select bibliography.

Kuch, Peter. *Yeats and Æ: The Antagonism That Unites Dear Friends*. Totowa, N.J.: Barnes & Noble, 1986. This work examines the relationship between Yeats and George Russell from their first meeting in art class to their split in 1908. Kuch provides excellent background on the inner workings of the London-Dublin esoteric worlds which shaped both men. Especially valuable is his ability to sort through the many branches of the esoteric tradition.

Loftus, Richard J. *Nationalism in Modern Anglo-Irish Poetry*. Madison: University of Wisconsin Press, 1964. Chapter 5, "The Land of Promise," is a substantial examination of Æ's attitudes toward Irish nationalism. His optimism turned to anger, then to disillusionment. Rarely did he include his private political feelings in his public verse. *The House of the Titans* is analyzed for nationalistic implications. Supplemented by notes, a bibliography, and an index.

Mercier, Vivian. "Victorian Evangelicalism and the Anglo-Irish Literary Revival." In *Literature and the Changing Ireland*, edited by Peter Connolly. Irish Literary Studies 9. Gerrards Cross, Bucks, Ireland: Colin Smythe, 1982. Evangelicalism is examined as the background to Æ's career. His father made Æ aware of the power of conversion, which occurred away from Evangelicalism to Theosophy for him. He helped to establish Theosophy as a sect similar in status to that of a Protestant Evangelical group. Includes notes and an index.

Summerfield, Henry. *That Myriad-Minded Man: A Biography of George William Russell, "A. E.," 1867-1935*. Gerrards Cross, Bucks, Ireland: Colin Smythe, 1975. Chapter 1 explains Russell's mysticism. His nationalism is then examined. Chapter 4 focuses on farm interests, and the following chapter describes his journalism from 1905 to 1914. Russell's pacifism is then posed against the violence of war in two chapters, and a final chapter covers his last years. Complemented by illustrations, notes, and an index.

John Harty III;
bibliography updated by the editors

CONRAD AIKEN

Born: Savannah, Georgia; August 5, 1889
Died: Savannah, Georgia; August 17, 1973

PRINCIPAL POETRY

Earth Triumphant and Other Tales in Verse, 1914
Turns and Movies and Other Tales in Verse, 1916
The Jig of Forslin, 1916
Nocturne of Remembered Spring and Other Poems, 1917
The Charnel Rose, 1918
Senlin: A Biography and Other Poems, 1918
The House of Dust, 1920
Punch: The Immortal Liar, 1921
Priapus and the Pool, 1922
The Pilgrimage of Festus, 1923
Changing Mind, 1925
Priapus and the Pool and Other Poems, 1925
Prelude, 1929

Selected Poems, 1929

John Deth: A Metaphysical Legend and Other Poems,
   1930

Gehenna, 1930

The Coming Forth by Day of Osiris Jones, 1931

Preludes for Memnon, 1931

And in the Hanging Gardens, 1933

Landscape West of Eden, 1934

Time in the Rock: Preludes to Definition, 1936

And in the Human Heart, 1940

Brownstone Eclogues and Other Poems, 1942

The Soldier: A Poem by Conrad Aiken, 1944

The Kid, 1947

Skylight One: Fifteen Poems, 1949

The Divine Pilgrim, 1949

Wake II, 1952

Collected Poems, 1953, second edition 1970

A Letter from Li Po and Other Poems, 1955

The Fluteplayer, 1956

Sheepfold Hill: Fifteen Poems, 1958

Selected Poems, 1961

The Morning Song of Lord Zero, 1963

A Seizure of Limericks, 1964

Cats and Bats and Things with Wings: Poems, 1965

The Clerk's Journal, 1971

A Little Who's Zoo of Mild Animals, 1977

OTHER LITERARY FORMS

Although best known as a poet, Conrad Aiken also
published five novels, six short-story collections, two
plays, a poetic autobiographical essay, two collections
of criticism, four books for children (including one of
limericks), and two anthologies of poetry.

ACHIEVEMENTS

From his mature years onward, Aiken was much
honored. In 1929, he received the Shelley Memorial
Award, and the following year, he received the Pulit-
zer Prize for *Selected Poems*. He was chosen to edit *A
Comprehensive Anthology of American Poetry* for The
Modern Library (1929) and published a revision in
1944. He continued to receive honors: a Guggenheim
Fellowship (1934); editor, *Twentieth Century American
Poetry*, for The Modern Library (1944); Poetry Consul-
tant, Library of Congress (1950-1952); National Book

Award for Poetry for *Collected Poems* (1954); Bollingen
Prize (1956); the Academy of American Poets Fellowship (1957); and Gold Medal for Poetry of the National
Institute of Arts and Letters (1958). A special issue of
Wake magazine (1952), in which there appeared new
and reprinted writing by Aiken and others, signaled a
step forward in the critical reappraisal of Aiken's contributions.

BIOGRAPHY

Conrad Aiken, born in Savannah, Georgia, in 1889,
was the oldest of three sons and one daughter. His father
was a surgeon, and the Aikens were well off, but the
family was fractured by strife. In "Obituary in Bitcherel," the last of his *Collected Poems* (1970), and in
Ushant: An Essay (1952), Aiken records the crescendo
of violence that tore his family apart. In "Obituary in
Bitcherel," Aiken gives himself a very good beginning,
with a distinguished father who was not only a physician
and surgeon but also a writer and painter and with a
mother, a New England beauty, whose father, William
James Potter, a Congregational minister, was a friend of
Ralph Waldo Emerson. Two Mayflower passengers and
six generations of the Delanos ran in Aiken's veins. His
parents reared him to appreciate literature and writing,
and he had happy hours of play besides. Then the parents seemed to turn against each other. The atmosphere
of the house became strained. Aiken was beaten,
barebacked, for reasons unknown. In his autobiography,
Ushant, he tells of the argument flaring up between his
parents early one morning, of his mother's half-smoth-
ered cry, of his father's voice counting to three, of the
handgun exploding twice, and of the two still bodies lying separately in the dim daylight of the room. Aiken
was about eleven and a half, and ever after the murder
and suicide he was to be in search of a literary consciousness that would do his parents credit.

Sent to live with a great-great aunt in New Bedford,
Massachusetts, Aiken entered Harvard University in
1907, but in protest at being placed on probation for irregular class attendance, he went on a six-month tour of
Europe; he did receive his Harvard degree in 1912. His
marriage, the first of three, took place a few days later.
After a year of honeymooning in Europe (to which he
was to return many times), he settled in Cambridge,

Conrad Aiken (Library of Congress)

Massachusetts, devoting his full time to writing on a small but independent income.

In 1914, with the publication of *Earth Triumphant and Other Tales in Verse*, Aiken began a search for poetic monuments to his parents' memory. Although he argued that there was no other possible judge of a poet's excellence than the consciousness of the poet himself, he did reach out to people. There were, for example, his onetime mentor, John Gould Fletcher; his Harvard classmate, T. S. Eliot; and his three children by his first wife. Wherever he took up residence, however, it was the "evolution" of his artistic consciousness, the legacy of his parents, that held first place in his thoughts. Living in England from 1922 to 1925, in Massachusetts, New York City, and again in Georgia, and living as a traveler, Aiken sang with a unique and solitary voice.

His single-minded purpose gained him early recognition. From 1910 to 1911, he published many pieces in the Harvard *Monthly* and the Harvard *Advocate*, of which he served as president. From 1916 to 1922, he was a critic, mainly of contemporary poets, for *The Poetry Journal*, *The New Republic*, and *The Dial*, to which

he was one of the contributing editors from 1917 to 1918. He also contributed to *Poetry* and the Chicago *Daily News*, among other periodicals. In the London *Mercury* and the London *Atheneum*, he published "Letters from America." He also published several volumes of poems during these years, and nearly thirty more thereafter.

There were interesting side excursions from Aiken's main road of poetry and criticism. He spent a year as an English tutor at Harvard (1927-1928) and wrote his play *Fear No More*, based on his short story "Mr. Arcularis." The play was performed in London in 1946, and in Washington, D.C., in 1951. In the 1930's, he conducted a summer school in painting and writing. In spite of his interludes, Aiken spent the last two decades of his life almost exclusively writing and revising his poems.

ANALYSIS

A poet and artist of the Second American Renaissance, Conrad Aiken pursued the theme of the poet alone, whose only true friends appear to be the characters of his writings. Technically, his poetry extends from the rhymes and measures of couplet and quatrain and blank and free verse to the more richly concentrated forms of the commemorative ode and "symphony"; the sonnet ("little song") and its sequence, such as "And in the Human Heart"; and the aubade ("morning song"), among a variety of experimental forms.

Aiken's experiments constantly remind readers of the tradition of meter, and especially of rhyme. Even his free verse uses enough rhyme to let one know that Aiken's sense of poetic tradition is important. Aiken is perhaps most admired for his exploration of music within poetic forms as he mixes iambs with polysyllables, ranging from five- to three-stress meters.

Conrad Aiken is part of a Romantic humanist tradition which seeks to heal the hurt of human bereavement and the failure of social revolution by substituting the idea of the creator God for the godly creator. The poet-hero shows that it is possible to achieve solitary pleasure in the "resurrected" imagination, and in spite of social failures and inadequacies, there is a type of poetry, a wry music of spiritual revolution, in which lyric narrative and dialogue resist social distress. Aiken creates the enduring mock- or antihero, seen best in Punch in his early writings and in the later figures of the Kid and of Lord Zero.

Aiken's monistic, dream view of life and art is expressed in his protagonists, who range from ironic middle-class types—Forslin and Senlin—to mock- and anti-hero types—Punch, John Deth, the Kid, and Lord Zero. In Aiken's mythology, death is a regulation, a point of genesis, perhaps because of the traumatic context of the deaths of Aiken's parents. Aiken's ironic rejoinder to death, the binding regulation on life, is the apotheosis of humankind through unity with godhead and nature in an endless cycle of death and rebirth, a pantheistic form of resurrection, as seen, for example, in Aiken's use of the phoenix in *The Morning Song of Lord Zero* and in another late poem, "Thee."

Aiken is a personal Romanticist. In his vaudeville poems, for example, which he wrote off and on well into his seventies, he tells of the sordid lives of the performers whose passions and violence catch the tonal quality of his own terrified childhood recollections. To what purpose the passion and the violence? the sad, wry music of Aiken's poetry seems to ask. Natural death is enough to contend with, without the horror of passion and murder.

Over the stratum of the reality of death, Aiken builds a dreamworld of resurrection in many forms, ranging from the would-be type of Christ, through middle-class "monarchs of all they survey," a Faustian puppet, a master demon and a vampire of the cyclic dance of death, various reincarnations of the American culture hero, to, finally, the apotheosis of man in the form of Lord Zero.

THE DIVINE PILGRIM

The Divine Pilgrim is a collection of six "symphonies": *The Charnel Rose, The Jig of Forslin, The House of Dust, Senlin: A Biography, The Pilgrimage of Festus*, all collected from earlier publications, and *Changing Mind*, which was added in 1925. Aiken spelled out his musical principle in "Counterpoint and Implication" (*Collected Poems*, "Notes"), reprinted as "Aiken, Conrad (1919)," in *A Reviewer's ABC: Collected Criticism Conrad Aiken from 1916 to the Present* (1958). His principle was to build each poem out of its key to emotional masses arranged so that each massing would set an elusively particular musical tone or subtheme to the words, and each masstone, or "sub-key," would dominate a

brief movement and its contrapuntal fellows until a "movement," a main section or part, had been stated, developed, and restated to give a general tonality out of the units and subunits of poetic composition.

THE CHARNEL ROSE

The Charnel Rose, in the traditional four-part division of the sonata and symphony, treats carnal love, idealistic or Romantic love, erotically mystical love, and, finally, purely mystical love in the crucifixion of Jesus Christ and his resurrection, which for Aiken is the symbol of flesh crucifying itself through its own lusts. At the end of the "symphony," the cycle of humanity is ready to begin again with carnal love. Throughout, the third-person narrator views women, phantoms, and the crucifying crowd as projections of his own frustrated dreams. The entire poem may be considered as having the standard sonata form, with the second main "movement" holding well to the andante tempo while weaving some andante texture into the last two "movements." The whole poem may be viewed as a musical theme with variations, as Aiken's tempos range from allegro quatrains to *allegro manon troppo*.

THE JIG OF FORSLIN

In *The Jig of Forslin*, Forslin is all man, an organic compound of the Latin *forsan* and *fors*, meaning "chanceling" or "weakling." Through all his dreams, ranging from the urge of his body to control his mind to his mind's struggle to control his body, he *is* a man of will, however misdirected. In the aquarium light of his imagination, his adopted personae—the suicidal juggler; the killer of both priest and inebriated sailor, as well as of his children, his wife, and her lover; the alluring lamia; the bodiless voice of Christ; the harlot's lover and the harlot herself—all can, by choice, be resurrected in humankind's dreams. This five-part poem employs both blank verse and free verse, rhymed and rhymeless. The poem is of an earlier, less sophisticated music than *The Charnel Rose* but is placed after it because, apparently, the imagery of *The Jig of Forslin* corresponds more closely to the imagery in *The House of Dust*, which comes next in *The Divine Pilgrim*.

THE HOUSE OF DUST

The House of Dust, is another four-part poem which Aiken has compared to a symphonic poem. This poem, however, emphasizes more programmatic detail, and sets forth humankind's innate ability to become divine by becoming divinely conscious of the individual lives of urban residents. The poem points ahead to the Metaphysical period in Aiken's work when, in *Preludes for Memnon* and *Time in the Rock: Preludes to Definition*, the poetic self examines traditional, polarizing, concepts of divinity, apparently dispenses with them, and then attempts to set up a new polarity, the self unto itself, in the continuing search for humankind's divine potential.

SENLIN: A BIOGRAPHY

Senlin: A Biography, is a three-part poem, which contains Aiken's most famous composition, the "Morning Song from Senlin" (section two of Part II). Senlin, whose name means "little old man," is an ironic or slightly comical middle-class imperturbable figure, who is potentially explosive and who shines like the sun as he rises from sleep in the morning. "Morning Song from Senlin" is a display of musical prosody, consisting of a variety of adapted ballad stanzas, refrains, and heroic quatrains. An evening ode of Senlin's (section three of Part I), in ternary order, inverts the usual Pindaric or even Cowleyan sequence, and finds its musical echoes in the refrains. Senlin, himself, is both a dreamer and everybody's dream.

THE PILGRIMAGE OF FESTUS

The Pilgrimage of Festus, in five parts and in rhymed free verse, is another step along the road to Lord Zero. Possessed of a Faustian thirst for ultimate knowledge, Festus searches out the world of temporal conquest and then that of spiritual power as he converses to no avail with Buddha, Mephistopheles, Confucius, and Christ. Finally, Festus hears a music that is so lovely that it must be the sign of eternal womanhood, the ultimate symbol of Romantic humanism. Old Man of the Rain, however, Festus's alter ego, soon disillusions him. The music comes from the instruments of a group of butchers on holiday who are still dressed in their spotted aprons. Festus emerges as a wry figure of paternalism in blithe search for truth, to be found only in his private self.

CHANGING MIND

Changing Mind is a poet's poem, in traditional four-part "music." Aiken's stated intention is to enunciate his newfound goal to help humankind "evolve" a higher consciousness pointing toward the divine, but he admits

that, as such a helper, he must "die daily" to self. A mixture of farce and brutality, this poem, which moves from free verse narrative and dialogue to prose and "prayer," advances Aiken from mere hedonism to a kind of creativity that recognizes its source in dust, which is the "true father."

JOHN DETH: A METAPHYSICAL LEGEND

John Deth is a rollicking, five-part Hudibrastic literary ballad about John Deth, the master of the death dance, and his two doxies, Millicent Piggistaile and Juliana Goatibed, demons all three. These death demons sleep and dream forever now in the mind of the poet but not until they have led many in the dance to death and have crucified the "god" of beauty itself, Venus Anadyomene. To Aiken, himself never sure of the total meaning of this poem, Deth seems to represent the negative, Piggistaile the positive pole of Aiken's being, while Goatibed stands for the conjoined consciousness of the two poles. Deth is Father Death, capable of using the power of unholy resurrection by word-magic, even as he can do to death by the word of his mouth, always assisted by his magic wand and by the walking dead, who serve as heralds of his deadly work. John Deth is also a grieving antihero, a Comus who, to lust, has added the dimension of death.

"THE ROOM" AND PRELUDES FOR MEMNON

"The Room," a marvelous blank verse ode in three stanzas, celebrates memory. An isolated single leaf is able to construct a great tree out of chaos through a reverse creation reflected in the reverse order of the stanzas. The mystic tree of the poem represents a cycle in which both life and death, joined by their intermediary, chaos, deserve praise for perpetuating the cycle. The same theme occurs in *Preludes for Memnon*, composed of sixty-three preludes, in which Aiken attempts to bring order out of chaos and death.

THE MORNING SONG OF LORD ZERO

In expanding and contracting lines of mainly free verse, rhymed and unrhymed, the fourteen poems of *The Morning Song of Lord Zero*, much of the time in dialogue, explore the image of the incarnate word of Romantic humanism, the "I" who has become Lord Zero. Lord Zero, however, is "The Island," death, into which the soul or self takes only a memory of love. The blessed isle of Romantic humanism here presents death as the ultimate identity.

A LITTLE WHO'S ZOO OF MILD ANIMALS

Finally, *A Little Who's Zoo of Mild Animals* mocks its own analysis of an evolved, portmanteau creation and consciousness. In the leaf there is already the seed, the branch, the trunk, and the root. In the heart of the child is the true beginning of heaven.

OTHER MAJOR WORKS

LONG FICTION: *Blue Voyage*, 1927; *Great Circle*, 1933; *King Coffin*, 1935; *A Heart for the Gods of Mexico*, 1939; *Conversation: Or, Pilgrim's Progress*, 1940; *The Collected Novels of Conrad Aiken*, 1964.

SHORT FICTION: *Bring! Bring! and Other Stories*, 1925; *Costumes by Eros*, 1928; *Among the Lost People*, 1934; *Short Stories*, 1950; *Collected Short Stories*, 1960; *Collected Short Stories of Conrad Aiken*, 1966.

PLAYS: *Mr. Arcularis: A Play*, pb. 1957 (first produced as *Fear No More*, 1946).

NONFICTION: *Skepticisms: Notes on Contemporary Poetry*, 1919; *Ushant: An Essay*, 1952; *A Reviewer's ABC: Collected Criticism of Conrad Aiken from 1916 to the Present*, 1958; *Selected Letters of Conrad Aiken*, 1978.

EDITED TEXTS: *A Comprehensive Anthology of American Poetry*, 1929, 1944; *Twentieth Century American Poetry*, 1944.

BIBLIOGRAPHY

Butscher, Edward. *Conrad Aiken, Poet of White Horse Vale*. Athens: University of Georgia Press, 1988. This 518-page biography is equipped with portraits, indexes, and a seven-page bibliography. Butscher attempts to examine both Aiken's flaws and achievements without exaggerating either. He covers Aiken's life through 1925 and traces the poet's relationships with other important literary figures of modernism.

Hoffman, Frederick John. *Conrad Aiken*. New York: Twayne, 1962. Hoffman's introduction to Aiken treats him as a representative American mind, one who explored and acutely expressed the problems of modern consciousness. Of the six chapters, the final four deal with the poetry. Hoffman holds that Aiken should be judged primarily as a poet. Contains notes, bibliographies, and an index.

Marten, Harry. *The Art of Knowing: The Poetry and Prose of Conrad Aiken*. Columbia: University of Missouri Press, 1988. Marten's book is a treatment of selected novels and significant narrative poems. He analyzes, for example, *Senlin: A Biography*, *Punch: The Immortal Liar*, *Preludes for Memnon*, and *Changing Mind*. Marten intends to illuminate Aiken's quest to understand the capabilities of the human mind. Includes an index and a five-page bibliography.

Martin, Jay. *Conrad Aiken: A Life of His Art*. Princeton, N.J.: Princeton University Press, 1962. Focuses on Aiken's growth and development as evidenced in his poetry and prose. The poetry is emphasized in this investigation, which uses his work in part to study how literary reputations have been achieved. A thorough index and notes.

Seigel, Catharine F. *The Fictive World of Conrad Aiken: A Celebration of Consciousness*. Dekalb: Northern Illinois University Press, 1993. Seigel shows a keen awareness of Aiken's agonizing over converting consciousness into a written account, preserving one's autonomy yet sharing one's experience with others. She enhances her study with a number of quotations from Aiken's correspondence.

Spivey, Ted R., and Arthur Waterman, eds. *Conrad Aiken: A Priest of Consciousness*. Georgia State Literary Studies 6. New York: AMS Press, 1989. The editors have selected essays that provide a variety of critical views on Aiken. Some of the articles discuss overall themes in the work, others interpret specific poems, such as "Mayflower" and "Hallowe'en." A special bibliographic section discusses works on Aiken. Contains a chronology, full notes, and an index.

Fred R. McFadden;
bibliography updated by the editors

ANNA AKHMATOVA

Anna Andreyevna Gorenko

Born: Bol'shoy Fontan, near Odessa, Russian Empire; June 23, 1889

Died: Domodedovo, near Moscow, U.S.S.R.; March 5, 1966

PRINCIPAL POETRY

Vecher, 1912

Chetki, 1914

Belaya staya, 1917

Podorozhnik, 1921

Anno Domini MCMXXI, 1922, 1923

Iz shesti knig, 1940

Izbrannye stikhotvoreniia, 1943

Stikhotvoreniia, 1958, 1961

Poema bez geroya, 1960 (*A Poem Without a Hero*, 1973)

Rekviem, 1963 (*Requiem*, 1964)

Beg vremeni, 1965

Sochineniya, 1965-1983 (3 volumes)

Poems of A., 1973

Selected Poems, 1976

Requiem, and Poem Without a Hero, 1976

You Will Hear Thunder, 1976

Anna Akhmatova: Poems, 1983

OTHER LITERARY FORMS

In addition to poetry, Anna Akhmatova wrote an unfinished play and many essays on Russian writers. Her spirited book *O Pushkine: Stat'i i zametki* (1977), published in its complete version posthumously, is one of the most discerning tributes to the greatest Russian poet by a fellow poet. Akhmatova also translated poems from the Old Egyptian, Hindu, Armenian, Chinese, French, Italian, and many other languages, most of these in collaboration with native speakers.

ACHIEVEMENTS

Anna Akhmatova enriched Russian literature immeasurably, not only with the quality of her poetry but also with the freshness and originality of her strong talent. Through Acmeism, a literary movement of which she was one of the founders and leading members, she effected a significant change of direction in Russian poetry in the second decade of the twentieth century. The Acmeists' insistence on clarity and precision of expression—much in the spirit of the Imagists, although the two movements developed independently of each other—represented a reaction against the intricate symbols and otherworldly preoccupations of the Symbolists. Akhmatova's youthful love poems brought her early fame, and her reputation was further enhanced during the long reign of terror in her country, through which she was able to preserve her dignity, both as a human being and as a poet. With Boris Pasternak, Osip Mandelstam, and Marina Tsvetayeva, Akhmatova is universally regarded as one of the four great poets of postrevolutionary Russia. Having been generously translated into English, Akhmatova's works are constantly gaining stature in world literature as well.

BIOGRAPHY

Anna Akhmatova—the pen name of Anna Andreyevna Gorenko—was born in a suburb of Odessa in 1889, into the family of a naval officer. Akhmatova be-

Anna Akhmatova

gan to write poetry when she was eleven, and her first poem was published in 1907. She achieved great popularity with her first books *Vecher* and *Chetki*. After joining the literary movement called Acmeism, she played an important part in it together with Osip Mandelstam and with her husband, Nikolay Gumilyov, from whom she was later divorced. During World War I and the Russian Revolution, Akhmatova stood by her people, even though she did not agree with the ideas and methods of the revolutionaries. Never politically inclined, she saw in the war and the revolution an evil that might eventually destroy the private world in which she had been able to address herself exclusively to her own problems. When the end of that world came, she refused to accept it, believing that she would be able to continue her sequestered life. She also refused to emigrate, saying that it took greater courage to stay behind and accept what came.

The effect of the revolution on her life and creativity was not immediately evident, for she subsequently published two more collections of poetry. When her former husband and fellow Acmeist Gumilyov was shot, however, Akhmatova realized that the new way of life was inimical to her own. Compelled to silence, she ceased to exist publicly, instead remaining an inner émigré for eighteen years and occupying herself mostly with writing essays and translating. This silence may have saved her life during the purges of the 1930's, although she was not spared agony while trying to ascertain the fate of her only son, a promising scholar of Asian history, who had been sent to a labor camp three times. Only World War II brought a change to Akhmatova's dreary and dangerous life. Like many Soviet writers and intellectuals, she once again sided with her people, suppressing her reservations and complaints. She spent the first several months of the war in besieged Leningrad and then was evacuated to Tashkent, where she stayed almost to the end of the war. In Tashkent, she was brought closer to the other part of her ancestry, for her grandmother, from whom she took her pen name, was a Tartar.

When the war was over and the authorities again resorted to repression, Akhmatova was among the first to be victimized. In a vitriolic speech by Andrei Zhdanov, the cultural dictator at that time, she and the satirist Mikhail Zoshchenko were singled out as examples of anti-Soviet attitudes among intellectuals and charged with harmful influence on the young. They were expelled from the Writers' Union, and their works ceased to be published. Thus, Akhmatova vanished from public view once again in 1946, this time involuntarily, and did not reappear until ten years later. In 1958, a slender collection of her poems was published as a sign of rehabilitation. A few more of her books were subsequently published, both at home and abroad, thus reinstating the poet as an active member of society.

During the last decade of her life, she wrote some of the best poetry of her career. Shortly before her death, she received two richly deserved accolades for her work. Ironically, the recognition came from abroad: She was awarded the prestigious Italian Etna Taormina Prize in 1964 and an honorary doctorate from Oxford University in 1965. Ravaged by long illness, she died in 1966, having preserved her dignity and independence by asking for and receiving a church funeral according to the Russian Orthodox rites. After her death, Akhmatova was almost unanimously eulogized as the finest woman poet in all of Russian literature.

ANALYSIS

Anna Akhmatova's poetry can conveniently be divided into three distinct periods: 1912 to 1923, 1940 to 1946, and 1956 to 1966 (with a few poems published in 1950). The interim periods were those of enforced silence. The first silence, from 1923 to 1940, came as a result of tacit admission on her part that the changed way of life in Russia was not fully acceptable to her. The second, from 1946 to 1956, was a direct result of the authorities' intervention. Needless to say, Akhmatova kept busy by further refining her poetry, by writing essays, and by translating.

VECHER AND CHETKI

Akhmatova's development as a poet can be traced from book to book. Her first books, *Vecher* and *Chetki*, impressed readers with the freshness of a young woman's concern about her feelings of love. In almost all the poems having love as a focal point, Akhmatova presents love from a woman's point of view, in a form resembling a diary. It is difficult to say whether the female voice in these poems belongs to the poet herself; probably it does, but in the last analysis it is immaterial. The beloved is almost always silent, never fully revealed or described, and at times he seems to be almost secondary—only a catalyst for the woman's feelings. She is so entranced by his mere presence that, in her anguish, she draws her "left-hand glove upon [her] right." The poet expresses the whole spectrum of love—from the playfulness of a young woman trying to dismay her partner (in order to prove that she, too, can wield some power over him) to moments of flaming passion.

To be sure, passion is presented implicitly, in the time-honored tradition of Russian literature, yet it is also vividly indicated in unique ways. As she says, "In human intimacy there is a secret boundary,/Neither the experience of being in love nor passion can cross it/ Though the lips be joined together in awful silence/ And the heart break asunder with love." Her fervent passion is coupled with fidelity to her partner, but as her loyalty is professed time and again, a note of frustration and a fear of incompatibility and rejection become noticeable. The prospect of unrequited love is confirmed by betrayal and parting. The ensuing feeling of loneliness leads to despair and withdrawal. The woman's reaction shows a mixture of anger, defiance, even resignation: "Be accursed . . ./ But I swear by the garden of angels/ By the holy icon I swear,/ By the passionate frenzy of our nights,/ I will never go back to you!" (These lines, incidentally, prompted Zhdanov, in his merciless attack many years later, to call Akhmatova "a nun and a harlot.") Thus, celebration, parting, and suffering receive equal play in Akhmatova's approach to love, although the ultimate outcome is a markedly unhappy one. Her love poetry is a vivid testimony both to the glories and to the miseries of her sex.

The feminine "I" of the poems seeks refuge, release, and salvation in religion, nature, and poetry. The refuge in religion is especially evident in *Chetki*. The work has a peculiar religious tone, pervaded, like Akhmatova's sentiments of love, with a mood of melancholy and inexplicable sadness. The persona seems to have found consolation for unhappiness in love when she says: "The King of Heaven has healed my/ Soul with the icy calm of love's/ Absence." Her prayers are mostly in the form of confession or intercession. It is easy to see, however,

that they are used primarily to compensate for her feeling of loneliness and weariness of life. Thus, privations and misfortunes are closely tied to her religious feelings; sin and atonement are inseparable, and her passions of the flesh are tempered by spiritual fervor. Akhmatova's poems with religious overtones have little in common with customary religious experience. They are also much more complex and psychologically laden than any of her other poetry.

BELAYA STAYA AND ANNO DOMINI MCMXXI

In Akhmatova's third collection, *Belaya staya*, a new theme joins those of love and religion: a presentiment of doom. Nourished by the horrors of war and revolution, this presentiment grows into a wake for a world on the verge of annihilation. As the revolution dragged on, Akhmatova's mood turned bleaker and more hopeless. She sought rapport with the events by writing poetry with political motifs but to no avail.

The poems in *Anno Domini MCMXXI* clearly reveal Akhmatova's state of mind and emotions at this difficult time, as well as her awareness that an era had come to an end. "All is sold, all is lost, all is plundered,/ Death's wing has flashed black on our sight,/ All's gnawed bare with sore, want, and sick longing," she laments in one poem. She refused to emigrate, however, knowing instinctively, as did Boris Pasternak many years later when he was threatened with expulsion from the Soviet Union, that for a poet to leave his or her native land is tantamount to a death worse than physical death. She did not hesitate to criticize those who had left their country in its worst hour: "Poor exile, you are like a prisoner/ To me, or one upon the bed/ Of sickness. Dark your road, O wanderer,/ Of wormwood smacks your alien bread." These lines have been quoted often by Soviet critics for propaganda purposes, although Akhmatova wrote them sincerely, as a poet who could not tear herself away from her own land.

WAR AND LOVE OF COUNTRY

In the poems in which Akhmatova grappled with the problems of present-day reality, a gradual shift away from intimate love poetry toward more worldly themes can be seen. This shift can be considered as an overture to another kind of Akhmatova's poetry. Tormented by the turbulent years of war and revolution, in which she made many personal sacrifices and witnessed many tragedies (the loss of friends, for example, including her former husband Nikolay Gumilyov), she was forced to face reality and to express her feelings and opinions about it. The silence imposed on her in 1923 only postponed further development in that direction.

When she was allowed to reappear shortly before World War II, she wrote little in her old idiom. In many poems written during the war, she extols the beauty of her land and the magnitude of the martyrdom of her people under attack by a ruthless enemy. Leningrad, the city of her life and of her dreams, is especially the object of her affection. Tsarskoe Selo—a settlement near Leningrad, which was the residence of the czars; the town of young Alexander Pushkin; and the town of Akhmatova's favorite poetry teacher Innokenty Annensky as well as of her own youth—remained vividly and forever etched in her memory, even when she saw it almost totally destroyed in the war.

Leningrad and Tsarskoe Selo were not the only places to which Akhmatova paid homage; indeed, all of Russia was her home. Her attitude toward her country is typical of many Russian intellectuals, who, despite a thick veneer of cosmopolitanism, still harbor a childlike, sentimental, and irrational love for their country. From her earliest poems to her last, Akhmatova expressed the same feeling for Russia, a strange mixture of abstract love for her country, on the one hand, and down-to-earth concern for its people, on the other. In the poem "Prayer," for example, she prays to the Lord to take even her child and to destroy "the sweet power of song" that she possesses if it would help to change "the storm cloud over Russia . . . into a nimbus ablaze."

This willingness to sacrifice what is dearest to her if it would benefit her country is no mere affectation—it is expressed with utmost sincerity and conviction. In a poem written almost thirty years later, "From an Airplane," she again expresses her love for her country in no less sincere terms: "It is all mine—and nothing can divide us,/ It is my soul, it is my body, too." Perhaps the most profound and meaningful testimony to her patriotism can be found in the poem "Native Land," written in the last years of her life. For her, her country was "the mud on our gumboots, the grit in our teeth . . . And we mill, and we mix, and we crumble/

This innocent earth at our feet,/ But we rest in this earth at the roots of the flowers,/ Which is why we so readily say: It is ours!"

Akhmatova did not limit her gaze to European Russia, where she was reared and where she spent most of her life. Through her experiences in Tashkent, the city in which her ancestors had resided, she acquired a great admiration for, and understanding of, the Asian mind and soul. A mystical bond with Asia inspired her to write some of her most beautiful descriptive poems, such as "From the Oriental Notebook."

REQUIEM

Nevertheless, Akhmatova could not close her eyes to the Soviet reality, in which she was personally caught in a most tragic way. In a unified cycle of poems, *Requiem*, a masterpiece unpublished in the Soviet Union until 1987, she expresses her deep sorrow not only about her personal loss but also about the suffering to which the Russian people were being subjected. *Requiem* was her closest approach to public castigation of the regime in her country. The tone for the entire work is set by the motto, which sadly admits that the circumstances are not those of a foreign country but, more personally, those of the poet's own country and people. In a short foreword in prose, Akhmatova tells how during the horrible years of the purges she spent seventeen months waiting in line in front of a prison in order to discover the fate of her son. Another woman recognized her and whispered, "Can you describe this?" "Yes, I can," Akhmatova replied.

She kept her promise by writing *Requiem*. Although much of it reflects the universal sorrow and despair of a mother on the verge of losing her son, it is the *injustice* of her suffering that most pains the poet. Using her personal sorrow to speak for all human beings who suffer unjustly, the poet created in *Requiem* a work of lasting value. Moreover, there is much encouragement to be gained from *Requiem*. The persona does not lose hope and courage. She perseveres, knowing that the victims are unjustly persecuted and that she is not alone in suffering. In the epilogue, she recalls the trying hours and the faces she has seen in those seventeen months; in her final words, she begs that her monument be erected in front of the prison where she has stood for "three hundred hours," so that the thawing snow from the face of her monument will glide like tears. Even if overt references to the political terror are overlooked, *Requiem* is still one of the twentieth century's most eloquent poetic testimonies to human tragedy.

A POEM WITHOUT A HERO AND FINAL POEMS

Akhmatova's poetry from the last decade of her life shows the greater maturity and wisdom of old age. Her approach to poetic themes is more epic and historical, with a deeper perspective. This mature poetry is also more philosophical and psychological. The best example is the autobiographical *A Poem Without a Hero*, a panoramic view of the previous century as it pertains to the present. It is a subtle and at times complex poem, difficult to fathom without a proper key.

In her last poems, she speaks as if she has realized that her active role is over and that nothing else can hurt her. Her work at this time shows a mixture of sadness, resignation, relief, and even slight bewilderment as to what life really is after more than seven decades of coping with it: "The grim epoch diverted me/ As if I were a river./ I have been given a different life. In a new bed/ The river now flows, past the old one,/ And I cannot find my shores. . . ." She finds solace in her increasing loneliness, contemplating the past, trying to reevaluate it and to find the correct perspective on it. In one of her last poems, written slightly more than a year before her death, she speaks of the "Supreme Mystery." It has been on her mind from the beginning, changing its face from period to period. In her early poetry, it was the mystery of the man-woman relationship. Later, it became the mystery of the man-to-man relationship, with the emphasis on the cruelty of man to man. In her last years, it became the mystery of the relationship of man to eternity, indeed, the mystery of the meaning of existence. Through such organic development, Akhmatova reached the pinnacle of her poetic power, the power found in Pasternak's late poetry and in the work of other great poets of the century.

FORM AND STYLE

The stylistic aspect of Akhmatova's poetry is just as important as the thematic one, if not more so. She shows several peculiarly Akhmatovian features. Above all, there is the narrative tone that points to a definite affinity with prose. Zhirmunski calls her entire oeuvre "a novel in verse." It is this affinity that enables her to switch eas-

ily from emotion to description. Connected with this skill is a dramatic quality, expressed either through inner monologue or dialogue. The second striking feature is the brief lyric form, usually consisting of three to four stanzas, rarely five to seven, and never more than seven. (Later in her career, Akhmatova wrote many poems in free verse.) Parallel to the brevity of form is a pronounced laconism: A few carefully selected details suffice to convey an entire picture. Akhmatova's economy of words, spare almost to the point of frugality, led her to the epigrammatic form and to fragmentation, understatement, and improvisation. As a result, her sentences are sometimes without a verb and even without a subject (that being quite possible in Russian). Another peculiarity is the concreteness of her images, especially with reference to space and time. She tells the reader exactly where and when, almost to the minute, the events in her poem take place. The colors are vividly and exactly given. She avoids metaphors, instead using pointed, explanatory epithets. Finally, her intonation, never scrupulously measured or regulated, is that of a syncopated rhythm, approaching the rhythm of some forms of folk poetry. Many of these stylistic features result from her adherence to the tenets of Acmeism, but many others are uniquely her own and are easily recognizable as such.

Of the poets who influenced her, Akhmatova herself admits indebtedness to Gavrila Derzhavin, Pushkin, and Annensky. The latter two can be said to have exerted the greatest influence on her, although traces of other poets' influences—Nikolai Nekrasov, Aleksandr Blok, Mikhail Kuzmin—can be found. Even Fyodor Dostoevski, who never wrote poetry, is sometimes mentioned as a possible source of influence. As for her impact on other poets, Akhmatova's influence, like that of her great contemporaries, Mandelstam, Pasternak, and Marina Tsvetayeva, is pervasive, elusive, impossible to measure. In her old age, she recognized the talent of Joseph Brodsky—then only twenty-two years old—and passed on her mantle, as Nadezhda Mandelstam has said, in a kind of poetic succession. Anna Akhmatova, "Tragic Queen Anna," as literary historian Alexander Werth calls her, is a poet without whom modern Russian literature is unthinkable and by whom world literature has been significantly enriched.

OTHER MAJOR WORK

NONFICTION: *O Pushkine: Stat'i i zametki*, 1977.

BIBLIOGRAPHY

Haight, Amanda. *Anna Akhmatova: A Poetic Pilgrimage*. New York: Oxford University Press, 1976. An excellent study of Akhmatova's poems by one of the best authorities on her work.

Ketchian, Sonia. *The Poetry of Anna Akhmatova: A Conquest of Time and Space*. Munich: Otto Sagner, 1986. This solid study places Akhmatova's poems in their historical perspective and examines their artistic merits. A thoroughly revised and enlarged dissertation on various aspects of Akhmatova's poetry.

Leiter, Sharon. *Akhmatova's Petersburg*. Philadelphia: University of Pennsylvania Press, 1983. A review of Akhmatova's life in her beloved St. Petersburg and of political circumstances providing the material for, and leading to, her poetry inspired by St. Petersburg. The book also discusses Akhmatova's vision of this city.

Nayman, Anatoly. *Remembering Anna Akhmatova*. Translated by Wendy Rosslyn. London: Peter Halban, 1989. A memoir about Akhmatova by a poet who knew her in her last years. The book provides many references to, and citations from, Akhmatova's poems.

Reeder, Roberta. *Anna Akhmatova: Poet and Prophet*. New York: St. Martin's Press, 1994. In the most extensive book in English on Akhmatova, Reeder discusses in scholarly fashion all facets of her life and work. Stressing the artistic aspects of her poems, the author also examines the political circumstances in which she had to live. A forty-six-page bibliography is particularly useful.

Rosslyn, Wendy. *The Prince, the Fool, and the Nunnery: The Religious Theme in the Early Poetry of Anna Akhmatova*. Brookfield, Vt.: Gower, 1984. A thorough analysis of Akmatova's early poetry written between 1909 and 1925, with the emphasis on the religious and love themes as expressed by the heroines of her poems. There are copious examples of such poems, both in Russian and in English.

Wells, David N. *Anna Akmatova: Her Poetry*. Oxford: Berg, 1996. Wells offers a succinct overview of Akhmatova's life and poetry from the beginnings to her later works. It is a penetrating study, with many citations from her poetry in both Russian and English, stressing her main achievements.

Vasa D. Mihailovich, updated by Mihailovich

RAFAEL ALBERTI

Born: Puerto de Santa María, Spain; December 16, 1902

Died: Puerto de Santa María, Spain; October 28, 1999

PRINCIPAL POETRY

Marinero en tierra, 1925
La amante, 1925
El alba del alhelí, 1927
Cal y canto, 1929
Sobre los ángeles, 1929 (*Concerning the Angels*, 1967)
Consignas, 1933
Verte y no verte, 1935 (*To See You and Not to See You*, 1946)
Poesía, 1924-1938, 1940
Entre el clavel y la espada, 1941
Pleamar, 1944
A la pintura, 1945
Retornos de lo vivo lejano, 1952
Baladas y canciones del Paraná, 1954 (*Ballads and Songs of the Parana*, 1988)
Poesías completas, 1961
Selected Poems, 1966 (Ben Belitt, translator)
The Owl's Insomnia, 1973
Alberti tal cual, 1978

OTHER LITERARY FORMS

Although Rafael Alberti established his reputation almost entirely on the basis of his poetry, he became involved in drama after emigrating to Argentina, writing plays of his own and adapting Miguel de Cervantes' *El cerco de Numancia* (c. 1585, discovered in 1784; *Numantia: A Tragedy*, 1870) for the modern stage in 1944.

Alberti's most notable achievement in prose, a work of considerable interest for the student of his poetry, was his autobiography, *La arboleda perdida* (1942; *The Lost Grove*, 1976). In addition, he was a talented painter and supplied illustrations for some of his later volumes.

ACHIEVEMENTS

Rafael Alberti had at once the ill luck and the singular good fortune to flourish during Spain's second great literary boom. Despite his acknowledged worth, he was overshadowed by several of his contemporaries—in particular, by Federico García Lorca. Although Alberti's name is likely to come up in any discussion of the famous *generación del 27*, or Generation of '27, he generally languishes near the end of the list. On the other hand, the extraordinary atmosphere of the times did much to foster his talents; even among the giants, he earned acceptance and respect. He may occasionally have been lost in the crowd, but it was a worthy crowd.

His first volume, *Marinero en tierra*, won Spain's National Prize for Literature in 1924, and throughout his long career, his virtuosity never faltered. Always a difficult poet, he never gave the impression that his obscurity stemmed from incompetence. His political ideology— Alberti was the first of his circle to embrace communism openly—led him to covet the role of "poet of the streets," but Alberti will be remembered more for his poems of exile, which capture better than any others the poignant aftermath of the Spanish Civil War.

Ultimately, Alberti stands out as a survivor. Many of his great contemporaries died in the civil war or simply lapsed into a prolonged silence. Despite his wholehearted involvement in the conflict, Alberti managed to persevere after his side lost and to renew his career. He continued to publish at an imposing rate, took up new activities, and became a force in the burgeoning literary life of Latin America, as evidenced by his winning of the Cervantes Prize, the Spanish-speaking world's highest literary honor, in 1983. Consistent in his adherence to communism, he received the Lenin Prize for his political verse in 1965. Oddly enough, then, Alberti emerges as a constant—an enduring figure in a world of flux, a practicing poet of consistent excellence during six decades.

BIOGRAPHY

Rafael Alberti was born December 16, 1902, near Cádiz in Andalusia, and his nostalgia for that region pervades much of his work. His genteel family had fallen on hard times, and Alberti's schoolmates made him painfully aware of his inferior status. In 1917, the family moved to Madrid, where Alberti devoted himself to painting in the Cubist manner, attaining some recognition. Illness forced him to retire to a sanatorium in the mountains—a stroke of luck, as it happened, for there he subsequently met such luminaries as García Lorca, Salvador Dalí, and Luis Buñuel and began seriously to write poetry. He won the National Prize for *Marinero en tierra*, his first volume, and thereby gained acceptance into the elite artistic circles of the day. Personal difficulties and an increasing awareness of the plight of his country moved Alberti to embrace communism. In 1930, he married María Teresa León, also a writer, and together they founded the revolutionary journal, *Octubre*, in 1934.

Alberti's new political credo enabled him to travel extensively and to encounter writers and artists from all parts of Europe and the Americas. After participating actively in the civil war, he emigrated to Argentina in 1940. There, he began to write for the theater, gave numerous readings, and resumed painting. Hard work and fatherhood—his daughter Aitana was born in 1941— preserved Alberti from embittered paralysis, and his production of poetry never slackened. Indeed, many of his readers believe that he reached his peak in the late 1940's.

In 1964, Alberti moved to Rome, where he lived until 1977, when he was finally able to return to Spain, after almost thirty-eight years in exile. He was welcomed by more than three hundred communists carrying red flags as he stepped off the airliner. "I'm not coming with a clenched fist," he said, "but with an open hand." He enjoyed a resurgence of popularity upon his return and proceeded to run for the Cortes, giving poetry readings instead of speeches, and won. Alberti resigned his seat after three months in order to devote himself to his art. He became a well-respected literary figure in his last

Rafael Alberti (Hulton Archive)

two decades in Spain; the lost Andalusian had returned home. He died there on October 28, 1999 from a lung ailment; he was ninety-six years old.

ANALYSIS

Throughout his long career, Rafael Alberti proved to be a remarkably versatile poet. His facility of composition enabled him to shift smoothly from fixed forms to free verse, even within the confines of a single poem. Whether composing neomedieval lyrics, Baroque sonnets, or Surreal free verse, he always managed to be authentic. His deep emotions, sometimes obscured by his sheer virtuosity, found expression in all modes. His technical skill did not allow him to stagnate: Commentators on Alberti agree in their praise of his astonishing technical mastery. He might continue in the same vein for three volumes, but he would invariably break new ground in the fourth. His massive corpus of poetry comprises a remarkable array of styles, themes, and moods.

Although he was a natural poet with little formal training, Alberti always kept abreast of current develop-

ments in his art—indeed, he kept himself in the vanguard. He associated with the best and brightest of his time and participated in their movements. When the luminaries of Spain reevaluated Luis de Góngora, Alberti wrote accomplished neo-Baroque poetry; when Dalí and Buñuel were introducing Surrealism in Spanish art and film, Alberti adapted its principles to Spanish poetry; when most of the intellectuals of Spain were resisting General Franciso Franco and embracing Communism, Alberti was the "poet of the streets." He remained withal a genuine and unique lyric voice. Even his political verses are not without poetic merit—an exception, to be sure. Alberti changed by adding and growing, never by discarding and replacing; thus, he became a richer talent with each new phase of his creative development.

Alberti's poetry is suffused with nostalgia. The circumstances of his life decreed that he should continually find himself longing for another time, a distant place, or a lost friend, and in his finest poems, he achieves an elegiac purity free of the obscurity and self-pity that mar his lesser works. From first to last, the sadness for things lost remains Alberti's great theme, one he explored more fully than any other poet of his generation.

Alberti was a poet who could grow without discarding his past. The youthful poet who composed marvelous lyrics persisted in the nostalgia of exile; the angry poet of the streets reasserted himself in diatribes against Yankee imperialism in Latin America. At ease in all forms and idioms, forever the Andalusian in exile, always growing in his art and his thought, Alberti wrote a staggering number of excellent poems. In the vast treasure trove of twentieth century Spanish poetry, he left a hoard of pearls and sapphires—hidden at times by the rubies and the emeralds, but worthy nevertheless.

MARINERO EN TIERRA

The doyens of Spanish letters received *Marinero en tierra* with immediate enthusiasm, and the young Alberti found himself a de facto member of the *generación del 27*, eligible to rub elbows with all the significant writers of the day. Although Alberti seems to have been happy in the mid-1920's, his early volumes glow with poignant nostalgia for the sea and the coasts of his native Andalusia. He expresses his longing in exquisite lyrics in the medieval tradition. Ben Belitt, introducing his translations collected in *Selected Poems*, confesses that he could find no way to render these lyrics in English. They depend entirely on a native tradition, the vast trove of popular verses from Spain's turbulent Middle Ages. Alberti's genius is such that the poems have no savor of pedantry or preciosity. Luis Monguió, in his introduction to Belitt's translations, suggests that "it is far from unlikely that they are being sung in the provinces today by many in complete ignorance of their debt to Rafael Alberti." The notion is a tribute both to the poet and to the tradition he understood so well.

The verses themselves may seem enigmatic, but only because the modern reader is accustomed to probe so far beneath the surface. One of the best of them, "Gimiendo" ("Groaning"), presents the plaint of a sailor who remembers that his shirt used to puff up in the wind whenever he saw the shore. The entire poem consists of only six brief lines; there is only one image, and only one point. That single image conveys a feeling close to the hearts of those born within smell of the sea—a need unfulfilled for Alberti. He speaks for all seamen who are marooned inland, the sailors on land.

"Pradoluengo," an aubade in the same style, is only seven lines long and conveys an equally simple message. The beloved to whom the poem is addressed is told that the cocks are crowing, that "we need cross only river waters, not the sea," and is urged to get up and come along. With all the richness of the genre, Alberti hints at a wealth of erotic possibilities and natural splendors. Only William Butler Yeats, in modern English poetry, matches this exquisite simplicity and feeling for tradition.

CAL Y CANTO

As noted above, Alberti took a leading role in the Góngora tricentennial of 1927, and many of the poems in *Cal y canto* owe much to the Baroque model. Here, Alberti reveals a new facet of his technical mastery, particularly in his handling of the sonnet, perhaps the most difficult of forms. "Amaranta," a sonnet that frequently appears in anthologies, shows how completely Alberti was able to assimilate the poetics of Góngora and to adapt them to the twentieth century. The octave describes, in ornate and lavish terms, the beauty of Amaranta; as with Góngora, the very exuberance of the description disquiets the reader. Her breasts, for example, are polished "as with the tongue of a greyhound." The sestet conceals the scorpion sting so often found in Góngora's conclusions: Solitude, personified, settles like a glowing coal between Amaranta and her lover. In this poem, Alberti displays his affinity with Góngora in two respects: an absolute control of his idiom and an obscurity that has deprived both poets of numerous readers. As Alberti himself remarked in his autobiography, "this was painterly poetry—plastic, linear, profiled, confined."

CONCERNING THE ANGELS

Concerning the Angels differs sharply from Alberti's previous work. Bouts of depression and a loss of faith in his former ideals drove him to abandon nostalgia and to confront despair. Suddenly, all the joy and tender sorrow of his early work is gone, replaced by anguish and self-pity. The revolution in content corresponds to a rebellion in form: Free verse prevails as more appropriate to the poet's state of mind than any traditional order. Alberti does not despair utterly, as Monguió indicates, but the overall tone of the collection is negative.

"Tres recuerdos del cielo" ("Three Memories of Heaven"), a tribute to the great Romantic poet Gustavo Adolfo Bécquer, constitutes a noteworthy exception to the depressing tone of the volume. Here, Alberti displays the subtlety and tenderness that characterize his work at its most appealing. Evoking a condition of being before time existed, Alberti recaptures the tenuous delicacy of Bécquer, the sense of the ineffable. The meeting between the lovers, for example, takes place in a world of clouds and moonlight: "When you, seeing me in nothingness/ Invented the first word." Alberti imitates Bécquer masterfully, at the same time finding a new way to express his own nostalgia.

"Three Memories of Heaven," however, is atypical of the collection. Virtually all the other poems treat of "angels" and ultimately of a world turned to wormwood and gall. "El ángel desengañado" ("The Angel Undeceived") debunks the ideals of the younger Alberti, particularly in its desolate conclusion: "I'm going to sleep./ No one is waiting for me." "El ángel de carbón" ("Angel of Coals") ends no less grimly: "And that octopus, love, in the shadow:/ evil, so evil." Several of the poems offer a kind of hope, but it is a wan hope, scarcely better than despair. Like the T. S. Eliot of "The Hollow Men," however, Alberti maintains his poetic control, even with the world withering away around him.

To See You and Not to See You

Two pivotal events in Alberti's life helped him out of this quagmire: meeting his future wife and becoming a communist. The political commitment, while it did little to benefit his poetry, provided him with a set of beliefs to fill the void within. Of his proletarian verse, one can say only that it is no worse than most political poetry. Like his friend and contemporary Pablo Neruda, Alberti mistook a sincere political commitment for an artistic imperative; like Neruda, he eventually returned to more personal themes, although he never wholly abandoned doctrinaire verse.

Even at the height of his political activism, however, Alberti was capable of devoting his gifts to the elegy; the death of Ignacio Sánchez Mejías in the bullring moved him to write the sonnet series that makes up *To See You and Not to See You* in 1935. The same tragedy also inspired Federico García Lorca to compose one of the most famous poems in the Spanish language, "Llanto por Ignacio Sánchez Mejías" ("Lament for Ignacio Sánchez Mejías"). A comparison of the two poems reveals the radical differences between these two superfi-

cially similar poets. García Lorca chants compellingly, "At five in the afternoon," evoking the drama of the moment and the awful immediacy of the bull. Alberti reflects on the bull's calfhood, its callow charges as it grew into the engine of destruction that destroyed Sánchez Mejías. García Lorca goes on to convey, in muted tones, his sense of loss. Alberti expresses that sense of loss in terms of distance: As his friend dies in the bullring, Alberti is sailing toward Romania on the Black Sea. The memory of the journey becomes permanently associated with the loss of the friend and thus a redoubled source of nostalgia.

In García Lorca's shadow

As usual, García Lorca enjoys the fame, and Alberti is lost in his shadow. No doubt García Lorca's elegy speaks more clearly and more movingly; it probably *is* better than its counterpart. Alberti himself admired the "Lament for Ignacio Sánchez Mejías" without reservation. The pattern, however, is only too familiar: Alberti, so like García Lorca in some ways, found himself outmatched at every turn while his friend and rival was still alive. Alberti wrote exquisite medieval lyrics, but García Lorca outdid him with the *Romancero gitano* (1928; *The Gypsy Ballads*, 1953). Alberti captured the essence of Andalusia, but the public identified Andalusia with García Lorca. Alberti wrote a noble and moving elegy for Ignacio Sánchez Mejías, but his rival composed such a marvelous lament that Alberti's has been neglected.

All this is not to imply conscious enmity between the two poets. Alberti had cause to envy his contemporary's fame, and his bitterness at playing a secondary role may have been reflected in *Concerning the Angels.* Indeed, although Alberti gave many indications, in verse and prose, of his profound regard for García Lorca, his relationship with the poet of Granada represents an analogue to the dilemma of his literary life. The competition must have stimulated him, but, because his poetry was less accessible and less dramatic in its impact, he tended to be eclipsed. After the Spanish Civil War, Alberti emigrated to Argentina, mourning his slain and dispersed comrades, including García Lorca, who was senselessly gunned down at the outset of the hostilities. The war poems in the Alberti canon compare favorably with any on that subject, not least because his lively imagination enabled him to look beyond the slaughter.

ENTRE EL CLAVEL Y LA ESPADA

For all his faith, the poet soon found himself across the Atlantic, listening to reports of World War II, picking up the pieces. Somehow he managed to recover and to emerge greater than ever. A poem from his first collection published outside Spain, *Entre el clavel y la espada* (between sword and carnation), sounds the keynote of his renewed art:

> After this willful derangement, this harassed
> and necessitous grammar by whose haste I must live,
> let the virginal word come back to me whole and
>   meticulous,
> and the virginal verb, justly placed with its rigorous
>   adjective.

The poem, written in Spain, anticipates the purity of Alberti's poetry in exile. The poet forgot neither the horrors he had seen nor his love for his homeland.

Another elegy deserves mention in this context. Written after news of the death of the great poet Antonio Machado, "De los álamos y los sauces" (from poplar and willow) captures the plight of Alberti and his fellow exiles in but a few lines. The man in the poem is caught up "in the life of his distant dead and hears them in the air." Thus, Alberti returns grimly to his leitmotif, nostalgia.

RETORNOS DE LO VIVO LEJANO

With his return to his nostalgic leitmotif, Alberti reached his full potential as a poet during the 1940's and 1950's. He poured forth volume after volume of consistently high quality. *Retornos de lo vivo lejano* (returns of the far and the living), a book wholly devoted to his most serviceable theme, may well be the finest volume of his career. The poems are at once accessible and mysterious, full of meaning on the surface and suggestive of unfathomed depths.

"Retornos del amor en una noche de verano" ("Returns: A Summer Night's Love") recalls in wondrous imagery the breathlessness of a time long past. For example, two pairs of lips, as they press together, become a silent carnation. "Retornos de Chopin a través de unas manos ya idas" ("Returns: Chopin by Way of Hands Now Gone") evokes some of the poet's earliest memories of his family. After many years, the poet is reunited with his brothers by an act of imagination, supported by the memory of Frédéric Chopin's music as played by the poet's mother. This is the quintessential Alberti, the master craftsman and the longing man in one.

A LA PINTURA

Amid the melancholy splendor of his poems of exile, Alberti distilled a curious volume entitled *A la pintura* (to painting). In contrast to all that Alberti lost in exile, painting stands as a rediscovered treasure, and the Alberti of the early 1920's comes face to face with the middle-aged émigré. The collection includes sonnets on the tools of painting, both human and inanimate; free-verse meditations on the primary colors; and poems on various painters, each in a style reminiscent of the artist's own. Beyond its intrinsic value, the volume reveals much about the mutual attraction of the two arts.

"BALLAD OF THE LOST ANDALUSIAN"

A poem from *Ballads and Songs of the Parana*, deserves special mention. "Balada del Andaluz perdido" ("Ballad of the Lost Andalusian"), as much as any single poem, reflects Alberti's self-image as a poet in exile. Written in terse, unrhymed couplets, it tells of a wandering Andalusian who watches the olives grow "by the banks of a different river." Sitting alone, he provokes curious questions from the Argentine onlookers on the opposite bank of the river, but he remains a mystery to them. Not so to the reader, who understands the pathos of the riderless horses, the memory of hatred, the loneliness. The final question admits of no answer and in fact needs none: "What will he do there, what is left to be done/ on the opposite side of the river, alone?"

OTHER MAJOR WORKS

PLAYS: *El hombre deshabitado*, pb. 1930; *El trébol floride*, pb. 1940; *El adefesio*, pb. 1944; *El cerco de Numancia*, pr. 1944 (adaptation of Miguel de Cervantes).

NONFICTION: *La arboleda perdida*, 1942 (*The Lost Grove*, 1976).

BIBLIOGRAPHY

Gagen, Derek. "Marinero en tierra: Alberti's first 'Libro organico de poemas'?" *Modern Language Review* 88, no. 1 (January, 1993): 91. Alberti's "Marinero en tierra" is examined in depth.

Havard, Robert. *The Crucified Mind: Rafael Alberti and the Surrealist Ethos in Spain*. London: Tamesis Books, 2001. A biographical and historical study of the life and works of Alberti.

Jiménez-Fajardo, Salvador. *Multiple Spaces: The Poetry of Rafael Alberti*. London: Tamesis Books, 1985. A critical analysis of Alberti's poetic works. Includes bibliographic references.

Manteiga, Robert C. *Poetry of Rafael Alberti: A Visual Approach*. London: Tamesis Books, 1978. A study of Alberti's literary style. Text is in English with poems in original Spanish. Includes bibliographic references.

Nantell, Judith. *Rafael Alberti's Poetry of the Thirties*. Athens: The University of Georgia Press, 1986. This study puts Alberti's work in historical and social context by analyzing the influences from a turbulent decade in which civil war erupts, ignites a European conflagration, and ends in societal crises. She discusses political poems that are not as memorable as his earlier works but deserve recognition for their artistic as well as social value.

Ugarte, Michael. *Shifting Ground: Spanish Civil War Exile Literature*. Durham: Duke University Press, 1989. Examination of the importance of Spanish exile literature during and after the civil war. The second section of the book explores the intellectual diaspora of the civil war, and an analysis of Alberti's *La arboleda perdida* is featured prominently.

Philip Krummrich; bibliography updated by Carole A. Champagne and Sarah Hilbert

---

RICHARD ALDINGTON

Born: Portsmouth, England; July 8, 1892
Died: Sury-en-Vaux, France; July 27, 1962

PRINCIPAL POETRY

Images (1910-1915), 1915, enlarged 1919
The Love of Myrrhine and Konalis, and Other Prose Poems, 1917
Reverie: A Little Book of Poems for H. D., 1917
Images of War: A Book of Poems, 1919
Images of Desire, 1919
War and Love, 1915-1918, 1919
The Berkshire Kennet, 1923
Collected Poems: 1915-1923, 1923
Exile and Other Poems, 1923
A Fool i' the Forest: A Phantasmagoria, 1924
Hark the Herald, 1928
The Eaten Heart, 1929
Collected Poems, 1929
A Dream in the Luxembourg, 1930
The Poems of Richard Aldington, 1934
Life Quest, 1935
The Crystal World, 1937
The Complete Poems of Richard Aldington, 1948

OTHER LITERARY FORMS

Richard Aldington established himself in the literary world of London as a youthful poet, but later in life he increasingly devoted his attention to prose fiction, translation, biography, and criticism. His first novel, *Death of a Hero* (1929), drew favorable attention, and it was followed in 1930 by *Roads to Glory*, a collection of thirteen short stories. Aldington continued to publish fiction until 1946, when his last novel, *The Romance of Casanova*, appeared.

From early in his career, Aldington was highly regarded as a translator. He translated from French *Remy de Gourmont: Selections from All His Works* (1929; 2 volumes), from Italian *The Decameron of Giovanni Boccaccio* (1930), from Classical Greek *Alcestis* (1930), and from Latin and Provençal.

Aldington wrote biographies of the Duke of Wellington (1943) and of Robert Louis Stevenson (1957), along with *Voltaire* (1925), *D. H. Lawrence: Portrait of a Genius But . . .* (1950), and *Lawrence of Arabia: A Biographical Enquiry* (1955), along with a substantial body of critical essays.

Other miscellaneous works include *Life for Life's Sake: A Book of Reminiscences* (1941) and *Pinorman: Personal Recollections of Norman Douglas, Pino Orioli, and Charles Prentice* (1954). Aldington also edited *The Viking Book of Poetry of the English-Speaking World* (1941).

ACHIEVEMENTS

Despite Aldington's extensive publications in criticism and in a variety of literary genres, he remains inextricably associated with the movement known as Imagism, of which he was certainly a founding member, along with the American poets H. D. (Hilda Doolittle) and Ezra Pound.

Although only twenty at the time Imagism was conceived (1912), Aldington found himself part of a mini-revolution against wordiness and imprecision in poetry, a revolution formulated in terms of advocacy of effective images and cogent free verse.

Aldington's later poems, though eliciting occasional praise from distinguished critics, actually did little to enhance the reputation he had earned as an Imagist. In 1947, Aldington was awarded the James Tait Black Memorial Prize for his biography of Wellington, and shortly before his death he was invited to Moscow, where his achievements were celebrated by the Soviet Writers' Union.

BIOGRAPHY

Edward Godfree Aldington, later known as Richard Aldington, was born on July 8, 1892, in Portsmouth, England, but spent most of his youth in Dover before enrolling at University College in London in 1910. A year later, his family having suffered from a financial reverse, Aldington left the college and went to work for a newspaper. He had already developed a keen interest in poetry and soon met others who shared his enthusiasm, including the Americans H. D. and Ezra Pound. Pound urged that the three promulgate their poetic affinities for precision, economy of language, striking images, and free verse, and Aldington and H. D. agreed, thus creating the literary movement known as Imagism.

Pound encouraged Harriet Monroe, editor of *Poetry*, a new literary magazine, to publish Imagist verse, and, in 1912, three poems by Aldington appeared, earning their author forty dollars and publicly establishing the twenty-year-old poet as a representative of the new movement. In London, Aldington met William Butler Yeats and other luminaries. He visited Paris and Italy and, in 1914, having married H. D. in the previous year, became assistant editor of a journal named *The Egoist*,

Richard Aldington (Library of Congress)

which developed into a significant outlet for Imagist productions. In the same year, ten of Aldington's poems were published in *Des Imagistes*, an anthology edited by Pound which also included poems by H. D., James Joyce, Ford Madox Ford, Amy Lowell, and William Carlos Williams, among others.

Aldington's first collection of his own work was *Images (1910-1915)*, which came out in 1915, by which time he had also embarked upon his long career of literary translation, publishing *The Poems of Anyte of Tegea* and *Latin Poems of the Renaissance* that year. In 1916, he volunteered for military service and saw action on the front until the end of the war. He was eventually discharged from service with the rank of captain. His experiences of the horrors of combat sent him back to England a changed man, and his marriage to H. D.—which had already suffered from their prolonged separation—proved unable to survive the challenge of their collective trauma. Though not officially divorced until 1938, Aldington and H. D. actually ended their marriage shortly after World War I.

Returning to London's literary life, Aldington resumed his career as poet and critic, accepting a position writing for the *Times Literary Supplement* and continuing to publish poems, translations, and criticism. He eventually decided, however, to move to the country, where he hoped to be able to work without distraction. This move was successful, and Aldington read, wrote, and translated diligently in his rural environment for several years, visiting Italy in 1922 and in 1926. In 1924, he published his first long poem, *A Fool i'the Forest: A Phantasmagoria*, which may be retrospectively regarded as a final departure from the Imagist lyrics of his youth. By 1927, Aldington was spending time in Paris, where he met Ernest Hemingway and Hart Crane, and, in 1928, he decided to leave England for good.

In 1929, Aldington published the novel *Death of a Hero*, which was based on his own experiences during World War I. This year also saw the appearance of another long poem, *The Eaten Heart*. Aldington remained in Italy and France during most of the next several years, with trips to Africa, Spain, and Portugal, and, as always, he worked steadily wherever he was. By the time European totalitarianism drove him from the Continent in 1935, Aldington had three more novels, another long poem, and a book of short stories in print, along with more translations.

With Benito Mussolini dominating Italy, Francisco Franco holding sway in Spain, and Adolf Hitler ruling Germany, Aldington, whose attitude toward Britain had not changed since 1928, looked westward. He crossed the Atlantic in 1935 and lived for several months in Tobago before moving to the United States, where he eventually took up residence in Connecticut. He had published *Life Quest*, a long poem, in 1935, and in 1937 he published a novel titled *Very Heaven* and his last long poem, *The Crystal World*.

Despite his initial enthusiasm for the United States, Aldington gradually became disenchanted with American life. In 1943 he published *The Duke, Being an Account of the Life and Achievements of Arthur Wellesley, 1st Duke of Wellington*, the Wellington biography which would later win Aldington the James Tait Black Memorial Prize. In 1944, he spent some time as a Hollywood

film writer, but, shortly after the war, he returned to France. In 1946, *The Romance of Casanova*, a novel, marked the end of Aldington's publication of fiction. From this point onward, though he remained industrious, his output was restricted to criticism and biography.

Aldington had been a personal friend of D. H. Lawrence and had always admired Lawrence's work, and in 1950 he issued *D. H. Lawrence, Portrait of a Genius But . . .* , a work which was followed by two publications which would damage Aldington's reputation and income for the rest of his life. *Pinorman: Personal Recollections of Norman Douglas, Pino Orioli, and Charles Prentice*, a memoir focused upon Aldington's old acquaintance Norman Douglas, aroused resentment among Douglas's friends and adherents, who regarded it as a betrayal on Aldington's part. Still more controversial was *Lawrence of Arabia: A Biographical Inquiry* (1955), which attacked the putative heroism, modesty, and truthfulness of a revered hero of World War I. Lawrence's admirers exerted some remarkable efforts to prevent the publication of this book, and, when it at length appeared, many of them engaged in vehement personal attacks on Aldington. These attacks caused a serious reduction in Aldington's royalties, as booksellers and publishers refused to handle his works, and he remained on the defensive and in financial difficulties for the rest of his life.

Aldington went on to publish *Introduction to Mistral* (1956), *Frauds* (1957), and *Portrait of a Rebel: The Life and Work of Robert Louis Stevenson* (1957). In 1962, he went to the Soviet Union at the invitation of the Soviet Writers' Union and was honored there for his contributions to literature. He died on July 27, 1962, near Sury-en-Vaux, France.

ANALYSIS

Richard Aldington's reputation as poet has been unduly shaped by the circumstances under which he published his early works. As one of the three original Imagists (along with Ezra Pound and H. D.), he at twenty (in 1912) was several years younger than his literary partners. Pound, already rather famous and something of a swashbuckler, aggressively cultivated the reputation of a trendsetter, and H. D.'s lyric gifts must have been enhanced in Aldington's eyes by her beauty. Pound and

H. D. had already been friends for years, so the young Aldington must have felt privileged to have been admitted to their circle and to have his work appreciated by them.

IMAGISM

It is clear that the famous principles of Imagism—directness, economy, and musical phrasing—are as frequently absent from Imagist poetry as they are present, and one must suspect the dogmatic hand of Pound in their formulation. Aldington's very early "Choricos" already suggests divergence from the movement's program:

> Brushing the fields with red-shod feet,
> With purple robe
> Searing the grass as with a sudden flame,
> Death,
> Thou hast come upon us.

Here there are colors ("red," "purple"), powerful verbs ("Brushing," "Searing"), alliteration, and assonance, but there is conspicuously no concrete image, and the absence of such an image works effectively to represent the mystery of death, whose certainty is more evident in inevitability than in visibility. Yet some conscious efforts were made by Aldington to focus on clear, arresting images. In "Round-Pond," he wrote:

> Water ruffled and speckled by galloping wind
> Which puffs and spurts it into tiny pashing breakers
> Dashed with lemon-yellow afternoon sunlight.
> The shining of the sun upon the water
> Is like a scattering of gold crocus petals
> In a long wavering irregular flight.

As pleasant and as exuberant as these lines are, they prepare no modernist jolt, for some lines later the poem concludes, "Even the cold wind is seeking a new mistress." This conclusion deflates the gentle pretensions of the preceding lines and seemingly defies the rigid seriousness of the announced program of Imagism.

Although Aldington's youthful work betrays influences that do not appear to have been fully integrated in his vision, his erudition and his sensitive ear for the music of language often helped him create his own voice. The Imagists' passion for classical poetry, tempered as it was by their experiments with English versions of Japanese poetry, combined in Aldington's case with his read-

ing of Walt Whitman and Algernon Charles Swinburne to produce insights that were first to be subjected to the psychological stress of front-line combat and later to the implications of Aldington's long recuperation from his wartime experiences. In 1915, Aldington was able to express emotional simplicity with his understated lines from "Epigrams": "She has new leaves/ After her dead flowers,/ Like the little almond tree/ Which the frost hurt." Yet, in the same collection, his rage about the pain of his childhood is elaborated at Whitmanesque length in a performance in which outrage consistently outdistances art:

> The bitterness, the misery, the wretchedness of childhood
> Put me out of love with God,
> I can't believe in God's goodness;
> I can believe
> In many avenging gods.

Though the doors to poetic recognition had been opened by his own talent as well as by the encouragement of his friends, Aldington was still developing a personal technique when the war came. World War I was a devastating experience for him, however, both as poet and as man. He wrote poems during and after the war in which some of his Imagist techniques are manifest, but it is in his collection *Exile and Other Poems* (1923) that the effects of the trauma of war are revealed. Recalling his grim life in combat in the poem "Eumenides," Aldington mused about

> That boot I kicked
> (It had a mouldy foot in it)
> The night K's head was smashed
> Like a rotten pear by a mortar.

The title of the poem, of course, refers to the monstrous Furies of Greek mythology, and Aldington was not to conquer his personal Furies until, at the end of the decade, he put his war experiences into prose with *Death of a Hero* and *Roads to Glory*, a sequence of short stories. *Exile and Other Poems*, in fact, marks the end of Aldington's effort to express himself artistically in short poems.

THE LONG POEMS

Aldington's first long poem, *A Fool i'the Forest*, was published in 1924. Subtitled *A Phantasmagoria*, the work combines a variety of poetic forms with narrative free verse to represent the psychomachia of the modern individual in crisis, evoking echoes of the past (William Shakespeare) and responding to contemporary poetry, notably that of T. S. Eliot. The shifting setting of the poem takes its protagonist from Greece to the trenches of France and finally back to London, where, his hopes defeated, he subsides into a conventional existence.

A Dream in the Luxembourg was written in 1928 but not immediately published. It was inspired by a love affair commenced at the time by Aldington, though it is notably devoid of the techniques generally considered poetic. Aldington published another of his long poems, *The Eaten Heart*, in 1929, and this poem also shows its author's rejection of conventional poetics. It focuses, as had *A Fool i'the Forest*, upon the fragmentation of modern existence, the dehumanization resulting from the rise of technology, and human isolation.

Life Quest, like Joyce's *Ulysses* (1922), evokes Homer's *Odyssey* (c. 800 B.C.E.; English translation, 1616), but the journey here also partakes of the religious qualities of the medieval quest. Aldington's hero makes his way at the end of the poem to Gibraltar, perhaps suggesting the poet's own decision to go to America.

Aldington's last long poem and last published poem, *The Crystal World*, appeared in 1937. Divided into two main sections, each with subsections, this poem marks both a return to lyricism and Aldington's own farewell to the composition of poetry. The poem explores the mystery and the promise of love, its frustrations and consummations. Aldington, now a middle-aged man and a veteran of more than war, ended his poetic career writing of love.

OTHER MAJOR WORKS

LONG FICTION: *Death of a Hero*, 1929; *The Colonel's Daughter*, 1931; *All Men Are Enemies*, 1933; *Women Must Work*, 1934; *Very Heaven*, 1937; *Seven Against Reeves*, 1938; *Rejected Guest*, 1939; *The Romance of Casanova*, 1946.

SHORT FICTION: *Roads to Glory*; 1930; *Soft Answers*, 1932.

PLAY: *Life of a Lady*, pb. 1936 (with Derek Patmore).

NONFICTION: *Voltaire*, 1925; *D. H. Lawrence: An Indiscretion*, 1927; *Remy de Gourmont: A Modern Man of Letters*, 1928; *Artifex: Sketches and Ideas*, 1935; *Life for Life's Sake:A Book of Reminiscences*, 1941; *The Duke, Being an Account of the Life and Achievements of Arthur Wellesley, 1st Duke of Wellington*, 1943; *Jane Austen*, 1948; *Four English Portraits, 1801-1851*, 1948; *D. H. Lawrence: Portrait of a Genius But . . .* , 1950; *Pinorman: Personal Recollections of Norman Douglas, Pino Orioli, and Charles Prentice*, 1954; *Lawrence of Arabia: A Biographical Inquiry*, 1955; *Introduction to Mistral*, 1956; *Frauds*, 1957; *Portrait of a Rebel: The Life and Work of Robert Louis Stevenson*, 1957.

TRANSLATIONS: *The Poems of Anyte of Tegea*, 1915; *Latin Poems of the Renaissance*, 1915; *Voyages to the Moon and the Sun*, 1923 (of Cyrano de Bergerac); *Dangerous Acquaintances*, 1924 (of Pierre Choderlos de Laclos's novel *Les Liaisons dangereuses*); *Candide and Other Romances*, 1927 (of Voltaire); *Fifty Romance Lyric Poems*, 1928; *Remy de Gourmont, Selections from All His Works*, 1929; *Alcestis*, 1930 (of Euripides); *The Decameron of Giovanni Boccaccio*, 1930.

EDITED TEXT: *The Viking Book of Poetry of the English-Speaking World*, 1941.

BIBLIOGRAPHY

Crawford, Fred D. *Richard Aldington and Lawrence of Arabia: A Cautionary Tale*. Carbondale: Southern Illinois University Press, 1998. A detailed description of the controversy arising from Richard Aldington's biography of T. E. Lawrence. The frequent quotations from Aldington provide an excellent portrait of his character in middle age, and other material gives insights into his life as poet.

Doyle, Charles, ed. *Richard Aldington: Reappraisals*. ELS Monograph Series 49. Victoria, B.C.: University of Victoria, 1990. A collection of essays that reconsider Aldington's reputation as poet, novelist, and writer of nonfiction. The assumption behind this collection is that Aldington was unjustly blacklisted as a result of his frank treatment of T. E. Lawrence.

Gates, Norman T., ed. *Richard Aldington: An Autobiography in Letters*. University Park: Pennsylvania

State University Press, 1992. An effort to display Aldington's temperament and experiences by means of selections from his correspondence.

Kershaw, Alister, and Frédéric-Jacques Temple, eds. *Richard Aldington: An Intimate Portrait*. Carbondale: Southern Illinois University Press, 1965. An anthology of favorable comments on Aldington from various distinguished persons, including T. S. Eliot, Lawrence Durrell, Sir Herbert Read, and C. P. Snow. Also contains an excellent bibliography of Aldington's writings.

Smith, Richard Eugene. *Richard Aldington*. Boston: G. K. Hall, 1977. A useful Twayne text with a chronology, comments on all Aldington's major works, and an annotated bibliography of secondary sources (most before 1977).

Robert W. Haynes

CLARIBEL ALEGRÍA

Born: Estelí, Nicaragua; May 12, 1924

PRINCIPAL POETRY

Anillo de silencio, 1948
Suite de amor, angustia y soledad, 1951
Vigilias, 1953
Acuario, 1955
Huésped de mi tiempo, 1961
Vía única, 1965
Aprendizaje, 1970
Pagaré a cobrar y otros poemas, 1973
Sobrevivo, 1978
Suma y sigue, 1981
Flores del volcán/Flowers from the Volcano, 1982 (parallel text in English and Spanish, trans. by Carolyn Forché)
Luisa en el país de la realidad, 1987 (*Luisa in Realityland*, 1987)
La mujer del rio Sumpul, 1987 (*Woman of the River*, 1989)
Y este poema-río, 1988
Fugues, 1993 (parallel text in English and Spanish, trans. by Darwin Flakoll)

Variaciones en clave de mí, 1993
Umbrales, 1996 (*Umbrales = Thresholds*, 1996; parallel text in English and Spanish, trans. by Flakoll)
Saudade, 1999 (*Saudade = Sorrow*, 1999; parallel text in English and Spanish, trans. by Forché)

OTHER LITERARY FORMS

Though primarily known as a poet, the prolific Claribel Alegría has published in a range of genres, sometimes in collaboration with her husband and principal translator, Darwin J. Flakoll. Alegría and Flakoll collaborated on the novel *Cenizas de Izalco* (1966; *Ashes of Izalco*, 1989), on a translation of the poems of Robert Graves (1981), on the anthology *New Voices of Hispanic America* (1962), and on the testimonials *Nicaragua: La revolución sandinista, una crónica política, 1855-1979* (1982; Nicaragua: the Sandinista revolution, a political chronicle, 1855-1979), *Para romper el silencio: Resistencia y lucha en las cárceles salvadoreñas* (1984; to break the silence: resistance and struggle in Salvadoran prisons), and *Fuga de Canto Grande* (1992; *Tunnel to Canto Grande*, 1996). Alegría has also published her own novellas, three of which are collected in *Album familiar* (1982, expanded edition 1986; *Family Album: Three Novellas*, 1991), as well as essays and children's literature. She has also edited poetry collections.

ACHIEVEMENTS

Claribel Alegría's novel of the 1932 massacre known as the Matanza, *Ashes of Izalco*, was a finalist in 1964 in the Biblioteca Breve contest, sponsored by the Spanish publishing house Seix Barral. In 1978 she won the prestigious Casa de las Américas Prize for her volume of poetry *Sobrevivo*. Perhaps most important, Alegría brought Central American literature, especially women's writing, to the attention of the American reader, and with it she brought a concern for the political situation in El Salvador and Nicaragua in particular. Her works have been translated into more than ten languages.

BIOGRAPHY

Claribel Alegría was born in Estelí, Nicaragua, to a Salvadoran mother and a Nicaraguan father, but her family soon moved to Santa Ana, El Salvador, because of the political problems her father suffered as a Sandino sympathizer. In 1932 she witnessed the Matanza, or massacre, of more than thirty thousand peasants slaughtered by government troops after a peaceful protest against the military dictatorship.

She published her first poems in 1941. In 1943 she went to the United States to attend a girls' school near New Orleans, Louisiana. She next attended George Washington University, where she met her husband, Darwin (Bud) J. Flakoll, a journalist who was studying for his master of arts degree. They married in December, 1947. In 1948, she was graduated and her first book of poetry, *Anillo de silencio*, was published in Mexico. Her first daughter, Maya, was born in Washington in 1949, followed by the birth of her twin daughters, Patricia and Karen, in Alexandria, Virginia, in 1950. In 1951, the family visited El Salvador briefly before moving to Mexico, where their circle included various writers and intellectuals, some living in exile like Alegría.

In 1953, the family moved to Santiago, Chile, where they lived for almost three years in order to work on an anthology (and translation) of Latin American writers

Claribel Alegría (© Miriam Berkley)

and poets, *New Voices of Hispanic America*, which introduced writers like Juan Rulfo and Julio Cortázar, who would later be part of the "boom" in Latin American literature. Her son Erik was born in Santiago in 1954. In 1956 the family returned to the United States, where Flakoll applied to the Foreign Service. In 1958 he was appointed second secretary to the U.S. Embassy in Montevideo, Uruguay. Two years later they were posted to Argentina. Disillusioned by the world of politics, her husband resigned from the foreign service, and in 1962 they moved to Paris, where they met many Latin American writers living in exile and worked on the first of many subsequent collaborations, producing her first novel, *Ashes of Izalco*, whose publication in Spain was delayed by censorship. In 1966, the family moved to Mallorca, where they lived for many years. In 1979, after the Sandinistas overthrew the dictatorship of Anastasio Somosa in Nicaragua, Alegría and her husband went to Nicaragua to do research for a testimonial on the revolution. In 1980, Archbishop Oscar Romero was assassinated in El Salvador. Alegría gave a poetic eulogy at the Sorbonne in Paris, and her criticism of government atrocities made her a political exile from her homeland. In 1983, they moved to Nicaragua. Flakoll died in 1995. Alegría continued to live in Nicaragua.

ANALYSIS

Claribel Alegría has often spoken in interviews of the writer's role as the voice of the voiceless, of poetry as a weapon against repression and oppression, against exploitation and injustice. She considers herself a feminist, which she defines as wanting equality for women and men, and both writes about women and promotes the work of women writers. Her poetry reflects her experience of exile, loss, and absence, often with a sense of nostalgia, or longing for a happier, more innocent past. Much of her work is at least partially autobiographical, and memory serves as a powerful means of preserving the past.

FLORES DEL VOLCÁN/FLOWERS FROM THE VOLCANO

This bilingual edition of Alegría's work was the first translation of one of her works into English. It is thanks to the efforts of the translator, prizewinning poet Carolyn Forché, that Alegría first came to the attention of the

American reader. Many of the poems chosen for this collection come from the 1978 collection *Sobrevivo*.

The title of the work is an indication of its contents: The volcano represents Central America as a region and El Salvador as a country, as part of the "ring of fire" of volcanoes that form a natural part of the geography, but the volcano also represents the eruption, violence, and death caused by the civil wars of the 1970's and 1980's in Nicaragua, Guatemala, and El Salvador, while flowers suggest beauty, hope, and life.

Alegría critiques the class structure in El Salvador in the title poem "Flowers from the Volcano," in which "the volcano's children/ flow down like lava/ with their bouquets of flowers," threatening the status quo of the well-to-do, "the owners of two-story houses/ protected from thieves by walls," who "drown their fears in whiskey." She remembers the dead in "Sorrow," with its "rosary of names," including Roque Dalton, the Salvadoran poet killed by government forces in 1975, and the Chilean folksinger Victor Jara, killed by security forces in the stadium of Santiago in 1973, along with many other Chileans.

Flowers from the Volcano contains some poems of nostalgic recollection of life in Santa Ana in simpler times, but the collection principally engages notions of class struggle and the brutal repression of liberty and life. As Forché notes in the volume's preface, five years passed between the summer that she and Alegría worked on the book and its publication, and in those five years "more than 40,000 people . . . died in El Salvador at the hands of security forces."

LUISA IN REALITYLAND

It is no wonder, then, Alegría commented in the poem "Personal Creed," from *Luisa in Realityland:*

> I don't know if I believe
> in the forgiveness
> of the Squadrons of Death
> but I do believe
> in the resurrection of the oppressed. . . .

Sometimes called a novel, or a "mixed-genre" work, *Luisa in Realityland* combines brief autobiographical anecdotes and vignettes with poetry to tell the story of a childhood and adolescence much like Alegría's in a country much like El Salvador. (The poems from this volume also form one section of the anthology *Y este poema-río.*)

For Luisa, like Alegría, the ceiba tree of her homeland is nearly mystical with meaning, "the sentinel/ of [her] childhood." Always present are the themes of exile and loss, as in "The Ceiba": "My absences/ have been lengthy/ innumerable. . . ./ They won't let me return." Alegría's politics are clear in these poems. In "Personal Creed" she states:

> I believe in my people
> who have been exploited
> for five hundred years

In "From the Bridge," the adult Luisa/Alegría looks back in time on the little girl and adolescent she once was, but now through the eyes of experience:

> Do you remember the massacre
> that left Izalco without menfolk?
> You were seven years old.
> How can I explain it to you
> nothing has changed
> and they keep killing people daily.

Despite the violence and pessimism of many of the poems, however, the book ends with an invitation to a "rebellious/ contagious peace," a "return to the future."

WOMAN OF THE RIVER

Many of the poems in *Woman of the River* directly confront the political situation of Central America and often condemn the influence of the United States and the U.S. presence there. In "The American Way of Death" Alegría criticizes America's response to people's desire for a better life:

> if you choose the guerrilla path,
> be careful,
> they'll kill you.
>
> If you combat your chaos
> through peace,
>
> .   .   .   .   .   .
> they'll kill you.
>
> If your skin is dark
>
> .   .   .   .   .   .
> slowly they'll kill you.

"The American Way of Life" contrasts skyscrapers with undocumented workers, wealth with wanton destruction, one dependent on the other. America, says Alegría, is a selfish "bitch" who "chews Salvadorans/ as if they were Chiclets/ chews up Nicaraguans." Perhaps here she refers to the massive U.S. funding of the war in El Salvador or the training of Salvadoran and Nicaraguan soldiers by the U.S. military.

The title poem "Woman of the River" testifies to the results of U.S. support of the war, telling the tale of a woman who survives the 1980 Sumpul River massacre with her baby and youngest son by hiding in the river for hours after the security troops have killed everyone in their path, including her other three children.

FUGUES

With the wars over in Central America, Alegría's later work became less political. In *Fugues*, the main themes are love, death, and aging. In "Mirror Image," for example, the poet considers the aging process, speaking to an alien, skull-like image superimposed on her own as it stares at her from the mirror:

> Why do you insist
> on showing me day after day
> these sockets
> that used to be my eyes?
>
> . . . .
>
> I traverse your skin
> to embrace the little girl
> who still resides in me

Fugues also contains a fascinating series of poems relating female mythological or historical figures to contemporary psychology. In "Letter to an Exile" the legendary Penelope (from Homer's epic ninth century B.C.E. poem the *Odyssey*) writes to her husband Odysseus, asking him please not to return home. Each of the Greek mythical figures Persephone, Demeter, Pandora, and Hecate has her own poem, as does Malinche, an Aztec interpreter and lover of the Spanish conqueror Hernán Cortés and the mother of the first Mexican. Each of the poems presents an interpretation from the woman's perspective rather than the usual interpretation *of* a woman by a man.

SORROW

Originally titled *Saudade*, this 1999 collection was written as a series of love poems to Alegría's dead husband. As her translator Carolyn Forché comments, *saudade* is "a Portuguese word for a vague and persistent desire for something that cannot be, a time other than the present time, a turning toward the past or future, a sadness and yearning beyond sorrow." *Saudade* means much more than the title *Sorrow* can express. The "Nostalgia" of *Fugues*, in which she leaves of being herself and begins forever "being us," becomes "Nostalgia II" in *Sorrow*, in which she ceases "being us" and again becomes "this I/ with its burden of winter/ and emptiness."

Yet the collection ends optimistically when the poet states that "sadness can't cope" with her. Although *Sorrow* does not have the political tone or content common to her earlier works, Alegría has not forgotten her rosary of names to remember the dead. As she says in "Every Time," the dead are resurrected when she names them. Just as she used her art as a weapon for the cause of justice and named the dead to keep them alive to memory, she now uses her art to keep her "deceased beloved" present.

OTHER MAJOR WORKS

LONG FICTION: *Cenizas de Izalco*, 1966 (with Darwin J. Flakoll; *Ashes of Izalco*, 1989); *El detén*, 1977; *Pueblo de Dios y de mandinga*, 1985; *Despierta mi bien, despierta*, 1986.

SHORT FICTION: *Album familiar*, 1982, expanded edition 1986 (*Family Album: Three Novellas*, 1991).

NONFICTION: *Nicaragua: La revolución sandinista, una crónica política, 1855-1979*, 1982 (with Darwin J. Flakoll); *No me agarran viva: La mujer salvadoreña en lucha*, 1983 (with Flakoll; *They Won't Take Me Alive: Salvadoran Women in Struggle for National Liberation*, 1987); *Para romper el silencio: Resistencia y lucha en las cárceles salvadoreñas*, 1984 (with Flakoll; *Fuga de Canto Grande*, 1992 (with Flakoll; *Tunnel to Canto Grande*, 1996); *Somoza: Expediente cerrado, la historia de un ajusticiamiento*, 1993 (with Flakoll; *Death of Somoza: The First Person Story of the Guerrillas Who Assassinated the Nicaraguan Dictator*, 1996).

TRANSLATION: *Cien poemas de Robert Graves*, 1981 (with Darwin J. Flakoll).

CHILDREN'S LITERATURE: *Tres cuentos*, 1958.

EDITED TEXTS: *New Voices of Hispanic America*, 1962 (with Darwin J. Flakoll); *Homenaje a El Salvador*, 1981; *On the Front Line: Guerrilla Poetry of El Salvador*, 1988 (translated with Flakoll).

BIBLIOGRAPHY

Aparicio, Yvette. "Reading Social Consciousness in Claribel Alegría's Early Poetry." *Cincinnati Romance Review* 18 (1999): 1-6. Contends that Alegría's earlier, more metaphorical and less overtly "resistant" poetry contains implicit social criticism and deals with issues of injustice and power relations in a more allegorical manner than her later overtly politicized poetry.

Beverly, John, and Marc Zimmerman. *Literature and Politics in the Central American Revolutions*. Austin: University of Texas Press, 1990. Traces the development of popular revolutionary poetry and testimonial narrative as reactions to historical events in Nicaragua and El Salvador, and the importance of revolutionary Salvadoran women poets such as Alegría.

Boschetto-Sandoval, Sandra M., and Marcia Phillips McGowan. *Claribel Alegría and Central American Literature: Critical Essays*. Athens: Ohio University Center for European Studies, 1994. An excellent collection of essays on Alegría's major works and themes. One essay specifically treats her poetry. Includes an interview with the poet and a chronology of her life and works, along with a bibliography of her publications and publications about her work.

Craft, Linda J. *Novels of Testimony and Resistance from Central America*. Gainesville: University of Florida Press, 1997. The chapter on Alegría examines two works written in collaboration with her husband, Darwin J. Flakoll, *Ashes of Izalco* and *They Won't Take Me Alive*, and the multigenre *Luisa in Realityland*.

McGowan, Marcia P. "Mapping a New Territory: *Luisa in Realityland*." *Letras Femeninas* 19, nos. 1/2 (Spring/Fall, 1993): 84-99. Considers *Luisa* a "new form of autobiographical discourse" that incorporates poetry, testimony, and elements of fiction.

Pearson, Carol E. *Gender, Genre, and Resistance in the Works of Lucha Corpi, Angela Mastretta, and Claribel Alegría*. Albuquerque: University of New Mexico, 1998. A readily available dissertation that examines the testimonial voice of Alegría's fiction (*Ashes of Izalco*), her nonfiction (*They Won't Take Me Alive*), and several volumes of poetry, including *Huésped de mi tiempo*, *Sobrevivo*, and *Y este poema-río*.

Sternbach, Nancy Saporta. "Remembering the Dead: Latin American Women's 'Testimonial' Discourse." *Latin American Perspectives* 18, no. 3 (Summer, 1991): 91-102. Examines the testimonial voice of prose and poetry in *They Won't Take Me Alive* and *Flores del Volcán/Flowers from the Volcano*.

Treacy, Mary Jane. "A Politics of the Word: Claribel Alegría's *Album familiar* and *Despierta mi bien, despierta*." *Intertexts* 1, no. 1 (Spring, 1997): 62-77. Discusses the "elite" or "bourgeois" woman as a marginalized "woman of porcelain," aware of her privileged status but not its political and economic underpinnings. In contrast to the passive bourgeois woman depicted in many of the female characters in novels by Isabel Allende, Rosario Ferré, and Teresa de la Parra, the two works by Alegría examined here portray "the struggles of the bourgeois woman to extricate herself from domesticity and to forge an independence through a 'progressive' political identity."

Linda Ledford-Miller

VICENTE ALEIXANDRE

Born: Seville, Spain; April 26, 1898
Died: Madrid, Spain; December 14, 1984

PRINCIPAL POETRY
Ámbito, 1928
Espadas como labios, 1932
La destrucción o el amor, 1935 (*Destruction or Love: A Selection*, 1976)
Pasión de la tierra, 1935, rev. ed. 1946
Sombra del paraíso, 1944 (*Shadow of Paradise*, 1987)
Mundo a solas, 1950 (*World Alone*, 1982)

Nacimiento último, 1953

Historia del corazón, 1954

Mis poemas mejores, 1956

Poesías completas, 1960

Picasso, 1961

En un vasto dominio, 1962

Retratos con nombre, 1965

Presencias, 1965

Poemas de la consumación, 1968

Sonido de la guerra, 1972

Diálogos del conocimiento, 1974

Poems, 1969

The Caves of Night: Poems, 1976

Twenty Poems, 1977

A Longing for Light: Selected Poems of Vicente Aleixandre, 1979

A Bird of Paper: Poems of Vicente Aleixandre, 1981

OTHER LITERARY FORMS

Vicente Aleixandre published a great number of prologues, critical letters, memoirs, and evocations of friends and literary figures, many of them later included or rewritten for his major prose work, *Los encuentros* (1958; the encounters). Aleixandre also made several speeches on poetry and poets, later published in pamphlet or book form.

ACHIEVEMENTS

After receiving the Nobel Prize for Literature in 1977, Vicente Aleixandre stated that the prize was "a response symbolic of the relation of a poet with all other men." In Aleixandre's own estimation, winning the Nobel was his only worthy achievement. All other influences on the development of poetry were insignificant compared to the poet's call to speak for his fellow humans.

The extent of Aleixandre's influence is considerable, however, even if he denied its importance. He was a member of the Royal Spanish Academy (1949), the Hispanic Society of America, the Academy of the Latin World, Paris, the Royal Academy of Fine Arts of San Telmo, Málaga, the Spanish American Academy of Bogotá, the Academy of Arts and Sciences of Puerto Rico, and, as of 1972, an Honorary Fellow of the American Association of Spanish and Portuguese.

All of these honors recognize Aleixandre's lifelong devotion to the production of a unified body of poetry. A member of the celebrated *generación del 27*, including Jorge Guillén, Pedro Salinas, Federico García Lorca, Rafael Alberti, and Gerardo Diego, Aleixandre was one of the central figures of Spanish Surrealism. Although influenced by André Breton and his circle, the Spanish Surrealists developed to a great extent independently of their French counterparts. While French Surrealism is significant for its worldwide impact on the arts, it produced a surprisingly small amount of lasting poetry. In contrast, Spanish Surrealism—both in Spain and, with notable local variations, in Latin America—constitutes one of the richest poetic traditions of the twentieth century, a tradition in which Aleixandre played a vital role.

BIOGRAPHY

Vicente Aleixandre Merlo was born on April 26, 1898, in Seville, Spain, the son of Cirilo Aleixandre Ballester, a railway engineer, and Elvira Merlo García de Pruneda, daughter of an upper-middle-class Andalusian family. Married in Madrid, Aleixandre's parents moved to Seville, the base for his father's travels with the Andalusian railway network. Four years after Aleixandre's birth, the family moved to Málaga, remaining there for seven years, spending their summers in a cottage on the beach at Pedregalejo a few miles from the city.

Aleixandre seems to have been very happy as a boy in Málaga, where he attended school, frequented the movie theater across the street from his house (he particularly liked the films of Max Linder), and read the Brothers Grimm and Hans Christian Andersen. Happy memories of Málaga and the nearby sea appear frequently in Aleixandre's poetry: He calls them "ciudad del paraíso" (city of paradise) and "mar del paraíso" (sea of paradise), respectively.

In 1911, the family moved to Madrid, where Aleixandre continued his studies at Teresiano School, but he found the strict requirements for the bachelor's degree tedious and preferred reading the books in his grandfather's library: classical and Romantic works and detective novels, especially those by Sir Arthur Conan Doyle. Aleixandre frequently visited the National Library, where he read novels and drama from Spain's Golden

Age to the *generación del 98*. During the summer of 1917, his friend Dámaso Alonso lent him a volume by Rubén Darío, a book which, Aleixandre said, revealed to him the passion of his life—poetry. The next year, he discovered the works of Antonio Machado and Juan Ramón Jiménez, as well as the Romantic world of Gustavo Adolfo Bécquer, and his interest in poetry was firmly established.

At the age of fifteen, Aleixandre began to study law and business administration, finishing the two programs in 1920. He became an assistant professor at the School of Commerce of Madrid and worked at night editing a journal of economics in which he published several articles on railroads. In 1921, he left his teaching post to work for the railway company, but when in 1925 he suffered an attack of renal tuberculosis, he dropped all professional and social activities, dedicating himself to his poetry, reading, and traveling with his family through Portugal, France, England, and diverse regions of Spain.

Aleixandre's first poems appeared in *Revista de occidente* (journal of the West) in 1926, and two years later his first collection, *Ámbito* (ambit) was published. In 1929, he discovered Sigmund Freud, James Joyce, and Arthur Rimbaud, and, although he suffered a relapse into his tubercular condition in 1932, this period of his life was very productive, resulting in three collections published between 1932 and 1935.

After the removal of his diseased kidney in 1932, Aleixandre retired to Miraflores de la Sierra to convalesce, but in 1933 he returned to Madrid. Carlos Bousoño reports that during this year, Aleixandre read French translations of the German Romantic writers Ludwig Tieck and Novalis, as well as *Les Romantiques allemands* (1933; a translation of Ricarda Huch's *Blüthezeit der Romantik*, 1899; the German Romantics). He completed this new spiritual phase with the lyric poetry of William Shakespeare, John Keats, Percy Bysshe Shelley, and William Wordsworth. In 1934, Aleixandre's mother died, and there were more travels through England, France, and Switzerland. During the years of the Spanish Civil War (1936-1939), Aleixandre was isolated from political turmoil, spending much of the time in convalescence after renewed bouts of illness. The death of his father in 1939 brought him even closer to his sister Concepción.

Aleixandre's work reflects his psychological and physiological state as a vitally passionate man and a chronically sick man, as a calm, patient man and a creative man. His poetic production has been sustained over a lifetime, although a great many years passed between his published collections. In his own words, "The poet dies only when the man dies. And then, his poetry lives forever."

ANALYSIS

In the work of Vicente Aleixandre's first period, the poet is interested primarily in terrible mythic elements of nature without people; he is chaotic, delirious, and grotesque. His is a kind of rebellion against the middle class that hems him in, but he is not yet aware that to save himself from its oppression he must transform his blind, ineffective rebellion into a conscious, efficient one. In his middle period, although Aleixandre continues to take refuge in myth to escape the horrible realities of the day, he faces them as he recalls his family and past, realizing that he cannot remain aloof from history, politics, and other realities when people believe in him. Finally, in his later work, the poet becomes academic, literary, cultured, and decorative. Gradually, finding historical and telluric man and his own dialectical reality, Aleixandre identifies with the public, and the amorous solidarity of the man and poet with all creation is complete.

The idea that love equals death is the leitmotif of almost all Aleixandre's poetry; it appears most clearly in his recurring images of the sea. In addition to repressed sexuality, a neurotic and somewhat limited group of fantasies recur throughout his oeuvre, many of them associated with the sea. His early years in Málaga impressed the sea on his consciousness, so that it became for him a symbol of youth, equated in turn with innocence, happiness, and his mother (in psychoanalytic dream interpretation, the sea often symbolizes the mother). His desire to return and merge with that happiness and all it represents implies his death as an individual, as he is absorbed by a larger unit. Intrauterine life, being premortal (except to the Church), is easily equated with postmortal life—life before birth equals life after death.

CENTRAL IMAGERY AND INFLUENCE

The sea occupies a high place in Aleixandre's poetic scale of values. Among the 336 poems of his *Poesías completas*, the sea appears 182 times; moreover, it is used as a central theme in sixteen poems. The sea, a recurring symbol or archetype which integrates all Aleixandre's characteristic themes, represents primitive, instinctive life, true values lost by modern civilized man and maintained by simple sea creatures, a constant interplay between Thanatos and Eros, and a variety of sensual, erotic states involving repressed sexuality. Often Aleixandre juxtaposes the sea with images of forest, beach, teeth, tongue, birds, sun, moon, and breast. The sea in Aleixandre's poetry is pathognomonic in its psychological connotations, rooted in the painful dynamic of Aleixandre's own life, although at times it evokes a happy, innocent childhood, much as the gypsy symbolized the childhood of García Lorca. Aleixandre disguises the relationship between the symbol and its meaning at unconscious levels; he distorts and represses it so that the symbols may lend themselves to many interpretations, which only psychoanalysis can fully reveal.

Indeed, a catharsis comparable to psychological analysis is accomplished by Aleixandre's poetry, except that here the patient ministers to himself; for example, unconscious forces account for the breast motif associated with the sea, one of Aleixandre's most constant neurotic projections. Throughout his poems, Aleixandre uses the sea as a surface on which to project his images, according to which it takes on various hues, colors, and attributes. It can be an "unstable sea," an "imperious sea," or a "contained sea," and it serves as the principal, though not the exclusive, vehicle for the projection of neurotic fantasies in which the poet employs symbols to convey meaning he might consciously wish to suppress. Aleixandre's sea imagery irrationally yet imaginatively challenges the reader's preconceptions, as the poet attempts deliberately or otherwise to recapture an unconscious knowledge and create a unity of perception.

Aleixandre's interest in Freudian analysis made him particularly receptive to Surrealism, yet he never accepted the "pure" Surrealism of André Breton. Breton defined Surrealism as a psychic automatism through which he proposed to express the real functioning of thought without control by reason and beyond all aesthetic or moral norms, revealing the relationship between the real and the imaginary. For Breton, perception and representation are products of the dissociation of a single original faculty which the eidetic image recognizes and which is to be found in the primitive and the child. The distinction between the subjective and the objective lost its value as the poet sought to engage in a kind of automatic writing. Aleixandre rejected the notion of automatic writing, but in his preoccupation with the subconscious and his powerful, irrational imagery, he introduced Surrealism to Spanish poetry, where it found extremely fertile soil.

ÁMBITO

Ámbito (ambit), Aleixandre's first collection, is related to the much later volume, *Shadow of Paradise*. *Ámbito*, composed of seven sections and eight "Nights" (including an initial and final "Night" and one "Sea"), contains classical and Gongoristic forms—not unexpected at the time, since the collection was composed partly during the tercentenary of Luis de Góngora y Argote, when Baroque formalism ruled the day. Nature is everywhere; although there is a faint reflection of the cosmic force, the poet is largely descriptive and objective in a somewhat traditional way. Here, he contemplates nature, while in later works he will seek to possess it and be one with it. Written during his first serious illness, the book sensually examines the fleeting aspects of time. Within his own boundary—the limits of his sickroom, where he lived a solitary existence—he waxed both tender and uncontrollably passionate. Yet *Ámbito*'s formal beauty, pleasure in the contemplation of nature, desire for perfection, and joy in life reflect both Juan Ramón Jiménez and Jorge Guillén more than the later Aleixandre. The poetry deals with the world of the senses, classic and cold at times but also warm and romantic. The elusive imagery resembles the reverberations of a musical instrument. The poet employs traditional ballad form instead of the free verse that he later came to use almost exclusively, and his ten- and six-syllable lines reveal his great sense of rhythm. In this volume of youthful love, Aleixandre delicately renders his love affair with nature, a love whose equations frequently resist logical interpretation.

ESPADAS COMO LABIOS

Begun in the summer of 1929, Aleixandre's second collection, *Espadas como labios* (swords like lips), concerns the central themes of life, death, and love—themes which the poet, in his moment of inspiration and suffering, views from a new perspective. An epigraph from Lord Byron, to the effect that the poet is "a babbler," serves notice that the volume eschews conventional "meaning." The work as originally presented was filled with poetic transpositions and capriciously arranged punctuation to help Aleixandre release what he considered his "interior fire." His intention was not to induce a surrealistic trance but to create a voluntary pattern of unusual images. Aleixandre, in his somewhat illogically and incoherently developed poetic structures, does not know exactly what theme he will develop. The diffuse emotion he creates in this confused and disturbed work gives rise to apparent indecision for the poet, which transfers to the reader. His liberty of form allows Aleixandre to cover a variety of subjects in a dream atmosphere that hovers between sensation and thought. *Espadas como labios*, in its examination of reality, petrifies it—or, as one critic phrases it, indulges in the immobilization of the moment. Aleixandre's bittersweet imagery of dead roses, coals of silence (because they lack life-giving flame), and other signs of loss and decay suggests a desire to embrace the reality of death.

DESTRUCTION OR LOVE

If *Espadas como labios*, despite its striking images, lacks imaginative coherence, Aleixandre's third collection, *Destruction or Love*, is an undisputed masterpiece. Here, in fifty-four poems divided into six parts, the poet offers a visionary transfiguration of the world in flux, a world of mystery and darkness whose basic fabric is erotic love. Aleixandre's universe is a place of cosmic and human passion, of frustrated and desperate clamor, and of unchained telluric forces that often prove fatal to man, absorbing him and destroying him. In Aleixandre's vision, men can obtain love only by destroying themselves and fusing with the cosmos, for human love is fleeting, and a final fusion with the earth will prove to be the most enduring love of all. Aleixandre excludes the life beyond and salvation. Absorbed in the living unity of nature, he acclaims a love without religious connotations. Aleixandre stresses the idea that the unity of the world includes man's works and his civilization, but they remain peripheral to the primary, instinctive life. Perhaps love can save him from society's mask—for love fuses all things, animal, vegetable, and mineral, into

one substance—but to achieve fusion, one must give up his limiting structures. Thus, the title of the volume is intended to signify not a choice between mutually exclusive alternatives (*either* destruction *or* love) but rather an identification (as when the subtitle of a book is introduced by the word "or").

In *Destruction or Love*, the animal and the vegetable worlds constantly interact with the thoughts and feelings of the poet. In virgin forests, ferocious beasts surround man, who seeks fruitlessly to find himself, half glimpsing his salvation in an identification with nature in all of its forms and thus affirming rather than denying love for all creation. Animals, the forest, and the sea live in intimate union with elementary forces of nature, and tender, small animals exist with large, destructive ones: the beetle and the scorpion with the cobra, the eagle, lions, and tigers. Thus, the tiger is an elastic fire of the forest, and the eagles resemble the ocean. Like other aspects of nature, such as the ocean, the moon, or the heavens, these animals may be virginal and innocent or terrible and destructive. In this vision of nature as a physical whole in which violence and love are complementary forces, everything attacks, destroys, and loves everything and, in so doing, loves, attacks, and destroys itself. Life is death. The limits between flora and fauna dissolve into a new unity; the sea's fish appear to be birds; foam is hair; a body becomes an ocean; a heart becomes a mountain; man may be metal or a lion. Like the mystic poets of old—who had to die in order to find eternal life—Aleixandre offers a mystic fusion or death with the sea and the maternal earth.

SHADOW OF PARADISE

Shadow of Paradise, begun in 1939 and finished in November, 1943, created a sensation among young poets even before its publication in book form; when it finally appeared in 1944, it won a wide and enthusiastic readership among the literary youth of the day. Here, Aleixandre returns to the innocent world of infancy, to a paradise beyond Original Sin and knowledge, to be one with the heavens and the creatures of the dawn. He evokes a Garden of Eden where he may find lost happiness in order to escape the evil world of man, its folly and malignity. The poet narcissistically reinvents his own reality, remembers it, or perhaps imaginatively recreates the world of childhood before the horrifying and inevitable loss of innocence. In his universe of serenity, order, and beauty, however, Aleixandre implies an awareness of the historical world, in which man must play his role. The tension between paradise and history is always just beneath the surface.

Shadow of Paradise is divided into six parts. Of its fifty-two poems, only a dozen have a definite metric form, but through them all there are patterns of association among rhythms of different kinds. The verse lines are of varying length, including hendecasyllables, pentasyllables, hexameters, exciting combinations of anapestic lines, and irregular meters. Avoiding monotony in his rhythmical movements by means of this prodigality of expression, Aleixandre uses exclamations, interrogatives, and an almost musical progression of scales to form a polyphonic richness. His fetish for rhythmic simplicity extends to his use of adjectives, which he occasionally employs adverbially and, rarely, in double or triple combination. Often his naked nouns convey his precise tone or mood; on other occasions, for special effect, he ends his poetic lines with a verb; infrequently, he employs gerundives experimentally.

HISTORIA DEL CORAZÓN

Of Aleixandre's later collections, the most important is *Historia del corazón* (history of the heart). Many underlying crosscurrents of thought and emotion can be found in this volume, but its central theme is the need for human solidarity and compassion for the victims of injustice. *Historia del corazón* reveals a dramatic change in Aleixandre's conception of man. Here, no longer the creature of telluric forces, man is defined by the dolorous round of daily experience. Likewise, Aleixandre's conception of poetry has changed: The poet, a man, becomes all men, destined to live and die, without the assurance of paradise or eternal life, in a world where death is always present. Nevertheless, the poet proclaims, it is not necessary to live desperate, solitary lives; he sings for all humankind of fleeting time, social love, and human solidarity. The poet recognizes that he is aging, but without despair, and empathizes with his neighbor, who must also stoically face the end.

OTHER MAJOR WORKS

NONFICTION: *Los encuentros*, 1958.
MISCELLANEOUS: *Obras completas*, 1977.

BIBLIOGRAPHY

Cabrera, Vicente, and Harriet Boyer, eds. *Critical Views on Vicente Aleixandre's Poetry*. Lincoln, Nebr.: Society of Spanish and Spanish-American Studies, 1979. Criticism and interpretation of Aleixandre's addresses, essays, lectures, and poetry. Includes selected poems in English translation.

Daydí-Tolson, Santiago, ed. *Vicente Aleixandre: A Critical Appraisal*. Ypsilanti, Mich.: Bilingual Press, 1981. A critical study of Aleixandre's work with a biographical introduction, extensively annotated bibliography, index, and Aleixandre's Nobel Prize acceptance lecture.

Harris, Derek. *Metal Butterflies and Poisonous Lights: The Language of Surrealism in Lorca, Alberti, Cernuda, and Aleixandre*. Anstruther, Fife, Scotland: La Sirena, 1998. History and criticism of Surrealism in Spanish literature, including the works of Aleixandre. Bibliography.

Ilie, P. *The Surrealist Mode in Spanish Literature*. Ann Arbor: University of Michigan Press, 1968. A study of Surrealism in Spanish literature. Includes bibliographic references.

Murphy, Daniel. *Vicente Aleixandre's Stream of Lyric Consciousness*. Lewisburg, Pa.: Bucknell University Press, 2001. Criticism and interpretation of Aleixandre's poetics, with bibliographical citations and index.

Schwartz, Kessel. *Vicente Aleixandre*. New York: Twayne, 1970. An introductory biography and critical analysis of selected works by Aleixandre.

Richard A. Mazzara;
bibliography updated by the editors

WILLIAM ALLINGHAM

Born: Ballyshannon, Ireland; March 19, 1824
Died: London, England; November 18, 1889

PRINCIPAL POETRY

Poems, 1850, enlarged 1861
Day and Night Songs, 1854, revised and enlarged 1855 (as *The Music Master, a Love Story, and Two Series of Day and Night Songs*)

Laurence Bloomfield in Ireland, 1864

Fifty Modern Poems, 1865

Songs, Ballads and Stories, 1877

Evil May-Day, 1882

Blackberries Picked off Many Bushes, 1884

Irish Songs and Poems, 1887

Rhymes for the Young Folk, 1887 (also known as
    Robin Redbreast, and Other Verses, 1930)

Flower Pieces and Other Poems, 1888

Life and Phantasy, 1889

By the Way: Verses, Fragments, and Notes, 1912

OTHER LITERARY FORMS

Although known primarily as a poet of light lyrics, William Allingham also wrote prose pieces and a diary. Few would deny that *William Allingham: A Diary* (1907) is one of the best literary diaries of the Victorian period. Primarily a product of his English years, it records conversations and encounters with an impressive array of

William Allingham (© Bettmann/Corbis)

eminent Victorian personalities. Alfred, Lord Tennyson, and Thomas Carlyle were intimates, and there is much about Robert Browning and Dante Gabriel Rossetti. Allingham's formal prose turns out to be surprisingly substantial. Starting in 1867, he wrote more than twenty travelogues for *Fraser's Magazine*. Narrated under the paronymatic pseudonym Patricius Walker, the travelogues are notable for their expository emphasis. The traveler will sometimes pass opinion on what he has seen in his wanderings (Wales, Scotland, provincial England, parts of the Continent), but for the most part he concentrates on describing scenery and reporting local customs and historical tidbits about the area. A selection of these pieces was later issued as *Rambles* (1873), while most of them were collected in the first two volumes of a posthumously published edition of his prose. The third volume of this work, *Varieties in Prose* (1893), contains Irish sketches and literary criticism.

ACHIEVEMENTS

William Allingham deserves the elusive label "Anglo-Irish." His reputation as a minor Victorian poet is largely the result of the popularity of a few frequently anthologized poems of Irish inspiration, subject matter, and sentiment. Like so many other "minor" literary figures, however, his historical significance goes beyond his accomplishment in any single genre. His foremost achievement is in lyric poetry. He had a knack for spinning songs and ballads. The most famous of these is "The Fairies," a delightful children's rhyme about the elvish world, which inevitably appears in anthologies of Irish verse. Also frequently anthologized is "The Winding Banks of Erne," a tender farewell to Ireland from an emigrant as he sets sail for the New World. Over the years, these two favorites have been included in most of the standard collections of Irish verse: Stopford A. Brooke and T. W. Rolleston's (1900), Padraic Colum's (1922), Lennox Robinson and Donagh MacDonagh's (1958), and Devin Garrity's (1965), among others. To complete their selection from Allingham's work, editors often include lyrics such as "A Dream" and "Four Ducks on a Pond," and ballads such as "Abbey Asaroe" and "The Maids of Elfin Mere."

A dozen or so preservable short poems from a canon of several hundred does not seem to be a very significant achievement. The quality of these poems is sufficiently high, however, to secure at least a minor position in Irish poetry, and, when considered in the light of Irish literary history, Allingham's stature grows substantially. As Ernest Boyd points out in *Ireland's Literary Renaissance* (1916), the third quarter of the nineteenth century was a transitional period in Irish literature, sandwiched between an earlier period of predominantly political verse and the later full renaissance led by William Butler Yeats and his circle. During this transitional period, there appeared a few poets who, though not of the first rank, were nevertheless serious, competent artists who celebrated Irish themes without lapsing into propaganda. Allingham was one of these, ranking alongside Aubry de Vere and just below Samuel Ferguson in importance. A country seeking to establish its cultural identity cannot afford to overlook the literary accomplishments of any of its native sons. Allingham helped to set the stage for the later flowering of Irish verse, and his historical importance was recognized by poets of the Irish Renaissance, particularly Katherine Tynan, William Butler Yeats, Lionel Johnson, and Padraic Colum.

Yeats above all is responsible for securing Allingham's modest niche in literary history. In an article entitled "A Poet We Have Neglected," Yeats gave an appreciation of Allingham's Irish songs and ballads, noting the poet's facility at capturing ephemeral moods and moments. "It is time," he declared, "for us over here to claim him as our own, and give him his due place among our sacred poets; to range his books beside Davis, Mangum, and Ferguson." Four years later he was writing to Tynan that "you, Ferguson and Allingham are, I think, the Irish poets who have done the largest quantity of fine work." In 1905, he put together and published a small selection of Allingham's best poems (*Sixteen Poems by William Allingham*). More important than Yeats's service to Allingham's reputation, however, is Allingham's influence on Yeats's own poetry. In 1904 Yeats wrote to Mrs. Allingham, "I am sometimes inclined to believe that he was my own master in verse, starting me in the way I have gone whether for good or evil." Allingham's success with ballads and songs encouraged Yeats to explore those genres during the early part of his career, and specific borrowings have been noticed by critics.

Allingham's short verse deserves wider recognition than its slight representation in anthologies seems to warrant. It is true that an enormous amount of inferior work must be waded through, but a reading of his entire canon reveals several dozen poems worth keeping in addition to the well-known ones. There is, for example, an interesting series of poems all entitled "Aeolian Harp." Although these poems are inspired more by English poetic convention than by "Irish scenes and Irish faces" (Yeats's phrase), they are nevertheless fairly successful imitations of the type of reflective poem for which Samuel Taylor Coleridge is known. Some of the sonnets, such as "Autumnal Sonnet" and "Winter Cloud," are very expressive, and there is even a sparkling translation of "The Cicada" from the *Greek Anthology* (first century C.E.). The most judicious twentieth century selection of Allingham's poetry is found in Geoffrey Taylor's anthology *Irish Poets of the Nineteenth Century* (1951), which contains about fifty pages of his shorter poetry. A selection that appeared in 1967 (*The Poems of William Allingham*, edited by John Hewitt) contains about twenty shorter poems, plus excerpts from longer ones.

Allingham's second major achievement was *Laurence Bloomfield in Ireland*, a long narrative in verse about Irish tenant-landlord relations in the mid-nineteenth century. Many later critics, including Taylor and Alan Warner, place *Laurence Bloomfield in Ireland* first on the list of Allingham's achievements. Yeats castigated it, as he did all of Allingham's longer poetry, but William Gladstone praised it and even quoted from it in the House of Commons. After reading it, Ivan Turgenev told a mutual friend, "I never understood Ireland before!" Allingham himself considered *Laurence Bloomfield in Ireland* his best work. The poem's modest popularity was partly owing to its contemporary subject matter and partly to its artistic strengths. It ran through several editions during Allingham's lifetime.

His third major area of achievement is his prose, including travelogues, occasional pieces, and a diary. Critic Sean McMahon labels Allingham's posthumously published *William Allingham: A Diary* his "greatest" work, ranking it above *Laurence Bloomfield in Ireland* and the lyrics.

BIOGRAPHY

William Allingham can be considered more quintessentially Anglo-Irish than other representative of that breed because he was truly poised between the two spheres. In his first thirty-nine years Ireland was his home; the last twenty-six were spent almost exclusively in England. Allingham's final visit to Ireland occurred as early as 1866, on the occasion of his father's funeral. The demarcation between the two lives, however, is not as clear as the mere circumstance of residence would seem to indicate. During the Irish years (1824-1863), he often visited England, where most of his friends and correspondents were. During the English years (1863-1889), his mind constantly returned to Ireland, as is evidenced in his writing and conversation.

Allingham was born in the western Ireland port town of Ballyshannon, County Donegal, situated at the mouth of the River Erne. Ballyshannon and vicinity would provide the setting for most of his well-known ballads and lyrics. His family was Protestant, having migrated from Hampshire more than two hundred years earlier. *William Allingham: A Diary* reports that his parents, William and Elizabeth, were both "undemonstrative," and his mother's early death in 1833 probably contributed to a curious personality trait observable in Allingham throughout his life—a simultaneous love of solitude and desire for companionship. "Has anyone walked alone as much as I?" he asked in his diary in 1865, and then immediately gave the counterpoint: "And who fonder of congenial company?"

His father, formerly a merchant, removed his son from a local boarding school at the age of thirteen and installed him as a clerk in the branch bank that he had managed for several years. Thenceforth Allingham educated himself at home during his spare time, no mean feat in the light of his later scholarship. When he was twenty-two, he secured a position in the Customs Service at eighty pounds a year, serving in Ballyshannon and other Ulster towns, and even for a short time on the Isle of Man. He assayed cargoes, visited shipwrecks, audited crew payrolls, no doubt did reams of paperwork, and, significantly, inspected fittings and provisions on immigrant ships heading for the United States. During those years he produced his first three volumes of poetry–*Poems, Day and Night Songs*, and *The Music Master, a Love Story, and Two Series of Day and Night Songs*—which, together, contain the core of his best ballads and lyrics.

Allingham's Irish period ended in 1863 when he transferred to the English port of Lymington, on the southern coast opposite the Isle of Wight. Long before this, however, he had become acquainted with England. Starting in 1847 he had made annual visits to London, eventually breaking into several different circles of artists. Through Leigh Hunt, Allingham met Carlyle; Coventry Patmore introduced him to Rossetti and the Pre-Raphaelites, as well as to Tennyson. During the early 1850's he was especially intimate with Rossetti, "whose friendship," he wrote in a dedication to one volume of his collected works, "brightened many years of my life, and whom I never can forget." Rossetti's letters to Allingham are numerous, interesting, and accessible (*The Letters of Rossetti to Allingham*, 1897, G. B. Hill, editor). The intimacy with Tennyson and with Carlyle deepened after Allingham's transfer to England. In 1864, he published *Laurence Bloomfield in Ireland*, much revised from its original form in *Fraser's Magazine*, and in 1865, *Fifty Modern Poems*. The latter must be considered more a product of his Irish period.

In 1870, acting upon Carlyle's advice, Allingham retired from the civil service to become subeditor of *Fraser's Magazine*, under J. A. Froude, whom he succeeded as editor in 1874. The same year he married Helen Paterson, an established watercolorist only half his age. They had three children. In 1879, Allingham retired permanently, moving to Witley, Surrey, in 1881, then to Hampstead in 1888, his final home. He had been awarded an annual civil pension of sixty pounds in 1864; it was increased to one hundred pounds in 1870. The last twenty years witnessed a decline in poetic output. *Songs, Ballads, and Stories* contains mostly work from previous volumes, though as a collection it may be the best single repository of Allingham's poetry. *Evil May-Day* will remain his least successful volume, mainly because of the heavy didactic nature of the title piece, which whines and frets in blank verse for some eight hundred lines. Ironically, the book also contains his most succinct lyric, the gem-like "Four Ducks on a Pond." His last major original production was *Blackberries Picked off Many Bushes*, composed entirely of short aphoristic verse.

ANALYSIS

As a poet, William Allingham will remain known primarily for his lyrics and for *Laurence Bloomfield in Ireland*. He had a lyric voice of unusual charm. He had an eye alert to local beauty. He had a heart sensitive to those passing emotions and thoughts, which, in the aggregate, form the very fabric of human experience. The voices that moved his voice to sing were principally Irish, though not exclusively so. He chose to live the latter third of his life in England; his temperament was largely English; he derived his sense of literary community and artistic purpose from English sources. What poetic strengths he did have are a product of his love for England and Ireland. Those strengths should not be underrated. "I am genuine though not great," he once wrote to a friend, adding "and my time will come."

The chief strengths of Allingham's best lyrics and songs are their simplicity and musicality. His themes are the universal ones: the joys and frustrations of romantic love, the many faces of nature, the quality of country life, humankind's ultimate relation to an indecipherable universe, memories of happier times, the supernatural, and death. His simplicity of style is typified by the following stanza from "The Lighthouse":

> The plunging storm flies fierce against the pane,
> And thrills our cottage with redoubled shocks:
> The chimney mutters and the rafters strain;
> Without, the breakers roar along the rocks.

As he does here, Allingham commonly uses familiar rhyme schemes, keeps syntax straight, and restrains metaphor to an unusual degree. His syntactical purity is such that the only departures from normal word order permitted are entirely conventional poetic inversions ("Many fine things had I glimpse of"). Even then he manages to avoid the grosser sort of inversion, as when the main verb is delayed until the end of the line for mere rhyme's sake ("Loud larks in ether sing"). Implicitly in several poems, explicitly in personal conversations, Allingham criticized the convoluted style of Robert Browning's poetry, friend though he was. Instead, in poetry (see "The Lyric Muse") and prose (*Rambles*, "To Dean Prior"), he holds up Robert Herrick as a model of lyricism. Not too much should be made of that, however, since the serious Allingham would never imitate the cavalier element in Herrick's verse, although he did approve of its "elegant naivete." One might discern an elegance, certainly a gracefulness, in the naïve treatment of idyllic love in the following lines:

> Oh! were my Love a country lass,
> That I might see her every day,
> And sit with her on hedgerow grass
> Beneath a bough of may.

Here as elsewhere in his most successful lyrics, Allingham keeps diction simple. Surely the freshness of lines such as these has some value today.

WILLIAM ALLINGHAM: A DIARY

The musical element is so omnipresent in Allingham's poetry that the distinction between song, lyric, and ballad is sometimes obscured. Many of his enduring poems tend toward song. To the simplicity of his poetry the musical element adds sweetness, or in some instances liveliness. *William Allingham: A Diary* records a conversation with William Makepeace Thackeray, in which Allingham wholeheartedly agrees with the novelist's dictum, "I want poetry to be musical, to run sweetly." It is not always easy, however, to determine whether the musical charm of a particular song derives from meter, rhyme, phonetic effects, or from a combination of the three. From *William Allingham: A Diary* and other prose writings it is apparent that Allingham considered meter to be the very soul of poetry. In fact, some of the most significant entries in his diary include those in which Tennyson and his Irish devotee discuss the technicalities of metrical effects. Lines such as "The pulse in his pillowed ear beat thick" (from "The Goblin Child of Ballyshannon") echo Tennyson both metrically and phonetically. Repetition of the haunting place-name "Asaroe" in "Abbey Asaroe" shows that Allingham could choose a word for its rhythm and sound; its precise placement in each stanza shows a talent for emphasis. On the other hand, rhyme is a prominent feature of Allingham's verse. Triplets, internal rhyme, and refrains are not uncommon.

FAIRY POEMS

Sprightly music, such as that which makes children laugh and sing, contributes in part to the popularity of Allingham's beloved fairy poems. Justly most famous of these is "The Fairies," with its traditional opening:

Up the airy mountain,
Down the rushy glen,
We daren't go a-hunting
For fear of little men.

Others, however, are almost as highly cherished. "Prince Brightkin," a rather long narrative, has some brilliant touches of whimsicality. In "The Lepruchan," the wee shoemaker escapes his captors by blowing snuff in their faces. In "The Fairy Dialogue," mischievous sprites confound housewives attempting to do their daily chores. It should be noted, however, that much of Allingham's verse contains an opposite charm, that of sweet sadness. Many of his descriptive poems, as well as many of the romantic lyrics, are tinged with a sense of regret, of longing for something unattainable. Allingham could sing in a minor key. This tendency derives partly from personal temperament, partly from the fashion of the times, partly from literary imitation of the Graveyard School or even the Spasmodic School of poetry. He might be said to have anticipated the tone of voice adopted by writers of the Celtic Twilight. For example, one, "Aeolian Harp," opens and closes with the question, "O what is gone from us, we fancied ours?" William Butler Yeats so appreciated the way the poem enshrouds its *sic transit* theme with a meditative plaintiveness that he included it in his selection of Allingham's verse.

INFLUENCE OF BALLADS

Allingham wrote only a handful of ballads, but his work was sufficiently crucial to establish him as a modern pioneer in this form. During his Irish period, study of the local folk ballad became a sort of hobby. He listened to balladeers at country market fairs, transcribed lyrics and melodies, and collected anonymous broadsheet ballads sold by hawkers. Next, he produced his own ballads, printed and circulated them as anonymous ha'penny broadsheets (a few of which have survived), and had the pleasure of hearing them sung in the streets and cottages of Ireland. Later, Yeats, Padraic Colum, and other poets of the Irish Renaissance took up the genre. Five of Allingham's broadsheet ballads were collected in the volume of 1855, which also has a preface describing the difficulties of adapting peasant Anglo-Irish idiom to verse. The best of these are "Lovely Mary Donnelly" and "The Girl's Lamentation." There is in the former poem a blind fiddler who, although sad because he could not see the pretty lass, "blessed himself he wasn't deaf" upon hearing her winsome voice. The girl's lament is for the perfidy of her lover, but also for her own loss of chastity, since "a maid again I can never be/ Till the red rose blooms on the willow tree." A third broadside ballad, "Kate O' Ballyshanny," belongs with these two in quality. Allingham also wrote a few literary ballads, perhaps imitating Rossetti or the Romantic poets. The best of these are "The Maids of Elfinmere," "The Abbot of Innisfallen," "Squire Curtis," and "St. Margaret's Eve."

POETIC DETRACTIONS

Allingham liked Herrick's lyrics for their simplicity "without flatness." The problem with his own verse is that most of it is both simple and flat. His failings as a poet, which, in Sean McMahon's phrase, keep him entrenched "on the foothills of Parnassus," are largely ones common to his period. Victorian oppressive seriousness, mediocrity of thought, and gushy sentimentality too often invade his poetry. At times the effusion of emotion becomes embarrassingly urgent:

Mine—Mine
O Heart, it is thine—
A look, a look of love!
O wonder! O magical charm!
Thou summer-night, silent and warm!

One is reminded of Percy Bysshe Shelley's "Indian Serenade." This tendency toward triteness extends past content into the realm of technique. For instance, eighteenth century poetic diction is resurrected and put to facile uses, so that one finds the earth to be "the whirling sphere," the night sky "the starry dome," and a field of wildflowers "the daisied lea."

Allingham's typical faults are magnified in his longer poems. "Evil May-Day" suffers especially from high seriousness. It is a philosophical discussion about the impact of science on traditional morality. The crisis of doubt, of the disorientation caused by a widespread questioning of creeds outworn, was a legitimate concern to Victorians, but Allingham's handling of it becomes painfully didactic. He treated the same issues more palatably in prose (see *Rambles*, "At Exeter," and "At Torquay"). "The Music Master," a tale about the tragic effects of prematurely severed love, suffers somewhat from sentimentality, but more so from lack of dramatic incident. Dante Gabriel Rossetti, who often asked Allingham for advice about his own poetry, wrote that "'The Music Master' is full of beauty and nobility, but I'm not sure it is not TOO noble or too resolutely healthy."

LAURENCE BLOOMFIELD IN IRELAND

The exception to this general awkwardness in the longer forms is *Laurence Bloomfield in Ireland*, which runs to nearly five thousand lines. Its fictionalized account of tenant-landlord relations provides a valuable sketch of economic and class struggles in rural Ireland a decade before the Land League and just prior to the first heated period of Fenian activity. The extreme right and extreme left are staked out by the reactionary landlords and the incendiary Ribbonmen respectively; the sensible, humane middle is occupied by Bloomfield (the ideal landlord) and the Dorans (the ideal peasant family). In outline form, the plot seems unpromisingly thin. Bloomfield, who has recently assumed control of his estate, is feeling his way cautiously into landlordism. He objects to the bigoted, self-servicing attitudes of the other landlords in the district, but as yet lacks the confidence to challenge the status quo. In addition, the secret societies are active in the district. Their activities, usually directed against the ruling class, range from the merely disruptive to the criminally violent. Neal Doran, a good lad, son of an aging tenant farmer, is drawn into the fringes of the insurgent movements. When he is arrested for fighting at a market fair, Pigot, the hardhearted agent for Bloomfield and other landlords, moves to evict the Dorans from the farm they had worked so hard to establish. It is then that Bloomfield acts decisively. Moved by the sight of the old man's grief, he dismisses Pigot, who is assassinated on his way home, and releases Doran. Time is telescoped in the latter section of the narrative: In the years to come, Bloomfield works hard at being the ideal landlord. He institutes revolutionary reforms, such as allowing tenants to buy their farms, and in general plays the enlightened, paternal ruler.

The poem's flaws are readily apparent. The lengthy coda, consisting of two whole books, seems tacked on, and occasionally a digression unnecessarily interrupts the flow of narrative. The poem was originally written under the pressure of monthly serial publication, which probably accounts for some of the structural flaws. After receiving proofs of Book 12 from *Fraser's Magazine*, Allingham confided in *William Allingham: A Diary*, "It's not properly compacted to plan, and never will be now." Another flaw is that Bloomfield, the central figure, is weakly drawn. The same might be said for the Dorans. Both are too pure to be believable. Nevertheless, a more pervasive and damaging problem is inconsistency in the quality of the verse.

The poem's strengths, however, far outweigh its weaknesses. In fact, virtually every modern critic writing on Allingham has given it high praise, particularly for its portraiture of Irish types and its many fine character sketches. The satiric portraits of the landlords in Book 2 are worthy of Alexander Pope. A wide spectrum of types is surveyed, from the haughty aristocrat to the licentious absentee to the clever usurer who hides his exploitation behind a surface of unctuous piety. Less barbed but equally effective are the portraits of clergymen, especially Father John Adair. The poem is also strong in its close observation of Irish life. Depicting "every-day Irish affairs" was a "ticklish literary experiment" (Preface, edition of 1864), but Allingham seems to have captured the essential fabric of life in his native Ballyshannon. To John Drinkwater, the poem is "second to none in the language as a description of peasant life and peasant nature" ("The poetry of William Allingham," *The New Ireland Review*, February, 1909). In this regard *Laurence Bloomfield in Ireland* is often compared to Oliver Goldsmith's "Deserted Village" and George Crabbe's "Borough." Allingham goes among the people, even into the most wretched hovel, showing their virtues and their vices. The description of the harvest fair in Book 9 is alive with sights and sounds—the throngs of people, traders' disputes, beggars' blessings, the flourish of Her Majesty's recruiting party—a sort of poetic Irish version of William Powell Frith's *Derby Day* (1858).

Dealing with potentially flammable political material, Allingham strives for a precarious neutrality. Actually, however, this noncommittal position is a fusion of conservative and liberal elements. Allingham was not an advocate of home rule. He felt that Ireland did not yet have the political experience or the administrative skills to assume such responsibility. On the other hand, his advocacy of peasant proprietorship of land (or at least increased security of tenancy) puts him firmly in the liberal camp.

BLACKBERRIES PICKED OFF MANY BUSHES

After *Laurence Bloomfield in Ireland* and *Fifty Modern Poems*, the quality and quantity of Allingham's verse fall off sharply. Yeats and others have seen this atrophy as evidence that his Muse was essentially Irish. Undeniably, the only substantial, entirely new poetic work of the English period was *Blackberries Picked off Many Bushes*. Many of its aphorisms and short satiric rhymes are very good, but as a whole they lack brilliance, and one suspects that reliance upon abbreviated modes indicates a faltering confidence in the ability to create more ambitious poetry.

OTHER MAJOR WORKS

PLAY: *Ashby Manor*, pb. 1883.

NONFICTION: *Rambles*, 1873; *Varieties in Prose*, 1893 (3 volumes); *William Allingham: A Diary*, 1907.

BIBLIOGRAPHY

Cronin, Anthony. *Heritage Now: Irish Literature in the English Language*. New York: St. Martin's Press, 1983. An excellent, concise review of Allingham's life, work, and importance in the poetic canon. The significance of Allingham's Irish heritage and his love of London are well explained and vividly rendered. Cronin also includes assessments of Allingham's poetry by his contemporaries.

Howe, M. L. "Notes on the Allingham Canon." *Philological Quarterly* 12 (July, 1933): 290-297. Howe offers a distinctly personal critique of Allingham's work. He defends "The Fairies" from critics who labeled it hastily written, reveals the history behind "The Maids of Elfen Mere," and untangles the relationships between Allingham, Dante Gabriel Rossetti, and William Morris. Howe also effectively argues the importance and grace of Allingham's overlooked dramas, essays, and short poems.

Hughes, Linda K. "The Poetics of Empire and Resistance: William Allingham's *Lawrence Bloomfield in Ireland*." *Victorian Poetry* 28, no. 2 (Summer, 1990): 103. Allingham's long narrative poem is discussed and analyzed in relation to the history of the English and the Irish peasants.

Husni, Samira Aghacy. "Incorrect References to William Allingham." *Notes and Queries* 30 (August, 1983): 296-298. An essential document for all Allingham scholars and students. Husni sets the record straight regarding common mistakes related to Allingham. These errors range from incorrect dates and titles of poems and books to generalizations about his poetry and relationships with contemporaries. Among those he finds guilty of errors are critics Katherine Tynan, Ifor Evans, and M. L. Howe.

Kavanagh, P. J. "Somewhat Surprising, Somewhat Surprised." *The Spectator* 283, no. 8941 (December 18, 1999): 71-72. A review of *William Allingham: A Diary* with some biographical information about Allingham's relationship with Thomas Carlyle and Alfred, Lord Tennyson.

Samuels Lasner, Mark. *William Allingham: A Biographical Study*. Philadelphia: Holmes, 1993. Lasner approaches Allingham by providing essential information with exceptionally rich notes on the production histories of the books, yet all this is presented in a humane style that serves as an excellent model of how to make an author bibliography both technically satisfactory and readable.

Warner, Allan. *William Allingham*. Lewisburg, Pa.: Bucknell University Press, 1975. Warner devotes his study to three aspects of Allingham: first, his narrative poem "Laurence Bloomfield in Ireland," second, his achievements as a lyric poet and writer of ballads and songs, and third, his prose as exemplified in *William Allingham: A Diary*. In each of these areas, Warner illustrates Allingham's real powers of observation, imagination, and reflection.

Welch, Robert. *Irish Poetry from Moore to Yeats*. Totowa, N.J.: Barnes & Noble Books, 1980. Welch examines Allingham in the context of his contemporaries—such as Thomas Moore, Jeremiah Joseph Callanan, and James Clarence Mangan—and the Irish poetic tradition. He skillfully guides the reader toward an appreciation of Allingham's objectivity, love of common life, political common sense, appreciation of nature, and, most important to Welch, his warmth and humanity.

Michael Case;
bibliography updated by the editors

JULIA ALVAREZ

Born: New York, New York; March 27, 1950

PRINCIPAL POETRY

Homecoming, 1984. revised and expanded 1996 (as
Homecoming: New and Collected Poems)
The Other Side/El Otro Lado, 1995

OTHER LITERARY FORMS

Alvarez has published several novels, her acclaimed
How the Garcia Girls Lost Their Accents (1991), *In the
Time of the Butterflies* (1994), *¡Yo!* (1996), and *In the
Name of Salome: A Novel* (2000); a collection of essays,
Something to Declare (1998); and children's books, in-
cluding *The Secret Footprints* (2000) and *How Tía Lola
Came to Stay* (2001). She has also edited a collection of
poetry, *Old Age Ain't for Sissies* (1979).

ACHIEVEMENTS

How the Garcia Sisters Lost Their Accents received
the PEN Oakland/Josephine Miles Book Award (1991)
and was selected as a Notable Book by both *The New
York Times* and the American Library Association
(1992). The critically acclaimed *In the Time of the Butterflies* was a finalist for the National Book Critics Circle Award for fiction (1995). Julia Alvarez won the La
Reina Press poetry award (1982), the Third Woman
Press first prize award for fiction (1986), and the General Electric Foundation award for young writers (1986).
Alvarez has received fellowships from the Bread Loaf
Writers' Conference (1986), the University of Illinois,
the National Endowment for the Arts (1987-1988), and
the Ingram Merril Foundation (1990).

BIOGRAPHY

Shortly after Julia Alvarez was born in New York
City, her family returned home to the Dominican Republic to live among their large, extended family. In
1960, her father took the family back to New York because he was wanted for his involvement in a failed plot
to overthrow dictator Rafael Trujillo. Thereafter, Alvarez lived in the United States, making visits to her extended family in the Dominican Republic. She married

and became the mother of two children. Along with her
husband, she became involved in the political life of the
Dominican Republic.

After two years at Connecticut College (1967-1969),
Alvarez transferred to Middlebury College, from which
she graduated summa cum laude with her bachelor's degree in 1971. She earned a master of fine arts degree
from Syracuse University (1975) and attended the Bread
Loaf School of English (1979-1980). Alvarez taught in
poetry-in-the-schools programs in Kentucky, Delaware,
and North Carolina (1979 and 1978). She has been an
instructor of English at Phillips Andover Academy in
Massachusetts (1979-1981), a visiting assistant professor of creative writing at the University of Vermont
(1981-1983), the Jenny McKean Moore Visiting Writer
at George Washington University (1984-1985), an assistant professor of English at the University of Illinois, Urbana (1985-1988), and an associate professor of English
at Middlebury College (1988-1999). Alvarez now devotes herself full-time to her writing.

Julia Alvarez

ANALYSIS

In her writing, Julia Alvarez says that she attempts

to move out into those other selves, other worlds. . . .
By allowing myself to be those mixtures and not having to choose or repress myself or cut myself off from
the other, I have become a citizen of the world.

She recalls disliking books as a child, except the tales of
the Arabian nights, or "one thousand one nights," which
she found to be full of both stories and power. She has
reflected that she

just knew words, stories, poems could keep me alive,
as they had my first teacher, Scheherazade. . . . And the
best part of the story is that we all have access to that
power in the meaning-making, story-telling Scheher-
azades of the books we read and the books we write.

The power of Alvarez's poetry is in the stories that it
tells, stories that transcend one place, one time, or one
person's experience.

Alvarez started her career as a poet and still thinks of
poetry as her first love. She also believes that being a
poet first has had an impact on her fiction, because
"writing poetry gives me a kind of intense particularity
about words. . . . [Writing is] a way of being in the
world, and the essence of it is paying attention." Attention to the minutiae of everyday life is one identifying
characteristic of Alvarez's poetic technique and a vehicle for bringing life and power to the everyday stories
she tells in her poems.

HOMECOMING: NEW AND COLLECTED POEMS

Referring to her career as a writer, Alvarez observes
that she found herself "turning more and more to writing
as the one place where I felt I belonged and could make
sense of myself, my life, all that was happening to me."
This is certainly true of the poems in *Homecoming: New
and Collected Poems*, which capture the ordinary aspects
of Alvarez's childhood and her identities as a young girl-
woman, daughter, immigrant, and finally grown woman
finding her artistic voice.

The book is organized into six sections: "Homecoming," "Housekeeping," "Heroines," "33," "Redwing Sonnets," "Last Night at Tía's," and "Afterward: Coming
Home to *Homecoming*," in which Alvarez comments on
the changes she made for her 1996 revised edition. The
1996 work includes the poems from the 1984 edition of
Homecoming, some of which have been revised to reflect her current perspectives more precisely. Alvarez
also added five sections that explore issues that have become important to her since the book's first publication.

While *Homecoming*'s central images—the events of
a "typical" household day such as cleaning, doing the
laundry, cooking, dusting, bed making, and ironing—
might be called commonplace or mundane, they are
ideal vehicles for exploring powerful, thought-provok-
ing issues. Alvarez accomplishes much more with such
simple scenes than merely chronicling a mother and
daughter's daily chores. These small household events
allow Alvarez to explore the tensions of family dynamics, the mother-daughter relationship, and the emotional
and physical awakening of a young girl to womanhood.

For example, "Storm Windows" not only shows a
mother hard at work securing their home but also demonstrates a young girl's need to separate from her
mother's protective and domineering grasp:

I wanted to mount that ladder,
. . .Then give a kick, unbuckling
her hands clasped about my ankles,
and sail up, beyond her reach,
her house, her yard, her mothering.

The mother-daughter relationship is complex, yet by
setting it among the commonplace events of women's
daily tasks, Alvarez creates an especially female canvas
on which to paint this dynamic and the roles that the
women in Alvarez's Dominican family fill. Despite the
everyday nature of their "chores," Alvarez reveals that
these women are the artists of the everyday: They bake,
select fabric, sew clothing. By definition, such women
create things that are designed for use—that will be used
up, works of art that will not last: pies, soups, dresses,
clean clothes, sparkling windows.

In "Woman's Work," Alvarez's mother challenges
her: "Who says woman's work isn't high art?/ She challenged as she scrubbed the bathroom tiles./ Keep house
as if the address were your heart." Ironically, although
Alvarez wanted to be different from her mother, wanted
to work away from home, she observes that, as a writer,
her work anchors her to her home, the very spot she
struggled to escape. She "did not want to be her counter-

part!/ I struck out . . . but became my mother's child:/ a woman working at home on her art,/ housekeeping paper as if it were her heart."

The book's remaining sections move away from the family home and sphere of influence. "Heroines" examines the importance of women's friendships ("Woman Friend"), the need for a woman to save herself rather than waiting for Prince Charming ("Against Cinderella"), and the value of the ordinary life ("Old Heroines").

When asked, "What kind of a woman/ are you?" the poet replies, "I wish I knew, I say, I wish/ I knew and could just put it into words." The sonnets of "33" chart her transition from youth to adult woman, introducing lovers and former lovers, identity crises, successes and failures, political concerns, suicidal times, fears of failure, writer's block, the conflicts associated with being an adult daughter, and the spiritual, emotional, and physical needs of an adult woman. While not always happy or pleasant, these poems make it clear that life's important realities require deep feeling, deep commitment, and a fair amount of pain. "Tell me what is it women want the most?" a man asks her, and this section concludes by powerfully articulating Alvarez's values:

> Sometimes the words are so close I am
> more who I am when I'm down on paper
> than anywhere else . . .
> Those of you lost and yearning to be free,
> who hear these words, take heart from me.
> I once was in as many drafts as you.
> But briefly, essentially, here I am.
> Who touches this poem touches a woman.

The next section, "Redwing Sonnets," describes the emerging writer—stronger, more self-assured and powerful—and demonstrates what the poet has "made" from that small girl first seen making beds with her mother. She has been turned into the inspiration for poetry: "I'm revising/ a poem I've tried for years to make as strong/ as I'm able." This voice is confident, deeply philosophical, and content. It knows what it is meant to do: "affirming that the saying of the world/ is what we're meant to do with chirps or words. . . ."

"Last Night at Tía's," the book's final section, integrates the present with the past: "Remember," says Alvarez, "remember was now the theme/ of all our conversations, the thread holding/ together what was left of our connection." Yet the conclusion of this poem is somewhat bleak: "We had become *the grown-ups* to our young,/ readying ourselves for the big deaths: our own,/ with the future shrieking in the garden,/ and the lighthouse beaming its useless light/ above the dark we navigate. . . ." Alvarez looks forward into a world from which it is impossible to regain the safety of childhood: ". . . but it was too late./ We had already strayed from that old world/ of the past we had shared with each other."

THE OTHER SIDE/EL OTRO LADO

These poems move from the simple, daily activities of family life, isolated from its Dominican heritage, to a more integrated consideration of how the child became the writer she is today. Like *Homecoming*, *The Other Side/El Otro Lado* relies heavily on autobiographical material; however, now Alvarez embraces her Dominican heritage, exploring the influence that her childhood and family heritage have had on her as a writer. Moreover, the voice speaking in this volume is more mature, more stable, more integrated.

The book contains six sections: "Bilingual Sestina," "The Gladys Poems," "Making Up the Past," "The Joe Poems," "The Other Side/*El Otro Lado*," and "Estel." While still a central theme, this time the family provides the framework within which Alvarez closely explores the ways in which her bicultural experience has shaped her development as both a writer and a women. The sections form a closed circle, with the first, "Bilingual Sestina," looking on the ways English, her second language, has constricted her as a writer. Alvarez says that there are experiences, knowledge, and ways of seeing the world that defy translation: "Some things I have to say aren't getting said/ in this snowy, blond, blue-eyed, gum-chewing English . . . *nombres* from that first world I can't translate from Spanish" ("Bilingual Sestina").

The book's remaining sections attempt to integrate these two languages—and the disparate parts of her life that they symbolize: the time before she and her family left the Dominican Republic for America; the period during which Alvarez was an "alien" in America, learning to "assimilate"; and the experience of returning "home" to the Dominican Republic after having lived as an American for many years. The end result of this quest for self-knowledge, self-acceptance, and a belief in the validity of her poetic voice is the final section, "The Other Side/*El Otro Lado*," a sequence purposely given a bilingual title to represent the integration of the old with the new, the Dominican with the American experiences, and the emergence of someone who can no longer go "home" to the Dominican Republic as a Dominican, no more than she can return from there to the United States and forget that she comes from Dominican roots. The poet has stepped through these shaping experiences in both the Dominican Republic and the United States to become a person comfortable in her own skin, comfortable being bicultural, no longer wanting to run back to a time that is inaccessible to her *because of* her experiences as an outsider, as a minority *in* America. She accepts who she is: an amalgam of *all* her life.

"Gladys" depicts life before Alvarez's father became endangered by the political upheavals in the Dominican Republic. As a child, Alvarez lived a life of relative privilege among her extended family, a position of safety and the isolation that money and influence can provide. The poems demonstrate these circumstances through contrasting pictures of the life of Gladys, Alvarez's nanny, and that of the Alvarez family.

In "Making Up the Past," "Exile" describes the family's flight to the United States, while "Sound Bites" offers glimpses of assimilation and struggle to assume a bilingual worldview: "There is nothing left to cry for,/ nothing but the story/ of our family's grand adventure/ from one language to another." In "Beginning Again," Alvarez works toward integrating the losses of the past that "can be, not just survived, but made into the matter/ of hope, made into song, not into a hatchet/ to cut off the offending parts, made into poems."

Yet it is not until "The Other Side/*El Otro Lado*" that Alvarez completes her transformation into a new person embodying both her Dominican past and her American present: "I know/ I won't be coming back to live/ in my ex-homeland. A border has closed like a choice/ I can't take back." By reexperiencing her first home now, as an adult, Alvarez discovers that her true identity lies in "a life of choice, a life of words."

The book concludes with "Estel," an enigmatic poem addressed to a mute village child whom Alvarez helped to escape the prison of her disability by enrolling her in a school for the deaf. Like Estel, Alvarez has been "mute," stricken with writer's block, unable to express her dual experiences, "a blank intelligence about to be filled/ with your new life." Yet through the school of her experiences she, too, has gained a voice, the proof of which is this book, *The Other Side/El Otro Lado*.

OTHER MAJOR WORKS

LONG FICTION: *How the Garcia Girls Lost Their Accents*, 1991; *In the Time of the Butterflies*, 1994; *¡Yo!*, 1996; *In the Name of Salome: A Novel*, 2000.

NONFICTION: *Something to Declare*, 1998.

CHILDREN'S LITERATURE: *The Secret Footprints*, 2000; *How Tía Lola Came to Stay*, 2001.

EDITED TEXT: *Old Age Ain't for Sissies*, 1979.

BIBLIOGRAPHY

Alvarez, Julia. "A Citizen of the World: An Interview with Julia Alvarez." In *Latina Self-Portraits: Interviews with Contemporary Women Writers*, edited by Bridget Kevane and Juanita Heredia. Albuquerque: University of New Mexico Press, 2000. Offers insight into background, politics, and various aspects of Alvarez's work as a poet and fiction writer.

_____. "Goodbye, Ms. Chips." In *Wise Women: Reflections of Teachers at Midlife*, edited by Phyllis R. Freeman and Jan Zlotnik Schmidt. New York: Routledge, 2000. Examines Alvarez's development as a writer and as a teacher of writing.

_____. "Julia Alvarez: 'A Clean Windshield.'" In *Passion and Craft: Interviews with Notable Writers*, edited by Bonnie Lyons and Bill Oliver. Urbana: University of Illinois Press, 1998. Alvarez discusses her writing career, influences on her work, and her political and literary philosophies.

_____. "An Unlikely Beginning for a Writer." In *Máscaras*, edited by Lucha Corpi. Berkeley, Calif.: Third Woman Press, 1997. Provides information on the life experiences that have influenced the themes and forms of Alvarez's work.

Rosenberg, Robert, ed. and director. *Women of Hope/ Latinas Abriendo Camino: Twelve Ground Breaking Latina Women*. Bread and Roses Cultural Project. Princeton, N.J.: Films for Humanities, 1996. Interviews a dozen Latina women, including writers Julia Alvarez and Sandra Cisneros.

Sirias, Silvio. *Julia Alvarez: A Critical Companion.* Westport, Conn.: Greenwood Press, 2001. A rare book-length introduction to Alvarez: her life, works, and historical context. Biblography, index.

Melissa E. Barth

YEHUDA AMICHAI

Born: Würzburg, Germany; May 3, 1924
Died: Jerusalem, Israel; September 22, 2000

PRINCIPAL POETRY

Akhshav u-ve-yamin aherim, 1955
Be-merhak shete tikvot, 1958
Shirim, 1948-1962, 1962
Akhshav ba-Ra'ash, 1968
Ve-lo 'almenat lizkor, 1971
Selected Poems, 1971
Me-ahore kol zel mistater osher gadol, 1974
Ha-zeman, 1978 (*Time*, 1979)
Shalyah gedolah, 1980 (*A Great Tranquillity: Questions and Answers*, 1980)
Love Poems, 1981
She'at ha-hessed, 1983
Me'adam ve-el adam tashav, 1985
The Selected Poetry of Yehuda Amichai, 1986, revised 1996
Poems of Jerusalem: A Bilingual Edition, 1988
Nof galui 'enayim/Open Eyed Land, 1992
Poems of Jerusalem and Love Poems: A Bilingual Edition, 1992
Yehuda Amichai: A Life of Poetry, 1948-1994, 1994
Akhziv, Kesaryah ve-ahavah ahat, 1996
Patuah sagur pattuah, 1998 (*Open Closed Open: Poems*, 2000)

OTHER LITERARY FORMS

Yehuda Amichai has written three volumes of fiction and a book for children. *Lo me-akhshav, lo mi-kan*, a novel, was published in Hebrew in Tel Aviv in 1963 and

translated into English as *Not of This Time, Not of This Place* in 1968. A collection of short stories, *Ba-ruah ha-nora'ah ha-zot*, was published in Tel Aviv in 1961; a translation of about half the stories appeared in English in 1984 under the title *The World Is a Room and Other Stories*. Amichai also wrote a play for the radio, titled *Pa'amonim ve-rakavot* (1968; pr. as *Bells and Trains*, 1966). Two of his plays, *No Man's Land* and *Masa' le-Ninveh* (journey to Nineveh) were performed in 1962 and 1964, respectively.

ACHIEVEMENTS

With Amir Gilboa, Abba Kovner, and Dan Pagis, Yehuda Amichai was a leading member of the first generation of Israeli poets. They were born in Europe and Hebrew was not their mother tongue, yet they came to Palestine and were soon writing in the resurrected tongue of Hebrew.

A continuous tradition of secular Hebrew poetry has existed since 1000 B.C.E., flourishing first in Spain, Portugal, Provence, Italy, and the Netherlands, migrating in the nineteenth century to Central and Eastern Europe. Yet the language that the poets used was literary rather than colloquial, and no one spoke it; the poet's Hebrew was largely derived from sacred texts. Amichai and his contemporaries were the first literary generation to use Hebrew as a vernacular. The new generation felt the need to break with the preceding poetic traditions, yet the new spoken language alone did not suffice as a literary instrument. It was this first generation that provided different models and showed how an everyday language–though still replete with biblical and Talmudic echoes—might be transformed into contemporary poetry.

Amichai was one of the leaders of this generation, and the various forms, tonalities, and influences which he introduced into Hebrew literature will have a lasting effect. As the critic Gabriel Josipovici has written, Amichai and his colleagues were European Jews first and Israelis second; the dreadful history of Europe and the Middle East in their lifetime forced them to contemplate their relationship to both Judaism and the State of Israel. Amichai's generation was unique in Hebrew literature, and of this group it is perhaps Amichai who explored the broadest range of poetic forms.

His poetry and prose were awarded the Shlonsky Prize, two Acum prizes, and the especially coveted Israel Prize. His radio play *Bells and Trains* won the first prize in Kol, the country's competition for original radio plays. While his country bestowed upon him its top honors, the Nobel Prize, which many felt he rightly deserved, eluded him. His own belief was that he had been passed over because the choice had become increasingly politicized.

BIOGRAPHY

Yehuda Amichai was born in Würzburg, Germany, in 1924. He grew up in an Orthodox Jewish home; his father was a shopkeeper, his grandfather a farmer. His mother tongue was German. Although he entered the government-sponsored Israelitische Volkschule at the age of six and learned to read and to write Hebrew, he did not begin to speak Hebrew until 1935, when he moved to Palestine with his parents and settled in Jerusalem. His outlook was influenced by the Socialist youth movement, to which most Jewish adolescents belonged in the Palestine of the 1930's and early 1940's. He fought with the British army in World War II, then with the Palmakh in the Israeli War of Independence of 1948. He also fought with the Israeli army in 1956 and 1973.

For most of his life, Amichai made his living as a schoolteacher and was a familiar figure on Jerusalem streets. His poetry was popular in Israel, and after the publication of his first book in 1955, his writing was an important source of supplemental income. Although there are fewer than three million readers of Hebrew in Israel, the collection of his early work, *Shirim, 1948-1962* (poems, 1948-1962), several times reprinted, has sold fifty thousand copies. Translations brought thousands of new readers and additional income for Amichai. He was a visiting poet at the University of California at Berkeley in 1971, and he frequently traveled abroad to give poetry readings.

Though he always served his country militarily when called, he came to view warfare ever more cynically and sadly. When he died, his passing was particularly lamented by the peace movement in Israel and Jewish America, which had come to view him as a spokesperson. He was survived by a much-loved second wife,

frequently celebrated in his poetry, two sons, and a daughter.

ANALYSIS

Yehuda Amichai was not a poet of a single major theme, and a variety of approaches to his work are open to the reader and critic. He was—perhaps above all—an autobiographical poet, yet it is also possible to consider him as a national poet whose personal concerns overlap those of his country. Amichai was one of the few poets of the late twentieth century who could be called genuinely popular, and it is important to consider the nature of his relationship to his audience. Other important features of Amichai's poetry are the apparent effortlessness of his poems, with their agile, attractive speaking voice and complex tone; his use of conceits (his early poetry especially has been called metaphysical) and his consistent success in finding striking, original metaphors; the rich variety of forms he tried, from quasi-Shakespearean sonnets to mock-heroic couplets and free verse; his emphasis on the concrete, palpable events of everyday life, as opposed to the abstract phraseology of ideologies and philosophers; and, finally, his love poetry, the major

Yehuda Amichai

theme of his work from the 1950's and 1960's. Today Amichai is recognized as the author of a body of work extremely varied, rich, and inventive in form. One of Amichai's most remarkable traits is that his poems have the ability to surprise.

AUTOBIOGRAPHICAL NATURE OF WORK

The autobiographical nature of Amichai's poetry was the cause of some attacks on his work. Spontaneous reference to his own experiences characterized his entire œuvre. The other, equally important, impulses are also present: the desire to describe what is real, immediate, and concrete and the need to reach out to his surroundings. In his second collection of poems, he wrote about his thirty-second birthday: "Thirty-two times I have put on the world/ and still it doesn't fit me./ It weighs me down,/ unlike the coat that now takes the shape of my body."

His references to himself were usually self-demeaning and rueful. He did not choose to present the "beautiful soul" held up for admiration by many contemporary American poets. The persona of his poems was always complex and viewed with levels of irony. Clearly there is no barrier between the speaker and his surroundings. Amichai's self—his autobiography—proves to be remarkably synoptic and inclusive. Always he saw himself not as an individual, but a human being against a rich, ambiguous backdrop of Hebrew history, European birth, and Israeli environment. Amichai described himself at home in Jerusalem in his poem "Travels of the Last Benjamin of Tudela":

> I've been patched together
> from many things, I've been gathered in different times,
> I've been assembled from spare parts, from disintegrating
> materials, from decomposing words. And already now,
> in the middle of my life, I'm beginning to return them
>   gradually.

The speaker of such a passage is intimate, his mind agile and far-reaching, never confined. The critic Robert Alter has stressed that archaeology was always one of Amichai's primary metaphors for his perception of the human condition; he saw both the individual self and history as an elaborate depositing of layers in which nothing is entirely buried from sight. There was also an uncanny overlapping between his own life and that of the country of Israel. He wrote in the poem titled "When I Was Young, the Whole Country Was Young":

> When I first fell in love, they proclaimed
> her independence, and when my hair
> fluttered in the breeze, so did her flags.
> When I fought in the war, she fought, when I got up
> she got up too, and when I sank
> she began to sink with me.

The combination of the two themes seems spontaneous and unstudied, always accompanied by humor, irony, and the special effortlessness that by the mid-1970's had become one of the most distinctive features of Amichai's poetry.

MATURE STYLE OF THE 1980'S

After 1980, Amichai fused the two themes to the point of self-parody. In "You Mustn't Show Weakness" he wrote: "This is the way things stand now:/ if I pull out the stopper/ after pampering myself in the bath,/ I'm afraid that all of Jerusalem, and with it the whole world,/ will drain out into the huge darkness." Although such a thought might have actually occurred to him while taking a bath, it is doubtful whether the passage could be called autobiographical; Amichai built a different, much more synoptic persona than the "I" of the earlier poems. This development is confirmed by a passage such as this: "If I'm a hedgehog, I'm a hedgehog in reverse,/ the spikes grow inward and stab./ And if I'm the prophet Ezekiel, I see/ in the Vision of the Chariot/ only the dung-spattered feet of oxen and the muddy wheels."

After the 1980's, it is no longer possible to speak of Amichai's poetry as predominantly autobiographical. He had achieved an inclusive view of the world in which the speaker's observations and his use of a first-person pronoun are strictly vehicles at the service of other concepts: of society and time, of reality, and of the world.

THE REALITY OF CONCRETE EXPERIENCE

Looking back from the vantage point of Amichai's mature style of the 1980's, it is clear that he always appreciated the reality of concrete, individual experience, and of the personalities of other people. For example, some poems were excellent portraits of women, especially "You Are So Small and Slight in the Rain," "The Sweet Breakdowns of Abigail," and the devastating and sensual "A Bride Without a Dowry," which ends:

And she's got a will of iron inside
that soft, self-indulgent flesh.
What a terrible bloodbath
she's preparing for herself.
What a Roman arena streaming with blood.

In another poem he wrote that as a child, when he banged his head on the door, he did not scream "Mama" or "God," but simply, "my head, my head," and "door, door." The meaning is clear: He always preferred solid, palpable reality to subjective notions.

LIMITS OF TRANSLATION

Gabriel Josipovici has written that, "like much postwar East European poetry, Amichai's is poetry which can travel"; that is, it is easily translated. His fluctuating tone, the humor, irony, and playfulness with words were extremely subtle; however, much is lost, both in style and content, in translation. Amichai's poetry remains powerful in the hands of such talented translators as Chana Bloch and Stephen Mitchell. But even they cannot fully render into English the complex historical stratifications of the Hebrew tongue. Words and images have acquired multiple resonances through the millennia, in biblical, talmudic, and cabbalistic writings.

An example of the limits of translation is the ending of "When a Man's Far Away from His Country," a wry, bitter poem whose subject is the quality of language. Not only in style but also in theme the tone and spoken rhythms are all-important. One translation, by Bloch, whose work has been justly praised, ends:

> In my words
> is the soul's garbage, the trash of lust,
> and dust and sweat. In this dry land even the water I drink
> between screams and mumblings of desire
> is urine,
> recycled back to me by a twisted route.

An English translation by Amichai himself reads:

> In my words there is garbage of soul
> and refuse of lust and dust and sweat.
> Even the water I drink in this dry land,
> between screams and memories of love,
> is urine recycled back to me
> through complicated circuits.

Amichai's version has one line less (like the original), a different system of emphases, stresses, and tonalities. In

the first translation, it would be difficult for the reader to divine that the "twisted route" could refer to the theme of memory, while the humorous "complicated circuits" clearly recalls the theme—and process—of memory. The stress on excretion in the first translation shifts the meaning.

Much is lost in even the best translations. As Robert Alter writes, "His Hebrew is often rich in sound play, wordplay, allusion, and other traits of virtuosity that are not readily evident in translation, and his language is a shifting mixture of colloquial and literary." Colloquial, spoken tone is important: Puns, employed seriously even by Hebrew prophets in the Bible, are either lost or misunderstood. Amichai was influenced by W. H. Auden: When he was a soldier in the British army, he found a Faber and Faber anthology of contemporary British and American poetry. Perhaps the best way for an English-speaking reader to have a sense of Amichai's verbal textures is to read the selections in *The Modern Hebrew Poem Itself* (1965), edited by Stanley Burnshaw, and the *Penguin Book of Hebrew Verse* (1981), edited by T. Carmi. These provide literal translations and full commentaries that give the English speaker an idea of the density of Amichai's style in the original Hebrew.

USE OF METAPHOR

One feature of Amichai's style much easier to translate is the use of metaphor. From the very beginning, Amichai was a virtuoso of metaphor. He seemed to produce metaphors effortlessly—perhaps too effortlessly, as some early poems became metaphorical tours de force. He could write about Jerusalem as "the Venice of God," or, in another context, as "An operation that was left open." A fig tree is "that brothel where ripe figs/ couple with wasps and are split to death." The metaphors were sometimes witty, as in "Jerusalem's a place where everyone remembers/ he's forgotten something/ but doesn't remember what it is" or "tears/ remain longer than whatever caused them." Yet the wit often is turned into profound meaning, as in this stanza:

> There are candles that remember for a full twenty-four
> hours,
> that's what the label says. And candles that remember
> for eight hours, and eternal candles
> that guarantee a man will be remembered by his children.

One of the vices of Amichai's poetry was that often he was willing to settle for easy metaphors. This might have been partly a result of his respect for solidity, for reality; as a young poet his posture was of assent, of necessary yet ironic acceptance. His concept of life was basically linear: "Our lives were stamped *To the last stop: one way*." He made a similar statement in another volume of poems: "I am always Cain:/ a fugitive and a vagabond before the deed that I won't do,/ or after the deed that/ can't be undone." This had its pious side; although he could be irreverent about God (Amichai ceased to believe in a deity at the age of fifteen), there was another, greater loyalty to his community: "When I was a child I sang in the synagogue choir,/ . . . and I'll go on singing/ till my heart breaks, first heart and second heart./ A Psalm." It required some time, perhaps two decades, for him to pass through the stage in which he thought of himself primarily as a vehicle—a head "like the heads of those senseless weeds" through which fate passes like wind from one place to another—to his later and far more dynamic, nonlinear version of history and life.

LOVE POEMS

It is in Amichai's earlier volumes that he was primarily a love poet. When he was in his twenties and thirties, it seemed as if the love of women, and especially one woman, was to be his overriding theme. Some of these poems express wonder at a woman's beauty and a concentrated dedication to sensual heterosexual love. He wrote: "I tried to go out into my times, and to know,/ but I didn't get further/ than the woman's body beside me."

Many of Amichai's love poems are very moving, and they are frequently anthologized. A bilingual collection was selected from his different volumes by Amichai himself and published as *Love Poems* in 1981. The poems are sensual, savage, nothing seems to be held back, and they range through a broad spectrum of emotions. "Six Songs for Tamar" and "Songs for a Woman" are especially beautiful. The note of wonder Amichai expresses could be very moving: "If you open your coat/ my love must widen." In many poems, however, there is a note not only of deep sadness but also of self-pity, as in the much-admired poem "A Pity. We Were Such a Good Invention," which ends:

A pity. We were such a good
and loving invention.
An airplane made from a man and a wife.
Wings and everything.
We hovered a little above the earth.

We even flew a little.

The note of mingled psychological realism and irony that became more pronounced as Amichai matured also crept into his verses contemplating love:

The singer of the Song of Songs sought his beloved so
long
and hard
that he lost his mind and went looking for her with a
simile
And fell in love with the images he himself had imagined.

Although the clipped, elegiac mood is obviously ironic, it spread from poem to poem and became obsessive, threatening to swamp Amichai's other concerns. Yet he grew and added new themes.

OPEN CLOSED OPEN

As a younger man, rejecting the jingoistic military phrases of a nation frequently embattled, Amichai had affirmed in verse his desire to die peacefully in his own bed rather than gloriously on the battlefield. In his last book, *Open Closed Open*, he reiterated this message, at the same time rejecting the burial practices of his Orthodox upbringing:

When I die I want only women to tend to me at the burial
society,
To do to my body what seems right in their pretty eyes and
clean out my ears from the
last words
I heard and wipe from my lips the last words I uttered
And rub my flesh with perfumed oil so as to anoint me the
King of Death for a single
day.

His last book also continued his lifelong argument with the God whose existence he doubted, a deity so negligent of his chosen people. The image of Jewish scholars reading the Torah aloud to God all year long, a portion each week, and then starting all over again the next year, called to his mind Scherherazade frantically talking to save her life. Jews, he suggested, hastened to put themselves in the hand of God merely to avoid that same punishing hand. In other lines he spoke of the Christian God as a suffering Jew and the Muslim God as an Arab Jew, still hoarse from the desert. Only the Jewish God seemed not really Jewish at all.

And he was ready to face head-on the Holocaust that his family had escaped by their early migration from Germany. How, he asked, could there be any desire to know God after Auschwitz? He observed that white smoke rises from Vatican chimneys when popes are chosen, while black smoke rose from Auschwitz crematoria to signify that "God has not yet chosen the Chosen People!"

Finally, Amichai was left to question one of the last verities of his life, the value and mission of the state of Israel. His chosen metaphor was the Huleh swamp, whose drainage had been an early article of Zionist pride. Later it was discovered that what had seemed a valiant land reclamation had been in fact an ecological disaster. The results of all human efforts seemed now equally uncertain.

While Amichai's last published poems conveyed a compassionate skepticism of all endeavor and despite war and world weariness, the poet did not totally abandon hope. Might it still be possible, he wondered, for Palestine and Israel to lay down their arms and, like their proverbial ancestors Ishmael and Isaac, come together after many grievances and bury their father Abraham in the Cave of Machpelah?

OTHER MAJOR WORKS

LONG FICTION: *Lo me-akhshav, lo mi-kan*, 1963 (*Not of This Time, Not of This Place*, 1968); *Mi yitneni malon*, 1971.

SHORT FICTION: *Ba-ruah ha-nora'ah ha-zot*, 1961; *The World Is a Room and Other Stories*, 1984.

PLAYS: *Masa' le-Ninveh*, pb. 1962, pr. 1964; *No Man's Land*, pr. 1962.

RADIO PLAY: *Pa'amonim ve-rakavot*, 1968 (pr. as *Bells and Trains*, 1966).

BIBLIOGRAPHY

Alter, Robert. "The Untranslatable Amichai." *Modern Hebrew Literature* 13 (Fall/Winter, 1994). A clear, succinct discussion of the problems of linguistic and cross-cultural translation, with attention to Hebrew writing in general and Amichai's verse in particular. Alter, who has discussed biblical translation in earlier writings, is well equipped to elucidate the multilayered cultural heritage of Israeli poetry.

Burnshaw, Stanley, T. Carmi, and Ezra Spicehandler, eds. *The Hebrew Poem Itself*. New York: Holt, Rinehart and Winston, 1965. An anthology of twentieth century Jewish poetry that provides, in addition to bilingual texts, transliterations of Hebrew poems into the Latin alphabet. A clarifying general introduction and perceptive analyses of individual poets and their verses are provided. The discussion of Amichai's poetry by Robert Friend stresses the poet's skill in transmuting the materials of his own life into universal statements.

Cohen, Joseph. *Voices of Israel: Essays and Interviews with Yehuda Amichai, A.B. Yehoshua, T. Carmi, Aharon Applefeld, and Amos Oz.* Albany: State University of New York Press, 1965. An examination of five "new wave" Israeli writers regarded as literary spokespersons for their nation. Both the introductory essays on the individual writers and the questions asked in their interviews highlight the special opportunities offered creative artists by the environment of Israel, a nation resurrected from antiquity, still precariously situated at a crossroads of global cultures.

Green, David B. "The Most Accessible Poet: Yehuda Amichai, 1924-2000." *The Jerusalem Report*, October 23, 2000. An obituary and overview of the achievements of Amichai, from a respected news magazine that surveys worldwide Jewry. Replete with facts and provocative observations, Green's article celebrates a beloved cultural hero of his nation.

Williams, C. K. "We Cannot Be Fooled, We Can Be Fooled." *New Republic*, July 3, 2000. Ostensibly a review of Amichai's last book published in English but actually an identification of the central themes of the poet's career. Green finds a clear "ethical focus" in the poet's work and places him within the grand tradition of Western humanistic letters, even while acknowledging the Hebraic sources.

John Carpenter, updated by Allene Phy-Olsen

A. R. AMMONS

Born: Near Whiteville, North Carolina; February 18, 1926

Died: Ithaca, New York; February 25, 2001

PRINCIPAL POETRY

Ommateum, with Doxology, 1955
Expressions of Sea Level, 1963
Corsons Inlet: A Book of Poems, 1965
Tape for the Turn of the Year, 1965
Northfield Poems, 1966
Selected Poems, 1968
Uplands, 1970
Briefings: Poems Small and Easy, 1971
Collected Poems, 1951-1971, 1972
Sphere: The Form of a Motion, 1974
Diversifications, 1975
The Snow Poems, 1977
The Selected Poems, 1951-1977, 1977
Highgate Road, 1977
Six-Piece Suite, 1979
Selected Longer Poems, 1980
A Coast of Trees, 1981
Worldly Hopes, 1982
Lake Effect Country, 1983
The Selected Poems: Expanded Edition, 1986
Sumerian Vistas, 1987
The Really Short Poems of A. R. Ammons, 1990
Garbage, 1993
The North Carolina Poems, 1994
Brink Road, 1996
Glare, 1997

OTHER LITERARY FORMS

Although A. R. Ammons is known primarily for his poetry, he also published reviews and essays. Central to an understanding of his work are "A Poem Is a Walk" and his short autobiographical reflection "I Couldn't Wait to Say the Word." Ammons's several published interviews, especially one by Cynthia Haythe, give additional insight into his poetics. *Set in Motion: Essays, Interviews, and Dialogues* (1996) collects his most important writings about poetry.

A. R. Ammons

ACHIEVEMENTS

Throughout a distinguished and prolific career, A. R. Ammons observed and presented the particulars of the world while projecting his longing for a sense of unity. He immersed himself in the flow of things, celebrating the world and the self that sees and probes it.

Ammons's work lies within the Emersonian tradition: He wrote from life without being a slave to any set poetic form. Yet, more than any other poet since Ralph Waldo Emerson, he developed a transcendentalism rooted in science and in a poetic that includes the self in the work. His epigrams, his short to moderate-length nature lyrics, and his long verse-essays are popular reading among poets.

His many awards include the Bread Loaf Writers' Conference Scholarship (1961), a Guggenheim Fellowship (1966), an American Academy of Arts and Letters Traveling Fellowship (1967), a National Endowment for the Arts grant (1969-1970), a Levinson Prize (1970), a National Book Award for *Collected Poems, 1951-1971* (1973), an honorary Litt.D. from

Wake Forest University (1973), the Bollingen Prize in Poetry for *Sphere: The Form of a Motion* (1974-1975), a National Book Critics Circle Award for *A Coast of Trees* (1981), a John D. and Catherine T. MacArthur Foundation Award (1981), and the North Carolina Award for Literature (1986). In 1990, he was inducted into the National Academy and Institute of Arts and Letters. In 1993, Ammons won a second National Book Award for *Garbage*, and he was also awarded the Poetry Society of America's Frost Medal for Distinguished Achievement in Poetry Over a Lifetime (1994) as well as the $100,000 Tanning Prize for mastery of his chosen art form (1998). Ammons is recognized as one of the most significant and original voices in twentieth century poetry.

Biography

Archie Randolph Ammons was born on February 18, 1926, near Whiteville, North Carolina, in a house bought by his grandfather and situated on the family farm. The main book in the house was the Bible. Ammons's early experiences on the farm, working the land, helped shape his imagination. The self in his poems appears most frequently in relation to the natural world he knew as a child.

He was his parents' fourth child. Three sisters were born before him and two brothers after; one sister lived for only two weeks, and both brothers died, one in infancy and the other at birth. Ammons remembered the deaths of his brothers, saying that they accounted in part for the undercurrent of loss and loneliness in his work.

Upon graduation from high school in 1943, Ammons took a job in the shipyard in Wilmington, North Carolina. In 1944, he joined the navy, spending nineteen months in service, including time in the South Pacific, where he began writing poems. Returning home after the war, Ammons attended Wake Forest College (his tuition paid for by the G.I. Bill) and graduated with a B.S. in 1949. That year he married Phyllis Plumbo and took a job as principal of an elementary school in the remote coastal community of Hatteras, North Carolina. From 1950 to 1952, he studied English at the University of California at Berkeley. In 1952, he took a position with his father-in-law's New Jersey medical glassware firm, a job he held for twelve years. He soon began to send poems to literary magazines, and in 1953 *The Hudson Review* accepted two of them. His first book of poetry, *Ommateum, with Doxology*, appeared in 1955. Eight years later, *Expressions of Sea Level* appeared. In 1964, he began teaching at Cornell University. Other books of poems followed, and in 1972 most of his poems were published as *Collected Poems, 1951-1971. Sphere: The Form of a Motion*, his poem of more than two thousand lines, published in 1974, gained for him the Bollingen Prize in Poetry for 1974-1975. Whitmanesque in its tendency toward democratic feeling, *Sphere* presents Ammons's aesthetic of continual motion and a musical affirmation of interdependence in the energy of all life. Ammons continued to be highly productive in his later years. *The North Carolina Poems* appeared in 1994; *Brink Road* was published in 1996; and his final book, *Glare*, appeared in 1997.

Ammons served for many years as the Goldwin Smith Professor of Poetry at Cornell University. In 1998, the university honored him with a celebration of his monumental achievement. He died from cancer in February of 2001, leaving behind his wife, his son John, and two grandchildren. Throughout his career, Ammons made frequent trips to eastern North Carolina, a place which figures prominently in his poems.

Analysis

In one of A. R. Ammons's early poems, "So I Said I Am Ezra," from *Ommateum, with Doxology*, the speaker is whipped over the landscape, driven, moved by the natural elements. He is at once ordered and disordered, close and far, balanced and unbalanced, and he exclaims: "So I Ezra went out into the night/ like a drift of sand." The line is representative of Ammons's entire body of work, for it announces a search through language in an attempt to mean and to be clear, and failing to succeed completely in such clarity, the line ends by affirming a presence of radiance.

Expressions of Sea Level

Ammons's poems have a tendency, like most contemporary poems, to take their own process, their own making, as a theme. Wanting to express something changeless and eternal, Ammons is constrained by his own intricate mortality. So in the title poem of *Expressions of Sea Level*, he presents the ocean as permanent and impermanent, as form and formlessness. He is interested in what man can and cannot know, giving full sway and expression to the ocean's activity: "See the dry casting of the beach worm/ dissolve at the delicate rising touch." The range and flow in Ammons's poetry, his search for balance, moved him to create his philosophical music, using a vocabulary drawn largely from everyday speech. He celebrates the need in every human being to discover a common experience in the least particular thing.

POEMS OF NORTH CAROLINA

Ammons attempts always to render visual details accurately. Some of the most moving poems in this regard are the poems inspired by his background in Columbus County, North Carolina. "Nelly Meyers" praises and celebrates a woman who lived on the farm where Ammons grew up; "Silver" records Ammons's love for and rapport with a mule he used for work. "Hardweed Path Going" tells of his life as a boy, doing chores on the farm, his playtime with a pet bird (a jo-reet) and a hog named Sparkle. These poems recreate Ammons's past, particularly his boyhood, which he renders in astonishingly realistic details.

CORSONS INLET

Ammons infuses the natural world with his own attuned sensibilities, acknowledging in the title poem of *Corsons Inlet* that "Overall is beyond me." The form of the poem is a walk over the dunes. What lives beyond his perception reassures, although he knows "that there is no finality of vision." Bafflement is a primary feeling in the poem, which may be studied for what it says about the relationship between logic and reason, imposed order and discovered order, art and life, reality and illusion, being and becoming. "Corsons Inlet" concludes the walk/quest on the note that "tomorrow a new walk is a new walk." Ammons's desire to say something clearly, therefore, is not so much a search for the word as it is an attempt to find original ways to make and shape poetry.

TAPE FOR THE TURN OF THE YEAR

With *Tape for the Turn of the Year*, Ammons writes a long, narrow poem on adding-machine paper. The poet improvises and spontaneously records his thoughts and moods in what resembles a poetic diary. In one place, he praises how writing gets done, suggesting that doing it is almost its own practical reward, as the speaker acknowledges in another poem, "Identity," "it is wonderful how things work."

MAJOR THEMES

By the mid-1960's, Ammons's major themes had emerged, his sensibility oscillating between extremes: formlessness-form, center-periphery, high-low, motion-stasis, order-disorder, one-many. One of his most constant themes has been the self in the work and in the world. He is concerned not only with the form of natural fact but also with form in the abstract sense, that is, with physical laws that govern the way individual entities act and behave. Ammons reaffirms the resonance of his subject, as in "The Eternal City," in which destruction must "accept into itself piece by piece all the old/ perfect human visions, all the old perfect loves."

Motion within diversity is perhaps Ammons's major theme. In "Saliences," from *Northfield Poems*, he discovers continuity in change. In "Snow Log," from *Uplands*, recognizing that nature's intentions cannot be known, he responds simply as an individual to what he sees in the winter scene: "I take it on myself:/ especially the fallen tree/ the snow picks/ out in the woods to show." In "The City Limits," from *Briefings*, a poem whose urban subject removes the speaker from nature, Ammons celebrates the "gold-skeined wings of flies swarming the dumped/ guts of a natural slaughter or the coil of shit."

COLLECTED POEMS, 1951-1971

Awarded the National Book Award for Poetry in 1973, *Collected Poems, 1951-1971* comprises most of Ammons's first six volumes, except for *Tape for the Turn of the Year* and three long verse-essays—"Extremes and Moderations," "Hibernaculum," and "Essay on Poetics." In "Extremes and Moderations" and "Hibernaculum," Ammons is a seer, lamenting humankind's abuse of the earth and appreciating the immediacy of a world that takes care of itself. "Essay on Poetics" considers the structural advantages and disadvantages of poetry. One reads this essay to appreciate more fully Ammons's views on writing.

SPHERE: THE FORM OF A MOTION

In perhaps his major work, the book-length poem *Sphere: The Form of a Motion*, Ammons explores motion and shape in a set form: sentences with no full stops, 155 sections of four tercets each. He relies on colons, perhaps suggesting a democratization and a flow. Shifting freely, sometimes abruptly, within a given stanza, phrase, or word, Ammons says, "I do not smooth into groups." Thus the book explores the nature of its own poetics, the poet searching everywhere for a language of clarity. In one place, he says that he is "sick of good poems." Wanting the smooth and raw together, Ammons reminds the reader that his prejudice against neat, traditional structures in poetry relates to the natural world where "the shapes nearest shapelessness awe us most, suggest the god." He regards a log, "rigid with shape," as "trivial." Ammons, therefore, makes his case for the poem of the open form as opposed to strong, traditional verses.

Ammons demythologizes poetics and language, while testifying to an Emersonian faith in the universe as flowing freely and spontaneously. At the same time, there is a counter feeling always working. He refers often to clarity and wants his poems to arrive and move forward "by a controlling motion, design, symmetry."

While he is writing the poem, commenting on it, writing himself into it, he shows his instinct for playfulness, for spoofing. This aspect of his work—the clowning humor—adds an inherent drama to his work, as critic Jerald Bullis has written:

> The tone of the poem or, I should say, of the voices of its "parts," ranges and range from that of the high and hard lyric, the crystalline and *as if* final saying, through a talky and often latinate professorial stance, to permutations of low tone: "bad" puns, catalogues that seem to have been lifted from a catalogue, and, in the example below, the high-pressure pitch-man tone of How-To scams: "Now, first of all, the way to write poems is just to start: it's like learning to walk or swim or ride the bicycle, you just go after it."

The poem goes on, praising the ability of man to write and to appreciate being alive.

Reverence for creation runs throughout *Sphere*, investing the work with a vision beyond and through the details of the poet's aesthetic. This religious strain has its source in Ammons's absolute reverence for the natural world. A religious vocabulary, then, is no surprise in his work and connects with his childhood, when church services and hymn-sings were dominant parts of his life. As in *Sphere*, he questions what is "true service," saying "it must be a service that is celebration, for we would celebrate even if we do not know what or how, and for He is bountiful if/ slow to protect and recalcitrant to keep." Ammons goes on to say: "What we can celebrate is the condition we are in, or we can renounce the condition/ we are in and celebrate a condition we might be in or ought/ to be in." Ammons fuses and plays on the relationship between creation and imagination, hoping and trying to discover "joy's surviving radiance." In the presence of this radiance—the hues and bends of Ammons's music—exist the crux of his aesthetic, his art and his being: the solitary man never surrendering as he is being imposed on and whipped about, as he writes in one of his earliest poems, "So I Said I am Ezra/ and the wind whipped my throat/ gaming for the sounds of my voice." Yet the self is not dwarfed by the world. Ammons understands his moral and aesthetic convictions and will not cease to assert them. Such desire allows the visionary in Ammons constantly to discover new ways to see and understand his life. In this regard, key words crop up often: "salience," "recalcitrant," "suasion," "periphery," "possibility," tentative words that tend to illuminate or seek the proper blend in experience. So *Sphere* ends as it began, clear and free of all encumbrances except the spoken voice: "we're ourselves: we're sailing." The ending is right for the "form of a motion," the sense of wonder and uncertainty going on beyond the finality of the poem. Past, present, and future are one, and the poem and its end recall Walt Whitman's absorption into the dirt in "Song of Myself."

THE SNOW POEMS

In *The Snow Poems*, Ammons continues his experimental attempt to arrange a poetic journal, recounting in lyrical splendor the concerns of daily life, including details about weather, sex, and the poet's attempt to write and to experience a dialogue between the specific and the general.

Ammons's work since the mid-1970's marks a return to the more visionary tendencies contained in his earlier terse, fierce lyrics of short or moderate length. "Progress Report" is an epigram from *Worldly Hopes:*

Now I'm
into things

so small
when I

say boo
I disappear

The words flow in natural motion.

LAKE EFFECT COUNTRY

Lake Effect Country continues Ammons's love of
form and motion. The whole book represents one body,
a place of water, a bed of lively recreation. In "Meeting
Place," for example, "The water nearing the ledge leans
down with/ grooved speed at the spill then,/ quickly
groundless in air." His vision comes from the coming together of the natural elements in the poem, rising and falling, moving and forming the disembodied voices that
are the real characters in his poems: "When I call out to
them/ as to the flowing bones in my naked self, is my/ address attribution's burden and abuse." "Meeting Place"
goes out "to summon/ the deep-lying fathers from myself,/ the spirits, feelings howling, appearing there."

A COAST OF TREES

A major contemporary poem is "Easter Morning,"
from *A Coast of Trees*. Based on the death in infancy of
the poet's younger brother, the poem is filled with reverence for the natural world, Ammons's memory ever enlarging with religious and natural resonances. "I have a
life that did not become,/ that turned aside and stopped,/
astonished." The poem carries the contradictory mysteries of the human condition—death, hope, and memory—
working together in a concrete and specific aesthetic.
Presented in the form of a walk, "Easter Morning" reveals the speaker caught in the motion, as two birds
"from the South" fly around, circle, change their ways,
and go on. The poem affirms, with the speaker in another poem called "Working with Tools," "I understand/
and won't give assertion up." Like Ezra going out "into
the night/ like a drift of sand," the poet celebrates "a
dance sacred as the sap in/ the trees . . . fresh as this par-
ticular/ flood of burn breaking across us now/ from the
sun." Though the dance is completed in a moment, it can
never be destroyed, because it has been re-created as the
imagination's grand dance.

SUMERIAN VISTAS

Another major contemporary poem is "The Ridge
Farm" from *Sumerian Vistas*. In fifty-one parts, the
poem renders the farm itself on a ridge, on the edge of
everything and nothing. Ammons's speaker joyfully re-
signs himself to the "highways" and the dammed-up
brooks. The implication is that poetry—like Nature—
breaks through and flows, exploring the motion and
shape of the farm's form. The farm itself is a concrete
place wherein Ammons explores the nature of poetics
and other realities.

THE REALLY SHORT POEMS OF A. R. AMMONS

In *The Really Short Poems of A. R. Ammons*, the poet
continues his necessity to really *see* the natural world.
That seeing becomes the poem; its motion, the story
moving through the images. The form and subject move
in a terse, fierce way as the poem discovers itself. In
"Winter Scene," for example, the natural world changes
radiantly when the jay takes over the leafless cherry tree.
The landscape transformed, the poet notes what he sees:
"then every branch// quivers and/ breaks out in blue
leaves." Motion formerly void of color brightens with
vision and sway.

GARBAGE

Many consider *Garbage* to be a capstone of Ammons's maturity. Inspired by a massive landfill along
Florida's portion of I-95, this book-length poem continues Ammons's contemplation of and reverence for
nature, this time positing the theme of regeneration following decay. It is a theme he applies to the human condition as well as to the sorry condition man has brought
to nature. According to David Lehman, in his profile
of Ammons published in the Summer, 1998, issue of
American Poet, Ammons was attracted to the garbage
mound for several reasons, including its geometry.
Writes Lehman, "The mound struck him as a hierarchical image, like a pyramid or the triangulation of a piece
of pie. The pointed top corresponded to unity, the base
to diversity. This paradigm of unity and diversity—and
the related philosophical question of "the one and the
many"—has been a constant feature of Ammons's work
from the start."

GLARE

Ammon's penchant for stretching out his thoughts
and words is nowhere as evident as in his 1997 volume,

Glare. Comprising two sections, "Strip" and "Scat Scan," and written in his familiar couplet style, it is a work that is self-deprecating and spontaneous. Ammons speaks of "finding the form of the process," and critics have noted that his apparent ambition in Glare was "to make the finished form of the poem indistinguishable from the process of composition." In doing so, it reveals an immediacy of experience and thought, a kind of poetry in real time. In "Strip," he writes, "I have plenty and/ give plenty away, why because here/ at nearly 70 stuff has bunched up/ with who knows how much space to/ spread out into." The themes of "Scat" are harder to discern. Overall, he uses twisted proverbs and recalls Robert Frost's poetry to sum up his life.

OTHER MAJOR WORK

NONFICTION: *Set in Motion: Essays, Interviews, and Dialogues*, 1996.

BIBLIOGRAPHY

Ammons, A. R.. "An Interview with A. R. Ammons." Interview by Cynthia Haythe. *Contemporary Literature* 21 (Spring, 1980): 173-190. Ammons responds to questions about his southernness and his "exile" in the North. He discusses *Sphere* and other poems, as well as his affinity with other contemporary poets.

Bloom, Harold, ed. *A. R. Ammons*. New York: Chelsea House, 1986. This volume contains eighteen essays on Ammons's work, plus an introductory essay by Bloom. Among the contributors are contemporary poets John Ashbery, Richard Howard, and John Hollander. Ammons himself offers an essay. Perhaps the central theme of all the essays is that Ammons, like Walt Whitman, is a solitary self in the world. The text is supplemented by a chronology, notes, a bibliography, acknowledgments, and an index.

Elder, John. *Imagining the Earth: Poetry and the Vision of Nature*. Urbana: University of Illinois Press, 1985. Elder writes about poets who remember and re-create the earth. His chapter on Ammons is called "Poetry and the Mind's Terrain." Elder's prose is clear and uncluttered; he presents Ammons from the fresh perspective of contemporary poets. Includes chapter notes and an index.

Hans, James S. *The Value(s) of Literature*. Albany: State University of New York Press, 1990. This book addresses the ethical aspects of literature by discussing three major American poets: Walt Whitman, Wallace Stevens, and A. R. Ammons. The chapter on Ammons is called "Ammons and the One: Many Mechanisms." In a concluding chapter, "The Aesthetic of Worldly Hopes," Hans speculates that one of the reasons poetry is not read widely in the United States is that it is "perceived to have nothing of ethical value inherent in it." What Hans calls "patterns of choice" exist in poems such as "Corsons Inlet" and "Essay on Poetics." Contains chapter notes.

Holder, Alan. *A. R. Ammons*. Boston: Twayne, 1978. This introductory book-length study presents Ammons's life and works through *Sphere*. The text is supplemented by a chronology, notes, a select bibliography (with annotated secondary sources), and an index.

Kirschten, Robert. *Approaching Prayer: Ritual and the Shape of Myth in A. R. Ammons and James Dickey*. Baton Rouge: Louisiana State University Press, 1998. A mythopoetic study of each author that focuses on ceremonial strategies, this analysis examines the nature of Ammons's interest in ancient Sumerian as well as other traditions.

Schneider, Steven P., ed. *Complexities of Motion: New Essays on A. R. Ammons's Long Poems*. Madison, N.J.: Fairleigh Dickenson University Press, 1999. Essays by Helen Vendler, Marjorie Perloff, and other major critics examine the genre of the long poem as individualized by Ammons. Rationale, shape, structure, and strategy are explored, along with recurrent themes.

Sciagaj, Leonard M. *Sustainable Poetry: Four American Ecopoets*. Lexington: University Press of Kentucky, 1999. Along with Ammons, discusses and compares Wendell Berry, Gary Snyder, and W. S. Merwin and their treatment of nature and environmental concerns in their works. Bibliographical references, index.

Spiegelman, Willard. *The Didactic Muse*. Princeton, N.J.: Princeton University Press, 1989. Spiegelman's chapter on Ammons is called "Myths of Concretion, Myths of Abstraction: The Case of A. R. Ammons." Spiegelman ranges over Ammons's work, particularly the longer poems through *Sumerian Vistas*. Spiegelman's concern is the relation between poetry and philosophy. He contends that Ammons's dominant conceit is motion: his attempt to find that place where the conscious and unconscious move, yet stay. The book is important to any student who wishes to see Ammons's work within the larger context of contemporary poetry.

Vendler, Helen, ed. *Voices and Visions: The Poet in America*. New York: Random House, 1987. A companion to *Voices and Visions*, a Public Broadcasting Service television series. In Calvin Bedient's essay on Walt Whitman, he discusses Ammons's *Sphere* within Whitman's energetic thrust out—toward a desire to create a motion within the American attraction for space, for going on, for expanding one's self in a larger world. The book contains pictures of poets, illustrations, notes on chapters, suggestions for further reading, notes on contributors, a list of illustrations, and an index.

Shelby Stephenson, updated by
Philip K. Jason and Sarah Hilbert

ANACREON

Born: Teos, Ionia, Asia Minor (now Sigacik, Turkey); c. 571 B.C.E.
Died: Athens, Greece; c. 490 B.C.E.

PRINCIPAL POETRY

Anacreon composed poems for oral performance, not posterity. He seems to have written no single book or collection of poems. For his complete poems in Greek, see *Poetae Melici Graeci*, 1962 (Denys Page, editor). The first English translation of Anacreon was *Anacreon Done into English out of the Original Greek*, 1683; later translations include *The Odes of Anacreon*, 1928 (Erastus Richardson, translator), and *Greek Lyric*, 1982 (David A. Campbell, translator).

OTHER LITERARY FORMS

Anacreon is remembered only for his poetry.

ACHIEVEMENTS

Included in the Alexandrine canon of nine Greek lyric poets, Anacreon has influenced generations of poets since classical times, although it is difficult to measure his influence precisely with such fragmentary texts. The surviving fragments show that Anacreon set a high standard for sophisticated, polished, short poems written in a variety of meters. While he appears to favor a combination of Glyconics and Pherecrateans in his extant verse, he is best known for the Anacreontic meter, an anaclastic Ionic dimeter to which he has given his name. He was probably most admired in antiquity for his love poems, his banquet poems, and his imagery and tropes, especially those dealing with Eros, which became standardized in later poetry.

Anacreon's style was copied by unknown Greek poets writing under his name; these spurious poems, usually called the Anacreonteia, survive in the *Palatine Anthology* and range in date from the Alexandrine period through late Byzantine times. The poetry of Horace and of other Roman lyric poets also shows conscious imitation of Anacreon, whose authentic works could still be read in Augustan Rome. Anacreon is better known in the modern world through the Anacreonteia than through his own works. The Anacreonteia, first printed in 1554, had a great influence upon several European literary schools; upon the French Renaissance poets Pierre de Ronsard and Rémy Belleau; upon such Italian lyric poets of the seventeenth and eighteenth centuries as Gabriello Chiabrera and Jacopo Vittorelli; upon such eighteenth century German poets as Friedrich von Hagedorn, Johann Gleim, and Johann Götz; and upon the British and Irish poets Robert Herrick, William Oldys, and Thomas Moore. These poets, often called Anacreontics, either made free translations of the Greek Anacreonteia into their own languages or wrote original poetry in the meter and style known as Anacreontic.

BIOGRAPHY

Anacreon's poetry reflects the aristocratic Greek society of the sixth century B.C.E. in which he lived. His was a society endangered by Persian encroachments on

Ionic Greece, as well as by internal political upheavals marked by the rise and fall of antiaristocratic tyrannies. Although little is known for certain about Anacreon's life, much can be conjectured from ancient citations and, to a lesser degree, from the remains of his own poetry.

Anacreon, son of Scythinus, was born in the Ionian city of Teos (now Sigacik, Turkey) about 571 B.C.E. Teos was seized by the Persian Harpagus soon after the fall of Sardis about 541 B.C.E. Many Teans, including Anacreon, escaped Persian rule by fleeing to Abdera on the coast of Thrace; fragments 391 P. and 419 P. may refer to this traumatic period in Anacreon's life. Anacreon's Thracian period is obscure; only a few fragments, including 417 P., reflect his experiences there. Anacreon's poetic reputation, however, certainly grew from that time, for he was at some point invited to the court of the Samian tyrant, Polycrates (ruled 540 to c. 522 B.C.E.), to tutor Polycrates' son in music and poetry.

Polycrates' political policy on Samos included a patronage of the arts which brought to the island not only Anacreon but also the West Greek poet, Ibycus of Rhegium, known for his choral song. Although Anacreon remained in Samos until the death of Polycrates and is said by ancient sources to have made frequent reference to the tyrant in his poetry, only a few allusions to events in Samos (348 P., 353 P., and 426 P.) can be found in Anacreon's extant fragments. The surviving poetry suggests that Anacreon had little enthusiasm for political themes; he preferred to write about love and wine. Although Anacreon's love poetry was addressed primarily to young boys, this provides meager evidence for the poet's biography, since homoeroticism was a conventional poetic theme in his society (as in, for example, Sappho's works).

With the fall of Polycrates about 522 B.C.E., Anacreon was brought to Athens by the Pisistratid Hipparchus, who, like Polycrates, practiced a policy of art patronage under the tyranny of his brother Hippias. Anacreon remained in Athens for the rest of his life, except for a brief interlude in Thessaly about 512 B.C.E., caused by the fall of the Pisistratids.

As he grew older, Anacreon introduced the theme of old age into his poetry, often combining it with his favorite themes of love and wine. It was for this type of poetry that he was best known in the aristocratic Athenian society for which he wrote. Anacreon's personality came to be so closely associated with love and wine that long after his death he was remembered as a drunken, amorous old man. Indeed, this may account for the ancient tradition that Anacreon died as a result of choking on a grape pip. Whatever the actual cause, Anacreon died probably about 490 B.C.E., since the ancients say that he lived past the age of eighty and that he lived long enough to experience the poetry of Aeschylus.

ANALYSIS

The Greek poetic tradition in which Anacreon wrote was a particularly rich one, tracing its origins to the oral songs of the Homeric period. It was in many ways a conservative tradition. It restricted certain genres to specific meters, such as epic to hexameter and invective to iambic, and depended to a great extent on stock epithets, formulas, and vocabulary from Homeric epic. Yet, at the same time, it was a tradition which encouraged experimentation and novelty of expression. Thus, beginning in the late eighth century B.C.E., lyric poetry, distinguished by the use of the first person, blossomed, especially in the Greek cities of Ionia and Aeolia, and produced Archilochus, Sappho, and Alcaeus in the seventh century B.C.E. All of these early lyric poets experimented with a poetic analysis of personal experience and emotion to which the late sixth century B.C.E. Anacreon was heir. While accepting the traditional metrical types and continuing the lyric proclivity toward self-expression and introspection, Anacreon brought to this poetry not so much new emotions and feelings as the skill of a meticulous craftsman who chose his words carefully and knew when to inject exaggeration and humor for the proper effect. Anacreon enriched Greek lyric with the novelties of a poetic experimenter who constantly sought new imagery and approaches for old themes. Certainly the themes of love and wine which dominate Anacreon's extant poetry are, for the most part, traditional. What is significant about Anacreon is that he strove to express these themes in new contexts and succeeded so well that the novel imagery and contexts he introduced, especially in the realm of love poetry, have generally become the clichés of later generations of poets.

357 P.

Anacreon's goal of novelty in a traditional context is demonstrated in 357 P., a prayer to Dionysus. The prayer form had early been recognized to be well suited to lyric expression; these prayers are meant not for public ceremony but for private performance. Sappho's "Ode to Aphrodite" had already used the prayer poem in a love context with great success, and Anacreon may here be following Sappho. Anacreon's prayer is divided into two parts: the invocation, in which the deity is addressed and described; and the entreaty, or the request made to the god. Anacreon's invocation, striking in that it does not mention the god's name, identifies Dionysus only by his habitual companions and haunts. Dionysus is described as playing on the lofty mountaintops with Eros, nymphs, and Aphrodite. Novelty of expression is achieved by the use of new rather than stock epithets for Dionysus's

companions. While the epithet "subduer," which Anacreon invents for Eros, is never used again in Greek literature, the concept of Eros as a tamer of men, which Anacreon implies through this epithet, is one which becomes commonplace in later lyric. Anacreon's descriptions of the nymphs as "blue-eyed" and Aphrodite as "rosy" are noteworthy both because these adjectives had never been applied to these deities before, and because they reflect another characteristic of Anacreon's style: a fondness for color contrasts. In a very few words, Anacreon is thus able to achieve a vivid, colorful, original description of Dionysus's world.

This formal invocation is followed by an equally formal entreaty. Anacreon maintains the solemnity of the prayer form here by employing standard expressions of entreaty: "I beseech you," "come kindly to us," and "hear our prayer." The climax to which the poem is leading is the specific request that the poet wants to make; the formality of structure and vocabulary suggests that the request is a serious one. Yet the next phrase, "be a good counselor to Cleobulus," shows that Anacreon is not serious. Anacreon's word for "good counselor," *sumbulus*, creates a pun on Cleobulus's name which is difficult to miss, since both Cleobulus and *sumbulus* are placed at the beginning of their respective lines. The humor of this phrase shatters the solemn tone of the prayer and prepares for the surprise of the last two lines, where Anacreon finally reveals that he is actually praying to Dionysus not for some lofty request, but for aid in a homosexual love affair. The manipulation of the prayer form to suit a love theme is already found in Sappho, but without the change in tone developed here. Sappho maintains in her poem an intensity of emotion which is not found in Anacreon. By adding a pun at the point when he is introducing the love theme, Anacreon empha-

The Greek poet Anacreon dismisses Cupid, who is dressed as a messenger boy. (Library of Congress)

sizes not his intense emotions but his artistic skill, his ability to control his poem through the careful selection of words.

359 P.

Cleobulus is featured in several other poems, including 359 P., which again shows Anacreon's interest in form rather than emotions. This love poem is a sequence of three parallel statements about Anacreon's relationship with Cleobulus. Each line begins with Cleobulus's name used in a different case ending and concludes with a different verb in the first person singular: "I love," "I am mad," and "I gaze." The grammatical trope is probably borrowed from Archilochus, who uses it in a political context. Anacreon's application of Archilochus's technique to love poetry reflects a de-emphasis of emotional intensity which is suggested by the verbal sequence, through which Anacreon moves from mad love for Cleobulus to mere gazing at the beloved. "I gaze at Cleobulus" suggests a distance between lover and beloved which is not evident in "I love Cleobulus." Such distance is critical to Anacreon's poetic stance, which is based on careful word study.

358 P.

Another of Anacreon's poems, 358 P., demonstrates not only his use of special descriptive words, but also his experimentation with new imagery. In this piece Anacreon describes Eros's invitation to play ball with a girl from Lesbos. Anacreon may here be inventing the image of Eros as the "ballplayer," a commonplace in later poets such as Apollonius and Meleager. The ball playing, possibly derived from Homer's *Odyssey* (c. 800 B.C.E. English translation, 1616), in which Nausicaa plays ball with her servant girls, is a successful variation on the traditional Greek theme of apple tossing (as in the story of Atalanta). The play here is a double entendre. Anacreon's fondness for color contrasts, noted above, is evident in this poem as well, and with even more effect. Eros's ball is "purple," a rich and expensive color in the ancient world, while Anacreon transfers an epithet of Dionysus, "golden-haired," to Eros. The girl, too, is described with colors; she is the girl "with the motley slippers." The final, and perhaps most important, color reference is to Anacreon's white hair, implying that the girl rejects Anacreon because he is too old. This incompatibility of love with old age, a theme repeated in Anac-

reon's extant corpus, is emphasized by the contrast of colors developed in the poem.

Old age, however, is not the only motive for the girl's rejection of Anacreon. She is from Lesbos and gapes after some "other" (female). To the modern reader this situation suggests an association of the island of Lesbos with female homosexuality which may not have been standard in Anacreon's day. Further, there is some ambiguity here, probably intentional, in the text. First, "female" is only grammatically understood and other nouns have been supplied, for example, "hair" (feminine in Greek), making the homosexuality theme more uncertain and, at the same time, enhancing the sexual double entendre. The epithet for Lesbos, "good to dwell in," is also ambiguous. While derived from a standard Homeric epithet for the island, this word is employed here with a meaning which is difficult to establish. The solemn Homeric word may simply be used, as David A. Campbell suggests, to contrast with the more playful tone of the poem as a whole. C. M. Bowra argues in *Greek Lyric Poetry from Alcman to Simonides* (1961) that the epithet, transposed to the girl, may suggest that she comes from a prosperous family and can pick and choose her mates. Bowra has also suggested that this epithet is a subtle dig at Lesbos, "well-established" in its sexual habits. Any and all of these interpretations may be correct, for in this poem, where Eros is depicted as a tease, perhaps the poet, too, is a tease through his use of ambiguity. Once again Anacreon is more interested in his poetic expression than in his emotions. Such a poetic distance from his emotions permits him to deal with sexual passion and with the frustrations of old age in a distinctively humorous way.

376 P.

Anacreon also demonstrates a concern with novelty and effect. The fragment 376 P. combines two of the poet's favorite topics, love and wine, in the context of a traditional love theme: the spurned lover's desperate leap from the Leucadian Cliff. Anacreon uses this theme in a new way. The poet states that the climb onto the rock is being made "again," indicating that this particular leap is not a suicide, but rather a repeated occurrence. The emphasis is not on the despair of unrequited love, but on the loss of self-control caused by love. This helplessness is further stressed by the dive which the poet takes in the second line. Finally, the poet mentions that he makes the plunge "drunk with love." Inebriety may already have been associated with the traditional leap from the Leucadian Cliff, but Anacreon appears to have transposed the theme into a significant metaphor which was not there before and which has not left love poetry since. "To be drunk with love" is certainly a comical exaggeration which suits Anacreon's theme of loss of self-control and which underscores his evident mastery over his poetry.

396 P.

Wine and love are also combined in 396 P., in which the poet addresses the cupbearer, who played a role of honor at Greek drinking parties, and asks for water and wine, which the Greeks mixed before drinking, as well as a garland of flowers, another common trapping of a Greek drinking song. Anacreon, however, adds something new to the drinking song by introducing a love theme. "Bring me these things," he says, "that I may box with Eros." The boxing metaphor is apparently an invention of Anacreon, who may have used it at least once more (in 346 P.). Eros, who was represented as a youth in the sixth century B.C.E. and was not transformed into an infant until the Hellenistic period, is thus fitted by Anacreon with another apt metaphor, that of boxing, an image appropriate to Eros's pain-inflicting capabilities.

417 P.

A final selection, 417 P., shows Anacreon not creating new imagery but rather using an old image in a strikingly new fashion. For the first time, perhaps, a lyric poet may be creating an entire poem out of a single metaphor, a comparison of women with mares, which had appeared earlier in the choral poetry of Alcman. Ibycus, Anacreon's poetic associate on Samos, also used the race-horse image for the lover controlled by Eros. In 417 P., however, Anacreon reverses Ibycus's imagery by making the girl the wild mare and himself the potential rider. The vocabulary of the poem is a remarkable combination of words with amatory undertones, such as "reins" and "mounter," and of elevated epic phraseology, such as "stubbornly" and "think me in no way wise" and "around the limits of the course."

These few examples of the surviving fragments of Anacreon's poetry suggest what a great loss the disappearance of his corpus has been. They demonstrate his consummate skill as a lyric poet who could manipulate poetic themes, imagery, vocabulary, and even his emotions for poetic effect. The reader of Anacreon, tantalized by the few extant fragments, must appreciate the poet's ironic position within literary tradition. A playfully original and prolific innovator, Anacreon became an authoritative model for many later poets, and, despite the ravages of time, he remains a major figure in literature through imitation by others rather than by the weight of his own writings.

BIBLIOGRAPHY

Campbell, David A. *The Golden Lyre: The Themes of Greek Lyric Poets*. London: Duckworth, 1983. Comments about Anacreon's work are scattered throughout a book devoted to exploring Greek poets' writing about subjects such as love, athletics, politics, friendship, gods and heroes, life and death, and the arts. Provides excellent insight into the ways Anacreon's poetry parallels or diverges from the work of other classical lyricists.

Frankel, Hermann. *Early Greek Poetry and Philosophy*. Oxford, England: Basil Blackwell, 1975. A section on Anacreon is included in this extensive study of the development of Greek literature. Selected poems are examined to illustrate the musical qualities of Anacreon's poetry and highlight his technique.

Kirkwood, G. M. *Early Greek Monody: The History of a Poetic Type*. Ithaca, N.Y.: Cornell University Press, 1974. Treats Anacreon as a major writer in the tradition of monody. Illustrates differences between his work and that of earlier monodists, and describes his influence on later writers, especially the Latin poet Horace.

O'Brien, John. *Anacreon Redivivus: A Study of Anacreontic Translation in Mid-Sixteenth Century France*. Ann Arbor: University of Michigan Press, 1995. Though concentrating on the work of scholars in only one century, this study provides useful insight into the ways Anacreon and his imitators have been read by later audiences. Carefully details the critical principles used by key translators who helped shape the canon of Anacreontic poetry in published form.

Rosenmeyer, Patricia A. *The Poetics of Imitation: Anacreon and the Anacreontic Tradition*. Cambridge, England: Cambridge University Press, 1992. Discusses the influence of Anacreon on his contemporaries and examines the way Anacreontic imitators have been discovered, translated, and evaluated. Contains a chapter on the poet's life and work, explicating individual works and exploring major themes in his corpus. Also examines the concept of imitation as a poetic device in ancient poetry.

Thomas J. Sienkewicz;
bibliography updated by Laurence W. Mazzeno

MAYA ANGELOU

Marguerite Johnson
Born: St. Louis, Missouri; April 4, 1928

PRINCIPAL POETRY

Just Give Me a Cool Drink of Water 'fore I Diiie,
1971
Oh Pray My Wings Are Gonna Fit Me Well, 1975
And Still I Rise, 1978
Shaker, Why Don't You Sing?, 1983
Poems: Maya Angelou, 1986
Now Sheba Sings the Song, 1987 (Tom Feelings, illustrator)
I Shall Not Be Moved: Poems, 1990
On the Pulse of Morning, 1993
The Complete Collected Poems of Maya Angelou,
1994
Phenomenal Woman: Four Poems Celebrating Women, 1994
A Brave and Startling Truth, 1995

OTHER LITERARY FORMS

In addition to being a poet, Maya Angelou is an essayist, playwright, screenwriter, and the author of children's books and other pieces of short fiction. Along with two volumes of her autobiography, her collection of essays *Even the Stars Look Lonesome* (1997) was on *The New York Times* best-seller list for ten consecutive weeks. Her two-act drama *The Least of These* was produced in Los Angeles in 1966. With her screenplay *Georgia, Georgia* she became, in 1972, the first African American woman to have an original screenplay produced. In 1974 she adapted Sophocles' *Aias* (early 440's B.C.E.; *Ajax,* 1729) for the modern stage. Her children's book *My Painted House, My Friendly Chicken, and Me* was published in 1994. Her works have been translated into at least ten languages.

ACHIEVEMENTS

Maya Angelou's work has garnered many prestigious awards. For her writing of the revue *Cabaret for Freedom,* which she and Godfrey Cambridge produced, directed, and performed in 1960 for the purpose of raising money for Martin Luther King, Jr.'s Southern Christian Leadership Conference (SCLC), she was named northern coordinator for the SCLC in 1959. She later worked with civil rights leader Malcolm X. Other honors include a nomination for a National Book Award (1970) for *I Know Why the Caged Bird Sings*; a Yale University fellowship (1970); a Pulitzer Prize nomination (1972, for *Just Give Me a Cool Drink of Water 'fore I Diiie*); Antoinette Perry ("Tony") Award nominations (1973 and 1977); a Rockefeller Foundation scholarship in Italy (1975); honorary degrees from Smith College (1975), Mills College (1975), Lawrence University (1976), and Wake Forest University (1977); the Woman of the Year in Communications award, and a listing as one of the one hundred most influential women, both bestowed by *Ladies' Home Journal* (1976); a Golden Eagle Award for documentary (1977); a Matrix Award from Women in Communications (1983); the North Carolina Award in Literature (1987); Distinguished Woman of North Carolina (1992); the Woman of the Year award from *Essence* magazine (1992); the Horatio Alger Award (1992); the Spingarn Medal (1993); a Grammy Award for Best Spoken Word or Non-Traditional Album (1994); the National Medal of Arts (2000); and the prestigious Order of Kilimanjaro Award from the National Association for the Advancement of Colored People (2001).

A high school graduate, Angelou has had honorary degrees bestowed upon her, and she was appointed Reynolds Professor of American Studies at Wake Forest University in Winston-Salem, North Carolina, in 1981. She read the poem she had composed in honor of the in-

Maya Angelou addresses an audience at the Gallagher-Bluedorn Performing Arts Center on the University of Northern Iowa campus in September of 2000.
(AP/Wide World Photos)

auguration of President Bill Clinton at the inaugural ceremonies in January, 1993; only one poet before her, Robert Frost, had been invited to read at an inauguration ceremony. In all, she has received more than thirty honorary degrees.

While many titles have been assigned to Angelou, one is especially significant to her: the modern female African American Proust. Angelou is known for addressing the world through the medium of her own life. The first volume of her autobiography made her the first African American woman to appear on nonfiction bestseller lists; four volumes followed the first.

BIOGRAPHY

Born Marguerite Johnson, re-christened Maya, and taking the professional name Angelou (an adaptation of the name of her first husband, Tosh Angelos), Maya Angelou studied music and dance with Martha Graham, Pearl Primus, and Ann Halprin. Her early career was as

an actress and singer, to which she quickly added the roles of civil rights worker (as the northern coordinator for the SCLC, 1959-1960), editor (as associate editor for the *Arab Observer*, 1961-1962), educator (beginning with the School of Music and Drama at the University of Ghana's Institute of African Studies, 1963-1966), and finally writer—first as a reporter for the *Ghanaian Times* (1963-1965). During the late 1960's and 1970's she taught at many colleges and universities in California and Kansas, accepting the post of Reynolds Professor at Wake Forest University in 1981. Since then she has also been a sought-after speaker and is in many respects regarded as America's unofficial poet laureate, although she had yet to receive that honor as of 2001.

She has told much of her own life's story in her five-volume autobiography. Undoubtedly, Angelou's legacy will be her writings: Although the best-selling *I Know Why the Caged Bird Sings* (1970) was censored, her excellent work as an author in all genres has kept her story before the world. Angelou's early years have been burned into the minds of numerous readers. An image from this work centers on three-year-old Marguerite and four-year-old Bailey Johnson aboard a train, alone, traveling from California to their grandmother's home in Stamps, Arkansas, after the breakup of their parents' marriage. The two children wore their names and their destination attached to their clothes. This locomotive quest for family is both a factual part of and an apt metaphor for the life of the world-famous poet. Her first feeling of being truly at home, she has said, came in Africa, after she accompanied her second husband to Egypt and then traveled to Ghana.

A second image from Angelou's childhood involves the seven-year-old's rape by her mother's boyfriend. When no legal punishment followed, the rapist was murdered, possibly by the victim's uncles. Guilt following this incident drove Angelou inward, and she began reading the great works of literature. Reading her way through the Stamps library, she fell in love with William Shakespeare and Paul Laurence Dunbar, among others. The child of a fractured nuclear family came to see herself as a child of the fractured human family.

By age thirteen Angelou had grown closer to her mother; at sixteen she became a mother herself. To earn a living for herself and her son Guy, she became a waitress, a singer, and a dancer. These and other occupations were followed by acting, directing, producing, and the hosting of television specials. She loved to dance, but when her knees began to suffer in her early twenties, she devoted her attention to her other love: writing. She began supporting herself through her writing in 1968. Her family came to include "sister friends" and "brother friends," as her troubled brother Bailey became lost in the worlds of substance abuse and prison. She married, but she has refused to attach a number to her marriages, as that might, she says, suggest frivolity, and she insists that she was never frivolous about marriage. To "brother friend" James Baldwin she gives much credit for her becoming an autobiographer. She assisted "brother friends" Martin Luther King, Jr., and Malcolm X in their work and pursued her own work to better the entire human family.

The hope that she found so significant in the 1960's is reflected in the poem she composed for Bill Clinton's presidential inauguration. The dream of King is evident in the words written and delivered by Angelou "on the pulse of [that] morning."

ANALYSIS

Asked in 1983 what she hoped to achieve as a writer, Maya Angelou answered, "to remind us that we are more alike [than un-alike], especially since I've grown up in racial turbulence and unfairness." Two 1990's poems reflect the dichotomy of her declaration: "Human Family" celebrates family likeness, and "Son to Mother" denounces wrongs inflicted by various branches of the human family. Angelou in her poetry dissects and resurrects humankind: She condemns its shamefulness and rejoices in its possibilities and its glories.

STILL RISING

"Some poets sing/ their melodies," writes Angelou in "Artful Pose," published in 1975, "tendering my nights/ sweetly." Angelou, in contrast, chooses to write "of lovers false" "and hateful wrath/ quickly." She adds the word "quickly" to balance and countermand "sweetly." Her style as she speaks to live audiences and to readers, whether her tone is optimistic or pessimistic, reveals a sense of "gusto." In 1982 she offered this bit of self-analysis:

If you enter a room of hostile strangers with gusto, there are few who can contain, preserve their hostility. . . . [I]t speaks immediately to the gusto in other people.

European American audiences applaud her and purchase her work even as she berates them: "You may write me down in history/ With your bitter, twisted lies," she says in the opening lines of one of her most famous poems, "Still I Rise."

"I'll play possum and close my eyes/ To your greater sins and my lesser lies," she writes in a jump-rope rhythm in "Bump d'Bump." "That way I share my nation's prize," she continues. "Call me a name from an ugly south/ Like liver lips and satchel mouth"; gusto, anger, and a challenge to humankind are integral ingredients of Angelou's poetry.

In "Man Bigot" Angelou writes,

> The man who is a bigot
> is the worst thing God has got

except his match, his woman,
who really is Ms. Begot.

Angelou is not unwilling to amuse as she challenges her audience. She did not leave the entertainment field behind when she turned to verse. Other entertaining and uplifting elements of her poetry are sass and the celebration of womanhood. "Men themselves have wondered/ What they see in me," says the speaker of "A Phenomenal Woman." A part of her mystery, she says, is in "the fire in my eyes," "the joy in my feet," and

> The grace of my style.
> I'm a woman
> Phenomenally.
> Phenomenal woman,
> That's me.

SASS AND ANGER

Sass is an element in 1978's "Still I Rise," but anger consistently tempers its speaker's joy. "Does my sassiness upset you?" and "Does my haughtiness offend you?" she asks her European American readers. "Out of the huts of history's shame/ I rise," says her African American speaker. In "Miss Scarlett, Mr. Rhett, and Other Latter-Day Saints," Angelou writes,

> Animated by the human sacrifice
> (Golgotha in black-face)
> Priests glow purely white on the
> bar-relief of a plantation shrine.

In "Slave Coffle" (1983) she speaks as a slave to whom "all the earth is horror," as the speaker realizes "Before the dawning,/ bright as grinning demons" that "life was gone."

While Angelou has claimed to interviewers to have mellowed since writing her first volume of poetry, her verse remains harsh to the reader's mind and ear. Shame and ignorance recur as significant themes. Pride, however, is at least as significant.

PRIDE IN ANCESTORS

In 1975 Angelou declared "Song for the Old Ones" her favorite poem. Her celebration of those who kept her race alive remained a favorite theme. Her 1990 volume of poetry, *I Shall Not Be Moved*, has as its title the chorus to the poem "Our Grandmothers." Her sense of pride in these old ones and her sense of kinship with them is

evident in the words she gives one of these grandmothers. To those who hurled ribbons of invective into the wind of history,

> She said, But my description cannot
> fit your tongue, for
> I have a certain way of being in this world,
> and I shall not, I shall not be moved.

In "Old Folks Laugh" (1990) she writes that old folks' laughter frees the world. The freedom that the grandmothers offer their children in "Our Grandmothers" is the freedom to be fully human: They tell them, "When you learn, teach. When you get, give."

"I laugh until I start to crying,/ When I think about my folks," says the speaker of "When I Think About Myself." Angelou's poetry shows that the stories of her people continued to fill and to break her heart. The title of the volume containing "Song for the Old Ones," *Oh Pray My Wings Are Gonna Fit Me Well*, seems, as does the title of her 1990 volume, *I Shall Not Be Moved*, to derive from her wish to be worthy of and to emulate the old ones.

That Angelou gives the final position in the 1990 volume to the poem dedicated to other, less great, old ones is significant, as is the idea of that poem: "When great souls die," she says in the final stanza,

> Our senses, restored, never
> to be the same, whisper to us.
> They existed. They existed.
> We can be. Be and be
> better. For they existed.

Unbelievable cruelty has given rise to unbelievable valor. Angelou cannot and will not forget the history of human cruelty as she feels that human beings must learn from their shared history. She continues to show human beings what they must learn that they can be better.

GUILT AND RESPONSIBILITY

Crucial to her overall idea is the shared guilt and responsibility of all history's survivors. In "I Almost Remember" (1975), the speaker recalls smiling and even laughing, but now

> Open night news-eyed I watch
> channels of hunger

written on children's faces
bursting bellies balloon
in the air of my day room.

The speaker's garden, television, and day room suggest the luxuries and the guilt of one of the "haves" as she/he witnesses the suffering of the "have-nots" on the "channels of hunger." Similarly, "Harlem Hopscotch," with a seemingly different tone and a hopscotch rhythm, shows children singing of "good things for the ones that's got." "Everybody for hisself," they continue. The pain of both the television viewer and the children reflects the suffering as well as the scarring of the human psyche.

"Take Time Out" challenges the acceptance of the status quo, challenging the attitude of all human players of life's game:

Use a minute
feel some sorrow
for the folks
who think tomorrow
is a place that they
can call up
on the phone.

The speaker of this poem asks that kindness be shown for the folk who thought that blindness was an illness that affected eyes alone. "We'd better see," says the speaker,

what all our
fearing and our
jeering and our
crying and
our lying
brought about.

Society is responsible for its children and for its own and its children's attitudes. As she shows in "Faces,"

the brown caramel days of youth
Reject the sun-sucked tit of
childhood mornings.
Poke a muzzle of war in the trust frozen eyes
of a favored doll.

This is what humanity has wrought and what it must not accept. Humankind must be rendered both human and kind, the poet seems to say.

NEW DREAMS

Angelou calls repeatedly on the human race to spare itself from suffering. "There's one thing that I cry for I believe enough to die for/ That is every man's responsibility to man," says the speaker of "On Working White Liberals." "Dare us new dreams, Columbus," says the speaker of "A Georgia Song" (1983). In "America" (1975) Angelou speaks of America's promise that "has never been mined": "Her proud declarations/ are leaves in the wind." The United States, says the speaker, "entraps her children/ with legends untrue." This country of such high promise—the promise that all are equally entitled to life, liberty, and the pursuit of happiness—has not yet been discovered. Its citizens are led by their poet laureate to see that it is high time that the discovery be made.

OTHER MAJOR WORKS

SHORT FICTION: *Ten Times Black*, 1972; *Confirmation: An Anthology of African American Women*, 1983; *Mrs. Flowers: A Moment of Friendship*, 1986.

PLAYS: *Cabaret for Freedom*, pr. 1960 (musical, with Godfrey Cambridge); *The Least of These*, pr. 1966; *Encounters*, pr. 1973; *Ajax*, pr. 1974 (adaptation of Sophocles' play); *And Still I Rise*, pr. 1976 (musical); *King*, pr. 1990 (musical; lyrics by Alistair Beaton, book by Lonne Elder III; music by Richard Blackford).

SCREENPLAYS: *Georgia, Georgia*, 1972; *All Day Long*, 1974.

TELEPLAYS: *Black, Blues, Black*, 1968 (ten episodes); *The Legacy*, 1976; *The Inheritors*, 1976; *I Know Why the Caged Bird Sings*, 1976 (with Leonora Thuna and Ralph B. Woolsey); *Sister, Sister*, 1982; *Brewster Place*, 1990.

NONFICTION: *I Know Why the Caged Bird Sings*, 1970; *Gather Together in My Name*, 1974; *Singin' and Swingin' and Gettin' Merry Like Christmas*, 1976; *The Heart of a Woman*, 1981; *All God's Children Need Traveling Shoes*, 1986; *Wouldn't Take Nothing for My Journey Now*, 1993; *Lessons in Living*, 1993; *Even the Stars Look Lonesome*, 1997; *A Song Flung Up to Heaven*, 2002.

CHILDREN'S LITERATURE: *Life Doesn't Frighten Me*, 1993 (poetry); *Soul Looks Back in Wonder*, 1993; *My Painted House, My Friendly Chicken, and Me*, 1994; *Kofi and His Magic*, 1996.

BIBLIOGRAPHY

Bloom, Harold, ed. *Maya Angelou*. Philadelphia, Pa.: Chelsea House, 1999. This selection of essays dealing with Angelou's poetry and prose broaches, among other subjects, the singular relationship of Angelou to her audience and her distinctively African American mode of literary expression.

Elliot, Jeffrey M., ed. *Conversations with Maya Angelou*. Jackson: University Press of Mississippi, 1989. This collection of informal interviews paints an appealing personal and intellectual portrait of the poet.

Guntern, Gottlieb, ed. *The Challenge of Creative Leadership*. London: Shepheard-Walwyn, 1997. Guntern's criteria for those who inspire others to move beyond mediocrity are explored in these philosophical pieces. Among these criteria are originality, elegance, and profundity.

Lisandrelli, Elaine Slivinski. *Maya Angelou: More Than a Poet*. Springfield, N.J.: Enslow, 1996. Lisandrelli discusses the flamboyance of Angelou, comparing her to the earlier African American author Zora Neale Hurston. Their hard work, optimism, perseverance, and belief in themselves are extolled.

Shapiro, Miles. *Maya Angelou*. New York: Chelsea House, 1994. A biography describing the life and work of the celebrated writer.

Williams, Mary E., ed. *Maya Angelou*. San Diego, Calif.: Greenhaven Press, 1997. This collection of essays by literary scholars and noted faculty offers diverse voices and approaches to Angelou's literary canon.

Judith K. Taylor, updated by the editors

INNOKENTY ANNENSKY

Born: Omsk, Siberia; August 20, 1856
Died: St. Petersburg, Russia; November 30, 1909

PRINCIPAL POETRY
Tikhie pesni, 1904
Kiparisovy larets, 1910 (*The Cypress Chest*, 1982)

OTHER LITERARY FORMS

In addition to his two collections of poetry, for which he is best remembered today, Innokenty Annensky wrote four tragedies and was a critic and pedagogue of note. His tragedies include *Melanippa-Filosof* (pb. 1901), *Tsar Iksion* (pb. 1902), *Laodamiia* (pb. 1906), and *Famira Kifared* (pb. 1913). Annensky's major critical effort consists of the essays constituting the two collections entitled *Kniga otrazhenii* (1906) and *Vtoraia kniga otrazhenii* (1909). They were reissued in a single volume in 1969. The remainder of Annensky's critical and pedagogical essays have never been collected in book form; they remain scattered throughout the Russian journals in which they first appeared.

ACHIEVEMENTS

Innokenty Annensky has always been considered a "poet's poet" because of the subtlety of his poetic imagery and the intricacy of his thought. In contrast to such contemporary poets as Aleksandr Blok and Konstantin Balmont, who were enormously popular in their own time, Annensky's main impact was rather on the aesthetic theory of Acmeism, one of the great Russian poetic schools of the twentieth century. Two gifted and famous Acmeists, Anna Akhmatova and Osip Mandelstam, were especially drawn to Annensky both as a poet and as a formulator of poetic doctrine.

Although he has often been regarded as a member of the older, "first generation" of Russian Symbolists (in contrast to the younger or "second generation"), Annensky does not truly fit into a particular category. His style can be designated as Symbolist insofar as his use of literary allusions is concerned, yet his worldview and aesthetic ideals, as well as his treatment of non-Symbolist stylistic elements, set him apart from this movement. Annensky differs from his contemporaries in his aesthetic independence. He is considered unique among twentieth century Russian poets in that he combined aspects of Symbolism with experimental stylistic devices to produce verse that cannot easily be labeled. He is regarded today as one of the more interesting and significant modern Russian poets, and he has a reputation far exceeding that which he enjoyed during his own lifetime.

BIOGRAPHY

Innokenty Fyodorovich Annensky was born in Omsk, Siberia, on August 20, 1856, but the family returned to St. Petersburg in 1858. Both parents having died when Annensky was quite young, he was reared by his brother, Nikolay Fyodorovich Annensky, publisher of the important journal *Russkoe bogatstvo*. Nikolay and his wife, Alexandra Nikitichna Annenskaya, held liberal political and social views typical of the positivistic thinkers of their generation.

Educated at home, possibly because his health was poor, Annensky mastered several foreign languages, including Latin and Greek. He completed a degree in philology at the University of St. Petersburg in 1879; in the same year, he married a widow named Dina Khmara-Barshchevskaya. The marriage was apparently a happy one; he was close to his two stepsons, and his own son Valentin was born in 1880.

Annensky embarked on his pedagogical career following graduation. After teaching Greek and Russian in several private institutions in St. Petersburg, he went to Kiev between 1890 and 1893, where he became director of the Pavel Galagan College. He returned to St. Petersburg in 1893, assuming the directorship of a high school there, and in 1896, he was appointed head of the famous lyceum at Tsarskoe Selo. It was during his tenure at Tsarskoe Selo that he issued his first volume of original verse and translations, *Tikhie pesni*; the book was virtually unnoticed by the critics.

Annensky's last post was as inspector of the St. Petersburg School District; he also lectured on classical literature at a private university for women. During this period, his friendship with the Acmeist poet and theoretician Nikolay Gumilyov gave him entrée into the literary world of St. Petersburg and brought him belated fame. Annensky died of a heart attack on November 30, 1909, the very day his retirement had been granted.

ANALYSIS

Innokenty Annensky's lyrics reflect an intimate knowledge of French poetry, particularly the verse of the Parnassians and the French Symbolists. Like many of these French poets, Annensky heeded Stéphane Mallarmé's dictum that to name was to destroy, while to suggest was to create. Like the French, Annensky concentrated a lyrical theme in one symbolically treated subject or in a complex of interconnected subjects. While he made use of symbol and suggestion, the fact that the lyrical theme was related to a single subject or a complex of related subjects lent greater impact to his poems.

Annensky's link with the French Symbolists was paralleled by his close ties with the Parnassians. The latter, particularly their principal poet, Théophile Gautier, advocated "art for art's sake" and the composition of a carefully constructed poetry equally removed from subjective emotions and contemporary events. The Parnassians also expressed a renewed interest in the classical world; indeed, the Parnassians had a greater impact on Annensky than did the Symbolists, for he shared with the former a cult of poetic form and a love of the word as such, as well as subscribing to their notion that there was no affinity between aesthetics and ethics.

Annensky's relationship with the Russian Symbolists is somewhat ambiguous for there was an absence of any kind of organizational tie or even any close relationship between him and representatives of the "new poetry." Unlike his contemporaries, he considered Symbolism to be an aesthetic system rather than a literary school. He neither rebelled against civic poetry, for example, as the Symbolists generally did, nor rejected his poetic heritage. Unlike the later Symbolists, he did not regard art as a means of mystical escape, maintaining that Symbolism was intended to be literature rather than a new form of universal religion.

The approximately five hundred lyrics that Annensky wrote are the center of his creative work and can be divided into six major themes: death, life, dream, nature, artistic creation, and time. The themes of death, life, dream, and nature are actually subordinate to that of time, which binds all of them together. In this very emphasis on temporality, Annensky transcended Symbolism and anticipated later poetic movements. His exemption of artistic creation from the strictures of time illustrates the enormous emphasis he placed on aesthetics.

Death played an important role in Annensky's verse, for he considered it as an ever-intruding end to a life without hope. He devoted a number of lyrics to this theme, one of the most important of which was "Siren' na kamne" ("Lilac on the Gravestone"). Here Annensky touches on the transitory nature of man's life, on the contrast between life and death, and on the awareness that the seemingly infinite possibilities of the intellect are thwarted by the intrusion of an awareness of physical death. Annensky's realization that death is a physical, inescapable end demonstrates his acceptance of the limitations of the material world and stresses thereby one of the most significant differences between him and the Symbolists.

"Depression" and "The Double"

One of Annensky's major themes is life. This category is dominated by lyrics about *toska* (depression, melancholy, or yearning personified), as exemplified by the poem "Toska" ("Depression"). The persona in "Depression" is an invalid, suspended, as it were, between life and death. The setting for the poem is a sickroom decorated with flowered wallpaper, around which flies hover. The unnaturalness of the surroundings, coupled with Annensky's frequent use of participles rather than finite verbs, separates both persona and reader from the normal, lively world of action and imprisons them in a static, banal realm. Like his poems on death, Annensky's lyrics about life are characterized by pessimism derived from his constant awareness of the limitations and frustrations of life.

In *The Influence of French Symbolism on Russian Poetry*, Georgette Donchin suggests that because the dream symbolizes an escape from reality, it was a common poetic theme for Russian Symbolists. The dream also occupies a special place in Annensky's poetry. Simon Karlinsky, in his 1966 essay "The Materiality of Annensky," argues that the dream represents a world divorced from the strictures of time, an alternative existence for the poet. Annensky's dream verses can be subdivided into three categories according to theme: disorientation, oblivion, and nightmare. In "Dvoinik" ("The Double"), the persona experiences a loss of orientation, with the primary differentiation of identity, that between the I and the non-I, blurred. Annensky's deliberate grammatical confusion of the first, second, and third persons destroys the normal distinctions between conversation and narration, even of existence. When the distinct separateness of the individual consciousness is eradicated, nothing is certain. Annensky has, in fact, placed the rest of the poem outside reality by erasing the conceptions of definite time and space, with all existence transformed into a dream.

Ephemerality and Death

In "Kogda b ne smert', a zabyt'e" ("If There Were Not Death, but Oblivion"), oblivion represents the cessation of time. It is a state divorced from temporality, which is seen in the poem as the creator and destroyer of beauty. The poet's awareness of the ephemerality of artistic as well as natural beauty is a source of torment for him; he is trapped by time and is doomed to solitude.

Unlike disorientation and oblivion, the nightmare threatens the sufferer with annihilation. In "Utro" ("Morning"), Annesky has erased the distinction between dream and reality, making the nightmare vividly real. When day comes at the end of the poem, it is not merely a unit of time but a symbol of the force of light against the power of darkness, good against evil, life against death.

Nature

Nature is the backdrop against which thoughts and emotions can be projected, the external mirror of human existence. As such, it constitutes a significant theme in Annensky's verse. The winter poem "Sneg" ("Snow") is characterized by a sharpness of line and by the specificity resulting from the repeated use of the definite demonstrative adjective *eto* (this). In addition to crispness of outline and color contrast, Annensky's employment of oxymoron makes his images clearer still. The clarity of nature has become a foil for the clarity of the thought of the persona.

"To a Poet"

In contrast to the later Symbolists, Annensky considered the poet a creator of clear, linear art. His divergence from the Symbolists is especially marked in the lyric "Poetu" ("To a Poet"), a lesson in how to write poetry. Annensky focuses on the importance of clarity and concreteness, opposing them to abstraction and indefiniteness. He asserts that poetry is a "science" governed by certain laws and is, within limits, exact, as the measuring triad of dimensions in the poem suggests. The figure with the triad is the Muse, who in turn symbolizes the art of classical Greece with its emphasis on clarity and beauty of form. The link with Greece is reinforced by the reference to Orpheus and the significance of form. The Muse is juxtaposed to veiled Isis, emblematic of the mystery and distortion of the later Symbolists. She perhaps stands for the figure of Eternal Wisdom that informed much of the philosophy of the Symbolist philosopher-poet Vladimir Soloviev. The poet is not an intermediary between the earth and a higher realm; he is not a seer or transmitter, but a writer.

"POETRY"

Like "To a Poet," "Poeziia" ("Poetry") is a meta-poem, in which art transcends the everyday world and allows the poet limited access to a realm of absolute beauty. The poem is set in the Sinai desert, a region of intense light and heat; the word "flaming" in the first line not only describes the concentrated heat of the desert but also carries the religious connotation of the fire that can purge sin and memory (as in Alexander Pushkin's famous poem "Prorok," "The Prophet"). Annensky personifies poetry in the last stanza, where he speaks of the "traces of Her sandals." The narrator never sees Poetry directly; he entreats Her, although not "knowing Her."

The desert can be seen here as a haven from society and from the decay of the established religion (in this case, Symbolism) from which the poet seeks to escape. Poetry is contrasted to the vision of Sophia (Eternal Wisdom) that Soloviev saw in Egypt, and the poem as a whole may well represent Annensky's escape from a burdensome, "official" school of poetry in his quest for pure art.

"THE STEEL CICADA"

Time is centrally important in Annensky's verse, for it is the regulator of the days and seasons, the ruler of life. Time connects and dominates all of Annensky's other themes, providing a focal point for understanding his conception of the material world and his emphasis on art. "Stalnaia cikada" ("The Steel Cicada") portrays time as an invention of the mind. In this lyric, Annensky has equated the timepiece with a cicada and has thus transformed it into something alive, thereby implying process and change. When the lid of the watch has been slammed shut in the last stanza, time has stopped. The intrusion of *toska*, having cut the poet off from external events (by shutting the watch lid), has stopped time.

Time, the medium of change, causes the alteration of moods and conditions that is the antithesis of depression. Annensky speeds up time through his poetic lexi-con, employing short phrases without enjambment to achieve a staccato effect. Near the end of the poem, the persona has become reconciled to the return of Depression; his companionship with the cicada is called a "miracle" that will last only for a minute. With the removal of the cicada comes the realization that the passing moment is beyond recall. The poet's attempt to escape from constancy into a realm of change that he has invented himself (symbolized throughout the poem by the watch, a mechanical object) has failed. In the end, he is the victim of his own immutability.

SYMBOLISM OF TIME

For Annensky, time symbolizes process and the final disintegration that characterizes life, nature, and death, while life represents the temporary immersion in process. It is the poet's realization of the relentless flow of time that produces the psychological state of depression, an awareness that the extreme limitations of existence are nevertheless the highest human achievement. Annensky's cognizance of depression amounts to a rejection of mysticism, separating him irrevocably from the later Symbolists. Time represents reality and is inescapable except through the momentary conquest by the mind and spirit of the artist.

USE OF PERSONIFICATION

Although he did not experiment in metrics and rhyme, Annensky was more adventurous stylistically in his employment of personification. He frequently capitalizes the first letter of a word denoting an object or abstract term to identify it with a human being, utilizing the simile and metaphor for the same purpose. Annensky's reliance on personification causes the reader to view nature, at least within the scope of these poems, as an extension of the conscious mind. His poetic universe centers on the mind, extends to artifacts, includes surrounding nature (especially the garden), and is limited only by the clouds. Beyond the clouds lies infinity, which cannot be understood and hence cannot be encompassed within the realm dominated by the mind. Because his universe can be considered as having a rational basis, Annensky should be regarded as a precursor of the rationalism of the Acmeists.

ROLE IN THE SYMBOLIST MOVEMENT

Although classified as a Symbolist by a number of critics, Annensky should rather be regarded as a transitional figure between Symbolism and later poetic developments in Russia. Annensky differs from the Symbolists in his use of conversational elements and in his preference for concrete, distinct objects as poetic images. Like his thematic emphasis on time, his predilection for the concrete and real as opposed to the abstract and mystical denotes an acceptance of the actual world. His literary orientation was toward new poets rather than toward those who were already established. His later poetry contains stylistic elements more compatible with Acmeism, even with Futurism, than with Symbolism.

Annensky's ambiguous position in relation to the Symbolists is underscored by his avoidance of the polemics characterizing the Symbolist school. This may have been partially a result of the fact that he was not a professional poet but instead was an educator who lacked sufficient time or opportunity to develop extensive personal contacts with the Symbolists. His abstention from the literary quarrels that were to climax in 1910, the year after his death, indicates an unwillingness to involve himself in the intricacies of literary battles. In addition, Annensky's avoidance of Symbolist polemics parallels his emphasis on poetry as an artistic phenomenon rather than a literary school. He believed that the intrinsic aesthetic value of poetry precluded its use as a vehicle. His abstention from mysticism and literary polemics resulted from a desire to preserve the integrity of the art and thus to prevent its prostitution to other ends.

INFLUENCE ON ACMEISTS

Annensky stood out from the poets of his time in devising a poetic world that was concrete rather than abstract, worldly rather than mystical. He employed personification and focused on images and objects that made his language concrete. Although he was interested in the musical elements of poetry, he emphasized its pictorial and visual aspects. He thus created a definitive background for the philosophical or aesthetic argument of a particular lyric. These factors, coupled with a respect for the intrinsic worth of art, relate him more closely to writers following him, particularly to such poets as the Acmeists, than to his contemporaries. In tracing the development of Russian poetry and, indeed, of Russian literature as a whole in the twentieth century, the pivotal position of Annensky and the great scope of his contribution must be taken into account.

OTHER MAJOR WORKS

PLAYS: *Melanippa-Filosof*, pb. 1901; *Tsar Iksion*, pb. 1902; *Laodamiia*, pb. 1906; *Famira Kifared*, pb. 1913.

NONFICTION: *Kniga otrazhenii*, 1906; *Vtoraia kniga otrazhenii*, 1909.

BIBLIOGRAPHY

Fedorov, Andrei V. *Innokentij Annenskij: Lichnost' i tvorchestvo*. Leningrad: Khudozhestvennaia literatura, 1984. A succinct and to-the-point biography by a leading Russian scholar on Annensky. It details the poet's life and discusses the essential aspects of his lyrics, prose, and plays, with the emphasis on poetry. In Russian.

Ljunggren, Anna. *At the Crossroads of Russian Modernism: Studies in Innokentij Annenskij's Poetics*. Stockholm: Almquist & Wicksell International, 1997. A thorough discussion of Annensky's poetry, addressing both the Russian and international links of his work, with the emphasis on how the French Symbolists were received and transformed by Annensky within the Russian Symbolist poetry. His poetics are discussed at length. His similarities with Boris Pasternak, Ivan Bunin, Vladislav Khodasevich, and Vladimir Nabokov are also discussed.

Setchkarev, Vsevolod. *Studies in the Life and Work of Innokenty Annensky*. The Hague: Mouton, 1963. This seminal work includes a biography and a discussion of Annensky's works and is one of the best on the subject. Setchkarev discusses in detail Annensky's rise to prominence and his contribution to the Russian literature of the first decade of the twentieth century. The author analyzes Annensky's significance in the second wave of Russian Symbolists. A must for the students of Annensky by a Russian scholar transplanted in the West.

Shubin, V. F., ed. *Innokentij Annenskij i russkaia kul'tura XX veka: Sbornik nauchnykh trudiov*. Sankt-Peterburg: AO, Arsis, 1996. A collection of fourteen studies of Annensky by leading Russian critics as well by foreign ones. The emphasis is on his poetry, relationship to and comparison with leading Russian poets of his time. In Russian.

Tucker, Janet G. *Innokentij Annenskij and the Acmeist Doctrine*. Columbus, Ohio: Slavica, 1986. In this studious examination of Annensky's poetry, the author analyzes the poet's contribution to the Symbolist poetry, the themes and devices of his poetry, his role as a literary critic, and, above all, his views of, and relationship to, the doctrine of Acmeism and his links with that movement. A valuable contribution to the critical evaluation of Annensky by a Western scholar.

Janet G. Tucker;
bibliography updated by Vasa D. Mihailovich

GUILLAUME APOLLINAIRE

Guillaume Albert Wladimir Alexandre Apollinaire de Kostrowitzky
Born: Rome, Italy; August 26, 1880
Died: Paris, France; November 9, 1918

PRINCIPAL POETRY
Le Bestiaire, 1911 (*Bestiary*, 1978)
Alcools: Poémes, 1898-1913, 1913 (*Alcools: Poems, 1898-1913*, 1964)
Calligrammes, 1918 (English translation, 1980)
Il y a, 1925
Le Guetteur mélancolique, 1952
Tendre comme le souvenir, 1952
Poèmes à Lou, 1955
Œuvres poétiques, 1956

OTHER LITERARY FORMS
Besides poetry, Guillaume Apollinaire wrote a number of prose works. Among the most significant of his short stories and novellas are *L'Enchanteur pourrissant* (1909; the putrescent enchanter), published by Henry Kahnweiler and illustrated with woodcuts by André Derain; *L'Hérésiarque et Cie.* (1910; *The Heresiarch and Co.*, 1965), a contender for the Prix Goncourt; and *Le Poète assassiné* (1916; *The Poet Assassinated*, 1923). They are contained in the Pléiade edition, *Œuvres en prose* (1977), edited by Michel Décaudin.

Apollinaire collaborated on numerous plays and cinema scripts. His best-known individual works in these genres are two proto-Surrealist plays in verse: *Les Mamelles de Tirésias* (*The Breasts of Tiresias*, 1961), first published in the magazine *SIC* in 1918, and *Couleur du temps* (the color of time), which first appeared in the *Nouvelle Revue française* in 1920. They are available in the Pléiade edition of *Œuvres poétiques* (1956). Apollinaire also published a great deal of art criticism and literary criticism in journals, newspapers, and other periodicals. In 1913, the articles published before that year were collected in *Peintres cubistes: Méditations esthétiques* (*The Cubist Painters: Aesthetic Meditations*, 1944). In 1918, *Mercure de France* published his famous manifesto "L'Esprit nouveau et les poètes" ("The New Spirit and the Poets"), which later appeared, along with many other articles, in *Chroniques d'art, 1902-1918* (1960), edited by L. C. Breunig. The same collection has been translated into English as *Apollinaire on Art: Essays and Reviews, 1902-1918* (1972).

Guillaume Apollinaire

ACHIEVEMENTS

After Guillaume Apollinaire, French poetry was never the same again. Writing at the end of the long Symbolist tradition, a tradition very apparent in his early works, Apollinaire moved into a new perception of the world and of poetry. In the world of his mature verse, spatial and temporal relations are radically altered. Apollinaire's was one of the first voices in French poetry to attempt to articulate the profound discontinuity and disorientation in modern society. At the same time, however, his works reflect hope, frequently ecstatic, in the promise of the future.

Apollinaire's sense of radical discontinuity was reflected in his formal innovations, analyzed in considerable depth by Jean-Claude Chevalier in *Alcools d'Apollinaire* (1970). Immediately before the publication of *Alcools*, Apollinaire went through the volume and removed all punctuation, a device which he continued to use in most of his later works. His most notable poems, such as "Zone," "Liens" ("Chains"), and "Les Fenêtres" ("Windows"), use free verse with irregular rhyme and rhythm; his most startling works are the picture poems of *Calligrammes*, a form which he falsely claimed to have invented. They consist of verses arranged to give both a visual and an auditory effect in an effort to create "simultaneity."

Like the cubists and other modern painters who sought to go beyond the traditional boundaries of space and time, Apollinaire desired to create the effect of simultaneity. This ambition is evident in "Zone," with its biographical, geographical, and historical discontinuity. In this single poem, the poet leaps from his pious childhood at the Collège Saint-Charles in Monaco to the wonders of modern aviation and back to the "herds" of buses "mooing" on the streets of Paris. Perhaps his most obvious achievement in simultaneity, though less profound, is in "Lundi rue Christine" ("Monday in Christine Street"), which records overheard bits of conversation in a "sinistre brasserie," a low-class café-restaurant that Apollinaire had frequented as early as 1903.

The friend and collaborator of many important painters during the exciting years in Paris just before World War I, Apollinaire began associating with artists when he met Pablo Picasso in 1904, after which he frequented the famous Bateau-Lavoir on the rue Ravignan with Max Jacob, André Derain, Maurice Vlaminck, Georges Braque, and others. After 1912, he moved into the world of art criticism, not always appreciated by the artists themselves, as critic Francis Steegmuller has noted. Not unrelated to this interest was Apollinaire's tumultuous liaison with Marie Laurencin from 1907 to 1912. He frequently inspired works and portraits by artists, including Laurencin, Henri Rousseau, and Picasso. Apollinaire's own works further testify to his links with painters: *Bestiary* was illustrated by Raoul Dufy, and "Windows" was the introductory poem to the catalog of the Robert Delaunay exhibit in 1912. His poems often parallel the work of the painters in their spirit of simultaneity; in their subjects, such as the *saltimbanques* of Picasso; and in their moods, such as those of Marc Chagall's dreamworld and inverted figures.

After 1916, Apollinaire became the "chef d'école," the leader of a new generation of poets and painters. Among them were Pierre Reverdy, Philippe Soupault, Jean Cocteau, André Breton, and Tristan Tzara. His own works appeared in the most avant-garde journals: Reverdy's *Nord-Sud*, Picabia's *391*, and Albert Birot's *SIC*. His lecture "The New Spirit and the Poets" called poets to a new prophetic vision, imploring them to create prodigies with their imagination like modern Merlins. Like Paul Claudel, Apollinaire regarded the poet as a creator. The modern poet, he believed, must use everything for his creation: new discoveries in science, in the subconscious and the dreamworld, and in the cinema and visual arts.

The Surrealists, in their desire to revolutionize art and literature, saw in Apollinaire their precursor. It was he who coined the word "surréaliste," in the preface to his drama in verse *The Breasts of Tiresias*. In it, he explains that an equivalent is not always an imitation, even as the wheel, though intended to facilitate transportation, is not a reproduction of the leg. Apollinaire conveys his message with a lighthearted tone, employing incongruous rhythms, parody, and sexual imagery. This is essentially the technique he employs in his most avant-garde poetry, and *The Breasts of Tiresias* echoes poems from "Ondes" ("Waves," the first part of *Calligrammes*) such as "Zone," "Le Brasier" ("The Brazier"), "Les Fiançailles" ("The Betrothal"), and "Le Larron" ("The Thief"). Thus, Apollinaire indicated the path to follow in revolutionizing poetry, although much of his work was in some respects traditional. Like Victor Hugo, he served subsequent poets chiefly as a guide rather than as a model, but it was his "esprit nouveau" that gave considerable impetus to a new form of modern poetry.

BIOGRAPHY

Born in Rome on August 26, 1880, Guillaume Albert Wladimir Alexandre Apollinaire de Kostrowitzky was an illegitimate child; in "The Thief," he says that his "father was a sphinx and his mother a night." In reality, his mother was a Polish adventurer of noble ancestry, Angelique Kostrowicka, known in Paris mostly as "Olga." His father's identity has never been definitively ascertained. The most plausible supposition points to Francesco Flugi d'Aspermont, a man from a noble Italian family which included many prelates. This theory is based on the careful investigation of biographer Marcel Adéma. Apollinaire's mysterious and involved parentage haunted the poet throughout his life, leaving unmistakable marks on his character and works.

Apollinaire received his only formal education at the Collège of Saint-Charles in Monaco and the Collège Stanislas at Cannes, from 1890 to 1897, where he acquired a solid grounding in religious and secular knowledge. Although his Catholic training was to remain firmly implanted in his memory and is evident in his poetry, he moved away from any outward adherence to religious beliefs after 1897. In 1899, he arrived in Paris, his home for most of the next nineteen years of his life and the center and inspiration of his literary activity. First, however, he made a significant trip to Germany's Rhineland in 1901, as tutor to Gabrielle, the daughter of the Viscountess of Milhau. There, he met and fell in love with Annie Playden, Gabrielle's English governess. This ill-fated romance and the beauty of the Rhineland inspired many of Apollinaire's early poems, which were later published in *Alcools*.

Apollinaire's return to Paris coincided with the beginning of friendships with artists and writers such as André Salmon, Alfred Jarry, Max Jacob, and especially Picasso. In 1903, he began his collaboration on many periodicals, which he continued throughout his lifetime. Most of his prose and poetry was first published in such journals, many of which—such as *Le Festin d'Esope*

and La Revue immoraliste—were of very short duration. His works appeared under several pseudonyms, of which "Apollinaire" was the most significant. Others included "Louise Lalame," "Lul," "Montade," and "Tyl." In 1907, he met Marie Laurencin, an artist, whose talent Apollinaire tended to exaggerate. Their liaison continued until 1912 and was an inspiration and a torment to both of them. During this period, Apollinaire was deeply marked by the false accusation that he was responsible for the theft of the *Mona Lisa* from the Louvre. A series of six poems in *Alcools*, "À la Santé" ("At the Santé") describes his brief stay in the prison of La Santé in Verlainian imagery.

The year 1912 marked Apollinaire's break with Laurencin and his definite espousal of modern art, of which he became a staunch proponent. During the two years preceding World War I, he gave lectures and wrote articles on modern art and prepared *Alcools* for publication. The beginning of the war, in 1914, was to Apollinaire a call to a mission. Although not a French citizen until the year 1916, he embraced with great enthusiasm his *métier de soldat* as an artilleryman and then as an infantryman, according an almost mystical dimension to his military service. His poetry of these first two years reveals the exaltation of war and the idealization of two women, "Lou" (Louise de Coligny-Châtillon) and Madeleine Pagès, to whom he was briefly engaged.

Wounded in the head in 1916, Apollinaire required surgery and was then discharged from the service. He returned to the world of literature and art with numerous articles, lectures, two plays, and a volume of poetry, *Calligrammes*. In May of 1918, he married Jacqueline Kolb ("Ruby"), the "jolie rousse" (pretty redhead) of the last poem in *Calligrammes*. The marriage was of short duration, however, as Apollinaire died of Spanish influenza on November 9 of the same year.

ANALYSIS

In his poetic style, Guillaume Apollinaire might be characterized as the last of the Symbolists and the first of the moderns. He is considered a revolutionary and a destroyer, yet the bulk of his work shows a deep influence of traditional symbolism, especially biblical, legendary, and mythical. Very knowledgeable in Roman Catholic doctrine from his years with the Marianists at

Monaco and Cannes, he uses extensive biblical imagery: Christ, the Virgin Mary, and the Holy Spirit in the form of a dove. Robert Couffignal has analyzed Apollinaire's religious imagery in detail and considers his comprehension of the Bible to be "a cascade of superficial weavings." Scott Bates sees the Last Judgment, with its apocalyptic implications, as central to Apollinaire's works. The concept of messianism and the advent of a new millennium is evident in both the early works and the war poems, which predict a new universe. In the Symbolist tradition, the poet is the seer of the new kingdom.

Many of Apollinaire's symbols are from the realm of legend and myth. Rosemonde, the idealized woman of the Middle Ages, is present in several poems, though she appears also as a prostitute. In "Merlin et la vielle femme" ("Merlin and the Old Woman"), the medieval seer foreshadows Apollinaire's vision of the future. Ancient mythology is the source for Orpheus, under whose sign *Bestiary* is written. Orpheus is also the symbol of Christ and the poet, as is Hermès Trismègiste. Ancient Egypt appears in frequent references to the Nile, the Israelites in bondage, and Pharaoh, the image of the poet himself. The fantastic abounds in Apollinaire's works: ghosts, diabolic characters, and phantoms, as found, for example, in "La Maison des Morts" ("The House of the Dead") and especially in the short stories.

Much of Apollinaire's early symbolism is directed toward the quest for self-knowledge; his choice of the name "Apollinaire" is a clue to his search. Though it was the name of his maternal grandfather and one of the names given to him at baptism, he seems to have chosen it for its reference to Apollo, the god of the sun. Indeed, solar imagery is central to his poetry, and the introductory poem of *Alcools*, "Zone," ends with the words "Soleil cou coupé" ("Sun cut throat"). Bates argues that the violent love-death relationship between the sun and night, with its corresponding symbolism, is as crucial to the interpretation of Apollinaire as it is to a reading of Gérard de Nerval or Stéphane Mallarmé. Along with love and death is death and resurrection. Apollinaire chooses the phoenix as a sign of rebirth and describes his own psychological and poetic resurrection in "The Brazier" and "The Betrothal," poems that he regarded as among his best. Fire seems to be his basic image, with

its multiple meanings of passion, destruction, and purification.

Passion as a flame dominated Apollinaire's life and poetry. Of the many women whom he loved, five in particular incarnated his violent passion and appear in his work: Playden and Laurencin in *Alcools*; Lou, Madeleine, and Jacqueline in *Calligrammes* and in several series of poems published after his death. Apollinaire is capable of expressing tender, idealistic love, as in the "Aubade chantée à Lætare un an passé" ("Aubade Sung to Lætare a Year Ago") section of the "La Chanson du mal-aimé" ("The Song of the Poorly Loved") and in "La Jolie Rousse" ("The Pretty Redhead"), which closes *Calligrammes*. In most cases, Apollinaire is the *mal-aimé*, and as he himself says, he is much less the poorly beloved than the one who loves poorly. His first three loves ended violently; his last was concluded by his death. Thus, the death of love is as important as its first manifestation, which for him resembles the shells bursting in the war.

Autumn is the season of the death of love, wistfully expressed in such nostalgic works as "L'Adieu" ("The Farewell") and "Automne" ("Autumn"). Because the end of love usually involved deep suffering for him, the image of mutilation is not uncommon. The beloved in "The Song of the Poorly Loved" has a scar on her neck, and the mannequins in "L'Émigrant de Landor Road" ("The Emigrant from Landor Road") are decapitated, much like the sun in "Zone." Apollinaire perceives love in its erotic sense, and in many cases he resorts to arcane symbolism, as in the seven swords in "The Song of the Poorly Loved." "Lul de Faltenin" ("Lul of Faltenin") is also typical, with its subtle erotic allusions. Such themes are more overt in Apollinaire's prose; indeed, Bates has compiled a glossary of erotic symbolism in the works of Apollinaire.

Apollinaire was both a lyric poet and a storyteller. In the lyric tradition, he writes of his emotions in images drawn from nature. His work is particularly rich in flora and fauna. *Bestiary* shows his familiarity with and affection for animals and his ability, like the fabulists, to see them as caricatures of people. *Alcools*, as the title indicates, often evokes grapes and wine; it also speaks of fir trees (in "Les Sapins") and falling leaves. "Zone" contains a catalog of birds, real and legendary. The Seine comes alive in Apollinaire's ever-popular "Le Pont Mirabeau" ("Mirabeau Bridge"). In *Calligrammes*, the poet often compares the explosion of shells to bursting buds.

Apollinaire was the author of many short stories, and he maintains a narrative flavor in his poetry. "The House of the Dead" was originally a short story, "L'Obituaire," and it reads like one. Many of the picture poems in *Calligrammes* tell a story; "Paysage" ("Landscape"), for example, portrays by means of typography a house, a tree, and two lovers, one of whom smokes a cigar that the reader can almost smell. Apollinaire's technique often involved improvisation, as in "Le Musicien de Saint-Merry" ("The Musician of Saint-Merry"). Although he claims almost total spontaneity, there are revised versions of many of his poems, and he frequently borrowed from himself, rearranging both lines and poems. In particular, Apollinaire tells stories of the modern city, imitating its new structures as Arthur Rimbaud did in his innovative patterns, and, like Charles Baudelaire, Apollinaire peoples his verse with the forgotten and the poor, the prostitutes and the clowns.

Apollinaire had a remarkable sense of humor, displayed in frequent word-plays, burlesques, and parodies. The briefest example of his use of puns is the one-line poem "Chantre" ("Singer"): "Et l'unique cordeau des trompettes marines" ("And the single string of marine trumpets"). *Cordeau*, when read aloud, might be *cor d'eau*, or "horn of water," another version of a marine trumpet, as well as *corps d'eau* (body of water) or even *cœur d'eau* (heart of water). The burlesque found in his short stories appears in poetry as dissonance, erotic puns, and irreverent parodies, such as in "Les Sept Epées" ("The Seven Swords") as well as in "The Thief," a poem that Bates interprets as parodying Christ. Apollinaire's lighthearted rhythm and obscure symbolism tend to prevent his verse from becoming offensive and convey a sense of freedom, discovery, and surprise.

BESTIARY

Bestiary is one of the most charming and accessible of Apollinaire's works. The idea for the poem probably came from Picasso in 1906, who was then doing woodcuts of animals. In 1908, Apollinaire published in a journal eighteen poems under the title "La Marchande des quatre saisons ou le bestiaire moderne" (the coster-

monger or the modern bestiary). When he prepared the final edition in 1911, with woodcuts by Raoul Dufy, he added twelve poems and replaced the merchant with Orpheus. According to mythology, Orpheus attracted wild beasts by playing on the lyre he had received from Mercury. He is the symbol of Gnosis and Neoplatonic Humanism and is also identified with Christ and poetry, in a mixture of mystical and sensual imagery.

Apollinaire himself wrote the notes to the volume and uses as its sign a Δ (the Greek letter delta) pierced by a unicorn. He interprets it to mean the delta of the Nile and all the legendary and biblical symbols of ancient Egypt, also suggesting a *D* for Deplanche, the publisher, in addition to the obvious sexual symbolism. He added the motto "J'émerveille" (I marvel), thus giving a fantastic aura to the work. Roger Little sees in the volume a "delicious and malicious" wit, with metamorphoses, syncretism, pride in poetry, carnal love, and mysticism. Like all Apollinaire's early works, it is full of self-analysis. In "La Souris" ("The Mouse"), the poet speaks of his twenty-eight years as "mal-vécus" ("poorly spent").

The animals represent human foibles; the peacock, for example, displays both his best and, unbeknownst to him, his worst. They also speak of love: the serpent, the Sirens, the dove, and Orpheus himself. They point to God and things divine: the dove, the bull, or, again, Orpheus. They speak of poetry: the horse, the tortoise, the elephant, and the caterpillar. For Apollinaire, poetry is a divine gift. He concludes his notes by observing that poets seek nothing but perfection, which is God himself. Poets, he says, have the right to expect after death the full knowledge of God, which is sublime beauty.

ALCOOLS

The most analyzed and the best known of Apollinaire's works is *Alcools*, a slender volume published in 1913 with the subtitle *Poèmes, 1898-1913*. A portrait of Apollinaire, an etching by Picasso, serves as the frontispiece. Apollinaire chose fifty-five of the many poems he had written from his eighteenth to his thirty-third year and assembled them in an order that has continued to fascinate and baffle critics. Michel Décaudin says that the order in *Alcools* is based entirely on the aesthetic and sentimental affinities felt by the author, or their discrete dissonances. Very few poems have dates, other than

"Rhénanes" (September, 1901, to May, 1902) and "At the Santé" (September, 1911); nevertheless, critics have succeeded in dating many, though not all, of the poems.

The poems have several centers, though not all of those from one group appear together. More than twenty were inspired by Apollinaire's trip to the Rhineland in 1901, including the nine in the cycle "Rhénanes." Several of these poems and some others, such as "The Song of the Poorly Loved," "Annie," and "The Emigrant from Landor Road," refer to his unhappy love affair with Playden. These poems and an interview with her as Mrs. Postings in 1951 by Robert Goffin and LeRoy Breunig are the only sources of information about this significant period in Apollinaire's life. Three poems, "Mirabeau Bridge," "Marie," and "Cors de chasse" ("Hunting Horns"), scattered throughout the volume, refer to Laurencin.

The poems exhibit great variety in form, tone, and subject matter. They range from the one-line "Chantre" to the seven-part "The Song of the Poorly Loved," the longest in the collection. Most of them have regular rhyme and rhythm, but "Zone" and "Vendémiaire," the first and the last, give evidence of technical experimentation. The poems range from witty ("The Synagogue") to nostalgic ("Autumn," "Hunting Horns"), from enigmatic ("The Brazier") to irreverent ("The Thief"). Critics have arranged them in various ways. Bates, for example, sees the volume as a "Dionysian-Apollonian dance of life in three major symbols: fire, shadow, alcools."

Apollinaire chose the beginning and concluding poems of the collection, "Zone" and "Vendémiaire," with great care. "Zone" is overtly autobiographical in a "Romantic-Symbolist" ambience, yet its instant leaps in space and time make it very modern. Also modern is the image of the city, where Apollinaire can see beauty in a poster, a traffic jam, and a group of frightened Jewish immigrants. The city is also the central focus in the concluding poem, "Vendémiaire" (the name given the month of vintage, September 22-October 21, in the revolutionary calendar), a hymn to the glory of Paris. The poet exuberantly proclaims his immortality and omnipresence: "I am drunk from having swallowed all the universe." Bates sees the end of the poem as a hymn to joy reminiscent of Walt Whitman and Friedrich Nietzsche.

The bizarre juxtapositions, the inner borrowings of lines from one poem to the next, and the absence of punctuation provoked various responses from critics. Cubists hailed Apollinaire as a great poet. Georges Duhamel, writing in the June 15, 1913, issue of *Mercure de France*, called the volume a junk shop. Critics such as Adéma, Décaudin, and Marie-Jeanne Durry analyze *Alcools* with depth and scholarship. They discover many platitudes and much mediocrity but find it redeemed by what Steegmuller identifies as a spirit of freedom.

CALLIGRAMMES

Intended as a sequel to *Alcools*, *Calligrammes* is much more unified than *Alcools*, yet its importance was seen only much later. It consists of six parts. The first part, "Waves," is the most innovative and was written before World War I in the frenzied stimulation of artistic activity in Paris. The other five contain poems inspired by the war and by the poet's love for Lou, Madeleine, and—in the final poem—his future wife, Jacqueline.

Philippe Renaud sees the difference between *Alcools* and "Waves" as one of nature rather than degree. Even the most enigmatic poems of *Alcools* follow a familiar plan, he maintains, whereas in "Waves" the reader is in unfamiliar territory, disoriented in space and time. In "Waves" one feels both the insecurity and the indefiniteness that can only be called "modern art." The introductory poem, "Chains," uses the elements recommended by Apollinaire in "The New Spirit and the Poets" yet remains anchored in the past. It leaps from the Tower of Babel to telegraph wires in disconcerting juxtapositions, speaking of man's eternal, frustrating quest for unity. In "The Windows," the window opens like an orange on Paris or in the tropics and flies on a rainbow across space and time.

Beginning with "Waves," and throughout *Calligrammes*, Apollinaire uses what he calls "ideograms," or picture poems. They are the most attractive pieces in the book, though not necessarily the most original. They became excellent vehicles for the war poems, where brevity and wit are essential. The theme of war dominates the majority of poems in *Calligrammes*. The war excited Apollinaire, promising a new universe. He experienced exhilaration as he saw shells exploding, comparing them in the poem "Merveilles de la guerre" ("Wonders of War"), to constellations and to women's hair, to dancers and to women in childbirth. He saw himself as the poet-hero, the omnipresent seer, the animator of the universe. In "La Tête étoilée" ("The Starry Head"), his wound was a crown of stars on his head.

Apollinaire was as dependent on love as he was on air, and he suffered greatly in the solitary trenches of France. His brief romance with Lou was intense and violent, as his pun on her name in "C'est Lou qu'on la nommait" ("They Called Her Lou") indicates; instead of "Lou," the word *loup* (which sounds the same in French but means "wolf") is used throughout the poem. In his poems to Madeleine, he devours images like a starving man. The anthology ends serenely as he addresses Jacqueline, "la jolie rousse," the woman destined to be his wife, as poetry was destined to be his life. This final poem is also his poetic testament, in which he bequeaths "vast and unknown kingdoms, new fires and the mystery of flowers to anyone willing to pick them."

OTHER MAJOR WORKS

LONG FICTION: *L'Enchanteur pourrissant*, 1909; *Le Poète assassiné*, 1916 (*The Poet Assassinated*, 1923).

SHORT FICTION: *L'Hérésiarque et Cie.*, 1910 (*The Heresiarch and Co.*, 1965).

PLAYS: *Les Mamelles de Tirésias*, pr. 1917 (*The Breasts of Tiresias*, 1961); *Couleur du temps*, pr. 1918.

NONFICTION: *Peintres cubistes: Méditations esthétiques*, 1913 (*The Cubist Painters: Aesthetic Meditations*, 1944); *Chroniques d'art, 1902-1918*, 1960 (*Apollinaire on Art: Essays and Reviews, 1902-1918*, 1972).

MISCELLANEOUS: *Œuvres complètes*, 1966 (8 volumes); *Œuvres en prose*, 1977 (Michel Décaudin, editor).

BIBLIOGRAPHY

Bohn, Willard. *The Aesthetics of Visual Poetry: 1914-1928*. Cambridge, England: Cambridge University Press, 1986. Chapter 3, "Apollinaire's Plastic Imagination," reveals the lyric innovations that Apollinaire brought to visual poetry with *Calligrammes*: new forms, new content, multiple figures in a unified composition, a dual sign system used to express a simultaneity, and a difficulty of reading that mirrors the act of creation. Chapter 4, "Toward a Calligram-mar," offers a sophisticated structural and statistical analysis of the calligrammes to demonstrate metonymy as the principal force binding the visual tropes, whereas metaphor and metonymy occur evenly in the verbal arena.

_____. *Apollinaire and the Faceless Man: The Creation and Evolution of a Modern Motif*. Rutherford, N.J.: Farleigh Dickinson University Press, 1991. Traces the history of Apollinaire's faceless man motif as a symbol of the human condition, from its roots in the poem "Le Musicien de Saint-Mercy" to its dissemination to the arts community through the unproduced pantomime "A quelle heure un train partira-t-il pour Paris?"

_____. *Apollinaire and the International Avant-Garde*. Albany: State University of New York Press, 1997. Chronicles the early artistic and critical reception of Apollinaire in Europe, North America, and Latin America. Especially interesting is the discussion of Argentina, exported through the Ultraism of Jorge Luis Borges, and Apollinaire's place in the revolutionary circles of Mexico.

Cornelius, Nathalie Goodisman. *A Semiotic Analysis of Guillaume Apollinaire's Mythology in "Alcools."* Berkeley Insights in Linguistics and Semiotics 17. New York: Peter Lang, 1995. Examines Apollinaire's use of linguistic and mythological fragmentation and reordering to mold his material into an entirely new system of signs that both encompasses and surpasses the old. Chapters give close semiotic readings of four poems: "Claire de lune," "Le Brasier," "Nuit rhëane," and "Vendémaine."

Matthews, Timothy. *Reading Apollinaire: Theories of Poetic Language*. Manchester: Manchester University Press, 1987. Uses a variety of historical, biographical, and stylistic approaches to offer an accessible point of entry into often difficult texts. Matthews's detailed discussion of *Alcools* focuses heavily on "L Adieu" and "Automne malade," which allows for a reading that may be transferred to the rest of the book. His chapter "Poetry, Painting, and Theory" offers a solid historical background that leads directly into his examination of *Calligrammes*.

Irma M. Kashuba;
bibliography updated by David Harrison Horton

APOLLONIUS RHODIUS

Born: Alexandria or Naucratis, Egypt; between 295
and 260 B.C.E.
Died: Alexandria, Egypt; late third century B.C.E.

PRINCIPAL POETRY
Argonautica, third century B.C.E. (English transla-
tion, 1780)
Ktiseis, third century B.C.E.

OTHER LITERARY FORMS

Apollonius Rhodius is credited with several works
besides the *Argonautica*. A collection of epigrams
passed under his name, but only one has survived. Besides these, he seems to have written a poem or group of
poems called *Ktiseis*, dealing with the founding of the
cities of Alexandria, Naucratis, Cnidos, Rhodes, and
Caunus; in this work, Apollonius might well have been
poaching on Callimachus's preserve, since he wrote
something similar. Apollonius also wrote philological
works in prose, including *Against Zenodotos* (third century B.C.E.). A variety of other works are attributed to
Apollonius, but it was not necessarily this Apollonius
who wrote them, since the name was a common one.

ACHIEVEMENTS

Apollonius Rhodius's principal work, the *Argonautica*, which has survived in revised form, is a deliberate
challenge to Callimachus's fundamental literary principle
that poems should be short, for it fills four lengthy books
with its 5,834 hexameter lines. It is a book of excellent
stories told in good verse rather than a regular and unified epic poem, and its merit lies in its episodes, notably
in the admirable recounting of the loves of Jason and
Medea, which fills the third book and part of the fourth.

BIOGRAPHY

The birth of Apollonius Rhodius is placed by scholars at various times between 295 and 260 B.C.E., and the
year of his death is equally uncertain. In fact, there is
very little information about his life available today.
There are two "lives" of Apollonius, both derived from
an earlier biography which is lost. From these one learns
that Apollonius was the son of one Silleus (or Illeus) and
was born either at Alexandria or Naucratis. Possibly, as
has been suggested, he was born at Naucratis and reared
in Alexandria.

Apollonius lived during the reign of the Ptolemies
and apparently was a pupil of Callimachus, the literary
dictator of the time, an author of frigid, learned poems
and a few highly polished epigrams and the originator of
the terse and generally true dictum that a big book is a
big nuisance. Apollonius's opinions on the subject of
lengthy poems were diametrically opposed to those of
Callimachus and, hence, heretical. At a youthful age, the
student-poet produced a long poem on the Argonautic
expedition. It was a complete failure, and in his shame
and distress, Apollonius left Alexandria and settled in
Rhodes. There he revised and polished, and perhaps
completed, his work. The Rhodians gave his book a far
more favorable reception. He was given Rhodian citizenship, hence the surname Rhodius, and was held in
high esteem. Years later, after the death of Callimachus,
Apollonius returned to Alexandria to a better reception;
indeed, one biographer reports that he followed Callimachus as head librarian there. He died in the late third
century B.C.E. and was buried near his old foe.

This traditional account of the life of Apollonius has
been questioned by modern scholarship. Callimachus
may never have been head librarian at Alexandria or
even the teacher of Apollonius. Indeed, Apollonius and
Callimachus may have been near contemporaries and
thus more likely to be literary opponents. Some scholars, for chronological reasons, deny the librarianship of
Apollonius, but it is clearly asserted by his biographer,
Suidas, and the arguments against it are not conclusive.

In spite of these uncertainties, it seems clear that
Apollonius's quarrel with Callimachus was a crucial
event in his life. This quarrel apparently arose from differences of literary aims and taste but degenerated into the
bitterest sort of personal strife. There are references to
the quarrel in the writings of both. Callimachus attacks
Apollonius in a passage at the end of his *Hymn to Apollo*
(third century B.C.E.), but he attacks Apollonius most vociferously in the *Ibis* (third century B.C.E.), which Ovid
imitated or perhaps translated in his poem of the same
name. On the part of Apollonius, there is a passage in
the third book of the *Argonautica* which is of a polemi-

cal nature and which stands out from the context, as well as a savage epigram attacking Callimachus. There is not enough data to determine the chronological order of the attacks and counterattacks. The *Ibis* has been thought to mark the termination of the feud on the curious ground that it was impossible for the abuse to go further.

ANALYSIS

The chief characteristics of Alexandrianism, of which Callimachus was the leading proponent, were refinement in diction, precision of form and meter, erudition which often degenerated into pedantry and obscurity, and avoidance of the commonplace in subject, sentiment, and allusion. Apollonius Rhodius shares some of these traits, and he seems to have written the *Argonautica* out of bravado, to show that he could indeed write an epic poem. The influence of the age, however, was too strong. Instead of a unified epic, there is merely a series of episodes. In the four books of his *Argonautica*, Apollonius tells of the quest for the Golden Fleece and especially of Jason and Medea. The same story was known to Homer and certainly belonged in the repertory of old epic. It provided a splendid source of thrilling adventures and opportunities for excursions into the unknown, a literary device that varied the more straightforward episodes of epic. It demanded, however, a heroic sense of human worth and of perilous action, and this was precisely what Apollonius lacked. His Jason is the faintest of phantoms; he could hardly be otherwise, inasmuch as Apollonius lived in the metropolitan society of Alexandria and had little idea of how to depict a hero. There were other defects as well. Apollonius never forgot that he was an antiquarian and therefore he liberally garnished his poem with tidbits of erudite information. This is deadly not only to the flow of the narrative but also to the actual poetry. The delight in learning for its own sake was an especially Alexandrian characteristic. Literary allusions seeped into Alexandrian poetry without poets quite noticing how cumbersome and distracting they were. Apollonius must have thought such allusions gave richness and dignity to his story, but ultimately, they make it tedious and pedantic.

ARGONAUTICA

Not until the Hellenistic age and Apollonius's *Argonautica* was there a complete epic presentation of the Thessalian or Argonautic cycle of legends, among the oldest in Greek mythology. Poetry in all its forms had time and again turned to the legend of the Argonauts and the local history of the many places connected with it. Thus, Apollonius was faced with a rich tradition with many partly contradictory variants.

Apollonius's composition exhibits a systematic arrangement of the subject matter. The first two books describe the voyage to the land of Colchis, the third relates the adventures leading to the winning of the Golden Fleece, while the fourth tells of the dangers of the flight and the return home. The stress on details, however, is variously distributed; there are rapid transitions, but there are also passages over which Apollonius had lingered lovingly, typical of the rejection of symmetry and the tendency to variety found elsewhere in Alexandrian poetry.

BOOK 1

While a proem with prayer formula is merely indicated at the beginning of book 1 and much of the preceding history is saved for later, the introductory passage offers an elaborate catalog of the Argonauts, geographically arranged in the manner of a circumnavigation and leading from the north of Greece to the east and west and then back to the north. The catalog tradition of ancient epic served as its model. The scenes of departure in Iolcus and on the beach at Pagasae are spun out in detail. Then follows the long series of stopping places and adventures on the way out, along the usual route to Colchis. For the voyage up to the treacherous passage through the Symplegades, which are thought to be at the entrance to the Pontus, the tradition had a number of effective, ready-made episodes upon which Apollonius elaborated successfully. First is the landing in Lemnos, where the women, under a curse of Aphrodite, have killed their husbands. Now, however, they are glad to entertain the Argonauts. The result is a delectable sojourn from which Heracles has to call his companions to action. That is followed by the initiation into the mysteries at Samothrace and the adventures in Cyzicus. Here the Argonauts give the Doliones effective help against evil giants only to become involved, through a misunderstanding, in a bitterly regretted nocturnal battle with their friends.

The next stop on the coast of Propontis provides the setting for the Hylas episode. When Apollonius tells how the beautiful youth Hylas is dragged down into a pool by a nymph who has fallen in love with him, he does it very well, since his dramatic economy avoids any kind of false pathos, and the reader witnesses the nymph's ruthless determination as she puts her arms around the boy who is stooping to get water. Heracles seeks Hylas in the woods and the Argonauts continue their voyage without him, since the sea-god Glaucus announces that the hero is destined to perform other deeds. This device eliminates from the narrative the greatest of the champions, beside whom the heroic Jason would pale by comparison.

BOOK 2

The story continues without a stop from book 1 to book 2, which begins with Pollux's boxing match with Amycus, a barbarian king. In Bithynia, the Argonauts come upon the blind king Phineus, who, in deep misery, is doing penance for some ancient offense. The winged sons of Boreas liberate him from the Harpies, the predatory storm spirits who rob him of every meal or defile it. As a reward, Phineus gives the Argonauts good advice for the rest of their voyage. The compositional significance of this preview is that it sums up the various minor episodes of the second half of the voyage. The passage through the Symplegades after a pigeon's test flight is depicted with dramatic power. Thereafter, the only sojourn worthy of mention is that on the island of Ares. There the Argonauts drive out the Stymphalian birds, and there they meet the sons of Phrixus. Their mother is Chalciope, Aeetes' daughter and the sister of Medea. Medea will play a significant role in the events in Colchis, thus the meeting in the island of Ares provides a dramatic link between the description of the voyage and the winning of the Golden Fleece.

BOOK 3

Book 3 starts with a new proem and portrays the events in Colchis by means of a technique which often resolves the action into parallel strands. Medea's decisive intervention is first motivated in a scene in which the goddesses Hera and Athena enjoin Aphrodite to have Eros do his work. Independent from this motivation, however, Medea's awakening love, her hard struggle between loyalty to her father's house and passion for the handsome stranger, is presented as a drama full of tension with the girl's soul as the stage. Apollonius is at

his best when he writes of love. What engages all his powers is not Jason's love for Medea (on which he leaves the reader uninstructed) but Medea's love for Jason, and it is this which makes book 3 of the *Argonautica* shine more brightly than the other three. Medea is still a girl, and she falls passionately in love at first sight. When she first sees Jason, he seems to her like Sirius rising from the ocean, and Apollonius, not without echoes of Sappho, describes how a mist covers Medea's eyes, her cheeks burn like fire, her knees are too weak to move, and she feels rooted to the earth. When, a little later, Medea helps him in his ordeals to win the Fleece, the light playing on his yellow hair makes her willing to tear the life out of her breast for him, and her heart melts like dew on roses in the morning. When their love is fulfilled, Medea is entirely absorbed in him, but when he plans to return to Greece and in his callous indifference is ready to leave her behind, the fierce side of her nature emerges, and she bursts into bitter remonstrances, chiding him for his ingratitude. If he really intends to desert her, she invokes disaster and vengeance on him and prays that the Furies will make him homeless. In this part of his poem, Apollonius tells one of the first surviving love stories in the world.

Alongside this love story runs a subplot concerning Chalciope, which leads to her intervention and to the decisive talk between the two sisters, Chalciope and Medea. The composition of book 3 is particularly careful. Developing in several stages, it progresses to the meeting of Medea and Jason, when he receives the magic ointment.

BOOK 4

Book 4, which begins with a brief invocation to the Muse, presents Apolonius with his most exciting challenge, to which he rises admirably. After receiving the magic ointment from Medea, Jason must yoke fire-breathing bulls, sow dragon's teeth, and destroy the armed men who spring out of them. Jason falls on the men like a shooting star, and the furrows are as filled with blood as runnels are with water. Apollonius presents the weird scene very vividly, capturing even the brilliant light shining from the armor and weapons. This struggle bears no resemblance to a Homeric battle, but, in its unearthly strangeness, it is convincing and complete. Apollonius glories in strangeness for its own sake, and it is this quality that makes him a pioneer of that kind of poetry which deals with remote and unfamiliar themes. The rest of book 4 describes the homeward voyage, two high points being the murder of Absyrtus, who has gone in pursuit of his sister Medea, and the marriage of Jason and Medea in the land of the Phaeacians. One of the most enchanting aspects of mythic geography is the way the return of the Argonauts was modified as the knowledge of foreign countries and seas increased, newly discovered facts and ancient mythic elements forming various and often grotesque combinations. After a series of less-than-dangerous adventures, the Argonauts return to Colchis.

Apollonius's epic has numerous qualities which depend largely on the literary and historical background of the work. Some readers find it pedantic, unpoetic, or dry, while others—and especially in recent times—are able to appreciate the truly poetical qualities of the *Argonautica*. In the first place, it should be clearly understood that the intellectual world in which this epic originated was separated from that of Homer by an immeasurable distance. When older poets molded the history of the heroic past for their people, they claimed that their verses imbued true events with splendor and permanence. In these events the gods were active everywhere; they were great spirits, inspiring faith and helpfully allying themselves with man or wrathfully striking out at him. By Apollonius's time, the living belief had become mythology or was proceeding toward this condition. Hardly anything can be said about Apolonius's personal religious feelings, but his attitude to tradition cannot have been very different from that of Callimachus. Apollonius's *stylos* was guided both by an erudite interest in mythical tradition and by a delight in the unfading beauty of its creations. Both can be discerned in his verse.

COMPARISONS TO HOMER

The tremendous distance from Homer's world is in exciting contrast with the fact that numerous and essential elements of ancient epic remain preserved. In Apollonius, the gods also act, but the very nature of the great Olympian scene at the opening of book 3 reveals the ornamental character of such passages. With Hera, Athena, and Eros a complete divine apparatus is developed, but Medea's love and its consequences are completely imaginable without it. Also, in the portrayal of the girl's emotional struggles, the poet can be recognized much more directly than in the conversations of the Olympians. While in Homer, man's actions are determined simultaneously by his own impulses and by the influence of the gods, in Apollonius this duality of motivation has resulted in separate spheres of action. The divine plot takes place on an upper stage; its connection with earthly happenings is neither indissoluble nor irrevocably necessary.

Apollonius retains important formal elements of Homeric epic. While he is sparing with metaphors, he uses similes with great frequency. Their free, Homeric spontaneity has been restricted in Apollonius in favor of a more direct bearing on the action, although the subject matter has been expanded in many directions. Illustrations of emotions by means of similes, found in the verse of Homer in rudimentary form, have been developed by Apollonius with great skill. Thus Medea's agitation and irresolution are elucidated by the image of the sun's ray which is reflected onto a wall by the ruffled surface of water. Apollonius also uses stock scenes, but he keeps recurrent formulas to a minimum. This is connected with another, fundamentally important observation. Apollonius's language is largely based on that of Homer. This does not mean that Apollonius accepted the tradition without due reflection or that he imitated it naïvely. Rather, the linguistic resources he borrowed are given new effectiveness through constant, well-planned variation, sometimes even by means of a shifting of the meaning.

The Homeric legacy, which functions as a sort of framework for the *Argonautica* with regard to themes and style, contrasts with the poem's Alexandrian element. Apollonius is a realist, although the term is to be taken in its broadest sense. In the final analysis, this realism is connected with the altered attitude toward myths, with the awareness of their illusory nature. Apollonius may be granted poetic ability, and there may be much that is praiseworthy in his work, but he was not truly a poet filled with the Muse; time and again, the reader is struck by the cool objectivity with which he describes legendary events. This also explains the great care he takes with motivation and establishment of cohesion.

Hellenist influences

The poet frequently accounts for contemporary customs by seeking explanations in early history, and in this way he links his own time with the mythical past. A true Hellenist, Apollonius devoted much of his poem to etiological matters, interspersing the narrative of the voyage with a wealth of such stories.

As a portrayer of emotions, especially of those which Eros brings to the human soul, Apollonius belongs entirely within the sphere of Hellenistic poetry. It has already been pointed out that his highest achievement was his description of Medea's pangs and doubts. After the long-winded description of the outward voyage, which at times sinks to the level of a learned guidebook, the realm of true poetry is entered. This is confirmed by the tremendous subsequent influence of book 3 in ancient literature. The characterization of Medea recalls Apollonius's predecessor Euripides in that the effective portrayal of individual emotion is more important than a finished portrait of a character. Medea the lovesick girl and Medea the great sorceress could not be readily combined in one description.

There is also an Alexandrian element in the many descriptions of nature which, in the traditional epic, would be unthinkable. Successful color effects are achieved in descriptions of seascapes, as in the sailing of the Argo when the dark flood foams under the beat of the oars, the men's armor flashes like fire in the morning light, and the long wake seems like a bright path in a green meadow. Apollonius also shares with the rest of Hellenistic art the discovery of children. The Eros of the celestial scenes of book 3, who in his day was a formidable god, has here been reduced to an ill-mannered boy. He is the epitome of the spoiled rascal who cheats his comrades at play and can be persuaded by his mother Aphrodite to perform a service only by means of an expensive present.

Apollonius cannot be characterized concisely. He proved himself to be a poet of considerable importance in several passages, but he was not completely successful in blending the rich epic tradition with his own creation. His fire was too weak to fuse all the heterogeneous elements into one whole.

Other major work

NONFICTION: *Against Zenodotos*, third century B.C.E.

Bibliography

Albis, Robert V. *Poet and Audience in the "Argonautica" of Apollonius.* Lanham, Md.: Rowman and Littlefield, 1996. This short study of the poet's major work concentrates on the rhetorical position of the poet relative to his audience, with significant attention paid to poetic performance as a point of scholarly inquiry. In addition, Albis examines the figure of the poet and the inscribed audience in the poem.

Beye, Charles Rowan. *Ancient Epic Poetry: Homer, Apollonius, Virgil.* Ithaca, N.Y.: Cornell University Press, 1993. The section on Apollonius examines his relationship to his literary patrons, including the Greek scholar Callimachus, and to the cultural milieu of ancient Alexandria. The study offers a significantly original interpretation of the *Argonautica* and counters ancient critical theories characterizing Apollonius's major work as both derivative and flawed.

Clauss, James Joseph. *The Best of the Argonauts: The Redefinition of the Epic Hero in Book One of Apollonius' "Argonautica."* Berkeley: University of California Press, 1993. This study presents the argument that Apollonius's major poem demonstrates a shift in the popular definition of heroism in ancient Greece, away from the notion of the protagonist as an autonomous superhero and toward later concepts of the protagonist as a tool of fate.

Hutchinson, G. O. *Hellenistic Poetry.* New York: Clarendon Press, 1988. This study adopts a necessarily broader view to position each of its subjects within the main currents of ancient Greek literature and culture and its impact on later Roman writers. The discussion of Apollonius Rhodius is fairly general.

Papanghelis, Theodore, and Antonios Renggkos. *A Companion to Apollonius Rhodius.* Boston: Brill, 2001. An anthology of scholarly articles borrowing heavily from various literary theories, this work examines subjects such as Hellenistic poetry and genres such as epic poetry and includes character studies of Jason and Medea.

Shelley P. Haley;
bibliography updated by Michael R. Meyers

JAMES APPLEWHITE

Born: Stantonsburg, North Carolina; August 8, 1935

PRINCIPAL POETRY

War Summer: Poems, 1972
Statues of the Grass, 1975
Following Gravity, 1980
Foreseeing the Journey, 1983
Ode to the Chinaberry Tree and Other Poems, 1986
River Writing: An Eno Journal, 1988
Lessons in Soaring, 1989
A History of the River, 1993
Daytime and Starlight, 1997

OTHER LITERARY FORMS

Poetry forms the main body of James Applewhite's work, but *Seas and Inland Journeys: Landscape and Consciousness from Wordsworth to Roethke* (1985) is a critical work in which Applewhite examines the subject which has been so important to his own poetry—the relationship of landscape to the poet's creative perceptions. The work gives particular attention to the Romantic poets William Wordsworth and Samuel Taylor Coleridge as well as to William Butler Yeats and Theodore Roethke. Applewhite also edited two volumes, *Brown Bag* (1971), with Anne Lloyd and Fred Chappell, and *Voices from Earth* (1971).

ACHIEVEMENTS

James Applewhite has been widely recognized as an important lyric poet whose work articulates the scenes and voices of the contemporary South, as his many awards attest. He received a Guggenheim Fellowship in 1976, the Associated Writing Programs' Contemporary Poetry Series Award in 1981, and the North Carolina Literary and Historical Association poetry award in 1981 and 1986. He received a prize in the *International Poetry Review* competition for 1982 and won the North Carolina Poetry Society award in 1990. He won the American Academy and Institute of Arts and Letters's Jean Stein Award in Poetry in 1992 and the North Carolina Award in Literature in 1993.

BIOGRAPHY

James Applewhite was born August 8, 1935, in Stantonsburg, North Carolina, a small rural town which, along with his family, has played an important role in the images and voices of his poetry. His grandfather was a farmer; his father owned a gasoline station, and Applewhite has frequently recorded the voices of the rural South from the men who worked for his father or who bought gasoline there and in the women like his mother, voices that shaped his understanding of the world. Growing up in a world at war also shaped the poet's consciousness, as did the constant sense of the Civil War, a painful event which seemed to the child to have occurred in the recent past.

Applewhite attended Duke University, receiving his B.A. degree in 1958, the M.A. in 1960, and the Ph.D. in 1969, eventually making his career there teaching English. It was during graduate study, especially during study of the Romantic poets, Applewhite said, that he discovered the power of poetry to address his sense of alienation.

ANALYSIS

James Applewhite's poetry validates the claim that Southern literature is often deeply rooted in place. Applewhite's work is steeped in North Carolina, both in Stantonsburg, a small town in the eastern part of the state, and in the area around Duke University and Durham. The sense of history has always been powerful in the South, and his own rootedness in the area has invited Applewhite to examine the relationship between past and present both in personal and historical terms. That relationship often produces a sense of duality that forms an important theme in Applewhite's work.

FOLLOWING GRAVITY

This early volume makes a good introduction to Applewhite's interests and themes. "Tobacco Men," "Drinking Music," "Elegy for a General Store," and "Rooster's Station" all look at the South of the poet's childhood. In the center of the volume, "My Grandmother's Life" uses images of water to link the poet to his grandparents as he seeks out their long-abandoned well. At the end of the volume, in the long poem "The Mary Tapes," a woman tells a tape recorder her life's history in country and town, a history which becomes emblematic of many lives in the "New South."

RIVER WRITING: AN ENO JOURNAL

Applewhite's *River Writing: An Eno Journal* (1988) chronicles a year of hiking and running along the Eno River, a nature preserve in the midst of the increasing urbanization of Durham and Chapel Hill. The poems detail the seasons and sights along the river, its cliffs and boulders, its kingfishers and beavers. The poems also insistently link the writer to his place in the setting, in both the present and past, just as the jonquils he picks in "The Sun's Tone" tie him to the grave of a woman who died in 1914 and yet resemble the jonquils he picks in "House of Seasons" to carry "Home to the living woman I love."

"Sleeping with Stars and Bulbs, Time and Its Signs" is the last poem in the collection. It marks the conclusion of Applewhite's year on the Eno and stands as a fine illustration of the level of lyricism many of the poems achieve. Camping beside the river in winter, the speaker thinks of the jonquil bulbs he dug from an abandoned homestead to plant at his own home. Even now, "each jonquil bulb/ . . . begins to unsheathe its single green claw/ Which will dig a yellow from night." He thinks of the relics of the past he has uncovered along the river, names and dates cut in trees, a "Model-T carcass"—all signs of those who came before him and reminders that others will follow. "All will come/ Round again, will be sounded." Even his own house will some day be a "branch-sketched cinder of rafters." Tonight, in this drowsy meditation, the speaker feels rooted in all he has experienced:

> I expand . . .
> To feel my huge shadow gravity-held,
> On the physical basis of all poetry,
> Nailed to earth's wheel by the stars.

LESSONS IN SOARING

Lessons in Soaring (1989) takes its themes from the life of the child who grew up in the rural South during World War II. Physically surrounded by a landscape of burgeoning life, he was also surrounded by adults whose focus was on the killing events abroad, where the technology of death superseded everything else.

Several poems in this collection blend imagery from the war with pictures of rural life, as in the volume's first poem, "The War Against Nature," which pictures the poet as a child watching for enemy aircraft from the observation tower in his father's service station. The adult narrator ponders the implications of the child's eagerness to see planes:

> Bored with a primordial green,
> We wanted experimental designs we'd seen,
>
> The fire it'd have meant had an enemy
> Plane appeared.

As the volunteer watchers gradually return to work on their farms, only the child is left, watching for the foreign shapes:

> Memorizing the chart of possible form:
> Messerschmitt, Wellington, workhorse Douglas.
> Ideas absolute as the blue emptiness.

Somehow the human designs of airplanes have taken on greater power to move the observer than even the absoluteness of the "blue emptiness," a phrase that hints at the emptiness of the human designs and their war against nature.

"The Memory of the Heart" asserts that the whole of the child's experience is written into his physical being. "Deciphering the Known Map" applies that idea to the geography of the family's world. It begins with town names from the family's history, goes on to a family cemetery, and widens its circles to the country music of Southern tastes. The very language of this world binds the speaker to it. At a rural general store of the sort still seen throughout the South, the speaker might

> Buy nabs and an orange drink.
> The speech I share
> With the guy behind the counter
> Is as thick as the creek's
> Low water.

The poem concludes at another family graveyard, where the speaker senses his own name on the gravestones. "Among the Old Stones" also deals with a family graveyard (a common interest among Southerners); here the setting leads the speaker to a meditation first on the speaker's relationship to the dead and then to the nature of the South and his place in it.

The realities of the modern South are often in tension with the South's romantic vision of itself both now and in its past, a tension that Applewhite articulates in "The Failure of Southern Representation." Here he considers the contradictions between the modern South of shopping centers and interstate highways and the fictional South of romanticized plantation life and the Civil War. The South of slavery and lynchings, the South of music, tobacco, and hurricanes—nothing can create a true picture of a place so riddled with opposites.

"A PLACE AND A VOICE" AND
"A CONVERSATION"

The long poem "A Place and a Voice" is addressed to the poet's mother in her old age, presenting her history in a collage of people, places, and events. The speaker has questions about them. Did her father recover from a buggy accident? Must a Methodist minister always be on the move? The questions suggest the mysteries that inevitably endure in any family's history. Sections 3 and 4 summarize the speaker's childhood in Stantonsburg, where he lived with his parents and brother near his paternal grandfather, enjoying the rich life of an active youth in a small town:

> Starved
> minds never lived in our house.
>
> Was it really the South? Life was
> rich, authentic.

In section 5, Applewhite imagines the tensions his mother endured in her strained relationship with her in-laws; section 6 records his own changing feelings toward his mother in his early maturity. Once she was the best listener to his stories; now he resents her claim on his imagination and simultaneously resents her absence, which leaves him feeling alone even when he is with his wife:

> I hated that you and a place were one,
> so vivid a myth, claustrophobic Eden,
> rich Atlantis in which to drown.

"The Conversation" makes a companion poem to "A Place and a Voice," this time addressed to Applewhite's father, cataloging his legacy as a former wrestler, garage owner, and wartime commander of the home guard. Now the son views his father in his old age; the rebellion of the son's adolescence has mellowed into affection. At the same time, he regrets what is lost: "I worship and regret the other figure,/ The god-king I once wished dead."

DAYTIME AND STARLIGHT

The first poem of *Daytime and Starlight* (1997), "My Grandparents Never Watched *Star Trek*," images the dualities that frequently form Applewhite's themes. Here he pictures the world of his grandparents, the wood-burning stove, the foods they preserved in mason jars, the sausages they made. Since the time he viewed that world as a boy, the world has changed, and he has changed in it. Televised space ships, real and fictional, have carried him away to another planet.

"Botanical Garden: The Coastal Plains" looks at the issue in another way, as the poet tours the coastal plains section of the university's botanical garden. It is a miniature of the land he was born into, but it cannot be the same. Its plants bear the same names, but these are labeled with neat tags. The poet's father is not there. Even the dangers that once attended the water moccasin have been tamed.

The volume contains a number of long-line poems, including several about a trip to Italy, new subject matter for Applewhite. Still, one sees in "Descending in St. Clements" the poet's ongoing interest in the relationship between past and present and in dualities. In this poem he is underground in an ancient temple of Mithras; above it the Christian basilica of St. Clement has been built; below it one can hear water rushing. The setting leads the poet to a meditation on the interconnectedness of the pagan god of bull sacrifices depicted at the lowest level and the depictions of Christ, who "shed blood of his own." Also pictured was the watery martyrdom of St. Clement, including fish and squid. The images and sound of water lead the tourist poet to contemplate the "higher miracle" which extinguished Mithras's flames, leaving that cellar temple as a "time-vein."

"Daytime and Starlight" is the volume's final poem. It pictures small-town North Carolina at dusk, a moment where time is always leaning into the past even while starlight ticks the world forward into its future.

OTHER MAJOR WORKS

NONFICTION: *Seas and Inland Journeys: Landscape and Consciousness from Wordsworth to Roethke*, 1985.

EDITED TEXTS: *Brown Bag*, 1971 (with Anne Lloyd and Fred Chappell); *Voices from Earth*, 1971.

BIBLIOGRAPHY

Applewhite, James. "Illegible Fields and Names in Marble." *Sewanee Review* 103 (1995): 522-537. This thoughtful autobiographical essay discusses the world that created Applewhite's poetic consciousness. The poet re-creates the world of Stantonsburg, where he grew up with his parents and many members of his father's family.

Gwynn, R. S. "What the Center Holds." *Hudson Review* 46, no. 4 (Winter, 1994): 741-750. In this lengthy review article, Gwynn discusses Applewhite's *A History of the River* as part of a general discussion of contemporary American poetry. He notes the poet's deep attachment to North Carolina and says that he can sometimes endow his subjects with "epic grandure," but he faults him for sometimes using imprecise imagery.

Lensing, George S. "Roads from Stantonsburg: The Poetry of James Applewhite." *The Southern Review* 31, no. 1 (1995): 139-161. Lensing discusses the relationship between Applewhite's native geography and his writing. He examines the forces of contemporary life which alienate the poet from the natural world and the unpretentious men who are the poet's heroes.

Levine, Philip. "A Conversation with Philip Levine." *TriQuarterly* 95 (Winter, 1995): 67-83. In this lengthy interview, Levine talks, among other things, about the importance of place for one who wants to write. Although he does not specifically discuss Applewhite, he offers readers an overview of the state of contemporary American poetry.

Publishers Weekly. Review of *A History of the River.* 240, no. 4 (January 24, 1993): 83. In this review, the author describes Applewhite's knowledge of his culture as "impressive" but says that his descriptions are sometimes "excessively nuanced."

Ann D. Garbett

LOUIS ARAGON

Born: Paris, France; October 3, 1897
Died: Paris, France; December 24, 1982

PRINCIPAL POETRY

Feu de joie, 1920
Le Mouvement perpétuel, 1925
La Grande Gaîté, 1929
Persécuté persécuteur, 1931
Hourra l'Oural, 1934
Le Crève-cœur, 1941
Brocéliande, 1942
Les Yeux d'Elsa, 1942
En Français dans le texte, 1943
Le Musée grévin, 1943
La Diane française, 1945
Le Nouveau Crève-cœur, 1948
Les Yeux et la mémoire, 1954
Le Roman inachevé, 1956
Elsa, 1959
Les Poètes, 1960
Le Fou d'Elsa, 1963
Les Chambres, 1969
Aux abords de Rome, 1981
Les Adieux et autres poèmes, 1982

OTHER LITERARY FORMS

Louis Aragon was one of the most prolific French authors of the twentieth century, and although lyric poetry was his first medium, to which he always returned as to a first love, he also produced many novels and volumes of essays. As a young man, he participated in the Surrealist movement, and his works of this period defy classification. In addition to the exercises known as "automatic writing," which had a considerable impact on his mature style in both prose and poetry, he wrote a number of Surrealist narratives combining elements of the novel (such as description and dialogue) and the essay. The most important of these, *Le Paysan de Paris* (1926; *Nightwalker*, 1970), is a long meditation on the author's ramblings in his native city and on the "modern sense of the mythic" inspired by its streets, shops, and parks.

Louis Aragon (Library of Congress)

In the 1930's, after his espousal of the Communist cause, Aragon began a series of novels under the general title of *Le Monde réel* (1934-1944), which follow the tenets of Socialist Realism. These are historical novels dealing with the corruption of bourgeois society and the rise of Communism. His later novels, however, beginning with *La Semaine sainte* (1958; *Holy Week*, 1961), show greater freedom of form and lack the explicit "message" characteristic of Socialist Realism; these later works incorporate an ongoing meditation on the novel as a literary form and on its relation to history and biography.

An important characteristic of Aragon's style that cuts across all his works of fiction and poetry is the use of spoken language as a model: His sentences reproduce the rhythms of speech, full of parentheses, syntactic breaks, and interjections, and his diction, especially in prose, is heavily interlarded with slang. This trait is true to some extent even of his essays, although the latter tend to be more formal to both diction and rhetorical strategy. His nonfiction works are voluminous, for he was an active journalist for much of his life, producing reviews and essays on politics, literature, and the visual arts for a variety of Surrealist and then Communist publications.

ACHIEVEMENTS

Like most writers who have taken strong political stands, Louis Aragon was, during the course of his lifetime, the object of much praise and blame that had little to do with the literary value of his work. This was especially true of his series of novels, *Le Monde réel*, which was hailed by his fellow Communists as a masterpiece and criticized by most non-Communist reviewers as contrived and doctrinaire. He was, with André Breton, one of the leaders of the Surrealist movement; his poetry after the mid-1940's combined elements of Romanticism and modernism, but his style evolved in a direction of its own and cannot be identified with that of any one school.

After his Surrealist period, during which he wrote for an intellectual elite, Aragon sought to make his work accessible to a wider public and often succeeded. The height of his popularity was achieved in the 1940's, when his poems played an important role in the French Resistance: written in traditional meters and using rhyme, so that they might more easily be sung, they became rallying cries for French patriots abroad and in occupied France. (Many of Aragon's poems have, in fact, been set to music by writers of popular songs, including Léo Ferré and George Brassens.) Beginning in the late 1950's, Aragon's work became much less overtly political, which contributed to its acceptance by non-Communist critics. At the time of his death in 1982, Aragon was considered even by his political opponents as a leading man of letters. Writers of lesser stature have been elected to the Académie Française, but Aragon never applied for membership, and it is hard to imagine such an ardent advocate of the common man, who used slang liberally in his own work, sitting in judgment on the purity of the French language.

For Aragon, who wrote his first "novel" at age six (and dictated a play to his aunt before he could write), writing was like breathing, a vital activity coextensive with living. He was a novelist whose eye (and ear) for telling detail never dulled, a poet whose lyric gifts did not diminish with age.

BIOGRAPHY

Until late in life, Louis Aragon was reticent about his childhood, and many biographical notices erroneously describe it as idyllic; in fact, his family (which consisted of his grandmother, mother, and two aunts) was obsessed with a concern for appearances that caused the boy considerable pain. The illegitimate son of a prominent political figure, Louis Andrieux, who chose the name Aragon for his son and acted as his legal guardian, Aragon was reared as his mother's younger brother, and although as a boy he guessed much of the truth, it was not until his twentieth year that he heard it from his mother (at the insistence of his father, who had previously insisted on her silence). Since his maternal grandfather had also deserted the family, his mother, Marguérite Toucas-Masillon, supported them all as best she could by painting china and running a boardinghouse. According to his biographer, Pierre Daix, the circumstances of Aragon's childhood left him with an instinctive sympathy for outsiders, especially women, and a great longing to be accepted as a full member of a group. This longing was first satisfied by his friendship with André Breton and later by Aragon's adherence to the Communist Party. (Indeed, his deep need to "belong" may help to account for his unswerving loyalty to the Party throughout the Stalinist era.)

Breton, whom he met in 1917, introduced Aragon to the circle of poets and artists that was to form the nucleus of the Dadaist and Surrealist movements. Horrified by the carnage of World War I (which Aragon had observed firsthand as a medic), these young people at first embraced the negative impulse of Dada, an absurdist movement founded in Zurich by Tristan Tzara. Their aim was to unmask the moral bankruptcy of the society that had tolerated such a war. Realizing that a philosophy of simple negation was ultimately sterile, Breton and Aragon broke away from the Dadaists and began to pursue the interest in the subconscious, which led them to Surrealism. Through the technique of automatic writing, they tried to suppress the rational faculty, or "censor," which inhibited free expression of subconscious impulses.

Politically, the Surrealists were anarchists, but as they became increasingly convinced that profound so-cial changes were necessary to free the imagination, a number of them, including Aragon, joined the French Communist Party. At about the same time (1928), Aragon met the Russian poet Vladimir Mayakovsky and his sister-in-law, the novelist Elsa Triolet, at the Coupole, a Paris café. As Aragon put it, describing his meeting with Elsa many years later, "We have been together ever since" (literally, "We have not left each other's side"). In Elsa, Aragon found the "woman of the future," who could be her husband's intellectual and social equal while sharing with him a love in which all the couple's aspirations were anchored. Aragon celebrated this love in countless poems spanning forty years; some of the most ecstatic were written when the two were in their sixties. Elsa introduced Aragon to Soviet Russia, which they visited together in the early 1930's; she also took part with him in the French Resistance during World War II, publishing clandestine newspapers and maintaining a network of anti-Fascist intellectuals. Although he followed the "party line" and tried to rationalize the Soviet pact with the Nazis, Aragon was an ardent French patriot; he was decorated for bravery in both world wars and wrote hymns of praise to the French "man (and woman) in the street," who became the heroes of the Resistance.

After the war, Aragon redoubled his activities on behalf of the Party, serving as editor of the Communist newspaper *Ce Soir* and completing his six-volume novel *Les Communistes* (1949-1951). In 1954, he became a permanent member of the Central Committee of the French Communist Party, and in 1957, the Soviet Union awarded him its highest decoration, the Lenin Peace Prize. He was vilified by many of his fellow intellectuals in France for failing to criticize Stalin; not until 1966, during the much-publicized trial of two Soviet writers, Andrei Sinyavsky and Yuli Daniel, did he venture to speak out against the notion that there could be a "criminality of opinion." In 1968, he joined with the French Communist Party as a whole in condemning the Russian invasion of Czechoslovakia. Throughout his life, Aragon continued to produce a steady stream of poetry, fiction, and essays. His wife's death in 1970 was a terrible blow, but he survived it and went on to write several more books in the twelve years that were left to him.

ANALYSIS

Despite the length of Louis Aragon's poetic career and the perceptible evolution of his style in the course of six decades, there is a remarkable unity in the corpus of his poetry. This unity results from stylistic as well as thematic continuities, for even when he turned from free verse to more traditional metric forms, he managed to preserve the fluency of spoken language. In fact, his most highly structured verse has some of the qualities of stream-of-consciousness narrative. There are a variety of reasons for this. Aragon began to write as a very young boy and continued writing, steadily and copiously, throughout his life. As critic Hubert Juin has observed, Aragon never needed to keep a journal or diary because "his work itself was his journal," into which he poured his eager questions and reflections on what most closely concerned him.

This confessional impulse was reinforced and given direction in Aragon's Surrealist period by experiments with automatic writing, a technique adapted for literary use primarily by Breton and Philippe Soupault. By writing quickly without revising and by resisting the impulse to edit or censor the flow of words, the Surrealists hoped to tap their subconscious minds and so to "save literature from rhetoric" (as Juin puts it). Literature was not all they hoped to save, moreover, for "rhetoric" had poisoned the social and political spheres as well; in liberating the subconscious, Aragon and his friends sought to break old and unjust patterns of thought and life. They also expected this powerful and hitherto untapped source to fuel the human imagination for the work of social renewal. Although Aragon repudiated the Surrealist attitude (which was basically anarchistic) when he embraced Communism as the pattern of the future, he never lost the stylistic freedom that automatic writing had fostered, nor did he become complacent about the "solution" he had found. Like his relationship with his wife, in which his hopes for the future were anchored, Aragon's Communism was a source of pain as well as of fulfillment: the deeper his love and commitment, the greater his vulnerability. Thus, poetry remained for him, as it had been in his youth, a form of questioning in which he explored the world and his relation to it.

There were, nevertheless, perceptible changes in Aragon's style during the course of his career. After the Dadaist and Surrealist periods, when he wrote mainly free verse (although there are metrically regular poems even in his early collections), Aragon turned to more traditional prosody—including rhyme—in the desire to make his verses singable. At the same time, he sought to renew and broaden the range of available rhymes by adopting new definitions of masculine and feminine rhyme based on pronunciation rather than on spelling. He also applied the notion of enjambment to rhyme, allowing not only the last syllable of a line but also the first letter or letters of the following line to count as constituent elements of a rhyme. Partly as a result of the conditions under which they were composed, Aragon's Resistance poems are for the most part short and self-contained, although *Le Musée grévin* (the wax museum) is a single long poem, and the pieces in *Brocéliande* are linked by allusions to the knights of the Arthurian cycle, whom Aragon saw as the symbolic counterparts of the Resistance fighters.

Aragon's postwar collections are more unified, and beginning with *Les Yeux et la mémoire* (eyes and memory), they might almost be described as book-length poems broken into short "chapters" of varying meters. Many of these "chapters," however, can stand alone as finished pieces; good examples are the love lyrics in *Le Fou d'Elsa* (some of which have been set to music, like the war poems) and the vignette from *Le Roman inachevé* (the unfinished romance) beginning "Marguerite, Madeleine, et Marie," which describes Aragon's mother and aunts—whom he thought of as his sisters—dressing for a dance. Within his longer sequences, Aragon skillfully uses shifts of meter to signal changes of mood and does not hesitate to lapse into prose when occasion warrants—for example, when, in *Le Roman inachevé*, he is suddenly overwhelmed by the weariness and pain of old age: "The verse breaks in my hands, my old hands, swollen and knotted with veins." Such disclaimers to the contrary, Aragon was never in greater control of his medium than in these poems of his old age, culminating in *Elsa, Le Fou d'Elsa* (Elsa's madman), and *Les Chambres* (the rooms). *Le Fou d'Elsa* is perhaps his greatest tour de force, a kind of epic (depicting the end of Muslim rule in Spain, with the fall of Granada in 1492) made up of hundreds of lyric pieces, along with some dialogue and prose commentary. As

Juin has remarked, Aragon tends to alternate between two tones, the epic and the elegiac, and *Le Fou d'Elsa* is a perfect vehicle for both. The grand scale of the book gives full sweep to Aragon's epic vision of past and future regimes, while the inserted lyrics preserve the reduced scale proper to elegy.

In order to appreciate the texture of Aragon's poetry—his characteristic interweaving of image and theme, diction and syntax—it is necessary to examine a few of his poems in detail. Choosing one poem from each of the three distinct phases of his career (the Surrealist, Resistance, and postwar periods), all dealing with his central theme, the love of a woman, makes it possible to demonstrate both the continuities and the changes in his poetry during the greater part of his career. All three poems are in his elegiac vein, the mode easiest to examine at close range and the most fertile for Aragon. The occasional false notes in his verse tend to be struck when he assumes the triumphalist pose of the committed Marxist. When he speaks of his wife, his very excesses suggest a shattering sincerity, especially when the subject is separation, age, or death.

"POEM TO SHOUT IN THE RUINS"

"Poème à crier dans les ruines" ("Poem to Shout in the Ruins"), although addressed to a woman, is not addressed to Elsa, whom Aragon had yet to meet when it was written. The poem records the bitterness of an affair that has recently ended and from which the poet seems to have expected more than his lover did. Like most of Aragon's work, the poem is heavily autobiographical; the woman involved was American heiress Nancy Cunard, with whom Aragon had lived for about a year, and the allusions to travel throughout the poem recall trips the couple had taken together. Although the poem opens with a passage that might be described as expository, and although it moves from particular details to a general observation and closes with a sort of reprise, it strikes the reader as more loosely organized than it actually is. This impression results from its rhythm being that of association—the train of thought created when a person dwells on a single topic for a sustained period of time. Because the topic is unhappy love and the bitterness of rejection, the process of association takes on an obsessive quality, and although the resulting monologue is ostensibly addressed to the lover, the title suggests that

neither she nor anyone else is expected to respond. The overall effect, then, is that of an *interior* monologue, and its power stems not from any cogency of argument (the "rhetoric" rejected by the Surrealists) but from the cumulative effects of obsessive repetition. Thus, the speaker's memories are evoked in a kind of litany ("I remember your shoulder/ I remember your elbow/ I remember your linen."); later, struck by the realization that memory implies the past tense, he piles up verbs in the *passé simple* (as in "Loved Was Came Caressed"), the tense used for completed action.

The lack of a rhetorical framework in the poem is paralleled by the absence of any central image or images. Although many arresting images appear, they are not linked in any design but remain isolated, reinforcing the sense of meaninglessness that has overwhelmed the speaker. The "little rented cars" and mirrors left unclaimed in a baggage room evoke the traveling the couple did together, which the speaker now sees as aimless. Some of the details given remain opaque because they have a private meaning that is not revealed ("Certain names are charged with a distant thunder"); others seem to be literary allusions, such as Mazeppa's ride (described in a poem by George Gordon, Lord Byron) and the bleeding trees, which to a reader who knows the works of Dante suggest that poet's "wood of the suicides." (Not until many years later did Aragon reveal that he had attempted suicide after the breakup with Cunard.)

The use of such arcane personal and literary allusions was a legacy of the Symbolist movement; as a young man, Aragon admired both Arthur Rimbaud and Stéphane Mallarmé, two of the most gifted Symbolists. The Surrealist approach to imagery evolved directly out of Symbolism in its more extreme forms, such as "Le Bateau ivre" ("The Drunken Boat") of Rimbaud and the *Chants de Maldoror* (1869) of Comte de Lautréamont. Despite its hopelessness, "Poem to Shout in the Ruins" conveys the almost hallucinatory power the Surrealists saw in imagery: its ability to charge ordinary things with mystery by appealing to the buried layers of the subconscious. "Familiar objects one by one were taking on . . . the ghostly look of escaped prisoners. . . ." The poem also suggests, however, that Aragon is not content merely to explore his subconscious; he hungers for a real connection to a real woman. In his desperate desire to prolong the liaison, he tries fitfully to make a "waltz" of the poem and asks the woman to join him, "since *something* must still connect us," in spitting on "what we have loved together." Despite its prevailing tone of negation and despair, the poem anticipates two central themes of Aragon's mature works: the belief that love between man and woman should be infinitely more than a source of casual gratification and the awareness of mortality (which the finality of parting suggests). This awareness is not morbid but tragic—the painful apprehension of death in a man whose loves and hopes were lavished on mortal existence.

"ELSA'S EYES"

"Les Yeux d'Elsa" ("Elsa's Eyes"), the opening poem in the collection of that name, is a good example of the metrically regular pieces Aragon produced in the 1940's (and continued to produce, together with free verse, until the end of his life). It is particularly characteristic in that, while each stanza has internal unity, the stanzas do not follow one another in a strictly necessary order; like those of a folk song or lyrical ballad, they offer a series of related insights or observations without logical or narrative progression. Many of Aragon's mature poems *do* exhibit such a progression (notably "Toi qui es la rose"—"You Who Are the Rose"), but in most cases it is subordinated to the kind of associative rhythm observed in "Poem to Shout in the Ruins."

The imagery of "Elsa's Eyes" is more unified than that of the earlier poem. Taking his wife's eyes as the point of departure, the poet offers a whole array of metaphors for their blueness (sky, ocean, wildflowers), brilliance (lightning, shooting stars), and depth (a well, far countries, and constellations). The last four stanzas are more closely linked than the preceding ones and culminate in an apocalyptic vision of Elsa's eyes surviving the end of the world. The poem as a whole, however, cannot be said to *build* to this climax; its power stems from the accumulation of images rather than from their arrangement. It should be noted that Aragon's Surrealist formation is still very much in evidence here, not only in the hallucinatory quality of his images but also in their obvious connection with subconscious desires and fears. The occasional obscurities are no longer the result of a deliberate use of private or literary allusions; Aragon was al-

ready writing with a wider public in mind. Nevertheless, he continued to evoke his own deepest desires and fears in language whose occasional ambiguity reflects the ambiguity of subconscious impulses.

A relatively new departure for Aragon in this period, the serious use of religious imagery, is reflected in the references to the Three Kings and the Mother of the Seven Sorrows in "Elsa's Eyes." Although reared a Catholic, Aragon became an atheist in his early youth and never professed any religious faith thereafter. During World War II, however, he was impressed by the courage of Christian resisters and acquired a certain respect for the faith that sustained them in the struggle against Fascism. For his own part, Aragon began to use the vocabulary of traditional religion to extol his wife. Thus, for example, in "Elsa's Eyes," Elsa is described as the Mother of the Seven Sorrows, an epithet of the Virgin Mary; at the same time, Elsa is assimilated by natural forces and survives the cataclysm of the last stanza like a mysterious deity. This is partly attributable to Aragon's rediscovery, at about this time, of the courtly love tradition in French poetry, in which the lady becomes the immediate object of the knight's worship, whether as a mediatrix (who shows the way to God) or as a substitute for God himself. Repeatedly in Aragon's postwar poetry, Elsa is endowed with godlike qualities, until, in *Le Fou d'Elsa*, a virtual apotheosis takes place: The "holy fool" for whom the book is named (a Muslim, not a Christian) is convicted of heresy for worshiping a woman—Elsa—who will not be born for four centuries.

Whenever he was questioned on the subject, Aragon insisted that his aim was not a deification of Elsa but the replacement of the transcendent God of traditional religions with a "real" object, a woman of flesh and blood who could serve as his partner in building the future. Thus, Elsa's madman tells his judge, "I can say of her what I cannot say of God: She exists, because she *will be*." At the same time, the imagery of "Elsa's Eyes" clearly indicates that on some level there is an impulse of genuine worship, compounded of love, fear, and awe, in the poet's relation to his wife; he turned to the courtly tradition because it struck a deep chord in him. From the very first stanza, Elsa is identified with forces of nature, not all of which are benevolent: "Your eyes are so deep that in stooping to drink/ I saw all suns reflected there/ All desperate men throw themselves there to die." In most of the early stanzas, emphasis is laid on her grief (presumably over the effects of war), which only enhances her beauty, but the insistence on her eyes also suggests that, like God, she is all-seeing. Aragon himself often referred to his wife as his conscience, and Bernard Lecherbonnier has suggested in *Le Cycle d'Elsa* (1974) that the circumstances of Aragon's upbringing created in him, first in regard to his mother and later in regard to his wife, "an obsession with self-justification that permitted the myth of god-as-love to crystallize around the person, and in particular the eyes, of Elsa." Such an attitude is especially suggested by the final images of the poem, that of "Paradise regained and relost a hundred times" and that of Elsa's eyes shining over the sea after the final "shipwreck" of the universe.

"YOU WHO ARE THE ROSE"

An attitude of worship can also be seen in "You Who Are the Rose" (from the collection entitled *Elsa*), but it is tempered considerably by the vulnerability of the rose, the central image around which the poem is built. Its tight construction makes this a somewhat uncharacteristic poem for Aragon, yet his technique is still that of association and accumulation rather than logical or rhetorical development. As in "Poem to Shout in the Ruins," short syntactic units give the impression of spoken (indeed, in this poem, almost breathless) language. With an obsessiveness reminiscent of the earlier poem, the speaker worries over the flowering of the rose, which he fears will not bloom "this year" because of frost, drought, or "some subterranean sickness." The poem has a clear dramatic structure: The tension of waiting builds steadily, with periodic breaks or breathing spaces marked by the one-line refrain "(*de*) *la rose*," until the miraculous flowering takes place and is welcomed with a sort of prayer. The images that accumulate along the way, evoked by the poet in a kind of incantation designed to call forth the rose, are all subordinated to this central image of flowering, yet by their startling juxtaposition and suggestiveness, they clearly reflect Aragon's Surrealist background. Thus, the dormant plant is compared to "a cross contradicting the tomb," while two lines later its roots are "like an insinuating hand beneath the sheets caressing the sleeping thighs of winter." The

use of alliteration is excessive—as when six words beginning with *gr-* appear in the space of three lines—and although this serves to emphasize the incantatory quality of the verse, to hostile critics it may look like simple bad taste. Hubert Juin, a friendly critic, freely acknowledges that a certain kind of bad taste is evident in Aragon; he ascribes it to the poet's "epic" orientation, his desire to include as much of the world as possible in his design, which precludes attention to every detail. It seems more to the point to recall that for the Surrealists, editing was a kind of dishonesty; by writing rapidly and not revising, they sought to lay bare what was most deeply buried in their psyches. What often saves Aragon from *préciosité*, or literary affectation, is the realism of this stream-of-consciousness technique. Caught up in the speaker's own anxiety or fantasy, the reader does not stop to criticize the occasional banalities and lapses of taste; he follows in the poet's wake, eager to see where the train of thought will lead.

The poignancy of "You Who Are the Rose," as of so many of Aragon's late poems, stems from the contrast between his exaggerated hopes—still virtually those of a young man—and the fact of old age, which threatens to deprive him of his wife and of his poetic voice. There is also, in some of his later work, a hint of sadness (although never of disillusionment) at the failure of Communism to fulfill its promise within his own lifetime. It is worth noting that in France the rose has long been associated with Socialist ideals; the poet's fear for his wife in "You Who Are the Rose" may be doubled by a tacit fear that the promise of Marxism will not be fulfilled. The two fears are related, moreover, because Aragon saw the harmony between husband and wife as the hope of the future, the cornerstone of a just and happy (Communist) society. His anguish is that of the idealist who rejects the possibility of transcendence: His "divinity" is mortal, like him. This helps to account for the fact that he continued to write with undiminished passion until the very end of his life, for poetry held out the only prospect of immortality in which he believed. The rose is mortal, but she has a name, and the poet can conjure with it (as his conclusion emphasizes: "O rose who are your being and your name"). What is more, Elsa Triolet was herself a writer, and in the preface to an edition combining her own and her husband's fiction, she described their mutually inspired work as the best possible memorial to their love. Aragon will probably be remembered primarily as the poet of Elsa—"Elsa's Madman," perhaps, in his anguished self-disclosure—but above all as Elsa's troubadour, an ecstatic love poet who insists on the possibility of earthly happiness because he has tasted it himself.

OTHER MAJOR WORKS

LONG FICTION: *Anicet: Ou, Le panorama*, 1921; *Les Aventures de Télémaque*, 1922 (*The Adventures of Telemachus*, 1988); *Le Paysan de Paris*, 1926 (*Nightwalker*, 1970); *Les Cloches de Bâle*, 1934 (*The Bells of Basel*, 1936); *Le Monde réel*, 1934-1944 (includes *Les Cloches de Bâle*, 1934; *Les Beaux Quartiers*, 1936; *Les Voyageurs de l'impériale*, 1942; and *Aurélien*, 1944); *Les Beaux Quartiers*, 1936 (*Residential Quarter*, 1938); *Les Voyageurs de l'impériale*, 1942 (*The Century Was Young*, 1941); *Aurélien*, 1944 (English translation, 1947); *Les Communistes*, 1949-1951; *La Semaine sainte*, 1958 (*Holy Week*, 1961); *La Mise à mort*, 1965; *Blanche: Ou, L'oubli*, 1967; *Théâtre/roman*, 1974.

SHORT FICTION: *Servitude et grandeur de français*, 1945; *Le Mentir-vrai*, 1981.

NONFICTION: *Le Traité du style*, 1928; *Pour une réalisme socialiste*, 1935; *L'Homme communiste*, 1946, 1953; *Introduction aux littératures soviétiques*, 1956; *J'abats mon jeu*, 1959; *Les Deux Géants: Histoire des États-Unis et de l'U.R.S.S.*, 1962-1964 (5 volumes; with André Maurois; partial translation *A History of the U.S.S.R. from Lenin to Khrushchev*, 1964); *Entretiens avec Francis Crémieux*, 1964; *Écrits sur l'art moderne*, 1981.

BIBLIOGRAPHY

Adereth, M. *Aragon, the Resistance Poems*. London: Grant & Cutler, 1985. A brief critical guide to Aragon's poetry.

_____. *Elsa Triolet and Louis Aragon: An Introduction to Their Interwoven Lives and Works*. Lewiston, N.Y.: Edwin Mellen Press, 1994. An introductory biography of Triolet and Aragon and their lives together including critical analysis of their work and a bibliography.

Becker, Lucille Frackman. *Louis Aragon*. New York: Twayne, 1971. An introductory biography of Aragon and critical analysis of selected works. Includes bibliographic references.

Josephson, Hannah, and Malcolm Cowley, eds. *Aragon, Poet of the French Resistance*. New York: Duell, Sloan and Pearce, 1945. A study of Aragon's poetic works produced between 1939 and 1945.

Lillian Doherty;
bibliography updated by the editors

JÁNOS ARANY

Born: Nagyszalonta, Hungary; March 2, 1817
Died: Budapest, Hungary; October 22, 1882

PRINCIPAL POETRY

Toldi, 1847 (English translation, 1914)
Murány ostroma, 1848
Katalin, 1850
Összes muvei, 1851-1868
Nagyidai cigányok, 1852
Toldi estéje, 1854 (*Toldi's Eve*, 1914)
Kisebb költeményei, 1856
Buda halála, 1864 (*The Death of King Buda*, 1936)
Arany János összes költeményei, 1867
Toldi szerelme, 1879 (*Toldi's Love*, 1976)
Arany János összes munkái, 1884-1885
Epics of the Hungarian Plain, 1976

OTHER LITERARY FORMS

János Arany's criticism and studies in Hungarian literature are in the best tradition of scholarship and remain useful. His translations of several of William Shakespeare's plays and of Aristophanes' comedies are outstanding in the history of Hungarian translations.

ACHIEVEMENTS

János Arany contributed to Hungarian literature a poetic style and language—in fact, a poetic tradition—that united the best elements of native Hungarian verse, based to a large degree on folk song and folk poetry, with the learned traditions of Western Europe, particularly the traditions of the Enlightenment and of Romanticism. The result was a poetry that, while retaining its distinctively Hungarian character, joined the larger conversation of European literature.

BIOGRAPHY

János Arany was born the last child of György Arany and the former Sára Megyeri in Nagyszalonta, Hungary (now known as Salonta, Romania). Taught to read by his father, Arany began his studies in 1828 at Nagyszalonta. In 1831, he became a tutor at the school there, and in 1833, he transferred to the gymnasium (high school) at Debrecen on a scholarship. He took a leave of absence to serve as tutor in Kisujszállas for about a year, and in 1836 left Debrecen without taking a degree. He settled in Nagyszalonta and became a teacher, later taking a post as notary. In 1840, he married Julianna Ercsey, the orphaned child of a lawyer. A daughter, Juliska, was born in 1841, and a son, László, in 1844.

Although originally Arany had intended to give up his literary aspirations and devote his energies to building a secure future for his family, the friendship of István Szilágyi, who became rector at Nagyszalonta in 1842, drew him into the literary world. Arany had read widely in popular Hungarian literature since his childhood and had been introduced to earlier as well as contemporary Hungarian literature at Debrecen, but Szilágyi encouraged him to continue his studies of English and other foreign authors. Arany learned English to be able to read the works in the original, and he later translated from this language as well as from German, Greek, Italian, and other languages. In 1845, Arany's poem "Az elveszett alkótmany" (the lost constitution) won a literary prize. In 1847, his *Toldi* won even greater acclaim, and he became increasingly involved in the literary life of the country, as well as in the events leading up to the Revolution of 1848. He ran for a seat in parliament but was defeated; he also served as a soldier during the siege of Arad.

After the defeat of the Hungarians by the combined forces of the Austrian and Russian empires, Arany, like most of his contemporaries, spent several months in hiding and naturally lost his teaching position. For a while, Count Lajos Tisza employed him as a tutor, and in 1851

he accepted a position as teacher in the gymnasium at Nagykörös. Arany never felt comfortable as a teacher, and in time the routine and the atmosphere of the small town depressed him. At first, however, there were brilliant colleagues who were similarly in hiding or exile during the years of terror, and he wrote a series of ballads, completed *Toldi's Eve* as well as several other narrative poems, and began the third poem of the Toldi trilogy, *Toldi's Love*. The notes for his lectures on Hungarian literature prepared at this time (never collected by him and published only after his death) show his sensitivity and the thorough critical and historical grasp he had of his subject.

In spite of his distance from the center of activity, Arany remained in close contact with literary developments. Recognition also came his way. On December 15, 1858, the Hungarian Academy of Sciences was allowed to resume its activity after a ten-year suspension, and Arany was elected a member. In his acceptance speech, he compared the epics of Miklós Zrinyi, a poet of the seventeenth century, with the work of Torquato Tasso. After repeated invitations by his friends to move to Budapest, Arany finally accepted the position of director of the Kisfaludy Társaság. In addition to administrative duties, he was active as an adviser and critic. He wrote a study on the Hungarian drama by József Katona, *Bánk bán* (1821, performed in 1833), and helped prepare Imre Madách's *Az ember tragédiája* (1861; the tragedy of man) for publication. Increasingly accepted as the unofficial laureate of Hungarian literature, he became secretary of the Academy of Sciences in 1865. He continued writing, although he was unable to complete many projects. The major poem he worked on in this period was what he hoped would be a national epic, *The Death of King Buda*. It was, moreover, a period during which Arany was active as a translator, rendering William Shakespeare, Aristophanes, and selections from many writers in other languages into Hungarian. He had the obligation to oversee the translation and publication of the complete works of Shakespeare and of Jean-Baptiste Molière, as well as a comprehensive edition of Hungarian folk literature.

In 1879, Arany's third request for retirement was finally accepted by the academy. In his last years, he enjoyed a resurgence of lyric power and, despite his ill health, was able to finish some earlier projects, notably *Toldi's Love*. He published his *Prózai dolgozatai* (1879; prose essays) and was increasingly involved in linguistic studies.

Arany died on October 22, 1882, several days before the unveiling of the statue of his friend, the poet Sandor Petőfi, that still stands by the Danube in one of the city's old squares. Arany was laid out in state in the main chamber of the academy and was eulogized by the important critics and poets of his day. His role as one of the major figures in Hungarian poetry and literary criticism, as well as a sensitive and learned molder of the language, continues to be recognized to this day.

ANALYSIS

János Arany was not the only writer engaged in the literary development of Hungary, nor was he the first. He built on medieval, Renaissance, and Baroque traditions, and his goals were shared by many of his contemporaries. His individual contribution rests above all on his knowledgeable and sensitive use of folk elements, his ability to recognize and reject undue foreign influence while using foreign models to enrich his own work, and his unerring sense of the forms and rhythms best suited to the Hungarian language. His affinity with the folkloric tradition, as well as his recognition of its role in preserving Hungarian cultural traditions, enabled him to put into practice the theories and plans of the reform movement. As a teacher and critic, he was further able to explain and elucidate reformist goals. He not only used native words but also explained their appropriateness and traced their history. He used meters based on folk song and wrote a thesis on Hungarian versification. Arguing that native themes and forms could equal the best in classical literature, he demonstrated this in his critical essays. Ever sensitive to literary developments abroad, he emphasized the need for literature to be realistic yet to avoid the excesses of naturalism; in his view, the poet should show not so much what is but rather its "heavenly counterpart."

"AZ ELVESZETT ALKÓTMANY"

In 1845, János Arany won the prize of the Kisfaludy Társaság with his mock-heroic epic, "Az elveszett alkótmany." He had begun writing it spontaneously and with no thought of publication, learning of the competi-

tion only when the poem was well under way. Although he was later to regret the unevenness and coarseness of the work, it deserves attention, for it shows Arany's use of supernatural machinery, which is rooted in Hungarian folklore and popular mythology—a device he borrowed from Mihály Vörösmarty and others but which Arany was to use effectively in later poems. His portrayal of the petty bickering between progressive and liberal political parties, no less than the high-handed and illegal actions of the party in power, indicates his political concerns. He suggests in the conclusion that only with a widening of the franchise, with the inclusion of all segments of the population in the political process can Hungarian institutions fulfill their proper role.

TOLDI

It was *Toldi*, however, that established Arany's literary reputation. As the enthusiastic Petőfi wrote: "Others receive the laurel leaf by leaf,/ For you an entire wreath must be given immediately." What Arany did was to create a folk-epic style that conveyed the life of the Hungarian Plain and the sense of history shared by the nation. Arany, who felt strongly that folk poetry should be the basis of the new national literary style, ennobled the genre by blending with it the qualities of the epic. Indebted to Petőfi's *János Vitéz* (1845; *János the Hero*, 1920), also a folk epic, which had appeared a year earlier, Arany nevertheless was responsible for innovations of his own. *Toldi* was written in the old narrative meter, the Hungarian Alexandrine or twelve-syllable hexameter line rather than in the simpler quatrain of the folk song. Arany's hero was an actual historical personage, while the poem's setting was based on the realistic verse chronicle by Péter Selymes Ilosvay; in contrast, Petőfi's *János the Hero* had a fairy-tale setting. In the handling of his sources and the characterization of his hero, Arany established the method he was to use in later poems.

Arany turns Ilosvay's sketchy tale about Miklós Toldi, a man of prodigious strength who won fame at the court of Lajos the Great (1342-1382), into a tightly organized poem in twelve cantos. Arany is careful to motivate each action and to fit each episode into his framework. Arany also concentrates on the hero's emergence as the king's champion rather than attempting to cover all of his life. He deliberately refrains from beginning his poem *in medias res* and filling in background through digressions and backtracking, a method he believed would have been incompatible with the spirit of folk poetry.

The action of the poem covers nine days and falls into two sections: Cantos 1 through 6 relate the crime of Toldi and give the reason for his leaving home to seek the favor of the king, while cantos 7 through 12 show how this is accomplished. Several episodes are intertwined, but all serve to illustrate the development of the hero's character.

In the course of a few days, Toldi emerges as a loyal, brave, generous, faithful, and compassionate man who uses his great strength for good—whether working in the fields or fighting in the lists. Arany, through an examination of Toldi's actions as well as of his underlying motivations, makes his hero representative of that which is best in the Hungarian character. Arany also makes him a representative of the entire nation, not restricting his ties to any one class; noble by birth, yet close to the peasants and servants on the farm, he embodies Arany's political views as well. In contrast to the affected, treacherous György, who seems to be both a parasite and a tyrant on his own land, Toldi is equally at home with the servants and at the court of the king.

Idealized and simplified in some respects, the hero retains many very human qualities. He is despondent and brooding when disappointed, gives way to anger quickly, and almost gives up while hiding in the swamp. On the other hand, he can rejoice with abandon as he celebrates the arrival of a gift from his mother and the opportunity to earn respect and recognition.

Arany's portrayal of Hungarian qualities, of the soul of the nation, as it were, is not, however, restricted to Toldi. Arany captures the essence of Hungarian life in his description of the activities of the people, whether in the fields or in the city, working or enjoying a festival. By projecting familiar details of the nineteenth century onto his fourteenth century setting, Arany was able, moreover, to give the epic a realism and intimacy it would otherwise have lacked. Far from being false to the medieval setting or an oversimplification of life in Buda and the court, this projection carries Arany's message that in the past, Hungarian society was more unified: Distinctions of rank were not chasms.

Like the overall concept and style of the poem, its language and form are based on folk literature. Arany, well aware of the power of native words, used these deliberately. He wished to make his poetry easily understood and enjoyed by all, but he also sought to introduce the *language* of the people, no less than their poetry and song, into Hungarian literature. An active language reformer, he felt that the written Hungarian language could be revitalized only by absorbing the pure speech of the common man, still rich in archaic words, local dialect, and variety. The form of *Toldi* is also rooted in folk poetry, for the Hungarian Alexandrine was the traditional verse of earlier narrative poems. It echoes the patterns of Hungarian speech and, as Arany showed, is capable of a wide range. In this first epic, Arany used the traditional accented line, divided by a caesura. Later, he was to use both accented and quantitative feet to fit the form to the theme.

POETRY OF THE 1850'S

Arany was deeply affected by the failure of the War of Independence, yet the early 1850's was one of his richer periods, even though many of the poems of this time are expressions of despair and disappointment. He not only criticized the newly evolving political and social life, but also questioned his own poetic style and creativity. In the two "Voitina levelei öccséhez" ("Voitina's Letters to His Brother"), he condemned the distortion of the folk style as well as the mere aping of foreign fashions, even as he himself sought the true possibilities of a popular national style. "Leteszem a lantot" ("I Lay Down the Lute"), an elegy for Petőfi, also expresses Arany's feeling that "he is no longer what he was,/ The better part has left him." No longer can he sing the hope of the future, nor can he even hope for the reward of immortality. The specter of the nation's death also haunted him in "Rachel" and "Rachel siralma" ("Rachael's Lament"). In "A nagyidai cigányok" ("The Gypsies of Nagyida"), he sought release from the disappointment and bitterness he felt at the failure of the revolution.

"FAMILY CIRCLE"

In his ballads and narrative poems, Arany continued to develop the folk style and to set his stories in a real time and place. He excelled in capturing the many moods of the life of the people, in painting intimate village scenes and establishing characterizations with a deft touch. A relatively short descriptive poem, "Családi kör" ("Family Circle"), illustrates this method in the compass of thirteen stanzas, but it was used no less effectively in the epics and the ballads. Arany describes a village evening, giving each element its due place while creating a domestic scene. As the village retires for the evening, the trees "nod," the bugs make a final sortie before becoming still, the frogs move "as if clods of earth had grown legs," and the bat and the owl take over their domain. He then moves closer to the farm to describe participants in the evening's activities: the cow, just milked, now feeding its calf; the playful cat; the inviting hearth guarded by the faithful dog; as well as the human inhabitants. A young girl is ironing her Sunday clothes; children listen to tales as they play or do their chores. A father returns from work and, putting his tools away, prepares for supper. Arany's attention to detail adds movement and drama to this still life; the father brings home from the fields a rabbit which the children immediately make their pet. As they sit down to the evening meal, a disabled veteran comes by, is welcomed as a member of the family, and yet is made to feel like an honored guest. After supper, he tells them stories of the war, and again it is through a comment here and there that the scenes are given dramatic tension. The father gently chides the young boy: The stranger's story is not fiction. The marriageable daughter asks about "her brother," yet the comment that she will wait another year before marrying gives a clue that her relationship to the lost youth is something different: It would be unseemly to question a stranger about a lover. The final lines return the scene to the calm mood of the opening ones. Night has now completely fallen; the frame is complete. The family drama portrayed here is universal, while rooted nevertheless in the Hungarian village.

Within this seemingly simple poem, one that rivals Petőfi's "Szeptember végén" ("At the End of September") as a literary masterpiece, Arany creates a little gem of realistic description in which each detail has its place and in which each seems uncontrived and follows from the preceding one as if without artifice. Arany also comments obliquely on Hungarian life in the 1850's: The veteran tells tales of the War of Independence, and the daughter's lost "brother" is a casualty of the war, dead or in hiding from the Austrians. It is interesting that this quintessentially Hungarian poem was inspired by Robert Burns's "The Cotter's Saturday Night." Thus, it provides a good example of Arany's successful assimilation of Western European influences.

BALLADS

The ballad, a form that in Arany's hands was to reach a height unsurpassed by anyone in world literature, interested him throughout his life. He believed that the ballad, while remaining within the lyric sphere, achieved objectivity; such a blending of lyric emotion and objective setting was not possible in any other form. In range, the ballad allowed him to explore both historical incidents and psychological tragedies and even to blend the two. He was familiar with German and Scottish ballads and borrowed judiciously from these as well as from the Hungarian ballads of Transylvania. In vocabulary and form, he explored the possibilities of the language and metrical variations. In theme, he gave his readers a feeling for their history. By portraying Hungarian history through words and actions with which his audience could easily identify, he reinforced the unity and continuity of the nation.

Arany's earlier ballads, whether on historical themes or dealing with private tragedy, are less elaborate than the later ones. "Rákocziné" ("Rákoczi's Wife") is still in the direct folk-narrative style. "Rozgonyiné" ("Rozgonyi's Wife") also turns to a historical incident, the rescue of King Sigismund from battle by Cicelle Rozgonyi, but the emphasis is on the beauty and bravery of the lady who joins her husband in battle.

"TÖRÖK BÁLINT" AND "SZONDI'S TWO PAGES"

The Turkish wars provided Arany with much material. In "Török Bálint," he recounts the treachery of the Turks, who lure the champion of the widowed queen of Lajos II and her infant son into Turkish territory, then imprison the queen's protector in Constantinople. The ballad focuses on the complicated political maneuverings of Bálint Török and the treachery of the monk György. The story is told through innuendo and dialogue: how the queen was beset by both the Habsburgs and the Turks; Török's plan seemingly to unite with the Turks to gain victory; the suggestion that the monk betrayed him when he was invited to the Turkish camp after the victory; and how—while Török was ostensibly a guest of the Turks—the Turks took the city and drove out the queen and her infant son. Others are given honors by the sultan—Brother György is appointed governor—but the hero is imprisoned. Through this tale, Arany not only depicts the fall of Buda, but also suggests the fateful division of the country, beset by both the Turks and the Habsburgs and forced to choose one or the other, or, as Bálint Török did, to try to play off one against the other.

"Szondi két apródja" ("Szondi's Two Pages") records the faithfulness of the pages who sing the deeds of their fallen master and refuse to leave his grave in spite of the promises and threats of the Turkish Ali. Interwoven with this song are the words of the Turkish messenger, who gradually loses his patience: All saw the battle, all recognize Szondi's heroism—but Ali will be angry if his offer is refused.

"THE WELSH BARDS"

In 1857, when Emperor Francis Joseph made a visit to Hungary and let it be known that he wished the poets to celebrate this event, Arany wrote "A walesi bardok" ("The Welsh Bards").

This ballad, based on a tradition that King Edward I of England had executed five hundred bards after his conquest of Wales, was a condemnation of the Habsburg ruler. Naturally, it was not published until later (1863), when the allusion was less obvious.

The ballad shows the influence of Scottish and medieval English models, which Arany had been studying for some time. The four-line stanza is in alternating iambic tetrameter and trimeter with an *abcb* rhyme scheme. Repetition and skillful variation are used both to move the narrative along and to paint the psychological mood. The scene is set with great economy, and the action is presented through dialogue. The opening lines, describing the triumphant march of the king, are repeated with significant variations at the beginning of each new section: "Edward the King, the English king/ Strides on his fallow horse/ Let's see, he says, just what the worth/ of the Welsh domains." He inquires about rivers and land and meadows ("Did the spilt patriot blood do it good?") and the people ("Are they happy . . . like the beast driven to the yoke?"). The courtiers assure him that all is well in words that echo the king's but with an ironic twist: "The people, the God-given people/ Are so happy here, Sire/ Its huts are silent, all silent/ Like so many barren graves."

The scene thus set in the first five stanzas is developed in the next section, which begins with the same two lines but intensifies the contrast between conqueror and conquered in the last two: "Edward the King, the English king/ Strides on his fallow horse/ Around him silence where'er he goes/ And a mute domain." The silence of the land puts its stamp on the banquet Edward holds that night, for the nobles sit in silence, and when Edward calls for song and toasts to celebrate his victory, "Words are choked, sound is suspended,/ Breath is caught" as an ancient bard rises. Arany presents three songs, or rather fragments of songs, for as each bard blesses the dead or curses Edward, he is sent to the stake. In the three songs, three different ages, three different styles are presented, symbolizing the united opposition of all. Edward flees the land, however, and in this final section, Arany gives the psychological retribution for the king's crime, which is not so much his conquest of the Welsh, but his presumption that the conquered should sing his praises: "Edward the King, the English king/ Gallops on his fallow steed,/ Around him burns earth and sky/ The entire Welsh domain." He is now fleeing a land that seems to be burning, yet it is only the fires of his own executioners. Nor does he find peace at home: All noise disturbs him, and drum, fife, and music will not drown out the curses of the Welsh banquet and the martyr-song of the five hundred.

CRIME AND THE SUPERNATURAL

Crime or sin upsets the balance of nature: It is this idea that lies at the heart of these ballads and dominates the series Arany wrote in 1877. In the late ballads, however, the scene is transferred to private life, and the crime itself becomes the focal point; the punishment often is more severe, and the role of the supernatural as a manifestation of spiritual disorder is more important. In "Éjfeli párbaj" ("Midnight Duel"), the Knight Bende's bride has been won in an unfair fight, and he has to duel with the ghost of his slain rival on three successive nights of the wedding festivities. Arany develops the mood gradually, from carefree joy to the bride's fear and the puzzling behavior of the host that forces the guests to leave. On the third night, Bende's guards watch as he hews and slashes the air, even killing some of them, thus fulfilling the ghostly foe's prediction that he will slay in the spirit, himself being a spirit. The interplay of the real and the imagined is at the core of the drama, as indeed it is in most of these ballads. Only the guilty see the supernatural forces, for these are projections of their own guilt and thus drive them mad.

In "Az ünneprontók" ("The Defilers of the Sabbath") and "Hídavatas" ("Bridge Dedication"), supernatural punishment is meted out to groups rather than to sinful individuals: Sunday revelers are forced by a demoniac bagpiper to perform a dance of death, and a procession of suicides jumps again from a newly built bridge. It is interesting to contrast the concentration and technical skill achieved here with the style of certain earlier ballads of sin and retribution: "A Hamis tanú" ("The False Witness"), "Ágnes Asszony" ("The Woman Agnes"), and "Bor Vitéz." In these earlier ballads, Arany tends to exploit the supernatural for its own sake, although in "The Woman Agnes," the protagonist's punishment takes place in her own unbalanced mind.

"Tengeri hántás" ("Corn Husking") and "Vörös Rébék" ("Red Barbara") rely on folklore and superstition to create an eerie world where human actions seem to be ruled by supernatural powers. In the first poem, the Halloween atmosphere of cornhusking and storytelling in the fields at night provides the background for a tale of illicit and tragic love. In the second, a snatch of a folk song serves as the leitmotif for a tale of infidelity and murder. "Tetemre hívas" ("Ordeal of the Bier") also has ancient beliefs at its core: A murdered youth begins to bleed in the presence of his lover, who, in a teasing mood, had given him the fatal dagger. While the narrative is relatively straightforward, the mood of intrigue and the grand medieval setting give the poem a mysterious quality. The climax, in which the girl suddenly goes mad with horror, achieves the surprising psychological realism of which the ballad form is capable.

The Death of King Buda

Throughout his life, Arany sought to create a popular national epic. The Toldi trilogy had not fulfilled these expectations fully, for it lacked the necessary historical component in the person of the central figure. The theme of the original settlement of Hungary would have been appropriate, but Arany found the historical and legendary material too limited. He projected events into an earlier period, that of the Hun conquest under the leadership of Attila. Originally, he planned a trilogy that would trace the fall of Attila and the fate of his son Csaba, who, according to legend, had led the remnant of Attila's forces back to their homeland, leaving a token force of Székelys in Transylvania. Their descendants later regained this patrimony and established the modern Hungarian state. Only the first poem, *The Death of King Buda*, was completed, but Arany did leave fragments of the other parts as well as several detailed outlines.

In *The Death of King Buda*, Arany united the archaic and the modern, the naïve and the sophisticated. He used a variety of sources and elements: Greek and Western history and legend, Eastern motifs in the tales and customs of the Huns, folklore, epic dreams and prophecies, even borrowings from *The Nibelungenlied* (c. 1200). All of these elements contributed to the realism of the poem, which was reinforced by Arany's attention to psychological conflicts.

Formally and stylistically, Arany broke new poetic ground in *The Death of King Buda*. In its form, the poem presents yet another variation of the Hungarian Alexandrine: The twelve-syllable line is an accented one with a definite caesura, and while Arany maintains the hexameter, two of the accented feet in each half are significantly stronger than the third, so that the line seems shorter and closer to ballad and other meters of folk poetry. The occasional alliteration enhances the archaic quality of the verse, although the couplet rhyme is maintained. In diction, Arany again turned to popular speech and to the Hungarian literary heritage. The numerous footnotes show how consciously he used both popular expressions and archaic forms and how carefully he researched chronicle and legend for each detail—but also the sound reasons he had for departing from these sources in any respect.

Late lyrics

Arany's late lyrics, written mostly in 1877, are characterized by introspection and a peaceful acceptance of life, particularly of his old age and its infirmities. Originally intended only for himself, they are intensely personal yet reveal the same values that inform his more public poems. Whatever their point of departure, these late poems are about his love for his homeland (particularly the scenes of his youth on the Alföld) and the changes he had experienced over the years. They capture the mood of quiet meditation in forms that are as rich as any he had used.

"A tölgyek alatt" ("Under the Oaks") is a meditative lyric in which Arany recalls happy hours spent under oak trees in his childhood as he rests under the oaks at his retreat on St. Margit Island. The poem's dominant mood is quiet and resigned, yet it gathers a variety of colors and scenes ranging from childhood games to the sunsets of old age. "Vásárban" ("At the Market") also serves as a release for the poet's homesickness for the Hungarian Plain: A wagon from this region with its load of wheat reminds him of the activities, the sights, and the sounds of the harvest, in which he, too, once participated. He also expresses the hope that after many sorrowful years, the region—and the country—will see better times. Personal comment and a concern for his country, both the "smaller one" and the larger nation, mingle naturally in these poems, as do the poet's childhood memories and the concerns of his old age.

LEGACY

Drawn almost reluctantly into a literary career, Arany left a legacy rich in both creative and critical works. It has been said that if Hungary were suddenly to disappear, its history and life (at least through the nineteenth century) could be reconstructed from Arany's works. In many ways, he is a *national* poet. One reason that he is not better known abroad is that, aside from the difficulty of translating his rich language, it is difficult to convey the Hungarian scenes, ideas, moods, and emotions of his verse without an overabundance of notes and commentary. Nevertheless, Arany was a poet who dealt with universal themes and general human problems. While the setting of his poetry reflects what he knew best, the ideas come from his wide reading and perceptive studies of the Western tradition. His critical works and his own practice showed how native Hungarian themes and concerns could be integrated into the body of Western literature. When he is approached from this comparative perspective, Arany can offer his wealth to the non-Hungarian reader as readily as he has been inspiring Hungarian readers for generations.

OTHER MAJOR WORKS

NONFICTION: *Prózai dolgozatai*, 1879; *Zrinyi és Tasso*, 1885.

TRANSLATIONS: *A Szent-Iván éji alóm*, 1864 (of William Shakespeare's play *A Midsummer Night's Dream*); *Hamlet, dán királyfi*, 1867 (of Shakespeare's play *Hamlet*); *János király*, 1867 (of Shakespeare's play *King John*); *Aristophanes vígjátékai*, 1880 (of Aristophanes).

MISCELLANEOUS: *Arany János hátrahagyott iratai és levelezése*, 1887-1889.

BIBLIOGRAPHY

Adams, Bernard. "Janos Arany and 'The Bards of Wales.'" *The Slavonic and East European Review* 77, no. 4 (October, 1999): 726-731. A critique of Janos Arany's poem "The Bards of Wales," concluding that the tale of the massacre of Welsh bards by Edward I of England is traditional rather than historically sound.

Balogh, László. *Az ihlet perce: A lírikus Arany János.* Budapest, Hungary: Tankönyvkiadó, 1983. One of the author's many studies of Hungarian literature. Published only in Hungarian, it is an expert critical interpretation of Arany's poetry with bibliographic references.

Reményi Jóseph. *Hungarian Writers and Literature.* New Brunswick, N.J.: Rutgers University Press, 1964. A history and critical study of Hungarian literature including the works of Arany. Includes bibliographic references.

Enikő Molnár Basa;
bibliography updated by the editors

ARCHILOCHUS

Born: Paros, Greece; c. 680 B.C.E.
Died: Paros (?), Greece; c. 640 B.C.E.

PRINCIPAL POETRY

Archilochus composed the earliest surviving first-person poetry in Western literature, especially hortatory and *iambus*, or blame, poetry. Probably intended for oral performance among a circle of friends or, sometimes, for cult-related and official occasions, the bulk of his poetry is hortatory or invective. He is also known to have produced hymns, including a "Hymn to Heracles," partially preserved, which is said to have been sung to victors at the Olympic Games. It is doubtful that Archilochus produced an edition of his poetry in the modern sense, but his work was written down either by the poet himself or by an unknown contemporary and was thus preserved. The first known text (which includes a commentary as well) was compiled by the Alexandrian scholar Aristarchus of Samothrace (c. 217-145 B.C.E.), who, in his canon of three Greek iambic writers, included Archilochus. Aristarchus's edition, which is lost, probably divided Archilochus's poems along traditional metrical lines, into iambic, elegiac, and lyric groupings. Archilochus's work survives in extensive fragments, mostly quotations from ancient writers, although several major papyrus and inscriptional finds in the twentieth century have greatly increased knowledge of the poet and his poetry. The most complete modern edition of Archilochus is that of Max Treu (*Archilochos*, 1959). The numerical references to Archilochus's corpus used by Treu and in this article are those of Ernst Diehl (*Anthologia Lyrica Graeca*, 3d ed. 1940). In 1975, an English translation by John Van Sickle of part of an epode by Archilochus appeared as the *Cologne Epode*.

OTHER LITERARY FORMS

Archilochus is remembered only for his poetry.

ACHIEVEMENTS

Archilochus was well known in antiquity as an innovator, especially in metrics. His metrical forms include iambic trimeter, elegiac couplets, trochaic tetrameter, epodes (poems in which a longer metrical unit is followed by a shorter one), and asynartete (verses consisting of two units having different rhythms). While he is traditionally said to have been the inventor of iambic and epodic poetry, it is possible that earlier poems in these meters failed to survive. Archilochus's technical innovations, rather, may be seen in the skilled combination of established meters in his epodes and asynartete. Archilochus writes mostly in an Ionic Greek, imbued with the language and especially the vocabulary of the epic tradition. In fact, he was frequently admired by the ancients for his successful imitation of Homer, and Ho-

meric influence, on both theme and vocabulary, can be seen in Archilochus's surviving fragments. The view that Archilochus is an anti-Homeric poet, at least in his rejection of epic standards and values, is increasingly questioned today. Archilochus's elegiac poems generally reflect the martial or hortatory themes found in other archaic Greek elegists, including Tyrtaeus and Theognis; elegy was not specifically associated with lament until the fifth century B.C.E. In general, Archilochus's poems are unbound by any rigid restriction of particular themes to particular meters. Not all his elegiacs are about war, and not all his iambics possess the invective or satirical mood to which that meter was restricted later in the Hellenistic period. Nearly all of Archilochus's poetry is written in the first person, and he has often been called the first European lyric poet. Modern scholars, however, are becoming increasingly convinced that Archilochus's invective poetry was part of an oral tradition of *iambus*, or Greek blame poetry, possibly cultic in origin and in performance and at least as old as the epic tradition, which used stock characters and the first-person persona in a conventional way. If this is true, Archilochus's "lyricism" in the modern sense of "expressing individual emotions" is much more formal and limited in scope than has heretofore been realized.

Archilochus's meters and style were imitated by later monodic Greek poets, including Alcaeus and Anacreon, but ancient admiration of Archilochus's skilled manipulation of meter was balanced by the poet's perhaps unjustified reputation for violent and abusive verse. The fifth century lyric poet Pindar himself criticized Archilochus for such violence in a Pythian ode. There is a suggestion that Archilochus was the butt of some later Greek comedy. Archilochus's poetry was evidently very influential on the iambics of the Hellenistic poet Callimachus, on the satirical poems of Catullus, and especially on the *Epodes* (c. 30 B.C.E.; English translation, 1638) of Horace. The poet was also the subject of several pieces in the *Palatine Anthology*. Archilochus's influence on more modern poets has been limited by the fragmentary preservation of his poetry.

BIOGRAPHY

A general biographical sketch of Archilochus can be drawn from the extant fragments, as well as from ancient sources which were clearly dependent for information on Archilochus's poetry. Particularly informative are several third and first century B.C.E. inscriptions which were recently found on Archilochus's native Paros and which are usually called the *Monumentum Archilochium*. These inscriptions were mounted in a sanctuary of Archilochus, the Archilocheion, founded in the third century B.C.E., and are evidence of the poet's posthumous appeal to the inhabitants of his birthplace. Unfortunately, nearly all the available biographical information concerning Archilochus must be qualified by its ultimate poetic source. While Archilochus does use the first-person persona and often provides apparent autobiographical information in his poetry, there is little that can be verified by independent sources. Modern scholars tend to argue that many of Archilochus's personal statements, especially in *iambus*, are actually conventions of the genre and provide little information about the life of the poet himself.

Even the dating of Archilochus is much debated. The poet's reference to a full eclipse of the sun in poem 74 D. suggests a date of either 711 or 648 B.C.E. The discovery in Thasos of the late seventh century tombstone of Archilochus's friend Glaucus (see, for example, poem 56 D.) makes the later period more likely for the poet's floruit. It is, therefore, probably safe to assume that Archilochus lived during the mid-seventh century B.C.E., perhaps from 680 to 640 B.C.E.

Traditionally, Archilochus is said to have been the son of Telesicles, a Parian aristocrat, and a slave woman, Enipo, but this bastard status may be a fictional poetic stance ("Enipo" may be derived from *enipe*, an epic word for "rebuke" or "invective"). It is fairly certain, however, that both Archilochus's life and his poetry reflect the history and rich Ionian tradition of Paros, the Aegean island on which he grew up. In the seventh century B.C.E., Paros organized a colony on the gold-rich island of Thasos, and it is probable that both Archilochus's father and the poet himself were involved in this venture. Mention of both islands occurs frequently in the surviving fragments. Archilochus's common martial themes mirror the military concerns of the Greek Archaic Age, when colonization and intense rivalry between city- and island-states led to frequent warfare. The tradition that Archilochus was a mercenary soldier may be a misinterpretation of his own poetry, but the evidence suggests that he was often called upon to fight, both for Paros and Thasos, against the Thracians, Euboeans, and Naxians. He is said to have been killed in battle by a Naxian named Corax, but this name, too (which means "crow"), may be derived from the invective tradition. The bulk of Archilochus's extant fragments do not support the antimilitaristic sentiment which some have noted in such poems as "On My Shield," but rather suggest the patriotic sentiments of an archaic Greek who knew his human weaknesses on the battlefield. Archilochus does not reject the martial world, but rather sees himself as a "soldier-poet."

The *Monumentum Archilochium* provides the mythic tale of how Archilochus as a boy met the Muses, who gave him a lyre in exchange for the cow which his father had sent him to sell. This etiology of Archilochus's poetic inspiration may have been derived from the poet's own work and is almost certainly an imitation of Hesiod's encounter with the Muses.

The best-known portion of Archilochus's poetry is concerned with his aborted engagement to Neobule, the daughter of Lycambes. According to tradition, Lycambes, said to have been an acquaintance of the poet's father, agreed to a match between Neobule and Archilochus. For unknown reasons, Lycambes later changed his mind, and Neobule married someone else. Much of Archilochus's invective poetry is directed against Lycambes and two of his daughters (the Lycambides), who are said to have hanged themselves as a result of the poet's bitter attacks. The entire Neobule story has by many scholars come to be considered spurious autobiographical material, despite the apparent confirmation of the tale suggested by a Hellenistic epitaph poem for the Lycambides. The suicide theme could be the result of the "killing-satire" tradition. In addition, the morphological relationship between Lyc-*amb*-es, i-*amb*-os, and dithyr-*amb*-os suggests to some modern scholars, including Martin West, that Lycambes and his daughters were not historical personages but rather stock characters in a traditional *iambus*, or blame poetry, possibly with some original cultic link with Dionysus and Demeter. The establishment of the Archilocheion sanctuary on Paros gives some confirmation of the poet's possible cultic connections.

ANALYSIS

Archilochus's poetry sprang from the rich oral poetic heritage of prehistoric and archaic Greece, and especially of Ionia. It was influenced not only by the impersonal, formulaic, epic tradition ending with Homer, but also by a parallel oral tradition of more personal expression which led, beginning with Archilochus in the mid-seventh century B.C.E., to Greek iambic, elegiac, and lyric poetry. It is probable that the invective mood, animated dialogues, and vivid expression of personal feelings which fill Archilochus's poems were not inventions of the poet, but rather his inheritance from the iambic and elegiac traditions, which Archilochus utilized in his own distinctive, usually unorthodox, manner. Interaction between the epic and lyric traditions is particularly evident in Archilochus's poetry, in which the poet not only uses but also often semantically transforms Homeric words, epithets, and even scenes. Archilochus's poetry is filled with metaphors that are often derived from Homeric, martial sources, but which are abrupt and violent in their poetic context; the much-discussed metaphor of a woman taking a town by storm through her beauty is one example.

Archilochus can also be seen to use conventional themes in unconventional ways: for example, his "On My Shield," in which he revises traditional military values; his unorthodox *propemptikon* or "bon voyage" poem (fragment 79a D.), which is really a wish for an evil voyage upon a personal enemy; and his seduction poetry, which has, at least once, in the *Cologne Epode*, an unconventional climax. His poetry also shows a fondness for animal fables in the tradition of Aesop; Archilochus uses these fables, often in unusual contexts, as brief metaphors or extended allegories. The biographical Archilochus may lie hidden behind the persona of his poetry, but the poetry itself reveals the talents of an original and unorthodox mind whose contributions to the Greek iambic and elegiac traditions are monumental. There may have been a lost "lyric" tradition before Archilochus, but through his personal, first-person poetry a distinctive form of poetic expression developed which lies at the beginning of the European lyric tradition.

The fragments of Archilochus's work reveal a dynamic poetry which creates, from the vocabulary and themes of the oral epic and iambic traditions, the impression of a personal voice upon which modern lyric poetry is ultimately based. It is especially through his unconventional use of standard words and concepts that Archilochus's style develops its forceful and unexpected turns of thought and expression. Although critical discussion of Archilochus's life and poetry may never be free from the controversies occasioned by the lack of primary evidence, enough of his work survives to show his original contributions to the European poetic tradition, especially in the areas of metrical experimentation, iambic or invective poetry, and lyric or first-person expression.

FRAGMENT 67A D.

Fragment 67a D. is a trochaic tetrameter example of the hortatory poem usually expressed in elegiacs and forms part of a thematic group in Archilochus's poetry on *tlesmosyne* or "endurance" (fragments 7 D., 68 D., and 58 D.). Significantly, this group is not bound to a particular meter and is composed of both elegiac and trochaic tetrameter. The exhortative theme is distinctive in 67a D. in that it is an introspective address to the poet's *thumos*, his "heart," rather than to another person (such as Glaucus in 68 D.). Address to one's own *thumos* and reflection on one's own state of mind are found in such epics as the *Odyssey* (c. 800 B.C.E.), but Archilochus's adaptation of this epic trope to the first-person persona reveals the ability to distance oneself from one's poetic persona, an ability which is essential to the lyric mode. In 67a D., Archilochus addresses his heart in a military or nautical context, as if his heart is under siege or at sea: "thrown into confusion" (*kukōmene*); "ward off" (*alexou*). The vocabulary is Homeric, but the context is original. The poet's advice to his heart is climaxed in lines four through six with a pair of parallel imperative phrases. The first pair, "don't in victory openly gloat" and "nor in defeat at home fall in grief," is balanced not only in sentiment but also in word order, where Greek participial references to victory (*nikōn*) and defeat (*nikētheis*) are completed in meter and in sense by the imperative forms "gloat" (*agalleo*) and "grieve" (*odureo*). In the second pair of imperative phrases, the emphasis is not so much on the contradictory imperatives "rejoice" (*chaire*) and "give sorrow" (*aschala*) or on the objects of these actions, "good fortune" (*chartoisin*) and "evils" (*kakoisin*), but on the adverbial qualification of these commands at the beginning of the last line, "at least not excessively" (*mē liēn*). This plea for moderation in the expression of emotion was a traditional archaic Greek sentiment, best known in the form of the Apollonian dictum "nothing in excess" (*mēden agan*), but Archilochus sums up this concept, in the rest of the last line, by a final imperative phrase semantically charged in a striking way: "Recognize what a rhythm of order controls human life."

Archilochus's use of *rhusmos*, an Ionic form of the Greek word *rhuthmos*, is ambiguous. The primary meaning of this word is "measure" or "order," but eventually the word developed a secondary meaning of flux, or change. Both meanings of the word may be operative in the poem and result in a paradoxical reading of the human situation: The order (*rhuthmos*) of human life is the constant change (*rhuthmos*) which Archilochus exhorts his heart to accept. Fragment 67a D. thus demonstrates Archilochus's original use of Homeric vocabulary and concepts as well as the hortatory mood of Greek elegy in a distinctive meter.

"ON MY SHIELD"

"On My Shield," composed of a pair of elegiac couplets, is Archilochus's best-known piece, in which he abandons his shield in battle. The shield, "untarnished by arms," that is, "brand-new," is left beside a bush where it is picked up by an enemy Saian (a Thracian). The poet's preference for saving his own life over keeping his shield (which he says he can always replace) has usually been interpreted as an outright rejection of epic, martial standards in favor of a more personal, self-centered attitude. Even in antiquity, this poem was contrasted with the Spartan woman's command to her man to return from battle "with his shield or on it," and Archilochus was known, derogatorily, as a *rhipsaspis*, or "shield-thrower," "deserter." Several later poets, including Alcaeus, Anacreon, and Horace, imitated this poem.

It should be noted, however, that, unlike some of his later imitators, Archilochus does not actually throw away his shield but rather hides it under a bush. Archilochus's act is not a frantic gesture in the midst of headlong flight but a calculated attempt to save his life and, possibly, his shield. The sentiment is certainly different from the Homeric battle standard but only in emphasis. Archilochus, whose military adventures clearly speak through these lines, is not spurning martial values, but rather placing his emphasis on the preservation of life instead of gear.

The noble value which the shield possesses in epic (for example, the importance of the shield of Achilles in the *Iliad*, c. 800 B.C.E.) is certainly undermined by Archilochus, who says of his shield that he can buy a "better one" (*ou kakiō*), but the underlying implication of this purchase is that Archilochus is prepared to enter battle again in the future. On the level of language, there appears to be a contrast in the poem between standard Homeric expressions and their unconventional contexts. The poet's lighthearted attitude toward the loss of his shield is reinforced in several ways. First, he uses the derogatory Homeric word *erretō* (to hell with it) in an emphatic position in reference to the shield. The epithet *amōmēton* (blameless), used for the lost shield, is also significant, for the poet's preference for a rare Homeric form of "blameless" instead of the more common epic form *amumona* is perhaps deliberately and comically unorthodox. Archilochus uses an even rarer form (*amōmon*) of this epithet in the *Cologne Epode*. Finally, the contrast between loss of shield and saving of life may be underscored by the possible phonological pun, unintelligible in translation, of *Saion* and *exesaosa*.

FRAGMENT 112 D.

Archilochus also expresses personal, unconventional views in an unconventional way in fragment 112 D., which is metrically an example of his asynartetic poems, using a combination of dactylic tetrameter, ithyphallic, and iambic trimeter catalectic. Here the poet is describing not a martial experience but an emotional one, but this personal theme is expressed in a vividly Homeric vocabulary: Eros (Passion), which in archaic Greek poetry was still an emotion rather than the anthropomorphic mythological figure (Cupid) of later periods, is "coiled beneath the heart" of Archilochus. The word *elustheis* (coiled) verbally recalls the epic scenes in which Odysseus was coiled beneath the Cyclops's sheep and Priam at Achilles' feet. In the second line, "Eros pours a thick mist over the poet's eyes," the words "pour" (*echeuen*) and "mist" (*achlun*) both invoke epic passages where the mist of death pours over a dying warrior. The Homeric vocabulary thus implies a vivid metaphor for Eros, which has a deathlike grasp on the poet and which is depicted, like death, as an external rather than an internal force. Archilochus continues this unconventional use of Homeric vocabulary in the last line, where Eros "steals the tender heart from his breast." Once again epic formulas for death are applied to Eros, but the epithet "tender" (*hapalas*) may be intentionally ambiguous; a secondary meaning of the word, "weak/ feeble," is perhaps implied by Archilochus as a subtle transformation of the Homeric epithet into a significant expression of the poet's helplessness in the face of violent passion.

COLOGNE EPODE

A papyrus find published as the *Cologne Epode* in 1975, not only added forty precious lines to the corpus of Archilochus but also has greatly advanced knowledge of the poet's epodic and invective style. This epode, a composition of iambic trimeters, hemiepes, and iambic dimeter, is most easily accessible in this English translation by John Van Sickle. The papyrus, the beginning of which is lost, appears to pick up in the middle of a dialogue between a man and a woman. The conversation is being narrated by the man. Only the last four lines of the woman's speech survive. The bulk of the extant poem is devoted to the man's response, "point by point," to the woman. The general background is an attempted seduction in which the woman argues against and the man for immediate physical union. The poem climaxes in a narration of sexual activity, the precise nature of which has been greatly debated. (Full intercourse and "heavy petting" are the apparent choices of interpretation.) A similar use of dialogue within narrative is employed by Archilochus in another recent papyrus find, which is also a seduction scene. The narrative in the *Cologne Epode* demonstrates Archilochus's skilled use of a structure well suited to the tone of Ionian *iambus*, the genre of personal expression and ridicule in which the poet is here operating.

The world of Homer is not far to seek, in both the vocabulary and themes of the *Cologne Epode*. The use of the matronym "daughter of Amphimedo" is good epic diction, and the phrase "I shall obey as you order" is another obvious example of Homeric phraseology. Thematically, the epode is a close iambic adaption of Hera's seduction of Zeus in the *Iliad*, book 14. The revelation in line 16 of the epode that Archilochus is probably talking to Neobule's sister makes the issue of autobiographical experience particularly pressing, but comparison of the epode to book 14 suggests that it is not so much the narration of a spontaneous and emotional event as it is an artistic, stylized variation of a Homeric seduction. The *Cologne Epode*, perhaps more than any other extant Archilochean fragment, suggests the presence of an artificial rather than an authentic first-person persona.

Formality is especially evident in the depiction of the female in a bucolic setting and the contrasting use of images from several archaic Greek professions and activities in an erotic context. While Archilochus's adaptation of the bucolic setting from Homer is evidenced by the fact that both poems associate sexual union with wildly blooming flowers, Archilochus has integrated this association of the female with the fertility of nature in a more basic way, into the very fiber of his vocabulary and imagery. The woman herself is described as "beautiful and tender" (*kalē tereina*), while her sister Neobule feels the brunt of Archilochus's invective in her description as a withered flower (*anthos d' aperruēke*). The final stage of this natural process is represented by the woman's late mother, Amphimedo, "who now is covered by the mouldering earth."

The concept and vocabulary, originally Homeric, is manipulated by Archilochus here into an unorthodox and subtle metaphor arguing in favor of the masculine demand of immediate sexual gratification. At the same time, the narrator disguises his eroticism behind references to various professions: rhetoric ("answering point by point"); architecture ("the coping stone" and "architrave"); navigation or horse racing ("I'll hold my course"); war ("reconnoitering"); wrestling ("seizing her"); and animal husbandry ("hasty bitch, blind pups"). The last reference, to an old Greek proverb, also underscores Archilochus's fondness for the use of animal fables as exempla. The proverb, arguing against hasty action, is a subtle ploy on the part of the narrator to disguise his own ambitions.

BIBLIOGRAPHY

Bartol, Krystyna. "Where Was Iambic Performed? Some Evidence from the Fourth Century B.C." *Classical Quarterly* 42, no. 1 (1992): 65. A discussion of the performance of iambic poetry in the fourth century B.C.E. Poems by Archilochus and Homer may have been presented during poetic competitions as suggested in a text by Heraclitus.

Burnett, Anne Pippin. *Three Archaic Poets: Archilochus, Alcaeus, Sappho*. Cambridge, Mass.: Harvard University Press, 1983. Explores the paradoxical career of Archilochus as both a professional solider and poet, the combination of "Ares and the Muses," as Burnett phrases it. This book also provides an even-handed view of Archilochus's use of obscenity in his poems. Burnett points out that during the time Archilochus was writing, obscenity was seen not as an end in itself but as part of ritual, verbal attacks on enemies. As such, Archilochus undoubtedly regarded his use of obscenity as a poet in the same way he considered his use of weapons as a warrior. Both were means to the same end: triumph over an adversary.

Davenport, Guy. Introduction to *Archilochos, Sappho, Alkman*. Berkeley: University of California Press, 1980. The placement of Archilochus among his contemporary poetic peers helps establish both his debt and contributions to the developing Greek poetic tradition. Davenport, who also translated and illustrated the selections in this volume, provides a brief but useful overview of Archilochus's place in early Greek literature, pointing out that "Archilochos is the second poet of the West" (after Homer). Since Davenport himself is both a creative writer and a scholar his translations tend to be more interesting than traditional, academic efforts.

Gerber, Douglas. Introduction to *Greek Iambic Poetry from the Seventh to the Fifth Centuries B.C.* Cambridge, Mass.: Harvard University Press, 1999. A solid essay which places Archilochus in the context of his times and his specific poetic genre. Douglas, who also provided the translations for the volume, offers a learned but accessible commentary on the techniques and methods of Greek verse of the period. Serving also as editor, Douglas has compiled a very useful volume.

Irwin, Elizabeth. "Biography, Fiction, and the Archilochaen Ainos." *Journal of Hellenic Studies* 118 (1998): 177-183. An examination of the historicity of characters in Archilochus's poetry. The question of the possible autobiographical nature of the poems remains open.

Rankin, H. D. *Archilochus of Peros*. Park Ridge, N.J.: Noyes Press, 1977. A good, in-depth review of the poet's career and achievements, with an emphasis on the themes and content of his verse. Rankin points out that Archilochus was the "first poet in our literary tradition to use sexuality in a conscious and deliberate way as a main theme in his poetry." Rankin's frank discussion of Archilochus's use of sexual themes and imagery helps the reader understand that the poet was not simply trying to shock the reader. In this and other areas, Rankin is especially helpful in his discussion of the role of poetry in Greek society of the time.

Will, Frederic. *Archilochos*. New York: Twayne, 1969. This volume provides a solid introduction to the study of the poet, his work, and his world. Since few of the basic facts known about the poet have changed—and little, in that sense, has been added—most of the material remains useful and can complement more recent works on Archilochus dealing more extensively with the interpretation of his work and his poetic techniques.

Thomas J. Sienkewicz;
bibliography updated by Michael Witkoski

LUDOVICO ARIOSTO

Born: Reggio Emilia, Italy; September 8, 1474
Died: Ferrara, Italy; July 6, 1533

PRINCIPAL POETRY
Orlando furioso, 1516, 1521, 1532 (English translation, 1591)
Satire, 1534 (written in 1517-1525; *Ariosto's Satyres*, 1608)
Cinque canti, 1545

OTHER LITERARY FORMS
Ludovico Ariosto was an influential verse dramatist of his time, following the form of the Latin comedies of

Plautus and Terence and rigorously adhering to the unities of time and place, though setting the plays in Ferrara and using the society of that city for his plots. His plays include *La cassaria* (1508; *The Coffer*, 1975), *I suppositi* (1509; *The Pretenders*, 1566), *Il negromante* (1520; *The Necromancer*, 1975), and *La Lena* (1528; *Lena*, 1975). His final play, "I studenti," written in 1533, was completed posthumously by his brother Gabriele and retitled *La scolastica* (1547; *The Students*, 1975).

ACHIEVEMENTS

Ludovico Ariosto was one of the greatest Italian poets, his supreme achievement being the long poem *Orlando furioso*. Many writers and thinkers of the Renaissance regarded *Orlando furioso* as one of the greatest works ever composed, and its influence lasted well into the Romantic period, though it is little read today. Although Ariosto's patrons, the Este family, did not fully recognize the importance of the poet who was under their care, Ariosto's epic poem established a proud, if fictitious, line of descent for the Estensi, pleased the court at Ferrara, and spread Ariosto's name across Europe; even bandits were said to hold him in awe. *Orlando furioso* captured the essence of Renaissance thought in its dynamic combination of classical form, fantasy, chivalry, medieval romance, irony, morality, and style. Fiercely independent as an artist, Ariosto obsessively wrote and rewrote his epic until it became, along with the works of Michelangelo, Leonardo da Vinci, and Raphael, one of the supreme artistic expressions of the Italian Renaissance.

BIOGRAPHY

Ludovico Ariosto was the son of Niccolo Ariosto, captain of the guard of Reggio Emilia, and vassal of the Duke of Ferrara. Niccolo was a stern father and a harsh ruler who was hated by the people of Reggio Emilia. In 1484, he moved to Ferrara with his ten children and set Ariosto to the study of law, despite the boy's inclination toward poetry. Ariosto resisted and was eventually permitted to study literature with Gregorio de Spoleto, until 1499, when Gregorio left for France as the tutor of Francesco Sforza. Ariosto was fluent in Latin (Horace became his favorite poet, exerting a significant influence on his later poetic forms and style), but, as a result of

Gregorio's departure and subsequent events, he never learned Greek, a failure which he regretted for the rest of his life. His first poetry was in Latin and earned the praise of Pietro Bembo, who urged him to continue writing in Latin. Ariosto, however, with his taste for simple things, preferred the vernacular and soon wrote only in Italian.

In 1500, Ariosto's father died and the young man was forced to take up the management of his mother's dowry and put aside his studies in order to care for his four brothers and five sisters. His dream of a simple life filled with humanistic studies was shattered; he found himself preoccupied with the banal tasks of finding positions for his younger brothers and administering the estate, an experience on which he would comment bitterly in his *Satire*. In 1502, he wrote a long Latin poem in honor of the marriage of Alfonso d'Este to Lucrezia Borgia and was rewarded with a captaincy in Reggio. He worked his way up to gentleman-in-waiting to Cardinal Ippolito d'Este, the brother of Duke Alfonso, and was sent on various diplomatic missions for the Este family. In 1509, for example, he went to Rome to seek the aid of Pope Julius II against Venice. On two other occasions, he visited the pope, trying to tighten the relationship between Julius and the Estensi, who were allied by marriage to Louis XII of France. Julius, however, became instrumental in driving the French from Italy with the League of Cambrai. Indeed, Ariosto irritated Julius so much that the pope threatened to have him tossed into the Tiber; he was forced to flee over the Apennines with Duke Alfonso in order to escape the consequences of Julius's fury.

In 1513, Ariosto visited the new pope, Leo X, who had been his friend as a cardinal, expecting the pope to become his patron. Leo, however, was a Medici (son of Lorenzo de' Medici), and that family hated the Estensi, so Ariosto went home empty-handed. In the same year, on his way home from a diplomatic mission in Florence, he began a long romantic attachment to Alessandra Benucci. He had carried on a number of previous romances, several leading to the birth of illegitimate children. One son, Virginio, born in 1509 to Orsolina Catinelli, became Ariosto's favorite and resided with Ariosto until the old man's death, even after Ariosto married Alessandra.

Ludovico Ariosto (Library of Congress)

In 1516, Ariosto completed his first version of *Orlando furioso* and dedicated it to his unappreciative patron, Ippolito. (The cardinal coarsely asked Ariosto where he had come up with all that foolishness.) Ariosto was thoroughly disillusioned with his patron, who, he suspected, gave him his pension to compensate the poet only for his life-threatening duties as a diplomatic messenger and not at all for his poetry. Furthermore, Ariosto was irregularly paid. A year later, when Ippolito was appointed bishop of Budapest, Ariosto pleaded his ill health, the poor health of his mother, and a desire to continue with his studies and refused to accompany Ippolito to Hungary. The poet was not disappointed when the angry cardinal released him from his service and even denied him an interview. Ariosto proudly said that if the cardinal had imagined he was buying a slave for a miserable seventy-five crowns a year, he was mistaken and could withdraw the pension.

Ariosto entered the service of Duke Alfonso and became governor of Garfagnana, a wild area between the provinces of Modena and Lucca, claimed by the Luchesi, Pisans, and Florentines. It had surrendered to the Estensi, however, and though given only halfhearted support by the duke, Ariosto proved himself a capable, honest, and diligent administrator. His letters to the duke from his headquarters in Castelnuovo show that, despite

his feeling of being in exile, he was a wise ruler in meting out justice, exacting tribute, and controlling the bandits. He was constantly called upon to settle squabbles, feuds, and complaints and to coax one faction to make peace with another. There is a story of his having been captured by bandits and taken to their chieftain. When the bandit leader discovered that he was addressing the author of *Orlando furioso*, he humbly apologized for his men's failure to show Ariosto the respect he deserved, a respect not shown even by his patrons. Ariosto did his best in extraordinarily difficult circumstances and was delighted when, after three years, he was allowed to return to Ferrara. One critic has observed that sending the gentle Ariosto to Garfagnana could be compared to Queen Victoria sending Tennyson to subdue a rebellion in Afghanistan; such were the absurdities of the patronage system.

Seeking a tranquil existence, Ariosto bought a vineyard in the Mirasole district with money he had set aside. He had always been frugal, and he built a small, simple house with a Latin motto on the facade: "Parva sed apta mihi, sed nulli obnoxia, sed non/ Sordida, parta meo sed tamen aere domus" ("A little house, but enough for me; to none unfriendly, not unclean, and bought with my own money"). Living with his son Virginio and his lame brother Gabriele, he was married to Alessandra Benucci (secretly, so that he could still collect his ecclesiastical income) and spent his time gardening, reading the Latin classics, writing comedies, and superintending their performance and the construction of a theater. He also made his third revision of *Orlando furioso*, increasing the number of cantos from forty to forty-six. When this task was completed, he traveled to Mantua to present a copy to Emperor Charles V, to whom the Estensi had become allied after abandoning the French. Charles appreciated the arts; allegedly, he once stooped to pick up Titian's brush, and there was a rumor that he intended to crown Ariosto in a special ceremony. This never came about, however, and the poet died of tuberculosis a year after his trip to Mantua. He was buried in the church of San Benedetto, though his remains were later transferred to the Biblioteca Comunale of Ferrara.

The posthumous success of Ariosto's great epic was extraordinary. It went through 180 editions in the sixteenth century, often in expensive illustrated formats. It was translated into all the languages of Europe and imitated in all of them.

Analysis

About 1494, Ludovico Ariosto began writing poetry, and, for about ten years, he wrote almost exclusively in Latin, primarily using the poetic forms of Catullus and Horace but influenced by many classical poets as well, including Albius Tibullus and Sextus Propertius. Although his verse in Latin is not equal in technical skill to that of Giovanni Pontano or Pietro Bembo, it has distinctive qualities, particularly its sincerity, which caused Bembo to urge Ariosto to continue writing in Latin. Ariosto's first published Latin ode, of 1494, is an Alcaic (the form most frequently employed by Horace), "Ad Philiroen" ("To Philiroe"). Written just as Charles VIII of France was about to invade Italy, it extols the blessings of peace and love. Catastrophe threatens, but it is good to lie under the trees gazing at Philiroe and listening to the murmur of a waterfall. Critic Francesco De Sanctis observes that Ariosto, in his Latin verse, thinks, feels, and writes like Horace. Political upheavals are not worth worrying about as long as one can wander in the fields in pursuit of Lydia, Lycoris, Phyllis, Glaura, or any other woman given a Latin pseudonym.

In these lyrics, such as "De puella," "De Lydia," "De Iulia," "De Glycere et Lycori," "De Megilla," and "De catella puellae," one immediately perceives the personality of Ariosto and the general aspiration of artists in the Renaissance to transcend ordinary events for the higher realms of art. Despite his diplomatic career, Ariosto always preferred a simple existence in unpretentious surroundings, but not until late in his life was he able to settle in his little house near Ferrara, where he could spend his time on poetry and gardening. His preference for this type of life is apparent even in his earliest works. He found no satisfaction in the complexities of court and politics and attempted to achieve classical serenity in the pleasures of nature, love, and poetic form. It hardly mattered to him whether Italy was tyrannized by a French king or an Italian one: Slavery is slavery.

Despite Bembo's advice, Ariosto preferred to write in the vernacular, though his lyrics in Italian are a great deal less sensuous than are their Latin counterparts.

Heavily influenced by Petrarch, the passions become Platonic, and the physicality of kisses and embraces is replaced by worshipful comparisons of the love object with divinity and the sun. Most of these poems are respectable but workmanlike imitations of Petrarch and are far from Ariosto's greatest work. The poet himself showed a great deal of indifference to the scattering of lyric poems he wrote throughout his life, never collecting and publishing them. He wrote in a number of forms: elegies, sonnets, canzones, madrigals, *capitoli*, and one eclogue. In the case of many poems ascribed to Ariosto, there are serious questions of authenticity. His most famous lyric poem is the sonnet "Non so s'io potro ben chiudere in rima" (I know not if I can ever close in rhyme), which touches on his falling in love with Alessandra in Florence on St. John's Day as the accession of Leo X was being celebrated.

Orlando furioso

Were it not for his great epic poem *Orlando furioso*, Ariosto would be regarded as no more than a minor poet whose lyrics influenced the French Pléiade and whose Roman-style comedies made a mark on Renaissance English drama through George Gascoigne, who adapted *Supposes* for the British stage in 1566, and William Shakespeare, who used part of it for the subplot of *The Taming of the Shrew* (c. 1594). *Orlando furioso*, however, is one of the great works of the Renaissance, dwarfing the numerous romances of other writers of that period. It served as a model for Cervantes' *Don Quixote* (1605, 1615) and Edmund Spenser's *The Faerie Queene* (1590, 1596). It influenced Bernardo Tasso's *Amadigi* (1560) and Torquato Tasso's *Gerusalemme liberata* (1581; *Jerusalem Delivered*, 1594, 1600). Robert Greene wrote a play entitled *The History of Orlando Furioso* (1594), and Shakespeare's *Much Ado About Nothing* (c. 1598) derives from an episode in Ariosto's epic. John Milton made some use of the poem, and *Orlando furioso* left its mark on the Romantic period as well, particularly on the poetry of George Gordon, Lord Byron. Sir Walter Scott faithfully read through *Orlando furioso* every year and relished the epithet bestowed upon him by Byron, who called him "the Ariosto of the north." Though not widely read today, *Orlando furioso* is nevertheless considered one of the masterpieces of the Italian Renaissance.

Ariosto's great poem began with his desire to complete the *Orlando innamorato* (1483, 1495; Roland in love) of the "Homer of Ferrara," Matteo Maria Boiardo. The Orlando of Boiardo's poem is descended from the hero of the Carolingian epic *Chanson de Roland* (eleventh century). Boiardo merged the traditions of the Arthurian romance with those of the Carolingian, and in his hands Orlando becomes much more than a warrior battling Saracens. The love theme of Arthurian romance assumes a dominant role, as the title reveals. The epic is complex, with supernatural events, subplots, battles with infidels and dragons, strange people and islands, fairies, giants, and the rescues of fair maidens. In the latter part of the poem, Boiardo intended to have the Saracen knight Ruggiero convert and marry Bradamante and to make them the ancestors of the Este family. Boiardo, however, died in the same year the French invaded Italy, and his Ruggiero remains Muslim and unmarried.

In 1506, Ariosto began *Orlando furioso* to complete Boiardo's epic, and over a lifetime of writing and revising, he proved himself the best Italian poet of the genre. As his predecessor had integrated the Carolingian and Arthurian traditions, so Ariosto added to them the classical tradition. Many critics have commented that the title of Ariosto's epic echoes Seneca's *Hercules furens* (first century C.E.). Ariosto's opening words, "I sing of knights and ladies, of love and arms, of courtly chivalry, of courageous deeds . . . ," are very close to the opening words of Vergil's *Aeneid* (29-19 B.C.E.): "Of the arms and the man I sing." In fulfilling Boiardo's intention to establish an illustrious lineage for the Estensi, Ariosto was also paralleling Vergil's attempt to establish a great ancestry for Augustus Caesar. The following line, "I shall tell of the anger, the fiery rage of young Agramante their king . . . ," is reminiscent of the opening of Homer's *Iliad* and the "wrath of Achilles." Critics have also noted the influence of Ovid, Lucan, and Statius on Ariosto's epic.

To summarize the story line of *Orlando furioso* would take many pages. The poem is longer than the *Iliad* (c. 800 B.C.E.) and the *Odyssey* (c. 800 B.C.E.) combined, and simply cataloging its characters is a major task. Some critics have therefore asserted that the poem is episodic and lacks unity. Most, however, point to the story of Ruggiero and Bradamante as the central plot around which the themes revolve, although many episodes seem to have no explicit connection with the conflicts between duty and love which constantly interfere with their relationship. Bradamante refuses to marry Ruggiero unless he converts to Christianity, and Ruggiero hesitates to do so while his lord Agramante is in danger. Later, Ruggiero becomes the friend of Leo, the man Bradamante's father had chosen to be her husband, and, out of loyalty, agrees to fight Bradamante in disguise, as Charlemagne has proclaimed that only he who defeats Bradamante in combat may marry her. Leo, however, asks Charlemagne to give his rights over her to Ruggiero (yet another act of selfless friendship and chivalry). As Ruggiero and Bradamante are being married, however, Rodomonte, a Muslim African king, calls Ruggiero an apostate, and they fight a duel. The poem ends with Rodomonte's condemned soul, in typical Renaissance style, blaspheming on its way to Hell.

Besides recounting the difficulties that Ruggiero and Bradamante must overcome in order to establish the Este line, *Orlando furioso* tells the story of Orlando, driven to madness by his love for Angelica, daughter of the emperor of Cathay, who has been sent to destroy the court of Charlemagne. Despite the title of the poem, his story seems secondary to that of Ruggiero. After Angelica flees Paris, Orlando searches the world for her, like a knight of the Round Table in quest of the Holy Grail, encountering various adventures along the way but always one step behind her. He rescues a woman from being sacrificed to a monster, for example, just after Ruggiero has lifted Angelica off the same island by means of the hippogriff, a flying horse.

Midway through the epic, Orlando goes mad—God's punishment for abandoning the Christian armies—and rampages naked across France. He stumbles across Angelica as she is about to set sail, but because of his state, they do not recognize each other, and Angelica sails out of the poem. Orlando swims across the Strait of Gibraltar to Africa and does not recover his senses until another madman, Astolfo, travels with St. John in Elijah's chariot of fire to the Moon, where all the things humankind has lost are collected. Astolfo recovers his own senses and puts Orlando's in a jar, so that he can transport them to Orlando. Restored, the knight devotes himself to the Christian cause and kills Agramante and several others in battles at Bizerta and Lipadusa.

This brief outline of the action of *Orlando furioso* can give only a partial idea of the epic's complexity. The range of Ariosto's imagination is enormous, and that the poem manages to maintain any coherence at all, considering its myriad characters and supernatural intrusions, is testimony to Ariosto's genius. Besides being unified by its major plots, the poem is unified by its warning to Christendom that its internecine troubles can only increase the Islamic threat. The Turkish advance into Europe was stopped only in 1529, four years before Ariosto's death, when the siege of Vienna was abandoned. The poet did not live to see the Battle of Lepanto in 1571, which ended the Ottoman threat to Europe, and throughout his life, the Turks seemed to be growing in power, while Christians squabbled among themselves.

Many critics argue that *Orlando furioso* is unified primarily by its style and tone rather than by its plot. With fantastic episodes occurring in every canto, Ariosto sustains the suspension of disbelief by deft use of details, imbuing scenes with the texture of familiar reality. He avoids the bombast and overt rhetorical flourishes that damage the style of so many epic poems of the period.

As De Sanctis points out, there are many tales concerning Ariosto's absentmindedness while composing the epic. It is said, for example, that he once walked halfway to Modena before remembering that he was still in his slippers. Few works of art in any age have been created with the intensity that Ariosto brought to *Orlando furioso*. As his satires prove, Ariosto took the role of the artist very seriously. Art was his faith; religion, morality, and patriotism were secondary. Ariosto's incessant reworking of the poem shows his artistic obsession with finding the ideal form for his creation. Just as Dante had captured the essence of the end of the Middle Ages, so Ariosto synthesized the essence of the Renaissance, merging classical form with medieval romance and balancing the ironic detachment of a poetic craftsman with an earthy sense of reality.

SATIRE

Between 1517 and 1525, Ariosto wrote seven verse epistles in tercets, modeled after Horace's *Sermones* (35 B.C.E.). Published posthumously, as *Satire*, because of the real people and situations mentioned in them, these poems reveal much of what is known of Ariosto's personality. Written to friends and relatives such as Bembo and Ariosto's brothers Alessandro and Galazio, the satires are autobiographical and use his personal experiences and observations to make larger moral generalizations. The writer's need for independence is expressed, corruption in the Church and court is exposed, and the dangers of ambition are shown in an Aesop-like fable of a pumpkin that climbs a pear tree. Other poems express Ariosto's regrets at not having completed his education, his views on marriage, his love for the simple life, and his unhappiness at being separated from his family by his patrons' business.

Frequently witty, the satires lack the aristocratic sophistication of Horace and often seem rambling and coarse. Instead of offering incisive observations on human weakness and foolishness, Ariosto often seems to be using the satires as a device to release his pent-up frustrations with a world that will not leave him alone. Nevertheless, the satires do tell a reader much about the atmosphere of the Italian Renaissance, especially the obsessive scrambling for power among noble families.

OTHER MAJOR WORKS

PLAYS: *La cassaria*, pr., pb. 1508, verse rev. pb. 1530 (*The Coffer*, 1975); *I suppositi*, pr. 1509 (*The Pretenders*, 1566); *I studenti*, wr. 1519 (completed by Gabriele Ariosto as *La scolastica*, pb. 1547, and completed by Virginio Ariosto as *L'imperfetta*, pr. c. 1556; *The Students*, 1975); *Il negromante*, wr. 1520, rev. pr., pb. 1529 (*The Necromancer*, 1975); *La Lena*, pr. 1528 (*Lena*, 1975); *The Comedies of Ariosto*, 1975 (includes the above).

BIBLIOGRAPHY

Ascoli, Albert R. *Ariosto's Bitter Harmony: Crisis and Evasion in the Italian Renaissance*. Princeton, N.J.: Princeton University Press, 1987. Ascoli's close reading of *Orlando* uncovers Ariosto's "poetics of concord and discord," the evasion of historical crises, and the relationship of this "text of crisis" to others of the genre.

Brand, Charles P. *Ludovico Ariosto*. Edinburgh: Edinburgh University Press, 1974. General introduction to Ariosto and *Orlando* designed as a guide to major themes (love, arms, and politics) and elements of method (narrative, poetics, and composition).

Carroll, Clare. *The "Orlando Furioso": A Stoic Comedy.* Tempe, Ariz.: MRTS, 1997. Analyzes the poem's stoic view of harmony through a dialectic of contradictory meanings (wisdom through madness, juxtaposition of excess and restraint) and the balance of the poem's structure. The poem is envisioned as "a miniature animated cosmos," an organism ordered yet changing, accomplished through the imagery of circle, wheel, ring, and *tondo*.

Finucci, Valeria, ed. *Renaissance Transactions: "Ariosto" and "Tasso."* Durham, N.C.: Duke University Press, 1999. Collection of six articles on *Orlando* by Ronald Martinez (Rinaldo's journey as epic and romance), Daniel Javitch (Ariosto's Vergilian use of arms and love), Katherine Hoffmann (his juxtaposition of honor and avarice in the criticism of courtly society), Finucci (the problematic masculinity of Jocondo and Astolfo), Eric Nicholson (early theatrical adaptations of *Orlando furioso*), and Constance Jordan (the woman warrior Bradamante).

Javitch, Daniel. *Proclaiming a Classic: The Canonization of "Orlando Furioso."* Princeton, N.J.: Princeton University Press, 1991. Studies sixteenth century reception of poem, how readers determined its literary value.

Wiggins, Peter D. *Figures in Ariosto's Tapestry: Character and Design in the "Orlando Furioso."* Baltimore: The Johns Hopkins University Press, 1986. Close intratextual analysis of major characters as coherent and naturalistic—if symbolic—creations.

J. Madison Davis;
bibliography updated by Joseph P. Byrne

MATTHEW ARNOLD

Born: Laleham, England; December 24, 1822
Died: Liverpool, England; April 15, 1888

PRINCIPAL POETRY
The Strayed Reveller and Other Poems, 1849
Empedocles on Etna and Other Poems, 1852
Poems, 1853

Poems, Second Series, 1855
Merope, 1858
New Poems, 1867
Poems, Collected Edition, 1869
Poetical Works of Matthew Arnold, 1890

OTHER LITERARY FORMS

Throughout his life Matthew Arnold wrote critical works on literature, culture, religion, and education which made him the foremost man of letters in Victorian England. This large body of prose is available in a standard edition: *The Complete Prose Works of Matthew Arnold* (1960-1976, R. H. Super, editor), with textual notes and commentary. Essays important to an understanding of Arnold's contribution to the discipline of literary criticism include *Preface to Poems* (1853), "Wordsworth," "The Study of Poetry," and "Literature and Science." "Culture and Anarchy" explains the philosophical positions and biases from which Arnold criticized literature and society. Also available are editions containing his letters and notebooks.

ACHIEVEMENTS

In 1840, while he was a student at Rugby, Matthew Arnold won the Poetry Prize for "Alaric at Rome," and three years later, then at Oxford University, he won the Newdigate Poetry Prize for "Cromwell." From this official recognition of his poetic gift, Arnold began a career that produced what T. S. Eliot calls in *The Use of Poetry and the Use of Criticism* (1933), "academic poetry in the best sense; the best fruit which can issue from the promise shown by the prize-poem." Yet Arnold wrote many poems which rise far above the merely academic, though popular interest in his poetry never approached the following of his more technically and expressively gifted contemporaries, Alfred, Lord Tennyson, and Robert Browning. Admittedly, Arnold's poems lack the polished texture that characterizes the great Victorian poetry; critics often complain about Arnold's lack of "ear." The novelist George Eliot, however, early recognized, in the *Westminster Review* (July, 1855), what has been increasingly the accepted opinion: "But when . . . we linger over a poem which contains some deep and fresh thought, we being to perceive poetic beauties—felicities of expression and description, which are too quiet and subdued to be seized at the first glance." Whatever his prosodic deficiencies, Arnold still composed several lyric and narrative poems which take their place with the best that the age produced.

In a century notable for elegies, "Thyrsis," for Arnold's friend Arthur Hugh Clough, ranks with *Adonais* (1821), "When Lilacs Last in the Dooryard Bloom'd" (1865), and *In Memoriam* (1850) as distinguished additions to the genre. "The Scholar-Gipsy" and "Dover Beach" contain the lyric energy and power which justify both their numerous anthology appearances and a body of criticism that places them among the most frequently explicated poems in the language.

In 1857, Arnold won election as professor of poetry at Oxford and, in 1862, was reelected to another five-year term. Receiving permission to abandon the customary Latin, Arnold delivered his lectures in English and invigorated the professorship with lectures ranging from the individual (Homer, Dante) to the topical ("The Literary Influence of Academies") to the broadly critical (*On the Study of Celtic Literature*, 1867). Though his critical writings on English culture, literature, and religion made him a controversial figure, Arnold gained respect in his post as inspector of schools, serving twice as assistant commissioner on official committees dispatched to study European schools, and eventually becoming a senior inspector in 1870, the same year in which Oxford conferred on him an honorary D.C.L. degree. In 1883, he visited the United States on a lecture tour which, though not triumphal, was at least a measure of his commanding stature as a critic and poet.

BIOGRAPHY

Matthew Arnold, born on Christmas Eve, 1822, at Laleham, England, was the second child and eldest son of five boys and four girls in the family of Dr. Thomas Arnold and his wife, Mary Penrose Arnold. At the time of the poet's birth, Dr. Arnold, a graduate of Oxford, was performing his duties as master at the school in Laleham, preparing himself intellectually and professionally for his appointment in 1828 as headmaster of Rugby, where he set about reforming the narrowly classical curriculum to include emphasis on language, history, and mathematics and to reflect his "broad church" liberalism, while insisting that his students maintain his

own high standards of discipline and moral conduct. Though his reformist views on both church and school invited attack from traditional quarters, Dr. Arnold exerted over his students, family, and English education a lingering influence after his premature death at the age of forty-seven.

Although there was an undoubtedly tense relationship between headmaster father and poetically inclined son (who, at times, neglected his studies and sported the dress and talk of a dandy), Arnold's elegiac tribute to his father in "Rugby Chapel" confirms his mature appreciation for Dr. Arnold's magisterial qualities of mind and conduct. Likewise, Arnold took a distinct pride in the Cornish ancestry of his mother, whose father was a clergyman named John Penrose and whose mother's maiden name was Trevenen. Arnold's interest in Celtic literature derived from this ancestral connection, received further stimulation from a trip to Brittany in 1859 to visit the schools, and finally resulted in the lectures *On the Study of Celtic Literature*. Whatever the exact influence of his parents, Matthew Arnold certainly felt the familial strains which, on the one side, tended toward the moral and intellectual honesty and practicality of the headmaster and, on the other, toward the imaginative and expressive charm of the Celtic mother.

Matthew Arnold (Library of Congress)

Arnold married Frances Lucy Wightman in 1851 after his celebrated infatuation, rendered in the "Switzerland" poems, for the beautiful "Marguerite," a woman now identified by Park Honan in *Matthew Arnold: A Life* (1981) as Mary Claude, "a descendant of French Protestant exiles" who came to live near the Arnold family home at Fox How. Matthew and Frances Lucy had six children, two daughters and four sons, in a happy marriage three times saddened by the early deaths of Basil at two, Thomas at sixteen, and William at eighteen.

Two years after his retirement from the wearying post of school inspector, Arnold entered in his diary, under the date of April 15, 1888, "Weep bitterly over the dead." That day, at Liverpool awaiting the arrival of his daughter and granddaughter from the United States, he collapsed from a heart attack and died.

ANALYSIS

A commonplace beginning for criticism of Matthew Arnold's poetry is one or another of his many well-known critical statements which provide a basis for showing how well or how poorly the critic's precept corresponds with the poet's practice. One must remember, however, that most of Arnold's best work as a poet preceded his finest work as a critic and that his letters reveal dissatisfaction with his poetic "fragments," as he called them. He did believe that his poems would have their "turn," just as Tennyson's and Browning's had, because they followed closely the trend of modern thinking. Indeed, Arnold's modernity—his sense of alienation, moral complexity, and humanistic values—makes his work, both critical and creative, a continuing presence in the literary world.

The sense of alienation which carries so much thematic weight in Arnold's poetry reaches back into his childhood. As a child, he wore a brace for a slightly bent leg. This had an isolating, restricting effect on a boy who enjoyed running and climbing. Also, he early realized the irony of numbers, because, as the second born, he found that his parents' time and attention did not easily spread over nine children, and, at fourteen, he spent what surely seemed like a year in exile at Winchester School. The need for attention influenced his pose as a dandy, and he probably enjoyed his reputation as an idler, especially in his circle of family and friends who upheld and practiced the Victorian principles of work and duty.

Of course, the religious and social atmosphere in which Arnold approached manhood conditioned his perception of the alienating forces at work in England: He entered Oxford during the Tractarian controversy that divided conservative and liberal elements in the Church of England, and he knew about the general economic and social discontent that separated the working class from the wealthy. With such factious elements at work—including the dispute between religion and science on the origin of earth and man—Arnold, facing his own lover's estrangement in "To Marguerite—Continued," could write with justifiable irony that "We mortal millions live alone." With good reason, then, Arnold formed his ideas on the wholesome effect of order and authority, of education and culture recommended in his prose—evident alike in that quest for unity, wholeness, and joy which, in the poems, his lyric and narrative speakers find so elusive.

In addition to the poems discussed below, the following poems are considered among Arnold's best work: "The Forsaken Merman," "The Strayed Reveller," "Palladium," "The Future," "A Dream," and "A Summer Night." Although Arnold's work has been very influential, even at its best it contains elements which can bother the modern reader, such as the over-reliance on interrogative and exclamatory sentences, giving to his ideas in the former case a weighty, rhetorical cast and, in the latter, an artificial rather than a natural emphasis. There is, however, a consistency in the melancholy, elegiac tone and in the modern concern with humankind's moral condition in a world where living a meaningful life has become increasingly difficult that makes Arnold's poetry rewarding reading.

"TO A FRIEND"

In the early sonnet "To a Friend," Arnold praises Sophocles, in one of his memorable lines, because he "saw life steadily, and saw it whole." "Wholeness" was the controlling thought behind the poet's vision: "an Idea of the world in order not be prevailed over by the world's multitudinousness," he tells Clough in a letter critical of the "episodes and ornamental work" that distract both poet and reader from a sense of unity. This unity of idea, in perception and execution, is necessary for poetry "to utter the truth," as Arnold says in his essay on William Wordsworth, because "poetry is at bottom a criticism of life . . . the greatness of a poet lies in his powerful and beautiful application of ideas to life,—to the question: How to live." For Arnold, this question is itself "a moral idea."

If Sophocles saw life "whole," he also, according to Arnold, saw it "steadily." For Arnold, Sophoclean steadiness implies two distinct but complementary processes. First, as physical steadiness, *seeing* is the broad sensory reaction to the range of stimuli associated with the poet's "Idea of the world." One may note, for example, the last six lines of "Mycerinus" with their heavy emphasis on auditory imagery—"mirth waxed loudest," "echoes came," "dull sound"—which perfectly conclude the preceding philosophical implications of six long years of reveling by King Mycerinus. These implications appear in a series of "it may be" possibilities, and the imagery underscores the essential uncertainty of the auditors ("wondering people") because the sounds are really once-removed "echoes," partly "Mix'd with the murmur of the moving Nile." There is an attempt to match appropriately the sensations with the subject.

The second point, related to physical steadiness, implies a type of mental fixity on the part of the observer, a disciplined exercise of consciousness operating throughout the temporal context of creative urge and eventual artistic fulfillment. Explaining the difficulty of this exercise for his own poetic practice, Arnold writes to Clough that "I can go thro: the imaginary process of mastering myself and the whole affair as it would then stand, but at the critical point I am too apt to hoist up the mainsail to the wind and let her drive." In short, Arnold recognizes a lack of mental fixity to accompany the poetic inspiration; he can, imaginatively, see the "whole," but, at the critical point of artistic execution, he lets go, becoming, at the expense of the whole, too insistent or expansive in one thematic or descriptive part. The lyric "Despondency" addresses this problem in the typically elegiac tone of Arnold's poetic voice. The lyric speaker says that "The thoughts that rain their steady glow/ Like stars on life's cold sea" have "never shone" for him. He has seen the thoughts which "light, like gleams, my spirit's sky," but they appear "once . . . hurry by/ And never come again." He laments the absence of that conscious persistence which preserves the "steady glow" of

thought bearing directly on the moral vastness of "life's cold sea."

In a more general way, seeing life steadily allies itself to the "spontaneity of consciousness" for which Arnold praises Hellenism in *Culture and Anarchy* (1869). This spontaneity suggests a physical and mental alertness which instantly responds to "life as it is," a consciousness prone to thinking but unencumbered by the predisposition to action which describes the force of "conduct and obedience" behind Hebraism, the other major tradition in Western civilization. Sophocles, the model Hellenist, possesses the "even-balanced soul" which holds in steady counterpoise the old dichotomy of thought and feeling, a pre-Christian possibility coming before the "triumph of Hebraism and humankind's moral impulses." Thus, as a letter to Clough shows, Arnold appreciates the burden of seeing steadily and whole for the modern poet whose subject matter is perforce a criticism of life, a burden compounded because "the poet's matter being the hitherto experience of the world, and his own, increases with every century." This "hitherto experience," both Hellenic and Hebraic, overlaying Arnold's own, accounts for his interest in remote, historical subjects such as "Mycerinus," "Empedocles on Etna," "Tristram and Iseult," "Sohrab and Rustum," and "Balder Dead"—which nevertheless contain critical implications for living morally, even joyfully, in the incipiently modern world of Victorian England.

POETIC DUALITIES

This "then and now" conception of the human experience has its analogues in the dualities which, as critics often note, Arnold's poems constantly explore: the moral and the amoral, the mind and the body, thought and feeling, the contemplative life and the active life, or, as scholar Douglas Bush labels them in *Matthew Arnold* (1971), the "Apollonian-Dionysian antinomy" of Arnold's ideas. Here again the dynamics for seeing steadily emerge because the poet must look simultaneously in polar directions, resisting all the while the temptation to "hoist up the mainsail to the wind and let her drive."

In his best poems, Arnold seeks the vantage point— call it a poetic situation—from which he can see steadily the dualities that, in the poem's thematic reconciliation, coalesce in the wholeness of the "Idea." Arnold warns, however, in the "Preface to Poems," against the poetic situations "from the representation of which, though accurate, no poetical enjoyment can be derived . . . those in which the suffering finds no vent in action . . . in which there is everything to be endured, nothing to be done." For Arnold, the problem of poetic situation means finding "a vent in action" which does not overwhelm the speculative nature of the idea, and the solution often comes in the form of the "quest," the symbolically active.

"THE SCHOLAR-GIPSY" AND "THYRSIS"

"The Scholar-Gipsy" is on a quest, "waiting for the spark from heaven to fall." When the spark falls, he can share with the world the secret art, learned from the "gipsy-crew," of ruling "the workings of men's brains." Until then, he wanders mysteriously from Berkshire Moors to Cumner Hills, pensively cast in an ageless "solitude," exempt from the "repeated shocks" and "strange disease of modern life." The shepherd who lyrically tells the scholar-gipsy's story speaks for the Victorians who also "await" the spark from heaven, but, with "heads o'ertax'd" and "palsied hearts," cannot acquire the immortalizing agency of a quest with "one aim, one business, one desire." The antithesis is clear: "Arnold's Gipsy," as Honan says, "represents stability in a world of flux and change, creative inwardness in a world of lassitude, stagnation, frustration, and dividedness." The shepherd, a part of the modern world but temporarily secluded in the imaginative distance of "this high field's dark corner," discovers the physical and mental steadiness to tell the story, to see concurrently the past and present, and to indict his society through the quest of the mythic wanderer.

"Thyrsis," a monody for Clough, follows the same stanza form and rhyme scheme of "The Scholar-Gipsy," continuing too the unifying strategy of the quest, this time for the "signal elm-tree" which has itself become a symbol for the perpetual existence of "our friend, the Gipsy-Scholar." In this way, Arnold aligns Clough with the legendary rover; Clough, however, unlike the Gipsy, "could not wait" the passing of the "storms that rage" in their fragmented society. With night descending, Corydon (Arnold's persona) sees, but does not achieve, the object of his quest; but he cries "Hear it, O Thyrsis, still our tree is there!" So lives the Gipsy-Scholar, so remains, in the symbolic activity of the quest, the idea of

hope: Corydon will "not despair." As in "The Scholar-Gipsy," Arnold turns the old genre of pastoral elegy to topical account, and the poem achieves a balanced steadiness, as much about Corydon as about Thyrsis, as much about hope as about despair, as much about life as about death.

The idea of the quest—or the hunt, or the journey—recurs again and again in Arnold's poetry, providing the "vent in action" required by the expanding idea. The journey may be inward, as in "The Buried Life," where Arnold says that humankind's impulse to know the "mystery" of his heart sends him delving into "his own breast." Here the poet tries to reconcile the dualities of outward "strife" (in "the world's most crowded streets") and inner "striving" (toward "the unregarded river of our life"). This self-questing journey, however, ironically needs the impetus of "a beloved hand laid in ours," "another's eyes read clear," and then, in the respite of love, one "becomes aware of his life's flow." There is, though faint, an optimistic strain rising through the modern sense of isolation, even permitting the poet, in "Resignation," to make a virtue of necessity by accepting "his sad lucidity of soul."

For Arnold, though, isolation and solitude are not similar; they represent yet another set of opposites: isolation, a state of rejection and loneliness, is to be shunned, while solitude, a state of reflection and inspiration, is to be sought. Away from the "sick hurry" of modern life, the poet in solitude achieves the steadiness of feeling and perception required for the aesthetic fulfillment of his idea. Arnold's lyric speakers enjoy solitude: the shepherd in "The Scholar-Gipsy" and "Thyrsis," or the lounger in Kensington Gardens who finds "peace for ever new" in the "lone, open glade," is analogous, in the "Austerity of Poetry," to the "hidden ground/ Of thought" within the Muse herself. Yet there is always the ironic danger: Empedocles, on the verge of suicide, drops his laurel bough because he is "weary of the solitude/ Where he who bears thee must abide." Arnold needs the creative succor of a solitude that carries over, as he says in "Quiet Work," into a life "Of toil unsever'd from tranquillity," a life that, even as Empedocles admits, still "leaves human effort scope." This "human effort" becomes the dynamics behind Arnold's own quest to focus and balance the idea with the action, to elevate and juxtapose the moral propositions of antagonistic extremes: life and death, love and hate, alliance and alienation.

"Stanzas from the Grande Chartreuse"

"Stanzas from the Grande Chartreuse" follows the typically Arnoldian pattern. The first sixty-five lines witness the sensory perception and steadiness of the speaker, his spontaneity of consciousness comprising a mixture of imagery—visual ("spectral vapours white"), auditory ("strangled sound"), tactile ("forms brush by"). There is the anticipatory journey or quest: "The bridge is cross'd, and slow we ride/ Through forest up the mountainside." Then, at line sixty-six, there is the idea, framed in the rhetorical question: "And what am I, that I am here?" The speaker admits that the object of his ultimate quest is really elsewhere, for the "rigorous teachers" of his youth "Show'd me the high, white star of Truth,/ There bade me gaze, and there aspire." That abstract quest, though, must temporarily defer to this cold physical journey to the Grande Chartreuse, a monastery in the French Alps, where the troubled speaker can shed his melancholy tears in the presence of a profound religious faith. No longer young and feeling caught in the forlorn void between the faiths of a past and future time, he is "wandering between two worlds, one dead,/ The other powerless to be born." The past age of faith, still ascetically practiced in the Carthusian monastery, and a desirable future age "which without hardness will be sage,/ And gay without frivolity" bracket a divisively inert time in which the sciolists talk, but, with their fathers' history of pain and grief as justification, "The Kings of modern thought are dumb."

Fraser Neiman, in *Matthew Arnold* (1968), summarizes the common emotional ground of the anchorite and Arnold: They both "turn to a quest for inward peace," but Arnold must find his in solitude, in the buried life, in quiet work, in, as Neiman says, "a profound inwardness . . . not incompatible with the world of activity." The poem concludes with images of "action and pleasure"—the "troops," the "hunters," the "gay dames" passing below the monastery—representing a life again rejected by the Carthusians but, as the reader infers, accepted by the speaker, who has had, at least, the catharsis of his tears. The emphasis, though, is on the idea, an idea which Arnold tries to see steadily and whole through the confrontation of opposites: the as-

cetic, contemplative life of anchorite, "Obermann," and the past at the top of the Etna-like mountain (where, one gathers, the "suffering finds no vent in action"), versus the secular, restless life of "Laughter and cries" at the bottom of the mountain where "Years hence, perhaps, may dawn an age,/ More fortunate." "Stanzas from the Grande Chartreuse" renders in setting, mood, and idea the predicament of the poet, expressed in Arnold's earlier poem, "Stanza in Memory of the Author of 'Obermann'":

> Ah! two desires toss about
> The poet's feverish blood.
> One drives him to the world without,
> And one to solitude.

"Dover Beach"

"Dover Beach" fits into the same structural pattern of imagery, idea, and resolution. The opening of the poem establishes the physical and mental awareness of the speaker, a person attuned to the sensory stimuli of the scene before him. The counterpointed imagery of sight and sound in the first verse paragraph divides as naturally as a Petrarchan sonnet: The visual imagery of the first eight lines suggests peace and serenity ("the moon lies fair," "the tranquil bay"), but the auditory imagery of the next six lines, signaled by the turn of the imperative "Listen!," introduces the "grating roar/ Of pebbles" which, in the climax of the paragraph, "Begin, and cease, and then again begin,/ With tremulous cadence slow, and bring/ The eternal note of sadness in." The Imagistic division, the modulated caesura, and the irregular pattern of end and internal rhymes provide the lyric energy leading up to the emotional dimension of sadness which the second verse paragraph quickly converts to the mental dimension of thought. In a transitional effect, the auditory imagery surrounding the "note of sadness" connects with the image of Sophocles who "long ago/ Heard it on the Aegaean," bringing "Into his mind the turbid ebb and flow/ Of human misery." Critics sometimes object to the shift in imagery from full to ebb tide, but the crucial thematic point lies not so much in the maintenance of parallel imagery as in the formulation of idea: "we/ Find also in the sound a thought/ Hearing it by this distant northern sea." Thus, the perception of dualities—full and ebb tide, present and past time, physical and metaphorical seas—prepares for the "then and now" structure of the third verse paragraph: the "Sea of Faith" was once full, like the tide at Dover, but the lyric speaker can "only hear/ Its melancholy, long, withdrawing roar."

The sociological interpretation, to select just one critical approach, maintains that the disillusioned speaker refers to the debate between religion and science then dominating the intellectual effort of so many Victorians. If the "Sea of Faith" came to full tide with the "triumph of Hebraism and humankind's moral impulses," the preceding image of Sophocles adds poignance to the speaker's resignation in the face of the constant factor of "human misery." Whereas Sophocles could, in an ancient world, see life steadily and see it whole in its tragic but nevertheless human consequences, the speaker enjoys no such certainty. The retreating Sea of Faith takes with it the moral and spiritual basis for "joy" and "love" and "peace." The speaker's own attempt to see modern life steadily and to see it whole, successful or not, as the individual critic may determine for himself, leads to the resolution of the lyric cry: "Ah, love, let us be true/ To one another!" The world may no longer offer the comfort of "joy" and "certitude" and "help for pain," but the lovers may create their own interpersonal world where such pleasures presumably exist.

Some critics fault the ending of "Dover Beach," which imaginatively transports the couple to "a darkling plain," leaving behind the sea imagery which guides the speaker's emotional and mental state throughout the poem. The ending, however, maintains the consistency of auditory imagery ("confused alarms," "armies clash") which concludes each of the preceding verse paragraphs, and the "struggle and flight" of the "ignorant armies" echo, in appropriately harsher terms, the "retreating" roar of the Sea of Faith. Furthermore, the principle of duality, carefully set up in the poem, works at the end: Physically, the lovers are still by the quiet, beautiful cliffs of Dover, but, figuratively, at an opposite extreme, they find themselves "as on a darkling plain."

OTHER MAJOR WORKS

PLAY: *Merope: A Tragedy*, pb. 1858.

NONFICTION: *Preface to Poems*, 1853; *On Translating Homer*, 1861; *Essays in Criticism*, 1865; *On the Study of Celtic Literature*, 1867; *Culture and Anarchy*, 1869; *Friendship's Garland*, 1871; *Literature and Dogma*, 1873; *God and the Bible*, 1875; *Last Essays on Church and Religion*, 1877; *Discourses in America*, 1885; *Civilization in the United States*, 1888; *Essays in Criticism, Second Series*, 1888; *The Complete Prose Works of Matthew Arnold*, 1960-1976 (R. H. Super, editor).

MISCELLANEOUS: *The Works of Matthew Arnold*, 1903-1904 (15 volumes).

BIBLIOGRAPHY

Bloom, Harold. *Matthew Arnold: Modern Critical Views*. New York: Chelsea House, 1987. Gathers together ten critical articles written between 1940 and 1986, representing a variety of critical approaches and analyzing the poetry and prose works of Matthew Arnold. Contains a chronology, a bibliography, and an index.

Dawson, Carl, ed. *Matthew Arnold, the Poetry: The Critical Heritage*. London: Routledge & Kegan Paul, 1973. Collects more than sixty reviews and essays written between 1849 and 1898. Gives a fascinating view of how Arnold was received and understood by his contemporaries. Presents some of the contexts to which his writing was responding. Contains an extensive bibliography and an index.

Hamilton, Ian. *A Gift Imprisoned: The Poetic Life of Matthew Arnold*. New York: Basic Books, 1999. The simple, fable-like structure of this account relies on the notion that Arnold wrote almost all his best poems before he wrote his best prose—an assumption that is a matter of scholarly dispute. Hamilton's achievement in this book is to have shifted attention away from Arnold's prose and back to his poetry.

Honan, Park. *Matthew Arnold: A Life*. New York: McGraw-Hill, 1981. A definitive biography of Arnold, accessible to the general reader and illuminating to the scholar. Most of this biographical information had never before appeared in print. The biography is lively, as well as thoroughly researched and documented. Includes a generous index.

Machann, Clinton. *Matthew Arnold: A Literary Life*. New York: St. Martin's Press, 1998. This study is a succinct and well-articulated exposition of Arnold's intellectual and literary concerns, spanning his career in chronological chapters. Emphasizes Arnold's achievement as an essayist: His ethical, interpretive, and instructional concerns are given full play, and due allowance is made for both the scope and limitations of his vision.

Mazzeno, Laurence W. *Matthew Arnold: The Critical Legacy*. Rochester, N.Y.: Camden House, 1999. Mazzeno surveys the critical response to Arnold. Resembling an annotated bibliography in that it treats its material item by item, this is a book for persons wanting to acquaint themselves with the scholarship on Arnold.

Neiman, Fraser. *Matthew Arnold*. New York: Twayne, 1968. This fine introduction to Arnold's wide-ranging work presents only enough biographical information to give shape and meaning to the analysis of Arnold's writing. Presents the study of Arnold's thought as a way into the study of mid-Victorian thought. Includes a chronology and a brief annotated bibliography.

Trilling, Lionel. *Matthew Arnold*. New York: W. W. Norton, 1939. Rev. ed. New York: Columbia University Press, 1949. This "intellectual biography" is an early but still unsurpassed study of Arnold's thought. Clear and insightful, it is a standard critical work on Arnold. Includes an extensive bibliography of early studies.

Ronald K. Giles;
bibliography updated by the editors

HANS ARP

Jean Arp

Born: Strasbourg, France; September 16, 1887
Died: Basel, Switzerland; June 7, 1966

PRINCIPAL POETRY

Die Wolkenpumpe, 1920
Der Pyramidenrock, 1924
Weisst du schwarzt du, 1930

Des taches dans le vide, 1937
Sciure de gamme, 1938
Muscheln und Schirme, 1939
Rire de coquille, 1944
Le Siège de l'air, 1946 (as Jean Arp)
On My Way: Poetry and Essays, 1912-1947, 1948
Auch das ist nur eine Wolke: Aus dem Jahren 1920 bis 1950, 1951
Beharte Herzen, Könige vor der Sintflut, 1953
Worträume und schwarze Sterne, 1953
Auf einem Bein, 1955
Unsern taglichen Traum, 1955
Le Voilier dans la forêt, 1957 (as Jean Arp)
Worte mit und ohne Anker, 1957
Mondsand, 1959
Vers le blanc infini, 1960 (as Jean Arp)
Sinnende Flammen, 1961
Gedichte, 1903-1939, 1963
Logbuch des Traumkapitäns, 1965
L'Ange et la rose, 1965 (as Jean Arp)
Le Soleil recerclé, 1966 (as Jean Arp)
Jours effeuillés, 1966 (as Jean Arp)
Arp on Arp, 1972 (poetry and prose)
Gedichte, 1939-1957, 1974

OTHER LITERARY FORMS

In addition to his large body of poetry, Hans Arp wrote a substantial number of lyrical and polemical essays, in which the metaphysical basis of his thought is given its clearest and most systematic expression. These essays are collected in *On My Way* (1948) and *Dreams and Projects* (1952). Arp also wrote about his fellow artists in *Onze peintres vus par Arp* (1949), a collection that helps to clarify the aesthetic values that influenced his own work as a plastic artist. Arp also published two works of fiction: *Le Blanc aux pieds de nègre* (1945), a collection of short stories, and *Tres inmensas novelas* (1935), short novels written in collaboration with the Chilean poet Vicente Huidobro.

ACHIEVEMENTS

Hans Arp actually has two reputations: one as a sculptor and painter of long-standing international fame, the other as a poet. Although his reputation as a plastic artist overshadowed his work as a poet during his lifetime, he is now recognized as an important and original contributor to the twentieth century literary avant-garde. As a literary artist, Arp is best known for his association with Dada and Surrealism. Together with Tristan Tzara, Hugo Ball, Richard Hülsenbeck, Marcel Janco, and Emmy Hennings, Arp was one of the earliest and most enthusiastic supporters of the Dada movement, which began in Zurich in February of 1916. In the 1950's and 1960's he erected sculpures for Harvard University, the University of Caracas, and the UNESCO Secretariat Building, the Brunswick Technische Hochschule, and Bonn University Libary. He also finished cement steles and walls for the Kunstgewerbeschule in Basel. In addition to these achievements, Hans Arp is best known for sculptures such as *Owl's Dream* (1936), *Chinese Shadow* (1947), *Muse's Amphora* (1959), and *Shepherd's Clouds* (1953). In 1954, he won the international prize for sculpture at the Venice Biennale.

BIOGRAPHY

Hans Arp, also known as Jean Arp, was born in Strasbourg on September 16, 1887. At the time of his birth, Alsace-Lorraine, the region in which Strasbourg lies, belonged to Germany, although culturally it was tied to France, to which it presently belongs. Arp's bilingualism, his equal ease with both French and German, which was a product of the history of this region, helps to account for the confusion concerning his Christian name. As Arp explained it, when he wrote in French, he called himself Jean Arp; when he wrote in German, he called himself Hans Arp. In his view, neither name was a pseudonym—the change was made simply for convenience, as one shifts from speaking one language to the other according to the language of the auditor.

This mingled French and German heritage was also reflected in Arp's home and social environment. His father, Pierre Guillaume Arp, who operated a cigar and cigarette factory in Strasbourg, was of Danish descent. His mother, Josephine Köberlé Arp, was of French descent. At home, Arp recalled, French was spoken. In the state-operated primary and secondary schools he attended, however, standard High German was used, and taught, the Alsace-Lorraine being at the time under German annexation. With his friends he spoke the Alsatian vernacular, a dialect of different derivation from the standard German used in education and for official business.

Arp's first published poem appeared in 1902, when he was only fifteen. Like most of his earliest poetry, it was written in the Alsatian dialect, although only two years later he had completed, in standard High German, a manuscript volume of poems. This manuscript, entitled "Logbuch," was unfortunately mislaid by the publisher to whom it was sent. Three poems by Arp in German did appear the same year, however, in *Das Neue Magazin*.

About 1904, Arp's involvement with the plastic arts began in earnest. He visited Paris for the first time, and for the next five years he studied art not only at Strasbourg but also in Weimar and Paris. In 1909, Arp, having served his artistic apprenticeship at various academies, moved with his family to Weggis, on the eastern shore of Lake Lucerne in Switzerland. In the five years Arp spent at Weggis, two important developments occured. Isolated from the influences of the academies and their avant-garde faddishness, Arp began to develop the personal aesthetic he called "concrete art," which was to influence the entire course of his career. In addition, he became acquainted with other artists who, like himself, were also pursuing personal aesthetics independent of the Paris academies. During this period, Arp exhibited his work with some of these artists, including Wassily Kandinsky and Paul Klee.

In 1914, Arp returned to Paris only to discover that war had been declared. Because his German money was suddenly valueless in France, and his German citizenship unwelcome, he promptly returned to neutral Zurich, and in order to avoid the draft, persuaded the authorities at the German consulate that he was mentally ill. In Zurich, Arp exhibited the abstract collages and tapestries which are the earliest examples of his work extant. In November of 1915, at an exhibition of his work with his friend and fellow artist Otto Van Rees, he met his future wife, Sophie Taeuber, an artist who was a native of Zurich.

In 1916, Arp and Taeuber participated in the activities of the newly formed Dada group, which met regularly at the Cabaret Voltaire. At this time, Arp produced bas-relief sculptures and woodcuts reflecting the developing aesthetic that he termed "concrete art." Unlike the earlier geometric productions of his abstract period, these reliefs and woodcuts were composed of asymmetrical curvilinear and bimorphic forms; they were, as Arp later explained, "direct creations," truly "concrete" art, not abstract representations of already existing forms. In 1921, Arp married Sophie, and together they collaborated on cut-paper collages and other plastic works. Arp also returned to writing poetry, producing a great number of poems in German which were collected in *Die Wolkenpumpe, Der Pyramidenrock*, and *Weisst du schwartz du*.

After the demise of Dada in 1924, Arp formed an increasingly close association with the Surrealist movement, and in 1926, he settled permanently in the Paris suburb of Meudon. Arp's first poem written directly in French was published in 1933, in the Surrealists' journal *Le Surréalisme au service de la révolution*, and his first collection of poems in French, *Des taches dans le vide* (splotches in space), appeared in 1937. At this time, Arp also began to create the free-form sculptures that he called "concretions," and that were to bring him international acclaim as a sculptor. He also began to experiment with a new type of "torn-paper" collage; his comments on these collages have often been linked to the Surrealist technique of "automatic writing." From this time on, Arp published poetry in both French and German, often translating originals from one language into the other, and in the process frequently introducing substantial changes.

In 1940, with the outbreak of World War II, the Arps fled south from Paris to Grasse to escape the German occupation, later managing to reach Zurich, in neutral Switzerland, in 1942. It was there that Sophie met with an accidental death on January 13, 1943, sending Arp into a deep depression that lingered for many years. Some of his most moving poems are beautiful evocations of Sophie's transforming influence upon his life.

After the war, Arp's growing fame as an important modern sculptor, as well as the increasing demand for exhibitions of his plastic works, allowed him to travel widely. During this period, he visited the United States, Mexico, Italy, Greece, Jordan, Israel, and Egypt.

In 1959, Arp married Marguerite Hagenbach, who had been a friend of Sophie in Zurich and had long admired Arp's work. In the remaining seven years of his life, Arp and Marguerite spent part of the year at their home in Meudon and the remainder at a second home near Locarno, in southern Switzerland. On June 7, 1966, Arp died at the age of seventy-eight, while away from home, in Basel.

ANALYSIS

Hans Arp was one of the founding members of the Dada movement, which had a broad impact on both art and literature in the early twentieth century. Dada's principal target was man's overestimation of reason. Its aim, Arp said, was "to destroy the reasonable deceptions of man," to expose "the fragility of life and human works" through the use of Dadaist humor, which would reveal "the natural and unreasonable order" of things. The poems of Arp's first collection, *Die Wolkenpumpe* (the cloud pump), date from this period, as does "Kaspar ist Tot" ("Kaspar Is Dead"), perhaps the most famous of all Dada poems. The Dada use of humor to reorient man's attitude toward the world was followed by Arp in these poems, where he began to develop his decidedly personal "Arpian humor."

Dada's critique of modern man, however, was not entirely destructive, despite the commonly held belief that it was a totally negative response to the world. Arp's own work is one of the best testaments to this fact. In order to rectify modern man's mistaken view of his place in the universe, Arp offered the notion of a "concrete art" that could transform both man and the world. His intention was "to save man from the most dangerous of follies: vanity . . . to simplify the life of man . . . to identify him with nature."

It was through his participation in the Dada group that Arp became acquainted with the Paris Surrealists, after he and his wife moved to the Paris suburb of Meudon in 1926, Arp frequently participated in Surrealist activities and contributed to their publications. Two important characteristics of Hans Arp's poetry distinguish it, however, from the work of other Dada and Surrealist poets: his highly personal humor and the metaphysical philosophy that underlies all his mature work.

Arp's humor achieves its effect by combining opposites: the celestial with the terrestrial, the eternal with the transitory, the sublime with the mundane, among others. That which comes from above—the celestial, the eternal, the sublime—sustains and nourishes man, while that which comes from below—the terrestrial, the transitory, the mundane—confuses and intoxicates him. Thus, Arp's conception of humor is connected with his metaphysical philosophy, which aims to restore the lost balance of forces in man. Arp uses humor in his work to destroy "the reasonable deceptions of man," which lead him to believe that he is "the summit of creation."

"KASPAR IS DEAD"

In Arp's view then, humor and metaphysics are not mutually exclusive, and elements of both are often present in a single work. A good example of this is the early poem "Kaspar Is Dead." The poem is written in the form of an elegy, and begins, as is customary in the genre, with a lament for the dead. The poem then proceeds to describe the remarkable accomplishments of the deceased, which seem superhuman in character: "who will conceal the burning banner in the cloud's pigtail now . . . who will entice the idyllic deer out of the petrified bag . . . who will blow the noses of ships umbrellas beekeepers ozone-spindles and bone the pyramids." It seems as if some golden age has passed: The link between man and nature has been broken by the death of Kaspar. At this realization, the speaker resumes his lament, but this time it seems even more self-conscious, and it includes a note of facetiousness: "alas alas alas our good kaspar is dead. goodness gracious me kaspar is dead." In the second half of the poem, the speaker turns to more generalized metaphysical speculation: "into what shape has your great wonderful soul migrated. are you a star now or a chain of water . . . or an udder of black light?" He despairs once again at the realization that, wherever he is and in whatever form, Kaspar can no longer reestablish for man the broken link between himself and nature. He has ceased to be human and has thus been liberated from the tragic condition of temporal consciousness that the speaker still suffers. The speaker concludes with resignation that it is man himself who is obligated to reestablish a proper relationship with nature; he cannot rely on anyone or anything else to do this for him, even such a heroic figure as Kaspar.

"I AM A HORSE"

One of Arp's most successful attacks on the reasonable deceptions of man is a poem of his early maturity entitled in German as "Ich bin ein Pferd," in French as "Je suis un cheval," and translated into English as "I Am a Horse." It is not man himself that is under attack but his vain rationality. The speaker of the poem is a reasoning horse, who resembles Jonathan Swift's Houyhnhnms. Investing a subhuman creature with the proud vanity of rational man creates an ironic situation reminiscent of the fable, in which talking animals are used to satirize particular forms of human folly. In this poem, however, it is the human beings who behave instinctively, emotionally, and impulsively—much to the disgust of the dignified horse, who observes the action from a detached perspective.

As the poem begins, the equine speaker is riding in a crowded passenger train, and "every seat is occupied by a lady with a man on her lap"—a most unpleasant sight to the snobbish, socially respectable horse. In addition to being crowded, the compartment is unbearably hot, and all the human passengers "eat nonstop." When the men suddenly begin to whine, unbuttoning the women's bodices and clutching their breasts, wanting to be suckled, the horse alone resists this primitive, uncivilized impulse, maintaining his proud composure. Yet, at the end of the poem, the detachment of the speaker, his feeling of superiority relative to the weak-willed humans with whom he shares the compartment, is revealed as a mere pose which disguises the same basic impulses behind the mask of rationality, for when he neighs loudly, "hnnnnn," he thinks proudly of "the six buttons of sex appeal" on his chest—"nicely aligned like the shiny buttons of a uniform." Through the agency of a reasoning horse, Arp presents a Dadaist fable which exposes the foolish vanity and isolation that has resulted from man's overestimation of his greatest creation—reason.

ARP'S WORLDVIEW

Arp's work consists of more than attacks on the reasonable deceptions of man and satires of his vain pride. Arp devoted a substantial portion of his mature work to communicating, in poetic images and symbols, his distinctive metaphysical philosophy, which has been called variously Platonic, Neoplatonic, Romantic, and Idealist. Arp's worldview eludes these categories; it is personal and intuitive in character, not critical and systematic.

When Arp spoke about the formation of his worldview, he associated it with two particular experiences. The first was the period of isolation he spent at

Weggis, which gave him the opportunity to cast aside the aesthetic of abstraction and formulate his theory of "concrete art." The second experience was his meeting Sophie Taeuber, whose work and life expressed in an intuitive way, free from self-consciousness, the reorientation of human values that Arp had been seeking.

"IN SPACE"

Arp's metaphysical beliefs, transformed into poetic images and symbols, appeared with increasing frequency in his poetry in the years following Sophie's death. One of the best of these metaphysical poems is "Dans le vide" ("In Space"), a moving, imaginative elegy written after the death of Arp's friend and fellow artist, Theo van Doesburg. In this poem, death is treated as cause for celebration, not mourning. When the poem begins, the soul of Arp's beloved friend—after having sojourned for a time in the transitory material world below—is preparing to leap out into the unknown, the eternal realm of unbounded space above. The soul, freed from the physical body, realizes that death is a return home, not an exile. This is reinforced by the fact that he enters space, the Above, in the fetal position—which is also the crouch he assumes in order to leap into space.

Refusing to see this death as a loss, Arp focuses on the freedom his friend is now able to enjoy for the first time, as he is joyously liberated from the demands of others. Doesburg now knows neither honor nor dishonor, censure nor obligation; he dwells blissfully alone, in an eternal realm of light. Arp had already described this state of blissful eternal existence in a much earlier poem entitled "Il chante il chante" ("He Sings He Sings"). It is in later poems such as "In Space" that Arp reached the height of his powers as a highly distinctive, imaginative, and lyrical poet.

OTHER MAJOR WORKS

LONG FICTION: *Tres inmensas novelas*, 1935 (with Vicente Huidobro)

SHORT FICTION: *Le Blanc aux pieds de nègre*, 1945.

NONFICTION: *Onze peintres vus par Arp*, 1949; *Dreams and Projects*, 1952; *Collected French Writings*, 1974.

MISCELLANEOUS: *Gesammelte Gedichte*, 1963-1984 (3 volumes).

BIBLIOGRAPHY
Fauchereau, Serge. *Hans Arp*. Translated by Kenneth Lyons. New York: Rizzoli, 1988. Biographical and critical introduction to Arp's artwork and poetry.

Last, R. W. *Hans Arp: The Poet of Dadaism*. Chester Springs, Pa.: Dufour, 1969. Critical interpretation of selected poetry by Arp. Includes translations of some of Arp's poems and bibliographic references.

Lemoine, Serge. *Dada*. Translated by Charles Lynn Clark. New York: Universe Books, 1987. Introduction to Dadaism with biographical information on Arp and other artists. Includes biblography.

Motherwell, Robert, ed. *The Dada Painters and Poets*. 2d ed. Cambridge, Mass.: Harvard University Press, 1989. A collection of texts and illustrations by Arp and others in the Dada movement with a critical bibliography by Bernard Karpel.

Richter, Hans. *Dada: Art and Anti-Art*. Translated by David Britt. New York: Thames and Hudson, 1997. A historical and biographical account of Dada by one of the artists involved in the movement. Includes bibliographical references and index.

Steven E. Colburn;
bibliography updated by the editors

JOHN ASHBERY

Born: Rochester, New York; July 28, 1927

PRINCIPAL POETRY
Turandot and Other Poems, 1953
Some Trees, 1956
The Tennis Court Oath, 1962
Rivers and Mountains, 1966
Selected Poems, 1967
The Double Dream of Spring, 1970
Three Poems, 1972
Self-Portrait in a Convex Mirror, 1975
Houseboat Days, 1977
As We Know, 1979
Shadow Train, 1981
A Wave, 1984

Selected Poems, 1985
April Galleons, 1987
Flow Chart, 1991
Hotel Lautrémont, 1992
Three Books: Poems, 1993
And the Stars Were Shining, 1994
Can You Hear, Bird: Poems, 1995
*The Mooring of Starting Out: The First Five Books
    of Poetry*, 1997
Wakefulness: Poems, 1998
Girls on the Run: A Poem, 1999
Your Name Here, 2000

OTHER LITERARY FORMS

Although known mainly as a poet, John Ashbery has produced a number of works in various genres. *A Nest of Ninnies* (1969) is a humorous novel about middle-class American life written by Ashbery in collaboration with James Schuyler. His plays include *The Compromise: Or, Queen of the Carabou* (pr. 1956) and *Three Plays* (pb. 1978). He also produced a volume of art criticism, *Reported Sightings: Art Chronicles, 1957-1987* (1989). His Charles Eliot Norton Lectures (given at Harvard University) were collected as *Other Traditions* (2000), an engaging volume of literary criticism about six eccentric poets.

ACHIEVEMENTS

John Ashbery won three major literary awards for *Self-Portrait in a Convex Mirror:* the National Book Award, the Pulitzer Prize, and the National Book Critics Circle Award. Ashbery has served as a member of two prestigious organizations, the American Academy and Institute of Arts and Letters and the National Academy of Arts and Sciences. Twice he has been honored with a Guggenheim Fellowship. In 1972, he won the Shelley Memorial Award. In 1982 Ashbery was awarded the Annual Fellowship of the Academy of American Poets, and in 1984 he received the important Bollingen Prize, awarded by Yale University. In 1985 he was named a winner of both a MacArthur Prize Fellowship and a Lenore Marshall Poetry Prize. He has also been awarded the Robert Frost Medal from the Poetry Society of America; the Gold Medal for Poetry from the American Academy of Arts and Letters; and, in 1992, the presti-

Pulitzer Prize winner John Ashbery in 1976. (AP/Wide World Photos)

gious Feltrinelli Prize from the *Academia Nazionale dei Lincei* in Rome, an award that dates back to the time of Galileo. In 2001, he was awarded the Wallace Stevens Award.

BIOGRAPHY

Born in Rochester, New York, in 1927, John Lawrence Ashbery grew up in rural Sodus, New York. He attended Deerfield Academy and Harvard University, where he became friends with poet Kenneth Koch. Ashbery received his B.A. from Harvard in 1949 and his M.A. from Columbia University in 1951. After leaving university life, Ashbery worked for various publishers in New York City until he moved to Paris in 1955. He remained in Paris until 1965, writing for the *New York Herald Tribune, Art International*, and *Art News*. From 1965 until 1972 Ashbery worked as executive editor for *Art News* in New York, before becoming a distinguished professor of writing at the Brooklyn College campus of the City University of New York. He has also taught at Harvard University. From 1988 to 1999 Ashbery served as a Chancellor of the Academy of American Poets, and he has been the Charles P. Stevenson, Jr., Professor of Languages and Literature at Bard College since 1990.

ANALYSIS

As a brief review of his biography would suggest, John Ashbery has had a considerable amount of exposure to the world of art and to the language of art criticism. Ashbery spent a full decade of his life in Paris, the art capital of Europe, where he read deeply in French poetry and immersed himself in the day-to-day life of French culture. Readers of Ashbery's poetry, then, should not be surprised to encounter references to art and occasional snatches of the French language as part of the poetic texts. For example, one of his poems is entitled "Le livre est sur la table." There are other titles in German, Latin, and Russian, and the poetry as a whole bristles with references from every department of highbrow, middlebrow, and lowbrow culture, including cartoons ("Daffy Duck in Hollywood"), silent movies ("The Lonedale Operator"), literature ("Sonnet," "A Long Novel," and "Thirty-seven Haiku"), history ("The Tennis Court Oath"), and linguistics ("The Plural of 'Jack-in-the-Box'").

Because of its unpredictable style and subject matter, Ashbery's poetry has managed to infuriate, befuddle, amuse, delight, and instruct its readers. His work remains some of the most difficult verse produced, for he refuses to provide the reader with a poetic "reality" that is any less complex than the "reality" of the world outside of poetry. Ashbery cannot be simplified or paraphrased, because his work has no "content" in the ordinary sense. His poetry is "about" the act of knowing, the process of imagining, the curious associational leaps made by the human mind as it experiences any given moment in time. To read Ashbery is to be teased into a whole range of possible meanings without finally settling on a single one. Although this openness might confuse the reader at the outset, the process of reading Ashbery becomes more pleasurable on each encounter. New meanings appear, and Ashbery's voice comes to seem strangely present, as if he were intoning directly into the reader's ear. These poems are filled with little verbal cues and signals aimed directly at the reader; many of the poems depend upon a complicated dialogue or interplay between the author and the reader (a technique he exploits masterfully in *Three Poems*). Thus his work is a kind of half-poetry, always requiring an active reader to make it whole. Ashbery achieves his trademark effect of apparent intimacy while simulating the very process of thought itself.

How Ashbery came to create this new kind of poetry is actually a subchapter in the general history of art and culture in the twentieth century. Certainly he benefited mightily from his study of other artists and thinkers. During his formative years in Paris, he absorbed the French language and the famous paintings of the Louvre while immersing himself in all kinds of printed matter: cheap pamphlets and paperback novels bought from the bookstalls, as well as journalistic prose (in French and English) and the rarefied language of art criticism (which he himself was producing).

In addition, it is clear that a strong line of influence connects Ashbery with writers such as Gertrude Stein, who used disjointed syntax and unorthodox grammar as part of her surrealistic poetry. He owes a clear debt also to Wallace Stevens, who taught him how to philosophize in poetry and also how to approach subjects obliquely. Stevens, also, was a great lover of French Impressionist painting and Symbolist poetry. From W. H. Auden, who chose Ashbery's *Some Trees* for the Yale Series of Younger Poets, Ashbery learned a conversational naturalness and a lyrical or musical way of phrasing. It might be argued that Ashbery, as a literate artist, was influenced by all the great thinkers of the century, but these poetic debts seem particularly obvious, especially in the early books. He probably learned something from Ludwig Wittgenstein's idea of language as a game, just as he must have responded to Jackson Pollock's expressionist paintings, which use paint in much the same way that Ashbery uses words. Something of the sheer shock value and unpredictability of musicians such as Igor Stravinsky, John Cage, and Anton Webern must have touched him also, since Ashbery is clearly fond of similar effects in his own poems.

These debts to the artistic pioneers of the twentieth century are most obvious in Ashbery's earlier books—that is, those preceding the publication of *Three Poems:*

Some Trees, *The Tennis Court Oath*, and *Rivers and Mountains*. All these books are relatively short and compact, typically containing one long or major poem, often positioned near the end of the volume.

Ashbery's characteristic wonder and inventiveness has proven a hallmark of the several volumes published since 1990. During that period, Ashbery wrote and published more and wrote more of the highest quality, than at any other time in his career. With Ashbery there is no limit to the possibilities inherent in human life and to the sheer fun of the mind's response to them. Regular readers of Ashbery will begin to inhabit a world that is larger, more unpredictable, and infinitely more interesting than anything they have known before.

THE TENNIS COURT OATH

In *The Tennis Court Oath*, the reader encounters the long quasi-epical poem entitled "Europe," a work related in overall form to T. S. Eliot's *The Waste Land* (1922) and to similar efforts by Ezra Pound, Hart Crane, and William Carlos Williams. In the most general terms, "Europe" here means the accumulated cultural wealth of European history and its ability—or inability—to help the creative artist in the twentieth century. The decay, or "wasteland," of Europe is juxtaposed to or "intercut" (in film terms) with a trivial story of two travelers, Pryor and Collins, whose unheroic status stands in sharp contrast to the old order. As the poem begins, the poet registers all these complex feelings, while focusing on the shocking blueness of the morning sky, here presented surrealistically:

> To employ her
> construction ball
> Morning fed on the
> light blue wood
> of the mouth

The wrecking ball of construction crews is one of the most visible symbols of the typical cityscape, suggesting simultaneously the twin processes of destruction and re-creation. The sudden, destructive impact of the steel ball approximates the elemental power of the morning light as it, too, rearranges and alters the city and all of its facets. The bystander is left openmouthed and speechless, like the sky itself. This analysis does not fully explicate Ashbery's lines, because, like all dream imagery, they resist final explication. One can describe their sug-

gestiveness and allusiveness, but the dream itself remains a mystery, as does this purely perceived moment of an ordinary morning in the city.

SOME TREES

More typical of Ashbery's early poems are "The Instruction Manual" (from *Some Trees*) and the title poem from *Rivers and Mountains*, each of which forces the reader to perform another kind of imaginative leaping, one that is different from the mere shock of the surreal. In "The Instruction Manual," the speaker is bored with his job of writing an instruction manual on the uses of a new metal and, instead, falls into a prolonged aesthetic daydream on the city of Guadalajara, Mexico, which he has never visited. He invents this city in magical detail for the rest of the poem. In like manner, the places described on a map and the map itself become utterly indistinguishable in "Rivers and Mountains," as if Ashbery were suggesting that one's most vivid moments are those that have been rescued or resurrected by the fertile powers of the poetic imagination. Ashbery always emphasizes the primacy of the imagination. In his view, the most vivid reality occurs in the poem itself, because that is the precise point where the inner and outer (spiritual and sensory) experiences of life actually intersect.

Two more of early poems bear analysis here, because they also illustrate the poetic techniques favored in many of Ashbery's later poems. "Le livre est sur la table" and "The Picture of Little J. A. in a Prospect of Flowers" (both found in *Some Trees*) are magnificent feats of imaginative power, and each operates on the same principle of aesthetic meditation. In each poem, the poet looks at reality through a work of art, or as if it were a work of art (in "The Picture of Little J. A. in a Prospect of Flowers" a photograph is the medium). The effect is largely the same, because the world is always transformed and made into a work of art by the conclusion of the poem. Wallace Stevens is probably the model for this kind of poem, in such works as "Thirteen Ways of Looking at a Blackbird" and "A Study of Two Pears." Other poets, particularly William Carlos Williams, Marianne Moore, and Elizabeth Bishop, were to involve themselves passionately in the writing of aesthetically oriented poems, and one can look to some of their pioneering work to explain the sureness and control of Ashbery's similar efforts.

In "Le livre est sur la table," Ashbery offers the reader a number of aesthetic propositions to contemplate, the most important of which is the notion that beauty results from a certain emptiness or from the placement of an object in an unusual or unaccustomed position. In both instances, the viewer is forced to see the object in a new way. Ashbery again underlines the power of the imagination, giving the example of an imaginary woman who comes alive in her stride, her hair, and her breasts as she is imagined. Most important of all is the artist who creates small artistic catalysts, new and strange relationships that haunt the perceiver with their beauty. Neither the sea nor a simple birdhouse can make for innovative art but placing them together in a fundamental relationship changes them forever:

> The young man places a bird-house
> Against the blue sea. He walks away
> And it remains. Now other
> Men appear, but they live in boxes.

The men in the boxes are the nonartists, who do not realize that the newly created sea is a highlighted thing. All along, the sea has been "writing" a message (with its waves and lines), but only the "young man" (the artist) can read it.

The other "young man," or artist figure, in *Some Trees* is Ashbery himself, described in the snapshot that serves as the aesthetic focal point for the autobiographical poem "The Picture of Little J. A. in a Prospect of Flowers." This little fellow has a head like a mushroom and stands comically before a bed of phlox, but he has the makings of a poet precisely because he appreciates the value of words—especially lost words, those tip-of-the-tongue utterances and slips of the tongue, in which the speaker strains to specify clear meaning. "The Picture of Little J. A. in a Prospect of Flowers" is a typical Ashbery performance, not merely because of its high aesthetic theme but also because of its inclusion of low comedy, irony, and parody. The epigraph—taken from Boris Pasternak's autobiography *Okhrannaya gramota* (1931; *A Safe-Conduct*, 1945)—seemingly contradicts the rest of the poem in what is the first of many jokes (Dick and Jane of childhood books become Dick and Genevieve, conversing in complicated Elizabethan sentences). Childhood is full of jokes and embarrassments,

like standing in front of the clicking shutter of a camera, but childhood can also be the beginning of the artist's journey: The poem ends by praising the imagination and its ability to rescue this early phase of life through the power of words. "The Picture of Little J. A. in a Prospect of Flowers" is a bittersweet portrait of a self-conscious and precocious young man who was destined to become a great artist.

THREE POEMS

Some of that greatness is evident on nearly every page of the book that many critics cite as Ashbery's masterpiece: *Three Poems*, a long, meditative work composed of three interlocking prose poems, "The New Spirit," "The System," and "The Recital," totaling 118 densely packed pages of text. Most of that text is written in prose, a highly interactive prose that constantly urges the reader forward, raises questions, voices doubts and suspicions, and generally plunges the reader headlong into a highly meditative process of thinking and reflecting. *Three Poems* is Ashbery at his most difficult and most satisfying, even though there is virtually no story or tidy paraphrase that can be made of the reading experience itself. Nevertheless, a few elusive details do emerge, and one dimly begins to realize that *Three Poems* is an oblique narrative that in general terms charts a deep relationship between two lovers, one that somehow founders, so that the narrator grows more and more self-possessed. The narrator becomes less and less likely to address the familiar "you" who is called upon again and again in the opening pages of the book. By the end the "you" has virtually disappeared, as if the loss of love might be charted by the absence of the "you" from pages where only the "I" can finally dominate.

The form of *Three Poems* deserves some attention, because the poems are cast in the form of prose, though their imagery, tonal shifts, and complicated rhythms all suggest poetic (not prosaic) form. To complicate matters even further, Ashbery originally published the second section of the work, "The System," in the *Paris Review* in 1971, the year before the whole work appeared in the form of a book. Ashbery specifically allowed "The System" to be published as a prose work, so by titling the whole three-part composition *Three Poems*, he seems to be teasing the reader again on the simplest level and at the same time calling attention to the arbitrariness of literary labels and taxonomy. As if all those complications were not enough, Ashbery carries the joke further by inserting several poems (or at least texts that look like poems) into the texture of the longer work. What counts in the end is the sustained act of mediation and empathy with the narrator which these manipulations of typeface and marginal format will induce in the reader.

The reader, facing *Three Poems*, has a Herculean task to perform: absorbing a long, oblique narrative that requires constant reflection, analysis, and thoughtful mediation. The difficulty is an intentional by-product of Ashbery's stated goal on the first page of the book: to leave out as much as possible in order to create a newer and truer form of communication. Any love story the reader could have encountered would have finally become banal; what Ashbery gives, however, cannot grow stale. To read *Three Poems* is to invent on every page the pain and exaltation that make up the essence of a love story. In that way, the "private" person of the book remains mysterious, as all lovers essentially must remain. Thus, one cannot summarize Ashbery's love story, but one can experience it vicariously.

In "The System," the second and most difficult part of the poem, the narrator becomes utterly preoccupied with himself. In "The New Spirit" even small details of urban life were associated with something the beloved had said or done; here, however, the details and the lover have disappeared. Instead, the narrator is trapped in a kind of mental labyrinth, or "system." In one memorable passage, he imagines the members of the human race boarding a train, which is, of course, their whole life. No one has any idea where the train is going or how fast it is moving. The passengers are ignorant of their journey and—the narrator insists—ignorant of their fundamental situation. The very core of their being is ignorance, yet they fail to recognize this crucial fact. Hence, the narrator views them with contempt.

Three Poems concludes on a lighter note, literally on notes of music, which offer a kind of deliverance for the narrator, who has been trapped in the labyrinth of his doleful thoughts. "The Recital" is important because Ashbery often sees music as an analogue to poetry. Indeed, at one point he had planned to become a musician, and music has remained a rich source of inspiration throughout his career. The power of music and its essen-

tial abstractness make a powerful appeal to the narrator, who at this juncture is exhausted by his Hamlet-like speculations. The poem ends, and with it the whole book, with a description of the power of music (and of art)—the power to inspire new beginnings and new possibilities. In a final jest, Ashbery offers the reader an ending that is actually a beginning: "There were new people watching and waiting, conjugating in this way the distance and emptiness, transforming the scarcely noticeable bleakness into something both intimate and noble." With this brilliant virtuoso effect, Ashbery concludes a poem that is at once a continuance of the great Western tradition of meditative writing (one that includes Saint John of the Cross and Sir Thomas Browne)—and a dramatically arresting rendition of how it feels to be alive in the last decades of the twentieth century. The old and the new come together in a synthesis that is as disturbing, fascinating, and elusive as the century that produced it.

Having reached a kind of artistic plateau with *Three Poems*, Ashbery's career took a new direction. In many ways, *Three Poems* occupies the kind of position in his life that *The Waste Land* did for Eliot. Both works explore psychological traumas and deeply sustained anguish; both plumb the depths of despair until a kind of spiritual nadir is reached. After Eliot completed *The Waste Land*, his work took on a new, spiritual dimension, culminating in the complex Christian poem he called *Four Quartets* (1943). Ashbery's work also changed after the publication of *Three Poems*, but he has not embraced Christian or even theistic belief; he has always insisted on a kind of agnostic or even atheistic vision of life, in which art supplants all conventional notions of divinity. Nevertheless, like Eliot, he has passed through the proverbial dark night of the soul, and his work after *Three Poems* is somehow more confident, less self-consciously experimental, and less opaque. The newer poetry is still impossible to paraphrase, but it is much more accessible and more readable (at least on first sight) than the most extravagant of the early poems, and its subject matter generally seems more central to human experience.

SELF-PORTRAIT IN A CONVEX MIRROR

All these tendencies culminate in a book that won the National Book Award, the Pulitzer Prize, and the National Book Critics Circle Award: *Self-Portrait in a Convex Mirror.* Those prizes and the book itself helped to put Ashbery on the literary map, so that he could no longer be summarily dismissed as an eccentric aesthete turning out brilliant but inaccessible work. Readers began to look more closely at what Ashbery was saying and to embrace his message (however complex) as never before.

"Self-Portrait in a Convex Mirror," the title poem, is a brilliant piece of autobiographical writing that does not reveal gritty details of Ashbery's personal life so much as his opinions about art and its power to transform the artist. Self-portraits are as old as art itself, but Ashbery as an art critic and former expatriate had encountered some especially powerful examples of the genre. He must have encountered the great self-portraits of Rembrandt van Rijn and Vincent Van Gogh, but the particular work that inspired this poem is a famous masterpiece of the High Renaissance, *Self-Portrait in a Convex Mirror* (1524) by Parmigianino (Girolamo Francesco Maria Mazzola), which now hangs in the Kunsthistorisches Museum in Vienna. Ashbery tells the reader that he encountered Parmigianino's famous painting in the summer of 1959, during a visit to Vienna. Parmigianino's self-portrait is uniquely circular in overall form and, as the title suggests, resulted from the artist's close inspection of his visage in a convex mirror, an optical device that creates interesting distortions of scale and distance. Parmigianino's hand, for example, is grossly exaggerated and dominates the foreground of the painting, while his head seems undersized and nearly childlike. It is possible that the Italian artist's childlike appearance appealed to Ashbery because it reminded him of the snapshot of little John Ashbery that had inspired his earlier, much shorter autobiographical lyric, "The Picture of Little J. A. in a Prospect of Flowers."

It is in the nature of self-portraits, then, to conceal and reveal simultaneously—hence the appropriateness of the convex mirror, whose powers of transformation and distortion apply equally to Parmigianino and Ashbery. The poet begins the poem by quoting and paying homage to Vasari, the first great art critic (Ashbery, too, had been an art critic at the time he saw the painting in Venice). Vasari explains the complicated arrangements that preceded Parmigianino's actual painting: the use of a barber's convex mirror and the necessity of having a carpenter prepare the circular wooden substratum of the painting. These operations are mere preliminaries, however, to the much more important work of the eyes themselves once the painting has been set up. The eyes cannot penetrate the artificial depth created by this strange mirroring device; therefore, everything that results is a kind of speculation—a word which derives from the Latin word for mirror, *speculum*, as Ashbery points out. Thus in the self-portrait one kind of "mirroring" leads to another; what one sees is not precisely what is there. To hold the paradox in the mind is to enter the world of the artist.

The argument that Ashbery then goes on to develop may perhaps be summarized by the adagelike statement that stability (or order) can be maintained in the presence of instability (or chaos). The movements of time, weather, Ping-Pong balls, and tree branches are all potential elements for the synthesizing and harmonizing power of art, no matter if it distorts something in the process. Perhaps the greatest distortion is that of stability; the stable simply cannot be found in nature, as Isaac Newton showed through his laws of thermodynamics. It is only in the mirror of art (a symbol also favored by William Shakespeare) that stability, order, and form may thrive. Since all art is by definition artificial, then, stability is an artifice, too.

Nevertheless, artistic stability is all the artist and the race of human beings can rely upon to reveal meaning in an otherwise meaningless space. So Parmigianino's Renaissance painting, like all art, is applicable to all future generations, and Ashbery borrows Parmigianino's technique of mirroring until the world seems to spin around him in a merry-go-round of papers, books, windows, trees, photographs, and desks, and "real life" itself becomes a kind of trick painting. Addressing the Italian master, Ashbery admits that the "uniform substance" or order in his life derives from the Italian genius: "My guide in these matters is your self."

He goes on to quote a contemporary art critic, Sydney Freedberg, who finds the idealized beauty and formal feeling of Parmigianino's self-portrait to depend on the very chaos Ashbery had earlier described. For Freedberg this instability is a collection of bizarre, unsettling aspects of reality which somehow the painting enfolds and harmonizes.

Readers might at this point recall similar discussions—though in radically different language—by John Keats, especially in his great mediation on art, "Ode on a Grecian Urn," which asks the reader to accept art precisely because it transforms the chaos and changeability of human life. Ultimately, this process results in a complete fusion of truth (or reality) and beauty (or art), in Keats's formulation. Ashbery is not Keats, but one has to note the similar posture of the two poets, both contemplating the power of art, both commencing with an art object (the Grecian urn and the Italian self-portrait) and concluding on a note of affirmation. For Ashbery the power of art is not only magnificent but terrifying, like a pistol primed for Russian roulette with only one bullet in the chamber. Art has the potential to "kill" our old perceptions. Some people might consider this power to be only a dream, but for Ashbery the power remains, and art becomes a kind of "waking dream" in the same unhappy world of human beings that Keats evokes in "Ode on a Grecian Urn." Even in the city, which Ashbery imagines as an insect with multifaceted eyes, art somehow survives. He envisions each person as a potential artist holding a symbolic piece of chalk, ready to begin a new self-portrait.

HOUSEBOAT DAYS

Ashbery continues with this more accessible (and essentially more affirmative) kind of poetry in the volume *Houseboat Days*, the title poem of which likens the mind and its vast storehouse of memory to a boardinghouse that is open to everyone, taking in boarders of every possible type and description. This metaphorical way of describing the sensory, intellectual, and imaginative powers of human beings is a valuable clue for understanding another poem in the volume, one of Ashbery's wittiest and most polished performances, "Daffy Duck in Hollywood," a poem that manages to be tender, lyrical, comic, outrageous, and serious without losing its sense of direction.

An obscure opera serves as a kind of grid or structural framework for this rather freewheeling poem. The poem begins with a stupefyingly absurd collection of mental odds and ends, the flotsam and jetsam of a highly cultured and sophisticated mind that also appreciates the artifacts of popular culture: an Italian opera, Rumford's Baking Powder, Speedy Gonzales, Daffy Duck, Elmer

Fudd, the Gadsden Purchase, Anaheim (California), pornographic photographs, and the comic-strip character Skeezix. All these apparent irrelevancies are entirely relevant, because they illustrate the random nature of the mind, its identity as a stream of consciousness. Yet these items are also a kind of dodge or subterfuge to block out images of a significant other, possibly a lover. Because of the odd way the mind works through the principle of association, however, these same cartoonlike images also remind the narrator of that other person.

As in so many of his other poems, Ashbery is again insisting that the only reality is the one human beings make, and he concludes by wisely noting that no one knows all the dimensions of this mental life or where the parts fit in. The goal, in Ashbery's opinion, is to keep "ambling" on; thus, each person might remain "intrigued" and open to all the extravagant invitations of life. The mind, with its interminable image-making, is strangely cut off from life, but when used properly (that is, aesthetically) it can lay hold of the abundant and unanticipated gifts that always surround and endow impoverished human beings.

A WAVE

This optimistic vein is apparent in most of *A Wave* but especially in the title poem, which seems to contrast crests of positive feelings with troughs of despair. The poem is a long discursive work in which Ashbery plays variations on one essential theme: that a fundamental feeling of security (not to be confused with superficial happiness), a deep and abiding sense of the goodness of life, can, in fact, sustain the person through the pain that life inevitably brings. In this poem human beings do have final control of their destiny, because they are supported by something powerfully akin to older notions of grace or faith. Having this power or "balm," as Ashbery terms it, no one is ever really stripped of autonomy: "we cannot be really naked/ Having this explanation."

APRIL GALLEONS

This mood of sustained hope continues in the exquisitely lyrical *April Galleons*, a book that, like *Houseboat Days*, relies on the metaphor of a boat as a vehicle for psychological as well as physical travel. Included is "Ice Storm," a poem that is highly original yet somehow manages to echo Robert Frost (especially "Birches" and

"Design"). As Frost did in "Birches," Ashbery describes winter ice in glittering detail. As Frost did in "Design," Ashbery questions the fate of small things that are out of their accustomed places, such as the rose he stumbles upon, growing beside a path entirely out of season. Yet none of these matters disturbs him fundamentally, because he is beginning to get his "bearings in this gloom and see how [he] could improve on the distraught situation all around me, in the darkness and tarnished earth."

AND THE STARS WERE SHINING

Ashbery's wit and virtuosity are often noted by critics, yet his humanity and intelligence are equally important facets of his work. In "And the Stars Were Shining," this fact becomes readily apparent when in many of the poems his wisdom of age is blended with a great and tender sadness and bursts of wit and vitality. The title poem harks back to the long poems of another age—Roman numerals mark its sections and its cadences recall a past era—but its direct and relaxed language brings it firmly into the late twentieth century. There are fifty-seven more poems in the volume, displaying Ashbery's characteristic wryness and filled with tragicomic snapshots of our time. The works are also philosophical, as he endeavors to find amusement as well as pain in his autumnal themed poems, including the title poem and "Token Resistance."

YOUR NAME HERE

The title of *Your Name Here* aptly hints at the volume's rambunctious, arbitrary themes and pell-mell performances: Poems include "Frogs and Gospels," "Full Tilt," "Here We Go Looby," "Amnesia Goes to the Ball," and "A Star Belched." While his poetic themes are capricious and whimsical, Ashbery's language is intricate, tightly constructed, rhythmic, and sinuous, with a serious undercurrent of memory, time, loss, angst, and desire. Thus, his tone is at once melancholic and comedic, best demonstrated in "What Is Written."

OTHER MAJOR WORKS

LONG FICTION: *A Nest of Ninnies*, 1969 (with James Schuyler).

PLAYS: *Everyman*, pr. 1951; *The Heroes*, pr. 1952; *The Compromise: Or, Queen of the Carabou*, pr. 1956; *The Philosopher*, pb. 1964; *Three Plays*, pb. 1978.

NONFICTION: *Reported Sightings: Art Chronicles, 1957-1987*, 1989; *Other Traditions*, 2000.

TRANSLATIONS: *Murder in Montarte*, 1960; *Melville*, 1960; *The Deadlier Sex*, 1961; *Alberto Giacometti*, 1971; *The Landscapes Behind the Door*, 1994.

BIBLIOGRAPHY

Carroll, Paul. *The Poem in Its Skin*. Chicago: Follett, 1968. One of the first books of poetry criticism to include a chapter on the poetry of Ashbery, Carroll's study contains a brilliant chapter entitled "If Only He Had Left the Finland Station," which explores one of the poet's early surrealist poems, "Leaving the Atocha Station." Carroll guides the reader through many possible responses to Ashbery.

Keller, Lynn. *Re-making It New: Contemporary Poetry and the Modernist Tradition*. New York: Cambridge University Press, 1987. "'We Must, We Must Be Moving On': Ashbery's Divergence from Stevens and Modernism" is the title of the very clearly written and cogently argued chapter in which Keller shows both Ashbery's debt to and divergence from Stevens, as well as his use of surrealism.

Malinowska, Barbara. *Dynamics of Being, Space, and Time in the Poetry of Czesław Miłosz and John Ashbery*. New York: Peter Lang, 2000. Malinowska provides a challenging discussion of poetic visions of reality in the works of Miłosz and Ashbery. She works with Martin Heidegger's philosophy of phenomenology and applies key Heideggerian terms—Dasein, space, time, and culture—to explore the reality created by or alluded to in their writings. Jargon-heavy but useful.

Schultz, Susan M., ed. *The Tribe of John: Ashbery and Contemporary Poetry*. Tuscaloosa: University of Alabama Press, 1995. Competent and inventive contributors examine the Ashbery legacy in fourteen essays on Ashbery and the generation of postmodern poets indebted to his achievement. Topics include Ashbery's landscapes, his love poetry, his later poetry, and his influence on such writers as Ann Lauterbach, Charles Bernstein, and William Bronk.

Shapiro, David. *John Ashbery: An Introduction to the Poetry*. New York: Columbia University Press, 1979. If students could read only one book on the poetry of Ashbery, then Shapiro's study, though now dated, would be an excellent choice: It is clearly written, intelligently organized, and generously documented. The book covers most of the early books and dwells considerably on *Some Trees*, *Three Poems*, and *Self-Portrait in a Convex Mirror*. This book has an excellent index and a short biography and bibliography.

Shoptaw, John. *On the Outside Looking Out: John Ashbery's Poetry*. Cambridge, Mass.: Harvard University Press, 1994. Abundant and detailed information about Ashbery's life, publication history, and manuscripts make the book valuable. It offers an intriguing but perhaps overworked and insufficiently proven argument that Ashbery's elusiveness derives from his homosexuality.

Stitt, Peter. *Uncertainty and Plenitude: Five Contemporary Poets*. Iowa City: University of Iowa Press, 1997. In "John Ashbery: The Poetics of Uncertainty," Stitt insists that Ashbery's poetry is about process and form, and that it does not release meaning in the traditional sense. The gnostic nature of truth is questioned, and indeterminacy is revealed. Stitt's effort is challenging and engaging.

Vendler, Helen H. *The Music of What Happens: Poems, Poets, and Critics*. Cambridge, Mass.: Harvard University Press, 1988. Vendler writes persuasively about Ashbery's subject matter, which she sees as similar to that of the great poet Keats. In her chapter on Ashbery and Louise Glück, she provides an especially detailed analysis of *Shadow Train* and *A Wave*.

Daniel L. Guillory,
updated by Philip K. Jason and Sarah Hilbert

MARGARET ATWOOD

Born: Ottawa, Ontario, Canada; November 18, 1939

PRINCIPAL POETRY

Double Persephone, 1961
The Circle Game, 1964 (single poem), 1966 (collection)
Kaleidoscopes Baroque: A Poem, 1965
Talismans for Children, 1965
Expeditions, 1966
Speeches for Dr. Frankenstein, 1966
The Animals in That Country, 1968
What Was in the Garden, 1969
The Journals of Susanna Moodie, 1970
Procedures for Underground, 1970
Power Politics, 1971
You Are Happy, 1974
Selected Poems, 1976
Two-Headed Poems, 1978
True Stories, 1981
Snake Poems, 1983
Interlunar, 1984
Selected Poems II: Poems Selected and New, 1976-1986, 1986
Selected Poems: 1966-1984, 1990
Poems, 1965-1975, 1991
Poems, 1976-1989, 1992
Morning in the Burned House, 1995
Eating Fire: Selected Poems 1965-1995, 1998

OTHER LITERARY FORMS

Margaret Atwood's publishing history is a testimonial to her remarkable productivity and versatility as a writer. As well as a poet, she is a novelist, a short-fiction writer, a children's author, an editor, and an essayist. *The Edible Woman* (1969), Atwood's first novel, defined the focus of her fiction: mainly satirical explorations of sexual politics, where self-deprecating female protagonists defend themselves against males, chiefly with the weapon of language. Other novels include *Surfacing* (1972), *Lady Oracle* (1976), *Life Before Man* (1979), *Bodily Harm* (1981), *Cat's Eye* (1988), *The Robber Bride* (1993), *Alias Grace* (1996), and *The Blind Assassin* (2000). *The Handmaid's Tale* (1985), a dystopian novel set in a postnuclear, monotheocratic Boston, where life is restricted by censorship and state control of reproduction, is the best known of Atwood's ten novels and was made into a commercial film of the same title, directed by Volker Schlondorff. *Dancing Girls and Other Stories* (1977) and *Bluebeard's Egg* (1983) are books of short fiction, as are *Wilderness Tips* (1991) and *Good Bones* (1992). Atwood has written four children's books: *Up in a Tree* (1978), which she also illustrated,

Margaret Atwood (© Washington Post; reprinted by permission of the D. C. Public Library)

Governor-General's Award for poetry in 1967. In that same year, Atwood's *The Animals in That Country* was awarded first prize in Canada's Centennial Commission Poetry Competition. The Chicago periodical *Poetry* awarded Atwood the Union Prize in 1969 and the Bess Hoskins Prize in 1974. Since that time Atwood's numerous awards and distinctions have been more for her work in fiction, nonfiction, and humanitarian affairs. She has received several honorary doctorates and many prestigious prizes, among them the Toronto Arts Award (1986), *Ms.* magazine's Woman of the Year for 1986, the Ida Nudel Humanitarian Award from the Canadian Jewish Congress, and the American Humanist of the Year Award for 1987. In fact, at one time or another, Atwood has won just about every literary award for Canadian writers. In 2000, Atwood won the Booker Prize for the best novel by a citizen of the United Kingdom or British Commonwealth.

Anna's Pet (1980), *For the Birds* (1990), and *Princess Prunella and the Purple Peanut* (1995). A nonfiction book for young readers is *Days of the Rebels: 1815-1840*, 1977.

Atwood's contributions to literary theory and criticism have also been significant. Her idiosyncratic, controversial, but well-researched *Survival: A Thematic Guide to Canadian Literature* (1972) is essential for the student interested in Atwood's version of the themes that have shaped Canadian creative writing over a century. Her *Second Words: Selected Critical Prose* (1982) is one of the first works of the feminist criticism that has since flourished in Canada. She also produced *Strange Things: The Malevolent North in Canadian Literature* (1995). A related title is *Negotiating with the Dead: A Writer on Writing* (2001).

ACHIEVEMENTS

Critical success and national and international acclaim have greeted Margaret Atwood's work since her first major publication, the poetry collection *The Circle Game* (1966). Poems from that collection were awarded the 1965 President's Medal for Poetry by the University of Western Ontario in 1966, and after commercial publication the collection won for Atwood the prestigious

BIOGRAPHY

Margaret Atwood was born into a family that encouraged inquiry and discovery. An important stimulus to her intellectual curiosity was certainly the family's yearly sojourns in the remote bush of northern Ontario and Quebec, where Atwood's father, an entomologist, carried out much of his study and research. It is likely that this environment shaped Atwood's ironic vision and her imagery. Atwood's writing, especially her poetry and her second novel, *Surfacing*, are permeated with her intimate knowledge of natural history and with her perception of the casual brutality with which the weak are sacrificed for the survival of the strong.

Studying between 1957 and 1961 for her undergraduate degree in English at Victoria College, University of Toronto, Atwood came under the influence of Canadian poet Jay MacPherson and especially of Northrop Frye, one of the twentieth century's preeminent critical theorists. They encouraged Atwood's early poetry and directed her toward biblical and mythological symbol and archetype, still strong forces in her writing.

Between 1961 and 1963, Atwood pursued graduate studies in English at Harvard University, receiving her M.A. in 1962. In 1963, she met fellow graduate student James Polk, whom she married in 1967, when, after a period of working, writing, and teaching, Atwood returned to Harvard to pursue a Ph.D. (beginning thesis work on the English metaphysical romance). In Canada, however, her burgeoning success as a writer and her involvement as a university teacher of creative writing soon superseded her formal studies.

In the early 1970's, Atwood traveled in Europe and then returned to Canada to continue writing and teaching. She became an editor at House of Anansi Press, one of the many Canadian publishing houses that sprang up in the fertile late 1960's to encourage young and sometimes experimental writers. She also met novelist Graeme Gibson, who may have influenced her own foray into experimental fiction, *Surfacing*. After her divorce from James Polk in 1973, Atwood moved with Gibson to rural Alliston, Ontario, where their daughter Jess was born in 1976.

Throughout the 1980's and 1990's, Atwood's overall output was steady, though she did not continue to produce very much new poetry. In the latter 1980's, Atwood made successful forays into the field of screenwriting for film and the musical theater. Her increased involvement with world social and political issues is evident in her vice-chairmanship of the Writers' Union of Canada and her presidency of P.E.N. International, where she has waged a vigorous battle against literary censorship. Her association with Amnesty International has prompted an increasingly strong expression of her moral vision. She has continued to publish regularly in Canadian, American, and European media and has received worldwide recognition as a major contemporary writer.

ANALYSIS

Margaret Atwood's poetry deals essentially with paradox and struggle in both art and life. Her first (and now generally inaccessible) chapbook of poetry, *Double Persephone*, contains the components of her vision, which she elucidates in her next nine poetry collections with more depth, conviction, and stylistic maturity, but whose elements she changes little. An overview of Atwood's poetry reveals patterns expressed through mythological and biblical allusion and recurring imagery relating to mutability, metamorphosis, near annihilation, and, ultimately, adaptation and definition. References to eyes, water, mirrors, glass, photographs, maps, and charts abound. The archetypal journey/quest motif is a vital component of Atwood's vision. It is worked out metaphorically in the historical context of European exploration and settlement of the Canadian wilderness, the pioneer's battle with alienation, loneliness, and the struggle to articulate a new self in a new world. If he masters the new "language," he will survive; his divided self will become whole. This life-and-death struggle is also carried out in the psychological arena of sexual politics. Much of Atwood's poetry (especially *Procedures for Underground* and *Power Politics*) explores—at first with anger, later with resignation, always with irony—the damage that men and women inflict on one another despite their interdependence. In Atwood's poetry, chaos is perceived as the center of things; it is the individual's quest, as both artist and natural being, to define order, meaning, and purpose—to survive.

THE CIRCLE GAME

The Circle Game, Atwood's first major poetry collection, represents the outset of an artistic and personal journey. The artist-poet (whose voice is personal, ironic, and female) struggles to shape chaos into order through language, whose enigmatic symbols she must master and control. Language is a set of tools, the key component of the poet's bag of tricks, packed for the (metaphoric) journey undertaken, for example, in *The Circle Game*'s "Evening Trainstation Before Departure":

> Here I am in
> a pause in space
> hunched on the edge
> of a tense suitcase.

Yet language is duplicitous; it is a weapon that can rebound against the poet herself. She is engaged in a constant struggle to interpret and communicate without being subsumed, as suggested in "The Sybil": "she calls to me with the many/ voices of the children/ not I want to die/ but You must die."

In life, chaos comprises process, flux, the temporal; the struggle for the individual is both to understand her own nature and to reconcile herself to the processes of nature, history, and culture. The external, natural world mirrors the self; it speaks the siren language of the primitive and lies in wait to ambush with casual cruelty human beings' fragile civility. Through recognition, struggle, and reconciliation, the individual can transcend his destructive self, mirrored in the natural world. Throughout *The Circle Game*, the self, both artistic and psychological, struggles to be born. The creative impulse is strong, the instinct for survival great, but *The Circle Game*'s "Journey to the Interior" says that the individual does not yet understand the ambiguous messages of either art or life and is in danger: "and words here are as pointless/ as calling in a vacant/ wilderness."

The opening poem, "This Is a Photograph of Me," presents a paradox. In the photograph, the speaker's image is barely discernible, suspended as if in a watery grave, yet awaiting redefinition, new birth: "I am in the lake, in the center/ of the picture, just under the surface." In "Camera," the artist is reviled for the impulse to capture life in a static form when the impulse to the kinesis, the process of life, is so compelling: "Camera man/ how can I love your glass eye? . . . that small black speck/ travelling towards the horizon/ at almost the speed of life/ is me." Who is "me"? It is the androgynous, divided self, defined metaphorically in the powerful poem "After the Flood, We." "We" are Deucalion and Phyrra, in Greek mythology the sole male and female survivors of the mythic flood, suspended over the misty shapelessness of the drowned old world, designated by Zeus as the only humans deserving of survival. The female speaker differentiates between "I" and "you," "you" being an intimate who is here (as elsewhere throughout Atwood's poetry) the male. These two are charged with creating a new world. The self-absorbed male is a casual progenitor, "tossing small pebbles/ at random over your shoulder," but the female persona perceives horror, a Frankenstein's monster rising up to overwhelm "the beauty of the morning." The threat to process and growth, both artistic and personal, is the strongest of perceived evils. A sense that the artist-speaker is not yet equal to the task, has not yet found the appropriate language, is particularly strong in "The Messenger," where

"a random face/ revolving outside the window" fades into oblivion because, the poem's ironic tone implies, the message is brought to the inappropriate recipient; the messenger shouts "desperate messages with his/ obliterated mouth/ in a silent language."

In *The Circle Game*, a game motif is evident in the titles and metaphoric significance of several poems ("Playing Cards," "An Attempted Solution for Chess Problems," and the collection's title poem). Intelligence, even cunning, is required. Knowing the divided self is the key to becoming the artist fit to pass on the message vital for survival. The collection's final poem, "The Settlers," suggests that perhaps success will come in laying the foundation for future understanding. The poet-narrator optimistically envisions their transformation through natural evolution into messages for the future, though understanding is still in doubt: "children run, with green/ smiles (not knowing/ where)." As yet the tools, the language, are lacking. The simple innocence of a children's circle game becomes weighted with foreboding; critic Rosemary Sullivan observes, "The narcissism of the circle game claims the narrator, and confines Atwood herself in its prisoning rhythms. We have yet to see the circle effectively broken."

THE ANIMALS IN THAT COUNTRY

The journey of discovery continues in *The Animals in That Country* and is undertaken in several metaphorical arenas: the natural, the historical, the cultural, and, above all, the arena of the self. Again, the artist-self is found wanting. Several poems such as "Provisions" and "The Surveyors" suggest that the pioneer brings the wrong equipment to the new world because he or she has a faulty concept of the terrain and its natural inhabitants. Later generations distance themselves as soon as possible from the natural interrelationship of human and animals, the hunt being transformed into a ritualized game and then an irrelevance, as the collection's title poem points out.

Self-definition in a modern cultural setting also eludes the speaker in this collection's poems. At its writing, Atwood was on the second of her two sojourns at Harvard. Her own dislocation in American society and her distaste (expressed in letters to friends and colleagues in Canada) for American materialism and the accelerating Vietnam War are expressed in poems such as "The Landlady" and "It Is Dangerous to Read Newspapers." Her sense of alienation, from both place and people, is sadly noted in "Roominghouse, Winter": "Tomorrow, when you come to dinner/ They will tell you I never lived here." An ironic view emerges in an encounter with a relief map of Canada in the poem "At the Tourist Centre in Boston." An increasingly irate narrator asks first herself and then the receptionist, "Do you see nothing/ watching you from under the water?// Was the sky ever that blue?// Who really lives there?" That series of ominous questions signals a return journey to the interior of both Canada and the still unmapped and undefined self.

The definitive exploration of humankind's relationship to the natural world, to history, and to their own warring selves takes place in two of the collection's most powerful poems, "A Night in the Royal Ontario Museum" and "Progressive Insanities of a Pioneer." In the former, the speaker is inadvertently locked in the museum, "this crazed man-made/ stone brain," and is compelled to undergo a metaphoric journey to the beginnings of natural and human history. The worst horror to contemplate is preexistence, nondefinition: "I am dragged to the mind's/ deadend, . . . lost/ among the mastodons." In "Progressive Insanities of a Pioneer" this struggle to redefine the self out of chaos is explored in a metaphorical battle between a pioneer and the wilderness. In seven sections, or chapters, the story of the pioneer's failure unfolds relentlessly, the poem's flat and terse diction underscoring the horror of his descent into insanity and death. Seeking to impose order on the perceived chaos of his surroundings, the pioneer fails to acknowledge the necessity of adapting to the wilderness rather than subjugating it. He does not learn the language; instead, he makes a futile effort to structure, to classify. He is doomed to failure and annihilation, drowning in a metaphorical flux of Leviathan proportions.

THE JOURNALS OF SUSANNA MOODIE

Success in these parallel journeys both into the physical wilderness and into the self is achieved, however, by the persona who informs and narrates Atwood's next collection of poems, *The Journals of Susanna Moodie.* J. W. Dunbar Moodie and his wife Susanna were impoverished English gentry who emigrated to Canada in

1832 and took up a land grant in the bush near what is now Peterborough, Ontario. Their seven-year sojourn in the bush before they settled in the town of Belleville was a searing experience for Susanna. Steeped in nineteenth century Romanticism and possessing to no small degree the arrogance of her class, Susanna arrived in Canada with the rosy expectations of vulnerable people unscrupulously lured from home by the promise of bountiful land, a temperate climate, congenial neighbors, and best of all, freedom from taxation. The harsh reality of life in the wilderness destroyed many; Susanna, though, was able to draw on a previously untapped toughness of spirit that eventually turned her from a homesick gentlewoman into a self-sufficient, grudgingly loyal Canadian who contributed much to a fledgling Canadian culture. She recorded her experiences in a pair of accounts entitled *Roughing It in the Bush: Or, Forest Life in Canada* (1852) and *Life in the Clearings Versus the Bush* (1853). In them, readers detect a duality of her attitude and personality that Atwood exploits to advantage in *The Journals of Susanna Moodie.* In her contemplation of the physical and spiritual wildernesses that confront her, Susanna's fear and despair is evident but so, increasingly, is a testy strength and a reluctant love for her new country.

The collection is divided into three sections that treat respectively Susanna's immigration, her sojourn in the bush, and her later years in Belleville and Toronto. Metaphorically, the "journals" chronicle the passages of Susanna's life: the rebirth and redefinition of the self that beginning in a new land requires; the trial by fire (in Susanna's case, literal) of life in the hostile wilderness; finally, reconciliation and death, where physical burial marks a spiritual intermingling with the new land, ironically becoming alien again through twentieth century urbanization.

In "Journal 1," Susanna repeatedly expresses the realization of her need for a new identity; familiar psychological landmarks are now irrelevant. In "Further Arrivals" she observes, "We left behind . . . our civilized/ distinctions// and entered a large darkness." At first she is threatened at every level, perceiving her husband as "the wereman," her "first neighbours" as "speaking a twisted dialect," and the wilderness as consciously malicious. Despite the familiar human instinct to order, catalog, and impose, Susanna recognizes the need for compromise: "Resolve: to be both tentative and hard to startle/ . . . in this area where my damaged knowing of the language means/ prediction is forever impossible." Susanna survives seven years of loneliness and physical hardship that transform her. She departs for Belleville with a sense that she does not yet fully understand her relationship with the wilderness. In "Departure from the Bush," she observes, "In time the animals/ arrived to inhabit me./ . . . There was something they almost taught me/ I came away not having learned." From the relatively civilized perspective of Belleville, Susanna contemplates the relationship between pioneer and wilderness with a mixture of bitterness and resignation. In the three "dream" poems of the "journal 2" section, she recognizes in the natural cycle the inexorable interrelationship of life and death (often violent) of which humankind is an integral part. Her own ambivalence is expressed in "The Double Voice": "Two voices/ took turns using my eyes"; while one saw "the rituals of seasons and rivers," the other pointed out "a dead dog/ jubilant with maggots." In "Journal 3," Susanna's reconciliation with her new self and with her harsh new land is completed; after her death, her defiant voice can still be heard over the roar of the twentieth century Toronto built over her bones. As Atwood says in the afterword to this collection, "Susanna Moodie has finally turned herself inside out, and has become the spirit of the land she once hated."

PROCEDURES FOR UNDERGROUND

Having left Susanna Moodie speaking prophetically from her underground grave, Atwood made the underground the shaping metaphor of her next poetry collection, *Procedures for Underground*. She returns to a theme that dominated *The Circle Game*: the power of the artist to shape and articulate both internal and external experience. Critic Jerome Rosenberg reminds readers of Atwood's observation that artists who experience the creative process make "a descent to the underworld"; the artist's role is a mystical and powerful one (and perhaps subversive, the collection's title suggests). The artist persona is set apart from ordinary human relationships, as a seer is, by the ability to interpret experience outside the literal. In the title poem, the expectations of the artist blessed (or cursed) with second sight are

grimly described: "Few will seek your help/ with love, none without fear."

The artist's compulsion to define, shape, interpret, and preserve permeates the collection's imagery. In "Three Desk Objects," the writer's tools are transformed by this purpose: "My cool machines/ . . . I am afraid to touch you/ I think you will cry out in pain// I think you will be warm, like skin." Many of the poems describe the capturing of images, meanings, and moments through a variety of artistic media. "Woman Skating" ends with "Over all I place/ a glass bell"; "Younger Sister, Going Swimming" has her dive recorded on the poet's paper; "Girl and Horse, 1928" and "Projected Slide of an Unknown Soldier" explore time and history through the "freeze-frame" of photography. Yet the artist fails to capture or interpret the "underground" aspect of the person. Human nature remains impenetrable, a language unlearned, a primeval mystery unsolved, as the poem "A Soul, Geologically" says. "Where do the words go/ when we have said them?" is the plaintive question in "A Small Cabin."

The most ominous note in the collection is struck by a poem that returns to the game motif of *The Circle Game* and makes a sad commentary on the passage from innocence to experience. In "Game After Supper," a memory of a happy children's game of twilight hide-and-seek turns macabre when the reader understands that the small child plays with spectral cousins long dead of diphtheria, and that the seeker is a threatening, anonymous male figure. "He will be an uncle,/ if we are lucky," comments the speaker wryly, but the sexual threat is clear, and the stage is set for the largely sexual struggle that provides the primary focus in Atwood's next collection. From here onward, her concern is more with external relationships; it is probably fair to say as well that this shift in focus marks the end of her most powerful work as a poet.

POWER POLITICS

Power Politics, written when Atwood's first marriage was breaking up, focuses primarily on human relationships, though Atwood's parallel concerns with humans in natural and social history and with interpreting the dual self are also strongly present. Specifically, *Power Politics* chronicles the destructive love-hate relationship that can exist between incompatible men and women. In this pessimistic collection, signals are missed, messages are misinterpreted, the battle is mutually lost. The menacing, shadowy "tall man" of "Game After Supper" resolves into an aggrieved male partner; the anguished female speaker explores their inability to fulfill each other sexually, intellectually, or spiritually. The inevitable failure of the relationship is evident from the collection's terse, vicious (and gratuitous) opening epigram: "you fit into me/ like a hook into an eye// a fish hook/ an open eye." The poems' titles provide an inexorable chronology of descent from love through suspicion, mutual betrayal, and accusation to sad resignation and parting. Much of the imagery is of battle; in the central, seven-section poem "They Are Hostile Nations," battle lines are drawn despite a perceived mutual need: "Instead we are opposite, we/ touch as though attacking." Ultimately, the speaker blames herself for bringing to bear the weight of her expectations, emotional and artistic, on a partner unable to carry them. In "Hesitation Outside the Door," she addresses him sadly: "Get out while it is/ open, while you still can." Yet in the final poem, "He Is Last Seen," the speaker mourns her partner's seeming escape "towards firm ground and safety" and away from the still-unresolved conflict underlying all Atwood's poetry thus far: that of the divided, unreconciled self.

YOU ARE HAPPY

In *You Are Happy*, progress is made toward the resolution of this conflict. The ironic, pessimistic tone of *Power Politics* continues in the opening section. Human relationships fail once again for both emotional and artistic reasons; they cannot withstand the double assault of misunderstanding and misinterpretation. Imagery of water, ice, mirrors, eyes, and particularly cameras still prevails, as "Newsreel: Man and Firing Squad" shows: "No more of these closeups, this agony/ taken just for the record anyway." Yet in the collection's middle sections, "Songs of the Transformed" and "Circe/ Mud Poems," the limitations of art in controlling and interpreting human nature and behavior are confronted. Through the voice of the sorceress Circe, a compelling character in Homer's *Odyssey* (c. 800 B.C.E.) who transformed men into swine, Atwood acknowledges the limitations of myth-making and the attraction of accepting life as it is, with its ambivalence and vitality: "I search instead for the others,/ the ones left over,/ the ones who

have escaped from these/ mythologies with barely their lives." This positive realization is reiterated in the collection's last section. In "Late August," a new mood of voluptuous acceptance and fruitfulness is evident: "The air is still/ warm, flesh moves over/ flesh, there is no// hurry."

In this collection, too, Atwood's poetic skills show new direction. She intersperses her familiar spare, short poetic forms with more fluid prose poems. Indeed, the early 1970's marked the beginning of Atwood's shift away from poetry toward prose writing; the themes and imagery in many poems are explored more fully in novels from the same periods. There was a hiatus of four years until *Two-Headed Poems* appeared.

TWO-HEADED POEMS

Interestingly, much of *Two-Headed Poems* relates closely in tone, theme, and imagery to *The Journals of Susanna Moodie*, but where the voice in the latter was objectified and dramatized as Moodie's, the voice in *Two-Headed Poems* is subjective and intimate. This relationship can perhaps be partly explained by the fact that Atwood gave birth to her daughter Jess in 1976, and her experience of motherhood is strongly reflected in this first collection of poems since her daughter's birth. There is a subtle softening of the irony of tone and vision and of terse diction, a perceptible turn toward acceptance rather than rejection. Now Atwood seems to have experienced personally, not only artistically, Moodie's sense of purpose and place in human history; Atwood too belongs to "the procession/ of old leathery mothers// passing the work from hand to hand,/ mother to daughter,// a long thread of red blood, not yet broken" ("A Red Shirt"). Poems such as "You Begin" reflect a renewed emotional and artistic purpose; "All Bread," with its motifs of sacrifice, sacrament, and Communion, expresses on one level acknowledgment of the rhythms of life and death inherent in nature, and on a parallel level the interdependence of the sexes, which marriage sanctifies. The poet has reconciled herself to the sometimes violent paradoxes that define life: natural, human, and artistic.

TRUE STORIES

That emerging attitude of acceptance is put to the test in *True Stories*. This collection is Atwood's poetic response to her increasing political commitment; its focus is even more external and marks a renewed emphasis on social themes less markedly evident in earlier collections such as *The Animals in That Country*. The generalized setting of many of the poems is the dusty, brutal, and brutalized countries of the Caribbean and Central America. The central group of poems in *True Stories* deals with political torture: The description of actual tortures is graphic, horrifying, emphasized rather than undercut by the spare, brutal, direct diction and imagery of Atwood's poetic style. Whether the original accounts themselves are true is a question with which Atwood grapples. In the three groups of poems in the collection (including a group of prose poems, "A True Romance") she examines the role of artist as witness-bearer, and the ironies inherent in the examination of truth and reality through art. As in *Two-Headed Poems*, there is a final expression of a tentative faith in and acceptance of life, for all its paradoxes. "Last Day" declares, "This egg/ in my hand is our last meal,/ you break it open and the sky/ turns orange again and the sun rises/ again and this is the last day again." The collection's final allusion, then, is to the egg, universal symbol of immortality and hope.

INTERLUNAR

After *Interlunar*, two books of selected poems have appeared, the first including twenty poems written in 1985-1986 and the second containing no new poems. Atwood's career has seen her turn almost exclusively to prose, perhaps best suited to the very public nature of her position as social arbiter and artistic guru of cultural life in Canada. Interestingly, *Interlunar* returns to the strongly mythological themes, characters, and imagery of her first collections of poems. From the first, the components of Atwood's complex vision have been clear; reading her poetry in chronological order is an odyssey through the maturing and honing of her artistic skills rather than through a definition and articulation of vision.

The mysticism suggested in *Interlunar*'s title is confirmed in the poems themselves. They are arranged in subtitled groups, a favorite device of Atwood; the most fascinating is "Snake Poems," which explores the symbolism of snakes throughout human cultural and religious history. This includes their association with darkness, evil, destructiveness, and the male principle, as well as with wisdom, knowledge, creativity, and the fe-

male principle. Above all, their association with resurrection (for their ability to shed their skins) is explored and viewed (especially in "Metempsychosis") with Atwood's customary ambivalence. Resurrection is also a central theme of the title group of poems, "Interlunar." Intimations of mortality are seen to be on the poet's mind in such poems as "Bedside," "Anchorage," and "Heart Test with an Echo Chamber"; the doubtful comfort of resurrection is ironically considered in a set of poems titled for and concerned with the mythological figures of Orpheus, Eurydice, and Persephone. So Atwood's poems and vision come full circle to her earliest poetic works, *Double Persephone* and *The Circle Game*.

The tone of the collection's title poem, "Interlunar," is uncharacteristically comforting and serene, the statement of a mature artist who recognizes that her odyssey toward understanding in art and life must be without end but need not be frightening: "Trust me. This darkness/ is a place you can enter and be/ as safe in as you are anywhere."

MORNING IN THE BURNED HOUSE

Morning in the Burned House is Atwood's first collection of new poems in a decade. It shows no falling off of skill or intensity and a continuation of all her familiar themes. The poems in this volume tend to a darker lyricism, a sharper awareness of mortality. While it is difficult to separate the personal from the political in Atwood's vision, the strongest newer poems seem to be those that are most intensely personal such as the series on the death of her father. In other poems, the satiric, sardonic, and sometimes outrageously feminist Atwood is very much in evidence.

OTHER MAJOR WORKS

LONG FICTION: *The Edible Woman*, 1969; *Surfacing*, 1972; *Lady Oracle*, 1976; *Life Before Man*, 1979; *Bodily Harm*, 1981; *The Handmaid's Tale*, 1985; *Cat's Eye*, 1988; *The Robber Bride*, 1993; *Alias Grace*, 1996; *The Blind Assassin*, 2000.

SHORT FICTION: *Dancing Girls and Other Stories*, 1977; *Bluebeard's Egg*, 1983; *Murder in the Dark: Short Fictions and Prose Poems*, 1983; *Wilderness Tips*, 1991; *Good Bones*, 1992 (pb. in U.S. as *Good Bones and Simple Murders*, 1994).

NONFICTION: *Survival: A Thematic Guide to Canadian Literature*, 1972; *Days of the Rebels: 1817-1840*, 1977; *Second Words: Selected Critical Prose*, 1982; *The CanLit Foodbook: From Pen to Palate, a Collection of Tasty Literary Fare*, 1987; *Margaret Atwood: Conversations*, 1990; *Strange Things: The Malevolent North in Canadian Literature*, 1995; *Deux sollicitudes: Entretiens*, 1996 (with Victor-Lévy Beaulieu; *Two Solicitudes: Conversations*, 1998); *Negotiating with the Dead: A Writer on Writing*, 2001.

CHILDREN'S LITERATURE: *Up in a Tree*, 1978; *Anna's Pet*, 1980 (with Joyce Barkhouse); *For the Birds*, 1990; *Princess Prunella and the Purple Peanut*, 1995 (with Maryann Kowalski).

EDITED TEXT: *The New Oxford Book of Canadian Verse in English*, 1982.

MISCELLANEOUS: *Murder in the Dark: Short Fictions and Prose Poems*, 1983.

BIBLIOGRAPHY

Davey, Frank. *Margaret Atwood: A Feminist Poetics.* Vancouver, B.C.: Talonbooks, 1984. Presented from a feminist perspective, this book is a nine-chapter examination of Atwood's language, patterns of thought, and imagery in her poetry and prose. The accompanying bibliography and index are thorough and useful.

Grace, Sherrill E., and Lorraine Weir, eds. *Margaret Atwood: Language, Text, and System.* Vancouver: University of British Columbia Press, 1983. These essays by nine different critics treat Atwood's poetry and prose, examining the "Atwood system," her themes, and her style from a variety of perspectives, including the feminist and the syntactical.

Howells, Coral Ann. *Margaret Atwood.* New York: St. Martin's Press, 1996. In this lively critical and biographical study, Howells elucidates issues that have energized all of Atwood's work: feminist issues, literary genres, and her own identity as a Canadian, a woman, and a writer. Focuses on the fiction.

McCombs, Judith, ed. *Critical Essays on Margaret Atwood.* Boston: G. K. Hall, 1988. This indispensable volume comprises thirty-two articles and essays, including reviews of all Atwood's poetry collections and assessments of patterns and themes in her poetry and prose. The entries are arranged in the chronological order of Atwood's primary works, beginning with *The Circle Game* and ending with *The Handmaid's Tale*. It includes a primary bibliography to 1986 and a thorough index. Judith McCombs's introduction provides an illuminating overview of Atwood's writing career and is a satisfying rationale for her choices of the critical pieces in the book.

McCombs, Judith, and Carole L. Palmer. *Margaret Atwood: A Reference Guide.* Boston: G. K. Hall, 1991. This chronological annotated bibliography of criticism traces Atwood's development through several creative stages. Clear, fair-minded annotations capture the diversity of opinion on her work. Includes important interviews.

Mallinson, Jean. "Margaret Atwood." In *Canadian Writers and Their Works: Poetry Series* 9, edited by Robert Lecker, Jack David, and Ellen Quigley. Downsview, Ont.: ECW Press, 1985. This study is divided into the four parts dictated by series format, with "Atwood's Works" the longest and most analytical. Mallinson provides insight into Atwood's poetry, considering as well the literary and critical influences on it. The concluding selected bibliography is useful.

Nischik, Reingard M., ed. *Margaret Atwood: Works and Impact.* Rochester, N.Y.: Camden House, 2000. This sturdy gathering of original (not reprinted) criticism includes Lothar Hönnighausen's comprehensive "Margaret Atwood's Poetry 1966-1995" as well as Ronald B. Hatch's "Margaret Atwood, the Land, and Ecology," which draws heavily on Atwood's poetry to make its case.

Stein, Karen F. *Margaret Atwood Revisited.* New York: Twayne, 1999. A lucid and thorough overview of Atwood's writing in all genres, including two fine chapters on the poetry which examine changes in mood, stance, and selfhood. Includes references and a selected bibliography. This volume supersedes an equally fine (though now outdated) volume in the same series, Jerome Rosenberg's *Margaret Atwood*, published in 1984.

Jill Rollins, updated by Philip K. Jason

W. H. AUDEN

Born: York, England; February 21, 1907
Died: Vienna, Austria; September 29, 1973

OTHER LITERARY FORMS

Though known primarily as a poet, W. H. Auden worked in a number of other forms, making him one of the most prolific and versatile poets of his generation. During the 1930's he wrote one play on his own—*The Dance of Death* (1933)—and collaborated on three others with his friend Christopher Isherwood. These retain their interest today both as period pieces and, to a lesser degree, as experimental stage dramas. The best of the plays, *The Dog Beneath the Skin: Or, Where Is Francis?* (1935), is an exuberant, wide-ranging work containing some of Auden's finest stage verse and illustrating many of his early intellectual preoccupations, including his interest in post-Freudian psychology. The other plays, *The Ascent of F6* (1936) and *On the Frontier* (1938), are of less interest, especially the latter, which is largely an anti-fascist propaganda piece. After the 1930's, Auden turned his dramatic interests toward the opera, writing his first libretto, *Paul Bunyan*, in 1941 for Benjamin Britten. (The work was not published until 1976, three years after Auden's death.) His better-known librettos, written in collaboration with Chester Kallman, are *The Rake's Progress* (1951), *Elegy for Young Lovers* (1961), *The Bassarids* (1966), and *Love's Labour's Lost* (1972). The assessment of the librettos and their relationship to the poetry has scarcely begun. Auden's prose writing, by contrast, has been quickly and widely recognized for its range, liveliness, and intelligence. His work includes dozens of essays, reviews, introductions, and lectures written over the span of his career. Many of his best pieces are gathered in *The Dyer's Hand and Other Essays* (1962) and *Forewords and Afterwords* (1973); other prose includes *The Enchafèd Flood* (1950) and *Secondary Worlds* (1969). In addition to his plays, librettos, and prose, Auden wrote for film and radio and worked extensively as an editor and translator. *Plays and Other Dramatic Writings by W. H. Auden, 1928-1938*, edited by Edward Mendelson, was published by Princeton University Press in 1988. It includes Auden's collaborations with Christopher Isherwood and works by Auden alone.

ACHIEVEMENTS

At a time when poets no longer enjoyed the wide readership they once did, W. H. Auden achieved a considerable popular success, his books selling well throughout his lifetime. He was also fortunate in having several sympathetic, intelligent critics to analyze and assess his work. It is true that Auden had his share of detractors, beginning, for example, in the 1930's with the negative response to his work in the influential journal *Scrutiny*, and, later, in two essays by Randall Jarrell tak-

W. H. Auden (© Jill Krementz)

ing him to task for his various ideological changes. Even today some argue that Auden's work is uneven or that his later poetry represents a serious decline from the brilliance he demonstrated in the 1930's. In a sense, his reputation has been granted grudgingly and, by some, with reservations. Despite all this, however, Auden is generally regarded today as one of the major poets of the twentieth century. Several of his lyrics are well established as standard anthology pieces—"Lullaby," "As I Walked Out One Evening," "In Memory of W. B. Yeats," "Musée des Beaux Arts,"—but his larger reputation may well rest not on the strength of individual poems but on the impressive range of thought and technical virtuosity found in his work as a whole.

Auden's poetry is quintessentially the work of a restless, probing intelligence committed to the idea that poise and clearheadedness are possible, indeed necessary, in a world beset by economic, social, and political chaos. Auden possessed, in the words of Chad Walsh, an "analytic power," an "ability to break a question down into its elements, to find new ways of putting familiar things together." "There is hardly an Auden poem," Walsh concludes, "that does not bespeak, and speak to,

the brain at work." Auden's intelligence, however, is rarely ponderous or pedantic, and part of his lasting achievement may be the blending of playfulness and seriousness that he managed to sustain in much of his best work.

While some may doubt the profundity of Auden's thinking, few question his technical virtuosity. No poet in recent times can match the range of traditional forms he used and often revitalized in his work—oratorio, eclogue, sestina, sonnet, villanelle, closet drama, verse epistle, and ode. Auden often boasted, perhaps with justification, that he had written successfully in every known meter. Perhaps even more than for his use of traditional literary forms, however, Auden is admired for his songs, which Monroe Spears sees as "his most distinctive accomplishment and his most popular." Auden borrowed from an array of musical forms, using irony and parody to transcend the limits of the genre in which he was working. His ballads are especially well regarded, as are many of the lyrics he wrote for the stage.

Over the course of his career Auden received numerous literary honors, beginning in 1937 with the King's Gold Medal for poetry. His other awards include Guggenheim Fellowships in 1942 and 1945; the Pulitzer Prize in 1948; the Bollingen Prize in 1954; the National Book Award in 1956; and the Austrian State Prize for European literature in 1966. From 1956 to 1960, Auden held the honorary position of professor of poetry at Oxford.

BIOGRAPHY

Wystan Hugh Auden was born in York, England, in 1907, the third and youngest son of George and Constance Auden. Before his youngest son was two years old, George Auden gave up a private medical practice in York and moved his family south to Birmingham, where Dr. Auden worked as the city's School Medical Officer. Auden's devout, middle-class family (both his parents were the children of clergymen) gave him a strong sense of traditional religious values and encouraged his early intellectual bent. His mother, Auden frequently said, was the strongest presence in his early years. He was particularly close to her and believed throughout his life that her influence was largely responsible for shaping his adult character.

His father, a widely educated man in both the humanities and sciences, acquainted his son at an early age with classical literature and Nordic myths, and encouraged his reading in poetry and fiction as well as scientific subjects, including medicine, geology, and mining. This early reading was supported by a close familiarity with nature, and Auden as a child developed a fascination for the landscape of limestone caves and abandoned mines that is recalled in several of his poems. Auden's first inclinations were, in fact, toward the scientific and natural rather than literary, and as a young boy he fancied himself a mining engineer. His interest in science continued throughout his life and is reflected in the frequent use of scientific ideas and images in his poetry, and accounts, perhaps, for the stance of clinical detachment found in his early work.

In 1915, Auden was sent as a boarder to St. Edmund's school in Surrey, and, after completing his studies there in 1920, attended Gresham's School, an institution known for its excellence in the sciences. While at Gresham's, Auden gradually came to acknowledge his homosexuality and to question many of his middle-class values and religious beliefs; by the time he left Gresham's, he had abandoned his faith. It was also during this period that Auden, at the suggestion of Robert Medley, began to write his first poems.

In 1925, Auden enrolled at Christ Church, Oxford, where he discovered a congenial social atmosphere far different from the repressive climate at Gresham's. He found in the young don Nevill Coghill a sympathetic, stimulating tutor who was soon informed of Auden's intentions to become a "great poet." After a year of reading in the sciences, Auden turned his interests to English studies and soon developed an enthusiasm for the then unfashionable poetry of the Anglo-Saxon period. This confirmed his preference for the Nordic-Germanic rather than Continental romance tradition, a bias evident in much of his early poetry and, later, in *The Age of Anxiety*, with its close imitation of Old English metric and alliterative patterns.

During the Oxford years and in the decade that followed, Auden was the central figure of a group of writers, including Cecil Day Lewis and Stephen Spender, who shared his liberal political leanings. The 1930's became a sort of golden decade for Auden, a time of intellectual excitement and artistic vitality. With various friends he traveled widely—to Iceland with Louis MacNeice, and to China with Christopher Isherwood. Both visits resulted in collaborative books containing poetry by Auden. In 1937 Auden went to Spain where he worked for the Loyalist cause in the Civil War, which had become a rallying cause for intellectuals of the time. His experience led to the writing of *Spain*, the celebrated political poem that Auden later rejected because of the "wicked doctrine" of its concluding lines; he purged the poem from most subsequent collections of his work. During the 1930's Auden was also active in his home country: He taught school from 1930 to 1935, helped found the Group Theatre in 1932, and published two volumes of poetry that secured for him a reputation as one of the most promising young poets of his generation. In 1935 he married Erika Mann, daughter of the German novelist Thomas Mann, in order to provide her with a British passport.

Auden's writing during the 1930's—both his poetry and the plays written in collaboration with Isherwood—largely constitutes a diagnosis of industrial English society in the midst of economic and moral decay. The diagnosis is made from the perspective of various ideologies that Auden adopted or toyed with during the late 1920's and 1930's—Freudian and post-Freudian psychology, Marxism, and liberal socialism.

In 1939, at the end of a full and brilliant decade, Auden and Isherwood decided to leave England permanently and move to the United States, which they had visited in the preceding year on their return trip from China. Auden's move to New York marked a major turning point in his life and career, for during this period he was gradually shifting away from many of his earlier intellectual convictions and moving toward a reaffirmation of his childhood faith; in October, 1940 he returned to the Anglican communion. Many of his poems in the 1940's record the gradual move toward Christianity, including, most explicitly, his Christmas oratorio, *For the Time Being*. Auden's concern for the ills of modern society did not end, however, with his affirmation of faith, for he pursued this concern in various ways in his poetry, most notably in *The Age of Anxiety*, whose title became a catch phrase for the war-torn decade in which it was written. During the 1940's Auden held teaching posts at several American colleges but continued to write prolifically, working chiefly on his ambitious longer poems.

Auden's life after the 1940's fell into a somewhat more staid routine. In the 1950's he began writing libretti with Chester Kallman, whom he had met shortly after his arrival in America; he and Kallman remained companions and collaborators until the end of Auden's life. From 1948 to 1957 Auden spent each spring and summer on the island of Ischia in the Tyrrhenian Sea, prompting some to suggest that he had entered a post-American phase in his career. Then, beginning in 1957 and for the remainder of his life, he stayed half of each year in New York and half in a converted farmhouse that he and Kallman purchased in the village of Kirchstetten, Austria. In a poem written at the time, Auden saw his departure from Ischia as a reaffirmation of his essential northernness. In Kirchstetten he settled into the happy domesticity celebrated in his *About the House* volume.

In 1972, his health failing, Auden decided to leave New York permanently and spend his winter season each year in a "grace and favour" cottage offered to him by the governing board of his old college, Christ Church, Oxford. As usual, he stayed the following spring and summer in Kirchstetten, and, on his way back to Oxford that fall, died of a heart attack in Vienna. He was buried, as he had wished, in Kirchstetten.

ANALYSIS

Read chronologically, W. H. Auden's poetry moves from alienation to integration; his work is a quest for wholeness, an escape from the isolated self, "where dwell/ Our howling appetites," into a community where the essential goodness of life is acknowledged despite the presence of sin. Over the course of his career, Auden's quest takes many forms, but his goal never varies; from beginning to end, he seeks to discover how love, in all its manifestations, can fulfill man's social and personal needs.

Auden began in the 1930's as a critic of his society, an outsider looking in and finding little to admire in what he saw. His early work is essentially a record of social ills; love is sought but rarely found. As he matures, however, Auden gradually becomes less of a diagnostician and more of a healer; he arrives eventually at a vision of love informed by human sympathy and, later, by religious belief. Once this vision is affirmed in his poetry, Auden again shifts direction, becoming more fully than before a comic poet, intent on celebrating the redemptive power of love and acknowledging the essential blessedness of life. These shifts in Auden's work are, of course, gradual and subtle rather than abrupt, but the division of his career into three phases provides a way to bring some sense of order to a body of work remarkable, above all else, for its diversity.

The early Auden is very much a poet of the 1930's—a time of economic depression and fascism, war and rumors of war. Faced with such a world, he adopts the pose of a clinical diagnostician anatomizing a troubled society. He sees the social and spiritual malaise of his time as a failure of communication; individuals are trapped inside themselves, unable to escape the forces of psychological and social repression that block the possibility of love.

"CONSIDER"

The poems that record Auden's diagnosis of his society are still considered by some to be his best. Although they are often bewildering to readers, they are admired for their energy and intensity, their brilliant, elusive surfaces. One of the most highly regarded of these early poems is "Consider," which illustrates Auden's early technical skill as well as his characteristic themes. The poem is divided into three verse paragraphs, each addressed to a different auditor by a speaker whose heightened theatrical language gives him an aloofness of tone which matches his arrogant message. Auden's voice in "Consider" typifies the detachment and impersonality of the early poems.

The first verse paragraph addresses the reader directly, asking that he "consider" a symbolic modern landscape "As the hawk sees it or the helmeted airman." From this great height, with the objective eye of the hawk, the speaker observes images of society on the verge of collapse: a cigarette end smoldering at the edge of a garden party; decadent vacationers at a winter resort, surrounded by signs of an impending war; and farmers "sitting in kitchens in the stormy fens." The vacationers, incapable of emotion, are "supplied with feelings by an efficient band," while the farmers, separated from them by physical distance and class barriers, yet equally lonely, listen to the same music on the wireless. Though explicitly social and political, the poem is also developed in personal and psychological terms; like the landscape, the individuals in the poem are "diseased," unable to establish genuine personal contacts.

Having drawn this grim picture of "our time," the speaker turns in the second verse paragraph to elucidate the psychological foundation of social ills, addressing, in the process, a "supreme Antagonist," who, according to Edward Mendelson, is the "*inner* enemy" that "personifies the fears and repressions that oppose love." The Antagonist finds an ample number of victims in the decadent society and spreads its evil, "scattering the people" and seizing them with "immeasurable neurotic dread." In this section, the poem's intense language and deliberate rhetorical excess are beautifully modulated, making the speaker aloof and detached yet with an edge of hysteria in his voice.

The final verse paragraph is addressed to the banker, the don, and the clergyman (representatives of the social elite), along with all others who seek happiness by following the "convolutions" of the distorted ego. The poem ends by warning the selfish and the elite of the inescapable psychological diseases that the Antagonist holds in store for them, diseases that will further destroy the possibility for love.

Auden's adaptation of various psychological theories in "Consider" is typical of his method in the 1930's, as is the detached clinical posture of the speaker and the explicit social and political concern voiced in the poem. Auden characteristically offers little hope and, given the extent of the ills he describes, his doing so might well have seemed facile. Auden's earliest poetry sometimes offers an idealized, vague notion of love as a healing force capable of breaking down repression and restoring social and personal relationships to their proper order. Usually, though, this message is faint and clearly secondary to the diagnostic aim of the poems.

"LULLABY" AND "AS I WALKED OUT ONE EVENING"

In two love poems written somewhat later than "Consider," Auden approaches more explicitly the view of love hinted at in the earliest poems. "Lullaby," his best-known lyric, ends with the speaker's hope that his beloved may be "watched by every human love." The poem's emphasis, however, rests on the transience of "human love": The arm upon which the sleeping lover rests is "faithless"; love is at best a temporary stay against loneliness. Likewise, in "As I Walked Out One Evening," Auden stresses the limitations of romantic and erotic love. "Time" lurks in the shadows and coughs when the lovers "would kiss," deflating the romantic delusions satirized at the beginning of the poem. Later, though, near the end, the chiming clocks of the city offer an injunction that suggests a new direction: "You shall love your crooked neighbor/With your crooked heart." Though undercut by a number of ironies, the love described here moves tentatively toward the vision of the 1940's. Even so, the "human love" that Auden evokes in the 1930's seems insufficient to resolve the social and personal ills diagnosed by his poetry.

During the 1930's, Auden gradually left behind the various ideologies he had seriously (and, perhaps, half-seriously) adopted during the decade. Humphrey Carpenter, Auden's biographer, suggests that these ideologies—Marxism, post-Freudianism, liberal humanism—all had in common a fundamental belief in the natural goodness of man. Near the end of the decade, Auden began to question his liberal humanism, partly because of its inability to offer, as he put it, "some reason why [Adolf Hitler] was utterly wrong." The reason he sought turned out to be in Christianity, particularly the doctrine of humankind's sinful nature and his need, because of that nature, for forgiveness and redemption. The quest for love that began in the early poetry thus grows in the 1940's into a quest for Christian love. There is, of course, no sudden shift in Auden's poetry as a result of the new direction in his thinking. Rather, at the end of the 1930's, he begins *gradually* to formulate this vision of *agape*; in a sense, he was already doing so in the two love poems examined above.

"HERMAN MELVILLE"

The poem "Herman Melville," though written a year before Auden "officially" rejoined the Church in 1940, demonstrates his thinking at this crucial period, a time which coincided with his arrival in the United States. The poem also suggests something of Auden's more relaxed, lucid style, a shift which began in the mid-1930's away from the verbal glitter and rhetorical intensity of poems such as "Consider." "Herman Melville" is thus a good example of Auden's thematic and stylistic direction in the shorter poems published during the 1940's.

In the poem Auden describes Melville's life and literary career as a metaphorical "gale" that had blown the novelist "Past the Cape Horn of sensible success" and "deafened him with thunder." Near the end of his life, after Melville had exorcised his demons, he "sailed into an extraordinary mildness," entering a domestic contentment where he discovered "new knowledge"—that "Evil is unspectacular and always human" (Auden develops a similar idea in "Musée des Beaux Arts") and "that we are introduced to Goodness every day." What Melville found, in essence, is what Auden himself was in the process of accepting—the universality of humankind's sinfulness and the possibility that goodness (that is, grace and redemption) can, in an unspectacular fashion, transform the corrupt present, enabling man to transcend his sinfulness.

At the end of the poem Auden describes Melville's exultation and surrender at his discovery of the transforming power of *agape*. The poem, while not autobiographical, certainly seems to be Auden's testing ground, his rehearsal of an idea that had been forming in his mind. Melville's discovery that his love had been "selfish" suggests perhaps that Auden has come full circle from his early poems, now denying completely the efficacy of eros, sexual-romantic love. Auden himself suggests, however, that this is not the case; writing for *Theology* in 1950, he argues that "agape is the fulfillment of eros, not its contradiction." Perhaps "Herman Melville" contains an early formulation of a position whose full complexity Auden had not yet resolved.

THE AGE OF ANXIETY

If "Herman Melville" records Auden's initial approach to Christianity, then *The Age of Anxiety* shows his response to a modern society at odds with the directives of *agape*. The poem is the longest of the four extended works Auden wrote in the 1940's. The bulk of his energy during the decade went into these poems, which were ambitious undertakings in an age when the long poem had all but died out. *The Age of Anxiety* is a "baroque eclogue," a pastoral form entirely incongruous with the poem's urban setting (New York) and its subject matter (four modern-day city dwellers during World War II). Auden also achieves irony with his imitation of Old English metric patterns. The contrast between an epic measure and the pettiness of modern life creates a mock-heroic tone.

The poem begins in a Third Avenue bar where four customers—Quant, Malin, Emble, and Rosetta—drink and discuss their lives. The conversation of these four representatives of modern man becomes an effort to find order in an age of chaos and disbelief. At the outset the characters drink in private corners of the bar, each dreaming (as Monroe Spears puts it) "of his own way of escape, but aware . . . of no recourse beyond the human level." Rosetta, for example, has "a favourite daydream" of "lovely innocent countrysides," while the youthful Emble dreams of success achieved only in a hollow "succession of sexual triumphs." The four dreamers eventually move out of their private corners and begin to discuss the war. As they grow more and more drunk their discussion turns, in the second part of the poem ("The Seven Ages"), to man, "the traveller through time . . . As he bumbles by from birth to death." Their analysis constitutes a psychological study of the maturation process of the individual and leads them to recognize their own failure in coming to terms with life. Their recognition is, however, only momentary, for in the poem's third section ("The Seven Stages") the four figures lapse into a drunken state of unconsciousness and travel over an allegorical dream landscape searching again for a solution of their own, and hence humankind's, dilemma.

Their journey, however, is doomed to fail, for they seek not spiritual enlightenment but a way of escaping it. The first six stages of their vision carry them through (and they believe away from) the anxiety and suffering of the world, but they are merely led deeper into themselves. The truth revealed in the dream is that the world and its anxieties—which they can only see in distortion—are unbearable for modern man. The egotism of the dreamer will not allow them salvation.

The first six stages of the dream explore every possible path of escape. In the seventh stage, however, all hope is lost. They are now, as Emble says, "miles" from any "workable world." The quest has taken them into a landscape of "ravenous unreals." As the chaos closes in on them they turn away from it, refusing to attempt the only true quest—the seeking of spiritual knowledge not in their own illusions but in the redemption of the present moment through a religious commitment. At the end of the poem Malin recognizes the failure of their journey. The moment is not redeemed, but the resolution of the poem defines their failure in Christian terms. In his final speech Malin describes modern humankind's unwillingness "to say Yes" to "That-Always-Opposite" who "Condescended to exist and to suffer death/ And, scorned on a scaffold, ensconced in His life/ The human household."

Thus the poem ends with humankind's refusal of *agape*, his resignation to loneliness, and his unwillingness to forgo egotism and accept the world as redeemed through the Incarnation. *The Age of Anxiety* takes up two main strands in Auden's work—the diagnosis of social and personal ills and the possibility of *agape* as a release from isolation. The four characters in this poem fail to achieve that release.

LATER YEARS

The Age of Anxiety brings to an end what some have called Auden's American period. From 1948 to the end of his life he spent half of each year abroad, and many of the poems of this time reflect the change of landscape. There is also a change in perspective, certainly not as radical as some of the earlier changes but a change nevertheless. Justin Replogle suggests that after 1950 Auden becomes an essentially comic poet whose emphasis shifts away from poetry as a repository for ideas. His work, says Replogle, "begins less to proclaim a belief than to celebrate one." The later poetry, then, is generally lighter in tone and technique than his earlier work, and Replogle's word "celebrate" is especially apt, for there are a variety of celebrations going on in the later work: of the natural world ("Bucolics"), of the five senses ("Precious Five"), of friends ("For Friends Only"), of the ordinary and domestic ("Thanksgiving for a Habitat"), and the earthly happiness ("In Praise of Limestone"). All these celebrations are enacted in *About the House*, a collection which typifies Auden's later style. The book celebrates the rooms of his converted farmhouse in Kirchstetten, Austria, becoming a sort of homage to domesticity.

ABOUT THE HOUSE

About the House is the work of a poet who, in a sense, has arrived. Auden's quest for love as a cure for humankind's ills took him in the 1930's to a landscape of desperation, isolation, and decay. Gradually he discovered a basis upon which, in the 1940's, he could build a vision of *agape*, a knowledge that, despite his sinfulness and guilt, man could be forgiven through grace; love was possible. In *About the House*, nearly forty years after his first poems appeared, the "cure" of love is still at the center of Auden's work; in his later work, however, the possibility of love is not so much proclaimed as celebrated.

"Tonight at Seven-Thirty," the dining-room poem in *About the House*, discusses with wit and charm the place where man enacts a ritual of celebration (the dinner party) that is nearly religious or mythical in its implications—the breaking of bread with friends. If many of Auden's poems call on man to love (often with didactic urgency), then the dining-room poem, like all of *About the House*, is informed by a gentle spirit of love. In one sense, the volume is a celebration of friendship; all the poems are dedicated to close friends, and several of them are addressed to people Auden loved. The *agape* proclaimed earlier now unobtrusively informs every poem as each room of the house becomes a celebration of some ordinary human activity—eating, sleeping, conversing, working.

"Tonight at Seven-Thirty" opens with a clever comparison of the eating habits of several species: plants ("one solitary continuous meal"), predators ("none of them play host") and man (who alone can "do the honors of a feast"). This definition is designed, first of all, to amuse; it nevertheless makes a serious point in asserting that only man—"Dame Kind's thoroughbred lunatic"—can invite a stranger to the table and serve him first. Auden celebrates humankind's capacity for kindness, ritual, and even good manners—another recurrent motif in the later poems.

OTHER MAJOR WORKS

PLAYS: *Paid on Both Sides: A Charade*, pb. 1930; *The Dance of Death*, pb. 1933; *The Dog Beneath the Skin: Or, Where Is Francis?*, pb. 1935 (with Christopher Isherwood); *The Ascent of F6*, pb. 1936 (with Isherwood); *On the Frontier*, pr., pb. 1938 (with Isherwood); *Paul Bunyan*, pr. 1941, pb. 1976 (libretto; music by Benjamin Britten); *The Rake's Progress*, pr.

pb. 1951 (libretto; with Kallman; music by Igor Stravinksy); *Delia: Or, A Masque of Night*, pb. 1953 (libretto; with Kallman; not set to music); *For the Time Being*, pr. 1959 (oratorio; musical setting by Martin David Levy); *Elegy for Young Lovers*, pr., pb. 1961 (libretto, with Kallman; music by Hans Werner Henze); *The Bassarids*, pr., pb. 1966 (libretto, with Kallman; music by Henze); *Love's Labour's Lost*, pb. 1972 (libretto, with Kallman); *The Entertainment of the Senses*, pr. 1974 (libretto; with Kallman; music by John Gardiner); *Plays and Other Dramatic Writings by W. H. Auden, 1928-1938*, pb. 1988.

NONFICTION: *The Enchafèd Flood*, 1950; *The Dyer's Hand and Other Essays*, 1962; *Selected Essays*, 1964; *Secondary Worlds*, 1969; *A Certain World*, 1970; *Forewords and Afterwords*, 1973.

EDITED TEXTS: *The Oxford Book of Light Verse*, 1938; *The Portable Greek Reader*, 1948; *Poets of the English Language*, 1950 (with Norman Holmes Pearson; 5 volumes); *The Faber Book of Modern American Verse*, 1956; *Selected Poems of Louis MacNeice*, 1964; *Nineteenth Century British Minor Poets*, 1966; *A Choice of Dryden's Verse*, 1973.

MISCELLANEOUS: *The English Auden: Poems, Essays, and Dramatic Writings, 1927-1939*, 1977 (Edward Mendelson, editor).

BIBLIOGRAPHY

Bloom, Harold, ed. *W. H. Auden: Modern Critical Views*. New York: Chelsea House, 1989. Arguably the most valuable anthology of Auden's criticism in print because of its comprehensive look at the life, times, and work of the poet, sometimes mistakenly considered a glib or arch-modern poet. Bloom has assembled essays that elucidate the biographical undercurrents of Auden's aesthetic vision with frank consideration of his homosexual relationships and conversion to Christianity. Included here is Edward Mendelson's seminal essay, "Auden's Revision of Modernism."

Callen, Edward. *Auden: A Carnival of Intellect*. New York: Oxford University Press, 1982. A skillful explication of Auden's main poetic themes, chronologically ordered from his 1930's interest in Romanticism to his later embracing of neoclassic aesthetics in the 1960's. Callen stresses Auden's misgivings about Romanticism's weakness in combatting fascism and violations of human individuality that he witnessed in writers such as William Butler Yeats and D. H. Lawrence.

Carpenter, Humphrey, *W. H. Auden: A Biography*. Boston: Houghton Mifflin, 1981. Carpenter had access to private and unpublished material in crafting this comprehensive and compelling critical biography of the poet. It is the key source to biographical detail that an Auden researcher should begin with to situate Auden's poetry within his world and worldview.

Fuller, John. *A Reader's Guide to W. H. Auden*. New York: Farrar, Straus & Giroux, 1970. Fuller has created a sensitive and invaluable guide to Auden's early and later works, offering clear and precise readings of difficult passages. Especially useful is Fuller's careful attention to many of the poet's allusions and influences.

_____. *W. H. Auden: A Commentary*. Princeton, N.J.: Princeton University Press, 1998. Brings to bear a great deal of erudition, along with meticulous critical attention, and covers the plays and libretti as well as the poetry. In this sense, it is indispensable for those readers who want to take Auden seriously, and at his word, on the concern for "truth" in writing.

Gingerich, Martin E. *W. H. Auden: A Reference Guide*. Boston: G. K. Hall, 1977. An immensely useful and annotated compendium of criticism of Auden's major poems through 1974. Auden's students will find this work indispensable in tracing the reception and appreciation of Auden through his early years as a poet to his posthumous reputation.

Mendelson, Edward. *Later Auden*. New York: Farrar, Strauss and Giroux, 1999. In discussing the verse, Mendelson concentrates not only on major works but also praises less well known, later poems. This is a major study of a poet whose cries against social injustice resound far beyond his time and place.

Spears, Monroe K., ed. *Auden: A Collection of Critical Essays*. Englewood Cliffs, N.J.: Prentice-Hall, 1964. This early compendium of Auden's criticism contains excellent exposition of well-known Auden poems and stands out for its inclusion of appreciations and contextualizations by Auden's fellow poets, including Cleanth Brooks and Marianne Moore. Also included are seminal articles by American critics Edmund Wilson ("Auden in America") and G. S. Fraser ("The Career of W. H. Auden") that provide essential biographical backgrounds to Auden's most productive periods of work.

Michael Hennessy;
bibliography updated by the editors

ROSE AUSLÄNDER

Rosalie Beatrice Ruth Scherzer

Born: Czernowitz, Bukovina (now Chernovtsy, Ukraine); May 11, 1901
Died: Düsseldorf, Germany; January 3, 1988

PRINCIPAL POETRY

Der Regenbogen, 1939
Blinder Sommer, 1965
36 Gerechte, 1967
Inventar, 1972
Ohne Visum, 1974
Andere Zeichen, 1975
Gesammelte Gedichte, first edition 1976, second expanded edition 1977
Noch ist Raum, 1976
Doppelspiel, 1977
Es ist alles anders, 1977
Selected Poems, 1977
Es bleibt noch viel zu sagen, 1978
Aschensommer, 1978
Mutterland, 1978
Ein Stück weiter, 1979
Einverständnis, 1980
Mein Atem heisst jetzt, 1981
Im Atemhaus wohnen, 1981
Einen Drachen reiten, 1981
Schatten im Spiegel, 1981 (in Hebrew)
Mein Venedig versinkt nicht, 1982
Südlich wartet ein wärmeres Land, 1982
So sicher atmet nur Tod, 1983
Gesammelte Werke in sieben Bänden, 1984-1985

Ich zähl die Sterne meiner Worte, 1985
Festtage in Manhattan, 1985
Brief aus Rosen, 1994
The Forbidden Tree: Englische Gedichte, 1995
Mother Tongue, 1995
Schattenwald, 1995

OTHER LITERARY FORMS

Rose Ausländer's reputation is based solely on her poetry. Volume 3 of her collected works, containing her writings from 1966 to 1975, includes several short prose pieces; volume 4, containing her writings from the year 1976, comprises, aside from her poetry, only one short autobiographical piece.

ACHIEVEMENTS

In 1957, the highly acclaimed poet Marianne Moore awarded Rose Ausländer the poetry prize of the Wagner College in New York. In 1967, Ausländer received the Meersburger Droste Prize; in 1977, the Ida Dehmel Prize and the Andreas Gryphius Prize; in 1978, the prize of the Federation of German Industry; and in 1980, the Roswitha Medal of the city of Bad Gandersheim.

BIOGRAPHY

Rose Ausländer was born Rosalie Beatrice Ruth Scherzer on May 11, 1901, to Jewish parents in Czernowitz, the capital of Bukovina. Her mother's name was Etie Binder and her father's, Sigmund Scherzer. Originally her father was supposed to become a rabbi, but later he decided to become a businessman. Until 1918, Bukovina was the easternmost part of the Habsburg Empire. The population of Czernowitz was about 110,000 and consisted of Germans, Romanians, Ukranians, Poles, and a large proportion of Jews. The Jewish population had assumed the role of preserving the German culture and of being an intermediary between it and the Slavic culture. As a child, Ausländer was educated in the German-Austrian school system, but she also learned Hebrew and Yiddish. Through her schooling she became acquainted with the German literary classics, especially those by Johann Wolfgang von Goethe, Friedrich Schiller, and Heinrich Heine. She enjoyed a harmonious childhood, which was filled with love toward her parents and her native country. With the advent of World War I and the Russian occupation of Czernowitz, however, this peaceful existence was abruptly terminated. Rose's family fled first to Bucharest and later to Vienna. There they led a life full of suffering and misery. As a result of the Versailles treaty, Bukovina became a part of Romania. The Scherzer family returned to their hometown, where Rose finished her secondary education and subsequently attended the University of Czernowitz, majoring in literature and philosophy. At the university, she became especially interested in Plato, Baruch Spinoza, and Constantin Brunner, a follower of Spinoza who lived in Berlin at that time. Later the teachings of Brunner were to become an integral part of her poetry.

Her studies and her active membership in literary circles exposed her to the poetry of Friedrich Hölderlin, Franz Kafka, Georg Trakl, Rainer Maria Rilke, Else Lasker-Schüler, and Gottfried Benn. Despite their distance from Vienna, the Jewish literary circles in Czernowitz had adopted the Viennese Karl Kraus as mentor. With the publication of the journal *Die Fackel* (the torch). Kraus had assumed the role of the "high priest of truth," the herald of an ethical humanism and poetry against nationalist chauvinism and the corruption of bureaucracy and politics.

In 1921, as a result of the worsening of the family's already dire financial situation following her father's death, Ausländer decided to emigrate to the United States. She emigrated with her childhood friend Ignaz Ausländer. After failing to establish themselves in Minneapolis-St. Paul, they settled in New York City, where they were married in 1923. Ausländer had a position in a bank, and her husband worked as a mechanic. The marriage was not to last; they separated in 1926 and were finally divorced in 1930. In 1924, Rose met Alfred Margul-Sperber, who later became the major sponsor of her poetry after her return to Czernowitz. In 1926, she became an American citizen and in 1927 visited Constantin Brunner in Berlin. She returned to New York in 1928, where she lived with Helios Hecht, a graphologist, writer, and editor of several periodicals. She published her first poems in the *Westlicher Herold-Kalender,* a Minneapolis publication, and later published a few poems in the *New Yorker Volkszeitung.* In 1931, she returned to Czernowitz with Helios Hecht and remained

there to care for her ailing mother. After her prolonged absence from the United States, her American citizenship was revoked in 1934. Eventually she and Helios Hecht separated.

Between 1931 and the outbreak of World War II, Ausländer published poems in various periodicals. Alfred Margul-Sperber arranged for the publication of her first volume of poetry, *Der Regenbogen* (the rainbow), despite the Romanian government's policy of suppressing non-Romanian literature. In 1941, the Germans occupied Czernowitz, forced the Jews to return to the old ghetto, and periodically deported groups to concentration camps in Transnistria. Ausländer and her mother escaped almost certain death by hiding from the Gestapo in basements where friends supplied them with food and clothes. The experience of persecution and underground existence was to become the motivating force behind her later poetry. In secret poetry-reading groups she met Paul Antschel, who later changed his name to Paul Celan. It was during this time that she came to believe in the existential function of poetry to preserve her own identity in a hostile world.

When the Soviet Union seized Bukovina after World War II, Ausländer, together with her mother and her brother's family, left Czernowitz for Bucharest. With the help of friends in the United States, she was able to obtain an immigration visa but only for herself; her family had to stay behind. In the fall of 1946 she arrived again in New York and found work as a translator and foreign-language secretary for a large shipping company. All of her attempts to obtain an immigration visa for her mother proved futile. The news of her mother's death in 1947 caused a psychological breakdown, after which for some time she wrote poetry only in English.

Although Ausländer became naturalized again in 1948, she never felt at home in New York. The American lifestyle remained alien to her. During a visit to Europe in 1957, she again saw Paul Celan, who had emigrated to Paris. He introduced her to contemporary European poetry, which resulted in the rebirth of her poetry in German. The new poems, however, were stripped of all harmonizing prosodic elements.

In 1961, in failing health, Ausländer could not continue her job and was forced to live on her Social Security income. In 1966, she received additional support from the West German government. By that time, she had once again returned to Europe, where she attempted unsuccessfully to settle in Vienna, which was to her the cultural center of the former Habsburg Empire. Finally she moved to Düsseldorf, West Germany, in 1965. The year 1965 was not only the date of the publication of her second volume of poetry, twenty-six years after her first one, but also the year of her belated reintroduction to a German audience. Although she could not return to her native country, she returned to her mother tongue, the only medium through which she could express her poetic message and establish a dialogue with an audience. In 1970, she moved into Nelly-Sachs-Haus, a Jewish home for the aged, which she made her permanent home. After a long illness and an increasing retreat from the outside world, she died in 1988. She left more than twenty thousand pages of manuscripts and typescripts, as well as numerous notebooks, material from which was used to form much of her posthumous collections.

ANALYSIS

Rose Ausländer did not become recognized as a major poet until the late 1960's and early 1970's, when volumes of her poetry appeared in rapid succession. At the same time, various German newspapers and magazines printed some of her poems, and her work appeared in anthologies as well. Because of the outbreak of World War II and her Jewish background, her early writings had never reached a sizable audience beyond her hometown. Not until her visit to Paul Celan in 1957, when she became acquainted with his elliptic hermetic style and that of his European contemporaries, did she adopt the curt, laconic manner of her mature poetry. In this style she vividly expressed the horrors of the Nazi persecution and her total desolation and despair, which continued even after the war, in her exile in the United States and later in Germany. Although the trauma of her persecution and exile was not diminished, she was able to transcend the pain of these experiences to reach a level beyond despair, a new affirmation of life and its riches—each object of which becomes the motif for a poem. Perhaps her hard-won message of consolation and redemption explains the increasing recognition of her achievements.

The titles of Rose Ausländer's collections, such as *Blinder Sommer* (blind summer), *Ohne Visum* (without

a visa), and *Aschensommer* (ash summer), like the images and motifs in the poems themselves, such as "ash," "smoke," and "dust," clearly reveal that Ausländer's poetry is directly linked to the Holocaust. She deeply identified with the suffering of her people. Even her first volume of poetry in 1939, however, reflected a troubled outlook on life. Here, nature, homeland, and love provide a refuge from a threatening reality, as the danger of national socialism loomed on the horizon. Despite their harmonizing prosodic elements, these early poems are characterized by a beginning awareness of the general crisis during these years. This awareness is put into the cosmogonic perspective of the world's fall from its original godlike state. Poetry became to Ausländer the only means of renewing this divine state. This concept is in direct accordance with Spinoza's philosophical theory of harmonizing microcosm and macrocosm. As acceptable as the harmonizing prosodic elements may be in this idealized conception, however, they are self-contradictory in the poems from the underground, appropriately titled *Ghettomotifs*. They first became available to a wider audience in volume 1 of *Gesammelte Werke*, containing the poetry from 1927 to 1956. The English poems written from 1948 to 1956 in the United States continue in this style, which Ausländer abandoned when she was confronted with the modern development of poetry during her 1957 visit to Europe.

HOLOCAUST AND PERSECUTION

Aside from the departure from rhyme and classical meters, her change in style can best be seen in the inclusion of the Holocaust into the cosmogonic process and in the reduction of the imagery to key words or constellations. The images of sun, stars, and earth lose all of their divine characteristics, and references to the Holocaust are so explicit that they evoke the absolute perversion and denaturalization of the human calling. "Ash-summer," "ash-rain" or "smoke is pouring out of the eyes of the cannibals" are only a few examples. The trauma of persecution is carried into the depiction of her experience of exile in the United States. The escape to freedom across the Atlantic resembles the never-ending search of the Flying Dutchman for a final resting place; the Nazi persecution is reenacted in America: "Men in Ku Klux Klan hoods, with swastikas and guns as weapons, surround you, the room smokes with danger"; the "ghetto-garb has not been discarded" despite a "fragrant" table full of food. This threat overshadows all personal relationships: "Can it be/ that I will see you again/ in April/ free of ashes?" The exile only reinforces the expulsion from paradise; the house turns into a prison, New York into a jungle, the subway into a funeral procession of war victims, and the summer heat of one hundred degrees evokes the image of the cremations in the concentration camps. Even more significant, the technology and modern civilization in New York are seen as symbols of the absolute denial of God.

YEARNING FOR HER HOMELAND

Against this background of persecution and exile, Ausländer's native country takes on the qualities of a fairy tale—it is a "once-upon-a-time home" representing a "once-upon-a-time existence"—or is mythologized as filled with the presence of God: "the Jordan river emptied into the Pruth" (the Pruth being the main river of Bukovina, the country of beech trees). Although political reality does not allow a physical return to her homeland, Ausländer's "always back to the Pruth" can only be a spiritual return to the full awareness of her cultural, religious, and family roots, to her beginnings; in its "utopian" fulfillment it would signify the unity of beginning and ending. The poet calls this state "the dwelling," in conscious or subconscious reference to the Kabbalistic *schechina*, which symbolizes the dwelling place of God's bride, or the lowest level of the sefiroth tree. She laments, "Flying on the air swing/ Europe America Europe// I do not dwell/ I only live"; her settling in Germany becomes merely another stage in her continuous exile.

The poet's desire to return to her homeland corresponds to that of the Jewish people to reestablish their homeland in Israel: "Phoenix/ my people/ cremated// risen/ among cypress and/ orange trees." To these "wandering brethren," to "Ahasver, the wandering Jew," she offers the Jewish greeting "Le Cháim": "We/ risen/ from the void/ . . . we are talking/ softly/ with risen/ brethren." Despite that bond, her social and national identity has been lost forever: "born without a visa to this world/ she never looks the other way/ people like us are always/ suspicious." For that reason poetry itself takes over the function of reestablishing a dwelling place that secures Ausländer's spiritual identity.

THE REDEMPTIVE PROCESS

Yet the creative poetic process had to build upon the foundation of annihilation and exile before any redemption and transfiguration could occur. As late as 1979, Ausländer maintained, in a poem: "I do not forget// my family roots/ mother's voice/ the first kiss/ the mountains of Bukovina/ the escape in World War I/ the suffering in Vienna/ the bombs in World War II// the invasion of the Nazis/ the anguish in the basement/ the doctor who saved our lives/ the bitter sweet America// Hölderlin Trakl Celan// my agony to write/ the compulsion to write/ still." In the strictest consistency with her fate, the redemptive process begins, "retracing my steps/ in the urn of memory," and culminates in a paradoxical statement that combines trauma and bliss: "Nothing is lost/ in the urn/ the ash is breathing." The ambiguity of this statement is heightened by the middle line being grammatically linked to both the first and the third lines. This grammatical linking is employed again in these lines: "how beautiful/ ash can blossom/ in the blood." Only by "losing herself in the jungle of words" can Ausländer "find herself again in the miracle of the word," ultimately God's Word, "my word/ born out of despair// out of the desperate hope/ that poetry/ is still possible." Only poetry can grant this renewed existence: "mother tongue is putting me together// mosaic of people" in a space "free of ashes/ among verses." Poetry offers renewed life, the divine breath of life that links past and future in a timeless present: "The past/ has composed me/ I have/ inherited the future// My breath is called/ NOW."

Such stances became more frequent in Ausländer's old age, possibly because the poet, being bedridden, had only poetry left as a means of self-affirmation: "My fatherland is dead/ they have buried it/ in fire// I live/ in my motherland/ the word"—an obvious play on the word "mother tongue," which has taken on the extreme existential function of being the only guarantor of Rose Ausländer's identity. Even then, this process does not entail an escape from reality but rather builds upon "professing to the earth and its dangerous secrets . . . to man I profess myself with all the words that create me." It is a reciprocal act which grants poetic identity by giving meaning to both man and life. For that reason, Ausländer can arrive at an otherwise unbelievable statement affirming the poetic process out of the annihilation of man: "Magnificent despite all/ dust of flesh// This light-birth/ in an eyelash womb/ Lips/ yes/ much remains/ to be said."

Ausländer has called the specific mode of this poetic process "this dual play/ flower words/ war stammering." It is a play of mediation or reconciliation between language and reality that might result in simplistic affirmation if the never forgotten point of departure were not to forbid such a reduction. On the contrary, this play takes on mystical proportions, striving for the redemption of the world by making it transparent to manifest its divine destiny. This interdependence between language and reality culminates in the image of the crystal, in which microcosm and macrocosm meet, in reverence to Spinoza, who was a lens maker as well as a philosopher: "My saint/ is called Benedict// He has/ polished/ the universe// Infinite crystal/ out of whose heart/ the light radiates."

Although the later poems, especially those after 1981, reduce the poetic process to such a degree that they can become manneristic, Ausländer's total poetic production clearly shows her to be among the most significant post-World War II poets. She has been able to find meaning in life despite the traumas she has experienced. Her "self-portrait" lists all the conditions that denied her the status of a regular member of society and at the same time testifies to poetry's power to transcend personal tragedy: "Jewish gypsy/ raised/ in the German language/ under the black and yellow flag// Borders pushed me/ to Latins Slavs/ Americans Germanic people// Europe/ in your womb/ I dream/ my next birth."

BIBLIOGRAPHY

Boase-Beier, Jean. "Translating Repetition." *Journal of European Studies* 24, no. 96 (December, 1994): 403. Any literary translation must involve a careful stylistic analysis of the source text, particularly the translation of poetry. The poem "Damit kein Licht uns liebe" by Rose Ausländer is translated.

Bower, Kathrin M. *Ethics and Remembrance in the Poetry of Nelly Sachs and Rose Ausländer.* Rochester, N.Y.: Camden House, 2000. Critical interpretation of the poetry of Sachs and Ausländer relating to the Jewish holocaust during the second world war. Includes extensive bibliographic references and an index.

Braun, Helmut. *"Ich bin fünftausend Jahre jung": Rose Ausländer zu ihrer Biographie.* Stuttgart, Germany: Radius, 1999. This biography includes an exhaustive bibliography. In German.

Friedericke, Elke P., and Elizabeth G. Ametsbichler, eds. *Women Writers in German-Speaking Countries. A Bio-Bibliographical Critical Source Book.* Westport, Conn.: Greenwood Publishing, 1997. Includes a chapter on Rose Ausländer and an introductory essay that examines the history of literature by women in German-speaking countries. Includes an extensive bibliography.

Glenn, Jerry. "Blumenworte/Kriegsgestammel: The Poetry of Rose Ausländer." *Modern Austrian Literature* 12, nos. 3/4 (1979). A brief critical study of selected poems by Ausländer.

Klaus Weissenberger; bibliography updated by the editors

KOFI AWOONOR

George Awoonor-Williams
Born: Weta, Ghana; March 13, 1935

PRINCIPAL POETRY

Rediscovery and Other Poems, 1964
Night of My Blood, 1971
Ride Me, Memory, 1973
The House by the Sea, 1978
Until the Morning After: Selected Poems, 1963-1985, 1987
Latin American and Caribbean Notebook, 1992

OTHER LITERARY FORMS

Kofi Awoonor is an accomplished writer in a range of genres. He has shown a lifelong interest in the oral poetry of his Ewe-speaking Anlo people and acted as translator of this culture's oral history and literature. His best-known work in this vein is his translation of three modern Ewe poets in *Guardians of the Sacred Word* (1974). He is well known as a political essayist, a role reflected in his larger nonfiction titles, which include *The Breast of the Earth: A Survey of the History, Cul-*

ture, and *Literature of Africa South of the Sahara* (1975), *The Ghana Revolution: Background Account from a Personal Perspective* (1984), and *Africa, the Marginalized Content* (1994). He is also a capable fiction writer, with works that include *This Earth, My Brother* (1971) and *Comes the Voyager at Last: A Tale of Return to Africa* (1992).

ACHIEVEMENTS

Kofi Awoonor has been honored with several awards and fellowships. He held Rockefeller, Longmans, and Fairfield Fellowships and won the University of Ghana's Gurrey Prize for creative writing in 1959 and for poetry in 1979, the National Book Council award for poetry in 1979, the 1988 Commonwealth Poetry Prize for the African region, and numerous other honors, including the Columbia University Translation Award, Brazil's Cruzeiro do Sol, and the Ghana Association of Writers Distinguished Author Award.

BIOGRAPHY

Kofi Awoonor's childhood was spent in the Volta region of Ghana near the seacoast town of Weta. Long a

Kofi Awoonor (© Thomas Bennett)

meeting place for the East and the West, both through agricultural commerce and the slave trade, the Weta area is also known for the strength of its traditional customs and the eloquence of its oral poets who speak the Ewe language. Such poems of Awoonor as "Night of My Blood" and "My Uncle, the Diviner Chieftain" show how deeply and personally the history and culture of his Anlo people influenced his formative years, despite the European surname Williams once appended to his African name (indeed, his first poems were published under the name George Awoonor-Williams). Though highly educated, Awoonor has never turned his back on the culture and beliefs that shaped his early years. In a 1975 interview, he said:

> As society progresses, this whole technological society in which we are living today, we tend to forget about those other mysterious areas of human experience. But hocus-pocus is part of our waking world. I believe strongly, very, very strongly, that I am never alone.

In a way, then, Awoonor's biography is that of a tribal man and cannot be separated from the history of his people. An understanding of his life should include an awareness of the traditions, for example, of the Ewe migration from the town of Notsie in present-day Togo, where the Ewe were held captive by an African tyrant, as well as some knowledge of how deeply the drumbeat penetrates every aspect of his life. While recognizing the holistic virtues of the "African way," Awoonor grew up knowing that all the evils of African life could not be attributed to colonialism.

Awoonor received his secondary education at the famous Achimota Secondary School near the capital city of Accra. At the University of Ghana at Legon, he won his first major literary recognition, the university's Gurrey Prize for the best original creative writing. After graduation, he lectured in English at the university from 1960 to 1963 before taking an appointment as a research fellow and lecturer in African literature at the university's pioneering Institute of African Studies. During the years that followed, he was constantly active, traveling to China, Russia, and Indonesia, editing the literary review *Okyeame*, acting as the managing director of the Ghana Film Corporation, and founding the Ghana Playhouse, where he worked as both producer and actor.

The overthrow of Ghananian president Kwame Nkrumah in 1966 coincided with Awoonor's decision to study abroad. In 1967, with the aid of a Longmans Fellowship, he went to the University of London, where he obtained a master's degree in modern English, focusing on the linguistic features of English in West Africa. A Farfield Fellowship brought him in 1968 to the University of California at Los Angeles. In 1969, he accepted a position at the State University of New York at Stony Brook, where he eventually obtained his doctorate and became chairman of the comparative literature program. Aside from brief trips to Europe and Africa, Awoonor did not leave the United States until 1975, when he ended his eight years of exile at the invitation of the Ghanaian head of state, Colonel Ignatius Kutu Acheampong, to become the chairman of the English department at the University of Ghana at Cape Coast. Awoonor's years in the United States were most productive: He published two volumes of poetry, a novel, a critical study of African literature, and an anthology of Ghanaian poets, which is also a seminal work on traditional oral poets.

Awoonor returned to Ghana with a number of ambitious projects in mind, including the launching of a publishing company, but political turmoil in Ghana interfered with his plans. The Ewe have a long history of nationalistic aspirations (because of arbitrary colonial boundaries, they are divided almost evenly between the present-day nations of Ghana and Togo), and Awoonor was linked to an Ewe military officer's alleged plot to overthrow the government of Ghana. On December 31, 1975, Awoonor was arrested for "harboring a fugitive" and placed in detention in Ussher Fort. His imprisonment lasted more than a year. His poems written during that period (later published in *The House by the Sea*) were smuggled out of prison and sent in letters to America, to one of his publishers, signed with such pseudonyms as I. H. A Birdcry. Following an international outcry and efforts by Amnesty International, Awoonor was released and, in 1977, was sent as Ghana's representative to the International Festival of African Arts and Culture (FESTAC) in Nigeria. In 1978, however, his home was surrounded by troops, and he escaped in the night, slipping over the border to Togo.

From 1978 to 1982, political turmoil continued in Ghana, with elections, coups, and the execution for political corruption of no fewer than three of Ghana's former heads of state, including Acheampong. During this period, Awoonor returned to Cape Coast as dean of the faculty of arts. In 1981, he was awarded a Rockefeller Foundation fellowship to further a study of "the moral perspective in the folktale and the modern novel in Africa."

A paucity of Awoonor's imaginative writings in the 1980's and 1990's attested to his growing involvement in government and foreign diplomacy. In 1989 he was appointed Ghana's Ambassador to Brazil, was reassigned to Cuba in 1988, and from 1990 to 1994 served as his country's permanent representative and ambassador to the United Nations.

ANALYSIS

Generally acknowledged as one of Africa's most exciting poets, Kofi Awoonor has been a significant presence since the publication in 1963 of his first poems, in Gerald Moore and Ulli Beier's *Modern Poetry from Africa*. His work is included in every anthology of contemporary African literature and has been translated into many languages, including Russian, French, Chinese, and German. His presence at various international forums on African literature and the awards he has won to encourage his continued study of oral traditions and contemporary African literature attest his stature, and he has been invited to read his poetry and discuss his work at colleges and universities throughout the United States, England, and Europe.

Although he is one of the most widely traveled contemporary African writers, Awoonor has maintained and continued to explore those links to his Ewe-speaking culture and language that make his poetry effective and unique. He has captured the feel and rhythms of traditional oral poetry in an English which, unlike that of such African poets as Christopher Okigbo and Wole Soyinka, is seldom obscure. In the words of one of Africa's foremost literary critics, Ezekiel Mphahlele (in his introduction to Awoonor's *Night of My Blood*), Awoonor's verse is "the truest poetry of Africa." As Mphahlele says, "Although Awoonor's poetry is packed with ideas, his gentle diction carries us there with its emotional drive, its traditional speech patterns. For all that, the poetry stays on the ground, avoiding any intellectual horseplay."

Whereas Christopher Okigbo (born in Nigeria in 1932 and killed in action with the Biafran Army in 1967), the most critically acclaimed African poet of Awoonor's generation, said that he wrote for other poets, Awoonor has sought a much broader audience, emulating, within the context of African and world literature, the role of the Ewe oral poets among their own people.

Awoonor has led a life exemplary of the committed writer, saying once that he "thrives on opposition and conflict" and stating early in his career that his pet aversions are "poseurs and hypocrites and righteousmen." Always political but never doctrinaire or propagandistic, he speaks with passion about the inequities of the world in a voice that avoids stridency. Indeed, his voice is often as gentle as a lover's, but his vision is unclouded by romanticism. His stance is closest, perhaps, to that of another well-traveled poet who addressed his verse to the common people—Pablo Neruda.

Awoonor's greatest accomplishment may lie in his synthesis of African ideas and Western experience. He reveres the philosophy of Africa yet moves in the technological world of the late twentieth century with ease, drawing from both cultures to forge a literary voice at once genuinely African and distinctly modern. Awoonor's language effects a similar synthesis, carrying the strong music of his native Ewe into English. (He continues to write in his native language, often doing first drafts in Ewe and producing both Ewe and English final versions.) Ewe is a highly tonal language, sung as much as spoken, with tonality determining the meaning of innumerable words. That Awoonor has made the transition from Ewe to English without sounding strained, stilted, or incomprehensible is almost an act of magic.

Awoonor's synthesis of language and ideas strengthens his expression of that "conflict between the old (traditional) and the new (foreign)" that the Nigerian critic Romanus Egudu rightly sees as characteristic of Awoonor's poetry. Indeed, there is a central theme that unifies all of Awoonor's works: the search for a new tomorrow in a recently independent Africa still confused by its bitter colonial past, a search for a synthesis of Western values and technology with the basically humanistic African culture that holds Awoonor's first allegiance. Awoonor, however, unlike many of his contemporaries, does not stop at that point of conflict. Instead,

he works toward a resolution, building a bridge to a new land which may not yet exist but which his work foresees, shaped from both past and present and based on the soil where ancestors are buried but never truly dead.

Awoonor's eloquent exhortation at the end of *The Breast of the Earth* serves as a concise statement of his poetic stance:

> Those who call for a total Europeanization of Africa are calling for cultural suicide. Those who are asking for a pure and pristine journey into the past are dreamers who must wake up. For in the center, somewhere between those two positions, lies the only possibility.

It is in that center, a center which *does* hold, that the poetry of Kofi Awoonor lives.

EARLY PERIOD

A useful key to understanding Kofi Awoonor's poems may be found in his own description in 1971 (pb. in *Palaver: Interviews with Five African Writers in Texas,* 1972) of his poetic development to date, which he divides into three phases "punctuated by my relationship to technique and my relationship to theme." The first phase, which Awoonor calls his apprenticeship, saw the creation of work that drew heavily on the tradition of the Ewe song, especially the dirge form. These laments—which have, as Awoonor puts it, a "lyrical structure with the repetitions of sections, segments, lines, along with an enormous, a stark and at times almost naive quality"—shaped his often anthologized "Songs of Sorrow" and "Song of War."

In the traditional Ewe dirge, the poet usually sings from the point of view of a man overwhelmed by the weight of life and by the enormity and inevitability of death. One should be careful, however, not to mistake this tone for one of total despair or hopelessness. An awareness of death is linked in African philosophy with an understanding that the departed ancestor's spirit still cares for the living left behind, and the bridge between life and death, or—to use a metaphor that both the Romans and the Ewe understand well—the ferry that crosses the river from the land of the living is a much more visible presence to the Ewe than to a contemporary Westerner. Awoonor's early poems fall squarely within that tradition and have images and even whole lines that are direct translations from the dirge poets of

Anlo. Thus, it is with a distinctly Ewe voice that Awoonor speaks in "Songs of Sorrow" when he writes:

> My people, I have been somewhere
> If I turn here, the rain beats me
> If I turn there, the sun burns me
> The firewood of this world
> Is only for those who can take heart
> That is why not all can gather it.

The poem's proverbial message is that suffering must be expected in any human life. It is only those who are able to "take heart," who continue to strive in the face of adversity, who can collect the firewood of the world, not merely surviving within the often hostile environment but husbanding it for their good and the good of others. The catalog of woes that follows—the loss of children, the extinction of great households, the fall of leaders ("the tree on which I lean is fallen")—is thus intended as a realistic appraisal of the worst events that might befall one. Knowing that these things can happen, the person of resolve should be inspired to strive that much harder.

"THE SEA EATS THE LAND AT HOME"

"The Sea Eats the Land at Home" also draws on the tradition of the lament, but it is a more original poem, one that points toward Awoonor's mature style. Blending wide personal experience with ancestral rhythms, the poem describes with photographic accuracy the erosion that has so often threatened the existence of the town of Weta. It captures the living presence of the sea, a capricious deity which men may propitiate but can never control. Awoonor has witnessed its capriciousness more than once (there are destroyed remnants of half a dozen breached seawalls in front of Fort Prinzenstein in Weta), and he has made it visible even to those who have never been to the coast. There is nothing vague or unclear in the poem. It moves with a slow, inexorable dignity that echoes the movement of the sea, ending with lines that resound like the ebb and flow of the waves: "In the sea that eats the land at home,/ Eats the whole land at home." It was a remarkable achievement for a young poet.

"THE WEAVER BIRD"

Awoonor's poems never operate on a single level. As in the traditional Anlo poems, where a leopard is never merely a leopard but may also be a number of other things, including death, an enemy, or the Ewe cult, Awoonor's references to nature are symbolic. Nowhere is this more clear than in "The Weaver Bird." These birds are found throughout Africa. In Ghana, they are brightly colored and raucous birds that make large colonies of finely constructed hanging nests. Beautiful yet obstreperous, creative yet crowding out the other birds in the environment—what better symbol for the colonizing European? At first, in Awoonor's poem, the weaver seems little more than a bird, even though it "built in our house/ And laid its eggs on our only tree." When the bird begins "Preaching salvation to us that owned the house," however, it is obvious that it represents the Christian missionary presence in Africa, a source of confusion for the true owners of the house. Awoonor's poem offers a powerful image of that clash of cultures in which the African is forced to conform to a European value system: "Its sermon is the divination of ourselves/ And our new horizons limit at its nest." Nevertheless, though their traditional ways have been sullied by the invaders, the poet and his people have not been defeated; indeed, the last lines of the poem might serve as an anthem for postcolonial Africa:

> We look for new homes every day,
> For new altars we strive to rebuild
> The old shrines defiled by the weaver's excrement.

"THE YEARS BEHIND": SECOND PHASE

The second phase of Awoonor's poetry is hinted at by "The Weaver Bird." Influenced by his study of Western literature, and particularly by the poetry of T. S. Eliot, Gerard Manley Hopkins, and William Butler Yeats, Awoonor began to write poems which embody in their linguistic texture as well as in their themes the collision of Western and African values.

In his second phase of poetry, Awoonor has said, he dealt "continuously with the theme of the conflict of cultures." The poetry is meant to be a commentary on the way the poet was torn in two by his allegiance to that side and his allegiance to this side, without this conflict ever being resolved. "The Years Behind" and "We Have Found a New Land" are two excellent examples. The former begins with lines that have the tone and diction of an English lyric, flowing with an almost artificial ease: "Age they say cannot wither the summer smiles/

nor will the trappings of our working clothes/ change into the glamour of high office./ Twenty-eight seasons have passed/ and the fleshy flushes of youth are receding/ before the residuary worm's dominion/ in the house of the fire-god." At that point, though, one third of the way into the poem, something begins to happen; the imagery leaves England far behind: "On the sacred stone with the neglected embers/ the cock-offering has fluttered and gone./ The palm-oil on the stone gods has turned green/ and the gods look on concerned and forgotten." The focus of the poem, then, is not on the poet's own approaching age but on the condition of his people and their gods, their culture. Though still alive, that culture is in neglect, while the speaker himself is in exile "among alien peoples whose songs are mingled with mine." What, then, can be done? The answer comes in the last four of the poem's twenty-three lines, with the beat and the wording of a traditional Anlo song. Neither working clothes nor the robes of high office are the proper garb for the poet. He must have a garment that is at once traditional and newly made, much as the famed Ewe weavers make kente cloth from the fine imported threads of England, embroidering it with old symbols that have proverbial connotations:

> Sew the old days for me, my fathers,
> Sew them that I may wear them
> for the feast that is coming,
> the feast of the new season that is coming.

"We Have Found a New Land"

A similar movement can be traced in "We Have Found a New Land," with its ironic image of "smart professionals in three piece" who find this Western costume inappropriate for their tropical homelands and begin "sweating away their humanity in driblets." They think they have "found a new land/ This side of eternity/ Where our blackness does not matter/ And our songs are dying on our lips." In their view, it is the poet—who wears traditional dress and speaks of the old ways, despite his Western education—who has "let the side down," their language reflecting their British overlay. The poet weeps for them—and for that part of himself which has not yet been reborn, for those who "have abjured the magic of being themselves." The conclusion of the poem again holds out a hope for a renewed future by looking to the past: "Reaching for the Stars we stop at the house/ of the Moon/ And pause to relearn the wisdom of our fathers."

"The Wayfarer Comes Home": third phase

In Awoonor's third phase of poetry, his political vision obtains a sense of urgency. Almost absent are poems in which he chooses only to reflect with a sense of detachment on politics, history, and culture. Most indicative of this change are the poems in *The House by the Sea*, which stem from his incarceration at Ussher Fort Prison (the "house" in the title referring to the prison). His words seem inspired by a larger vision, an experience of political repression and cultural genocide, and he urges action in word and deed.

In this phase, his stylistic preference turns to the long poem. In the more than four hundred lines of "The Wayfarer Comes Home," the imprisoned poet looks far beyond the borders of his native Ghana to witness a worldwide struggle for human dignity. Like Awoonor's other long poems, "Night of My Blood" (which retells the story of the Ewe migration), "I Heard a Bird Cry," and "Hymn to My Dumb Earth," "The Wayfarer Comes Home" makes great use of Ewe rhythms, at times even breaking into the native language itself. Like "Hymn to My Dumb Earth," the poem modulates between a prose rhythm tone and a stress rhythm, but this is not a departure from Awoonor's traditional roots. Interestingly enough, this seemingly modern structure, with something like reportage flowing into song (reminiscent of the works of Robert Duncan and Allen Ginsberg), characterizes the Ewe technique in poetry, whereby the cantor makes his address to the audience and then swings into the story.

The unifying image of "The Wayfarer Comes Home" is the "evil animal," the creature that has been created by colonialism, by the misuse of power, by human greed. The poet sees his mission as destroying that beast and prophesies its demise. At the end of the poem, when the poet-hunter—whose vision has ranged throughout the world seeking that empowering feminine presence that is his one true love and his native land—predicts his eventual triumph, it is a triumph for all humanity, one which all human beings should strive for and celebrate.

Until the Morning After

Until the Morning After: Selected Poems, 1963-1985 collects a range of Awoonor's poetry from his earliest published work, *Rediscovery and Other Poems*, through *The House by the Sea* and contains nine previously unpublished poems, some of which are translations of works originally composed in Ewe. These new poems mirror Awoonor's lifelong preoccupation with "life's tears" or "life's winds and fate." In typical Awoonor and Ewe dirge tradition, there is hope beyond death. Life itself is seen as the ultimate "act of faith." The collection also includes a brief autobiographical appendix explaining his relationship with language and writing. *Until the Morning After* helps trace Awoonor's development as a poet, from his early lyrics about nature and heritage, through his politically oriented period formed by his experiences in prison. The title of the volume is based on Awoonor's belief in the basic human need for freedom, and two of his later poems explain that freedom is so important that death will be postponed "until the morning after" it is finally achieved.

LATIN AMERICAN AND CARIBBEAN NOTEBOOK

Awoonor's role as a foreign diplomat and his travels in Brazil, Cuba, and Nicaragua inspired his collection titled *Latin American and Caribbean Notebook*. He takes a defensive and self-accusatory tone here, calling himself "the braggart loudmouth boastful/ uncertain diplomat" ("Rio de Janeiro: Fearful and Lovely City") who serves other countries while his own is being wrecked by corrupt politics and criminals. His feelings of displacement among victims of the black diaspora in other lands—for example, Brazilian squatters or African gardeners in England—is palpable. He notes an ironic solidarity with those who have fallen from the regal anestral glories of their African heritage "down the vast saharas of my history." Coupled with his self-scrutinizing pieces are those that adulate revolutionary heroes of Nicaragua and Cuba and a number of poems that are nostalgic love lyrics ("Time Revisited," "Distant Home Country," "Lover's Song," "Readings and Musings"). In the love poems he reflects upon time and aging and melds childhood memories with the everyday business of a diplomat, condemned to lonely beds in distant cities.

OTHER MAJOR WORKS

LONG FICTION: *This Earth, My Brother*, 1971; *Comes the Voyager at Last: A Tale of Return to Africa*, 1992.

NONFICTION: *The Breast of the Earth: A Survey of the History, Culture, and Literature of Africa South of the Sahara*, 1975; *Fire in the Valley: Ewe Folktales*, 1983; *The Ghana Revolution: Background Account from a Personal Perspective*, 1984; *Africa, the Marginalized Continent*, 1994.

EDITED TEXT: *Message: Poems from Ghana*, 1970 (with G. Adali-Mortty).

TRANSLATIONS: *Guardians of the Sacred Word: Ewe Poetry*, 1974; *When Sorrow-Song Descends on You*, 1981 (of Vinoko Akpalu).

BIBLIOGRAPHY

Egudu, Romanus. *Four Modern West African Poets*. New York: NOK Publishers, 1977. Examines the etiology of conflict in the poetry of Kofi Awoonor and cultural oppression in the poetry of Christopher Okigbo, John Pepper Clark, and Lenrie Peters.

Goldblatt, John. "African Literature: The Common Tongue—A Conversation with Kofi Awoonor." *Transition* 75/76 (1997): 358. Golblatt interviews Kofi Awoonor and explores the roots and commonalities in African literature.

Lindfors, Bernth, ed. *Palaver: Interviews with Five African Writers in Texas*. Austin: African and Afro-American Research Institute, University of Texas, 1972. Explores literary criticism of African literature through interviews with Chinua Achebe, John Pepper Clark, Dennis Brutus, Ezekial Mphahlele, and Kofi Awoonor.

Morrell, Karen L., ed. *In Person: Achebe, Awoonor, and Soyinka at the University of Washington*. Seattle: African Studies Program, Institute for Comparative and Foreign Area Studies, University of Washington, 1975. Presents interviews with and literary criticism of Kofi Awoonor, Chinua Achebe, and Wole Soyinka.

Ojaide, Tanure. "New Trends in Modern African Poetry." *Research in African Literatures* 26, no. 1 (Spring, 1995): 4. Examines the way in which younger African poets have rejected many of the poetic practices associated with the early Christopher Okigbo, Kofi Awoonor, Wole Soyinka, and others. Among the characteristics of the new poetry are the national experience, indigenous and oral modes, and a loosening and diversification of language.

Roscoe, Adrian A. *Mother Is Gold: A Study in West African Literature*. Cambridge, England: Cambridge University Press, 1971. Examines the roots and historical criticism of a range of West African authors, including Kofi Awoonor. Includes bibliography.

Wilkinson, Jane. *Talking with African Writers: Interviews with African Poets, Playwrights, and Novelists*. Studies in African Literature. London: J. Currey, 1992. Provides a series of interviews—Kofi Awoonor among them—and a discussion of the history and criticism of African literature. Includes bibliographical references and index.

Zell, Hans M., et al. *A New Reader's Guide to African Literature*. Rev. ed. New York: Africana Publishing Company, 1983. Traces the history and theory of African literature.

Joseph Bruchac, revised by Sarah Hilbert

B

MIHÁLY BABITS

Born: Szekszárd, Hungary; November 26, 1883
Died: Budapest, Hungary; August 4, 1941

Levelek Irisz koszorújából, 1909
Herceg, hátha megjön a tél is!, 1911
Recitativ, 1916
Pávatollak: Műfordítások, 1920
Jónás könyve, 1940
Hátrahagyott versei, 1941
Vlogatott művei, 1959
Összegyűjtött versei, 1963

OTHER LITERARY FORMS

Although best known for his lyric poetry, Mihály Babits was also among the outstanding essayists of modern Hungary, and his novels and short stories were important expressions of the Hungarian intellectuals' search for their place in a changing society. Equally familiar with the history of European and Hungarian culture, the formal and contextual problems of literature from Homer to the moderns, and the literary struggles of his own times, Babits wrote essays on topics ranging from Henri Bergson and Friedrich Nietzsche to folk literature. Especially revealing of his attitude toward the responsibility of creative artists is his 1928 essay, *Az írástudók árulása* (the treason of the intellectuals), which took its topic as well as its title from Julien Benda's *La Trahison des clercs* (1927). Babits's awareness of the intellectual and artistic ferment of the twentieth century is evidenced by the numerous reviews and critical essays he published.

Babits's novels and short stories are marked by the lyrical approach to prose characteristic of his generation. His short novel *A gólyakalifa* (1916; *The Nightmare*, 1966) is heavily garlanded with the Freudian trappings of the period, particularly with notions concerning dreams and split personalities. The novel *Timár Virgil fia* (1922; the son of Virgil Timár) is closer to the author's own experiences, as it deals with the life of a teacher-priest whose conflict with the urban world ends in tragic isolation, while *Kártyavár* (1923; house of cards) offers a repulsive picture of modern Budapest and its corrupting influence on human character. Babits's best novel is *Halálfiai* (1927; the condemned), an obituary-like tableau of his own generation, a Hungarian *Buddenbrooks* in which embezzlers, small-town curmudgeons, susceptible wives, and representatives of the emerging urban bourgeoisie are masterfully presented. *Elza pilóta vagy a tökéletes társadalom* (1933; Elza the pilot, or the perfect society) is a witty, stylistically elegant, though somewhat anemic utopian novel which takes place in "the forty-second year of the next war," and which is graced by an emphasis on two lasting human values: peace and decency.

Babits's translating activities began as mere philological excursions into other literatures, in part to satisfy his curiosity, and in part to assist him in finding his own voice. In time, however, he developed into one of the most significant modern Hungarian translators, with a range that included classical Greek drama and medieval Latin verse as well as the works of Dante, William Shakespeare, Johann Wolfgang von Goethe, George Meredith, Edgar Allan Poe, Oscar Wilde, and Charles Baudelaire. The impressionistic ease of Babits's early translations was replaced by a disciplined striving for precision and faithfulness.

It should be mentioned among the lasting contributions of Babits that, as the curator of the Baumgarten Foundation and as the editor of the journal *Nyugat*, he exercised great refining, moderating, and encouraging influence on his contemporaries and on younger generations of writers as well.

ACHIEVEMENTS

Mihály Babits, the lyric poet of "restless classicism," embodied the modern synthesis of the Hungarian spirit with the great European values. His only major award came in 1940, when he won the San Remo Prize from the Italian government for his translation of Dante's *La divina commedia* (c. 1320; *The Divine Comedy*). While his humanistic orientation and moral stand remained consistent throughout his life, the marginal nature of his background, combined with the events of his times, presented him with a weighty dilemma: His liberal erudition made him break with the provincialism of the late nineteenth century and urged him to lead his culture toward an acceptance of Western European trends, but his innate idealism made him lean toward conservatism and reinforced his view of literature as an "elite function," independent of any social utility. His writings represent the highest level of urban liberalism in Hungarian literature. Standing on the ground of a humanism which was declared anachronistic and unrealistic by many of his contemporaries, Babits defended the cultural values he considered timeless, against all onslaughts, from Right and Left alike. His experimentation with form and his meticulous craftsmanship enabled him to become one of the most accomplished masters of Hungarian literature. During his declining years, Babits became a living cultural symbol in his country: He dared to produce intellectual writings in an age when the cult of spontaneous life-energy was approaching its peak and young geniuses openly raged against the artistic validity of intellect.

BIOGRAPHY

Mihály Babits was born the only son of an intellectual Roman Catholic family. His father, a circuit judge, was assigned to Budapest and the city of Pécs before he died in 1898. Thus, young Babits became acquainted with various parts of Hungary but always considered Transdanubia (or, as he preferred to call it, Pannonia, after the ancient Roman territory) as his home region. From 1901, he studied at the University of Budapest, majoring in Hungarian and Latin. During his school years, he began to write poetry, and among his best friends he could count Dezső Kosztolányi and Gyula Juhász, who were also to become outstanding poets. After receiving his diploma in 1906, Babits taught in high schools in Szeged, in Fogaras (Transylvania), and in one of the workers' districts of Budapest. His poems were first published in 1902, and by 1908 he was one of the chief contributors to the new literary journal *Nyugat*. During the years preceding World War I, he published several volumes of poetry, read voraciously to acquire a broad European background, and began to translate the

classics. He was opposed to the war from its beginning, and his pacifism became ever more outspoken. The nationalist press of the period attacked him, and one of his poems, "Fortissimo," provoked the confiscation of the journal in which it appeared.

Although decidedly apolitical, Babits welcomed the Revolution of 1918, seeing in it the end of Hungary's participation in the war and the birth of a national republic. As the revolution was quickly taken over by Hungary's handful of Bolsheviks, however, he became disappointed and aloof, even though the short-lived Republic of Councils appointed him professor of world literature at the University of Budapest. His acceptance of this position was harshly criticized in certain quarters during the subsequent years of counterrevolutionary backlash, but by that time his position as one of the central figures in Hungarian cultural life was established.

In 1921, Babits married Ilona Tanner, who (under the name Sophie Török) was herself an accomplished poet. At their summer home, in one of the most picturesque parts of Hungary, they entertained many of the country's best writers and poets. In 1927, Babits was appointed curator of the prestigious Baumgarten Foundation, which had as its aim the aiding of impoverished young writers and artists. This meant not only that his financial situation improved but also that he became perhaps the preeminent literary arbiter in the country—a role that was confirmed when he became the editor of *Nyugat*.

The 1930's brought a series of painful and destructive illnesses to Babits: first polyarthritis, later cancer of the larynx. The frail man underwent dangerous operations which proved to be only half successful. During the last years of his life, he was able to communicate only with the aid of his "talking notebooks." In spite of his illnesses, however, he remained active. In 1940, he was awarded the San Remo Prize by the Italian government for his translation of Dante's *The Divine Comedy* (c. 1320) and subsequently he was elected a member of the Hungarian Academy of Sciences. He died of cancer in 1941.

ANALYSIS

The first volumes of the young Mihály Babits, *Levelek Irisz koszorújából* (leaves from Iris's wreath) and *Herceg, hátha megjön a tél is!* (prince, what if the winter comes?), contain poems representing the best of Hungarian *fin de siècle* aestheticism and secessionist tendencies. Babits rejected both the lyrical approach of his contemporaries—who, in the tradition of Hungarian populism, relied on the anecdotal retelling of subjective experiences—and the pathos of the neo-Romantics. The most frequent object of his early poetry is a cultural experience treated in an intellectualized manner; his own feelings appear only indirectly and in a highly generalized form. Another notable trait of Babits's youthful poetry is its playful richness and variety of tone. The poet refuses to reveal his feverish inner turmoil, his painful loneliness, and his internal conflict between thought and action. He hides behind a number of veils: now a scene from Hindu mythology, now a figure of the Roman Silver Age, now an episode from modern life—many worlds, many styles, many ways of looking at human existence. The poet's touch makes the rather ponderous Hungarian words dance in exciting configurations. Babits's verse can be read in a number of ways, not only because of the virtuoso arrangement of rhyme and rhythm but also because of the shimmering sound and sense of every word within the lines. Perhaps more than any of his Hungarian predecessors, Babits maintained a strong connection with the fine arts, not merely in his themes and images but also in his approach to literature. His stance as a craftsman was consciously chosen to distinguish himself from the multitude of spontaneous and pseudospontaneous versifiers.

Despite his experimental playfulness, Babits's poems are always thoughtful, often philosophical; they are also among the most eloquent expressions of the *fin de siècle*'s characteristic moods: nostalgia, dissatisfaction, and a superstitious, almost mystical *Weltangst*. There are also powerful streaks of Satanism and sin consciousness in his poetry. This strain in Babits's work is not attributable to the poet's personal experience, for he led a quiet, almost ascetic life; rather, it can be viewed as an expression of "preventive guilt," resulting from the purity of his soul: While he recoiled from the touch of the vulgar, he was at the same time attracted by it.

Babits considered himself one of the last descendants of the great Hungarian poets of the nineteenth century and refused to bow to the "vulgar" democratism of his age. His sentences, therefore, remain among the weightiest in Hungarian literature; the poet crammed them with colorful and unusual words, arranged so that the reader is forced to read the lines rapidly, without relaxing his intellectual excitement. If they are to yield their full meaning, though, the sentences have to be broken down and dissolved, somewhat like those of the English sonneteers. As in the work of his great contemporary, Endre Ady, the sentences in Babits's verse have a larger function than simply conveying the idea: With their solidity or elusive airiness, their zigzagging speed or ponderous pace, they are meant to express the atmosphere and the emotional content of the poetic text.

There was a perceptible conflict between the young poet and the culture of Hungary under a dual monarchy, but this was scarcely manifested in writings of social or political content. The overwhelming presence of subjective elements, the almost total exclusion of reality, the adoration of the past, and an emphatic cultivation of Nietzschean individualism are all indicative of Babits's desire to evade having to deal with the present, even at the risk of becoming isolated.

World War I

The years of World War I brought significant changes in Babits's poetry. "The cool glitter of classical contemplation" is gone from the poems written during this period. The style is now simpler and closer to everyday experience, while the poet's active pacifism also forced him to discontinue his flirtation with irrationalism. Babits remained immune to the radical fervor which infected many of his contemporaries, but his desire for peace was passionate and, at times, militant. After he claimed, in one of his poems, that he would rather shed blood for the little finger of his beloved than for any flag or cause, the nationalistic press of the period attacked him sharply. This did not stop the poet from repeating his cry for peace: "Let it end!" The signs pointing toward a great social upheaval in Hungary filled him with hope and enthusiasm: "The world is not a plaything! Here, one must see and create!" Soon, however, it became obvious that he viewed the events of 1919 (the "mud and blood of the revolution," in the words of a Hungarian historian) with increasing apprehension. Hope in the passing of the chaos permeates his writings after 1919, and, in a characteristically bitter image, he compares political ideologies to "slow-acting poisons."

POSTWAR CHANGES

In words as well as deeds, Babits put a distance between himself and public affairs during the post-World War I decades. "Fence in your property!" was his *ars poetica*; he sought to preserve his islandlike independence and remain aloof from politics, which interested him only as "a threatening force, which may seriously interfere with my life." Nevertheless, Babits's withdrawal into the shell of love (as represented by his 1921 marriage, and by the frequent get-togethers with a small circle of friends) cannot be classified as a frightened retreat. In stating his conviction that it is "better not to understand one's age and to be left behind" (repeated later as "noble souls do not pay obeisance to their immediate environments"), Babits remained consistent with his elitist conception of art. As the spiritual leader, later editor, of *Nyugat*, and as the curator of the prestigious Baumgarten Foundation, he remained uncompromising in upholding the highest artistic standards, and he refused to treat literature as a social force, or as a propaganda tool. At the same time, there were anticapitalist pieces among his poems ("The Mice of Babylon") and, realizing that the age of *fin de siècle* individualism was ended, he was enthusiastic about the rise of a socially and politically active neopopulist trend in Hungarian literature. Even his hitherto dormant nationalism was aroused, and in several poems he eloquently pleaded the cause of his nation.

The form of Babits's poetry now changed. The craftsman gave up strict rhyme and rhythm, and assumed the freer style of expressionism, while his sentences became more puritanical, almost democratic in their spareness. He became more aware of the dominance of concrete experience, and registered this with sad resignation, because he could never become a vitalist. The main motive of his poems remains the primacy and freedom of the human spirit over matter, a message he often conveyed with the resignation of a wounded combatant.

JÓNÁS KÖNYVE

With Europe shifting toward the Right and the ascent of Fascism, even Babits found it impossible to remain aloof. He was forced to take sides for moral and intellectual reasons. His condemnation of anything cheap, low-grade, and vulgar—which had made him lose faith in the Bolshevik experiment—was turned against the rising tide of another ideological madness, foreboding new horrors for his continent. He began to revise his views but had no time to complete this task; illness and suffering—which are the topics of several late works in Babits's oeuvre—sapped his energy during his final years. In *Jónás könyve* (the book of Jonah), a confessional allegory on the biblical theme, Babits appears chastened and repentant of his earlier idealism and aloofness: "The wicked find their cronies among the silent!" The most eloquent testimony of the poet, however, is perhaps best summed up in these lines from one of his essays:

I still believe in human reason. I am still convinced that, as far as it reaches, it faithfully serves that which it cannot comprehend, . . . and that the poem will not suffer but improve if it is constructed by human intellect (as long as the Owner watches over the Architect!). Europe has experienced years of mindless horror: Let the age of reason come forth!

OTHER MAJOR WORKS

LONG FICTION: *A gólyakalifa*, 1916 (*The Nightmare*, 1966); *Timár Virgil fia*, 1922; *Kártyavár*, 1923; *Halálfiai*, 1927; *Elza pilóta vagy a tökéletes társadalom*, 1933.

NONFICTION: *Az írástudók árulása*, 1928; *Esszék, Danulmányok*, 1978 (2 volumes).

TRANSLATION: *Dante Romédiája*, 1913, 1920, 1923, 1939 (of Dante's *Divine Comedy*)

MISCELLANEOUS: *Összegyűjtött munkái*, 1937-1939 (collected works, including prose and poetry).

BIBLIOGRAPHY

Basa, Eniko Molnár, ed. *Hungarian Literature*. New York: Griffon House, 1993. A historical overview that provides some background to the life and work of Babits. Includes bibliographic references.

Csányi, László. *Babits átváltozásai*. Budapest: Akadémiai Kiadó, 1990. Thorough biography of Babits with bibliographic references. In Hungarian.

Czigány, Lóránt. *The Oxford History of Hungarian Literature from the Earliest Times to the Present*. New York: Oxford University Press, 1983. A critical and historical overview of Hungarian literature. Includes bibliographic references and an index.

Lengyel, Balázs. "A Poet's Place: Mihály Babits." *The New Hungarian Quarterly* 24, no. 90 (Summer, 1983). A brief critical study of the poetic works of Babits.

Remenyi, Joseph. "Mihály Babits." *World Literature Today* 63, no. 2 (Spring, 1989): 186. In his poetry, Babits reflects the introspective uneasiness of the modern man and his attempts to find meaning in the meaningless life.

András Boros-Kazai

JIMMY SANTIAGO BACA

Born: Sante Fe, New Mexico; January 2, 1952

PRINCIPAL POETRY

Immigrants in Our Own Land, 1979
Swords of Darkness, 1981
What's Happening, 1982
Poems Taken from My Yard, 1986
Martín; &, Meditations on the South Valley, 1987
Black Mesa Poems, 1989
Set This Book on Fire, 1999
Que Linda la Brisa, 2000 (with Benjamin Alier Sáenz; photographs by James Drake)
Healing Earthquakes: A Love Story in Poems, 2001

OTHER LITERARY FORMS

Jimmy Santiago Baca has drawn extensively on the difficult circumstances of his early years and on his involvement with the social and political concerns of his cultural community in his poetry. The autobiographical orientation of his writing often results in a placing of prose commentary amid poetry. Similarly, in his memoir *Working in the Dark: Reflections of a Poet of the Barrio* (1992), essays and reflective accounts of his experiences are blended with passages of poetic intensity. His contributions to collections such as *Between the Lines: Letters Between Undocumented Mexican and Central American Immigrants and Their Families and Friends* (1995)

and *Undoing Time: American Prisoners in Their Own Words* (2000) continue in this mode. *A Place to Stand: The Making of a Poet* (2001) is a recollective re-creation of his youth, adolescence, and years in prison. He also coedited *The Heat: Lives and Legends of Steelworkers* (2001) and wrote, as well as coproduced, the film *Bound by Honor* (1993; released on video as *Blood in, Blood Out*). The letters that Baca and Denise Levertov exchanged between 1976 and 1987 were issued by the Stanford University Library Department of Special Collections in 1998.

Baca took part in several extensive conversations with interviewers during the 1990's, including a discussion with John Keene, which was published in *Callaloo* (1994); an interview with Robert Stuart for the National Public Radio program *Fresh Air* (1993), in which he also reads several poems; an interview with Gabriel Melendez for the *Las Americas Journal* (1990); and an interview with Rudy Miera (1993) that appeared on the official Baca Web site (www.swcp.com/~baca).

ACHIEVEMENTS

Jimmy Santiago Baca has been recognized for his efforts with a National Endowment for the Arts Literary Fellowship (1986), the Pushcart Prize (1988), the American Book Award (1989), and the International Hispanic Heritage Award (1990). He has also served as the Wallace Stevens Professor at Yale (1989) and held the Regents Berkeley Chair at the University of California (1990), and he was the winner of the International Poetry competition at Taos, New Mexico, in 1996 and 1997.

BIOGRAPHY

Jimmy Santiago Baca was born into the chaos of a fractious family living in an adobe shack on the outskirts of Sante Fe in 1952. His father, Damacio Baca, of Apache and Yaqui lineage, and his mother, Cecilia Padilla, a woman with a Hispanic background, left him with his *Indio* grandparents when he was two. Baca stayed with them for three years, then was placed in a boy's home, then foster care, before drifting onto the streets of Albuquerque's barrio at thirteen. In and out of detention and correction facilities, he was in prison at seventeen when he "confirmed" or recognized his iden-

Jimmy Santiago Baca (Lawrence Benton, Courtesy of New Directions)

tity as a Chicano after leafing through a stolen book, *Four Hundred Fifty Years of Chicano History in Pictures*, the only kind of text he could understand, because he was functionally illiterate. Speaking of his father, but alluding to his own situation at that time, he observed, "He was everything that was bad in America. He was brown, spoke Spanish, was from a Native American background, had no education."

In a characteristic act of defiance, he took a guard's schoolbook, glanced at it, and realized that "sounds created music in me and happiness" as he gradually enunciated some lines of a poem by William Wordsworth. Recalling that he was a *vato loco* (crazy dude) serving a five-year term in a federal prison on drug charges, he began a self-directed program of personal education that rapidly led to an explosion of creative energy. Within a short time, he was writing poetry about his current expe-

riences and his troubled past, composing letters for other inmates, and listening to the stories of older men whose stories "made barrio life come alive." A number of his poems were published in the magazine *New Karui*, and with the assistance of Denise Levertov, a prominent poet and social activist, Baca was able to produce a chapbook, *Jimmy Santiago Baca*, in 1978.

Released from prison, Baca traveled to North Carolina to live with Virginia Love Long, with whom he had been corresponding, then returned to Albuquerque, where he worked as a janitor at a treatment center for abused teenagers. There, he met Beatrice Narcisco, a therapist who recognized that, in spite of his unsettled nature, "he was great with children," and they were married six months later. During the 1980's, Baca began to build a national reputation as a poet and graduated from the University of New Mexico in 1984, but he was unable to completely withdraw from drug addiction. *Martín; &, Meditations on the South Valley*, the first of three books which Baca published with the eminent New Directions press, won the Before Columbus Foundation American Book Award, which led to teaching opportunities at Yale and the University of California, Berkeley.

In 1993, Baca cowrote and produced the film *Bound by Honor* and spent much of the 1990's living with his family on the Black Mesa of Albuquerque's South Valley, editing and contributing to various anthologies concerned with issues he cared about, producing films, and reading poetry throughout the Southwest. At the end of the decade he published two compact books of poetry, the intensely personal *Set This Book on Fire* and a collaboration with the photographer James Drake and the poet Benjamin Alier Sáenz, *Que Linda la Brisa* (2000), which included Baca's eight-part searing re-creation of the flow of consciousness of transsexual prostitutes living on the fringes of society. In the twenty-first century, Baca continued to work extensively with at-risk youth in workshops, read his poetry throughout the United States, and declared himself "back in action after a long sabbatical from the publishing world," issuing from Grove/Atlantic a memoir that concentrated on his life inside a maximum security prison, *A Place to Stand: The Making of a Poet* (2001), and a new book of poems, *Healing Earthquakes: A Love Story in Poems* (2001), tracing the course of a romantic relationship from beginning to end.

ANALYSIS

Describing himself as a "detribalized Apache"—a man born and raised outside the predominant social patterns of American life—Jimmy Santiago Baca has based his poetry on a commitment to the presentation and preservation of a marginalized, degraded, and often silent segment of American society. Speaking about his utilization of Chicano motifs in his work, he has said that one can "be successful in this society and still offer it all the resources that come from [one's] culture." His faith in the latent redemptive energy inherent in the production of poetry, an act he regards as responsible for his own survival and which he feels can restore dignity to other people who have struggled with destabilizing psychic states, has enabled him to explore and express conditions of extreme mental and emotional duress. His work, frequently autobiographical in nature, charts a course from near total despair through periods of reversal and dejection toward a life of real accomplishment in literary and social terms.

In conversations about his work, Baca has consistently stressed his belief that poetry is the ultimate act of self-creation, explaining that he has been able to overcome the very grim circumstances of his youth and teen years through a poetic process of anguished rebirth that he says "gives you a brief view of the intense beauty of life." Because his work deals with the most sordid aspects of existence, the "intense beauty" is not reduced or trivialized by easy emotion or appeals to bogus and shallow sentimentality. Contrary to William Butler Yeats's observation in "The Second Coming" that "the worst/ Are full of passionate intensity," Baca's poetry is an endorsement of the redemptive, inspiring qualities that passion communicated through appropriate language can generate. The "passionate intensity" of Baca's work has lost none of its fiery energy or inventive brilliance.

IMMIGRANTS IN OUR OWN LAND AND EARLY POEMS

In his first collection from New Directions, Baca chose a title that expressed his position as an outsider, challenging a dominant culture which had effectively forced his community into a "protective" silence. Most of the poems were written while Baca was in prison, detailing a life in jail often set in sharp contrast with dreams of "the handsome world" outside. The title poem delineates the ways in which inmates establish their own close fraternity of cooperation, and it is characteristic of the ingenuity and methods of endurance to which a beleaguered cohort of society has resorted for survival.

The poems about incarceration are candid and explicit without being brutal, as Baca is not trying to shock a more genteel audience. Their intent is to inform, and the clear-eyed way in which Baca describes his life and the people he met is intriguing without being sensationalistic or falsely romantic. Many of the poems ("In My Land," "So Mexicans Are Taking Jobs from Americans") are specifically political without being polemical, with Baca's stance introducing an element of humor that ameliorates his justified anger. The exuberance of his mocking but ultimately idealistic "The New Warden" is an indication of his unquenchable thirst for a better life and of the guarded optimism that informs his accounts of hard times and hard men.

MARTÍN; &, MEDITATIONS ON THE SOUTH VALLEY

Denise Levertov, who was instrumental in bringing Baca's early work into print, wrote in her eloquent introduction to *Martín; &, Meditations on the South Valley* that the poem "draws upon elements in Baca's own history, but does not duplicate them."

The volume consists of two long narrative poems about Baca's semifictionalized figure, who follows a path similar to the author's in a quest for a stable family and a real home. Along the course of this archetypal journey, the narrator passes through a period of personal desolation, a barren, desert landscape, and then on toward a fertile valley, where he establishes a secure place to dwell. The second half of the volume opens with the destruction by fire of the house that represents Martín's initial removal from the poverty of the past, and then proceeds as Martín returns to the barrio, the place of his worst experiences as a young man. Now, seen from a different perspective, the barrio offers a harsh but penetrating vision of beauty that Martín recognizes as one of the sources of the lyric element found in all his work. The poem closes with the reconstruction of the house destroyed by fire and the impulse to write poems to replace the ones lost in the blaze, including the separate poems in the book itself.

Baca called the poem "the rediscovery of who I was" and noted that it marked his reemergence into the world after years lost to drug addiction. He designed the poem as an attempt to portray the full scope of a Chicano civilization as opposed to the "official" depiction, "a long poem that could describe what happened here in the last twenty years." Poet Gary Soto described the poem as "a sort of *Ironweed* of the West," with many Spanish words, including abundant street slang, that conveyed the unique flavor of a region essentially invisible prior to the work of Baca and others of his generation.

BLACK MESA POEMS

The Black Mesa near Albuquerque was sacred ground to the Isleta tribal group, Baca's *Indio* ancestors, and in the poems in the book of that name, Baca celebrates the geological features of the land and the generations who lived there. "My book is a homage to the people of the South Valley," Baca observed, "a gift of gratitude for keeping the culture alive." By honoring the Chicano community which he regards as his true spiritual home, Baca traces his evolution from anger on the edge of a violence he feels will always be in his soul to a position where he can accept his obligations as a husband and father.

The endurance and ingenuity of the people he writes about in many poems offer examples of maturity and persistence in situations at least equal to Baca's own troubled past. In the anthologized "Green Chile," Baca's tribute to his grandmother, who raised him in his early years, the poet uses the ubiquitous plant, which lends "historical grandeur" to homes and vegetable stands, as a symbol of cultural richness and vividly describes the pleasures involved in the preparation and consumption of a food that permits people to take part in "this old, beautiful ritual" central to Chicano life.

SET THIS BOOK ON FIRE

During the latter part of the 1990's, Baca published his first collection in a decade and contributed an eight-part sequence to accompany photographs by James Drake. *Set This Book on Fire* is divided into three parts, each beginning with a poem—"IN '78," "IN '88," "IN '98"—that sets a tone for the following decade. The initial section is a retrospective consideration of Baca's prison years, centered around the poem "THIS DARK

SIDE," which Baca acknowledges "has always haunted me." He identifies this psychic demon as something that has been "fiercely adamant in its opposition/ to all the good I create." The manner in which he has been able to resist his "dark side" is discussed in "THE DAY I STOPPED" ("being an alien to myself") and several other poems that conclude the section.

Part 2 is a heartfelt evocation of people who have been close to him and a poignant examination of the contrary impulses to be near his family and to return to a vagabond life. Part 3 is a reflective meditation on what it means to be a poet with the poems gathered in a narrative that touches on some of his experiences in elite universities and at times when he "took [his] songs to the gutter to sing them to drunks." The disjunction between poetic ambition and the actuality of the poet's life runs through this section like a dark rhythm, summarized in the last poem, "WHY AND WHEN AND HOW," which concludes with an ongoing query about dreams when "we heard angels/ whisper once in our sleep," which have devolved into moments when words "scatter/ like crumbs on the floor."

QUE LINDA LA BRISA

The eight linked poems in *Que Linda la Brisa* are an effort by a man who admits that he comes "from a macho side" to "get into somebody's skin" who is the polar opposite. The poems are an attempt to understand the psychology of transvestites from the Mexican interior who are working as entertainers in saloons in Juárez. The poem "Smoking Mirrors" begins in the mind of "A hybrid flower/ Of honey and poison,/ half moon half sun," who is "In constant conflict." Baca's ability to understand something of this condition is a consequence of his own internal divisions, and his capacity to appreciate the position of someone on the margins of society owes something to his own heritage as a man born of a cultural confluence marginalized in many ways by "mainstream" America.

OTHER MAJOR WORKS

SCREENPLAY: *Bound by Honor*, 1993 (with Floyd Mutrux and Ross Thomas).

NONFICTION: *Working in the Dark: Reflections of a Poet of the Barrio*, 1992; *A Place to Stand: The Making of a Poet*, 2001.

BIBLIOGRAPHY

Coppola, Vincent. "The Moon in Jimmy Baca." *Esquire*, June, 1993, 48-56. A revealing profile that links the poet's life with his work.

Gish, Robert Franklin. *Beyond Bounds: Cross-Cultural Essays on Anglo, American Indian, and Chicano Literature*. Albuquerque: University of New Mexico Press, 1996. Contains an informative essay on Baca's use of the myth of the legendary city of Aztlán and his consideration of the sociology of the border.

Levertov, Denise. Introduction to *Martín; &, Meditations on the South Valley*. New York: New Directions, 1987. An extremely incisive discussion by the poet who was instrumental in helping Baca publish his work.

Rector, Liam. "The Documentary of What Is." *Hudson Review* 41 (Summer, 1989): 393-400. One of the best literary analyses of Baca's poetic methods.

Schubnell, Mathias. "The Inner Landscape of the Self in Jimmy Santiago Baca's *Martín; &, Meditations on the South Valley*." *Southwestern American Literature* 21 (1995): 167-173. Focuses on the personal and autobiographical elements.

Leon Lewis

INGEBORG BACHMANN

Born: Klagenfurt, Austria; June 25, 1926
Died: Rome, Italy; October 17, 1973

PRINCIPAL POETRY

Die gestundete Zeit, 1953
Anrufung des grossen Bären, 1956
Gedichte, Erzählungen, Hörspiel, Essays, 1964
Werke: In 4 Bänden, 1978
Die Gedichte, 1981
In the Storm of Roses: Selected Poems, 1986

OTHER LITERARY FORMS

In addition to her poetry, Ingeborg Bachmann published two radio plays, three volumes of short stories, and a novel. Much of her prose concerns the role of women in search of their own identity. Bachmann also collaborated with the composer Hans Werner Henze, writing the librettos for his operas *Der Prinz von Homburg* (pb. 1960; the prince of Homburg) and *Der junge Lord* (pb. 1965; *The Young Milford*, 1967). She was praised by critics as a librettist of great talent. Bachmann's other publications include essays in which she discusses her poetic theory.

ACHIEVEMENTS

Ingeborg Bachmann attracted and fascinated readers and critics alike during her short life and has continued to do so since her untimely death in 1973. Bachmann's work has been praised as great and pure poetry, and she has been compared with such towering figures of German poetry as Friedrich Gottlieb Klopstock, Friedrich Hölderlin, and Rainer Maria Rilke. At the same time, the critic Peter Demetz has charged that her verse is marred by a "gauche combination of high polish and utterly sentimental *Kitsch*," and her metaphors have been labeled vague, justifying almost any interpretation.

It cannot be denied that Bachmann's personality and her life, shrouded in mystery to this day, have attracted at least as much attention as her work. After her appearance in 1952 at a meeting of Gruppe 47 (group 47), an influential circle of postwar writers, followed in turn by a story about her in *Der Spiegel*, Germany's mass-circulation newsmagazine (similar to *Time* magazine), Bachmann could never rid herself of her image as a beautiful blonde who had become, of all things, a writer—sensuous yet intellectual, a cosmopolite from a provincial town in Austria, succeeding in a world traditionally dominated by males. When, after her death, her colleagues Günter Grass, Uwe Johnson, and Max Frisch began writing about her, Bachmann, who had already become a legend of sorts, gained increasing recognition as a significant figure in postwar German literature.

Bachmann's appeal derived from a happy fusion of traditional and modern elements. The older generation of readers, reared on Hölderlin and Georg Trakl, appreciated her classical German, while the younger critics welcomed her linguistic experiments, controlled as they were, and what Peter Demetz has called her "hard, dry poems in the manner of the older Brecht." It was, however, mainly because of their themes that Bachmann's poems struck the nerve of their time. In a period when Germans were busy reconstructing their country and enjoying the fresh fruits of the so-called economic miracle, she sent out warning signals of approaching doom. In imploring tones, she attempts to remind her readers that the end of time is near—the titles of her first two volumes, *Die gestundete Zeit* (borrowed time) and *Anrufung des grossen Bären* (evocation of the great bear), are such signals. The poems in these collections clearly define the situation: "Borrowed time, now recalled, grows visible on the horizon"; the "creature of cloudlike fur . . . with tired flanks, and the sharp, half-bared teeth stands threateningly in the sky." In the same breath, however, Bachmann exuberantly announces her readiness for life: "Nothing more beautiful under the sun than to be under the sun. . . ." Bachmann's combination of apocalyptic vision and lyrical affirmation compelled the attention of her generation.

While Bachmann's poems must be understood as products of their time and seen in their historical and cultural context, they have universal and timeless appeal. Bachmann's existential concern, her warnings not to succumb to comfortable adjustment, and the unique poetic quality of her language will continue to capture the imagination of readers.

BIOGRAPHY

The daughter of a schoolteacher, Ingeborg Bachmann grew up in her native Klagenfurt, the capital city of Austria's southernmost province, Carinthia. If the fictional account of *Jugend in einer österreichischen Stadt* (1961; youth in an Austrian town) is any indication, Bachmann's childhood and youth were not particularly happy. Perhaps this accounts for her reticence concerning that period of her life. She does mention the traumatic days of March, 1938, when Adolf Hitler annexed Austria and the German army triumphantly marched into Klagenfurt with most of her countrymen applauding enthusiastically. Otherwise, very little is known about Bachmann's life before the age of twenty-three.

Bachmann initially studied law but soon took up philosophy at the universities of Innsbruck, Graz, and Vienna. In 1950, she received her doctorate with a dissertation on the critical reception of Martin Heidegger's existential philosophy. In 1950 and 1951, she traveled to London and Paris. For two years, she was a member of the editorial staff of Radio Rot-Weiss-Rot, the American-sponsored radio station in Vienna. In 1952, she gave her first reading at a meeting of Gruppe 47.

After the success of her first two books of poetry, Bachmann chose to take up the life of a freelance writer, residing in Rome for many years. Her visit to the United States in 1955, at the invitation of Harvard University, provided the background for the American setting of her highly successful radio play, *Der gute Gott von Manhattan* (1958; the good god of Manhattan). From 1959 to 1960, Bachmann was the first guest lecturer in poetics at the University of Frankfurt. She was awarded many of the important literary prizes of her time, including the Great Austrian State Prize in 1968.

Bachmann died in 1973, following a somewhat mysterious fire in her Rome residence. Five years later, her collected works were published in four volumes by Piper Verlag in Munich. The tenth anniversary of her death sparked renewed interest in Bachmann and was the occasion for many symposia throughout the world on her work.

Ingeborg Bachmann (Courtesy of R. Piper & Co.)

ANALYSIS

With love and joy, departure and death as her prevalent themes, it seems safe to say that Ingeborg Bachmann stays well within the conventions of poetry. Nor is her message novel; after all, the end of the world has been proclaimed many times before in poetry. Bachmann tells her readers solemnly that "the great cargo of the summer" is ready to be sent off and that they must all accept the inevitable end. Time is only borrowed, if one is to believe the ominous title of her first collection of poems. The titles of many of her poems are ciphers of farewell: "Ausfahrt" ("Departure"), "Fall ab, Herz" ("Fall Away, Heart"), "Das Spiel ist aus" ("The Game Is Over"), "Lieder auf der Flucht" ("Songs in Flight"). Indeed, Bachmann's poetry constitutes a "manual for farewells," as George Schoolfield has put it.

Images of night, darkness, ice, and shadow abound in Bachmann's verse. Upon closer inspection, however, one also discovers an entirely different set of images: warmth, summer, sunlight, plant growth. While all these images may look conventional at first glance, one soon discovers that Bachmann has a very private mythological system and that most of her images have meaning only within that system. Many critics have attempted to decode Bachmann's verse; perhaps the most persuasive reading is that of Hans Egon Holthusen, who sees two basic attitudes reflected in Bachmann's poetry. One must agree with his diagnosis that there is a tension between hope and despair or joy and anguish in the fabric of nearly every poem by Bachmann.

DIE GESTUNDETE ZEIT

Bachmann's "dark" or "negative" images are ciphers for what Holthusen calls her "elegiac" consciousness (in contrast to her "panegyric" consciousness, as reflected in her "positive" imagery). Images of ice, snow, cold, or barren landscape represent restricting elements in life, such as the impossibility of communication between lovers. Particularly in her first volume, *Die gestundete Zeit*, Bachmann frequently writes about the coldness of time. The poem "Curriculum Vitae," for example, evokes a winter landscape. In it, life is imaged as a quest for a path laid between ice skeletons. Even in Bachmann's love poems, there are repeated images of snow, ice, and cold.

Such imagery must be related to Bachmann's worldview. Although there are those who see her poems as reflections of a blurry *Weltschmerz* trimmed in beautiful language, her pessimism was earned by experience and reflected a concrete historical situation. Bachmann herself protested frequently against the mere culinary enjoyment of her poetry. Rather, she wanted her poems to be understood as a reaction to the unprecedented horrors of World War II.

"EARLY NOON"

This intention is clear in "Früher Mittag" ("Early Noon"), a major poem of her first collection. In this poem, there are numerous references to Germany's recent past. Having been offered a platter on which is displayed the German heart, Bachmann's lyrical traveler opens the heart, looks inside, and reflects on what he finds: Germany's misuse of idealism and its efforts to disguise the past with what George Schoolfield has called the "simple heartiness of the beer-garden." Fragments of a song by Franz Schubert and a poem by Johann Wolfgang von Goethe, cherished treasures of the German musical and literary heritage, are interspersed with Bachmann's lines reminding the reader, all too painfully, of the aesthetic component of the German mind. In their context, these quotations sound like parodies, for Germany, in the poem, is a beheaded angel, and yesterday's hangmen drink from the golden goblet of Goethe's "Der König in Thule"—who, one must know, was "faithful unto the grave."

The message could not be lost on the German (or Austrian) reader of the poem. After all, loyalty was a key word with which many of Hitler's henchmen defended their actions. Later in the poem, Bachmann conjures up Fyodor Dostoevski's *Zapiski iz myortvogo doma* (1861-1862; *House of the Dead*), provoking visions of Germany as a Siberian labor camp, with all the old jailers still in power—a not-so-subtle reminder that many of Germany's war criminals went free, had their civil rights and privileges restored, and even, in some cases, once again enjoyed positions of power.

"Early Noon" clearly demonstrates that Bachmann did not wish to retreat into a realm of private memories or to hide behind fairy tales, as some critics have charged. On the contrary, it should be mentioned here that even many of her love poems are not as private as they may at first appear. Love, too, is shown as a victim of the modern age. Communication is no longer possible. The poem "Nebelland" ("Fog Land"), for example, is set in the winter. The lost lover is seen as a fish. The speaker is being driven away by ice floes, symbols of despair and desolation.

Although her poems can be related to their historical situation, Bachmann was not, strictly speaking, a political poet. Her methodological approach to language was based on her study of the philosopher Ludwig Wittgenstein. Attempting to discover the limits of human understanding, Bachmann, in "Early Noon," questions the effectiveness of the poetic word. "Where Germany's soil blackens the sky," she writes, "the cloud searches for words and fills the crater with silence. . . ." Silence, the ultimate vanishing point of a poem? In "Early Morning," Bachmann clings to the hope that the unspeakable may still be said. The poem concludes with the words: "The unutterable, gently uttered, goes over the land: it is already noon." As Schoolfield explains, "unutterable" is an abstract noun with two implications. Unspeakable crimes and unutterable beauty come to mind, and beyond these connotations lies a hint that there are problems the complexity of which defies expression.

It should be pointed out that Bachmann's skeptical attitude toward language reflects an Austrian tradition whose roots lie in the linguistic and philosophical dilemmas of the turn of the century. Hugo von Hofmannsthal, in his celebrated *Brief des Lord Chandos* (pb. in a journal as "Ein Brief" in 1902, pb. in book form in 1905; *Letter of Lord Chandos*, 1952), expressed his despair at the ineffectiveness of poetic language. In "Early Noon," an echo of the famous last sentence of Wittgenstein's *Tractatus Logico-Philosophicus* (1922) can be heard: "What one cannot speak of, one must keep silent about."

"AUTUMN MANEUVERS"

Many of the poems in Bachmann's first collection read—in the apt formulation of George Schoolfield—like a *vade mecum* of instruction for dealing with a brief phase of European history. One such poem is "Herbstmanöver" ("Autumn Maneuvers"). In it, Bachmann addresses German readers of the 1950's. They may find personal pleasures by traveling to the most exotic lands, but they will still be afflicted by twinges of guilt—guilt that they will not be able to dispel by claiming that they are not at home.

"BORROWED TIME"

Another such poem is "Die gestundete Zeit" ("Borrowed Time"). When time actually does run out and appears on the horizon, "your beloved," Bachmann writes, "sinks into the sand, which rises to her wandering hair, choking her into silence and finding her mortal, willing to part after each embrace." Once again, the imagery of this poem and its symbols, drawn from nature, should not be regarded as mere ornamentation but rather as integral elements in a "complex totality operating on the outer boundaries of meaning." Again, an individual is shown as being incapable of communication and falling into silence.

"EVOCATION OF THE GREAT BEAR"

One of Bachmann's best-known poems is "Anrufung des grossen Bären" ("Evocation of the Great Bear"). It has been anthologized many times and has provoked numerous interpretations. In spite of its fairy-tale-like introduction and atmosphere, it suggests many parallels with contemporary history.

In the first stanza, the image of a shaggy bear blends with that of the Ursa Major of the stars. The mighty old bear is about to break loose and destroy all of those shepherds, representatives of humankind who have, maliciously or mischievously, invoked him, knowing full well that he would destroy them and their flock, thus bringing about their predicament. In the second stanza, the bear becomes a symbolic bear, and the earth itself becomes a pinecone with which he plays, testing it between his teeth, rolling it between the trees, and grabbing it with his paws—all this symbolizing man's precarious position. A warning follows in the last two stanzas: Contribute to the church and keep the blind man (who shows the bear at carnivals) happy, so that he will not let the beast loose. The bear could still crush all cones, all worlds that have fallen from the trees of the universe. Biblical parallels suggest themselves here: the story of the Last Judgment, the Fall of Man.

In the final analysis, no single interpretation is possible. The total effect of Bachmann's symbolic vocabulary in this poem is to leave the reader in doubt about its exact meaning.

THE VALUE OF POETRY

Bachmann's entire oeuvre can be interpreted as a transformation of inner conflict into art. In a speech of thanks to the donors of an award she received, Bachmann spoke in the following terms of the function of the poet:

> We extend our possibilities in the interplay between the impossible and the possible. It is important for us to create this tension, we grow on it, we look toward a goal, which becomes more distant the closer we get.

In this speech, Bachmann expresses a certain ambivalence about the role of the poet. She vacillates between a firm belief in the eternal value of poetry and poetic language and a sense of its ultimate futility. In the end, the latter prevailed, and she virtually gave up poetry. The few poems that Bachmann wrote after 1956 and published in various magazines all revolve around her doubts about the validity of poetic language. The final poem of her collection *Anrufung des grossen Bären*, titled "Ihr Worte," ends with two ambiguous lines that are indicative of her crisis: "Kein Sterbenswort, Ihr Worte!" (not one more death-prone word, you words!).

Ingeborg Bachmann has been called a poet-thinker. As such, she made heavy demands upon herself, and her work likewise demands much from her readers. Bachmann's readiness to confront, using exemplary lyric language, the issues of Germany's dark historical past as well as the universal problems of modern man has secured for her a permanent position among the great poets of German literature.

OTHER MAJOR WORKS

LONG FICTION: *Malina*, 1971 (English translation, 1989)

SHORT FICTION: *Das dreissigste Jahr*, 1961 (*The Thirtieth Year*, 1964); *Jugend in einer österreichischen Stadt*, 1961; *Simultan: Neue Erzählungen*, 1972 (*Three Paths to the Lake*, 1989).

PLAYS: *Die Zikaden*, pb. 1955 (radio play); *Der gute Gott von Manhattan*, pb. 1958 (radio play); *Der Prinz von Homburg*, pb. 1960 (libretto); *Der junge Lord*, pb. 1965 (libretto; *The Young Milford*, 1967).

BIBLIOGRAPHY

Achberger, Karen. *Understanding Ingeborg Bachmann*. Columbia: University of South Carolina Press, 1995. The first biography of Bachmann in English offers interpretation of her poetry, radio plays, librettos, critical writings, and prose. Achberger is a leading critic and has published a number of articles on Bachmann.

Demetz, Peter. "Ingeborg Bachmann." In *Postwar German Literature: A Critical Introduction*. New York: Pegasus, 1970. A brief introduction to Bachmann's work.

Ezergailis, Inta. *Woman Writers: The Divided Self*. Bonn, Germany: H. Grundmann, 1982. Critical analysis of prose by Ingeborg Bachmann and other authors. Includes bibliographic references.

Gölz, Sabine I. *The Split Scene of Reading*. Atlantic Highlands, N.J.: Humanities Press, 1998. Criticism and interpretation of Ingeborg Bachmann and Franz Kafka's writing with an emphasis on the influence of Jacques Derrida and Friedrich Nietzsche. Includes an extensive bibliography.

Gudrun, Brokoph-Mauch, and Annette Daigger, eds. *Ingeborg Bachmann: Neue Richtungen in der Forschung?* Ingbert, Germany: Röhrig, 1995. A collection of critical essays on Bachmann in German with a section of essays in English.

Lyon, James K. "The Poetry of Ingeborg Bachmann: A Primeval Impulse in the Modern Wasteland." *German Life and Letters* 17 (April, 1964): 206-215. A critical analysis of selected poems by Bachmann.

Schoolfield, George C. "Ingeborg Bachmann." In *Essays on Contemporary Literature*, edited by Brian Keith-Smith. London: Oswald Wolff, 1969. A critical study of Bachmann's oeuvre.

Jürgen Koppensteiner;
bibliography updated by the editors

DAVID BAKER

Born: Bangor, Maine; December 27, 1954

PRINCIPAL POETRY

Laws of the Land, 1981
Summer Sleep, 1984

Haunts, 1985
Sweet Home, Saturday Night, 1991
After the Reunion, 1994
Holding Katherine, 1996 (with Ann Townsend)
The Truth About Small Towns, 1998
Changeable Thunder, 2001

OTHER LITERARY FORMS

Aside from his poetry, David Baker has published a book of criticism about poetry for the University of Arkansas Press: *Heresy and the Ideal: On Contemporary Poetry* (2000). More than a decade of critical essays and reviews about the work of modern American poets are included in this collection. Baker edited *Meter in English: A Critical Engagement* (1996), written by and for practicing poets.

With his wife, poet Ann Townsend, Baker published *Holding Katherine* (1996), a chapbook about the birth of their daughter. He also published the chapbook *Summer Sleep* (1984). The poem "Trees in the Night" was translated into French for the Belgium magazine *Inédit* in 1993. Baker's work has appeared in a variety of anthologies as well as literary magazines such as the *New Yorker, Atlantic Monthly, American Scholar*, and *Poetry*.

ACHIEVEMENTS

David Baker has been awarded grants and fellowships from the Guggenheim Memorial Foundation, the National Endowment for the Arts, the Poetry Society of America, the Ohio Arts Council, and the Society of Midland Authors. He has been honored with a Pushcart Prize and *Mid-America Review*'s James Wright Prize for Poetry. He was selected the 1991 poet of the year by the Ohio Poetry Association. Formerly awarded a student fellowship in 1989 to the famed Bread Loaf Writers' Conference, Baker was named a member of its faculty in 2001. He has participated in numerous national writers' conferences and judged national poetry contests, including those sponsored by the *Kenyon Review*, where he became poetry editor. Baker is a member of the National Books Critics Circle and sits on the advisory boards of the literary journal *Pleiades* and of Zoo Press, publisher of emerging poets, playwrights, and essayists.

BIOGRAPHY

Born in Bangor, Maine, while his father, Donald, was stationed at the now-closed Dow Air Force Base, David Anthony Baker moved with his parents and younger brother Phil to Macon, Missouri, when his father accepted a job with the highway department. Donald Baker was transferred to the state capital of Missouri, Jefferson City, in 1960. David spent his childhood camping and fishing. He went mushroom hunting and learned to identify sea fossils in limestone dynamited by the highway department. An athlete and popular student in high school, Baker and his fellow students in the jazz band cut a record. Baker, a guitarist, took courses in music theory, where he developed his ear for rhythm and harmony.

Gaining experience by playing locally at diners and clubs, Baker, still in high school, performed at the Kansas City Jazz Festival. Immediately following his 1973 graduation, he played banjo for two months in the musical *Hello, Dolly!* at the Cork County Opera House in Ireland and seriously considered a career as a musician. That fall, Baker enrolled in Central Missouri State University (CMSU).

At CMSU, Baker took a course from English professor Bob Jones, who introduced him to poetry. After deciding to teach English in the high school from which he had graduated, Baker enrolled in every English course the university offered but one. Having taken several advanced placement courses in high school, Baker was able to complete his B.A. and M.A. degrees by 1977. A year earlier, he had published a prose poem, "Stories in the Land," in Northeast Missouri State (now Truman State) University's newly established *Chariton Review*. After receiving his master's degree, Baker accepted a position teaching at Jefferson City High School and in 1978 married Charlotte Miller. His early publication encouraged Baker to continue writing, but the demands of high school teaching did not leave him as much time as he needed to do so.

In 1979, Baker accepted a research fellowship at the University of Utah, attracted by its American studies and creative writing programs. At Utah, Baker worked under poet Dave Smith, who often marked Baker's early poetry with different colored inks to show literal, figurative, and potential meanings. During his first two years at Utah, Baker completed a manuscript, *Laws of the Land*, and was urged to submit it to Ahsahta Press. The book, published in 1981, became the core of his dissertation. Baker received his Ph.D. in English in 1983.

Baker refused several tenure track positions to accept a visiting professorship at Kenyon College, home of the *Kenyon Review*. Besides teaching literature and fiction-writing classes, Baker worked as an assistant editor on the *Review*. In 1984, the end of his visiting professorship coincided with the end of his marriage. Baker accepted a tenure track position at Denison University in Granville, Ohio, where he, in 1996, was granted the Thomas B. Fordam Endowed Chair in Creative Writing. Baker met his second wife, Ann Townsend, in Ohio. They married in 1987 and had a daughter, Katherine.

ANALYSIS

David Baker's poetry reflects the influence of time and space in rural communities and the relationships they contain. In images of landscape, and in stories of long-term personal relationships, Baker consistently writes about a future that encroaches on the past. His poetry, rooted in the architecture of human community, tells of the deep histories and small towns that influence his readers' lives. Baker's poems, written in various forms (he is an expert sonneteer) as well as in free verse, offer an extended and verifiable memory of objects and events, even those not always visible to all of his readers or recollected by them.

Empires, and the villages within them, last when time (permanence, custom) and space (expansion, progress) are held in balance; they decay when either time or space is overemphasized. The United States, with its bias toward growth and expansion, depends on the work of poets like Baker, who recall the archeology of specific places and remind their audience of the value of a private history.

LAWS OF THE LAND

Baker's earliest collection illustrates the emotional attachment to landscape that would later suffuse his work. "Stories in the Land," a prose poem about fossil hunting on Missouri Highway 63, tells readers that "words" found "among the rocks" speak to those who will listen. The land Baker writes of in "History as

Place" records the past and is "formed/ by the shape of its dead," by what has lived before.

The carefully metered poems in this collection recall the landscapes of not only Missouri but also Utah and, by incorporating the writing of the eighteenth century spiritual naturalist William Bartram, a lagoon in Florida. The landscapes are connected because Baker shows what the people who live in these landscapes have in common. Bartram, in "Ephemerae," watches the future poet, who watches Bartram "in the sweet/ shade of the past." Baker's family members mentioned in the poem "Antioch Church and Cemetery, 1840-1972," who worked in "the old pit mines," foreshadow the miners mentioned in Utah's "Peabody #7 Strip Mine."

Dave Smith, Baker's former teacher and mentor, writes in the introduction to *Laws of the Land* that Baker wanders the landscape so that his readers may "behold . . . the hope for" and the "idea of home." Indeed, the idea of home, of how long-term relationships influence readers' lives, is like a watermark on the pages of the poems here.

SWEET HOME, SATURDAY NIGHT

Ten years after his first collection, Baker published what writer and *Georgia Review* columnist Judith Kitchen called a "tour de force—as exciting as Eliot's *Waste Land* in its mix of voices, its fractured sensibility, and its visionary sweep." In this, his third book, the poet analyzes the home he was part of even as he is separating himself from it. Missouri is the home where the poet hears "the oldest voices . . . aching again," saying "This is the living we make. This is our love and pain." Missouri is where the poet fondly recalls attending baseball games in the late 1960's and cheering with his family for the St. Louis Cardinals ("never more perfect than now").

The book's twenty-two-page title poem recalls a Saturday night on "August 15, 1977" at the "Com-On-Inn, Rt. 63, Missouri," where the poet is the lead guitarist in a band playing Lynyrd Skynyrd's "Sweet Home Alabama" as he simultaneously sits at a "solitary corner table" watching the band play. The modernist structure of the poem counterpoints the voices of an observer (the sense of the poet as observer emerges in this poem; later work will expand this theme), a participant, a singer, and a postmodern analyst. This integration of voices and the rhythms in which they overlap underscore the sense of meter Baker learned as a musician. In fact, lyrics from familiar songs accompany Baker's own lyrics throughout this book, and the integration, as Baker writes in "Dixie," a long poem written in septets or seven-line stanzas, "signals the going-on of things."

AFTER THE REUNION

In his fourth book, published in 1994, Baker combines his themes of landscape, home, and the relationships that "connect and so sustain" them. The title poem concerns a family reunion in spring ("The lilac hedge let go its whole bushel of odors") so enjoyable that the poet wants to "keep loving" even though his love is "doomed as a rose." The poems center around Baker's Missouri home and the family that lives and dies there. "What could be sweeter/ than the company of family" the poet writes in "Music in the Smokehouse," a long poem that moves from the poet's past where he was too young to "walk through the doorway" of an uncle's smokehouse where relatives are singing, dancing, and loving each other, to the present, where the poet, an adult, still waits "for someone to let me inside." These are poems about the duration of a home, the architecture of a family, and the poet's struggle to use his private history to love, again.

THE TRUTH ABOUT SMALL TOWNS

Published in 1998, this volume, highlighted by Baker's graceful stanzas and his use of contemporary sonnets, tells of time spent with a grandmother at her cast-iron stove, and, in "Home," of the mother who would like him to "come back in." Continuing to explain the pull of land and family, "Dust to Dust" asks, "Who would guess it takes this long to come home?"

Landscape and one's relationship to it contribute to "Treatise on Touch," a nineteen-stanza poem written in quatrains. The poem details how the poet watches his wife's response to not only being tested in a physician's office for nerve damage but also revisiting the convent school grounds of the Sisters of Divine Providence in Pittsburgh, Pennsylvania, where she becomes "a child/ again watched by . . . watchers." Baker noticeably expands one theme in this collection; he is much more open to showing that he observes, or bears witness to, the past and the present. "Still-Hildreth Sanatorium, 1936" describes a grandmother who worked as a nurse in a "mansion-// turned-sickhouse" in Macon, Missouri, before she lay dying in her daughter's house in Jefferson City. The poem recounts Baker's own suffering of

chronic fatigue syndrome, a disease that causes him to die, yet not die, "each night" and imagine his grandmother coming to his room to offer comfort.

As one theme surfaces, another begins to submerge. Though he continues to write about specific places, Baker mentions fewer place names. The private history that has informed Baker's poetry is beginning to go public.

"MIDWEST: ODE"

Baker's Horatian ode, or song, in memory of the poet William Matthews, who died in 1997, first appeared in *The Georgia Review*. The poem not only shows the influence of classical poets, such as Horace and Pindar, but also continues the poet's themes of landscape, history, and human relationships.

Baker praises the Amish way of life, with its "field things hand-wrought" and "piecework quilts." The landscape in this poem is Charm, Ohio, an Amish village in the east central part of the state that holds a Saturday morning market described as "the meeting point/ of many worlds." Again Baker is a witness, this time to the "bearded" Amish "men in mud boots/ and city kids tugging on a goat rope." The poet recognizes that here in this small village, he can observe continuity and discontinuity—the past and the present—in the Amish families who sell their farm produce as they always have and the buyers from the cities and towns "who stare/ and smile." This later poem best exemplifies Baker's belief that "poetry tells you how to live with conflict and with multiplicity."

OTHER MAJOR WORKS

NONFICTION: *Heresy and the Ideal: On Contemporary Poetry*, 2000.

EDITED TEXT: *Meter in English: A Critical Engagement*, 1996.

BIBLIOGRAPHY

Collins, Floyd. "Transience and the Lyric Impulse." *The Gettysburg Review* 12, no. 4 (Winter, 2000): 702-719. After providing a definition and brief discussion of lyric poetry, Collins reviews the work of three contemporary American poets, including Baker, who, Collins says, captures everyday life in well-crafted lyric poems that reclaim personal history. The basis for his discussion is Baker's *The Truth About Small Towns*.

Dobberstein, Michael. "Review: *Laws of the Land*," by David Baker. *The Chariton Review*, Spring, 1983. Dobberstein reviews Baker's first book in considerable detail, relating Baker's poetry to the work of William Bartram, calling the poems a tribute to Bartram's spirit. The reviewer finds a solitude and stillness in the poet's voice.

Genoways, Ted. "Our Town." *Boston Book Review*, May, 1999. The reviewer examines several poems from *The Truth About Small Towns*, quoting them at length to illustrate Baker's technical skill. Genoways comments on Baker's graceful and elegant love poems.

Kitchen, Judith. "For the Moment: Essential Disguises." *The Georgia Review* 46, no. 3 (Fall, 1992): 554-572. Kitchen praises the display of technical skill and postmodern sensibility she finds in *Sweet Home, Saturday Night*. Explaining how all of the poems in the book lead to the title poem, Kitchen remarks that Baker's poetry unifies many aspects of the contemporary self.

Lea, Sydney. "Aging White Men." *The Southern Review* 30, no. 4 (Autumn, 1995): 957-973. Lea carefully distinguishes the poems that are in his view the strongest in *After the Reunion*—he calls the title poem "near-perfect"—explaining that Baker has a distinct voice in a consumerist culture and is "on the cusp of major achievement."

Reiter, Thomas. "Review: *Haunts*," by David Baker. *Quarterly West*, Spring, 1986. Reiter points out that Baker's poetry deals with the personal and the familial, and that this collection is "direct and radiant."

Ginger Jones

JOHN BALABAN

Born: Philadelphia, Pennsylvania; December 2, 1943

PRINCIPAL POETRY

After Our War, 1974
Scrisori de peste mare/Letters from Across the Sea, 1979
Blue Mountain, 1982
Words for My Daughter, 1991
Locusts at the Edge of Summer: New and Selected Poems, 1997

OTHER LITERARY FORMS

Apart from his volumes of poetry, John Balaban published a novel, *Coming Down Again* (1985; revised 1989); a juvenile fable, *The Hawk's Tale* (1988); and several nonfiction books about his Vietnam experience. These include *Vietnam: The Land We Never Knew* (1989) and a memoir, *Remembering Heaven's Face: A Moral Witness in Vietnam* (1991). With coeditor Nguyen Qui Duc, Balaban edited a collection of seventeen short stories, *Vietnam: A Traveler's Literary Companion* (1996). He also wrote a screenplay titled *Children of an Evil Hour*, which was produced in 1969.

ACHIEVEMENTS

John Balaban's deep concern for humanity on the brink of annihilation, which he witnessed during the Vietnam War, is the hallmark of his poetry. Although he explored other areas of human experience, both geographically and historically, as well as his own inner world, the Vietnam factor stayed with him as a sounding board for whatever else came under his scrutiny. In three decades of steady publication his work accumulated the needful critical mass to secure him an enduring place among the very best poets writing in the United States at the dawn of the twenty-first century.

Among his numerous awards and honors, his first book of poetry (published in the United States), *After Our War*, received the Laughlin Award from the Academy of American Poets in 1974 and was nominated for the National Book Award for poetry. His third book, *Words for My Daughter*, was a National Poetry Series Selection, while his fourth book of poetry, *Locusts at the Edge of Summer*, was nominated for the National Book Award and won the Poetry Society of America's William Carlos Williams Award. Balaban was also the recipient of literary distinctions or prizes in Romania, the Steaua Prize of the Romanian Writers' Union (1978) and the Prize for Poetry at the Lucian Blaga International Poetry Festival (1999). In Bulgaria he won the Vaptsarov Medal given by the Union of Bulgarian Writers (1980). In Romania he held a Fulbright-Hayes Lectureship for 1976-1977 and, in 1979, a Fulbright Distinguished Visiting Lectureship. After his alternative military service was completed in 1969, he visited Vietnam in 1971 to work on his translation of folk poetry, in 1985 to study the institutions of the unified country, and in 1989 he lectured for a few days at the University of Hanoi.

Between 1994 and 1997 he was president of the American Literary Translators Association. He was awarded two Pushcart Prizes, for his *Hudson Review* essay "Doing Good" (1978-1979) and for his poem "For the Missing in Action" (1990), originally published in *Ploughshares* and collected in *Words for My Daughter.* Balaban won the National Artist Award of the Phi Kappa Phi Honor Society for 2001-2004. Balaban contributed poems, translations, essays and reviews to such periodicals as *The American Scholar, Asian Art and Culture, Hudson Review, Modern Poetry in Translation, Sewanee Review, Southern Review, Steaua* (Cluj-Napoca, Romania), and *Triquarterly.*

BIOGRAPHY

John Balaban was born to Romanian immigrant parents, Phillip and Alice (Georgies) Balaban. The name Balaban has been traced to a Polish count who led a force against the Turks in about 1510. Both of the poet's parents were of peasant stock. Balaban's father, Filip Balaban, was born in Lovrin, a village in the Banat, while his mother, Alexandra Georgies, came from a nearby village in southwestern Transylvania. The population was predominantly Romanian in the countryside. However, the people did not enjoy any civic rights and freedoms. Balaban's parents met in 1930 in the United States, having immigrated with their respective families before World War I. They married and had two children, a girl and a boy, and their assimilation was quick and thorough.

Balaban showed an early bent toward the humanities and became a student at Pennsylvania State University, majoring in English. In 1966 he received his bachelor's degree with the highest honors. This secured a much-coveted place at Harvard University, where the next year he earned his master's degree. He accepted a position with the International Voluntary Services, a predecessor of the Peace Corps, which fulfilled his alternative ser-

vice as a conscientious objector during the Vietnam War. As a graduate of Harvard, he was appointed instructor in literature and descriptive linguistics at the University of Can Tho in South Vietnam (1967-1968).

The next year he served as field representative for the Committee of Responsibility to Save War-Burned and War-Injured Children, a Boston-based group that offered hospital care to children. It was at this time that he met his future wife Lana (Lonnie) Flanagan, a teacher. Between 1970 and 1992 he taught English and creative writing at his alma mater, Pennsylvania State University, during which time he taught twice as a Fulbright lecturer in Romanian universities.

From 1992 to 2000 he was professor of English at the University of Miami. In 2000 he was appointed professor of English and poet-in-residence at North Carolina State University in Raleigh. In the early 1980's his only child, a daughter, Tally, was born. A westward trip across the United States, during which he hitchhiked through the desert in order to escape the "technological sublime," helped him cope with his memories of Vietnam. What happened during that trip was recorded in *Blue Mountain. Words for My Daughter* continues the attempt to contain and make sense of the past and offer wisdom and guidance to his daughter.

ANALYSIS

John Balaban's main contribution to American poetry is rooted in his unique experience as an eyewitness of and conscientious objector to the mass destruction of the rural population in Vietnam. The uncompromising picture he so powerfully paints deals with the plight of the indiscriminate war casualties among children, women, and elderly peasants. Some were caught in the crossfire between the belligerent armies, but more often than not, they were victims of "collateral damage."

Balaban's was not a straightforward journalistic account but instead a young humanist's response. In order to develop a rapport with the centuries-long tradition of Vietnamese folk and written poetry, he went back to Vietnam in 1971 and became fluent in the language of this tradition. His superb craft was steeled from within by a sense of urgency and outrage, and many of his later experiences yielded a poetry, the richness of which was informed by those early traumatic events.

"AFTER OUR WAR"

"After Our War," the concluding piece of Balaban's first volume of poetry, is a meditation in the wake of the peace agreement signed on January 27, 1973, in Paris, between the United States and North Vietnam. According to that agreement, the United States military would withdraw from the conflict. The poem opens with an apocalyptic vision:

> After our war, the dismembered bits
> —all those pierced eyes, ear slivers, jaw splinters,
> gouged lips, odd tibias, skin flaps, and toes—
> came squinting, wobbling, jabbering back.
> The genitals, of course, were the most bizarre,
> inching along roads like glowworms and slugs.

The tone is bemused, detached, and slightly ironic. The concreteness and specificity of the depiction mark the intensity of the experience. After more details of a like nature, the reader is shocked into the realization that:

> Since all things naturally return to their source,
> these snags and tatters arrived, with immigrant uncertainty,
> in the United States.

The poem concludes with a sequence of questions:

> After the war, with such Cheshire cats grinning in our
>   trees,
> will the ancient tales still tell us new truths?
> Will the myriad world surrender new metaphor?
> After our war, how will love speak?

In "Gerontion," T. S. Eliot had asked a somewhat similar question: "After such knowledge, what forgiveness?" However, there is a significant difference here: Balaban's knowledge was steeped in the nightmare of history. Under such circumstances, the poet asks, is it worthwhile to seek after new truths, mediated by new metaphors? Art seems helpless and impotent in the face of twentieth century genocide.

"SITTING ON BLUE MOUNTAIN . . ."

A poem from Balaban's 1982 volume, "Sitting on Blue Mountain, Watching the Birds Fly South and Thinking of St. Julien Ravenel Childs," throws some further light on the topic of war and violence in the United States. Sitting, watching, thinking aloud, and apparently addressing the person mentioned in the title is a common stance for Balaban. The poem bears an omi-nous motto lifted from Mrs. St. Julian Ravenel's book on the city of Charleston, South Carolina:

> *If the new is, or shall be, better,*
> *purer, braver or higher, it will be well.*
> *This is the tale of the old and* it is done.

While there may be some hope for the future, the past is beyond mending. Forgetful of human history for the moment, the first stanza is about migratory birds heading south toward the Carolinas. After a Whitmanesque catalog, the poet stops and asks himself: "Are these birds worth a whole stanza? Sure,/ they point our noses south; our hearts, to memory."

The entire second stanza is a splendid account of the burgeoning Civil War, the secession of South Carolina, and the battering of Fort Sumter. The character mentioned in the title is the grandson of the author from whose book the motto has been culled, a southerner steeped in the colonial mentality of the slave-owning class. He addresses this man, who could be the poet's brother or his grandfather,

> In 1922, you soldiered in Santo Domingo.
> With Marines led by a latter General Lee
> you chased bandits through riverine jungles
> and saved the cane crop for a New York bank.

The next stanza casts the same doubt as to the scope and potency of poetry: "We live in a world with a simple sense of use/ that doesn't include poetry and musings." Yet in spite of that, the poet declares himself a prisoner of his vocation and craft. He cannot abandon himself to other pursuits, as his addressee cannot escape his delusions. The poem ends on a resigned note, with an implicit comparison between the Blue Mountain of the poet's sublime idealism and the Atlantis of his interlocutor's incurable "dynastic mind."

"WORDS FOR MY DAUGHTER"

A solution to the dilemmas that occupy the poet is attempted in "Words for My Daughter," a frequently anthologized poem. The title recalls William Butler Yeats's "A Prayer for My Daughter," and a comparison of the two poems yields some insight. Balaban seems to be aware that there is no point in sheltering one's offspring from the harsh reality of living. Yeats's prayer, in contrast, is directed toward God, entreating him to protect, insulate, and endow his infant daughter with the graceful arts of gentility. The middle-class Balaban writes to his daughter an account of his own rough childhood environment, thereby educating her in the difficult art of survival. At the same moment, he becomes aware of the healing power he feels as he holds his daughter, which triggers a renewal of hope in his alienated self.

OTHER MAJOR WORKS

LONG FICTION: *Coming Down Again*, 1985, revised 1989.

SCREENPLAY: *Children of an Evil Hour*, 1969.

NONFICTION: *Vietnam: The Land We Never Knew*, 1989; *Remembering Heaven's Face: A Moral Witness in Vietnam*, 1991.

CHILDREN'S LITERATURE: *The Hawk's Tale*, 1988.

TRANSLATIONS: *Ca Dao Vietnam: A Bilingual Anthology of Vietnamese Folk Poetry*, 1974; *Vietnam: A Traveler's Literary Companion*, 1996; *Spring Essence: The Poetry of Ho Xuan Huong*, 2000.

BIBLIOGRAPHY

Beidler, Philip D. *Re-writing America: Vietnam Authors in Their Generation*. Athens: University of Georgia Press, 1991. The collection *After Our War* announces Balaban's sense of the crucial role of the Vietnam poet in remaking Americans' collective cultural experience of this conflict.

Erhart, W. D. "Soldier-Poets of the Vietnam War." In *America Rediscovered: Critical Essays on Literature and Film of the Vietnam War*, edited by Owen W. Gilman, Jr., and Lorrie Smith. New York: Garland, 1990. Describes the lengths Balaban went to in order to absorb the culture of Vietnam, including learning the language and even becoming wounded.

Minar, Scott. *"Words for My Daughter* by John Balaban." Review of *Words for My Daughter. Mid-American Review* 12, no. 2 (1992). Balaban is revealed as a man trying desperately to cope with the memories of this ugly episode in American history.

Rignalda, Don. *Fighting and Writing the Vietnam War.* Jackson: University Press of Mississippi, 1994. Balaban brings Vietnam home to the United States and Americans, while also seeing a more global perspective on the conflict.

Smith, Lorrie. "Resistance and Revision by Vietnam War Veterans." In *Fourteen Landing Zones: Approaches to Vietnam War Literature*, edited by Philip K. Jason. Iowa City: University of Iowa Press, 1991. Balaban implicates the reader in the decision to fight in Vietnam by calling it "our" war.

Stefan Stoenescu

AMIRI BARAKA

Everett LeRoi Jones

Born: Newark, New Jersey; October 7, 1934

PRINCIPAL POETRY

Preface to a Twenty Volume Suicide Note, 1961
The Dead Lecturer, 1964
Black Art, 1966
A Poem for Black Hearts, 1967
Black Magic: Sabotage, Target Study, Black Art—Collected Poetry, 1961-1967, 1969
It's Nation Time, 1970
In Our Terribleness: Some Elements and Meaning in Black Style, 1970
Spirit Reach, 1972
Afrikan Revolution, 1973
Hard Facts, 1975
Selected Poetry of Amiri Baraka/LeRoi Jones, 1979
Reggae or Not!, 1981
Wise, Why's, Y's, 1995
Transbluesency: The Selected Poems of Amiri Baraka, 1995
Funk Lore: New Poems, 1984-1995, 1996

OTHER LITERARY FORMS

Amiri Baraka is a protean literary figure, equally well known for his poetry, drama, and essays. In addition, he has written short stories and experimental fiction. Baraka's early plays, notably *Dutchman* (1964), *The Slave* (1964), and *The Toilet* (1964), were produced under his given name, LeRoi Jones, and derive from his period of involvement with the New York City avant-garde. Baraka's critical and political prose has appeared in many collections, and throughout his career he has also been active as an anthologist of African American literature.

ACHIEVEMENTS

Amiri Baraka has been the recipient of many awards and honors. He won the Longview Best Essay of the Year award (1961) for his essay "Cuba Libre"; the John Whitney Foundation fellowship for poetry and fiction (1962); the Obie Award for Best American Off-Broadway Play of 1964 for *Dutchman*; a Guggenheim Fellowship (1965-1966); second prize in the International Art Festival of Dakar (1966) for his play *The Slave*; a National Endowment for the Arts grant (1966); a doctorate of humane letters from Malcolm X College in Chicago (1972); appointment as a Rockefeller Foundation Fellow in drama (1981); a National Endowment for the Arts poetry award (1981); a New Jersey Council for the Arts award (1982); the American Book Award (Before Columbus Foundation) for *Confirmation: An Anthology of African-American Women* (1983); a PEN-Faulkner Award (1989); the Langston Hughes Medal (1989) for his outstanding contributions to literature; Italy's Ferroni Award and Foreign Poet Award (1993); and the Playwright's Award from the Black Drama Festival of Winston-Salem, North Carolina, in 1997.

BIOGRAPHY

Amiri Baraka, as he has been known since 1967, was born Everett LeRoi Jones into a black middle-class family in Newark, New Jersey. An excellent student whose parents encouraged his intellectual interests, Jones was graduated from Howard University of Washington, D.C., in 1954 at the age of nineteen. After spending two years in the United States Air Force, primarily in Puerto Rico, he moved to Greenwich Village, where he embarked on his literary career in 1957. During the early stage of his career, Jones associated closely with numerous white avant-garde poets, including Robert Creeley, Allen Ginsberg, Robert Duncan, and Dianne DiPrima, with whom he founded the American Theatre for Poets in 1961. Marrying Hettie Cohen, a white woman with whom he edited the magazine *Yugen* from 1958 to 1963,

Amiri Baraka (Library of Congress)

Jones established himself as an important young poet, critic, and editor. Among the many magazines to which he contributed was *Downbeat*, the jazz journal where he first developed many of the musical interests which were to have such a large impact on his later poetry. The political interests which were to dominate Jones's later work were unmistakably present as early as 1960 when he toured Cuba with a group of black intellectuals. This event sparked his perception of the United States as a corrupt bourgeois society and seems particularly significant in relation to his later socialist emphasis. Jones's growing political interest conditioned his first produced plays, including the Obie Award-winning *Dutchman* (1964), which anticipated the first major transformation of Jones's life.

Separating from Hettie Cohen and severing ties with his white associates, Jones moved from the Village to Harlem in 1965. Turning his attention to direct action within the black community, he founded the Black Arts Theatre and School in Harlem and, following his return to his native city in 1966, the Spirit House in Newark. After marrying a black woman, Sylvia Robinson (Amina Baraka) in 1966, Jones adopted his new name, which means "Prince" (Ameer) "the blessed one" (Baraka), along with the honorary title of "Imamu." Over the next half dozen years, Baraka helped found and develop the Black Community Development and Defense Organization, the Congress of African Peoples (convened in Atlanta in 1970), and the National Black Political Convention (convened in Gary, Indiana, in 1972). As a leading spokesman of the Black Arts movement, Baraka provided support for young black poets and playwrights, including Larry Neal, Ed Bullins, Marvin X, and Ron Milner. During the Newark uprising/riot of 1967, Baraka was arrested for unlawful possession of firearms. Although he was convicted and given the maximum sentence after the judge read his poem "Black People!" as an example of incitement to riot, Baraka was later cleared on appeal.

Baraka supported Kenneth A. Gibson's campaign to become the first black mayor of Newark in 1970, but he later broke with Gibson over what he perceived as the bourgeois values of the administration. This disillusionment with black politics within the American system, combined with Baraka's attendance at the Sixth Pan-African Conference at Dar es Salaam in 1974, precipitated the subsequent stage of his political evolution. While not abandoning his commitment to confronting the special problems of African Americans in the United States, Baraka came to interpret these problems within the framework of an overarching Marxist-Leninist-Maoist philosophy. In conjunction with this second transformation, Baraka dropped the title "Imamu" and changed the name of his Newark publishing firm from "Jihad" to "People's War."

Baraka has continued to teach, lecture, and conduct workshops, and he is noted not only for his writings but also for his influence on young writers and social critics. He is the editor of *Black Nation*, the organ of the League of Revolutionary Struggle, a Marxist organization. His influence extends far beyond African American culture and politics to embrace other people of color. Native American writer Maurice Kenney, for example, credited

Baraka for teaching ethnic writers how to open doors to important venues for their writing, to "claim and take" their place at the cultural forefront.

ANALYSIS

Amiri Baraka's importance as a poet rests on both the diversity of his work and the singular intensity of his Black Nationalist period. In fact, Baraka's diversity gave his nationalist poetry a symbolic significance with personal, political, and aesthetic dimensions. Perhaps his most substantial achievement is his ability to force reconsideration of the relationship between the artist, his work, its audience, and the encompassing social context. Reconstructing his own vision of this relationship both at the beginning and at the end of the nationalist period, Baraka has increasingly stressed the necessity for an art that will alter the context and increase the real freedom of both artist and community.

During his Black Nationalist period, Baraka concentrated on exposing the unstated racist premises of Euro-American art and developing an alternative "Black Aesthetic." In part because he had demonstrated mastery of Euro-American poetic modes, Baraka's Black Nationalist philosophy commanded an unusual degree of white attention. Coming from an unknown poet, his militant poetry might well have been dismissed as a naïve kind of propaganda. It did, in fact, alienate many of his earlier admirers, who came to see him as an embodiment of the civil disorders of the mid-1960's. On a more profound level, however, he spurred many to ponder the complex logic of his transformation and to reassess the political implications of their own aesthetic stances.

Even as his relationship with the "mainstream" audience underwent this metamorphosis, his call for a militant, and if necessary violent, response to American racism received an affirmative answer from many younger African American writers. Challenging them to speak directly to and for the African American community, Baraka pursued the implications of his demand and employed his poetry as a direct political force. His subsequent turn to a socialist position, reflecting his growing conviction that simple nationalism unintentionally contributed to capitalist oppression, forced many Black Nationalists to reassess their own positions. Though Baraka again alienated much of his audience, he continued to generate serious debate on central issues. Throughout his career, but especially in the 1960's and early 1970's, Baraka has exerted a combined political and aesthetic influence matched by few other figures in American literary history.

Baraka's poetry falls into three distinctive periods, each reflecting an attempt to find a philosophy capable of responding adequately to a corrupt culture. The voice of each period is shaped in accord with a different set of assumptions concerning the nature of the cultural corruption, the proper orientation toward political action, and the poet's relationship with his audience. During his early period, Baraka built an essentially aesthetic response on premises shared primarily with white poets and intellectuals. Although Baraka always recognized the importance of his racial and economic heritage, the intricate philosophical voice of the early period sounds highly individualistic in comparison with his later work. During his middle Black Nationalist period, Baraka shifted his emphasis to the racial dimension of American culture. The associated voice—much more accessible, though not nearly so simple as it first appears—reflects Baraka's desire to relate primarily to the African American community. During his third Marxist-Leninist-Maoist period, Baraka adopted a less emotionally charged voice in accord with his stance as a scientific analyst of capitalist corruption.

Differing from the voices of the earlier periods, which assumed an equality between Baraka and his audience, whether based on aesthetic awareness or racial experience, this socialist voice frequently takes on the didactic tones of a teacher lecturing an audience unaware of its potential identity as a revolutionary proletariat. The diversity of Baraka's work makes it extremely difficult to find a vocabulary equally relevant to the complex postmodernism of *Preface to a Twenty Volume Suicide Note*, the militant nationalism of *Black Magic*, and the uncompromising economic analysis of *Hard Facts*. Nevertheless, Baraka is not three different people. Anticipations and echoes of each voice occur during each period. Throughout his career several constants emerge, most notably a philosophical refusal to conform to the demands of a corrupt culture and an emphasis on the oral/musical nature of the poetic experience.

"DUNCAN SPOKE OF A PROCESS"

Baraka's early work emphasizes the relationship between psychological experience, vocal rhythm, and the poetic line. This aesthetic adapts and develops those of Euro-American poets such as Robert Duncan, Robert Creeley, and Charles Olson, whose essay "Projective Verse" states many of the general premises of the group with which Baraka associated. Olson insists on "the possibilities of breath" as the central element of "Open" verse and develops the idea that "FORM IS NEVER MORE THAN THE EXTENSION OF CONTENT." Given this aesthetic, the poetic voice should embody the precise rhythm and emphasis of the poet's immediate experience and perception.

The poem "Duncan Spoke of a Process" both explicitly recognizes Baraka's aesthetic affinities (he also inscribed poems to Gary Snyder, Allen Ginsberg, and Michael McClure during this period) and analyzes the experience and premises shaping his voice. The poem typifies Baraka's early work in that it is philosophical, abstract, and nonracial. While it may obliquely relate to Baraka's experience as a black man, it is equally accessible to a reader whose emotional state derives from different specific circumstances. In addition, it typifies the early work in its intimation of the deep dissatisfaction with Euro-American culture which led to Baraka's later political development.

Assuming an audience familiar with Duncan, Baraka meditates on the emotional and intellectual implications of his work and revises its aesthetic in accord with his own perceptions. Although he repeats the word "repeat" three times in the first stanza, he is not simply repeating Duncan's words. The poem most closely resembles Duncan in its syntax, which mirrors the hesitations of a consciousness struggling to embody a natural process, to find words which repeat experience "as a day repeats/ its color." Frequently "sentences" consist of a string of perceptual units with ambiguous syntactic relationships. Many sentences contain no concrete images ("Before that, what came easiest"); the images that do occur are in relation to poetic consciousness rather than external "reality." Like Duncan's, Baraka's landscape is part psychological, part mythic or archetypal. The image of unidentified people traveling across the "greenest earth" represents his struggle to unite these landscapes, to bring the nurturing archetypal world to life in the persona's mind.

The remainder of the poem, however, emphasizes the persona's inability to achieve this rejuvenating unity. He insists that all abstract ideas and assumptions be validated in relation to memory (of psychological states rather than of external experiences). His memory, however, confronts him with an internal wasteland, "a heap of broken feeling." Starting with this consuming feeling of loss—whether of lover, childhood innocence, affinity with Duncan, or spiritual resiliency remains purposefully ambiguous—the persona's process leads him increasingly toward solipsism. No longer able to distinguish between "love" and "opinion," he feels no sense of the reality of past connections; even the archetypal Eden seems to be an illusion. Existing "where there/ is nothing, save myself," he is unable to "fill" that suffering self. The isolation of the word "myself" in its own line emphasizes the isolation which momentarily overwhelms the persona. Paradoxically, the line expressing the moment of existential terror intimates the pure merging of voice and consciousness associated with the processes of nature in the first stanza.

Perhaps because of this resemblance, the moment generates in the persona a resolve to reestablish contact with the external world. His determination, however, collapses in a way which, at least in retrospect, seems to anticipate Baraka's later political development. His first reaction to the existential terror is a perception of what he "love[s] most." Rather than reassuring him, however, this engenders a cynical determination—perhaps reflecting the continuing sense of loss—that he will "not/ leave what futile lies/ I have." In a context where "love" is a "futile lie," the persona's subsequent decision to "go out to/ what is most beautiful" demands ironic revaluation. The irony increases when the persona derives his conception of the "beautiful" from the platitudinous appeal to nobility of "some noncombatant Greek/ or soft Italian prince," the originators of the Machiavellian slavocracy of Euro-American culture. The persona's concluding questions anticipate the insistence on social and political processes which characterizes Baraka's later works: "And which one/ is truly/ to rule here? And/ what country is this?" Duncan spoke of a process which was essentially mythic, natural, and psychological. While

mirroring this process, Baraka's internal processes are clearly carrying him toward the political arena where questions concerning control and possession are central rather than subordinate.

MASKS AND "CROW JANE"

Throughout his early work, Baraka tries on a variety of personas, indicating a fascination with masks which provides the center for some of his most interesting early work. The "Crow Jane" sequence, echoing both William Butler Yeats's "Crazy Jane" poems and a blues composition by Mississippi Joe Williams, focuses on the limits of social masking. "Crow Jane," a white woman unconsciously adopting the old Jim Crow racial patterns, attempts to escape her role in "straight" America only to find herself a "wet lady of no image." Even more uncompromising in its dissatisfaction with masks which take their meaning from Euro-American cultural patterns, "An Agony. As New." develops the image of a persona being burned within a mask of "white hot metal." Tormented by the constrictions of a corrupt, mechanical white role, the persona feels himself "inside someone/ who hates me." Although that someone can easily be seen as a white self tormenting a black soul, the poem is not developed in explicitly racial terms. It could apply, for example, to a homosexual living a "straight" life or a businessman on the verge of a breakdown. Its implications are clear, however; inexorably, the agony leads to the final line consisting only of the word "screams." Again, the "projective" merging of voice and experience is pure, but the echoes of the scream sound in a voice which is no longer intended for the ears of the white avant-garde.

Baraka's nationalist voice, collective where the earlier voice was individualistic, aspires to a specifically "black" purity. Even while assuming the role of teacher, Baraka claims authority for his voice only to the extent that it reflects the strength and values of his African American heritage. In "Leroy" he offers up his old voice to the black community, urging it to "pick me apart and take the/ useful parts, the sweet meat of my feelings. And leave/ the bitter . . . rotten white parts/ alone." The alienation associated with Euro-American culture, expressed in the word "alone" as a line by itself, contrasts with the expansive sense of connection felt by the Amiri who rejects the masks of his predecessor "Leroy."

It would be misleading, however, to suggest that Baraka simply rejects all masks imposed by white society in order to reveal his "true" black face. Even while rebelling against the masks associated with his avant-garde personas, Baraka continues to explore the potential of masking in relation to his new orientation. This exploration takes two distinct forms, both designed to bring Baraka closer to the black community. First, he realizes that his own family background distances him from the "black angels" and "strong nigger feeling" described in "Leroy." Even while envisioning Leroy's mother "getting into/ new blues, from the old ones," he sees her "hypnotizing" him as she stares into "the future of the soul." In relation to African American culture, the future of the black bourgeoisie appears increasingly white and alienated. To become "purely black," Baraka must to some extent mask the influence of his class origins. Second, the mask itself is a central image in both African and African American culture. Invoking both the ritual knowledge of Africa and the survival strategy of the black South, the mask has been exploited in African American literature from Charles Waddell Chesnutt and Langston Hughes through Ralph Ellison and William Melvin Kelley. To speak with a black voice, Baraka must, like Brer Rabbit, present a variety of shifting surfaces, both to defend against and to attack the predatory forces of his environment.

MUSIC

These shifting surfaces are extremely elusive, deriving their meaning as much from audience as from speaker. Using musical forms and images as primary points of reference, Baraka explores this relationship between group and individual voices. His music criticism frequently refers to the primacy in African American culture of the "call and response" mode of work songs and spirituals. Playing off this dynamic, many of Baraka's nationalist poems identify his individual voice with that of a group leader calling for an affirmative response from his community. "Three Movements and a Coda," for example, concludes: "These are songs if you have the/ music." Baraka can provide lyrics, but if they are to come alive as songs, the music must be provided by the participation of a responsive community. The conclusion of "Black Art" makes it clear that this music is more than a purely aesthetic response: "Let the world

be a Black Poem/ And Let All Black People Speak This Poem/ Silently/ or LOUD." If the world is to be a poem for the black community, a political response must accompany the aesthetic one.

SHAKING READERS INTO POLITICAL ACTION

Determining the precise nature of the desired response demands an awareness of the differing implications of Baraka's poetry when interpreted in relation to white and black cultural traditions. Euro-American reactions to Baraka's nationalist voice tend to attribute even its most extreme statements to the poet himself, dismissing the possibility that he is wearing a mask for political purposes. This is particularly significant in relation to the poems in which Baraka appears to suggest random violence against whites. "Three Movements and a Coda" presents the image of looting a drugstore as a guerrilla attack on the "Vampire Nazis." "Black People!" includes the exhortation: "you can't steal nothin' from a white man, he's already stole it he owes/ you anything you want, even his life." The same poem, using profanity as "magic words," pictures looting as a "magic dance in the street."

VIOLENCE

Frequently, Baraka pictures violence in graphic images of "smashing at jelly-white faces" or "cracking steel knuckles in a jewlady's mouth." Given the unqualified intensity of these images, it hardly seems surprising that many white and less militant black readers dismiss the Baraka of this period as a reverse racist forwarding the very modes of thought he ostensibly rejects. In essence, they take the call which concludes "A Poem Some People Will Have to Understand" on a literal level. When Baraka asks "Will the machinegunners please step forward," they respond that a military race war can end only in catastrophe for both races.

As the title of the poem suggests, however, the call should not be interpreted simplistically. To be understood, it must be seen in the context of Baraka's view of the historical response of African Americans to racist oppression. Describing a society in which "the wheel, and the wheels, wont let us alone," he points out that blacks have "awaited the coming of a natural/ phenomenon" to effect a release. Only after repeating "But none has come" three times does Baraka summon the "machinegunners." The call sounds Baraka's response to what he sees as the traditional passivity of the African American community. Recognizing that practically all black experience involves direct contact with psychological racism tied to economic exploitation, Baraka treats these shared experiences hyperbolically in order to shake his community into political action. Placed in a social context where violent group rebellion has been the exception, there is much less chance than most white readers believe that his words will be acted on literally. The use of this aesthetic of calculated overstatement demonstrates Baraka's willingness to use the tradition of masking for a new set of political purposes. Where the form of most African American masks has been dictated by their relationship to white psychology, however, Baraka shapes his new masks to elicit response from blacks. Far from oversimplifying his awareness in the nationalist period, Baraka demonstrates his developing sense of the complexity of poetry designed to function in a real social and political context.

The contextual complexity, however, adds a new dimension of seriousness to attacks on Baraka's use of anti-Semitism and racism as rhetorical strategies. Baraka negotiates extremely treacherous territory when and if he expects readers to concentrate on his desire to "Clean out the world for virtue and love" in the same poem ("Black Art") which endorses "poems that kill . . . Setting fire and death to/ whitie's ass." A similar apparent paradox occurs in "Black People!" which says both "Take their lives if need be" and "let's make a world we want black children to grow and learn in." Baraka's aesthetic approach, which vests ultimate authority in the authenticating response, raises the problematic possibility that the audience's real social actions will authenticate the destructive rhetoric rather than the constructive vision.

BLACK NATIONALISM

Baraka attempts to diminish this possibility by developing his constructive vision in celebratory nationalist poems such as "It's Nation Time" and "Africa Africa Africa," which introduce a new musical/chant mode to his work. Exhortations such as "Black Art," which, like Baraka's earlier work, manipulate punctuation and syntax to express fully the urgency of an emotional experience, also anticipate the chant poems by introducing oratorical elements reflecting participation in communal ritual. "A Poem for Black Hearts," for example, varies the opening phrase "For Malcolm's eyes" to establish a focal point for audience response. "For Malcolm's words," "For Malcolm's heart," and similar phrases provide a kind of drum beat for Baraka's meditation on the fallen leader.

In "It's Nation Time" and "Africa Africa Africa" this drumbeat, clearly the constitutive structural element, often sounds explicitly: "Boom/ Boom/ BOOOM/ Boom." Writing primarily in short lines echoing these single drumbeats, Baraka uses reiteration and rhythmical variation to stress his vision of Pan-African unity. The first thirteen lines of "Africa Africa Africa" include no words other than "Africa" and "Africans." Anticipating Baraka's developing interest in reggae music, these poems call for the transformation of the old forms of African American culture into those of a new Pan-African sensibility. "It's Nation Time" phrases this call: "get up rastus for real to be rasta fari." Baraka rejects those "rastus" figures content to wear the passive masks imposed on Africans unaware of their heritage, and celebrates the rastafarians, a Caribbean sect associated strongly with reggae.

"AM/ TRAK"

The most effective poems of Baraka's socialist period redirect the music of these nationalist chants in an attempt to lead the proletariat, black and white, to a new awareness of the implications of its own experience. "Am/ Trak," Baraka's celebration of John Coltrane, attempts to chart this new social and aesthetic awareness by relating Baraka's poetic processes to those of the great jazz saxophonist. Beginning with a section which, like 'Trane's" piercing high notes, merges "History Love Scream," Baraka explores the origins of Coltrane's art, which combines individual intensity and the communal response of the bars and churches of Coltrane's Philadelphia. At once purely black and more highly aware than any single voice from the community, Coltrane's voice combines "The vectors from all sources—slavery, renaissance/ bop Charlie Parker/ nigger absolute supersane screams against reality."

Just as Coltrane's voice incorporates and surpasses that of Charlie "Yardbird" Parker, Baraka's incorporates Coltrane's and places it in a wider socialist perspective. Meditating on the aesthetic "difficulty" of both Coltrane's experimental sounds and his own philosophical works, Baraka considers the threat of losing the communal response: "'Trane you blows too long.'/ Screaming niggers drop out yr solos." Of course, the phrase "drop out" is ambiguous: Even as the audience refuses to make the effort to comprehend the call, the call perfectly expresses the implications of the audience's experience. Such a call, Baraka insists, can never simply fade into silence. Rather, it will receive a response from artists such as Thelonius Monk, the jazz pianist who played "Street gospel intellectual mystic survival codes." Coltrane's audience, according to Baraka, consists largely of fellow artists able to perceive the depths of his involvement with black reality.

By associating his own voice with Coltrane's, Baraka points to the developing distance between himself and his wider audience, a distance reflecting his shift to a socialist stance. The poem's final section, especially, is much more politically explicit than either the previous sections or Coltrane's music. As he does in numerous poems of the period, including "Dictatorship of the Proletariat" and "Class Struggle in Music," Baraka insists that the capitalist economic system bears full responsibility for the aesthetic and political corruption of American life. Seeing that "the money lord hovers oer us," he concludes that "only socialism brought by revolution/ can win." Meditating on Coltrane's death in relation to the Newark disorders, Baraka responds to his music as an implicit call for the socialist revolution which will "Be reality alive in motion in flame to change." The intensity of the call for change is unmistakable, in both Coltrane's music and Baraka's poetry. Baraka's identification of the change with "socialism brought by revolution," however, seems abstract and unconvincing in contrast, perhaps because of the relative flatness of diction.

As in many of the poems of the socialist period, Baraka's rhetorical strategy seems unclear. "Am/ Trak" contains few indications that the last section should be seen as some type of intricate mask. In fact, American socialist writing both lacks a dominant tradition of masking and tends to reject philosophically anything other than direct confrontation. Still, Baraka certainly retains his knowledge of the African American tradition of masking and has the ability to adjust his voice in accord with shifting social contexts. His extreme didactic stance may be intended as much to spark debate as to enforce agreement. The direct attacks on Don L. Lee (Haki R. Madhubuti) and Nikki Giovanni that occur in Baraka's works, however, suggest that such an interpretation may be overly ingenuous and that Baraka does in fact seek total agreement.

SOCIALIST VOICE

No simple aesthetic analysis suffices to explain either Baraka's new poetic voice or his difficulty in calling forth an affirmative response from either the artistic or the working-class community. Lines such as "This is the dictatorship of the proletariat/ the total domination of society by the working class" can easily be dismissed as lacking either the intellectual complexity or the emotional power of Baraka's earlier work. Such a dismissal, however, risks avoiding the issue of cultural conditioning, which Baraka now sees as central. Arguing that capitalist control of the media deforms both the proletariat's image of itself as a revolutionary force and its response to a "pure" socialist art, Baraka attempts to shatter the psychological barriers through techniques of reiteration similar to those used in the nationalist poetry. His relationship with the proletariat audience, however, generates a new set of political and aesthetic problems. While the nationalist voice assumed authority only insofar as it was validated by the experience of the African American community, the socialist voice must take on the additional burden of convincing the proletarian audience that its interpretation of its own experience had been "incorrect." If the community does not respond to Baraka's voice as its own, the problem lies with a brainwashed response rather than with a tainted call (the source of the problem in "Leroy"). As a result, Baraka frequently adopts a "lecturer's" voice to provide the "hard facts" which will overcome resistance to political action by proving that capitalism deceives the proletariat into accepting a "dictatorship of the minority."

The lack of response to his poems based on this aesthetic may simply reflect the accuracy of his analysis of the problem. What is certain is that Baraka remains determined to resist corruption in whatever form he perceives it, and that he continues to search for a voice like the one described in "Class Struggle in Music (2)," a voice which "even reached you."

OTHER MAJOR WORKS

LONG FICTION: *The System of Dante's Hell*, 1965.

SHORT FICTION: *Tales*, 1967; *The Fiction of LeRoi Jones/Amiri Baraka*, 2000.

PLAYS: *A Good Girl Is Hard to Find*, pr. 1958; *Dante*, pr. 1961; *The Baptism*, pr. 1964; *Dutchman*, pr., pb. 1964; *The Slave*, pr., pb. 1964; *The Baptism*, pr. 1964; *The Toilet*, pr., pb. 1964; *Experimental Death Unit #1*, pr. 1965; *J-E-L-L-O*, pr. 1965; *The Death of Malcolm X*, pr. 1965, pb. 1969; *A Black Mass*, pr. 1966; *Arm Yourself, or Harm Yourself*, pr., pb. 1967; *Great Goodness of Life (A Coon Show)*, pr. 1967; *Madheart: Morality Drama*, pr. 1967; *Slave Ship: A Historical Pageant*, pr., pb. 1967; *Board of Education*, pr. 1968; *Home on the Range*, pr. 1968; *Junkies Are Full of (SHHH . . .)*, pr. *1968*; *Resurrection in Life*, pr. 1969; *Bloodrites*, pr. 1970; *Black Dada Nihilism*, pr. 1971; *Columbia the Gem of the Ocean*, pr. 1973; *A Recent Killing*, pr. 1973; *The New Ark's A-Moverin*, pr. 1974; *The Sidnee Poet Heroical*, pr. 1975 (as *The Sidney Poet Heroical*, pb. 1979); *America More or Less*, pr. 1976; *S-1*, pr. 1976; *The Motion of History*, pr. 1977; *What Was the Relationship of the Lone Ranger to the Means of Production?*, pr., pb. 1979; *Dim Cracker Party Convention*, pr. 1980; *Boy and Tarzan Appear in a Clearing*, pr. 1981; *Money: A Jazz Opera*, pr. 1982; *Song: A One Act Play About the Relationship of Art to Real Life*, pr. 1983; *Primitive World*, pr. 1984; *The Life and Life of Bumpy Johnson*, pr. 1991; *Meeting Lillie*, pr. 1993.

SCREENPLAYS: *Dutchman*, 1967; *Black Spring*, 1968; *A Fable*, 1971; *Supercoon*, 1971.

NONFICTION: *"Cuba Libre,"* 1961; *Blues People: Negro Music in White America*, 1963; *Home: Social Essays*, 1966; *The New Nationalism*, 1962; *Black Music*, 1968; *A Black Value System*, 1970; *Strategy and Tactics of a Pan-African Nationalist Party*, 1971; *Kawaida Studies: The New Nationalism*, 1971; *Raise Race Rays Raze: Essays Since 1965*, 1971; *Crisis in Boston!*, 1974; *The Creation of the New Ark*, 1975; *The Autobiography of LeRoi Jones/Amiri Baraka*, 1984; *Daggers and Javelins: Essays*, 1984; *The Artist and Social Responsibility*, 1986; *The Music: Reflections on Jazz and Blues*, 1987 (with Amina Baraka); *Jesse Jackson and Black People*, 1994; *Conversa-* *tions with Amiri Baraka*, 1994 (Charlie Reilly, ed.); *Eulogies*, 1996.

EDITED TEXTS: *The Moderns: New Fiction in America*, 1963; *Black Fire: An Anthology of Afro-American Writing*, 1968 (with Larry Neal); *African Congress: A Documentary of the First Modern Pan-African Congress*, 1972; *Confirmation: An Anthology of African-American Women*, 1983 (with Amina Baraka).

MISCELLANEOUS: *Selected Plays and Prose*, 1979; *The LeRoi Jones/Amiri Baraka Reader*, 1991.

BIBLIOGRAPHY

Baker, Houston A., Jr. *The Journey Back: Issues in Black Literature and Criticism*. Chicago: University of Chicago Press, 1980. Traces the evolution from the "elegant despair" of Baraka's early poems to his later Black Nationalism. Baker sees Baraka's transformation as groundbreaking, pivotal in the development of a "Black Aesthetic" that would define itself apart from the Western white canon. The reader must use the index to find references to Baraka, as the chapters are organized historically rather than by authors considered.

Baraka, Amiri. *Conversations with Amiri Baraka*. Edited by Charlie Reilly. Jackson: University Press of Mississippi, 1994. Offers insights into the black experience through Baraka's experiences during the turbulent later half of the twentieth century, from his ghetto life in the 1940's through the Black Nationalist movement of the 1970's to his intellectual life in the 1990's. Baraka critiques and elucidates his works and underscores his belief in the connection between art and social criticism.

_____ [Jones, LeRoi]. "Philistinism and the Negro Writer." In *Anger, and Beyond: The Negro Writer in the United States*, edited with an introduction by Herbert Hill. New York: Harper & Row, 1966. This essay is useful to the student of Baraka as an articulation in prose of the commitments that were being made simultaneously in the poetry. The tone is rather quiet and reasoned, relative to Baraka's later rhetoric, but the radical central theme is clear: "The Negro writer can only survive by refusing to become a white man."

Benston, Kimberly W., ed. *Imamu Amiri Baraka (LeRoi Jones): A Collection of Critical Essays*. Englewood Cliffs, N.J.: Prentice-Hall, 1978. Benston, who has written a full-length work on Baraka (*Baraka: The Renegade and the Mask*, 1976), brings together essays that shed light on various aspects of his poetry and drama. Includes a bibliography.

Brown, Lloyd Wellesley. *Amiri Baraka*. Boston: Twayne, 1980. By a scholar who specializes in African, African American, and Western Indian literary studies, this is the standard critical piece on Baraka's poetic achievement. Provides a bibliography and a index.

Gibson, Donald B., ed. *Five Black Writers: Essays on Wright, Ellison, Baldwin, Hughes, and LeRoi Jones*. New York: University Press, 1970. Particularly valuable for setting Baraka in context of other major African American writers of the twentieth century. The assessment of him in the introduction, moreover, places him firmly within the wider literary culture and argues that as of 1970 he had not yet become a "social activist" in his poems and plays. In one chapter Stephen Schneck takes an unflattering look at Baraka's contradictory political statements and maneuverings, while in another, "Black Man as Victim," Donald P. Costello explores Baraka's early plays.

Hudson, Theodore. *From LeRoi Jones to Amiri Baraka: The Literary Works*. Durham, N.C.: Duke University Press, 1973. This sympathetic work provides a biographical chapter based on interviews with Baraka and his parents. Other chapters examine his nonfiction, fiction, poetry, and drama; his philosophical stance is surveyed in one chapter, his forms and styles in another. Notes and an index are provided, along with a bibliography that lists primary and secondary works through the early 1970's.

Johnson, Charles. *Being and Race: Black Writing Since 1970*. Bloomington: Indiana University Press, 1988. Places Baraka in the tradition of Negritude and credits him as having "for the most part established the style of Cultural Nationalist poetics in the period between 1960 and 1970—for an entire generation of writers." Examines his "art-as-weapon" philosophy and his influence on Ntozake Shange. There is no chapter devoted to Baraka, so the reader must consult the index.

Lacey, Henry C. *To Raise, Destroy, and Create: The Poetry, Drama, and Fiction of Imamu Amiri Baraka (LeRoi Jones)*. Troy, N.Y.: Whitston, 1981. As the subtitle indicates, this is a wide-ranging study that attempts to do justice to Baraka's work in several genres. Bibliographical references are included as well as an index.

Watts, Jerry Gafio. *Amiri Baraka: The Politics and Art of a Black Intellectual*. New York: New York University Press, 2001. The focus of this tome of more than six hundred pages is on the intellectual development of Baraka from bohemian writer in Greenwich Village to militant Black Nationalist to Marxist. Baraka does not escape the author's criticism for his political oversimplification and polemicism, at the same time outlining his influence on other writers and contrasting him with other black activists and political figures.

Woodard, K. Komozi. *A Nation Within a Nation: Amiri Baraka (LeRoi Jones) and Black Power Politics*. Chapel Hill: University of North Carolina Press, 1999. Revises the common view of Baraka as an extremist, arguing that he became a seasoned political veteran who brought together divergent black factions.

Craig Werner;
bibliography updated by the editors

MARY BARNARD

Born: Vancouver, Washington; December 6, 1909

PRINCIPAL POETRY

Cool Country in *Five Young American Poets*, 1940
A Few Poems, 1952
Collected Poems, 1979
Time and the White Tigress, 1986

OTHER LITERARY FORMS

While Mary Barnard's principal genre is poetry, she has also worked with translations from the Greek, most notably in her well-known *Sappho: A New Trans-*

lation (1958). The bulk of her fiction, published in widely read periodicals in the 1950's, is as yet uncollected, though *Three Fables* appeared in 1983. Her essays from her research into Sappho, *The Mythmakers* (1966), also inform her poetry collection *Time and the White Tigress*. Perhaps her best-known work, aside from the poetry, is the autobiography *Assault on Mount Helicon: A Literary Memoir* (1984), which features portraits of many of the chief figures in modern American literature but especially of Ezra Pound and William Carlos Williams.

ACHIEVEMENTS

Mary Barnard's work shows the influence of the modernists transposed to a minor key. While it lacks the cosmopolitan effusiveness of Ezra Pound or the cultural skeet-shooting of T. S. Eliot or the secret ambition of William Carlos Williams, it nevertheless sets forth a legitimate agenda and succeeds in convincing its readers that while it is small as an oeuvre, it is by no means slight. Moreover, the scope belies the small size. If one believes with Samuel Taylor Coleridge that one of the distinguishing characteristics of high art is its ability to pack maximum content into minimum space, then the miniatures of Mary Barnard offer more aesthetic satisfaction than their collective heft would suggest. By invoking the mythical within the ordinary and the everyday within the mythical, she has created a resonant parallel device for treating the subjects of her choice: childhood, the meaning of change, the pervasiveness of limits, man's relation to nature and to his past, and the fate of women.

While she has written essays and fiction as well as translating from the Greek, these endeavors provide—to use one of her favorite images—a spring from which to enlarge and refresh her poetry. In its classical approach to hidden truths about human nature, it bears resemblance to such earlier writers as Leonie Adams and Louise Bogan. Her translations of Sappho show what can be done to breathe life into revered but seldom-read classics, and the autobiographical *Assault on Mount Helicon* is an important and engaging document of literary history and literary survival from one who wrote from "the far shore" but was nevertheless in the midst of one of the great cultural revolutions of modern times.

BIOGRAPHY

Born of parents who moved west from Indiana, a move inspired in part by the Lewis and Clark Exposition of 1905, Mary Barnard was born on December 6, 1909, in Vancouver, Washington. Her father ran a lumber mill, and Barnard was able to grow up happily in congenial surroundings. Her parents encouraged her early interest in poetry, and Barnard—unusual for her time—attended Reed College, where she took creative writing courses and was graduated in 1932.

Twice during the 1930's, Barnard took up summer residencies at Yaddo in upstate New York and met a number of writers, including Muriel Rukeyser, Kenneth Fearing, Eleanor Clark, and Delmore Schwartz. It was during this decade that she also began corresponding with Ezra Pound and William Carlos Williams, who further encouraged her. In 1935, she won the Levinson Prize from *Poetry* magazine, and her poems were first collected in New Directions' *Five Young American Poets* in 1940. From 1939 to 1943, she worked as curator of the poetry collection at the University of Buffalo, and from 1943 to 1950, she worked as a research assistant to Carl Van Doren and wrote fiction that appeared in such periodicals as *The Saturday Review of Literature, The Kenyon Review*, and *Harper's Bazaar. A Few Poems* appeared from Reed College in 1952, and in the mid-1950's she worked on her translations of Sappho. In 1957, simultaneously with their acceptance, she moved back to the West Coast and settled in Portland, Oregon. Her collection of essays, *The Mythmakers*, appeared in 1966.

The 1979 publication of her *Collected Poems* brought Barnard's poetry to the attention of a new generation of readers. Both this book and her memoir, *Assault on Mount Helicon*, were widely reviewed and warmly received. *Time and the White Tigress* won the 1986 Western States Book Award for Poetry and prompted the jury to cite it as "an impressive achievement from a distinguished writer, and an admirable new American poem."

ANALYSIS

Mary Barnard's poetic output, while quite slim, nevertheless spans and reflects more than half a century of involvement in the art. Her brief, solicitous early lyrics delineate the natural world of the Pacific Northwest with quiet precision, while her later poems reveal her increasing interest in mythological models. Devoid of gimmick and rhetoric, they are as unassuming and as well made as Shaker furniture. The world described in the earlier poems is a world in transition—mostly gone, a remote place of springs and rivers, of meadows and deer, where railroads provide the transfusions of people and goods necessary for a human population to flourish. The later poems cease to reflect a period aspect and, with increasing awareness and confidence in her powers, rely more heavily on invention than recollection. The dominant elements throughout are water and earth rather than air or fire.

COLLECTED POEMS

Collected Poems opens in childhood, not a childhood toggled to personal memory, but a childhood that any adult might imagine as belonging to a young girl. In "Playroom," there is

> mournfulness of muddy playgrounds,
> raw smell of rubbers and wrapped lunches
> when little girls stand in a circle singing
> of windows and of lovers.

The lives within the playground sing of the life beyond their experience and place, just as the mature poet sings of her "beyond," the past:

> Hearing them, no one could tell
> why they sing sadly, but there is in their voices
> the pathos of all handed-down garments
> hanging loosely on small bodies.

The poem suggests that life itself is a process of outgrowing "garments," that the provisional is the domain of the living. Thus, the girls "sing sadly," not because they understand this condition but because, literally, they embody it.

If the girls have to content themselves with hand-me-downs, a young girl in "The Fitting" must contend with a "trio of hags . . . with cold hands" who roam over her young body and "compress withered lips upon pins" in order to produce a dress for her. They are the three Fates, who determine the quality and duration of life. As they fit the girl, "The knocking of hammers comes/ from beyond the still window curtain. . . ." Some portion of the future, pertinent to others, is being constructed, but her

hands will make nothing: "Her life is confined here, in this depth/ in the well of the mirrors." The poem ends with the soft snipping of scissors and pulled threads—also not to be hers—lying on the carpet. The tiny separations imparted by the scissors suggest many more consequential leave-takings to come.

The understanding of limitations of which the young may only have vague intimations, and their delineation, drawn from images in the natural world, are the subjects of many of Barnard's poems. To define a limit, to put a form to what is already form, is to pay it authentic homage. One of the most elemental limits and the source of centuries of solemn meditation from Homer to Wallace Stevens is the seashore. The sea, as a self-sufficient, obverse universe, confronts people both with their otherness, with respect to their mutually incompatible biologies, and with their own "shores," beyond which begins the vast Not-me, a country about which they are impelled to educate themselves, education being the development of commerce between the two realms. Yet their bodies feel a distant affinity to that otherness not easily accessible to language. As the Metaphysical poet Thomas Traherne noted, humanity is "both with moons and tides."

"SHORELINE"

In "Shoreline," one of Barnard's longer poems (and her first published poem), the poet states flatly, "Sand is the beginning and the end/ of our dominion." Yet "The way to the dunes is easy," as children, who have not yet transformed the sea and land, water and earth, into concepts, instinctively know: "their bodies glow/ in the cold wash of the beach." When they return from the beach, "They are unmoved by fears/ that breed in darkening kitchens at sundown/ following storm. . . ." Barnard asserts of the shoreline: "This, then, is the country of our choice." The operative word here is "choice," for one would have thought that limitation was, on the contrary, merely the country of necessity. By choice, however, one stands by the shore "and long[s] for islands"; thus, in some measure, one equally and consciously partakes of one's limitations as well. As one gets older, on the other hand, and one's choices dwindle in the face of increased experience, "We lose the childish avarice of horizons." The poem ends with the refrain, "sand/ is the beginning and the end/ of our dominion," though with a different line break, as if to suggest its shifting against "our dominion." One hears a gentle corrective here both to the infinitude of William Blake's sand and, prophetically, to the sonorous "dominion" of which death shall have none in Dylan Thomas. Barnard's poem seems more thoughtfully located in the actual experiences of people, less in the seductive undertow of language.

Those childhoods, suspended in the ancestral and the domestic, however unique they may seem to the individual and web-spun consciousness of children, carry with them the evidence of their lineages. This evidence, which bespeaks generations of labor needed to produce the child into its time, is present everywhere but especially in those objects that address the body, as in "Beds": "The carved oak headboards of ancestral beds tilt/ like foundered decks from fog at the mouth of the river." The lovely image of care and protection is addressed specifically to the body, whose vulnerability reaches its apex at night. Fear—of being abducted (into the night, into the future, into death)—alternates with remembered or implied assurances of protection:

Lulla, lulla, will there be, will there
   always be a place to sleep when smoke gathers in the
      rafters?
. . . .
Lulla, lulla. Flood after flood. When the beds float
   downstream, will there be a place to sleep, Matthew, Mark?

Unlike the children's playground, the sanctuary of the bed is permanent, even obligingly providing, although somewhat transformed, humanity's last "resting place." Consequently, the bones' sanctuary posture is the horizontal, and it is through this "angle" that one can see that the eternal nature of the forms links people from biology to biography to history, from their bodies to those of their ancestors and of all humankind:

The feathers of my grandmothers' beds melted into
   earlier darkness
as, bone to earth, I lay down. A trail that leads out, leads
   back.
Leads back, anyway, one night or another, bone to earth.

"THE RAPIDS"

Limits, which provide Barnard with so much of her subject matter, are not inert barriers but, because

they are "our choice," are rather actively engaged in transformations. In "The Rapids," the poet focuses on the distinction between the boundary as limit and as transformer: "No country is so gracious to us/ as that which kept its contours while we forgot them. . . ." The precisely placed "gracious" suggests how accommodating a contour a boundary can manage to be to satisfy one's need for orientation and security. At the same time, it is an agency of change: "The water we saw broken upon the rapids/ has dragged silt through marshland/ and mingled with the embittered streams of the sea."

In the last stanza of this three-stanza poem, Barnard telescopes the stationary and the moving into a single image of "ungatherable blossoms floating by the . . . rock." These "have flung light in my face, have made promises/ in unceasing undertone." The promises are guarantees made subliminally that one will be at home in the world, or at least that one can recover his home. "Alienation"—one of the most self-incriminating buzzwords of the twentieth century—and all the philosophical ramifications tangled up with it, are, after all, of human manufacture, and while the mind can surely suffer from alienation, it can also break out of it in an instant. Such an instant constitutes the poetic moment of this and other of Barnard's poems.

"WINTER EVENING"

Being at home in the world means also adjusting to its cyclic nature, which involves death. Usually, human beings do all they can to insulate themselves from its blows, and when the time comes when they can no longer do that, they remember, if they still can, the traditional loophole, lamentation, channeling their sorrow, paying homage, and letting off the steam of outrage and fear all at once. The ability and courage to confront death (of others and one's own) is inversely proportional to the amount of insulation one has accumulated (in the twentieth century, quite a lot). In "Winter Evening," Barnard examines the mythical place of death, for mythological treatment tends to "naturalize" death and so render it less psychically damaging by treating it as an equal partner in the scheme of things. On the other hand, modern middle-class living has tried, in countless ways and to its detriment, to dust its hands of the unflattering fact of terminal being:

> In the mountains, it is said,
> the deer are dying by hundreds.
> We know nothing of that
> in the suburbs.

Doubtless, suburban life has what passes for myths, too, but these are not "ancestral myth," the myth of origins. Rather, "our century/ clings to the novel./ Coffee and novels." Only the train whistles "howl against death/ . . . like Lear in his heartbreak,/ savage as a new myth." Lear, in his vanity, also upset a primordial set of precedents and suffered madness and death for his trouble. The odd juxtaposition of Lear (though, appropriately, Lear is a winter king) and the suburbanites clearly boosts the latter into a mythical realm of danger, for the forces involved are huge and indifferent to human willfulness. The leveling snow that is the immediate cause of the animals' deaths goes on quietly covering all the houses in the town.

"THE SPRING"

While Barnard has clearly absorbed the image-based tenets of Pound and Williams, she most clearly follows the homegrown variety of Williams. In the slyly self-referential "The Spring," Barnard follows the course— one is tempted to say "career"—of a spring, "a mere trickle," as it "whispers" out from under a boulder and fills, first, a pond, then travels (somehow keeping its integrity as a separate spring as it does so) over a spillway, fills another pond, and then falls between trees "to find its fate in the river." The poet concludes,

> Nameless, it has two little ponds
> to its credit, like a poet
> with two small collections of verse.
>
> For this I celebrate it.

Executed in Williams-style tercets, the poem concerns the question of poetic identity, as the simile makes clear. It is also a self-celebration, for the spring is a decidedly naturalistic image and so in Barnard's canon gets a de facto seal of approval. From the boulder of obscurity to the river of judgment, the stream has avoided dilution, just as a poet with two small collections will, one hopes, have avoided assimilation. To the untrained eye, however, the spring's continuity, its purposefulness, will be invisible: At the point that it is a pond, it *is* a pond; at the river, the river. Guiding her own stream be-

tween the "tall cottonwoods" of Pound and Williams (as one would imagine) becomes a matter of integrity that she does not need to spell out, just as it is an act of homage in form and feeling.

"INHERITANCE"

Barnard's revival ("arrival" might more accurately indicate the tone of her reception) in the late 1970's was to a considerable degree enhanced by her feminist principles. "Inheritance" addresses the theme of the woman's largely uncommemorated contribution to the settling of America:

> Spoon clink fell to axe-chink
> falling along the Ohio. These women
> made their beds, God bless them,
> in the wandering, dreamed, hoped-for
> Hesperides, their graves
> in permanent places.

The poet admits that, indeed, she was left no tangible inheritance, only pride, and not even pride, but the memory of it, which she identifies as "armor/ . . . against time and men and women." The final placement of women in the list of the enemies of women is a fine idea, and the poem, armored, ends on that note. Barnard obviously believes that one of the chief battles of feminism must be fought on the field of memory, and indeed much of feminist work has been in rectifying the obscured and mystified history of the sex and in transferring future custodianship to women.

"PERSEPHONE"

Barnard's reading of the classics, from which emerged her translations of Sappho, shows up in poems such as "Persephone." Here, the poet disposes of the hierarchical view of the surface as implicitly preferable to the underworld:

> I loved like a mole. There were
> subterranean flat stone stairways
> to columns supporting the earth and its
> daffodils. Or shall we say, to the facade
> of the hiding place of earth's treasure?

Nostalgia has no place in the erection of hell: "Homesickness here/ is for the raw working and scars of the surface. . . ." Persephone will make do with what is at hand and will not be enticed into living by "hunger—to which/ . . . surrender is death." She will return to the surface, but not by giving in to her hunger for it. Rather, she will have her pride, and presumably the memory of it, to strengthen her for her return:

> How many times it is said to the living,
> Conquer hunger! If you
> want to go back, up, up where the sun falls
> warm on flowering rock and make garlands again.

Barnard puts an effective feminist spin on Persephone's self-denial: Neither the hunger for the world nor the conquering of it is tinged with the desire to return to men (they are conspicuously absent from the poem); rather, Persephone's desire is "to make garlands again."

"ONDINE"

The image of another "buried" woman appears in "Ondine." Here, the speaker has invited the mermaid into her house to eat, but instead of eating, she sits weeping and blames the speaker for stealing driftwood to burn, a charge the speaker denies. At this, the mermaid stands up and wrings her hair "so that the water made a sudden splash/ on the round rug by the door" and leaves to return to the sea. The speaker throws the knot of wood where the mermaid had sat into the fire ("I beat it out with a poker/ in the soft ash"). At length, she comes to regret her fit of anger:

> Now I am frightened on the shore at night,
> and all the phosphorescent swells that rise
> come towards me with the threat of her dark eyes
> with a cold firelight in them . . .

Her sense of self-reproach at her inability to establish any but the most cursory of relationships with the strange creature gives way to anxiety and guilt. The poem ends with an apocalyptic image that hints at the psychological forces involved in her failure:

> Should she return and bring her sisters with her,
> the withdrawing tide
> would leave a long pool in my bed.
> There would be nothing more of me this side
>
> the melting foamline of the latest wave.

"FABLE FROM THE CAYOOSH COUNTRY"

It is in her mythological voice that Barnard most comfortably addresses the larger themes. In one of these,

"Fable from the Cayoosh Country," the subject is the power and influence of language. The poet and an unnamed companion lie beside a lake in a pastoral setting. Aware of the nature surrounding them, their thought "pushed forward into the margins of silence/ . . . the boundaries of an inarticulate world." Falling asleep, she dreams of being a missionary of language to the beasts:

> I preached the blessing of the noun and verb,
> but all was lost in the furred ear of the bear,
> in the expressive ear of the young doe.
> What the doe said with her ear, I understood.
> What I said, she obviously did not.

Exasperated, she hurls her grammar books into a pool that immediately begins to address her. It relates the story of a time when all nature could speak with the eloquence that human beings have, but found it was a curse, not a blessing:

> . . . The blade of this tool, useless for digging, chopping,
> shearing, they used against each other with such zeal
> they all but accomplished their own extermination.

The creatures of nature therefore "abandoned speech" yet "retained cries expressive of emotion,/ as rage,/ or love." The pool adds, "They have never seen any cause to repent their decision." The speaker then dreams that the lake has risen over them and confesses, "My consternation was that of a poet, whose love/ if not his living was gravely endangered." She wakes and, finding the lake in place as before, wonders whether it is not a pity that it had not, in fact, flooded over them. As a visionary poem, "Fable from the Cayoosh Country" locates in language not the tool that binds human beings together in a mutually satisfying quest for articulation, but a tempting means to allow oneself to become separate from nature and from one's self. Unfortunately, language cannot police its abuses. In fact, it is not usually aware of them until the harm has been done. Obviously, the poem is a retelling of the Fall, and the striving after language (not in the sense of naming but in the proud rise to eloquence) becomes an activity inappropriate to either Paradise or redemption, the beasts having already fallen and redeemed their natures through a return to the inarticulate. The triumph and burden of language being the human lot, however, the wish to do as the beasts do becomes moot, as language is, for humankind, an irreversible phenomenon.

"LETHE"

Another fine poem that speculates on erasure (and mentioned approvingly by Ezra Pound) considers the return to the tabula rasa of the soul recycled and made ready for reincarnation by the waters of Lethe. The soul in "Lethe" pauses over the waters and ponders the enormous human loss necessary to prepare the soul for return to earth:

> Will a few drops on the tongue
> like a whirling flood submerge cities,
> like a sea, grind pillars to sand?
> Will it wash the color from the lips and the eyes
> beloved? It were a thousand pities
> thus to dissolve
> the delicate sculpture of a lifted hand. . . .

The cost of such forgetting, is, for a poet, unbearable, even as it is inevitable. Oblivion is the exact enemy of art, just as Satan is the enemy of virtue, and the poet, "hesitant, unwilling to drink," is ennobled by her resistance.

TIME AND THE WHITE TIGRESS

Time and the White Tigress is a series of verse essays (Barnard refers to it as a single long poem) about the celestial and natural cycles and their impact on humanity's understanding of its place in the cosmos. Harking back to her classical studies and the archaeological arcana of *The Mythmakers*, the poems present, complete with contextual notes, a rationale for the capture and implementation of time as a series of demarcations suitable to the use of custom, since there is "no society without customs. . . ." Hence, the possession of knowledge about time is power inasmuch as it gives its possessor(s) knowledge of the cycles through which one conducts one's life:

> A rhythm established by moon after moon,
> tide after tide, and year after year
> has formed the framework for all our cultures,
> a pattern of custom that echoes the pattern
> woven by time in the heavens.

Principally, it is to the ancient astronomers, whose priestly function it was to observe and mime the activities of the sky, that beginnings of mythology can be traced: the Twins (dark and light), the signs of the Zodiac, the gods and goddesses of the ancient religions. Yet far from pushing mythology deeper into the mists, Barnard shows that the sky watchers were pragmatic sages who interpreted the heavens in ingenious and economic ways and set the stage for the growth of civilization, from the role of priests and kings to the use and democratization of time to the techniques of mythologizing as a form of advancing out of the darkness. Miming her own subjects, she writes,

> We are following here the spoor
> of a White Tigress who prowled
> Time's hinterlands. . . .
>
> . . . .
>
> Her teats, dripping a moon-milk,
> suckled the Twins. The savor,
> still on our tongues, is fading.
>
> Here, a pug-mark in the path.
> There, bent grass where she crouched.
> From this I construct a tigress?
>
> A mythical one?
> Perhaps. Why
> should we cease to make myths?

One of Barnard's achievements is a conscious invention and perpetuation of myths, which are the "necessary fictions" by which human beings try to invoke principles of memory and harmony in their otherwise partial and painful existence through time's indifferent hallways.

OTHER MAJOR WORKS

SHORT FICTION: *Three Fables*, 1983.

NONFICTION: *The Mythmakers*, 1966; *Assault on Mount Helicon: A Literary Memoir*, 1984; *Nantucket Genesis: The Tale of My Life*, 1988; *The Diary of an Optimist*, 1995.

TRANSLATION: *Sappho: A New Translation*, 1958.

BIBLIOGRAPHY

Fantazzi, Charles E. Review of *The Myth of Apollo and Daphne from Ovid to Quevedo*, by Mary Barnard. *Choice* 25 (September, 1987): 112. Fantazzi comments on Barnard's highly learned book of comparative literature, which traces the story of Apollo and Daphne from Ovid to the Spanish Golden Age.

Barnard's facility with myth is apparent here, as it is in her poetry. Gives an idea of the breadth of Barnard's accomplishment as a writer.

Helle, Anita. "Dialogue with Mary Barnard." *Northwest Review* 20, nos. 2/3 (1982): 188-198. Few biographical sources on Mary Barnard exist, therefore this interview is very important. Barnard explains that she uses myth to reveal lost history, especially the history of women in Western society. Interesting for all students.

Swift, John. "Separations." *Northwest Review* 18, no. 3 (1980): 114-119. Swift explains Barnard's attempt to separate the idea of boundaries as limits and the notion of limits as powers that enable transformation. This is related to Barnard's connection with the land of the Pacific Northwest.

Van Cleve, Jane. "A Personal View of Mary Barnard." *Northwest Review* 18, no. 3 (1980): 105-113. Barnard's work did not find a large audience until the late 1970's, when feminist writing came into vogue. Van Cleve discusses how Barnard's poetry affects Van Cleve as a woman.

Whitman, Ruth. Review of *Time and the White Tigress*, by Mary Barnard. *Choice* 24 (December, 1986): 620. Whitman calls Barnard's book of poetry "extraordinary." She describes how it weaves comparative mythology with comparative science in a beautiful, simple way. Provides students with a helpful overview and understanding of Barnard's book. Informative for all students.

David Rigsbee;
bibliography updated by the editors

CHARLES BAUDELAIRE

Born: Paris, France; April 9, 1821
Died: Paris, France; August 31, 1867

PRINCIPAL POETRY

Les Fleurs du mal, 1857, 1861, 1868 (*Flowers of Evil*, 1931)
Les Épaves, 1866
Petits Poèmes en prose, 1869 (also known as *Le Spleen de Paris*; *Poems in Prose*, 1905, also known as *Paris Spleen, 1869*, 1947)

OTHER LITERARY FORMS

Collections of Charles Baudelaire's essays on literature, art, aesthetics, and drugs appeared under the titles *Les Paradis artificiels* (1860), *Curiosités esthétiques* (1868), and *L'Art romantique* (1868). Baudelaire also published translations of several volumes of the prose works of Edgar Allan Poe. The most convenient edition of most of his works is the Pléiade edition, *Œuvres complètes* (1961), edited by Yves Le Dantec and Claude Pichois.

ACHIEVEMENTS

Although Baudelaire is sometimes grouped with the Symbolists, a movement that constituted itself more than a decade after his death, Baudelaire himself neither belonged to nor founded a school. It is probably fair, however, to designate him as one of the earliest exponents of modernism. He constantly sought, in both literature and painting, works that expressed a beauty specific to the reality of the moment, even if that reality was unpleasant or bizarre. His corrosive irony, his suggestive understatement of the metaphoric sense of his images, and his aggressive use of material drawn from the prosaic side of life have had a lasting success and influence. Movements as diverse as Symbolism, Dadaism, and the Italian neorealist cinema have claimed descent from his work.

BIOGRAPHY

Charles-Pierre Baudelaire was born in Paris on April 9, 1821. His father, Joseph-François, was of modest origin but well educated, for he attended seminary and became a priest before the Revolution. Well connected, he became preceptor to the children of the Duke of Choiseul-Praslin and, as a painter, was personally acquainted with Enlightenment figures such as Condorcet and Cabanis. After the Revolution, having left the priesthood, Joseph-François Baudelaire worked on the administrative staff of the French senate. Caroline Archenbaut-Defayis, Baudelaire's mother, was thirty-four years younger than his father. Widowed, she remarried when her son was six years old. Baudelaire's stepfather, Jacques

Aupick, was a career military officer who had him placed in a series of boarding schools, first in Lyons, when the child was nine, and then in Paris, at fifteen. The choice of schools permitted Baudelaire to be near his mother as the Aupick household moved in response to the officer's promotions.

As an adolescent, Baudelaire was friendly, religious, and studious. He won prizes in Latin verse composition (one of the poems in *Flowers of Evil* is in Latin). He seems to have had few serious disputes with his stepfather until after obtaining the *baccalauréat* in 1839. After that, however, the now successful general became progressively the object of Baudelaire's dislike and even hatred. Disapproving of the young man's friends and conduct, the general sent him on a long boat trip toward India, but Baudelaire, once embarked, refused to go farther than Mauritius. When Baudelaire reached legal majority in 1842, he broke with the Aupicks and lived prodigally on the money he inherited from his father. The life of ease of the young literary dandy lasted only two years, however, for the Aupicks had Baudelaire placed under conservatorship in 1844 on the grounds

Charles Baudelaire (Library of Congress)

that he was incapable of managing his money. This deprivation of his full personal freedom had a devastating effect on Baudelaire, who attempted suicide the following year. Upon his recovery, he apparently resolved to write copiously and seriously, contributing to various reviews, especially *L'Artiste* and *Le Corsaire-Satan*.

Baudelaire was widely acquainted with important Romantic authors, including Charles Sainte-Beuve, Théophile Gautier, Hugo, Gérard de Nerval, Théodore de Banville, Petrus Borel (the Wolf-man), and Champfleury. He was also close to the active painters of his day and spent much of his time in their studios. His essays on expositions and on individual artists, especially Eugène Delacroix and Constantin Guys, actually occupy twice as many pages in the complete works as his literary criticism. More intermittently, Baudelaire was involved in the political life of his day, manning the barricades in the 1848 Revolution and distributing political tracts. His love of order, or rather his aspiration to order and hatred of disorder, kept him from fitting into the revolutionary cause, and his hatred of the bourgeoisie prevented him from siding with the conservatives.

By 1845, Baudelaire was already announcing a forthcoming volume of poetry, under the title "Les Lesbiennes." In 1848, he claimed to be working on a volume called "Les Limbes." Finally, in 1855, he settled on the title *Flowers of Evil*. When it appeared in 1857, the collection provoked a scandal that led to the prosecution of the poet and the publisher. Six of the poems were suppressed, and the poet was fined.

The death of General Aupick a few months before the appearance of *Flowers of Evil* led Baudelaire to a reconciliation with his mother. Although he never succeeded in putting his life in what he called "order," living within his means and avoiding debts, his attempt to heal his rift with his respectable middle-class origins may explain the increasingly Christian and even Catholic orientation of his ideas in the last decade of his life. In 1866, while visiting Brussels, Baudelaire was stricken with partial paralysis and became aphasic. He died in Paris after more than a year of suffering.

ANALYSIS

Although Charles Baudelaire was close to the major Romantic artists and poets, his work announced something new and difficult to describe. Baudelaire did not introduce a fundamentally new aesthetic principle but made important changes in the proportions of idealism and realism, formal beauty and attention to ideas, social commitment and alienation from society—all categories through which the Romantic poets had expressed their conception of literary art. More than most Romantics, he wrote poetry based on the ugliness of urban life and drew an intense beauty from the prosaic and the unspeakable. Although major Romantics, including Victor Hugo, had broken down many restrictions on subjects that could be treated in poetry, Baudelaire went further, choosing such topics as crime, disease, and prostitution as his points of departure. While many Romantics suggest a transcendent redemptive quality in art, a spiritual enlightenment that gives readers a kind of religious or social pathway to liberation, Baudelaire tantalizes the reader with religious hope but then pulls it away, suggesting that all hope is in the moment of artistic insight and not in the real future.

The image of the poet as prophet or spiritually superior dreamer, typical of Hugo or Alfred de Vigny, flickers occasionally through Baudelaire's work, but it generally yields to an image of the poet as a sensitive and marginal individual whose only superiority to his contemporaries is his consciousness of his corruption and decadence, something Baudelaire expressed as "conscience [or consciousness] in the midst of evil." Baudelaire thus prepared the way for the decadent poets, and for those poets of the twentieth century who conceived of their work as primarily individual and not social. In this regard, it is significant that Baudelaire introduced Edgar Allan Poe to the French. Poe subsequently came to be a major influence on Stéphane Mallarmé and Paul Valéry and even played a role in contemporary French psychoanalysis.

In terms of poetic form, Baudelaire's major innovation was undoubtedly in the prose poem, which existed before him but achieved status as a major form principally through *Paris Spleen, 1869*. In his verse, Baudelaire often used the highly restrictive "fixed forms" with their set repetition of certain verses, such as the *pantoum*, in which the second and fourth verses of one stanza become the first and third of the following four-verse unit. Such forms were common among the Ro-

mantics, but Baudelaire's combination of this formal perfection with surprising and even shocking subjects produces a dissonant and unforgettable music. Baudelaire thus avoids the pitfalls of the school of "art for art's sake," which he denounced for its exclusive attachment to surface beauty.

FLOWERS OF EVIL

Baudelaire insisted that *Flowers of Evil* should be read as a structured whole and not as a random collection of verse. Whatever one may think about the authority of such claims, the six major divisions of the book, beginning with the longest section, eighty-five poems, titled "Spleen et idéal" ("Spleen and Ideal"), and ending with the six poems of "La Mort" ("Death"), seem to outline a thematic and perhaps even chronological passage from aspirations toward a transcendence of pain, suffering, and evil (in the earliest section) through the exploration of various kinds of intoxication or escape—glimpsed in the sections "Le Vin" ("Wine"), "Flowers of Evil," and "Révolte" ("Rebellion")—only to end in death, seen itself as a form of escape from the disappointments or boredom of this world.

"TO THE READER"

Throughout *Flowers of Evil*, a major theme is the uncovering of man's own contradictions, hypocrisies, desires, and crimes: all the aspects of life and fantasy that the respectable middle class hides. In the very first poem of the book, "Au lecteur" ("To the Reader"), Baudelaire establishes an unusual relationship with his public. The poem begins with a list of vices—stupidity, error, sin, and stinginess—but instead of reproaching humanity and urging the reader to reform, the poet finishes the sentence with an independent clause containing a remarkable simile: "We feed our nice remorse,/ As beggars nourish their lice." Over this humanity presides the Devil, described two stanzas later as the magician, not Hermes but Satan Trismegistus (three-times great), who turns the rich metal of the will into vapor like an alchemist working backwards. Building toward what will apparently be a crescendo of vice, Baudelaire, in stanza 7, lists sins that man would commit if he had the courage (such as rape, poisoning, stabbing, and arson) and then points to a still greater vice, which he names only three stanzas later in the conclusion: boredom (*ennui*). In the poem's striking concluding lines, Baudelaire claims that the reader knows this "delicate monster," and then calls the reader "Hypocritical reader, my likeness, my brother!"

This strange poem, borrowing so much of its vocabulary and rhetoric from the tradition of religious exhortation, does not choose between good and evil. Instead, it promotes a third term into what is usually a simple dilemma: Boredom, as the greatest of vices, is an aesthetic concept that replaces traditional moral concepts of evil as that which must be avoided at all costs, a vice which "could swallow the world in a yawn." In religious verse, the address to the reader as a brother is part of a call, first to recognize a common weakness and, second, to repent. Baudelaire does make an avowal of similarity but calls for an aesthetic rather than an ethical response.

"BEACONS"

The largest part of *Flowers of Evil* evokes a struggle against boredom through the artistic use of the ugliness of everyday life and ordinary, even abject, passions. The poem "Les Phares" ("Beacons") is an enumeration of eight great painters, including Peter Paul Rubens, Rembrandt, and Michelangelo, not as a celebration of human greatness but as a testimony to human sentiment and sensation, predominantly in the negative. Rubens is described, for example, as a "Pillow of fresh flesh where one cannot love" and Rembrandt as a "sad hospital full of murmuring." The last three stanzas seem at first to point to a religious purpose in this art which depicts a swarming, nightmare-ridden humanity, for Baudelaire uses terms from religion: malediction, blasphemy, *Te Deum*. Humankind's art is called a "divine opium," but this drug is not offered upward as incense to the Deity. It is, rather, an opium for human hearts. The purpose of art is ambiguous in this conclusion, for it is the best testimony to human dignity but is destined to die at the edge of God's eternity. In the historical context of French Romanticism, this vision of art serves at least to set Baudelaire apart from the partisans of "art for art's sake," a movement that Baudelaire himself called the "Plastic school." Clearly, the visual beauty of the paintings alluded to is not their primary characteristic in "Beacons." These works of art are great because of their representative quality and for the tension between their beauty and the suffering on which they are based.

"A CARCASS"

The paradoxical search for an art that draws its beauty from ugliness and suffering appears in a spectacular way in another of the early poems of *Flowers of Evil*, titled "Une Charogne" ("A Carcass"). Baudelaire's particular delight in the shocking combination of refined form with a crude and repugnant subject is noticeable in the very organization of the stanzas. There are twelve units of four lines each: The first and third lines of each stanza are rhyming Alexandrines (twelve-syllable lines), while the second and fourth lines are rhyming octosyllables. This division imposes a rhythm that heightens the contrast between refined gentleness and sickening sensations. As a whole, the poem is a monologue addressed to a person or character whom the speaker calls "my soul." Although there is a certain ambiguity about the significance of the term (it could represent a division of the self into two parts, a common Baudelairean theme), the poet's "soul" assumes the role of a woman to whom he speaks in words of endearment. He also recalls, however, the discovery, one summer morning, of a carcass lying near a pathway.

The poem's opening stanza illustrates the way in which a tension is created between contrasting tones. The first two lines are addressed to the soul in terms that allow one to expect some pretty image, something that would fit the context of a beautiful, mild summer morning. The end of the second Alexandrine, however, names the object: a "foul carcass." The discovery occurs as the speaker and his soul are coming around a bend in the path (*détour*), which parallels the transition from the first half of the stanza to the somewhat startling second half. The next eight stanzas continue to tell about the discovery of this cadaver in a tone that alternates, sometimes within stanzas and sometimes from one stanza to the next, between a distant aesthetic contemplation and a crude and immediate repulsion. The fourth stanza starts with a presentation of the point of view of the sky witnessing the "blossoming" of the carcass as if it were a flower, while the next two lines ("The stench was so strong that you thought you would faint on the grass") take a distinctly human point of view, even rather sadistically delighting in the soul's weakness. The speaker's reaction is represented as quite different, much closer to that attributed to the sky. In stanza 7, he compares the sounds coming from the carcass, eaten by organisms of decomposition, to flowing water and wind and to the sound of grain being winnowed. Not only does this comparison permit the poet to find beauty in ugliness, but it also permits him to pay homage to the bucolic poetry of the Renaissance (exemplified in such poems as Joachim du Bellay's "D'un vanneur de blé aux vents" ("From a Winnower to the Winds"), showing that classical themes can be presented in a thoroughly modern way.

In the following stanza, the speaker's drift continues from a purely aesthetic contemplation of the object to a comparison of the carcass to an artist's preliminary sketch in the artist's memory. This reverie is broken off in the ninth stanza by the return to the supposed summer morning scene and the recollection that a dog was waiting for the couple to leave so that he could get her meat.

The last three stanzas are quite different, for they depart from the scene, which is in the past, and look forward to the future of the speaker's beloved "soul," foreseeing the time when she will be like that carcass. Yet, even in this section (a form of *envoi*, a traditional closing message to the addressee of a poem), the alteration of tone continues. In the tenth stanza, where the speaker declares "You will be like this filth," he still continues to refer to her as "my angel and my passion." This contrast leads toward the final stanza in which Baudelaire, again recalling the poetry of the French Renaissance, proclaims the immortality of his poetry ("I have kept the form and divine essence/ Of my decomposed loves") in contrast to the fleshly mortality of his "soul," his beloved.

It is impossible to assert that this conclusion is a straightforward poetic doctrine. Perhaps the poet, after having cast the "soul" in the paradoxical role of decomposition, is exercising a final irony toward his own poetry. In any case, it is clear that "A Carcass" represents Baudelaire's reworking of traditional texts from classical and Renaissance tradition. His way of using the tradition sets him apart from those Romantics he called the Pagan school, who preferred to assume the posture of outright return to pre-Christian belief by denying historical evolution. One reason Baudelaire objected to this position was that he himself possessed a deeply tormented Christian character, described by some as Jansenist (that is, as belonging to the most severe, pessimistic, and ascetic form of seventeenth and eighteenth century French Catholicism), penetrated by the sense of sin and guilt. He could not imagine a simple return to classical "innocence." Baudelaire also had an acute sense of the passage of time and of historical change. In calling the work of the neopagans "a disgusting and useless pastiche," he was implicitly drawing attention to his own use of antiquity in a resolutely modernist manner, one that did not copy the ancients but assimilated their ideas into a representation of the reality of modern life.

"THE SWAN"

The poignancy that Baudelaire achieves with such an approach can be seen in his "Le Cygne" ("The Swan"), dedicated, like two other poems in the section "Tableaux parisiens" ("Parisian Pictures"), to Victor Hugo, a deep believer in the historical movement of poetry. "The Swan" is divided into two numbered parts, one of seven and the other of six stanzas. In the first section, the speaker begins by addressing the legendary figure Andromache, the Trojan Hector's widow, captive in the city of Epirus. The Parisian speaker's memory, he says, has been made pregnant by the thought of the "lying Simoïs swelled by your tears." This allusion to the legends of Troy is the key to understanding the rest of the first part of the poem, most of which seems merely to tell of an event in the speaker's own life, an event without apparent connection with Andromache. He was walking across the new Carrousel Square when he recalled a menagerie that once stood on that spot. A swan had escaped from its cage and was bathing its wings in the dust of a gutter.

The allusion to Andromache is now clearer, for the "lying" Simoïs was a replica in Epirus of the small river that once flowed at the foot of the walls of Troy. In an attempt to make the widow happier, her captors had constructed this imitation, described by Baudelaire as "lying" because it is not only false but actively and disappointingly deceitful. It can never replace the Simoïs but can only remind Andromache of the discrepancy between past and present. In the second part of the poem, Baudelaire explains the multiple analogy that had been left implicit in the first part. Returning to the present (the first part had been composed of three chronological layers: the legendary past of Andromache, the moment when the speaker saw the swan, and the approximate present in which he recollects the swan), he exclaims, "Paris changes! but nothing in my melancholy/ Has moved!"

What had seemed in the first part to be a comparison only between the widow and the swan now includes the speaker. Each of the three has an immovable memory on the inside—the speaker compares his to rocks—which cannot match the mutable outside world. This dissonance between mind and world is expressed not only in the image of the swan but also, more subtly and pathetically, in the temporal organization of the poem. Between the time he saw the swan and the time of the creation of the poem, the swan has vanished and the old Carrousel has been changed into the new. The chronological layering of the text has the same function as the simile. Furthermore, the changes in Paris, composed of monumental constructions of carved stone, give the city an ironic and metaphoric significance. Monuments, like the palace of the Louvre near which the menagerie stood, are usually associated with memory. They are meant to last longer than individuals. Here, however, the city represents change. Baudelaire has thus united a commonplace of certain Romantic poets (the indifference of nature to man's suffering) with a classical poetry of cities (Troy, Epirus, Rome) to produce a thoroughly modern poetic idiom.

The conclusion of "The Swan" continues the interplay of literary allusion, for it opens still further the analogy involving Andromache, the swan, and the poet to include an African woman exiled in a northern climate, sailors, captives, and the conquered. There is a decidedly epic quality to this expansion of the analogy to include vast numbers of modern exiles. Baudelaire did not, unlike many Romantics, believe in long poems, and he seems here to be condensing the grandeur of the epic into the brevity of the personal lyric. The many components of this epic analogy, stretching from Andromache to the suggestively open-ended last line ("Of captives, of the conquered . . . of still others!"), are reminiscent of the multiple symbolic figures (the artists) of "Beacons." With this latter poem "The Swan" also shares the vision of suffering as a defining characteristic of life, for exiles "Suck at the breast of Sorrow as if she were a good wolf." This image is a way of tying in the Roman epic of Romulus and Remus while emphasizing the voluntary or consoling aspect of pain and suffering.

SUFFERING

Suffering, inflicted on others or on oneself, is a frequent theme in *Flowers of Evil* and is linked to learning and self-awareness. In "Heautontimoroumenos" (a Greek term for "the executioner of oneself," borrowed from a comedy of Terence), the speaker declares himself a "dissonance in the divine symphony" on account of the irony that eats away at him. In the most remarkable stanza, he declares in part, "I am the wound and the knife!/ I am the blow and the cheek!" In the poem immediately following, "L'Irrémédiable" ("The Irreparable"), after briefly tracing the fall of an ideal being from Heaven into Hell, Baudelaire evokes a "Somber and clear tête-à-tête/ A heart become its own mirror!" This division of the self into two sides, each looking at the other, is then described metaphorically as a "Well of truth, clear and black/ Where a pale star trembles." Although, here, knowledge is stressed more than the pain that is so fiercely displayed in "Heautontimoroumenos," pain must be the outcome of self-examination in this "well of truth" because the inward discovery is the sentiment of a fall from a higher state, an "irreparable" decadence. Yet, there is a tension here between the claim to total clarity and the image of the well, for the latter promises depths which can never be coextensive with the mirroring surface. Working back from this tension, one can see that the whole poem is full of terms for depth, darkness, and entrapment. The lucidity toward which the poem tends will never be complete, for consciousness can only discover the extent, apparently infinite, of its deprivation.

"THE TRIP"

The concluding note of *Flowers of Evil*, the section called "Death," is a reminder of this perpetual quest for new discovery, even at the price of horror. In fact, the last stanza of the concluding poem, "Le Voyage" ("The Trip"), is based on the concept of depth that had already appeared in "The Irreparable": "Plunge into the deeps of the abyss, Hell or Heaven, that difference/ Into the depth of the Unknown to find something *new*!" Here the preoccupation with boredom as supreme evil in "To the Reader" appears coupled with the themes of knowledge and discovery that constitute much of the other sections.

"The Trip" is a kind of summary in dialogue of *Flowers of Evil*, beginning with the childlike hope of discovery in the exploration of the real world. When asked later what they discovered, the travelers say that no city they discovered was ever as interesting as the cities they imagined in the shapes of clouds. Then, in passages that seem to recall the "Parisian Pictures," "Wine," and "Rebellion," the world of human sin is sketched out as a monotonous mirror in which man sees his own image, "An oasis of horror in a desert of boredom!" The only hope is in death itself, addressed in the last two stanzas as a ship's captain. He alone holds out a balm for our boredom, which itself results from an unresolvable tension between the aspirations of the heart and the outside world, ostensibly a mirror but actually an incomplete reflection because it can capture only actions and not intentions.

PARIS SPLEEN, 1869

Baudelaire's collection of prose poems, *Paris Spleen, 1869*, is thematically very similar to *Flowers of Evil*. The prose pieces, however, have greater means to establish a situation for the poetic speaker and to accumulate aspects of life that seem "realistic" but serve ultimately to reveal figurative meanings in the most ordinary surroundings, a process sometimes called "correspondences" after the title of one of Baudelaire's verse poems. Frequently, as in "Le Gâteau" ("The Cake"), Baudelaire dramatically alters the situation of the poetic speaker so that he is not a representative of dissatisfaction with the world but an amazed spectator of the subjectivity of desire. In "The Cake," a traveler finds himself in a country where his plain bread is called "cake," unleashing a fratricidal war for its possession. In "Le Joujou du pauvre" ("The Poor Child's Plaything"), he discovers two children playing on opposite sides of a fence. One child is rich and has a meticulously crafted doll while the other holds his toy in a little cage. It is a living rat. Although these texts include elements of diction, characterization, and setting typical of fiction in the realist or naturalist vein, Baudelaire always suggests a larger significance that makes the scene or incident figurative. In "The Poor Child's Plaything," the fence between the children is referred to as a symbolic barrier, and the rat is described as a toy drawn from life itself. Baudelaire specifies the metaphoric meaning much less in the prose poems than in his verse. One can, however, easily view the rat as a synecdoche for Baudelaire's aesthetic, based on drawing beauty from those aspects of life that are most repulsive.

OTHER MAJOR WORKS

LONG FICTION: *La Fanfarlo*, 1847.

NONFICTION: *Les Paradis artificiels*, 1860 (partial translation as *Artificial Paradises: On Hashish and Wine as a Means of Expanding Individuality*, 1971); *Curiosités esthétiques*, 1868; *L'Art romantique*, 1868; *Mon cœur mis à nu*, 1887 (*My Heart Laid Bare*, 1950); *The Letters of Baudelaire*, 1927; *My Heart Laid Bare and Other Prose Writings*, 1951; *Baudelaire on Poe*, 1952; *The Mirror of Art*, 1955; *Intimate Journals*, 1957; *The Painter of Modern Life and Other Essays*, 1964; *Baudelaire as Literary Critic*, 1964; *Art in Paris, 1845-1862: Salons and Other Exhibitions*, 1965.

TRANSLATIONS: *Histoires extraordinaires*, 1856 (of Edgar Allan Poe's short stories); *Nouvelles Histoires extraordinaires*, 1857 (of Poe's short stories); *Aventures d'Arthur Gordon Pym*, 1858 (of Poe's novel); *Eureka*, 1864 (of Poe's poem); *Histoires grotesques et sérieuses*, 1864 (of Poe's tales).

MISCELLANEOUS: *Œuvres complètes*, 1868-1873 (7 volumes), revised 1961.

BIBLIOGRAPHY

Blood, Susan. *Baudelaire and the Aesthetics of Bad Faith*. Stanford, Calif.: Stanford University Press, 1997. Examines the role of Baudelaire in the history of modernism and the development of the modernist consciousness. Detailed analysis of the poetry, especially its relationship to Baudelaire's writings on caricature and the problem of its "secret architecture." Also examines the nature of Baudelaire's symbolism.

Evans, Margery A. *Baudelaire and Intertextuality*. Cambridge, England: Cambridge University Press, 1993. Study of *Paris Spleen, 1869*, which validates its reassessment as a work that rivals the success of *Les Fleurs du mal*. Sees these prose poems as hybrid works that set themselves up for comparison with the novel as much as with lyric poetry.

Hyslop, Lois Boe. *Charles Baudelaire Revisited*. New York: Twayne, 1992. Useful and uncomplicated general introduction to the life and work of Baudelaire. Sees Baudelaire as transforming his emotional torment into aesthetic form, and as finding both beauty and spiritual revelations within the dark side of modernity. Discusses *Paris Spleen, 1869* and *Flowers of Evil* as major works and pays much attention to Baudelaire's theories of art. Includes a chronology and bibliography.

Leakey, F. W. *Baudelaire: "Les Fleurs du mal."* Cambridge, England: Cambridge University Press, 1992. Thorough, appreciative, and thoughtful introduction to *Flowers of Evil*, with particular attention to the sociopolitical context in which the poems were written. Includes a detailed discussion of individual poems and a bibliography.

Thompson, William J., ed. *Understanding "Les Fleurs du mal."* Nashville, Tenn.: Vanderbilt University Press, 1997. Collection of sixteen essays by various authors on *Flowers of Evil*, with the express purpose of giving students a clear, scholarly introduction to the poems. Each essay selects one particular poem for detailed discussion, and the analysis may be theoretical or textual. Essays represent a variety of critical perspectives, including feminist, Jungian, sociopolitical and structuralist.

John D. Lyons;
bibliography updated by Margaret Boe Birns

ROBIN BECKER

Born: Philadelphia, Pennsylvania; March 7, 1951

PRINCIPAL POETRY

Personal Effects, 1976 (with Helena Minton and Marilyn Zuckerman)
Backtalk, 1982
Giacometti's Dog, 1990
All-American Girl, 1996
The Horse Fair: Poems, 2000

OTHER LITERARY FORMS

As a poetry editor for the *Women's Review of Books*, Robin Becker has published numerous articles reviewing scholarly works on Elizabeth Bishop. Two such articles, reviewing Bonnie Costello's *Elizabeth Bishop: Questions of Mastery* (1991) and Lorrie Goldensohn's *Elizabeth Bishop: The Biography of a Poetry* (1992), appeared in the periodical *Women's Review of Books* (July, 1992). Becker has published other book reviews in *Belles Lettres*, *The Boston Globe*, *The Boston Review*, and *Prairie Schooner*.

ACHIEVEMENTS

Robin Becker has been honored many times for her work and has achieved a reputation as one of America's premier lesbian poets. She has received several fellowships: a Massachusetts Artist Foundation Fellowship in Poetry (1985), a fellowship in poetry from the National Endowment for the Arts (1990), and a fellowship from the Bunting Institute of Radcliffe College (1995-1996). She received Lambda Literary Awards for *All-American Girl* and *The Horse Fair*. Other literary honors have included the Virginia Faulkner Prize for Excellence in Writing from *Prairie Schooner* (1997), a position as visiting scholar at the Center for Lesbian and Gay Studies at the City University of New York (1998), and an invitation to serve as the William Steeple Davis Artist-in-Residence (2000-2001).

BIOGRAPHY

Robin Becker was born March 7, 1951, in Philadelphia, Pennsylvania, to realtors Benjamin Becker and Ann Weiner Becker. She entered Boston University in 1969, earning her B.A. in 1973 and her M.A. in 1976. Her teaching career has been long and varied: She taught at Massachusetts Institute of Technology, first as a lecturer in creative writing and humanistic studies (1977-1983) and then as an assistant professor of exposition and rhetoric (1983-1987); she was a writer-in-residence for the Wyoming Council on the Arts, in Sheridan, and the Writers' Place, in Madison, Wisconsin (both in 1991). She was a visiting professor of writing at Kent State University (1992) and Pennsylvania State University (1993-1994); an *American Poetry Review* scholar-in-residence at Central High School, in Philadelphia (1994); and an associate professor of English and Women's Studies at Pennsylvania State University (beginning in 1994). Besides her teaching, Becker has been active in other areas: She was co-coordinator of a reading series at New Words Bookstore (1981-1983), served as poetry editor for *Women's Review of Books* and as a member of the board of directors of Associated Writing Programs (1992-1995), and, during the 1998-1999 academic year, was a visiting scholar at the Center for Lesbian and Gay Studies at the City University of New York.

ANALYSIS

Throughout Robin Becker's poetry there is a sense of alienation and otherness. As a woman, as a Jew, and as a lesbian, Becker has faced the difficulties of living in an essentially male, Christian, heterosexual America with humor, intelligence, and tenacity. Her writing is specifically intended to honor and explore issues of sexual identity: "I write about issues dealing with sexual identity, relationships, and Jewish identity."

PERSONAL EFFECTS

Becker's first collection of poems gives the reader a glimpse of the poet's lifetime journey of self-discovery. Just as in later books, the poet writes verse celebrating her grandmother, examining her emergent sexuality, relating her childhood experiences, and discovering the breadth and scope of the wider world. Despite being fully aware of the differences between the dominant culture and her own, private, sensibilities, Becker stands unafraid. She accepts her Jewishness, her homosexuality, and her femininity in strong yet graceful lines.

BACKTALK

Backtalk is a volume exploring the often complex relationship between family members, friends, lovers, and pets. It describes the balances created between people and their loved ones, between people and the places they travel, and between people and their memories. These poems sort out the complexities of existence: "I remember the globe that was a pencil sharpener," says the speaker in "A Long Distance":

> I remember standing in the lunchroom
> & trying to figure out
> how I could be standing in the lunchroom
> & standing on the earth which was the globe.

The pencil sharpener—a small, concrete, graspable object—is connected to the larger idea of the world beneath her feet—an idea hard to fathom but easy to experience. This difficulty of conception yet ease of experience describes not only standing on earth but also the emotions of love and worship. As described by one critic in the *Valley Advocate*, Becker's poems tell truths of the gut and the groin. They are one half of a dialogue; communication from one individual to another rather than the meditation of a solitary individual; literally, the poems are "talking back."

GIACOMETTI'S DOG

Each poem in Becker's third book of verse, *Giacometti's Dog*, is a tribute to the impact of her visual imagery. Many of the poems, particularly "Grief," which recounts the suicide of Becker's sister, and "Good Dog," which refers to the accidental death of her beloved pet, are paeans to the sorrows of her life. The feelings expressed are raw and unrestrained, but Becker uses the very details of her works as a purgative. These poems, widely ranging in their emotional content, give voice to loss, guilt, and erotic yearning and describe the consolation that love, creativity, and friendship can provide. Becker seems to gain in wisdom as she travels, and her desire to understand the cultures of Europe and the American Southwest give the poems a depth rarely found in "travel poems."

In "The Children's Concert," Becker reminisces, guiltily, about how she tormented her younger sister into believing that the monthly concerts to which their mother took them were in reality a temporary distraction intended to hide maternal abandonment. The cultural value of the concerts is lost in the face of the younger girl's panic, but it is not until Becker's sister's suicide years later that Becker regrets her actions. "Grief," too, expresses Becker's unswerving self-condemnation as openly as "the kindness of the rabbi I remember now." The poem moves from a Philadelphia cemetery to Florence and Venice, Italy, comparing Becker's sister's life to "a place I visited by boat." Becker finds that only in the distance of poetry can she gain some kind of peace and contentment.

ALL-AMERICAN GIRL

Becker's fourth book of verse, *All-American Girl*, has the greatest scope of geographical distance of her early works. Many places—the site of a Quaker meeting in Philadelphia; a drugstore in Buffalo, Wyoming; pueblos in the American Southwest—are only a few of the vast distances traveled in the scope of this small volume, which also explores the vastness of inner space. Becker drives from Taos to Sante Fe, goes "contra" dancing in New Hampshire, dresses up as Peter Pan and "flies" onstage. Her movements are quick, sure, and far-reaching. The only constant is her voice, daring the reader to follow her further into her vision and pain. Every poem describes a revolution, a breakup, a sorrow. Love ends, families dissolve, childhood innocence is ended.

All-American Girl, like *Giacometti's Dog*, describes loss and acceptance of loss. Becker seems to struggle for order and strives to make sense out of the chaos of her life. "The Star Show," with its chaotic universe, is no more out-of-control than Becker; its planetarium commentator who "[throws] stars across the sky, [flings] meteors/ carelessly . . ./ . . . punctur[ing] the darkness with white bullets" is no more destructive than the forces that make Becker's life difficult. Becker truly is an all-American girl: She loves her dog and horses, enjoys the vigorous exercise of skiing, hiking, and skinny-dipping at midnight. She finds pleasure in her femininity, although she wishes that she could enjoy the benefits of being male:

> . . . the boy across the street
> who hung upside down from a tree and didn't care
> that his shirt fluttered over his bare chest.

But all of these things pale beside the death of her sister and the dissolution of her grieving family.

This fourth book follows the pattern set by her third, *Giacometti's Dog*, in that she revisits her Philadelphia childhood, her Jewish family, her constant travel, and her blossoming homosexuality. Both volumes are anecdotal in flavor and tend toward the humorous, but *All-American Girl* more thoroughly examines Becker's growth as a lesbian. It is more erotic in tone and, though often droll, reflects more deeply on the pain of embracing an "alternative lifestyle." "Philadelphia, 1955," for example, shows the young Becker

> . . . in a nightgown
> closes the door and walks barefoot
> on the black grass. Stars have grouped

> like families into their fixed relations.
> She welcomes the great indifference
> of the street. . . .

That "indifference" demonstrates the distance she feels between the silently sleeping families and her burgeoning desires: "Everything that is her own is suddenly here revealed, separate as her body." "A History of Sexual Preference" further demonstrates this new, proud sexuality in a way that the poems in *Giacometti's Dog* failed to do. Becker, in her quest for equal rights for women, casts herself as "seventeen and tired of fighting for freedom/ and the rights of men." She is preparing her own declaration of independence and is "already dreaming of Boston—/ city of women." It is here that Becker and her girlfriend have their first sexual encounter, "in a hotel room on Rittenhouse Square":

> And I am happy as the young
> Tom Jefferson, unbuttoning my collar, imagining his
>   power,
> considering my healthy body, how I might use it in the
>   service
> of the country of my pleasure.

Thus, Becker's restless travel makes sense; she is converting her inner pain into movement. Though love fails and families suffer, she knows that greater wisdom awaits those who seek it. In "Shopping" she says that "If things don't work out/ I'll buy the belt/ with the fashionable silver buckle," acknowledging the frivolous ways in which women use clothing to control their internal suffering: "I'll do what my mother did/ after she buried my sister:/ outfitted herself in an elegant suit/ for the rest of her life." The outside clothing, Becker comments, controls the inner torment even though, as she further notes in "Santo Domingo Feast Day," "there are no remedies for great sorrow . . . only dancing and chanting, listening and waiting."

THE HORSE FAIR

In *The Horse Fair*, Becker questions the nature of citizenship; she examines the ways in which we, as human beings, market our bodies, our ideas, our belongings. She describes how marginalized individuals alternate between their public and private personae in their everyday lives. Unlike previous volumes, *The Horse Fair* speaks with many voices. Beginning with Rosa Bonheur, the nineteenth century French painter who created the painting that inspired the book's title, Becker describes a woman caught up by the pain of her culture. In another poem, Becker becomes Charlotte Salomon, child of German Jews, killed by the Nazis at twenty-six. In this portrait, Becker establishes a parallel structure that compares sections of the Rosh Hashanah and Yom Kippur services with stanzas that mourn her sister's death and stanzas that celebrate nontraditional families. Organized around long meditations, other poems show Becker's dexterity with formal verse (she uses the sestina and sonnet forms with ease) and free verse.

The Horse Fair serves as the instrument with which Becker explores anti-Semitism, cross-dressing, and homosexuality—the sexual preference of both Becker and Bonheur. The volume presents the reader with the marketplace, the communal spaces where purchases of self and lifestyle are made. The best part of Becker's poems is how much the world is with her in these lyrics; characters, histories, animals, places, and things crowd onto the pages, inscribing them with living, breathing voices.

BIBLIOGRAPHY

Ciuraru, Carmela. "The Horse Fair." *The New York Times Book Review*, September 24, 2000. Ciuraru describes Becker as "honest" in describing her Judaism, complicated relationships, and unconventional sexuality. She presents to the reader a poet who fearlessly confronts events and emotions. She defines Becker's poems as paeans to animals, lovers, and family members, who have taught her the more important lessons in life.

Frank, Allen. "*Giacometti's Dog*." Review of *Giacometti's Dog. Poet Lore* 85, no. 4 (Winter, 1990/1991): 49. Frank celebrates the tenacity of Becker's vision in this book review. He establishes the fluidity of her verse while recognizing the sometimes brutal impact of the described scenarios.

Grosholz, Emily. "Flint and Iron." *The Hudson Review* 53, no. 3 (Autumn, 2000). Grosholtz compares Becker's poetry with the "fire" created from the clashing of divergent parts of Becker's life—the "flint" and "iron." She describes the revolutionary spirit that fuels Becker's poetry while still acknowledging the delicacy of her work.

Schwartz, Patricia Roth. "Profound Pitt Poets." *Lambda Book Report* 9, no. 2 (September, 2000). Characterizing Becker as a thoroughly erudite and often-witty lesbian, Schwartz honors Becker, now a professor at Pennsylvania State University, for her five books of poetry and her National Endowment for the Arts fellowship. Schwartz confirms that Becker has chosen not to be simply a lesbian poet but has instead achieved a larger artistic acceptance without compromising her lesbian identity. She comments on knowing Becker personally and seeing her work mature from *Backtalk*, where the focus is her relationships, her sister's suicide, her family, and her own often-troubled past, through *Giacometti's Dog* and *All-American Girl*, where the focus is more complex.

Shomer, Enid. "Hungry for the World." *The Women's Review of Books* 18, no. 1 (October, 2000). Shomer, commenting that Becker's poems reflect the poet's sexual and social identity in startlingly apt metaphors, describes the poet's careful handling of the widely varying scenery in *The Horse Fair*. The Philadelphia of Becker's girlhood, her ancestral links to the shtetls of Eastern Europe, the mesas of New Mexico (one of her favorite landscapes), and the towns and people of Italy meet and meld in "surprising satisfying juxtapositions." She describes Becker's poetic technique as combining irony and directness.

Ullman, Leslie. "The Heart's Difficult Speech." *The Kenyon Review* 17, no. 1 (Winter, 1995). In the *Kenyon Review*, poet Ullman notes that Becker writes "with a gentleness, calmness, and frank sensuality that makes her poems refreshing and wise." She describes Becker's poems as not only affirming the condition of love (be it lesbian, gay, or heterosexual) but also detailing the struggle of learning to love.

Yannone, Sandra. Review of *All-American Girl. Prairie Schooner* 72, no. 4 (Winter, 1998): 195-198. Yannone describes Becker's work as roving the terrain of loss and grief: the streets of Becker's childhood in Philadelphia, where she courts other women; the arid deserts of the Southwest, where she examines her childless, often partnerless life; and the romantic tapestry of Italy, where she struggles as an outsider to make a life with other women.

Julia M. Meyers

SAMUEL BECKETT

Born: Foxrock, Ireland; April 13, 1906
Died: Paris, France; December 22, 1989

PRINCIPAL POETRY

Whoroscope, 1930
Echo's Bones and Other Precipitates, 1935
Poems in English, 1961
Collected Poems in English and French, 1977

OTHER LITERARY FORMS

Samuel Beckett is far better known for his fiction and plays than for his poetry, even though it was as a poet that he began his writing career. In fact, Beckett explored almost every literary form, writing in English and in French. His early fiction, the collection of stories *More Pricks than Kicks* (1934) and the novels *Murphy* (1938) and *Watt* (1953), was written originally in English, but his best-known fictions, including the trilogy of *Molloy* (1951; English translation, 1955), *Malone meurt* (1951; *Malone Dies, 1956*), and *L'Innomable* (1953; *The Unnamable*, 1958), and *Comment c'est* (1961; *How It Is*, 1964) and *Le Dèpeupleur* (1971; *The Lost Ones*, 1972) were written and published originally in French. From the beginning, Beckett's greatest strength was as an innovator, writing prose works which do not seem to fit easily into traditional categories but which extend the possibilities of contemporary fiction and which have had a profound influence on the writers who have followed him.

Beckett was also a writer of plays, and, when his name is mentioned, most people think of *En attendant Godot* (pb. 1952; *Waiting for Godot*, 1954). This difficult theatrical work met with astounding success on stages throughout the world, and it is still Beckett's best-known and most-discussed piece. Other works for the stage, *Fin de partie: Suivi de Acte sans paroles* (pr., pb. 1957; music by John Beckett; *Endgame: A Play in One Act, Followed by Act Without Words: A Mime for One Player*, 1958); *Krapp's Last Tape* (pr., pb. 1958), *Happy Days* (pr., pb. 1961), and *Rockaby* (pr., pb. 1981), to name only a few, have extended the possibilities of live theater. His *Collected Shorter Plays* was published in 1984.

Never content to restrict himself to a single medium, Beckett demonstrated that radio and television can serve as vehicles for serious drama with radio plays such as *All That Fall* (1957), *Cascando* (1963), and *Words and Music* (1962), and television scripts such as *Eh Joe* (1966). Beckett also wrote the screenplay for the short movie *Film* (1965), produced and directed by Alan Schneider and starring Buster Keaton. Like the novels and the plays, these works for the mass media tapped new possibilities and pointed out new directions which other younger writers are only now beginning to explore.

Early in his career, Beckett also showed that he was a brilliant critic of the arts, writing on the fiction of James Joyce and Marcel Proust and on the paintings of his longtime friend Bram van Velde. In addition to translating his own works, he has translated other writers, including Robert Pinget, Paul Eluard, Alain Bosquet, and Sebastien Chamfort from the French and *An Anthology of Mexican Poetry* (1958) from the Spanish. His English version of Arthur Rimbaud's "Le Bateau ivre" (The Drunken Boat), done in the 1930's but lost for many years and rediscovered and published for the first time only in the 1977 *Collected Poems in English and French*, is masterful, but his best-known translation is of Guillaume Apollinaire's "Zone" (1972), a long poem that addresses many of Beckett's own themes and which opens with a line that could well characterize Beckett's efforts in all forms: "In the end you are weary of this ancient world."

ACHIEVEMENTS

When the Swedish Academy selected Samuel Beckett to receive the Nobel Prize in Literature in 1969, the award only confirmed what critics and readers had known for some time: that he is one of the most important literary figures of the late twentieth century. Few authors in the history of literature have attracted as much critical attention as Beckett, and with good reason; he is both an important figure in his own right and a transitional thinker whose writings mark the end of modernism and the beginning of a new sensibility, postmodernism. The modernists of the early twentieth century—James Joyce, W. H. Auden, Virginia Woolf, Marcel Proust, and others—were stunned by the absur-

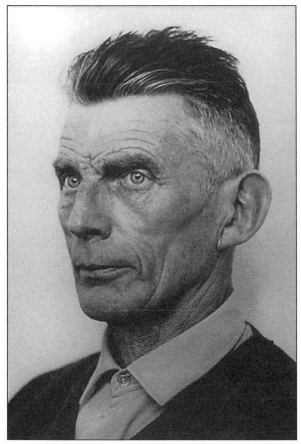

Samuel Beckett, Nobel Prize laureate in literature for 1969.
(© The Nobel Foundation)

Joyce could revel in the possibilities and textures of the written word, Beckett could not. Instead, he reduced his fictions, his plays, and his poems to the barest elements, and, throughout his career, he tried to rejoin art and life in his own way. For the pre-modernists, art imitated the world beyond the human mind. The modernists rejected this idea of imitation, and so did Beckett. Instead, his art reflects the inner world, the world of the human voice, the only world human beings can ever really experience. In the pre-modern era, art was successful if it depicted some truth about the world. For the modernists, art succeeded only on its own terms, regardless of the world beyond the scope of the arts. For Beckett, art never succeeds. It is a necessary failure which never manages to link the inner mind to outer reality. As such, art is an exercise in courage, foredoomed to failure, like human life itself. Human beings are human beings not because they can give meaning to the world or because they can retreat into aesthetics but because they can recognize that their world is meaningless and that their lives are leading them only toward death; yet they must continue to live and strive. As a philosopher of failure, Beckett was the first thinker of the post-modern age.

BIOGRAPHY

Samuel Barclay Beckett grew up in a suburb of Dublin, Ireland, a Protestant in a Catholic country and therefore something of an exile in his own land. He attended Trinity College in Dublin, where he discovered his talent for languages and studied English, French, and Italian. He taught for two terms at Campbell College in Belfast and then, in 1928, traveled to Paris, where he lectured in English at the ècole Normale Supèrieure. It was during this tenure that he met his countryman James Joyce. Beckett returned to Ireland to teach four terms at Trinity College, but, in 1932, after much consideration and anguish, he left the teaching profession for good, convinced that he could not survive as a writer in academe. For the next five years, he wandered through Europe, and, in 1937, he settled in Paris permanently. It was in Paris that Beckett died in 1989, at the age of eighty-three.

There were probably many reasons for Beckett's self-imposed exile and for his decision to write in a language not his by birth, but surely one reason was the in-

dity of their world. Previous generations had filled that world with philosophical, religious, and political meanings, but their orderly vision of reality no longer seemed to apply to life in the early 1900's. The modernists lacked the faith of their forebears; they had experienced the chaos of the modern world with its potential for global war and the destruction of civilization, and they believed that the order of reality was a fiction, that life was unknowable. In response to their doubts, they turned literature in upon itself, separating it from life, creating an art for its own sake. These writers trusted in language to create new meanings, new knowledge, and a separate, artistic human universe.

As a young man, Beckett also experienced this sense of absurdity and meaninglessness in the modern world, but, unlike his modernist predecessors, he could not even muster faith in his art or in language. Thus, while fluence of Joyce, who recommended exile for artists. It would be difficult to overestimate the effect that Joyce had on Beckett's life and work. In the late 1930's, the younger Irishman was an intimate member of Joyce's inner circle. He worked on a translation of Joyce's "Anna Livia Plurabelle" into French, took dictation for his friend, wrote a critical study of Joyce's writings, ran errands for the Irish master, and even attracted the romantic interest of Joyce's daughter, Lucia. Apparently, Joyce thought a great deal of Beckett, and Beckett looked upon Joyce as a consummate master, so that it is possible he decided to write in French in order to avoid the language which, in his own mind, Joyce had all but exhausted.

As Beckett grew older and developed as a writer, Joyce's influence began to weaken, and, in many ways, Beckett's later style—spare, flat, reduced to the barest elements—is the antithesis of Joyce's rich, punning, heavily textured prose. Beckett also rejected Joyce's "Irishness" in favor of characters and settings without specific nationality or history. In the early poetry, however, the influence of Joyce and Ireland is still strong, and, in fact, it was in his poems that Beckett first began to work through Joyce's voice and to discover his own.

ANALYSIS

Whoroscope was Samuel Beckett's first major publication. It is a long poem, written originally in English, and published in book form by the Hours Press after winning a prize offered by the publisher for the best poem on the subject of time. The first-person narrator of the work is René Descartes, the seventeenth century French philosopher, mathematician, and scientist, and the poem is so full of obscure allusions to his life and times that, at the publisher's request, Beckett added a page and a half of notes to the ninety-eight-line piece. In fact, the notes are almost as interesting as the poem itself, and, without them, it is unlikely that the average reader would even recognize Descartes as the speaker.

WHOROSCOPE

Whoroscope is an important poem not only because it marked Beckett's official entry into the literary world but also because it introduced the basic themes that continued to occupy him as a writer and thinker. Clearly,

Beckett himself recognized this fact, because he chose to keep this early work intact in the subsequent collections of his poetry, *Poems in English* and *Collected Poems in English and French*, which include all the works discussed here. In many ways, *Whoroscope* is quite unlike the author's later writings. The structure of the piece is open, without rhyme or regular meter. The poem shows the influence of the French surrealists in its associative juxtaposition of images, but the influence of Joyce is also apparent in the punning title and in the body of the text.

On first reading, it is not at all obvious that this is a poem about time. From the opening line, Descartes rambles on, apparently at random, about various events in his life, without respect for chronology or even historical accuracy. In the closing section, it becomes clear that the philosopher is on his deathbed and that his ramblings are the result of illness and fever. In a sense, his life is flashing before his eyes. He is trying to grasp the fullness of time at the moment of his death, and a closer reading shows that the sequence of memories is not random at all but associative, each a memory leading to the next— not in chronological order but in the order dictated by Descartes's subjective thought process.

In fact, the poem is very much about time—the time of a man's life and the attempt to recapture lost time in the instant before time runs out. The Joycean influence in Descartes's stream-of-consciousness narrative is evident, but it is also obvious that Beckett has learned a great deal from Marcel Proust's *A la recherche du temps perdu* (1913-1927, *Remembrance of Things Past*), which the young Beckett knew well—so well, in fact, that in 1931 he published *Proust*, a book-length study of this French masterwork.

Whoroscope, then, is about time as the great destroyer, time that eats up a man's life and leads only to death. It is important to remember, however, that this poem is about the lifetime of a particular man, Descartes, and there is good reason for Beckett's choice of this philosopher as his narrator. Like Beckett himself, Descartes was a transitional figure, the father of modern philosophy and the opponent of Aristotelian scholasticism. He and his contemporaries initiated a new age in Western civilization, an age that is only now passing away, and, in his poem, Beckett pays tribute to other great thinkers such as Galileo and Francis Bacon, who directed Western thought into the era of science and rationalism.

Descartes was a great builder, but he was also a great destroyer of the philosophies of the past, and, in the poem, he speaks with pride of "throwing/ Jesuits out of the skylight." He devoted his life to the development of a new system of thought, but, in so doing, he also undermined the Aristotelian metaphysics that had served as the basis of European philosophy for centuries. Ironically, while Descartes was destroying his predecessors, the time of his own life was destroying him.

This is one of the key themes of Beckett's work: the fact that death comes to all living things, without reason, without justice, regardless of whether one is innocent or guilty. As Beckett writes in a later, untitled poem, man lives "the space of a door/ that opens and shuts." He is born to die; he is dying even in the womb, losing time from the moment of conception, and there is nothing that can stop or even delay this process. Each man's life cancels itself, moment by moment.

The historical Descartes died while in the service of Queen Christina of Sweden, a harsh woman who forced the aging philosopher to call upon her at five o'clock each morning although he had been in the habit of staying in bed until midday all his life. This change in his routine, coupled with the northern weather, led to his final illness. In the poem, the fictional Descartes refers to Queen Christina as "Rahab of the snows." Rahab was a biblical harlot mentioned in *The Divine Comedy* (c. 1320) of Dante (whom Beckett has called "the only poet"), and so it would seem that the Queen is the whore of the title. In his notes to the poem, Beckett points out that Descartes kept his birthday secret so that no astrologer could cast his horoscope. The philosopher was opposed to such mysticism, not only because it was unscientific but because he felt that many people let their entire lives be dictated by astrology; he even knew of two young men who had allowed themselves to die simply because their horoscopes had predicted death for them. With this knowledge, the Joycean pun of the title becomes clear. Queen Christina, the harlot, has cast Descartes's death, which was present from the moment of his birth. His "whoroscope" is her prediction of his inevitable end.

This theme of the inevitability of death, of death as a necessary function of birth, runs through the poem in the form of a recurring motif. Again in the notes, Beckett explains that Descartes liked his morning omelette to be made from eggs that had been hatched from eight to ten days—that is, eggs in which the embryo was partially developed. Time and again in the poem he asks about his morning eggs: "How long did she womb it, the feathery one? . . . How rich she smells,/ this abortion of a fledgling!"

For Beckett, the egg is the symbol of the fetus conceived only to die, its brief span of life lived out in the instant between nonexistence and nonexistence. The time of the egg is the time of the philosopher as well. As with all human beings, Descartes is dying before he has even really lived, and, like the fledgling in the egg, he is dying for no purpose, simply because that is the way things are.

Beckett explored the themes of the inevitability of death and the meaninglessness of life time and again in his works, but he has always coupled these themes with another: the necessity of going on, of raging against the inevitable, of refusing to accept man's fate. In the poem "Serena III," he insists that human beings must "keep on the move/ keep on the move," and, in *Whoroscope*, he depicts Descartes first as angry, cursing his fate, then as begging for another chance at a life he has never managed to understand, a "second/ starless inscrutable hour." There is no reason for him to go on, and yet, as a human being, he must.

For Beckett, man must die, but he must also live and think and speak, as Descartes does, even to the last possible instant. He must live in his own inner world which is always dying, and he must also live in the outer world which will live on after him and which, therefore, is not his. This theme of the conflict between the inner and the outer worlds which runs through Beckett's later work is present in *Whoroscope* as well. The very structure of the poem, which follows the philosopher's associative thinking, places the narrative within Descartes's inner mind, though in the end it moves to the outer world, to "Christina the ripper" and to her court physician, Weulles, who is attending to Descartes in his last moments. In his inner world, Descartes is alive and reliving his past, but it is the outer world which is leading him to inevitable death. Descartes devoted his life to trying to understand the outer world, but the very foundation of his thought, the dictum "cogito, ergo sum" ("I think, therefore I am") trapped him within his own subjectivity, and generations of later philosophers have tried to understand how one can move from the certainty of the "cogito" to the world beyond which is not oneself. The "cogito," the single point of certainty in the Cartesian philosophy of doubt, is the fulcrum of modern Western philosophy, and yet it restricts the thinker to his own inner world, to what Beckett calls, in his poem "The Vulture," "the sky/ of my skull."

For Beckett, it is impossible for man to come to know the world beyond his skull, that very world in which he must live and die. In the play *Endgame*, the characters Hamm and Clov live within a skull-like structure; Hamm is blind, and Clov can see the world only through two eyelike windows which restrict his vision. In the short novel *The Lost Ones* an entire society lives and passes away within a huge white dome, a skull. In *Whoroscope*, Descartes can know his inner world, but the outer world remains "inscrutable." He knows that he thinks and, therefore, that he is, but he does not know why. He wants to know the truth and to speak it, but the "cogito" cannot lead him to knowledge of the outer world. In the poem, he mentions St. Augustine, who also sought a single point of certainty in a world in which everything was open to question, and found that the only thing he could be sure of was that he could be deceived. The Descartes of the poem states the Augustinian dictum as "Fallor, ergo sum!" ("I am deceived, therefore I am"). At the moment of death, this certainty seems truer to the philosopher than his own "cogito." To be a man is to be deceived, to fail, and, for a human being, courage is the courage to fail. Man is man only insofar as he knows that failure is inevitable and yet keeps going in spite of that knowledge.

ECHO'S BONES AND OTHER PRECIPITATES

There is another important Beckett theme which surfaces only briefly in *Whoroscope* but which becomes the main focus of the author's second collection of poems, *Echo's Bones and Other Precipitates:* the theme of the impossibility of love in the face of absurdity and death. For Beckett, love is another of man's basic needs, as important as the quest for meaning, and as futile. The Des-

cartes poem touched on the theme only briefly, in the philosopher's memory of a little cross-eyed girl who was his childhood playmate and who reminds him of his only daughter, Francine, who died of scarlet fever at the age of six. The implication is that love always ends, if not now, then late; and, like the rest of life, love is both essential and hopeless, necessary and frightening. Knowing that love is impossible, pretending that it is not, man loves, and that love is the source of his pain but also of his life.

The poems of *Echo's Bones and Other Precipitates* differ from *Whoroscope* not only because they focus on love but also because the narrator is not a fictional version of a historical character but the author himself. The title of the collection comes from Ovid's *Metamorphosis* (before 8 C.E.), from the story of Echo, who, after being spurned by Narcissus, lets herself wither away until only her bones and voice remain. The connection between Ovid's tale and Beckett's theme of love is clear, but the story of Echo also provides the poet with two of his favorite images: the inevitability of death and the survival of the voice.

Most of the titles and forms of the poems in this collection are based on the songs of the troubadours which Beckett knew well and which attracted him no doubt because they were songs of love and, often, of loss, and also because the troubadours were usually wanderers and exiles, like Beckett himself and like the narrators of most of these poems. The work "Enueg I" draws its title from the traditional Provençal lament or complaint, and, as might be expected, it is a complaint of love. In the poem, the narrator leaves the nursing home where his beloved is dying of tuberculosis ("Exeo in a spasm/ tired of my darling's red sputum") and wanders through Dublin, traveling in a wide circle. He finds that the world is full of images of death ("a dying barge," "the stillborn evening," "the tattered sky like an ink of pestilence") and that he cannot forget his beloved or the fate of their love. Of course, these signs of death are not really present in the outer world; they reflect the narrator's inner life, the only life he can know, and, like Descartes, he rages against what he knows to be true as his own blood forms a "clot of anger."

There is no romance in Beckett's lament, only the all-encompassing awareness of mortality. Love and romance are like "the silk of the seas and the arctic flowers/ that do not exist," figments of the imagination that lose all sense of reality in the face of "the banner of meat bleeding."

The narrator keeps moving, however, and throughout the poem he has contact with others, with a small boy and "a wearish old man," an archetypal Beckett character, "scuttling along between a crutch and a stick,/ his stump caught up horribly, like a claw, under his breech, smoking." These meetings show the continuing possibility of human contact, even in a dying world; they also make clear the need for going on even in the face of futility. Perhaps the others, like the narrator, are also moving in circles, but circular movement is still movement, and even the old man, crippled and in pain, does not remain motionless, does not give up.

"Sanies I" is also modeled on a Provençal form; the title is derived from a Latin term meaning "morbid discharge." For Beckett, writing is such a discharge, a residue, a "precipitate." It is a by-product of living and dying, but it is also that which remains, like Echo's voice.

Like the narrator of "Enueg I," the narrator of "Sanies I" is a wanderer in the process of completing a circle; in this case, he is returning home to Ireland after traveling in Europe, apparently in Germany, for his speech is full of Germanic terms. Like later Beckett protagonists, he rides a bicycle, and he describes himself as "a Ritter," a German knight, and, therefore, a somewhat ironic hero, though perhaps the only kind of hero who remains in the postmodern age: the hero who keeps moving. He has been wandering for a long time, and he says that he is "müüüüüüüüüde now." The German "müde" means "tired," but the extended "ü" sound also gives a sense of boredom, an essential element in most of Beckett's work. Clearly, the narrator is both tired and bored, and, as a result, he is "bound for home like a good boy." Thinking about home and his parents, he recalls his birth and longs for that sweet oblivion of the womb: "Ah to be back in the caul now with no trusts/ no fingers no spoilt love."

This is a key passage. "The caul" to which the narrator would like to return is a fetal membrane covering the head, and, according to folklore, the child who is born with a caul is born to good luck. The implication here, however, is that the best of luck is never to have been

born at all and, therefore, to have avoided "trusts" and "spoilt loves," those exercises in futility. The unborn child also has "no fingers," and one without fingers cannot, and therefore need not, travel on a bicycle as the narrator does. Even better, one without fingers cannot write, no matter how strongly he might feel the need to do so.

Of course, the narrator no longer has the option of not being born. He is "tired now hair ebbing gums ebbing ebbing home," and yet he approaches his hometown like a "Stürmer," German slang for "lady-killer." It would seem that, despite his "spoilt loves," he is prepared for love again, and, indeed, he sees his beloved waiting for him. "I see main verb at last/ her whom alone in the accusative/ I have dismounted to love." In German, the "main verb" comes at the end of the sentence, and in this sentence that word is "love." At the last moment, however, the narrator sends the girl away ("get along with you now"), refusing to make the mistake his parents made by bringing another being into the world. Although one cannot return to the peace of the womb, one can at least refuse to pass on the curse of life to another.

If "Sanies I" is about nonexistence in the womb (the Cartesian egg), and if "Enueg I" is about nonexistence in the tomb, the title poem of the collection brings these two notions together. "Echo's Bones" is a short lyric that restates Beckett's key themes in capsule form. The first word of the poem is "asylum," a reference to the womb, but this is an "asylum under my tread," a shelter underground, a tomb. Like those in the womb, those in the tomb are beyond the confusions and pains of living now that they have run the gauntlet of life, "the gantelope of sense and nonsense." Only now, in death, are they free to be themselves, "taken by the maggots for what they are," and what they are is fleshless bone, without love or dreams and without the need to keep striving. The title of the poem, however, is a reminder that something more than bone remains: the voice. The words may be only a "morbid discharge," but, like Echo's voice, they survive.

"SOMETHING THERE"

Leaping ahead four decades to "Something There," a poem composed in 1974, the reader finds that the author's voice has changed, although his key themes remain. Here the lines are short and direct, flat and prosaic. There are no obscure allusions, no Joycean puns. The "something there" of the title is "something outside/ the head," and this contrast of inner and outer worlds returns the reader to *Whoroscope* and to the Cartesian dilemma of subjectivity which cannot reach beyond itself. The poem tries to reach that "something" in the only way it can, through words, but "at the faint sound so brief/ it is gone." The reality beyond the inner mind disappears as soon as the words of the mind try to grasp it, and so language, in the end, describes only the inner world which becomes something like a womb and a tomb in the midst of life. The inner world is not life, and yet, despite the fact that man cannot reach beyond his inner self to comprehend the "something outside/ the head," still he must try to do so, and the sign of his failure is language, the voice which always remains.

One can argue that Beckett's view of existence is largely negative. On the other hand, however, it is important to remember that he was influenced greatly by the medieval theologians who argued that truth, in the person of God, is beyond positive statement and that man can know the truth only in the negative, by describing what it is not. Beckett seems to have taken the same approach. It is true that he wrote about the curse of life, but he did so beautifully, raging against the inevitability of silence. The beauty of his work is the beauty of the human will to live in the face of death. Beckett sings the praises of those who say, with the nameless, formless, faceless narrator of *The Unnamable:* "I can't go on, I'll go on."

OTHER MAJOR WORKS

LONG FICTION: *Murphy*, 1938; *Molloy*, 1951 (English translation, 1955); *Malone meurt*, 1951 (*Malone Dies*, 1956); *L'Innommable*, 1953 (*The Unnamable*, 1958); *Watt*, 1953; *Comment c'est*, 1961 (*How It Is*, 1964); *Mercier et Camier*, 1970 (*Mercier and Camier*, 1974); *Le Dèpeupleur*, 1971 (*The Lost Ones*, 1972); *Company*, 1980; *Mal vu mal dit*, 1981 (*Ill Seen Ill Said*, 1981); *Worstward Ho*, 1983.

SHORT FICTION: *More Pricks than Kicks*, 1934; *Nouvelles et textes pour rien*, 1955 (*Stories and Texts for Nothing*, 1967); *No's Knife: Collected Shorter Prose 1947-1966*, 1967; *First Love and Other Shorts*, 1974; *Pour finir encore et autres foirades*, 1976 (*Fizzles*, 1976).

PLAYS: *En attendant Godot*, pb. 1952 (*Waiting for Godot*, 1954); *Fin de partie: Suivi de Acte sans paroles*, pr., pb. 1957 (music by John Beckett; *Endgame: A Play in One Act, Followed by Act Without Words: A Mime for One Player*, 1958); *Krapp's Last Tape*, pr., pb. 1958; *Act Without Words II*, pr., pb. 1960 (one-act mime); *Happy Days*, pr., pb. 1961; *Play*, pr., pb. 1963 (English translation, 1964); *Come and Go: Dramaticule*, pr., pb. 1965 (one scene; English translation, 1967); *That Time*, pr., pb. 1976; *Footfalls*, pr., pb. 1976; *Ends and Odds*, pb. 1976; *A Piece of Monologue*, pr. 1979; *Rockaby*, pr., pb. 1981; *Ohio Impromptu*, pr. 1981; *Catastrophe*, pr. 1982; *Company*, pr. 1983; *Collected Shorter Plays*, pb. 1984.

SCREENPLAY: *Film*, 1965.

TELEPLAYS: *Eh Joe*, 1966 (*Dis Joe*, 1967); *Not I*, 1972; *Tryst*, 1976; *Shades*, 1977; *Quad*, 1981.

RADIO PLAYS: *All That Fall*, 1957, revised 1968; *Embers*, 1959; *Words and Music*, 1962 (music by John Beckett); *Cascando*, 1963 (music by Marcel Mihalovici).

NONFICTION: *Proust*, 1931.

TRANSLATION: *An Anthology of Mexican Poetry*, 1958 (Octavio Paz, editor).

MISCELLANEOUS: *I Can't Go On, I'll Go On: A Selection from Samuel Beckett's Work*, 1976 (Richard Seaver, editor).

BIBLIOGRAPHY

Alvarez, Alfred. *Samuel Beckett*. New York: Viking Press, 1973. Alvarez discusses Beckett's literary output and argues that he is creative for the originality with which he restates the same case in unexpected ways. This good introduction to a difficult writer identifies Beckett's themes as expressing "a message of undifferentiated gloom . . . and a spirit of pure desolation." Really a praise of Beckett, not a criticism.

Bair, Deirdre. *Beckett: A Biography*. New York: Harcourt Brace Jovanovich, 1978. This unauthorized biographical account follows Beckett from his childhood in Ireland through his years in Paris. It covers his relationships with James Joyce, his family, and others, and it examines the autobiographical influences on his work. This interpretive biography tends to trivialize the mysterious universality of Beckett's life and work. Bair interviewed Beckett, his friends, and his colleagues and was given access to correspondences hitherto unpublished. Not without its detractors, this is the first full biography of the writer.

Beckett, Samuel. *No Author Better Served: The Correspondence of Samuel Beckett and Alan Schneider.* Edited by Maurice Harmon. Cambridge, Mass.: Harvard University Press, 1998. The letters not only include discussions of many issues surrounding the plays, but, more important, they bring alive the playwright's moment-by-moment intentions with respect to the feelings elicited. In effect, Beckett's letters provide a study guide to the plays, a guide originally intended for directors, not actors or audience.

Bryden, Mary. *Samuel Beckett and the Idea of God.* New York: St. Martin's Press, 1998. The strength of Bryden's book is the very limitation of its method: to show that though Beckett may have despised God, at least he did not ignore His scriptures, acolytes, ministers, priests, theologians, or mystics. What she has labored to produce is an indispensable compendium, virtually a concordance, of religious reference in Beckett.

Esslin, Martin, ed. *Samuel Beckett: A Collection of Critical Essays.* Englewood Cliffs, N.J.: Prentice-Hall, 1965. This collection includes a survey of Beckett's verse by John Gould Fletcher and is an excellent reference book on Beckett with material from Beckett's leading critics and observers. These essays are definitely mid-twentieth century opinions and reflect Esslin's own philosophical bent toward existentialism.

Harvey, Lawrence E. *Samuel Beckett: Poet and Critic.* Princeton, N.J.: Princeton University Press, 1970. This study, devoted almost entirely to Beckett's poetry, looks at the early writing from 1929 to 1949. It combines analyses of the poems with comments on the young Beckett based on conversations with the

author and unpublished manuscripts. A thoughtful examination of Beckett's poetry, it analyzes Beckett's first poem, *Whoroscope*, and points out the early incarnation of Beckett's philosophical disposition and the roots of his future characters.

Kaelin, Eugene F. *The Unhappy Consciousness: The Poetic Plight of Samuel Beckett.* Boston: D. Reidel, 1981. Characterizing Beckett as a philosophical writer, Kaelin analyzes his creative work from a phenomenological, structuralist point of view attempting to show the degree to which the philosophical structures of Beckett's works have changed. Comparisons and references to Georg Wilhelm Friedrich Hegel, Martin Heidegger, Jean-Paul Sartre and Maurice Merleau-Ponty are discussed.

Kenner, Hugh. *Samuel Beckett: A Critical Study.* Berkeley: University of California Press, 1973. This edition of a 1961 study contains a supplementary chapter and explores Beckett's themes with careful readings of all the existing material up to the date of publication. Beckett's relationships to Marcel Proust and James Joyce as well as Homer, Vergil, Dante, philology, René Descartes and phenomenology are examined. This "classical" study of Beckett also notes what he has done with the forms of drama and the novel.

Mercier, Vivian. *Beckett/Beckett.* New York: Oxford University Press, 1977. Each chapter sets up a dialectic to explore the dualistic elements found in Beckett's work, including Ireland/The World, Gentleman/Tramp, Classicism/Absurdism, Painting/Music, and Woman/Man, ending with an epilogue on Intellect and Emotion. This study of polarities looks at Beckett on the basis of his own dichotomies as a guide to his methods and meanings.

Pilling, John. *Beckett Before Godot.* New York: Cambridge University Press, 1998. Pilling writes with authority on the early years of Beckett's literary activity. He goes beyond the many critical studies to undertake a discussion of the works that precede *Waiting for Godot* in the breadth and depth of attention he gives to unpublished manuscripts and correspondence.

Welch D. Everman;
bibliography updated by the editors

GUSTAVO ADOLFO BÉCQUER

Born: Seville, Spain; February 17, 1836
Died: Madrid, Spain; December 22, 1870

PRINCIPAL POETRY

Rimas, 1871 (*Poems*, 1891; better known as *The Rhymes*, 1898)

OTHER LITERARY FORMS

Although Gustavo Adolfo Bécquer's fame rests mainly on his only volume of poetry, *The Rhymes*, he was also a notable prose writer. Bécquer demonstrated his talent at an early age with the publication of *Historia de los templos de España* (1857; a history of Spain's temples), an ambitious project of which only the first volume, a study of the churches of Toledo, was completed. Posterity has recognized the greater value of a variety of prose works which appeared in Madrid's newspapers and magazines during Bécquer's lifetime. Outstanding among these works are the newspaper letters published under the heading *Cartas desde mi celda* (1864; *From My Cell*, 1924). They were written from Veruela's monastery in Aragón, where the author had gone to seek relief for his failing health. In these "letters," Bécquer pours out his moral biography, revealing himself to be a religious man who is both aware of the problems of his surroundings and sensitive to the legends and traditions he hears from shepherds and rovers in the northeast of Spain.

Also of great importance among Bécquer's prose works are the four *Cartas literarias a una mujer* (1860-1861; *Letters to an Unknown Woman*, 1924) and the prologue to the book *La Soledad* (1861) by his friend Augusto Ferrán. In these works, Bécquer expresses his ideas about love, literature in general, and, above all, poetry. In his prologue to Ferrán's book, Bécquer categorizes his own poetic production as the kind that is "natural, brief, dry, that which germinates in the soul like an electric spark, touches the feelings with a word and flees...."

Bécquer's most celebrated prose works were his more than twenty legends, *Leyendas* (1858-1864). The themes of these prose tales do not differ substantially from those of the tales in verse typical of the Romantic movement in Spain and throughout Europe; they reveal a taste for the macabre, for medieval settings and exotic lore. What differentiates Bécquer's legends from the verse narratives and plays of the Duque de Rivas and José Zorrilla is their greater emphasis on the mysterious, the uncanny, the supernatural.

ACHIEVEMENTS

Gustavo Adolfo Bécquer achieved fame only after his death. Although in his last years he was beginning to be recognized as a good journalist and an excellent prose writer, he was virtually unknown as a poet; only a handful of his poems were published during his lifetime.

Bécquer's recognition as a poet began with the publication of *The Rhymes* one year after his death. By 1881, when the third edition of his poems was published, Bécquer was acknowledged as an important poet, and his fame was spreading throughout the Hispanic world. Since that time, Bécquer's reputation has grown steadily; his verse has achieved both critical acclaim and an extraordinary popular appeal. Indeed, after Miguel Cervantes' *Don Quixote de la Mancha* (1605, 1615), no literary work has had as many editions in Spanish as Bécquer's *The Rhymes*. In the last 150 years, no Spanish poem has touched as many hearts or has been recited and memorized as often as "Rime of the Swallows," and in that period, no poet has surpassed Bécquer's influence on Hispanic poetry. All the movements, groups, and poetic generations that have come after Bécquer in Hispanic literature have been indebted, directly or indirectly, to his innovations.

BIOGRAPHY

Gustavo Adolfo Bécquer was born in Seville, in the south of Spain, on February 17, 1836, the son of José María Domínguez Insausti, a painter, and Joaquina Bastida Vargas. The surname Bécquer had come to Spain from Flanders during the seventeenth century as Becker. Although the direct line of the name had ended with the poet's great-grandmother, the whole family was still known as the Bécquers. One month before young Bécquer turned five, his father died, and four years later his mother died also, leaving Bécquer and his seven brothers to the responsibility of their surviving relatives.

While under the care of his mother's uncle, Don Juan de Vargas, Bécquer began to study at the Colegio de San Telmo in Seville, in order to become a sea pilot. When this school was closed a short time later, he went to live with his godmother, Doña Manuela Monchay. It was decided that Bécquer should take up his late father's profession, and he began to study painting at the school of the Sevillian artist Antonio Cabral Bajarano. Bécquer devoted his free time to reading in his godmother's library, where he developed his preference for Horace and for the Spanish Romantic José Zorrilla and where he became fond of literary studies in general.

Bécquer also studied painting with his uncle Joaquín Domínguez Bécquer. Nevertheless, his interest in literature had continued to grow, and when his uncle expressed doubts about Bécquer's potential to become a great artist, Bécquer decided, in 1854—against his godmother's advice—to go to Madrid and seek his fortune as a writer.

If in Seville Bécquer had found little happiness, he found even less in Madrid, where he always had economic difficulties and where he was soon diagnosed as having tuberculosis, the sickness that would take him to an early grave. Bécquer quickly ran out of the little money he had brought from Seville, and when he could no longer pay rent in the boardinghouse of Doña Soledad, she generously allowed him to continue residing there anyway. During his early years in Madrid, he worked in collaboration with various friends, turning out translations from French and writing original dramas and *zarzuelas* (musicals). These pieces for the stage, largely hackwork, did not command good payment, and some were not even produced. Needing to find another source of income, Bécquer obtained an insignificant position as a public servant, but he was soon fired, after being caught during working hours drawing a picture of William Shakespeare's Ophelia. In those days, he also contributed to a number of Madrid's newspapers and magazines, and he even tried, unsuccessfully, to found some new ones. These activities neither produced sufficient income for a comfortable life nor contributed to Bécquer's fame, since his works were often published without his name.

In the year 1858, Bécquer began to publish his "legends" in the newspapers of Madrid; in the same year, he met Julia Espín, a beautiful girl who later became an opera singer. It is said that, although Bécquer's love for this girl was unrequited, she inspired many of the entries in *The Rhymes*. It was at this time that Bécquer experienced his first health crisis. In 1859, a poem later included in *The Rhymes* was published under the title "Imitación de Byron" ("Imitation of Byron"); it was the first of fifteen of *The Rhymes* that appeared in Madrid periodicals during Bécquer's lifetime.

In 1860, Bécquer began publishing *Letters to an Unknown Woman* in serial form and met Casta Esteban Navarro, his doctor's daughter, whom Bécquer married the following year; the marriage would eventually produce two sons. In that same year, Bécquer's brother, Valeriano, a notable painter, came with his two children to live in Madrid and soon moved in with Gustavo and his wife. Throughout his married life, the poet and his wife spent several periods near Soria, where his father-in-law had a house. Between 1863 and 1864, Bécquer spent eight months living in the monastery of Veruela, where he wrote the letters in *From My Cell*. On several occasions, Bécquer and Valeriano took long trips to various parts of Spain, during which the artist would paint typical local scenes while the writer would take notes for his own works or would write articles for newspapers.

The year 1864 marked a change in Bécquer's life. He was appointed to a higher civil-service position with a better salary, but a change in the government caused him to lose the job a year later. Soon, however, yet another change in the government resulted in his reappointment to the job, where he worked until 1868, when the revolution that dethroned Isabella II took place. In the same year, Bécquer separated from his wife. Taking his two children, he went to live with Valeriano in Toledo, where he supposedly wrote the last poems for the book *The Rhymes*. A year later, they all returned to Madrid, and Bécquer resumed his journalistic work for the newspaper *La ilustración de Madrid*, where he was appointed editor in 1870. In September of that year, Valeriano died, and almost immediately Bécquer's wife repentantly returned to live with him and their children. Soon, the poet's health took a turn for the worse, and he died on December 22, 1870, at the age of thirty-four.

After Bécquer's death, his friend appointed a committee to publish his works. The committee collected his prose works which had appeared in the periodicals of Madrid and published them with the seventy-six poems from the manuscript of *The Rhymes*. This first edition of Bécquer's works was published in 1871, one year after his death.

ANALYSIS

The poems that made Gustavo Adolfo Bécquer famous, and that make up practically his entire production, are those included in his book *The Rhymes*. Only eight or ten other poems have been found, almost all juvenilia and not of high quality. When Bécquer's friends published the first edition of his works in 1871, *The Rhymes* consisted of seventy-six untitled poems as well as the previously published prose works. Another manuscript of the collection was later found, containing three more poems, for a total of seventy-nine. The discovery and publication of other poems raised the number to ninety-four, but later it was proved that many of the new poems actually had been written by Bécquer's contemporaries or had been fraudulently attributed to him.

The single most important influence on Bécquer's poetry was Heinrich Heine, whose impact on Bécquer is universally acknowledged. In addition, critics have pointed out a wide variety of lesser influences, ranging from Lord Byron and Edgar Allan Poe to the German poets Johann Wolfgang von Goethe, Friedrich Schiller, and Anastasius Grün (pseudonym of Anton Alexander, count of Auersperg) and the Spanish poets Eulogio Florentino Sanz (the translator of Heine into Spanish), José María de Larrea, and Augusto Ferrán. Nevertheless, Bécquer's poetic genius was so powerful that he was capable of fusing these influences with that of the popular Andalusian tradition to create his own distinctive style.

The most important characteristics of Bécquer's poetry are its simplicity and its suggestive, ethereal inwardness. It should be noted that the great majority of his poems are very short; his verse lines are generally short as well, and he prefers assonance to rhyme. Bécquer's language is elegant but simple, lacking exotic and high-sounding words, and he uses a minimum of rhetorical techniques. His preference for suggestion rather than explicit statement is reflected in his frequent

use of incorporeal motifs such as waves of light, the vibration of air, murmurs, thoughts, clouds, and sounds. Anecdotes are absent from his poetry, except for some extremely short ones that are indispensable to the communication of emotions. Nature appears in his poems impressionistically, mirroring the poet's interior drama. Above all, Bécquer is an eminently subjective poet who uses his poetry to express his inner feelings with almost complete indifference to the objective reality of the world.

The above-mentioned characteristics, as well as others, place Bécquer as a precursor of the Symbolist movement. Traditionally, he has been considered a late Romantic, and to a certain extent this classification is correct. In Bécquer's poetry, it is easy to observe the cult of the individual, the exaggerated sensitivity, the centering of the world on the subjectivity of the poet—all typical of the Romantic movement. Nevertheless, these characteristics appear in Bécquer in conjunction with others that typify the Symbolism of Stéphane Mallarmé, Paul Verlaine, and Arthur Rimbaud. For Bécquer, emotions or feelings are the true object of poetry. Feelings cannot be expressed with exact and precise words, and to represent his interior world, the poet must rely on suggestion and evocative symbolism. In the first poem in *The Rhymes*, Bécquer says that he would like to express the "gigantic and strange hymnal" that he knows, by "taming the rebel, and miserly language,/ with words that are at the same time/ sighs and laughs, colors and notes." In these lines, it can be seen that Bécquer conceived of the possibility of the correspondence of sensations, also typical of Symbolism. For him, as for the Symbolists, there is an ideal, absolute, and perfect world, of which the familiar physical world is an imperfect representation, significant not for itself but only for the impressions of a higher reality that it conveys. Finally, Bécquer, like the Symbolists, made frequent allusions to music and struggled to make his language as musical as possible.

THE RHYMES

In the manuscript of *The Rhymes*, the poems do not follow a chronological order; indeed, they seem to follow no logical order at all. The most widely accepted critical opinion is that, having lost the original manuscript (which he gave to a friend for publication right before the revolution of 1868), Bécquer had to reconstruct the collection from memory, adding some new poems. It is speculated that in the new copy, the majority of the poems appear in the order in which the poet remembered them, interspersed with those newly created. In any case, when Bécquer's friends decided to publish his works, they rearranged the poems, placing them in the order in which they have appeared in all of their subsequent publications.

The sequence imposed on the poems, justifiably or not, gives the collection a "plot." Early poems in the sequence reflect the enthusiasm of a young poet who seeks to explain the mystery of his art and who discovers the mysterious connections between poetry and love. In later poems, however, celebration of love gives way to disillusionment with the beloved. In the final poems in the sequence, the poet is increasingly preoccupied with death.

Thus, with few exceptions, the poems collected in *The Rhymes* can be divided into four sequential groups. The first group consists of poems that consider the poet per se and the nature of poetry; the second, of poems dealing with love; the third, of poems expressing disillusionment with love; and the fourth, of poems dealing with anguish and death.

Included in the first group are poems 1 through 8— except for poem 6 (a pathetic description of Shakespeare's Ophelia)—and poem 21. In poems 2 and 5, Bécquer focuses his attention on the poet per se, trying to explain what it means to be a poet and to describe the intimate nature of the poetic spirit. In the first of these two poems, Bécquer employs a series of similes to define himself both as a poet and as a human being. To suggest the narrow limits of man's control over his own destiny, Bécquer imagines himself to be an arrow, a dry leaf, a wave, and a ray of light, saying in the last stanza that he is crossing the world "by accident," "without thinking/ where I am coming from nor where/ my steps will take me." In poem 5, Bécquer portrays the poet as a vase containing the poetic spirit, described as an "unknown essence," a "mysterious perfume." Throughout the poem, Bécquer tries to determine the nature of that spirit. He identifies it in another series of beautiful similes where the objects of comparison are almost always immaterial and vague, with the clouds, the waking of a

star, the blue of the sea, a note from a lute, and so on. This poem introduces an important idea in Bécquer's poetics: Poetry is the marvelous reduction of ideas and feelings to words and verbal forms. The poetic spirit is described as the "bridge that crosses the abyss," as "the unknown stair/ that connects heaven and earth," and as "the invisible/ ring that holds together/ the world of forms with the world of ideas."

The remaining poems of the first group attempt to explain the mystery of poetry. Poem 1 declares that poetry is "a hymn" that cannot be confined by words and that the poet can communicate fully only with his beloved. Here again, one notes the identification of poetry with feelings and the insistence that feelings cannot be explained but can be communicated only emotionally. These same notions lie behind the succinct affirmation of poem 21, repeated by countless lovers of the Hispanic world since it was first published: Bécquer answers his beloved's question, "What is poetry?" with the simple statement, "Poetry is you."

The second group of poems, those dealing with love, includes poems 9 through 29, except for 21 (already placed in the first group) and 26 (which is closely related to the poems in the third group). Some of these poems can be considered as a series of gallant phrases forming beautiful madrigals appropriate for address to young ladies. Among them are poem 12, written to a green-eyed girl; poem 13 (the first of Bécquer's poems to have appeared in a newspaper, titled "Imitation of Byron"), composed for a blue-eyed girl; and poem 19, addressed to a girl who has the purity of a white lily. Some of the poems in this group have the charm, brevity, and sparkling shine of the *coplas* (ballads) from the Andalusian region; among these are poems 17 and 20.

In almost all the remaining poems of the second group, Bécquer appears as the poet of love, but of love as a superior and absolute feeling. Poems 9 and 10 show the universality of love. The former attempts to present all of nature as loving, and the latter describes how everything is transformed when love passes by. In poems 11 and 15, Bécquer realizes that love and the beloved for whom he searches are ideal entities of an absolute perfection and beauty that cannot exist in tangible reality. In the first of these two poems, two girls appear, one brunette and the other blond, and each in turn asks the poet if it is she for whom he is looking, to which he answers no. Then comes an unreal girl, "a vague ghost made of mist and light," incorporeal and intangible, who is incapable of loving him; immediately, the poet shows his preference for this ethereal figure, crying "Oh come, come you!" In poem 15, the ideal beloved is a "curled ribbon of light foam," a "sonorous rumor/ of a golden harp," and the poet runs madly after her, "after a shadow/ after the fervent daughter/ of a vision."

The beloved becomes corporeal in only a few poems of the second group. In poem 14, the poet sees "two eyes, yours, nothing else," and he feels that they irresistibly attract him. In poem 18, the entire physical woman appears "fatigued by the dancing" and "leaning on my arm," and in poem 29, the poet and his beloved are reading the episode of Paolo and Francesca in Dante's *La divina commedia* (c. 1320; *The Divine Comedy*) when suddenly they turn their heads at the same time: "our eyes met/ and a kiss was heard." Finally, in this second group, there is a poem that expresses the realization of love. In a typical series of incorporeal images, Bécquer says that his and his beloved's souls are "two red tongues of fire" that reunite and "form only one flame," "two notes that the hand pulls at the same time from the lute," "two streams of vapor" that join to form only "one white cloud," "two ideas born at the same time," and "two echoes that fuse with one another."

The third group of poems in *The Rhymes*, those expressing disillusionment with love, includes poems 30 through 51 as well as poem 26. Although in these poems Bécquer continues talking about love, the ideal and sublime love of the poet has decayed, ending in failure and producing great disappointment, disenchantment, and sorrow. Bécquer speaks scornfully of feminine inconstancy in a few poems, but without the note of sarcasm characteristic of Heine. In Bécquer, sorrow produces only a fine irony, which at times leads him to insinuate that women are valuable only for their physical beauty. In poem 34, after describing in detail the beauty of a woman, the poet faces the fact that she is "stupid." Bécquer resolves this conflict by saying that, as long as she stays quiet, her intelligence is of no concern to him, since "what she does not say, will always be of greater value/ than what any other woman could tell me." Similarly, in poem 39, the poet enumerates the character

flaws of a woman, only to end up stressing his preference for physical beauty by saying, "but . . . / she is so beautiful!"

The most interesting and intense poems of this third group are those in which the poet expresses his sorrow at the failure of his love. Some of them also seem to be the most autobiographical, although the impression given by the poems of *The Rhymes* is that all of them were the result of experiences lived by their author. Poem 41 appears to allude to the incompatibility between Bécquer and his wife, although it could refer to another woman. Its three brief stanzas present the poet and his beloved as opposing forces: the hurricane and the tower, the ocean and the rock, the beautiful girl and the haughty man. In each instance, the conclusion is the desolate phrase, "it could not be." The next poem, number 42, describes the moment when "a loyal friend" tells the poet a piece of "news" not mentioned in the poem. The last lines, in which the poet expresses his gratitude, would seem rather prosaic if the author had not earlier shown the intensity of his sorrow by saying, "then I understood why one cries,/ and then I understood why one kills."

The fourth and last group of poems in *The Rhymes*, those preoccupied with anguish and death, includes poems 52 through 76. In general, the poems of this group seem to be more detached from autobiographical experience, less charged with emotional intensity. Perhaps for this very reason, they are pervaded by a haunting lyricism.

One of the most famous poems ever written in Spanish is poem 53, the "Rime of the Swallows," which has been read and memorized by one generation after another. The poem expresses the brevity and the irreversibility of life and the unique value of every experience. The poet admits that the "dark swallows will return," but not "those that learned our names," "those . . . will not return!" He acknowledges that there will be flowers again on the honeysuckle tree, but not "those decorated with dew/ whose drops we used to see trembling," "those . . . will not return!" Finally, he concedes that "the fervent words of love/ will sound again in your ears," but "as I have loved you, . . . do not deceive yourself/ nobody will love you like that!"

The last poems in the collection are dominated by the theme of death. When the poet asks himself about his origin and his end in poem 66, he ends his expression of radical loneliness by affirming that his grave will be "where forgetfulness lives." In poem 71, he hears a voice calling him in his sleep, and he concludes that "somebody/ whom I loved has died!" In another of his most famous poems, which is also the longest in the book, Bécquer describes the funeral of a girl, repeating at the end of each stanza, "my God, how lonely stay the dead!" The same experience may have inspired poems 74 and 76. In poem 74, it seems that he sees a dead woman, and at the spectacle of death his soul is filled with "a fervent desire": "as the abyss attracts, that mystery/ was dragging me towards itself." At the same time, the angels that are engraved on the door seem to speak to him: "the threshold of this door only God trespasses." In poem 74, which concludes the volume, Bécquer again describes the funeral of a woman and expresses his own wish to rest from the struggles of life: "oh what love so quiet that of death/ what sleep so calm that of the sepulchre."

OTHER MAJOR WORKS

SHORT FICTION: *Leyendas*, serial 1858-1864 (selections translated in *Terrible Tales: Spanish*, 1891; also in *Romantic Legends of Spain*, 1909).

NONFICTION: *Historia de los templos de España*, 1857; *Cartas literarias a una mujer*, serial 1860-1861 (*Letters to an Unknown Woman*, 1924); *Cartas desde mi celda*, 1864 (*From My Cell*, 1924).

MISCELLANEOUS: *Obras*, 1871; *The Infinite Passion: Being the Celebrated "Rimas" and the "Letters to an Unknown Woman,"* 1924 (includes *Rimas*, *Letters to an Unknown Woman*, and *From My Cell*); *Legends, Tales, and Poems*, 1907; *Legends and Letters*, 1995.

BIBLIOGRAPHY

Bynum, B. Brant. *The Romantic Imagination in the Works of Gustavo Adolfo Bécquer*. Chapel Hill: University of North Carolina Press, 1993. Interpretation of Bécquer's work with an introduction to Romantisicm and an extensive bibliography.

Havard, Robert. *From Romanticism to Surrealism: Seven Spanish Poets*. Totowa, N.J.: Barnes & Noble, 1988. Brief biography and critical analysis of Span-

ish poets of the nineteenth and twentieth centuries. Includes bibliographic references.

Mizrahi, Irene. *La poética dialógica de Bécquer*. Atlanta, Ga.: Rodopi, 1998. The author's principal objective in this critical analysis is to establish Bécquer as a poet whose works undermine previous literary and philosophical motifs and anticipate those to come. Published in Spanish.

Rogelio A. de la Torre;
bibliography updated by the editors

THOMAS LOVELL BEDDOES

Born: Clifton, England; June 30, 1803
Died: Basel, Switzerland; January 26, 1849

PRINCIPAL POETRY
The Improvisatore, 1821
The Poems, Posthumous and Collected, of Thomas Lovell Beddoes, 1851
The Poetical Works of Thomas Lovell Beddoes, 1890
The Poems of Thomas Lovell Beddoes, 1907
Selected Poems, 1976

OTHER LITERARY FORMS

During his lifetime, Thomas Lovell Beddoes published only one volume of poetry, one play, scattered incidental poems, and a few newspaper articles written in German. His most substantial publications, *The Improvisatore* and the play *The Bride's Tragedy* (1822), appeared when he was very young. The poems were published at Oxford; the play appeared on the London stage.

ACHIEVEMENTS

Thomas Lovell Beddoes was recognized during his lifetime as a promising young lyrical dramatist who never fulfilled the early expectations he raised. The one volume of poems and the single play—virtually all of his work to be published during his lifetime—appeared while he was an undergraduate. They attracted sufficient attention to earn him the acquaintance and support of a small circle of London literary figures including Mary Shelley and William Godwin. Throughout the remainder of his life, however, Beddoes became increasingly aloof from literary "insiders." He gained a modest notoriety on the Continent for the fiery radicalism which caused him repeated conflicts with the authorities.

In the twentieth century, a number of scholars returned to Beddoes's work (most of it unpublished before his death, much of it never finished) with a new seriousness which gave him a firm though not exalted reputation among late Romantic (or early Victorian) writers. Beddoes is no longer seen as a mere anachronism, writing Elizabethan plays out of their time. Rather, he is seen as a man of deeply romantic temperament who tried to ground his commitment to the imagination in a rigorously scientific account of the human faculties. His failure to integrate these opposing tendencies resulted in strong tensions which generated a few powerful poetic characters and a poignant imagery in his work. The same tensions perhaps also contributed to the mood of despair which ended in his suicide.

BIOGRAPHY

Born at Clifton, England, Thomas Lovell Beddoes grew up under the shadow of a distinguished father (usually referred to as "Dr. Beddoes" to avoid confusion with the poet). Dr. Beddoes had been the friend of Erasmus Darwin, Samuel Taylor Coleridge, and other celebrated figures. The poet also grew up in the reflected fame of his aunt—the novelist Maria Edgeworth.

As a schoolboy at Charterhouse, Beddoes was a precocious student of the classics. There he wrote a juvenile short story, "Scaroni: Or, The Mysterious Cave" and also, apparently, some plays no longer extant. At Pembroke College, Oxford, Beddoes distinguished himself both as a student and as a writer. The success of *The Improvisatore* and *The Bride's Tragedy* led him to believe that he might expect a future in letters. He did not then know that he had already published the last significant work he would ever see in print. In 1825, after taking his degree in classics, Beddoes went abroad to improve his German and to scoop the cream of German learning at a time when both letters and the sciences were enjoying a burst of brilliance in Germany. In fact,

however, Beddoes was never to return to England except for short interludes.

At Göttingen University he polished the manuscripts of *Torrismond* (1851) and *The Second Brother* (1851) and tried to complete the project which was to occupy him for the rest of his life: *Death's Jest-Book* (1850). Failing in his attempt to complete these projects, Beddoes attempted suicide in 1829. In the same year, he was expelled by the university court on charges of drunken and disorderly behavior. His fortunes grew still more turbulent after he had transferred to the University of Würzburg: desultory composition, occasional political articles for the *Volksblatt*, a revolutionary speech at Gaibach, deportation from Munich, imprisonment for debt at Würzburg, a move to Zurich. In Switzerland he found a temporarily safe haven and entered the University at Zurich in 1833, remaining there until 1837.

During the period of his German studies, Beddoes had become increasingly absorbed by a scientific interest which finally led to a degree in physiology. Thus, he can be seen as an interesting case of the nineteenth century polymath, trying fiercely to hold the humane and scientific cultures together in his own mind, on the eve of Matthew Arnold's and T. H. Huxley's open acknowledgment that classical and scientific education had become adversarial. Beddoes himself seems to have practiced his dissections in the futile hope of finding some undiscovered organ which could authenticate the arguments for human immortality, thus grounding metaphysics in physics.

Beddoes continued to create social difficulties for himself through both his political radicalism and his casual disregard for bourgeois conventions. In 1839, he experienced a continuing conflict with the Zurich police over his lack of a residence permit. In 1840, he moved to Berlin and attended the university. Back in Zurich in 1845, he was fined for disturbing the peace. He traveled to Frankfurt, where he suffered a long illness brought on by an infection he incurred while dissecting. After a brief trip to England, he went to Basel, Switzerland. On the morning following his arrival there, Thomas Beddoes deliberately opened an artery in his left leg. Six months later, after recuperating from the second attempt on his own life, Beddoes died—most likely a suicide—on January 26, 1849—too early in the year to enjoy the fall of Metternich and the broad victory of radicals throughout Europe. He was forty-five years old.

The fate of Beddoes's manuscripts is one of the most curious in literary history. Hours before his death he bequeathed all of his papers to his English friend T. F. Kelsall. Kelsall, in turn, left the extensive collection of largely unpublished Beddoes manuscripts to Robert Browning; Browning showed them to Edmund Gosse and Dykes Campbell, both of whom laid the foundation for modern critical studies by transcribing extensively from what they saw. At his own death, Browning left the black box containing the Beddoes materials to his son, Robert Waring "Pen" Browning. At the subsequent sale of Pen Browning's estate, the "Browning Box" of Beddoes papers did not appear. Its fate is still a mystery.

ANALYSIS

Thomas Lovell Beddoes's poetry (including his verse drama) focuses on three subjects: love, death, and madness. There is a constant theme: Love offers an entrance to the charmed world where spirit and nature are one; yet, just when love asserts its claims and some ideal of joy seems realizable, either madness or death intrudes with an ironic laugh to snatch away that love—the best hope that human beings have for something approximating transcendence. The reader is left with an ironic ambivalence toward the expectations of the spirit. Those expectations are linked ever more tightly, as Beddoes's poetry unfolds, with the mocking ironies (death and madness) which give the lie to dreams of love, immortality, and transcendence. Beddoes's ambivalence toward his own dream of immortality is partly a result of his progressively deeper commitment to scientific inquiry, with its rigorous rules of evidence. It is also in part a reflection of the ambivalence of the whole age. John Herschel, William Whewell, and Augustus De Morgan were all Victorian scientists, for example, who wrote highly romantic poetry. Charles Darwin enjoyed a wide reading in imaginative literature. Yet, it was becoming progressively clear that the specializations of scientific thought would soon put an end to the ideal fusion of science and the humanities which Beddoes sought.

The main body of Beddoes's work shows the ambivalence which he felt about all of the great themes of literature: love, the meaning of suffering, the significance of everyday life, the possibilities for some sort of redemptive experience, the hope for immortality. The fragmentation of his work, his desultory efforts to polish and finish it, his inability to commit himself to a dramatic poem with sufficient force to work it through, all suggest Beddoes's dilemma. He was a man whose learning and instincts were grounded in the classical past, a man who loved the great sureties of the great poets. In his own age, however, and in his own mind, those sureties were being eroded by a secular skepticism which denied him the assurance and joy of the old world, yet revealed no credible options for a man of the spirit living in an empirical and pragmatic age. Before Matthew Arnold, Beddoes was "caught between two worlds,/ One dead, the other powerless to be born." Before Kafka, he sensed the abyss which underlies everyday experience. Biographies can never, of course, reconstruct all of the sorrows, the intense impressions, of a private man who lived long ago. It is clear enough from his work itself, however, that Beddoes believed that the illusions of a sacred and mythopoeic world were breaking up, that the losses to be suffered would throw enormous stress on the devices of sanity, and that in the end, Death would mock the illusions, the losses, and even the madness itself by keeping its eternal secret.

THE IMPROVISATORE

Such ambivalence appears as early as *The Improvisatore* and grows progressively more profound and ironic all the way through his work, culminating in *Death's Jest-Book. The Improvisatore* is a series of three ballad-like tales which suffer from a trite and overheated romanticism. These tales were published when Beddoes was eighteen, and they reflect his early quest for a lyrical style which would give voice to his yearnings for a mythopoeic, spiritual world. His images, however, are often clichés: "'Twas as though Flora had been sporting there,/ And dropped some jewels from her loosened hair." Sometimes the images are absurd conceits, similar to those of the metaphysical poets two centuries earlier: "Her mouth!—Oh pardon me, thou coral cave,/ Prison of fluttering sighs . . . if I fail to tell/ The Beauty and the grace, that in thee dwell."

These early tales share in common the themes listed above: love, madness, and death. In each ballad, youthful or infant love loses its object—a sweetheart, a parent.

This loss starkly transforms the protagonist. The youthful sense of a charmed and summertime reality gives way to a madness expressed in images of a horrific supernaturalism. The only escape from that madness is into death.

THE BRIDE'S TRAGEDY AND THE SECOND BROTHER

The Bride's Tragedy and *The Second Brother* are more accomplished than *The Improvisatore*. There are fewer clichés. Still, these plays too might be thought melodramatic except that the romanticism is less feverish, and Beddoes's ability to control his lyricism, his characterizations, and his plot construction have clearly matured. In *The Bride's Tragedy*, Hesperus is secretly married to Floribel. Orlando, son of the Duke, also loves Floribel but knows nothing of the marriage. He imprisons Hesperus's father and offers Hesperus his (Orlando's) sister in order to have Floribel for himself. Trapped (and jealous), Hesperus murders his secret wife. What enables this play to transcend such a melodramatic plot is a more mature lyricism, as in the song "Poor Old Pilgrim Misery" where the strong feelings of Hesperus are not merely enunciated (as Beddoes had enunciated emotions in *The Improvisatore*) but suggested through controlled images: "Beneath the silent moon he sits,/ a listening to the screech owl's cry,/ and the cold wind's goblin prate."

In 1825, Beddoes published his translation of some of J. C. F. Schiller's philosophic letters (their first translation into English) in *The Oxford Quarterly Magazine*. His preface reveals the depth of the bifurcation of his own mind. "We seldom attain truth otherwise than by extremes; we must first exhaust error, and often madness before we end our toil at the far goal of calm wisdom." By this time his enthusiasms—poetry and science—have been polarized into a rigorous dialectic. His effort to integrate them is failing. His extremes are tending toward madness. He further claims that "scepticism and free-thinking are the feverish paroxysm of the human spirit, and must, by the very . . . concussion which they cause . . . help to confirm the health [of the soul]." His assurance on this point seems a romantic's whistling in the dark of rationalist doubt. Consider, for example, his translation of Schiller's first letter, Julius to Raphael: "There is nothing holy but truth. What reason acknowledges is truth . . . I have sacrificed all my opinions. . . . My reason is now my all; my only security for diversity, virtue, immortality." Beddoes has set himself on an irreversible track. During the whole course of his writing he will find, like Julius, no earnest for love, wholeness, nor peace.

Beddoes's lyrical poems may be grouped under the headings Juvenilia (1818-1821), Outidana (1821-1825), The Ivory Gate (1830-1839), German Poems (1837-1845), and Lost Poems (1843-1848). These headings are used in H. W. Donner's definitive one-volume edition of Beddoes's complete works. Although the topics are various, a selected list of titles suggests how closely the lyrical poems are tied to the major themes already identified: "Threnody," "Fragments of a Dirge," "Epitaph," "The Tree of Life," "Dirge and Hymeneal," "Lament of Thanatos," "Thanatos to Kenelm," "The Last Judgment," "The Phantom-Wooer," and others of the same sort.

DEATH'S JEST-BOOK

The poem "Dream Pedlary," written for use in *Death's Jest-Book*, is typical of the mature Beddoes. It consists of five stanzas, the first of ten lines, rhyming *ababccaaab*, and the remaining four of nine lines each, rhyming *ababccaab*. Because some of the rhyming words are carried from one stanza to the next, a spare economy of form emerges which is well-suited to the stark theme of the poem. The poem begins with a question: "If there were dreams to sell,/ What would you buy?" Beddoes then offers images of various dreams for sale. In the first stanza, these dreams are described as "merry and sad," but in the second stanza the image chosen is a sad one, "a cottage lone and still." In the next stanza, the dream for sale is a "spell to call the buried," which gives way in the fourth stanza to the dream that "there are no ghosts to raise./ Out of death lead no ways." The last stanza expresses a death wish ("lie as I will do/ And breathe thy last") because the fear that death is a void at least validates the claim that "all dreams are made true"; that is, all dreams are only dreams and therefore truly dreams. The images have progressed from merry and sad dreams, through solitude (the lone cottage), to the dream of ghosts, to the dream of a nihilistic void where there are no ghosts. This terrible finality is so unthinkable to Beddoes that it draws and fascinates him.

No other work of Beddoes has achieved as high a standing with critics as *Death's Jest-Book*. He worked on this poetic drama for more than twenty years, and it was still unpublished at his death. This macabre play provides a historical link between the revenge tragedy of the Renaissance and the tale of terror in modern times. It strings together a powerful series of images: the court jester (Isbrand) in cap and bells who is driven by the wish for revenge to try to usurp the throne of Münsterberg; a conjuration scene in which the Duke opens the tomb of his wife only to find there the ghost of a man he has murdered; and a dance of death consisting of painted figures who actually descend from the wall to act out a grotesque masque.

The play has the eloquence, the ghosts, and the strong-willed characters of an Elizabethan swashbuckler, but it also hints at the nihilism of a modern tale of terror. It is this latter fact which sets it apart from contemporaneous gothic tales such as those of Ann Radcliffe. The macabre events of *Death's Jest-Book*, such as the conjuration scene in a derelict Gothic cathedral, suggest the possibility that behind the terrors there lies no supernatural law of justice or piety, but rather a lawless abyss just a finger-reach beyond everyday normalcy. The critic John Agar believes that Isbrand's tragedy is that he aspires to be a hero, not a villain (his motive, after all was to avenge his father's and his brother's deaths), but—lacking an adequate sense of his own limits—he becomes as evil as he had hoped to be good. Good intentions, it might be observed, do not save us in a naturalistic world where there is no omnipotent judge to weigh them.

Although the images of horror in the play are fairly conventional—a ghost (Wolfram, Isbrand's murdered brother), the skeletal *danse macabre*—nevertheless Beddoes's keenly spiritual sensibility, faced with the persuasions of a rigorous skepticism, suffers much as Franz Kafka suffered from a tormenting recognition that life, love, kingdoms, even efforts at revenge, may be nothing but a macabre joke—Death's Jest. The characters in Beddoes's play sustain the conventional hope that death is only a mask for immortality: "Death is old and half worn out: Are there no chinks in it?" Yet death keeps its mocking secret as these stage directions show: "The Deaths . . . come out of the walls, and dance fantas-

tically to a rattling music . . . ; some seat themselves at the table and drink with mocking gestures." Later, as Isbrand dies, having briefly occupied the usurped throne, the ghost of his brother places the cap and bells upon his head again. All are absurd fools in *Death's Jest-Book*.

OTHER MAJOR WORKS

PLAYS: *The Bride's Tragedy*, pr., pb. 1822; *Death's Jest-Book*, pb. 1850.

NONFICTION: *The Letters of Thomas Lovell Beddoes*, 1894.

MISCELLANEOUS: *The Complete Works of Thomas Lovell Beddoes*, 1928; *The Works of Thomas Lovell Beddoes*, 1935 (H. W. Donner, editor).

BIBLIOGRAPHY

Donner, H. W. *The Browning Box: Or, The Life and Works of Thomas Lovell Beddoes*. London: Oxford University Press, 1935. A collection of letters about Beddoes's life and poetry, by friends and admirers. The odd title refers to the box of materials given to Robert Browning after Beddoes's death. The box has disappeared, but "probably all the letters of real importance" survived through transcriptions.

_____. *Thomas Lovell Beddoes: The Making of a Poet*. Oxford: Basil Blackwell, 1935. This comprehensive study of Beddoes's life and times balances biography with literary interpretation. Contains an informative introduction on nineteenth century theater and the influence of Elizabethan drama on Romantic poetry. A conclusion summarizes Beddoes's aesthetics. Illustrated.

Snow, Royall H. *Thomas Lovell Beddoes: Eccentric and Poet*. New York: Covici-Friede, 1928. This early biographical study concentrates on the poet's morbidity as his defining characteristic. Somewhat dated, especially in the ways it deals with the literature. Contains an annotated bibliography of Beddoes's books and periodical publications.

Thompson, James R. *Thomas Lovell Beddoes*. Boston: Twayne, 1985. The most useful critical introduction to Beddoes. Includes a brief biography, a chronology, and a selected bibliography. Follows Beddoes's career from the early poems of Shelleyan and gothic derivation, through his growing interest in Jacobean drama and his satiric verse dramas, to his mature work obsessed with death.

Watkins, Daniel P. "Thomas Lovell Beddoes' *The Bride's Tragedy* and the Situation of Romantic Drama." *Studies in English Literature, 1500-1900* 29 (Autumn, 1989): 699-712. Considers Beddoes's poetic drama as a work of gothic horror on the order of Mary Wollstonecraft Shelley's *Frankenstein*. Watkins utilizes historical analysis to show that Beddoes's concerns are less a throwback to Jacobean drama than an essentially Romantic "desire for a return to an aristocratic feudal" order.

L. Robert Stevens;
bibliography updated by the editors

PATRICIA BEER

Born: Exmouth, Devon, England; November 4, 1924
Died: Honiton, England; August 15, 1999

PRINCIPAL POETRY

Loss of the Magyar and Other Poems, 1959
The Survivors, 1963
Just Like the Resurrection, 1967
The Estuary, 1971
Driving West, 1975
Selected Poems, 1979
The Lie of the Land, 1983
Collected Poems, 1988
Friend of Heraclitus, 1993
Autumn, 1997

OTHER LITERARY FORMS

Aside from her poetry, Patricia Beer published two books of criticism, *An Introduction to the Metaphysical Poets* (1972) and *Reader, I Married Him* (1974), the latter being a study of the female characters in the works of Jane Austen, Charlotte Brontë, Elizabeth Gaskell, and George Eliot. She also published a book of fiction, *Moon's Ottery* (1978), and a nonfictional account of her childhood, *Mrs. Beer's House* (1968). The latter pro-

vides insights into the poet's development and serves as a gloss for much of her poetry, particularly that which is rooted in her childhood experiences. Although her publications reveal a variety of interests and a willingness to work in various literary forms, Beer's most significant writing and the principal focus of her energies was her poetry.

ACHIEVEMENTS

Patricia Beer won few formal honors in her lifetime. In 1958 she won second prize in the Cheltenham Festival of Art and Literature for *Loss of the Magyar and Other Poems*. She was also a Fellow of the Royal Society of Literature. While she is not as widely known in the United States as some of her British contemporaries, she achieved a solid reputation in her native England as a deft craftsperson and a poet of genuine perception. Her accomplishments become even more significant when one considers how few of her fellow poets in the British Isles are women. Certainly, the poets with the widest reputations—Philip Larkin, Ted Hughes, and Dannie Abse, to name only a few—are all men. In this context, Beer occupied a position of considerable importance.

BIOGRAPHY

Patricia Beer was born November 4, 1924, in Devon, England, and is a member of the first generation in England to have ready access to higher education through the state school system. Coming from a working-class background, she made her way through the state schools by excelling at her studies. As a native of Devon with a pronounced Devonian accent, she remembered being drilled by elocutionists who were determined to teach her proper speech. She resisted the instruction and retained the accent that no doubt exerted an influence, however subtle, on her poetry. She left home to study at Exeter University but graduated with a bachelor's degree from the University of London and received another bachelor's degree from St. Hugh's College at Oxford University. After graduation she embarked on a teaching career and was a lecturer in English at the University of Padua in Italy, where she stayed from 1946 to 1948 before moving on to the British Institute and then the Ministero Aeronautica, both in Rome. By 1953 Beer moved back to England and began writing in earnest.

She supported herself in a series of odd jobs through the 1950's but in 1962 went back to teaching in a post at the University of London. She lectured there for several years and married her second husband, John Damien Parsons, in 1964. In 1968 she chose to make writing her full-time profession. By that time, she had already seen several of her books published, including *Loss of the Magyar and Other Poems.*

She would eventually divide her time between homes in Hampstead Heath (London) and Devon, considering her continued connection with the place of her birth an element essential to her creativity. She continued to write poetry and literary criticism in the years leading to her death and in the late 1990's contributed to the *London Review of Books.* She died in 1999 from a stroke.

ANALYSIS

As a child, Beer was strongly influenced by the Plymouth Brethren Church, a loosely structured, fundamentalist sect that flourished amid the working and lower-middle classes. Its principal theology was a strict moral code and a dependence on literal interpretation of the Bible. Beer recalled vividly the extemporaneous hellfire sermons and the hymns offering salvation, and these bits of childhood found their way into her poetry. In a larger context, the pervasive sense of death that she experienced regularly at the church services may well have afforded the main impetus for her poetry. In much of her work, she was preoccupied with death, and she frequently commented that she wrote poems against death. The relationship between her religious upbringing and her craft was a complex one, but there is little doubt that Beer's fundamentalist training helped to form her as a poet.

Beer's childhood in Devon and her experiences in the Plymouth Brethren Church afforded her abundant material for poetry and a unique point of view. Just as her semirural Devonian background accounts for the rustic quality of much of her work, her childhood among the Plymouth Brethren, as well as the death of her mother when Beer was fourteen, helps to explain her ambivalent attitude toward death, a mixture of fascination and fear. It is this subtle but fundamental tension that underlies some of her most successful poems.

While Beer explored feminist themes in her work, her tone was without rancor and she was rarely polemical. Rather, she typically presented her poems in a calm and understated voice. She was also not a single-issue poet and so did not feel bound to champion a feminist cause in every line of every poem, thereby avoiding the trap into which politically aroused poets have frequently fallen. Beer commented that she wanted equality, not superiority, and that such a position precludes any kind of attack on the male establishment.

It would be a mistake, however, to view Beer only in the role of feminist poet; she transcended any such narrow category in both her aspirations and her accomplishments. Her voice was as unique and genuine as that of Hughes or Larkin, and her carefully crafted poems are an important contribution to contemporary British poetry. At her best, she invited comparison with Elizabeth Bishop, for she has the same perceptive eye, the same gift for the exact image. A poem such as "Spanish Balcony," with its moon suspended "uselessly, in the smooth sky/ White and rumpled like a vaccination mark," is as precise and evocative as Bishop's celebrated description of the rainbow trout in "The Fish." The controlling mind behind the poem is sure and accurate.

SELECTED POEMS

The publication of *Selected Poems* in 1979 marked an important milestone in Patricia Beer's career. In addition to winning for her the kind of recognition she had long deserved, it provided her with the opportunity to assess her own development and to select from twenty years of writing the poetry that she most wanted to preserve. Significantly, she included only eight poems from her first two books, *Loss of the Magyar and Other Poems* and *The Survivors.* Although she was in her thirties when those books were published, she later regarded them as juvenilia. Those early books, in Beer's assessment, lack conviction, an authentic voice. Beer's major development as a writer involved a movement toward the more personal and autobiographical. Along the way, she abandoned her reliance on mythology and consciously tried to pare down her style, seeking simplicity and directness.

Ironically, Beer grew distrustful of the spareness that characterized her writing and turned to a language that she regarded as more heightened. She did not, however, regard this as a return to her earlier style but rather as a progression into a kind of language that would have a more immediate impact on the reader. It seems that, during the middle part of her career, Beer was trying to find some point of balance between her initial work and her subsequent reaction to it. She later began to seek a marriage of technique and inspiration, and the fifteen "New Poems" that constitute the final section of *Selected Poems* suggest that she found it.

DEATH

It has often been remarked that the two most common themes in poetry are the possibility of love and the inevitability of death, so it is perhaps unremarkable to find a poet dealing with either of these matters. Even so, Beer's preoccupation with death was noteworthy because she succeeded in capturing so much of the ambivalence that most people have toward it—the attraction and repulsion of the unknown. This viewpoint is effectively communicated in a short poem titled "Dilemma," in which Beer projected two possible role models for herself. The first is a Buddhist monk who screams so loudly when seven brigands approach to murder him that businessmen in Peking can hear him twenty miles away. The second is "the Queen in corny historical plays," who fixes her hair, forgives everybody, and moves to the executioner's block "With only a sidelong glance/ At the man with the axe." The monk and the queen represent two attitudes toward death—resistance and acquiescence—and Beer is free to choose the one she wishes to adopt. Thus, the poem's final line is a question: "Which ought I to be?" On the surface, this poem appears to be very simple, but it compresses a great deal of thought and attempts to bridge a gap as wide as the one between William Cullen Bryant's advice in "Thanatopsis" to embrace death gently like a sleeper and Dylan Thomas's exhortation to his father not to go "gentle into that good night."

"THE CLOCK"

A variation on this theme is found in "The Clock," an excellent example of Beer's mastery of syllabics and her skillful employment of sounds, particularly assonance. She was most adept at using and then defusing the irresistible iambic trimeter in her six-syllable lines, as in the following pair: "Where once a pendulum/ Thudded like a cart-horse." The regularity of meter is effectively bro-

ken by an abundance of stresses, as though the thudding horse himself had broken in, and the entire poem is carried forward by the subtle suggestion of rhyme as exemplified by the four end-words in the fourth stanza: "this," "is," "death," "stairs." It is no accident that "death" stands out so starkly among the off-rhymes, because that is where Beer wished to put the stress, on obtrusive death itself. In this fashion, she made form and content work together in a most remarkable way. The focus of the poem is an old clock that stops every few days when its weights catch on the case. The old saying that "A stopped clock foretells death" leads Beer to speculate about the symbolic meaning of the event and she finds a lesson of her own in such folklore: "Obviously/ Death cannot come each time/ The clock stops. It may be/ Good practice to think so." The malfunctioning clock, then, becomes an important element in a rehearsal for death. As in "Dilemma," where Beer tried to decide how she will face death when it finally arrives, she is preparing herself for the inevitable, for the moment when time will truly stop for her. In a very real sense, Beer's poetry in general is a kind of rehearsal for death. She herself acknowledged that the impetus behind her decision to write poetry was her fear of dying.

"THE EYES OF THE WORLD"

Initially, Beer's horror of death was somewhat mitigated by a fantasy of becoming famous and having thousands of people mourn her passing. The vehicle for her fame, decided upon when she was only eight years old, was to be poetry. She "Turned poet for a lying-in-state/ As though comfort came from cut flowers," a decision that she examined at length in "The Eyes of the World." Somehow, to her child's mind, having the world take note of her death would make the event less terrifying: "Something like this I felt might make it/ Tolerable: if everyone would stare/ At my last breaths and speak about them." She envied the fame of kings, of men on the moon, of Leda and Mary and the martyrs Latimer and Ridley, all seared into the consciousness of millions and thus given a kind of immortality.

The fantasy passed, however, when she matured and began to view the world more cynically, suspecting that the watchers were more likely to notice flaws and weaknesses than accomplishments. Further, she suspected that "The audience shut their eyes before we/ Shut ours," insensitive to another person's death or unable to see the process through to completion. The poem ends with the following reflection on the eyes of the world: "I cannot imagine now/ Why I believed they were the answer." As Beer discovered, the true answer to her fear of death was not to become famous but to learn to write about her fears. She found that she could not chase them away in the glare of public recognition but could embrace them privately and learn to live with them. Poems such as "Concert at Long Melford Church" and "After Death" show her bravely coming to terms with what she most feared. If the truce is shaky and the question of how to face death when it arrives remains unresolved, Beer nevertheless expanded her personal and poetic boundaries by confronting head-on what she most wished to flee.

"CALLED HOME"

Related to the poems about death are Beer's poems about religion, particularly so since the religious group on which she focused is the death-obsessed Plymouth Brethren of her childhood. In "Called Home," the title recalls something that "the Plymouth Brethren used to say/ When someone died." The phrase creates a picture of "eternal domesticity," which was intended to be comforting, assuring the congregation that families would be reunited after death, as in the hymns "Shall We Gather at the River?" and "In the Sweet By-and-By." Having lost her ability to accept this simple picture of life after death, Beer claimed that "Loving an atheist is my hope currently." She wanted an "Ally who will keep noncompany/ With me in a non-life, a fellow tombstone." The rejection of her previous belief and the adoption of a nihilistic view of life and death were integral to Beer's struggle. In order to come to terms with death she imagined it at its most horrible, and this necessitated relinquishing the convenient crutches offered by the church and courageously confronting nothingness in its plainest form, not draped in domestic imagery.

"ARMS"

The loss of faith is also treated in "Arms," but without the cynical, intellectual toughness that characterizes "Called Home." Indeed, "Arms" is poignant precisely because Beer gave in somewhat to her emotions and looked back on the lost faith of her childhood with sorrow and regret. She recalled that her innocent reliance

on the "Everlasting Arms" gradually gave way to nightmare visions of drowned animals "Holding each other like bars" and then remembered her grandfather sinking with his brig in the North Sea, his arms around his son, "Protector, up to his knees/ In death, and that was the last/ That anyone saw of him." The poem progresses from a child's concern with the mortality of animals to an understanding that humans, even her grandfather, share in that mortality, and the immortal arms of her childhood belief become the ineffectual arms of her grandfather, disappearing forever beneath the waves.

AUTOBIOGRAPHY

Beer's poems of death have immediacy because of their autobiographical nature, because the poet was willing to expose herself. The details of poems such as "The Clock," "The Eyes of the World," and "Arms" are factually accurate. The clock that stops every few days did exist; Beer did decide to become a poet when she was eight because she thought fame would help her accept death; and her grandfather went down with his brig, the *Magyar*, and was last seen by the only survivor with his arms around his son and the water rising.

Getting the facts down, however, was not Beer's final objective. She was after the truth behind the facts, and it is that truth that produces a response in the reader. Beer was, in the best sense of the term, a confessional poet, because her view always penetrated through the self to the larger background. Her movement as a poet was steadily away from the detached, manufactured poem toward the autobiographical, and as the poetry became more sharply focused on the immediate self rather than on the self's past, Beer was likely to draw nearer to the confessional vein. Instinctively wary of the confessional poem, Beer's progress toward it was slow. There were, after all, the dangers of becoming too self-involved, too obscure, and Beer resisted the mode because of these potential hazards. Nevertheless, she seemed irresistibly led to write more and more about her immediate life. She thoroughly explored and exploited the material of her childhood, and so it is only natural that she turned her attention to her present self. Her best poems are those that risk an intense look at the self.

THE ESTUARY

In the title poem of her fourth book, *The Estuary*, Beer looked intensely at herself and effectively brought together past and present as she reflected on the body of water that separated the two towns of her childhood—Exmouth, her father's home, and Torquay, her mother's place of origin. She found in the division a symbol not only of the distance between her mother and father in terms of their personalities but also of her own character, which was a combination of attributes inherited from both parents. On one side "stiff fields of corn grow/ To the hilltop, are draped over/ It surrealistically." On the other side, small white boats lean sideways twice a day as the tide goes out and comes in and "the sea pulls away their prop." One side is covered with lush and vigorous growth, while the other is represented by fragile boats that seem as susceptible to the intermittent tides as people are to fate or chance.

A reader does not need to know a great deal about Beer's background to appreciate the geographical metaphor, though some knowledge of her childhood may enhance one's understanding of the poem. It is clear from the poem itself that Beer was forced by circumstances to move from a normal life on one side of the river to "a house where all was not well" on the other. The poem does not indicate, however, just what the circumstances were nor why things were not well on the other side, focusing on effect and leaving the cause unspecified. There is no exposition to reveal that the move was precipitated by the death of Beer's mother when Beer was fourteen and that she crossed the river to live with relatives because her father seemed unable to manage his children alone.

With this information in hand, a reader may better understand the source of the poem, but the significant details of the poem itself operate independent of any such biographical footnotes. By dealing with the effects of the move rather than its causes, Beer was able to take a highly personal experience and give it a more general significance. The estuary, rather than remaining a simple fact of Beer's childhood, became a symbolic boundary that everyone must cross, and the move was not simply from Exmouth to Torquay but from childhood to adulthood, from the dreamlike growth on one side to a more conscious life on the tides of the other. The opposing banks are innocence and experience, and the move from one to the other is archetypal. Underscoring this symbolism is the estuary itself, the meeting place of fresh

and salt water. The flow of the individual river into the sea parallels the movement of the child from her small, self-involved world into the larger community of responsibility.

"SELF-HELP"

Beer used essentially the same technique in "Self-Help," employing her personal experiences as a telescope through which the larger world can be viewed. Meditating on the fact that she "was brought up on notions of self-help," she realized that she got where she is because she believed "that if/ You didn't help yourself in worldly matters/ Nobody else was at all likely to." She struggled alone and enjoyed her success alone, sitting on her sofa in Hampstead Village listening to the threatening noises of all those on the streets outside who wanted desperately to help themselves as well. She separated herself from the "Cockney accents" and "bathless flats," virtually becoming a living example of the model described in books on self-help, "Practising lawful self-advancement, preaching/ It, enjoying its rewards." Yet behind her smugness and her sense of separation, she feels a bond with all those who have not succeeded in helping themselves. She sees that "through/ The white comfortable mist a wind blows holes/ Lays bare the quagmire reaching for us all./ Whispers how soon we could be shouting 'Help.'" What she sensed is the common link of death, and she realized that despite her accomplishments she could never raise herself beyond the quagmire that reaches out for everyone. If there was truth in this perception, there is also humility, for Beer put her successes into context and implicitly undertood how small they look in terms of the ultimate struggle. In the final sense, she was alone, and yet, paradoxically, she was united with everyone. Death is the great separator, but it is also the great leveler, mindless of class distinctions and accomplishments.

Although Beer herself rejected the confessional label, poems such as "The Estuary" and "Self-Help" work as the best confessional poems have always worked, by using the personal details of the poet's life to discover larger meanings. Beer preferred to call her poems in this vein autobiographical, perhaps because the term "confessional" has come to connote obscurity and tedious self-involvement. Whatever label the poems are given, they unquestionably transcend the limitations of the purely personal, for Beer masterfully used her experiences and emotions as a bridge to the common ground shared by her and the reader. The personal is always a means to an end and never an end in itself. In fact, Beer's strengths as a poet seem to increase in direct proportion to her willingness to exploit her personal life for poetic material.

"FEMALE, EXTINCT" AND "HOME"

Beer knew, too, how to approach sensitive topics, not by taking a position and arguing directly but by presenting a point of view obliquely, subtly. Her skills in this area were clearly on display in "Female, Extinct." The female of the title is never identified by species, and her wired-together rib cage and "bony gloves" with no marrow in them could belong to any vertebrate animal. The reference to "her sons, little dragons" suggests something reptilian, but the term "little dragons" is appositional and may be meant figuratively rather than literally. Now on display in the museum, the female once "Stood up with hundreds/ As if to bellow/ The Hallelujah Chorus." As a reconstructed artifact she seems to be saying something else: "Her passionate jaws/ Shout 'Give me time.'" This may well be a poem about the primordial struggle to survive, but it may just as well be about the more contemporary efforts of women to overcome their symbolic extinction. Beer created the possibility of the latter reading by leaving the type of female unspecified. Quite probably, she intended the poem to function on both levels of meaning, for the real point of the poem is the implied connection between the two kinds of females.

Equally subtle and effective is a short poem titled "Home." Here, the speaker, presumably a woman, looks out from her house, "as warm/ And secure as bathwater." Curiously, her sense of responsibility begins with a rejection of that responsibility. She discovers that she cannot remove herself from the world of human suffering, and she is beginning to understand that home has a larger significance than the safe house in which she would prefer to seal herself.

Both "Female, Extinct" and "Home" may be regarded as feminist poems because both address issues of great concern to women. The first may be taken as an implied warning of a present danger and the second as a charge to move beyond the walls of home into the surrounding world. Because she did not argue a position, she avoids the didactic and the abrasive, and her point of view seeps slowly into the reader's receptive consciousness.

Indeed, perhaps the best word to describe Beer's poetry in general is "understated." Whether writing about death, her childhood, or topics of a political nature, Beer's characteristic voice is one of composure. This is not to say that her poems are lacking in vitality; quite the opposite, for she has learned that the disparity between her calm perceptions and the themes derived from them creates a great deal of energy. One often has the sense that in Beer's poetry things have been defused, only to find upon reflection that a small explosion has occurred in the mind.

OTHER MAJOR WORKS

LONG FICTION: *Moon's Ottery*, 1978; *The Star Cross Ferry*, 1991.

NONFICTION: *Mrs. Beer's House*, 1968; *An Introduction to the Metaphysical Poets*, 1972; *Reader, I Married Him*, 1974.

BIBLIOGRAPHY

Beer, Patricia. *Mrs. Beer's House*. London: Macmillan, 1968. This is Beer's autobiography, the main source of public information about her life. Easy to read and an essential source for any student of the poet.

Montefiore, Janet. "Autumn." *The Times Literary Supplement*, October 9, 1998, p. 37. A critical review of Beer's *Autumn*.

Ravo, Nick. "Batrica Beer, 79, Poet Who Explored Religion." *The New York Times*, August 23, 1999, p. 9. An obituary with brief biographical information.

Skelton, Robin. "Leaders and Others: Some New British Poetry." *Kenyon Review* 30, no. 5 (1968): 689-696. Skelton reviews Beer's volume *Just Like the Resurrection* and discusses it in comparison with the work of Ted Hughes and Thom Gunn, two other British poets who also published collections at that time. Interesting in that it offers a rare look at how Beer's contemporaries perceived her at that point in her career.

Neal Bowers

APHRA BEHN

Born: England; July(?), 1640
Died: London, England; April 16, 1689

PRINCIPAL POETRY

*Poems upon Several Occasions, with A Voyage to
the Island of Love*, 1684 (adaptation of Abbé
Paul Tallemant's *Le Voyage de l'isle d'amour*)
*Miscellany: Being a Collection of Poems by Several
Hands*, 1685 (includes works by others)

OTHER LITERARY FORMS

Although Aphra Behn wrote more than a dozen separate pieces of fiction that critics of her day called novels, only a portion may legitimately be labeled as such.
Principal among these is her most noted work of fiction,
Oroonoko: Or, The History of the Royal Slave (1688);
others worthy of consideration are *Agnes de Castro*
(1688), *The Fair Jilt: Or, The History of Prince Tarquin
and Miranda* (1688), *The History of the Nun: Or, The
Fair Vow-Breaker* (1689), and *The Nun: Or, The Perjured Beauty* (1697). During her lifetime, Behn established her literary reputation by writing for the London
stage, creating more than fifteen plays.

ACHIEVEMENTS

Critics may defend Aphra Behn's talent for drama
and prose fiction as worthy of recognition beside that of
her male contemporaries. As a writer of verse, however,
she cannot claim a place among the poets of the first
rank. This does not mean that her poetry has no value for
the critic, the literary historian, or the general reader; on
the contrary, her occasional verse is no worse than the
political pieces of her colleagues (with the exception of
John Dryden), while the songs and poems from her
plays reflect her ability to manipulate verse as reinforce-
ment for dramatic theme and setting.

In the nineteenth century, such poet-essayists as
Leigh Hunt, Edmund Gosse, and Algernon Swinburne
recoiled initially from what they saw in Behn's occasional verse as indelicate and indecent language. They
recovered sufficiently to find some merit in her songs.
Hunt bemoaned her association with the rakes of the

Aphra Behn (Library of Congress)

age, yet praised the songs as "natural and cordial, written in a masculine style, yet womanly withal." Gosse
dubbed her "the George Sand of the Restoration"—an
obvious reference that had nothing whatsoever to do
with her literary abilities—although "she possessed an
indisputable touch of lyric genius." Swinburne looked
hard at a single poem, "Love in fantastic triumph sate,"
and concluded that "the virtuous Aphra towers above
her sex in the passionate grace and splendid elegance of
that melodious and magnificent song. . . ." The most attractive quality of her lyrical pieces is their spontaneity,
demonstrating to the reader (or the theatergoer) that the
best poetry need not be anchored to learning, but can
succeed because the lines are memorable, singable, and
direct.

In her public verse, Behn had to compete with a large
number of poets who tended to be more skilled mechanics and versifiers than she, and all of whom sought the
same limited patronage and political favors as she. She
found herself at a disadvantage because of her sex,
which meant, simply, that her occasional verse did not

always reach the widest possible audience. For example, such pieces as "A Pindarick on the Death of Charles II" (1685) and "A Congratulatory Poem to Her Most Sacred Majesty" (1688) may appear stiff and lacking in sincerity, but certainly no more so than the verses on the same subjects written by her contemporaries.

Her elegy on the death of Edmund Waller and her other contributions to a volume in memory of the departed poet in 1688 do, however, reflect a deep feeling of sorrow because of the occasion; these poems serve as a transition to her private verse, representing perhaps the highest level of Behn's poetic achievement. In "The Disappointment," for example, she reveals herself as a woman whose real desires have been obscured by frivolity and professionalism and who realizes that her laborious life is drawing to a close. The importance of such poems is that they provide the deepest insight into Behn; they draw a picture of the poet far more honestly and realistically than do the rumors, allusions, and innuendos set forth in countless biographical sketches and critical commentaries.

BIOGRAPHY

Although the details surrounding the life of Aphra Behn have at least become stabilized, they have not always been clear. Her earliest biographer, the poet Charles Gildon (1665-1724), maintained that she was born at Canterbury, in Kent, the daughter of a man named Johnson. In 1884, however, Edmund Gosse discovered a marginal note in a manuscript belonging to the poet Anne Finch, Countess of Winchelsea (1661-1720), revealing that Behn had actually been born at Wye, near Canterbury, the daughter of a barber—which John Johnson certainly was not. The countess's note receives support from an entry in the parish register of the Saints Gregory and Martin Church, Wye, to the effect that Ayfara Amis, daughter of John and Amy Amis, was baptized there on July 10, 1640. Apparently Johnson, related to Lord Francis Willoughby of Parham, adopted the girl, although no one seems certain of the exact year. Nevertheless, Ayfara Amis accompanied her stepparents on a journey to Surinam (later Dutch Guiana) in 1658, Lord Willoughby having appointed Johnson to serve as deputy governor of his extensive holdings there. Unfortunately, the new deputy died on the

voyage; his widow and children proceeded to Surinam and took up residence at St. John's, one of Willoughby's plantations. The exact length of their stay has yet to be determined; later biographers, though, have settled upon the summer of 1663 as the most probable date of return. The family's tenure at St. John's forms the background of Behn's most celebrated production, her novel *Oroonoko*.

By 1665, the young woman was established in London, married to a wealthy Dutch merchant (or at least a merchant of Dutch ancestry) who may well have had connections in or around the court of Charles II. In 1665 came the Great Plague and the death of Behn's husband; his death proved disastrous for his widow. For unknown reasons, the Dutch merchant left her nothing of substance—with the possible exception of his connections at court. Charles II, in the midst of his first war against the Dutch, hired Behn as a secret agent to spy against Holland; for that purpose, she proceeded to Antwerp. There she contacted another agent, William Scott, from whom she received various pieces of military information for forwarding to London. Although her work earned her little acknowledgment and even less money, Behn did conceive of the pseudonym "Astrea," the name under which she published most of her poetry. Essentially, the venture into foreign intrigue proved a dismal failure for her; she had to borrow money and pawn her few valuables to pay her debts and provide passage back to England.

Once home, early in 1667, Behn found no relief from her desperate financial situation. Her creditors threatened prison, and the government ministers who had employed her refused any payment for espionage service rendered. Prison followed, most probably at Caronne House, South Lambeth, although again the specifics of time and length of term are lacking. Behn's later biographers speculate that she may have been aided in her release by John Hoyle (died 1692)—a lawyer of Gray's Inn, a wit and an intellectual, at times an active homosexual, the principal subject and reason for Behn's sonnets, and the man with whom the writer carried on a long romance. In fact, Hoyle, to whom she refers often in her poems, is the only one of Behn's supposed lovers who can be identified with any certainty. When she finally gained her release from prison, she determined to dedicate the rest of her life to pleasure and to letters, to trust her own devices rather than to rely upon others whom she could not trust.

Behn launched her career as a dramatist in late December, 1670, at the New Duke's Theatre in Little Lincoln's Inn Fields, London. Her tragicomedy, *The Forced Marriage: Or, The Jealous Bridegroom* (1670), ran for six nights and included in the cast nineteen-year-old Thomas Otway, the playwright-to-be only recently down from Christ Church, Oxford. The neophyte bungled his lines, and with that his acting career came to a quick halt. Because of the length of the run, however, Behn, as was the practice, received the entire profit from the third performance; she could now begin to function as an independent artist. She followed her first effort in the spring of 1671 with a comedy, *The Amorous Prince: Or, The Curious Husband*, again at the New Duke's; another comedy, *The Dutch Lover*, came to Drury Lane in February, 1673, and by the time of her anonymous comedy, *The Rover: Or, The Banished Cavaliers, Part I*, in 1677, she had secured her reputation. Now she mixed easily with the likes of Thomas Killigrew, Edward Ravenscroft, the Earl of Rochester, Edmund Waller, and the poet laureate, John Dryden—who would publish her rough translations from Ovid in 1683. With the reputation came offers for witty prologues and epilogues for others' plays, as well as what she desired more than anything—money. A confrontation, however, with the earl of Shaftesbury and the newly formed Whigs during the religiopolitical controversies of 1678, when she offended the opponents of Charles II in a satirical prologue to an anonymous play, *Romulus and Hersilia*, brought her once again to the brink of economic hardship; for the next five years, she was forced to abandon writing for the stage.

Fortunately, Behn could find other outlets for her art in popular fiction and occasional verse, although neither proved as profitable as the stage. Her series of *Love Letters Between a Nobleman and His Sister* (1683-1687) and *Poems upon Several Occasions* were well received, but the meager financial returns could not keep pace with her social expenses. When she did return to the stage in 1686 with a comedy, *The Lucky Chance: Or, An Alderman's Bargain*, she met with only moderate success and much public abuse. *The Emperor of the Moon*, produced the following season, fared somewhat better, although the London audience had seemingly lost its stomach for a woman playwright with Tory sympathies.

She continued to write fiction and verse, but sickness and the death of her one true artistic friend, Edmund Waller, both occurring in October, 1688, did little to inspire confidence in her attitudes toward life or art. Five days following the coronation of William III and Mary, on April 16, 1689, Aphra Behn died, the result, according to Gildon, of incompetent surgery. Nevertheless, she had risen high enough to merit burial in Westminster Abbey; in fact, her memorial, interestingly enough, lies near that of the famous actress Anne Bracegirdle (died 1748), whose acting skills prolonged Behn's popularity well after the playwright's death. The fitting epitaph to Behn was provided by her lover, John Hoyle, who declared: "Here lies proof that wit can never be/ Defense against mortality."

ANALYSIS

The history of English poetry during the Restoration of Charles II and the reign of James II seems to have no room for Aphra Behn. The reasons, all having little or nothing to do with her true poetic abilities, are fairly obvious. To form a composite of the Restoration poet, one must begin with an outline of a gentle*man* who wrote verse for other gentle*men* and a few literate ladies, who directed his efforts to a select group of coffeehouse and drawing-room wits, who wrote about politics, religion, scientific achievement, or war. He wrote poetry to amuse and to entertain, and even, on occasion, to instruct. He also wrote verse to attack or to appease his audience, those very persons who served as his readers *and* his critics. Thus, the Restoration poet vied with his colleagues for recognition and patronage—even for political position, favor, and prestige. He hurled epithets and obscenities at his rivals, and they quickly retorted. Of course, that was all done in public view, upon the pages of broadsheets and miscellanies.

Reflect, for a moment, upon the career of John Dryden (1631-1700), who dominated the London literary scene during the last quarter of the seventeenth century. He stood far above his contemporaries and fulfilled the practical function of the Restoration man of letters: the poet, dramatist, and essayist who focused upon whatever subject or form happened to be current at a particular moment. Dryden succeeded because he understood his art, the demands of the times upon that art, and the arena in which he (as artist and man) had to compete. Around 1662 to 1663 he married Lady Elizabeth Howard, daughter of the Earl of Berkshire and sister of Sir Robert Howard. Sir Robert introduced the poet to the reestablished nobility, soon to become his readers and his patrons. In 1662, Dryden joined the Royal Society, mainly to study philosophy, mathematics, and reason, in order "to be a complete and excellent poet." One result, in 1663, was a poem in honor of Dr. Walter Charleton (1619-1707), physician to Charles II; the poet praised the new scientific spirit brought on by the new age and lauded the efforts of the Royal Society and its support of such geniuses as Robert Boyle and Sir Isaac Newton. In February, 1663, *The Wild Gallant*, the first of Dryden's twenty-eight plays, appeared on the stage; although the comedy was essentially a failure, it marked the beginning of an extremely successful career, for Dryden quickly recognized the Restoration theater as the most immediate outlet for his art.

Certainly Dryden became involved in the major religious and political controversies of his day, both personally and poetically, and his fortunes fluctuated as a result. His reputation, however—as critic, dramatist, and poet laureate of England—had been secured, and he remained England's most outstanding, most complete writer. As a poet, he headed a diverse group of artists who, although not consistently his equals, could compete with him in limited areas: the classicists of the Restoration, carryovers from an earlier age—Edmund Waller and Abraham Cowley; the satirists—Samuel Butler, John Oldham, Sir Charles Sedley, the earls of Rochester and Dorset; the dramatists—William Wycherley, Sir George Etherege, Nathaniel Lee, Thomas Otway, William Congreve, George Farquhar, and Aphra Behn.

The point to be made is that unlike Dryden and his male counterparts, Behn had little time and even less opportunity to develop as a poet. Her sex prevented her from fitting the prototype of the Restoration poet; she lacked access to the spheres of social and political influence, mastery of classical languages and their related disciplines, and the luxury of writing when and what she

pleased. The need for money loomed large as her primary motive, and, as had Dryden, she looked to the London stage for revenue and reputation. She certainly viewed herself as a poet, but her best poetry seems to exist within the context of her plays.

One problem in discussing Behn's poetry is that one cannot always catalog with confidence those pieces attributed to her and written by others. Also, there is confusion regarding those pieces actually written by her but attributed to others. For example, as late as 1926, and again in 1933, two different editors of quite distinct editions of the earl of Rochester's poetry erroneously assigned three of Behn's poems to Rochester, and that error remained uncorrected until 1939. Textual matters aside, however, Behn's poetry still provides substantive issues for critical discussion. Commentators have traditionally favored the songs from her plays, maintaining that the grace and spontaneity of these pieces rise above the artificiality of the longer verses—the latter weighed down by convention and lack of inspiration. True, her major poem (at least in terms of its length) of two thousand lines, *A Voyage to the Island of Love*, while carrying the romantic allegory to extremes, does succeed in its purpose: a poetic paraphrase of the French original, and nothing more. Indeed, Behn, as a playwright, no doubt viewed poetry as a diversion and exercise; she considered both activities useful and important, and both provided added dimensions to her art. She was certainly not a great poet; but few during her time were. Her poetic success, then, must be measured in terms of her competence, for which she may, in all honesty, receive high marks and be entitled to a permanent place on the roster of poets.

ABDELAZAR

At the head of the list are two songs from the play *Abdelazar: Or, The Moor's Revenge* (1676), the first a sixteen-line lyric known by its opening, "Love in fantastic triumph sate." Despite the trite (even by Restoration standards) dramatic setting—the usurper who murders his trusting sovereign and puts to death all who block his path to the throne—the poem reflects pure, personal feeling, as the poet laments over the misery of unrequited love. Behn depicts Love as a "strange tyrannic power" that dominates the amorous world; there is nothing terribly complicated, in either the sound or the sense of the language, for she relies upon simple sighs, tears, pride, cruelty, and fear. In the end, the poem succeeds because it goes directly to the central issue of the poet's personal unhappiness. "But my poor heart alone is harmed,/ Whilst thine the victor is, and free." The other song from *Abdelazar* is a dialogue between a nymph and her swain. The young lady, cognizant of the brevity of "a lover's day," begs her lover to make haste; the swain, in company with shepherds, shepherdesses, and pipes, quickly responds. He bears a stray lamb of hers, which he has caught so that she may chastise the creature ("with one angry look from thy fair eyes") for having wandered from the flock. The analogy between man and beast is obvious and nothing more need be said; the swain begs her to hurry, for "how very short a lover's day!"

SONGS AND ELEGIES

There are other songs of equal or slightly less merit, and they all seem to contain variations on the same themes. In one, "'Tis not your saying that you love," the speaker urges her lover to cease his talk of love and, simply, love her; otherwise, she will no longer be able to live. Another, a song from Lycidus beginning "A thousand martyrs I have made," mocks "the fools that whine for love" and unmasks the fashion of those who, on the surface, appear deeply wounded by the torments of love when they actually seek nothing from love but its shallow pleasures. In a third song, "When Jemmy first began to love," Behn returns to the shepherd and his flock motif. On this occasion, the nymph, overpowered by Jemmy's songs, kisses, and general air of happiness, gives herself completely to him. Then the call to arms beckons; Jemmy exchanges his sheep hooks for a sword, his pipes for warlike sounds, and, perhaps, his bracelets for wounds. At the end, the poor nymph must mourn, but for whom it is not certain: for the departed Jemmy or for herself, who must endure without him? Finally, in one of the longest of her so-called songs, a 140-line narrative titled "The Disappointment," Behn introduces some of the indelicacies and indiscretions of which Victorian critics and biographers accused her. By late seventeenth century standards, the piece is indeed graphic (although certainly not vulgar or even indecent); but it nevertheless succeeds in demonstrating how excessive pleasure can easily turn to pain.

Although Behn, whether by choice or situation, kept outside the arena of poetic competition of the sort engaged in by Dryden and his rivals, she managed to establish personal relationships with the major figures of her age. Dryden always treated her with civility and even kindness, and there are those who maintain that a piece often attributed to Behn—"On Mr. Dryden, Renegade," and beginning "Scorning religion all thy lifetime past,/ And now embracing popery at last"—was not of her making. In addition, she remained on friendly terms with Thomas Otway, Edward Ravenscroft, Edmund Waller, and the earl of Rochester.

"ON THE DEATH OF THE LATE EARL OF ROCHESTER"

Behn wrote elegies for Waller and Rochester, and both poems are well suited to their occasion; yet they are two distinctly different poems. "On the Death of the Late Earl of Rochester" (wr. 1680, pb. 1685) is an appeal to the world to mourn the loss of a great and multifaceted personality: The muses must mourn the passing of a wit, youths must mourn the end of a "dear instructing rage" against foolishness, maidens the loss of a Heaven-sent lover, the little gods of love the loss of a divine lover, and the unhappy world the passage of a great man. Draped in its pastoral and classical mantles, the poem glorifies a subject not entirely worthy of glorification; yet, if the reader can momentarily forget about Rochester, the piece is not entirely without merit. After all, the poet did demonstrate that she knew how to write a competent elegy.

"ON THE DEATH OF EDMUND WALLER"

More than seven years later, on October 21, 1687, the aged poet Edmund Waller died, and again Behn penned an elegiac response, titled "On the Death of Edmund Waller." Her circumstances, however, had changed considerably since the passing of Rochester in July, 1680. Her health was poor, her finances low, her literary reputation not very secure. Apparently she had to write the piece in some haste, specifically for a collection of poems dedicated to Waller and written by his friends. Finally, Behn was deeply affected by Waller's death and chose the opportunity to associate that event with her own situation—that of the struggling, ailing, and aging (although she was then only forty-seven) artist. Thus, she sets the melancholy tone at the outset by identifying herself as "I, who by toils of sickness, am become/ Almost as near as thou art to a tomb." Throughout, she inserts references to an untuned and ignorant world, the muses' dark land, the low ebb of sense, the scanty gratitude and fickle love of the unthinking crowd—all of which seem more appropriate to her private and professional life than to Waller's. Still, the poem is not an unusual example of the elegy; Behn was not the first poet to announce her own personal problems while calling upon the world to mourn the loss of a notable person.

Midway through the elegy to Waller, Behn provides a clue that may well reveal her purpose as a poet and, further, may help to establish her legitimacy within the genre. She writes of a pre-Wallerian world of meaningless learning, wherein dull and obscure declamations prevented the blossoming of sensitive poets and true poetry and produced nothing that was "great and gay." During those barren years, she laments, there existed only thoughtless labor, devoid of instruction, pleasure, and (most important) passion. In a word, "the poets knew not Love." Such expressions and sentiments may appear, on the surface, as attempts to elevate the memory of her subject; in reality, they serve well to underline her own concerns for poetry as a means of bringing harmony to disorder, comfort to discord, love to insensitivity. As a woman, she looked upon a poetic field dominated by masculine activity and masculine expression, by masculine attitudes and masculine ideals. Where, she must certainly have asked herself, could one find the appropriate context in which to convey to an audience composed of both males *and* females those passions peculiar to her sex and to her person?

Whether she actually found the form in which to house that passion—or whether she even possessed the craft and the intellect to express it—is difficult to determine. One problem, of course, is that Behn did not write a sufficient quantity of poetry outside of her plays and novels to allow for a reasonable judgment. Nevertheless, she never ceased trying to pour forth the pain and the love that dominated her emotions. She wrote (as in "'Tis not your saying that you love") that actions, not words, must reinforce declarations of love, for only love itself can sustain life. Without love, there is no life. Throughout her poems, that conclusion reverberates from line to line: Love is a triumph, a lover's day is short, the death of one partner means the spiritual (and automatic) death of the one remaining; a lover's soul is made of love, while the completion of an empty (and thus meaningless) *act* of love leaves a lover "half dead and breathless."

EXOTIC SETTINGS

Perhaps the most interesting aspect of Behn's poetry is her taste for exotic settings. These backdrops appear to contradict her very way of life. Behn was a woman of the city, of the urban social and intellectual center of a nation that had only recently undergone political trauma and change. She belonged to the theater, the drawing room, the coffeehouse, the palace—even to the boudoir. Not many of those settings, however, found their way into her poetry. Instead, she selected for her poetic environments a composite that she called the "amorous world" ("Love in fantastic triumph sate"), complete with listening birds, feeding flocks, the aromatic boughs and fruit of a juniper tree, trembling limbs, yielding grass, crystal dew, a lone thicket made for love, and flowers bathed in the morning dew.

Even the obviously human subjects, both alive and dead, rarely walk the streets of the town or meditate in the quiet of their own earthly gardens. Thus, Dryden, in the midst of religious disorientation, wanders about upon the wings of his own shame, in search of "Moses' God"; Rochester flies, quick as departing light, upon the fragrance of softly falling roses; and Waller, a heaven-born genius, is described as having rescued the chosen tribe of poetry from the Egyptian night. Of course, in the last two instances, Behn wrote elegies, which naturally allowed her departed subjects greater room for celestial meanderings. Love, however, had to be relieved from its earthly, banal confines. Love was very much Behn's *real* subject as a poet, but she was never prepared to discuss it within the context of the harsh and often ugly realities of her own time and place.

OTHER MAJOR WORKS

LONG FICTION: *Love Letters Between a Nobleman and His Sister*, 1683-1687 (3 volumes); *Oroonoko: Or, The History of the Royal Slave*, 1688; *Agnes de Castro*, 1688; *The Fair Jilt: Or, The History of Prince Tarquin and Miranda*, 1688; *The History of the Nun:*

Or, The Fair Vow-Breaker, 1689; *The Lucky Mistake*, 1689; *The Nun: Or, The Perjured Beauty*, 1697; *The Adventure of the Black Lady*, 1698; *The Wandering Beauty*, 1698.

PLAYS: *The Forced Marriage: Or, The Jealous Bridegroom*, pr. 1670; *The Amorous Prince: Or, The Curious Husband*, pr., pb. 1671; *The Dutch Lover*, pr., pb. 1673; *Abdelazar: Or, The Moor's Revenge*, pr. 1676; *The Town-Fop: Or, Sir Timothy Tawdry*, pr. 1676; *The Debauchee*, pr. 1677; *The Rover: Or, The Banished Cavaliers, Part I*, pr., pb. 1677, *Part II*, pr., pb. 1681; *Sir Patient Fancy*, pr., pb. 1678; *The Feigned Courtesans: Or, A Night's Intrigue*, pr., pb. 1679; *The Young King: Or, The Mistake*, pr. 1679; *The Roundheads: Or, The Good Old Cause*, pr. 1681; *The City Heiress: Or, Sir Timothy Treat-All*, pr., pb. 1682; *The Lucky Chance: Or, An Alderman's Bargain*, pr. 1686; *The Emperor of the Moon*, pr., pb. 1687; *The Widow Ranter: Or, The History of Bacon of Virginia*, pr. 1689; *The Younger Brother: Or, The Amorous Jilt*, pr., pb. 1696.

TRANSLATIONS: *Aesop's Fables*, 1687 (with Francis Barlow); *Of Trees*, 1689 (of book 6 of Abraham Cowley's *Sex libri plantarum*).

MISCELLANEOUS: *La Montre: Or, The Lover's Watch*, 1686 (prose and verse); *The Case for the Watch*, 1686 (prose and verse); *Lycidus: Or, The Lover in Fashion*, 1688 (prose and verse; includes works by others); *The Lady's Looking-Glass, to Dress Herself By: Or, The Art of Charming*, 1697 (prose and verse); *The Works of Aphra Behn*, 1915, 1967 (6 volumes; Montague Summers, editor).

BIBLIOGRAPHY

Carnell, Rachel K. "Subverting Tragic Conventions: Aphra Behn's Turn to the Novel." *Studies in the Novel* 31, no. 2 (Summer, 1998): 133-151. Carnell discusses strategies employed by Behn to counter the blatantly misogynistic resistance to her participation in political exchange. In later life, she turned to writing tragedies and to writing them not as drama but as prose fiction.

Duffy, Maureen. *The Passionate Shepherdess: Aphra Behn, 1640-1689*. London: Jonathan Cape, 1977. This reliable, scholarly examination of Aphra Behn and the Restoration period in which she wrote informs readers about the social and political life that governed Behn's style. Duffy treats Behn as a serious artist, not as the superficial, almost unknown figure that earlier biographers painted. Generously illustrated with portraits, maps, and drawings of theaters.

Gardiner, Judith Kegan. "Aphra Behn: Sexuality and Self-Respect." *Women's Studies Quarterly* 7 (1980): 67-78. Gardiner's useful study contrasts Behn's attitudes toward sex, as shown in her poetry and plays, with those of male writers of her time. She finds in Behn, who was as much a Restoration character as the men, a more wholesome attitude toward sexual power games, impotence, and erotic wit. Behn seeks "a cavalier balance in independent sexuality capable of mutual pleasure and mutual response."

Goreau, Angeline. *Reconstructing Aphra: A Social Biography of Aphra Behn*. New York: Dial Press, 1980. Goreau attempts to recover a heroic life in the story of the first woman to earn her living by her pen. The contradictions of a woman trying to be both independent and competitive in the theater world and at the same time trying to live the feminine roles of lover and wife occupy Goreau's attention throughout the study. Presents the political background and the social scene of fashionable London in the 1660's and 1670's. Includes sixteen pages of portraits and theater scenes.

Link, Frederick M. *Aphra Behn*. New York: Twayne, 1968. A thorough account of the sum of Behn's work: plays, poetry, stories, novels, and translations from the French. Behn's criticism of social conditions, forced marriage and economic dependency of women, colonial oppression, and slavery are all treated in the analysis of her writings. Augmented by a chronology, notes, a bibliography, and an index.

Rivero, Albert J. "Aphra Behn's *Oroonoko* and the 'Blank Spaces' of Colonial Fictions." *Studies in English Literature, 1500-1900* 39, no. 3 (Summer, 1999): 443-462. Rivero discusses Joseph Conrad's *Heart of Darkness* (1902) and Aphra Behn's *Oroonoko*. Both feature a protagonist who, beginning as civilized, goes spectacularly native, and both attempt to preserve hierarchies of race and class, while representing the impossibility of doing so in chaotic colonial settings.

Woodcock, George. *Aphra Behn: The English Sappho.* 1948. Reprint. Montreal: Black Rose, 1989. First published in 1948 in England, this book is now reprinted in its entirety with a short introduction by the author. Woodcock reflects that since writing the original version, he has come to see Behn less as a revolutionary and more as a participant in her times. Reviews the history of the debate about her childhood in Central America, her life as a spy, her prison experience, her career as a playwright, and her years of success.

Samuel J. Rogal;
bibliography updated by the editors

BEN BELITT

Born: New York, New York; May 2, 1911

PRINCIPAL POETRY

The Five-Fold Mesh, 1938
Wilderness Stair, 1955
The Enemy Joy: New and Selected Poems, 1964
Nowhere but Light: Poems, 1964-1969, 1970
The Double Witness: Poems, 1970-1976, 1977
Possessions: New and Selected Poems, 1985
This Scribe, My Hand: The Complete Poems of Ben Belitt, 1998

OTHER LITERARY FORMS

Ben Belitt, a major translator of verse into English, translated works by Arthur Rimbaud, Jorge Luis Borges, Federico García Lorca, Rafael Alberti, and, preeminently, Pablo Neruda. He has also written about both the problems of translation and poetics in general.

ACHIEVEMENTS

Belitt's poetry is, by common assent, difficult, owing to its casual erudition, allusiveness, exacting vocabulary, and compact figuration. He has so assiduously avoided

being a public poet that his reserve seems an explanation of why his work is not more anthologized. Nevertheless, his poetry has not escaped recognition: Belitt has received the Shelley Memorial Award (1936), the Oscar Blumenthal Award (1957), the National Institute of Arts and Letters Award (1965), and the Russell Loines Award (1981). He has twice been a candidate for the National Book Award (in poetry and in translation), and he is a past recipient of fellowships and grants from the Guggenheim Foundation and the National Endowment for the Arts.

BIOGRAPHY

Ben Belitt was born in New York City in 1911, the son of a teacher, Lewis, and Ida Lewitt Belitt. He earned his bachelor's, master's, and doctoral degrees at the University of Virginia and served in the U.S. Army during World War II.

Belitt joined the faculty of Bennington College (Vermont) in 1938; he has remained on Bennington's faculty since and continues to teach on an occasional basis. He has preferred a provincial to an urban setting for what he has called his "obsessional" writing habits. His poems and translations, however, reveal the least provincial of men. In 1936 and 1937, while still working on a doctoral degree (which he never finished) at the University of Virginia, he served as an assistant literary editor of *The Nation*, and late in World War II he served with the U.S. Army Department of Historical Films.

Belitt was orphaned early in life after the death of his father and subsequent abandonment by his mother. He and his sisters returned to their mother after her remarriage, but Belitt felt permanently isolated where family was concerned. He is not a confessional sort of poet, but this experience and its consequences are presented in his poem "Orphaning" and elsewhere.

ANALYSIS

From the outset, Ben Belitt's poetry has been aurally remarkable. Though his first volume was excessively alliterative and was spoken in a too-mannered voice, it revealed a poet whose first priority was control of traditional forms, in terms of meter and stanza. He managed this with a fluent prosody driven equally by the line and the sentence. Since then, Belitt has written a freer verse in accommodating his times and the dictates of his own sensibility. His genius for linking the sounds of words abides, however, and he would rather risk verbal excess than speak flatly.

Belitt's imagination is demanding. Images and the terms of his similes and metaphors are brought together rapidly in his work. The reader may feel that some unimaginable step by which the poet mediated the associations has been left out. Moreover, Belitt requires intellectual rigor from his reader. Often, he brings an immediately realized object or event into relation with historical figures and their ideas. His practice assumes that these unions are self-evident.

PLACE

Perhaps more than anything else, Belitt's poems strive to realize and throw light upon the nature of place and his response to place, which originates in alienation and need, moves on to solace and immersion and thence to a mature acceptance of rootlessness. (The reader who interprets this as the displacement of childhood anxieties overlooks the philosophical richness of Belitt's mind.) This enterprise is only roughly chronological in his work, as Belitt works by perpetually reconnoitering the old ground of his thought. As he goes, place is always complex, sometimes consoling, sometimes inscrutable, sometimes antagonistic; it can be all of these at once.

The reader sees then that place, though sharply focused and delineated by Belitt, is rendered in an essentially impressionistic manner and stands more for the poet's metaphysical and aesthetic probings than for its own pictorial value. Thus his common practice of envisioning place through contrasting entities like stone and tree, gem and flower, desert and water, is deeply related to his existential struggle to achieve, without self-delusion or the consolations of defunct mythologies, stable and abiding worldview. It is not surprising that such a poet would eventually write a book titled *Nowhere but Light*, having touched with clarity the innumerable dark places of his outer and inner landscapes.

THE FIVE-FOLD MESH

In a prefatory note to *The Five-Fold Mesh*, Belitt speaks of two of its sequences, "Many Cradles" and "In Time of Armament," as dealing, respectively, with a "problem in orientation" and an "expanding record of change." The whole collection he sees as moving from "simple responses to the natural world" to "usable relationships between the personal and the contemporary world." This is the case. The poet is lost in the face of absolute flux. His "contemporary world" is not rife with technological paraphernalia; it is the psychological state of incertitude in the province of metaphysics and value. Thus he says in "The Unregenerate": "Cherish this disbelief/ For final truth, although the end be grief." The "heart," he argues, should confront and "accept this thing" (disbelief); the mind has been long aware of it. This collection then is largely about the heart and mind's taking up the "problem in orientation" to utter mutability.

Many of the poems, to test the poet's integrity, confront suffering and death. In these provinces mutability is most vexing and makes disbelief small consolation. "John Keats, Surgeon" is preeminent in this category. It goes beneath the ceaselessly kindling fever of that poet's tubercular dying to discover first his broken heart and then his great integrity. He sees every impulse of Keats as rejecting the balm of easy, traditional consolation (the "kindly unguent") and, equally, any kind of nepenthe. Better to treasure the merciless truth, a poet's duty, and be left with the "ruined heartbeat ailing still." This is the archetypal spirit of the poet, who must be surgeon to himself. Yet if darkness and this tragic unconsolability mark much of the collection, it is noteworthy that Belitt closes with the more hopeful touches of "Battery Park: High Noon." Here the controlled and behatted individual of workaday lower Manhattan is pulled irresistibly toward the allurements of nature's ancient condition by a concert of spring's forces.

WILDERNESS STAIR

Wilderness Stair continues in a dark vein, its concluding sequence of war poems contributing largely to that effect. There is, however, much balance of joy and despondency here, an "equilibrium" in Belitt's lexicon.

Four sequences make up the volume. The first, "Departures," dominates by length. Its main body is a tour of places, each a blend of antithetical features that usually astound by their grace on the one hand and their starkness on the other. A maple in a Vermont quarry constitutes the wholeness of fragile fruitfulness and hard duration. A dead bull in a Mexican bull ring testifies to the commingling of dark and light: the "hilt . . . in a column of gristle" but also "Dionysus drowsing in a meadow." The second section, "The Habit of Angels," suggests transcendence and entails a struggle with the inner conflict created by the world's wildness. Belitt is moved by the call of moral rectitude, sent to one sensually engaged upon the "wilderness stair." (Stairwells and ladders, venues of psychological and spiritual ascent and descent, make up much of Belitt's terrain.) Yet his testament is, finally, an affirmation of the worldly stance, there being a "void at the sheer of the stair" and a fading godhead at the "place of the rock and the ladder."

The third section, "Karamazov," gets at the wish to murder the father. It is a tribute to Fyodor Dostoevski, like Keats esteemed by Belitt, and an exploration of the oedipal urge. Certainly, the section has biographical overtones but is very distanced in accepting a mother's peaceful counsel, which leads to the poet's generic blessing of the father.

Four grim war poems make up "In Agamemnon's Color." A paratrooper's "Descent in a Parachute" renders his fall a traumatic birth. Fumbling the cord ("on his broken navel"), what he had expected to be easeful becomes only a terrifying "question" in "his brute and downward waste." "The Spool" is a cinematic account of a day at war. The most rhetorically straightforward poem in Belitt's whole corpus, it is a narrative of filmed action, beginning with the routine of the morning march and ending with the field surgeon's rubber-gloved hands poised above a "nerveless and saline wound." The surgeon's "mouth rejects contemplation" as Belitt mines a dark vein.

THE ENEMY JOY

Belitt's title for his third collection, *The Enemy Joy*, comes from a poem published in *The Five-Fold Mesh* that is reprinted there, though not among the new poems. It is significantly positioned, however, as the book's final piece. The paradoxical title refers to Belitt's sense that joy is always accompanied by its antagonist. In the poem, which is basic to understanding the continued balancing of the contrarieties of place in the new work, a bird "in jackal country" sings "for pure delight." The bird suggests Thomas Hardy's darkling thrush, but Hardy's bird seemed to announce some

hope of which Hardy remained unaware. Belitt's bird sings "the enemy joy as it were grief"; its utterance is powerful, manifold, and paradoxically evident to Belitt. Simply put, this bird is the spirit of Keats, of the "Ode on Melancholy."

Thus, a quite productive orientation to the new poems may be to approach them in terms of aesthetics or of art understood as worldview, though life per se is nowhere shunned by Belitt. "Battle-Piece," a poem in five parts, is not simply an extension of the interest in war that was the finale to *Wilderness Stair*. It is an envisioning of Paolo Uccello's painting *Battaglia di San Romano* (1456-1460). Belitt regards the "champion" of the field as awaiting some interpretation of the deadly event. The poet concludes simply with "Nothing responded." This is not just colloquial; this is the veritable "nada" of a nihilistic insight. It is the artistic representation, ostensibly by Uccello but really by Belitt, of that "nerveless wound" speaking in the face of the surgeon's stilled mouth. In the penultimate line of this brilliant sequence, Belitt uses the word "placeless" with a cunning ambiguity. In one of its principal designations, it states the irreducible position of the artist. He is the poem's "Begetter," whose vision goes beyond the "landscape." He is the one to "fight that battle after the battle,/ Inward and naked." A commensurate realization caps "Memorial Hospital: Outpatient," dedicated to a physician. It is conveyed by the utterance "There is nowhere but light."

NOWHERE BUT LIGHT

That line, of course, prefigures the title of Belitt's fourth volume. It derives, as mentioned, from his steady effort to illuminate the darkness of the world and of his experience. *Nowhere but Light* also points, however, to the acceptance of a placeless condition, to some vanquishing of an old desire. The zone of his concern shifts here to being itself. Indeed, the first line of the first poem is merely "To be." Yet place, especially contrastive place, though differently regarded, remains important.

Thus the sequence titled "Antipodal Man" comes to a head in "Siesta: Mexico/Vermont." (The term "antipodal man" appears here.) Like many of Belitt's poems, this one suggests the Hartford/Florida and Nova Scotia/Brazil frames of reference of Wallace Stevens and Elizabeth Bishop. All have required antitheses of climate and topography for their work. Yet here it is the light of a dual setting, glimpsed in siesta, that dominates and grants the "antipodal man" his bearing. He enters simultaneously "the tropic/ and the polar fires." There is a mystic, albeit humanistic, dimension to this; the poem is about the rarefied human experience in which the poet enters fire and circles "the precision/ of a moment." Specific place yields to archetypal place, which yields to light, which yields to an enlightened moment.

The volume's first poem, one of Belitt's finest, "The Orange Tree," sets the stage for such experience. Belitt meditates on the idea that if one can "live in the spirit" perhaps it is a state analogous to "the orange's scent/ in the orange tree." It is the marriage of the palpable tree and the ephemeral scent that excites the poet's imagination. In tying that union to conceivable spirituality, he arrives at a synesthetic figure in which the tree's branch, then twig, then leafage lead irrepressibly to the "sunburst of white in the leaves," which he calls "the odor's epiphany." Scent inhabits color. This natural epiphany dictates a paring of excess to Belitt, a search for the "minimal." The epiphany and its lesson stand as emblems of the questing and goal particular to this collection that, with *The Enemy Joy*, considerably broadens Belitt's use of his materials and his idea of his art.

THE DOUBLE WITNESS

Belitt continues to explore his isolation in *The Double Witness*, though he employs "we" more than before. The title comes from the opening poem, "Xerox," wherein an "original" man lies down upon a copy machine's glass to double all that was "lonely, essential, unique." In witty prayerfulness, he calls from the machine's inky pit, "Forgive our duplicity." Belitt uses the volume to track the individual into the species, locating a range of doubles. The poems are worlds of mirroring.

The volume's key piece is the sequence "This Scribe My Hand," about Belitt's relation to Keats, which is represented by the contact of their pens' nibs as Keats writes on the underside of Belitt's page. Its exquisite realization of psychological pain does not check its despair and nihilistic feeling. These become the dominant tones of the volume's final section, where "chaos" rules and the mundane lament that "nothing will happen to-

day" is a refrain. Belitt's despair is attributable to his continuing appraisal of his art, which—especially in "This Scribe My Hand"—grows utterly pessimistic in this volume. He feels his own work as posthumous and envisions Keats writing his own solitude "in water" on his side of the page. He sees that "something murderous flows/ from that page," a silence that stills their language and is the fate of which they are the double witness. He calls the silence "mortal."

These are the poems of a poet's most extreme crisis, come inexorably to haunt his sixties. They give us suicides, exiles, and deep anxiety about the poet's own enterprise. Belitt's skill in connecting detail within and between them, his management of paradox and the forthrightness of his self-questioning, all preserve integrity in a volume menaced by disintegration. Belitt has always considered poetry his talisman. That these poems so thoroughly doubt themselves philosophically yet remain so exquisitely executed suggests that for Belitt the true poem of the chaotic, even one written against itself, retains its talismanic power.

POSSESSIONS

There are only twelve new poems in *Possessions*. They are not easily characterized, as each picks up on some dominant strain long at work. "Graffiti" is a "vandal's dream" in which Belitt writes himself large and pervasively, in his "double initials," on a subway's every surface. It is, first, an absurd fantasy of a literary status denied and, second, a dealing with the commensurate sense that his work has only posthumous prospects. "Walker" is an old woman's revery of dancing as she stands, shut in and stalled, before her doorframe, which holds the image of Candlewood Mountain at an impossible distance. Belitt does not let her drift into a nostalgic past; rather, he makes up the fantastic satisfaction of her longing from her present condition. "Walker" belongs to a group that takes the difficult lives of elderly women as subject. It originates with the excellent "Charwoman" (*The Five-Fold Mesh*) and comes to full development both here and in "A Suicide: Paran Creek" (*The Double Witness*).

The poem titled "Possessions" glimpses King Tutankhamen's realization that grave robbers have done him out of the wherewithal of his immortality. Belitt takes the point to heart, seeing his own desire through the boy king's. Each of the volume's poems ties in with "Possessions" in some way. The quite dissimilar "Sumac" ends with a remark about how the "marauders move in," and the subterranean setting of "Graffiti" is characterized as "the tomb-robber's darkness."

"On Paran Creek" and "Voyage of the *Beagle*" get finely at Henry David Thoreau's and Charles Darwin's probing to discover precisely why certain particulars and not others constitute the world. The poems relate to "Possessions" and its spiritual search to locate and possess what can bestow some abiding meaning on human existence. Belitt knows that nothing can be so possessed except in illusion, and that everyone is robbed even of that, one way or another. Though *Possessions* is a small volume, it is not skimpy. It is a plenitude from the lively mind of a poet in his seventies.

OTHER MAJOR WORKS

NONFICTION: *Four Poems by Rimbaud: The Problem of Translation*, 1947; *Adam's Dream: A Preface to Translation*, 1978; *The Forgèd Feature: Toward a Poetics of Uncertainty—New and Selected Essays*, 1995.

TRANSLATIONS: *Poet in New York*, 1955 (of Federico García Lorca); *Selected Poems of Pablo Neruda*, 1961; *Juan de Mairena*, 1963 (of Antonio Machado); *Selected Poems of Rafael Alberti*, 1965; *Poems from the Canto General*, 1968 (with Alastair Reid; of Neruda); *A New Decade: Poems, 1958-1967*, 1969 (of Neruda); *New Poems, 1968-1970*, 1972 (of Neruda); *Splendor and Death of Joaquin Murieta*, 1972 (of Neruda); *A la pintura*, 1972 (of Alberti); *Jorge Luis Borges: Selected Poems*, 1972; *Five Decades: Poems, 1925-1970*, 1974 (of Neruda); *Skystones*, 1981 (of Neruda); *The New York Poems: Poet in New York/Earth and Moon*, 1982 (of Federico García Lorca); *Late and Posthumous Poems, 1968-1974*, 1988 (of Neruda).

BIBLIOGRAPHY

Goldensohn, Lorrie. "Witnessing Belitt." *Salmagundi* 44 (1979): 182-196. Analyzes Belitt's habit of "cannibalizing" prior books so as to enrich his current approach to a theme, a habit that goes beyond the borrowing of a line or image; it entails whole poems, which when newly placed revisit, enlarge, and reshape a concern. Also offers insight into Belitt's "gloominess" and spirituality.

Landis, Joan Hutton. "A Wild 'Severity': Toward a Reading of Ben Belitt." In *Contemporary Poetry in America*, edited by Robert Boyers. New York: Schocken, 1974. Excellent overview of Belitt's work (excepting the new poems in *Possessions*) links the poet's dominant attitude to Keats's "melancholy." Treats also the recurrent balancing of opposites in the poems, whether the rock and flower of the world or the joy and despair of humanity.

Nemerov, Howard. "The Fascination of What's Difficult." In *Reflexions on Poetry and Poetics*. New Brunswick, N.J.: Rutgers University Press, 1972. Nemerov argues the efficacy of Belitt's difficulty grasped verbal associations and demanding vocabulary. He sees Belitt's typical manner as a blending of "great elaboration" and "great intensity" (conciseness) and contends that one must read "around" rather than "through" his lyrics and see them in combination.

Salmagundi 87 (1990): 3-231. An indispensable issue devoted to readings of Belitt's poems. Mary Kinzie's "A Servant's Cenotaph" is broadest in scope, taking up the whole of *The Double Witness* and noting that there as elsewhere Belitt's "vision of human experience is fateful and symbolic." Hugh Kenner's "Meditations on 'Possessions'" deals with Belitt's predilections for lists and the "rite" of naming. He sees these characteristics as the poet's means for manifesting both the intense particularity of things and the dilemma of valuing what one is attached to but cannot possess. Terence Diggory's "On Ben Belitt's 'The Bathers: A Triptych'" discusses the poet's work as frequently conscious of itself as art. It characterizes Belitt's particularly rich way of revealing the division between the work and the object it contemplates.

David M. Heaton;
bibliography updated by the editors

MARVIN BELL

Born: New York, New York; August 3, 1937

PRINCIPAL POETRY

Things We Dreamt We Died For, 1966
A Probable Volume of Dreams, 1969
Escape into You, 1971
Residue of Song, 1974
Stars Which See, Stars Which Do Not See, 1977
These Green-Going-to-Yellow, 1981
*Drawn by Stones, by Earth, by Things That Have
    Been in the Fire*, 1984
New and Selected Poems, 1987
Iris of Creation, 1990
A Marvin Bell Reader: Selected Poetry and Poems,
    1994
The Book of the Dead Man, 1994
Ardor: The Book of the Dead Man, Volume 2, 1997

OTHER LITERARY FORMS

Although Marvin Bell published mainly poetry, he also wrote essays about poetry in *Old Snow Just Melting: Essays and Interviews* (1983). Bell also collaborated with poet William Stafford on two books: *Segues: A Correspondence in Poetry* (1983), and *Annie-Over* (1988). He also made a sound recording of *The Self and the Mulberry Tree* (1977), for the Watershed Foundation. His poetry has appeared in many anthologies, and in 1998 he published some of his collected poems in *Wednesday: Selected Poems, 1966-1997*, in Ireland.

Bell has extensive editing experience, first with *Statements* (1959-1964), which he founded, and later as poetry editor for *North American Review* (1964-1969), and *Iowa Review* (1969-1971). Partly because of his long association with the *Iowa Review* and the University of Iowa, he was twice interviewed at length by the editors of the *Iowa Review:* in the winter edition of 1981 and in the fall issue of 2000.

ACHIEVEMENTS

Beginning in 1966, Marvin Bell published a volume of poetry approximately every three years and has just as steadily acquired critical acclaim. He won the James Laughlin Award from the Academy of American Poets for *A Probable Volume of Dreams* in 1969, the Bess Hokin Award from *Poetry*, the Emily Clark Balch Prize from the *Virginia Quarterly Review* in 1970, and the prestigious Literature Award from the Academy of Arts and Letters in 1994. He was also the recipient of a Guggenheim Fellowship (1976) and National Endowment for the Arts Fellowships (1978 and 1984). He has twice held Senior Fulbright Scholarships (Yugoslavia, 1983; Australia, 1986) and has served as visiting professor at several universities. In 1986 his alma mater, Alfred University, awarded him the Lh.D., and in 2000 he was named the first poet laureate in Iowa.

BIOGRAPHY

Marvin Hartley Bell was born in New York City but spent his childhood in Center Moriches, a small Long Island town sixty miles from Manhattan. His parents, Saul and Belle Bell, were the children of Russian Jews who had emigrated to escape persecution. In his boyhood Bell played on soccer, baseball, and basketball teams, became a ham radio operator, and played the trumpet in a jazz group. His early writing experience consisted of writing a column about school events for the local weekly newspaper.

After high school, Bell attended Alfred University in upstate New York. There he continued with his trumpet playing in the university orchestra; worked for the yearbook and *Fiat Lux*, the weekly newspaper, which he edited his senior year; and became interested in ceramics and photography. Bell was initially more attracted to journalism than to literature, and when he found appropriate political causes (discriminatory clauses in sororities and fraternities, for example), he wrote and mimeographed an underground newsletter. After graduation from Alfred, Bell enrolled in the graduate journalism school at Syracuse University, where he met Al Sampson, who became a lifelong friend, and Mary (Mickey) Mammosser, who became his first wife. The couple then moved to Rochester, where they founded *Statements*, a journal that enabled them to include both literature and photography.

At the urging of Al Sampson, who was now studying literature at the University of Chicago, the Bells moved to Chicago in 1958. Bell enrolled in the M.A. program in English at the University of Chicago, continued to publish *Statements* (five issues ultimately appeared), wrote poems, and did still photography. His marriage to Mickey ended after the birth of their son Nathan, who stayed with Bell. He later married Dorothy Murphy, with whom he had another son, Jason, in 1966. Bell comments, "My story since 1960 is forever woven together with the stories of Dorothy, Nathan, and Jason." The three often appear in Bell's poems.

While in Chicago, Bell took a writing seminar with John Logan, who had encouraged Bell to contribute an article and a photograph to *Choice*, which Logan had just founded. When Logan recommended the Writers' Workshop in Iowa, Bell applied for the doctoral program at the University of Iowa and was accepted. Studying with Donald Justice and Paul Engel, Bell writes, "In the midst of a swirl of literary fellowship, I still felt that I was following my own road." Bell, however, left Iowa to go on active duty with the Army (he had been in the ROTC program at Alfred) in 1965. After his military tour of duty Bell returned

Marvin Bell (© Erik Borg)

to Iowa City, where he taught with Donald Justice and George Starbuck in the Writers' Workshop. After 1966, when his first volume of poems appeared, Bell published a poetry volume about every three years, while also serving as poetry editor for the *North American Review* (1964-1969) and the *Iowa Review* (1969-1971). He continued to teach at Iowa but also taught abroad and at other universities in the United States. After 1985 he divided his time between Iowa and Port Townsend, Washington, where he bought a house. In the 1990's a series of fellowships took him to several universities and colleges including the University of the Redlands, in 1991 to 1993; St. Mary's College of California in 1994-1995, Nebraska-Wesleyan University in 1996-1997, and Pacific University in 1996-1997. He frequently acts as judge for various writing competitions. In 2000 he was named poet laureate of Iowa.

ANALYSIS

The dominant themes and motivations of Marvin Bell's poetry perhaps can be best understood by hearing him speak of his own work. Discussing his personal aesthetic, he told Wayne Dodd and Stanley Plumly in an *Ohio Review* interview, "I would like to write poetry which finds salvation in the physical world and the here and now and which defines the soul, if you will, in terms of emotional depth, and that emotional depth in terms of the physical world and the world of human relationships." Indeed, Bell is a poet of the family and the relationships within. He writes of his father, his wives, his sons, and himself in a dynamic interaction of love and loss, accomplishment, and fear of alienation. These are subjects that demand maturity and constant evaluation. Bell's oeuvre highlights his ability to understand the durability of the human heart. As a son of a Jew who immigrated from the Ukraine, Bell writes of distance and reconciliation between people, often touching on his complex relationship to his heritage.

And while concern with the self and its relationships provides a focal point in Bell's early poetry, many of his poems have crystallized around a reflection on the self in relation to nature, evident in collections such as *Stars Which See, Stars Which Do Not See*. Growing up among farmers, Bell has always felt nature to be an integral part of his life. The rural life that so fascinated other writers during the 1960's back-to-nature movement was not Bell's inspiration. Rather, nature forms a critical backdrop for events and relationships in his life, and in that sense, he says, "I *am* interested in allowing nature to have the place in my poems that it always had in my life."

He notes that

contemporary American poetry has been tiresome in its discovery of the individual self, over and over and over, and its discovery of emotions that, indeed, we all have: loneliness, fear, despair, ennui. . . . I think it can get tiresome when the discovery of such emotions is more or less all the content there is to a poem. I think, as I may not always have thought, that the only way out of the self is to concentrate on others and on things outside the self.

Thus, Bell has evolved his ability to perceive and praise small wonders in a quiet and reserved fashion and, as one critic noted, "has found within his *own* voice that American voice, and with it the ability to write convincingly about the smallest details of a personal history."

A PROBABLE VOLUME OF DREAMS

"An Afterword to My Father," which ironically begins *A Probable Volume of Dreams*, is a fairly typical early Bell poem. The "probable" part of the book's title and the placement of an "afterword" at the beginning of a poem reflect Bell's characteristic ambiguity and uncertainty.

> Not so much "enough,"
> there is more to be done,
> yes, and to be done with.
>
> You were the sun and moon.
> Now darkness loves me;
> the lights come on.

Here Bell uses cliches, an allusion ("done") to Donne, and metaphors (father as sun and moon). What remains to be "done" must also be "done with," moved beyond. The father, a recurrent image in Bell's poems, *was* the poet's source of light; the darkness that follows the father's death *now* provides light, but what is illumined is not stated, nor is it necessarily positive.

ESCAPE INTO YOU

Escape into You chronicles the breaking up of a marriage and a poet's gradual coming to terms not only with a wife and sons, but with himself. As Arthur Oberg puts it, the poems describe "a poetic self that is still learning to bury the dead and to walk among the living." "Homage to the Runner," also the title of a column Bell wrote, is about running, one of Bell's athletic outlets, but also about poetry and how poetry affects others. Running and poetry both involve "pain," and "the love of form is a black occasion/ through which some light must show/ in a hundred years of commitment." While there is "some light," the occasion is "black." The runner and poet "ache" to end the race and poem, which begin in darkness, but there "is no finish; you can stop [running or writing] for no one," not even family, as much as you care for them.

RESIDUE OF SONG

Residue of Song contains thirteen poems to Bell's father and concerns loneliness. "Residue of Song" begins by stating that "you were writing a long poem, yes,/ about marriage, called 'On Loneliness.'" Like the "probable" in his *A Probable Volume of Dreams*, the "residue" also undercuts its subject matter. In fact, in "Residue of Dreams" "you" decide not to write the poem. In Bell's poem it is the speaker who is the lonely one as he describes a woman's egotism and violence and his callous responses to her; but, as is usually the case with Bell, the poem ends in bittersweet acceptance of the "residue" in a relationship:

> Your cries,
> for ecstatic madness, are not sadder than some things.
> From the residue of song, I have barely said my love again,
> as if for the last time, believing that you will leave me.

The use of "barely" and "as if" is part of Bell's tendency to qualify, to undercut, and to leave meaning implied but not defined.

STARS WHICH SEE, STARS WHICH DO NOT SEE

Stars Which See, Stars Which Do Not See contains poems about Dorothy, Bell's wife, but also includes several poems about poetry. In his "To a Solitary Reader," an allusion to William Wordsworth's poem about the solitary reaper, Bell discusses the development of his poetry: "If once he slept with Donne/ (happily) now he sleeps/ with Williams/ the old Williams." Bell thereby indicates his movement from John Donne's metaphysical style to William Carlos Williams's stress on a poem being, rather than meaning. The remainder of the poem distinguishes between "memory," which is what we "are" in the sense that "they/ think they know us," and what our "being" is, that which is inexplicable, without meaning. The poem concludes, "Time's determinant./ Once I knew you." Bell leaves behind certainty and memory and instead embraces the idea that nothing can be "known."

THESE GREEN-GOING-TO-YELLOW

In the title poem of *These Green-Going-to Yellow* the poet states, "I'm raising the emotional ante" by attempting to align himself with nature, particularly the leaves of a gingko tree someone planted in New York City. The poem concerns people's perspectives on life and asks if they really see beauty. Of course, the answer is "no." People look down "not to look up" and "look at the middles of things." Comfortable with mediocrity, like the seasons, people go from green to yellow, age like autumn, and lose their creative powers. Bell declares that people's perspective would be different "if we truly thought that we were gods." This line denies people even an erroneous presumption about their place in the universe, but in his acceptance of the situation Bell somehow remains "green." He has said, "I started out green and I intended to remain so."

DEAD MAN POEMS

In the Dead Man poems in *The Book of the Dead Man* and *Ardor: The Book of the Dead Man, Volume 2*, Bell moves in a new direction, adopting a persona or mask that he often denies but on at least one occasion accepts: "He was my particular and my universal./ I leave it to the future to say why." The Dead Man has enabled Bell to erase distinctions such as the one between life and death. In "About the Dead Man" the poet writes, "He [the Dead Man] thinks himself alive because he has no future." Statements like this, especially when they are preceded by and followed by other seemingly unrelated statements, would appear to be incredibly complicated, but Bell asserts that they are complex, rather than complicated. Complexity, for him, is "the fabric of life and the character of emotion." In his poetry things "connect," even if the connections are not always apparent to the reader.

The "Baby Hamlet" poem in this section embodies Bell's ideas about complexity, which requires "a fusion of many elements, some of them seemingly disparate, even contradictory." Hamlet's indecision is fused with the world's indecision, its "hopeless pacifism" and the "Platonic ideal carried to its logical inconclusion." According to Bell, "It doesn't seem a stretch to me to parallel Hamlet's indecision with the world's reluctance to act early and decisively against the Nazis." After all, "events occur while waiting for the news./ Or stuck in moral neutral."

OTHER MAJOR WORKS

NONFICTION: *Old Snow Just Melting: Essays and Interviews*, 1983.

MISCELLANEOUS: *Segues: A Correspondence in Poetry*, 1983 (with William Stafford); *Annie-Over*, 1988 (with Stafford).

BIBLIOGRAPHY

Bell, Marvin. "An Interview with Marvin Bell." Interview by David Hamilton. *Iowa Review* 30 (Fall, 2000): 3-22. Because Bell was the first poetry editor for the *Iowa Review*, which interviewed him in 1981, this review provides an excellent overview of Bell's writing career. Hamilton discusses the development of the Dead Man poems, beginning with *Iris of Creation* (1990) with later appearances in *A Marvin Bell Reader* (1994). These lead to *The Book of the Dead Man* and *Ardor*. The Resurrected Dead Man first appeared in *Wednesday* (1997), published in Ireland. Hamilton describes the Dead Man as "an archetypal figure with sacramental dimensions." Bell distinguishes between the two figures by stating that a Dead Man poem is a field, but a Resurrected Dead Man poem is a path: "I go first. If you want to follow me, you have to stay on the path."

_____. "My Twenties in Chicago: A Memoir." *Triquarterly* 60 (Spring/Summer, 1984): 118-126. Bell's vivid account of the years 1958 to 1961, which he spent in the artistic neighborhood of Hyde Park in Chicago. Bell describes the "activist" nature of the neighborhood, his growing involvement with photography, his M.A. writing classes at the University of Chicago, and his many colleagues, friends, and teachers. John Logan, poet and professor, is discussed at length. Of special interest is his discussion of the Chicago artistic and literary scene, including the work of several prominent Beat poets such as Jack Kerouac, Allen Ginsberg, and Gregory Corso.

Jackson, Richard. "Containing the Other: Marvin Bell's Recent Poetry." *The North American Poetry Review* 280 (January/February, 1995): 45-48. Jackson focuses on *The Book of the Dead Man*, which he finds rich in complexity. For Jackson, Bell extends his emphasis on inclusiveness and counterpointing in the Dead Man poems. The book begins with poems about feeling and sensing, moves to dreams and the psychic life, and concludes "with two poems about our relation to the cosmos." Jackson finds in Bell's poetry the joy of life.

Kitchen, Judith. "'I Gotta Use Words. . . .'" *The Georgia Review* 51 (Winter, 1997): 756. Kitchen believes that in the Dead Man Bell has found "a liberating spirit, someone who could serve his poetic innovation." She finds *Ardor*, not surprisingly, more passionate than *The Book of the Dead Man* and sees Bell moving from a forward look at death to a backward look at life. As a result, she claims, the poems in the later book to be a cohesive whole, to be able to create a contextual world and then provide a "take" on that world. For her, Bell is sending poetry into new and original territory.

Thomas L. Erskine,
updated by Sarah Hilbert

HILAIRE BELLOC

Born: La Celle-Saint-Cloud, France; July 27, 1870
Died: Guildford, England; July 16, 1953

PRINCIPAL POETRY

Verses and Sonnets, 1896
The Bad Child's Book of Beasts, 1896
More Beasts for Worse Children, 1897

The Modern Traveller, 1898
A Moral Alphabet, 1899
Cautionary Tales for Children, 1907
Verses, 1910
More Peers, 1911
Sonnets and Verse, 1923, 1938
New Cautionary Tales, 1930
Sonnets and Verse, 1954 (Reginald Jebb, editor)
The Verse, 1954 (W. N. Roughead, editor)

OTHER LITERARY FORMS

Hilaire Belloc was a prolific and popular writer of prose. He is identified primarily as a historian and defender of the Roman Catholic religion, but he wrote history, biography, travel, literary criticism, church history and religious doctrine, political theory, and translation, as well as some autobiographical travel books which are difficult to categorize. In all, he wrote more than 150 books, as well as many book reviews and magazine articles. His prose and poetry both show a wide range of themes and forms.

Belloc was one of a number of Catholic writers of the period, including Francis Thompson, Gerard Manley Hopkins, Alice Meynell, and G. K. Chesterton. He wrote rebuttals to views of his Church held by the historians Edward Gibbon, H. G. Wells, and George Coulton, but he could also see its imperfections, remarking to a friend that such an institution could not have lasted a fortnight if it had not been divine.

ACHIEVEMENTS

Although he was a man of letters in many genres, Hilaire Belloc often said in later years that he hoped to be remembered for his poetry. He wrote more than 170 poems in all and was a writer of both light and serious verse. Much of the former was intended for children, but it appealed to adults as well. The first edition of *The Bad Child's Book of Beasts* (1896) sold out in four days, and four thousand copies were sold in three months. This was followed by other nonsense books which were much praised. *The Spectator* ranked his satirical and comic verse with Edward Lear's, and Sir Arthur Quiller-Couch commended it.

A volume of Belloc's serious poetry also appeared in 1896, and it increased in size in succeeding editions.

Belloc was said by Desmond McCarthy to be the most underrated of poets. At a dinner in his honor on his sixtieth birthday, Chesterton said that such a ceremony "might have been fitting thousands of years ago at the festival of a great Greek poet," and that "Belloc's sonnets and strong verse would remain like the cups and carved epics of the Greeks."

In later years, his poetry has been generally neglected, although the serious poems include many beautiful works. This neglect is probably the result of three circumstances. First, his themes and forms were traditional and classical rather than avant-garde. Second, his reputation as a prose writer made his poems seem secondary. Third, some of his best poems were not published in his collections of poetry until 1938. This was true of many of his epigrams and of the Juliet poems, which had been privately printed. His "Heroic Poem in Praise of Wine" probably has been his most admired work.

Hilaire Belloc in 1904. (Hulton Archive)

BIOGRAPHY

Joseph Hilaire Pierre Belloc was born in 1870 in La Celle-Saint-Cloud, near Paris, of a French father and an English mother. He was called Hilaire after his grandfather, a celebrated painter. His father died when he was a baby, and, after his mother suffered financial reverses when he was eight years old, they moved to England, his home in Sussex becoming a major influence in his life. He wrote his first poem when he was eight years old. In 1882, he was sent to the Oratory School at Edgbaston, a boarding school that had been established by Cardinal Newman. While he did not like school, he nevertheless learned the classics, took parts in Latin plays, and won a prize in his last year. After leaving school, he considered joining the French Navy, since he loved sailing, but he studied for only a term at the Collège Stanislas at Paris before finding it too restrictive. He was then apprenticed to a farmer to learn to be a land agent, but that did not work out either. He then turned to journalism and edited a weekly paper called *The Lamp*, in which some of his early poems appeared. Other early poems appeared in *The Irish Monthly* and *Merrie England*.

In 1889, he fell in love with Elodie Hogan, an Irish American visiting Europe with her family whom he met at his mother's house. Belloc wanted to marry her, but she returned to California. He followed her to the United States in 1890, and made his way westward laboriously, often on foot, selling sketches to pay his way. Elodie's mother did not favor the marriage, and Elodie considered becoming a nun. She persuaded Belloc to take the military training required of all French citizens. When he returned east, she sent him a letter refusing his proposal. He did join the Battery of the Eighth Regiment of Artillery at Toul, serving from November, 1891, to August, 1892, and very much enjoyed military life.

Although Catholics were not yet formally permitted to attend Oxford or Cambridge, Belloc became a student at Balloil College, Oxford, helped financially by his sister and her husband-to-be. In October, 1892, he received a history scholarship. During his three years at Oxford, he received the Brackenbury Prize for history, took a brilliant first, became President of the Union, and walked from Oxford to London in record time. He was deeply disappointed, however, that he did not receive a history fellowship, especially since it was awarded to another Catholic for the first time since the Reformation.

Elodie entered the convent, but soon left, suffering from physical and nervous disorders. In 1896, Belloc went again to California, where they were married on June 16 despite Elodie's mother's objections; Belloc also did some lecturing while he was in the United States. The couple then lived in Oxford, where Belloc published his first collection of poems. He earned money by tutoring, giving University Extension lectures, and writing books, including *The Bad Child's Book of Beasts* (1896). He wrote political articles and gave speeches for Liberal candidates. He wanted to apply for the Professorship of History at Glasgow University, but that university did not favor a Catholic and prevailed upon Elodie to discourage him from applying.

In 1902, Belloc became an English citizen, and in 1906, he entered Parliament as the Liberal member from South Salford. Although he saw the House of Commons as a place of corruption and hypocrisy, he was reelected as an Independent.

He founded a weekly review, *The Eye Witness*. He moved from Oxford to Cheyne Walk, and then in 1906 to King's Land, a house in Sussex near Horsham, where he enjoyed his four children and his many friends, including the Chesterton brothers. His wife, whose literary judgment he greatly respected, died at forty-three in 1914, and ever after he dressed in black and used black-bordered stationery. He traveled frequently to the continent to study the scenes of his historical works. Unable to get an active appointment in World War I, he spent some time writing articles concerning the war.

He became ill in 1941 after his youngest son died in military service and had a stroke at the beginning of the next year, from which he recovered slowly. He died on July 16, 1953, just short of his eighty-third year.

ANALYSIS

Belloc enjoyed playing with various forms of verse while adhering to the ideals of the classics. His range was unusual: He could write, with almost equal facility, a heroic poem or an epigram, a sonnet or a ballade, a satire or a piece of nonsense verse.

What Hilaire Belloc praised in others' verse he tried to achieve in his own. He said, in a preface to Ruth

Pitter's poetry, that the classical spirit, which involved "rhythmic effect without emphatic lilt," subtlety without obvious complexity, and artistry without artifice, was almost unknown in his time. In his preface to D. B. Wyndham Lewis's book on François Villon, he remarked that the clarity, relief, and vigor mentioned by Lewis were qualities of "hardness," explaining that the marks of hardness were inevitability, the sense that to change a line would be to destroy it; a sense of sequence, of smooth linking; and economy of speech. Belloc's most successful poems, particularly his epigrams, have this intensity.

"HEROIC POEM IN PRAISE OF WINE"

Belloc was classical in his ideals but innovative in his practice. His classicism bore poetic fruit in his "Heroic Poem in Praise of Wine," probably his best-known poem. The work (which was influenced by the French writer Clèment Marot's vineyard song) was finished in 1928, although fragments of it had appeared earlier. Although it is a poem of praise treating a subject in an exalted way, Belloc the classicist is careful to refer to it as a heroic poem rather than an ode, for it is written in neither the Pindaric nor the Horatian form. The poem changes direction several times and ranges from heroic to mock-heroic.

The first stanza begins in the classical convoluted manner with infinitives of purpose, followed by several lines giving appositives for wine, and finally, five lines below the infinitives, the material to which they refer, an admonition to the Ausonian Muse. The stanza thus incorporates the classical statement of theme with the invocation of the Muse. The invocation to the Ausonian Muse, however, is amusing, since there was no Muse of lower Italy, thus making the reader suspect a partly humorous purpose in the elaborate beginning. The poet personifies wine as a mysterious friend of humanity, begetter of the arts and avenger of wrongs, and he calls upon the Muse to praise and enthrone it.

In the second stanza, the poet requests the Muse to sing of how the Charioteer from Asia with his panthers and the thyrsus twirling came to Greece. The wine of the first stanza has become Dionysus the god. Belloc achieves a sense of anticipation in his description of the ill-at-ease sea, the sudden glory of the mountain, the luminous sky, and the wind with the wonderful word that goes before the pageantlike progress. The group becomes a "something" or a shining cloud as it passes over the land; but everywhere it goes there is the miracle of the creation of vines, exuberantly portrayed with a double exclamation. The god is not named here; he is only alluded to by his characteristics. The next stanza shows the vines spreading everywhere, even as far as Africa, but also covering human habitations, thus being both wide and deep, exotic and domestic. In the next section, the day ends with Dionysus completing his journey, going from Spain to Ocean, where Hercules adores him. The author alludes to Hercules, expecting that his readers will have read of the Pillars of Hercules. The next section consists of only a single line, set off for emphasis, stating that the wine is better than riches or power.

The poet then seems to see people who breathe foul air from a well that is oozing slime along the floor of Hell and asks a rhetorical question concerning their identification—rhetorical because he answers it himself. They are the brood of sin, the cursed water-drinkers, and he says with ironic humor that their mothers must have been gin-sodden. This section is mock-heroic and satirical; Belloc attempts to guess their genealogy in the classical manner, calling them white slugs, an apt use of insect imagery to indicate their lack of vitality and character. Those who drink water instead of wine must, by implication, disapprove of it. Thus he uses the explosive "What!" to show indignation that the human race that was exiled from Paradise should have to suffer an evil (these people) with every good (the wine). In the next stanza, he says that even these filthy creatures were permitted to exist in the shadow of the bright Lord, an ambiguous term probably meaning Christ or Dionysus. Like John Milton, Belloc blends classical motifs with such Christian ones as Paradise. Whoever is contaminated by these creatures is condemned to drink the beverage of beasts. In the next section, the poet declares that the grapes are raised in vain for such as these in the various wine-growing regions to which he refers and, again proceeding in the negative, says that it is not for them "the mighty task/ Of bottling God the Father in a flask." The imagery is once more ambiguous, ostensibly Christian but possibly classical. He compares the dull, lifeless behavior of the water-

drinkers with the inspired creativity of the wine-drinkers, who have companions in their sleep, as Dionysus had Ariadne. He exports the reader to forget the water-drinkers, to form the Dionysian ring and let Io sing. The inclusion of Io in the poem is appropriate since her frenzied condition produced by the gadfly sent by Hera was akin to the divine frenzy of the followers of Dionysus; furthermore, Io was an ancestor of Semele, the mother of Dionysus.

In the next stanza, Belloc addresses Dionysus directly as "Father Linaean" and entreats him not to abandon ruined humanity, as the other gods have done, attributing both architectural elements and rhyme to the god. The following stanza praises the god in three lines stating his powers of enlightening seers, making statues live, and making the grapes swell. In a pastoral strain, he wishes a peaceful life for a farmer; but, knowing that this is not possible, he remembers that all must face their passion (a Christian concept) and gives examples of ironic unsung tragedies.

The last stanza dramatizes old age and death in a series of images. He, too, having wasted long labor, will leave the sun and walk with the shadows, will look at the plain, not at the mountain, and will be alone with nothingness before him. The image of God becomes a military one, understandable in Belloc, who loved the military life: His Comrade-Commander (Christ) will drink with him in His Father's Kingdom. When the hour of death comes, Belloc says, let his youth appear with a chalice bearing an engraved blessing for his dying lips. His youth is here personified to provide a contrast to his age, but the image of a youth with a chalice also suggests Dionysus, who was portrayed as a youth in later representations, one of whose attributes was the *kantharos*, a large two-handled goblet. Dionysus was associated with death and the afterlife through the story of his descent into the underworld to rescue his mother and, in Thrace and in Orphic mythology, his death and resurrection. The ending of the poem would seem to be Christian in its references to wine as sacramental, although the image of wine as his last companion and of wine as raising the divine is not necessarily so. Belloc skillfully blended Christian and classical references in this unusual poem. His sonnet XXXVI in praise of wine ascribed its creation to the Christian God, who made men vintners as well as bakers so that they could have the sacraments. Belloc, it may be added, also wrote several drinking songs.

"ON A DEAD HOSTESS"

The epigram is another classical form employed by Belloc, possessing that element of hardness that he so much admired. He achieved great economy in his use of comparisons. "On a Dead Hostess" begins with an explicit comparison of the subject to other people in this "bad" world by stating two superlatives. The hostess is lovelier than all others and better than everyone else; she has smilingly bid her guests goodnight and gone to her rest, a metaphor for her quiet death, mentioned only in the title. Belloc achieved delicacy here by implying rather than stating. In some of his epigrams suitable for inscriptions on sundials, the shadow represents death, as in one which says that "Loss and Possession, Death and Life are one,/ There falls no shadow where there falls no sun." In a few words, he conveys the idea of the positive inherent in the negative, the theme of John Keats's "Ode to Melancholy." In some of his humorous sundial epigrams, the sundials identify themselves as such and make some wry comment, such as that it makes a "botch/ Of what is done far better by a watch," and "I am a sundial/ Ordinary words/ Cannot express my thoughts on birds."

EPIGRAMS AND BALLADS

The epigrams were generally published for the first time in the collected poems of 1938, while the epigrammatic Juliet poems were privately printed in 1920 and 1934. Thus, some of these poems have not been as accessible as some of his lesser efforts. Many of the Juliet poems are compliments, some of them making use of classical allusions. In "The little owl that Juliet loved is dead," he explains that Pallas Athene took him, since "Aphrodite should not keep her bird," thus identifying Juliet with Aphrodite. In "On a Sleeping Friend," he declares that when she awakens, Dawn shall break over Lethe, the river of forgetfulness.

Belloc experimented with French forms, particularly the ballade and triolet. The triolet, which rhymes *abaaabab*, lines 1, 4, and 7 being identical, is appropriate for playful praise, but Belloc used it for more serious themes. The triolet beginning "The young, the lovely and the wise" says that they are intent on their going and

do not seem to notice him. This makes him wonder about "my losing and my owing," presumably the things he has lost and the things he intended. In addition to the repetition of line 1 in lines 4 and 7, line 2 is repeated as line 8, thus giving the poem a strong echoic quality. Delicacy is also achieved by ambiguity; the reader is not exactly sure what is meant by the young's "going." It may be their going out into the world, being on their own. The young people are certain that they know where they are going, paying no attention to others. On the other hand, their "going" may be their death, to which the young are indifferent but about which older people are very much concerned.

"YOUR LIFE IS LIKE A LITTLE WINTER'S DAY"

Belloc considered the sonnet to be the "prime test of a poet," as he said in his book *Milton* (1935). The sonnet "Your life is like a little winter's day" has a delicacy comparable to "The young, the lovely and the wise," and again an ambiguity contributes to the delicacy. It speaks directly to the reader, using "you" throughout, giving unusual immediacy to the subject of death. In the first line, the poet compares "your" life to a "little" day in winter, while the second line elaborates with a mention of a "sad" sun rising late and setting early; thus life seems sad and wintry. The third line questions your going away, since you have just come; and the fourth line elaborates, saying that your going makes evening instead of noon. The reader is thus likened to the winter sun, and the theme of departure is introduced. The next quatrain compares life to something else that is "little," a flute lamenting far away, beyond the willows. Willow trees are associated with sorrow and death. "A long way off" at the beginning of line 6 is repeated at the beginning of line 7, and because the music is far away, only its memory is left in the breeze. The poet implies that life is faintly heard, like the flute. The octave is Shakespearean in form, but the sestet reverses the usual rhyming couplet at the end, placing it at the beginning of the sestet. The sestet's rhyme scheme is *eefggf*, enabling another rhyming couplet, *gg*, to appear where it is hardly expected, before the last line. The sense of reversal and paradox of the rhyme scheme conveys the ironic nature of the subject matter. The third comparison here is that life is like a pitiful farewell that is wept in a dream, with only shadows present. Belloc's ending is couched in religious terms, calling the farewell a benediction that has no fruit except a consecrated silence. The benediction or farewell is whispered and comes too late, so that there is no response to it. The three comparisons, a little day in winter, a flute playing at a great distance, and a farewell made too late in a dream, all contribute to the sense of being incomplete. Life is unfulfilled, fleeting, and inconsequential, and the reference is not only to life in general but to "your" life. This discrepancy between expectation and actuality is reinforced by the unexpected rhyme scheme.

"THE END OF THE ROAD" AND "TO DIVES"

Belloc also experimented by trying to make the rhythm of a poem simulate the action. "The End of the Road" is a poem about the successful completion of Belloc's difficult journey to Rome and is reminiscent of the Carmina Burana of the Middle Ages. He manages to portray a rollicking hike by using many variations of the word "walked," by inverting the subject, and by making trochaic lines with a tripping meter: "Walked I, went I, paced I, tripped I." He goes on in that way for eleven lines, changes to Latin, then back again to English, calling on the major, doubtful, and minor prophets, among others. Another poem in which he tries to imitate motion by meter is his "Tarantella," in which he simulates the beat of the dance with short lines and internal rhymes.

Belloc's inventiveness extended to his satirical poems. "To Dives," the name meaning "rich man" in Latin, was inspired by Belloc's indignation at instances of unjust social and financial influence; it was written a week after Sir Henry Colville, Commander of the Ninth Division in South Africa, was dismissed without court martial or public investigation. Unlike the fiery directness of some of his other satirical poems, including the sonnet "Almighty God, whose justice like a sun," which speaks indignantly of the plight of the poor, Belloc in "To Dives" adopts the manner of Horatian rather than Juvenalian satire. He satirizes himself as well as his subject, saying to Dives that when they both go to Hell, Dives will stagger under his pack. Charon the ferryman will tell Dives that his baggage must go overboard.

There are many humorous touches here, including the formal address and the many possessions, including the fifteen kinds of boots for town, and the gifts for those already there, such as the working model of a burning farm to give to the little Belials, as well as the three biscuits for Cerberus. Dives assures Belloc that he will not burn with him, though he will have to leave his possessions behind and enter Hell as tattered and bare as his father was when he pushed a wheelbarrow (Belloc's smirk at the *nouveau riche*). When Charon sees how lightly the poet is provided with such things as honor, laughter, debts, and trust in God, he lets him pass, having tried to write poetry himself.

The poem ends with the rhetorical question to Dives as to who will look foolish, Dives, Belloc, or Charon. The answer is uncertain because "They order things so damnably in hell." Here Belloc has placed a contemporary rich man in the classical underworld and contrasted him with a poet. Yet he represents himself as going there as well.

OTHER MAJOR WORKS

NONFICTION: *Paris*, 1900; *Robespierre*, 1901; *The Path to Rome*, 1902; *Avril*, 1904; *The Catholic Church and Historical Truth*, 1908; *Marie Antoinette*, 1909; *The Pyrenees*, 1909; *The French Revolution*, 1911; *The Four Men*, 1912; *The Servile State*, 1912; *The Cruise of the "Nona,"* 1925; *A History of England*, 1925-1941; *The Catholic Church and History*, 1926; *Milton*, 1935; *On the Place of Gilbert Chesterton in English Letters*, 1940.

BIBLIOGRAPHY

Cheyette, Bryan. *Constructions of "the Jew" in English Literature and Society*. New York: Cambridge University Press, 1993. Less focused on such overtly prejudiced writers as Ezra Pound and Wyndham Lewis, Cheyette concentrates on Matthew Arnold, Anthony Trollope, George Eliot, John Buchan, Rudyard Kipling, George Bernard Shaw, H. G. Wells, Hilaire Belloc, G. K. Chesterton, James Joyce, and T. S. Eliot. Includes an extensive bibliography of published and unpublished material.

Corrin, Jay P. *G. K. Chesterton and Hilaire Belloc: The Battle Against Modernity*. Athens: Ohio University Press, 1981. Two champions of "democratic anarchy" are juxtaposed as writers and polemicists in an exploration that illuminates both of their careers.

Corrin ably demonstrates the near inseparability of intellect and theological commitment of the two allies, while offering good expositions of the histories, fiction, and poetry of the lesser known Belloc.

McCarthy, John Patrick. "Hilaire Belloc and the French Revolution." *Modern Age* 35, no. 3 (Spring, 1993): 251-257. The appraisal of Belloc as a champion of the counter-revolution is generally accepted by scholars, but McCarthy challenges that assumption, citing Belloc's belief in first principles and in democracy and asserting that he was sympathetic even to violent revolution.

_____. *Hilaire Belloc: Edwardian Radical*. Indianapolis: Liberty Press, 1978. McCarthy's concern is to elucidate Belloc's career as a political conservative who opposes statism and the growing intervention of government in the private lives of individuals. This resourceful volume explains the relationship between Belloc's politics and economics, and his poetics, while offering an apologia for reading Belloc in the present.

Markel, Michael H. *Hilaire Belloc*. Boston: Twayne, 1982. Markel provides a sympathetic overview of Belloc's life and a mostly thorough exposition of his major and minor works. This source is the best starting place for gaining a sense of the breadth of Belloc's writing career and political commitments. Markel's bibliography of primary and secondary sources is succinct, but valuable.

Speaight, Robert. *The Life of Hilaire Belloc*. New York: Farrar, Straus & Cudahy, 1957. Until A. N. Wilson's 1984 biography, this volume was the authoritative biography of Belloc, offering the facts of his life and the best available exposition and critique of his wide-ranging oeuvre. It remains a helpful starting place for Belloc's life and times even if its mid-century judgments about Belloc's work—as an "authorized biography"—have been superseded by later scholarly perspective.

Wilson, A. N. *Hilaire Belloc*. New York: Atheneum, 1984. A renowned novelist and biographer, Wilson provides researchers with an impeccable source of critical biographical material. Using Belloc's letters and manuscripts previously unavailable, Wilson places Belloc and his writing within his historical

milieu with affection and candor, refusing to ignore the darker side of Belloc's sympathies with the anti-Semitism of the 1930's and 1940's.

Rosemary Ascherl;
bibliography updated by the editors

PIETRO BEMBO

Born: Venice, Italy; May 20, 1470
Died: Rome, Italy; January 18, 1547

PRINCIPAL POETRY

Gli Asolani, 1505 (includes poems and prose; English translation, 1954)
Rime per festa carnascialesca, 1507
Rime, 1530
Carmina, 1533
Opere, 1729

OTHER LITERARY FORMS

Pietro Bembo wrote a range of nonfiction titles, many of which presented literary criticism, including *De Aetna* (1496), *De imitatione* (1514), *Prose della volgar lingua* (1525), *De Guidobaldo liber* or *De Urbini ducibus* (1530), and *Epistolae familiares libri VII* (1552).

ACHIEVEMENTS

The influence of Pietro Bembo on his contemporaries and on the Italian language far outstripped his talent as a writer. The literary dictator of Italy for more than fifty years, he was dubbed the foster father of the Italian language, and authors whose names are more familiar than his sent him their manuscripts for corrections and improvements. Bembo did not fail to partake of the best his era had to offer. He lived in the Florence of Lorenzo de' Medici, the Venice of Aldus Manutius, and the Rome of Pope Leo X. Bellini and Titian painted portraits of him. He was a friend of Lucrezia Borgia, Isabella d'Este, Raphael, Poliziano, Ludovico Ariosto, Desiderius Erasmus, and Pietro Aretino, and both friend and literary mentor to Gaspara Stampa, Vittoria Colonna, and Veronica Gambara. Giangiorgio Trissino,

Colonna, and Ariosto, among many others, wrote sonnets to him. He wrote two of the most famous essays of his century and the best Petrarchan verse.

Bembo is credited with having heterosexualized the concept of Platonic love. For the ancient Greeks, Platonic love was not love between the sexes but a philosophical idea based on heroic friendship, and what was so called by the Neoplatonists was still essentially the same as, for example, the relationship of Marsilio Ficino and Guido Cavalcanti, or of Giovanni Pico della Mirandola and Girolamo Benivieni. The Neoplatonic idealism that inspired Bembo and his style of balanced moderation determined an important pattern in the Renaissance poetry of several countries until the early Baroque.

Bembo restored Petrarchanism to its original luster and form by providing an unmistakably elegant standard by which the excesses of such conceitful poets as Il Chariteo, Antonio Tebaldeo, Serafino Aquilano, and Panfilo Sasso (who stressed the obvious and inferior elements of Petrarch's poetry rather than its deeper and less readily imitable perfections) could be judged as inferior. The prose style of *Gli Asolani* is equally elegant. Bembo was always an imitator, but he could judge better than others who and which elements were worthiest of imitation. As his poetry is modeled after Petrarch, his prose is modeled on the classicizing prose of the *Ameto* of Boccaccio. The Italian of *Gli Asolani* is indeed a new classic language, as if its author had been writing in Latin.

If readers did not become familiar with the Neoplatonism, the revised Petrarchanism, and the lapidary stylistics of Bembo from *Gli Asolani*, they read the words put into his mouth in the fourth book of Castiglione's *The Courtier*, a work of deeper insight than Bembo's, and his name was subsequently associated with all the characteristics that Castiglione attributed to him. Bembo, who is present in all the dialogues of *The Courtier*, assumes a leading role when the Duchess asks him to expound on what kind of love is appropriate for a courtier. Despite what his American translator Rudolph B. Gottfried calls the raillery and worldliness apparent in *Gli Asolani*, Bembo waxes almost mystical as he defines the Neoplatonic doctrine of love for Castiglione. He speaks of the divine origin of beauty, the distinction between the worlds of sense and intellect, and the various steps by which sensual love for a woman is finally transformed into spiritual love for God.

Perhaps Bembo at the age of fifty-eight simply allowed himself to appear more Platonic than he had been in his earlier years. The fifty *Rime per festa carnascialesca* that he composed for the Carnival at Urbino in 1507 (reworked by the Spaniard Juan Boscan in his own long poem, *Octava rima*, omitting certain stanzas whose licentiousness was unsuited to Spanish taste) urge Duchess Isabella Gonzaga and her sister-in-law Emilia Pia not to deny themselves the joys of love and are anything but Platonic. Even in *Gli Asolani*, published some twenty years before *The Courtier*, Perottino's attack on, and Gismondo's eulogy of, earthly love are more convincing than Lavinello's shorter Platonic resolution of the problem in book 3. While Castiglione uses some of the same arguments that are advanced in *Gli Asolani*, he also adds material that makes Bembo more Platonic than he appears in his own works; indeed, Bembo's Platonism in *Gli Asolani* is more literary than philosophical. The fact remains, however, that without Bembo, the finer art of Castiglione might never have emerged.

BIOGRAPHY

Pietro Bembo, the son of Venetian vice-doge and senator Bernardo Bembo and his wife, Elena Morosina, was born in Venice in 1470. Bembo acquired a more thorough knowledge of Tuscan than would have otherwise been possible, because his father, a member of Ficino's Academy, took him to Florence when he was eight years old. Proud of the boy's facility with languages, his father sent him to Messina to study under Constantine Lascaris in 1492. Bembo stayed in Sicily for two years, years of intense study which he fondly remembered all of his life. Later, he studied philosophy at Padua under Pietro Pomponazzi, for whom Bembo would later intercede to save him from condemnation by the Lateran Council.

In 1498, Bembo's father went to Ferrara as Venetian coruler and took Pietro with him, hoping to acquaint him at long last with affairs of state. There he became intimate with Jacopo Sadoleto and Ercole Strozzi, and was appreciated by Duke Ercole of Ferrara. When Duke

Ercole's son and heir Alfonso married Lucrezia Borgia in 1502, Bembo became friendly with her as well, and there developed between the two of them a deep friendship that may or may not have been Platonic.

On leaving Ferrara, Bembo returned to Venice, where he helped the printer Aldus Manutius form a learned academy and, in 1501, prepared for him the text of Petrarch's *Canzoniere* (wr. 1374, pb. 1470), as well as the first Aldine copy of *La divina commedia* (c. 1320; *The Divine Comedy*), published under the title *Terza rima* in 1502. Bembo and Aldus are credited with establishing the use of the apostrophe, the period, and the comma in modern printing.

Tall and handsome, witty and learned, a writer of verse in three languages (Italian, Latin, and Greek), Bembo was in his prime when he moved to Urbino in 1506. Until 1511, he was a member of the court circle of Urbino, which, under Duke Guidobaldo Montefeltro and his wife Elisabetta Gonzaga, rivaled Ferrara in social, artistic, and literary brilliance and which included such figures as the dramatist Bernardo Bibbiena, Giuliano de' Medici, Ottaviano Fregoso (later doge of Genoa), Louis of Canossa (later papal nuncio to France), and sundry other poets, musicians, and visitors. It was this refined circle that Castiglione idealized in *The Courtier*, and it was to Bembo that he gave the most distinguished role in the dialogue to discourse upon the nature of Platonic Love.

In 1512, Bembo accompanied Giuliano de' Medici to Rome, and when Giuliano's brother became Pope Leo X in 1513, Bembo was given duties as Leo's secretary, a post he shared with his old friend and fellow student Sadoleto. Bembo was precisely the man to make Leo's life more agreeable by flattering his superficial tastes and by directing the faculties of his highly cultured mind to frivolous, if intellectual, amusements. The position afforded Bembo the opportunity to display his greatest talent, composing papal documents and letters in very polished Latin. It was also during these papal years that Bembo was most aggressively Ciceronian in his controversy with Poliziano and Erasmus.

In 1519, Bembo's debt-ridden father died, and Bembo left the Vatican to spend most of the next year between Venice and Padua. In April, 1521, wearied after nearly thirty years of continual court life, harried by ill-ness, and depressed by the deaths of many of his good friends in Rome the previous year (Raphael, the banker Agostino Chigi, and Bibbiena had all died in 1520), he resigned his secretaryship and retired to his villa Noniamo near Padua. There, he entertained himself collecting manuscripts (his library, particularly rich in the works of the Provençal poets and Petrarch, passed after his death to Urbino and thence to the Vatican), experimenting with horticulture, and following the example of Horace and Vergil in appreciating the charms of country life. He was living with Morosina (Ambrogia della Torre), whom he had met in Rome in 1513 when she was barely sixteen (his ecclesiastical responsibilities and aspirations had precluded marriage), and was much concerned with the education of their three children, Lucilio, Torquato, and Elena. In 1530, he was appointed historiographer of the Venetian Republic, succeeding Andreas Navigero, and later, librarian of St. Mark's.

After the death of his beloved Morosina in August, 1535, Bembo embraced a more austere life, gave up his classical interests, and devoted himself to scriptural and patristic readings. Pope Paul III made him a cardinal in 1539, when he was sixty-nine years of age. In 1541, he was given the bishopric of Gubbio, where he moved in 1543. In 1544, he was given the rich see of Bergamo, but he never moved there. During these last years of life, Bembo seems to have taken great interest in the reforming views of Cardinal Pole and Vittoria Colonna at Viterbo—so much so that after his death, his name was found on the list of suspects of the Roman Inquisition.

In March of 1544, Bembo moved back to Rome, where he lived until his death in 1547 after a fall from his horse. He was buried in the Church of the Minerva between Popes Leo X and Clement VII. Olimpia Morata wrote the following words for him in Greek: "Bembo is no more. . . . He dies, and with him, disappears the splendid genius of eloquence; Cicero seems to have passed away a second time into the dark shadows."

ANALYSIS

Bembo's poems were borrowed, translated, and clearly plagiarized by subsequent generations of European writers. Among Italian poets, his greatest disciple was Giovanni Della Casa. In England, Sir Thomas Wyatt paraphrased "Voi me poneste in foco" ("Lady,

You've Set Me All Afire") from *Gli Asolani*, representing it as his own work, and Thomas Lodge included translations from Bembo in his *Phillis* poems. Because the principles of scansion are the same in Italian as in Spanish, Spanish poets such as Torres Naharro, Juan Boscan, and Luis de Léon were especially avid imitators of Bembo's verse, and Bembo's poem "Quand'io penso al martire" ("Madrigal") found its way into no less a work than *Don Quixote de la Mancha* (1605, 1615). Francisco de Sá de Miranda, who spent time in Italy in the 1520's and became acquainted with Bembo, introduced Petrarchan imagery in Portugal and ultimately influenced the style of Luis de Camões. The epitaph Bembo wrote for Jacopo Sannazzaro, "De sacro cineri flores. Hic ille Maroni/ Syncerus, musa proximus ut tumulo" (Give to the sacred ashes flowers. Here Maro/ In Muse Sincerus neighbors as in tomb) was copied on Edmund Spenser's tomb in Westminster Abbey.

As a native Venetian and an affiliate of the Papal Court who endorsed the Florentine dialect, Bembo did not see himself as a pacesetter. He had observed that the majority of older exemplary writers were native Tuscans, but he mistakenly considered himself the successor of such non-Tuscan writers as Pietro de Crescenzi and Guido delle Colonne of Messina. Actually, their works had been composed in Latin and translated anonymously by Tuscan scribes. It was not until the decision of Jacopo Sannazzaro, a Neopolitan, to write his highly successful *Arcadia* (1504) in Tuscan that the precedent of the Tuscan dialect as a vehicle for non-Tuscan writers was set. In the wake of Sannazzaro, Bembo proclaimed the preeminence of fourteenth century Tuscan; his views prevailed, and the influence of his prescriptive attitude on the subsequent development of Italian literature can hardly be exaggerated. Ludovico Ariosto, for example, undertook a massive revision of *Orlando furioso* (1516, 1521, 1532) after the appearance of Bembo's *Prose della volgar lingua*. He attempted to bring his Italian closer to the precepts of Bembo by doubling consonants, modifying his use of the article (*il* for *el, lo* before impure *s*), and revising verb forms. In a letter to Bembo dated February 23, 1531, Ariosto announced his intention of coming to Padua to consult him on stylistic matters. Ariosto gave Bembo a permanent tribute in the body of his masterpiece:

I see Pietro Bembo here,
Him who our pure and dulcet speech set free
From the base vulgar usage, and made clear
By his example what it ought to be.

GLI ASOLANI

Gli Asolani is a treatise on love in three books, with sixteen poems (canzones, canzonets, and one double sestina) interspersed in the text. The canzonets do not qualify as madrigals, even by Pietro Bembo's own broad definition in *Prose della volgar lingua*, but in *Italian Poets of the Renaissance*, Joseph Tusiani nevertheless gives to one of them, "Quand'io penso al martire," the title "Madrigal." The treatise takes its name from the Castello d'Asolo, belonging to Caterina Cornaro, the former queen of Cyprus, in the mountains north of Venice, which also served as the poetic inspiration of Robert Browning, who made it the scene of "Pippa Passes" and finished there the collection of lyrics titled "Asolando." Bembo wrote the treatise between 1497 and 1502, recast the work in 1503 and 1504, and published it in 1505, with a dedication to Lucrezia Borgia. The three principal speakers are three young Venetian gentlemen, Perottino, Gismondo, and Lavinello, and their ladies, Lisa, Sabinetta, and Berenice, all members of the court under fictitious names. Praises of the Asolan circle run through the work, and the picture of the six novices, sauntering through shade and sunlight under the vines of a leafy pergola or seated on the grass listening to a deftly stroked lute, retains its freshness even for the modern reader.

The discussion revolves around the question of whether love is a good or a bad thing. Gismondo maintains that it is good, and Perottino counters that it is bad with an argument that occupies the entire first book. Berenice refuses to accept his conclusion, whereupon Perottino recites a list of love's casualties (Pyramus and Thisbe, Murrha and Byblis, Medea, Tarquin) and supports his argument by singing songs of his own composition. Perottino's tale of sighs and wretchedness is also punctuated with questions on punning etymologies, such as the relationship of *amare* (to love) and *amaro* (bitter), *donna* (lady) and *danno* (damage), *giovani* (young men) and *giovano* (they help).

One of the poems he recites, translated by Tusiani as "Madrigal," is "Quand'io penso al martire," which traces how the lover is forced by Love to stand before the sea of bitterness, where, once facing death, he is so happy to be relieved of his first burden that he feels like living again. In another, which Perottino recites in a voice "which would move stones," "Lady, You've Set Me All Afire," the poet admits that he is not as angry at the lady who caused his discomfort as he is at Love and at himself for allowing himself to be in Love's thrall.

In book 2, Gismondo refutes the arguments of Perottino, concluding that love is not only good but also the source of all that is good in life. In the canzonet "Non si vedrà giammai stanca né sazia" (O love, my lord, faint and forworn this pen), Gismondo thanks Love for leading him to seek the skies and for giving his speech a music sweet. It is to Love that the poet owes his happy life and his pure and joyous thoughts.

On the third afternoon, the Queen and some other guests join the six, and Lavinello assumes a conciliatory position between Perottino and Gismondo, arguing that love can be good if it is worthy love of a good object; that love is evil if it is love of an evil object and evil as well if it is unworthy love of a good object. Love is the search for beauty, and beauty, physical or mental, is a grace, which derives from good proportion, compatibility, and harmony of the various elements. Halfway through Lavinello's argument and after he recites three poems, he introduces a conversation he claims to have had with a hermit that morning. If love is to be good, the hermit tells Lavinello, it must arise from true beauty, beauty that is divine and immortal.

All in all, *Gli Asolani* has little that is original. From Petrarch, Bembo derived the first and second books and the first half of the third book, while the hermit's conversation is mainly from Dante; despite the Neoplatonic label attached to Bembo, only a few tidbits are borrowed from Platonic theory. Although some of its individual passages are beautiful, on the whole the work holds little appeal for the modern reader. Bembo makes no attempt to develop an independent philosophy apart from Ficino's theory of Platonism, nor does Bembo, except in the second book, try to relate it to practical problems, regarding it as a thing beautiful in itself, a charming abstraction shining in its distant and rarefied air.

RIME

The poetry in *Rime* is thoroughly Petrarchan in form (sonnets, canzones, *ballate*), phrasing (eyes brighter than the sun, the calming smile, the ivory hands), imagery (love as the impious lord, the lover as the ship battered by the storm, the song of birds expressive of the pain of love), and content (the request to God for the power to resist love, lamentation for the ruthlessness of love, regret for allowing oneself to be caught by love). Bembo's poetry demonstrates a more refined taste than that of earlier imitators of Petrarch, but it still lacks originality by modern standards. Bembo's most famous sonnet, "Crin d'oro crespo" ("A Curly Hair of Gold"), is a catalog of his lady's attributes that ends with a line taken almost verbatim from Petrarch: "Grazie, ch'a poche il ciel largo destina" ("Graces that on few women heaven freely bestows").

While Petrarch was keenly and painfully aware of both the transitory nature of man's existence and the profane power of love to deflect him from his true devotion to God, these themes did not particularly interest Bembo. There is some religious poetry among his sonnets, but it is rather facile; indeed, Bembo wrote to the Duchess of Urbino on March 20, 1504, that the thought of heavenly things had never occupied him much and did not occupy him then at all. He is supposed to have undergone a conversion after the death of Morosina, but until then he had blithely accumulated ecclesiastical benefits without in the least renouncing earthly pleasures. In his sonnet, "O Sol, di cui questo bel sol è raggio" (O sun, of whom this beautiful sun is a glimmer), written probably in 1538, he asks God to look upon his soul, "to sweep away the ancient fog," and to keep his soul safe from the injuries of the world. In "Signor, quella pietà, che ti constrinse" (Lord, that mercy which bound you), the reader is impressed with the familiarity that Bembo affects in order to bargain for his salvation, which may be due to the earlier date of its composition (1510). In "Signor, che per giovar si chiama Giove" (Lord, who for your help, are called Jove), written in 1528, he plays flippantly upon the similarity of the verb *giovare* (to help) and the name of the pagan deity *Giove* (Jove).

OCCASIONAL POEMS

Bembo wrote many occasional poems, such as to celebrate the birth of a friend's son or the exploits of an unidentified "conqueror of Naples." He had a knack for converting an ordinary incident into a subtle vignette. In "Ove romita e stanca si sedea" (where tired and alone she sat), the poet, like a thief burning with hope and fear, surprises his beloved as she is lost in thought and perhaps even talking to herself. She is mildly upset that he has seen her so absorbed, and he is possessed by tenderness to have seen her so. His elegies on the death of persons dear to him are counted among his best poems; unlike so many of his Petrarchan exercises, they do not lack spontaneous emotion. "Donna, di cui begli occhi alto diletto" (lady, whose beautiful eyes gave such delight) is one of his many sonnets on the death of his mistress Morosina, and "Adunque m'hai tu pur, in sul fiorire" ("On the Death of His Brother") was penned in memory of his brother Carlo, who died at the age of thirty-two in 1503.

LATIN POEMS

Bembo also wrote Latin poetry. His hexameter poem "Benacus" is a description of Lago di Garda, and he also wrote epitaphs in Latin for many of his contemporaries. In his epitaph for Poliziano, whose death in 1494 followed close upon that of his patron, Lorenzo de' Medici, Bembo tells how death struck him while he wept, breaking his heartstrings in the middle of his sighs, and dubs him in the last line as "master of the Ausonian [Italian] lyre." Two elegiac poems, "Priapus" and "Faunus ad nympheum flumen," are remarkable for their pagan approach to morality; his masterpiece in elegiac meter is "De Galeso et Maximo," about a boy, Galesus, who wrongs his master, Maximus, who, as the epigraph explains, is a great man in Rome and may possibly represent Pope Leo X himself. When Maximus is confronted with the boy's misdeed, the boy does not apologize but rather runs to clasp the neck of his angry master, raining kisses upon him. Bembo concludes: "Still doubting, Maximus? Change place with me:/ Gladly I'd bear such infidelity."

The influence of Bembo was so strong that an entire half century (1500-1550) has been designated by many critics as the "Bembist period." His support of the vernacular as the equal of Latin, and his support of the Florentine dialect over competing dialects, determined in no small way the course of Italian literature. As a poet, he refurbished the Petrarchan tradition, and

he was instrumental in the spread of Neoplatonism. While it is true that his influence on literature was out of proportion to the value of his literary output, Bembo inspired a fierce loyalty in his contemporaries, and his precepts commanded a vigorous authority long after his death.

OTHER MAJOR WORKS

NONFICTION: *De Aetna*, 1496; *De imitatione*, 1514 (literary criticism); *Prose della volgar lingua*, 1525 (literary criticism); *De Guidobaldo liber* or *De Urbini ducibus*, 1530; *De Virgilii Culice et Terentii fabulis*, 1530; *Epistolarum Leonis X nomine scriptarum libri XVI*, 1535; *Lettere*, 1548-1553 (4 volumes); *Rerum Venetarum historiae libri XII*, 1551; *Epistolae familiares libri VII*, 1552.

MISCELLANEOUS: *Gli Asolani*, 1505 (includes prose and poetry; English translation, 1954); *Prose e rime di Pietro Bembo*, 1960 (prose and poetry).

BIBLIOGRAPHY

Brand, Peter, and Lino Pertile, eds. *The Cambridge History of Italian Literature*. New York: Cambridge University Press, 1996. In "Bembo and the Classicist Tradition," Anthony Oldcorn sketches the broad influence of Bembo on the likes of Michelangelo, Della Casa, Torquato Tasso, and contemporary women poets, such as Gaspara Stampa. Presents Bembo's establishment of *bembismo* and the debate it sparked.

McLaughlin, Martin L. *Literary Imitation in the Italian Renaissance: The Theory and Practice of Literary Imitation from Dante to Bembo*. Oxford: Clarendon Press, 1995. The final chapter outlines the 1512 literary dispute between Bembo and Pico della Mirandola. McLaughlin examines Bembo's defense of strict Ciceronian formalism, in opposition to eclectic or syncretic developments in Latin or the vernacular, and his "literary credo," which is applicable to all his subsequent critical work.

Raffini, Christine. *Marsiglio Ficino, Pietro Bembo, Baldassare Castiglione: Philosophical, Aesthetic, and Political Approaches in Renaissance Platonism*. New York: Peter Lang, 1998. This is a short, chronological treatment of Bembo's life and major works with an emphasis on his impact on contemporary poets and scholars. Platonism is treated but lightly.

Robb, Nesca A. *Neoplatonism in the Italian Renaissance*. London: Allen and Unwin, 1935. In the chapter on the *trattato d'amore*, Robb analyses *Gli Ascolani* as a Neoplatonic treatise on love in a courtly setting and a prototype of its genre.

Wilkins, Ernest H. *A History of Italian Literature*. Cambridge, Mass.: Harvard University Press, 1974. Wilkins's short chapter on "Bembo" places him squarely in the tumultuous years of the early sixteenth century. His life and major works are discussed chronologically, if briefly, and his later influence is asserted.

Jack Shreve;
bibliography updated by Joseph P. Byrne

STEPHEN VINCENT BENÉT

Born: Bethlehem, Pennsylvania; July 22, 1898
Died: New York, New York; March 13, 1943

PRINCIPAL POETRY

Five Men and Pompey, 1915
Young Adventure, 1918
Heavens and Earth, 1920
King David, 1923
Tiger Joy, 1925
John Brown's Body, 1928
Ballads and Poems, 1915-1930, 1931
A Book of Americans, 1933 (with Rosemary Carr Benét)
Burning City, 1936
The Ballad of the Duke's Mercy, 1939
Western Star, 1943

OTHER LITERARY FORMS

Stephen Vincent Benét made his major contribution to literature as a poet and primarily as the author of the book-length poem *John Brown's Body*. Benét was a prolific writer in several genres, however, and his canon includes short stories, novels, radio scripts, and nonfiction.

His short stories are collected in *Thirteen O'Clock* (1937) and *Tales Before Midnight* (1939). The first collection contains the well-known "The Devil and Daniel Webster," which he adapted as a play, opera, and film script. He wrote several novels: *The Beginning of Wisdom* (1921), *Young People's Pride* (1922), *Jean Huguenot* (1923), *Spanish Bayonet* (1926), and *James Shore's Daughter* (1934). Benét chose to support himself and his family as a writer and, as a result, his short stories and novels often were hack work churned out for whoever would pay him the most money.

He also composed radio scripts, collected in *We Stand United, and Other Radio Scripts* (1945), plays, and a short history. These writings were propagandistic, wartime efforts that he felt he had to do no matter what the effect on his literary reputation.

The best collections of his works are the two-volume hardback edition, *Selected Works of Stephen Vincent Benét*

Stephen Vincent Benét (Library of Congress)

(1942; Basil Davenport, editor), and the paperback edition, *Stephen Vincent Benét: Selected Poetry and Prose*, also edited by Davenport (1942).

ACHIEVEMENTS

Stephen Vincent Benét's achievements began early in his life. In 1915, when he was only seventeen years old, he made his first professional sale of a poem—to *The New Republic*—and published his first book of poems (*Five Men and Pompey*). He published his second book of poems (*Young Adventure*) in 1918 just before he was twenty years old. Between 1916 and 1918, while at Yale, he was, first, on the editorial board of the *Yale Literary Magazine*, and then chairman. He received a traveling fellowship from Yale in 1920 that enabled him to go to Paris, where he completed his first novel, *The Beginning of Wisdom*.

Benét received many literary and academic awards throughout his life, and he was popular with the public. His collection of poems *King David* received *The Nation*'s poetry prize in 1923, when he was twenty-five years old. A Guggenheim Fellowship allowed him to return to Paris, where he worked on *John Brown's Body*. In 1929, a year after the publication of *John Brown's Body*, when he was thirty-one years old, he received the prestigious Pulitzer Prize for poetry and became famous overnight.

He accepted the editorship of the Yale Series of Younger Poets competition in 1933, and in 1935 he began regular reviewing for the New York *Herald Tribune* and the *Saturday Review of Literature*. He was elected to the National Institute of Arts and Letters in 1929 and to the American Academy of Arts and Letters in 1938, and he received the Theodore Roosevelt Medal for literary accomplishment in 1933. Benét won the O. Henry Memorial Prize for the best American short story of the year several times; among his winning stories were "The Devil and Daniel Webster" and "Freedom's a Hard-Bought Thing." Finally, he received posthumously the Gold Medal for Literature from the National Institute of Arts and Letters and the Pulitzer Prize a second time for the unfinished epic poem *Western Star*.

BIOGRAPHY

Stephen Vincent Benét was born July 22, 1898, in Bethlehem, Pennsylvania. His parents were Frances Neill Rose Benét and James Walker Benét, Captain of Ordnance, United States Army, a man with poetic and literary tastes. Stephen was their third child and second son; his sister and brother were Laura Benét and William Rose Benét, who were both active in the literary world. Well-read from his youth and thoroughly educated, Benét began writing early in his life.

During his childhood, his family moved throughout the United States because of his father's position in the Army. Benét and his family were at the Vatervliet, New York, Arsenal from 1899 until 1904; the Rock Island, Illinois, Arsenal during 1904; the Benicia, California, Arsenal from 1905 until 1911; and the Augusta, Georgia, Arsenal from 1911 until he was graduated from a coeducational academy and entered Yale College in 1915. There he was with such undergraduates as Archibald MacLeish, Thornton Wilder, Philip Barry, and John Farrar. He left Yale after completing his junior year in 1918 to enlist in the Army, but was honorably discharged because of his bad eyesight. After working briefly for the State Department in Washington, D.C., he reentered Yale. Benét received his B.A. degree in 1919 and his M.A. degree in 1920. At that time, he was given a traveling fellowship by Yale and went to Paris, where he completed his first novel.

Unlike other expatriates in Paris, Benét was not disillusioned or dissatisfied with America; he went to Paris because he could live there cheaply. He was very patriotic and loved his country deeply. While in Paris, he met Rosemary Carr; about a year later, in 1921, they were married in her hometown of Chicago. Their marriage was a happy one, producing three children: Stephanie Jane, born in 1924; Thomas Carr, born in 1925; and Rachel, born in 1931.

Benét earned his living by writing. In order to support his family, he was often forced to devote less time than he would have liked to his serious writing—rather than concentrating on his poetry, he sometimes had to spend time and energy writing short stories and novels that would bring in money. Although *John Brown's Body* generated substantial sales, he lost most of his capital in the crash of 1929 and never again enjoyed financial security.

When World War II broke out, fiercely loyal to democracy, he felt compelled to contribute to the war effort as much as he could. As a result, in the early 1940's he devoted much of his time and energy to writing propagandistic radio scripts and other needed pieces.

During Benét's most creative years, he was handicapped by poor health; from 1930 until his death in 1943, he suffered from arthritis of the spine and other illnesses. He was hospitalized for several weeks in 1939 for a nervous breakdown caused by overwork. On March 13, 1943, when he was forty-four years old, he died in his wife's arms following a heart attack.

ANALYSIS

In the nineteenth century, Walt Whitman called for a national poet for America and sought to be that poet. While he envisioned himself as the poet working in his shirt sleeves among the people and read by the population at large, he was never really a poet of the people, absorbed by the people. Ironically, Stephen Vincent Benét became the poet that Whitman wanted to be. Although Benét's approach as a poet was a literary, academic one, his poetry was widely read and popular with the public.

Using American legends, tales, songs, and history, he was most effective writing in epic and narrative forms, especially the folk ballad. Benét's primary weakness is related to his strength. He lacks originality; he takes not only his subjects but also his techniques from other sources. In his first published poems, a series of dramatic monologues called *Five Men and Pompey*, the influence of Robert Browning and Edward Arlington Robinson is evident. As Donald Heiney indicates in *Recent American Literature* (1958), Benét never developed a single stylistic quality that was his own.

His poetry, particularly *John Brown's Body*, is nevertheless worth reading for its presentation of American folklore and history. As Benét himself indicated in a foreword to *John Brown's Body*, poetry, unlike prose, tells its story through rhyme and meter. By using such a method to tell stories and convey ideas, the poet can cause the reader to feel more deeply and to see more clearly; thus, the poet's work will remain in the reader's memory.

TIGER JOY

Benét's strengths are evident in the volume preceding *John Brown's Body*, *Tiger Joy*. The best poems in this collection include an octave of sonnets, "The Golden Corpse," and two very good ballads "The Mountain Whippoorwill" and "The Ballad of William Sycamore."

In "The Mountain Whippoorwill: Or, How Hill-Billy Jim Won the Great Fiddlers' Prize," subtitled "A Georgia Romance," Benét uses the dialect of the inhabitants of the Georgia hills. The rhythm of the poem suggests the music that is produced as Big Tom Sargent, Little Jimmy Weezer, Old Dan Wheeling, and Hill-Billy Jim attempt to win the first prize at the Georgia Fiddlers' Show. The mountain whippoorwill serves as a unifying element; initially, the whippoorwill is supposedly the mother of Hill-Billy Jim, the narrator, but then becomes symbolic of him as fiddler and of his genius.

"THE BALLAD OF WILLIAM SYCAMORE"

"The Ballad of William Sycamore," one of Benét's frequently anthologized poems, is the autobiography of William Sycamore, an archetype of the pioneer. The son of a Kentucky mountaineer, Sycamore was born outdoors near a stream and a tall green fir. Following a childhood during which he learned his woodsman's skills from his father, he and his wife were part of the westward movement; he lost his eldest son at the Alamo and his youngest at Custer's last stand, and died with his boots on. At the end of the poem he tells the builders of towns to go play with the towns where they had hoped to fence him in. He has escaped them and their towns, and now sleeps with the buffalo. According to Heiney, the poem differs from the traditional ballad primarily in that it is written in the first person and covers Sycamore's life from his birth to his death.

JOHN BROWN'S BODY

John Brown's Body, a book-length narrative poem, became immediately popular with the American public when it was published in 1928; it was the poem that established his position in American literature. Although many critics have complained that a major weakness of the poem is a lack of unity, Parry Stroud points out, in *Stephen Vincent Benét* (1962), several ways in which the epic is unified—through the characters, through the symbolism, and through the consistent and purposeful use of several meters.

First, John Brown himself and the imaginary characters representing the major regional areas of America serve to unify the poem. Jack Ellyat, a Connecticut boy who enlists in the Union Army, is the counterpart of Clay Wingate, a Southerner from Wingate Hall, Georgia. Ellyat eventually marries Melora Vilas, who, with her father, stands for the border states and the West. At the end of the war Wingate also marries the woman he loves, the Southern belle Sally Dupre. There are several other minor fictional characters typifying various regions and classes in America: Lucy Weatherby, a Southern coquette; Spade, a slave who runs away; Cudjo, a slave who remains loyal to the Wingates; Jake Diefer, a stolid Pennsylvania farmer for whom Spade works after the war; Luke Breckinridge, an illiterate Tennessee mountaineer who fights for the South; and Shippey, a spy for the North. The war resolves the fates of most of these fictional characters.

Parry Stroud disagrees with the many critics who believe that Benét's style disrupts the unity of the poem. Benét uses three basic meters: traditional blank verse, heroic couplets, and what Benét called his "long rough line." This versatile long line approximates the rhythm of everyday speech more than traditional meters do. Benét also uses rhythmic prose and lyrics. In the foreword that he wrote for the poem in 1941, he states that he intentionally used a variety of meters. For example, he used a light, swift meter for the episodes concerning Clay Wingate, the Southerner, to suggest dancing, riding, and other aspects of Southern culture.

In the foreword, Benét indicates that the poem deals with events associated with the Civil War, beginning just before John Brown's raid on Harpers Ferry and ending just after the close of the war and the assassination of Abraham Lincoln. Although he did not intend to write a formal history of the Civil War, he did want the poem to show how the events presented affected different Americans; he was concerned with the Americans of the North and South as well as those of the East and West.

By describing the American landscape and people, Benét gives American historical events a reality greater than mere names and dates can confer. He believed that the people living during the Civil War encountered problems similar to those of his time and that the decisions they made then had a great effect upon future generations of Americans.

Growing out of Benét's fondness for his country, *John Brown's Body* will have a permanent place in American literature because it is an epic having uniquely American themes and qualities. He researched the historical details of the war extensively, but he also understood the human complexities involved. Exhibiting a high level of narrative skill, Benét presented five of the most crucial years in American history, poetically interpreting part of the great heritage of America.

WESTERN STAR

Western Star, a fragmentary work, which was to have been another epic like *John Brown's Body*, was published after Benét's death in 1943. He had begun writing it previous to World War II, but upon the entry of America in the war, he put it aside, planning to resume work on it when peace was achieved. *Western Star* was to have been Benét's interpretation of the settlement of the United States and of the westward movement of frontier life. He intended to present frontier life in a way similar to that he had used to present the Civil War in *John Brown's Body*—by using actual events and both actual and imaginary persons for his characters. Unfortunately, his early death prevented his completing this work.

OTHER MAJOR WORKS

LONG FICTION: *The Beginning of Wisdom*, 1921; *Young People's Pride*, 1922; *Jean Huguenot*, 1923; *Spanish Bayonet*, 1926; *James Shore's Daughter*, 1934.

SHORT FICTION: *Thirteen O'Clock*, 1937; *Tales Before Midnight*, 1939; *Twenty-five Short Stories*, 1943.

PLAYS: *Nerves*, pr. 1924 (with John Chipman Farrar); *That Awful Mrs. Eaton*, pr. 1924 (with Farrar); *The Headless Horseman*, pr. 1937; *The Devil and Daniel Webster*, pr. 1938.

RADIO PLAYS: *We Stand United, and Other Radio Scripts*, 1945.

NONFICTION: *America*, 1944; *Stephen Vincent Benét on Writing: A Great Writer's Letters of Advice to a Young Beginner*, 1946; *Selected Letters of Stephen Vincent Benét*, 1960.

MISCELLANEOUS: *Selected Works of Stephen Vincent Benét*, 1942 (Basil Davenport, editor); *Stephen Vincent Benét: Selected Poetry and Prose*, 1942 (Basil Davenport, editor); *The Last Circle*, 1946.

BIBLIOGRAPHY

Davenport, Basil. Introduction to *Stephen Vincent Benét: Selected Poetry and Prose*. New York: Rinehart, 1960. Davenport's short essay is a good overview of Benét's life and literature for those unfamiliar with his writing. He stresses how unusual Benét's Americanism seemed during a time when Paris overflowed with expatriates cynical of American idealism. The poet is seen as essentially a romantic, able to show extraordinary feeling for his subjects.

Fenton, Charles A. *Stephen Vincent Benét: The Life and Times of an American Man of Letters, 1898-1943*. New Haven, Conn.: Yale University Press, 1958. Based chiefly on several interviews with friends and relatives and on Benét's own writings, this detailed biography paints an admirable and sympathetic portrait of a struggling writer striving to live according to his literary conscience. The few critical evaluations of Benét's writings show insight. The 440-page text includes an index and several illustrations.

LaFarge, Christopher. "The Narrative Poetry of Stephen Vincent Benét." *Saturday Review* 27 (1944): 106-108. LaFarge presents a glowing evaluation of Benét, seeing him as an enduring and timely writer who contributed much to the political writing of his day. Benét is lauded for his complex patterns of rhythm, meter, and form and for his rich characterization, but most of all for his clear style that makes his work accessible to the general reader.

Stroud, Parry. *Stephen Vincent Benét*. New York: Twayne, 1962. This work is an informative critical study of Benét, focusing on liberalism and patriotism as it appears in his best writings. Stroud's close and thorough readings help place Benét in historical and literary perspective, emphasizing his contemporary relevance. The 173-page book is arranged by genre and includes a chronology of Benét's life, a selected annotated bibliography, and an index.

Wells, Henry W. "Stephen Vincent Benét." *College English* 5 (1943): 8-13. Written soon after Benét's death, this critical survey of the author's major works, *John Brown's Body* and *Western Star*, strikes an elegiac tone, although a negative one. Wells mostly examines possible reasons for Benét's waning reputation as a poet, but also deals briefly with his achievements and skill.

Sherry G. Southard;
bibliography updated by the editors

GOTTFRIED BENN

Born: Mansfeld, Germany; May 2, 1886
Died: Berlin, East Germany; August 7, 1956

PRINCIPAL POETRY

Morgue und andere Gedichte, 1912
Söhne, 1913
Fleisch, 1917
Schutt, 1924
Spaltung, 1925
Betäubung, 1925
Gesammelte Gedichte, 1927
Ausgewählte Gedichte, 1911-1936, 1936
Gedichte, 1936
Zweiundzwanzig Gedichte, 1943
Statische Gedichte, 1948
Trunkene Flut, 1949
Fragmente, 1951
Frühe Lyrik und Dramen, 1952
Destillationen, 1953
Aprèslude, 1955
Gesammelte Gedichte, 1956
Primäre Tage: Gedichte und Fragmente aus dem Nachlass, 1958
Primal Vision, 1958
Gedichte aus dem Nachlass, 1960
Gottfried Benn: Selected Poems, 1970
Gottfried Benn: The Unreconstructed Expressionist, 1972
Sämtliche Gedichte, 1998

OTHER LITERARY FORMS

Gottfried Benn was primarily a poet, but he did write some significant works in other genres, most notably a collection of novellas, *Gehirne* (1916; brains); a novel,

Roman des Phänotyp (1944; novel of the phenotype); the essay *Goethe und die Naturwissenschaften* (1949; Goethe and the natural sciences); his autobiography, *Doppelleben* (1950; double life); and a theoretical treatise, *Probleme der Lyrik* (1951; problems of lyric poetry). His writings also include other prose and dramatic works.

ACHIEVEMENTS

No other German poet exemplifies as fully as Gottfried Benn the emergence of the modern tradition within postwar German literature. His radical aesthetic as well as his political affiliations have made Benn a controversial figure. He was the "phenotype" of his age—that is, the exemplary representation of the intellectual and spiritual condition of his times. As such, Benn can be viewed not only as a remarkable poet, but also as an important figure of twentieth century German *Geistesgeschichte*.

Benn's early work (until about 1920) was known only to a relatively small circle of readers. Indeed, it was only after World War II, in the last decade of his life, that Benn achieved fame. His achievements were acknowledged in 1951, when he was awarded the Georg Büchner Prize in literature. For years prior to this time, Benn had been blacklisted, as it were, as a result of his short-lived infatuation with Nazism. Because of the public commentary to which he had been subjected, Benn was reluctant to reenter public life. He did publish again, however, and in the years before his death a generation of poets in search of a tradition flocked around him like disciples around a master. What were the reasons for Benn's appeal?

The years of Nazi control had yielded a vast wasteland in German literature. Indeed, the historical events of the twentieth century, in particular as they affected Germany, intensified the general philosophical disorientation of the immediate postwar period. Marxism was no real alternative for the West; Existentialism prevailed instead, based in large measure on the writings of Martin Heidegger and Jean-Paul Sartre. In this context, Benn's theory of art as a metaphysical act had considerable authority. For postwar poets in search of a new way of writing, Benn provided a transition from the various offshoots of French Symbolism and German expressionism to contemporary modernism.

BIOGRAPHY

Gottfried Benn was born on May 2, 1886, the son of a Protestant minister. He studied philosophy and theology at the University of Marburg and later studied medicine at the University of Berlin. He completed his medical degree in 1910 and was awarded first prize for his thesis on the etiology of epilepsy in puberty. Benn worked as a pathologist and serologist in Berlin, where he became friends with several expressionist poets, the most important of whom was Else Lasker-Schüler. Benn also set up medical practice in Berlin, and his first volume of poetry, *Morgue und andere Gedichte* (morgue and other poems), clearly shows the influence of his scientific and medical training: The cold and unforgiving objectivity and precision of medical and surgical technique inform these poems, with their shocking portrayal of brutality and morbidity.

In 1914, Benn traveled briefly to the United States. Upon his return, he was drafted into the military medical corps, serving as an officer in Belgium before returning to Berlin in 1917. These years, contrary to what one might expect, were extremely productive for Benn as a writer, and he later noted that during the following years, on the whole relatively uneventful for him, he constantly drew for inspiration on his experiences in Belgium.

In 1933, Benn filled the position of which Heinrich Mann had been relieved, section president of the Prussian Academy. Later, Benn became director for the Department of Literature. In April of the same year, he gave a radio talk, "Der neue Staat und die Intellektuellen" ("The New State and the Intellectuals"), clearly in response to a letter from Klaus Mann, the son of Thomas Mann, who wrote from the south of France. It is true that Benn initially embraced National Socialism in 1933. He greeted the political doctrines of the Nazis as a means for overcoming the stagnation and nihilism of Western civilization, but he soon regretted his participation and withdrew into silence.

In 1935, Benn left Berlin and headed for Hannover. It was Benn's early poetry which gave rise to the debate on expressionism carried in the émigré paper *Das Wort*, printed in Moscow. In the ensuing years, Benn had a run-in with W. Willrich, a party loyalist who labeled Benn a "cultural Bolshevist" and tried to have Benn effectively "removed" from public life. Ironically, only the intervention of Heinrich Himmler himself stayed Willrich's attempts. Benn remained in the army medical service from 1935 until the end of the war. After 1948, he enjoyed a new phase of poetic creativity, and his poetry eventually achieved recognition throughout Europe.

ANALYSIS

Both poetically and existentially, Gottfried Benn resided at the crossroads of two significant traditions. At the turn of the century, the natural sciences exercised a substantial "claim to truth" and provided influential paradigms of thought. For many of Benn's generation, however, scientific study had entered a rapid phase of entropy—it was seen no longer to answer questions meaningfully from the humanist point of view. In fact, one could even say that the "scientific approach" was seen by many to "explain" the universe inadequately, precisely because it did not pose the right questions. In Germany, the most significant manifestation of this dissatisfaction with the scientific paradigm took place under the rubric of "expressionism," which in many respects carried on the tradition of German Romanticism. The tension exemplified in the conflict between Benn's scientific training and his early intoxication with expressionism came to play an important role in the development of his aesthetic theory and poetry.

A concept basic to Benn's thought was his conviction that humankind necessarily "suffered consciousness." He attributed this suffering to modern overintellectualization: "The brain is our fate, our consignment and our curse." The modern consciousness fragments the totality of the world into its conceptual categories; reality is particled past meaningful comprehension; and the loss of man's capacity to perceive relationships points ineluctably in the direction of nihilistic resignation. During the years from 1921 to 1932, Benn studied the works of Johann Wolfgang von Goethe, Friedrich Nietzsche, Oswald Spengler, Carl G. Jung, Ernst Troeltsch, and Gotthold Lessing, and through his study of prehistory, paleontology, and myth, he developed his own notions of art, reality, and the self.

In Benn's conceptual framework, the inner space once occupied by the premodern sense of harmony and totality is now filled with a kind of nostalgic longing. By somehow penetrating and deactivating the rational consciousness, Benn hoped to return (momentarily) to archetypal, primal, and prelogical experience. Benn identified this act as "hyperemic metaphysics"—that is, an intensified state of perception (such as that induced by intoxication, dream visions, or hallucinations), which he then applied exponentially to derive his "hyperemic theory of the poetic," or primal moments of poetic creativity.

It is necessary to see how Benn viewed the creative process in order to understand his poetry. According to Benn, the creative process required first "an inarticulate, creative nucleus, a psychic substance"; second, words familiar to the poet which "stand at his disposal" and are "suited to him personally"; and third, a "thread of Ariadne, which leads him with absolute certainty out of this bipolar tension"—that is, the tension between the psychic substance and the "word." This amalgam constitutes the basic creative situation for Benn.

"BEAUTIFUL YOUTH"

One of his first poems, "Schöne Jugend" ("Beautiful Youth"), perhaps best illustrates Benn's early cynicism. The poem describes the dissection of the body of a young (and possibly at one time "beautiful") girl, whose decomposed mouth and esophagus are perfunctorily noted, as is the nest of young rats discovered beneath the diaphragm, "one little sister" of which lay dead while the others lived off the liver and kidneys—"drank the cold blood and had/ spent here a beautiful youth." A quick death awaits the rats: "They were thrown all together in the water. Ah, how their little snouts did squeal!" It becomes obvious that the "beautiful youth" to which the title refers is not that of the young girl, as the reader is intended to assume, but rather of the rats.

"ONE WORD"

A good example of Benn's preoccupation with the capacity of language to "fascinate," and in so doing to give momentary vision to meaning within meaninglessness (form from chaos), is his poem "Ein Wort" ("One Word"). This poem is about the fact that words and sentences can be transmuted into *chiffres*, from which rise life and meaning. The effect can be such as to halt the sun and silence the spheres, as everything focuses for the moment on the primal catalyst, the single word. The word, however, is transitory, brilliant but short-lived, and already in the second and last strophe of this brief poem it is gone, leaving behind it the self and the world once again apart and distinct, alone in the dark, empty space surrounding them. Perhaps this paraphrase of Benn's poem gives an idea of how Benn viewed the magic of the poetic word, its unique ability to stand (and consequently place the reader/listener) outside the "normal" conceptual categories of time and space. It communicates truth as a bolt of lightning momentarily illuminating the sky.

"LOST SELF"

The radical dissolution of meaning with the evaporation of the word's spellbinding aura, as this last poem illustrates, aligns with Benn's view of the disintegration of reality in general. Nowhere are the consequences of this loss of reality for the individual given more poignant expression than in Benn's poem "Verlorenes Ich" ("Lost Self"). Benn applies the terminology of modern science as an explanation of the radical alienation of the modern self. The strictly scientific explanation of the universe does not adequately explain the vicissitudes of human existence. Benn does not envision a return to a previous form of existence, since that is an impossibility, nor does he seek refuge in a Christian answer, positing God as the source of an otherwise incomprehensible universe. Neither, however, is his stance one of resignation or of *l'art pour l'art*, even though he is often reproached for both. Instead, his predicament always centers on the struggle for human meaning and significance. The solution to this existential dilemma, he finds, is manifested in the intellectual and spiritual acts that human beings can perform, among these the creative act of giving form. "The artist," wrote Benn, "is the only one who copes with things, who decides their destiny."

"DEPARTURE"

It is true that Benn felt that all good poetry is "addressed to no one," and that he expressly refuted the possibility of poetry having any public function. To castigate Benn for an unconscionable aestheticism, though, would not be accurate or just. He does not cast aside the question of ethical responsibility; if he did, one would not expect to find such an obsession with what constitutes the essence of humanity, above all with the existential-poetic confrontation with Being. To explore this problem further, it is illuminating to consider a highly auto-

biographical poem by Benn, "Abschied" ("Departure"), contained originally in a cycle of poems Benn referred to as "Biographische Gedichte" ("Biographical Poems") and first published in *Zweiundzwanzig Gedichte* (twenty-two poems). Formally, the poem is a classic example of artistic control: four strophes of eight lines each in iambic pentameter, with alternating feminine and masculine rhymes in an *ababcdcd* scheme. Structurally, the poem constitutes a tightly organized unit: Its formal principles interact with its themes—namely, the schizophrenic existence of the persona and the acknowledged taking leave from the old Self.

The topos of parting (*Abschied*) is itself an interesting one within German poetry; one may recall the significant example of Goethe's "Willkommen und Abschied" ("Greeting and Parting"). Benn's poem, however, does not deal with the separation of two individuals—two lovers, for example. Instead, it describes a separation of the persona, a division of the Self into a former "You" and a present "I." The You represents the part of the individual which belongs to a world of the past, while the I attempts to grasp and develop within the poem the process of alienation to which it has been subjected. The first strophe outlines the relationship of the former to the present Self by employing a series of metaphors, while the second strophe probes the cause of the schism and relates the sole recourse as perceived by the persona. The link between past and present—memory—becomes the topic of the third strophe, and finally the poem moves toward a further degree of estrangement, concluding with a note of sadness and melancholy typical of Benn.

The subject of each independent clause in the first strophe is the pronoun "you," and initially it is the active subject, while the "I" remains the passive object. The relationship is established via a metaphor: "You fill me as does blood the fresh wound,/ and run down its dark path." The image of the wound operates on the physical plane to suggest impairment, disease, decay. Later, in the third strophe, this physical affliction is seen to be present on a psychological plane as well. The adjective describing the wound, "fresh," can be read two ways. On the one hand, it accentuates the grotesque nature of the wound by showing it in its first moments when blood flows most freely. On the other hand, "fresh" can suggest "recent." The reader is thus made privy to the suffering of the persona as it takes place. The metaphor of the wound encompasses the first two lines of the poem. The dark trace of the blood is more than merely graphic realism; it evokes an aura of mysterious origin. Blood is the life-sustaining fluid, and its escape from the wound enacts the kind of exposure that the "deep self" of the persona endures. Its dark hue contrasts with the "day of minutiae," the "heavenly light" of the third strophe, and "a high light" in the third line of the last strophe. Its opaqueness suggests obscurity and impregnability. The persona's flight into silence at the end of the second strophe ("you must take your silence, travel downward/ to night and sorrow and the roses late") gives image to the inexpressibility of the "deep self."

The night setting maintains the motif of darkness found in the "dark path" on the second line. The hour corresponds to dusk and evinces the twilight of the former self, the You. The atmosphere of darkness surrounding the You continues to dominate, although it retreats for the moment with the appearance of roses in the following line. While this imagery is initially perplexing (because it does not seem to cooperate with the earlier metaphor of the wound), under the assumption that the You represents a former state of naïve harmony and quietude, the rose will be seen to bloom now only with difficulty, indicating the suffering connected with the memory of the persona's previous unified existence.

In the second strophe, the self-reflection intensifies, resulting in a kind of linguistic breakdown: The abstract nouns lack contact with reality and no longer illustrate the tendency toward analogous thought, as in the first five lines; no finite verb appears from lines six to eight, leaving the explication static and ineffective. Significantly, it is the second strophe which introduces the idea of alienation. Its cause is seen as the absence of a homogeneous reality, as a craze of pluralities (Benn speaks of "realities"). Resistance against this disembodying centrifugal force is sustained within the act of composing the poem itself, in the creative act which circles around the "deep self" in an attempt to describe it with more accuracy than simple, or even scientific, language can yield. "The form *is* the poem," Benn wrote elsewhere, stating the crux of his aesthetic.

In spite of the alienation from the "deep self," it is only this region that can satisfy the needs of the persona. This part of the Self, however, is (linguistically) impregnable, and silence represents the only alternative. The poem ends as "a last day" (Benn's own advancing age), which "plays its game, and feels its light and without/ memory goes down—everything is said." Such a poetic stance is rooted in the modernist poetic tradition. Benn acknowledges that no word or sign can now reveal that for which he searches; they are but symbols of the essential thing.

Had the persona no memory of itself, then no tension or conflict would result. The plague of consciousness is such, however, that it disrupts the fluidity of expression. This is represented throughout the poem by frequent dashes, colons, and question marks. Sentences and thoughts are left incomplete, fragmented; punctuation replaces words and becomes itself a frustrated sign or symbol of the inexpressible. The "deep self" evades all intellectualization.

In his epoch-making address, *Probleme der Lyrik*, Benn postulated that

> not one of even the great poets of our time has left behind more than six or eight complete poems. The rest may be interesting from the point of view of biography and the author's development, but only a few are content in themselves, illuminating from within themselves, full of lasting fascination—and so, for these six poems, [there are] thirty to fifty years of asceticism, suffering, and struggle.

Even according to Benn's own stringent definitions, he deserves to be acknowledged as a great poet.

OTHER MAJOR WORKS

LONG FICTION: *Roman des Phänotyp*, 1944.

SHORT FICTION: *Gehirne*, 1916; *Provoziertes Leben: Eine Auswahl aus den Prosaschriften*, 1955.

NONFICTION: *Fazit der Perspektiven*, 1930; *Nach dem Nihilismus*, 1932; *Der neue Staat und die Intellektuellen*, 1933; *Kunst und Macht*, 1943; *Goethe und die Naturwissenschaften*, 1949; *Doppelleben*, 1950; *Essays*, 1951; *Probleme der Lyrik*, 1951.

MISCELLANEOUS: *Die gesammelten Schriften*, 1922; *Gesammelte Prosa*, 1928; *Ausdruckswelt: Essays and*

Aphorismen, 1949; *Frühe Prosa und Reden*, 1950; *Gesammelte Werke in vier Bänden*, 1958-1960 (4 volumes).

BIBLIOGRAPHY

Alter, Reinhard. *Gottfried Benn: The Artist and Politics (1910-1934)*. Bern, Switzerland: Herbert Lang, 1976. A biography including the history of German politics and literature in Benn's time.

Benn, Gottfried. *Briefe*. Edited by Harald Steinhagen, Jürgen Schröder, Friedrich Wilhelm Oelze, Paul Hindemith, and Ann Clark Fehn. Wiesbaden, Germany: Limes-Verlag, 1977. Three volumes of Benn's correspondence with bibliographic references and an index.

Dierick, Augustinus Petrus. *Gottfried Benn and His Critics: Major Interpretations, 1912-1992*. Columbia, S.C.: Camden House, 1992. Critical interpretation and history by an expert in German expressionist literature. Includes an exhaustive bibliography.

Hamburger, Michael. *Reason and Energy: Studies in German Literature*. Rev. ed. London: Weidenfeld & Nicolson, 1970. A critical and historical study of German literature in the nineteenth and twentieth centuries. Includes bibliographic references.

Roche, Mark William. *Gottfried Benn's Static*. Chapel Hill: University of North Carolina Press, 1991. Intellectual and historical interpretation of Benn's poetry with bibliography and index.

Richard Spuler;
bibliography updated by the editors

THOMAS BERNHARD

Born: Heerlen, The Netherlands; February 10, 1931
Died: Gmunden, Austria; February 12, 1989

PRINCIPAL POETRY
Auf der Erde und in der Hölle, 1957
In hora mortis, 1957
Unter dem Eisen des Mondes, 1958
Die Irren-die Häftlinge, 1962

Contemporary German Poetry, 1964 (includes selections of his poetry in English translation)

OTHER LITERARY FORMS

Thomas Bernhard's reputation rests primarily on his fiction and his memoirs. His first novel, *Frost* (1963), won critical acclaim, and his subsequent novels, novellas, and stories have brought him most of the significant literary prizes awarded in the German-speaking world. Among Bernhard's novels are *Verstörung* (1967; *Gargoyles*, 1970; literally translated, "derangement"); *Das Kalkwerk* (1970; *The Lime Works*, 1973); and *Korrektur* (1975; *Correction*, 1979). Bernhard's memoirs, regarded by many critics as semifictional, present autobiographical material in the monomaniacal voice of his fictional narrators. This ongoing sequence includes *Die Ursache: Eine Andeutung* (1975; the cause), *Der Keller: Eine Entziehung* (1976; the cellar), *Der Atem: Eine Entscheidung* (1978; the breath), *Die Kalte: Eine Isolation* (1981; the cold), *Ein Kind* (1982; a child), and *Wittgenstein's Neffe: Eine Freundschaft* (1982; *Wittgenstein's Nephew: A Friendship*, 1986).

The premiere of Bernhard's first play, *Ein Fest für Boris* (1970), created a small sensation, and since then more than ten of his plays have been produced, some of them at the Salzburg Festival; among them are *Die Macht der Gewohnheit* (1974; *The Force of Habit*, 1976) and *Über allen Gipfeln ist Ruh: Ein deutscher Dichterag um 1980* (1981).

ACHIEVEMENTS

Critic George Steiner has described Thomas Bernhard as "the most original, concentrated novelist writing in German." The locution "writing in German" is significant, for Bernhard's achievements must be seen in the context of the Austrian literary tradition. Bernhard occupies a special position in contemporary Austrian literature. Unlike most Austrian writers of recent fame, he does not belong to a group, such as the Wiener Gruppe or the group at the Forum Stadtpark in Graz, nor can he be identified with any of the prevailing literary factions. Yet if Bernhard is a nonconformist—in his personal life as well as in his writing—he is nevertheless a typical Austrian author, rooted in the Austrian literary tradition, despite the fact that he rejects "Austria" as a political and ethnic abstraction and even blames her for much of his existential anguish. This distinctively Austrian tradition is characterized by several features, the foremost of which is a morbid preoccupation with death, and in particular with suicide.

Another facet of this tradition can be traced to the Baroque period and manifests itself as an inclination to give form preference over substance—to value the way something is expressed more highly than what is said. Other Baroque contributions to the Austrian tradition clearly visible in Bernhard's work are the *memento mori* theme and the typically Austrian response to this reminder of the imminence of death, the *carpe diem* motif. Yet another Baroque ingredient is the recurring metaphor of the *theatrum mundi*—the notion that the world is a stage upon which all humans must perform their roles. It is no accident that Bernhard has increasingly devoted himself to the theater in the 1970's and 1980's and that critics have noted in his works affinities with Hugo von Hofmannsthal and Franz Kafka.

Austrian literature has a long tradition of complaining about the conservative artistic attitudes of the Austrians and about the narrowness of the country's intellectual life. This complaint, which is surely not exclusively Austrian, appears in the works and in the private utterances of Wolfgang Amadeus Mozart, Franz Grillparzer, Sigmund Freud, and Arthur Schnitzler, to name only a few, and a frighteningly large number of Austrian artists and intellectuals were driven to suicide or into exile by this feeling of rejection and claustrophobia. Bernhard expresses this notion with obsessive force in many of his works. He did not grant interviews and lived in virtual isolation on a farm in a secluded valley, rejecting most involvement in the social life of the Austrian literary scene.

Finally, Bernhard is firmly entrenched in an Austrian tradition of language skepticism associated with Hofmannsthal, Ludwig Wittgenstein, and Theodore Mauthner. Bernhard's entire oeuvre is informed by a profound distrust of language as an efficacious artistic or communicative tool. The influence of Wittgenstein, most explicit in the novel *Correction*, in which one of the characters is modeled after him, and in the memoir *Wittgenstein's Nephew*, is of particular significance in Bernhard's development. Bernhard treats Wittgenstein

Thomas Bernhard

with a mixture of reverence and savage irony, and the philosopher's ideas are implicit in all Bernhard's works. One of the key phrases in *Gargoyles* is an implicit response to the famous aphorism which concludes Wittgenstein's *Tractatus Logico-Philosophicus* (1922); Bernhard writes: "The words we use really do not exist any longer. . . . But it is also no longer possible to be completely silent." Bernhard shares this belief with many contemporary Austrian writers, including Peter Handke.

While Bernhard's verse is not his most significant contribution to Austrian literature—four slim volumes containing some 150 poems are an insufficient basis for such a claim—it did provide Bernhard with an early testing ground for his literary talent. Critics so far have not paid much attention to Bernhard, the poet, although this neglect is not justified. At their worst, the poems are a youthful testimony to early poetic influences and to eclectic readings in nineteenth century European philosophy. At their best, they are lyrical precursors of Bernhard's fiction, foreshadowing the linguistic experiments of his early prose and introducing the themes of his mature work, such as death, the desertion of God, impotence in the face of suffering, the world as prison and insane asylum, rural decay, urban decadence, and the impossibility of communication. Bernhard's poetry is sure to be given increased critical attention.

BIOGRAPHY

Biographical data, particularly of Thomas Bernhard's early life, must be considered with some caution, as many of these "facts" have been excerpted from the author's autobiographical writings and from a letter to the editor of an anthology, published in 1954—a letter which Bernhard had not intended to make public.

Bernhard was born on February 10, 1931, the illegitimate son of an Austrian carpenter. Bernhard's mother was the daughter of an eccentric Austrian writer, Johannes Freumbichler. In the strictly Catholic, rural Austrian environment, an illegitimate birth would have created quite a stir, and so Bernhard was born in a convent near Maastrich, Netherlands, where his mother had to remain in service to defray the cost of the birth of her son. Much of Bernhard's childhood was spent with his maternal grandparents near Salzburg. He formed a strong attachment to his grandfather, who became the dominating personal and intellectual influence of his early life, as described in Bernhard's memoir, *Ein Kind*. In Freumbichler's house, the young Bernhard met Ödön von Horvath and Carl Zuckmayer; Zuckmayer later wrote encouraging and thoughtful reviews of the young man's first volumes of poetry. Bernhard's grandfather, who had received the highest Austrian literary award, mainly for his novel *Philomena Ellenhub* (1937), was an avid reader of the German writers and philosophers of the later nineteenth century and was particularly fond of Michel de Montaigne. Bernhard claimed to have read Arthur Schopenhauer in Freumbichler's study and to have discovered then for the first time "the impossibility of saying the truth and the inability of transcending human existence."

In 1938, Bernhard's family—his mother was then married to a man who was not Bernhard's father— moved to Traunstein, Bavaria, where the boy had his first music lessons. Music has played an important part in Bernhard's life; much of his literary vocabulary is taken from musical terminology, and he speaks in terms of the theory of musical composition when he discusses the structure of some of his works. In 1943, the boy was sent to a Nazi-sympathizing boarding school in Salzburg. After the war, the school was taken over by the Roman Catholic Church, but Bernhard claims not to have noticed any difference. In his memoir *Die Ursache*, he deals extensively with this depressing period in his life.

In 1946, Bernhard's family was forced to leave Germany and moved to Salzburg. Soon after that, Bernhard quit school and apprenticed himself to a grocery merchant. His relationship with his stepfather deteriorated, and finally the working conditions in the wet storage cellar of his employer (described in his memoir *Der Keller*) caused Bernhard to contract first pleurisy and then a severe lung disease. The next four years, a hellish period described in the memoirs *Der Atem* and *Die Kalte*, were spent being shuttled between hospitals and sanatoriums; in 1949, Bernhard's grandfather was taken to the same hospital where the young man himself lay in a bathroom in the section for the terminally ill. During the following year, both Bernhard's grandfather and his mother died, and he also learned that his natural father had died in 1943 in the turmoil of the war. It was at this time, while confined to the bed of a hospital for pulmonary diseases, that Bernhard began to write. He is convinced that this activity prevented him from succumbing to insanity or suicide and eventually cured him of his illness.

In 1951, Bernhard received a scholarship to attend the music academy in Vienna, but since the stipend covered only his tuition, he was forced to work as garbage collector, luggage porter, and attendant to a seventy-year-old insane woman whom he cared for until her death. He often slept in railroad cars and in abandoned air-raid shelters; his move to the Mozarteum in Salzburg in 1952 was a welcome change. At the Mozarteum, he did considerable acting and directing in addition to his musical studies and earned his way by working for a local newspaper, mainly as a court reporter and an art critic. In the period from 1952 to 1956, Bernhard also submitted his first poems and short stories to various publishers and to literary contests, but with no success. In 1955 and 1956, he interrupted his studies at the Mozarteum to travel around Europe; he was graduated in 1957 after completing a thesis on Antonin Artaud and Bertolt Brecht. In that year, Bernhard also published his first two volumes of poetry, followed by his third collection in 1958. During the next five years, he tried to make his living as a freelance writer in Vienna and Carinthia; he traveled frequently and also spent a short time as librarian at the Austrian Cultural Institute in London.

Discouraged by his continuous failure to gain recognition as a writer—again and again his submissions did not find favor with the judges of literary contests awarding prestigious and lucrative prizes—Bernhard decided to emigrate to South Africa. Allegedly on the very day he was ready to embark from Venice, he received notice that his first novel, *Frost*, had been accepted for publication. Official recognition and prizes followed in rapid succession, most notably the Austrian State Prize in 1968, when he shocked the dignitaries with his polemical acceptance speech. He died in Gmunden, Austria, on February 12, 1989.

ANALYSIS

Thomas Bernhard's biography offers a temptation to the critical reader of his work. It is easy to conclude—as many critics have—that his chaotic, parentless childhood, the rootless life of his adolescence, the loss of all of those he loved, and his own near-fatal illness are the direct causes of the grim worldview expressed in his novels and plays, and are responsible for the melancholy tone of his poems. Such a view is contradicted by the fact that Bernhard's journalistic work, which is chronologically closest to the period from 1950 to 1952, the most depressing years of his life, shows few traces of this pervasive pessimism. The articles and reviews of that time are full of praise for contemporary artists; they speak of the regenerative beauty of the Salzburg region and comment favorably on the value of regional Austrian culture. The tone of these articles is low-key, often a little sad, but still full of *joie de vivre* compared to that of his early poems, which appeared in 1957. Further study of Bernhard's life and his published and unpublished work of the years from 1950 to 1957 is needed to explain the struggling author's change in outlook.

AUF DER ERDE UND IN DER HÖLLE

Bernhard's first collection of poems, *Auf der Erde und in der Hölle*, was published in 1957 in an edition of one thousand. It contains seventy-one poems grouped into five thematic sections; many of these poems have since been included in anthologies of contemporary German and Austrian poetry. Bernhard himself claims to have been influenced mainly by Walt Whitman, Georg Trakl, and Charles Péguy—the latter supplies the motto for the volume—but one also hears echoes of Paul Celan and Charles Baudelaire, as well as of William Blake's more hellish visions.

"Der Tag der Gesichter" appears as a separate poem before the first section and sets the tone for the entire volume: The "Earth" and the "Hell" of the title are not to be understood as separate locations but as identical places. The poet acknowledges his complicity in the decay, suffering, and death that are all around him. He anticipates shudderingly the apocalyptic "day of visions" when he will be shown Hell, reproduced for the reader in the following seventy poems. It is Earth as Inferno that the poet sees. *Auf der Erde und in der Hölle* offers a vision of Hell without any glimpses of Heaven. The five sections of the volume systematically deny any relief from this view and reject any traditional redemptive imagery.

The journey through Hell—the reluctant reader is led by the guilt-ridden poet—begins in the traditional "dark wood," the rural region of Bernhard's ancestors. There is no pastoral tranquillity, however, in this "other world behind the trees." This area has changed drastically since the time of the poet's great-grandfather. Now, there is decay, despair, and other harbingers of death in the form of frost, crows, and blackbirds. The black farm soil prophesies a wintry death; schnapps, fame, and love are insufficient anesthesia for loneliness and the sense of complicity in the sad state of the world. What is the poet to do, cast out from this destroyed Eden into the night? The brave front he puts up at times—as in the great poem "Crows," which ends with the line "But I am not afraid"—cannot be maintained for long, and he crosses the river to find "another world."

There, he finds the "burnt-out cities" of the second section—Vienna, Paris, Venice, Chioggia—cities which one can no longer shore against one's ruins. Wherever the journey leads, the poet encounters night, death, the pale, unapproachable ghosts of his ancestors, and anterooms to Hell. Attempts at cleansing through penitence on Ash Wednesday (Bernhard knows T. S. Eliot very well) are ineffectual.

In the last section, "Rückkehr in eine Liebe," the poet expresses the wish to be able to return to his "love," represented by his rural village, the memory of his parents, and nature, but even the first poem of the section, "Yeats war nicht dabei," indicates that he cannot go home again. The fields do not accept his name, the trees withdraw their roots, and no one offers him a bed and a jug with drink.

Auf der Erde und in der Hölle is a remarkable first collection of poems. Clearly, there are literary debts, but Zuckmayer's judgment, that these poems show the mark of the great modern artists and originate from the same artistic background as the music of Béla Bartók, is accurate.

IN HORA MORTIS

Bernhard's second collection of poems, *In hora mortis*, also appeared in 1957. The title is taken from the Latin text of the "Hail Mary," in which the Holy Virgin is asked to intercede for all sinners in the hour of death. The volume, much slimmer than *Auf der Erde und in der Hölle*, is dedicated to "my only and true friend G. L. whom I met at the right moment." "G. L." is almost certainly the young Austrian composer Gerhard Lampersberg, who had apparently taken in the despondent writer for some time between 1957 and 1959. Bernhard always speaks in negative terms of the Church and of religion, but it appears that the time he spent in a Catholic boarding school left him with the wish to come to terms with that facet of his childhood. It is even more likely that his self-confessed interest in Blaise Pascal's *Pensées* (1670; English translation, 1688) and his early acquaintance with the writings of Schopenhauer and Montaigne are responsible for the persistent religious stratum in his early work.

In hora mortis has the structure of a prayer—it is quite possible that Pascal's "Prayer in Sickness" is the model—and employs frequent direct appeals to "my God" and "my Lord." These appeals are not always submissive in tone; the first line of the collection, "Wild grows the flower of my anger," indicates the mood of the poet. Rebellion, outrage, and disappointment in an elusive God dominates the early parts of the volume; later, the tone changes to hopelessness and to the Schopenhauer-like recognition that redemption is only possible when the rebellious will to live has been subdued. It can

be assumed that the poetic experience in this slim volume closely parallels Bernhard's wrestling for a spiritual and intellectual position during the time of his near-fatal illness.

In these poems, Bernhard does not as closely identify himself with his literary models as in *Auf der Erde und in der Hölle*. His poetry here approaches that of his contemporaries Ingeborg Bachmann, Christine Busta, and Christine Lavant in its imperious appeals to a *Dieu abscondit*. Bernhard's early verse depicts a desolate universe through which man is condemned to wander aimlessly, incapable of bringing any relief to the universal suffering, unable to stop the general decay, but also unable to resign himself completely to this condition. The language is emotional, the imagery flowery, and the tone still echoes the plaintive cries of the expressionists. Bernhard's next collection of poems, however, published in 1958, marked a transition from subjective lyrical expressionism to the maniacal "objectivity" of his prose.

UNTER DEM EISEN DES MONDES

In *Unter dem Eisen des Mondes* (under the iron of the moon), Bernhard broke completely with his poetic models. The fifty-seven untitled poems in this volume severely reduce the use of the first person in an attempt to objectify the lyrical "I" of *Auf der Erde und in der Hölle* and *In hora mortis*. The title is taken from Georg Büchner's play *Woyzeck* (1879; English translation, 1927), from the scene in which the protagonist is about to stab his fiancé; to her observation, "How red the moon rises!" He replies with the words "like a bloody blade" (*Eisen*).

This bloody moon casts a grim light; there is not even the elusive hope for redemption still expressed in *In hora mortis*, nor the faint prospect of a "return to love." Images are no longer used as objective correlatives of the poet's subjective feelings but take on a physical and metaphysical reality of their own. The reader can no longer escape by rejecting Bernhard's night visions as sentimental exaggerations of a paranoid, tortured soul but must deal with an intellectual position. The symbolism of the four seasons which runs through the whole volume further serves this purpose.

Unter dem Eisen des Mondes was the penultimate step in Bernhard's development from lyric poet to novelist. The symbolic code of these poems and their syntactic structure anticipates the forms of his early prose, particularly of his first novel, *Frost*. Apart from some poems published in the magazine *Akzente* in 1968, but probably written before 1963, Bernhard published only one more, very small volume of poetry before abandoning verse after the success of his first novel.

Published in 1962 by a small Klagenfurt publisher in an edition of only 120 copies, *Die Irren-die Häftlinge* does not appear in many Bernhard bibliographies. The critic Manfred Mixner considers it the last and most important stage of Bernhard's early creative period. The left-hand pages of this collection contain "Die Irren," a poem of fifteen stanzas; on the right-hand pages appears "Die Häftlinge," a poem of twenty-two stanzas. Both are interrupted by aphoristic prose sentences which appear to be quotations, but no source is indicated. Some of these sentences seem like remarks by a distant observer concerning the "madmen" and "prisoners" who are the subjects of these two long poems.

Madmen and prisoners (their prisons are often metaphorical) are the central characters of Bernhard's novels and plays. In his later work, Bernhard reiterates his conviction that the human condition is best defined as incarceration. Most of his characters are trapped by the narrowness of their physical, cultural, or geographical prisons. Only "insane" people are sensitive enough to recognize the inevitability of their fate as prisoners, from which they try to find relief in interminable cascades of tautological ruminations. The "sane" people live as animals, unthinking, trapped in lies and clichés.

DIE IRREN-DIE HÄFTLINGE

In *Die Irren-die Häftlinge*, Bernhard anticipates the recurring themes of his prose. The madmen are anonymous, deprived of their individuality by being addressed only by the symptoms of their condition. Their fate is not presented from their subjective standpoint as lyrical narrators; instead, they are viewed by an impersonal observer who registers their hate, their torture, and their indignation as if seen through the peephole of their cells and who punctuates his observations with aphorisms on rationality. With this virtually forgotten volume, Bernhard found the logical transition from poetry to the novel; he abandoned the emotive stance of the lyrical "I" and assumed the role of an omniscient, clinical observer who presents

the twitchings of his tortured madmen and prisoners in the manner of a painstakingly arranged medical report.

The small but growing number of Bernhard scholars have devoted themselves almost exclusively to his fiction, his memoirs, and his plays, neglecting his journalism and paying scant attention to his poetry. Bernhard's verse deserves to be read for its own considerable achievements rather than as a mere preface to his fiction.

OTHER MAJOR WORKS

LONG FICTION: *Frost*, 1963; *Verstörung*, 1967 (*Gargoyles*, 1970); *Das Kalkwerk*, 1970 (*The Lime Works*, 1973); *Korrektur*, 1975 (*Correction*, 1979); *Beton*, 1982 (*Concrete*, 1984); *Der Untergeher*, 1983 (*The Loser*, 1991); *Holzfällen: Eine Erregung*, 1984 (*Woodcutters*, 1987); *Alte Meister*, 1985 (*Old Masters*, 1989); *Auslöschung: Ein Zerfall*, 1986 (*Extinction*, 1995).

SHORT FICTION: *Amras*, 1964; *Prosa*, 1967; *Ungenach*, 1968; *An der Baumgrenze: Erzählungen*, 1969; *Ereignisse*, 1969; *Watten: Ein Nachlass*, 1969; *Gehen*, 1971; *Midland in Stilfs: Drei Erzählungen*, 1971; *Der Stimmenimitator*, 1978 (*The Voice Imitator*, 1997).

PLAYS: *Ein Fest für Boris*, pr., pb. 1970; *Der Ignorant und der Wahnsinnige*, pr., pb. 1972; *Die Jagdgesellschaft*, pr., pb. 1974; *Die Macht der Gewohnheit*, pr., pb. 1974 (*The Force of Habit*, 1976); *Der Präsident*, pr., pb. 1975 (*The President*, 1982); *Minetti: Ein Porträt des Künstlers als alter Mann*, pr. 1976; *Die Berühmten*, pr., pb. 1976; *Immanuel Kant*, pr., pb. 1978; *Der Weltverbesserer*, pb. 1979; *Vor dem Ruhestand*, pb. 1979 (*Eve of Retirement*, 1982); *Über allen Gipfeln ist Ruh: Ein deutscher Dichtertag um 1980*, pb. 1981; *Am Ziel*, pb. 1981; *Der Schein trügt*, pb. 1983; *Ritter, Dene, Voss*, pb. 1984; *Elisabeth II*, pb. 1987; *Heldenplatz*, pb. 1988.

NONFICTION: *Die Ursache: Eine Andeutung*, 1975; *Der Keller: Eine Entziehung*, 1976; *Der Atem: Eine Entscheidung*, 1978; *Die Kalte: Eine Isolation*, 1981; *Ein Kind*, 1982; *Wittgensteins Neffe: Eine Freundschaft*, 1982 (*Wittgenstein's Nephew: A Friendship*, 1986); *Gathering Evidence*, 1985 (English translation of the first five autobiographical works listed above; includes *An Indication of the Cause*; *The Cellar: An Escape*; *Breath: A Decision*; *In the Cold*; and *A Child*).

BIBLIOGRAPHY

Dowden, Stephen D. *Understanding Thomas Bernhard.* Columbia: University of South Carolina Press, 1991. Biography and criticism by an expert in German modernist literature with bibliographic references.

Konzett, Matthias. *The Rhetoric of National Dissent in Thomas Bernhard, Peter Handke, and Elfriede Jelinek.* Rochester, N.Y.: Camden House, 2000. Focuses on the new literary strategies with which Thomas Bernhard and other Austrian writers engage their readers in critical self-perception each with a unique model of dissent. Includes bibliography and index.

Martin, Charles W. *The Nihilism of Thomas Bernhard: The Portrayal of Existential and Social Problems in His Prose Works.* Atlanta, Ga.: Rodopi, 1995. Examines the nihilistic basis of Bernhard's writing and traces developments in the author's writing. Includes bibliography and index.

Franz G. Blaha;
bibliography updated by the editors

WENDELL BERRY

Born: Henry County, Kentucky; August 5, 1934

PRINCIPAL POETRY

November Twenty-six, Nineteen Hundred Sixty-three, 1963
The Broken Ground, 1964
Openings, 1968
Findings, 1969
Farming: A Hand Book, 1970
The Country of Marriage, 1973
An Eastward Look, 1974
To What Listens, 1975
Horses, 1975
Sayings and Doings, 1975
The Kentucky River: Two Poems, 1976
There Is Singing Around Me, 1976
Three Memorial Poems, 1976
Clearing, 1977
The Gift of Gravity, 1979
A Part, 1980
The Wheel, 1982
Collected Poems: 1957-1982, 1985
Sabbaths, 1987
Traveling at Home, 1989
Sabbaths 1987-1990, 1992
Entries, 1994
The Farm, 1995
The Selected Poems of Wendell Berry, 1998
A Timbered Choir: The Sabbath Poems 1979-1997, 1998

OTHER LITERARY FORMS

In addition to poetry, Wendell Berry has written nonfiction, fiction, essays, and a biography of Harland Hubbard.

ACHIEVEMENTS

Wendell Berry first achieved regional and then national prominence as a poet, essayist, and novelist who writes about the small tobacco farmers of his fictional Port William community in northern Kentucky. As a poet, Berry has published widely since 1957, in small magazines, poetry volumes, private printings, and a collected edition of his verse in 1985. In 1971 he won an award from the National Institute of Arts and letters. In 1999 he won a T. S. Eliot Award and the Thomas Merton Award. His major topics are the land, the family, and the community, especially the way that each has been affected by greed and indifference. Berry is a deeply traditional poet in theme and form, celebrating a timeless agrarian cycle of planting and harvest. He affirms a strong sense of place and ancestral inheritance, stemming from local family ties stretching back almost two centuries. His values are a curious blend of conservative and radical, combining a strong commitment to marriage and family with a pacifist stance and criticism of corporate exploitation of rural Appalachia. His voice is that of the farmer-poet, husband, father, and lover. For many readers and critics, he has reached the stature of a major contemporary philosopher.

BIOGRAPHY

Born in Henry County, Kentucky, on August 5, 1934, Wendell Berry grew up in a family of strong-willed, independent-minded readers and thinkers. His father, John M. Berry, was an attorney and a leader of the Burley Tobacco Growers Association. After attending the University of Kentucky for his bachelor's and master's degrees, Berry was married and taught for a year at Georgetown College in Kentucky. He then accepted a Wallace Stegner Fellowship in creative writing (1958-1959) at Stanford University. A Guggenheim Foundation award allowed him to travel to Europe in 1962 before he returned to teach English at New York University from 1962 to 1964. Berry wrote a moving elegy for President John F. Kennedy that won critical praise, and his first poetry volume, *The Broken Ground*, appeared in 1964.

Berry and his family returned to Kentucky in 1964, when he was appointed to the English Department at the University of Kentucky in Lexington. He purchased Lane's Landing Farm in Port Royal in 1965 and moved back to his native county, where he has continued to farm and write. Berry has also served as a contributing editor to Rodale Press. He and his wife, Tanya (Amyx) Berry, raised two children, Mary and Pryor Clifford, on that farm.

ANALYSIS

Wendell Berry is a poet of deep conviction. Like Henry David Thoreau, he has felt a need to reestablish himself from the ground up by articulating the ecological and economic principles by which he would live, and by trying to live and write in accordance with those principles. He has striven to achieve a rigorous moral and aesthetic simplicity in his work by reworking the same basic themes and insights; the proper place of human life in the larger natural cycle of life, death, and renewal; the dignity of work, labor, and vocation; the central importance of marriage and family commitments; the articulation of the human and natural history of his native region; and precise, lyrical descriptions of the native flora and fauna of his region, especially of the birds, trees, and wildflowers. Expanding on these basic themes, he has included elegies to family members and friends, topical and occasional poems (especially antiwar poems expressing his strong pacifist convictions), didactic poems expressing his environmental beliefs, and a surprising number of religious poems expressing a deeply felt but nondenominational faith.

One finds in Berry's verse a continual effort to unify life, work, and art within a coherent philosophy or vision. Put simply, that vision includes a regional sensibility, a farming avocation, a poetic voice of the farmer-husband-lover-environmentalist, and a strong commitment to a localized environmental ethic. His most notable persona is the "Mad Farmer," though it is not clear why he is "mad"—does Berry mean passionate, exuberant, or merely eccentric? From childhood, Berry always hoped to become a farmer, and his verse celebrates the life of the land. His vision, however, is that of diminishment: of the land, of the community, and even of his art. In his literary works, Berry expresses nostalgia for the kind of small-scale, labor-intensive tobacco farming that was practiced in his region before World War II. His style of unmechanized organic farming is practiced today mainly by the Amish and the Mennonites. Berry has admitted that farming his hilly, eroded land has not been profitable, and while it may be ethically admirable to restore damaged land to production, it is generally not economically feasible without another source of income.

One senses in Berry's poetry a keen awareness of living in a fallen world, to be redeemed, if at all, through hard work, disciplined self-knowledge, and a gradual healing of the land. Yet though he is a lyric poet, too often his lyrics do not sing: His muse is Delphic rather than Orphic, prophetic instead of lyrical. His verse is carefully worked and thoughtful but burdened at times by didacticism. The Berry persona is often detached and impersonal, preoccupied with its own sensibility or with an environmental theme. His lyrics are often descriptive meditations in which too little happens aside from the registration of impressions on the poet's sensibility. The simplicity of his verse becomes drab, colorless, even oppressive at times. It needs to be lightened by a sense of humor, a sense of proportion, and awareness of others. Sometimes his lyrics seem sanctimonious or

Wendell Berry (© Dan Carraco, courtesy of North Point Press)

self-righteous. His verse echoes the rhetorical question of Robert Frost's "The Oven Bird"—"What to make of a diminished thing?"—and the answer seems uncertain.

Berry first published many of his poems in literary journals or small magazines or specialty presses, so that original editions of his works are often hard to find. His individual poetry volumes were published first with Harcourt Brace (*The Broken Ground, Openings, Farming: A Hand Book, The Country of Marriage*, and *Clearing*) and later with North Point Press (*A Part, The Wheel, Collected Poems*, and *Sabbaths*). The pieces in *Collected Poems* are selected from each volume, but the collection is not entirely inclusive. Yet he has added some important poems, such as the contents of the volume *Findings* (1969), which was originally published by a small specialty press and is out of print.

Wendell Berry's poetry marks him as one of the most important contemporary American nature poets. His sense of the sacredness and interdependence of all life places him within the tradition of Ralph Waldo Emerson, Walt Whitman, and Henry David Thoreau. He is also one of the foremost American regional writers, in-

sisting that his poetry be firmly rooted in a sense of place. His poetry reflects the same deep concern for the natural environment and for sound conservation and farming practices that is evident in his essays and fiction. His emphasis on marriage, family, and community allows him to affirm these necessary human bonds. His poems reflect his loyalty to his native region, his love of farming, his view of marriage as a sacrament, and his deep awareness of the beauty and wonder of the natural world.

ELEGIAC POETRY

Though Berry had been publishing poems in literary magazines and journals since the mid-1950's, his first critical recognition came in 1964, with the appearance of *The Broken Ground*, his first poetry volume, and *November Twenty-six, Nineteen Hundred Sixty-three*, his elegy for John F. Kennedy, which first appeared in the December 21, 1963, issue of the *Nation*. Berry's elegy, which was accompanied by woodcuts by Ben Shahn, has been called the most successful commemoration of Kennedy's death. Though written in free-verse form, Berry's elegy makes use of a traditional stanzaic organization and refrain and incorporates the traditional elegiac cycle of grief, mourning, the funeral procession, the interment, and the apotheosis of the subject's memory. Berry's interest in the elegy was also apparent in "Elegy," the opening poem in *The Broken Ground*. Other elegiac works include "Three Elegiac Poems" (*Findings*), "In Memory: Stuart Engol" (*Openings*), and "Requiem" and "Elegy" (*The Wheel*). Death is always present in Berry's work, but it is presented naturalistically, without a compensating *carpe diem* theme or renewal except in the natural cycle of life.

THE BROKEN GROUND

The Broken Ground is a collection of thirty-one free-verse lyrics with a distinctly regional flavor, twenty of which were later included in his *Collected Poems*. Many of these poems first appeared in *Stylus, Poetry, The Nation*, and *The Prairie Schooner*. This early collection introduces the Berry voice and some of his major themes: the cycle of life and death, a sensitivity to place, pastoral subject matter, and recurring images of water, the Kentucky River, and the hilly, pastoral landscape of north-central Kentucky. His language is terse, intense, and compressed, his style imagistic and at times almost epigrammatic. The stylistic influence of William Carlos Williams and the Orientalism of Kenneth Rexroth seem apparent in these early poems. Berry's sharp, sculpted images also recall those of his friend and fellow poet Gary Snyder. Some of the poems seem curiously detached and impersonal. They are animated by no great myths, legends, or events, aside from the figures of Daniel Boone and other early settlers. Instead, the poems are intensely private, detached, and descriptive. Although many of them are set in his native Kentucky, the Berry persona seems curiously detached from members of his local community beyond his family. One does not find the social engagement Williams shows in his Patterson poems, a warmth that came from his lifelong involvement as a local pediatrician. Instead, the Berry persona seems solitary and austere: too much the detached observer, quiet and understated, though perhaps not intending to project a sense of social isolation. The parallels with Williams are instructive: While Williams was a practicing local physician whose poetry often reflects his sympathetic understanding of his patients and their families, Berry presents himself as a working farmer whose poetry reflects his love of his work. What redeems Berry's poems is his love of farming and the rhythms of physical labor: its purposefulness, its physicality, and its tangible rewards.

LOST PARADISE AS THEME

There is a mythic vision in Berry's poems of a lost, primeval paradise, a fall from grace, and a guarded hope in work, discipline, and renewal. "Paradise might have appeared here," he announces in "The Aristocracy," but instead he finds a wealthy old dowager airing her cat. Like Robert Frost's pastoral world of a diminished New England landscape, Berry's Kentucky River Valley has suffered from neglect and abuse. The moments of grace are few—bird songs, the return of spring, the cycle of the seasons, glimpses of the natural order—and death is always present. Like Frost, Berry has chosen to make a "strategic retreat" to a pastoral world in which the poet-farmer can take stock of his resources, but his sensibility differs from Frost's. For Frost, the sense of diminishment came from the abandonment of farms in rural New England after the Civil War, while for Berry the sense of loss comes from environmental despoilation of the Cumberland plateau, first by careless

farming practices and later by timber interests and the big coal companies.

Berry's version of the Paradise Lost myth centers on the massive environmental destruction visited upon the Cumberland region by absentee corporate owners. He has been radicalized by Kentucky's legacy of corrupt government and indifference to environmental concerns, which has left the region virtually a Third World economy, based upon cheap, large-scale mineral extraction with little regard for the human or environmental consequences of pit or surface mining. The practice of strip-mining has been particularly devastating to the land and water resources. Living downstream from the despoiled hills and polluted creeks of Appalachia, Berry has seen at first hand the flooding and water pollution that have occurred on the Kentucky River.

THE KENTUCKY RIVER AND FINDINGS

As Berry recounts in *The Kentucky River*, the first white settlers who entered the Kentucky territory were unable to respond to the richness and abundance of natural resources except by exploitation. Hence, in "July, 1773," the first of the "Three Kentucky River Poems," young Sam Adams fires heedlessly into a herd of peacefully grazing buffalo at a salt lick.

Not only did the publication of Berry's *Collected Poems* in 1985 permit the republishing of nearly two hundred poems from his previous eight volumes, many of which were by then out of print, but it also allowed him to select which poems he could retain and which he would drop from those early volumes. Among Berry's best early work was the sequence of three long poems from *Findings*. "The Design of a House" is a poem about beginnings and intentions, the conscious fabrication of a dwelling and a marriage relationship that had previously existed merely as a vague dream or desire, and a wish to reestablish roots in one's native place. It becomes a nuptial poem, the speaker's dedication of his love to his wife, Tanya, and his daughter, Mary, and the continuation of their life together. The design of their house comes to signify the design of their family relationship.

The second poem in *Findings*, "The Handing Down," continues this theme of family and place, this time in terms of an old man's memories and reflections, his sense of satisfaction with the life he has led, as expressed through conversations with his grandson. The speaker in this poem recalls Jack Beecham, the protagonist of Berry's novel *The Memory of Old Jack* (1974). Both the poem and the novel have to do with an old man's preparations for death, his gradual letting go of life through the memories that run through his mind. The third part of *Findings*, "Three Elegiac Poems," commemorates the death of the old man, which the speaker hopes will occur quietly at home, away from the sterile coldness and isolation of hospital wards and the indifference of physicians.

CELEBRATION OF NATURE AND LAND

Openings, *Farming: A Hand Book*, *The Country of Marriage*, and *Clearing* celebrate his return to Kentucky and the satisfaction he found in taking up farming. After living in California, Europe, and New York City, he came to appreciate the possibilities of writing about his native region. Berry was particularly impressed with the hill farms of Tuscany, around Florence, which showed him that such "marginal land" might remain productive for many centuries with the proper care and attention. The quality of these farms led him to rethink the possibilities of hill farming in his native Kentucky. As he indicates in the autographical title essay in *The Long-Legged House* (1969), he kept feeling himself drawn back home, particularly to the small cabin built on the Kentucky River by his uncle Curran Matthews. After it was flooded, Berry moved this house farther up the riverbank and rebuilt it to create his writer's study.

Berry's poems in these middle volumes show a new depth of craft and responsiveness to nature. They celebrate the values of land and nature, family and community, marital love and devotion. They are quietly attentive to the cycle of seasons, of the organic cycles of growth and decay, of the subtle beauty of the native flora and fauna. As philosopher, visionary, and political activist, his "Mad Farmer" persona speaks out against war, wastefulness, and environmental destruction. He dreams of a new, gentler orientation to the land that will encourage people to cherish and preserve their natural heritage. He finds deep spiritual sustenance as he reflects on the beauty and fitness of the natural order and the richness of the present moment.

Berry's poems are broadly pastoral in orientation, but they reflect the Kentucky frontier tradition of pioneer homesteading and yeoman farming rather than artificial literary tradition. Some pastoral themes evident in his work include an idealization of the simple life, an implied city-country contrast, a yearning for a past "golden age" of rural life, a celebration of the seasonal tasks of farming life, a strong affirmation of small-scale, organic farming, and an identification of the poet with his native region.

OPENINGS

In *Openings*, the poem "The Thought of Something Else" announces the speaker's desire to leave the city for country life, but first he must make peace with the legacy of the past, which he does in "My Great-Grandfather's Slaves." The next three poems are autumnal in tone, establishing the speaker within a seasonal cycle. In "The Snake," he comes upon a small reptile preparing for winter hibernation. The "living cold" of the snake, replete with its engorged meal, parallels the contented winter solitude of the speaker in the next poem, "The Cold." The starkly descriptive "Winter Rain" leads to "March Snow" and "April Woods: Morning," which resemble haiku in their delicate imagery. In "The Porch over the River," the speaker establishes himself in his riverside writer's cabin, like the classical Chinese poet Du Fu. In "The Dream," he imagines the surrounding countryside restored to its pristine beauty, unspoiled by greed or acquisitiveness. The tree celebrated in "The Sycamore," a venerable specimen whose gnarled trunk is scarred by lightning, becomes a symbol of natural resiliency. Like the tree, the poet wishes that he might be shaped and nurtured by his native place. The longest and most abstract piece, "Window Poems," is composed of twenty-seven sections that reflect the speaker's changing moods as he watches the shifting patterns of river scenery from his study window. "Grace" and "A Discipline" reflect the strength the speaker draws from nature, allowing him to withstand the destructiveness of his culture, in which people are at war with the environment, one another, and themselves.

FARMING: A HAND BOOK AND THE COUNTRY OF MARRIAGE

Farming: A Hand Book and *The Country of Marriage* are less solitary in mood. They introduce the colorful persona of the "Mad Farmer," an exuberant, Bunyanesque figure who flaunts social conventions in

"The Mad Farmer's Revolution" and "The Contrariness of the Mad Farmer," dances in the streets in "The Mad Farmer in the City," and—through his prayers, sayings, satisfactions, and manifestos—offers a wry and humorous commentary on Berry's own views as expressed in his books and essays. "The Birth," a dramatic dialogue, constitutes an interesting departure from Berry's customary lyrical verse. A group of farmers, up late with lambing on a cold winter night, unexpectedly come upon a couple and child who have taken sanctuary in their barn for their own nativity. Berry's poem captures the cadences and flavor of ordinary country talk, in which more is implied than said.

Berry's poems are noted for quiet attentiveness to surroundings, almost as if the speaker tried to make himself part of his habitat. His farmer persona is a keen naturalist, carefully observing the seasonal behavior of the birds and animals. His speaker is especially attuned to bird songs, and the variety of birds mentioned in his poems is notable—kingfishers, song sparrows, phoebes, herons, wild geese, finches, wrens, chickadees, cardinals, titmice, and warblers. Implicit in his poems is a sense of grace and renewal, a deep satisfaction and contentment.

Berry's relationship with his wife and children has been central to his task of renewal as a pastoral poet. An accomplished love poet, Berry has written many poems to his wife Tanya, on the anniversaries of their marriage or to express his gratitude for their common life. For his children, too, Berry has written poems on their births, comings of age, and marriages, and on the births of grandchildren. In "The Gathering," the speaker recalls that he now holds his son in his arms the way his father held him. In "The Country of Marriage," farming and marriage serve as complementary and inseparable extensions of each other. Husbandry and marriage are recurring tropes in Berry's poetry, illustrated in clearing fields, sowing crops, planting a garden, tending livestock, mowing hay, and taking in the harvest. He celebrates farming as a labor of love, the work of regeneration and fecundity that is at once vital and procreative.

CLEARING

The poems in *Clearing* articulate Berry's sense of region and place. "Where" is a long pastoral meditation on the history and ownership of the fifty-acre farm, Lane's

Landing, which the Berrys purchased between 1965 and 1968. The history of the farm provides a case study in attitudes toward stewardship and land use, from the earliest settlers to the developer from whom Berry bought the farm. The transition from wilderness to settlement to worn-out land rehearses an ecological myth of the fall from primeval abundance to reckless waste and decay. Berry presents the history of his farm as a parable of the American frontier and an indictment of the reckless habits that quickly exhausted the land's natural richness and abundance. "Where" is both a personal credo and a contemporary ecological statement of what needs to be done, both in terms of land management and in changing cultural attitudes toward the land.

A PART

Berry's next two poetry volumes, *A Part* and *The Wheel*, reflect in their titles his deepening ecological awareness. *A Part* includes short pastoral lyrics; some religious verse; translations of two poems by the sixteenth century French poet Pierre de Ronsard; "Three Kentucky River Poems," a narrative triptych based in part on historical accounts of the McAfee brothers' 1773 expedition into Kentucky; and "Horses," a verse tribute to the skills of working draft horses, in which Berry excoriates tractors and internal combustion engines for destroying the quiet pleasures of farming.

THE WHEEL

The Wheel takes its title image from the mandela, or "wheel of life," of which Sir Albert Howard speaks in his classic study *An Agricultural Testament* (1943), which influenced Berry's thinking about organic farming. This collection is a book of elegies of remembrance and praise, celebrating the continuities of birth, growth, maturity, death, and decay. An increasing self-assurance is evident in Berry's voice, a relaxed, self-confident voice free of anxiety. His verse forms also become more formal, with an increased use of rhyme and regular stanzaic form, though he still seems to prefer a short line.

"Elegy," one of Berry's finest poems, appears in this collection. A pastoral elegy, it is one of a series of three poems dedicated to Owen Flood, whom Berry honors as a teacher and friend. The first poem, "Requiem," announces his passing, though his spirit remains in the fields he had tended. "Elegy" pays tribute to the quality of Flood's life in eight sections, invoking the spirits of the dead to reaffirm the traditional values that Flood embodied: duty, loyalty, perseverance, honesty, hard work, endurance, and self-reliance. It reaffirms the continuity of the generations within a permanent, stable agricultural order. There is a sense of recycling human life, as nature recycles organic materials back into the soil to create the fertile organic humus of the soil. The poem also celebrates human permanences: marriage, work, friendship, love, fidelity, and death. The dominant image is of life as a dance within the circle of life, implying closure, completeness, and inclusion. "Elegy" affirms farm labor as an honorable calling, true to the biblical injunction to live by the sweat of one's brow. The opening line of the poem reaffirms an implicit purpose in all Berry's work: "To be at home on its native ground." The poem honors the elders of the community who were the speaker's teachers, including Flood, and concludes with the affirmation that "the best teachers teach more/ than they know. By their deaths/ they teach most."

Another important poem in this collection, "The Gift of Gravity," reaffirms the life-sustaining cycles of sunlight, photosynthesis, growth, decay, and death. The poem announces its major theme, "gravity is grace," with the dominant image of the river of life and the return of all life to its source. There is an almost mystical unity conveyed in the opening lines: "All that passes descends,/ and ascends again unseen/ into the light." Two other poems, "The Wheel" and "The Dance," affirm the interlocking unities that knit the community together in festive celebrations of song and dance.

Dissatisfied with Harcourt Brace, Berry changed publishers in the early 1980's, moving to North Point Press, a small publisher in Berkeley, California. One immediate result was the issuing of his *Recollected Essays, 1965-1980* (1981), and *Collected Poems*. Including the better part of his first eight volumes of poetry, the *Collected Poems* is certainly the definitive volume for the reader of Berry's verse.

SABBATHS

Sabbaths marks something of a departure in tone and style from Berry's earlier work. It is at once more formal, more structured, and more overtly religious in its sensibility. The forty-six poems in this collection were written over a six-year period, from 1979 to 1985.

The poems are untitled, arranged by year, and identified only by their first line. There are quiet, restrained, almost metaphysical meditations that incorporate a number of lines from Scripture. Here Berry makes use of traditional rhyme and meter. These poems show a deep, nonsectarian religious sensibility, akin to the personal faith of the New England Transcendentalist poets—especially Emily Dickinson. Like Dickinson, Berry applies Christian tropes to nature to imply a natural religion. The many allusions to Eden, Paradise, worship, hymns, song, grace, gift, Maker, heaven, resurrection, darkness, and light invoke a kind of prophetic vision of a new earth, healed and reborn—a paradise regained. Berry again describes the primal fertility and richness of the Kentucky landscape before it was ruined by the rapacious settlers. His poems combine a moral awareness of a deep wrong done to the earth by human greed and ignorance with an ecological awareness of the need for a change that can come only from within. His poems offer a dichotomized moral vision of nature as basically innocent and human nature as the source of evil.

The overall theme of *Sabbaths* is the need for rest and renewal—both within human hearts and in the natural world. People need to take time away from their heedless ravaging of the environment to try to understand and appreciate the earth's beauty and strength. Berry calls for the cultivation of a different kind of sensibility—less inclined to impose human will on nature and more inclined to appreciate the natural world on its own terms, as a kind of heaven on earth. Berry weaves many scriptural allusions into his poems, quoting from the Psalms, the Old Testament prophets, and the New Testament. The poems manage to convey a deep meditative sensibility without making any formal religious affirmations except by implication. The speaker comes across as a deeply thoughtful but independent spirit, reverent but unchurched. One finds in *Sabbaths* a new blend of spiritual and ecological awareness, a sense of life, of the earth, of the land, as worthy of the deepest veneration. This meditative cycle of poems is extended in *A Timbered Choir.*

OTHER MAJOR WORKS

LONG FICTION: *Nathan Coulter*, 1960, rev. 1985; *A Place on Earth*, 1967, rev. 1983; *The Memory of Old*

Jack, 1974; *Remembering*, 1988; *A World Lost*, 1996; *Jayber Crow*, 2000.

SHORT FICTION: *The Wild Birds*, 1986; *Fidelity: Five Stories*, 1993.

NONFICTION: *The Long-Legged House*, 1969; *The Hidden Wound*, 1970; *The Unforeseen Wilderness*, 1971; *A Continuous Harmony*, 1972; *The Unsettling of America*, 1977; *Recollected Essays, 1965-1980*, 1981; *The Gift of Good Land*, 1981; *Standing by Words*, 1983; *Home Economics*, 1987; *What Are People For?*, 1990; *Harland Hubbard: Life and Work*, 1990; *Sex, Economy, Freedom, and Community: Eight Essays*, 1994; *Another Turn of the Crank*, 1996; *Life Is a Miracle: An Essay Against Modern Superstition*, 2000.

BIBLIOGRAPHY

Angyal, Andrew J. *Wendell Berry*. New York: Macmillan Library Reference, 1995. This study, which provides an examination of Berry's entire career, includes Angyal's 1991 interview with Berry. Angyal argues that Berry's advocacy of traditional rural life is both balanced and sharpened with an informed ecological vision and deep understanding of the complex relationships among the individual, the family, the community, and the environment. One chapter is exclusively devoted to Berry's poetry.

Basney, Lionel. "Having Your Meaning at Hand: Work in Snyder and Berry." In *Word, Self, Poem: Essays on Contemporary Poetry from the Jubilation of Poets*, edited by Leonard M. Trawick. Kent, Ohio: Kent State University Press, 1990. Discusses Berry's early volumes as articulating a work ethic that is rooted in a person's interaction with a particular place, with a sense of community, and with an uneasy Christian sacramental vision.

Cornell, Daniel. "*The Country of Marriage:* Wendell Berry's Personal Political Vision." *Southern Literary Journal* 16 (Fall, 1983): 59-70. Through a close reading of the poems in *The Country of Marriage*, Cornell offers a thoughtful examination of the thematic implications of Berry's pastoral metaphors. Cornell locates Berry within an agrarian populist tradition that defies conventional conservative or liberal labels.

Freeman, Russell G. *Wendell Berry: A Bibliography*. Lexington: University of Kentucky Libraries, 1992. This is the place to begin straightening out the history of Berry's nonstop, multigenre publishing career.

Hicks, Jack. "Wendell Berry's Husband to the World: *A Place on Earth*." *American Literature* 51 (May, 1979): 238-254. In perhaps the best critical overview of Berry's earlier work, Hicks examines the farmer-countryman vision in Berry's fiction, stressing the need of atonement for past neglect or abuse of the land and discussing the strengths and weaknesses of Berry's protagonists—especially Mat Feltner—as farmers, husbands, and parents. Hicks traces thematic connections between Berry's essays, poetry, and fiction.

Knott, John R. "Into the Woods with Wendell Berry." *Essays in Literature* 23 (Spring, 1996): 124-140. Knott draws upon both Berry's fiction and poetry to explore the role of the wilderness in his works, noting the more hopeful tone of later volumes.

Merchant, Paul, ed. *Wendell Berry*. Lewiston, Idaho: Confluence Press, 1991. This is a collection of appreciations by several writers, including Wallace Stegner, Terry Tempest Williams, Donald Hall, and Gary Snyder. The observations of Hall and Snyder are particularly useful in gauging Berry's poetry.

Nibbelink, Herman. "Thoreau and Wendell Berry: Bachelor and Husband of Nature." *South Atlantic Quarterly* 84 (Spring, 1985): 127-140. Another study of the farmer-husbandry theme in Berry's work. Nibbelink traces the influence of Thoreau in Berry's work and contrasts Thoreau's appreciation of wildness with Berry's preference for cultivated land as the difference between naturalist and farmer.

Sciagaj, Leonard M. *Sustainable Poetry: Four American Ecopoets*. Lexington, University Press of Kentucky, 1999. Along with Berry, discusses and compares A. R. Ammons, Gary Snyder, and W. S. Merwin and their treatment of nature and environmental concerns in their works. Bibliographical references, index.

Slovic, Scott. "Coming Home to 'The Camp': Wendell Berry's Watchfulness." In *Seeking Awareness in American Nature Writing: Henry Thoreau, Annie*

Dillard, Edward Abbey, Wendell Berry, Barry Lopez, by Slovic. Salt Lake City: University of Utah Press, 1992. A fine appreciation of Berry's naturalist, ecological vision. The larger study places Berry within an important American tradition.

Weiland, Steven. "Wendell Berry: Culture and Fidelity." *Iowa Review* 10 (Winter, 1979): 99-104. Weiland points out that Berry's values, though seemingly personal and domestic, are nevertheless radical in their political implications.

Andrew J. Angyal,
updated by Philip K. Jason

JOHN BERRYMAN

Born: McAlester, Oklahoma; October 25, 1914
Died: Minneapolis, Minnesota; January 7, 1972

PRINCIPAL POETRY

Five Young American Poets, 1940 (with others)
Poems, 1942
The Dispossessed, 1948
Homage to Mistress Bradstreet, 1956
His Thought Made Pockets and the Plane Buckt, 1958
Seventy-seven Dream Songs, 1964
Short Poems, 1967
Berryman's Sonnets, 1967
His Toy, His Dream, His Rest, 1968
The Dream Songs, 1969
Love and Fame, 1970, 1972
Delusions, Etc. of John Berryman, 1972
Henry's Fate and Other Poems, 1977
Collected Poems, 1937-1971, 1989

OTHER LITERARY FORMS

In addition to his poetry, John Berryman produced a considerable number of reviews and critical pieces. A posthumous collection, *The Freedom of the Poet* (1976), gathers a representative sample of his criticism, published and unpublished. Berryman did not produce much prose fiction, preferring to use verse as a narrative vehicle. He did, however, write several short stories, and an unfinished novel, *Recovery* (1973), was published as he left it at his death. Other critical writing includes *Stephen Crane* (1950), a critical biography with a psychological slant, and *The Arts of Reading* (1960), a collection of essays coauthored with Ralph Ross and Allen Tate. Berryman also edited a 1960 edition of Thomas Nashe's *The Unfortunate Traveller: Or, The Life of Jack Wilton*. Berryman may be heard reading his poems on several recordings produced by the Library of Congress.

ACHIEVEMENTS

In *Beyond All This Fiddle* (1968) A. Alvarez remarks that

> John Berryman is one of those poets whom you either love or loathe. Yet even the loathers have grudgingly to admit that the man is extraordinary . . . with a queer, distinct voice of his own.

No doubt, there are "loathers" who would apply "extraordinary" in no laudable sense, and who would use

John Berryman (© Tom Berthiaume, courtesy of Farrar, Straus & Giroux, Inc.)

far cruder adjectives than "queer" and "distinct" in describing Berryman's voice. Still, decades after his death, Berryman's place in modern poetry seems as secure as that of any of his contemporaries, living or dead—Robert Lowell, Delmore Schwartz, Richard Wilbur, Adrienne Rich, or W. D. Snodgrass. Though he died a most unsatisfied man, his poetic career certainly brought him his share of recognition and praise: the Levinson and Guarantors Prizes from *Poetry* and the Shelley Memorial Award, 1948; the University of Chicago's Harriet Monroe Poetry Prize, 1957; the Brandies Creative Arts Award, 1960; the National Institute of Arts and Letters' Loines Award for Poetry, 1964; the Pulitzer Prize in Poetry for *Seventy-seven Dream Songs*, 1965; an Academy of American Poets fellowship in 1966; and both the National Book Award and the Bollingen Prize (shared with Karl Shapiro) for *His Toy, His Dream, His Rest*, 1969. In addition, he won grants and fellowships from such organizations as the Guggenheim Foundation (1952, 1966), the Rockefeller Foundation (1944), the National Institute of Arts and Letters (1950), and the Academy of American Poets (1966). He was much in demand for public readings, even though, especially toward the end of his career, his alcoholism and unpredictable personality made some of these appearances traumatic for both poet and audience.

In his poetry, Berryman moved from an ordered, restrained style, imitative of William Butler Yeats and W. H. Auden, to a passionate, energetic, deeply personal mode of expression, held in check—though just barely in places—by skilled attention to rhythm and sound. So decisive was this movement that comparing such early poems as "Winter Landscape" with a random sample from his later work, *The Dream Songs*, is almost like comparing two different poets. It is easy enough to look back at Berryman's early work and find it too poised, too urbane and academic. A number of critics, however, have objected to much of his later work, finding in it too little restraint and much too large a dose of the poet's raw experience. He is placed by some, with Anne Sexton and Lowell, in the "confessional school." The label does not quite apply, for Berryman's work at its best— and, unfortunately, he did frequently allow it to be published at its worst—remained for him a means of using personal experience to get at human experience. He

retained too much formal control to be considered a "Beat" and was too inventive in his use of language to be classed with the vernacular mode of William Carlos Williams. Whatever else may be said about him, Berryman is one of the most individual voices in twentieth century American poetry.

In spite of his successes, however, it is difficult not to wonder whether Berryman has been overpraised. His *Homage to Mistress Bradstreet*, for example, was extolled by Robert Fitzgerald (*The American Review*, Autumn, 1960) as "the poem of his generation," while Edmund Wilson, solicited for a back-cover blurb for a 1968 paperback edition of the poem, responded with, "the most distinguished long poem by an American since *The Waste Land*." There must certainly be a middle stance, somewhere between overpraise and Stanton Coblentz's view that "*Seventy-seven Dream Songs* has all the imaginative fervor of a cash register." Such a moderate perspective would see Berryman as a major poet of his generation, and view *Seventy-seven Dream Songs* as one of the major poetic events of the 1960's. His *Collected Poems, 1937-1971*, was published in 1989.

Biography

John Berryman was born John Allyn Smith, in McAlester, Oklahoma, the eldest son of a banker and a schoolteacher. His early childhood, spent in various small Oklahoma towns, was normal enough until his father's work took the family to live in Tampa, Florida; marital problems developed and the boy's father became increasingly troubled and unstable. In June, 1926, he shot himself in the chest at the family's vacation home across Tampa Bay. Young John heard the shot just outside his window—one sharp report that would echo through his consciousness for the rest of his life. When the boy's mother moved to New York and remarried, his name was changed to John Allyn McAlpin Berryman. Berryman wrote many letters to his mother as an adult, which were published as *We Dream of Honour: John Berryman's Letters to His Mother* in 1988.

Berryman attended a Connecticut prep school, South Kent; though he showed great intellectual promise, he was only intermittently moved to apply it. He was graduated in 1933 and went on to Columbia University in New York. There he felt much more at home academically and socially, and there he began a lifelong friendship with Mark Van Doren, who, by Berryman's account, was the first person to inspire and encourage him to be a poet. Not long after this association began, Berryman published his first poem, an elegy on Edwin Arlington Robinson, in the *Nation*. In 1936 he received his bachelor's degree from Columbia, Phi Beta Kappa, and won the University's Kellett Fellowship, which he used to pursue further studies at Clare College, Cambridge University. Academically, his Cambridge experience was extremely rewarding. In 1937, he served as Oldham Shakespeare Scholar, and received a bachelor of arts degree in 1938. His social contacts were rewarding, to say the least, including as they did William Butler Yeats, W. H. Auden, and Dylan Thomas.

Back in New York, Berryman was a friend of another young poet, Delmore Schwartz, and became poetry editor of the *Nation*. His teaching career began in 1939 at Wayne State University in Detroit. After a year there, Berryman took a position at Harvard, where he remained until 1943. During this time, his first published collection of poems appeared in *Five Young American Poets* (1940). His work was well received, as were the poems of another promising young talent, Randall Jarrell. In 1942 Berryman published a self-contained selection, *Poems*. On October 24 of the same year, he married Eileen Patricia Mulligan. From 1943 to 1951, Berryman lectured in creative writing at Princeton, taking time out frequently, with the help of grants and fellowships, to write poetry and criticism, as well as a few short stories. In 1948 he published a new book of poems, *The Dispossessed*, which was received more politely than enthusiastically. His most significant work while at Princeton was his critical study, *Stephen Crane*. His psychoanalytic approach was not popular with most reviewers, but the book, on the whole, attracted a good deal of praise.

In 1951 Berryman accepted a one-year position as Elliston Lecturer in Poetry at the University of Cincinnati and spent the next academic year in Europe with the help of a Guggenheim Fellowship. While in Europe he completed the poem that, upon its publication in 1956, would bring him his first great critical success as a poet—*Homage to Mistress Bradstreet*. The price of this success, however, was high. Berryman later cited his preoccupation with the poem, coupled with an increasing dependence on alcohol, as the cause of his separation in 1953 from his first wife. Certainly, the marriage had not been helped by an intense, guilt-ridden love affair in which Berryman had indulged during the summer of 1947, an affair portrayed in painful detail in the sequence *Berryman's Sonnets*. In the meantime, however, Berryman's academic and literary careers proceeded without serious hindrance. In the fall of 1954, having spent the preceding spring and summer semesters, respectively, at the University of Iowa and at Harvard, he began his long tenure as a professor of humanities at the University of Minnesota in Minneapolis, where he became a popular, if eccentric, academic figure. In 1969 he received the university's most prestigious faculty award, a Regents' Professorship, and he remained on the faculty there until his death.

In 1956, Berryman divorced Eileen and married Ann Levine, who gave birth to a son in 1957. The marriage lasted only until 1959. When he again remarried, in 1961, it was to Kathleen Donahue, twenty-five years his junior. In the same year he lectured at Indiana University, then moved on, in 1962, to a visiting professorship at Boon University. During that year, Kathleen gave birth to a daughter, Martha. In 1965, Berryman won the Pulitzer Prize for *Seventy-seven Dream Songs*; his place as a major contemporary poet seemed secure. He had begun work on these "songs" around 1955, and continued to work in this form for nearly twenty years, publishing in 1968 *His Toy, His Dream, His Rest*, a collection of 308 more poems that won the National Book Award in 1969. The two volumes were combined in *The Dream Songs* (1969).

The 1960's were a time of triumph for Berryman. The decade saw, along with *The Dream Songs*, the long-delayed publication of *Berryman's Sonnets*, and of *Short Poems*, a compilation of the earlier collections, *The Dispossessed* and *His Thought Made Pockets and the Plane Buckt*, with the addition of "Formal Elegy," a poem on the death of John F. Kennedy. Yet, the kind of success that most poets only dream of left Berryman dissatisfied and unfulfilled. His drinking problem became more serious than ever, interfering not only with his family life but with his professional responsibilities as well, disrupting classes and public readings, much to the dismay of students, admirers, and colleagues.

Berryman's next book of poems, *Love and Fame*, did not fare well with the critics, and the poet took their disapproval hard. He had been, by this time, in and out of alcoholic treatment programs, and, while he had found some consolation in a renewal of his Roman Catholic faith, he could not overcome the addiction to alcohol; drinking had for too long been, in Joel Conarroe's words, "both stabilizer and destroyer, midwife and coroner, focuser and depressant." He spent many weeks of 1971 in the alcohol treatment facility at St. Mary's Hospital in Minneapolis, the hospital that provided the setting for *Recovery*. He remained, however, busy. He prepared a new book of poems for publication, and his plans for work included a translation of Sophocles and a book or two on Shakespeare. Unfortunately, the prospect of hard work, the comfort of family and friends, his affection for his daughters, Martha and Sarah—these were not enough.

On January 7, 1972, readers of the *St. Paul Dispatch* were greeted with the front page headline: "Poet Berryman Leaps to Death." That afternoon, Berryman had thrown himself some one hundred feet from the railing of a bridge in Minneapolis; his body was recovered from among the rocks on the frozen west bank of the Mississippi. In a circumstance worthy of the most bitterly ironic of his poems, the only identification he carried was a blank check.

After a Requiem Mass, he was buried in Resurrection Cemetery in St. Paul.

ANALYSIS

In his essay "Tradition and the Individual Talent," T. S. Eliot asserts that

> the more perfect the artist, the more completely separate in him will be the man who suffers and the mind which creates; the more perfectly will the mind digest and transmute the passions which are its material.

Poetry, to Eliot, is "not a turning loose of emotion, but an escape from emotion; it is not the expression of personality, but an escape from personality." Regardless of what Eliot's critical stock is worth these days, there is an essential truth in what he says. Of course, poetry has brought to its readers the sweetest joys and the bitterest sorrows that human flesh is heir to, from "sweet silent thought" to "barbaric yawp." To the extent, however, that a poet presents his passions to the reader undigested, untransmuted, he damages the quality of his work *as poetry*. The more loudly personality speaks in a poem, the more art is forced to falter, to stutter. The poem—and the poet, and the reader—suffers.

To the extent to which "the man who suffers" and "the mind which creates" are not kept separate, to that extent will that poet's art be imperfect. A case in point is John Berryman. There is much in his work that is brilliant; since his death, his stature has grown. There is no denying that he suffered much in his life, and risked much, dared much, in his poetry. What he was never really able to do was to find the voice and mode that would allow him, not to banish personality from his poems but to keep personality from getting in the way, from obstructing the proper work of the poem.

BERRYMAN'S SONNETS

Berryman's Sonnets, though unpublished until 1967, was mostly written some twenty years earlier. These poems are the poet's first sustained use of what may be called his "mature style," much of his previous work being rather derivative. The 115 sonnets form a sequence that recounts the guilty particulars of an adulterous love affair between a hard-drinking academic named Berryman and a harder-drinking woman named Lise, with the respectively wronged wife and husband in supporting roles. The affair, as the sonnets record it, is a curious mixture of sex, Scotch, and Bach (Lise's favorite, her lover preferring Mozart), punctuated by allusions right out of a graduate seminar, from the Old Testament to E. E. Cummings.

In form, the sonnets are Petrarchan, with here and there an additional fifteenth line. In his adherence, more or less, to the stanzaic and metric demands of the sonnet, Berryman pays a sort of homage to earlier practioners of the form. At the same time, he is attempting to forge a mode of expression that is anything but Petrarchan, in spite of the fact that, as Hayden Carruth pointed out in a review in *Poetry* (May, 1968), the poems "touch every outworn convention of the sonnet sequence—love, lust, jealousy, separation, time, death, the immortality of art, etc." Carruth points out in the same review that "the stylistic root of *The Dream Songs*" is present in the sonnets, with those attributes that came to be trademarks of Berryman's style—"archaic spelling, fantastically complex diction, tortuous syntax, formalism, a witty and ironic attitude toward prosody generally." A concentrated if somewhat mild example of how Berryman combines any number of these traits within a few lines is the octet of "Sonnet 49":

> One note, a daisy, and a photograph,
> To slake this siege of weeks without you, all.
> Your dawn-eyed envoy, welcome as Seconal,
> To call you faithful . . . now this cenotaph,
> A shabby mummy flower. Note I keep safe,
> Nothing, on a ration slip a social scrawl—
> Not that it didn't forth some pages call
> Of my analysis, one grim paragraph.

There are enjoyable juxtapositions here. Outdated words such as "slake" and "cenotaph," the oversweetness of "dawn-eyed envoy," ranged about the all-too-contemporary simile, "welcome as Seconal," are no accident. There is an irreverent literary mind at work here, orchestrating intentionally a little out of tune. It is harder to appreciate or justify a phrase such as "not that it didn't forth some pages call/ Of my analysis." Such syntax is a high price to pay for a rhyme, and much more extreme examples could be cited.

On the whole, the sequence is successful, but the seeds of Berryman's eventual undoing are here. The confessional nature of the poems (Berryman did experience just such an affair in 1947, and required a good deal of psychoanalysis afterward) makes it plain enough why their publication was delayed so long, but it also leads the reader to wonder whether they should have been published at all. In his attempts to work within a fairly strict form, he shows a tendency to force rhyme and overburden meter. His literary name-dropping ("O if my syncrisis/ Teases you, briefer than Propertius' in/ This paraphrase by Pound—to whom I owe three letters"), private allusions, and inside jokes present a dangerous intrusion of the idiosyncratic, the personal. With more shaping, more revision, more distance generally, the sequence could have been much more artistically successful than it is. Perhaps part of Berryman's intention was to get the thing on paper "as it was," to share his raw feelings with the reader. The best of the sonnets, by their wit and craft, speak against such a supposition. They contain, as a group, too much undigested Berryman to be placed, as some have placed them, beside the sonnets of William Shakespeare. Lise is all too actual, "barefoot . . . on the bare floor riveted to Bach," no Dark Lady. Further, while Shakespeare's sonnets have much to say about love, loss, youth, age, success, and failure, they tell the reader little if anything about William Shakespeare, while Berryman's sonnets reveal more than one may care to know about Berryman.

HOMAGE TO MISTRESS BRADSTREET

Not long after the strenuous summer of the sonnets, Berryman began a poem on the seventeenth century American Puritan poet, Anne Bradstreet. Part of the initial task was to find the right stanza for the job; an eight-line stanza suggested itself, the pattern of feet running 5-5-3-4-5-5-3-6, with a rhyme scheme of *abcbddba*. Neither meter nor rhyme is adhered to inflexibly in the resulting poem, *Homage to Mistress Bradstreet*, but for the most part Berryman succeeded in his choice of a stanza "both flexible and grave, intense and quiet, able to deal with matter both high and low." He achieves beautiful effects in the fifty-seven stanzas of this poem. The birth of Bradstreet's first child after several years of barrenness is portrayed in images wonderfully right: "I press with horrible joy down/ my back cracks like a wrist." The words sweep forward, charged with the urgency of this experience, "and it passes the wretched trap whelming and I am me/ drencht & powerful, I did it with my body!/ One proud tug greens Heaven. . . ." In fact, some of the most touching moments in the poem focus on Bradstreet and her children, whether the occasion be death, as in stanza 41, "Moonrise, and frightening hoots. 'Mother,/ how *long* will I be dead?'" or nothing more than a loose tooth, as in stanza 42: "When by me in the dusk my child sits down/ I am myself. Simon, if it's that loose,/ let me wiggle it out./ You'll get a bigger one there, & bite." Moving outdoors, away from the hearth, there are lovely scenes of natural description: "Outside the New World winters in grand dark/ white air lashing high thro' the virgin stands/ foxes down foxholes sigh. . . ."

Berryman, however, has his problems with the poem. As in the sonnets, he sometimes tangles his syntax unnecessarily: "So were ill/ many as one day we could have no sermons." To write "so were ill many" instead of "so many were ill," without even the excuse of a stubbornly kept rhyme scheme, seems at best eccentric, at worst, sloppy. As in the sonnets, also, there is an unfinished quality about the poem. Tangled phrasing, the inconsistent use of a rather carefully established rhyme scheme—these in spite of the fact that Berryman spent years on the poem, even blamed the demise of his first marriage partly upon the intense effort that the work required. One may wonder, in spite of his long labors, whether he relinquished it to the public a bit unfinished.

The major flaw in *Homage to Mistress Bradstreet*, however, has not so much to do with details of diction or prosody. Anne Bradstreet was, by historical accounts, a happily married, deeply religious woman, devoted to her husband and children, who happened to write poetry. Berryman needed for his poem a passionately suffering artist, plagued by religious doubt, resentful of her husband and family, thwarted in her dream of artistic commitment, so he altered the historical Bradstreet to suit his purposes. This reshaping of history is necessary for the centerpiece of the poem—a seduction scene between a modern poet and a woman three hundred years buried. In an understandably surrealistic dialogue, the poet speaks his love for the poor, tormented Anne in a rather far-fetched variation of the designing rake's "Let me take you away from all this." Bradstreet (Berryman's, that is) is tempted to religious doubt, to extramarital dalliance (she *does* ask the poet for a kiss), to despair over her misunderstood lot. Her domestic commitments, however, overrule her temptations, and the poem ends with the modern poet standing before Bradstreet's grave and uttering words that are supposed to be touching and solemn, but which somehow fail to convince:

I must pretend to leave you . . . O all your ages at the
    mercy of my loves
together lie at once, forever or
so long as I happen.
In the rain of pain & departure, still
Love has no body and presides the sun . . . Hover, utter,
    still
a sourcing whom my lost candle like the firefly loves.

The rhyming of "still" with itself is a nice touch, and "the rain of pain & departure" rings true, but the passage has a disturbing, self-conscious quality that is not at all helped by a reference, in one of the closing stanzas, to contemporary (post-World War II) anxieties—"races murder, foxholes hold men,/reactor piles wage slow upon the wet brain rime."

The foregoing summary oversimplifies and leaves much unsaid. In all fairness, there are a good many brilliant moments in Berryman's poem, but, as a whole, *Homage to Mistress Bradstreet* is somewhat less than brilliant. John Frederick Nims, reviewing the poem in *The Prairie Schooner*, termed it a "gallant failure," finding it "magnificent and absurd, mature and adolescent, grave and hysterical, meticulous and slovenly." In the end, his major complaint is that the poem,

> purportedly concerned with Anne Bradstreet . . . is really about "the poet" himself, his romantic and exacerbated personality, his sense of loneliness, his need for a mistress, confidante, confessor. One might think there would be more satisfactory candidates for the triple role among the living.

Nims's position is persuasively put and strikes at the heart of what is wrong with *Homage to Mistress Bradstreet*. Rather than conveying any true homage to this first American poet, Berryman lets his own personality, his own needs and concerns, dominate the stage, to the extent that the Bradstreet of his poem becomes a just version of himself. Far from "escaping personality," to recall Eliot's term, Berryman forces Bradstreet into the mold of his own personality.

THE DREAM SONGS

From "Berryman" of the sonnets, to "the poet" of *Homage to Mistress Bradstreet*, Berryman moved on to "Henry," the narrator and protagonist of *The Dream Songs*, the sequence of 385 poems that is considered to be his major work. Berryman apparently began with the notion of writing another long poem, about as long as Hart Crane's *The Bridge* (1930). What resulted, however, was something closer to Ezra Pound's *Cantos* (1925-1972). At the center of the poems is a character known variously as Henry House, Henry Cat, Pussycat, and Mr. Bones. Within flexibly formal songs of three sestets apiece, Berryman reveals Henry's trials and sufferings, which in many cases are the reader's as well. Too often, however, the songs are about Berryman.

There is real feeling in *The Dream Songs*. Too much suffering, however, spread not at all thinly over seven thousand lines and interspersed with proportionately more of the same sort of name-dropping and private allusion encountered in the sonnets, becomes oppressive and even boring. There are wonderful moments, notably in the elegies for dead friends—Jarrell, Schwartz, Sylvia Plath. The obsession with suicide that laces many of the poems is lent a special poignance when considered in the light of Berryman's father's, then his own, suicide. Not surprisingly, Henry's father took his life when he was young. Still, readers must be very interested in Berryman as a person to wade through these 385 poems, for Berryman is once again the center of attention, the "star" of his own epic, despite his coy disclaimer that Henry is "not the poet, not me."

In his continuing inability to distance himself sufficiently from his poetry, Berryman places the reader in an awkward position. In *The Personal Heresy: A Controversy* (1939), C. S. Lewis describes the necessity of keeping one's response to a poem separate from one's response to the personality of the poet, a task that Berryman makes unfairly difficult. When readers mix the two, says Lewis, they offend both poet and poem. "Is there, in social life," he asks, "a grosser incivility than that of thinking about the man who addresses us instead of thinking about what he says?" No, says Lewis, "We must go to books for that which books can give us—to be interested, delighted, or amused, to be made merry or to be made wise." As for personalities, living or dead, the response should be some "species of love," be it "veneration, pity," or something in between.

Berryman's personality is hard to love, easier to pity, but what is truly to be pitied is the fact that, had his skills as a poet been a match for his troubled personality, he would without question have been one of the greatest poets of his time.

OTHER MAJOR WORKS

LONG FICTION: *Recovery*, 1973.

NONFICTION: *Stephen Crane*, 1950; *The Arts of Reading*, 1960 (with Ralph Ross and Allen Tate); *The*

Freedom of the Poet, 1976; *We Dream of Honour: John Berryman's Letters to His Mother*, 1988.

MISCELLANEOUS: *The Unfortunate Traveller: Or, The Life of Jack Wilton*, 1960 (edited text).

BIBLIOGRAPHY

Bloom, Harold, ed. *John Berryman: Modern Critical Views*. New York: Chelsea House, 1989. Collects twelve critical essays on Berryman's poetry, representing a variety of approaches. Contains a good index, a chronology, and a bibliography.

Conarroe, Joel. *John Berryman: An Introduction to the Poetry*. Columbia Introductions to Twentieth Century American Poetry. New York: Columbia University Press, 1977. Written after Berryman's death but before his unpublished writings were made available to scholars, this study presents a brief biography followed by insightful explications of representative poems.

Haffenden, John. *John Berryman: A Critical Commentary*. New York: New York University Press, 1980. This rather dense study examines Berryman's major poetry, showing the connections between Berryman's personal and poetic challenges. Although students may find this work difficult, they will be enlightened by the extensive reproductions of Berryman's drafts, notes, and diary entries. Includes a composition chronology and an index.

_____. *The Life of John Berryman*. Boston: Routledge & Kegan Paul, 1982. This long and sometimes difficult volume draws heavily on Berryman's unpublished diaries, letters, and notes to tell the story of the poet's life from his father's suicide to his own. The contrast between Berryman's artistic successes and personal failures is at the center of this unblinking biography.

_____, ed. *Berryman's Shakespeare: Essays, Letters, and Other Writings by John Berryman*. New York: Farrar, Strauss, and Giroux, 1999. In this collection of Berryman's best short writings on Shakespeare, he explores the complex power of England's greatest dramatist and how knowledge of his work might be enlarged. An intimate, intricate view of Shakespeare's work.

Halliday, E. M. *John Berryman and the Thirties: A Memoir.* Amherst: University of Massachusetts Press, 1987. A close friend of Berryman, Halliday presents his recollections of his friendship with Berryman from 1933 to 1943. An account of college life in the 1930's, glimpses of other writers, and excerpts from Berryman's letters to Halliday make this a touching and fascinating memoir.

Hirsch, Edward. "One Life, One Writing! The Middle Generation." *The American Poetry Review* 29, no. 5 (September/October, 2000): 11-16. The quest for identity is a key theme in the poetry of Randall Jarrell, Elizabeth Bishop, Robert Lowell, Delmore Schwartz, Theodore Roethke, and John Berrymore. Hirsch examines their poetry and finds in each a deep sympathy, an attentive regard, an overwhelming and overwhelmed reverence for all living things.

Linebarger, J. M. *John Berryman.* New York: Twayne, 1974. After a brief biographical chapter, Linebarger examines Berryman's poetry, dividing it into four periods. This fine introduction to Berryman's work is perhaps the best available for the common reader. The volume includes a chronology, an annotated bibliography, and an index, but contains few quotations from the poetry.

Mariani, Paul. *Dream Song: The Life of John Berryman.* New York: William Morrow, 1990. This highly readable biography conveys at every point Mariani's admiration for Berryman. As he traces Berryman's brilliant and tragic life, Mariani does not flinch from what was unattractive about the poet. Instead, he describes with respect Berryman's struggles to overcome his weaknesses. Includes extensive quotations from letters, essays, and poems, and numerous photographs.

Thomas, Harry. *Berryman's Understanding: Reflections on the Poetry of John Berryman.* Boston: Northeastern University Press, 1988. A collection of critical essays, reviews, interviews, and memoirs. Covers the canonical criticism of Berryman's work and the uses of that criticism to document the ongoing work of intelligent, imaginative reading.

*Richard A. Eichwald;
bibliography updated by the editors*

JOHN BETJEMAN

Born: London, England; August 28, 1906
Died: Trebetherick, Cornwall, England; May 19, 1984

PRINCIPAL POETRY
Mount Zion: Or, In Touch with the Infinite, 1931
Continual Dew: A Little Book of Bourgeois Verse, 1937
Old Lights for New Chancels: Verses Topographical and Amatory, 1940
Slick but Not Streamlined, 1947 (W. H. Auden, editor)
Selected Poems, 1948 (John Sparrow, editor)
A Few Late Chrysanthemums, 1954
Poems in the Porch, 1954
Collected Poems, 1958, 3d ed. 1970 (as *John Betjeman's Collected Poems*)
Summoned by Bells, 1960
A Ring of Bells, 1962 (Irene Slade, editor)
High and Low, 1966
A Nip in the Air, 1974
Ten Late Chrysanthemums, 1975
Uncollected Poems, 1982

OTHER LITERARY FORMS

Hand in hand with John Betjeman's lifelong commitment to poetry went an equal dedication to the preservation of the best of English architecture, particularly that of the nineteenth century. Throughout his life, he was intent upon opening the eyes of the public to the glories of Victorian architecture, and he and his friends John Piper (the painter) and Osbert Lancaster (the cartoonist) pursued this cause with such dedication and enthusiasm that they have probably done more to influence public taste in this area than anyone since John Ruskin. Such overriding interest in the quality of modern urban life, and, more specifically, its aesthetic excellence or excesses, is to be seen again and again in Betjeman's prose.

In 1933, soon after publication of his first volume of verse, he published *Ghastly Good Taste: Or, A Depressing Story of the Rise and Fall of English Architecture.*

This work was followed in 1944 by *John Piper*, and then, in the 1950's and early 1960's, a spate of books on landscape and architecture (listed below) as well as various Shell Guides: *First and Last Loves*, essays on architecture (1952); *The English Town in the Last Hundred Years* (1956); *Collins' Guide to English Parish Churches* (1958); *English Churches* (1964, with B. F. L. Clarke). *Betjeman's Cornwall* was published in 1984. He also edited a number of anthologies that illustrate his interests, including *English, Scottish, and Welsh Landscape* (1944), a collection of poetry edited with Geoffrey Taylor; he also collaborated with Taylor in editing *English Love Poems* (1957). In 1959, *Altar and Pew: Church of England Verses*, edited by Betjeman, was published, and in 1963 *A Wealth of Poetry*, edited with Winifred Hudley, was issued.

Betjeman was also an accomplished and sometimes inspired broadcaster, whether reading his own poems or describing and discussing architecture, and, for the most part, he wrote his own scripts. Unfortunately, none of his broadcasts has been published in book form, although such a book would probably prove to be as popular as his poetry and essays.

ACHIEVEMENTS

John Betjeman's most notable though least tangible achievement was to make poetry accessible once more to the reading public. Until the publication of his *Collected Poems* in 1958, he was largely unknown; the publication of this volume by John Murray proved to be something of a literary phenomenon. Compiled and with an introduction by the earl of Birkenhead, it sold so quickly that it had to be reprinted three times within the month. It has been said that in the history of the John Murray publishing firm, nothing like it had been known since the publication of George Gordon, Lord Byron's *Childe Harold's Pilgrimage* in 1812, when copies were sold to a clamoring crowd through the windows of the publisher's house on Albemarle Street. The most recent poetic success of unparalleled magnitude was that of Alfred, Lord Tennyson in the mid-nineteenth century. So far-reaching was the effect of the publication of this volume that in 1959, when applicants interviewed for entry into an English School at a modern university were asked to name a modern poet, it is said that they would

automatically answer "Betjeman." Prior to this, the most popular answer had been "T. S. Eliot."

It is impossible to explain fully the wide appeal of Betjeman's poetry. At the time it came to the fore, the Movement poets (Philip Larkin, John Wain, Kingsley Amis, and others, to be found in D. J. Enright's 1955 anthology *Poets of the 1950's*) were engaged in a philosophical reaction against the neo-Romanticism of the 1940's, typified by the vogue for the work of Edith Sitwell and the Dylan Thomas cult which emerged after that gifted writer's death in America in 1953.

It must have been extremely galling for these poets, engaged in stringent academic opposition to the tyranny of the iambic pentameter and attempting to purge poetry of the lush metaphor and hyperbole of neo-Romanticism, to witness the meteoric rise to fame of a poet such as Betjeman. It is still true that a taste for Betjeman's poetry is regarded with suspicion in some academic and intellectual circles. John Wain, for example, gave voice to a ponderous and unfavorable judgment of Betjeman's verse autobiography *Summoned by Bells* when it was published in 1960, and when Philip Larkin, perhaps the best known of the Movement poets, expressed his own admiration for Betjeman's poetry, he too was greeted with disapprobation. Nevertheless, Betjeman's poetry continued to outsell that of others.

It may be that Betjeman's poetic contemporaries have regarded Betjeman with suspicion and dislike because of the force of an argument advanced by Robert Graves in his idiosyncratic but fascinating book *The Crowning Privilege* (1955)—that is, that poetry is not in itself commercial, so that poetry books which sell do not truly contain poetry. It may also be that the overwhelming success of a poet with an instantly recognizable poetic voice, who lauds and celebrates the mores of a way of life which has virtually vanished in the face of the inexorable march of progress, is not thought to be seemly by more stringent and muscular writers.

Whatever the reasons for Betjeman's success and the scant respect with which his work is sometimes treated by more "serious" poets, there is no doubt that he was extensively honored, not only by the literary establishment but also by the country's ruling elite, by professional and academic bodies, and by an abiding public recognition and popularity.

His *Selected Poems* won the Heinemann Award; he also won the Foyle Poetry Prize twice, the Duff Cooper Prize, and the Queen's Gold Medal for Poetry. He was a member of the Royal Commission on Historical Monuments in England from 1970 until 1976. He was made an Honorary Fellow of Keble College, Oxford, in 1972, and of Magdalen College, Oxford, in 1975. He was also an honorary LL.D. of the University of Aberdeen, an Honorary Litt.D. of the Universities of Oxford, Reading, Birmingham, Exeter, Liverpool, Hull, and of City University, and an Honorary Associate of the Royal Institute of British Architects (ARIBA).

In 1960, he was awarded a CBE, followed by a C.Lit. in 1968; in 1969, he was knighted; and in 1972 he became poet laureate, that is, official court poet, responsible for writing poems for state occasions such as the investiture of the prince of Wales and the marriage of the prince of Wales to the Lady Diana Spencer. As poet laureate, he followed such distinguished practitioners of the art as William Wordsworth, Alfred, Lord Tennyson, and John Masefield.

Betjeman restored the status of poetry to a level where people who would never normally consider opening a book of verse were actually prevailed upon to pay for the privilege of reading his work. When William Wordsworth (with Samuel Taylor Coleridge) published *Lyrical Ballads* in 1798, his expressed intention was to restore the status of the poet to that of "a man speaking to men," as well as to "exalt and transfigure the natural and the common." More than a hundred years later, with no publicity and no stated poetic philosophy, John Betjeman succeeded in both of those aims—perhaps unconsciously, but undeniably.

BIOGRAPHY

John Betjeman was one of those poets who are profoundly affected by their childhood environment. He was born in London in the early years of the twentieth century, into a class-ridden society, where even small differences in income were important in measuring a family's neighborhood status. This would probably have passed unnoticed had Betjeman been a less observant and sensitive child. As it is, although it is obvious from his poetry that none of the finer nuances of middle-class snobbishness escaped his eye, it is unclear whether these

small cruelties were profoundly hurtful or whether the objectivity of the artist was already sufficiently developed to protect him. Certainly there is no bitterness in his poetry, so probably the latter explanation is the correct one. He recounts many of the events of his early life in *Summoned by Bells*, transporting the reader back in time to an England reminiscent of the world depicted by Arthur Conan Doyle, Edith Nesbit, and John Galsworthy.

After leaving Oxford without attaining a degree, Betjeman supported himself by teaching, while continuing to write both poetry and topographical essays. In *Summoned by Bells*, he states quite clearly that as soon as he could read and write he knew that he must strive to become a poet. Despite the disappointment that he caused his father by refusing to take his place in the family business, he was always true to that early ambition.

He married in 1933 and had a son and a daughter, although domestic considerations are not of primary importance in his work. His sense of place and his eye for the eccentricities of the English character were far more important to him.

Betjeman was named poet laureate in 1972. Although the post is bestowed as an accolade, it was probably a strain for a craftsman-poet such as Betjeman to have been expected to produce odes and hymns to order. He never found inspiration in the machinations of the higher echelons of humankind, but rather in the idiosyncrasies of its middle ranks. When he entered his seventies and was afflicted by ill health, he was no longer able to write as freely as he once had. Betjeman died in Trebetherick, Cornwall, in 1984. It is to be hoped that his later work, which cannot be judged as anywhere near his best, is not allowed to obscure the very real value and artistic achievement of his most productive middle years.

ANALYSIS

It is somehow appropriate that the first item in the 1958 volume of John Betjeman's *Collected Poems* should be "Death in Leamington," for this poem touches upon many of the themes which preoccupied him. Although he has been sometimes accused of facility, both because of the traditional rhyme and rhythms of his work and because of his tendency to stress the light-hearted and humorous, it soon becomes obvious to the reader that he was as aware of "the skull beneath the skin" as any apparently more serious writer.

DEATH THEME

"Death in Leamington" deals with the death of an elderly person in the subdued atmosphere of an unfashionable English spa town, at a time when the town is almost as dead as the ostensible subject of the poem. The title is ambiguous, as is much of Betjeman's work. He equates the death of a person, and even of a generation, with the death and decay of their surroundings and traditions, and it is clear that he laments the passing of both.

For a poet who is often referred to as "lighthearted" and "humorous," he is surprisingly often to be found writing on the subject of death. Indeed, in his introduction to Betjeman's *Collected Poems*, the Earl of Birkenhead compares him in this respect with Samuel Johnson. "On a Portrait of a Deaf Man," "Before the Anaesthetic: Or, A Real Fright," "Exeter," "Inevitable," "N. W. 5 & N. 6," and "Saint Cadoc" are only a few of the other poems in which he touches upon various aspects of man's attitude toward his own mortality.

A particularly striking poem on this theme is "The Heart of Thomas Hardy," which is written with a degree of bathos and black humor. It describes the heart of Thomas Hardy as "a little thumping fig," a flight of poetic fancy which in itself should serve to ensure Betjeman's literary immortality. He goes on to describe the Mayor of Casterbridge, Jude the Obscure, Tess of the D'Urbervilles, and other products of Hardy's imagination coming to life and leaving their graves to confront their creator in the chancel of Stinsford Church. The poem is something of a literary joke, but it also illustrates Betjeman's interest in the supernatural. There are several other ghosts and eerie incidents described in his poetry, notably in "A Lincolnshire Tale" and the "Sir John Piers" poem sequence, the latter being among the finest in Betjeman's canon.

It would be wholly wrong to place too much emphasis on this darker side of Betjeman's work—indeed, many critics deal with it by the simple expedient of ignoring it; thus they feel justified in dismissing Betjeman as a nostalgic, sentimental apologist for a vanished

Empire-building middle class. To achieve a balanced view of his work, however, it is necessary to explore all of his primary themes, and it is undeniable that there is a somber thread in the fabric of his work.

A LIGHTHEARTED ATTRACTION TO WOMEN

Of course it would be equally wrong to ignore the lighter side of his poetry, especially when that is probably what initially attracts the casual reader to Betjeman's writing. The most frequently anthologized of his poems are those which describe his attraction toward large, athletic women—Miss Joan Hunter Dunn (in "A Subaltern's Love-Song"), Pam (in "Pot Pourri from a Surrey Garden"), and Myfanwy (in "Myfanwy" and "Myfanwy at Oxford"). These ideal women and his attitude toward them come together in "The Olympic Girl," where, after eulogizing at some length this perfect and unattainable young woman, he concludes sadly: "Little, alas, to you I mean,/ For I am bald and old and green." This sentiment, in various forms, appears ever more often in Betjeman's work and strikes a distinctly Prufrockian note. At first glance, T. S. Eliot and Betjeman seem to have little in common; in the early Betjeman, however, it is possible to detect an awareness of Eliot; for example, "Clash Went the Billiard Balls" is very reminiscent of the concluding section of "A Game of Chess" from *The Waste Land* (1922), and Betjeman's personae frequently recall "The Love Song of J. Alfred Prufrock."

CHARACTERS OF EXPERIENCE

Eliot's smoky, desolate urban landscapes are not so far removed from Betjeman's "Slough," or even from his "Middlesex." Nor are Betjeman's delicately observed characters so far removed from Eliot's less personal portraits. The difference is, perhaps, that Eliot's characters are observed, while Betjeman's are experienced. It certainly takes much more intellectual effort to come to terms with Eliot, and perhaps this effort exerts a distancing effect upon the reader, maintaining a welcome emotional detachment. It is much more difficult to maintain detachment from Betjeman's work. He was not a poet much given to analysis and metaphysical themes. Perhaps that is why he is often ignored by critics; they may admit to enjoying his poetry but are unprepared to acknowledge that in writing poetry which is comprehensible, and also of consistently high quality, he has achieved anything worthwhile.

NATURE POEMS

Because Betjeman was often to be heard giving broadcasts and lectures on architecture and aspects of the British countryside which were especially dear to him, he is perhaps most commonly thought of as a "nature," or, more specifically, a "landscape" poet. Yet he was not a nature poet in the Wordsworthian sense. Where he excelled was in his ability to express his delight in a particular area and a particular type of scenery, and to convey that delight to the reader. "Ireland with Emily" is an excellent example of this strain in his work; it is a poem which evokes country life in southern Ireland brilliantly, as, in a different mood, does "A Lament for Moira McCavendish." "Matlock Bath," from the collection *High and Low*, is another such poem, describing life in the nonconformist industrial Midlands of England. In other poems he describes the Cornish coast and various parts of London, especially those areas near Highgate, where he spent his childhood and about which he writes at length in his verse autobiography, *Summoned by Bells*.

HUMOR AS SATIRE

It is impossible to discuss the work of John Betjeman fully without reference to his humor, yet a laborious treatment of this topic is the easiest way of rendering the humor itself ineffective and unfunny. Suffice to say that much of Betjeman's poetry has a considerable element of humor, but that it would be wrong to regard him as merely a funny writer. His humor always has a purpose, and often, as in "A Lincolnshire Tale," he uses humor for special effect, combining it with a degree of the macabre to make the reader chuckle and then shudder.

His best-known and most anthologized poems, such as "Hunter Trials" and "How to Get on in Society," are those which satirize various easily recognizable aspects of English middle-class life. "How to Get on in Society" covers much the same ground as Nancy Mitford does in *Noblesse Oblige* (1956)—that is, the distinction between "U" (university) and "non-U." The speaker in the poem is distinctly "non-U," but with "U" aspirations. Betjeman cleverly picks up all the social and linguistic pointers and strings them together to create a picture of a type of person in a social milieu recognizable to the English reader; yet he does so through only a few simple lines of conversation. Of course the poem is very much of its time; language change constantly, and such a poem written today

would obviously have very different nuances. The same is not true of "Hunter Trials," which applies as much to horse-mad little girls now as it did when it was written.

SEX AND LOVE

Betjeman was always interested in social distinctions—"Group Life: Letchworth" is an earlier example of his keen eye for the extreme and the ridiculous. It concludes with a reference to the cult of free love which flourished in some sections of English society, apparently in the wake of D. H. Lawrence. It has been suggested that Betjeman had a very ambivalent attitude toward sex, being able to deal with it effectively in his work only by making it funny. Leaving aside the thought that often the antics of human beings in love are very amusing to the detached observer, it seems unfair to dismiss Betjeman's subtleties so lightly. In "Group Life: Letchworth," he satirizes one aspect of the English attitude toward sexuality. In "Indoor Games near Newbury," he deals with a quite different, pre-sexual love, and in "Beside the Seaside," the agony of adolescent love. Later, in such poems as "Senex" and "Late Flowering Lust," he takes an ironic, sometimes metaphysical look at the immutability of emotions as the flesh ages. He touches the same topic in "Sun and Fun," and it is part of his strength that he maintains his integrity of tone whether writing about a view he admires or a state of affairs which he obviously deplores. This is possibly why some critics seem to disapprove when he strays from the more familiar descriptive and social poetry to write about emotions. Critics are as likely to be alarmed by change as anyone else, but there is no need to think that change is necessarily always for the worse. In Betjeman's case, he merely showed that he could write about most things with skill, insight, and sympathy.

LEGACY

It is difficult to assess the achievement of Betjeman, who had great public success yet remained outside the mainstream of English poetry. Unlike Eliot or Dylan Thomas, Betjeman inspired no school of poets who either imitate or react unfavorably to him. Yet he is widely read and admired, both by the general public (many of whom would never consider reading poetry if it were not for Betjeman) and by other poets. As Kenneth Allott has pointed out in *The Penguin Book of Contemporary Verse* (1962), a poet who won the admiration of W. H. Auden in one poetic generation and of Philip Larkin in another may well rest content. What is certain is that Betjeman's was a strong and individual poetic voice, whose influence, by virtue of his very popularity, has been far-reaching. Reading his work must make readers aware of both the beauties which surround them and the influences which conspire to threaten those beauties. To speak of the morality of art is to venture onto dangerous ground, yet in writing skillfully in a way which encourages readers to view humankind with tolerance and understanding, and the environment with respect, Betjeman must be thought of as a good poet in both senses of the word.

OTHER MAJOR WORKS

NONFICTION: *Ghastly Good Taste: Or, A Depressing Story of the Rise and Fall of English Architecture*, 1933; *John Piper*, 1944; *First and Last Loves*, 1952; *The English Town in the Last Hundred Years*, 1956; *Collins' Guide to English Parish Churches*, 1958; *English Churches*, 1964 (with B. F. L. Clarke); *Betjeman's Cornwall*, 1984; *John Betjeman: Letters*, 1994-1995 (2 volumes); *John Betjeman: Coming Home*, 1997.

EDITED TEXTS: *English, Scottish, and Welsh Landscape*, 1944 (with Geoffrey Taylor); *English Love Poems*, 1957 (with Taylor); *Altar and Pew: Church of England Verses*, 1959; *A Wealth of Poetry*, 1963 (with Winifred Hudley).

BIBLIOGRAPHY

Betjeman, John. *Letters*. Edited by Candida Lycett Green. 2 vols. London: Methuen, 1994. This comprehensive collection reveals many intimate details about the life of John Betjeman, including the depth of his affection for his friends, his religious sentiment, and his relationship with his wife and Elizabeth Cavendish. Covers letters written between 1926 and 1984.

Delany, Frank. *Betjeman Country*. London: John Murray, 1983. This remarkable travel book combines biographical commentary on Betjeman with excerpts from the poet's poems and numerous photographs of the places connected with the poems of Betjeman. Includes a primary bibliography.

Harvey, Geoffrey. "John Betjeman: An Odeon Flashes Fire." In *The Romantic Tradition in Modern British Poetry*. New York: St. Martin's Press, 1986. This provocative, informative study rejects the assessment of Betjeman as a minor establishment poet. Harvey views him as a "consistently subversive force in modern verse"—a committed writer mindful of a real audience.

McDermott, John V. "Betjeman's 'The Arrest of Oscar Wilde at the Cadogan Hotel.'" *The Explicator* 57, no. 3 (Spring, 1999): 165-166. McDermott argues that Betjeman's poem, which seems at first to be a singular assault on the character of Oscar Wilde but proceeds, by subtle implication, to condemn the society that held Wilde up to scorn.

Press, John. *John Betjeman*. London: Longman, 1974. This monograph, an excellent introduction to Betjeman, includes concise sections on his life, his prose works, and his poetry: themes and character, the shorter poems, and the poet's autobiographical poem *Summoned by Bells*. Supplemented by a select bibliography that emphasizes primary works and a three-quarter-page photograph.

Taylor-Martin, Patrick. *John Betjeman: His Life and Work*. London: Allen Lane, 1983. This excellent study of Betjeman is a useful balance of critical commentary and biography. Taylor-Martin views Betjeman as a serious writer, not a light versifier. The text is supplemented by a select bibliography—primary texts, secondary books, and articles—and a list of his recordings. No index.

Tolley, A. J. "The Old Order and the New: Louis MacNeice and John Betjeman." In *The Poetry of the Thirties*. New York: St. Martin's Press, 1975. This useful study examines the poet's collections published in the 1930's, measuring Betjeman against Louis MacNeice and other poets of the 1930's. Tolley's views on the tone of Betjeman's poetry are particularly insightful.

Vestey, Michael. "Betjeman Recalled." *The Spectator* 278, no. 8793 (February 8, 1997): 52-53. Vestey reminisces about an interview with Betjeman, which took place in the 1970's. The article follows on the heels of a Radio Two program, *Softly Croons the Radiogram*, in which Betjeman's collaboration with composer Jim Parker to set his poetry to music was discussed.

Vivien Stableford;
bibliography updated by the editors

FRANK BIDART

Born: Bakersfield, California; May 27, 1939

PRINCIPAL POETRY

Golden State, 1973
The Book of the Body, 1977
The Sacrifice, 1983
In the Western Night: Collected Poems, 1965-1990, 1990
Desire, 1997

OTHER LITERARY FORMS

Frank Bidart is known primarily for his poetry. He also coedited the monumental *Collected Poems of Robert Lowell* (2001).

ACHIEVEMENTS

Deeply engaged in the moral issues of both personal and cultural guilt, Frank Bidart's poetry has won praise for the intensity with which it documents the struggle between the limits imposed by the body and the ideals envisioned by the mind. In 1981, Bidart won the *Paris Review*'s first Bernard F. Conner Prize for his long poem "The War of Vaslav Nijinsky." This extended dramatic monologue highlights Bidart's unique talents: an unsettling insight into the psychology of guilt and anger, a singular style of narrative poetry based on abstract speech with little reliance on traditional poetic devices, and a thematic focus on the suffering occasioned by humankind's ambiguous intermixture of body and spirit. In 1998, *Desire* won both the Bobbitt Prize given by the Library of Congress and the Theodore Roethke Memorial Prize. Bidart's work has also won him the Shelley Award of the Poetry Society of America (1997), the Lannan Literary Award (1998), and the Wallace Stevens Award of the Academy of American Poets (2000).

BIOGRAPHY

Frank Leon Bidart, Jr., was born in 1939 in Bakersfield, California, where he grew up, in his words, "obsessed with his parents." After he was graduated from the University of California at Riverside, he attended graduate school at Harvard University. He formed a close relationship with poet Robert Lowell while residing in Cambridge, Massachusetts, and soon after began to write poetry with a style and content distinctive from those of his illustrious mentor. Bidart settled in Cambridge to undertake a teaching career at Wellesley College.

ANALYSIS

Frank Bidart's poetry is decidedly original in style and content. Thematically, his work resembles confessional poetry, since it is obsessed with the family drama along with the attendant guilt and longing for forgiveness. Like Robert Lowell's groundbreaking *Life Studies* (1959), Bidart's poetry abounds with autobiographical revelations of sexual perversion and neurotic family dynamics; like Lowell, Bidart develops personae that dramatically present these topics with an excruciating anguish that often borders on insanity. Unlike Lowell, however, Bidart presents the guilt and suffering of the mind embedded in the raging emotions and chaotic desires of the body with singular directness.

Whereas Lowell's poetic style has a rhetorical eloquence fashioned from the New Critical techniques of irony, fragmentation, and detailed imagery, Bidart's develops directly from an impassioned narrative voice that is abstract rather than particular, flatly prosaic rather than rhythmically colloquial. In Bidart's poetry, the line breaks and the idiosyncratic punctuation function to reproduce the "pauses, emphases, urgencies and languors in the voice." Often the syntax is complex; sometimes sentences stretch over a page or more and are rife with qualifications and contradictions, all signs of an active mind that, though speaking with the eloquence of polite, educated conversation, is in the grip of strong emotion. Bidart's dependence on an articulate, abstract style risks prosaic blandness, but the reward is a remarkably faithful fastening of his distinctive voice to the page.

GOLDEN STATE

Bidart's first collection, *Golden State*, begins with the poem "Herbert White," a dramatic monologue prefiguring the thematic focus on insanity and morality in his prizewinning poem "The War of Vaslav Nijinsky," published ten years later in *The Sacrifice*. At first the eponymous narrator of "Herbert White" views his murder and rape of a young child as morally justifiable because the act comes from a unity of body and desire: "When I hit her on the head, it was good." From this point of view, however, life is "without sharpness, richness or line." Only when White splits his awareness from his physical desires does suffering, and hence morality, commence:

> —Hell came when I saw
>   MYSELF . . .
>   and couldn't stand
> what I see. . . .

Coordinate with White's separation from and feeling of revulsion for the body and natural processes is the advent of Bidart's characteristic stylistic devices. Before the foregoing lines occur, the verse in "Herbert White" is irregular, but when the narrator's split consciousness focuses on the agony of parental rejection, the gnawing guilt of his familial relationships, his sexual perversity, and the suffering occasioned by his body's unbridled instincts, the line breaks become directly reflective of emotional urgency and certain words, such as "MYSELF," are capitalized in order to reproduce the sonic dynamics of impassioned speech. Significantly, the suffering and the guilt cannot be ameliorated by appeal to a higher plane of understanding such as that normally supplied by religion. Devoid of absolutes, the narrator's voice exists only in the domain of his suffering, a voice universalized by the sound, grammar, and vocabulary of the relentless anguish of self-awareness.

The autobiographical poem "Golden State" reveals one of the sources of the emotional distress pervading Bidart's poetry: his father, a millionaire farmer described in the poem as "the unhappiest man/ I have ever known well." The father's unhappiness results not only from his pathetic desire to be a film star, cowboy, or empire builder but also from a "radical disaffection/ from the very possibilities/ of human life." Disconnected from himself and from his family, the father demonstrates to the poet that the search for connections is both initiated and frustrated by the family:

>   The exacerbation
> of this seeming *necessity*
> for connection—;
>   you and mother taught me

there's little that's redemptive or useful
in natural affections. . . .

Bidart is subject to the compelling human need to make something—some meaning, some pattern—out of these natural affections, but he finds little assistance from the conventional means toward establishing a relationship between his life and a larger realm of understanding. In section 4 of "Golden State," Bidart considers and rejects the efficacy of what his education has given him as an aid to understanding the mysterious hold his father wields on his innermost being: "the lies/ of mere, neat poetry"; his readings of Carl Jung that "never get to the bottom/ of what is, or was"; and the very "patterns and paradigms" of his Harvard studies that are rendered effete by his father's sarcasm, "How are all these bastards at Harvard?" Mere objective insight is rejected in section 5, and section 7 demonstrates the inadequacy of psychiatry to effect a reconciliation between the son and his memories of his dead father. Prayer is discovered to be ineffective in section 8. Only by entering into the words of his poem "to become not merely/ a speaker, the 'eye,' but a character" can Bidart represent the actual shape of his inner life. It is precisely in order to represent his inner life that Bidart has developed poetic techniques that eschew the artificiality of traditional prosody, with its dependence on meter, metaphor, image, and irony. Bidart's poetry demands directness, a physical entering of the self into the poem, an embodiment, that reifies the relentless agony and violence of human experience.

THE BOOK OF THE BODY

The Book of the Body, Bidart's next collection of poetry, presents the poet's sheer disgust at having to enter aesthetically into "the stump-filled material world// things; bodies;/ CRAP." These lines are from the first poem of the book, titled "The Arc," which sets the collection's pervasive tone of physical laceration (the poem's narrator has lost his arm as a result of a senseless accident) and bodily anxiety ("I'm/ embarrassed to take my shirt off"). An arc could geometrically be part of the unity of a circle, but in this poem an arc is seen as irremediably cut off from wholeness, as is the arm of the amputee-narrator; it is an unredeemed segment of time, like a person's life bounded by its birth date and death date between parentheses. Unable to transcend the suffering of his limited physical existence, the narrator can achieve only the equivocal resolution of contemplating "how Paris is still the city of Louis XVI and/ Robespierre, how blood, amputation, and rubble// give her dimension, resonance, and grace."

Having explored his obsession with his father in *Golden State*, Bidart now turns to his mother in the poem "Elegy." References to laceration abound: the chewing done by his mother's pet dog Belafont, his mother's reply of "gelding" to the narrator's ambition to become a priest, a love affair that leads to abortion, the envisioning of death and memory as "a razor-blade without a handle." Especially interesting is the interconnection made between being cut off from a satisfying relationship with his mother as well as himself and discussions of impotent mouths and mutilated breasts. When dreaming of the dog Belafont, the narrator recalls how the dog attempted to kiss him, but "carefully avoiding the mouth, as/ taught." In the section grotesquely entitled "Pruning," his mother exclaims, "I'd rather die than let them/ take off a breast." Mouths that cannot make contact, breasts that are threatened with excision indicate a lack of connection with the physical world as matter, "mother."

A morbid rejection of matter and of eating, an act that implicates the self in matter, forms a large portion of the theme of Bidart's great dramatic monologue from *The Book of the Body*, "Ellen West." Assuming the mask of the anorectic Ellen West, Bidart dramatizes how acquiring a body that is the image of the soul necessitates destroying that very body. To West, food is inextricably entangled with sex, death, and the material world:

> Even as a child,
> I saw that the "natural" process of aging
> is for one's middle to thicken—
> one's skin to blotch;
>
> as happened to my mother.
> And her mother.
> *I loathed "Nature."*

Only by opposing the body—as, in the poem, did Maria Callas, the great opera singer, when she drastically trimmed her once-ample body by sixty pounds, illustrat-

ing how her soul "loved eating the flesh from her bones"—can an ideal approaching great art be realized. Such an art records the unending struggle of the spirit to embody and manifest itself in a medium that it finds repulsive. Finally, each attempt to reconcile the body and the spirit heightens a hunger that neither food nor ink, the food of art, can satisfy. At the end of the poem, West poisons her body to achieve the ideal self that the world has sought to poison through food.

THE SACRIFICE

Although Ellen West sacrifices her body for an ideal in "Ellen West," that ideal cannot be directly embodied in art, for art as physical representation partakes of the body, not the soul. What can be recorded is the struggle itself, the sacrifice—and that is the central theme of Bidart's next book, *The Sacrifice*.

One of the major poems in *The Sacrifice*, "Confessional," extends the thematic conflict of an earlier poem centered on Bidart's mother, "Elegy." In "Confessional," the body, the material world, presents a terrain on which it is impossible for mother and son to find harmony, for in the physical world dwell anger and unredeemable guilt occasioned by Bidart's memory of his childhood predatory wish to supplant both his father and his stepfather in his mother's affections, a situation exacerbated by the mother's excessive emotional dependence on him when he was a child. In an extreme contrast to the condition between the poet and his mother, sections from *The Confessions of Saint Augustine* (c. 397-400) that depict the relationship between Saint Augustine and his mother, Monica, constitute a major portion of the poem. Like Bidart in his childhood, Augustine supplanted his own father to the extent that Monica wished to be buried next to him, not her husband. The unbridgeable gap between Augustine and his mother, on one hand, and Bidart and his mother, on the other, results from Augustine and Monica's ability within the framework of the Christian mythos to transcend the "tumult of the flesh" and ascend to "the WISDOM that is our SOURCE and GROUND." Entangled in the confusions and desires of the body, Bidart's poetry cannot appeal to a higher level of meaning, however strongly craved: "*Man needs a metaphysics;/ he cannot have one.*" As in the poem "Genesis," a reworking of the first two books of the Bible into Bidart's poetic voice, not only did God rest after the days of creation, but God also "ceased." In the absence of an absolute, no anagogic, no symbolic function of language can mend the chasm between the mutually exclusive pairs: Augustine and his mother with their harmonious heavenly vision, Bidart and his mother with their "unappeasable anger, and remorse."

Also contained in *The Sacrifice* is the remarkable long poem "The War of Vaslav Nijinsky," a dramatic monologue in the persona of Vaslav Nijinsky (1890-1950), a famous dancer who had a formidable talent to turn his body into symbol. Nijinsky is presented as a figure that would—as Friedrich Nietzsche did in his unconditional acceptance of eternal return and thus the cycles of physical existence—say yes to life, were it not for his realization that he is not Nietzsche but the "bride of Christ." The dowry of the bride of Christ is an unrelenting guilt that leads to the rejection of life. There is no relief from this guilt, for "God was silent.// Everything was SILENT." Love, religion, philosophy, art, and mythology cannot assuage Nijinsky's insight that "All life exists// at the expense of other life" and that war is a given of life. Only sacrifice serves to atone for the guilt and suffering of the world, and Nijinsky, therefore, according to Bidart, danced "the Nineteenth Century's/ guilt," World War I, on January 19, 1919, in order to redeem, or perhaps destroy, the earth. Like Ellen West, Nijinsky can overcome the body and, by extension, earthly existence only through annihilation of the body. At the end of the poem, Nijinsky feels a "need to be as low down as possible" in his bed at an asylum in Zurich, Switzerland. He has sacrificed his body to his art.

IN THE WESTERN NIGHT

Bidart's publication of his first three books plus two previously unpublished collections in *In the Western Night: Collected Poems, 1965-1990* confronts the reader with an odd ordering of these works: A new collection, *In the Western Night*, precedes the three previously published books, which are in reverse chronological order, and another new collection, *The First Hour of the Night*, ends the entire poetry collection. A possible reason for this arrangement is that *In the Western Night* underscores a theme that has been muted in the previous works, a theme that revalues those works and resolves it-

self in the final collection, *The First Hour of the Night*. In his 1990 review of *In the Western Night*, Denis Donoghue noted that "several of Bidart's most urgent poems are, in some sense that is hard to describe, mystical." Odd as it may sound, Bidart's earthbound poetry possibly conceals a strong mystical impulse that intuits meaning beneath or beyond physical appearance. Such a mystical theme is strongly suggested in the first poem of the volume, "To the Dead":

once we'd been battered by the gorilla

we searched the walls, the intricately carved impenetrable panelling

for a button, lever, latch

that unlocks a secret door that reveals at last the secret chambers,

CORRIDORS within WALLS

(the disenthralling, necessary, dreamed structure beneath the structure we see,)

After the poem's "we" have been battered by the gorilla-like physical life, a secret chamber hidden behind the veil of material appearance is revealed. This innermost structure is "disenthralling," liberating from the prison of the body and the material world.

The working out of the mystical implications of "To the Dead" occurs, as it should, in the last poem in *In the Western Night*, "The First Hour of the Night." Perhaps Bidart's most ambitious poem, it balances the Western philosophical tradition against the poet's personal feelings of guilt, putting in equilibrium both "*wound* and *balm*." The occasion of the poem is the return of the poet to the house of a dead friend, at the invitation of the friend's son. The son and the poet discover that they share a sense of unresolved guilt: the son over the death of his father, the poet over the death of a pony that had been his close companion when he was young. Late that night, the poet retires to the guest bedroom and dreams two dreams. In one dream he enters into an etching of *The School of Athens* by the Renaissance painter Raphael, which presents the ancient philosophers unified around the opposing but balanced gestures of Aristotle, representing matter, and Plato, representing spirit. Before entering into this painting in a dream state, the poet describes the panorama from an intellectual, objective point of view that sees a Janus-like unity in the divided philosophical positions of the ancient philosophers. Once embodied in the dream, however, the poet is weighed down by humiliation and guilt and strives unsuccessfully to regain a sense of unity. Philosophers who lived and wrote after the execution of Raphael's painting join the original group, bringing a cacophony of opinions that result in irreparable chaos. Finally, the poet awakes from this dream into "the desolation of/ HISTORY's/ leprosy,–*LEPROSY* of SPIRIT."

The first dream ends in Bidart's customary vision of spirit hopelessly mired in a diseased, repulsive physical state. In the second dream, the poet discovers that he has been carrying the entrails of his pet pony on his back ever since the animal died (when the poet was nine). Entrails not only suggest eating and the processes of the body but also haruspication, the divination of spirit. For the first time in Bidart's poetry, the mouth, the agent of eating and sexuality, joins with the breast, no longer seen as repulsive as it was in "Elegy" from *The Book of the Body:*

> hungry, SUCKING mouths stretched toward
> swollen, distended udders that I saw must be
>
> painful *unless* sucked—;
>
> . . . RECIPROCITY,—
>
>   I thought,—
>
>   *not the chick*
>   *within*
> *the egg, who by eating its way*
> *out, must DESTROY the egg to become itself . . .*

Destroying in order to become, the way of sacrifice, is abandoned in favor of reciprocity, the interpenetration of matter and spirit. Thus "The First Hour of the Night" ends with a tentative glimmer of transformation possible in the physical world.

Although his later work intimates a conditional transcendence, the bulk of Bidart's poetry to this point envisions the self trapped in history, sunk in the body, devoid of wholeness. Like an animal in a snare, the frustrated spirit experiences only torment, rage, grief, and guilt. The language of his poetry seldom soars, but remains earthbound, flat, prosaic, lexically abstract.

DESIRE

Many of the same features characterize Bidart's next book, *Desire*, published to much acclaim after a period of silence. There is, in this prizewinning collection, less flatness and more lyricism, though it is indeed a dark lyricism. These poems draw heavily upon the history of the Roman Empire and upon Greek and Roman mythology, arguing in various ways that one is what one desires. Is desire, or will, only an illusion, or is it a dependable, controlled spring for action? Is it destiny? Bidart wrestles profoundly with such questions, enlarging the spiritual questing evident in his earlier work. More than half of *Desire* is taken up by a contemporary masterpiece, "The Second Hour of the Night," which may be Bidart's most significant achievement and one of the great meditative-dramatic poems of the late twentieth century. It recounts the story of Myrrah, the mother of Adonis, whose desire led her to sleep with her father, after which she found both life and death unbearable. The gods transform her into a tree: "She must/ submit, lose her body to an alien/ body not chosen, as the source of ecstasy is/ not chosen." Bidart's poetry documents the contemporary moral and psychological state of humankind, often through the vehicle of classical allusion, with such excruciating intensity that it resonates in the depths of every reader.

OTHER MAJOR WORK

EDITED TEXT: *Collected Poems of Robert Lowell*, 2001.

BIBLIOGRAPHY

Bergman, Susan. "Frank Bidart's Personae: The Anterior 'I.'" *Pequod*, no. 43 (2000): 100-111. Bidart's dramatic or persona poems are based on the stance that "self precedes and centers expression." Bergman underscores what is unique in Bidart's version of the vogue for persona poems, providing excellent close readings of many key passages.

Birkerts, Sven. *The Electric Life: Essays on Modern Poetry.* New York: William Morrow, 1989. In his chapter "Frank Bidart," Birkerts comments on how

Bidart's dualistic conception of body and spirit is enlarged to encompass the guilt of Western humankind. Tracing a progression from "Ellen West" to "The War of Vaslav Nijinsky," Birkerts not only addresses the widening of Bidart's themes to include a more general religious point of view but also comments on the interrelation of these themes and Bidart's distinctive style.

Crenshaw, Brad. "The Sin of the Body: Frank Bidart's Human Bondage." *Chicago Review* 33 (Spring, 1983): 57-70. This article contains an insightful discussion of "Ellen West" and clarifies Bidart's construction of an art that presents the ethical paradox of carnality. Bradshaw discusses how Bidart has contracted human ethics within bodily limits, so that customary morality with its exaltation of the spirit becomes severely modified.

Donoghue, Denis. "The Visible and the Invisible." *The New Republic* 202 (May 14, 1990): 40-45. This extensive review of *In the Western Night* traces Bidart's rather deviatory development toward a quasi-mystical sense of personal experience. Interestingly, Donoghue connects the typography of Bidart's dramatic monologues with his longing to escape the lure of mystical states. Donoghue also demonstrates that Ezra Pound, not Robert Lowell, should be viewed as Bidart's artistic mentor.

Gray, Jeff. "'Necessary Thought': Frank Bidart and the Post-Confessional." *Contemporary Literature* 34 (Winter, 1993): 714-738. Focusing on *In the Western Night*, Gray considers the postmodern nature of Bidart's work. Several close readings underpin arguments about the nature of subjectivity and textuality in this twenty-five-year collection.

Pinsky, Robert. *The Situation of Poetry: Contemporary Poetry and Its Traditions*. Princeton, N.J.: Princeton University Press, 1976. In his overview of poetry of the 1970's, Pinsky gives an early recognition of Bidart's stylistic achievement. He praises Bidart's *Golden State* for taking the risk of rhetorical flatness in order to reproduce a genuine sense of the speaker's voice.

Williamson, Alan. *Introspection and Contemporary Poetry*. Cambridge, Mass.: Harvard University Press, 1984. As part of the chapter "The Future of Personal Poetry," Williamson argues that Bidart is an emotionally moving and artistically significant poet because he speaks from the wholeness of his life. Although employing an abstract poetic style, Bidart, Williamson avers, never becomes vague or dematerialized, but vividly dramatizes the tragic interplay of aggression and guilt.

Kenneth Gibbs,
updated by Philip K. Jason

WOLF BIERMANN

Born: Hamburg, Germany; November 15, 1936

PRINCIPAL POETRY

Die Drahtharfe: Balladen, Gedichte, Lieder, 1965 (*The Wire Harp: Ballads, Poems, Songs*, 1968)
Mit Marx- und Engelszungen: Gedichte, Balladen, Lieder, 1968
Für meine Genossen: Hetzlieder, Gedichte, Balladen, 1972
Deutschland: Ein Wintermärchen, 1972
Nachlass I, 1977
Poems and Ballads, 1977
Preussischer Ikarus: Lieder, Balladen, Gedichte, Prosa, 1978
Verdrehte Welt—das seh' ich gerne: Lieder, Balladen, Gedichte, Prosa, 1982
Alle Lieder, 1991
Alle Gedichte, 1995
Paradies uff Erden: Ein Berliner Bilderbogen, 1999

OTHER LITERARY FORMS

Most of Wolf Biermann's published work consists of poems and songs. This fact reflects his conviction that poetry, especially song, provides the most appropriate and effective means of conveying the intensely personal and political content of his work. Biermann's other writings reinforce this strong political emphasis. These writings include several collections of essays, university lectures on the writing of poetry and songs, children's books, and a play. The play *Der Dra-Dra: Die grosse*

Drachentöterschau in acht Akten mit Musik (1970; the dra-dra: the great dragon-killer show in eight acts with music), is an adaptation of the fairy-tale comedy *Drakon* (1943; *The Dragon*, 1963) by the Russian playwright Yevgeny Schwartz and concerns the fate of a city-state ruled by a dragon. In Biermann's hands, it becomes a political parable about the specter of Stalinism in Eastern Europe. In addition, Biermann has translated numerous poems and songs by other poets into German, most notably the long Yiddish poem on the fate of the Jews of Eastern Europe by the Polish-Jewish writer Yitzak Katzenelson, *Grosser Gesang vom ausgerotteten jüdischen Volk* (1994; great song of the exterminated Jewish people).

ACHIEVEMENTS

Wolf Biermann is perhaps the best-known living German-language poet. The success of his books—*The Wire Harp* became a best-selling book of German poetry in the postwar era—and the popularity of his more than twenty recordings provide ample evidence of this.

Several factors have contributed to Biermann's renown. There is, first, the political controversy which has surrounded him since he first fell into disfavor with cultural authorities in East Germany in the early 1960's. While his problems with the party bureaucracy led very quickly to an absolute publication and performance ban in the East, his identification with opposition forces in East Germany served to increase his notoriety, particularly in the West. It is ironic that, although Biermann's work was never to reach a large audience in the socialist East—depending as it did upon the circulation of underground manuscripts and tapes—his poetry and recordings were widely distributed and discussed in capitalist West Germany. Not surprisingly, Biermann's outspoken and often uncomfortable political views kept him in the public eye during much of his thirteen years of western "exile" and continued to do so after the two Germanys reunited in 1990.

Another factor has played an even more central role in Biermann's popularity as a poet. He is a people's poet in every sense of the word, a fact reflected in the everyday language, themes, and imagery of his poetry. His preference for simple, traditional forms, such as the German folk song and the ballad, and his use of music as a vehicle for his texts have enhanced the strong populist appeal of his work.

Biermann's strong identification with the traditions of the German folk song and the political song places him somewhat outside the mainstream of contemporary German-language poetry, with its greater emphasis on sophisticated aesthetic and literary values. Nevertheless, the strength and vitality of Biermann's language and imagery effectively rebut the notion that the populist orientation of his work lessens its significance in any way, and his poems are clearly among the most provocative being written in Germany today.

Biermann has been awarded numerous prizes in including Germany's most prestigious literary prize in the Georg Büchner Prize in 1991. Other major prizes include the Berlin Art Prize for Literature (the Theodor Fontane Prize) in 1969; the Jacques Offenbach Prize of the City of Cologne (for his achievement as a composer and performer of the contemporary political song) in 1974; the Friedrich Hölderlin Prize of the City of Homburg in 1989; the Eduard Mörike Prize in 1991; the Heinrich Heine Prize of the City of Düsseldorf in 1993; and the National Prize of the German National Foundation in 1998.

BIOGRAPHY

Wolf Biermann comes from a Communist, working-class family tradition. His father, Dagobert Biermann, a Jewish worker on the Hamburg docks, joined the Communist Party in 1921 and was active in the anti-Fascist resistance of the early and mid-1930's. Arrested in 1937 for his role in sabotaging arms shipments to Francisco Franco's Spain, he was sent in 1942 to Auschwitz, where he was put to death in 1943. Although Biermann hardly knew his father, he was reared by his mother and grandmother, both active Communists, in the spirit and image of the elder Biermann. This legacy of political activism and Communism would have a profound effect upon Biermann's life.

In the spirit of his father, Biermann left his native Hamburg in 1953 to join in the socialist experiment under way in East Germany. There, he finished his high school education and, from 1955 to 1957, studied political economy at Humboldt University in East Berlin. In 1957, he interrupted his studies to take a position as a dramatic assistant at Bertolt Brecht's theater, the *Berliner Ensemble*. Although Brecht had died the previous year, this confrontation with his work was of great importance in Biermann's development. During this period, too, he met Brecht's friend and collaborator, the composer Hanns Eisler, whose musical influence is readily apparent in Biermann's songs.

The years from 1960 to 1964 represent a particularly significant period in Biermann's life. He had returned to the university in 1959 to study philosophy and mathematics, but his studies were gradually replaced by an ever-greater emphasis upon his artistic interests. In 1960, at the relatively late age of twenty-three, he began to write and compose his first songs. The songs written after the building of the Berlin Wall in 1961 concentrated more and more upon the discrepancy between the promise and the reality of socialism in East Germany and quickly drew the attention of cultural authorities.

In 1961-1962, Biermann helped to found the Berlin Worker and Student Theater and wrote his first dramatic effort for its scheduled opening. His unpublished play "Berliner Brautgang," a love story set amid the political tensions of the newly divided city, was never performed. Before its premiere, the theater was closed by authorities and Biermann was placed under a performance ban. The ban was lifted again in 1963, but Biermann was excluded from the Socialist Unity Party, in which he had been a candidate for membership.

During a brief period of relative cultural freedom in 1964, Biermann began to make a name for himself as a writer and performer of political songs. He was allowed to undertake a concert tour of West Germany, which established his reputation there as one of East Germany's leading young poets, and which led subsequently to the 1965 publication in the West of his first book of poems, issued by a leftist publishing house. This brief cultural thaw, however, ended for Biermann as abruptly as it had begun; at the Eleventh Party Congress in 1965, his poetry was attacked for its "dangerous" subjectivity and its "anti-Communist" slant, and he was placed under a second absolute publication and performance ban.

For the next eleven years, Biermann lived as a "nonperson" in his homeland: There was no possibility for public discussion or performance of his work, much less publication; he was under constant surveillance; his friends were subjected to various forms of official intimidation. Surprisingly, during this period he was allowed to continue to publish and record his work for release in the West. His reputation grew as he, together with his close friend, the physicist and philosopher Robert Havemann, became the focus and primary symbols of intellectual opposition in East Germany.

As early as 1972, Biermann was offered the chance to emigrate to the West, but he was adamant in his refusal to leave his chosen land. Unexpectedly, Biermann was allowed in 1976 to accept an invitation from West German unionists for a concert tour of several major cities. Following the first concert, in Cologne, he was notified that his East German citizenship had been revoked and that he would not be allowed to return home. This calculated move by the Party resulted in an unprecedented protest among artists and intellectuals in the East and had far-reaching consequences for oppositional elements there. Over the next several years, numerous East German writers and artists chose or were forced to emigrate to the West. For many of those who remained, Biermann's expatriation served to solidify and unite their opposition to the East German regime.

Following his expatriation in 1976, Bierman steadfastly resisted the attempts in the West to cast him in the role of an anti-Communist dissident. While affirming still his preference for socialism and the East German homeland now closed to him, he began immediately to immerse himself in the political and social reality of his new home. The dislocation of being "exiled" in the West, which often severely interrupted the work of other East German writers who later came to West Germany, seemed to have little effect on Biermann. Indeed, the thirteen years of western "exile" (1977-1990) brought an increase in artistic productivity, as evidenced in several new volumes of poetry and songs, new recordings, and a busy concert schedule throughout Germany, Western Europe, and Scandinavia. In 1983, Biermann also spent three months in the United States as a guest professor at the Ohio State University.

Despite this public notoriety and success, the early and mid-1980's was a period of profound artistic and personal crisis for Biermann. In 1980 he retreated from the demands of his public life and concert schedule and spent the majority of the next one and one-half years in relative isolation in Paris. From the distance of Paris, he struggled to understand better his new German-German identity as a poet-singer who was at home in both the East and the West yet fully at home in neither. This period of artistic self-questioning was followed by the traumatic collapse of his marriage. In keeping with the intensely personal nature of his work, this personal crisis occupied a central place in the poetry, songs, and concerts of the mid-1980's.

The fall of the Berlin Wall in 1989 and German unification the following year ushered in a new phase in Biermann's biography. As the poet who perhaps more than any other had come to personify divided Germany, he now took up a prominent position in the public discussion of Germany and its future. His return to East Germany in December of 1989 to give a concert in Leipzig was a media event, and the concert was carried by both East and West German television. Throughout the early 1990's Biermann was seen and heard from—especially in articles for newspapers—on a regular basis.

Biermann's essays reflect his return to a public involvement with political issues. Typically outspoken and unconventional, they contain some of the most stimulating contributions to the public discussion of German unity, the legacy of the former East Germany, and the issues raised by the Gulf War. From 1992 to 1995 Biermann lectured on the of writing poetry and song as a guest professor at the Heinrich Heine University in Düsseldorf, and in 1997-1998 he returned to Berlin for one year as a fellow at the prestigious Wissenschaftskolleg.

Although free to resettle in Berlin after German unification in 1990, Biermann chose to remain in Hamburg, the city of his father, together with his second wife, Pamela Biermann.

ANALYSIS

Wolf Biermann is a political poet. He follows in the tradition of François Villon, Heinrich Heine, Kurt Tucholsky, and Bertolt Brecht, with whom he shares both an acute political awareness and a biting, aggressive wit. As with these forerunners, art, life, and politics are virtually inseparable in Biermann's work. He is, as one collection of critical essays refers to him in its title, a "Liedermacher und Sozialist," both a "maker of songs"

and a dedicated socialist; his poetry records with great feeling his own political struggle as a socialist poet and his personal political fate as a renegade and exile.

Biermann's connection with the tradition of Heine and Brecht is apparent. He is the prototypical "troublesome" poet, unwanted and rejected by his homeland—a homeland which he "loves" and "hates" in nearly equal degrees. In a recurring image in his early poetry, Biermann portrays himself as the embattled but unrelenting poet caught in the no-man's-land between East and West, as the poet balanced precariously on the Wall—neither understood nor at home in either Germany. He is torn as Germany itself is torn, not between socialism and capitalism—for his political position as a socialist is clear—but torn by the disparity between Germany's promise and its reality. He is both the victim and the uncompromising critic of this disparity, which is given concrete form in his poetry in the image of the Berlin Wall.

This intense intermingling of the personal with the political is central to all Biermann's poetry and provides the key to its understanding. One cannot separate the poetry from the man and his experience, or hope to understand it fully outside the political and historical context of his personal struggle. Although his poems and songs display a rich variety of themes, Biermann's central concerns may be summarized under three broad headings: Germany's fascist legacy, division, and unification; the unfulfilled promise of socialism; and the poet's celebration of life despite its many contradictions. As these themes suggest, the poetry often exhibits an antithetical structure built upon the contradictions and antagonisms which Biermann perceives around him—antagonisms between the real and the possible, between that which exists and that which remains to be done, and, ultimately, between the forces of quiescence, stagnation, and death and those of life. The conflict expressed in the major themes is mirrored in Biermann's own mixed feelings regarding the world around him. These reactions are expressed in a broad range of tones, from anger and bitterness to ecstatic celebration. Biermann's poems are alternately sad and accusatory, aggressive and subdued, but there remains in them always a determined optimism and a fundamental affirmation of life.

THE WIRE HARP

Biermann's first collection of poetry, *The Wire Harp*, introduces many of the central themes and formal hallmarks of his work. His preference for a simple lyrical style and for everyday rather than literary language is clearly demonstrated here, as is his reliance upon traditional lyrical forms and rhymed verse. He reacts in these poems both to the broader world—as in his critically optimistic picture of socialism in the "Buckower Balladen" ("Buckow Ballads") and in his indictment of American racism in "Ballade von dem Briefträger William L. Moore" ("Ballad of the Letter-Carrier William L. Moore")—and to the more immediate personal world of his loves, his joys, and his sorrows, as illustrated in the "Berlin" poems of this volume. Included under the heading "Portraits" are tributes to both Brecht and Eisler, as well as the well-known "Ballade auf den Dichter François Villon" ("Ballad on the Poet François Villon"). Here, Biermann celebrates the rude and drunken Frenchman with whom he so obviously identifies. He, like his "brother" Villon, is always in trouble with the authorities, and he never tires of ridiculing their petty fears. In this poem, Biermann is at his provocative best, and he revels in the impudent, mocking tone of his great predecessor.

In the group of poems titled "Beschwichtigungen und Revisionen" ("Reassurances and Revisions"), Biermann addresses his ambivalent relationship to the Communist Party. He alternately asserts his role as the critical outsider in "Rücksichtslose Schimpferei" ("Reckless Abuse") and affirms his solidarity of purpose with his comrades in "An die alten Genossen" ("To the Old Comrades"). These poems characteristically illustrate Biermann's defiant subjectivity and his refusal to accept the Party's demand for artistic and political conformity. In the poem "Tischrede des Dichters" ("The Poet's Table Speech"), Biermann presents his criticisms by means of a simple culinary metaphor: He complains that his comrades reject his rich and varied cuisine, preferring instead their bland "single-course dinner of happiness." The tone of the poem is assertive and yet conciliatory as Biermann defends his role as critic and argues for greater artistic tolerance.

MIT MARX- UND ENGELSZUNGEN

In the poems and songs of his second collection, *Mit Marx- und Engelszungen* (with the tongues of Marx and Engels—or angels) Biermann continues his attack upon the blandness of officially sanctioned literature. There is, however, a discernible difference in tone in these poems. Although the poet's voice is no less insistent here, the tone has become more earnest and betrays some hint of the bitterness and frustration which have come of Biermann's prolonged isolation. In the love songs included in this volume, Biermann celebrates life and love, combining traditional images of spring and hope with good-humored earthiness. The poems express the poet's hope against the background of his personal political struggle, and they represent an attempt to counteract his growing sadness.

In one of the last songs in the collection, Biermann finds the source of this sadness in the deep division of Germany itself. He concludes his poem "Es senkt das deutsche Dunkel" ("The German Darkness Falls") with the paradoxical assertion that, though he lives in the "better half" of this divided land, he feels "double the pain." This doubly intense pain is the pain of hopes betrayed, a theme which comes to play an ever-greater role in his work.

DEUTSCHLAND: EIN WINTERMÄRCHEN

The idea for Biermann's long narrative poem *Deutschland: Ein Wintermärchen* (Germany, a winter's tale) was taken from Heine's verse satire of the same title, which appeared in 1844. Biermann's poem was written in 1965 shortly after a visit to his native Hamburg, where he had stopped during his Western concert tour the year before. Biermann uses the occasion of his trip, as Heine had done more than one hundred years earlier, to reflect satirically upon Germany's current political "misery" as mirrored now in the country's political division. He has retained both the tone and the simple folksong verse (four-line stanzas rhyming *abab*) of the original, and he consciously imitates and parallels Heine's masterpiece at every turn.

The return to this "foreign" homeland evokes a mixed response in Biermann. Though he views the "German question" from the perspective of a socialist, critical of Western capitalism, he does not gloss over the heritage of Stalinism in Eastern Europe. He concludes his "winter's tale" with the important programmatic poem "Gesang für meine Genossen" ("Song for My Comrades"), which summarizes the political focus of his entire work, a work which he characterizes here as "das Lied von der verratenen Revolution" (the song of the revolution betrayed). The poem illustrates a central paradox of Biermann's work: the fact that he devastatingly criticizes that which he loves. The Party is the object of simultaneously his love and his hate, for it represents both the future hope of socialism and its dogmatic inflexibility and bureaucratic stagnation.

FÜR MEINE GENOSSEN

The poetry of Biermann's third collection, *Für meine Genossen* (for my comrades), documents the "crimes" of which he was accused in East Germany. Organized under five headings corresponding to sections of the East German penal code, the poems are presented as evidence of his "misdemeanors," "slander," "agitation," and "irresponsibility," but also of the "extenuating circumstances." Biermann defends his "crimes" by placing them in the context in which he prefers to view them: Each section of the collection begins with an appropriately "heretical" quotation from Karl Marx, Vladimir Ilich Lenin, or Rosa Luxemburg that supports Biermann's view of revolutionary art and its function in socialist society.

The poems and songs of *Für meine Genossen* continue in the vein of Biermann's earlier collections. The theme of betrayal—the betrayal of the revolution by the Party, and the betrayal of hope by the friends who have given up the fight—is especially prominent and is recorded in emotions ranging from impatience and anger to profound sorrow. The melancholy undertone, present to some extent in the earlier poetry, is more pronounced here, and the songs have lost much of the playfulness of the early years. The ballad, in Biermann's view a proper instrument of "agitation," maintains its formal preeminence in his work, but is complemented here by highly self-conscious and reflective poems that expand his range of expression.

PREUSSISCHER IKARUS

Biermann's experimentation with new forms and themes alongside the old is carried a step further in the book *Preussischer Ikarus* (Prussian Icarus). This volume was published after Biermann's expatriation in 1976, and includes both poems written in the East and others written in and from the perspective of his Western exile. Together with the familiar East German motifs of the earlier collections, there are a variety of new, specifically Western themes. Biermann responds here not only to the problem of his exile but to the Western German political scene as well—to the misdirected terrorism of the Baader-Meinhof era and the disarray and ineffectiveness of the West German Left.

The title for the collection is taken from the poem "Ballade vom preussischer Ikarus" (ballad of the Prussian Icarus), which closes the first half of the book. In the poem, Biermann projects himself into the role of a modern Icarus weighed down by the heavy iron wings of Prussian tradition—a tradition of authoritarianism and unquestioning obedience that continues to throttle the socialist revolution in the East. The West, however, offers Biermann no solace; the poems that close the second half of the volume portray the ostensibly "free" and "democratic" West as merely the other side of the same German coin.

VERDREHTE WELT

In this collection of poems, songs, and ballads, Biermann struggles to find his bearings in the West. As in *Preussischer Ikarus*, political themes remain in the forefront and many of the poems address topical issues: labor unrest and the 1980 elections in West Germany, environmental concerns, and the suppression of the Solidarity movement in Poland. The poetry dealing with Poland is significant in Biermann's work for the clear break with Communism that it signals. It is a difficult emotional step for the poet, who in the poem "Schuften" (scoundrels) dreams of wrestling with the ghost of his father over his public critique of Communism's failure.

Despite Biermann's continuing political engagement, the poetry of *Verdrehte Welt* (world turned on its head) betrays a more complicated and less ideological view of the world, one that admits to not having all of the answers. The long poem "À Paris" (in Paris) describes Biermann's attempt to come to terms with his new western identity. He is no longer the Socialist "dragon-slayer" of old, a role that his western exile denies him; but neither is he at home in the inconsequential leftist "ghetto" to which the western media would assign him. From the healing distance of Paris, Biermann learns to accept a dual German identity outside the confining pull of ideology. From this position he is able again to write from his life experience rather than merely in response to the issues of the day. Biermann's most compelling poetry arises where personal experience and political reality intersect for him. Thus, for example, the apparently private, family poem "Willkommenslied für Marie" (song of welcome for Marie), written at the birth of his daughter, reflects both the father's joy at her birth and his consciousness of a threatening world, with its "forest of weapons" and its ruined environment, that imperils her future.

AFFENFELS UND BARRIKADE

Affenfels and Barrikade (1986) is Biermann's most personal and least political book. It clearly carries the mark of the collapse of his marriage, which affects both the tone and the content of the poems and songs. The title of this mixed-genre collection contains Biermann's ironic assessment of human life on the planet, determined by human beings' animal nature—captured in the image of the "Affenfels" (monkey rock) of human, especially sexual, relations—and by human attempts, inspired by human reason, to change and improve it—symbolized in the "Barrikade," that is, the political barricades on which the battles for change are fought. In contrast to the earlier collections, these poems and songs reveal an unsure and less assertive, even at times a despairing, poet.

The collection opens with the song "Pardon" (pardon me!), a clever account of his contented discontent living in the West. Each of the poet's claims to be doing fine in his new life in the West is immediately contradicted (Pardon!) by a qualifying addition. Thus he sings that he is "living still"—well, he really meant to say, he is "not yet dead"; he has every thing he needs,—well, come to think of it, he is actually in dire need. In this manner, Biermann announces a central theme of the collection: learning to live in this less-than-perfect and often contradictory world.

In the long poem "Vom Lesen in den Innereien" (reading in my innards), Biermann offers a self-critical assessment of his first ten years in West Germany. His experience in this time, both personal and political, has freed him from many of the illusions with which he arrived ten years earlier. Communism in eastern Europe is "dead," incapable of the reform he had agitated for in his early work; similarly, he no longer places much hope

in the ability of art and poetry to bring about change in the world. Rummaging through his "innards," he derides his utopian optimism of earlier days and refers to his present-day role in the West as an "artist for hire," a "dragon-slayer armed with a lyre" who is astounded to find that the dragon (money and capitalism) has come to reside in him. In the West, he, like other poets, finds himself asking of his poetry, "Will it sell?" when in the East he used to ask, "Will it be banned?" Despite this new tone of self-doubt, the poem ends with an affirmation of the path he has taken and must continue to follow. He will continue to walk in the footsteps of his father and of the Jewish and Communist dead of his father's generation who will not allow him to escape their grasp and the responsibility it holds for him. Thus the poem ends with the repeated refrain, "I'm on my way," a way from which he cannot be deterred, neither by the "applause of my enemies" nor by the "hate of my friends."

PARADIES UFF ERDEN

Nearly fourteen years transpired between the publication of *Affenfels und Barrikade* and the release of *Paradies uff Erden* (paradise on earth) in 1999. Relatively few new songs and poems appear in either of the two compilations of poetry that Biermann issued in the early and mid-1990's, a fact that reflects his high-profile participation in various public debates during these years. As suggested by its subtitle, meaning "a Berlin picture album," the new collection consists almost entirely of poems and songs about Berlin. Almost all of them were written in 1997 and 1998, during a year that Biermann spent at Berlin's Wissenschaftskolleg, where he had planned to continue his work on the translation of William Shakespeare's sonnets. Instead, he found himself drawn out into the city, the eastern half of which had been his home from 1953 until 1976. As Biermann writes in the afterword, the book represents his retaking possession of his beloved second home, a claim that is reinforced by the many poems in which present and past, personal and poltical history intersect for him in Berlin.

Partly because of the more reflective, even occasionally nostalgic tone of some of the poems, *Paradies uff Erden* displays a literary quality somewhat at odds with Biermann's rough-edged image as a political poet. This is not to say that the firebrand poet is absent here; under the heading "Pasquille," Biermann delivers more of his trademark attacks on the stupidity he finds around him. In the song "Journaille" (yellow press), for example, he is on the offensive against the irresponsible German boulevard press and its smear tactics, while in another, "Einem Hirten ins Gebetbuch" (into a shepherd's prayer-book), he attacks the wrong-headed logic of a Lutheran pastor-politician's proposal to destroy the files that the former East German state security agency kept on its citizens. In other poems, however, a different tone emerges. In "Güterbahnh of Grunewald" (Grunewald freight yard), the poet invites an aged Holocaust survivor and friend from Israel to return to the scene of the crime, to Berlin and the freight yard from which many of Berlin's Jews began their journey to the Nazi death camps; it is not perfect here, he argues, but in the new unified country the Germans have made progress in confronting their past. Returning to his old neighborhood in East Berlin, he is struck now, for the first time, by the absence of Jews in what before World War II had been the hub of Jewish life in Berlin. This and other absurdities are to be found "Im Steinbruch der Zeit" (in the quarry of time) as this poem is titled; understanding them is crucial to Germany's future, for "the future will be decided/ in the struggle over the past."

Despite Berlin's central place in his life and memory, Biermann takes leave of the city in the poem "Adieu, Berlin." His absence, however, will not keep him from getting involved in the affairs of the new "Berlin Republic." In an image reminiscent of his early poetry, he portrays himself as the crowing cock-rooster who can make any "dung-heap," regardless of its location, into the "center of this world." The more reflective tone of the Berlin poems and songs may signal yet another transition in Biermann's career, one that ushers in a more literary and less public phase in his poetry and writing. It will be very surprising, however, if Biermann, in his own words here a "burned child, ever in search of fire," is not to be heard from regularly and vociferously well into the future.

OTHER MAJOR WORKS

PLAY: *Der Dra-Dra: Die grosse Drachentöterschau in acht Akten mit Musik*, pb. 1970.

CHILDREN'S LITERATURE: *Das Märchen vom kleinen Herrn Moritz*, 1972; *Das Märchen von dem Mädchen mit dem Holzbein*, 1979.

NONFICTION: *Klartexte im Getümmel: 13 Jahre im Westen*, 1990; *Über das Geld und andere Herzensdinge: Prosaische Versuche über Deutschland*, 1991; *Der Sturz des Dädalus: Oder, Eizes für die Eingeborenen der Fidschi-Inseln über den IM Judas Ischariot und den Kuddelmuddel in Deutschland seit dem Golfkrieg*, 1992; *Wie man Verse macht und Lieder: Eine Poetik in acht Gängen*, 1997.

TRANSLATIONS: *Berichte aus dem sozialistischen Lager*, 1972; *Grosser Gesang vom ausgerotteten jüdischen Volk*, 1994 (of Yitzak Katzenelson's poem).

MISCELLANEOUS: *Affenfels und Barrikade: Gedichte, Lieder, Balladen*, 1986.

BIBLIOGRAPHY

Arnold, Heinz Ludwig, ed. *Wolf Biermann*. 2d ed. Munich: Edition Text und Kritik, 1980. A collection of essays by leading scholars that examine Biermann's poetry both before and after his expulsion from East Germany. In German.

Flores, John. "Wolf Biermann." In *Poetry in East Germany: Adjustments, Visions, and Provocations, 1945-1970*. New Haven, Conn.: Yale University Press, 1971. An introduction to Biermann and his early poetry in English; includes several translations of Biermann's poems and songs.

Rosellini, Jay. *Wolf Biermann*. Munich: C. H. Beck, 1992. One of the most comprehensive studies of Biermann's work. Includes a detailed account of Biermann's life and its relation to his poetry up to the end of 1991.

Rothschild, Thomas, ed. *Wolf Biermann: Liedermacher und Sozialist*. Reinbek bei Hamburg, Germany: Rowohlt, 1976. A collection of essays and articles that provides an excellent introduction to the poet's poetry and songs up to the time of his expatriation from East Germany. In German.

Shreve, John. *Nur wer sich ändert, bleibt sich treu: Wolf Biermann im Westen*. New York: Peter Lang, 1989. A scholarly study of Biermann's poetry during his western "exile" from 1977 until 1989. The author makes a strong case for continuity of focus in Biermann's poetry during a difficult period of transition to life in West Germany. In German.

James R. Reece, updated by Reece

EARLE BIRNEY

Born: Calgary, Alberta, Canada; May 13, 1904
Died: Toronto, Ontario, Canada; September 3, 1995

PRINCIPAL POETRY

David and Other Poems, 1942
Now Is Time, 1945
The Strait of Anian, 1948
Trial of a City and Other Verse, 1952
Ice Cod Bell or Stone, 1962
Near False Creek Mouth, 1964
Selected Poems, 1940-1966, 1966
The Poems of Earle Birney, 1969
Pnomes, Jukollages and Other Stunzas, 1969
Rag and Bone Shop, 1971
What's So Big About Green?, 1973
The Bear on the Delhi Road, 1973
The Collected Poems of Earle Birney, 1975
The Rugged and the Moving Times, 1976
Ghost in the Wheels: Selected Poems, 1920-1976,
    1977
Fall by Fury, 1978
The Mammoth Corridors, 1980
Copernican Fix, 1985
Last Makings, 1991

OTHER LITERARY FORMS

Earle Birney, like many contemporary Canadian poets, both created and explicated the tradition of his country's writings. He wrote or edited more than two dozen volumes, including poetry, fiction, drama, criticism, and anthologies, as well as nearly a hundred short stories, pamphlets, essays, reviews, and articles. The novels *Turvey* (1949), which won the Stephen Leacock medal for humor, and *Down the Long Table* (1955) are well worth reading for an appreciation of Birney's sense of style. Of

his critical articles and books, *The Creative Writer* (1966), *The Cow Jumped over the Moon: The Writing and Reading of Poetry* (1972), and *Spreading Time* (1980) are the most notable collections, for they offer invaluable insights into Birney's poetry.

ACHIEVEMENTS

Earle Birney's career has been laced with numerous honors. He won the Governor-General's medal for poetry in 1942 for *David and Other Poems* and in 1945 for *Now Is Time*, the Stephen Leacock Medal for Humour in 1949 for *Turvey*, the Borestone Mountain prize in 1951, a Canadian government fellowship to France in 1953, the Lorne Pierce Gold Medal from the Royal Society of Canada in 1953, and the President's Medal for Poetry from the University of Western Ontario in 1954. He was given a Nuffield fellowship in 1958-1959 and Canada Council traveling fellowships throughout the 1960's and 1970's to most of the world regions, including Latin America, Australia, West and East Africa, Europe, and South Asia. Additionally, he won the Canada Council Medal for services to arts in 1968 and a Canada Council senior arts fellowship from 1978 to 1980. He was named Officer of the Order of Canada in 1981 and received an honorary degree from University of British Columbia in 1987.

BIOGRAPHY

Alfred Earle Birney was born on May 13, 1904, in Calgary, Alberta, which was then a part of the Northwest Territories. He spent his youth in Calgary, Banff, and Creston, British Columbia, was graduated from Creston High School in 1920, and then worked at a variety of jobs to earn money for university. By 1926, he had been graduated from the University of British Columbia with first-class honors in English literature, and that autumn he entered the University of Toronto as a Leonard Graduate Fellow. During the next year, he concentrated on Old and Middle English, and his studies led to his later imitations of the Anglo-Saxon line in "Anglo-Saxon Street" and "Mappemounde." He was graduated with an M.A. in 1927 and was married the same year.

From 1927 to 1934, he studied at the University of California as well as in Toronto. Two years later, he completed his Ph.D. thesis, "Chaucer's Irony," and received his degree from the University of Toronto. During the years 1936 to 1940, Birney acted as the literary editor of *The Canadian Forum*, writing numerous articles for this journal. When World War II began, Birney served overseas in the Canadian Armed Forces as a personnel officer. He would later use this experience as the basis for his comic war novel *Turvey*.

In 1945, at the end of the war, he was appointed professor of English at the University of British Columbia. While at UBC, he was instrumental in establishing the first Department of Creative Writing at a Canadian university. Once the program was set up, he invited American poets such as Charles Olson, Robert Creeley, and Robert Duncan to teach there. To some extent, these writers would greatly affect Birney's view of poetics; in particular, they expounded theories about spacing, breath, and projective verse which led Birney to revise many of his own ideas about these matters. Birney followed their direction, although he did not become a disciple of the Black Mountain movement. By 1963, Birney had become the chairman of the Department of Creative Writing and also editor of *Prism International*. In 1964, Birney left UBC to become writer-in-residence at such institutions across Canada as the universities of Toronto, Waterloo, and Western Ontario. In 1968, as a Canada Council Fellow, he traveled to Australia, New Zealand, and other parts of the world; some of his best poetry deals with these experiences.

After 1969, Birney devoted his time primarily to his writing, leaving his career as an educator behind him. In the middle and late 1970's, he concentrated most of his energy on recording the developments in Canadian writing which he witnessed during his lifetime. In March of 1987 he suffered a serious heart attack and two months later had an almost fatal stroke. He decreased his writing considerably, although he continued to serve as a contributor of plays, talks, and readings to CBC "Transcanada" radio programs—which he had been doing since 1945—until his death in 1995 and made frequent appearances on CBC television panels during this span of time as well.

Analysis

Earle Birney's poetry reflects and summarizes the ambiguities, inconsistencies, and changes in direction in Canadian writing during the second half of the twentieth century. His central achievement was simple: He brought Canadian poetry from traditional conservatism through modernism and, finally, to postmodernism. As a result, his mere presence on the Canadian literary scene generated everything from respect to contempt. No writer in Canada stirred as much controversy about the nature, direction, and accomplishment of Canadian poetry; Birney will always be remembered and acknowledged. Literary nationalism had been the catchphrase of Canadian writing, but when it arrived in the form of Earle Birney, Canadians discovered a contentious, outspoken gentleman who shocked the literary establishment.

The most distinguishing characteristic of Earle Birney's poetry is its diversity. Birney cannot be associated with any single place, with any single movement (either political, social, or poetic), or with any single theme—he wrote about everything that interested him at the moment it interested him. The result may be a solitary poem quickly forgotten or an entire book of experiments immediately abandoned after publication. Birney's chameleon-like nature forced commentators to

Earle Birney

discuss his work in large, broad generalizations. Yet, Birney's achievement does have a center, and that center rested in his belief that the future was always open and that nothing was ever quite finished or complete or final.

Permanence, for Birney, was an illusion; only death had finality. The recurring images of death, loss, and failure, suggested particularly in the autumnal imagery of his early and middle poetry, are present to emphasize that only one force defeats, or at least temporarily overcomes, death: the creative power inherent in the individual. In conjunction with his firm belief in the inward potential of the individual's creative energy, Birney maintained that art, like anything else, must be the expression of creative change. For these reasons, he would revise, alter, and completely transform an earlier poem to accommodate and reflect the changes he sensed in his world.

A volume of Birney's poems might include forms as diverse as pastiche, allegory, Anglo-Saxon forms, narrative and reflective poems, lyrics, limericks, found poems, and concrete or "shapomes" (poems which rely, almost wholly, on their visual, rather than verbal, effect). No single volume amassing all the various forms Birney used would be satisfactory, for Birney often not only changed and revised poems for later editions but entirely transformed their format and design, as well. A linear poem in one edition may appear in the next as a "shapome." In his *Selected Poems, 1940-1966*, Birney added dates after each poem to indicate the impermanence of his own "final" selection. "North of Superior," for example, is followed by the dates 1926-1945. Which is the "real" version? The poem of 1926 (or was this merely the first draft?) or the poem of 1945? Such questions can hardly be answered when the reader thinks of the poem "Mammorial Stunzas for Aimee Simple McFarcin," dated "Toronto 1932-San Francisco 1934" but first printed in 1959, then reprinted in a wholly transformed shape in 1966. The only possible complete and satisfactory edition of Birney's work would include all the versions of the revised and restructured poems, introduced by the following heading: The "final" version of any poem in this edition rests in the invisible creative energy suggested by every visible act of imagination (that is, every altered poem) included here.

"DAVID"

Analysis of Birney's work inevitably begins with his first major poem, "David," a narrative which records the last day of "youth" in the mountains. Although the poem is entitled "David," it is centrally about Bobby, the narrator. Bobby possesses a naïve and sentimental view of Nature, and David attempts to teach his younger friend the necessity of living in a world where beauty and magnificence have value only when death is recognized as both necessary and inevitable. The lyricism and descriptive detail in the poem move the reader most forcefully at the moments when death and beauty are inextricably entwined in the passages of description.

The climax of the poem is reached when David falls to a ledge far below. Bobby's error has caused the mishap, although David, now crippled, does not press the blame upon his friend. Instead, David asks Bobby to demonstrate that he has grasped the principle of necessary death by pushing him off the ledge so that he will not have to live as an invalid. Bobby finally responds to David's requests. The conclusion of the poem focuses on Bobby's need to reorient and reevaluate his own outlook and attitudes, which he cannot do. For Bobby, Nature is now frightening, horrific, and repugnant. Ironically, David has died for nothing; Bobby's idealism has simply turned to blind pessimism. The poem, however, forcefully depicts man's need to incorporate not only new values but also values which may initially seem incomprehensible and alien. Bobby may fail, but the reader clearly sees that Birney favored David's vision of life, for it allows for both beauty and death without fear.

The initial publication of the poem created a shock, and for years Birney was inundated by letters asking him if he had once pushed a friend off a cliff. The confusion between literature and reality may seem humorous to the more experienced reader, but the fact that such letters were written and sent testifies to the impact of the poem. The same narrative, in later years, however, stirred an even greater debate. Birney suddenly modernized it. He stripped the poem of punctuation and inserted spaces for commas, semicolons, and periods. The argument about the purpose and significance of the changes continues even now: Can a traditional poem be "modernized" by simply omitting punctuation? Such a process, for the modern purist, defies any sense of organic form or poetic necessity. For many, Birney's revision was superficial tinkering.

The attacks on the so-called facile alterations of the poem are valid if one accepts the notion that poems of the past must remain in the past, but Birney would not accept that notion. He boldly challenged his detractors to explain their principles, even if they did not have the patience to listen to his reasoning. For Birney, no poem could be imprisoned in the abstraction called "the past": Every poem is read in the present; it is experienced in the present, and the sensibility of the present is attuned to verse without punctuation. Neither the sensibility which was at work in the "older" version nor the audience for whom it was intended still exists. The old must be pushed over the cliff to its death; the new must be incorporated.

Birney did not receive acceptance on this point, but, whatever a reader's attitude, an understanding of the poet's principles clarifies why Birney so markedly shifted and shifted again, even in experimental forms. In "Anglo-Saxon Street," for example, he created his best-known satire by using Old English stress and modern "kennings." In "Billboards Build Freedom of Choice," he used a variation of Olson's projective verse but, at the same time, sported with the ambiguities inherent in the slang of the 1950's and early 1960's. In "There Are Delicacies," he created a concrete poem that resembles a timepiece in order to remind a woman that there is only so much time for love. In a book called *What's So Big About Green?*, the poet had the words themselves printed in green ink to accompany his theme in visual form: Everything is capable of greenness, freshness, vitality, and rebirth. Birney's constant insistence upon the dynamics of change was not an idle or frivolous gesture; the philosophy gave direction and unity to all he wrote.

"TRIAL OF A CITY: A PUBLIC HEARING INTO THE PROPOSED DAMNATION OF VANCOUVER"

The philosophy of change, or the all too common lack of it, often led Birney to lash out with forceful and even vitriolic satires and parodies. Even in these works, Birney's central vision is not lost to anger or outrage. The work "Trial of a City: A Public Hearing into the Proposed Damnation of Vancouver" excellently illustrates the point. The work is a madcap fantasy of the future, the setting a kangaroo court wherein the sentence

has already been pronounced, although the case is tried afterward. The powers that be can see no reason for halting the annihilation of the city until a common housewife enters. She stands for the forces of creation and meaning and love. For her, there is neither causality nor inevitable end. Creative response to the moment, her presence insists, allows for life, passion, and continuance. For her, all human "freedom is renewable each moment," but only if the individual exercises his creative energy to embrace and accept.

The theme of "Trial of a City," then, despite its harsh attack on the stultified values of society (represented by the traditionalist, Mr. Legion), was typical of Birney's larger concerns. In form, the work also bore the marks of Birney's experimentalism, including everything from typographical idiosyncrasies in the manner of E. E. Cummings to the use of diction and thought echoing W. H. Auden.

Through the years, Birney gradually incorporated into his own work all the various developments in poetry since the 1930's and 1940's. His rhetoric based on image shifted to a rhetoric of voice, and from there to a rhetoric of visual design. At times, the ability to accommodate such disparate poetic modes resulted in profoundly moving verse dealing with man's place in a hostile world, as in "Mappemounde," and in delightful typographical humor, as in "Appeal to a Lady with a Diaper." Often, however, the all too predictable pursuit of novelty wears thin, and Birney's work becomes tiresome.

The tiresome poems cannot be reread, and therein lies their greatest weakness. On first reading, the timepiece design of the poem "There Are Delicacies" enchants; on the second reading, it bores. The language, the essence of the poetic craft, has been treated too lightly; the reverberations have been too easily lost. One can admire Birney's effort to be consistent, one can sympathize with his healthy and reinvigorating outlook, one can admire the notion that creative acts are always required and always possible, but one cannot always summon the energy to rejoice at poems that seem flat and stale once the novelty has worn off.

In the poems that can be reread, Birney's theme, form, language, typography, and verse form (be they traditional or modern) create fulfilling, enriching experiences. Anyone interested in poetry can read them, for the literary devices enhance the texture of the poems rather than point to themselves as being present and active (thereby inadvertently drawing the reader's eye from the true center of the poem—the content). The most important poems in this category may be loosely called Birney's "travel poems"; they deserve special attention.

TRAVEL POEMS

Birney was not a regional poet. This point is significant, for the term "travel poem" is used here to encompass all poems wherein Birney's speaker is on the road, in a train, or in a new city, be that city in Canada or Japan. The poems have great force because usually, although not always, the reader, by the end of the poem, knows more than the person who did the traveling. Since the reader can measure both the speaker and what he thinks, as well as the atmosphere and history of the place visited, that reader is often in a privileged position to judge and evaluate both the ridiculous and the redeeming in human nature. This striking effect in the travel poems was the consequence of Birney's masterful control of both his speaker and his setting. Some of the best of the travel poems are "For George Lamming," "Arrivals," "The Bear on the Delhi Road," "Cartagena de Indias," "El Greco," "November Walk Near False Creek Mouth," and "A Walk in Kyoto." In these and the other travel poems, Birney concentrated on his favorite topic, the moment of needed creative impulse, and the speaker usually discovers his creative force as he reflects upon his experience.

"FOR GEORGE LAMMING"

"For George Lamming" best illustrates how Birney concentrated on the moment of change. The free-verse poem, lacking punctuation, suggests fluidity and freedom from beginning to end. It deals with the speaker's sudden insight into an experience he had in Kingston, Jamaica, where, invited to a party, he found himself totally in harmony with all who were there. More than "rum happy," he did not even recognize his joy until he looked in the mirror; then his face "assaulted" him. He was the only white among five or six black couples, and despite the color barrier, the history of black tensions, and the racial prejudice of the ages, these people had allowed him to share "unchallenged" their friendship and intimacy. The speaker will always feel "grateful" for

having been allowed, even temporarily, to escape the prison of his own skin and his own prejudices (although he had not recognized them until that moment).

This summary of the poem slips over the numerous subtleties of the "master" and "slave" imagery used throughout (for language itself requires one to "risk words," although they are such "dull/ servants") to make a central point about Birney's artistry at its best: Creative insight, for Birney, represented the moment of transcendence of the narrow self. Imagination, in its largest sense, was, for Birney, an act or ability which is not confined to poets or to poetry; it was the act of sympathetic insight and understanding available to all people at all times, provided they transcend themselves. If Birney, at times, insisted too loudly, if he pressed his experiments too often, if he revised and altered and again altered too persistently—these were merely the signs of his sincerity and consistency. Every altered and modified poem Birney presented can be, and probably should be, read as his unaltering embrace of constant change through individual creative gestures. As such, the poetry of Earle Birney is a testament of one man's unshakable conviction that human growth, development, and perfection are possible.

OTHER MAJOR WORKS

LONG FICTION: *Turvey*, 1949; *Down the Long Table*, 1955.

SHORT FICTION: *Big Bird in the Bush*, 1978.

PLAY: *The Damnation of Vancouver: A Comedy in Seven Episodes*, pb. 1952.

NONFICTION: *The Creative Writer*, 1966; *The Cow Jumped over the Moon: The Writing and Reading of Poetry*, 1972; *Spreading Time*, 1980; *Essays on Chaucerian Irony*, 1985.

EDITED TEXTS: *Twentieth Century Canadian Poetry*, 1953; *New Voices*, 1956; *Selected Poems of Malcolm Lowry*, 1962.

RADIO PLAY: *Words on Waves*, 1985.

BIBLIOGRAPHY

Adams, Ian. "Marginality and Tradition: Earle Birney and Wilson Harris." *Journal of Commonwealth Literature* 24, no. 1 (1989): 88. Several works from Birney and Guyanese poet Wilson Harris are discussed. Both writers are generally credited with a major role in the establishment of a modern literature authentic of their region, and both view themselves as doing so out of a position of cultural marginality.

Aichinger, Peter. *Earle Birney*. Boston: Twayne, 1979. This introductory study looks at Birney's criticisms of capitalism, modern culture, and militarism. Divided thematically with chapters on biographical background, satire, love and death, myth, nature, poetic technique, and politics, the book concentrates on Birney's poetry over his criticism and prose fiction. The cynicism, raunchiness, and invective in Birney's later work are considered in a negative light. Contains an annotated bibliography of primary and secondary sources, as well as notes to the text.

Cameron, Elspeth. *Earle Birney: A Life*. Toronto, Ont.: Viking, 1994. A biography that attempts to get at the many men that Birney was: poet, novelist, soldier, journalist, academic, and world traveler. Cameron also covers his romantic life. In so doing, she calls upon the copious materials (including hundreds of letters) archived at the University of Toronto.

Fink, Howard, et al. *Perspectives on Earle Birney*. Downsview, Ont.: ECW Press, 1981. A reassessment of Birney by eminent critics and authors, this collection was originally published as a special issue on Earle Birney in *Essays on Canadian Writing* 21 (Spring, 1981). Pieces of Birney's poetry are interspersed with observations on his radio drama, Chaucerian scholarship, and political prose.

Latham, David. "From the Hazel Bough of Yeats: Birney's Masterpiece." *Canadian Poetry: Studies, Documents, Reviews* 21 (Fall/Winter, 1987): 52-58. Latham traces the influence of W. B. Yeats's "Song of the Wandering Aengus" on Birney's "From the Hazel Bough," a poem Birney considered his masterpiece.

Lecker, Robert, Jack David, and Ellen Quigley, eds. *Canadian Writers and Their Works*. Downsview, Ont.: ECW Press, 1985. This collection of essays includes an article on Birney by Peter Aichinger, which contains a short introduction to Birney's life, his traditions and worldview, and a critical overview. It looks specifically at the alliterative verse, lyric poetry, ex-

perimental verse, and the narrative poems. Includes extensive notes that contain bibliographical references and a select bibliography that lists primary and secondary sources.

Nesbitt, Bruce, ed. *Earle Birney: Critical Views on Canadian Writers*. New York: McGraw-Hill, 1974. This collection of representative critical essays on Birney contains both positive and negative reviews and critical essays on Birney's craft and creativity mixed with a number of his prose pieces. The useful introduction gives an overview and appreciation, while in an epilogue, Birney himself reflects on his career and responds to some of the critical appraisals in the essays.

Ed Jewinski;
bibliography updated by the editors

ELIZABETH BISHOP

Born: Worcester, Massachusetts; February 8, 1911
Died: Boston, Massachusetts; October 6, 1979

PRINCIPAL POETRY
North and South, 1946
Poems: North and South—A Cold Spring, 1955
Questions of Travel, 1965
The Ballad of the Burglar of Babylon, 1968
The Complete Poems, 1969
Geography III, 1976
The Complete Poems, 1927-1979, 1983

OTHER LITERARY FORMS

In addition to her poetry, Elizabeth Bishop wrote short stories and other prose pieces. She is also known for her translations of Portuguese and Latin American writers. *The Collected Prose*, edited and introduced by Robert Giroux, was published in 1984. It includes "In the Village," an autobiographical revelation of Bishop's youthful vision of, and later adult perspective on, her mother's brief return home from a mental hospital. Like her poetry, Bishop's prose is marked by precise observation and a somewhat withdrawn narrator, although the prose works reveal much more about Bishop's life than the poetry does. Editor Giroux has suggested that this was one reason many of the pieces were unpublished during her lifetime. *The Collected Prose* also includes Bishop's observations of other cultures and provides clues as to why she chose to live in Brazil for so many years.

ACHIEVEMENTS

Elizabeth Bishop was often honored for her poetry. She was honored by the Library of Congress in 1949-1950 as poet laureate. Among many awards and prizes, she received the 1956 Pulitzer Prize for Poetry and the 1970 National Book Award for Poetry. Yet, as John Ashbery said, in seconding her presentation as the winner of the *Books Abroad*/Neustadt International Prize for Literature in 1976, she is a "writer's writer." Despite her continuing presence for more than thirty years as a major American poet, Bishop never achieved great popular success. Perhaps the delicacy of much of her writing, her restrained style, and her ambiguous questioning and testing of experience made her more difficult and less

Elizabeth Bishop (© Thomas Victor, courtesy of Farrar, Straus & Giroux, Inc.)

approachable than poets with showier technique or more explicit philosophies.

Bishop's place in American poetry, in the company of such poets as Marianne Moore, Wallace Stevens, and Richard Wilbur, is among the celebrators and commemorators of the things of this world, in her steady conviction that by bringing the light of poetic intelligence, the mind's eye, on those things, she would enrich her readers' understanding of them and of themselves.

BIOGRAPHY

Elizabeth Bishop is a poet of geography, as the titles of her books testify, and her life itself was mapped out by travels and visits as surely as is her poetry. Eight months after Bishop's birth in Massachusetts, her father died. Four years later, her mother suffered a nervous breakdown and was hospitalized, first outside Boston, and later in her native Canada.

Elizabeth was taken to Nova Scotia, where she spent much of her youth with her grandmother; later, she lived for a time with an aunt in Massachusetts. Although her mother did not die until 1934, Bishop did not see her again after a brief visit home from the hospital in 1916—the subject of "In the Village."

For the rest of her life, Bishop traveled: in Canada, in Europe, in North and South America. She formed friendships with many writers: Robert Lowell, Octavio Paz, and especially Marianne Moore, who read drafts of many of her poems and offered suggestions. In 1951, Bishop began a trip around South America, but during a stop in Brazil she suffered an allergic reaction to some food she had eaten and became ill. After recovery, she remained in Brazil for almost twenty years. During the last decade of her life, she continued to travel and to spend time in Latin America, but she settled in the United States, teaching frequently at Harvard, until her death in 1979.

ANALYSIS

In her early poem "The Map," Bishop writes that "More delicate than the historians' are the map-makers' colors." Her best poetry, although only indirectly autobiographical, is built from those mapmakers' colors. Nova Scotian and New England seascapes and Brazilian and Parisian landscapes become the geography of her poetry. At the same time, her own lack of permanent roots and her sense of herself as an observer suggest the lack of social relationships one feels in Bishop's poetry, for it is a poetry of observation, not of interaction, of people as outcasts, exiles, and onlookers, not as social beings. The relationships that count are with the land and sea, with primal elements, with the geography of Bishop's world.

For critics, and certainly for other poets—those as different as Marianne Moore and Robert Lowell, or Randall Jarrell and John Ashbery—Elizabeth Bishop is a voice of influence and authority. Writing with great assurance and sophistication from the beginning of her career, she achieved in her earliest poetry a quiet, though often playful, tone, a probing examination of reality, an exactness of language, and a lucidity of vision that mark all of her best poetry. Her later poetry is slightly more relaxed than her earlier, the formal patterns often less rigorous; but her concern and her careful eye never waver. Because of the severity of her self-criticism, her collected poems, although relatively few in number, are of a remarkably even quality.

History, writes Bishop in "Objects and Apparitions," is the opposite of art, for history creates ruins, while the artist, out of ruins, out of "minimal, incoherent fragments," simply creates. Bishop's poetry is a collection of objects and apparitions, of scenes viewed and imagined, made for the moment into a coherent whole. The imaginary iceberg in the poem of that name is a part of a scene "a sailor'd give his eyes for," and Bishop asks that surrender of her readers. Her poetry, like the iceberg, behooves the soul to see. Inner and outer realities are in her poetry made visible, made one.

"SANDPIPER"

In Elizabeth Bishop's poem "Sandpiper," the title bird runs along the shore, ignoring the sea that roars on his left and the beach that "hisses" on his right, disregarding the interrupting sheets of water that wash across his toes, sucking the sand back to sea. His attention is focused. He is watching the sand between his toes; "a student of [William] Blake," he attempts to see the world in each of those grains. The poet is ironic about the bird's obsessions: He is "finical"; in looking at these details he ignores the great sweeps of sea and land on either side of

him. For every point in time when the world is clear, there is another when it is a mist. The poet seems to chide the bird in his darting search for "something, something, something," but then in the last two lines of the poem the irony subsides; as Bishop carefully enumerates the varied and beautiful colors of the grains of sand, she joins the bird in his attentiveness. The reward, the something one can hope to find, lies simply in the rich and multivalent beauty of what one sees. It is not the reward of certainty or conviction, but of discovery that comes through focused attention.

The irony in the poem is self-mocking, for the bird is a metaphor for Bishop, its vision like her own, its situation that of many of her poetic personaes. "Sandpiper" may call to mind such Robert Frost poems as "Neither out Far nor in Deep" or "For Once, Then, Something," with their perplexity about inward and outward vision and man's attempt to fix his sight on something, to create surety out of his surroundings. It may also suggest such other Bishop poems as "Cape Breton," where the birds turn their backs to the mainland, sometimes falling off the cliffs onto rocks below. Bishop does share with Frost his absorption by nature and its ambiguities, the ironic tone, and the tight poetic form that masks the "controlled panic" that the sandpiper-poet feels. Frost, however, is in a darker line of American writers: His emphasis is on the transitoriness of the vision, the shallowness of the sea into which one gazes, the ease with which even the most fleeting vision is erased. For Frost's poet-bird, "The Oven Bird," the nature he observes in midsummer is already ninety percent diminished. Bishop, rather, prefers the triumph of one's seeing at all. In her well-known poem "The Fish," when the persona finally looks into the eyes of the fish she has caught— eyes, the poet notes, larger but "shallower" than her own—the fish's eyes return the stare. The persona, herself now caught, rapt, stares and stares until "victory fill[s] up" the boat, and all the world becomes "rainbow, rainbow, rainbow." Like the rainbow of colors that the sandpiper discovers, the poet here discovers beauty; the victory is the triumph of vision.

Like the sandpiper, then, Bishop is an obsessive observer. As a poet, her greatest strength is her pictorial accuracy. Whether her subject is as familiar as a fish, a rooster, or a filling station, or as strange as a Brazilian interior or a moose in the headlights of a bus, she enables the reader to see. The world for the sandpiper is sometimes "minute and vast and clear," and because Bishop observes the details so lucidly, her vision becomes truly vast. She is, like Frost, a lover of synecdoche; for her, the particulars entail the whole. Nature is the matter of Bishop's art; to make her readers see, to enable them to read the world around them, is her purpose. In "Seascape," what the poet finds in nature, its potential richness, is already like "a cartoon by Raphael for a tapestry for a Pope." All that Bishop must accomplish, then, as she writes in "The Fish," is simply "the tipping/ of an object toward the light."

"OBJECTS AND APPARITIONS"

Although the world for the sandpiper is sometimes clear, it is also sometimes a mist, and Bishop describes a more clouded vision as well. She translated a poem by Paz, "Objects and Apparitions," that might indicate the fuller matter of her own work; the objects are those details, the grains of sand that reveal the world once they are tipped toward the light. The apparitions occur when one sees the world through the mist and when one turns vision inward, as in the world of dreams. Here, too, the goal is bringing clarity to the vision—and the vision to clarity. As Bishop writes in "The Weed," about drops of dew that fall from a weed onto a dreamer's face, "each drop contained a light,/ a small, illuminated scene."

Objects and apparitions, mist and vision, land and sea, history and geography, travel and home, ascent and fall, dawn and night—these oppositions supply the tension in Bishop's poetry. The tensions are never resolved by giving way; in Bishop's world, one is a reflection of the other, and "reflection" becomes a frequent pun: that of a mirror and that of thought. Similarly, inspection, introspection, and insight suggest her doubled vision. In "Paris, 7 A.M.," looking down into the courtyard of a Paris house, the poet writes, "It is like introspection/ to stare inside," and there is again the double meaning of looking inside the court and inside oneself.

VERBS OF SIGHT AND "THE MAN-MOTH"

No verbs are more prevalent or important in Bishop's poetry than those of sight: Look, watch, see, stare, she admonishes the reader. From "The Imaginary Iceberg," near the beginning of her first book, which compares an iceberg to the soul, both "self-made from elements least visible," and which insists that icebergs "behoove" the soul "to see them so," to "Objects and Apparitions" near the end of her last book, in which the poet suggests that in Joseph Cornell's art "my words became visible," one must first of all see; and the end of all art, plastic and verbal, is to make that which is invisible—too familiar to be noticed, too small to be important, too strange to be comprehended—visible.

In "The Man-Moth," the normal human being of the first stanza cannot even see the moon, but after the man-moth comes above ground and climbs a skyscraper, trying to climb out through the moon, which he thinks is a hole in the sky, he falls back and returns to life below ground, riding the subway backward through his memories and dreams. The poet addresses the readers, cautioning them to examine the man-moth's eye, from which a tear falls. If the "you" is not paying attention, the man-moth will swallow his tear and his most valuable possession will be lost, but "if you watch," he will give it up, cool and pure, and the fruit of his vision will be shared.

QUESTIONS OF TRAVEL

To see the world afresh, even as briefly as does the man-moth, to gain that bitter tear of knowledge, one must, according to Bishop, change perspectives. In *Questions of Travel*, people hurry to the Southern Hemisphere "to see the sun the other way around." In "Love Lies Sleeping," the head of one sleeper has fallen over the edge of the bed, so that to his eyes the world is "inverted and distorted." Then the poet reconsiders: "distorted and revealed," for the hope is that now the sleeper sees, although a last line suggests that such sight is no certainty. When one lies down, Bishop writes in "Sleeping Standing Up," the world turns ninety degrees and the new perspective brings "recumbent" thoughts to mind and vision. The equally ambiguous title, however, implies either that thoughts are already available when one is upright or, less positively, that one may remain unattentive while erect.

The world is also inverted in "Insomnia," where the moon stares at itself in a mirror. In Bishop's lovely, playful poem "The Gentleman of Shalott," the title character thinks himself only half, his other symmetrical half a reflection, an imagined mirror down his center. His state is precarious, for if the mirror should slip, the symmetry would be destroyed, and yet he finds the uncertainty "exhilarating" and thrives on the sense of "re-adjustment."

"OVER 2000 ILLUSTRATIONS AND A COMPLETE CONCORDANCE"

The changing of perspectives that permits sight is the theme of Bishop's "Over 2000 Illustrations and a Complete Concordance." The poet is looking at the illustrations in a gazetteer, comparing the engraved and serious pictures in the book with her remembered travels. In the first section of the poem, the poet lists the illustrations, the familiar, even tired Seven Wonders of the World, moving away from the objects pictured to details of the renderings, until finally the "eye drops" away from the real illustrations which spread out and dissolve into a series of reflections on past travels. These too begin with the familiar: with Canada and the sound of goats, through Rome, to Mexico, to Marrakech. Then, finally, she goes to a holy grave, which, rather than reassuring the viewer, frightens her, as an amused Arab looks on. Abruptly, the poet is back in the world of books, but this time her vision is on the Bible, where everything is "connected by 'and' and 'and.'" She opens the book, feeling the gilt of the edges flake off on her fingertips, and then asks, "Why couldn't we have seen/ this old Nativity while we were at it?" The colloquial last words comprise a casual pun, implying physical presence or accidental benefit. The next four lines describe the nativity scene, but while the details are familiar enough, Bishop's language defamiliarizes them.

The poet ends with the statement that had she been there she would have "looked and looked our infant sight away"—another pun rich with possibilities. Is it that she would have looked repeatedly, so that the scene would have yielded meaning and she could have left satisfied? Do the lines mean to look away, as if the fire that breaks in the vision is too strong for human sight? The gazetteer into which the poet first looked, that record of human travels, has given way to scripture; physical pictures have given way to reflected visions and reflections, which, like the imaginary iceberg, behoove the soul to see.

"THE RIVERMAN"

Bishop participates in the traditional New England notion that nature is a gazetteer, a geography, a book to be read. In her poem "The Riverman," the speaker gets up in the night—night and dawn, two times of uncertain light, are favorite times in Bishop's poetic world—called by a river spirit, though at first the dolphin-spirit is only "glimpsed." The speaker follows and wades into the river, where a door opens. Smoke rises like mist, and another spirit speaks in a language the narrator does not know but understands "like a dog/ although I can't speak it yet." Every night he goes back to the river, to study its language. He needs a "virgin mirror," a fresh way of seeing, but all he finds are spoiled. "Look," he says significantly, "it stands to reason" that everything one needs can be obtained from the river, which draws from the land "the remedy." The image of rivers and seas drawing, sucking the land persists in Bishop's poetry. The unknown that her poems scrutinize draws the known into it. The river sucks the earth "like a child," and the riverman, like the poet, must study the earth and the river to read them and find the remedy of sight.

PICTORIAL POETRY

Not only do the spirits of nature speak, but so too for Bishop does art itself. Her poetry is pictorial not only in the sense of giving vivid descriptions of natural phenomena but also in its use of artificial objects to reflect on the self-referential aspect of art. Nature is like art, the seascape a "cartoon," but the arts are like one another as well. Bishop is firmly in the *ut pictura poesis* tradition—as is a painting, so a poem—and in the narrower *ekphrastic* tradition: Art, like nature, speaks.

In "Large Bad Picture," the picture is an uncle's painting, and after five stanzas describing the artist's attempt to be important by drawing everything oversized—miles of cliffs hundreds of feet high, hundreds of birds—the painting, at least in the narrator's mind, becomes audible, and she can hear the birds crying.

In the much later "Poem," Bishop looks at another but much smaller painting by the same uncle (a sketch for a larger one? she asks), and this time the painting speaks to her memory. Examining the brushstrokes in a detached and slightly contemptuous manner, she suddenly exclaims, "Heavens, I recognize the place, I know it!" The voice of her mother enters, and then she concludes, "Our visions coincided"; life and memory have merged in this painting as in this poem: "how touching in detail/ —the little that we get for free."

"THE MONUMENT"

Most explicitly in "The Monument," she addresses someone, asking her auditor to "see the monument." The listener is confused: the assemblage of boxes, turned catty-corner one upon the other, the thin poles hanging out at the top, the wooden background of sea made from board and sky made from other boards: "Why do they make no sound? . . . What is that?" The narrator responds with "It is the monument," but the other is not convinced that it is truly art. The voice of the poet again answers, insisting that the monument be seen as "artifact of wood" which "holds together better than sea or cloud or sand could." Acknowledging the limitations, the crudeness of it, the questions it cannot answer, she continues that it shelters "what is within"—presenting the familiar ambiguity: within the monument or within the viewer? Sculpture or poem, monument or painting, says the poet, all are of wood; that is, all are artifacts made from nature, artifacts that hold together. She concludes, "Watch it closely."

Thus, for Bishop, shifting perspectives to watch the natural landscape (what she quotes Sir Kenneth Clark as calling "tapestried landscape") and the internal landscape of dream and recollection are both the matter and the manner of art, of all arts, which hold the world together while one's attention is focused. The struggle is to see; the victory is in so seeing.

POEMS OF QUESTIONING

Yet Bishop's poetry is not unequivocally optimistic or affirmative. There are finally more ambiguities than certainties, and—like her double-edged puns—questions, rhetorical and conversational, are at the heart of these poems. Bishop's ambiguity is not that of unresolved layers of meaning in the poetry, but in the unresolvable nature of the world she tests. "Which is which?" she asks about memory and life in "Poem." "What has he done?" the poet asks of a chastised dog in the last poem of *Geography III*. "Can countries pick their colors?" she asks in "The Map." *Questions of Travel* begins with a poem questioning whether this new country, Brazil, will yield "complete comprehension"; it is followed by another poem which asks whether the poet should not have stayed at home: "Must we dream our dreams/ and have them, too?" Bishop poses more questions than she answers. Indeed, at the end of "Faus-tina," Faustina is poised above the dying woman she has cared for, facing the final questions of the meaning that death gives to life: Freedom or nightmare?, it begins, but the question becomes "proliferative," and the poet says that "There is no way of telling./ The eyes say only either."

Knowledge, like the sea, like tears, is salty and bitter, and even answering the questions, achieving a measure of knowledge, is no guarantee of permanence. Language, like music, drifts out of hearing. In "View of the Capitol from the Library of Congress," even the music of a brass band "doesn't quite come through." The morning breaks in "Anaphora" with so much music that it seems meant for an "ineffable creature." When he appears, however, he is merely human, a tired victim of his humanity, even at dawn. Yet, even though knowledge for Bishop is bitter, is fleeting, though the world is often inscrutable or inexplicable, hers is finally a poetry of hope. Even "Anaphora" moves from morning to night, though from fatigue to a punning "endless assent."

POETIC FORM

Bishop's poetry is often controlled by elaborate formal patterns of sight and sound. She makes masterful use of such forms as the sestina and villanelle, avoiding the appearance of mere exercise by the naturalness and wit of the repetitions and the depth of the scene. In "The Burglar of Babylon," she adopts the ballad form to tell the story of a victim of poverty who is destroyed by his society and of those "observers" who watch through binoculars without ever seeing the drama that is unfolding. Her favorite sound devices are alliteration and consonance. In "The Map," for example, the first four lines include "shadowed," "shadows," "shallows," "showing"; "edges" rhymes with "ledges," "water" alliterates with "weeds." The repetition of sounds not only suggests the patterning that the poet finds in the map, but also the slipperiness of sounds in "shadows"/"shallows" indicates the ease with which one vision of reality gives place to another. The fifth line begins with another question: "Does the land lean down to lift the sea?," the repeated sound changing to a glide. "Along the fine tan sandy shelf/ is the land tugging at the sea from under?" repeats the patterning of questions and the *sh* and *l* alliteration, but the internal rhyme of "tan" and "sandy," so close that it momentarily disrupts the rhythm and the plosive alliteration of "tan" and "tugging," implies more strain.

Being at the same time a pictorialist, Bishop depends heavily on images. Again in "The Map," Norway is a hare that "runs south in agitation." The peninsulas "take the water between thumb and finger/ like women feeling for the smoothness of yard-goods." The reader is brought up short by the aptness of these images, the familiar invigorated. On the map, Labrador is yellow, "where the moony Eskimo/ has oiled it." In the late poem "In the Waiting Room," a young Elizabeth sits in a dentist's waiting room, reading through a *National Geographic*, looking at pictures of the scenes from around the world. The experience causes the young girl to ask who she is, what is her identity and her similarity, not only with those strange people in the magazine but also with the strangers there in the room with her, and with her Aunt Consuela, whose scream she hears from the inner room. Bishop's poetry is like the pictures in that magazine; its images offer another geography, so that readers question again their own identity.

USE OF CONCEIT

This sense of seeing oneself in others, of doubled vision and reflected identities, leads to another of Bishop's favorite devices, the conceit. In "Wading at Wellfleet," the waves of the sea, glittering and knifelike, are like the wheels of Assyrian chariots with their sharp knives affixed, attacking warriors and waders alike. In "The Imaginary Iceberg," the iceberg is first an actor, then a jewel, and finally the soul, the shifting of elaborated conceits duplicating the ambiguous nature of the iceberg. The roads that lead to the city in "From the Country to the City" are stripes on a harlequin's tights, and the poem a conceit with the city the clown's head and heart, its neon lights beckoning the traveler. Dreams are armored tanks in "Sleeping Standing Up," letting one do "many a dangerous thing," protected. In the late prose piece "12 O'Clock News," each item on a desk becomes something else: the gooseneck lamp, a moon; the typewriter eraser, a unicyclist with bristly hair; the ashtray, a graveyard full of twisted bodies of soldiers.

Formal control, a gently ironic but appreciative tone, a keen eye—these are hallmarks of Bishop's poetry. They reveal as well her limitation as a poet: a deficiency of passion. The poetry is so carefully controlled, the patterns so tight, the reality tested so shifting, and the testing so detached, that intensity of feeling is minimized. Bishop, in "Objects and Apparitions," quotes the painter Edgar Degas, "'One has to commit a painting . . . the way one commits a crime.'" As Richard Wilbur, the writer whom she most resembles, has pointed out, Degas loved grace and energy, strain coupled with beauty. Strain is absent in Bishop's work.

CHARACTER SKETCHES

Although there are wonderful character sketches among her poems, the poetry seems curiously underpopulated. "Manuelzinho" is a beautiful portrait of a character whose account books have turned to dream books, an infuriating sort whose numbers, the decimals omitted, run slantwise across the page. "Crusoe in England" describes a man suddenly removed from the place that made him reexamine his existence. These are people, but observers and outsiders, themselves observed. The Unbeliever sleeps alone at the top of a mast, his only companions a cloud and a gull. The Burglar of Babylon flees a society that kills him. Cootchie is dead, as is Arthur in "First Death in Nova Scotia," and Faustina tends the dying. Crusoe is without his Friday, and in "Sestina," although a grandmother jokes with a child, it is silence that one hears, absence that is present. There is little love in Bishop's poetry. It is true that at the end of "Manuelzinho," the narrator confesses that she loves her maddening tenant "all I can,/ I think. Or do I?" It is true that at the end of "Filling Station," the grubby, but "comfy" design of the family-owned station suggests that "Somebody loves us all," but this love is detached and observed, not felt. Even in "Four Poems," the most acutely personal of Bishop's poems and the only ones about romantic love, the subject is lost love, the conversation internal. "Love should be put into action!" screams a hermit at the end of "Chemin de Fer," but his only answer is an echo.

OTHER MAJOR WORKS

SHORT FICTION: "In the Village," in *Questions of Travel*, 1965.

NONFICTION: *The Diary of "Helena Morley,"* 1957 (translation of Alice Brant's *Minha Vida de Menina*); *Brazil*, 1962 (with the editors of *Life*); *One Art: Letters*, 1994.

CHILDREN'S LITERATURE: *The Battle of the Burglar of Babylon*, 1968.

EDITED TEXT: *An Anthology of Twentieth Century Brazilian Poetry*, 1972 (with Emanuel Brasil).

MISCELLANEOUS: *The Collected Prose*, 1984.

BIBLIOGRAPHY

Bishop, Elizabeth. *Conversations with Elizabeth Bishop*. Edited by George Monteiro. Jackson: University Press of Mississippi, 1996. These interviews with Bishop reveal the unusual artistic spheres in which she moved. Monteiro's lucid introduction respects the complexities of both Bishop and her repressive historical moment.

Bloom, Harold. *Elizabeth Bishop: Modern Critical Views*. New York: Chelsea House, 1985. Bloom has gathered fifteen previously published articles on separate poems and on Bishop's poetry as a whole, as well as a new article, "At Home with Loss" by Joanne Feit Diehl, on Bishop's relationship to the American Transcendentalists. "The Armadillo," "Roosters," and "In the Waiting Room" are some of the poems treated separately. A chronology and a bibliography complete this useful collection of criticism from the 1970's and early 1980's.

Costello, Bonnie. *Elizabeth Bishop: Questions of Mastery*. Cambridge, Mass.: Harvard University Press, 1991. Provides a comprehensive view of Bishop's visual strategies and poetics, grouping poems along thematic lines in each chapter. She examines the poet's relationship to spirituality, memory, and the natural world by exploring her metrical and rhetorical devices.

Goldensohn, Lorrie. *Elizabeth Bishop: The Biography of a Poetry*. New York: Columbia University Press, 1992. Analyzing Bishop's life through the lens of her verse, Goldensohn probes the lesbianism and alcoholism that Bishop wished to conceal in her life, and examines the role that Brazil played in shaping Bishop's works.

Harrison, Victoria. *Elizabeth Bishop's Poetics of Intimacy*. New York: Cambridge University Press, 1993. Harrison's application of critical theory to Bishop's work reveals new facets of Bishop's art. She examines Bishop's language, poetics, and prosody via postmodern theory, including feminism and cultural anthropology. Takes advantage of the ample manuscript materials available.

Kalstone, David. *Becoming a Poet: Elizabeth Bishop with Marianne Moore and Robert Lowell*. New York: Farrar, Straus & Giroux, 1989. In a 1977 work, *Five Temperaments*, Kalstone wrote of Bishop and other poets. This book, completed after Kalstone's death, keeps Bishop at the center with many quotations from her correspondence with Marianne Moore (the first long section) and Robert Lowell (the second long section). Includes a preface by Robert Hemenway, an afterword by James Merrill, notes, and an index.

Millier, Brett C. *Elizabeth Bishop: Life and the Memory of It*. Berkeley: University of California Press, 1993. The first critical biography of Bishop, this resource combines the subject's life and writings. Numerous notebook entries and letters are uncovered as sources for later poems, and Bishop's alcoholism is discussed.

Mullen, Richard. "Elizabeth Bishop's Surrealist Inheritance." *American Literature: A Journal of Literary History, Criticism, and Bibliography* 54 (1982). The liberating inheritance of Surrealist poetry allowed Bishop to "explore the workings of the unconscious and the interplay between conscious perception and dream." After a brief description of Surrealist poetics, Mullen shows how Bishop differs in holding on to the form and reality of the observed object while also expressing its strangeness or dreamlike quality. Mullen uses Bishop's prose poems as examples of dreamscape and the natural world brought together.

Parker, Robert Dale. *The Unbeliever: The Poetry of Elizabeth Bishop*. Urbana: University of Illinois Press, 1988. Parker has the advantage of a longer view of Bishop's writings and criticism. His wide grasp of her life and work leads him to shape her development into three stages: poems of wish and expectation, resignation into poems of place, and finally, as is natural with maturity, poems of retrospection. He focuses on the major poems in each area, with a last chapter on the later poems, some of which, such as "The Moose," had been in her mind for twenty years. Includes particularly fine notes and an index.

Schwartz, Lloyd, and Sybil P. Estess. *Elizabeth Bishop and Her Art*. Ann Arbor: University of Michigan Press, 1983. This indispensable source gathers critical articles from many admirers, as well as interviews, introductions at poetry readings, explications of specific poems, and a bibliography (1933-1981). Some of Bishop's journal passages demonstrate why she is a preeminent American poet—her realism, common sense, lack of self-pity over losses—as James Merrill calls her, "our greatest national treasure."

Stevenson, Anne. *Elizabeth Bishop*. New York: Twayne, 1966. Although outdated, this important first biography places Bishop in her time as a modernist in relation to other twentieth century artists. It emphasizes her technical skills, moral preoccupations, and acceptance of the terms of contemporary philosophy and science—uncertainty and ambiguity. Supplemented by notes and an index.

Travisano, Thomas. *Elizabeth Bishop: Her Artistic Development*. Charlottesville: University Press of Virginia, 1988. This comprehensive study of Bishop's career traces the evolution of her prose and poetry through three phases. The first, "Prison," uses enclosure as its metaphor; the second, "Travel," breaks through into engagement with people and places; and the third, "History," reconciles her life of loss and displacement to a calm, mature mood of courage and humor. Complemented by a chronology, a bibliography, and an index.

Howard Faulkner;
bibliography updated by the editors

JOHN PEALE BISHOP

Born: Charles Town, West Virginia; May 21, 1892
Died: Hyannis, Massachusetts; April 4, 1944

PRINCIPAL POETRY

Green Fruit, 1917
The Undertaker's Garland, 1922 (includes poetry and stories; with Edmund Wilson)

Now with His Love, 1933
Minute Particulars, 1935
Selected Poems, 1941
The Collected Poems of John Peale Bishop, 1948

OTHER LITERARY FORMS

The literary reputation John Peale Bishop retains is connected almost solely to his work as a poet, but he was also involved in journalism as a editor for *Vanity Fair* (1922), and wrote for that magazine in the 1920's. He produced a volume of short stories, *Many Thousands Gone*, in 1931 and a novel, *Act of Darkness*, in 1935.

ACHIEVEMENTS

John Peale Bishop was a member of the literary establishment of New York in the early 1920's but spent most of the decade living in Europe. He never won a major prize for his work, but in 1931, the short story "Many Thousands Gone" won the *Scribner's Magazine* annual short-story prize. He was respected as a critic, and in 1940 he worked as the poetry reviewer for the periodical *The Nation*.

In 1943 he was honored by the appointment as resident fellow at the Library of Congress in Washington, but ill health forced him to resign; he died soon after.

BIOGRAPHY

John Peale Bishop was born in Charles Town, West Virginia, to a family of substantial wealth. He began writing poetry in his late teen years; *Harper's Weekly* published a poem by him in 1912, a year before he entered Princeton University. He came to university somewhat later than most because of serious illness in his late youth. At Princeton, he was part of the literary coterie which included F. Scott Fitzgerald. Upon graduation in 1917, he took a commission in the U.S. army and served until the end of World War I.

In 1920 he became a prominent member of the new York City literary circle, working as an editor of *Vanity Fair* as well as writing poems, reviews, and comic pieces. He married Margaret Hutchins in 1922, and they went off to tour Europe. In 1924 they returned to New York, and Bishop worked in the office of Paramount Pictures. He also contributed occasional work to New York magazines. Dissatisfied with intellectual life in the

United States, he returned to Europe, living in a chateau in rural France, but he continued to write for American publications. While there he published a book of short stories and a book of poems, *Now with His Love* (1933).

Bishop returned to America in 1933, living for a short time in Connecticut, then in New Orleans. In 1935 he settled on Cape Cod, where he wrote some of his best poems. The December, 1940, death of F. Scott Fitzgerald was remembered in "The Hours," and a series of somber, sonorous poems followed. Constantly troubled by serious illness, he worked when he was able, in New York in the Office of the Coordinator of Inter-American Affairs and in editorial work. In 1942, his health forced him to return to Cape Cod. In 1943, he tried to work at the Library of Congress with the poet Archibald MacLeish but suffered a heart attack soon after his arrival. He returned to the Cape, where he continued to write poetry. He died in Hyannis Hospital on April 4, 1944.

ANALYSIS

The reputation of poets is often fragile, dependent upon changes in taste for certain themes, tonalities, and technical enthusiasms. This is particularly true of John Peale Bishop (who was ruefully aware of it), for he was rarely chosen for poetry anthologies and of little interest to the critics.

His major limitations were his lack of a singular voice or an individual style. His early poetry was influenced by several nineteenth century poets, including John Keats, Percy Bysshe Shelley, and Algernon Charles Swinburne, and his later work revealed an enthusiasm for the twentieth century poets William Butler Yeats, T. S. Eliot, and Ezra Pound. His poems are often clever but lack originality (a touchstone for artistic praise) and that indefinable artistic sense of power that marks the great poet. His later poetry, however, often manages interesting ideas and possesses a laconic tone that is attractive.

"SPEAKING OF POETRY"

The first poem in his 1933 collection *Now with His Love* uses a central problem of William Shakespeare's *Othello, the Moor of Venice* (1604) as a metaphor for the relation of poetry to ordinary life. How can Desdemona, so civilized and cultivated, so delicate and fastidious, be attracted to the rough animality of Othello? Unlike most twentieth century lyric poets, Bishop does not quite answer the question, although the poem is reminiscent of the problem poems of Yeats and W. H. Auden in which some final solution is reached.

Desdemona represents, for Bishop, the intellect, the world of European culture, restraint, and the feminine, while Othello represents the emotions, the dark uncivilized African, the male. "For though Othello had his blood from kings/ his ancestry was barbarous, his ways African,/ his speech uncouth." Bishop explores the nature of their coming together in a way which suggests that such is how art is made, in a coming together of the traditions and disciplines of the form wedded to the unconscious, the wayward, dark aspects of the poetic imagination.

It is a tonally tough poem, cool in its comparison of the act of artistic creation with the sexual attraction of Desdemona "small and fair,/ delicate as a grasshopper" and Othello, "his weight resilient as a Barbary stallion's." All the trappings of "poetic" language that mar so many of Bishop's early poems are left behind here for an informal, angular verse, with intimate conversational simplicity. The question of how culture is related to ordinary life was common with Bishop and shows up most successfully in his later work in *Minute Particulars* (1935) in "The Freize" and "Your Chase Had a Beast in View," in which the artist is praised for the ability to bring order and meaning out of humanity's base existence.

NOW WITH HIS LOVE

Bishop had a wide range of subject matter, and in the 1933 collection *Now with His Love* he faces the horror of his service in World War I, juxtaposing the innocence of daily life behind the battle lines with the existential facts of daily slaughter. His gift for the description of the indifferently beautiful world of nature makes the facts of life even more intensely sad. The dead are buried close to their billets in "In the Dordogne":

> the young men rotted
> under the shadow of the tower
> in a land of small clear silent streams
> where the coming on of evening is
> the letting down of blue and azure veils
> over the clear and silent streams
> delicately bordered by poplars.

The senselessness of the fighting is conveyed not by heroic posturing or heightened emotion but rather by a distasteful rigor and a recognition of the sad foolishness of the idealizations of the young men. Relentless in tone and intelligent candor, bone thin in its refusal to glorify, it is war poetry of considerable power.

"Young Men Dead" is a powerful evocation of three boys slain in France, one who might have become a formidable man in time, one a great lover "who had so many dears/ Enjoyed to the core," and "Newlin who hadn't one/ To answer his shy desire." However different they may be, they are "blanketed in the mould." The emotional tightness of the poem, the terse bleakness of the memory is brought to a deadening conclusion in the muted admission that "I who have most reason/ Remember them only when the sun/ is at his dullest season."

"Fiametta" and "Metamorphoses of M"

These two poems are also from *Now with His Love*. Bishop wrote love lyrics from early in his career, but it was only in his later years that he was consistently able to find an economical, intensely direct way to deal with the subject. He did, however, show signs of power early on, as in "Fiametta," written in the early 1920's. The poem is metrically very strict for the first two six-line stanzas; the final stanza is somewhat looser and provides a pleasing contrast. It is a poem that displays how technically skilled Bishop was at an early age. It is a simple song of outright adoration of female beauty, full of color and sensitive evocations of sexual excitement: "In a gown the color of flowers;/ Her small breasts shine through the silken stuff/ Like raindrops after showers." The poem is not without a glint of wit: "Whatever her flaws, my lady/ Has no fault in her young body."

In 1933, this sexual adoration appears again, with even greater success, in "Metamorphoses of M." This poem is strongly reminiscent of Yeats but remains a successful evocation of adoration of the female. In this love poem written on the morning after a night of sexual pleasure, the lover contemplates the beauty fit for Venetian craftsmen to adorn. "I could have sworn Venetian artisans/ Had all night been awake, painting in gold,/ To set your beauty on appropriate heels."

Bishop, deeply lettered in literature and history, often subtly infuses his poetry with cultural references, and Shakespeare's Cleopatra is hinted at in "Your beauty is not used" as the lover marvels at the unspoiled perfection of the loved one. There is also a touch of the Metaphysical poets in his logic-chopping consideration of the woman, sexually active, yet so beautiful that a kind of virginity surrounds her. "Though you have lain/ A thousand nights upon my bed, you rise/ Always so splendidly renewed that I have thought" that "even the unicorn" would be "so marvelled by virginity/ That he would come, trotting and mild,/ To lay his head upon your fragrant lap/ And be surprised."

"A Subject of Sea Change"

The longer poems, gathered in *The Collected Poems of John Peale Bishop* (1948) under the subtitle *Uncollected Poems, 1937-1945*, are examples of his ability to sometimes, but not always, organize his work with a happy conjunction of technical and aesthetic success. "Sea Change" was the name of the house he had built on Cape Cod, the name coming from Shakespeare's *The Tempest* (1611) in a passage describing the act of drowning, an act in which all is changed forever. In the poem "A Subject of Sea Change," the speaker reflects upon life, public and private, as he looks out to the shore and the rolling sea. Bishop had considerable sensitivity in the description of nature, and the beginning section places the house within the beach landscape. "I have built my house amid sea-bitten green,/ Among the pitch pines of a dispersed wood." The time is ominous, that of World War II: "I hear the great bombs drop." Humanity's limited hold on time, and its failures, are put into the context of the long run, of the ability to accept failure and responsibility, but to maintain a sense of life having meaning.

> Time is man's tragic responsibility
> And on his back he bears
> Both the prolific and destroying years.
> . . . he must surround each act
> With scruples that will hold intact
> Not merely his own, but human, dignity.

"The Hours"

Something of similar thoughtfulness and tender passion can be seen in "The Hours," the elegy written on the death of F. Scott Fitzgerald. The Cape Cod landscape is used with relentless force in pastoral sympathy. "The sky is overcast,/ And shuddering cold as snow the shoreward blast./ And in the marsh, like a sea astray, now/ Waters brim." John Milton's "Lycidas" may be the inspiration behind the poem, but Milton had never met the young man who was the subject of that poem, nor had the boy done anything significant with his life. By contrast, Bishop was an intimate of Fitzgerald, and Fitzgerald was one of the finest American novelists of his time. The poem has an intimacy that Milton's poem lacks: "None had such promise then, and none/ Your scapegrace wit or your disarming grace." The poem concludes in acceptance of eternal loss. "I cannot pluck you bays,/ Though here the bay grows wild. For fugitive/ As surpassed fame the leaves this sea-wind frays/ Why should I promise what I cannot give?"

OTHER MAJOR WORKS

LONG FICTION: *Act of Darkness*, 1935.

SHORT FICTION: *Many Thousands Gone*, 1931.

NONFICTION: *The Collected Essays of John Peale Bishop*, 1948; *The Republic of Letters in America: The Correspondence of John Peale Bishop and Allen Tate*, 1981.

EDITED TEXT: *American Harvest*, 1942 (with Allen Tate).

BIBLIOGRAPHY

Arrowsmith, William. "An Artist's Estate." *Hudson Review* 2 (1949): 118-127. A short account of the Bishop poetry and its relation to early twentieth century literary movements.

Bier, Jesse. *A Critical Biography of John Peale Bishop*. Ann Arbor, Mich.: University Microfilms, 1957. This thesis for Princeton University is one of the rare biographical works on Bishop.

Frank, Joseph. "The Achievement of John Peale Bishop." *Minnesota Review* 2 (1962): 325-344. Bishop often used mythological themes in his poetry; Joseph spends considerable time on that aspect of the work but also examines the later poetry with considerable sensitivity.

Hyman, Stanly Edgar. "Notes on the Organic Unity of John Peale Bishop." *Accent* 4 (1949): 102-113. A comment upon the complexity of some of the poetry.

Spindler, Elizabeth Carroll. *John Peale Bishop: A Biography*. Morgantown: West Virginia University Press, 1980. Includes bibliographical references, index.

Tate, Allen. "A Note on Bishop's Poetry." *Southern Review* 1 (1935): 357-364. Tate, a good poet and distinguished critic, was Bishop's closet literary confidante and a personal friend; his judgment of the Bishop work is probably the best available.

Tate, Allen, and John Peale Bishop. *The Republic of Letters in America: The Correspondence of John Peale Bishop and Allen Tate*. Lexington: University Press of Kentucky, 1981. The sparsity of criticism of Bishop's work can, in part, be alleviated by his long personal and critical correspondence with fellow poet Allen Tate. They discuss the problem of making art in America.

White, Robert Lee. *John Peale Bishop*. 1966. Reprint. Detroit: Gale Group, 1983. A widely accessible, full-length study of the poet. It is sensible and thorough, dealing with his life and his full range of literary endeavors. A good source for student study.

Charles H. Pullen

PAUL BLACKBURN

Born: St. Albans, Vermont; November 24, 1926
Died: Cortland, New York; September 13, 1971

PRINCIPAL POETRY

The Dissolving Fabric, 1955

Brooklyn-Manhattan Transit: A Bouquet for Flatbush, 1960

The Nets, 1961

Poem of the Cid, 1966 (translation)

Sixteen Sloppy Haiku and a Lyric for Robert Reardon, 1966

Sing-Song, 1966

The Reardon Poems, 1967

The Cities, 1967

In. On. Or About the Premises: Being a Small Book of Poems, 1968

Two New Poems, 1969

Three Dreams and an Old Poem, 1970
Gin: Four Journal Pieces, 1970
The Assassination of President McKinley, 1970
The Journals: Blue Mounds Entries, 1971
Early Selected y Mas: Poems, 1949-1966, 1972
The Journals, 1975 (Robert Kelly, editor)
Halfway down the Coast: Poems and Snapshots, 1975
By Ear, 1978
Against the Silences, 1980
The Selection of Heaven, 1980
The Collected Poems of Paul Blackburn, 1985

OTHER LITERARY FORMS

Paul Blackburn was an ambitious translator, not only of such modern Spanish-language writers as Federico García Lorca, Julio Cortázar, and Octavio Paz, but also of the medieval troubadours, who had some influence on his own verse. Although his work in the Provençal poets was primarily finished by the late 1950's, Blackburn continued to revise his translations for the rest of his life. The substantial manuscript was eventually

Paul Blackburn (© Thomas Victor)

edited by his friend, the scholar of medieval literature George Economou, and published posthumously as *Proensa: An Anthology of Troubadour Poetry* (1978).

ACHIEVEMENTS

Appreciated as a translator, Paul Blackburn limited his reputation as a poet during his lifetime by publishing only a small portion of his poetry and then in very limited editions. His position in literary history can be appreciated through the inevitable comparison with Frank O'Hara. Both poets were born, and graduated from college, in the same years; both were celebrators of the city, primarily New York, in verse that revealed their awareness of centuries of literary history at the same time that they were pursuing some of the more radical modernist innovations in poetic structure and idiom; and both bodies of work reveal warm, generous, witty sensibilities; unfortunately, both poets also died young. Blackburn and O'Hara were, in fact, simultaneously experimenting with the open-form poem, the poem that strives to convey the immediacy of life by presenting the poet's situation, observations, and responses as directly and precisely as possible, according to the chronology of the events themselves as they happened, thus giving the illusion of both inclusiveness and inconclusiveness. The mediating consciousness that shapes and judges experience, that yields a crafted, discursive, linearly logical development of images progressing to a closure that both evolves from and unifies them, is seemingly denied. O'Hara's affinities, however, are with the French: the post-Symbolists Pierre Reverdy and Guillaume Apollinaire, and the Surrealists. Consequently, his "lunch poems" retain a sense of a consciousness willing and directing, a gesture akin to that of the analogical subconscious managing the flow of his "automatic" texts. Blackburn, on the other hand, places the reader almost completely in reality, in the experience itself, perhaps because he is working within the more objectivist American tradition.

Blackburn readily acknowledged that Ezra Pound had the most influence upon his work, along with William Carlos Williams, whom he first encountered through the poetry of Robert Creeley. Charles Olson's essay "Projective Verse" (1950) provided added incentive, as did the poetry of Louis Zukofsky. Blackburn worked in the modernist poetic technique pioneered by Pound and Williams, and E. E. Cummings and T. S. Eliot as well, and defined in 1945 by Joseph Frank in a seminal essay as "spatial form." This technique complements a nondiscursive content by replacing the linear conventions of typographically recorded language, appropriate to discursive content, with a two-dimensional, spatially oriented presentation. The unconventional spacing of words or phrases can establish rhythm by indicating length of pause between verbal elements, and calculated rather than conventional line endings can provide emphasis whenever strategically desirable. Blackburn consistently avails himself of both of these features of spatial form, as did his predecessors.

His unique contribution to modernist poetics, however, is to utilize juxtaposition, the primary aspect of spatial form that yields thematic meaning, in the spontaneous, open-form poem of immediate experience to convey definite, if subtle, complex meanings within verse that appears simply to be recording random observations of the ongoing flow of life. The placing of material in different areas on the page according to subject does not merely isolate particular experiences, preserving their phenomenal integrity, but also facilitates a more profound kind of relationship between them. When Blackburn is at his best, he is shrewdly choosing for a given poem inherently related experiences that comment upon one another, yet describing them with complete fidelity to their objective reality and presenting them nonchalantly, extemporaneously, as if they are insignificant coincidences. In this way, Blackburn creates in his poems a living world of joyous activity and sensuous appearance that is nevertheless intrinsically meaningful.

Blackburn was aware, however, that a poem is not merely a written, visual product, but also a spoken, aural event. What made Blackburn the complete poet, the virtuoso, was the other great influence on his poetic career besides Pound: the troubadours. Music in poetry was for Blackburn at once formal, the orchestration of material for thematic and emotional impact, and aural, the rhythm and sound of the language itself. To be sure, Blackburn, like his contemporaries, sought American speech rhythms and conversational diction, an aesthetic inaugurated by Walt Whitman. Blackburn had a fine

ear for colloquialisms and slang, but that ear was also trained by Provençal. Consequently, the play of assonance, consonance, internal rhyme, off-rhyme, and rhythmic nuance inspired by troubadour lyric can be found at times alternating, or even blending, with modern idiom, for atmosphere, emphasis, or wit. Blackburn's range of diction, in fact, enables him to enliven his poetry with irony and humor, formal diction and slang clashing unexpectedly. Despite the minimalist tendencies of many of his contemporaries to strip poetry of all rhetorical beauty, Blackburn found ways to preserve the varied aural richness of language.

The troubadours may also be responsible, along with Blackburn's avowed Mediterranean sensibility, for the one quality of his poetry that is very rare in English verse: the comfortable ease, the relaxed poise, with which he treats the erotic. Cummings was, of course, always aware of the shock that he was creating with his references to sexual love. John Donne and even Robert Herrick are self-conscious by comparison. One would have to go back to Geoffrey Chaucer for a similar natural acceptance of sensuality. Certainly Blackburn's stature as an American poet is enhanced, not diminished, by such a foreign influence as Provençal poetry. A melting-pot culture remains vital by renewing component cultures latent in its native tradition, a program that Pound, as well as Eliot, followed. As Blackburn deliberately takes his place in the tradition of poetry from the Middle Ages on through his work with the troubadours, so he openly acknowledges a similar tradition of modern poetry by occasionally parodying or quoting poets of the immediate past, including Pound, Williams, Eliot, Robert Frost, Walt Whitman, William Butler Yeats, and Gerard Manley Hopkins.

This inclusive view of the modern poetic tradition is indicative of the richness of Blackburn's own poetry: its technical innovations with spatial form, sound and rhythm, and diction; its thematic and emotional range; and its ability to perceive, in the immediate and the personal, the general and the universal. Blackburn's verse is always grounded in private experience, yet it expresses the common concerns of humanity. He is able to structure the immediate without violating it, whereas others of his generation were only able, or simply content, to record. Thus, poetry for him is never therapy through confession, or a notebook of fragments from his reading, or a self-absorbed diary. When one speaks of significant postwar poets, one cannot with any justice mention any one of his contemporaries, no matter how well-respected at the present time, without mentioning Blackburn's name in the same breath.

BIOGRAPHY

Paul Blackburn was the son of the poet Frances Frost. Having been reared in Vermont, New Hampshire, South Carolina, and New York City, he attended New York University and the University of Wisconsin, where he received a B.A. degree in 1950. While at Wisconsin, Blackburn began corresponding with Ezra Pound, whose poetry he admired, and then occasionally visited Pound in St. Elizabeths Hospital, Washington, D.C. At Pound's suggestion, Blackburn began writing to Robert Creeley, who eventually published his poems in the *Black Mountain Review* and put him in touch with Cid Corman, who, in turn, published Blackburn's poems in *Origin* (a quarterly for the creative) and introduced him to Charles Olson, though Blackburn was never to study or teach at Black Mountain College. Pound also encouraged Blackburn's interest in the troubadours, which began when Blackburn encountered Pound's own quotations and imitations of Provençal verse in *Personae* (1909) and the *Cantos* (1925-1972). In 1953 Blackburn published a small volume of translations through Creeley's Divers Press, the early *Proensa*, that earned him a Fulbright scholarship in 1954 to do research in Provençal poetry at the University of Toulouse in southern France, and he returned as *lecteur américain* the following year. He remained in Europe, principally in Málaga, Spain, and Bañalbufar, Mallorca, with Winifred McCarthy, whom he married in 1954, until 1957, when they returned to New York.

For the next ten years in New York City, in addition to writing and translating, Blackburn worked to establish a sense of community among the poets centered on St. Mark's Church in the Bowery. As well as offering help and encouragement, he organized and tape-recorded weekly poetry readings at the church. His efforts eventually led to the funded Poetry Project at St. Mark's in 1967. He also conducted a "Poet's Hour" on radio station WBAI. In 1963 he was divorced from his first wife and married Sara Golden; that marriage also ended in divorce in 1967, around the time that he was poet-in-residence at the Aspen Writers' Workshop in Colorado. That year also saw the appearance of his most widely circulated collection of poems, *The Cities*, published by Grove Press. Toward the end of 1967, he returned to Europe on a Guggenheim Fellowship, where he met Joan Miller, whom he married in 1968, and with whom he had a son. In September, 1970, he assumed a teaching position at the state college in Cortland, New York, where he died of cancer the following year.

ANALYSIS

Because Paul Blackburn is a poet of immediate observation and spontaneous response, his poetry thrives on particular places. His work, however, is not rooted in a specific geographical location that is transformed into a frame of mind, as is Frost's New England, or that is elevated to a latter-day myth, as is Williams's Paterson. Blackburn's places are the environments in which he happens to be: a town plaza, a boat at sea, a wooded hill, a city street, a subway car, a tavern, a luncheonette, a kitchen, a bedroom. He would often generate a poem by immersing himself in his surroundings until man and place were one, the identification stirring in him a particular thought or emotion, a combination of his mood and the suggestion of that particular rush of outside activity. Although his thematic preoccupations and technical goals remain fairly uniform throughout the course of his work, he did tend to prefer certain themes and to express certain emotions through certain techniques when he was living in European cities, and others when he was living in New York. Perhaps because he could see sheep grazing in the town square in Málaga or burros passing through Bañalbufar, when Blackburn was living in Europe he often considered the relationship between man and nature through such concepts as freedom, mutability, eternity, and religiosity; love is portrayed as sentiment. Perhaps because his mind was on the troubadours, living with his hands on their manuscripts near Provence, Blackburn's European poetry tends to be meditative and pensive, the soundplay more melodious, the language more metaphorical. When he was living in New York, on the other hand, in the densely populated modern city, where concrete substituted for grass, Blackburn focused on interpersonal relations, including friendship, complicity, estrangement, and anonymity; love becomes erotic energy. In a city whose traffic rushes and whose subway rumbles and roars, Blackburn's poetry becomes more immediate and involved, conversational and witty; sound is orchestrated for dissonance; metaphor, if resorted to at all, is unexpected, shocking; but the occasional use of symbol is retained.

EARLY SELECTED Y MAS

Blackburn is best read, then, chronologically, according to the place where he was living and writing. The dates given for the poems gathered in *Early Selected y Mas*, which includes the small, early books of limited circulation, makes such a reading possible for most of the first half of his work. In the poetry written or set in Europe between 1954 and 1958, Blackburn explores man's existence as a creature both fundamentally a part of nature, with its physicality and sensuousness, and separate through his consciousness, will, and ephemerality.

In "A Permanence," Blackburn uses the seven-star constellation "the bear" to present nature as an eternal force separate from man: The bear "is there/ even in the day, when we do not see him." Nevertheless, man cannot help responding to nature's perpetually changing life, being natural himself. The lovers in "The Hour," for example, are "hungering" not only for food but also for the first sign of spring after a long winter: They sit "listening to the warm gnawing in their stomach/ the warm wind/ through the blossoms blowing." These lines exemplify the rich grammatical ambiguity made possible by spatial form: The appetites for food and for seasonal renewal are associated not only by repetition of the adjective "warm" but also by the possibility that "wind" as well as "gnawing" can be the object of the preposition "to," modifying "listening."

Separation from and unity with nature are confronted simultaneously in "Light." Initially, man and sea are only linguistically related through a simile; day moves inevitably into night, but an effort of the will is required for human action: "My thought drifts like the sea/ No grip between it and my act." By the end of the poem, however, the dark, drifting sea complements and then merges with the poet's gloomy mood. The assertion is metaphoric, but the poet's mind and his perceptual experience have indeed become one: "The sea flashes up in the night/ to touch and darken my sea."

"MESTROVIĆ AND THE TREES"

From this contemplation of the relationship between man and nature a religious sense develops, as expressed in "Mestrović and the Trees." For Blackburn, a feeling for the divine is unavoidable: "You never get passed the wood" where "The beginnings of things are shown." Religion for him is a matter of origins, and this poem is Blackburn's own version of the cosmological argument. From man's own existence, which cannot be denied—"Yes we are"—he moves back to origins—"Our mother and father," and by implication, Adam and Eve—to their origin, in nature, through God: "So these trees stand there, our/ image, the god's image." The trees "stand there/ naked" just as man enters the world, his unity with nature now binding him also to the divine. By using the lower case for God and preceding his name with the definite article, Blackburn indicates that his religion is natural rather than orthodox. Although Blackburn is certain of the existence of the divine, its nature remains an enigma.

"HOW TO GET THROUGH REALITY"

This mystery, essential to Blackburn's religious experience, is in itself sacred for him and not to be violated by forms and formulas that he considers to be ultimately human fabrications, at best mere approximations of the divine. In "How to Get Through Reality," Blackburn insists upon the separation, epistemological despite a metaphysical complicity, between the temporal and the divine, that is, "Those who work with us . . . who create us from our stone." An impenetrable glass wall separates the two realms, and he celebrates the divine only in the most general of ways, aesthetically: "Our beauty under glass is your reality, unreachable/ sliding our gift to you." The insistence upon the unintelligibility of the divine is portrayed grammatically with a sentence that ends incompletely just at the point God is to be named: "Beauty is the daily renewal in the eyes of." Feeling, the basis of his perception of beauty, provides his only sense of the divine: "One could kick the glass out, no?/ No./ Pass through." Breaking the glass, transcending the temporal, for direct communication with and precise knowledge of the supernatural is impossible; only intimations, illuminations, can pass through the transparency of the glass. A similar warning is sounded in "Suspension," where the poet's vision of the moon is obscured by tree branches: "—Shall I climb up and get it down?/ —No. Leave it alone."

"Ritual I"

As a consequence, Blackburn's attitude toward orthodox religious forms—language, ceremony, observance—is ambivalent. "Ritual I" presents a religious "Procession," as it moves "with candles" from the church through the various streets of the Spanish town to the chant of "Ave Maria." Because the "fiesta" does not "celebrate," but rather "reenacts" the "event," "*time emerges*." Blackburn is observing that the religious ritual is "a timeless gesture" because its origin cannot be traced or dated, because it has been perpetuated throughout the course of history, and because it creates anew the event each time it is performed. Through this persistence of religion, this infinite renewal, this timelessness, human time is made possible: The participants too are renewed along with the ritual. Blackburn continues, however, to enlarge the concept of ritual to encompass secular as well as religious life. Midway through the poem a "lady tourist/ . . . joined the procession"; she appeared an "anomaly": "Instead of a rosary, carried/ a white pocketbook." After this secular irregularity in the religious ceremony, Blackburn immediately introduces what appear to be irregularities of subject in a poem describing a sacred ritual: He tells the reader that he rises everyday "in the dawn light"; he eats "Meat every Thursday/ when the calf/ is killed"; he gets "Mail from the bus at 4:30/ fresh milk at 5." What Blackburn is implying through these juxtapositions is that our everyday lives are composed of rituals that renew life on a daily basis, that make life itself possible. The "german anthropologist," then, "her poor self at the end of the line," is really not at a terminal point; for life, like this yearly ritual, is a perpetual process of renewal, a series of rebirths: "End of a timeless act of the peoples of the earth," hardly an end at all.

"Ritual IV"

In poetry written after Blackburn's return to New York in 1957, the religious and the secular merge for him to the point where his rituals consist entirely of various activities repeated on a daily basis. Religion becomes the celebration of life, since the divine is immanent in the world itself. In "Ritual IV," for example, Blackburn juxtaposes a description of plants growing in his kitchen with a reenactment of a Saturday morning breakfast with his wife, in order to express the unity of all living things. "You sit here smiling at/ me and the young plants," as the "beams" of sunlight reveal the "dust" that "float[s]" from the plants to them. The poet concludes: "Everything/ grows,/ and rests."

"Lines, Trees, and Words"

Having united the sacred and profane to such a degree, Blackburn occasionally grows impatient with orthodox ceremony. In "Lines, Trees, and Words," walking through a park and overhearing children singing a hymn off-key, a friend observes how they are mutilating "it." Blackburn, however, willfully misunderstands the referent of the pronoun to be the divine and replies, "Don't we all." Any verbal attempt to embody the spiritual will result in such travesty: "Give the child words, give him/ words, he will use them." Characteristically, the poem ends with the preferred indefinite, natural, religious note: "How the trees hang down from the sky." At times, Blackburn will even imply that the more Puritanical strain in orthodox religion might very well obstruct his and others' more spontaneous celebration of the divine through joyous living, as in "Ash Wednesday, 1965."

"The Purse Seine"

Most of the poetry that Blackburn wrote between 1958 and 1967 had New York City for its setting and focused intimately on human psychology: the ways in which people relate to one another, how they react to the world in which they find themselves, and how they regard their own personalities and bodies. In Blackburn's love poems of this period, two symbols, fishing nets and the sea, continually recur, helping him to express his vision of love as unavoidable and overwhelming, as the persistent tide of the sea, and therefore frightening, threatening, as the confining fishing net, at first unnoticed. Love for Blackburn is a force that one can resist only for so long; then one gives in wholeheartedly, though with trepidation. "The Purse Seine" accumulates a number of aquatic images that express this ambivalence: what "gulls" "do that looks so beautiful, is/ hunt"; at once they are "crying freedom, crying carrion"; the eye of the gull, merging with that of his lover, "frightens," for both are the "beautiful killer"; "the net/ is tight," and then "The purse closes" and "we drown/ in sight of/ I love you and you love me." In "Park Poem," the poet reels from "the first shock of leaves their alliance with love"—the complicity of nature in romance. "How to Get up off It" is a contemporaneous poem that juxtaposes several random events ultimately related to the persistence of love in nature, and thus in human beings. The poet begins the poem by recalling a mountain climber's words: "Am I ready for this mountain?" As "they go up," so does the poet climb love's mountain, sitting with his second wife in front of the Public Library, next to a girl writing a letter to her boyfriend; they are passed by a couple holding hands who wave to them and then witness a mating dance: "The pigeons never seem to tire/ of the game," and neither do people, as the events recorded in the poem demonstrate.

"CALL IT THE NET" AND "THE NET OF MOON"

Depending upon his mood, Blackburn can portray love as simply the drive of blind passion that results in a loss of freedom through its satisfaction. In such poems as "Call It the Net," love is a "silken trap . . . the net of lust." In "The Sea and the Shadow," that "damned sea" of sexuality will drive him back to his lover despite his anger at her; the waves become the rhythm of the sexual act: "I will come into your belly and make it a sea rolling against me." At other times, however, sexual love will be a joyous occasion, as in "lower case poem": "of that spring tide i sing/ clutched to one another." At such times, as Blackburn explains in "The Net of Moon," the lovers have achieved a union of the physical and the spiritual, "a just balance be-/ tween the emotion and the motion of the wave on the bay," lust being transformed into love. What Blackburn finds most striking, in the end, is the inevitable nature of both sexuality and love. Upon seeing a pretty girl on the street in "The Tides," the poet exclaims: "Terrible indeed is the house of heaven in the mind." After recalling the act of love, "its flood/ its ebb," the poet can only conclude: "What the man must do/ what the woman must do."

EROTIC POEMS

Blackburn accepts, as a natural dimension of human relations, this constant attraction between men and women, which exists as much on the physical as on the emotional level. Rather than trying to resist or repress the erotic impulse, Blackburn celebrates it in a series of erotic poems unique in the language. Never vulgar, tawdry, or exhibitionistic, they involve a drama of emotion as well as of desire, for Blackburn portrays the woman as well as the man being caught in the erotic moment and enjoying it with equal relish. This mutual, if often covert, complicity results in a sense of the erotic as all-pervasive and joyous rather than predatory or compromising. These poems are usually contemporaneous with the events and feelings they describe and involve witty shifts of tone through incongruous diction, ranging from colloquial ("all very chummy") to tabloid cliché ("the hotbed of assignation") to scientific jargon ("hypotenuse," "trajectory").

Two of his best erotic poems appear in *Brooklyn-Manhattan Transit*, for the subway is one of the more likely places to afford the modern troubadour an opportunity to admire the feminine. In "The Once-Over," a pretty blond woman is being appreciated by the poet and the other riders of the car. According to the poet, however, she is deliberately inviting their admiration: She is "standing/ tho there are seats"; "Only a stolid young man . . . does not know he is being assaulted"; "She has us and we her." In "Clickety-Clack," Blackburn is reading out loud a blatantly erotic passage from one of Lawrence Ferlinghetti's poems on the subway car, much to the amusement (and arousal) of a young lady, despite her frown, as the negative prefix split by the line ending from the rest of its root word indicates: She "began to stare dis-/ approvingly and wiggle." "The Slogan" records the provocative stroll of a "wellknit blonde in a blue knit dress" past a group of utility workers, Blackburn describing her walk with terms borrowed from physics. "Hands" portrays a girl entering her room and going to open a window with her boyfriend in pursuit, "bringing/ one thing up, & another down." Even in "The Assassination of President McKinley," the opportunistic proprietor of the drapery shop is not the only one who enjoys "the last rite/ for the assassinated Mr. McKinley."

AGAINST THE SILENCES

Blackburn's one long cycle of poems on love, published posthumously as *Against the Silences*, was written between 1963 and 1967, and deals with the dissolution of his second marriage. The cycle moves from uneasy marital contentment ("knowing we love one another/ sometime," from "The Second Message"), to the beginning of estrangement ("the thought dissolves & only/ fact remains," from "Slippers, Anyone?"), to argument resulting from a misunderstanding of the husband's deepest personal allegiances ("The Value"), to the wife's infidelity ("What Is It, Love?"), and finally to divorce ("Scenario for a Walk-On," in which the poet depicts the separation as the ending of a film). The sequence recalls George Meredith's *Modern Love* (1862), a series of fifty sixteen-line sonnets portraying the psychological dilemmas of an unhappy married couple through dramatic monologue or silent rumination, written the year after Meredith's divorce from his first wife. Because Blackburn's poems focus specifically on the intimate details of his own marriage, automatically recorded in the contemporaneous open-form poem of immediate experience, his cycle has somewhat greater emotional range and depth than Meredith's, which is a more conscious attempt to generalize from personal experience about the condition of romantic love in the modern world, as the title suggests.

In *Against the Silences*, the complexity of the beleaguered husband's feelings is captured in poems that often portray several conflicting emotions at once: confusion, frustration, pain, humiliation, anger, disgust, fear, loneliness. The subtle role that sexual passion assumes in the relationship is also treated. In the early "So Deep We Never Got," the poet wishes his wife to make love to him as a reassurance of her affection: Resorting to a favorite symbol, he needs to be with her "chest-deep in the surf/ and those waves coming and coming." In "Monday, Monday," however, the husband uses an offer of sex in an attempt to keep his wife from meeting her lover, but the response remains the same throughout the poem: "away,/ her body pushed me away." In this sequence, Blackburn's idea of love as a net to which one deliberately surrenders oneself attains its most explicit statement. Although staying with his wife was always an "act of will" ("The Second Message"), "reasons of choice" are "so obscure" that the process of choice can never ensure happiness; he can only "choose and fear and live it thru" ("Accident"). The result is equally ironic: The possessor of another in love becomes "possessed" by that very love ("The Price").

ELEGIES

If Blackburn adds a new genre to English-language verse, or revives one long defunct, through his erotic poems he contributes to an ongoing tradition with his elegies, which he composed throughout his career. In "The Mint Quality" (1961), the poet attempts to "Sing/ straight as I can" about the death of a vivacious young woman by first giving the details of her automobile accident in France and then presenting her monologue to her friends from the other side of death. The poem becomes ironic when Christiane assures them that "*next time*" she will "*wait til the middle of life/ know what you know/ just to understand.*" The poem began with the poet, at middle age, professing his complete incomprehension of the cycle of life and death: "two friends' wives/ are near their term and large./ . . . One/ girl is dead. No choice."

THE REARDON POEMS

The Reardon Poems is a sequence of seven poems written in memory of Blackburn's friend Robert Reardon: "Bluegrass" presents the unsuccessful operation to save his life; "The Writer" tells of Reardon's vocation, novelist; "The Husband" treats his relationship with his wife and presents her disorientation and loneliness; "Sixteen Sloppy Haiku" are brief glimpses or thoughts of Reardon's last days of life; "The List" consists of Reardon's last rites, as specified by him before his death; and "St. Mark's-in-the-Bouwerie" is an elegy proper on death, its inexplicability amidst life ("When there's nothing anyone can do,/ reality/ comes on fast or slow"). "Seventeen Nights Later at McSorley's" is the epilogue, employing recorded conversation with great thematic effect; Blackburn is speaking to Reardon's former roommate in the hospital:

> You won't see him again, sez I
> "No?"
> No. You're well again? Mazeltov.
> "No?"
> No.

Perhaps Blackburn's finest elegy is "December Journal: 1968," on the death of his third wife's father, in which practically all of his formal poetic resources come into play. The poem begins with the telephone call informing them of the death and moves through grief and tears to the wake and funeral in a passage in which breakfast and the Eucharist are superimposed; to a meditation on the mystery of life and death, creation and destruction, inspired by an open journal on alchemy lying before the poet; and finally to lovemaking and a renewal of domestic patterns ("'You have to get up and move the car.'/ I existed again, I/ was married to my wife!"). Inspired by his alchemical reading, the poet realizes that life mysteriously renews itself within materials that compose rock; that is, life dwells in and is sustained by essentially inanimate matter, a theme first heard in "How to Get Through Reality." This miracle, and the miracle of the living child in his wife's womb, has by the end of the poem put him at ease.

OTHER MAJOR WORKS

TRANSLATIONS: *Proensa*, 1953; *End of the Game and Other Stories*, 1967 (of Julio Cortázar); *Hunk of Skin*, 1968 (of Pablo Picasso); *Cronopios and Famas*, 1969 (of Cortázar); *The Treasure of the Muleteer and Other Spanish Tales*, 1974 (of Antonio Jimenez-Landi); *Peire Vidal*, 1972; *Guillem de Poitou: His Eleven Extant Poems*, 1976; *Proensa: An Anthology of Troubadour Poetry*, 1978; *Lorca/Blackburn: Poems of Federico García Lorca Chosen and Translated by Paul Blackburn*, 1979.

NONFICTION: "Das Kennerbuch," 1953; "Writing for the Ear," 1960; "The American Duende," 1962; "The Grinding Down," 1963.

BIBLIOGRAPHY

Malkoff, Karl. *Crowell's Handbook of Contemporary American Poetry*. New York: Thomas Y. Crowell, 1973. The entry on Blackburn lists him not only as a Black Mountain Poet but also as a Projectivist, although like most Projectivists, his poetry is individualistic. Mentions his long sojourns abroad and discusses two of his works, *The Cities* and *The Nets*. Other than some insightful comments about Projectivist poetry—for example, that there is no real distinction between the inner and outer world—there is little noteworthy criticism here.

Marowski, Daniel G., and Roger Matuz, eds. *Contemporary Literary Criticism*. Vol. 43. Detroit: Gale Research, 1987. Lists Blackburn as a noted translator,

scholar, and poet, whose poetry combines structural experimentation with colloquial forms. This combination creates a "visual, aural, and psychological reading experience." Gathers together some fine reviews of Blackburn's work, in particular critical commentary of his most widely acclaimed work, *The Journals*. Also notes that since the posthumous publication of *The Collected Poems of Paul Blackburn*, his verse has attracted a wider audience and has undergone critical reevaluation.

Rosenthal, M. L. Review of *The Cities*, by Paul Blackburn. *Poetry* 114 (May, 1969): 129-130. Comments on Blackburn's love of American lingo and his emphasis on the quality of movement, both of which lend his poems qualities of "humor and sensuality." Appreciates Blackburn's focus on the process of the poet's involvement in the poem as a "disciplining subject of the poem, as well as its range in action."

Stephens, Michael. "Common Speech and Complex Forms." *The Nation* 223 (September 4, 1976): 189-190. Reviews *The Cities, The Journals*, and *Halfway down the Coast*, which he considers a suitable introduction to Blackburn. Notes that the possibility of death that Blackburn explores in *Halfway* becomes the reality of dying in *The Journals*. Commends Blackburn for his ability to appreciate "overheard cadences in common speech," which he says is indicative of Blackburn's love of people.

William Skaff;
bibliography updated by the editors

WILLIAM BLAKE

Born: London, England; November 28, 1757
Died: London, England; August 12, 1827

PRINCIPAL POETRY
Poetical Sketches, 1783
There Is No Natural Religion, 1788
All Religions Are One, 1788
Songs of Innocence, 1789

The Book of Thel, 1789
The Marriage of Heaven and Hell, 1790
The French Revolution, wr. 1791, pb. 1913
America: A Prophecy, 1793
Visions of the Daughters of Albion, 1793
Songs of Innocence and of Experience, 1794
Europe: A Prophecy, 1794
The [First] Book of Urizen, 1794
The Song of Los, 1795
The Book of Ahania, 1795
The Book of Los, 1795
Vala: Or, The Four Zoas, wr. 1795-1804, pb. 1963
   (best known as *The Four Zoas*)
Milton: A Poem, 1804-1808
Jerusalem: The Emanation of the Giant Albion, 1804-
   1820
The Poems of William Blake, 1971

OTHER LITERARY FORMS

William Blake's prose includes *An Island in the Moon* (wr. c. 1784), *To the Public: Prospectus* (1793), *A Descriptive Catalogue* (1809), marginalia, and letters. It is almost a given with Blake scholarship and criticism that the interrelation of poetry and design is vital. David V. Erdman's *The Illuminated Blake* (1975) includes all of Blake's illuminated works, text, and design, with a plate-by-plate commentary.

ACHIEVEMENTS

William Blake's reputation during his lifetime was not a fraction of what it is today. He worked hard at his trade, that of engraving, but his style was not in fashion, and his commissions were few. His poverty and the laborious process of producing his own illuminated books for sale prevented him from producing more than two hundred copies of his own work in his lifetime. Even the *Songs of Innocence and of Experience*, which he sold sporadically throughout his career, remained virtually unnoticed by his contemporaries. What little reputation he had among his contemporaries was as an artist, ingenious but no doubt mad.

In 1863, Alexander Gilchrist's biography of Blake did much to establish Blake's reputation as an artist and a poet. The Yeats-Ellis edition of Blake (1893) further enhanced his fame, not as a forgotten painter and poet,

but as a purveyor of esoteric lore. Accurate transcription of Blake's texts began only in the twentieth century with the work of Geoffrey Keynes. Modern critical work was pioneered by S. Foster Damon in 1924, but it was not until Northrop Frye's *Fearful Symmetry* in 1947 that Blake's work was treated as a comprehensible, symmetrical whole.

A poet-artist who imaginatively remolds his own age and its traditions and then produces poetry, engravings, and paintings within that re-created world is a poet-artist who will attract a wide variety of readers. Blake's profound understanding of the ways in which man deals with the warring contraries within his mind has become a fertile source for modern psychology. Carl Jung referred to Blake as a visionary poet who had achieved contact with the potent wellspring of the unconscious. Blake's devotion to a humanistic apocalypse created through the display of exuberant energies and expanded imaginative perceptions has been an inspiration to two generations of twentieth century writers: first D. H. Lawrence, E. M. Forster, William Butler Yeats, and Aldous Huxley, and later, Norman O. Brown, Allen Ginsberg, Theodore Roszak, Colin Wilson, and John Gardner, among others. If a poet can be judged by the quality and quantity of the attention he receives, Blake certainly rose in the twentieth century from a vague precursor of Romanticism to one of the six major English Romantic poets.

BIOGRAPHY

William Blake was born in Carnaby Market, London, on November 28, 1757. By the age of four, he was having visions: God put his head through the window to look at him, angels walked among the haymakers, and a tree was starred with angels. The visionary child was spared the rigors of formal schooling and learned to read and write at home. He attended a drawing school for four years and in 1772 began a seven-year apprenticeship to James Basire, engraver. He had already begun three years before to write the lyrics which were later printed in *Poetical Sketches*. It was not as a poet, however, that he would make his living but as an engraver who also could do original designs. The Gothic style of engraving which he learned from Basire was unfortunately somewhat passé. In later years, Blake had to sit

William Blake (Library of Congress)

back and watch other engravers receive commissions to execute his own designs.

At the age of twenty-two, Blake became a student of the Royal Academy, which meant that he could draw from models, living and antique, and attend lectures and exhibitions for six years. The politics of the day, as well as a spreading evangelical fervor, infused his life as an artist-poet. Blake was part of the 1780 Gordon Riots and was present at the burning of Newgate Prison. He was a vehement supporter of the French Revolution and attended radical gatherings which included William Godwin, Thomas Paine, Mary Wollstonecraft Shelley, and Joseph Priestley. Through John Flaxman, Blake developed an interest in Swedenborgianism. The doctrines of Emanuel Swedenborg seemed both to attract and to repel Blake. *The Marriage of Heaven and Hell* launched an attack on this movement.

In 1782, Blake married Catherine Boucher, whose life apparently became one with his. He tried his hand at running a printshop, but in 1785 it failed. He continued to make a meager living on commissions for designs and engravings, but these were the work of other men. In

1800, he moved to Felpham near Chichester at the invitation of William Hayley, a minor poet, who attempted for the next three years to guide Blake's life into a financially lucrative mold. Blake returned as impoverished as ever to London in 1803, never to leave it again. In 1804, he was tried for sedition and was acquitted. It is ironic that Blake was not being tried for his pervasive iconoclasm, thoughts expressed in his unpublished work which would have set the eighteenth century on its head, but because a drunk had falsely accused him. In 1809, he had his one and only exhibition of sixteen paintings, an exhibition ignored by everyone except one reviewer, who attacked it viciously.

If the political and religious spirit of this period inspired Blake, it also worked against his prosperity as an engraver. Few in England during the Napoleonic wars could afford the luxury of commissioning the work of an engraver. In the last ten years of his life, Blake attracted the attention of a group of young painters whose admiration doubtless enriched this period of increasing poverty. On August 12, 1827, Blake died singing of the glories he saw in heaven.

ANALYSIS

William Blake's focus is primarily on inner states; the drama of the later books has been called a *psychomachia*, a drama of the divided psyche. In Blake's world, man was once integrated but suffered a Fall when reason sought to dominate the other faculties. The disequilibrium of the psyche, its reduced perception, is the creator of the natural world as it is now known.

CONTRARIES: THE MARRIAGE OF HEAVEN AND HELL

The notion of "contraries" as defined and developed in *The Marriage of Heaven and Hell* provides a dialectical basis for the regeneration of this psyche. Contraries are to be understood as psychic or mental opposites which exist in a regenerated state, a redeemed paradisiacal state of unlimited energy and unbounded perception. Blake has in his total work depicted the progress to regeneration based on a conflict between contraries. Once contraries are accepted, energy is created, progress is inevitable, and reintegration occurs.

Blake's paradisiacal man differs from fallen man only in that he is aware of his divinity. Paradisiacal man perceives the majesty of the imagination, the passions, the reason, and the senses. The imagination in the redeemed state is called Urthona, and after the Fall, Los. Urthona represents that fourfold, unbounded vision which is the normal attribute of the redeemed man. Such vision is not bound by the particulars it produces through contraction, nor is it bound by the unity it perceives when it expands. Blake, in the imagination's true and saving role as poet, envisions the external world with a fourfold vision. Luvah, the passions or love, is represented after the Fall by Jesus, who puts on the robes of love to preserve some hint of divine love in the fallen world. Urizen, the zoa of reason, is the necessary boundary of energy, the wisdom which supplied form to the energies released by the other contraries. In the fallen world, he is the primary usurper of the dominion of other faculties. Tharmas, the zoa of the senses, has, in his paradisiacal form, unrestrained capacity to expand or contract his senses. In the fallen state, these senses remain but in an enervated condition. Sexuality, the sense of touch shared by two, is a means by which fallen man can regain his paradisiacal stature, but it is unfortunately a suppressed sense. The Blakean Fall which all the personified contraries suffer is a Fall from the divine state to the blind state, to the state where none of their powers are free to express themselves beyond the severe limitations of excessive reason. Each of the contraries has his allotted place in the Fall; each sins either through commission or omission.

Contraries remain a concern of Blake from *The Marriage of Heaven and Hell* to the later prophecies: *The Four Zoas*, *Milton*, and *Jerusalem*. The metaphysic of contraries, the theoretical doctrine, is never denied. The opposition of energy to reason, however, dramatized in the Orc cycle, is no longer Blake's "main act" in the later books. From Night IX in *The Four Zoas* onward, Los, who embodies something akin to the Romantic concept of the sympathetic imagination, becomes the agent of regeneration. It is he who can project himself into the existence of his polar opposite, can accept the existence of that contrary in the act of self-annihilation and consequently forgive. Thus, the theory of contraries has not altered; any contrary can assume a selfhood in conflict with dialectic progression itself. Los preserves the dialectic while Orc maintains a hierarchy.

INNOCENCE AND EXPERIENCE

Blake's concern with the earthly states of Innocence and Experience, with a fallen body and its contraries, has been associated with religious apocalypse. Blake's apocalypse involves a progression from Innocence to Experience and an acceptance of the contraries in those states. An acceptance of contraries would lead to the destruction of false perception and disequilibrium and eventually to a complete resurrection of the fallen body. Man would again possess divine proportions through a progressive development of his own nature rather than through obedience to the supposed laws of an external deity. Through the faculty of imagination Blake intuits the divinity of man, the falseness of society, and the falseness of laws based upon societal behavior. He perceives the spiritual essence of man, displaying therefore a spiritual rather than a rational brand of humanism. Blake's assumption that man is a fallen god makes his psychology more than a psychology; and it makes his humanism an apocalyptic humanism. His diagnosis of the divided psyche becomes a revelation, and his therapy, an apocalypse. Blake himself dons the mantle of a prophet.

Able to see God and his angels at the age of four, Blake gave precedence in his life to vision over the natural world. He would continue to see through and not with the eye, and what he saw he would draw in bold outline as ineluctable truth. Ultimately, even the heterodoxy of Swedenborgianism was an encroachment upon the supremacy of his own contact with the spiritual world. Early inspired by the revolutionary spirit of the times, he continued throughout his life to advocate a psychic revolution within each person which would lead to regeneration.

ARCHETYPAL THEMES

Blake's mission throughout his work is always apocalyptic, although he creates a political terrain in the Lambeth books (*The [First] Book of Urizen*, *The Book of Ahania*, *The Book of Los*, and *The Song of Los*) and a psychological one in his later prophecies (*The Four Zoas*, *Milton*, and *Jerusalem*). His focus moves from a political-societal revolution of apocalyptic proportions to a psychic, perceptual regeneration of each individual person. It is the regenerated person who can perceive both a unity beyond all diversity and a diversity within that unity.

Songs of Innocence and of Experience demonstrates Blake's concern for individual human life, in particular its course from innocence to experience. What are the destructive forces operating early upon man, upon his childhood, which ultimately imprison him and lead to "mind-forged manacles"? In *Songs of Innocence*, a glimpse of energies is uncircumscribed, of what man was and again could be if he rightly freed himself from a limited perception and repressed energies.

The later poems, *The Four Zoas*, *Milton*, and *Jerusalem*, are large-scale epics whose focus is a particularly Romantic one—epistemological and ontological transformation. Los, hero of the imagination, is not a hero who affirms the values of a culture, nor are his strengths and virtues uniformly admired by that culture. Like traditional epics, Blake's epics begin *in medias res*, but because the natural world is usually seen unclearly, it is worthless to speak of its beginning, middle, or end. The reader who enters the world of Blake's epics enters a psychic world, becomes a "mental traveller," and in his purest states reaches heights traditionally reserved for deity in the Judeo-Christian tradition and deities in the epics of Homer and Vergil.

Blake's work is not unconnected with the natural world, but he attempts to bracket out all but the irreducible elements of the archetypal, individual human life. Paradoxically, Blake's work is characterized by less structural context than that of any poet of whom one could readily think; yet that work is such a dramatic reaction to the eighteenth century and such a dramatic revelation of the new Romanticism that it is unrivaled as an intense portrait of both sensibilities.

MAN IMAGINING

In reaction to John Locke's view that the perceiver is separated from the world because of his incapacity to do more than apprehend the secondary qualities of objects, Blake asserted the supremacy of individual perception. Man perceiving is man imagining, an act which encompasses the totality of an individual's energies and personality. What is perceived is dependent upon the imaginative act. The world can only be construed imaginatively. Man, Blake held, can only apprehend the infinity within him through his imagination. The London of Blake's poem of that name is a pitiable place because man's imagination, his poetic genius, is repressed. London is at every moment available for imaginative transformation; so is every object in the natural world. In this view of imagination, Blake foreshadows Samuel Taylor Coleridge and especially Percy Bysshe Shelley and attacks the rationalism of the eighteenth century. The metaphysics of Francis Bacon, Isaac Newton, and Locke were despicable because they elevated rationality and denied imagination, thus standing in the way of regeneration.

Besides disagreeing with the philosophy and psychology of his own day, Blake criticized traditional religious and aesthetic views. Man's fallen perception created the world, not in seven days, but in what became a moment in time. Jesus was a man of revitalized perceptions, a man fully conscious of his unlimited energies. Jesus was thus a supranatural man, one who had achieved the kind of regeneration that Blake felt it was in every person's power to achieve. In art, Blake applauded the firm outline of Michelangelo and Raphael and despised the indeterminacy of Rubens and Titian. The artist who apprehended with strong imagination drew boldly because the truth was clearly perceived. Socially and politically, Blake, unlike Coleridge and William Wordsworth, remained unreconciled to the status quo. Blake's revolutionary zeal, most pronounced in the Lambeth books, remained undiminished, urging him to portray error so that it could be cast out. Only Shelley equals Blake's faith in poetic genius to transform the very nature of man and thus the very nature of the world he perceives.

SONGS OF INNOCENCE AND OF EXPERIENCE

Songs of Innocence and of Experience shows "the two contrary states of the human soul." The contraries cited in *The Marriage of Heaven and Hell* are "Attraction and Repulsion, Reason and Energy, Love and Hate. . . ." Since, however, these songs are not sung outside either Innocence or Experience but from within those states, the contraries are not fully presented in their ideal forms. The songs are from corrupted states and portray disproportionate contraries. Theoretically, each contrary state acts as a corrective to the other, and contraries in the *Songs of Innocence and of Experience* are suggested either in the text of the poem or in the accompanying design.

The introduction song to the *Songs of Innocence and*

of Experience is a good example not only of Blake's view of the role of Innocence and Experience in regeneration but also of the complexity of these seemingly simple songs. This song manages in its twenty lines to present a transition from absolute sensuous Innocence to a recognition of Experience and finally a transition to a higher state. The first stanza presents an almost complete picture of absolute carefree innocence. The adjective "wild" may imply a condemnation of an aspect of absolute Innocence. Because Blake believed that Experience brings an indispensable consciousness of one's actions so that choice becomes possible, the essential flaw in the state of Innocence is that it does not provide the child with alternatives.

The second stanza of this lyric presents the image of the lamb, a symbol of Christ. The lamb, while creating the image of the Innocence of Christ, also exhibits the equally true image of Christ crucified. It is this symbol of Experience which brings tears to the child, and on a psychological level, the child is emerging from a "wild" unconscious realm to a realm of consciousness, of Experience.

The third stanza presents two interesting additions: The pipe is replaced by human song and the child weeps with joy. The pipe had first produced laughter and then tears, but it is the human voice which elicits the oxymoronic reaction of joyful weeping. It is only in the human form that the attributes of the two contrary states of Innocence and Experience can exist harmoniously. "Piping down the valley wild" had brought unconstrained laughter, while the figure of the Christ-lamb had brought a more tearful vision of Experience; yet in stanza three, such contrary reactions exist, unresolved but coexistent, as do the contrary states which foster them.

The fourth stanza alludes to the loss of childhood through the disappearance of the child of the poem and implies that the elemental properties of Innocence remain after the departure of the physical state of childhood. By plucking the hollow reed, Blake, the piper and singer, reveals a move toward creation which is fully realized in the last stanza. From the vision of Experience of stanza two, and the acceptance of the necessary contrary states of Innocence and Experience through their inherent qualities, laughter and tears, presented in stanza three, Blake has reached the higher plateau of

conscious selflessness described in stanzas four and five. Through the act of creation, the conscious selfless act, which intends to give joy to every child, the conscious selflessness of Blake's paradisiacal reintegrated state is achieved.

THE BOOK OF THEL

In *The Book of Thel*, Thel, a young girl in Innocence, is fearful of advancing to a state of Experience. Lily, Cloud, Clay, and Worm, symbols of innocence and experience, try to allay her fears. Experience may contain key contraries in extreme form; it may be the wrath of the father and the restraint of morality and the curtailment of vision, but it is a state which provides Thel her only opportunity of advancement, of completion and eventual salvation. Experience is a necessary step to the "peace and raptures holy" described by the Cloud. Thel, however, surveys the traditional misfortune of Experience—mortality. She finds no meaningful comfort in the Lily's belief that from Experience, from death, one flourishes "in eternal vales." Thel laments the consciousness that is hers when she takes a trial step into Experience. She finds morality, which represses sexual energy, unbearable. Thus, in spite of the eventual "peace and raptures holy" which Thel can proceed to from a state of Experience, her first look at that state proves too much for her. She flees Experience and consciousness to the vales of Har, the land of superannuated children, described in the poem *Tiriel*; it is a land of unfulfilled innocents who have refused to graduate into the world of Experience. A *Songs of Innocence* poem, "The Lamb," and a *Songs of Experience* poem, "The Tyger," depict the nature of perception in those states and the contraries which abide in each state. The poems may be viewed as "contrary poems."

The questions of the child in "The Lamb" are not the reason's questions but imagination's—questions he can answer because he has perceived the identity of himself, the lamb, and God. The equation is formed thus: The lamb is Christ the lamb; the child is Christ as a child; and the lamb and child are therefore joined by their mutual identity with Christ. In Innocence, all life is perceived as one and holy. Since there are two contrary states of the human soul and "The Lamb" is a product of only one, Innocence, it is not possible to conclude that this poem depicts Blake's paradisiacal state. The vines in the design are twisting about the sapling on both sides of the engraving, indicating in traditional symbolism the importance of going beyond childhood into Experience. If the child-speaker can see all life as one, can imaginatively perceive the whole, he cannot perceive the particularity, the diversity, which comprises that unity, which Experience's reason so meticulously numbers and analyzes. Even as the adult speaker of "The Tyger" can see only a fragmented world which his imagination is too weak to unify, so the child-speaker cannot see the fragments that comprise the world.

The spontaneity and carefree abandon of the lamb in Innocence can in Experience no longer be perceived in the form of a lamb. The perceiver in Experience fears the energy of Innocence and therefore shapes it into a form which his reason has deemed frightening—that of a tiger. This form which the tiger of the poem "The Tyger" possesses is symmetrical, its symmetry lying in its perfect relationship with the energy it contains. It is only a "fearful symmetry" to the perceiver in Experience who is riddled with the prejudices of Experience, prejudices regarding what is good and what is evil, what is rational and what is irrational, or wild. The moral hierarchy of Experience—good is good and evil is evil—does not permit the perceiver in Experience to perceive a Keatsian "fineness" in the tiger, a marvelous interrelationship of form and energy.

The reader goes back and forth in this poem from a vision of the energies of the unconscious mind to a perception of the boundaries of those energies. It is the mixture of energy and boundary which the speaker-perceiver finds disturbing. The tiger in the first stanza is seen as a burning figure in the night, perhaps symbolizing the burning vibrant passions repressed in the darkened areas of the mind. The tiger perceived by the speaker can live only in the dark since both reason and moral hierarchy have relegated it to that realm. The tiger is, in its energies, in its fire, too great for the conscious mind to accept; yet, like a recurrent nightmare, the tiger burns brightly and cannot be altogether denied. The tiger cannot be quietly integrated into the personality of the speaker-perceiver without doing severe damage to the structure of self carefully fabricated by reason and moral hierarchy. Rather than transform himself, question himself, the speaker-perceiver questions the tiger's creator.

What creator could possibly give form to such uncontrollable energy? How can such energy be satisfactorily bounded? The perceiver in Experience assumes that such energy as the tiger represents can be denied only through repression. It cannot be given necessary form; it must be perceived as having a fearful rather than a fine form. This speaker turns questioner and by his questioning reveals his subservience to analytical reason.

The questioner proceeds under the assumption that no creation can be greater than its creator, that in some way the dangerous, fearful energies of the tiger are amenable to that creator, are somehow part of that creator. Where is such a creator to be found? More specifically, where are those burning energies to be found in the spiritual realm? The questioner is already convinced that the creation of the tiger is a presumptuous act and he therefore concludes that Satan is the great presumer. This tiger is, therefore, in the questioner-perceiver's mind, Satan's work, a hellish creation forged in the fires not of Blake's Hell but of a traditional Hell.

The final questions to be asked are merely rhetorical. The questioner has decided that *his* creator could never have created the tiger. The creator involved here has dared to create the tiger. There exists here a Manichaean split, a desperate attempt to answer the problem of the existence of evil. Part of man has been made by God and that part is good, while Satan has made the evil part of man, the part symbolized by the tiger. The only symbol of energy that the questioner-perceiver is prepared to face is that of the lamb. Yet, while the lamb sufficed in Innocence as representative of certain energies, it is no longer indicative of the growth of energy which is a mature person's in Experience. The tiger of Experience expresses the symbolic balance of energy and reason, fire and form; however, only a perceiver whose energies are brought from Innocence and matured in Experience under the guidance of reason in necessary proportions can perceive that balance. This uncorrupted perceiver can see the child lying down with the tiger, as in "A Little Girl Found." That tiger is the perfect symbol of the balance of contraries and is perceived as such; the tiger of "The Tyger" is also a perfect symbol but improperly perceived.

THE MARRIAGE OF HEAVEN AND HELL

The *raison d'être* of the incorporation of all contraries as they are perceived in the two contrary states, Innocence and Experience, is provided in *The Marriage of Heaven and Hell*. It fulfills more than a mere metaphysical role. It is the foundation of Blake's prophecy, the basis not of extended system but of vision. *The Marriage of Heaven and Hell* preserves the whole body of contraries by a relentless attack upon all divisive factors. Dualism in all areas is negated and the suppressed half of the fallen body, represented by the suppressed division of contraries, is supported and affirmed in opposition to the deadening voices of the "Angels."

The framework of *The Marriage of Heaven and Hell* is traditional Judeo-Christian religion and morality. Blake completely alters and destroys this traditional structure and replaces it with an equal acceptance of the two contrary states of the human soul and their inherent contraries. Energies which are indigenous to childhood must take their place alongside the necessary contraries of Experience—reason, repulsion, and hate. The traditional moral hierarchy of good over evil allows one state and its contraries to have ascendancy over the other. Blake boldly adopts the standard nomenclature and marries good and evil as true opposites, essential contraries. Both the passive and active traits of man's nature are assumed. Rather than an exclusive emphasis on good, as in the Judeo-Christian ethic, or evil, as in sadism, Blake seeks the reintegration of the unity of man through the opposition of these strategic contraries. Once Blake's doctrine of contraries as presented in *The Marriage of Heaven and Hell* is understood, it becomes clearer what *Songs of Innocence and of Experience* is describing, what the basis of Orc's battle on behalf of energy in the Lambeth books is, and in what way Los preserves the contraries in the later books.

The Marriage of Heaven and Hell is a theoretical base for Blake's vision; however, the form of the work is by no means expository. It presents a dialectic of contraries in dialectical form. Blake's dialectic is not a system of reason in the Hegelian sense, not a system leading to an external synthesis and to the creation of new contraries. Blake's dialectic is composed of contraries immanent in the human personality, contraries which do not change but which generate increasing energy.

In the "Argument" section, "keeping the perilous path" refers to primal unity, Blakean primal unity, and means maintaining all contraries. The man in the vale maintains the dialectic between conscious and unconscious mind. In Blake's view, once the "path is planted," once the Fall has occurred, man must journey forward, through Innocence and Experience to reintegration.

In Plate 3, Blake declares the immanence of contraries within the human personality and denies the moral dualism of the Judeo-Christian ethic. These contraries are not illusory; their opposition is real, but one contrary does not subsume or upset another. No hierarchy is imposed. The energies which are traditionally classified as "good" are not superior to the energies traditionally classified as "evil." Neither is the reverse true, since Blake is no disciple of the Marquis de Sade. In Blake's view, the hierarchy of morality is particularly insidious since it prevents man from espousing contraries and achieving the progression resulting from that act.

In Plate 4, Blake indicates that the contraries transcend the dualism of body and soul. It is the Devil who proclaims the body as the only portion of the soul, and thus Blake's Devil is his hero, his spokesman. This identification of the soul with the observable, physical body, when combined with Blake's notion of progression based on a dialectic of contraries, implies that although the body is a mere portion of the soul, its most debased portion, it is the only medium available to man by which an amplified body, a spiritual body or soul, can be reached. Contraries existing within the body which are perceived in this fallen world are accepted in pursuit of "ideal" or amplified contraries. In Blake's view, the body and its contraries are sacred.

In Plates 5 and 6, Blake's Devil says that energies are too often repressed. The person who represses his energies in turn suppresses the energies of others. Plate 5 begins the "Proverbs of Hell" section. The proverbs are designed to strengthen the imagination of the reader so that the dynamic of contraries is perceived. Once the reader perceives imaginatively the reality of this dynamic, the dynamic is maintained and energy ensues. Ever-increasing energy leads to ever-expanding perception, and perception, for Blake, ultimately determines ontology. The Proverbs of Hell are pithy "consciousness raisers," each demonstrating the dynamic or dialectic of contraries in both content and form.

Plate 11 continues Blake's assault on the priesthood. In Plates 12 and 13, Blake allies himself with the prophets, Isaiah and Ezekiel—voices of "firm persuasion" and "honest indignation." In Plates 14 and 15, Blake describes the creative process that produced *The Marriage of Heaven and Hell*. He further defines the psychic terrain in Plate 16 by presenting two groups, "Prolific" and "Devourer," that can be seen as personified categories incorporating all dichotomies previously discussed in *The Marriage of Heaven and Hell*; Devil-Evil-Energy-Hell are subsumed by the Prolific, and Angel-Good-Reason-Heaven are subsumed by the Devourer. Plates 17 to 20 contain Blake's "fantastic" satirical drama between an Angel and Blake, as Devil. Limited or bounded perception creates a world and an end for itself that a liberated, diabolical perception can alter in the twinkling of an eye. The Angel perceives such a world of error because he has no sense of the dynamic interplay of contraries, no idea that "Opposition is true Friendship."

THE FRENCH REVOLUTION

Some of the political implications of Blake's doctrines in *The Marriage of Heaven and Hell* are evident in *The French Revolution*. This poem of twenty pages, posthumously published, has no accompanying designs and was written for the radical publisher Joseph Johnson. It is conjectured that by 1791 it was dangerous for an Englishman to express a revolutionary enthusiasm inspired by the French Revolution. Blake's own political radicalism is not in this poem couched in symbolic terms and therefore he may have had second thoughts about printing it and risking imprisonment. Blake chronicles, with ample poetic license, the period in France from June 19 to July 15, when the king's troops were dispersed. Louis XVI and his nobles debate their course of action in the light of the growing revolution outside, and they finally decide to remove the troops surrounding Paris. In Blake's telling, this decision represents a renewed perception on the part of the king and his nobles. The Bastille, a symbol of political repression, consequently falls. In actuality, the Bastille fell before the decision was made to remove the king's troops.

AMERICA: A PROPHECY

There is more of what will become Blake's completed mythology in *America: A Prophecy* than there is in *The French Revolution*. Besides historical characters such as George Washington, Benjamin Franklin, and

Thomas Paine, Blake here introduces Orc and Urizen, personifications of revolutionary energy and reason. In a preludium or preface, Vala, the shadowy female who symbolizes North America, is in chains. Her liberation occurs through her sexual relations with the fiery Orc. To Blake, therefore, a successful American revolution is not only political but also sexual. George III is the Angel of Albion (England) who worships Urizen and Urizen's law of the Ten Commandments. These two attempt to saturate America with their own diseases by sending a plague across the Atlantic to America. However, the plague is countered by the revolutionary zeal of Orc, who replaces the oppressions of Urizen with genuine political and sexual freedom. All Europe is affected by this revolution, but England, seeking the protection of Urizen, hurries to rebuild the gates of repression, the gates of moral good and evil and a dominant rationality.

Blake's Orc, revolutionary energy, successfully counters Urizen ("your reason") just as the French Revolution countered the Ancient Regime. However, the French Revolution lost its revolutionary energy in the tyranny of Napoleonic France. It became obvious to Blake that historical, political solutions—revolutions—could not effect a break in the historical cycle, a break that would be an apocalypse. Thus, in *The Four Zoas*, Orc becomes a destructive force in nature, an opponent of reason totally oblivious to reason's importance on a regenerated scale. Orc becomes as tied to the natural, unregenerated cycle as Vala, the embodiment of the natural process itself.

Although Urizen is easily defeated by Orc in *America*, he remains an important character in Blake's myth. He is at once Nobodaddy, a comical, ridiculous father figure, and the Ancient of Days, depicted with grandeur in the frontispiece to *Europe: A Prophecy*. Urizen represents the urge to structure and systematize, to reduce all to rational terms. In the language of our own day, he recognizes only what can be quantified, and, like a good logical positivist, seeks empirical referents to instill meaning in words.

EUROPE: A PROPHECY

Europe can be viewed as a continuation of *America* in which revolutionary zeal has been replaced by a repressive conservatism which binds both energies and perceptions. The time is the birth of Jesus, a time of possible regeneration through his example. This possibility is not realized and the world falls into a long sleep, an eighteen-hundred-year sleep of Nature. Los, the poetic genius, naïvely rejoices in a promise of peace while Urizen is attempting to rule outside his own domain; and Los's female counterpart, Enitharmon, is a victim of Urizen's dominion and seeks to bind sexual love with moral law. Urizen solidifies his rule, his brazen book of law which ignores imagination, forgiveness, and the necessity of self-annihilation. Edmund Burke and William Pitt, represented by the characters Palamabron and Rintrah, are also under the dominion of Urizen and Enitharmon. The revolutionary spirit of the youth of England is doomed. Pitt-Rintrah three times attempts to lead England to war, into total devastation. In Blake's view, however, Sir Isaac Newton and his system are the real beginning of devastation in England. Newton's blast on the trumpet does not lead to glorious apocalypse but to death-in-life. Enitharmon wakes and calls her perverted children to her—materialism, delusion, hypocrisy, sensualism, and seduction. The poem ends with Orc inspiring the French Revolution, the spirit of which will be challenged by a Urizenic England. Los, the poetic genius, summons his sons to the coming strife, but it is as yet unclear what his precise role will be. That role is defined in *The Four Zoas*, *Milton*, and *Jerusalem*.

THE [FIRST] BOOK OF URIZEN AND THE BOOK OF LOS

In *The [First] Book of Urizen* and *The Book of Los*, Blake does not present a cryptic intermingling of history and myth but rather a first attempt at describing his cosmogony and theogony. *The Book of Los* tells the story of the Fall from Los's point of view and *The [First] Book of Urizen* from Urizen's point of view. Thus, the texts interconnect and gloss each other. The Fall is a fall into creation, one precipitated by Urizen's desire for painless joy, for laws binding everything, for "One King, one God, one Law." Urizen's usurpation of power is clearly an act of the Selfhood, a condition in which the legitimacy and importance of other energies are not recognized.

Los, as imagination, is the epistemological faculty, by which truth or error is perceived. Urizen's revolt on behalf of reason skews perception and plunges Los into the Fall. The world of time and space, the Natural World, is formed by Los, and both Los and Urizen, fallen, are bound to this Natural World. A fall into sexuality follows the fall into materiality. Sexuality is subject to moral constraints. Science is a woven "woof" which is created to hide the void. Orc is born but his youthful exuberance is bound by the perversions of the Net of Religion, a direct product of the perverted dream of Reason. Urizen explores the dens of the material world and observes the shrunken nature of a humanity which has completely forgotten its eternal life.

THE SONG OF LOS

The Song of Los can be viewed as the mythological framework for *America* and *Europe*. The first part of Los's song, "Africa," recounts history leading up to George III—Guardian Prince of Albion's war against the Americans, as depicted in *America*. What exists here is also a historical counterpart to the mythology presented in *The [First] Book of Urizen* and *The Book of Los*. Dark delusion was given Moses on Sinai, abstract law to Pythagoras, Socrates, and Plato, a wretched gospel to Jesus, and the reprehensible Philosophy of the Five Senses to Newton and Locke. The second section, "Asia," is a continuation of *Europe*; it does not speak of events but of the psychological-physiological consequences of Urizen's reign. King, Priest, and Counsellor can only restrain, dismay, and ruin humanity in the service of Urizen. Orc rages over France, but the earth seems too shrunken, humankind too imprisoned to heed. Again, Orc himself, as revolutionary energy, is a questionable savior, since he is described as a serpent. The energy of the French Revolution had become debased, and although Blake hoped for a renewal of its original energies, he was already too skeptical of revolution to present Orc as a hero.

THE BOOK OF AHANIA

The Book of Ahania takes its name from Urizen's female counterpart or emanation, who comes into existence when Fuzon, an Orc-like figure, battles Urizen. Urizen immediately calls Ahania sin, hides her, and suffers jealousy. Ahania becomes the "mother of Pestilence," the kind of pestilence that is a result of a sexuality restrained by the moral law. Urizen's mind, totally victimized by a repressive rationality and the resulting morality, breeds monsters. From the blood of one of these monsters, Urizen forms a bow and shoots a rock at

Fuzon, killing him. Fuzon is pictured as a revolutionary who has assumed the seat of tyranny previously occupied by Urizen. Urizen nails Fuzon to a tree, an act which imitates the death of Christ, Christ as rebel. Fuzon dies because he has not broken the material cycle and is thus vulnerable to the repressive laws of the material world. In the same fashion, the creators of the French Revolution failed to achieve a significant ontological and epistemological revolution and therefore became ensnared once again in nets of mystery which led to the Reign of Terror. Fuzon and the French Revolutionaries achieve no true revolution and fall victim to the "black rock" which is formed by a mind whose energies are repressed in the name of reason and its countless offshoots.

VISIONS OF THE DAUGHTERS OF ALBION

One of the ways to Blakean regeneration is through sexuality, specifically through a reassimilation of the female emanation and the re-creation of the Edenic androgynous body. In *Visions of the Daughters of Albion*, Oothoon is a female emanation; Theotormon is her male counterpart and a victim of a repressive moral code; Bromion is a spokesman of that code. Sexually, Oothoon represents the Prolific; the Devourer equivalent, the opposing sexual nature, must be created in Experience. Jerusalem, in the poem *Jerusalem*, becomes that female emanation cognizant of the nature of the regenerated, androgynous body, and she has gained that knowledge in Experience.

Oothoon is raped by Bromion, and Theotormon treats her like a harlot because she has been raped. Oothoon's imagination gives her a vision of her intrinsic sexual nature. Her vision is of the body, the sexual body no less, a body that is not distinct from the soul. In her newfound identity, Oothoon tries to bring Theotormon to the same vision, tries to bring him beyond the moral categories; but Theotormon demands a rational proof for all living things. Why, he asks implicitly, should he believe Oothoon is pure when the moral code clearly states that she is not pure? Bromion declares that only what can be perceived by the five senses has merit. Oothoon attacks priests and their restraining moral ethic but finally gives up trying to win Theotormon to her newly liberated vision. Her comprehension of the warped picture of sexuality in Experience as demonstrated by

Theotormon and Bromion causes her to conclude that Experience has nothing to offer. Although she is not blinded regarding her own sexual nature, she is unable to reunite with Theotormon, male sexuality, and is denied a vision of sexuality based on energies of both Innocence and Experience. Thus, sexual relations, androgyny, and regeneration are denied both Oothoon and Theotormon.

THE FOUR ZOAS

The Four Zoas is an unengraved poem written in two overlapping stages. The main characters, Luvah, Urizen, Tharmas, and Urthona, are the "zoas" of the human personality, each representing an inherent, indivisible quality of the human personality. However, these characters are true characters and not mere allegorical representations. *The Four Zoas* is Blake's account of a split in the Edenic personality of Man, called Albion, of a Fall into the cycle of the natural world, and of the labors of Los, the imagination, to reunite and regenerate the four zoas. This poem is both a historical drama inevitably unfolded in time and space and a psychological drama, one in which time and space have no validity. As a historical drama, the poem lends itself to the kinds of historical connections made in *Europe* or *America*, but this is not a consistent base from which to read the poem, nor will expectations of a conventional narrative structure be at all fruitful.

The poem begins when Luvah and Vala rush from the loins and into the heart and on to the brain, where they replace Urizen's ordering of the body's life with their own cyclical, generative ordering. This sleeping man, Albion, who has within him the whole world—the powers to contract and expand—wakes up in Night VIII of the poem. Albion was asleep because he was in repose in Beulah, a state of threefold perception between Eden (fourfold perception) and Generation (twofold perception). To be in Beulah is to be at rest from the dynamic interplay of contraries of Eden, Blake's paradisiacal state. The aura of Eden pervades Beulah but the threat of the lower state, Generation, is always present. A fall into a reduced perception is always imminent. In *The Four Zoas* that fall occurs. The fall into Generation is a fall into the natural world; it is Blake's version of the biblical Fall.

In the state of Generation, Urizen declares himself God; the "mundane shell," the material world, is built, and Jesus appears and is sacrificed so that regeneration can become possible. Jesus is identified with Luvah, love, with Orc, revolutionary energy battling Urizen in the Lambeth Books, and with Albion, Universal Man. Under Jesus's inspiration, Los perceives the errors of the Fall and begins to build Jerusalem, a spiritual freedom in which regeneration is possible. From Night IX in *The Four Zoas* onward into *Milton* and *Jerusalem*, Los, who embodies something akin to the Romantic concept of sympathetic imagination, becomes the agent of regeneration. It is Los who can project himself into the existence of his contrary, can accept the existence of that contrary in the act of "self-annihilation," and can consequently forgive. Thus, in the later books, the theory of contraries is not altered; any contrary can assume a selfhood in conflict with dialectical progression itself. Los preserves the dialectic, while Orc maintains a hierarchy—"saviour" and "villain."

MILTON

The historical John Milton is revived in Blake's *Milton* so that he can experience a personal self-annihilation which leads to the incorporation of his Spectre, Satan. Blake's Milton is a Milton of energy and imagination, a Milton determined to correct his view (expressed in *Paradise Lost*, 1667) that love "hath his seat in Reason." Through self-annihilation, Blake's Milton acknowledges the validity of Reason, his Spectre. Once Milton is united with his Spectre, he can preach effectively to the public. The repression of the reasoning power is peculiar only to the Blakean "heroes," such as Blake's Milton. Outside this Blakean world, in the world of Innocence and Experience, the reasoning power is not repressed but assumes the role of usurper, a faculty of mind which has overridden the powers of all other faculties. Reason as Blake perceived it in the eighteenth century was in complete control. It is this unrepressed, dominant, reasoning power which Milton calls a "Negation." The reasoning power which Blake's Milton finally accepts is reason as Spectre, not as Negation, reason in its Edenic proportions.

An act of self-annihilation also precipitates the union of female emanation and the fallen male principle. Blake's Milton is reconciled with his emanation, Ololon. What Blake's Milton undergoes here becomes a precedent for what Los and other contraries will undergo. In annihilating his Selfhood, the Los-Blake-Devil Selfhood, Blake's Milton shows that reason is a necessary contrary, that man is not ruled by energies alone. The Spectre as reason has been accepted and Blake's Milton attains an expanded perception. His emanation perceives her power fade. In "delighting in his delight," they are again one in sexuality.

Blake's Milton enables the contraries to be saved, enables a dynamic interplay of contraries once again to take place. In contrast, Orc's obdurate maintenance of his own Selfhood and his denial of Urizen's reality in any proportions did not preserve Edenic contraries and could not therefore lead to regeneration. Blake's Milton achieves self-annihilation through forgiveness, itself based upon the imagination. It is Los, the imagination, who perceives the dialectic of contraries and recognizes the message of continued forgiveness. It is Los, the imagination, who is employed by each contrary in recognition of its polar opposite.

JERUSALEM

In *Jerusalem*, Los and the Spectre of Urthona take center stage. Los addresses his Spectre as "my Pride & Self-righteousness," indicating that the Spectre's presence tends to affirm Los's obdurate Selfhood. Throughout *Jerusalem*, the reader witnesses a "compensatory" relationship between the Spectre and Los, although the Spectre seems to be "watching his time with glowing eyes to leap upon his prey." In Chapter IV, Los ends this continuing struggle with his Spectre by accepting it. Once Los, identified here with Blake, becomes one with his Spectre, he appears to Albion, fallen humankind, in the form of Jesus and preaches forgiveness based on imaginative identification and self-annihilation. Jesus-Los annihilates himself before Albion and thus points to the necessary destruction of the Selfhood. Overwhelmed by this act, imaginatively caught in Jesus-Los's sacrifice, the albatross drops from Albion's neck, and it is the Selfhood. This is the apocalyptic moment when Albion, like the phoenix, descends to the flames and rises anew. Regeneration is intimately connected with self-annihilation, as it was in *Milton*.

Albion's emanation, Jerusalem, is also spiritual freedom. A reassimilation of Jerusalem generates a climate of freedom in which contraries can interact. Jerusalem as an emanation is beyond morality. She represents the whole of life, but a fallen Albion applies "one law" to her. Because of this application of a rigid "one law," a rigid hierarchical ethic, Jerusalem is separated from Albion. A female emanation repressed becomes a tyrant. Blake gives readers a close view of this "proud Virgin-Harlot," whom he calls Vala. The Vala whom Blake presents is corrupt, since she stands for restraint in all areas, especially moral, as opposed to Jerusalem-as-liberty. The Vala figure, advocate of a repressive morality, both tempts and lures, and also upholds the sense of sin. She thus becomes woman-as-tyrant. She is the femme fatale who incites desire but never acts. Such a morality turns love into prostitution, the free lover into a prostitute.

Again, Los, the imagination, perceives the validity of Jesus's word to Jerusalem regarding forgiveness, annihilation, and regeneration. Los applies what he has learned, unites with his own Spectre, and sends him forth to preach the methods of regeneration—forgiveness and self-annihilation. Albion regains his Jerusalem; spiritual freedom once again exists; and England itself has apocalyptically become Jerusalem, the city of God.

OTHER MAJOR WORKS

FICTION: *An Island in the Moon*, wr. c. 1784, pb. 1987; *To the Public: Prospectus*, 1793.

NONFICTION: *A Descriptive Catalogue*, 1809.

ILLUSTRATIONS AND ENGRAVINGS: *The Complaint and the Consolation: Or, Night Thoughts, by Edward Young*, 1797; *Blair's Grave*, 1808; *The Prologue and Characters of Chaucer's Pilgrims*, 1812; *The Pastorals of Virgil*, 1821; *Illustrations of the Book of Job*, 1825; *Illustrations of Dante*, 1827.

BIBLIOGRAPHY

Blake, William. *William Blake: The Illuminated Books*. New York: Thames & Hudson, 2000. Blake is better known as a poet than as a painter, but this book makes a strong case that Blake's poems reveal only half of Blake the artist. An introduction by David Bindman tells how Blake, trained as an engraver, invented a technique for printing word and image together.

Bloom, Harold, ed. *William Blake*. New York: Chelsea House, 1985. Includes thirteen previously published essays or extracts from longer works, with the aim of providing a representative selection of criticism from 1950 to 1980. The essays are of varying difficulty, but no student should miss the contributions of Northrop Frye (overview of Blake's myth), David E. Erdman (Blake and contemporary politics), Robert F. Gleckner (point of view in *Songs of Innocence and of Experience*), W. J. T. Mitchell (Blake's composite art), and Leopold Damrosch, Jr. (Los and apocalypse).

Bruder, Helen P. *William Blake and the Daughters of Albion*. New York: St. Martin's Press, 1997. Bruder's overt concern is with issues of "women, sexuality, gender, and sexual difference," but her book is perhaps better regarded as a reassessment of Blake's relation to popular culture. Bruder presents a thorough and astute reception history. Includes a bibliography and an index.

Frye, Northrop. *Fearful Symmetry: A Study of William Blake*. Princeton, N.J.: Princeton University Press, 1947. It would be difficult to overestimate the importance of this brilliant and endlessly stimulating book, which reveals perhaps for the first time the full extent of Blake's genius. Frye interprets Blake's myth in terms of archetypal symbolic structures, which he also finds underlying much Western literature and mythology. Almost all later writers have been indebted to Frye, although some contemporary Blake critics are wary of being too captured by his ideas.

Larrissy, Edward. *William Blake*. Oxford, England: Basil Blackwell, 1985. Blake's reputation was strongly affected by the revolution in critical theory that swept through literary studies in the 1970's and 1980's, and this introductory study is useful because it applies these developments to Blake's poems in a way that is intelligible to beginning students. Larrissy emphasizes Blake's political radicalism without ignoring the spiritual aspects of his thought. One drawback to the book is that it undervalues Blake's later works and covers them only briefly.

Lindsay, David W. *Blake: Songs of Innocence and Experience*. London: Macmillan, 1989. A very informative, if brief, introduction that examines a range of critical approaches to *Songs of Innocence and of Experience*. Lindsay's impartial discussions of different interpretations of selected poems will be useful for readers who want a concise survey of the field. The second part of the book gives attention to eight *Songs of Experience* in the context of Blake's other works. Includes a full and up-to-date bibliography.

Percival, Milton O. *William Blake's Circle of Destiny*. 1938. Reprint. New York: Octagon Books, 1977. This introduction to Blake's prophetic books has stood the test of time. Percival demonstrates that Blake's myth was firmly rooted in a traditional body of thought that included Neoplatonism, Kabala, alchemy, Gnosticism, and individual thinkers such as Jakob Böhme, Paracelsus, Emanuel Swedenborg, and Plotinus. This book should be read as a balance to the works of Bloom, Frye, and Erdman, who all minimized the esoteric aspects of Blake's thought.

Joseph Natoli;
bibliography updated by the editors

ALEKSANDR BLOK

Born: St. Petersburg, Russia; November 28, 1880
Died: Petrograd, U.S.S.R.; August 7, 1921

PRINCIPAL POETRY

Stikhi o prekrasnoy dame, 1904
Nechayannaya radost, 1907
Snezhnaya maska, 1907
Zemlya v snegu, 1908
Nochyne chasy, 1911
Skazki, 1912
Krugly god, 1913
Stikhi o Rossii, 1915
Sobraniye stikhotvoreniy i teatr v 4 kigakh, 1916 (4 volumes; includes the poetic cycles *Puzyri zemli*, *Gorod*, *Faina*, etc.)
Solovinyy sad, 1918
Skify, 1918 (*The Scythians*, 1982)
Dvenadtsat, 1918 (*The Twelve*, 1920)
Iamby: Sovremennye stikhi, 1907-1914, 1919
Sedoe utro, 1920
Za granyu proshlykh dnei, 1920

Vozmezdie, 1922 (wr. 1910-1921)
Poems of A. B., 1968
Selected Poems, 1972

OTHER LITERARY FORMS

Aleksandr Blok wrote three lyrical plays, the first of which, *Balaganchik* (1906; *The Puppet Show*, 1963), was staged immediately and widely. The second, *Korol' na ploshchadi*, written in 1906 (*The King in the Square*, 1934), although its material was absorbed into other works. *Roza i krest* (1922; *The Rose and the Cross*, 1936) was popular in print, had more than two hundred rehearsals at the Moscow Art Theater, but was never publicly staged. Several additional dramatic monologues failed before presentation. Blok also wrote critical essays on poetry and drama, wrote a series of articles dealing with the role of the intelligentsia in Russian cultural development, translated several plays from French and German for stage production, and edited his mother's translation of the letters of Gustave Flaubert.

Aleksandr Blok (Library of Congress)

Much of his work was reissued in various collections during his lifetime, and posthumous editions, including diaries, letters, and notebooks, have appeared regularly. A scholarly collected works in nine volumes has been completed in the Soviet Union.

ACHIEVEMENTS

Aleksandr Blok was the leading Russian Symbolist and is universally regarded as one of the most important Russian poets of the twentieth century. The Symbolists were interested in poetic reform in order to reshape the partly sentimental, partly social-oriented poetic idiom of the second half of the nineteenth century. They favored a return to mysticism, albeit with modern overtones, free from the rational tenor of the scientific age. The movement's early exponents, notably Konstantin Balmont and Valery Bryusov, incorporated French Symbolist ideas into their work, but when Blok began to write at the turn of the century, Symbolism was no longer a single unit. It had disintegrated into literary factions which reflected the movement's precepts in their own way. Though Blok paid homage to the search for spiritual values, his mysticism owes as much to the writings of his uncle, the religious philosopher Vladimir Solovyov, as to Stéphane Mallarmé, with whom he shared the striving to give shape to the "music of the spheres," the elusive entities beyond reality.

In contrast to his eccentric fellow Symbolists and the equally whimsical linguistic experimenters of other movements, Blok stood out as a contemplative, sincere individual whose philosophical concerns were as important as the language used to express them. He attached an almost metaphysical significance to the creative power of the poet, and this belief in the transcendental quality of art led him to reach beyond the partisan interests of his contemporaries to create a solid, coherent poetical system reminiscent of the "golden age" of Alexander Pushkin, Mikhail Lermontov, and Fyodor Tyutchev almost a century earlier. Blok's considerable talent and natural sense of rhythm facilitated the realization of these aspirations, resulting in an amazing output during twenty years of literary activity. Thematically, Blok brought the cult of the Eternal Feminine to Russia, using the concept as focal point in his search for spiritual unity. The immense range of this vision, incorporating, among others, the Virgin Mary, Holy Sophia, Mother Russia, Blok's wife, and St. Petersburg prostitutes, permitted the poet to extend early mystical longings to the concrete realities of his own life and to revolutionary changes. His verse cycles dedicated to his native land, his perceptive essays on the role of the intelligentsia, and his refusal to emigrate during the famines of the Civil War brought him deference from all segments of the Russian public. Stylistically, he honored the conventions of the past by building on existing rhyme schemes in much of his work, even as he changed from the traditional counting of syllables in a metric foot to modern tonic verse patterns.

Blok's poetry appealed to fellow poets, critics, and the public at large alike. He managed to avoid censorial confrontations with both prerevolutionary and postrevolutionary regimes to emerge as the most esteemed writer of the Silver Age, at once a preserver of tradition and a precursor of modern poetry. His work is widely translated and discussed abroad, while he remains a respected literary figure in Russia.

BIOGRAPHY

The artistically, academically, and socially illustrious family into which Aleksandr Blok was born on November 16, 1880, contributed significantly to his poetic development and success. His maternal grandfather was the prominent botanist and rector of St. Petersburg University, Andrey Beketov, and his grandmother was an editor and translator—from English, French, and German—of artistic and scientific works. Blok's mother, one of the prime influences on his life, wrote poetry herself and established a reputation as a translator of French literature. Several other female members of the family were also engaged in literary activity, especially the interpretation of French writers to the Russian public, thus exposing Blok early to the ideas of European literature. The Blok side of the family consisted of outstanding professional people, though tainted with a strain of insanity which affected Blok's father, a law professor at Warsaw University. Blok believed that his father's mental instability contributed to his own frequent despondency. Blok's parents, highly individualistic and incompatible in personality, did not remain together for long. The poet was born in his mother's ancestral home and reared by a household of solicitous women, who nourished both his physical and artistic development until age eleven, when he was finally enrolled in a boys' school. By that time, he had already written poems, coedited an informal family journal, and taken part in domestic theatricals. Blok's lifelong attachment to the feminine principle in his poetry, and his first book of verse specifically devoted to that concept, may well reflect the influence of the women in the Beketov household.

In 1898, Blok entered the Law School of St. Petersburg, but changed three years later to the philology department, from which he was graduated in 1906. In 1903, he published his first verses and married the daughter of the scientist Dmitry Mendelyev, a family friend. He had also become interested in mystic philosophy, contributing essays to the Religious-Philosophical Society, of which he was a member. By the time his first verses were printed, he had amassed more than six hundred poems, most of which found ready acceptance after his debut. From this point on, a steady stream of poems, dramas, and essays issued from Blok's pen with seeming effortlessness. In 1904, the collection *Stikhi o prekrasnoy dame* appeared, to be followed in 1907 by his second book, *Nechayannaya radost*, and several plays. Under the influence of his mystical beliefs, Blok had transferred the cult of a divine feminine vision to his wife Lyubov, an aspiring actress, to whom many of the "Beautiful Lady" poems were dedicated. Blok's close friend and fellow mystic, the poet Andrey Bely, carried this adoration to extremes, causing family disharmony. Blok's wife rejected all mysticism, lived a life of her own, and bore a short-lived son conceived in an extramarital liaison. Nevertheless, the couple remained together as trusted friends. Blok to the end admired, needed, and relied on Lyubov's strong, earthy personality, as he had earlier relied on his mother and grandmother.

The shattered idealism of Blok's marriage and the miscarried 1905 uprising drew the poet away from the otherworldly themes of his early work. As he developed a more skeptical, practical outlook, he immersed himself in the street life of St. Petersburg, giving himself up to several passions. His infatuation with Natalia Volokhova, an actress in his play *The Puppet Show*, inspired the verse cycles *Snezhnaya maska* (the snow mask) and "Faina," which are among his finest works. A happier love affair with the opera singer Lyubov Delmas in 1914 engendered the cycle "Karmen."

Blok made five journeys abroad. As a young man, he accompanied his mother twice to Germany. Later, in 1909, he traveled with his wife to Italy and transformed his impressions of that country into the group of "Italyanskie stikhi." In 1911, the Bloks toured Europe, which provided inspiration for the verse tale *Solovinyy sad* and the play *The Rose and the Cross*, reflecting experiences on the Basque coast and in Brittany respectively. A nagging feeling of guilt about having neglected his father is reflected in the unfinished epic "Vozmezdie" (retribution).

Blok's political involvements were minor, though controversial. His ideas on the state of the country were published in *Rossia i intelligentsia* (1918), a series of essays spanning a decade. Blok accuses his own upper class of having created a cultural schism by looking to Europe while slighting its own people and heritage. This negative attitude toward the existing ruling circles encouraged him not to condemn the revolution, though he did not welcome it enthusiastically. A stint at the front contributed to his unhappiness, as he saw the philosophical unity sought in his work disappear in the ravages of war and revolution. He served briefly on a provisional government commission investigating suspect czarist officials, then composed his best-known and most controversial poem, *The Twelve*, which depicts a murderous Red Army detachment as disciples to an ineffectual, effeminate Christ. The equally provocative *Skify* (the Scythians) followed a few days later. Between 1918 and his death on August 7, 1921, Blok wrote little, though he continued work on "Vozmezdie." The Bolshevik government, grateful for his conciliatory stance, printed and reissued many of his works and appointed him to several literature boards and artistic commissions. Through these activities his material circumstances were less desperate than those of his fellow citizens, but his health declined quickly just the same. Depression and doubts about the future of his country hastened his end. Russia's artistic, literary, and governing elite and more than a thousand people followed his coffin in recognition of his cultural contributions.

ANALYSIS

Aleksandr Blok sought to give a metaphysical dimension to his poetry by creating a persona that pays homage to a supernatural ideal, in his own words "an essence possessed of an independent existence." This ideal is usually represented by the concept of the Eternal Feminine, which takes on a range of embodiments in the various stages of Blok's development. Initially, he depicted an ephemeral, distant spirit, "the Beautiful Lady," whose presence the poet perceives in almost every poem, but who is never made manifest. As Blok matured, his mental discipline, inquiring mind, and sensuous disposition prompted him to alter the image, until it became more of a literary device and less of a religious inspiration. While the vision retained some of its ethereal, purifying characteristics in later works, it also assumed demoniac, physically alluring aspects. In many other poems, desperate city women, whose misfortunes Blok ascertained from newspapers, represent the feminine ideal, as do the poet's female friends and relatives. The persona's attitude to the changing image is ambiguous. He is inexplicably and fatally drawn to some embodiments, observing others wistfully and indifferently. Eventually, social pressures, war, and revolution drew Blok further from the transcendental sphere, causing him to blend his vision with the concept of Mother Russia. Blok then saw "the Beautiful Lady" in the lined faces of praying peasant women and urban prostitutes, and even in the Russian landscape. A final attempt to revive the religious dimension of the image occurs in the revolutionary poem *The Twelve* in which an effeminate, Christ-like ghost silently and gently accompanies marauding Bolshevik revolutionaries.

Blok was the forerunner of modern Russian poetry. He replaced the realistic, low-quality verse of the second half of the nineteenth century with a new lyricism, to which he gave a mystical dimension. Technically, he freed Russian verse from rigid meter and led the way to modern tonic patterns. The social upheavals of his era are reflected in his work, but always subordinate to artistic requirements. Blok appealed to all segments of the public and continues to be popular at home and abroad.

"GOROD" AND "ARFY I SKRIPKI"

Although the Eternal Feminine is a constant in Blok's work, it does not exhaust his poetic themes. After witnessing the bloodbath of the unsuccessful 1905 uprising in St. Petersburg, he devoted an entire cycle, "Gorod," to his hometown. Only a few of these poems express political observations; most of them deal with the darker aspects of street life. Feelings of impending catastrophe, both personal and societal, pervade the poetic atmosphere. The later cycle "Strashny mir" (a terrible world) extends this theme of urban degradation and misery. In one of the sections of the cycle, "Plyaski smerti" (dances of death), which echoes Charles Baudelaire's "Danse Macabre," Blok evokes the disintegration of his society, which the persona views in the shape of a corpse, no longer believing in transcendence, while soulless St. Petersburg citizens dance their own deaths through empty lives. In the seventy-two-poem cycle "Arfy i skripki" (harps and violins), Blok endeavors to link poetry to music, and several of his verses were later set to music. He manages to reproduce the rhythm of ballads, romances, and factory and folk songs in these and many other poems. Finally, the unfinished epic "Vozmezdie" is a lyrical chronicle of his family's and nation's destiny. Blok's general poetic mood ranges from mystical belief and idealistic expectation to false rapture, skeptical, even cynical visions of life, and eventually sadness, despair, and critical aloofness.

POETIC STYLE

Stylistically, Blok stands between the traditional syllabic meter and modern tonic patterns. In his earlier work, metric regularity and exact rhyme dominate, to be followed by syllabotonic verse and experiments with *vers libre*. His rhymes become approximate, until he evolves a very modern, conversational style. Typically, his line has three stresses, interrupted by one or two unstressed syllables, but his rather extensive output shows great stress and syllable diversity within the line. He favors lexical repetition and occasionally repeats the first stanza as the last, with slight lexical change, to achieve a musical effect. Not the least of his skills is to transform vague, mystical notions into concise, elegant verse. Blok's poetry is more accessible than the linguistic experiments of the Futurists and other innovators, and theme or thought are not as completely subordinated to technique. This accessibility, achieved with no loss of artistic quality, and the generally held belief that he recreated the great poetic traditions of the nineteenth century, give him a fame and exposure not matched by other modern Russian poets.

CELEBRATION OF THE ETERNAL FEMININE

Blok's celebration of a feminine ideal is a twentieth century version of earlier cults, encompassing the Gnostic image of Holy Sophia, the adoration of the Virgin Mary in its various guises, Dante's devotion to Beatrice, and Johann Wolfgang von Goethe's evocation of the Eternal Feminine in *Faust* (1808). Blok was not directly influenced by Western manifestations of the concept, though he employed all of them. His interest in the symbol came from the writings of the mystic philosopher Vladimir Solovyov, who incorporated Holy Sophia into his ideological system. Blok called his ideal more generally "the Beautiful Lady," devoting not only his first collection, *Stikhi o prekrasnoy dame*, to her, but extending the vision in diverse guises in all major subsequent work. His choice of an ancient symbol was influenced by the belief that familiar, even proverbial concepts, call forth deeper emotions than newly created metaphors. The more than three hundred poems of his first collection portray the Beautiful Lady as a godlike essence which can never assume concrete, earthly shape, but is accessible in spirit to the perceptive poetic persona. The image thus appears in fleeting poses, in the flickering of a candle, the rustle of a curtain, a breeze, or simply as a felt presence. Particularly prominent is Blok's evocation of a distant shadow: "I waited for You. But Your shadow hovered/ In the distance, in the fields . . ." or "You are leaving into crimson sunset/ Into endless circles."

In this semblance, the Beautiful Lady is sometimes an elemental, an almost pagan spirit, enveloped in mists and twilight, floating by in a snowflake or glistening in a star. She appears as a figure in a song and is herself a song, perceived in snatches of distant melodies. In line with traditional symbolism, she is frequently represented by a radiant light: "I wait. Unexpectedly a door will open,/ And vanishing light will fall on me." The association with light extends naturally to religious settings, in which the Beautiful Lady is an incarnation of the Virgin. She is anticipated by the persona at the temple entrance: "The church steps are illuminated/ Their stones alive—and waiting for Your steps," and immediately perceived within: "Holy Lady, how caress-

ing the candles,/ How comforting Your features." The poems tend to follow a rigid scheme: a physical setting empty of other people, the persona's anticipation, his ritualistic incantations, resulting in perception of the vision.

Blok often used dark/light contrasts to separate image from persona and the rest of the world. In a well-known poem of this type, "I Go into Darkened Temples," the worshiper waits in the dim edifice, contemplating the flickering candle before the icon of the Virgin. The intense longing produces a state of excitement, in which real or imaginary creaks, rustles, and movements translate into a perception of her presence. The icon seems to come alive as the worshiper falls into a trance, engulfed by dreams and fairy-tale images. The final impression is an instant of joy and relief. These verses are not so much a lyrical diary, though Blok designated them as such, as they are a glimpse of his spiritual search. The intensity of his emotions carries a hint of immaturity, even sentimentality, which is redeemed, however, by the careful transmutation of the ecstasy into a restrained poetic idiom, and by the gossamer quality of the dreamlike reflections.

Several factors led the poet to change the image and thus extend the range of his spiritual odyssey. The idea of constant longing and expectation, interrupted only by vague, insubstantial moments of revelation, failed to satisfy the poet on a permanent basis. Doubt in the validity of his adoration, even in the existence of the Beautiful Lady and impatience with her remoteness already appear in the first collection. Blok sees himself as her "Obscure slave, filled with inspiration/ Praising You. But You don't know him." He also reproaches her: "You are different, mute, faceless,/ Hidden away. You bewitch in silence." In the end, he challenges the symbol more directly: "You are holy, but I don't believe You." In one of Blok's most quoted poems, "I Have a Premonition of You," he fearfully anticipates other embodiments: "The entire heaven is on fire, and Your appearance near,/ But I am terrified that You will change your visage." The changes were inevitable in the light of the poet's determination to transfer some of the mystique to his fiancé Lyubov, who became his wife in 1904. This attempt at earthly incarnation miscarried, for while he implored Lyubov to serve as his inspiration, addressing her with the same capitalized "You" often lavished on the Beautiful Lady, she refused all mysticism and insisted on an ordinary flesh-and-blood relationship.

NECHAYANNAYA RADOST

Blok's second book, *Nechayannaya radost* (unexpected joy), features an altered image of the Beautiful Lady. The thirteen-poem lead cycle "Puzyry zemli" identifies the symbol with the Macbethian witches, described by William Shakespeare: "The earth has bubbles, as the water hath/ And these are of them." Religious adoration is here replaced by riotous cavorting amid the demons of the St. Petersburg marshes. The second cycle of the book, "Nochnaya fialka," a fantastic tale composed in 1905-1906, expands this underground involvement. A new version of the Eternal Feminine appears in the form of a graceful but lethally poisonous flower princess. The dreamer-poet leaves his city and friends to venture far into a swampy netherworld, where he encounters a faceless, ageless vegetable female. This sweet-smelling woman flower eternally spins, casting her devastating marsh breath over others, while she herself blooms in the poisonous atmosphere. The sleepy hero perceives distant echoes of a happier land, now forever lost to him. The style of "Nochnaya fialka" demonstrates Blok's increasing technical mastery. Though he preserves traditional regular rhythm, he uses free verse and uneven rhyme and syllable schemes. This poem is considered one of Blok's best.

In Blok's subsequent collections, the Eternal Feminine assumes whatever aspect suits the poetic theme. When casting his unrequited love for Natalia Volokhova into verse in the cycle *Snezhnaya maska*, the vision becomes a glacial force, indifferently condemning the persona to a frozen wasteland. In "Faina," she is a cruelly teasing gypsy. Blok's most famous poems feature other embodiments of the ideal. In "The Stranger," she is a prostitute, uncannily reflecting the purity and mystery of the Beautiful Lady, and in "A Girl Sang in a Church Choir," she is a young singer transformed into a ray of light, promising salvation, while the piercing cries of a child reveal her deception. When the poet does make contact with his vision, the encounter is usually unsatisfactory or violent, as in "Humiliation," where the persona wrestles with a prostitute and shouts in despair: "I am neither your husband, nor bridegroom, nor friend!/

So go ahead, my erstwhile angel and plunge/ Your sharp French heel into my heart."

THE TWELVE

Blok's most controversial manifestation of a divine vision occurs in the final stanza of his revolutionary poem *The Twelve*. Technically, *The Twelve* is a masterpiece. It pits the icy, howling snowstorm of the revolution against the vulnerable population, seen as unsure of its footing and slipping on the ice. All segments of society confront and attempt to hurdle the Bolshevik snowdrift. A fur-clad upper-class lady fails and lies prostrate; a fat-bellied priest attempts to squeeze by furtively; a bourgeois stands undecided at the crossroad; an intellectual shouts his dissent; a peasant woman, not understanding the political event, succeeds in clambering across the snowdrift. Prostitutes using incongruous political jargon establish union fees for their services. These scenes are background for the main drama dealing with twelve Red Army men who think they safeguard the revolution, but really loot and kill. One of them murders his lover in a jealous rage, only to be overcome by religious scruples and feelings of guilt. At poem's end, the revolutionaries continue on their violent path, boldly asserting their freedom from religion, but—unknown to them—they are led by the shadowy, gentle, garlanded figure of an effeminate Christ, whose unexpected appearance transmutes the marauders into the twelve disciples. Blok was vilified by both the Left and the Right for this inexplicable ending, but insisted that his poetic instinct dictated it. The controversy over this image for a long time obscured appreciation of the poem's exquisite artistic craftsmanship. Blok wrote very little after *The Twelve*.

OTHER MAJOR WORKS

PLAYS: *Balaganchik*, pr. 1906 (*The Puppet Show*, 1963); *Korol' na ploshchadi*, wr. 1906, pb. 1907 (*The King in the Square*, 1934); *Pesnya sudby*, pb. 1909 (*The Song of Fate*, 1938); *Ramzes*, pb. 1921; *Roza i krest*, pb. 1922 (*The Rose and the Cross*, 1936).

NONFICTION: *Rossia i intelligentsia*, 1918; *Katilina*, 1919; *O simvolizme*, 1921 (*On Symbolism*, 1975); *Pis'ma Aleksandra Bloka*, 1925; *Pis'ma Aleksandra Bloka k rodnym*, 1927; *Dnevnik Al. Bloka, 1911-1913*, 1928; *Dnevnik Al. Bloka, 1917-1921*, 1928;

Zapisnye knizhki Al. Bloka, 1930; *Pis'ma Al. Bloka k E. P. Ivanovu*, 1936; *Aleksandr Blok i Andrey Bely: Perepiska*, 1940.

Bibliography

Berberova, Nina. *Aleksandr Blok: A Life*. Translated by Robyn Marsack. New York: George Braziller, 1996. A biography originally published in 1996 by Carcanet Press Limited, Britian, and by Alyscamps Press, France.

Hackel, Sergei. *The Poet and the Revolution: Aleksandr Blok's "The Twelve."* Oxford: Clarendon Press, 1975. One of the best analyses of the contents and form of Blok's best-known work, "The Twelve." It covers the background of the poem, its characters, especially Jesus Christ, and the formalistic aspects.

Hellman, Ben. *Poets of Hope and Despair: The Russian Symbolists in War and Revolution, 1914-1918*. Helsinki: Institute for Russian and East European Studies, 1995. Surveys and compares the work of half a dozen Russian symbolists of the World War I period, including Blok. Includes bibliographical references.

Kisch, Sir Cecil. *Alexander Block, Prophet of a Revolution*. London: Weidenfeld & Nicolson, 1960. The first study of Blok in English, a combination of biography and critical evaluation. A somewhat old-fashioned biography, but still very useful.

Pyman, Avril. *The Life of Aleksandr Blok: The Release of Harmony, 1908-1921*. Oxford: Oxford University Press, 1980. One of the most exhaustive treatments of Blok as a man and a writer by a leading scholar of Russian literature. The emphasis is on biography, but there are also discussions of Blok's poems. Excellent illustrations.

Reeve, F. D. *Alexander Blok: Between Image and Idea*. New York: Columbia University Press, 1962. A good study, with extensive but selective bibliography.

Sloane, David A. *Aleksandr Blok and the Dynamics of the Lyric Cycles*. Columbus, Ohio: Slavica, 1987. A penetrating study of Blok's lyrics, especially of his tendency to write in cycles throughout his career.

Vickery, Walter, ed. *Aleksandr Blok Centennial Conference*. Columbus, Ohio: Slavica, 1984. A collection of twenty-one essays on various aspects of Blok's life and work, prepared for a seminar in Chapel Hill, North Carolina, in 1981, the centennial of Blok's birth. The topics tend to concentrate on the stylistic elements of his poetry and other aspects of Blok's portrait.

Vogel, Lucy, ed. *Blok: An Anthology of Essays and Memoirs*. Ann Arbor, Mich.: Ardis, 1982. A collection of informative memoirs by Blok's acquaintances, including his wife Lyubov Mendeleeva, Maxim Gorky, Osip Mandelstam, and Boris Pasternak. Includes a twenty-six-page bibliography.

Margot K. Frank;
bibliography updated by Vasa D. Mihailovich

Edmund Blunden

Born: London, England; November 1, 1896
Died: Long Melford, Suffolk, England; January 20, 1974

Principal poetry

Poems, 1914
The Harbingers, 1916
Pastorals: A Book of Verses, 1916
The Waggoner and Other Poems, 1920
The Shepherd and Other Poems of Peace and War, 1922
To Nature: New Poems, 1923
English Poems, 1925
Masks of Time: A New Collection of Poems, Principally Meditative, 1925
Retreat, 1928
Undertones of War, 1928
Near and Far: New Poems, 1929
The Poems of Edmund Blunden, 1914-1930, 1930
To Themis: Poems on Famous Trials, with Other Pieces, 1931
Halfway House: A Miscellany of New Poems, 1932
Choice or Chance: New Poems, 1934
An Elegy and Other Poems, 1937
Poems, 1930-1940, 1940
Shells by a Stream: New Poems, 1944
After the Bombing and Other Short Poems, 1949

Poems of Many Years, 1957
A Hong Kong House, 1962
Eleven Poems, 1965
Selected Poems, 1982
Overtones of War, 1996

OTHER LITERARY FORMS

Edmund Blunden's reputation as a major British poet is founded primarily, and perhaps unfairly, on the poems he wrote about his service in World War I. Similarly, his popular prose works were connected to his wartime experiences. His most famous prose work, *Undertones of War* (which includes a section of poems at the end), is one of the least vituperative of postwar British memoirs. Blunden's wartime experiences also featured prominently in the novel *We'll Shift Our Ground: Or, Two on a Tour* (1933), written in collaboration with Sylva Norman, in which two central characters visit the former battlefields of Flanders.

In contrast to his poetry and popular prose, Blunden's scholarly writing consisted primarily of biographies of important British literary figures—including Percy Bysshe Shelley, Lord Byron, and Charles Lamb—and rather impressionistic literary criticism. His scholarly approach was to focus on an author's life in order to understand his or her writings. Toward this end, Blunden wrote studies of a wide variety of major English poets, including the seventeenth century poet Henry Vaughan (1927), the Romantic poets Leigh Hunt (1930) and Shelley (1946), the Romantic essayist Charles Lamb (1933), the early modern poet and novelist Thomas Hardy (1942), and fellow World War I poet Wilfred Owen (1931).

ACHIEVEMENTS

Edmund Blunden's formal honors had little to do with his war poetry. In 1950, for example, Blunden was elected an honorary member of the Japan Academy, mainly for his educational work with the United Kingdom Liaison Mission in Tokyo after World War II. In 1963, the Japanese government awarded Blunden the Order of the Rising Sun, Third Class. Blunden's greatest honor had to do with his work in education and criticism: In 1966, he was elected Professor of Poetry at Oxford.

BIOGRAPHY

Although he was born in London, England, Edmund Charles Blunden's early years were spent in Yalding, a small English village, where his father was employed as a schoolmaster. For the next thirteen years, Blunden's experience of life was formed in Yalding, where the age-old rhythms of agriculture held sway. In 1909, Blunden entered Christ College, a public school in London. Already endowed with both scholarly interests and a desire to write, Blunden won the Senior Classics scholarship to Queen's College, Oxford, in 1914. As it did for many in his generation, World War I interrupted Blunden's further studies.

In 1915, Blunden took a commission in the Royal Sussex Regiment and was in active service until 1917. Although two books of his poetry were accepted for publication before enlisting—*The Harbingers* and *Pastorals: A Book of Verses*—Blunden developed his poetic voice during active service. After the war and a brief stint at Oxford, he soon joined the staff of the *Athenaeum*, a literary journal. For most of the next four decades, Blunden's work life oscillated between literary journalism and teaching. For instance, a teaching post at Merton College, Oxford, lasted from 1931 to 1941 and was immediately followed by a job with the *Times Literary Supplement*, from 1941 to 1947.

From 1947 until his retirement in 1964, Blunden lived in Asia, first working in Japan and later taking a professorship of English literature at the University of Hong Kong. In 1966, after returning to England, Blunden was elected Professor of Poetry at Oxford University, a post he almost rejected because of ill health. By the early 1970's, the long-term effects of his war wounds forced him to retire from active life. He died in Long Melford, Suffolk, England, on January 20, 1974.

ANALYSIS

In *Heroes' Twilight* (1965, 1996), a study of World War I literature, the critic Bernard Bergonzi emphasizes the literariness of the average British officer, who "had received a classical education and [was] very well read in English poetry, so that [William] Shakespeare and [John] Milton, [William] Wordsworth and [John] Keats would be constantly quoted or alluded to when they wrote about the war." However true this observation may be of others, it is perfectly suited to Edmund Blunden. Blunden was the epitome of the well-educated, humane, and literary-minded British officer of World War I. Support for this argument comes in Blunden's *Undertones of War* when Blunden's commanding officer summons him to headquarters to express his admiration upon learning that a published author serves under him. The respect accorded poetry is almost unbelievable until one considers Bergonzi's further point about the value of poetry during the war. Poetry provided "a sense of identity and continuity, a means of accommodating to life in a bizarre world as well as a source of consolation." As a form of shared experience and as a form of therapy, poetry helped many British soldiers endure the barbaric conditions they faced.

In the 1960's, Bergonzi pointed out that Blunden could be distinguished from his contemporaries by "the intensity of his absorption in the countryside." Blunden was almost always considered a nature poet; that is, his interest lay in representing the interconnection between humans and the natural world. The critical status of nature poetry varies greatly over time; correspondingly, Edmund Blunden's critical reputation also varied. During the late 1920's and early 1930's, he was compared unfavorably to more experimental poets like T. S. Eliot and Ezra Pound; in the mid-1960's, his poetry seemed hopelessly old-fashioned to many Oxford University undergraduates, who vocally opposed his candidacy for Professor of Poetry. It is questionable whether either set of critics truly understood the value of nature for Edmund Blunden. Nature was to Blunden a complex and compelling subject for poetry.

NATURE AS THE ART OF GOD

The strongest of Blunden's reasons for writing nature poetry was to convey his deep love for the English countryside. As Bergonzi points out, "He knows the country with a deep knowledge and a deep love and it pervades the whole structure of his mind and feelings." This sense of deep intermingling of nature and the human mind is central to Blunden's poetry. In another critical study of Blunden's work, Thomas Mallon makes the same point, writing, "Poetry's chief task in describing nature [is] to capture its spirit, to communicate those feelings it gave to man." In a public address, Blunden

endorsed the belief that "Nature hath made one World, and Art another. In brief, all things are artificial; for Nature is the Art of God." Thus, through his poetry Blunden could posit himself within this process of creation and understand more deeply the proper relationship of human beings, nature, and God. Seen in this way, Blunden's poetry is classifiable in terms of a series of interpenetrations of human beings and nature: the effect of nature on the human being, the effects of war on nature, the effect of war on humanity, and, finally, the effect of humans on nature.

POEMS, 1914-1930

This collection of previously published works contains some of Blunden's earliest and most accessible poems. Blunden often offered a straightforward view of nature as therapy for suffering humanity, particularly those who are facing death during war. In "The Pagoda," the speaker dwells on the crumbled building and the animals that inhabit it:

> The small robin reconnoitres,
> Unabashed the woodmouse loiters:
>   Brown owls hoot at shadow-fall
>   And deathwatch ticks and beetles drone.

Apart from a few suggestive words such as "reconnoiters," there is little to suggest that the speaker is in active service during wartime. Blunden pointed out, however, that the poem was provoked by a visit to "some château in ruins" near the front. It is characteristic of much of his earlier poetry that war should be almost entirely absent; for nature to provide therapy, it must first allow the sufferer to distance himself or herself from the war.

As Blunden puts it in "Bleue Maison," the speaker longs to

> attune [his] dull soul, . . .
> To the contentment of this countryside
> Where man is not for ever killing man
> But quiet days like these calm waters glide.

This poetic landscape is described in blissful terms that become even more clear as the speaker continues:

> And I will praise the blue flax in the rye,
> And pathway bindweed's trumpet-like attire,
> Pink rest-harrow and curlock's glistening eye,
> And poppies flaring like St. Elmo's fire.

There is little sense in this poem that nature here has suffered from the war; in fact, the landscape of "Bleue Maison" is almost unaffected by the war.

A similar sense of nature as a place of spiritual healing is presented in "Mont de Cassel," although the frightful fact of the war does intrude on this speaker's consciousness:

> Here on the sunnier scarp of the hill let us rest,
> And hoard the hastening hour
> Find a mercy unexpressed
> In the chance wild flower.

The mercy that the speaker seeks is unexpressed, unvoiced, but still present. In fact, as the speaker later puts it, the merciful therapy provided by the flower and "other things so small and unregarded" reduces the war to "a leering ghost now shriven."

Blunden frequently returned to the concept of nature as a place of healing in his poetry, yet many of his later poems present a different sense of the interpenetration of the natural and the human worlds. In some of his later poems, particularly those written after World War I, Blunden describes nature as scarred and suffering. In this second sense of the overall theme, Blunden shows the effect of war on nature. By "nature," Blunden does not mean untamed wilderness, but rather landscape and the plants and creatures that cling to existence in the face of human destructiveness.

THE SHEPHERD

In *The Shepherd and other Poems of Peace and War*, published in 1922, Blunden's emphasis on the effect of war on nature is stated both clearly and emphatically. For instance, in the short work "A Farm Near Zillebeke," a rural home becomes a victim of the war:

> The Line is all hushed—on a sudden anon
> The fool bullets clack and guns mouth again.
> I stood in the yard of a house that must die,
> And still the black hame was stacked by the door,
> And harness still hung there, and the dray waited by.

The depersonalization of the soldiers, "The Line," contrasts with the humanized "house that must die." In a poetic gesture reaching back to the Romantic period, Blunden uses the landscape to underscore the emotional significance of the moment.

This technique, called the pathetic fallacy by Samuel Taylor Coleridge and others, appears in another poem from the same collection, "1916 Seen from 1921." This poem turns on a central irony: The speaker, who has survived the war, is hardly alive spiritually. It is strongly implied that the speaker suffers from a form of guilt that is common in people who have survived harrowing and deadly experiences. Those who survived the war often felt guilty for living and would fruitlessly wonder why they lived on while so many others died. In this poem, the speaker clearly manifests this guilt:

> Dead as the men I loved, [I] wait while life drags
>
> Its wounded length from those sad streets of war
> Into green places here . . .

The speaker implies that he was most alive during active service. The intensity of life during wartime cannot be replicated in peacetime, and the speaker cannot find solace in nature. The green places once "were my own;/ But now what once was mine is mine no more." The sense of guilt shouts down the voice of nature: "the charred stub outspeaks the living tree."

UNDERTONES OF WAR

At the end of his prose memoir of the war, *Undertones of War*, Blunden included a series of poems, most of which were published between 1918 and 1928. In them, Blunden clearly demonstrates the effect that war has had on human beings. As in "1916 Seen from 1921," survivor's guilt figures prominently in some poems, but not all. In poems like "II Peter ii 22," Blunden offers a thoroughly negative representation of the postwar world to the returning veteran. In this poem, the speaker castigates a society in which

> slinking Slyness rules the roost
> And brags and pimps

and in which

> Quarrel with her hissing tongue
> And hen's eye gobbles gross along
>   To snap that prey
>   That marched away
> To save her carcass, better hung.

To this observer, the postwar society is corrupt and little understands or appreciates the sacrifices that World War I demanded of the British soldier.

"AT THE GREAT WALL OF CHINA"

If society ignores the sacrifice of the soldier, Blunden certainly did not. In the later poem "At the Great Wall of China," published in *Poems of Many Years* (1957), the poet describes the wall clearly and concisely, pointing out its structure and fortifications, yet finds himself thinking more about the lonely sentry who stood guard long ago:

> But I half know at this bleak turret here,
> In snow-dimmed moonlight where sure answers quail,
> This new-set sentry of a long-dead year,
> This boy almost, trembling lest he may fail
> To espy the ruseful raiders, and his mind
> Torn with sharp love of the home left far behind.

Understanding Blunden's life, it is tempting to interpret this poem as a disguised representation of his own feelings while standing guard in the trenches of the western front. However, the import of this poem is more universal: Its overall sense is to convey the tragedy of war in compelling human terms and to offer nature as solace, victim, and alternative.

OTHER MAJOR WORKS

LONG FICTION: *We'll Shift Our Ground: Or, Two on a Tour*, 1933 (with Sylva Norman).

NONFICTION: *On the Poems of Henry Vaughan: Characteristics and Imitations*, 1927; *Undertones of War*, 1928; *Leigh Hunt and His Circle*, 1930; *The Poems of Wilfred Owen*, 1931; *Votive Tablets*, 1931; *Charles Lamb and His Contemporaries*, 1933; *The Mind's Eye*, 1934; *Edward Gibbon and His Age*, 1935; *English Villages*, 1941; *Thomas Hardy*, 1942; *Shelley: A Life Story*, 1946.

BIBLIOGRAPHY

Barlow, Adrian. *The Great War in British Literature.* Cambridge: Cambridge University Press, 2000. Although intended more for the student reader, this short book does an effective job of overviewing the major issues faced by British writers like Vera Brittain, Robert Graves, Richard Aldington, and Edmund Blunden.

Bergonzi, Bernard. *Heroes' Twilight: A Study of the Literature of the Great War.* 1965. Reprint. Manchester, England: Carcanet, 1996. Bergonzi's book was one of the first critical studies of its subject written for the nonacademic. This work postulates that British writers represented the war in terms of a "complex fusion of tradition and unprecedented reality."

Cross, Tim, ed. *Lost Voices of World War I.* Iowa City: University of Iowa Press, 1990. A moving anthology of poetry and other short works by writers who were killed in the conflict; enhancing its value is the wide coverage, including writers from England, France, the United States, Germany, Italy, Austria, and the Turkish Empire. The only major nation it excludes is Russia. It includes a fine introduction by Robert Wohl, a leading scholar of modernism, who offers valuable insight into how Blunden's British contemporaries felt about literature and the role it plays in society.

Hibbard, Dominic. *The First World War.* London: Macmillan, 1990. This work offers a chronological study of the war seen through the eyes of the writers who represented it at the time and much later. Generally, Hibbard does not focus much attention on Blunden, although he does point out that writers were far from univocal in their treatment of the war; responses ranged from the kind produced by Blunden to the gossipy cynicism and outrage of Robert Graves and Siegfried Sassoon.

Mallon, Thomas. *Edmund Blunden.* Boston: Twayne, 1983. Like other works in the Twayne series, this study of Blunden is a fine starting point for general readers who are unfamiliar with the poet or his poetry.

Webb, Barry. *Edmund Blunden: A Biography.* New Haven, Conn.: Yale University Press, 1990. This biography goes into great detail about the difficulties he faced in finding suitable work and domestic happiness; the general picture that emerges is of a thoroughly decent, kindly man who made the best of the worst possible experiences.

Michael R. Meyers

ROBERT BLY

Born: Madison, Minnesota; December 23, 1926

PRINCIPAL POETRY

The Lion's Tail and Eyes: Poems Written Out of Laziness and Silence, 1962 (with James Wright and William Duffy)
Silence in the Snowy Fields, 1962
The Light Around the Body, 1967
The Teeth Mother Naked at Last, 1970
Jumping Out of Bed, 1973
Sleepers Joining Hands, 1973
Point Reyes Poems, 1974
Old Man Rubbing His Eyes, 1974
The Morning Glory, 1975
This Body Is Made of Camphor and Gopherwood, 1977
This Tree Will Be Here for a Thousand Years, 1979
The Man in the Black Coat Turns, 1981
Out of the Rolling Ocean, and Other Love Poems, 1984
Loving a Woman in Two Worlds, 1985
Selected Poems, 1986
The Apple Found in the Plowing, 1989
What Have I Ever Lost by Dying: Collected Prose Poems, 1992
Meditations on the Insatiable Soul, 1994
Eating the Honey of Words: New and Selected Poems, 1999
Morning Poems, 2000
The Night Abraham Called to the Stars, 2001

Robert Bly (© Jerry Bauer, courtesy of HarperCollins)

OTHER LITERARY FORMS

Robert Bly has been a prolific critic, translator, and anthologist. His work in these areas complements his poetic accomplishments and was a significant influence on the internationalization of the literary community in the last third of the twentieth century. His most important works include translations of the poems of Georg Trakl, Juan Ramón Jiménez, Pablo Neruda, Tomas Tranströmer, and Antonio Machado. He has also called attention to the work of other poets through anthologies: *News of the Universe: Poems of Twofold Consciousness* (1980), *The Winged Life: The Poetic Voice of Henry David Thoreau* (1986), *The Rag and Bone Shop of the Heart: Poems for Men* (1993), and *The Soul Is Here for Its Own Joy: Sacred Poems from Many Cultures* (1995).

Bly's writings about the practice of poetry have been published as *Leaping Poetry: An Idea with Poems and Translations* (1975) and *American Poetry: Wildness and Domesticity* (1990). His social criticism has ranged from *A Poetry Reading Against the Vietnam War* (1966, with David Ray) to *Iron John: A Book About Men* (1990), the best-seller that became a primer for the men's movement of the 1990's. It was followed by similarly controversial studies, including *The Spirit Boy and the Insatiable Soul* (1994) and *The Sibling Society* (1996).

ACHIEVEMENTS

Robert Bly is the central poet of his generation. His wide-ranging achievements in poetry, criticism, and translation, as well as his work as editor and itinerant apologist for poetry and various social causes, have made him one of the most conspicuous, ubiquitous, and controversial poets in the United States since the mid-1960's. His significance and influence extend well beyond his own work.

Bly's various accomplishments have been rewarded by a Fulbright Fellowship for translation (1956-1957), the Amy Lowell Traveling Fellowship (1964), two Guggenheim fellowships (1965 and 1972), and a Rockefeller Foundation Grant (1967). In 1968 *The Light Around the Body*, his most controversial collection of poetry, won the National Book Award. In 2000, Bly was presented with the McKnight Distinguished Artist Award.

BIOGRAPHY

Born in the small farming community of Madison, Minnesota, Robert Bly grew up, as he said, a "Lutheran Boy-god." He attended a one-room school in his early years. Upon graduation from high school, he enlisted in the navy, where he first became interested in poetry. After the war, Bly enrolled at St. Olaf's College in Northfield, Minnesota, but after only one year there, he transferred to Harvard University. At Harvard he read "the dominant books" of contemporary American poetry, associated with other young writers (among them John Ashbery, Frank O'Hara, Kenneth Koch, Adrienne Rich, and Donald Hall), worked on *The Harvard Advocate* (which he edited in his senior year), delivered the class poem, and graduated magna cum laude in 1950.

Having decided to be a poet, and seeking solitude, Bly moved back to Minnesota; then, in 1951, still "longing for 'the depths,'" he moved to New York City, where he lived alone for several years, reading widely and writing his early poems. In 1953 he moved to Cambridge, Massachusetts, and in 1954 to Iowa City, where he enrolled in the creative writing program at the University of Iowa. His M.A. thesis consisted of a short collection of poems titled "Steps Toward Poverty and Death" (1956). Bly was married to Carolyn McLean in 1955, and in 1956 they moved to Oslo, Norway, via a Fulbright grant. In Norway, Bly sought out his family roots, read widely, and translated contemporary Norwegian poetry.

In 1957, back in Minnesota, living now on the family farm, Bly continued his work as a translator. In 1958 he founded a magazine, *The Fifties* (which would become *The Sixties, The Seventies*, and *The Eighties*), in which he published his translations and early literary criticism. His first book of poetry, "Poems for the Ascension of J. P. Morgan," he did not publish, but in 1962 he published two books: *The Lion's Tail and Eyes: Poems Written Out of Laziness and Silence* (written with his friends James Wright and William Duffy), and *Silence in the Snowy Fields*, his first independent book of poetry.

By the mid-1960's Bly was actively engaged in the anti-Vietnam War movement. He and David Ray formed a group called American Writers Against the Vietnam War, and they published an anthology titled *A Poetry Reading Against the Vietnam War* (1966). Bly attended draft card turn-ins, and he demonstrated at the Pentagon in 1967. When his second book of poems, *The Light Around the Body*—filled with his outspoken poems against the war—won the National Book Award in 1968, Bly donated the prize money to the draft resistance.

During the 1970's, Bly's interests and activities diversified considerably. He studied Sigmund Freud, Carl Jung, Eastern meditation, myths and fairy tales, philosophy, and psychology. He organized conferences on "Great Mother and New Father" culture and consciousness. Bly's poetry, social commentary, and literary criticism during this period reflected his wide-ranging interests. By this point in his career, he said, he believed that he had "gotten about half-way to the great poem."

In 1979 Bly and his wife of more than twenty-five years were divorced. In 1980 he was married to Ruth Ray; they moved to Moose Lake, Minnesota, and lived there for ten years before moving to Minneapolis in 1990.

During the 1980's and 1990's, Bly continued to work at a rapid pace, writing and publishing widely in several genres, translating, giving readings throughout the United States and overseas, and holding meetings and seminars for groups of women and men. His books during and since the 1980's document as well as anything the life and activities of this exceedingly visible and yet, finally, extremely private individual.

ANALYSIS

Since Robert Bly has habitually brought his wide-ranging interests in literary history, myth, fairy tales, philosophy, psychology, politics, social concerns, and poetry past and present into his own work, his poetry reflects these interests and is enriched by them. Furthermore, because he has been prolific and unsystematic, even at times seemingly self-contradictory, he is extremely difficult to categorize and analyze. Nevertheless, it is possible—indeed necessary—to consider Bly's poetry in terms of the series of various phases it has gone through. These phases, although they are also reflected in Bly's other writings and involvements, are, finally, most evident in his poetry.

SILENCE IN THE SNOWY FIELDS

Bly's first published book of poetry, *Silence in the Snowy Fields*, remains one of the best examples of his deepest obsession: the notion that a personal, private, almost mystical aura adheres to and inheres with the simplest things in the universe—old boards, for example, or a snowflake fallen into a horse's mane. These things, observed in the silence of contemplation and set down honestly and simply in poems, may, Bly believes, inform human beings anew of some sense of complicity, even communion, they have always had with the world, but have forgotten. Bly's focus has caused his work to be labeled Deep Image poetry. In a 1981 essay, "Recognizing Image as a Form of Intelligence," he explained the term's application to his work: "When a poet creates a true image, he is gaining knowledge; he is bringing up into consciousness a connection that has been largely forgotten." In this sense, these early poems provide the reader with the re-created experience of Bly's own epiphanic moments in the silences of "snowy fields," and they become his means of sharing such silences with his readers.

The epigraph to *Silence in the Snowy Fields*, "We are all asleep in the outward man," from the seventeenth century German mystic Jacob Boehme, points up both the structural and the thematic principles upon which Bly builds his book. The three sections of the book suggest a literal and a mental journey. The second, central section, "Awakening," contains twenty-three of the forty-four poems in the book and serves as a structural and thematic transition from "Eleven Poems of Solitude," the first section, to the final section, "Silence on the Roads," which sends both book and reader, via the central "awakening," outward into the world. The soli-

tude and contemplative silence of this first book, then, prepare both poet and reader for the larger world of Bly's work.

THE LIGHT AROUND THE BODY

The way the world impinges on private life is immediately evident in Bly's next book, *The Light Around the Body*. This is his most famous (or for some, most infamous) book. Like *Silence in the Snowy Fields*, *The Light Around the Body* shows the strong influence of Boehme (four of the five sections of the book have epigraphs from Boehme), especially in terms of the dichotomy of the inward and the outward person, the "two languages," one might argue, of Bly's first two books. If *Silence in the Snowy Fields* deals primarily with the inward being, clearly the focus of *The Light Around the Body* is on the outward being—here seen specifically in a world at war.

The Light Around the Body was published in the midst of the American obsession with the Vietnam War, and most of the poems in it are concerned with that war, directly or indirectly. The third section of the book (following sections titled "The Two Worlds" and "The Various Arts of Poverty and Cruelty") is specifically titled "The Vietnam War." This is the most definitive, the most outspoken and condemnatory group of poems—by Bly or anyone else—on the war in Vietnam. Bly reserves his harshest criticism for American involvement in the war. He does not mince words, and he names names: "Men like [Dean] Rusk are not men:/ They are bombs waiting to be loaded in a darkened hangar" ("Asian Peace Offers Rejected Without Publication").

Perhaps the most famous poem Bly has written is also his most definitive criticism of the Vietnam War. In "Counting Small-Boned Bodies," the speaker of the poem has been charged with keeping the grisly count of war casualties to be reported on the evening news. Shocked by the mounting death tolls, he finds himself trying to imagine ways to minimize these terrifying statistics. The refrain that runs through the poem is, "If we could only make the bodies smaller." The implication is that if the bodies could be made smaller, then people might, through some insane logic, be able to argue the war away. Bly's poems in *The Light Around the Body* ensure that the war will never be forgotten or forgiven.

The last two sections of *The Light Around the Body* ("In Praise of Grief" and "A Body Not Yet Born") move back "inward" from the "outward" world of the war, just as the first two sections of the book had moved "outward" from the "inward" world of *Silence in the Snowy Fields*. Since the war, however, this new inward world can never again ignore or fail to acknowledge the outward world. Therefore, Bly writes "in praise of grief" as a way of getting through, psychologically speaking, both outward and inward conflicts.

The first three poems of the fourth section of the book define a progression back toward a place of rest, calm, peace. In the third poem the body is described as "awakening" again and finding "nourishment" in the death scenes it has witnessed. Such a psychic regeneration, which parallels the inevitable regeneration of nature after a battle, is what is needed to repair the damage the war has done if people are to be restored to full human nature. Thus, in the final section of the book, although the new body is not yet fully born, it is moving toward birth, or rebirth.

Finally, then, although *The Light Around the Body* will no doubt be most often remembered for the overt antiwar poems in it, from the point of view of Bly's developing poetic philosophy it is best seen as a description of the transition from the outer world back into the inner world.

Sleepers Joining Hands

The psychological movement first suggested and then begun in *The Light Around the Body* is followed further inward by Bly's next important book, *Sleepers Joining Hands*. This book contains three distinctly different sections. The first section consists of a series of short lyric poems. Beginning with "Six Winter Privacy Poems," it comes to a climax with a long poem, "The Teeth Mother Naked at Last," Bly's final, psychological response to the war in Vietnam.

The second section of *Sleepers Joining Hands* consists of an essay in which Bly documents many of the philosophical ideas and psychological themes with which he has long been obsessed and which he has addressed (and will continue to address) both in his poetry and in his criticism. Bly here summarizes his thinking in terms of Jungian psychology, father and mother consciousness, the theory of the three brains, and other ideas that he groups together as "mad generalizations." This essay, although it is far from systematic, remains an important summary of the sources of many of Bly's most important poems and ideas.

Thus, although *Sleepers Joining Hands* does not contain Bly's most important poetry, it does discuss much of the theory behind that poetry, and it is an extremely important book. In the central essay, Bly describes in detail the way in which "mother consciousness" has come to replay "father consciousness" during the last several centuries. Four "force fields" make up the Great Mother (or Magna Mater), which, according to Bly, is now "moving again in the psyche." The Teeth Mother, one of these force fields, attempts to destroy psychic life. She has been most evident in the Vietnam War and has caused the "inward" harm that that war has brought to the world. "The Teeth Mother Naked at Last," the climactic poem in the first section of *Sleepers Joining Hands*, like the earlier antiwar poems in *The Light Around the Body*, describes the conditions of psychic reality in terms of the presence of the Teeth Mother. It argues that once the Teeth Mother is acknowledged ("naked at last"), she can be dealt with and responded to, and then the outward physical world can be effectively reconnected with the inward psychic or spiritual world.

"Sleepers Joining Hands," the long title poem that constitutes the collection's third section, is an elaborate and challenging poem, a kind of dream journal/journey with overt Jungian trappings. Thematically, it constantly shifts back and forth between dreamed and awakened states. These thematic shifts are evidenced in the structure of the poem. The poem as a whole is a kind of religious quest based in large part on the Prodigal Son story—one of the great paradigms of the journey motif in Western culture. At the end of the poem, bringing to climax so many of his themes, Bly provides "An Extra Joyful Chorus for Those/ Who Have Read This Far" in which "all the sleepers in the world join hands."

The Morning Glory

The next several books in Bly's canon consist of prose poems. Bly believes that when a culture begins to lose sight of specific goals, it moves dangerously close to abstraction, and that such abstraction is reflected in the poetry of the time. Prose poetry, then, often appears as a way of avoiding too much abstraction. Whether this theory holds up historically or not, it certainly can be made to apply in Bly's case, even if only after the fact—

the theory having been invented to explain the practice. Certainly, there is ample reason to think that Bly judged that his own work, influenced by the events the world was witnessing, was moving dangerously toward "abstraction," perhaps most conspicuously so in *Sleepers Joining Hands*. For whatever reason, then, Bly turned, in the middle of his career, to the genre of the prose poem. His prose poems of this period are extremely strong work, arguably his strongest poetry.

The two most important collections of prose poems are *The Morning Glory* (which includes as its central section the ten-poem sequence "Point Reyes Poems," published separately the year before, and one of the strongest sequences of poems Bly has written) and *This Body Is Made of Camphor and Gopherwood*. These poems move "deeply into the visible," as the old occult saying Bly quotes as epigraph to *The Morning Glory* demands, and they are poems written "in a low voice to someone he is sure is listening," as Bly suggested they should be in his essay "What the Prose Poem Carries with It" (1977).

The Morning Glory, like *Silence in the Snowy Fields*, contains forty-four poems, suggestive of a new beginning in Bly's career. The poems follow a rather typical pattern. They begin in the most offhand ways, frequently with the speaker alone outdoors, prepared, through his openness to possibilities, for whatever he may find there. These poems are journeys; they move from the known to the unknown. Therefore, what can be learned from them is often difficult to analyze, especially since Bly frequently only suggests what it is or might be. Indeed, often it seems to be something that the body comes to know and only later—if at all—the mind comprehends. In this sense these are poems of preparation, and they frequently imply apocalyptic possibilities.

The Morning Glory ends with several poems that describe transformations. One of the most important of these, "Christmas Eve Service at Midnight at St. Michael's," involves the personal life of the poet, who, six months after his only brother has been killed in an automobile accident, attends a Christmas Eve service with his parents. He and his parents take Communion together and hear the Christian message. Coming so soon after his brother's death, however, this message is "confusing," since the poet knows that "we take our bodies with us when we go." The poem ends in a reverie of transfiguration in which a man (both brother and Christ), with a chest wound, flies out and off over the water like a large bird.

THIS BODY IS MADE OF CAMPHOR AND GOPHERWOOD

The basic "religious" theme begun in *The Morning Glory* is continued in *This Body Is Made of Camphor and Gopherwood*. Here Bly writes overtly religious meditations, thus picking up again the aura of the sacred that has been important in his work since the beginning. Indeed, this book immediately reminds the reader of *Silence in the Snowy Fields*, both thematically and in terms of Bly's basic source material.

There are twenty poems in *This Body Is Made of Camphor and Gopherwood*; they are divided into two thematic units. The first ten poems describe, often through dreams, visions, or dream-visions, "what is missing." Not surprisingly, given this theme, Bly frequently uses the metaphor of sleep and awakening. Indeed, the first poem in the book begins, "When I wake." This awakening is both a literal and an imaginative or metaphoric awakening, and it signals at the outset the book's chief concern.

The second section of the book is filled with intensely heightened, almost ecstatic, visionary poems. The crucial transitional poems in *This Body Is Made of Camphor and Gopherwood*—which is itself a crucial transition in Bly's canon—are "Walking to the Next Farm" and "The Origin of the Praise of God." "Walking to the Next Farm" describes the culmination of the transition "this body" has been going through as the poet, his eyes wild, feels "as if a new body were rising" within him. This new body and the energy it contains are further described and defined in the other central poem, "The Origin of the Praise of God." It begins with exactly the same words that begin several other poems in this book: "My friend, this body." This poem, in the words of Ralph J. Mills, Jr., "a visionary hymn to the body, . . . dramatizes [the] experience of the inner deity" and thus is the paradigm of the entire prose-poem sequence. By the end of the book, this visionary, mystical, yet still fully physical body is finally fully formed and is "ready to sing" both the poems already heard and the poems ahead.

THIS TREE WILL BE HERE FOR A THOUSAND YEARS

This Tree Will Be Here for a Thousand Years is a second collection of "snowy fields" poems. Bly said that it should be understood as a companion volume to *Silence in the Snowy Fields*. In this sense, then, *This Tree Will Be Here for a Thousand Years* is a specific, overt attempt on Bly's part to return to his beginnings. Just as it is a return, however, it is also a new beginning in the middle of his career. Bly is clearly a poet obsessed with a need for constant renewal, and in many ways each of his books, although taking a different direction, also retraces each earlier journey from a different vantage point.

Yet perhaps it is not surprising that, although *This Tree Will Be Here for a Thousand Years* is a new beginning for Bly, it is also a darker beginning, a darker journey than the journey he took in *Silence in the Snowy Fields*. Here the journey envisions its end. This, then, is the book of a man facing his mortality, his death, and walking confidently toward it. As Bly puts it in one of these poems, "there are eternities near." At the same time, there is the inevitable paradox that poems outlive the poet who has written them—and, thus, even poems that speak of death outlive the death of their speaker.

THE MAN IN THE BLACK COAT TURNS

Two later books may be seen as companions to each other: *The Man in the Black Coat Turns* and *Loving a Woman in Two Worlds*. Like *This Tree Will Be Here for a Thousand Years*, these books circle back to Bly's beginnings at the same time that they set out on new journeys. Furthermore, these books are among the most personal and private he has published, and thus they are particularly immediate and revealing.

The Man in the Black Coat Turns is divided into three sections, the central section, as in *The Morning Glory* and *This Body Is Made of Camphor and Gopherwood*, being made up of prose poems. The prose poems here, however, are different from their predecessors in being much more clearly related to Bly's personal experiences; as he says in the first of them, "Many times in poems I have escaped—from myself. . . . Now more and more I long for what I cannot escape from" ("Eleven O'Clock at Night").

More than anything else, the poems in *The Man in the Black Coat Turns* are poems about men. The domi-

nant theme of the book is the father-son relationship. This theme and its association with the book's title is immediately, and doubly, announced at the outset of the book, in the first two poems, "Snowbanks North of the House" and "For My Son, Noah, Ten Years Old," as Bly works the lines of relationship through the generations of his own family: from his father to himself as son, then, as father, through himself to his own son, Noah. The third poem, "The Prodigal Son," places the personal family references into a larger context by relating them to father and son in the New Testament parable. In the final poem in this first section of the book, "Mourning Pablo Neruda," Bly extends the father-son relationship again—this time to include one of his own important poetic "father figures," Pablo Neruda, a poet he has often translated.

The final section of *The Man in the Black Coat Turns* draws all these themes together in "The Grief of Men." This poem is clearly the climactic thesis piece for the whole book. There are, however, a number of important poems grouped together in this last section: "Words Rising," "A Meditation on Philosophy," "My Father's Wedding," "Fifty Males Sitting Together," "Crazy Carlson's Meadow," and "Kneeling Down to Look into a Culvert." In the last of these poems, via the account of a symbolic, ritualized sacrificial death, the poet completes his preparations for another new life.

LOVING A WOMAN IN TWO WORLDS

The poems of *Loving a Woman in Two Worlds* are, for the most part, short—almost half of them contain fewer than eight lines, and eleven of them are only four lines long. Technically speaking, however, this book contains poems in most of the forms and with most of the themes Bly has worked in and with throughout his career. In this sense the collection is rather a tour de force. Many of these poems of *Loving a Woman in Two Worlds* are love poems, and some of them are quite explicitly sexual. The book can be read in terms of the stages of a love relationship. These are poems that focus on the female, on the male and female together, and on the way the man and the woman together share "a third body" beyond themselves, a body they have made "a promise to love."

This book thus charts another version of the "body not yet born" journey with which Bly began his poetry.

In the final poem in *Loving a Woman in Two Worlds*, Bly, speaking not only to one individual, but also to all of his readers, writes, "I love you with what in me is unfinished.// . . . with what . . . is still/ changing."

SELECTED POEMS

In the 1986 *Selected Poems*, in addition to poems from all of Bly's previous major collections (some of the poems have been revised, in some cases extensively), he has included some early, previously uncollected poems. A brief essay introduces each of the sectional groupings of this book. *Selected Poems*, then, is a compact, convenient collection, and it succinctly represents Robert Bly in the many individual phases of his work.

MORNING POEMS

Bly's later collections continue to develop, without any loss of power, his distinctive vision and manner. *Morning Poems* is something of a departure, revealing a rich vein of humor and growing out of the discipline of writing a poem a day before getting on with any other matters. These poems capture the speaker's amazement at newness, the splendor of reawakening, and they also do their share of mourning. In an unexpected and powerful sequence, Bly presents an imagined interchange with Wallace Stevens.

THE NIGHT ABRAHAM CALLED TO THE STARS

In *The Night Abraham Called to the Stars*, Bly enjoys the leaps of the Islamic ghazal, a form in which each stanza can exist as an independent poem. At once chaotic and closed, these poems, with their leaping shifts of focus, underscore the great range of Bly's curiosity, his reasonable argument against reason, his quest for a mystical simplicity and unity that does not deny the power of the particular. Biblical allusions permeate this collection, as do historical references and legends. As ever, Bly oscillates between the generic and the generative.

OTHER MAJOR WORKS

NONFICTION: *A Poetry Reading Against the Vietnam War*, 1966 (with David Ray); *Leaping Poetry: An Idea with Poems and Translations*, 1975; *Talking All Morning*, 1980; *American Poetry: Wildness and Domesticity*, 1990; *Iron John: A Book About Men*, 1990; *The Spirit Boy and the Insatiable Soul*, 1994; *The Sibling Society*, 1996; *The Maiden King: The Re-*union of Masculine and Feminine*, 1998 (with Marion Woodman); *Write More, Sell More*, 1999.

TRANSLATIONS: *Twenty Poems of Georg Trakl*, 1961 (with James Wright); *Forty Poems*, 1967 (of Juan Ramón Jiménez); *Hunger*, 1967 (of Knut Hamsun's novel); *I Do Best Alone at Night: Poems*, 1968 (of Gunnar Ekelöf); *Neruda and Vallejo: Selected Poems*, 1971; *Ten Sonnets to Orpheus*, 1972 (of Rainer Maria Rilke); *Lorca and Jiménez: Selected Poems*, 1973; *Friends, You Drank Some Darkness: Three Swedish Poets, Harry Martinson, Gunnar Ekelöf, and Tomas Tranströmer*, 1975; *Twenty Poems*, 1977 (of Rolf Jacobsen); *The Kabir Book: Forty-four of the Ecstatic Poems of Kabir*, 1977; *Truth Barriers: Poems*, 1980 (of Tomas Tranströmer); *Selected Poems of Rainer Maria Rilke*, 1981; *Times Alone: Selected Poems of Antonio Machado*, 1983.

EDITED TEXTS: *A Poetry Reading Against the Vietnam War*, 1966; *News of the Universe: Poems of Twofold Consciousness*, 1980; *The Winged Life: The Poetic Voice of Henry David Thoreau*, 1986; *The Rag and Bone Shop of the Heart: Poems for Men*, 1993; *The Soul Is Here for Its Own Joy: Sacred Poems from Many Cultures*, 1995.

BIBLIOGRAPHY

Davis, William V. *Robert Bly: The Poet and His Critics*. Columbia, S.C.: Camden House, 1994. This chronological study traces the twists and turns of Bly's reputation, accounting for both the aesthetic and nonaesthetic components of critical judgments.

_____. *Understanding Robert Bly*. Columbia: University of South Carolina Press, 1988. A book-length study of Bly's poetic career, geared to an understanding of the chronological development and ongoing significance of Bly's life and work through a detailed analysis of individual poems and an in-depth consideration of each of the major books. Includes a primary and secondary bibliography and an index.

Jones, Richard, and Kate Daniels, eds. *Of Solitude and Silence: Writings on Robert Bly*. Boston: Beacon Press, 1981. A miscellany of materials on Bly, including essays, memoirs, poems, notes, and documents, as well as new poems and translations by

Bly. Includes an extensive primary and secondary bibliography but no index.

Nelson, Howard. *Robert Bly: An Introduction to the Poetry.* New York: Columbia University Press, 1984. A detailed critical introduction to and analysis of Bly's career through *The Man in the Black Coat Turns*, stressing the way in which his various theories illuminate his poems. Includes a chronology of his life, a primary and secondary bibliography, and an index.

Peseroff, Joyce, ed. *Robert Bly: When Sleepers Awake.* Ann Arbor: University of Michigan Press, 1984. A substantial collection of reviews and essays (including several previously unpublished) on Bly and his work through *The Man in the Black Coat Turns.* Includes an extensive primary and secondary bibliography but no index.

Quetchenbach, Bernard W. *Back from the Far Field: American Nature Poetry in the Late Twentieth Century.* Charlottesville: University of Virginia Press, 2000. In a lengthy chapter on Bly, the author explores Bly's concept of a true humanity, including his insistence that consciousness be linked to the environment or disaster will follow.

Sugg, Richard P. *Robert Bly.* Boston: Twayne, 1986. An introductory critical overview of Bly's work and career (stressing a Jungian interpretation), through *The Man in the Black Coat Turns.* (*Loving a Woman in Two Worlds* and *Selected Poems* are mentioned in passing.) Includes a selected bibliography of primary and secondary sources and an index.

William V. Davis,
updated by Philip K. Jason

JOHANNES BOBROWSKI

Born: Tilsit, East Prussia, Germany (now Sovetsk, Russia); April 9, 1917
Died: East Berlin, East Germany; September 2, 1965

PRINCIPAL POETRY
Sarmatische Zeit, 1961
Schattenland Ströme, 1962
Shadow Land: Selected Poems, 1966
Wetterzeichen, 1966
Im Windgesträuch, 1970
The White Mirror: Poems, 1993

OTHER LITERARY FORMS

Although Johannes Bobrowski is remembered primarily for his poetry, he did publish two critically acclaimed experimental novels: *Levins Mühle: 34 Sätze über meinen Grossvater* (1964; *Levin's Mill,* 1970) and *Litauische Claviere* (1966; Lithuanian pianos). He also wrote several short stories, which are collected in the following volumes: *Boehlendorff und andere Erzählungen* (1965; Boehlendorff and other stories), *Mäusefest und andere Erzählungen* (1965; festival of the mice and other stories), and *Der Mahner* (1967; *I Taste Bitterness,* 1970). Working as a reader at an East German publishing house, he had the opportunity to edit books by others, including collections of legends and poetry. Recordings of several of his poems are available.

ACHIEVEMENTS

Johannes Bobrowski belonged to that generation of East German poets who matured late artistically, since their creative development was interrupted by the events of World War II and the founding of a new state. When Bobrowski finally published his first slender volumes in the early 1960's, they caused a great deal of excitement in both East and West Germany, for he was recognized as a major talent. His thematic concerns were new and provocative, and his unique style, based in part on classical German modes yet stripped to the bare linguistic essentials, was rich in metaphor and allegory. For his poetic accomplishments he was awarded the prestigious prize of the Group 47 in 1962, a prize given only to the most promising new authors in the German-speaking world. In the same year, he won the Alma-Johanna-Koenig Prize in Vienna. For his novel *Levin's Mill,* he was awarded the Heinrich Mann Prize of the East Berlin Academy of the Arts and the international Charles Veillon Prize from Switzerland, both in 1965. He was posthumously granted the East German F. C. Weiskopf Prize in 1967.

Together with Erich Arendt and Peter Huchel, Bobrowski is credited with giving a new direction and inspiration to East German poetry, which until his time was rather bogged down in the principles of Socialist Realism and the Brechtian tradition. Bobrowski showed his own generation and younger, emerging poets that artistic integrity and genuine creativity and diversity were possible within the framework of a Socialist state. He also called attention to the great classical German heritage, which had been largely forgotten in the postwar years, and to the most recent developments in West German and foreign poetry. About ten years later, in the early 1970's, his name was again invoked by younger authors in East Germany who sought a new means of aesthetic expression. Although Bobrowski was notably absent from literary anthologies and histories in East Germany immediately after his death, he is today given a place of honor in the literary canon there and is recognized as a humanitarian author who strove for Socialist ideals. In West Germany, more emphasis is placed on an appreciation of his style. He is often mentioned in connection with Günter Eich and Paul Celan, who, like Bobrowski, employed a reduced and concentrated lexical inventory, to the point of being hermetic or even opaque, and who at the same time did not shy away from combining mythological elements with autobiographical and contemporary references.

BIOGRAPHY

Johannes Bobrowski was born in a German town in East Prussia, not far from Lithuania; his father was a German railroad employee of Polish descent. Bobrowski spent his childhood in the small village of Mozischken and frequently visited his grandparents on their farm in the country. It was at this time that he learned much about the culture and history of the Slavic peoples who lived across the border. In 1928, the family moved to Königsberg (later called Kaliningrad), where Bobrowski attended a college-preparatory high school. In school, he was particularly attracted to the disciplines of music and painting; one of his teachers there was the writer Ernst Wiechert. In 1937, the family moved again, this time to Berlin, where Bobrowski began to study art history.

In 1939, Bobrowski was conscripted into military service. During World War II, he served as a soldier in France, Poland, and northern Russia, but he was also a member of the Bekennende Kirche (the Confessing Church), a Protestant resistance group. He was taken prisoner of war in 1945 and remained in Russian captivity until 1949; he was held in the regions of the Don and middle Volga Rivers and did forced labor as a coal miner. He returned to East Berlin in 1949, and in 1950 he began working as a reader at the publishing house Union Verlag, affiliated with the Lutheran Church. He remained there until his death, resulting from complications after an appendicitis operation, in 1965.

Bobrowski began writing poetry in 1941, when he was stationed at Lake Ilmen, and a few of his poems were published in the "inner emigration" magazine *Das innere Reich*. He did not write much again until the early 1950's. His first poems after the war appeared in 1954 in the East German literary magazine *Sinn und Form*, which was edited by his friend Peter Huchel. Bobrowski continued to write sporadically after this literary debut, but he did not feel that his style had matured sufficiently until the early 1960's, when he published his first two volumes of poetry. He completed work on *Wetterzeichen*

Johannes Bobrowski (© Lufti Özkök)

(signs of the weather), but it did not appear until after his death. *Im Windgesträuch* (in the wind bushes), appeared in 1970, containing poems of lesser quality which were written between 1953 and 1964.

ANALYSIS

Many of Johannes Bobrowski's poems, as he often stated, have as their central theme the relationship between the Germans and their neighbors to the East, the Slavic peoples. Because he grew up along the river Memel, where these two cultures merge, Bobrowski was particularly sensitive to this issue. From the days of the Order of the Teutonic Knights in the Middle Ages, the Germans had treated these people very badly, and the history of their relations is marred by war, repression, and murder. Bobrowski the poet recalls these atrocities, lest contemporary Germans forget to atone for their past misdeeds.

SARMATIA

To accomplish this goal, Bobrowski uses the concept of Sarmatia, a vague term applied by ancient historians and geographers to the area that he has in mind—namely, the territory between Finland and southern Russia from the Baltic to the Black Sea. He populates his Sarmatia with a host of various personages: ancient gods, legendary figures, and historical personalities. Bobrowski thus creates a mythology of sorts in order to come to terms with the German past, but it is not a well-defined mythology, and one can discern its full richness only by studying his poems as a totality.

Thus, when one reads about the ancient gods Perkun and Pikoll in "Pruzzische Elegie" ("Prussian Elegy"), about the great Lithuanian ruler Wilna in "Anruf" ("Appeal") or in "Wilna," about the legendary sunken city of Kiteshgorod in "Erzählung" ("Story"), or about Russian writer Isaac Babel in "Holunderblüte" ("Elderblossom"), one confronts only one aspect of Bobrowski's poetic world. History is treated as myth and myth as history. The reader must be willing to mingle and combine past and present, the real and the fictional, in order to form a coherent concept of the historical development Bobrowski has in mind.

LAYERS OF HISTORY

This historical dimension of Bobrowski's poetry offers a key to understanding his works. His poems contain five intertwined temporal layers: ancient times, in which the Slavic or Sarmatian tribes were free to determine their own existence and live in close harmony with nature; past centuries of conflict with the German invaders; the horrors of World War II, which Bobrowski had personally experienced; the present time, in which one must rectify old wrongs; and a future era, in which all men will live in communion with one another. It is often difficult to separate these layers, particularly when the reader finds many confusing temporal references within a single poem, yet this very ambiguity accounts for the richness of Bobrowski's verse; the various layers illuminate one another and promote an understanding of historical and cultural processes.

Moreover, these poems transcend their historical occasion, offering profound general insights into man's inhumanity to man on a global scale and forcefully arguing the need for reconciliation and the end of barbarism. They can thus be read and appreciated by persons from various cultural backgrounds and different eras. This rich philosophical content of the poems also explains how Bobrowski, as a Christian non-Marxist, was able to survive and publish in East Germany. He was seen as a seer or prophet who pointed out the errors of the past and the way to achieve the future brotherhood of all men—one of the proclaimed goals of the communist state. In a manner similar to the historical process he was describing, Bobrowski's poetry underwent a noticeable thematic development or progression: His first poems are concerned primarily with the fantastic landscape of Sarmatia; later poems include historical events and persons from the recent and distant past; and finally, Bobrowski arrives at a discussion of the problems of his present-day Berlin.

POEMS OF HONOR AND REMEMBRANCE

Not all Bobrowski poems deal with Sarmatia. A few treat the themes of love and death, not with any specificity, but in general philosophical terms. Two other categories, however, must be discussed in greater detail. The first contains poems written in honor or in memory of other artists with whom Bobrowski feels some affinity, such as François Villon, Joseph Conrad, Dylan Thomas, Marc Chagall, Johann Georg Hamann, Friedrich Gottlieb Klopstock, Gertrud Kolmar, Friedrich Hölderlin, Else Lasker-Schüler, Nelly Sachs, Wolfgang Amadeus Mozart, Johann Sebastian Bach, Christian Domelaitis, and J. R. M. Lenz. These "portrait poems" are not biographical or artistic summaries, but rather impressions of the artists or their lives. Bobrowski merely takes one aspect or feature of the artist and explains why he admires it or considers it important for his work. Thus, in the poem "An Klopstock" ("To Klopstock"), Bobrowski praises Klopstock's notion that one must recall the past and atone for former transgressions. (Bobrowski considered Klopstock to be his "taskmaster," both stylistically and thematically.) In "Hamann," he praises the eighteenth century poet for collecting and preserving ancient tales and legends. (Bobrowski was greatly influenced by Hamann while still in school and felt that Hamann's life's goals were similar to his own. He had been collecting material for years for a monograph on Hamann but was unable to complete it because of his premature death.) In the poems "Else Lasker-Schüler" and "An Nelly Sachs" ("To Nelly Sachs"), Bobrowski points to the suffering these poets endured because they were Jewish, a suffering similar to that of the Jews living in Sarmatia. Bobrowski shared with all of these artists a deep humanistic commitment to his fellowman and a concern for suffering in the world.

METAPOETRY: "ALWAYS TO BE NAMED" AND "LANGUAGE"

Another significant category of Bobrowski's poems, though by no means large, could be termed "metapoetry." In these poems, Bobrowski describes his concept of poetic language and poetic communication. Two of these poems are especially paradigmatic: "Immer zu benennen" ("Always to Be Named") and "Sprache" ("Language"). Here, Bobrowski shows that he believes in an almost mystical relationship between the word and the thing named, that the word somehow captures the spirit of the thing or the person to which it refers. This idea plays an important role in Bobrowski's mythology, for objects, particularly from nature, take on a new significance: They become part of man, part of his past and his relationship to other men. Thus, not only history is important for an understanding of man's advance into the future, but also words and nature, for by means of these two elements

men can communicate with one another and prepare themselves for what is to come. This is for Bobrowski the highest sense of poetry—it speaks to the reader on several levels and raises his degree of consciousness. Poetry does not, Bobrowski claims, move the reader to bold political or social acts.

NATURE AS SYMBOL

Because of his emphasis on man's relationship to nature through language, and because he believed that man's harmony with nature, which was somehow lost in the past, must be regained in order to save the human race, Bobrowski's work has often been referred to as nature poetry. This description is valid only to a certain extent. It is true that Bobrowski does employ a great number of recurring nature motifs in his poetry, most frequently rivers, birds, trees, fish, stones, wolves, light, and darkness. These motifs, however, are not an evocation of nature per se. They do not merely conjure up the beauty of landscapes to be admired and enjoyed, but rather they function as symbols within the overriding thematics of the poem. Although they have varying connotations, Bobrowski generally uses these motifs to connect man to nature and to show how man is part of the natural historical process. The objects of nature remain constant throughout historical change, says Bobrowski, and so, too, does man's soul. If man can rid himself of the barbarous acts of war and violence and return to his primeval natural state, he will have reached his ultimate goal. This strong concern for the human and communal element is what sets Bobrowski's poems apart from traditional nature poetry.

POETIC MINIMALISM

Bobrowski's symbolic treatment of nature is only one aspect of his laconic style. The most striking feature of his poetry is the reduction of the linguistic material to an extreme minimum. Frequently, lines consist of merely a word or two each, and the length of the line is very irregular. Bobrowski often employs sentence fragments consisting of a single word, and longer syntactic units are usually broken up into several lines, interrupting the semantic flow.

The breaking of the poem into small phrases gives primacy to the individual word and lends the poetic message an aspect far different from what it would possess were it written in prose or even conventional poetic style. The free rhythms are sometimes fairly regular, so that the reader is often reminded of the odes and elegies of previous centuries. Bobrowski's concentrated and abbreviated style demands the active participation of the reader, who must fill in the missing material and make the appropriate associations and connections, a process similar to that through which one tries to remember events of the distant past. Such a difficult procedure tends at times to weaken the thematic impact of the poem, but as Fritz Minde points out in an article on Bobrowski, the poems can indeed be decoded with the help of published biographical and historical material; their difficult construction mimics the deformed and incoherent structure of reality.

STRUCTURE

In *Poetry in East Germany*, John Flores suggests a method by which this decoding can be performed. He believes that most of Bobrowski's poems have three parts or stages. In the first, or introductory, part, the author relies chiefly on nouns, employed in an uncertain, staccato fashion. He is setting the mood for the poem by using the naming process described above. The reader is uncertain and somewhat confused. In the second stage, spatial and temporal connections begin to appear. The style is more reflective and narrative, and nouns are linked with verbs. The thematic thrust of the poem begins to take shape. In the final stage, the staccato mode is reintroduced, but here the verb prevails. The author unleashes his thoughts and ideas in a torrent of words. These thoughts have been building in intensity throughout the poem, and they all come together in the end in a desperate cry for recognition.

LEGACY

The difficult and cryptic nature of many of Bobrowski's poems raises the question of his place in literary history. Was he a true member of the avant-garde, a forerunner of or participant in the reductive "linguistic" movement of contemporary German poetry? No, he did not use language as a collection of building blocks devoid of meaning. Instead, he can be seen as part of the movement toward radical reduction of language that began around 1910 with the expressionists in Germany and that insisted on a language free of all decadent cultural encrustations. Such a purification of language became all the more necessary after the abuses

of the Nazi years. At the same time, however, Bobrowski went beyond this essentially negative program, offering in his verse substantive arguments in favor of a new and better world.

OTHER MAJOR WORKS

LONG FICTION: *Levins Mühle: 34 Sätze über meinen Grossvater*, 1964 (*Levin's Mill*, 1970); *Litauische Claviere*, 1966.

SHORT FICTION: *Boehlendorff und andere Erzählungen*, 1965; *Mäusefest und andere Erzählungen*, 1965; *Der Mahner*, 1967 (*I Taste Bitterness*, 1970).

BIBLIOGRAPHY

Bridgwater, Patrick. "The Poetry of Johannes Bobrowski." *Forum for Modern Language Studies* 2 (1966): 320-334. A critical study of Bobrowski's poetic works.

Flores, John. *Poetry in East Germany: Adjustments, Visions, and Provocations, 1945-1970.* New Haven, Conn.: Yale University Press, 1971. A history and critical analysis of poetry in postwar East Germany including the works of Bobrowski during this period. Includes bibliographic references.

Glenn, Jerry. "An Introduction to the Poetry of Johannes Bobrowski." *The Germanic Review* 41 (1966): 45-56. A brief critical assessment of Bobrowski's poetic works.

Keith-Smith, Brian. *Johannes Bobrowski.* London: Wolff, 1970. Introductory biography with selected poetry and prose in English translation. Includes bibliography.

Scrase, David. *Understanding Johannes Bobrowski.* Columbia: University of South Carolina Press, 1995. Critical interpretation and brief biography by a specialist in German and Austrian art and literature. Includes bibliography.

Wieczorek, John P. *Between Sarmatia and Socialism: The Life and Works of Johannes Bobrowski.* Atlanta, Ga.: Rodopi, 1999. Examines the chronological development of Bobrowski's 'Sarmatian' works and places them within the context of a biography of his career.

Robert Acker;
bibliography updated by the editors

LOUISE BOGAN

Born: Livermore Falls, Maine; August 11, 1897
Died: New York, New York; February 4, 1970

PRINCIPAL POETRY

Body of This Death, 1923
Dark Summer, 1929
The Sleeping Fury, 1937
Poems and New Poems, 1941
Collected Poems 1923-1953, 1954
The Blue Estuaries: Poems 1923-1968, 1968, 1977

OTHER LITERARY FORMS

There are two collections of Louise Bogan's criticism, most of it consisting of articles and reviews from her many years with *The New Yorker:* The posthumously published *A Poet's Alphabet* (1970), edited by Robert Phelps and Ruth Limmer, contains all the pieces from *Selected Criticism* (1955) plus other writings previously uncollected. Bogan's brief history of modern American poetry, *Achievement in American Poetry*, appeared in 1951. Her translations include *The Glass Bees* by Ernst Jünger (1960, with Elizabeth Mayer), and three works of Johann Wolfgang von Goethe: *Elective Affinities* (1963), *The Sorrows of Young Werther* (1971), and *Novella* (1971); she also edited a translation of *The Journal of Jules Renard* (1964). Ruth Limmer, Bogan's friend and literary executor, also brought out two posthumous collections of personal writings: *What the Woman Lived: Selected Letters of Louise Bogan 1920-1970* (1973) and *Journey Around My Room* (1980), a chronological selection from diaries, letters, and other published and unpublished papers.

ACHIEVEMENTS

Louise Bogan devoted her life to poetry in writing, criticism, reviews, lectures, and consulting, and she was recognized with "all the honors that are an honor" for a poet in America. Early in her career she was awarded the John Reed Memorial Prize by *Poetry* magazine; a Guggenheim Fellowship followed. In subsequent years she received the Helen Haire Levinson Prize from *Poetry*, the Harriet Monroe Award from the University of Chicago, the Poet Laureate Consultant in Poetry given through the Library of Congress, the Bollingen Prize, the Academy of American Poets Fellowship, and the Senior Creative Arts Award from Brandeis University. Western College for Women and Colby College bestowed honorary degrees. She was elected a Fellow in American Letters of the Library of Congress, a member of the Institute of Arts and Letters, and a member of the American Academy of Arts and Letters.

These honors came in recognition of a substantial body of prose as well as poetry. From 1931 until 1968, Bogan regularly reviewed poetry for *The New Yorker*, contributing notes and reviews on twenty to forty books of poetry every year. Her published criticism helped shape the taste of generations of readers. Less well known but also influential was Bogan's second career as teacher, lecturer, and poet-in-residence. In 1944, she delivered the Hopwood Lecture at the University of Michigan, and for the next twenty-five years she lectured and taught at universities from Connecticut to Arizona and Washington State to Arkansas.

Bogan never cultivated popularity, and, despite the many academic and official honors, popular acclaim for her work has been scant. She received neither the Pulitzer Prize nor the National Book Award. More puzzling has been the neglect by the academic establishment; few scholars have undertaken the thorough examination of her work that has been accorded such contemporaries as Theodore Roethke and Marianne Moore. In the late 1970's, however, stimulated by feminist criticism and an awakening interest in women authors, literary scholars began more extensive studies of Bogan's works.

BIOGRAPHY

About the details of her life, Louise Bogan maintained a deliberate and consistent reticence. Yet she also claimed that she had written a searching account of her life; it was all in her poetry, she said, with only the vulgar particulars omitted. The information available about her life substantiates her claim.

The earliest theme to emerge in Bogan's life is the struggle for order amidst chaos and violence. She was born in Livermore Falls, Maine, on August 11, 1897, the second child and only daughter of Mary Helen Shields and Daniel J. Bogan. During the next twelve years the

Louise Bogan (© Bettmann/Corbis)

family lived variously in Milton and Manchester, New Hampshire, and in Ballardvale, Massachusetts, before settling, in 1910, in Boston. Life was characterized by extremes of physical and psychological violence between the parents, and between mother and children. While Bogan's father is almost totally absent from her recollections, her mother, a woman of elegance, taste, and ferocious temper, imposed an unpredictable and almost overwhelming presence on the young girl's life. There are startling gaps in memory: an unexplained year in a convent boarding school, two days of blindness at the age of eight. The convent year, the boarding house in Ballardvale, and an art teacher in Boston, however, represented relief from the constant struggle for sanity and order in the chaotic Bogan household. As a child, Louise relished the soothing atmosphere of order, cleanliness, and competence found in the boarding house, and later the enchantment of Miss Cooper's studio with its precious trinkets and carefully ordered tools. During her teens, Bogan's five years at Boston's Girls' Latin School enlarged her experience of both discipline and disorder; it was here that she received the thorough classical education she treasured so, and here that she encountered

firsthand the vigorous New England Protestant bigotry against the Irish. To her classmates, Bogan was a "Mick," and she kept this consciousness of class distinctions throughout her life. The revelation must have amazed the girl steeped in a rich and intricate Catholicism. During this period of childhood and youth, which ended with marriage after one year at Boston University, she began to write.

In 1916, against the strong objections of her mother, Bogan forfeited her scholarship to Radcliffe and married Curt Alexander, a private in the Army. Her overriding motive was escape from a constricting life, but that illusion was very short-lived. Exactly one year after joining her husband in Panama, where she gave birth to a daughter, Maidie, Bogan returned with the child to Boston. Later, she and Alexander attempted to revive the marriage, living first near Portland, Maine, and later in Hoboken, New Jersey; all they had in common, Bogan recalled, was sex. She began to publish more, establishing a literary life as part of the Greenwich Village artistic milieu, and eventually the two separated. In 1918, Bogan's brother Charles was killed in France, and two years later Curt Alexander died. In 1923 her first collection, *Body of This Death*, came out.

The next twelve years of her life reflected a pattern of increasing professional skill and discipline together with a persistently troubled personal life. From 1925 to 1937 she was married to Raymond Holden. The relationship was stormy, not least because of Holden's infidelities, and marked by a series of moves—to Santa Fe, to Hillsdale, to various addresses in New York City. Material losses took a toll: In 1929 the Holdens' house burned, destroying books, pictures, and manuscripts, and in 1935, while she was separated from Holden, Bogan was evicted from her apartment. In 1937 her mother died. During this period of her life Bogan was hospitalized twice for depression and nervous collapse. She later speculated on the relationship between childhood experience and memory and the many upheavals of her young adult life, locating the beginning of her depression in a visit to the earliest neighborhood the Bogans had lived in after coming to Boston. She continued writing; in 1937, *The Sleeping Fury* appeared.

The period 1937 to 1965 marked a time of maturity, productivity, and fulfillment. In 1937, Bogan moved to the New York apartment that would be her home thenceforth. Three volumes of poetry, as well as two critical works, an anthology, and translations were published. Awards and honors came almost yearly, along with invitations to lecture, read, and consult.

Turmoil and controversy reappeared in her life in 1965, when another depression resulted in hospitalization. The 1960's also saw Bogan's first public political activity, when she took part in the protests against the war in Vietnam. She continued lecturing, reading, and reviewing until, at the age of seventy-two, she resigned from her position as poetry reviewer for *The New Yorker.* Her last collection of poems, *The Blue Estuaries,* appeared in 1968, and she completed the compilation of her reviews that was published as *A Poet's Alphabet.* On February 4, 1970, Louise Bogan died alone in her New York apartment.

ANALYSIS

Louise Bogan's well-known reticence about the details of her personal life extended to her poetry. She said that she had written down her experience in detail, omitting only the rough and vulgar facts. This dichotomy of fact and experience lies at the heart of her poems: They are about experience, not about facts. Four basic thematic concerns emerge in Bogan's work. Many poems center on women or womanhood. This was a theme to which Bogan returned often in her criticism, and her history of modern American poetry is one of the few to acknowledge the contributions of women. A second theme emerges in the many poems that explore the universal human condition of fleshly existence and the disasters and delights of love. Another preoccupation is art, the process of making art, and the artist and his commitment. Finally, the struggle of the mind and spirit for sanity and consolation in the face of insanity, chaos, and meaninglessness inspired the greatest of her poems.

WOMEN AS THEME

"Women" may be Bogan's most frequently anthologized poem, and it has certainly troubled feminist critics more than any other. The poem is cast as a diatribe by a male speaker who generalizes about women as "they." This catalog of faults outlines the stereotype of "woman" that Bogan herself referred to impatiently in

several of her essays. The speaker's harsh tone modulates toward pity for women's habit of using their own benevolence against themselves, but he does not speculate on the causes of the many flaws in women. Neither did Bogan, as evidence by her letters and criticism: She inherited, without question, the Victorian and Romantic view that applied the dichotomies of emotion and intellect to woman and man, respectively, and then raised those parallel associations to the status of natural law.

In her poems, however, Bogan's perception of stereotypes of gender reflects a more complex vision. "The Romantic," for example, mocks the sentimental ideal of the passionless woman. The romantic had sought to impose his vision of femininity on the young woman and lost both woman and ideal. In both "Women" and "The Romantic" the poet distances herself from the subject. In the first a presumptively male voice discourses, not about any real woman but about the idea of women, while in the second a voice of unspecified gender addresses a man about a woman who has vanished.

Other poems confront more directly the particular heartaches, upheavals, and joys of being a woman, but in these, too, the approach is ordered and the thought kept coherent by various techniques of distancing. In each of the three poems, "The Changed Woman," "Chanson un peu naïve," and "For a Marriage," an anonymous speaker talks about a woman who also remains unspecified and anonymous. "Chanson un peu naïve" expresses an ironic, despairing pity at the destructive results of frequent childbearing and an apparent self-deception that permits its continuance. In "For a Marriage," a dispassionate onlooker reflects on intimacy as a sharing of pain, in this instance the woman's revelation of her pain to be shared by her husband. "The Changed Woman" is more obscure, referring perhaps to a miscarriage or abortion; the quality of the experience, the dream denied and driven, supersedes factual references. Another treatment of the theme is "The Crossed Apple": Here an older person, man or woman, directly addresses a young girl and offers the gift of an apple. The poem invokes the creation myth in Genesis, as the voice suggests that eating the fruit means knowledge as well as sustenance: She will taste more than fruit, blossom, sun, or air.

Such distancing brings order to the chaotic, impulsive, often outrageous realities of women's lives, placing those realities within the bounds of an art that can illuminate and make them meaningful. Those poems in which Bogan uses a woman's voice to articulate a woman's point of view also find means to distance and thus order her subject. "Men Loved Wholly Beyond Wisdom" generalizes about men and women according to familiar stereotypes. For the first five lines women love and therefore demand love excessively, and in the remaining eight lines, the speaker resorts to harsh suppression of her emotions as the solution to the dilemma presented by her feelings and her perceptions of them. "Girl's Song" implies the same problem: The speaker addresses the man who has abandoned her in favor of another woman who, it is implied, will likewise love him in a sacrificial, even destructive way. While this poem expresses resignation rather than the fierce despair of "Men Loved Wholly Beyond Wisdom," the view of women's nature and circumstances is the same: Women love excessively, to their sorrow and destruction.

WOMEN IN LATER POETRY

Both of the foregoing poems come from Bogan's early work, and they, like many of the early poems, express the tension between matter and form, instinct and reason, in terms of the relationships between women and men. In three poems published much later in her life she spoke less generally and more directly in the persona of a particular woman with a specific history.

In "The Sorcerer's Daughter" and "Little Lobelia's Song," women speak of their own experience, and both poems spring from recognition of that most fundamental of connections, the relationship between parent and child. The sorcerer's daughter, who can read signs and auguries, finds herself bound to an unfortunate fate. The poem echoes the prophetic pessimism of "Cassandra" without the formal restraint and emotional tension of the earlier poem. "The Sorcerer's Daughter" is no tragedy; from her father the speaker inherits, chiefly, bad luck. In "Little Lobelia's Song" the piteous, helpless, inarticulate voice is an infant addressing its mother. Reflections on Bogan's tumultuous relationship with her own mother are inevitable, although the poem contains no details. The speaker's expression of identity with its mother, and the agony of separation, invite Freudian interpretation. Bogan's own acquaintance with modern psychology emerged from experience as well as theory, and the poem, published

not long after her last stay in a mental hospital, is one of a group of three including "Psychiatrist's Song." Seldom did Bogan permit expression of such unalloyed pathos, yet the poem achieves power precisely through its rigid form and the distancing created by the artificial persona; the poet even succeeds with that commonest of clichés, flower as metaphor for child.

"Masked Woman's Song," the third poem of this trilogy, speaks most specifically yet most enigmatically about Bogan's own experience. While the other poems use personas as disguise, the masked woman acknowledges her disguise and thus disarms skepticism. The singer seems to disown her previous sense of the value of artistic and moral order. The poem contains more physical description than most: The man is tall, has a worn face and roped arms. These are matters of fact, not experience, and the poem remains virtually impenetrable. The poet has moved beyond the classical values and virtues to a realm so resistant to description that it defies metaphor, where the familiar images of male and female no longer serve.

LOVE AS THEME

As is already evident, Bogan made love in its many varieties a major theme in her poetry. She framed her exposition generally in the Renaissance terms of flesh and spirit, passion and reason. The classical understanding of passion, derived from *passio* (suffering, submission) and related to "passive," regarded the lusts of the flesh not as mere sentiment or feeling but as the fundamental, chaotic, instinctual life of man that provides all force for ongoing life and regeneration, but that also constantly moves to overwhelm and subsume the cognitive being. Thus, the great human enterprise is to balance and harmonize both the instinctual and the mental, the flesh and the spirit.

Bogan's poems express disdain for excess in either direction. In "Several Voices out of a Cloud" the drunks, drug-takers, and perverts receive the laurel, for they have—whatever their flaws—been committed, they have used their creative energy. The pallid, the lifeless, punks, trimmers, and nice people—all of those who denied life in favor of empty form—forgo eternity. The conception, the thesis, and even the terminology are Dantean.

Two poems about men suggest the peculiar dangers of trying to avoid confrontation with passion. In "The

Frightened Man" the speaker explains that he feared the rich mouth and so kissed the thin; even this contact proved too much as she waxed while he weakened. His shattered image of the docile woman implies a self-destructive loathing of the real and the fleshly. "Man Alone" explores the subtle complexities of this solipsistic position. The man of the title seems to exist in a hall of mirrors; unable to confront and acknowledge the common humanity and individual otherness of his fellow human beings, he persists in a state of autistic rage. Literally and figuratively he cannot face another person. The man does not suffer an excess but rather a perversion; passion misplaced has devolved into self-absorbed rage and infatuate isolation.

Most of Bogan's poetic statements on the subject of passionate love decry its excesses. She acknowledged and even emphasized the urgency of fleshly desire, but rarely celebrated it for itself. In her poems, giving oneself to overwhelming passion means capitulation, not liberation. Variations on this theme are played in "Women," in "Men Loved Wholly Beyond Wisdom," in "Chanson un peu naïve," and in "Girl's Song." Bogan's clearest critique of excessive love is in "Rhyme," with its echoes of William Shakespeare's sonnet, "The expense of spirit in a waste of shame." In Bogan's poem a lover recollects a former love, addressing the absent one in a tone of wry nostalgia. The speaker articulates the Renaissance perception of excessive love as a form of idolatry, yet also acknowledges the nourishing function that passion can have, for the loved one had been heart's feast to the lover.

"Second Song" and "At a Party" describe the destructiveness of undisciplined love. In "Second Song" the speaker bids farewell to passion, which has garnered mere trinkets and a poisoned spiritual food. The speaker has undergone passion, has suffered it in the classical sense, as a pensioner, and so chooses to become detached from it. Like the speakers in "Rhyme" and "Second Song," the voice in "At a Party" has no specified gender; nor does this persona speak from behind mask or disguise, as do the speakers in many poems about women. When she spoke most directly, Bogan framed her persona as androgynous. This is a Renaissance ideal; one image for the integration of opposing dualities was the figure of the androgyne. "At a Party," however, treats the more cosmic theme of the corruption of nature that can follow from worship of the flesh. The speaker observes a dizzy, drunken revelry that ignorantly mocks the ordered progress of the stars, and then orders flesh to assert primacy over spirit and proclaim the tyranny of the material and the final corruption of value and beauty. Against this projected debacle the speaker then invokes malice and enmity, which may bring salvation. The philosophy and the images recall John Donne and Dante: Disorder and perversion affront the natural order of the universe and require stern correctives.

ART AS THEME

While Bogan's poems on the subject of love consistently treat the hazards and disasters of passion, models of harmonious, productive love exist mainly in the ideal implied by negative examples. The integration of duality, a fruitful union of passion and intellect, is imaged not in the lover, but in the artist.

Bogan expressed more than once her faith in art as a means to sanity and salvation in her troubled personal world, and two of her poems on art specifically explore the great power she attributed to it. "M., Singing" celebrates the capacity of art to articulate the unspeakable. The speaker finds that the melancholy words and subtle music of M.'s song cause the soul's hidden demons to step forth into the light of day. This is healing music, for these corrupt creatures abandon their unseen work of destruction and become subject to rational examination in human space; evil can be neutralized. "Song for a Slight Voice" returns to the theme of possessive love. The discipline of art, the speaker implies, has overcome the exigencies of passion, and the lover's stubborn heart will become an instrument for music, will hear the dance. Art can triumph over witless passion.

In two poems that explore the traditional theme of nature versus art, however, Bogan does not offer a clearcut statement of superiority for either side. "To an Artist, To Take Heart" is an epigram in which the speaker contrasts the violent ends of Shakespeare's characters Hamlet, Othello, and Coriolanus with the peaceful death of the author who outlived them all. Neither nature nor art wins supremacy, but each finds its fulfillment. The speaker's wry view of the artist as parent to his creations is adumbrated in the title: The work of art does not kill the artist, for the author lives even though his characters die. Verb tenses, however, signify the reverse: "Shakespeare died" in the past, once and for all, whereas "Hamlet, Othello, Coriolanus fall" in the present, as the creation lives after the creator dies.

"Animal, Vegetable, Mineral" is an uncharacteristically long poem of sixty-five lines in rhymed five-line stanzas. It is a meditation on the subject of cross-pollination, which is a work of nature; but it takes as its starting point art objects twice removed from the natural world: a publication of color plates depicting glass models of flowers. Both language and subject matter point to the pervasive theme of cross-pollination, or integration, of nature and art, instinct and mind. Blossoms are Gothic or Baroque, bees are *Empire*. The precise workings of instinct and of natural functions stimulate thought in the human mind, here represented by Charles Darwin, and provide occasion for almost incomprehensible devotion to craft in the work of the Blaschkas, the Czech family of glassblowers who worked for fifty years to produce the botanical models. The speaker remains awed by cross-pollination of science, art, and nature: It is the process itself that is valuable, unfathomable, a loud mystery.

Like "Animal, Vegetable, Mineral," "Roman Fountain" and "Italian Morning"—two poems set in Italy—take visual art as their theme. The first emphasizes the process of making art while the latter focuses on the work of art. Each, too, expresses a quintessential Renaissance theme, the triumph of art over time. In "Roman Fountain" the speaker is a poet sustained and reinvigorated upon seeing water rising and falling in an ornate fountain. The gushing, noisy, ceaselessly moving water fructifies and enlivens the poet's imagination, but it does so because it has been shaped and directed by the carefully wrought fountain created by hands long dead. This perfect union of nature and art elates and inspires the poet. In "Italian Morning," on the other hand, the work of art confronts the speaker with human mortality. Two people awaken in an ornately decorated room, and the calm, silent presence of the painted fruit and flowers conveys a sense of timelessness. In contrast, the speaker's perception of time—placing the hour, naming the year—indicates a paradoxical poverty in human life: Time evaporates in the act of being possessed.

These poems suggest a mystical dimension to art that is made even more explicit in two others, "The Alche-mist" and "Musician." In the former the alchemist speaker represents the artist who has taken his own self as the base material for transmutation. The alchemist renounces material life and its rewards in search of a wholly spiritual existence and pleasure. Mere breathing will become the vehicle for ecstasy. The connection between breath and transcendent contemplation occurs in mystical traditions of both East and West; in the case of Bogan's alchemist the long search culminates in a vision of reality stripped of illusion, of pure substance without the accident of meaning.

"Musician" portrays process and performance in terms similar to some types of Zen Buddhist aesthetics. Musician and instrument join to produce harmony so effortless and perfect that it seems the instrument has a life of its own. The agent is subsumed in perfect art. Like the figure of the androgyne, the image of the musician with instrument represented to the Renaissance mind the perfect dynamic balance of material and spiritual, matter and form. This ideal of vital integration of opposites pervades Bogan's poems about art, most clearly in the many poems centering on the image of the musician.

PSYCHOLOGY AS THEME

Bogan's preoccupation with the achievement of balance, harmony, and fruitfulness through reconciliation of opposites receives its finest expression in the poems that present most explicitly the struggle of the human mind to avert chaos and integrate impulse. Two poems that take a merely clinical look at the issue, "Evening in the Sanitarium" and "Psychiatrist's Song," recall her own experiences with the institutional view of mental illness. These poems are closer to the factual end of the fact-experience continuum, as is "Animal, Vegetable, Mineral," and all three are also very discursive and formally loose by comparison with her other works. For Bogan, it was formal rigor that produced the tension needed to convey intensity of thought and feeling.

Four poems deserve special notice as preeminent expressions of this struggle of the spirit. "Exhortation," "Simple Autumnal," "Kept," and "Henceforth, from the Mind" focus in turn on hate, grief, renunciation, and sublimation as healing powers.

"Exhortation" further elaborates the ideas expressed in "At a Party": The person who is conscious and moral and therefore alive lives in a world of the walking dead—the callous and the ignorant who are impervious to insight or ethics. In material terms, the latter always wins; success and failure rather than good or evil are the terms on which they operate. The speaker in the poem counsels detachment as the only remedy for the thinking, feeling person. The listener is advised to renounce both joy and rage, to leave behind the comforts of love and grief, and to cultivate indifference. This is a harsh doctrine, uncongenial to a vision of man as naturally good or perfectible. It has been called stoic; certainly, it accords with the Catholic philosophy of Bogan's early education, which emphasized the fall of man and a resultant debility of spirit. At the heart of the poem lies a crucial distinction, however: The living dead, preoccupied with trivia and sated with insolence, exist in a state of moribund sterility, passionless and bleak. The speaker's renunciation of passion and rage, grief and joy, does not deny these elements of human life, but rather requires a full realization (in its root meaning) of them. Discipline and detachment, superficially similar to indifference, sustain life in the face of mere repression and ignorance.

"Simple Autumnal," one of Bogan's few sonnets, makes a contrasting assertion: Grief denied repudiates both life and death. The speaker compares delayed autumn with delayed grief; time is frozen and so is life. The maturing process seems to come to a standstill in nature as it mirrors the person who refuses grief, so that nature takes on the static character of art and is therefore unnatural. Sorrow could heal, fulfilling life's intent, but feelings remains unreachable. The poem expresses the experience of living death referred to in "Exhortation," but with one difference: In "Simple Autumnal" the speaker comprehends the situation of lifelessness fully, and suffers intensely thereby. The sense of the poem recalls many of Emily Dickinson's works, in particular those such as "Pain Has an Element of Blank" which explore the experience of unreleased pain.

Reminiscent of Dickinson also is the emphasis on renunciation in "Kept." Again, the speaker takes up the theme of movement versus stasis, life against lifelessness. Those who would cling to the past as represented by its artifacts, dolls, and toys, will never be free of it. Nostalgia can trap one in everlasting childishness, for the past must be destroyed in order to be the past. Growth and maturity can occur only in the passage of time. Without the process of growth a reverse process takes place: The person existing in an artificial world diminishes and indeed begins to metamorphosize until only an object remains. As in the two preceding poems, sanity is a function of conscious, heartfelt, and disciplined submission to the natural processes of life and death, growth and decay.

In "Henceforth, from the Mind," Bogan reaches beyond the pain of discipline and renunciation to affirm the final achievement of sublimation. The speaker does not advocate substitution or repression, as the notion of sublimation is often wrongly understood. It is real joy that will spring from the mind, from the tongue—the selfsame exaltation that the younger person ascribes to passion. The form of the poem harmonizes with this theme. The forward motion of the first two stanzas takes momentum from the "henceforth" that begins each and from the emphatic reversal of verb and subject in the two main clauses; the repetition of the rhyming couplets ending each stanza counterbalances this same forward motion. The last two stanzas mirror in their form the perfect transmutation of the material and spiritual that the poem asserts. In a single twelve-line sentence as convoluted as the image of the shell in the first line, syntactical momentum builds until the verb and—finally—the subject appear at the *end* of the sentence, which is also the end of the poem. This reversal of the usual sentence structure is itself a form of echoing: The sea and earth that will henceforth be known from their echoes within memory and imagination sound back to the resonating shell in a grammatical spiral that imitates the convolvulus's physical shape. The shell encloses the ocean, echoing a knowledge of that sea from which it is itself sundered. Sound and motion prevail in the rocking, cradling rhythms of bell and wave, the music of transcendent illumination, echoing through the depths within depths of perfect harmony.

OTHER MAJOR WORKS

NONFICTION: *Achievement in American Poetry*, 1951; *Selected Criticism: Prose, Poetry*, 1955; *A Poet's Alphabet: Reflections on the Literary Art and Vocation*, 1970; *What the Woman Lived: Selected Letters of Louise Bogan, 1920-1970*, 1973; *Journey Around My Room: The Autobiography of Louise Bogan*, 1980.

TRANSLATIONS: *The Glass Bees*, 1960 (of Ernest Jünger; with Elizabeth Mayer); *Elective Affinities*, 1963 (of Johann Wolfgang von Goethe; with Mayer); *Journal*, 1964 (of Jules Renard; with Elizabeth Roget); *The Sorrows of Young Werther*, 1971 (of Goethe); *Novella*, 1971 (of Goethe).

EDITED TEXTS: *The Golden Journey: Poems for Young People*, 1965 (compiled with William Jay Smith).

BIBLIOGRAPHY

Bowles, Gloria. *Louise Bogan's Aesthetic of Limitation*. Bloomington: Indiana University Press, 1987. Bowles uses a feminist perspective to examine Bogan and her work and asserts that the poet's "limitation" results from her notion of what she could and could not do within the male literary tradition. The author identifies Bogan as a modernist and explores a variety of influences—including William Butler Yeats and the Symbolists—on her poetry.

Collins, Martha, ed. *Critical Essays on Louise Bogan*. Boston: G. K. Hall, 1984. The first collection of scholarly essays on Bogan ever published. The writings of fellow poets, including Ford Madox Ford and W. H. Auden, represent the majority of the thirty-five essays. Topics discussed are varied and range from the tendencies to misunderstand Bogan's work to feminist responses to her poetry. Collins has written an extensive and enlightening introduction.

Dodd, Elizabeth Caroline. *The Veiled Mirror and the Woman Poet: H. D., Louise Bogan, Elizabeth Bishop, and Louise Glück*. Columbia: University of Missouri Press, 1992. In this study Dodd identifies a strain in women's poetry she calls "personal classicism": poetry grounded in the writer's private experience yet characterized by formal and tonal restraint. Includes a bibliography and an index.

Frank, Elizabeth. *Louise Bogan: A Portrait*. New York: Alfred A. Knopf, 1985. Although this book is intended for the general reader, it will also satisfy and inform Bogan scholars. Frank deftly examines the relationship between Bogan's life and work, utilizing a variety of sources, including letters, diaries, recollections of people who knew her, and unpub-

lished and uncollected works. The author is eminently qualified for this ambitious work, as she has studied Bogan for many years.

Knox, Claire E. *Louise Bogan: A Reference Source*. London: Scarecrow, 1990. Knox draws on files of *The New Yorker* (where Bogan was poetry editor from 1931 to 1969), the Berg Collection at the New York Public Library, collected materials at Harvard and Amherst Universities, and the Library of Congress (where Bogan was consultant in poetry) to compile this exhaustive, annotated bibliography on Bogan.

Ridgeway, Jaqueline. *Louise Bogan*. Boston: Twayne, 1984. This ambitious book explores childhood experiences that influenced Bogan's poetry, the symbols that express her poetic statements, and her use of the formal lyric style long after it had fallen out of favor with her contemporaries. Ridgeway also examines a rarely discussed topic: Bogan's influence on other poets.

Simmons, Thomas. *Erotic Reckonings: Mastery and Apprenticeship in the Work of Poets and Lovers*. Urbana: University of Illinois, 1994. Examines the mentor-apprenticeship relationships between three pairs of twentieth century poets: Ezra Pound and H. D., Yvor Winters and Janet Lewis, and Louise Bogan and Theodore Roethke. Explores the force of biographical and literary events on the mentor, then traces the mentor's impact on the apprentice.

Helen Jaskoski;
bibliography updated by the editors

EAVAN BOLAND

Born: Dublin, Ireland; September 24, 1944

PRINCIPAL POETRY
Twenty-three Poems, 1962
New Territory, 1967
The War Horse, 1975
In Her Own Image, 1980
Introducing Eavan Boland, 1981

Night Feed, 1982
The Journey and Other Poems, 1987
Selected Poems, 1989
Outside History: Selected Poems, 1980-1990, 1990
In a Time of Violence, 1994
Collected Poems, 1995 (pb. in U.S. as *An Origin Like Water: Collected Poems, 1967-1987*, 1996)
The Lost Land, 1998
Against Love Poetry, 2001

OTHER LITERARY FORMS

Eavan Boland collaborated with Micheál Mac Liammóir on the critical study *W. B. Yeats and His World* (1971). Boland has contributed essays in journals such as the *American Poetry Review*; she also reviews regularly for the *Irish Times* and has published a volume of prose called *Object Lessons: The Life of the Woman and the Poet in Our Time* (1995). With Mark Strand, she prepared the anthology *The Making of a Poem* (2000).

ACHIEVEMENTS

Ireland has produced a generation of distinguished poets since 1960, and the most celebrated of them have been men. Seamus Heaney is the best known of this group of poets to American audiences, but the reputations of Thomas Kinsella, Derek Mahon, Michael Longley, Paul Muldoon, and Tom Paulin continue to grow. Poetry by contemporary Irishwomen is also a significant part of the Irish literary scene. Eavan Boland is one of a group of notable women poets including Medbh McGuckian, Eithne Strong, and Eilean Ni Chuilleanain. In an essay published in 1987, "The Woman Poet: Her Dilemma," Boland indicates her particular concern with the special problems of being a woman and a poet. Male stereotypes about the role of women in society continue to be very strong in Ireland and make Irishwomen less confident about their creative abilities. Women must contend as well with another potentially depersonalizing pressure, that of feminist ideology, which urges women toward another sort of conformity. Boland and the other poets mentioned above have managed to overcome both obstacles and develop personal voices. Boland is on the board of the Irish Arts Council and a member of the Irish Academy of Letters. She is a winner of the Lannan Award for Poetry (1994).

BIOGRAPHY

Eavan Boland was born on September 24, 1944, in Dublin, Ireland. Her parents were Frederick Boland and Frances Kelly Boland. Her father was a distinguished Irish diplomat who served as Irish ambassador to Great Britain (1950-1956) and to the United States (1956-1964). Her mother was a painter who had studied in Paris in the 1930's. Boland's interest in painting as a subject for poetry can be traced to her mother's encouragement. Because of her father's diplomatic career, Boland was educated in Dublin, London, and New York. From 1962 to 1966, she attended Trinity College, Dublin; beginning in 1967, she taught at Trinity College for a year. In 1968, she received the Macauley Fellowship for poetry.

In the 1980's, Boland reviewed regularly for the arts section of the *Irish Times*. In 1987, she held a visiting fellowship at Bowdoin College. She married Kevin Casey, a novelist, with whom she had two children: Sarah, born in 1975, and Eavan, born in 1978.

Boland began writing poetry in Dublin in the early 1960's. She recalls this early period: ". . . scribbling po-

Eavan Boland (Allison Otto, courtesy of *Stanford Daily*)

ems in boarding school, reading Yeats after lights out, revelling in the poetry on the course. . . . Dublin was a coherent space then, a small circumference in which to . . . become a poet. . . . The last European city. The last literary smallholding." After her marriage, Boland left academe and moved out of Dublin and into the suburbs to become "wife, mother, and housewife." *In Her Own Image* and *Night Feed* focus on Boland's domestic life in the suburbs and especially on her sense of womanhood. In the 1990's, Boland taught at several universities in the United States. She became a professor at Stanford University in 1995, chairing the Creative Writing Program from 1995 to 2000.

ANALYSIS

Hearth and history provide a context for the poetry of Eavan Boland. She is inspired by both the domestic and the cultural. Her subjects are the alienating suburban places which encourage one to forget one's cultural roots, her children with their typically Irish names, demystified horses in Dublin streets that can still evoke the old glories from time to time, and the old Irish stories themselves, which at times may be vivid and evocative and at others may be mere nostalgia. Boland's distinctly female perspective is achieved in several poems about painting which note the dominance of male painters in the history of art from the Renaissance to the Impressionists, painters such as Jan van Eyck, Edgar Degas, Jean Auguste Dominique Ingres, and Auguste Renoir. Women were painted by these artists in traditional domestic or agrarian postures. Boland perceives woman as far less sanitized and submissive. Her collection *In Her Own Image* introduces such taboo subjects as anorexia, mastectomy, masturbation, and menstruation.

IN HER OWN IMAGE AND NIGHT FEED

Two of Boland's works, *In Her Own Image* and *Night Feed*, deal exclusively with the subject of woman. *Night Feed* for the most part examines suburban woman and chronicles the daily routine of a Dublin housewife in a positive way. The book has poems about babies' diapers, about washing machines, about feeding babies. The cover has an idyllic drawing of a mother feeding a child. The other volume, however, *In Her Own Image*, published two years before *Night Feed*, seems written

by a different person. Its candid and detailed treatment of taboo subjects contrasts sharply with the idyllic world of *Night Feed*. Boland's ability to present both worlds testifies to her poetic maturity.

The need for connection is a major theme in Boland's poetry. Aware of traditional connections in Irish and classical myths, she longs for an earlier period when such ties came instinctively. Her sense of loss with respect to these traditional connections extends beyond mythology to Irish history as well, even to Irish history in the twentieth century. Modern-day Dubliners have been cut off from the sustaining power of myth and history. Their lives, therefore, seem empty and superficial. Surrounded with the shards of a lost culture they cannot piece together these shards into a coherent system.

The alienation of the modern urban Irish from their cultural roots is the subject of Boland's poem "The New Pastoral." She considers alienation from a woman's perspective. Aware of the myths that have traditionally sustained males, Boland desires equivalent myths for females. She longs for a "new pastoral" which will celebrate women's ideals, but she finds none. She encounters many domestic "signs," but they do not "signify" for her. She has a vague sense of once having participated in a coherent ritual, of having "danced once/ on a frieze." Now, however, she has no access to the myth. Men seem to have easier access to their cultural roots than women do. The legends of the cavemen contain flint, fire, and wheel, which allowed man "to read his world." Later in history, men had pastoral poems to define and celebrate their place in the world. A woman has no similar defining and consoling rituals and possesses no equivalent cultural signs. She seems a "displaced person/ in a pastoral chaos," unable to create a "new pastoral." Surrounded by domestic signs, "lamb's knuckle," "the washer," "a stink/ of nappies," "the greasy/ bacon flitch," she still has no access to myth. Hints of connection do not provide a unified myth:

> I feel
> there was a past,
> there was a pastoral
> and these
> chance sights—
> what are they all
> but late amnesias

of a rite
I danced once
on a frieze?

The final image of the dancer on the frieze echoes both John Keats's Grecian urn and William Butler Yeats's dancers and golden bird. The contemporary poet, however, has lost contact. Paradoxically, the poem constitutes the "new pastoral" which it claims is beyond its reach. The final allusion to the dancer on the frieze transforms the mundane objects of domestic life into something more significant, something sacred.

Boland seems in conflict over whether women should simply conform to male stereotypes for women or should resist these pressures to lead "lesser lives," to attend to "hearth not history." Many poems in *Night Feed* accept this "lesser" destiny, poems such as "Night Feed," "Hymn," and "In the Garden." The several poems in this volume which deal with paintings, "Domestic Interior," "Fruit on a Straight-Sided Tray," "Degas's Laundresses," "Woman Posing (After Ingres)," "On Renoir's 'The Grape-Pickers,'" all deal with paintings by male painters which portray women in traditional domestic or rural roles. The women in these paintings appear content with their "lesser lives." Poems such as "It's a Woman's World" seem less accepting, however, more in the spirit of *In Her Own Image*, which vigorously rejects basing one's identity on male stereotypes. "It's a Woman's World" complements "The New Pastoral" in its desire for a balance between hearth and history.

as far as history goes
we were never
on the scene of the crime. . . .
And still no page
scores the low music
of our outrage.

Women have had no important roles in history, Boland asserts. They produce "low music," rather than heroic music. Nevertheless, women can have an intuitive connection with their own "starry mystery," their own cosmic identity. The women in those paintings apparently pursuing their "lesser lives," may have a sense of "greater lives." The male world (including male artists) must be kept in the dark about this, must keep believing that nothing mythic is being experienced.

That woman there,
craned to the starry mystery
is merely getting a breath
of evening air,
while this one here—
her mouth
a burning plume—
she's no fire-eater,
just my frosty neighbour
coming home.

The "woman's world" and the "starry mysteries" are presented far less romantically in Boland's volume *In Her Own Image*. The poems in this volume refuse to conform to male stereotypes of woman as happy domestic partner. They explore male-female conflicts in the deepest and most intimate psychic places. The title *In Her Own Image* indicates the volume's concern with the problem of "identity." Boland wishes to be an individual, free to determine her own life, but other forces seek to control her, to make her conform to female stereotypes. A woman should be perfect, unchanging, youthful, pure, in short, should be ideal. Male-dominated society does not wish women to explore their own deepest desires. Women transform these social messages into the voice of their own consciences, or, in Sigmund Freud's terms, their own superegos: "Thou shalt not get fat!" "Thou shalt not get old!" "Thou shalt not get curious."

These naysaying inner voices dominate the first three poems of *In Her Own Image:* "Tirade for the Mimic Muse," "In Her Own Image," and "In His Own Image." The "mimic muse" in the first poem urges the speaker to "make up," to conceal aging with cosmetics. The illustration for this poem shows a chunky and unkempt woman gazing into a mirror and seeing a perfect version of herself, thin, unwrinkled, physically fit. The phrase "her own image" in the second poem refers to another idealization, the "image" of perfection which the speaker carries around inside herself. She finally frees herself from this psychic burden by planting it outside in the garden. The illustration shows a naked woman bending over a small coffin. The third poem, "In His Own Image," considers the pressures of a husband's expectations on a wife's sense of self. The speaker in this third poem does not try to reshape her features with makeup.

She is battered into a new shape by a drunken husband. No illustration appears with this poem.

The speaker's "tirade" in "Tirade for the Mimic Muse" begins at once and establishes the intensely hostile tone of much of *In Her Own Image:* "I've caught you out. You slut. You fat trout." She despises the impulse in herself to conform to a stereotype, to disguise the physical signs of time passing: "the lizarding of eyelids," "the whiskering of nipples," "the slow betrayals of our bedroom mirrors." In the final section of the poem, the authentic self has suppressed those conforming impulses: "I, who mazed my way to womanhood/ Through all your halls of mirrors, making faces." Now the mirror's glass is cracked. The speaker promises a true vision of the world, but the vision will not be idyllic: "I will show you true reflections, terrors." Terrors preoccupy Boland for much of this book.

"In Her Own Image" and "In His Own Image" deal with different aspects of the "perfect woman." The first poem has a much less hostile tone than does "Tirade for the Mimic Muse." The speaker seems less threatened by the self-image from which she wishes to distance herself. Images of gold and amethyst and jasmine run through the poem. Despite the less hostile tone, Boland regards this "image" as a burdensome idealization which must be purged for psychic health: "She is not myself/ anymore." The speaker plants this "image" in the garden outside: "I will bed her,/ She will bloom there," safely removed from consciousness. The poem "In His Own Image" is full of anxiety. The speaker cannot find her center, her identity. Potential signs of identity lie all around her, but she cannot interpret them:

> Celery feathers, . . .
> bacon flitch, . . .
> kettle's paunch, . . .
> these were all I had to go on, . . .
> meagre proofs of myself.

A drunken husband responds to his wife's identity crisis by pounding her into his own desired "shape."

> He splits my lip with his fist,
> shadows my eye with a blow,
> knuckles my neck to its proper angle.
> What a perfectionist!
> His are a sculptor's hands:

> they summon
> form from the void,
> they bring
> me to myself again.
> I am a new woman.

How different are these two methods of coping with psychic conflict. In "In Her Own Image," the speaker plants her old self lovingly in the garden. In "In His Own Image," the drunken husband reshapes his wife's features with violent hands. The wife in the second poem says that she is now a "new woman." If one reads this volume as a single poem, as Boland evidently intends that one should (all the illustrations have the same person as their subject), one understands that the desperate tone of other poems in the book derives from the suffering of this reshaped "new woman," victim of male exploitation.

The next four poems of *In Her Own Image* deal with very private subjects familiar to women but not often treated in published poems: anorexia, mastectomy, masturbation, and menstruation. Both the poems and Constance Hart's drawings are startlingly frank. The poet wants readers to experience "woman" in a more complete way, to realize the dark side of being female. The poems further illustrate Boland's sense of alienation from cultural myths or myths of identity. She desires connections, but she knows that she is unlikely to have them. She is therefore left with images which signify chaos rather than coherence, absence rather than presence, emptiness rather than fullness.

Two of the four poems, "Anorexia" and "Mastectomy," read like field reports from the battle of the sexes. The other two poems, "Solitary" and "Menses," have a female perspective but are also full of conflict. In the illustrations for "Anorexia," a very determined, extremely thin, naked woman, arms folded, looks disapprovingly at a fat woman lolling on a couch. An anorectic woman continues to believe that she is fat, despite the fact that she is a virtual skeleton. Boland introduces a religious level in the first three lines: "Flesh is heretic./ My body is a witch./ I am burning it." The conviction that her body is a witch runs through the whole poem. Here, in an extreme form, is the traditional Roman Catholic view that soul and body are separate. The body must be punished because, since the Fall, it has been the dwelling place of the devil. The soul must suppress the body in order for the soul to be saved. This tradition provides the anorectic with a religious reason for starving herself. In this poem, she revels in the opportunity to "torch" her body: "Now the bitch is burning." A presence even more disturbing than the witch is introduced in the second half of the poem, a ghostly male presence whom the anorectic speaker desires to please. To please this unnamed male presence, the speaker must become thin, so thin that she can somehow return to the womb imagined here paradoxically as male: "I will slip/ back into him again/ as if I had never been away." This return to the male womb will atone for the sin of being born a woman, with "hips and breasts/ and lips and heat/ and sweat and fat and greed."

In "Mastectomy," male-female conflict predominates. Male surgeons, envious of a woman's breasts (an effective transformation of the male-centered Freudian paradigm), cut off a breast and carry it away with them. The shocking drawing shows one gowned male surgeon passing the breast on a serving dish to another gowned male surgeon. The woman who has experienced this physical and psychological violation cries despairingly "I flatten to their looting." The sympathetic words of the surgeon before the operation belie the sinister act of removing the breast. It can now become part of male fantasy, as a symbol of primal nourishment and primal home:

> So they have taken off
> what slaked them first,
> what they have hated since:
> blue-veined
> white-domed
> home
> of wonder
> and the wetness
> of their dreams.

The next two poems, "Solitary" and "Menses," deal with equally private aspects of a woman's life, autoeroticism and menstruation. "Solitary" has a celebratory attitude toward self-arousal. The drawing shows a relaxed naked female figure lying on her stomach. Religious imagery is used in this poem as it is in "Anorexia," but here the body is worshiped rather than feared. The only negative aspect of "Solitary" is its solitude. The female

speaker is unconnected with another person. Solitary pleasures are intense but less so than the pleasures of intercourse. The reader is taken on a journey from arousal to orgasm to postorgasmic tranquillity. The religious language at first seems gratuitous but then perfectly appropriate. The speaker affirms the holiness of her body: "An oratory of dark,/ a chapel of unreason." She has a few moments of panic as the old words of warning flash into her mind: "You could die for this./ The gods could make you blind." These warnings do not deter her, however, from this sacred rite:

> how my cry
> blasphemes
> light and dark,
> screams
> land from sea,
> makes word flesh
> that now makes me
> animal.

During this period of arousal and climax, her "flesh summers," but then it returns again to winter: "I winter/ into sleep." "Menses" deals with the private act of menstruation. A cosmic female voice addresses the speaker as menstruation begins, attempting to focus her attention solely on the natural powers working in her body. The speaker resists this effort. She feels simultaneously "sick of it" and drawn to this process. She struggles to retain her freedom. "Only my mind is free," she says. Her body is taken over by tidal forces. "I am bloated with her waters./ I am barren with her blood." At the end of the poem, the speaker seems more accepting of this natural cycle. She reflects on two other cycles which she has experienced, childbirth and intercourse. All three cycles, she begins to see, make her a new person: "I am bright and original."

The final three poems of *In Her Own Image*, "Witching," "Exhibitionist," and "Making-up," return to the theme that "Myths/ are made by men" (from "Making-up"). Much of a woman's life is spent reacting to male stereotypes. In "Witching," Boland further explores the idea of woman-as-witch, which was introduced in "Anorexia." Historically, women accused by men of being witches were doomed. The charges were usually either trumped-up or trivial. Boland's witch fantasizes about turning the table on her male persecutors and burning them first:

> I will
> reserve
> their arson,
> make
> a pyre
> of my haunch . . .
> the stench
> of my crotch

It is a grim but fitting fate for these male witch-burners. Another male stereotype, woman-as-stripper, is treated in the poem "Exhibitionist." This poem has the last accompanying drawing, a vulnerable young woman pulling her dress up over her head and naked to those watching her, perhaps as Boland feels naked toward those who have read through this volume. The male observers in "Exhibitionist" have in mind only gratifying their lusts. The speaker detests this exploitation and hopes to have a deeper impact on these leering males, hopes to touch them spiritually with her shining flesh:

> my dark plan:
> Into the gutter
> of their lusts
> I burn
> the shine
> of my flesh.

The final poem, "Making-up," returns to the theme of "Tirade for the Mimic Muse," that women must alter their appearances to please men, but that men have no such demands placed upon them. The poem rehearses a litany of transformations of the speaker's "naked face." "Myths/ are made by men," this poem asserts. The goddesses men imagine can never be completely captured by that "naked face." A woman's natural appearance inevitably has flaws. Women are encouraged by men to disguise these flaws to make themselves look perfect. From these "rouge pots," a goddess comes forth, at least in men's eyes. Women should really know better.

> Mine are the rouge pots,
> the hot pinks, . . .
> out of which
> I dawn.

Eavan Boland is determined to make poetry out of her domestic life. *In Her Own Image* and *Night Feed* indicate that she has turned to the very ordinary subjects of hearth, rather than to the larger subjects of history, which she explored in her earlier volumes *New Territory* and *The War Horse*. In "The Woman Poet: Her Dilemma," Boland admits to uncertainty about this new orientation. She is encouraged especially, however, by the example of French and Dutch genre painters, whose work she calls "unglamorous, workaday, authentic," possessing both ordinariness and vision: "The hare in its muslin bag, the crusty loaf, the women fixed between menial tasks and human dreams." In her own equally ordinary domestic life, she believes that she has found a personal voice.

THE JOURNEY AND OTHER POEMS

Boland's next major collection, *The Journey and Other Poems*, explores more fully the poetic implications of this uncertainty. *In Her Own Image* and *Night Feed* offer opposed accounts of Boland's concerns as a woman and a writer, the former vehemently critical and openly outraged at sexual injustices, the latter more generously idyllic and positive about the domestic side of her femininity. In *The Journey and Other Poems*, Boland incorporates this ambivalence into the fabric of her poems, channeling the tension between her contrary aspects into an antithetical lyric energy; each piece, that is, derives its form and force from a doubleness in the poet's mind, an impulse to be at once critical and affirmative. Instead of lamenting her inner confusions and contradictions, however, Boland builds a new sense of the lyric poem and engages with renewed vigor the vexed questions of gender, tradition, and myth that characterize her work.

The collection is divided into three sections, forming a triptych. In traditional religious painting, a triptych is composed of three canvases, side by side, the outer two either elaborating upon or supporting visually the central portion, which usually contains the main subject of the work. In *The Journey and Other Poems*, the first and third sections comment upon, refocus, and expand the thematically dense matter of the central section, which contains "The Journey"—one of Boland's finest lyric achievements—and its "Envoi." Furthermore, Boland uses the structure of the triptych to underscore the ambivalence she feels. In the first section, the reader encounters memorial and idyll; in the third section, one finds the opposite, a vehement critique of inherited sexual mores and the patriarchal "tradition." Only in the central portion of the volume, "The Journey," does Boland take on both aspects at once and attempt, not to reconcile one to the other, but to reanimate and reenergize what she calls a dying, diminished poetic language.

The volume opens with a nostalgic tribute to the poet's mother, "I Remember." Boland recalls her mother's studio, and her almost irrepressible need, as a child exploring that room, "to touch, to handle, to dismantle it,/ the mystery." Boland longs for the mystery of innocence and the childlike wonder of a lost time— before the harsh realities of Irish economics and suburban alienation had taken root—when the world seemed balanced, "composed" and beautiful; but in the poem that world is veiled and hidden from her, like the otherworldly elegance of her mother's "French Empire chairs" over which opaque cotton sheets have been draped. Similarly, in "The Oral Tradition," when Boland overhears two women exchanging gossip—figures who, emblematically, "were standing in shadow"—she longs for "a musical sub-text," an "oral song" which seems only to express itself in "fragments and innuendoes," which nevertheless resonate with "a sense/ suddenly of truth." Boland wants to discover the archetypal "truth" buried under opaque surfaces, and, as she says in "Suburban Woman: A Detail," to find traces of the lost "goddess" within her instinctive, feminine memory. She expresses her need to be "healed into myth" through poetry and to recover the deeply ingrained, basic "patterns" of her womanhood.

The third section, on the other hand, works negatively, upsetting traditional myths of the archetypal feminine. In "Listen. This Is the Noise of Myth," Boland starts to recount a "story" of "a man and woman," setting the stage for a traditional version of domestic order, but she becomes self-conscious and critical, calling her own methods into question, making her characters— especially the woman—into "fugitives" from their traditional roles. Boland proposes to "set truth to rights," defiantly dismantling the old stories. She laments that even she must put "the same mirrors on the old magic" and return to the "old romances." Despite the sweet lure of

storytelling, Boland wants to remake her own role as an author, and though she finds herself repeatedly thwarted by the "consolations of the craft," she struggles on.

Several poems in the third section echo Boland's other work. "Tirade for the Lyric Muse" recalls her "Tirade for the Mimic Muse," but here the subject is plastic surgery. The speaker addresses a sister "in the crime," an epithet which suggests a fellow poet, but one who, for Boland, has betrayed herself and her implicit commitment to "truth" by having the ordinary "surface" of her face altered to conform to a false notion of "skin deep" beauty. The true "music" of poetry, for Boland, cannot be captured by outward conformity to the "cruel" standards of a male world. Poems such as "Fond Memory" and "An Irish Childhood in England: 1951" respond to lyrics such as "I Remember" in the first section, rejecting nostalgia and finding in Boland's own indelible Irishness a sense of exile and insecurity. To be an English-speaking Irish native is to be a perpetual outcast. Irishness, for Boland, represents her own inability to settle upon a given set of values or a certain appearance of "truth"; her nationality, paradoxically, undermines easy acceptance of the safe "myths" she craves.

If the first section works to rediscover the force of myth, and the last section to dismantle the false safety net of traditional roles, the central portion—"The Journey"—springs directly from a double impulse. "The Journey" is a dream-vision, a description of a mental journey to the underworld undertaken in the poet's dreams. Many medieval poets, including Geoffrey Chaucer, wrote dream-visions. Like these poets, Boland depicts herself falling asleep over an open book of classical poetry. This connection to tradition, both medieval and ancient, is important to the poem, which describes a poetics, an account of how poems are or ought to be written. Boland searches for a new, vital form of writing. She begins by stating angrily that "there has never . . . been a poem to an antibiotic. . . ." She questions what is the proper subject for poetry, introducing antibiotics as something about which no one would bother to write. She espouses the ordinary and the domestic rather than the ethereal of the "unblemished" as a basis for poetry. In order to heal us, and to repair our diminished relationship to "the language," poetry must look with renewed energy to the particulars of everyday life.

In her dream, Boland descends with Sappho—the greatest ancient female poet, whom she has been reading—to the land of the dead, where she meets the ghosts of mothers and housewives, women in whose experiences Boland has been trying to discover her mythical roots. Boland pleads with her mentor to let her "be their witnesses," but she is told that what she has seen is "beyond speech." She awakens, only to find "nothing was changed," despite her vision of "truth," and she weeps. This poetic "misery," taken up in the poem's "Envoi," comes from disappointment at being incapable of resuscitating the lost myths of womanhood, the anxiety of trying to bless "the ordinary" or to sanctify "the common" without the comfort of a traditionally sanctioned muse. Boland's work, to revive the feminine in poetry, results in a difficult mixture of discovery, desire, dissatisfaction, and rage. "The Journey" is a complex poem, and one of Boland's best works. It expresses both a naïve, dreamy faith in the power of myth and "truth" and a severe self-consciousness that calls the elements of her feminine identity into question. The ability to dwell poetically upon such a problematic duplicity in a single poem truly indicates Boland's literary accomplishment.

IN A TIME OF VIOLENCE AND THE LOST LAND

Similar concerns, sometimes more deeply and darkly wrought, sometimes inscribed with a tonic humor, permeate Boland's poems of the 1990's. *In a Time of Violence* uses unusual and risky strategies to clarify the personal/political weave in Boland's vision. All those who lack autonomy are ultimately susceptible to victimhood and violence. This equation pertains to gender, nationhood, and any other form of identification. In *The Lost Land*, she continues to explore the issues and emotions both of exile and colonial victimhood. These are especially the burdens of "Colony," a major poem that makes up the first half of the book. Colonization, we learn, is not just an act of governments, but an act of individuals—any exercise of power and dominance at the expense of the independence of others. It even applies to the relationships of parents and children, husbands and wives. However, these echoes weave their way more noticeably through the shorter poems in the collection. Along with the losses of place that Boland records, "place" having political, cultural, and psychic significance, she expresses here the loss of motherhood—another "place" of position that vanishes with time. Boland's constantly growing artistry, her ability to fasten upon the telling concrete detail, and her hard-won personal and public authority make this collection a pinnacle in a career that yet has far to go.

OTHER MAJOR WORKS

NONFICTION: *W. B. Yeats and His World*, 1971 (with Micheál Mac Liammóir); *Object Lessons: The Life of the Woman and the Poet in Our Time*, 1995.

EDITED TEXT: *The Making of a Poem*, 2000 (with Mark Strand).

BIBLIOGRAPHY

Boland, Eavan. "The Serinette Principle: The Lyric in Contemporary Poetry." *Parnassus* 15, no. 2 (1989): 7-25. Boland writes obliquely about her own poetic practice in relation to her American contemporaries. The lyric poem, she argues, should achieve the "serinette" principle, a complex idea which is emblematized by the eighteenth century hand-organs used to teach caged birds to sing; that is, the lyric must, however tenuously, liberate the reader's limited perception from the narrow confines of time. The new lyric, epitomized for Boland by the work of Jorie Graham and Robert Hass, recognizes the time-honored impulse of song but has "reshaped [its] contents." Boland looks to such work for plasticity, experiment, and expansiveness.

Gonzalez, Alexander G., ed. *Contemporary Irish Women Poets: Some Male Perspectives*. Westport, Conn.: Greenwood Press, 1999. Enthusiastic responses by male critics to a wide range of Irish women poets include two strong essays on Boland: Thomas C. Foster's "In from the Margin: Eavan Boland's 'Outside History' Sequence" and Peter Kupillas's "Bringing It All Back Home: Unity and Meaning in Eavan Boland's 'Domestic Interior' Sequence." Selected bibliography.

Keen, Paul. "The Doubled Edge: Identity and Alterity in the Poetry of Eavan Boland and Nuala Ni Dhomhnaill." *Mosaic* 33, no. 3 (2000): 14-34. Setting his investigation within the political and cultural upheavals in contemporary Ireland, Keen attends to

Boland's theoretical writings to approach her poems. He sees her as rewriting Irish myths about the country and women rather subverting them. Several key poems examined with clarity and compassionate care. The comparative approach is fruitful.

McElroy, James. "The Contemporary Fe/Male Poet: A Preliminary Reading." In *New Irish Writing*, edited by James Brophy and Eamon Grennan. Boston: Twayne, 1989. McElroy examines the same trio of writers as Johnston with considerably more depth. In particular, he defends Boland against critical charges of "stridency" and overstatement, arguing that her recurrent confrontations with the Irish domestic woman constitute a crucial part of her poetics of recovery and renewal, and that her willful reiterations of "female miseries" form a powerful catalog of matters that must be treated emphatically if Irish poetry is to recover its potency.

McGuinness, Arthur E. "Hearth and History: Poetry by Contemporary Irish Women." In *Cultural Contexts and Literary Idioms in Contemporary Irish Literature*, edited by Michael Kenneally. Totowa, N.J.: Barnes & Noble Books, 1988. McGuinness redresses an imbalance in the critical treatment of Irish women poets, contrasting McGuckian, Boland, and Eithne Strong. He examines the theme of "hearth and history," troublesome issues of domesticity and culture. He finds in Boland's work a "distinctively feminine perspective" on taboo subjects such as masturbation and anorexia. Boland dwells on present-day alienation from mythical connectedness and longs for the instinctive spiritual balance of an earlier period in Irish history.

Reizbaum, Marilyn. "An Interview with Eavan Boland." *Contemporary Literature* 30, no. 4 (1989): 470-479. Boland discusses women's poetry, feminism, Ireland, Yeats, tradition, and the muse. Her comments are accessible to all readers and useful for understanding her poetry.

Kevin McNeilly and Arthur E. McGuinness,
updated by Philip K. Jason

YVES BONNEFOY

Born: Tours, France; June 24, 1923

PRINCIPAL POETRY

Traité du pianiste, 1946

Anti-Platon, 1947

Du mouvement et de l'immobilité de Douve, 1953 (*On the Motion and Immobility of Douve*, 1968; Galway Kinnell, translator)

Hier régnant désert, 1958

Pierre écrite, 1965 (*Words in Stone*, 1976)

Selected Poems, 1968

L'Ordalie, 1975

Dans le leurre du seuil, 1975 (*The Lure of the Threshold*, 1985)

Rue traversière, 1977

Trois Remarques sur la couleur, 1977

Poèmes, 1978

Poems, 1959-1975, 1985

Things Dying, Things Newborn: Selected Poems, 1985

Ce qui fut sans lumière, 1987 (*In the Shadow's Light*, 1991)

Début et fin de la neige, 1991

Early Poems, 1947-1959, 1991

New and Selected Poems, 1995

Le Cœur-espace, 2001

Les Planches courbes, 2001

OTHER LITERARY FORMS

Yves Bonnefoy has distinguished in the fields of art criticism and literary criticism. He is also renowned as a translator of William Shakespeare's plays into French. His essays on art span the entire range from Byzantine to contemporary, from studies of the Renaissance and the Baroque to such works as Bonnefoy's *Alberto Giacometti: Biographie d'une œuvre* (1991; *Alberto Giacometti: A Biography of His Work*, 1991), on the twentieth century Italian sculptor. Bonnefoy is not simply an academic critic; some of his most moving prose writing is that which ties the experience of the artist to the interior experience of the imaginative writer. In *L'Arrière-pays* (1972; the hinterland), for example, he combines insightful discussions of classical Renaissance paintings with meditations on the sources of inspiration he draws from his own childhood. The title's *arrière-pays* (which brings to mind *arrière-plan*, the background in a painting, and which means, roughly, "back country") allows for an extended meditation on the figures in the backgrounds of classic paintings and the feeling of well-being which Bonnefoy has experienced in his childhood and in his many travels.

This interior experience is Bonnefoy's major focus in his literary criticism as well, from the essays in *L'Improbable et autres essais* (1959, 1980; "The Improbable" and other essays) to the monograph *Rimbaud par lui-même* (1961; *Rimbaud*, 1973) to the collections *Le Nuage rouge* (1977; the red cloud) and *La Présence et l'image* (1983; the presence of the image). Bonnefoy returns again and again to the idea that the images a poet uses, while in some sense unreal, are able to lead the reader to what he calls the "true place" of poetry. Thus the line "Ô Saisons, ô châteaux" (Oh Seasons, oh castles), which begins the famous poem by Rimbaud, becomes for Bonnefoy both a utopian dream and a reality which can be reached through language.

The philosophical issues that the poet locates in his artistic and literary researches are, in turn, fed back into his poetry, with the result that the poetry and the critical works come to mirror each other's concerns. His collection of lectures, *Lieux et destins de l'image: Un Cours de poétique au Collège de France, 1981-1993* (1999) is perhaps the most comprehensive compilation of his poetics to date.

ACHIEVEMENTS

Yves Bonnefoy is one of the most highly admired poets to reach maturity in France in the post-World War II period, and many would identify him as the most important French poet-intellectual at the turn of the twenty-first century. His early work had the character of being challenging and even hermetic, but it struck a chord with a whole generation of readers and poets. His poetry has always maintained the quality of being highly meditated and serious to its purpose. While his preoccupations are philosophical—death, the existence of the loved one, the place of truth—his poetic language is highly imaged and moves equally in the realms of beauty and truth.

The close association Bonnefoy has always maintained with visual artists who are his contemporaries has given him a high prominence in the art world as well. Though he maintains a teaching position in literature, he has tended more and more in his later career to pursue his interests in art and the theory of culture. His writings on art are prized both for what they say about individual artists and for the high level of reflection they bring to the subject of creativity.

Bonnefoy's nomination to the Chair of Comparative Studies of the Poetic Function at the Collège de France in 1981 confirmed his position as one of France's leading poets and intellectual figures. A regular affiliation with Yale University and visiting professorships at other American universities ensured Bonnefoy's prominence among American academic circles as well; he was awarded an honorary doctorate by the University of Chicago in 1988. He was also honored, in 1992, with an exhibition of his manuscripts and other documents at the Bibliothèque Nationale, Paris. His many other awards include the Grand Prix de Poésie from the French Academy (1981), the Grand Prix Société des Gens de Lettres (1987), the Bennett Award from *The Hudson Review*, in which may of his poems and essays have appeared (1988), the Bourse Goncourt (1991), the Prix Balzac (1995), the Prix Del Duca (1995), the Prix National de Poésie (1996), and the Mutsuoko Shiki Prize (2000).

BIOGRAPHY

Yves Bonnefoy was born on June 24, 1923, in Tours, France. His mother was a nurse and later a schoolteacher; his father died when Bonnefoy was thirteen. His early life was divided between the working-class surroundings of Tours and the rural home of his maternal grandfather, a schoolteacher and natural intellectual who had a great influence on the boy, and in many ways Bonnefoy considered his grandparents' home his own true home. He studied in Tours and at the University of Poitiers, primarily chemistry and mathematics.

Bonnefoy moved to Paris in 1943 to continue his scientific studies, but once there he found that his interests moved more toward poetry and philosophy. He sought out what remained of the Surrealist group—André

Breton in particular—and, though his formal association with it was brief, he formed many important friendships with young artists and poets, including Egyptian francophone Surrealist Georges Henin. Bonnefoy married, edited a review, and studied widely different subjects, eventually taking a degree by writing a thesis on Charles Baudelaire and Søren Kierkegaard. This combined interest in poetry and philosophy has remained with him during his entire career.

Bonnefoy accepted jobs in Paris as a mathematics and science teacher, escaping the draft for "compulsory labor" during World War II because the war ended before he was called. During this time he was reading the poetry of Paul Éluard, whose influence, according to Bonnefoy, "tempered the influences of Baudelaire and Valéry." In politics, he was a Trotskyite, and having broken away from Breton's influence he and friends edited a journal, *La Revolution, La Nuit*. He was poor during these years and benefitted from his sister's influence as a secretary at the Sorbonne in that she found him a job there, which allowed him to attend lectures and apply for research grants. These, in turn, allowed him to travel. He began to publish his poems and art criticism as well. Subsequently he earned a living teaching at universities, both in France and in the United States, becoming a professor of comparative poetics and department chair at the Collège de France in 1981.

In 1981, at the inauguration ceremony of his being named a department chair at the Collège de France, his highly publicized lecture "La Présence et l'image" (presence and the image) became a major statement for his particular style of intermixing philosophy and literature. Throughout his working career, Bonnefoy has traveled widely, especially in pursuing his growing interest in art, art history, and the theory of culture. He is recognized as one of the most important poets of his generation. In 2001, he was working on a forthcoming collection of poems tentatively titled "La Pluie d'été" (summer rain).

ANALYSIS

From the beginning of his poetic career, Yves Bonnefoy's work has sounded the note of a serious pursuit of the truths which language reveals. His early divergence from the later figures of the Surrealist movement in France seems to have been provoked by what he perceived as a lack of purpose in their pursuits. For Bonnefoy, poetic language, above all, is a place or a function which grants access to the truths of existence. The path to those truths may of necessity be a difficult one, but once one is on that path, there can be no turning back. Bonnefoy is a highly original and engaging writer of criticism in which he explores these issues, but it has always been in his poetry that he has sought to discover their ground.

ANTI-PLATON

The early works *Anti-Platon* and *On the Motion and Immobility of Douve* introduce his poetry of high seriousness and announce a break from Surrealist practice. If Bonnefoy declares early his stance "against Plato," as the title of the first collection states, it is to restore the real dimension of experience, this object here and now, over against any sort of Platonic ideal. By extension, the importance of this real object leads Bonnefoy to examine the importance of this real life, here and now, in its affective dimension. Perhaps paradoxically, the importance of life emerges fully only when one confronts the actual death of someone. The poems in the second collection take up this theme; they are also the poems which established Bonnefoy as one of the most important poets of his generation.

ON THE MOTION AND IMMOBILITY OF DOUVE

The figure of Douve in Bonnefoy's second collection is based on a young girl of his acquaintance who died a sudden and tragic death. (He gives her name only in a later collection; see below.) As the form in the poems alternates between highly organized quatrains and looser prose-poem utterances, so the investigation in the poems moves between the image of the dead young woman and death in general. As the sequence progresses, the speaker seeks to discover his own destiny based on an identification with the words of the young woman. In this work, death is present in the form of a person who is no longer there. She is troubling, however, because she poses the question of existence, of essence, of being. It is by means of this questioning that the poet discovers his own means of expression. More even than the torment of mourning, there seems to emerge the injunction to silence as the most accurate means of representing death.

There is a progression, then, in the poems of this collection as far as the identification of the poet with the figure of the dead woman by means of her speech. When she speaks in the first part of the collection, it is in the past tense, and she speaks of natural forces, wind and cold. The poet-speaker sees her, however, and as a result there is a separation, the separation of death. The only way to overcome this separation is by the identification involved in speaking. Changing to the present tense, the speaker says, "Douve je parle en toi" (Douve, I speak in you):

> Et si grand soit le froid qui monte de ton être,
> Si brûlant soit le gel de notre intimité,
> Douve, je parle en toi; et je t'enserre
> Dans l'acte de connaître et de nommer.

> (And though great cold rises in your being,
> However burning the frost of our intimacy
> Douve, I speak in you; and I enshroud you
> In the act of knowing and of naming.)

This is one of the strong moments of identification and the beginning of poetic creation, as Bonnefoy describes it in his essay "The Act and the Place of Poetry": "So Dante who has lost her, will *name* Beatrice." Over against the natural forces that are imaged here as present because of her death, the act of naming and of knowing restores a certain presence to the lost loved one. Even so, this is a first stage: Far from being consoling, it leads the poet to the point of anguish.

The central part of the collection, "Douve parle" (Douve speaks), begins with this identification in speaking, "ce cri sur moi vient de moi" (this cry above me comes from me). Paradoxically, in the series of poems bearing the title "Douve speaks," she finishes by saying: "Que le verbe s'éteigne" (Let the verb be extinguished). That which one must recognize in oneself as death surpasses the function of speech. The poet enters this region of contradiction when he says: "Je parle dans ton sang" (I speak in your blood).

This progression reaches its completion in the injunction, which the figure of the woman makes to the speaker, to remain silent. The poem which begins "Mais que se taise" (But that one be silent) requires silence above all of the one "Qui parle pour moi" (Who speaks for me). In the following poems, she is even more direct, saying simply, "Tais-toi" (remain silent; shut up). The speaker finds himself in a place of radical transformations, during a time of anguish and of struggle: "Quand la lumière enfin s'est faite vent et nuit" (When the light at last has become wind and night). The figure of the dead woman has led the speaker to a privileged place of being, where the poet not only recognizes himself in his own expression but also is faced with his own anguish, his authentic attitude toward death.

HIER RÉGNANT DÉSERT

The collected edition of Bonnefoy's poetry *Poèmes* of 1978 added three important collections to the earlier work, *Hier régnant désert* (yesterday the desert reigning), *Words in Stone*, and *The Lure of the Threshold*. These collections continue to explore the areas mapped out by Bonnefoy's earlier work. The tone is serious and the subject matter highly philosophical. Death is a constant presence and is confronted continually for what it tells about existence. In the first of these later collections, *Hier régnant désert*, Bonnefoy returns again to the Douve figure, although here, at least in one poem, she is named—Kathleen Ferrier. The same contradictions between a conflicted natural universe and a tragic sense of human destiny are confronted again in the elemental terms: face, voice. Whereas to see an image of the dead young woman leads to separation, an identification with her voice allows for the poet to discover his own utterance. As he says in "À la voix de Kathleen Ferrier" (to the voice of Kathleen Ferrier):

> Je célèbre la voix mêlée de couleur grise
> Qui hésite aux lointains du chant qui s'est perdu
> Comme si au delà de toute forme pure
> Tremblât un autre chant et le seul absolu.

> (I celebrate the voice mixed with grey color
> Which hesitates in the sung distances of what is lost
> As if beyond every pure form
> Trembled another song and the only absolute.)

This poem is more insistently philosophical than any examined hereto. The voice that is celebrated seems to have lost all contact with the merely human as it moves toward the realms of pure being.

WORDS IN STONE

Even the poems ostensibly concerned with inanimate objects bear their burden of existence, as does this short poem from *Words in Stone*, "Une Pierre" (a stone):

Il désirait, sans connaître,
II a péri, sans avoir.
Arbres, fumées,
Toutes lignes de vent et de déception
Furent son gîte.
Infiniment
II n'a étreint que sa mort.

(It desired, without knowing
It perished, without having.
Trees, smoke,
All lines of wind and of deception
Were its shelter
Infinitely
It only grasped its death.)

This deceptively simple poem about a stone carries a weight of thought and image balanced off in a skillful suspension. It may or may not carry direct reference to Jean-Paul Sartre's existential philosophy, which affirmed the stone's interiority and self-identity over time while denying these same inherent qualities to the human subject. Bonnefoy's turn on the idea here is to introject the tragic sense into the simple being of the stone. Bereft of the human qualities of knowing or having, it was at one with nature and alone to face death.

POÈMES

Bonnefoy's later poems in the collected volume *Poèmes* trace a dialectic between the tragic sense of human destiny, as presented in Douve's words, and the introjected tragedy of nature just examined in the poem from *Words in Stone*. The difference in the later works is in their form. From the short, often highly formal, verse of his early career, Bonnefoy here moves to a more expanded utterance. Though the poems are longer, however, there is a greater degree of fragmentation. It is as though the silence which was so important thematically in the speech of Douve has been refigured in the form of the poem itself. From the highly wrought, lapidary form of the early work has emerged a laconic style, hinting at what the speaker cannot say.

Into the atmosphere of charged philosophical speculation—in effect, a dialogue between being and nonbeing—Bonnefoy brings a new element of disjunction and, ultimately, of mystery, as in these lines from "Deux Barques" (two boats): "Étoiles, répandues./ Le ciel, un lit défait, une naissance." (Stars, spread out./ The sky, an unmade bed, a birth.) The traditional analysis of metaphor in terms of "tenor" and "vehicle" becomes very difficult with lines such as these. How is one to decide what is the content of the statement and what is the rhetorical trapping? Here the stars could be the vehicle for an image having as its content the beginning of human life. In like manner, the heavens could be the content and the bed an image to describe the appearance of stars, with birth as an added metaphorical element. As this example makes clear, Bonnefoy's long meditations on the power of language to investigate the central issues of existence remain as intense in his later work as in his earlier poetry.

In all of Bonnefoy's work, an extremely restricted vocabulary is used to describe the conflicts between nature and human existence. Words such as "stone" and "fire," "wind" and "star," take on an elemental sense rather than being merely descriptive. These word elements are placed in the context of laconic statements, each statement offering but a hint of the overall movement in the poem. This overall movement in turn is established through the cumulative force of these elemental images placed into disjunctive and often contradictory sequences. Almost always, a mood of high seriousness is the result. The simplest language thus becomes a language of tragic dimensions. The elemental forces at work in the poem's image sequences reflect directly on the human dimension of existence. Bonnefoy places hard demands on the conceptual capabilities of his readers. He is clearly uninterested in easy sentiment or pleasing verses. His poetry presents a continual invitation to join in the struggle out of which the truths of existence emerge.

In the final poem of his collected edition, "L'Épars, l'indivisible" (the sparse, the indivisible), an anaphoric repetition is utilized, with the first word of most stanzas being "Oui" (yes). Under the general structuring principle of affirmation, the seemingly most opposite elements are joined. One section reads simply: "Oui, par la mort,/ Oui, par la vie sans fin" (Yes, through death,/ Yes, through life without end). Affirming opposites in this manner runs the risk of affirming nothing, but again the cumulative effect of the contradictions is to lead to a synthesis of values. Two sections later, the speaker states: "Oui, par même l'erreur,/ Qui va,// Oui, par le bonheur simple, la voix brisée." (Yes, even through error,/ Which passes,// Yes, through simple happiness, the broken voice.) Bonnefoy does not seek easy resolution or unexamined pleasures. When he speaks of happiness in the same breath with a broken voice, however, the force of the image goes beyond the conceptual setting up of paradoxes. Happiness which leads to a broken voice is happiness that carries with it a strong emotion and the force of personal history. These deceptively simple images are weighted with complex and achieved emotion.

The figure of Yves Bonnefoy the poet is closely allied to that of Bonnefoy the thinker. His researches into art, literature, and the sources of creativity in life history have always been motivated by a search for truth which can then find form and be expressed in his poetry. This is not to say that reading Bonnefoy's poetry is the equivalent of reading his essays and criticism or that the philosophical underpinnings of the works are presented in a predigested or easily digestible form. His highly imaged poems show a consistent concern for poetic image and emotion. As a result, the reality they possess is one which adds to experience. The highly wrought, imaginatively charged poems of Yves Bonnefoy reveal the common origins of thinking and of poetry. By posing the central questions of existence, they are timeless. They are also of a pressing timeliness in that they recall the reader to being in the present.

OTHER MAJOR WORKS

NONFICTION: *Peintures murales de la France gothique*, 1954; *L'Improbable et autres essais*, 1959, 1980; *La Seconde Simplicité*, 1961; *Rimbaud par lui-même*, 1961 (*Rimbaud*, 1973); *La Poésie française et le principe d'identité*, 1967; *Miró*, 1964 (English translation, 1967); *Un Rêve fait à Mantoue*, 1967; *Rome 1630: L'Horizon du premier baroque*, 1970; *L'Arrière-pays*, 1972; *Le Nuage rouge*, 1977; *Entretiens sur la poésie*, 1981; *La Présence et l'image*, 1983; *La Vérité de Parole*, 1988; *The Act and the Place of Poetry: Selected Essays*, 1989; *Alberto Giacometti: Biographie d'une œuvre*, 1991 (*Alberto Giacometti: A Biography of His Work*, 1991); *La Vie errante, suivi de Une autre Époque de*

l'écriture, 1993; *Dessin, couleur, et lumière*, 1995; *The Lure and the Truth of Painting: Selected Essays on Art*, 1995; *Théâtre et poésie: Shakespeare et Yeats*, 1998; *Lieux et destins de l'image: Un Cours de poétique au Collège de France, 1981-1993*, 1999; *La Communauté des traducteurs*, 2000.

TRANSLATIONS: *Une Chemise de nuit de flanelle*, 1951 (of Leonora Carrington); *1 Henri IV, Jules César, Hamlet, Le Conte d'hiver, Vénus et Adonis, Le Viol de Lucrèce*, 1957-1960 (6 volumes; of William Shakespeare); *Jules César, Hamlet, Le Roi Lear, Roméo et Juliette, Macbeth*, 1960-1983 (5 volumes; of Shakespeare); *La Tempête*, 1997 (of Shakespeare).

EDITED TEXTS: *Dictionnaire des mythologies et des religions des sociétés traditionnelles et du monde antique*, 1981 (*Mythologies*, 1991); *Roman and European Mythologies*, 1992; *Greek and Egyptian Mythologies*, 1992; *Asian Mythologies*, 1993; *American, African, and Old European Mythologies*, 1993.

BIBLIOGRAPHY

Caws, Mary Ann. *Yves Bonnefoy*. Boston: Twayne, 1984. A rare book-length work in English that introduces Bonnefoy's life and works to students. Bibliography.

Fink, Michèle. *Yves Bonnefoy: Le Simple et le sens*. Paris: Corti, 1989. In French.

Lawler, James. "'La Neige Piétinée est la seule rose': Poetry and Truth in Yves Bonnefoy." *L'Esprit Créateur* 32, no. 2 (Summer, 1992): 43-53. Analysis of Bonnefoy's work.

Naughton, John T. *The Poetics of Yves Bonnefoy*. Chicago: University of Chicago Press, 1984. Along with that of Caws, one of the few book-length studies in English devoted to Bonnefoy's poetics. The reviewer for *Choice*, J. Labat, noted that Naughton's "numerous notes contain a wealth of scholarly information. The broadly selected bibliography includes the latest publications by and about the poet. Index of names and titles. This study should be acquired by every academic library and teacher of Bonnefoy's work."

Petterson, James. *Postwar Figures of L'Ephemer: Yves Bonnefoy, Louis-Rene de Forets, Jacques Dupin, Andre Du Bouchet*. Bucknell University Press, 2000.

Pinet-Thélot, Livane. *Yves Bonnefoy: Ou, L'Expérience de L'Etranger.* The subtitle translates as "the experience of the foreigner." This brief (142-page) monograph focuses on certain aspects of Bonnefoy's poetics. In French.

Thélot, Jérôme. *La Poétique d'Yves Bonnefoy.* Geneva: Droz, 1983. Criticism and interpretation of Bonnefoy's works. In French.

Peter Baker,
updated by Gordon Walters
and Christina J. Moose

PHILIP BOOTH

Born: Hanover, New Hampshire; October 8, 1925

PRINCIPAL POETRY

Letter from a Distant Land, 1957
The Islanders, 1961
Weathers and Edges, 1966
Margins: A Sequence of New and Selected Poems, 1970
Available Light, 1976
Before Sleep, 1980
Relations: Selected Poems, 1950-1985, 1986
Selves: New Poems, 1990
Pairs: New Poems, 1994
Lifelines: Selected Poems, 1950-1999, 1999
Crossing, 2001 (juvenile)

OTHER LITERARY FORMS

Philip Booth's poetry forms the basis of his literary reputation. He has given readings of his works on both radio and television, and he has edited several volumes of poetry. His essay collection *Trying to Say It: Outlooks and Insights on How Poems Happen* appeared in 1996.

ACHIEVEMENTS

The finely crafted poetry of Philip Booth has a strong, clear connection with his ancestral home of Castine, Maine, a colonial coastal village of fewer than seven hundred year-round residents. Through his poetry, Booth has carefully captured this place; he is at home with its blustery winters, its tides and charts, its starkness, its dry humor, its sparse, homely conversation, and its flora, fauna, and animals. Yet, like Emily Dickinson, through an intimate closeness with one place, the poet speaks of a common humanity and universal themes.

Booth's poems move from engaging openings to clear, satisfying conclusions and are meticulously placed in each volume, moving toward a final resolution of their themes. Booth husbands his language, but his poems hold a richness of meaning and look with curiosity and wonder at the miracle of human life. The poet, whose works have been translated into French, Portuguese, Finnish, Dutch, and Italian, and have been lauded by fellow poet Maxine Kumin as having a "wonderfully consistent tone," is recognized as one of the best of late twentieth century writers.

His first collection of poems, *Letter from a Distant Land*, won the 1956 Lamont Prize of the Academy of American Poets. Additional honors include Guggenheim and Rockefeller fellowships, grants from the National Institute of Arts and Letters and from the National Endowment for the Arts, and awards from *Poetry, Saturday Review, The Virginia Quarterly Review*, and *Poetry Northwest*. In 1983, Booth was elected a fellow of the Academy of American Poets. His 1986 collection *Relations* earned for him the Maurice English Poetry Award. In 2001, Booth was awarded the Poets' Prize by the Academy of American Poets.

BIOGRAPHY

As his poetry suggests, Philip Booth is a New Englander, a man of Down East sensibilities and humor. Born in 1925 in Hanover, New Hampshire, to a Dartmouth English professor and his wife, and having grown up both in New Hampshire and in Maine, he settled in the white-clapboard, black-shuttered, 130-year-old house in Castine, Maine, which has belonged to his family for five generations. Thomas Jefferson appointed Booth's maternal great-great-grandfather to serve as customs collector in Castine two hundred years before, and the Greek revival house on Main Street where the poet would reside has belonged to his mother's family for nearly a century.

Booth received his undergraduate degree at Dartmouth College in New Hampshire; there, as a freshman in a noncredit seminar during the summer of 1943, he met Robert Frost, who acted as an occasional grandfather for Booth's three daughters during the early years of his marriage (in 1946, to Margaret Tillman). Booth was graduated from Dartmouth in 1947, taught at Bowdoin College in Maine in 1949, and then stopped teaching for a while. He hoped to be a novelist and, to pay the bills for the next four years, worked in both Vermont and New Hampshire at jobs that included a stint in Dartmouth's admissions office, work as a traveling ski-book salesman, and some time in a carpentry shop. After deciding that he was not a good storyteller but rather a good wordsmith, Booth turned his attention to writing poetry. He earned his master's degree at Syracuse University, and for the next twenty-five years he served as senior poet in the creative writing program there. During these years he edited several volumes of *Syracuse Poems*.

Since the early 1950's, Booth has published poetry in many leading literary magazines and journals, including

Philip Booth (© Rollie McKenna)

Harper's, *The Kenyon Review*, *The New Yorker*, and *Saturday Review*.

ANALYSIS

Philip Booth's list of accomplishments is impressive, and his reputation is international, but he is, most of all, a humanist speaking to an individual audience, one person at a time. Although he is widely identified as a regional poet who writes of life in a harsh, cold northern climate, Booth's subjects cover the whole range of human experience. The powerful forces of nature and how humans relate to them play prominently in his work, but his poems also speak of other human concerns: love, sex, marriage, children, aging, poverty, death, and the mysteries of existence. In his earliest collection, *Letter from a Distant Land*, his poetic patterns are fairly traditional; however, as one moves to his later poems, one finds less attention to traditional form and sometimes an abandonment of rhyme and stanza. In all Booth's works, one senses the struggle of form and matter; his themes are of human loneliness and vulnerability set against the impersonal forces of nature. This struggle is never fully reconciled, but the poet examines the need for the coexistence of humankind and the natural world.

LETTER FROM A DISTANT LAND

In the sonnet "Good Friday, 1954," which appears in *Letter from a Distant Land*, the number of lines and the rhyme scheme follow the traditional pattern, but the poet uses slant rhyme, with "lodged" and "judged" ending the sixth and eighth lines. The poem's final line reveals Booth's closeness to the New England school headed by Robert Frost and its belief in the moral function of poetry: "To spike a rumor sacrifice a man." "The Wilding," another early poem, issues a springtime call to love; Booth plays on the sexual suggestiveness of jack-in-the-pulpits and maidenhair fern. E. E. Cummings's playfulness is echoed in "a sweet fern questionmark/ whorls green as green is today,/ and ferns ask no answer a swallow/ can't fly." The youthful joy and exuberance of this poem fill the reader with hope and expectation. Another early poem, "First Lesson," instructs a daughter about trusting the father who is cradling her head in the "cup" of his hand as he gently urges her to learn to swim. Just as the swimmer learns to trust the sea, a person can learn to survive by remembering experiences that, like the sea, "will hold you." "Chart 1203" captures the essence of sailing's allure and challenge in saying of the sailor, "He knows the chart is not the sea." The Atlantic coast is threatening, Booth says, only for the sailor who is not familiar with its eccentricities and relies on charts and maps alone to guide him. The sailor must have "local knowledge of shoal/ or ledge." The poem celebrates the thrill of meeting a challenge and surviving through a combination of good luck and skill.

The volume's title poem, "Letter from a Distant Land," combines slant rhyme and true rhyme. The poem, a lengthy meditation about the area around Henry David Thoreau's Walden Pond and the changes it has undergone since the nineteenth century, is written in terza rima, with long sentences and a doubly alternating rhyme scheme. The rhyme and meter are, nevertheless, so subtle, with approximate combinations such as "desk" and "risk," that the reader hardly notices them. In this way the poem does have the flavor of a letter written from a distant land to a friend, with themes of the connectedness of writer and reader, the natural world and human values.

WEATHERS AND EDGES

In *Weathers and Edges*, New England voices speak with terse language and dry humor. The arrangement of the poems moves from works such as "Heart of Darkness," which deals with large human concerns, to personal poems of private experience such as "Cleaning Out the Garage," and then outward again to a series of sea poems set on the Maine coast. The reader of "Heart of Darkness" is struck by the short lines arranged as a column on the page: The poem itself is presented as "some sort of base/ to start out from." The stanza arrangement in "Cleaning Out the Garage" is less lean. Filling out the page, its four stanzas move from nine to ten to eleven and finally to twelve lines, ironically accumulating lines as the garage is cleaned out and its contents diminished, and ending with an almost Frostian moral: The speaker has learned, after discarding all the "useless stuff" stored since his boyhood, "how to let go what won't do." "Report from the Scene," an immediate description of the effects of severe local thunderstorms on boats moored in a Maine harbor, is arranged in eleven two-line stanzas; in it, the forces of nature seem nearly overwhelming, but two people "with reflex love" reach for each other and face the storm. The individuals

watching the violent storm are an image of human vulnerability in the face of natural forces, but as the two reach out toward each other, they and the storm are able to coexist.

AVAILABLE LIGHT

Several works in *Available Light* try to come to terms with harsh winters, the freeze of a late spring, the poet's Puritan need to take inventory constantly, and the nearly mystical experience of a dream. "Entry," a terse, honed poem that is skinny on the page, describes bitter cold weather that has lasted for four days, drifted snow coming in large flakes, and a "small sun." The poet's words "quicken," or give life to, the silence and allow an entry for him, suggesting Booth's fascination with the life-giving power of words. "Adding It Up" uses what light is available as the speaker's mind begins to open up before dawn, while he lies in bed tallying his life and its concerns. As his mind opens and he meticulously counts, his body prepares for the first humorously ordinary job of the day: "cleaning up after/ an old-maid Basset in heat." With humor the speaker looks at himself and inventories his Puritan characteristics: being sorry, worrying, counting.

Set against such straightforwardness, "Dreamscape" has a visionary quality in its carefully shaped free verse. In contrast to "Supposition with Qualification," in which the speaker struggles with wanting to give himself up to experience, the speaker in "Dreamscape" lets the dream experience take control of the poem. The opening stanza describes the familiar road to town as the speaker has "always" known it: the steep hill, the filled-in old British canal, the spruce trees, the five houses. The certainty of "always," however, is denied by the vision of the road in the dream. In the second stanza, beginning with the word "but," the poet presents the road in his dream, with the left side now cleared into pasture in which "miniature bison" are kneeling. Avoiding the questioning of experience found in some of Booth's earlier works, he neither can nor wants to explain this dreamscape. The organic process of the poem takes on a life of its own, offering a sharing of the dream's experience and suggesting the chance that this dream experience opens up a wholly new perspective.

"How to See Deer" comments directly on the subtler theme of an earlier poem, "Shag." "Shag" first describes the poet's observations of seven cormorants (shags), follows with ruminations about what ornithologists say regarding their strange flights, and concludes as the poet continues to observe and to row "as if/ on vacation from knowledge." Here Booth has tried to let the experience speak for itself, and to avoid explaining it or generalizing from it. "How to See Deer" makes a similar point, but much more overtly, in contrast to Booth's usual practice: by advising, if one purposely sets out to see deer—or, by extension, to experience anything—that the deer will not be seen. Serendipity is a factor; however, taking "your good time," trusting "your quick nature," learning to listen and to observe, to "see/ what you see," will permit one to experience joy. Perceptions and experiences cannot be forced; if, however, one is alert and receptive, one is able to participate in life.

BEFORE SLEEP

Like Booth's earlier works, *Before Sleep* is divided into parts, but they are concurrent rather than consecutive, with tightly woven interaction. These pieces are separated into poems and "Night Notes": The forty-three poems appear on numbered pages indicated in the table of contents; the eighteen "Night Notes," offering commentaries on the poems to which they are juxtaposed, appear between listed poem titles and are not given page numbers. The collection's title, reminiscent of the famous Frost poem "Stopping by Woods on a Snowy Evening," brings to mind the long sleep of death. The poems themselves, however, offer meditations on how to live life. There are no formal stanzaic patterns here; rhyme and even approximate rhyme are absent. Figurative language is also sparse; Booth uses mostly simple words and gives particular attention to the word "nothing," which exists by itself, contradicting the view—held by Booth in his early years—that nothing exists in isolation.

The opening poem, "Not to Tell Lies," describes a man who wishes to strip life down to the barest essentials. Initially, the lines are short, but they quickly become longer, only to shorten again to the single word "lies." This arrangement is striking, for it suggests a wedge used to force the truth into a limited space, without anything extraneous. The poet is coming to terms with his age, having reached his sixth decade and returned to live year-round in the ancestral Maine home. Items in his upstairs room, "which corners late sun," include a schoo-

ner model, the portrait of a daughter, a rock brought from Amchitka by the speaker's doctor, an ancestor's photograph, and books by Henry David Thoreau and Herman Melville—men who also made outward and inward journeys. As in earlier poems, Booth uses sea metaphors—for example, his bed has been:

> moored . . .
> perpendicular to the North wall,
> whenever he rests his head is compassed barely west
> of Polaris

All the poem's other words catalog what he has gathered and sorted through "in order not/ to tell/ lies." Following this poem, and integral to its meaning, is a "night note" introducing the idea of "nothing." The room just described is nothing, Booth says, when separated from the life he lives within it; the person, the poet, is more "vital" than the room, and his "virtue" is "not/ in my own life to live/ as if nothing/ were more important."

As the collection progresses, one senses the nothingness of death but also the meaning and sometimes the meaninglessness of life. "The House in the Trees," the collection's final entry, pictures a continuous moving toward life, affirming the possibility of continuing to build for the future, although, like the house "in the process/ of being built," the poet's life and art may not reach complete fulfillment before his death. In this process, in the sense of "constantly being arrived at," life and art are affirmed.

RELATIONS

The title poem of *Relations* is a poem of affirmation; the speaker does not deny life's uncertainties, but wonders at the miracle of each moment, amazed at the movement of the spheres,

> . . . by how
>   to each other
>   we're held, we keep
>
>   from spinning out
>   by how to each other
>   we hold.

The staggered placement of the poem's lines suggests how each line relates to those that follow and precede it. "From broken dreams," says the poem, "we wake to every day's/ brave history." That all persons do this, that history involves experience, and perhaps as well that opening oneself to each day's experience is "brave" indicate the commonality of persons, their dependence on one another. As the poem progresses, the speaker becomes more personal, naming his village's zip code, 04421, and a specific woman. Janet, the town's postmaster, is "spun into light" by the planets' movements, as all people are. Moving from the specific person in Castine to the inclusive "we" once more, Booth combines thanksgivings for his peninsular village and, by extension, for life.

Relations includes selections from all Booth's previous collections, as well as thirty-one new poems. The later works use terse Down East language, slanted syllables, and simple Anglo-Saxon diction, omitting rhyme and meter. The fragmentation of short lines and stanzas gives these poems a conversational quality. Woven into these works is the theme of human isolation but also of love and connectedness with the world, for the poet often looks to nature for answers and for the reassurance of order. The title poem, "Relations," explores relationships not only of people to one another over space and time but also among lines in a poem, of words to other words, and of the limits the poet imposes on them. These poems do not offer certainties for the reader, but rather uncertainties, as the poet struggles to find his way through questions such as "Where did I come from?" and "Where am I going?" Booth speaks of this searching as a "coming to terms" with experience, and of human relationships as giving meaning to life.

Originally published in *Margins*, "Supposition with Qualification" questions the eternal mystery of being. The speaker discusses a man who "if he could say it" certainly meant to do so, but who is never clear about what "it" means. Instead, the man intended to say "how it felt when he let himself/ feel." It is, however, difficult for him to let himself feel anything without allowing his mind to get in the way. The poem includes several question words: "what," "how," "when." Even with the need to know suggested by these words, the man does not want to intellectualize but to feel, to "give himself up," although the qualification itself, "if he could say it," suggests his inability to do so, as well as the human need to question and articulate experience.

"The Man on the Wharf," which is arranged in direct two-line stanzas, describes a man, drunk with Jim Beam whiskey, who has lost his woman. He watches another man shuck clams; although he does not know why he watches, one senses in him a questioning about his life and his loss: He "swallows no answer/ but questions in bourbon this seeming harbor." "Seeming harbor" questions what is real and what is imagined, while the man turns to perhaps the most fundamental source for answers in the poem's concluding lines: "The sea is all he can ask."

"The Stranding" journeys inward, as the first-person speaker puts his eyes to the eyes of his own skull to look through both pairs of eyes into his own head, only to find a "stranding," a sense of being left alone in a helpless position, of being separated from his essential self. The speaker, though, can hardly see himself, and, when he considers calling to his inner self by name, he realizes that the inner self whom he can barely see is listening to porpoises, not to the self on the outside calling to him. Perhaps in answer to the universal question "Who am I?" the speaker finds isolation. In simple, carefully sharpened language arranged in stanzas of three short lines each, the poem successfully creates the effect of the speaker explaining to an individual listener what happened as he searched for himself.

Reminding one of David Wagoner's "Return to the Swamp," "The Question Poem" also deals with eternals. What does the wind mean? What "sudden discipline" determines the course of birds' migrations? Do the seabirds fish for answers, too? No answers are offered, but, like any human being, the speaker finds it impossible to imagine a world in which he himself is absent. He does seem to find some hint of a response to his questions in the mysteries of the sea and its creatures as they move in their carefully ordered, delicately balanced relationships to one another.

SELVES

Booth alludes to the theme of *Selves* in *Vermont Academy Life* (Fall/Winter, 1979/1980): "I read because . . . my many selves . . . need to experience other lives." In *Selves*, once again, he presents beautifully moving, tightly made, sometimes humorous poems that employ a minimum of figurative language. The volume's prologue, from Wallace Stevens's *Esthétique du*

Mal (1945), introduces the theme of the many selves within each human being. Participation in these poems allows the reader to become part of the creative process and, in turn, to begin to discover his or her own many selves. The poems combine philosophical speculation about universal mysteries with ordinary, mundane topics such as losing a glove, splitting wood with a wedge and an ax, and spreading manure. While commenting on each person's inability to feel another's feelings completely, and while expressing concern for the future given past and present ecological disasters, these poems give thanks for life, music, sex, food, and relationships, for awareness, consciousness, and wonder. Traditional rhyming and restrictive forms are eschewed in favor of the comfortable patterns of common speech, so that these works are very accessible.

The epigraph poem "Reaching In," with parallels from physics and probability theory, expresses deep concern with and respect for how each reader experiences the poem. Booth asks his readers to "weigh each word before you believe me"; there is an implied reward for the reader who follows this directive. The first "reaching" in the poem is that of the physicist who reaches in to measure momentum. The second use of the word is literal: The poet reaches through the dark at night on his way to the bathroom, and like the physicist's changing of the photon's position, the poet's "feet displace the shape of the dark." The third "reaching" is internal but also cosmic: "Reaching in, I trembled the landscape." The unusual transitive use of "trembled" continues the opening image. The word "you" in stanza 3 begins in reference to a particular person but subsequently moves to the individual reader and beyond. This poem suggests how to experience the poems that follow.

Some of the poems in part 1 are eloquent pictures of rural poverty. With simple, direct language "Poor" describes the impossibility of planning ahead when one has very little. Moose Coombs has never been able to afford the time to seek out seasoned wood for heating the kitchen stove. Instead he has brought home green wood, which burns too intensely and coats the chimney with creosote; the result is a sudden fire that destroys his wife and his house. There are no metaphors here, but the ordinary language brings the event home and shows its pointless tragedy.

In "Civilities," with humor, fondness, and appreciation, the poet turns to his grandmother's knowledge of "right words, and which/ to use when." Without ever using the four-letter word for excrement, Booth makes it humorously present. His portraits of Mr. Bowden delivering and of Mrs. Hooke paying for "spring dressing" are painted with tender humor and fond respect, as the poet, years later, prepares the same perennial garden they tended with "lovely dark clouds of cowdung."

Further poems in this volume speak of the isolation of aging, of survival, and of the hopefulness of life. "Fallback" poignantly describes an elderly couple imprisoned in a home for the aged. Concrete, direct language brings home the predicament of the old couple, who have been together for sixty-two years. They are now perfunctorily tended by a young nurse who "looks like a grebe" and who cannot and probably does not care to know the elderly woman's tender memories of love and caring: how her husband in years past spread out his jacket for picnics and how they "made love/ in the sweetfern high on an island." The husband's mind is now gone, and the wife's body is impossibly frail, but the memories are sturdy and real.

"Provisions," in reaction to a book on survival tactics left on an airplane, speaks against the directions it offers about what to take when one is dealing with a nuclear disaster and agrees only with the advice "Leave objects behind" (especially, Booth says, the survival book itself). His advice, instead, is to take poems, Thoreau, the memory of a tune by Bach, and sustaining memories. As the old woman in "Fallback" finds, it is the experiences of life that will sustain one.

The final piece in the collection, "Presence," is a poem of wonder. In simple, two-line stanzas, the poet speaks of the singular mystery "that we are here, here at all." The very title suggests an almost worshipful attitude toward life, that there is a being, a presence, a hint of a supernatural influence felt nearby. "Presence" offers the opportunity for joy in life, brief as it is, and an affirmation of being.

LIFELINES

In *Lifelines*, the new poems comprise a final section. In this grouping, Booth enjoys more than even the formal play that is his hallmark, though with a continuing loosening of exterior borders. Understandably, many of these poems (as do several in *Pairs*) flirt with the impingement of aging. Memories have further to travel. Losses pile up. Yet Booth's clipped, dignified style—and his occasional humor—hold despair in check. A long poem, "Reach Road: *In Medias Res*," follows an old mailman over the rural route he has traversed for decades, defined by the familiar blend of nature and neighborhood. His larger route, his lifepath, takes the mailman and the reader in and out of the books that define another kind of journey, the life of intellect and art that is Booth's own. At once narrative and meditative, "Reach Road" is a late marvel in a career of many marvels. It is a brilliant, if premature, review of Booth's territory—a summation.

While all Booth's poetry explores the struggle and isolation of human existence, his ultimate response to both is positive. He embraces the old but important observation of John Donne that we are all, with our fears, affirmations, sorrow, and happiness, joined in the large human family. We are part of one another, and we share in the sorrows, mysteries, and joys of life. Booth's poems, with their universal themes and simple language, enlarge and expand that life.

OTHER MAJOR WORK

NONFICTION: *Trying to Say It: Outlooks and Insights on How Poems Happen*, 1996.

BIBLIOGRAPHY

Booth, Philip. Interview by Rachel Berghash. *The American Poetry Review* 18 (May/June, 1989): 37-39. This interview was conducted in Maine for radio station WBAI in New York City and was aired in two parts in August, 1986. The poet discusses his sense of place and roots in Castine, offering some biographical information. He also talks about his views on survival, his philosophy of poetry, and his largest collection, *Relations*.

_____. Interview by Stephen Dunn. *New England Review and Bread Loaf Quarterly* 9 (Winter, 1986): 134-158. Dunn is one of the four former students to whom Booth dedicated *Selves* and from whom the poet says he is still learning. This interview, conducted in the Booth ancestral home, offers good insight into the poems of Booth's seventh volume, *Relations*.

Phillips, Robert. "Utterly Unlike." *Hudson Review* 52, no. 4 (Winter, 1999): 689-697. Phillips contrasts Booth's style and thematic focus in *Lifelines* with Levine's *The Mercy* and Mary Jo Salter's *A Kiss in Space* in this celebration of poetic diversity.

Rotella, Guy L. *Three Contemporary Poets of New England: William Meredith, Philip Booth, and Peter Davison*. Boston: Twayne, 1983. Rotella places Booth in a New England regional context alongside Meredith and Davison, providing biographical information along with analysis of the poetry. Includes an index and a bibliography.

Taylor, John. Review of *Lifelines: Selected Poems, 1950-1999*. *Poetry* 177, no. 1 (January, 2001): 272-273. Taylor notes that Booth's realism is often overcast with a dreaminess that invites introspection and meditation. Booth's poetry "seeks to reconcile mystical questioning with a precise examination of the outside world."

Tillinghast, Richard. "Stars and Departures, Hummingbirds and Statues." *Poetry* 166, no. 5 (August, 1995): 295-297. Booth's *Pairs* is matched up with Mark Strand's *Dark Harbor*. Tillinghast appreciates Booth's Yankee sensibility, his close and convincing observation, and the way in which he avoids forcing his material into thematic clusters or sequences. The poet's sensibility *is* the theme. Tillinghast enjoys Booth's humor as well.

Linda K. Martinez,
updated by Philip K. Jason

EDGAR BOWERS

Born: Rome, Georgia; March 2, 1924
Died: San Francisco, California; February 4, 2000

PRINCIPAL POETRY

The Form of Loss, 1956
The Astronomers, 1965
Living Together, 1973
For Louis Pasteur, 1989
Collected Poems, 1997

OTHER LITERARY FORMS

Edgar Bowers is known primarily for his poetry.

ACHIEVEMENTS

Edgar Bowers's poetry was championed by Yvor Winters, who offered the first critiques of Bowers's poetry in his critical book *Forms of Discovery* (1967). Winters's analysis was based on Bowers's first two books, *The Form of Loss* (1956) and *The Astronomers* (1965). Winters was drawn to Bowers's imagery, his word choice, and his capable use of meter. He noted that Bowers's "vision" was shaped by many factors, including the war, his reading, and his intellectual interests. In his *Lives of the Poets* (1998), Michael Schmidt includes Bowers as one of the representative poets of the modern era and notes the influence on Winters on Bowers's style, describing the "harsh discipline" of Winters's teaching of poetry writing as having produced rigorously formal poetry linked to stoicism.

Bowers received many awards and honors in his career. In 1950 he was awarded a Fulbright Fellowship for study in England. In 1955, he won the Swallow Press Prize for Poetry. He received two Guggenheim Fellowships, in 1958 and 1969. In 1989, Bowers won both the Bolligen Prize and the Harriet Monroe Prize for excellence in poetry.

BIOGRAPHY

Edgar Bowers was born in Rome, Georgia, to William Edgar Bowers and Grace Anderson Bowers. His father, who was from South Carolina, graduated from Clemson University, served in World War I, briefly taught at Virginia Polytechnic University, and ended his career as a nurseryman in Stone Mountain, Georgia. His mother was a graduate of Agnes Scott College and a native of Iowa. She was a schoolteacher and an accomplished painter. Bowers had one sister, Eleanor, who predeceased him.

Between 1943 and 1946, Bowers, who was a French and German major at the University of North Carolina, served in the U.S. Army with the 101st Airborne's unit in counterintelligence. His role included service in Germany, where he acted as a translator and where he saw many scenes of devastation and despair. These would figure later in the sensibility of his poetry. After his tour ended, Bowers returned to finish his education on the G.I. Bill. He earned his B.A. in 1947 and enrolled in the Stanford M.A. program, where he would study with poet-critic Yvor Winters. He earned his degree in 1949 and followed that with a Ph.D. from Stanford in 1953. Bowers went on to teach at Duke University and Harpur College. In 1958, he joined the English faculty at the University of California at Santa Barbara, from which he would retire in 1991. He then moved to San Francisco where he died of lymphatic cancer on February 4, 2000.

ANALYSIS

Edgar Bowers's poetry has been praised for its technical skill, its smooth integration of philosophical ideas, and its intellectual rigor. He was described by Dick Davis, a fellow poet and professor of Persian at Ohio State University, as "a cerebral poet," while the *Oxford Companion to Poetry* states Bowers's poetry shows "great intellectual sophistication" as he writes "with unmannered dexterity."

Bowers's greatest achievement was in his use of blank verse for poetry on contemporary themes and issues. Bowers kept aspects of the Elizabethan style, such as that of Ben Jonson, alive in his poetry. He wrote on a range of subjects, effectively blending elements of past literary traditions with contemporary concerns. He could be characterized as a poet of World War II in the sense that the war remained central to his writing. As late as the "New Poems" in the *Collected Poems* (1997), Bowers dealt with the way the war had changed his perceptions of life. Technically, he is a postwar poet having published his first book of verse, written after the war, in 1956. Bowers never attempted to reconcile the war's experiences with his situation, nor did he moralize about the wrongs of war. His use of the war was as setting and a platform for deeper reflection on human nature and the way circumstances affect the course of life.

For someone who was counted in the company of such notable poets as Howard Nemerov and Louis Simpson, Bowers received little critical attention after the publication of Yvor Winters's 1967 book that discussed him. Bowers's verse is the work of a serious observer of himself and human nature. The poetry is marked by its keen attention to details in both physical and abstract nature. The poems have great range and of-

Edgar Bowers (© Miriam Berkley)

ten accumulate information from various sources, which enables the poems to appeal to a variety of readers.

THE FORM OF LOSS

Published in 1956, *The Form of Loss* has twenty-six poems composed between 1947 and 1955. "To the Reader," which opens the collection, and "To this Book" were the last poems written in 1955. The primary images in the book are derived from nature. Bowers uses the image of snow, for example, to show mutability.

The Form of Loss demonstrates Bowers's use of rhetorical figures, stanza forms, rhymes, and meters in an unobtrusive manner in these poems based on his travels, his Army experiences, and his personal life. In the poem "Dark Earth and Summer," Bowers uses an alternating rhyme in the quatrains to counterpoint the words in the unrhymed lines to great effect. "To W. A. Mozart" is based on the time Bowers found himself in a German castle, where he was able to play a tune on Mozart's own clavier.

Other poems in the collection are topical, bringing together Bowers's interests in the lives of his friends, historical subjects, and the arts. "The Prince," a poem praised by Winters, combines the themes which dominate the book—time, loss, perception, and perspective—with a formal elegance and expertise. The poem is a dramatic monologue spoken by a father whose son has been executed as a spy in wartime. The title of the collection comes from "The Prince" as he says, "My son, who was the heir/ To every hope and trust grew out of caring,/ Into the form of loss as I had done,/ And then betrayed me who betrayed him first."

THE ASTRONOMERS

Bowers's 1965 collection of fifteen poems was dedicated to his mother and his aunts, who were formative influences in his education. The majority of these poems were written in Santa Barbara, after Bowers assumed his faculty position. Blank verse dominates the collection as rhyme recedes and the poems become more conversational and evenly paced.

Death and the passage of time continue as important themes in this book. Two poems that stand out in this book are the sonnet "The Mirror," in which the poet-speaker addresses his father and their similarities in personality, and "Autumn Shade," a poem of ten numbered sections. The poem describes the sensations of coming home, the loss of innocence associated with aging, lost childhood, and the passage of time as the personality of the speaker has been changed by time, death, and experiences. The poem is rich in natural imagery, philosophical concepts, and lived experience.

LIVING TOGETHER

Bowers's third book is concentrated on the theme of love lost. Not based on any one experience, the poems are an assimilation of all people's experiences of sadness when relationships fail. The poems were composed between 1964 and 1971 in Santa Barbara.

"Living Together" in eight lines provides the themes of memory, love, loss, and loyalty. The poem "Wandering" charts the breakup of a relationship and ends with the speaker both literally sick in bed with the flu and emotionally heartsick. This is one instance of Bowers's use of comic or situational irony. "Insomnia" is a fine ten-line poem about the speaker's insomnia and his hope to wake up one morning with "the need to have no need." This collection shows Bowers's mastery of the shorter lyric, rich with formal elegance and vivid language.

For Louis Pasteur

Of all his books, Bowers declared *For Louis Pasteur* (1989) his favorite for its technical skill, its variety in the use of blank verse for many diverse themes, and its alliance with his own interests. This is the book that best represents Edgar Bowers. The cover of the book is a painting by Bowers's mother, "The Big Oak."

The collection is divided into three numbered sections. Part 1 contains the title poem and two sequences of short poems—"Thirteen Views of Santa Barbara" (with its allusion to Wallace Stevens's "Thirteen Ways of Looking at a Blackbird")—and "Witnesses," in which Old Testament people—Adam, Eve, Cain, Noah, and Jacob— have a say about creation. "Thirteen Views" begins with the highly visual poem "Hang Gliding," which uses language of flight and falling to connect the picture of the hang glider "leaping out from the fartherest ridge" with the soldier's memory of being a parachutist. Falling would have killed both these men, who hang precariously on the wind.

The second section of the book is composed of seven poems. These include a description of Dick Davis reading his poetry, with an emphasis on how he sounds when he reads and how the reading stops time and the noises of the environment in Los Angeles. "Mary" is a long narrative about Bowers's aunt, and "Elegy: Walking the Line" begins, "Every month or so, Sundays, we walked the line." It largely describes in rich visual language walking through the nursery on Stone Mountain and remembering all that happened there as well as the family that called it home.

The third section of the book has five poems on subjects that merge philosophical concepts with historical moments. The central poem of this section is "Chaco Canyon," which is at once topographical, experiential, and philosophical as the canyon is likened to Plato's cave from which knowledge of the world came.

The themes of this book advance those of the previous books with a new emphasis on ordering experiences and memories to make life less chaotic. The opening lines of "For Louis Pasteur" set the tone for the rest of the book as the speaker ponders: "How shall a genera-

tion know its story/ Of it will know no other?" This is elaborated on in stanza two, "How shall my generation tell its story?" These are the seminal questions of Bowers's oeuvre and express what he is trying to accomplish in his poetry. As a poet who served in World War II, Bowers seeks to answer questions raised by subsequent generations about the meaning of war and such experience in everyday life.

The elegant poem "In Defense of Poetry," which ends the collection, begins, "Childhood taught us illusion," and it proceeds from there to address the theme of forms of deception, which Winters had first noticed in Bowers's verse. Here movies, books, and education emphasizing self-esteem are the culprits in the false sense of security and accomplishment people have. In the final lines, the poet looking around at these people of the suburbs sees in his mind's eye Polish families on the trains to their deaths. Without saying anything more than just what the memory flash is the poem effectively makes its point about the fragility of human life and civilization.

Collected Poems

Bowers's final book is a compilation of the previous books in total, but they are presented in reverse chronological order. The effect of this structure is to allow the reader to hear the different voices in Bowers's poetry and to chart its evolution from the present to the past. When the reader comes to *The Form of Loss*, it is clear how Bowers moved beyond his early rigorous use of form to create a more subtly crafted poem in which rhyme, meter, and rhetorical devices become a necessary extension of expressing the ideas of the poems. Taken together, one sees continuity in Bowers's interests and the development of traditional themes over time. From last to first book, the impression of Bowers's poetry is that it is a consistent exploration of universal ideas couched in a range of experiences.

The book opens with twenty-five new poems under eleven titles. There is one lyric sequence called "Mazes" which is composed of fourteen poems on time, space, nature, and ideas. "New Poems" opens with a long lyric in memory of John Finlay, a poet who died of AIDS. The second poem, "Clear-seeing," about a clairvoyant in Germany during the war, complements the two poles of Bowers's poetic experiences: now and then. Other poems address preparing for death and remembrances.

The poem "The Poet Orders His Tomb," with its allusion to Robert Browning's "The Archbishop Orders His Tomb," opens with an appeal to art historian Erwin Panofsky to design a tomb rich with animal imagery and symbols. As the poem speeds along in rhymed quatrains, stanza 8 provides a glimpse at Bowers's definition of his role as a poet: "I who have sought time's memory afoot,/ Grateful for every root/ Of trees that fill the garden with their fruit,/ Their fragrance and their shade?"

As these stanzas suggest, Bowers's poetry is not easily reducible to a core set of stylistic preferences or themes. He showed great skill with the short lyric, stanzas, and the long narrative. Significantly, he extended the possibilities for blank verse as a tool for poets wanting to write meaningful poetry in a formal mode. His themes were varied, but they seem to center on such concepts as loyalty, love, honor, courage, and beauty.

BIBLIOGRAPHY

Akard, Jeffery, and Joshua Odell. *A Bibliography of the Published Works of Edgar Bowers*. Barth Bibliographies 3. Santa Barbara, Calif.: J. Akard, 1988. Provides technical descriptions of the books published before 1988 and includes listings of the periodicals in which many of the poems were first published. Bowers provided a chronology for the poems as well.

Davis, Dick. "The Mystery of Consciousness: A Tribute to the Poet Edgar Bowers." *Poets and Writers*, July/August, 2000, 14-19. A tribute and analysis of some of Bowers poetry by his friend Dick Davis.

Schmidt, Michael. *Lives of the Poets*. London: Weidenfeld & Nicolson, 1998. Places Bowers in the context of a discussion of Yvor Winters's poetry and notes the influence of Winters on Bowers's use of language and uses of poetic form.

Winters, Yvor. *Forms of Discovery*. Denver: Alan Swallow Press, 1967. Winters studies Bowers's first two books and analyzes their strengths and weaknesses. Winters also edited two collections of poetry in which he included Bowers's verse: *Poets of the Pacific* (1949; second series) and *Quest for Reality* (with Kenneth Fields, 1969).

Beverly Schneller

WILLIAM LISLE BOWLES

Born: Kings Sutton, Northamptonshire, England; September 24, 1762
Died: Salisbury, Wiltshire, England; April 7, 1850

PRINCIPAL POETRY

Fourteen Sonnets, 1789, enlarged 1794, enlarged 1796, enlarged 1798
Verses to John Howard, 1789
The Grave of Howard, 1790
Verses on the Benevolent Institution of the Philanthropic Society, for Protecting and Educating the Children of Vagrants and Criminals, 1790
A Poetical Address to the Right Honourable Edmund Burke, 1791
Elegy Written at the Hot-Wells, Bristol, 1791
Monody, Written at Matlock, 1791
Elegiac Stanzas, Written During Sickness at Bath, 1796
Hope: An Allegorical Sketch, 1796
St. Michael's Mount, 1798
Coombe Ellen, 1798
Song of the Battle of the Nile, 1799
Poems, 1801
The Sorrows of Switzerland, 1801
The Picture, 1803
The Spirit of Discovery: Or, The Conquest of the Ocean, 1804
Bowden Hill, 1806
The Little Villager's Verse Book, 1806, 1837 (juvenile)
Poems, 1809
The Missionary, 1813
The Grave of the Last Saxon, 1822
Ellen Gray, 1823
Days Departed, 1828
St. John in Patmos, 1832
Scenes and Shadows, 1835

OTHER LITERARY FORMS

Although best known as a poet, William Lisle Bowles also published an edition of Alexander Pope, pamphlets of literary criticism regarding Pope (in a famous controversy with Lord Byron and others), sermons, antiquarian works, and an autobiographical fragment. A number of his letters are also extant (see Garland Greever's edition of them), but he is more memorably preserved in the recollections of others, as Thomas Moore and Samuel Taylor Coleridge fondly described and preserved his eccentricities.

ACHIEVEMENTS

Few people today regard William Lisle Bowles as a major poet, and some would speak contemptuously of him, for all his enormous output. Sharply contrasting with a modern sophisticated dismissal of his work, however, was the immediate and forceful influence that Bowles exerted upon the first generation of British Romantic poets, including William Wordsworth, Robert Southey, Charles Lamb, and above all Samuel Taylor Coleridge. For them he was the herald of a new sensibility, almost a Vergil to follow beyond the desiccated landscape of neoclassical detachment into a richer vale of fresh response and honest moralizing. Having been educated in part by the poets he inspired, modern readers find it hard to appreciate Bowles's originality. Largely because he was transitional to better poets than himself, Bowles now appears to be of historical interest only. He is frequently omitted from modern anthologies altogether and appears in some literary histories only as a footnote to Coleridge.

BIOGRAPHY

William Lisle Bowles was born on September 24, 1762, at Kings Sutton, Northamptonshire (his father's vicarage), the son and grandson of clergymen and the eldest of seven children. At seven he moved with his parents to Uphill, Somerset; on the journey southward young Bowles saw the Severn Valley and derived from it a lifelong association of poetry with picturesque scenery.

From 1775 to 1781 Bowles was educated at Winchester School under Dr. Joseph Warton, who had written an essay critical of Alexander Pope and was a pre-Romantic advocate of descriptive poetry. Warton's feeling for nature, dislike of neoclassical rules, and knowledge of Vergil impressed Bowles (see his "Monody on the Death of Dr. Warton," 1819), who thereafter followed and enlarged upon Warton's precepts. In 1781 Bowles went on to Trinity College, Oxford, where his master, Thomas Warton, Joseph's brother, further reinforced Bowles's dislike of neoclassicism and preference for lyric poetry, the ode and sonnet in particular. Bowles wrote "On Leaving Winchester School," his first important poem, retrospectively in 1782.

His record at Oxford was that of an unusually able student. In 1782, for example, Bowles won a scholarship that sustained him for the next five years. In 1783 his "Calpe Obsessa" (on the Siege of Gibraltar) was the Latin prize poem. Three years later, however, in 1786, Bowles's father died, leaving the family in difficult financial straits. Though Bowles received his B.A. degree the next year, his engagement to a niece of Sir Samuel Romilly appeared imprudent to her parents and was summarily broken off. In his disappointment, Bowles elected to travel through northern England, Scotland, Belgium, Germany, and Switzerland. While thus relieved, he composed a series of sonnets; published in 1789 at Bath as *Fourteen Sonnets*, they quickly made him famous.

Wordsworth, on vacation from Cambridge, read Bowles's sonnets that Christmas in London, as he was walking the streets with his brother John, and (as Mary Moorman has it in her biography of Wordsworth), "their graceful melancholy, dwelling on the memories of beloved places, at once made a strong appeal." Bowles's influence on Wordsworth is traceable in the latter's work from *Descriptive Sketches* (1793) to "Lines Composed a Few Miles Above Tintern Abbey" (1798). The first edition of Bowles's sonnets that Wordsworth read, however, was a rarity, for only one hundred copies were published. There soon followed a second edition (also 1789) containing twenty-one sonnets, which Coleridge read—he was then a seventeen-year-old schoolboy at Christ's Hospital—and transcribed endlessly for his literary friends. As J. Shawcross has remarked, "in Bowles's sonnets Coleridge found the first genuinely unconventional treatment of Nature, the first genuine stimulus to an understanding of her 'perpetual revelation'" (*Biographia Literaria*, 1817). One of those to whom Coleridge sent Bowles's sonnets was Robert Southey, who soon shared his enthusiasm for them. "Buy Bowles poems, and study them well," he advised a friend in 1794.

"They will teach you to write better, and give you infinite pleasure." Bowles was a major influence on Coleridge and his circle from 1789 to 1797, and these years were also the Wiltshire parson's most prolific.

The *Fourteen Sonnets* proved to be a remarkable success. Following the first and second editions of 1789, there was a third in 1794 containing twenty-seven sonnets and thirteen other poems. The fourth edition of 1796 was little changed, but the fifth (1796; two new poems) and sixth (1798; thirty sonnets and sixteen other poems, including *Hope*) both contained additions and plates. Less significant, except as evidence of Bowles's continuing popularity, were editions seven (1800), eight (1801), nine (1805), and ten (1809). Coleridge followed the earlier editions as they appeared and even wrote Bowles (whom he visited in September, 1797) to comment on his various omissions and emendations.

Coleridge acknowledged his own profound indebtedness to Bowles in a sonnet of December, 1794, "To the Rev. W. L. Bowles," which was printed in the *Morning Chronicle*, a London newspaper, on the day after Christmas, together with a note from Coleridge praising Bowles's sonnets XIII ("At a Convent"), XIX, and XXV as "compositions of, perhaps, unrivalled merit." In *Poems on Various Subjects* (1796), Coleridge reprinted his Bowles sonnet in a revised form. That same year he also published *A Sheet of Sonnets*, twenty-eight in all, designed to be bound up with Bowles's own, which Coleridge praised effusively in his preface. By 1802, however, Coleridge was no longer satisfied with Bowles, who had "indeed the *sensibility* of a poet," but "not the *Passion* of a great Poet" (*Collected Letters*, 1956-1959).

Having met with considerable success, Bowles published much during these years. Among the poems added to later editions of his sonnets, for example, were humanitarian verses on John Howard, slavery, and the American Indian. His *Verses on the Benevolent Institution of the Philanthropic Society* (1790) furnished the epigraph to Southey's "Botany Bay Eclogues" (written in 1794). Bowles's *Elegy Written at the Hot-Wells, Bristol* was translated into French by Madame de Staël, who also admired his sonnets and *The Spirit of Discovery*. Both *Elegy Written at the Hot-Wells, Bristol* and *Monody, Written at Matlock* continued the strain of poetic

melancholy that Bowles inherited from Thomas Gray and then applied to Romantic settings. He also wrote elegiac tributes to fellow clergymen during these years, as well as melancholy reflections occasioned by his own serious illness in December, 1795, from which the allegorical poem called *Hope* resulted. Writing to John Thewall in November, 1796 (the poem had actually appeared a few weeks before the year of its imprint), Coleridge found *Hope* to be a poem "without plan or meaning, but the component parts are divine." In addition to Bowles's own sickness, there had been that of Harriet Wake, his fiancé, who died a year following their engagement, in 1793. In 1797, Bowles married Magdeline Wake, his dead fiancé's younger sister.

Though his influence on Coleridge's circle was now waning (Coleridge's visit that year had been disillusioning), Bowles came before the public as an established author, producing a series of longer poems: *Hope* in 1796; *Coombe Ellen* and *St. Michael's Mount* in 1798; *Song of the Battle of the Nile* in 1799; the seventh edition of his *Sonnets* (including *Hope* and a preface), in 1800; *The Sorrows of Switzerland* in 1801; *The Picture* in 1803; and *The Spirit of Discovery* in 1804. It was a remarkably prolific sequence of now-forgotten poems.

In 1804 Bowles was appointed vicar at Bremhill, Wiltshire, where he continued to live for most of his remaining years. He was also appointed prebendary of Salisbury Cathedral and spent some time there every year. Bowles's sonnets continued to be popular, and he published yet another long poem in an eighteenth century mode (*Bowden Hill*) but quickly gained a new and more controversial reputation with his ten-volume edition of Pope and his essay on Pope's "Poetical Character" in 1806. His views on Pope were criticized in the *Edinburgh Review* of January, 1808, and Lord Byron (influenced by the review) satirized Bowles in the anonymous first edition of *English Bards, and Scotch Reviewers* (1809), though John Cam Hobhouse wrote the actual lines on Bowles. In the acknowledged second edition (1809) Byron substituted lines of his own on Bowles, castigating him for opposing Pope, ridiculing his long poems ("Stick to thy sonnets, man!—at least they sell"), and jibing erroneously at an episode from *The Spirit of Discovery*, a poem which Byron had not seen at firsthand, as he admitted to Bowles three years later. Relations after 1812 were cordial, and Bowles even proposed that Byron add some lines (he did not) to Bowles's forthcoming long poem *The Missionary*. This latest effort, though it had four editions, was dismissed by George Daniel in *The Modern Dunciad* (1814): "While Bowles exists," he asked, "can satire want a dunce?" Similarly, John Hamilton Reynolds characterized Bowles as a gabbling goose in *The Champion* of April 7, 1816, and Bowles's outraged reply of May 12 did nothing to improve his reputation. That same year Coleridge visited Bowles at Bremhill and had the temerity to correct his poems, for which he was hardly forgiven. The public, it seemed, had tired of Bowles and his evangelistic inanities.

Nevertheless, it was Coleridge who paid Bowles the tribute that immortalized him in literary history. In Chapter 1 of *Biographia Literaria*, Coleridge specifically recalled his first acquaintance with Bowles's sonnets in 1789 and how, with almost equal delight, he later read three or four more publications by the same author, including *Monody, Written at Matlock* and *Hope*. Bowles and Cowper were, for Coleridge, "the first who combined natural thoughts with natural diction; the first who reconciled the heart with the head." Coleridge also stated that Bowles's works "were of great advantage in the formation and establishment of my taste and critical opinions." Thus was the Wiltshire poet defended against his critics. Though later ones have often found Coleridge's enthusiasm for Bowles inexplicable, his words are clear enough. Perhaps some of Coleridge's generosity toward Bowles reflected the assistance that Bowles had given him (through Byron) toward the publication of *Sibylline Leaves* (1817).

After 1817, Bowles was closely associated with Thomas Moore, of Sloperton Cottage (a three-hour walk from Bremhill), who has left a fine record of Bowles's eccentricities. In February, 1818, for example, Moore and his wife spent three or four days with Bowles at Bremhill and observed: "What an odd fellow it is! and how narrowly, by being a *genius*, he has escaped being set down for a *fool*!" But, Moore went on, "he is an excellent creature notwithstanding." That September, Moore praised Bowles in his diary as a delightful "mixture of talent and simplicity," then repeated his earlier opinion about Bowles's poetry almost word for word.

That October, as well, Bowles seemed to Moore "the most delightful of all existing parsons or poets," for all his genius and blundering alike. There are brief glimpses in Moore also of Louisa Stuart Costello (1799-1877), the artist and poet whom Bowles had taken as his protégé. She is best known in literary history for *Songs of a Stranger* (1825), which was dedicated to Bowles. Her *Specimens of the Early Poetry of France* (1835) was dedicated to Moore.

The controversy over Pope began in earnest in 1819, when Thomas Campbell's *Specimens of the English Poets* appeared, championing Pope. Bowles immediately replied with a pamphlet essay on "The Invariable Principles of Poetry" (1819) addressed specifically to Campbell, whose remarks on Pope had been excerpted by the *Morning Chronicle* as an answer to Bowles. Bowles's pamphlet, originally intended as a public letter to Moore, was supposedly dictated by its author to a waiter in the bar of the White Hart pub, Salisbury. In all, Bowles wrote six pamphlets pertaining to the Pope controversy, two of them in response to letters from Byron. J. J. Van Rennes has listed twenty-nine publications generated by the controversy as a whole.

In the thirty years remaining to him, Bowles published six more volumes of poetry, including *The Grave of the Last Saxon, Ellen Gray, Days Departed, St. John in Patmos, Scenes and Shadows* (with an autobiographical fragment), and, for children, *The Little Villager's Verse Book*; none, except perhaps the last, had enduring merit. His more important medium in his later years was prose, and his most characteristic product the sermon. However welcome they may have been as guidance, Bowles's sermons seem not to have had more than local impact. Bowles remained productive until 1844, when the death of his wife crushed him. In January, 1845, he resigned his vicarate at Bremhill and retired to Salisbury, where he endured five years of senile helplessness until his death on April 7, 1850.

ANALYSIS

SONNETS

William Lisle Bowles was, with Thomas Warton and Charlotte Smith, among those who in the late eighteenth century sought to revive the sonnet form. His own sonnets are particularly noteworthy for their responsiveness to landscape. Their diction was influential, though less original than one might think, as some investigation of late eighteenth century descriptive poetry and the picturesque travel effusions of William Gilpin (1724-1804) confirm. If Bowles borrowed from other writers, however, greater writers borrowed from him. Thus, "To the River Wensbeck" is echoed by Samuel Taylor Coleridge in "Kubla Khan" and "Dejection: An Ode" (line 96). Similarly, Bowles's sonnet "To the River Itchin" influenced Coleridge's "To the River Otter," and his poem "On Leaving Winchester School" probably inspired two similar poems, "Sonnet: On Quitting School for College" and "Absence. Farewell Ode on Quitting School for Jesus College, Cambridge," by the better poet. Though ostensibly dated 1788, Coleridge's "Sonnet: To the Autumnal Moon" is almost surely an imitation of Bowles, just as Coleridge's "Anthem for the Children of Christ's Hospital" is an adaptation of Bowles's "Verses on the Philanthropic Society." Coleridge's sonnet "Pain" should also be compared with Bowles's sonnet XI, "At Ostend," to which it is indebted. Coleridge was not only indebted to Bowles for imagery, phrases, and subjects, but for attitudes as well. Thus, Bowles's early poems are topographical and melancholic, with time his major theme. He then moved toward more outgoing, humanitarian utterances and eventually to public manifestos full of noble sentiments but of no other lasting interest.

In Bowles's later sonnets, written after 1789 (when John Milton's influence on him became more evident), the diction is less stilted and of some historical importance. Sonnets XXIII to XXVII, for example, probably influenced William Wordsworth's "Tintern Abbey," which specifically echoes XXVII ("On Revisiting Oxford"). Sonnets XX and XXII anticipate the imagery of Percy Bysshe Shelley. Bowles was among the first of the minor descriptive poets to abandon much of eighteenth century diction in favor of a fresher, more experiential imagery, even if his own was weak, occasionally trite, moralistic, and too often encumbered by personification. Granting that Bowles failed to achieve poetry of lasting distinction himself, his own work still pointed toward the heights that Wordsworth and Coleridge achieved. While Wordsworth's pronouncements in his preface to *Lyrical Ballads* (the edition of 1800) do not always re-

flect his own poetic practices, they are surprisingly like a pro-and-con discussion of Bowles.

MONODY, WRITTEN AT MATLOCK

Unfortunately, Bowles failed to develop as a poet beyond the promise of his later sonnets. His longer and more pretentious poems attracted readers in their day, but now seem disappointingly flat. Among the best of them is *Monody, Written at Matlock*, which was a favorite with Coleridge. In it, an eighteenth century mind saturated with the melancholy of Thomas Gray confronts the Romantic landscape of the peak. Though a monody is normally a lament or dirge, often about another poet's death, it is hard to see what Bowles had to be so gloomy about, as there seems to be little connection between the landscape and his reflections, which are the expected ones of a poet revisiting a scene of his youth. There is, however, no better poem to compare with Wordsworth's "Tintern Abbey" to help one see both the conventionality and the originality of Wordsworth's masterpiece.

THE PICTURE

A second longer poem of interest is *The Picture*, which (like Wordsworth's "Elegiac Stanzas") is based on a painting owned by Sir George Beaumont—in this case, a landscape by Peter Paul Rubens. Compared with Bowles's sonnets, *The Picture* already seems heavy-handed and regressive. It is still an interesting attempt at landscape aesthetics, however, and gathers within a single poem many of Bowles's characteristic pieties. Finally, there are good things in both *Coombe Ellen* and *St. Michael's Mount*, though the poems are overly long, easily outrunning their inspiration. Even at this early date, Bowles had begun to display his characteristic faults of insipidity, loquaciousness, and unoriginality.

THE SPIRIT OF DISCOVERY

Bowles's longest poem (in five books) is *The Spirit of Discovery*, which, beginning with Noah, moves from the Egyptians, the Phoenicians, the Babylonians, and the Greeks to the discoveries of Columbus and Captain Cook. An appended prose analysis sufficiently describes the poem, which is a curious mixture of heroic aspiration and credulity. While several of the Romantic poets, including Southey and Rogers, were attracted to Columbus and the age of exploration, only Coleridge (who preceded all of them) created major poetry on the theme, with *The Rime of the Ancient Mariner* (1798). Bowles's *The Spirit of Discovery*, with all its length and notes, is a pretentious failure, as were his works that followed. The only other work requiring mention is *The Missionary*, a long poem in eight cantos about Spaniards and Indians in South America; showing the influence of Wordsworth, Robert Southey, and Sir Walter Scott, it involved some new techniques and was popular for a time.

OTHER MAJOR WORKS

PLAY: *The Ark: A Dramatic Oratorio*, pb. 1824.

NONFICTION: Pamphlets on the Pope controversy, 1819-1826; *Illustrations of Those Stipendous Monuments of Celtic Antiquity Avebury and Silbury, and Their Mysterious Origin Traced*, 1827; *Hermes Britannicus*, 1828; *The Parochial History of Bremhill*, 1828; *The Life of Thomas Ken, D.D.*, 1830; *Annals and Antiquities of Lacock Abbey*, 1835; sermons and pamphlets on religious controversies, various dates, to 1838; *A Wiltshire Parson and His Friends: The Correspondence of William Lisle Bowles*, 1926 (Garland Greever, editor).

BIBLIOGRAPHY

Little, Geoffrey, and Elizabeth Hall. "Coleridge's 'To the Rev. W. L. Bowles': Another Version?" *The Review of English Studies: A Quarterly Journal of English Literature and the English Language* 32 (May, 1981): 193-196. This fine assessment of Bowles's poetry offers an illuminating overview of Bowles's poetic development.

Modiano, Raimonda. "Coleridge and Wordsworth: The Ethics of Gift Exchange and Literary Ownership." *The Wordsworth Circle* 20 (Spring, 1989): 113-120. In this comprehensive essay, Modiano provides informative coverage of English literature from 1800 to 1899 and examines the views of Coleridge, Wordsworth, and Bowles.

Rennes, Jacob Johan van. *Bowles, Byron, and the Pope-Controversy*. New York: Haskell House, 1966. Bowles, who is referred to here as a "sonneteer of no mean deserts," edited a volume of Alexander Pope's works. In his edition, Bowles criticized Pope, which prompted George Gordon, Lord Byron to leap to his defense. This volume chronicles the correspondence that surrounded this controversy and provides useful background of Bowles and his contemporaries.

Vinson, James, ed. *Great Writers of the English Language*. 3 vols. New York: St. Martin's Press, 1979. The entry on Bowles, by Tony Bareham, calls him a second-rank poet, without much individuality. Nevertheless, he acknowledges that Bowles was carefully competent with an eye for details, and notes the popularity of *Fourteen Sonnets*, which restored dignity to a verse form that had been "neglected for the last two generations."

Wu, Duncan. "Wordsworth's Readings of Bowles." *Notes and Queries* 36 (June, 1989): 166-167. A perceptive and thorough reading of Bowles's poetry makes this essay worth consulting. Central to an appreciation and understanding of Bowles's imagination.

Dennis R. Dean

ANNE BRADSTREET

Born: Northampton, England; 1612(?)

Died: Andover, Massachusetts Bay Colony; September 16, 1672

PRINCIPAL POETRY

The Tenth Muse Lately Sprung Up in America: Or, Several Poems Compiled with Great Variety of Wit and Learning, Full of Delight, 1650, revised and enlarged 1678 (as *Several Poems Compiled with Great Variety of Wit and Learning, Full of Delight*)

OTHER LITERARY FORMS

Anne Bradstreet's published collection of 1650 and its revised edition of 1678 consist entirely of poetry, and her reputation rests on her poems. She left in manuscript the prose "Meditations Divine and Morall" (short, pithy proverbs) and a brief autobiography written especially for her children.

ACHIEVEMENTS

Anne Bradstreet and Edward Taylor are the two foremost Colonial American poets. They form a classic study in contrasts: She was emotional, he cerebral; she secular, he spiritual; she feminine, he masculine; she stylistically straightforward, he complex; she generically varied, he generically limited; she well known by her contemporaries, he little known until the twentieth century. These are only generalizations; however, they suggest a special problem that Bradstreet criticism has overcome: the inability to divorce her work from biographical, historical, and personal elements.

One of Bradstreet's distinctive poetic strengths is her generic variety. She wrote epics ("The Four Monarchies" and the "Quaternions"), dialogues ("A Dialogue Between Old England and New," among others), love lyrics, public elegies (on Sir Philip Sidney, Guillaume de Salluste Du Bartas, and her parents, for example), private elegies (on her grandchildren and daughter-in-law), a long meditative poem ("Contemplations"), and religious verse. Few other Puritan poets successfully tackled so many genres.

Although Bradstreet's contemporaries admired her early imitative poetry ("The Four Monarchies," the "Quaternions," and the elegies on Sidney, Du Bartas, and Queen Elizabeth I), her later personal poetry is what endures (and endears). Poems included in *The Tenth Muse Lately Sprung Up in America* fall within an essentially Renaissance tradition, while those in *Several Poems Compiled with Great Variety of Wit and Learning, Full of Delight* initiate a distinctive tradition of *American* literature. Bradstreet's love poems to her husband are admired for their wit, intricate construction, emotional force, and frank admission of the physical side of marriage: As she says in "To my Dear and Loving Husband," "If ever two were one, then surely we./ If ever man were lov'd by wife, then thee." Bradstreet's personal elegies on her grandchildren skillfully dramatize the Puritans' unremitting battle between worldliness (grieving for the dead) and unworldliness (rejoicing in their salvation). However, her masterpiece is probably her long meditative poem "Contemplations," praised for its maturity, complexity, and lyricism. Her love poems, personal elegies, and "Contemplations" reveal the human side of Puritanism from a woman's vantage point.

BIOGRAPHY

Through her poetic voices, Anne Bradstreet assumes a clear (but complex) presence, yet factual data about her are surprisingly scant. Joseph McElrath, editor of *The Complete Works of Anne Bradstreet* (1981), shows that even her birth date is uncertain. She was probably born in 1612 in Northampton, England, but may have been born as late as 1613, one of Thomas Dudley and Dorothy Yorke's six children.

In 1619 the family moved to Sempringham, where Dudley became steward to the earl of Lincoln. Both Thomas Dudley and his employer allowed the prospective poet an unusually good education for a woman. Scholars even speculate that she had access to the earl's library. There she may have read staples of humanism: William

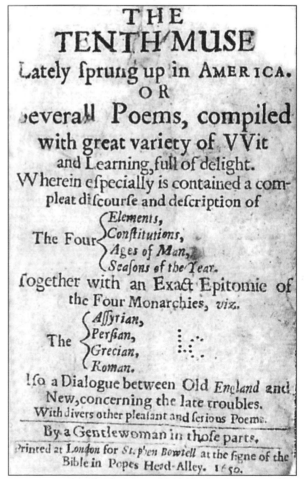

The title page from Anne Bradstreet's The Tenth Muse, *published in 1650.*
(Library of Congress)

Shakespeare, Sir Philip Sidney, Sir Walter Ralegh, Du Bartas, and Cervantes. In 1621, Simon Bradstreet joined the earl's household to assist Dudley; but in 1624, the Dudleys moved to Boston, England, and Simon Bradstreet left to work for the countess of Warwick.

When the poet was about sixteen, as she records in her autobiographical prose, "the Lord layd his hand sore upon me & smott mee with the small pox." After her recovery in 1628, she and Simon Bradstreet married, and two years later, the Dudley and Bradstreet families left for America aboard the *Arbella*.

For Anne Bradstreet, the transition was not entirely smooth, and her prose autobiography speaks of "a new World and new manners at which my heart rose. But after I was convinced it was the way of God, I submitted to it & joined to the chh., at Boston." After brief spells in Salem, Boston, Cambridge, and Ipswich, the Bradstreets moved to North Andover, Massachusetts Bay Colony, where Anne Bradstreet reared eight children, wrote, and shared her husband's life as he rose from judge to governor of the colony. Although the poet was susceptible to many illnesses and was childless for several years, her supremely happy marriage compensated for, and helped her to overcome, these "trials."

As the governor's wife, Bradstreet enjoyed a socioeconomic status conducive to writing. In the mid-1640's, Bradstreet had completed the poems which appeared in her first collection. Bradstreet herself did not supervise their printing; John Woodbridge, her brother-in-law, probably carried the manuscript to London, where it was published in 1650. Bradstreet expresses mixed feelings about its publication, largely because of the printing errors. The poem "The Author to Her Book" mildly chides "friends, less wise than true" who exposed the work "to publick view." Poems in the collection are mainly public in tone and content, while those in her second collection (published posthumously in 1678) are mainly private and personal.

Bradstreet was a known, respected, and loved poet in both the Old and New Worlds. Her death in 1672 called forth elegies and eulogies. These lines from the preface to *The Tenth Muse Lately Sprung Up in America*, probably written by Woodbridge, best convey Bradstreet's qualities: "It is the Work of a Woman, honoured, and esteemed where she lives, for her gracious demeanour, her

eminent parts, her pious conversation, her courteous disposition, [and] her exact diligence in her place."

ANALYSIS

Anne Bradstreet wrote poetry from the 1640's to her death in 1672. Naturally, her work developed and deepened over this thirty-year period. The critic Kenneth Requa's distinction between her public and private poetic voices (in "Anne Bradstreet's Poetic Voices," *Early American Literature*, XII, 1977) is a useful way to assess her poetic development. Her public voice, which dominates the early poetry, is eulogistic, imitative, self-conscious, and less controlled in metaphor and structure. Most of the poems in *The Tenth Muse Lately Sprung Up in America* illustrate these traits. Her private voice—more evident in *Several Poems Compiled with Great Variety of Wit and Learning, Full of Delight*—is often elegiac, original, self-confident, and better controlled in metaphor and structure. Any attempt to divide Bradstreet's work into phases has its dangers. Here, however, it is convenient to consider representative elegies from three roughly chronological stages: "poetic" involvement, conventional involvement, and personal involvement.

FIRST PHASE

Almost all the verse in her first collection conveys Bradstreet's public, poetic involvement. Specifically, in secular poems such as the "Quaternions," "The Four Monarchies," and the elegies on famous Elizabethans, Bradstreet as professional poet or bard dominates and controls. "In Honour of Du Bartas" (1641) contains the typical Renaissance characteristics of public content, imitative style, classical allusions, and secular eulogy. The poem's content could hardly be more public, since it dutifully details the accomplishments of Bradstreet's mentor Du Bartas—his learning, valor, wit, and literary skill. Although Bradstreet contrasts her meager poetic powers with Du Bartas's unlimited powers, her involvement is not personal; rather, it eventually points a favorite moral for Renaissance poets. No matter how bad the writer, the dead person (in this case a poet, too) will "live" in the poem's lines. The "Quaternions"—a quartet of long poems on the four elements, the four humors, the four ages of man, and the four seasons—and the interminable rhymed history "The Four Monarchies" are similarly public in content.

An extension of public content and bardic involvement is imitative style. For example, "In Honour of Du Bartas" contains conventional images like the simile comparing Bradstreet's muse to a child, the hyperbole declaring that Du Bartas's fame will last "while starres do stand," and the oxymoron in "senslesse Sences." Although Bradstreet's early imitative style is skillful, it hinders her from expressing the unique voice of her later work. Furthermore, tradition compels her to scatter her public poems with classical allusions. In the three elegies on Du Bartas, Sidney, and Queen Elizabeth I, these allusions are a conventional part of the Renaissance pastoral elegy, and in the "Quaternions" they imitate the medieval/Renaissance debates.

Finally, these lengthy early poems may contain secular eulogy, also a characteristic of the pastoral elegy, and hyperbole, common in the debate form. The opening lines of "In Honour of Du Bartas," for example, state that Du Bartas is "matchlesse knowne" among contemporary poets. In such a richly literary age, Bradstreet obviously uses hyperbole and eulogy to emphasize Du Bartas's greatness for her.

SECOND PHASE

The second phase—conventional involvement—includes religious poems within a public or orthodox context. In many ways this is a transitional voice, for some poems recall the imitativeness and bardic self-consciousness of the first phase, while others anticipate the domestic content and individual voice of the third phase. A few poems (such as "David's Lamentations for Saul" and "Of the vanity of all worldly creatures") are from *The Tenth Muse Lately Sprung Up in America*; more are from her second collection (the elegies on Thomas and Dorothy Dudley and "The Flesh and the Spirit," for example). In this poetry, Bradstreet moves closer to mainstream Puritan verse. The elegies on her parents are conventionally formal and fit the pattern of the New England funeral elegy, whose hallmark was public praise of the dead one's life and virtues to overcome personal grief. "The Flesh and the Spirit," "As weary pilgrim now at rest," and "Of the vanity of all worldly creatures" treat the theme of worldliness versus unworldliness generally and impersonally to reach orthodox conclusions.

Bradstreet's elegy on her father, "To the memory of my dear and ever honoured Father Thomas Dudley," begins with an apparently personal touch: Bradstreet's claim to write from filial duty, not custom. Even so, as she reminds her readers, this filial duty allows her to praise her father's virtues fully and publicly, not partially and privately. In later elegies, Bradstreet does not explain so defensively why she follows certain conventions; indeed, she frequently modifies or ignores them. In this early elegy, however, these conventions constrain Bradstreet's own voice so that she writes forced lines such as these: "In manners pleasant and severe/ The Good him lov'd, the bad did fear,/ And when his time with years was spent/ If some rejoyc'd, more did lament." Lacking are the emotional force, personal involvement, and dramatic struggle between flesh and spirit found in the later poems.

Another characteristic apparent in the second phase is Bradstreet's use of fairly standard poetic structure. "The Flesh and the Spirit," for example, is in dialogue/debate form, while "As weary pilgrim, now at rest" and "Of the vanity of all worldly creatures"—both meditations—examine the battle between body and soul to attain the eternal peace that only Christ's love will bring. "David's Lamentations for Saul" is a versified retelling of the scriptural story. Bradstreet's epitaphs on her mother and father, as already stated, follow the form of the Puritan elegy.

Standard, often biblical, imagery is another distinct aspect of the second phase. While this imagery is to some extent present in the earlier and later phases, it is particularly evident in the middle stage. In the first stage, Bradstreet's images are traditionally Renaissance, and in the third stage, they are biblical but infused with emotive and personal force. The elegy on Thomas Dudley illustrates the traditionally biblical images found in phase two: Dudley has a "Mansion" prepared above; and, like a ripe shock of wheat, he is mown by the sickle Death and is then stored safely. The other orthodox poems also use biblical images almost exclusively.

Appropriately, in these poems, Bradstreet generally excludes the personal voice. Only "As weary pilgrim, now at rest," the theme of which is the heaven-bound soul housed within the "Corrupt Carcasse," succeeds in combining the general and individual situations. Universality and individuality form the special strength of Bradstreet's masterpiece, "Contemplations." This thirty-three-verse meditative poem fits best into the second stage because of its spiritual content. Given the poem's importance, however, it must be discussed separately. Bradstreet skillfully evokes a dramatic scene—she walks at dusk in the countryside—then uses it to explore the relationships among man, God, and nature.

In stanzas one to seven, the poet acknowledges nature's potency and majesty by looking first at an oak tree and then at the sun. If they are glorious, she muses, how much more glorious must their creator be? Stanzas eight to twenty recall man's creation and fall, extending from Adam and Eve to Cain and Abel and finally to Bradstreet's own day. The answer to man's misery, however, is not nature worship. Instead, man must acknowledge that God made him alone for immortality. In stanzas twenty-one to twenty-eight, the poet considers the amoral delight of nature—the elm, the river, the fish, and the nightingale—incapable of the tortures of free will. Stanzas twenty-nine to thirty-three show that beyond the natural cycle, only man ("This lump of wretchedness, of sin and sorrow," as the poet states) can be resurrected within the divine cycle.

"Contemplations" contains some of Bradstreet's most original and inspired poetry within the three-part structure of the seventeenth century meditation. These parts correspond to the mental faculties of memory, understanding, and will. In the first part, the person creates or recalls a scene; in the second part, he analyzes its spiritual significance; and last, he responds emotionally *and* intellectually by prayer and devotion. Clearly, these are the three basic structural elements of "Contemplations." Although Bradstreet ultimately returns to orthodoxy, this poem is no mere religious exercise; it is "the most finished and musical of her religious poems."

THIRD PHASE

The third phase of Bradstreet's poetry includes love lyrics, elegies on grandchildren and a daughter-in-law, and other works inspired by private matters (the burning of Bradstreet's house, the publication of her first collection, the poet's eight children). Yet, unlike the poems of the previous stage, which are overwhelmingly spiritual, the poems of the third phase are primarily secular. If they deal with religious matters—as the elegies do, for example—it is within a personal context. One critic calls Bradstreet "the worldly Puritan," and these late poems show the material face of Puritanism. Bradstreet's personal involvement affects structure, tone, rhythm, and metaphor. "In memory of my dear grand-child Elizabeth Bradstreet" illustrates many of these changes.

Because she was more comfortable writing of private matters in a private voice, Bradstreet's poetic structure arises naturally from content and context. The elegy on Elizabeth, for instance, divides into two seven-line stanzas (it is a variation of the sonnet form). In stanza one, the poet says farewell to her grandchild and questions why she should be sad since little Elizabeth is in Heaven. In stanza two, Bradstreet explains that nature's products perish only when they are ripe; therefore, if a newly blown "bud" perishes, it must be God's doing. The structure aptly complements the poet's grief, disbelief, and final resignation. Both stanzas effortlessly follow the rhyme scheme *ababccc*. Bradstreet's love poems are also constructed in an intricate but uncontrived way. Both poems titled "Another [Letter to Her Husband]" show careful attention to structure. The first poem of this title personifies the sun and follows the sun's daily course; the second ties together three images and puns suggesting marital harmony (*dear/deer, heart/hart*, and *hind/hind*).

A marked difference in the poetry of the third phase is its tone. Instead of sounding self-conscious, bookish, derivative, overambitious, or staunchly orthodox, Bradstreet's later poetry is poised, personal, original, modest, and unwilling to accept orthodoxy without question. Another tonal change is subtlety, which the elegy on Elizabeth illustrates well. Throughout the poem Bradstreet hovers between the worldly response of grief and the unworldly one of acceptance. This uneasy balance, finally resolved when Bradstreet accepts God's will, makes the elegy especially poignant. The poet's other late elegies on her grandchildren Anne and Simon and her daughter-in-law Mercy are also poignant. The secular love poetry that Bradstreet wrote to her husband—often while he was away on business—conveys playfulness, longing, and, above all, boundless love. The tone of Bradstreet's late poetry tends to be more varied and complex than the tone of her early poetry, the only notable exception being "Contemplations," placed in phase two.

Bradstreet's rhythm reflects her increased poetic self-confidence. Gone are the strained lines and rhythms characteristic of the "Quaternions" and "The Four Monarchies"; instead, the opening lines of Bradstreet's elegy on Elizabeth show how private subject matter lends itself to natural, personal expression: "Farewel dear babe, my hearts too much content,/ Farewel sweet babe, the pleasure of mine eye,/ Farewel fair flower that for a space was lent,/ Then ta'en away unto Eternity." The delicate antithesis in lines one to three and the repetition of "Farewel" add emotional force to the content and emphasize Bradstreet's difficulty in accepting Elizabeth's death. The other late elegies are rhythmically varied and use antithesis to underscore life's ever-present duality: flesh/spirit, worldliness/unworldliness. For example, within the elegy on three-year-old Anne, Bradstreet conveys her problem in coming to terms with yet another grandchild's death when she uses this forced, monosyllabic rhythm, "More fool then I to look on that was lent./ As if mine own, when thus impermanent." The love poetry is also written with special attention to rhythmic variety.

The poet's metaphoric language in the later works is free of bookishness and imitativeness. She does not resort to classical allusions or literary images but chooses familiar, often domestic or biblical, metaphors. In the elegy on Elizabeth, the entire second stanza comprises a series of images drawn from nature. Bradstreet heightens her grandchild's death by saying how unnatural it is compared to the natural cycle of trees, fruit, corn, and grass. The love poetry draws on nature images too—the sun, fish, deer, and rivers, for instance. In her late personal poetry, Bradstreet also feels comfortable using some extended images. "The Author to Her Book," for example, extends the metaphor of Bradstreet's relationship as author/mother to her book/child, while "In reference to her Children, 23 June 1659" humorously compares Bradstreet and her children to a mother hen and her chicks. These images are original in the sense that they arise in an unaffected, apparently spontaneous, way. They are not original in the sense of being innovative.

The elegies on Du Bartas, Thomas Dudley, and Elizabeth Bradstreet are representative of stages in Bradstreet's poetic career. Her poetry has always been known, but now, more than ever, critics agree on her importance as one of the two foremost Colonial poets. Until recently, scholarship focused on biographical and historical concerns. Modern criticism, on the other hand, concentrates on structure, style, theme, and text. This move toward aesthetic analysis has deepened scholarly appreciation of Bradstreet's talent. In addition, the rise of women's studies ensures her place as a significant female voice in American poetry. She has stood the test of time as "a writer of unquestionably major stature."

OTHER MAJOR WORKS

MISCELLANEOUS: *The Complete Works of Anne Bradstreet*, 1981 (Joseph R. McElrath and Allan P. Robb, editors).

BIBLIOGRAPHY

Cowell, Pattie, and Ann Stanford, eds. *Critical Essays on Anne Bradstreet*. Boston: G. K. Hall, 1983. An excellent collection of essays by a variety of Bradstreet scholars. Part 1 includes criticism from the Colonial period to the twentieth century. The essays cover issues as diverse as Bradstreet's role in the American female literary tradition, the role of religion in the poet's life and work, and her inventive use of language.

Hammond, Jeffrey. *Sinful Self, Saintly Self*. Athens: University of Georgia Press, 1993. Solidly grounded in scholarship, this study compares works by Bradstreet, Michael Wigglesworth, and Edward Taylor. Hammond finds unexpected resemblances in the ways in which these three Puritan poets responded to their projected audiences. Clearly written and carefully documented.

Martin, Wendy. *An American Triptych: Anne Bradstreet, Emily Dickinson, Adrienne Rich*. Chapel Hill: University of North Carolina Press, 1984. Examines how the American experience has been transformed in the works of three American women poets. The section on Bradstreet focuses on the relationship between the poet's commitment to the religious values of her culture and her desire to create an alternative vision in her art.

Piercy, Josephine K. *Anne Bradstreet*. New York: Twayne, 1965. This 145-page work attempts to remedy Bradstreet's critical neglect by arguing that her poetry is important not only as a historical phenomenon but also as a real contribution to American literature. Analyzes the effects of Bradstreet's spiritual growth and struggle with orthodoxy in her poetry and prose and outlines the poet's development as a writer from imitative apprenticeship to maturity. Contains extensive notes and a bibliography.

Scheick, William J. *Authority and Female Authorship in Colonial America.* Lexington: University Press of Kentucky, 1998. Scheick searches for aesthetic and thematic dissonance in texts such as Mary English's acrostic poem or Elizabeth Ashbridge's autobiography. The choice of authors spans a provocatively wide sample of women's writing, including Bradstreet's.

Stanford, Ann. *Anne Bradstreet: The Worldly Puritan.* New York: Burt Franklin, 1974. Written as an introduction to the works of Bradstreet. Discusses the body of the author's poetry in the light of the prevailing literary forms and examines how Bradstreet fashioned these forms into a personal voice for argument between the world she knew and the greater world she envisioned. Contains extensive notes, a bibliography, and appendices.

Tyler, Moses C. *A History of American Literature During the Colonial Period.* New York: G. P. Putnam's Sons, 1897. Although the work is dated, Tyler remains one of the best historians and critics of American literature of the colonial period. Tyler is one of the earliest critics to give full recognition to Bradstreet's writing.

White, Elizabeth Wade. *Anne Bradstreet: The Tenth Muse.* New York: Oxford University Press, 1971. Although Bradstreet's writing became the object of increasing interest and discussion in the twentieth century, White maintains that her life and historical background have been neglected. Calls Bradstreet the first resident poet of English-speaking North America and the first significant British poet. In this first full-length biography of Anne Bradstreet, White uses Bradstreet's writings to find a key to unlock her complex personality. Contains numerous illustrations, an appendix, and a bibliography.

K. Z. Derounian;
bibliography updated by the editors

EDWARD KAMAU BRATHWAITE

Born: Bridgetown, Barbados, West Indies; May 11, 1930

PRINCIPAL POETRY

Rights of Passage, 1967
Masks, 1968
Islands, 1969
The Arrivants: A New World Trilogy, 1973 (includes *Rights of Passage*, *Masks*, and *Islands*)
Other Exiles, 1975
Days and Nights, 1975
Black + Blues, 1977
Mother Poem, 1977
Word Making Man: A Poem for Nicólas Guillèn, 1979
Sun Poem, 1982
Third World Poems, 1983
Jah Music, 1986
X/Self, 1987

Edward Kamau Brathwaite

OTHER LITERARY FORMS

Edward Kamau Brathwaite has published scores of books, articles, and reviews as a historian and literary critic. Among his historical studies are *The Development of Creole Society in Jamaica, 1770-1820* (1971), which was his dissertation in college in the sixties, one chapter of which was expanded and published as *Folk Culture of Slaves in Jamaica* (1970); *Contradictory Omens* (1974); *Caribbean Man in Space and Time* (1974); and *History of the Voice* (1984). His historical studies have delineated the historical pressures that have shaped present-day Caribbean life. He is particularly interested in the transmission of African culture to the New World, the "'little' tradition of the ex-slave," and its promise to serve as a "basis for creative reconstruction" in postemancipation, postcolonial Creole society. His literary criticism has sought out the presence of African traditions in Caribbean literature and has helped to develop a vigorous, indigenous school of West Indian criticism. Brathwaite's work as poet, critic, and historian has made available to a wide audience the rich cultural heritage of Caribbean people.

ACHIEVEMENTS

Edward Kamau Brathwaite is one of the most popular and critically acclaimed writers to emerge in the West Indies during the remarkable period in the region's history and literature following World War II. He epitomizes the intensified ethnic and national awareness of his generation of writers—which includes Derek Walcott, Wilson Harris, Michael Anthony, Martin Carter, Samuel Selvon, John Hearne, and Austin Clarke, to name several of the more prominent—whose writing seeks to correct the destructive effects of colonialism on West Indian sensibility.

For his efforts, Brathwaite has earned a number of honors. He won an Arts Council of Great Britain bursary in 1967, a Camden Arts Festival prize in 1967, a Cholmondeley Award in 1970 for *Islands*, a Guggen-

heim fellowship in 1972, a City of Nairobi Fellowship in 1972, the Bussa Award in 1973, a Casa de las Americas Prize for Poetry in 1976, a Fulbright Fellowship in 1982, and an Institute of Jamaica Musgrave Medal in 1983. He is also winner of the prestigious Neustadt International Prize for Literature.

BIOGRAPHY

Lawson Edward Kamau Brathwaite was born in Bridgetown, Barbados, on May 11, 1930, the son of Hilton Brathwaite and Beryl Gill Brathwaite. He enrolled at Harrison College in Barbados, but won the Barbados Scholarship in 1949, enabling him the next year to read history at Pembroke College, University of Cambridge, England. He received an honors degree in 1953 and the Certificate of Education in 1955.

His earliest published poems appeared in the literary journal *Bim*, beginning in 1950. The poems of that decade, some of which are collected in *Other Exiles* and, in revised form, in *The Arrivants*, portray an estranged world fallen from grace, a world that can be redeemed through poetic vision—a creative faith that sustains the more complex fashionings of his later work. Brathwaite shared with other West Indian writers of his generation a strong sense of the impossibility of a creative life in the Caribbean, and the equal impossibility of maintaining identity in exile in England or North America. That crisis of the present he understood as a product of his island's cultural heritage fragmented among its several sources: European, African, Amerindian, and Asian.

His reading of history at Cambridge heightened both his sense of the European culture which had been the dominant official culture of the West Indies and his need to understand the African culture that had come with the slaves on the Middle Passage. His search led him to Africa, where from 1955 to 1962 he served as an education officer in Kwame Nkrumah's Ghana. His career in Ghana (and in Togoland in 1956-1957 as United Nations Plebiscite Officer) provided the historical and local images that became *Masks*, the pivotal book of *The Arrivants*. In Ghana, he established a children's theater and wrote several plays for children (*Four Plays for Primary Schools*, 1961, and *Odale's Choice*, 1962). He married Doris Welcome in 1960, and he has a son, Michael Kwesi Brathwaite.

Brathwaite returned to the West Indies after an exile of twelve years to assume a post as Resident Tutor at the University of the West Indies in St. Lucia (1962-1963) and to produce programs for the Windward Islands Broadcasting Service. His return to the Caribbean supplied the "centre" that his poetry had lacked:

> I had, at that moment of return, completed the triangular trade of my historical origins. West Africa had given me a sense of place, of belonging; and that place . . . was the West Indies. My absence and travels, at the same time, had given me a sense of movement and restlessness—rootlessness. It was, I recognized, particularly the condition of the Negro of the West Indies and the New World.

The exploration of that sense of belonging and rootlessness in personal and historic terms is the motive for Brathwaite's subsequent work in poetry, history, and literary criticism. He began in 1963 as lecturer in history at the University of the West Indies at Kingston, Jamaica; he became a professor of social and cultural history there. He earned his Ph.D. at the University of Sussex in England (1965-1968). His dissertation became *The Development of Creole Society in Jamaica, 1770-1820*, a study of the assimilation of cultures by various groups within the colonial hierarchy.

His poetry continues to explore the cultural heritage of the West Indies in historical and personal terms. During the 1980's Brathwaite continued to produce important literary criticism and poetry collections. The death of Brathwaite's wife, Doris, in 1986 marked a critical juncture in his career. The shock came in the midst of a series of publications that year: a retrospective collection of essays (*Roots: Essays in Caribbean Literature*); a retrospective collection of poems (*Jah Music*); and Doris's own labor of love, the bibliography *EKB: His Published Prose and Poetry, 1948-1986*. Another blow came in 1988, when hurricane Gilbert virtually destroyed Brathwaite's house and buried most of his library in mud, entombing an unequaled collection of Caribbean writing as well as Brathwaite's own papers. Even more harrowing was a 1990 break-in and physical attack against Brathwaite in his Marley Manor apartment in Kingston, Jamaica. These events helped in his decision to leave Jamaica in 1991, when he began his tenure at New York University, teaching comparative literature.

ANALYSIS

Brathwaite's aim, as he has described it, is to "transcend and heal" the fragmented culture of his dispossessed people through his poetry, reexamining the whole history of the black diaspora in a search for cultural wholeness in contemporary Caribbean life. Brathwaite offers his poetry as a corrective to the twin problems of the West Indian: dispossession of history and of language. The West Indian writer labors in a culture whose history has been distorted by prejudice and malice, the modern version of which is the commonplace notion, after James Anthony Froude and V. S. Naipaul, that nothing was created or achieved in the West Indies. The Afro-Caribbean's history is the record of being uprooted, displaced, enslaved, dominated, and finally abandoned. Brathwaite's reclamation of racial pride centers on rectifying the significance of the Middle Passage not as the destroyer but as the transmitter of culture.

The second problem that the writer confronts, that of language, is an aspect of cultural dispossession. The diversity of Creole languages, hybrids of many African and European tongues, reinforces the insularity of the individual and devalues the expressively rich languages that the people use in their nonofficial, personal, most intimate lives. Brathwaite's poems in Bajun dialect extend the folk traditions of Claude McKay and Louise Bennett and ground his work in the lives of the people for and about whom he writes.

The problem of language, however, is not a matter of choosing the Creole over the metropolitan language. It is a deeply political and spiritual problem, since, as Brathwaite writes, it was with language that the slave was "most successfully imprisoned by the master, and through his (mis)use of it that he most effectively rebelled." With nearly all other means of attaining personal liberty denied, the slave's last, irrevocable instrument of resistance and rebellion was language. For Brathwaite, a West Indian writer, Caliban in William Shakespeare's *The Tempest* (1611), written at the beginning of England's experiment in empire, is the archetype of the slave who turns his borrowed language against his master. To turn his instrument of rebellion into one of creation is Brathwaite's task.

"CALIBAN"

Accordingly, in his poem "Caliban" (*The Arrivants*), Brathwaite's persona begins by celebrating the morning of December 2, 1956, the start of the Cuban Revolution, which remains a symbol of self-determination in the region. In the second section of the poem, Brathwaite adapts Shakespeare's "'Ban Ban Caliban,'/ Has a new master" curse-chant to the hold of a slave ship, articulating a spirit of resistance which turns in the final section to an assertion of endurance. At the end of the poem, the slaves' nightly limbo on deck becomes the religious ceremony—the seed of African culture carried to the New World—of the assembled tribes, who are able to raise their ancestral gods and be for the moment a whole people.

NATION LANGUAGE

What he achieves in "Caliban" Brathwaite achieves in his poetry at large: He uses his languages, both Creole and metropolitan English, to define the selfhood of the group in positive terms, contrary to the negations of the colonizers. "Within the folk tradition," Brathwaite writes, "language was (and is) a creative act in itself; the word was held to contain a secret power." His term "nation language" (defined in *History of the Voice*) for the language of the people brought to the Caribbean, as opposed to the official language of the colonial power, has profoundly influenced the theory and criticism of African American literature. Brathwaite continues in *Mother Poem* and *Sun Poem* to explore the resources of both his native Bajun dialect and contemporary standard English. In his poetry, the power of the word is to conjure, to evoke, to punish, to celebrate, to mourn, to love. He uses language boldly as one who seeks its deepest power: to reveal and heal the wounds of history.

Edward Kamau Brathwaite's early poetry in *Bim*, collected later in *Other Exiles*, with its themes of anxiety and alienation, changed under the search for racial and cultural identity while in exile. Brathwaite became surer of his European heritage while he was a student in England and recovered the remnants of his African heritage while working in Ghana. Those two great cultures, in conflict in the New World for the last four centuries, are the forces that shape Brathwaite's personal and racial history and the poetics through which he renders his quest for wholeness.

He is equally indebted to the Euro-American literary tradition through the work of T. S. Eliot and to the Afro-West Indian tradition through the work of Aimé Césaire. Brathwaite draws upon Eliot's musical form in *Four Quartets* (1943) for his own use of musical forms developed in stages of the black diaspora—work song, shanto, shango hymn, spiritual, blues, jazz, calypso, ska, and reggae—for his poetic rendering of historic and lyric moments. He also draws his aesthetic for rendering modern industrial and mercantile society in the United States and the Caribbean from Eliot's *The Waste Land* (1922). From Césaire's *Cahier d'un retour au pays natal* (1968; *Notebook of the Return to My Native Land*, 1995), Brathwaite derives the epic and dialectical structure of his trilogy as well as the surrealistic heightening of language that propels the movement from the reality of the Caribbean as wasteland to the vision of the Caribbean as promised land.

THE ARRIVANTS

That movement can be discerned in the three books of *The Arrivants* through the poet's reconstruction of racial history and his tracing of his personal history. *Rights of Passage*, the first book of the trilogy, contains the restless isolation of his early life in Barbados that sends him into exile in England and Africa, as well as a recollection of the first phase of the black diaspora, the advent of the slave trade and the Middle Passage. The original dispersal of tribes from Ethiopia to West Africa, as well as his own search for his African origins, is the subject of *Masks*. In *Islands*, racial and personal history merge in the exile's return to the West Indies. The fruits of that return will become manifest in his planned second trilogy.

Readers of *The Arrivants* who focus on its historical dimension figure Brathwaite as the epic poet of the black diaspora, while those who focus on the autobiography make him the hero of the poem. Taking both approaches as valid, with the binocular vision that the poem requires, one can see that the central figure of the rootless, alienated West Indian in exile and in search of home is the only possible kind of hero for a West Indian epic. That questing poet's voice is, however, often transformed into the voice of a precolonial African being fired upon by a white slaver; the Rastafarian Brother

Man; Uncle Tom; a *houngan* invoking Legba; or some other historic or mythic figure. Brathwaite's use of personas, or masks, derives equally from the traditions of Greek drama (dramatic monologue) and African religious practice (chant or invocation). One communal soul speaks in a multiplicity of guises, and the poet thereby re-creates not only his own quest as victim and hero but also the larger racial consciousness in which he participates. The poet's many masks enable him to reconstruct his own life and the brutal history that created "new soil, new souls, new ancestors" out of the ashes of the past.

Combining racial history and personal quest in *The Arrivants*, Brathwaite has fashioned a contemporary West Indian myth. It is not the myth of history petrified into "progress" but that of a people's endurance through cycles of brutal oppression. Across centuries, across the ocean, and across the three books of this poem, images, characters, and events overlie one another to defy the myth of progress, leading in the poem only to heaven swaying in the reinforced girders of New York, and to the God of capitalism floating in a soundless, airtight glass bubble of an office, a prisoner of his own creation. For the "gods" who tread the earth below, myth is cyclical, and it attaches them to the earth through the "souls" of their feet in repetitions of exodus and arrival.

The trilogy begins with one tribe's ancient crossing of the Sahara desert, their wagons and camels left where they had fallen, and their arrival at a place where "cool/ dew falls/ in the evening." They build villages, but the cattle towns breed flies and flies breed plague, and another journey begins, for across the "dried out gut" of the riverbed, a mirage shimmers where

> trees are
> cool, there
> leaves are
> green, there
> burns the dream
> of a fountain,
> garden of odours,
> soft alleyways.

This is the repeated pattern of their history: exodus across desert, savanna, ocean; in caravan, ship, or jet

plane; visitations of plague, pestilence, famine, slavery, poverty, ignorance, volcanoes, flood. The promised land is always elsewhere, across the parched riverbed ("Prelude") or in the bountiful fields of England, not in Barbados ("The Cracked Mother").

The connections between history and biography and the difficult process of destroying the colonial heritage in favor of a more creative mode of life are evident in the six poems that constitute the "Limbo" section of *Islands*. In "The Cracked Mother," the first poem of "Limbo," the dissociation of the West Indian's sensibility—regarding attitudes toward self, race, and country—threatens to paralyze the poet's dialectical movement toward a sustaining vision. The poet's rejection of his native land in favor of England is an acceptance of the colonial's position of inferiority. That attitude is instilled in young West Indians, such historians as Walter Rodney, Frantz Fanon, and Brathwaite have argued, by the system of colonial education that taught an alien and alienating value system. The debilitating effects of such an education are the subject of "The Cracked Mother." The three nuns who take the child from his mother to school appear as "black specks . . . / Santa Marias with black silk sails." The metaphor equates the nuns' coming with that of Columbus and anticipates the violence that followed, especially in the image of the nuns' habits as the sails of death ships. With her child gone, the mother speaks in the second part of the poem as a broken ("cracked") woman reduced to muttering children's word-games which serve as the vehicle for her pain:

> See?
> She saw
> the sea . . .
> I saw
> you take
> my children . . .
> You gave your
> beads, you
> took
> my children . . .
> Christ on the Cross
> your cruel laws teach
> only to divide us
> and we are lost.

History provides the useful equation of nuns' habits with sails and the nuns' rosary with the beads that Columbus gave to the inhabitants of his "discovered" lands, but it is Brathwaite's own biography that turns metaphor into revelation in the last two parts of the poem, showing how ruinous the colonial mentality is, even to the point of rejecting the earth under one's feet (another "cracked mother") because it is not England.

Brathwaite's corrective begins in "Shepherd," the second poem of the "Limbo" section. Having recalled the damage of his early education and having felt again some of the old abhorrence of the colonial for himself, the poet returns to the African drumbeats of *Masks* to chant a service of possession or reconnection with the gods of his ancestors. The poet then addresses his peers in proverbs, as would an elder to his tribe:

> But you do not understand.
> For there is an absence of truth
> like a good tooth drawn from the tight skull
> like the wave's tune gone from the ship's hull
> there is sand
> but no desert where water can learn of its loveliness.

The people have gifts for the gods but do not give them, yet the gods are everywhere and waiting. Moving in *Islands* toward the regeneration promised in *Masks*, Brathwaite continues with "Caliban" to explore the potential for liberty inherent in the Cuban Revolution, then moves at the moment of triumph back into the slave ship and the limbo that contained the seeds of African religion and identity.

The "Limbo" section ends with the beautiful poem "Islands," which proposes the alternatives that are always present in every moment of Caribbean history: "So looking through a map/ of the islands, you see/ . . . the sun's/ slums: if you hate/ us. Jewels,/ if there is delight/ in your eyes." The same dichotomy of vision has surrounded every event and personage in the poem, all infolded upon the crucial event of the Middle Passage: Did it destroy a people or create one? Brathwaite's account of the voyage in "New World A-Comin'" promises "new worlds, new waters, new/ harbours" on the one hand, and on the other, "the flesh and the flies, the whips and the fixed/ fear of pain in this chained and welcoming port."

The gods have crossed with the slaves to new soil, and the poet has returned to the origin of his race to discover his communal selfhood in African rite, which requires participation by all to welcome the god who will visit one of them. *The Arrivants* is a long historical and autobiographical poem, and it is also a rite of passage for the poet-priest who invites the god to ride him. Brathwaite's incantatory poems in *Masks* are his learning of the priest's ways, which restores his spirit in *Islands*. The refrain "*Attibon Legba/ Ouvri bayi pou'moi*" (Negus) is the Voodoo *houngon*'s prayer to the gatekeeper god Legba to open the door to the other gods. The prayer is answered in the final poem "*Jou'vert*" ("I Open"), where Legba promises

> hearts
> no longer bound
> to black and bitter
> ashes in the ground
> now waking
> making
> making with their
> rhythms some-
> thing torn
> and new.

MOTHER POEM

In *Mother Poem*, the first book of Brathwaite's planned second trilogy, the central figure is not the restless poet but the mother he has left and returned to, the source of his life. The types of motherhood established in "The Cracked Mother" (*The Arrivants*) are reiterated here as the poet's human mother and his motherland, Barbados. Both "mothers" are established in the first poem, "Alpha," the origin. Barbados is the mother-island of porous limestone (thus absorbing all influence of weather and history), cut by ancient watercourses that have dried up in sterility. Her dead streams can be revived only by the transfigured human mother who "rains upon the island with her loud voices/ with her grey hairs/ with her green love." The transfiguration that occurs in the last lines of the book must wait, however, for the woman to endure the dream-killing, soul-killing life of the island that is dominated by "the man who possesses us all," the merchant, the modern agent of bondage ("name-tracks").

The mother is his victim, no matter whether she "sits and calls on jesus name" waiting for her husband to come home from work with lungs covered with jute from the sugar sacks, or whether she goes out after his death to sell calico cloth, half-soled shoes, and biscuits, or persuades her daughter to sell herself to the man who is waiting: "It int hard, leh me tell you/ jess sad/ so come darlin chile/ leh me tell he you ready you steady you go" ("Woo/ Dove").

She gets no help from her men, who are crippled, destroyed, frightened, or sick from their lives of bondage to the merchant. One man goes to Montreal to work for nine years and sends back nothing ("Woo/ Dove") and another goes to work for life in the local plantation, brings nothing home, and loses three fingers in the canegrinder ("Milkweed"). Nor does she receive comfort from her children, "wearing dark glasses/ hearing aids/ leaning on wine" ("Tear or pear shape"), who were educated by Chalkstick the teacher, a satirical composite of the colonial educator whose job is to see that his pupils "don't clap their hands, shake their heads, tap their feet" or "push bones through each others' congolese nostrils" ("Lix"). Nor does her help come from her sisters ("Dais" and "Nights"), or from her Christianity ("Sam Lord").

Rather, the restoration of her powers as life-giver begins in the guttural, elemental, incantatory uttering of "Nametracks," where, as a slave-mother beaten by her owner, she reminds herself and her huddled children in dark monosyllables like the word-game of "The Cracked Mother" that they will endure while "e di go/ e go di/ e go dead," that despite all his power, he "nevver maim what me." Her eyes rise from the plot of land she has bought with her meager earnings, the land that has sustained her and her children, to the whole island and a vision of revolutionary solidarity with her people: "de merchants got de money/ but de people got de men" ("Peace Fire"). With full realization that her child will be born to the life of "broken islands/ broken homes" ("Mid/Life"), in "Driftwood," the human mother still chooses to suffer the "pour of her flesh into their mould of bone." The poem ends with the mother re-created in clay by the potter who can work again, in stone by the sculptor whose skill has returned, and in her words gathered by the poet as rain gathering in the dry pools flows once more past the ruins of the slave and colonial world, refreshing and renewing the ancient life of the island.

SUN POEM

Brathwaite's second volume on Bajun life moves from *Mother Poem*'s focus on the female characters (and character) of the island to the male principle of the tropical sun and of the various sons of Barbados. The pun of sun/son is derived from a number of historical and mythological associations, including that of Christianity (Brathwaite renames himself Adam as the boy-hero of the poem, and spells the pronoun "his" as "ihs" or Iesu Hominum Salvator) and various African traditions. The sun, for instance, contains "megalleons of light," the invented word associating it with the Egyptian god Ra's sun-ship, the galleons of European explorers, and the enormous nuclear energy that eclipses or perhaps anticipates the holocaust that Western man has in his power. The complexity of the sun/son as controlling metaphor, as it evokes various ethnic and historical images, extends through time and geographic space the significance of the narrative, even as it complements and completes the female principle of *Mother Poem*.

The mythologies evoked in the poem contribute to the meaning of the life of the son Adam, as he begins to understand the West Indian male's sunlike course of ascent, dominance, and descent, played out through the rituals of boyhood games and identity-seeking, adolescence, adult sexual experience, marriage and paternity, and finally death. In an early encounter, Adam wrestles the bully Batto underwater in a life-or-death rite of passage that initiates him into the comradeship of his peers, but which, Brathwaite suggests, fails (as the other games that "had little meaning" fail) to prepare him for the struggles of adult manhood ("Son"). The types of fathers portrayed ("Clips") fall into roles available from Christian, bourgeois, and Rastafarian cultures that are equally dead-ended. These fathers are unable to pass on to their sons any mode of fulfilling identity or action, even as in his soliloquy the father laments his own diminishment, his being displaced as the head of his family by his own son.

The central incidents of Adam's life introduce him to the cares and costs of adulthood. On his Sunday school trip to the Atlantic coast he enters the adult world, in part by hearing the story of Bussa's slave rebellion, a story of the painful price one pays for asserting his personhood ("Noom"). He conducts his courtship of Esse ("Return of the Sun") with a blithe but growing awareness of the consequences of one's sexual life in determining social and political roles ("Fleches"). The death of Adam's grandfather ("Indigone"), the final event in the poem, reveals to him the cyclical nature of manhood in which he begins to locate himself: "and i looked up to see my father's eye: wheeling/ towards his father/ now as i his sun moved upward to his eye." The cultural determinants of dispossession and lack of identity that so condition the natural progress and decline of masculine life are transcended in the poem's ultimate vision of a world capable of beginning anew. The final section ("Son") returns to the cosmic, creative domain of the poem's invocation ("Red Rising"), but with a clarified focus on creation and growth as the first principles of the natural and hence human world. The image of emerging coral returns the reader to the genesis of the island at the beginning of *Mother Poem* ("Rock Seed"), completing the cycle of the poems with the "coming up coming up coming up" of his "thrilldren" to people a world renewed.

MIDDLE PASSAGES

A collection of fourteen poems, *Middle Passages* has a running theme regarding the effects of slavery on Caribbean culture and on the world. The title also seems to evoke the grief caused by his wife's death in 1986, an event he personally referred to as "middle passages" in his book with excerpts from his personal diary, *The Zea Mexican Diary* (1993). Thus the title also suggests a spiritual passage that death entails for both the dead and the living. Journeys, especially those to African roots, is a recurring theme in this volume.

"Columbe" suggests the beauty that Christopher Columbus and his entourage must have discovered upon their arrival in the Caribbean: "Yello pouis/ blazed like pollen and thin waterfalls suspended in the green." Told from the perspective of an island inhabitant watching the arrival, it also asks whether Columbus understood the violence to which his discovery would lead: "But did his vision/ fashion as he watched the shore/ the slaughter that his soldiers/ furthered here?"

Music and musicians are a strong presence in the collection as well. "Duke Playing the Piano at 70" pictures Duke Ellington's wrinkled hands as alligator skins gliding along a keyboard. Brathwaite uses a number of devices to evoke a sense of music to the printed page. Several poems call on the rhythm and cadence of different instruments to heighten the theme at hand: "Flutes" lyrically describes the sounds of bamboo flutes, while "Soweto," written about the Soweto massacre, draws on the rhythm of drums.

The history of violence against Africa plays a dominant role here, as it does in so many of Brathwaite's literary works. "The Visibility Trigger" surveys European history of using guns to kill and subdue Third World peoples. Another, "Stone," is dedicated to Mickey Smith, a poet and political activist who was "stoned to death on Stony Hill, Kingston" in 1983.

OTHER MAJOR WORKS

SHORT FICTION: *DreamStories*, 1994.

PLAYS: *Four Plays for Primary Schools*, pr. 1961; *Odale's Choice*, pr. 1962, pb. 1967.

NONFICTION: *Folk Culture of Slaves in Jamaica*, 1970; *The Development of Creole Society in Jamaica, 1770-1820*, 1971; *Contradictory Omens: Cultural Diversity and Integration in the Caribbean*, 1974; *Caribbean Man in Space and Time*, 1974; *Our Ancestral Heritage: A Bibliography of the Roots of Culture in the English-Speaking Caribbean*, 1976; *Wars of Respect: Nanny, Sam Sharpe, and the Struggle for People's Liberation*, 1977; *Barbados Poetry, 1661-1979: A Checklist*, 1979; *Jamaica Poetry: A Checklist*, 1979; *The Colonial Encounter: Language*, 1984; *History of the Voice: The Development of Nation Language in Anglophone Caribbean Poetry*, 1984; *Roots: Essays in Caribbean Literature*, 1986; *The Zea Mexican Diary*, 1993.

BIBLIOGRAPHY

Brown, Stuart. *The Art of Kamau Brathwaite*. Bridgend, Mid Glamorgan, Wales: Seren, 1995. A book of critical essays that includes some of the most informed and cogent ways to approach Brathwaite's varied body of work. It also has the distinction of looking at most of that corpus, allowing the reader to discover Brathwaite the critic, the historian, the poet, and the essayist.

Gowda, H. H. Anniah. "Creation in the Poetic Development of Kamau Brathwaite." *World Literature Today* 68, no. 4 (Autumn, 1994): 691. The poetry of Kamau Brathwaite is examined. He insists on the sense and value of the inheritance of the West Indies and is keen on discovering the West Indian Voice in creative arts.

McWatt, Mark A. "Edward Kamau Brathwaite." In *Fifty Caribbean Writers*, edited by Daryl Cumber Dance. New York: Greenwood Press, 1986. While this study traces the shift of the West Indies from "wasteland" to "promised land" in Brathwaite's poetry, it more importantly recounts the critical debate over the relative merits of the poetry of Brathwaite and Derek A. Walcott in relation to West Indian society.

Povey, John. "The Search for Identity in Edward Brathwaite's *The Arrivants*." *World Literature Written in English* 27 (1987): 275-289. Povey details both the historical causes of the lack of a coherent regional identity and Brathwaite's exploration of European and African elements that have shaped the region. Povey studies autobiographical aspects of *The Arrivants*, in particular the reversal of the route of the slave trade that Brathwaite's own career has made.

Rohlehr, Gordon. "'Megalleons of Light': Edward Brathwaite's *Sun Poem*." *Jamaica Journal* 16 (1983): 81-87. Rohlehr draws together *Mother Poem* and *Sun Poem* in reading their parallel movements, passages, and themes. Those poems revive the redemptive view of history taken in *The Arrivants*. Rohlehr expertly delineates the patterns of imagery and their thematic relations, particularly in the poem's depiction of the West Indian's distorted self-image and cultural dispossession.

_____. *Pathfinder: Black Awakening in "The Arrivants" of Edward Kamau Brathwaite*. Tunapuna, Trinidad: Gordon Rohlehr, 1981. This lengthy work is an indispensable companion to *The Arrivants*. Rohlehr's commentary is compendious and meticulous. It clarifies what the poem's language and syn-

tax leave obscure to a non-West-Indian reader, and identifies the poem's references unfailingly, including the many musical references that are essential to Brathwaite's technique. Lack of an index, however, hampers efforts to locate specific topics.

Ten Kortenaar, Neil. "Where the Atlantic Meets the Caribbean: Kamau Brathwaite's *The Arrivants* and T. S. Elliot's *The Waste Land*." *Research in African Literatures* 27, no. 4 (Winter, 1996): 15-27. Brathwaite has acknowledged T. S. Eliot as a poetic precursor. Parallels between Brathwaite's trilogy *The Arrivants* and Eliot's *The Waste Land* are examined.

Thomas, Sue. "Sexual Politics in Edward Brathwaite's *Mother Poem* and *Sun Poem*." *Kunapipi* 9 (1987): 33-43. In her seminal feminist reading, Thomas analyzes the sexual politics inherent in the poet's portrayal of, and commentary on, racial and sexual stereotypes. She finds Brathwaite's ideology to be patriarchal, with the liberated husband supplanting the colonizer in a continuing subordination of the West Indian woman.

Torres-Saillant, Silvio. *Caribbean Poetic: Towards an Aesthetic of West Indian Literature*. New York: Cambridge University Press, 1997. The author makes the assertions that there should be a new system of canon formation and that Caribbean discourse in European languages is a discrete entity. Offers scholarly, in-depth studies of Edward Kamau Brathwaite, René Depestre, and Pedro Mir.

Williams, Emily Allen. "Whose Words Are These? Lost Heritage and Search for Self in Edward Brathwaite's Poetry." *CLA Journal* 40 (September, 1996): 104-108. Williams examines the search for identity in Braithwaite's work. She asserts that Brathwaite's poetry moves readers through a world of dichotomized existence brought on by the ravages of European colonization and acts as a song for the disenfranchised.

World Literature Today 68, no. 4 (Autumn, 1994). An entire issue is devoted to an examination of Brathwaite's contribution to the literary world and to West Indies studies.

Robert Bensen,
updated by Sarah Hilbert

BERTOLT BRECHT

Born: Augsburg, Germany; February 10, 1898
Died: East Berlin, East Germany; August 14, 1956

PRINCIPAL POETRY

Hauspostille, 1927, 1951 (*Manual of Piety*, 1966)
Lieder, Gedichte, Chöre, 1934 (*Songs, Poems, Choruses*, 1976)
Svendborger Gedichte, 1939 (*Svendborg Poems*, 1976)
Selected Poems, 1947
Hundert Gedichte, 1951 (*A Hundred Poems*, 1976)
Gedichte und Lieder, 1956 (*Poems and Songs*, 1976)
Gedichte, 1960-1965 (9 volumes)
Poems, 1913-1956, 1976 (includes *Buckower Elegies*)
Bad Time for Poetry: 152 Poems and Songs, 1995

OTHER LITERARY FORMS

A prolific writer, Bertolt Brecht experimented with several literary forms and subjected nearly everything he wrote to painstaking revision. He first became known as a dramatist when he won the distinguished Kleist Prize in 1922 for his plays *Baal* (wr. 1918, pb. 1922; English translation, 1963), *Trommeln in der Nacht* (wr. 1919-1920, pr., pb. 1922; *Drums in the Night*, 1961), and *Im Dickicht der Städte* (pr. 1923; *In the Jungle of Cities*, 1961), and he remains perhaps best known for plays such as *Mutter Courage und ihre Kinder* (1941; *Mother Courage and Her Children*, 1941) and his groundbreaking operas *Die Dreigroschenoper* (1928; *The Threepenny Opera*, 1949) and *Aufstieg und Fall der Stadt Mahagonny* (pb. 1929; libretto; *Rise and Fall of the City of Mahagonny*, 1957). His longer prose works include the novels *Der Dreigroschenroman* (1934; *The Threepenny Novel*, 1937, 1956) and *Die Geschäfte des Herrn Julius Caesar* (1956; the affairs of Mr. Julius Caesar). Brecht also wrote about eighty short stories, as well as essays in his *Arbeitsjournal* (1938-1955, 1973; work journal).

ACHIEVEMENTS

Just as he would have it, Bertolt Brecht remains today a controversial figure. His literary works, his poli-

Bertolt Brecht in 1976. (Hulton Archive)

tics, and his biography spark disagreement, but one thing is clear: Brecht belongs among the great writers of the twentieth century, and certainly among the great modern poets. When Brecht died, Lion Feuchtwanger praised him as the only originator of the German language in the twentieth century.

Brecht was a bit of a showman (he was immediately recognizable in Berlin with his leather jacket, his proletarian cap, and his nickel-rimmed glasses), but he was always more interested in what people thought of his work than in what they thought of him. Eric Bentley, for example, has called Brecht's *Manual of Piety* "one of the best of all books of modern poems." Brecht's initial success on the stage in 1922, the year in which he won the Kleist Prize, was echoed in 1928 with the sensational premiere of *The Threepenny Opera* in Berlin. Toward the end of his life, Brecht was awarded the East German National Prize (1951), the highest distinction conferred by the German Democratic Republic on one of its citizens. In 1954, he became vice president of the East German Academy of Arts. One year before his death, he traveled to Moscow to accept the Stalin Peace Prize.

Without a doubt, Brecht is best known for his concept of the epic theater and his staging and acting technique of *Verfremdung* (alienation). He sought the intellectual rather than the emotional engagement of the audience, and his propensity for didactic structure rather than sentimental discourse is evident in his poetry as well. Brecht embraced Karl Marx's thesis that "it is not a matter of interpreting the world, but of changing it." His anti-Aristotelian theater concentrated on the factual and sober depiction of human and social conflicts, but with humorous alienation and alienating humor. To do serious theater today without acknowledging Brecht in some way is nearly impossible.

An assessment of Brecht's achievements cannot overlook his relation to literary tradition. Brecht "borrowed" freely from his predecessors, and he frequently chose the forms of parody or satire to make his readers aware of historical change and social contradictions. His candid speech did not always win favor: Because of his antiwar poem "Legende vom toten Soldaten" ("Legend of the Dead Soldier"), which was appended to his play *Drums in the Night*, Brecht was high on the Nazis' list of undesirables. It must be ranked among Brecht's accomplishments that, with his pen, he fought doggedly against the forces of evil and injustice which he saw embodied in the figure of Adolf Hitler and in the Nazi regime. The intensity and range of Brecht's voice as an essayist and dramatist have long been recognized; in contrast, because of the publication history of his poetry, it is only since Brecht's death that the power and scope of his lyric voice have begun to be appreciated.

BIOGRAPHY

Eugen Bertolt Friedrich Brecht was born into a comfortable middle-class home. His father, the manager of a paper factory, was Catholic; his mother, Protestant. Brecht was reared in the Lutheran faith. Before long, he turned strongly against religion, but the language of Martin Luther's translation of the Bible continued to influence Brecht throughout his life. A local Augsburg newspaper carried his first poems and essays in 1914, under the pen name "Berthold Eugen." Brecht dropped

the mask in 1916 with the publication of his poem "Das Lied der Eisenbahntruppe von Fort Donald" ("Song of the Fort Donald Railroad Gang"), in the same local paper.

A restless and arrogant student ("I did not succeed in being of any appreciable help to my teachers"), Brecht enrolled in the University of Munich in 1917. There, he claimed to study medicine (as his father wished) and learned to play the guitar (less to his father's liking, no doubt). He completed a brief term of military service in 1918 as a medical orderly in a hospital for patients suffering from venereal disease. (It was in this year that Brecht wrote the "Legend of the Dead Soldier.") In Munich, Brecht soon became more interested in the local cabarets than in the study of medicine. He especially enjoyed the comedian Karl Valentin, who, along with Frank Wedekind, became an important influence on Brecht's literary development. He turned increasingly to literature and began taking seminars at the university with Professor Arthur Kutscher in 1918; he wrote the first version of *Baal* between March and June of the same year. Brecht traveled to Berlin in 1920; the city impressed him, but he returned to Munich after failing to make substantial literary contacts.

Brecht was to make one more trip to Berlin before finally moving there in 1924. From then until 1933, he spent his time in the capital and cultural center of Germany. In 1926, he first became acquainted with the writings of Marx; in its profound impact on his work, Brecht's discovery of Marx could be compared to Friedrich Schiller's reading of Immanuel Kant. At the time, Brecht was working on the play "Wheat" (to be staged by Erwin Piscator), and he wanted to understand how the exchange market worked. In the short run, his effort proved futile: "From every point of view," he wrote, "the grain market remained one impenetrable jungle." The consequences of his study, however, were far-reaching. His planned drama was never completed. Instead, he began to read Marx intensely: "It was only then that my own jumbled practical experiences and impressions came clearly into focus." Brecht's conversion to the principles of communism had begun. What followed in its literary wake were the operas and several strongly didactic plays in the early 1930's. Brecht, the eminent political poet, wisely left Germany on February

28, 1933, the day after the burning of the Reichstag. Several years of exile ensued.

"Changing countries more often than shoes," as Brecht reflected once, he eventually found his way to a place near Svendborg in Denmark, after traveling through Prague, Zurich, Lugano, and Paris. In Denmark, Brecht was—for the time being, anyway—relatively settled. Still, he remained acutely sensitive toward "escape routes" (images of doors are frequent in the poetry of his exile). He traveled to Moscow and New York in 1935, to London in 1936, and to Paris in the next year. With the threat of Nazi invasion looming large, Brecht left Denmark for Sweden in 1939 and settled near Stockholm. Before long, this sanctuary, too, appeared endangered by the Nazis. Brecht fled to the United States in 1941.

Brecht's life in exile, coupled with his fascination for the exotic, drew him in particular to the Chinese poet, Po Chü-yi, whose work he had come to know through the translation of Arthur Waley. In America, Brecht was particularly conscious of his displacement; having settled in Santa Monica near Hollywood, he never felt comfortable in the "tinsel town." His productivity slackened somewhat during his American years, though he collaborated with artists of the stature of Fritz Lang and Charles Laughton. On October 30, 1947, the day after he appeared before the House Un-American Activities Committee, Brecht flew to Paris and shortly thereafter moved to Switzerland.

Brecht's second wife, the accomplished actress Helene Weigel, was an Austrian citizen, and it is most likely for this reason that Brecht acquired Austrian citizenship as well, even though he finally settled in East Berlin in 1949. There, until his death in 1956, Brecht worked with the Berlin Ensemble. Meanwhile, his Austrian citizenship allowed his work to remain accessible to all the German-speaking countries (Brecht was also shrewd about the business and politics of publication). As he wished, Brecht's death was accorded a quiet ceremony. He lies buried in an old cemetery not far from his apartment, near the graves of G. F. W. Hegel and Johann Gottlieb Fichte.

ANALYSIS

It is important to note that Bertolt Brecht's creativity as a poet resulted less from any inclination toward intro-

spection than from his desire to communicate with others. Against the prevailing tone of German poetry in the 1920's, at least as it was represented by Rainer Maria Rilke, Hugo von Hofmannsthal, and Stefan George, Brecht's poetic voice startled and shocked his readers. "These poems [of Rilke and others] tell ordinary people nothing, sometimes comprehensibly, sometimes incomprehensibly," he wrote in his youth. One of Brecht's main objections to this style of poetry was that its sense of artistic order hid rather than disclosed the chaos he saw in modern life. For this reason, Brecht eventually came to see rhyme and rhythm as obstructive and to prefer "Rhymeless Verse with Irregular Rhythms," as the title of an essay in 1939 reads. As basic to Brecht's poems as their consideration of the reader is his notion of functionality. He first articulated this concept in 1927 when asked to judge a poetry contest which had brought more than four hundred entries. Brecht read them all and awarded no prize. Instead, he acknowledged an unsubmitted poem from a little-known writer, appreciating its simplicity, its engaging choice of topics, its melodiousness, and its documentary value. The notion that "all great poems have the value of documents" was central to Brecht's thought. Writing poetry was, for Brecht, no "mere expression," but a "social function of a wholly contradictory and alterable kind, conditioned by history and in turn conditioning it."

Brecht wrote his poems in, as he called it, "a kind of Basic German." His sensitivity for the "gestic" power of language was nurtured by his fondness for Luther's Bible (the term Brecht uses, *Gestus*, is difficult to render adequately in English: John Willet identifies it with "gesture" and "gist," attitude and point). At the root of Brecht's poetry, indeed all of his work, are the notions of clarity ("The truth is concrete" was Brecht's favorite maxim from Hegel) and functionality. Form, of which Brecht was a master and not a slave, was a means toward an end, that being enlightenment. In tracing Brecht's poetic development, one can see how the forms and motifs change against the backdrop of these guiding concepts.

One attribute of the term "gestic" is that of performance. Brecht was always concerned with delivery (it is central to his theory of the epic theater), and his early poetry is characterized by its close links with song. Indeed, most of Brecht's early poems were written to be accompanied by the guitar. Verse and melody often came about simultaneously, the rhythm of the words combining with the flow of the song. It is not surprising that Brecht's early poems acknowledge such traditional forms as legends, ballads, and chronicles. He was aware that no poet who considered himself important was composing ballads at that time, and this fact, too, may have intrigued the young iconoclast. What drew Brecht to these older poetic forms was their attention to adventure, to nature, and to the role of the heroic individual. Brecht rejuvenated a tired literary tradition by turning to the works of François Villon and Rudyard Kipling. Brecht's ballads mark a decisive turning point in the history of that genre.

"SONG OF THE FORT DONALD RAILROAD GANG"

"Song of the Fort Donald Railroad Gang," written in 1916, exhibits Brecht's youthful keenness for the frontier spirit. It relates the struggle and demise of a railroad crew laying track in the wilderness of Ohio. The portrayal of nature as rugged and indifferent marks a distinct switch for Brecht from the mediocre war poems he had been writing earlier. A common denominator, however, was the element of destructive force. This poem leads, step by inevitable step, through six strophes toward the culminating catastrophe. Initially, nature tolerates the intruders, who can be seen as pilgrims of modern progress pitted against the dense forests, "forever soulless." With the onset of torrential rains, the tolerance of nature becomes indifference, but the railroad gang forges on. Striking up a song within a song, they take to singing in the night to keep themselves awake and posted of the dangers posed by the downpour and the swelling waters. For them, escape is not an option. Death simply comes, and comes simply, leaving only the echo of their melody: "The trains scream rushing over them alongside Lake Erie/ And the wind at that spot sings a stupid melody." A stupid melody? What has happened to these modern "heroes"? There are no modern heroes, Brecht answers—and this in the poetic form which traditionally extols them. Brecht debunks their melody, uses the ballad to put an end to the balladesque hero. Death and nature prevail.

"REMEMBERING MARIE A."

Death and nature, along with murder and love, are the elemental themes distinguishing Brecht's early po-

ems. He was wont to treat these perennial subjects, though, in nontraditional ways. He does this with great effect in what is ostensibly a love poem, "Erinnerung an die Maria A." ("Remembering Marie A."), written in 1920 and later included in *Manual of Piety*. It is more lyrical than the balladesque forms Brecht had already mastered, but it does not get lost in sentimentality. Instead, Brecht achieves a parody of the melancholy youth remembering an early love, and in its attitude it is quintessential Brecht. What the speaker in the poem actually recalls is less his "love so pale and silent/ As if she were a dream that must not fade," than it is "a cloud my eyes dwelt long upon/ It was quite white and very high above us/ Then I looked up, and found that it had gone." Not even the woman's face remains present for Brecht's persona, only her kiss, and "As for the kiss, I'd long ago forgot it/ But for the cloud that floated in the sky." The idyllic atmosphere of the first strophe turns out to be nothing but cliché.

What Brecht does with the element of time in this poem is essential to its overall effect. He establishes an internal relationship on three levels: first, the love affair, located in the past; second, the passage of time, the forgetting which wastes all memory; third, the making present, by means of the cloud, that September day long ago. The tension Brecht succeeds in creating between these different levels has ironic consequences. For one, his use of verb tenses renders as present what is actually narrated in the past tense, while the grammatical past tense functions on the level of present time. The hierarchy of experiences is also switched: the backdrop of nature, the embodiment of everything transitory, can be remembered, while the primary experience (or what convention dictates should be the primary experience)—namely, the relationship between the lovers—falls prey to bad memory. Ultimately, it is a poem about the inconstancy of feeling and the mistrust between people which renders meaningful and lasting relationships problematic. It treats an old theme originally; where others write poems directed toward those lovers in the present, those passed away, those absent, or even those expected in the future, Brecht writes of the lover forgotten.

"OF POOR B.B."

"I, Bertolt Brecht, came out of the black forests." So begins Brecht's famous autobiographical poem, "Vom armen B.B." ("Of Poor B.B."), first written in 1922, later revised when he was preparing *Manual of Piety* for publication. It was composed during a period when Brecht had his feet mostly in Augsburg and Munich, but his mind mostly in Berlin. The poem marks a turning point for Brecht. He leaves behind the ballad form and takes up the theme of the city. Nature in the raw yields to the irrepressible life of the big city, although neither locus is ever idealized. Written literally while under way (apparently on a train to Berlin), the poem is about where one feels at home, "one" in this instance being no one but Brecht himself. "In the asphalt city I'm at home," he admits, and he goes on to describe the daily routine of city dwellers, situating himself in their midst: "I put on/ A hard hat because that's what they do./ I say: they are animals with a quite peculiar smell/ And I say: does it matter? I am too." The poem is full of cynicism and despair. The poet admits that he is undependable and remains convinced that all that will remain of the cities is what passed through them—that is, the wind: "And after us there will come: nothing worth talking about." Thematically, the change of emphasis in "Of Poor B.B." prepares the way for later poems. Formally, the delivery of the poem is less dependent upon melody (song) and relies on the premise of conversation between poet and reader.

"IN DARK TIMES"

Brecht's poems of the 1930's reveal a heightened awareness of the function of the poet with regard to his readership. He had made this point quite polemically already in 1927 as the judge of the poetry contest noted above. The poem, he claimed, had functional value. Looking for the functional lyric caused Brecht to seek a new style and idiom. The often-quoted poem "In finsteren Zeiten" ("In Dark Times"), written in 1937 during Brecht's exile in Denmark, attests his self conscious task as responsible poet. Brecht imagines what people will later say about these "dark times." "They won't say: when the child skimmed a flat stone across the rapids/ But: when the great wars were being prepared for." History, in other words, will ride along on the backs of the little people—as Brecht makes clear in "Fragen eines lesenden Arbeiters" ("Questions from a Worker Who Reads")—but what remain visible are only the "great powers." In the face of this adversity, Brecht

remarks with chagrin: "However, they won't say: the times were dark/ Rather: why were their poets silent?"

"BAD TIME FOR POETRY"

Brecht refused to be silent. His "Schlechte Zeit für Lyrik" ("Bad Time for Poetry"), written in 1939, is a personally revealing poem about his own internal struggle to reconcile aesthetic demands with demands of social responsibility: "In my poetry a rhyme/ Would seem to me almost insolent." Still, as Brecht wrote in his essay on poetry and logic, also from the 1930's, "we cannot get along without the concept of beauty." The poem "Bad Time for Poetry" thus concludes:

> Inside me contend
> Delight at the apple tree in blossom
> And horror at the house-painter's speeches.
> But only the second
> Drives me to my desk.

Brecht seldom mentioned Hitler by name, preferring to call him only "the house-painter," ridiculing Hitler's artistic pretentions.

"LEGEND OF THE ORIGIN OF THE BOOK TAO-TÊ-CHING ON LAO-TZÛ'S ROAD INTO EXILE"

To appreciate Brecht's aesthetic sensitivities, one must realize that he saw the felicitous poem as one in which "feeling and reason work together in total harmony." For Brecht, too, there was no distinction between learning and pleasure, and thus a didactic poem was also cause for aesthetic pleasure. The sensual pleasure derived from knowledge is an important aspect of the title figure of Brecht's play *Leben des Galilei* (1943; *The Life of Galileo*, 1960). What to do with knowledge and wisdom was another question which, for Brecht, followed inevitably. He answered it in his poem "Legende von der Entstehung des Buches Taoteking" ("Legend of the Origin of the Book Tao-Tê-Ching on Lao-tzû's Road into Exile") written in 1938 and included in the *Svendborg Poems*.

This poem is a highly successful combination of Brecht's earlier fascination with legends, the ballad-esque narrative, and the aesthetics of functional poetry. It relates the journey of Lao-tzû, "seventy and getting brittle," from his country, where "goodness had been weakening a little/ And the wickedness was gaining ground anew" (a topic of immediate interest to the exile

Brecht). Brecht does not puzzle over Lao-tzû's decision to leave; it is not even an issue. He states simply: "So he buckled his shoe." (One recalls Brecht's line that he had "changed countries more often than shoes.") Lao-tzû needs little for the journey: books, pipe, and bread (note here the relation between knowledge and sensual pleasure). After four days, he and the boy accompanying him come across a customs official at the border: "'What valuables have you to declare here?'/ And the boy leading the ox explained: 'The old man taught'/ Nothing at all, in short." The customs official, however, is intrigued by the boy's modest assertion that the old man "'learned how quite soft water, by attrition/ Over the years will grind strong rocks away./ In other words, that hardness must lose the day.'" The official shouts to them before they are able to move on and requires them to dictate what it was the old man had to say about the water: "'I'm not at all important/ Who wins or loses interests me, though./ If you've found out, say so.'" The old man obliges him ("'Those who ask questions deserve answers'"), and he and the boy settle down for a week, the customs man providing them with food. When the dictation is finally done, "the boy handed over what they'd written./ Eighty-one sayings." This is the wisdom of Lao-Tzû, for which posterity has been grateful, but Brecht is quick to point out that "the honor should not be restricted/ To the sage whose name is clearly writ./ For a wise man's wisdom needs to be extracted./ So the customs man deserves his bit./ It was he who called for it."

Brecht's return to rhyme in this poem is consistent with its ballad form. Where rhyme no longer sufficed for what was to be said, Brecht applied his theory of rhymeless verse with irregular rhythms. He had already used this style occasionally in the 1920's but mastered it fully in the poetry of the 1930's and 1940's; the form corresponded to Brecht's perception of a society at odds with itself, and it dominated his later lyrical writings.

BUCKOWER ELEGIES

Brecht's later poetry tends to be at once more intimate and more epigrammatic than his earlier work. This late style is best illustrated in his last group of poems, the *Buckower Elegien* (*Buckower Elegies*), written in 1953. The poems are concise evidence of Brecht's fascination with the fragmentary nature of the lyric, which he

viewed as an appeal to the reader. Many of the poems mimic the open form of the riddle, with a strong central image, as in "Der Radwechsel" ("Changing the Wheel"). In six brief lines, Brecht observes how a driver changes a wheel. He voices his own dissatisfaction with his course in life ("I do not like the place I have come from./ I do not like the place I am going to"). Brecht characteristically leaves this poem open toward the future: "Why with impatience do I/ Watch him changing the wheel?"

The critic Joachim Müller has written that "In all its phases and in all its forms, Brecht's poetry is neither exclusively subjective confession, nor simply an agitator's call to arms; every confession becomes an appeal to human activity, and every appeal, however it may alienate us by its satire or its polemics, springs from the deep emotion of a rational heart that sees all conditions in the world dialectically and that always sides with what is human against every inhumanity."

OTHER MAJOR WORKS

LONG FICTION: *Der Dreigroschenroman*, 1934 (*The Threepenny Novel*, 1937, 1956); *Die Geschäfte des Herrn Julius Caesar*, 1956.

SHORT FICTION: *Kalendergeschichten*, 1948 (*Tales from the Calendar*, 1961); *Geschichten vom Herrn Keuner*, 1958; *Me-ti: Buch der Wendungen*, 1965; *Prosa*, 1965 (5 volumes); *Collected Stories*, 1998.

PLAYS: *Baal*, wr. 1918, pb. 1922 (English translation, 1963); *Trommeln in der Nacht*, wr. 1919-1920, pr., pb. 1922 (*Drums in the Night*, 1961); *Die Hochzeit*, wr. 1919, pr. 1926 (also known as *Die Keinbürgerhochzeit*; *The Wedding*, 1970); *Im Dickicht der Städte*, pr. 1923 (*In the Jungle of Cities*, 1961); *Leben Eduards des Zweiten von England*, pr., pb. 1924 (with Lion Feuchtwanger; based on Christopher Marlowe's play *Edward II*; *Edward II*, 1966); *Mann ist Mann*, pr. 1926 (*A Man's a Man*, 1961); *Die Dreigroschenoper*, pr. 1928 (libretto; based on John Gay's play *The Beggar's Opera*; *The Threepenny Opera*, 1949); *Aufstieg und Fall der Stadt Mahagonny*, pb. 1929 (libretto; *Rise and Fall of the City of Mahagonny*, 1957); *Das Badener Lehrstück vom Einverständnis*, pr. 1929 (*The Didactic Play of Baden: On Consent*, 1960); *Happy End*, pb. 1929 (lyrics with

Elisabeth Hauptmann); *Der Ozeanflug*, pr., pb. 1929 (radio play; *The Flight of the Lindberghs*, 1930); *Die Ausnahme und die Regel*, wr. 1930, pb. 1937 (*The Exception and the Rule*, 1954); *Der Jasager*, pr. 1930 (based on the Japanese No play *Taniko*; *He Who Said Yes*, 1946); *Die Massnahme*, pr. 1930 (libretto; *The Measures Taken*, 1960); *Die heilige Johanna der Schlachthöfe*, pb. 1931 (*St. Joan of the Stockyards*, 1956); *Der Neinsager*, pb. 1931 (*He Who Said No*, 1946); *Die Mutter*, pr., pb. 1932 (based on Maxim Gorky's novel *Mat*; *The Mother*, 1965); *Die Sieben Todsünden der Kleinbürger*, pr. 1933 (cantata; *The Seven Deadly Sins*, 1961); *Die Horatier und die Kuriatier*, wr. 1934, pb. 1938 (*The Horatians and the Curatians*, 1947); *Die Rundköpfe und die Spitzköpfe*, pr. 1935 (based on William Shakespeare's play *Measure for Measure*; *The Roundheads and the Peakheads*, 1937); *Die Gewehre der Frau Carrar*, pr., pb. 1937 (*Señora Carrar's Rifles*, 1938); *Furcht und Elend des dritten Reiches*, pr. 1938 (*The Private Life of the Master Race*, 1944); *Leben des Galilei*, first version, pr. 1943; second version (in English), pr. 1947; third version (in German), pr. 1955, pb. 1952; third version, pb. 1955, rev. 1957 (*The Life of Galileo*, 1960); *Der gute Mensch von Sezuan*, wr. 1938-1940, pr. 1943 (*The Good Woman of Setzuan*, 1948); *Das Verhör des Lukullus*, pr. 1940 (radio play), pb. 1940 (libretto; *The Trial of Lucullus*, 1943); *Herr Puntila und sein Knecht, Matti*, wr. 1940, pr. 1948 (*Mr. Puntila and His Hired Man, Matti*, 1976); *Der aufhaltsame Aufstieg des Arturo Ui*, wr. 1941, pb. 1957 (*The Resistible Rise of Arturo Ui*, 1972); *Mutter Courage und ihre Kinder*, pr. 1941 (based on Hans Jakob Christoffel von Grimmelshausen's *Der abenteuerliche Simplicissimus*; *Mother Courage and Her Children*, 1941); *Die Gesichte der Simone Machard*, wr. 1941-1943, pb. 1956 (with Feuchtwanger; *The Visions of Simone Machard*, 1961); *Schweyk im zweiten Weltkrieg*, wr. 1941-1943, pb. 1957 (based on Jaroslav Hašek's novel *Osudy dobrého vojáka Švejka ve svetove války*; *Schweyk in the Second World War*, 1975); *Der kaukasische Kreidekreis*, wr. 1944-1945, pr. in English 1948, pb. 1949 (based on Li Hsing-dao's play *The Circle of Chalk*; *The Caucasian Chalk Circle*, 1948); *Die Antigone des Sophokles*, pr., pb.

1948; *Die Tage der Commune*, wr. 1948-1949, pr. 1956 (based on Nordahl Grieg's *Nederlaget*; *The Days of the Commune*, 1971); *Der Hofmeister*, pr. 1950 (adaptation of Jacob Lenz's *Der Hofmeister*; *The Tutor*, 1972); *Turandot: Oder, Der Kongress der Weisswäscher*, wr. 1950-1954, pr. 1970; *Der Prozess der Jeanne d'Arc zu Rouen, 1431*, pr. 1952 (based on Anna Seghers's radio play; *The Trial of Jeanne d'Arc at Rouen, 1431*, 1972); *Coriolan*, wr. 1952-1953, pb. 1959 (adaptation of William Shakespeare's play *Coriolanus*; *Coriolanus*, 1972); *Don Juan*, pr. 1953 (based on Molière's *Don Juan*; English translation, 1972); *Pauken und Trompeten*, pb. 1956 (adaptation of George Farquhar's *The Recruiting Officer*; *Trumpets and Drums*, 1972); *Collected Plays*, pb. 1994.

NONFICTION: *Der Messingkauf*, 1937-1951 (*The Messingkauf Dialogues*, 1965); *Arbeitsjournal*, 1938-1955, 1973 (3 volumes); *Kleines Organon für das Theater*, 1948 (*A Little Organum for the Theater*, 1951); *Brecht on Theatre*, 1964 (John Willett, editor); *Schriften zum Theater*, 1964-1967 (7 volumes); *Tagebücher, 1920-1922*, 1975 (*Diaries, 1920-1922*, 1979); *Letters*, 1990; *Bertolt Brecht Journals*, 1993; *Brecht on Film and Radio*, 2000.

SCREENPLAYS: *Kuhle Wampe*, 1932 (English translation, 1933); *Hangmen Also Die*, 1943; *Das Lied der Ströme*, 1954; *Herr Puntila und sein Knecht Matti*, 1955.

BIBLIOGRAPHY

Bentley, Eric. *Bentley on Brecht*. New York: Applause, 1998. Noted Brecht scholar subsumes two earlier works on the German poet-playwright covering his knowledge of Brecht from 1942-1948. Cogently examines Brecht's stagecraft and dramatic theory, his position as a poet, his influence, and fifteen of his plays (including their production). Contains personal reminiscences and includes an index to Brechtian works and characters and two bibliographies.

Eddershaw, Margaret. *Performing Brecht: Forty Years of British Performance*. London: Routledge, 1996. Analyzes how British performances from the 1950's to the 1990's have been influenced and shaped by Brecht's dramatic theories, his own practice and productions, and changing views of the plays' meanings.

Included are case studies of three 1990's productions.

Esslin, Martin. *Brecht: A Choice of Evils*. London: Methuen, 1984. Valuable early political biography and critical study of the complicated writer, encompassing his relations with the Communist Party and the influence of Marxism in his work. Contains chronology of Brecht's life, descriptive list of his works, and a bibliography.

Fuegi, John. *Brecht and Company: Sex, Politics, and the Making of the Modern Drama*. New York: Grove, 1994. Controversial detailed biography portraying Brecht as an exploiter and stealer of the work of friends, lovers, and collaborators. Fuegi claims much of Brecht's work was contributed by uncredited female collaborators such as writer Elizabeth Haupmann, actress-journalist Ruth Berlau, and actress Grete Steffin. Includes index.

Martin, Carol, and Henry Bial. *Brecht Sourcebook*. London: Routledge, 2000. Collection of protean essays in three sections: Brecht's key theories, his theories in practice, and, most successful, the adoption of his ideas internationally.

Spiers, Ronald. *Bertolt Brecht*. New York: St. Martin's, 1987. A readable reference for students and teachers and a fine guide as to how Brecht's plays worked on stage. Contains material on Brecht's life, his development as a dramatist, and his plays from the 1920's through his major works. Interesting focus on how Brecht's theories have been translated into live theater.

Richard Spuler;
bibliography updated by Christian H. Moe

ANDRÉ BRETON

Born: Tinchebray, France; February 19, 1896
Died: Paris, France; September 28, 1966

PRINCIPAL POETRY
Mont de piété, 1919
Clair de terre, 1923

L'Union libre, 1931 (*Free Union*, 1982)
Le Revolver à cheveux blancs, 1932
L'Air de l'eau, 1934
Fata Morgana, 1941 (English translation, 1982)
Pleine marge, 1943
Young Cherry Trees Secured Against Hares, 1946
Ode à Charles Fourier, 1947 (*Ode to Charles Fourier*, 1970)
Poèmes, 1948
Poésie et autre, 1960
Selected Poems, 1969
Poems of André Breton, 1982 (includes *Free Union*, *Fata Morgana*, and other selected poems)

OTHER LITERARY FORMS

André Breton published many experimental works during his career, some of which were written in collaboration with friends. *Les Champs magnétiques* (1921; magnetic fields), the first Surrealist text to employ the technique of "automatic" writing, was done with Philippe Soupault. *L'Immaculée Conception* (1930; immaculate conception), an attempt to simulate the thought processes of various types of insanity, was written with Paul Éluard. Among the basic Surrealist documents were several works by Breton alone, such as *Poisson soluble* (1924; soluble fish) and *Les Vases communicants* (1932; the communicating vessels), which mixed lyrical elements with philosophical speculations cast in the form of prose, as well as the numerous polemical manifestos such as *Manifeste du surréalisme* (1924; *Manifesto of Surrealism*, 1969) and *Second Manifeste du surréalisme* (1930; *Second Manifeste of Surrealism*, 1969). Breton's numerous essays were also collected in three volumes: *Les Pas perdus* (1924; the lost steps), *Point du jour* (1934), and *Perspective cavalière* (1970). Convenient selections from Breton's prose in English translation have appeared in *Les Manifestes du surréalisme* (1955; *Manifestoes of Surrealism*, 1969), translated by Richard Seaver and Helen R. Lane, and *What Is Surrealism? Selected Writings* (1978), edited by Franklin Rosemont.

ACHIEVEMENTS

Above all, André Breton will be remembered as the founder and leader of the Surrealist movement. Of all the avant-garde movements which rocked the foundations of the arts at the beginning of the twentieth century, Surrealism has had perhaps the greatest and longest-lived impact. Surrealism, created in Paris in 1924 by André Breton and a small group of friends, was the last inheritor of a long series of "isms," including Dadaism, German expressionism, French and Spanish cubism, Italian Futurism, and Anglo-American Imagism and Vorticism, which attempted to transform modern man's conception of the world through artistic innovation. Under the leadership of Breton, Surrealism became the most mature expression of this developing sensibility, not only because of its relatively well developed underlying philosophy—which was both far-reaching and systematic in nature—but also because it eventually came to have the greatest international scope of all of these movements and because it stimulated the production of a vast body of work of great diversity in all the major artistic genres—poetry, fiction, drama, philosophy, painting, sculpture, and film.

BIOGRAPHY

André Breton was born on February 19, 1896, in Tinchebray, a small inland town in the old French province of Normandy. The family soon moved, however, to the fishing port of Lorient, in Brittany, on the Atlantic

André Breton

coast of France. This seaside environment was particularly important later in the poet's life. When Breton first began to write in 1914, his highly imaginative lyrical poems expressed the wondrous abundance of nature and were often filled with images of sea life and other details evoking the maritime setting of his youth—which contrasted sharply with his life in Paris.

Breton was an only child, and his parents seemingly had an unusually strong influence on his personality. His father, who was a merchant, seems almost a prototype of the complacent, self-satisfied bourgeois that the Surrealists were later to attack as the epitome of the social conformity they rejected. Breton's mother, whom he described as straitlaced, puritanical, and harsh in her response to any suggestion of impropriety, must have also been responsible, to a large degree, for his later hatred of restraint and his provocative attitude toward anything he considered conventional.

Being the only child of a comfortably situated family, Breton had much attention lavished on him, and, naturally, his parents had great ambitions for him. He attended school in Paris from 1907 until his graduation in 1912, entering the Sorbonne in 1913 to study medicine. This contact with medicine was also important for the later development of the poet and is reflected in Breton's diverse poetic vocabulary. Even more important, however, was the experience which resulted when Breton was sent to work at the neurological center of the hospital at Nantes during World War I instead of into combat. Breton's experiences as a medical assistant during the war—first at Nantes and later at the psychiatric center at Saint-Dizier, to which he was transferred in 1917—introduced the young, impressionable poet to the bizarre aberrations of mental illness.

During this period, Breton was exposed not only to the diverse forms of mental illness from which the soldiers suffered but also to the theories upon which the practical measures used to treat them were based. Among the most important of these theories were those of Jean-Martin Charcot, Sigmund Freud, and Pierre Janet, each of which contributed an important element to the formulation of Breton's view of the operation, structure, and purpose of the human mind. From Charcot's work, Breton learned of the unlocking of the will through the use of hypnosis and saw some of the dramatic cures it was able to effect. From Freud's work, he learned about the existence of the unconscious, its role in determining mental health, and the method of dream interpretation by which one could reveal its secrets to the dreamer. From Janet's work, he learned about the existence of "psychic automatism" and the means by which it might be evoked—which eventually resulted in his own experiments with automatic writing.

These influences were reflected in three important ways in Breton's later work. First, they resulted in the two important prose experiments in automatic writing that he produced: *Les Champs magnétiques*, written with Philippe Soupault, and *Poisson soluble*, which Breton created alone. The second product of his wartime experience was the novel *Nadja* (1928; English translation, 1960), which describes the encounter of an autobiographical persona with a mysterious woman who suffers a bizarre and debilitating psychosis. The third product of these influences was *L'Immaculée Conception*, a series of writings undertaken with Paul Éluard, with the purpose of simulating, in verbal form, the thought processes of various types of insanity.

Following the war, Breton came under the influence of Dadaism, which by then had moved its base of operation from Zurich to Paris. The heyday of Dada in Paris was brief, however, lasting from January of 1920 until July of 1923. In the meantime, beginning in May of 1921, Breton and some of his friends were forming a new group whose optimistic attitude toward life, experiments with new methods of literary composition, and increasingly systematic philosophical orientation was in marked contrast to Dada's attitude of nihilistic despair. Breton later called this period, which extended from May of 1921 until October of 1924—when the first *Manifesto of Surrealism* was published—the "intuitive phase" of Surrealism. The publication of this first manifesto established, in an explicit way, a new aesthetic and a profoundly optimistic, imaginative conception of the world which its author, André Breton, named "Surrealism." The intense period of Surrealist creative activity, which began at that time and continued unabated until the appearance of the *Second Manifesto of Surrealism* in 1930, Breton was later to call the "reasoning phase" of Surrealism. This period culminated in the appearance of *Les Vases communicants*, a series of lyrical philosophical discourses expressing in mature, fully developed form the central ideas of the Surrealist philosophy and aesthetic.

The period following 1930, the year of the second manifesto, was characterized by two developments. One of these was the Surrealists' increasing involvement with the Communist International movement. The second development was, in a direct sense, an outgrowth of the first, for it was also during this period that Surrealism was disseminated on a worldwide scale and gained adherents outside Western Europe in many places where it was seen as the artistic concomitant of Marxist revolutionary philosophy. This period, which might be called, with some small injustice, the "dogmatic phase" of Surrealism, lasted until the outbreak of World War II. In 1941, Breton left France and lived for five years in New York. When he returned to Paris in 1946, Surrealism was effectively dead, although with those few friends of the original group who still remained, and with the growing support of countless other self-acknowledged "Surrealists" in many other countries where their dream had been carried, André Breton lived on as the universally acknowledged magus of Surrealism until his death on September 28, 1966, in Paris.

ANALYSIS

André Breton's poetry forms a relatively small though important part of his total literary output, being dwarfed in quantity by his lengthy experiments in prose and his numerous polemical writings. His poetry, from the first published collection, *Mont de piété* (mount of piety), to his last major poetic work, *Ode to Charles Fourier*, shows a remarkable consistency of style. As a poet, Breton is best known for his remarkable imagery— which, at its best, expresses the powerful ability of the imagination to reconcile basic human drives and desires with the material conditions of reality and, at its worst, lapses into bizarre forms of irrationality which are incomprehensible to all but the poet himself.

In general terms, Breton's poetic imagery is characterized by comparisons which yoke together extremely disparate objects, by the sudden, sometimes violent shifting of context as the poet moves from one image to the next, and by an extremely indirect method of expressing comparisons between objects. It is these three qualities, above all, which give his poetic imagery the appearance of being spontaneous rather than deliberate. As critics have shown, however, much to Breton's credit as a poet, this initial impression is a misleading one.

Breton's imagery is reinforced by other prominent aspects of his style, one of which might be called "devices of syntactic derangement." These devices range from the use of simple paradoxes involving logical and semantic contradictions, to syntactic ambiguity involving multiple or imprecise grammatical modification, to much more unsettling contradictions of reference—where the referent of a speech act is left unidentified, is deliberately misidentified, or is made ambiguous.

One other important element of Breton's style which helps to support the dramatic effect of his poetic images on his readers is his diction, which is characterized by two principal traits. The first of these is the extremely wide range of his vocabulary, which frequently includes the use of words from anatomical, zoological, botanical, and technical contexts that are unfamiliar to most readers of poetry. The second important trait of his diction is the tendency to use words in specialized, atypical ways that emphasize (and often create) their figurative meanings over their denotations. These qualities have two important effects on Breton's work: The first helps make possible his imagery of violent contrasts, and the second is, to a large degree, responsible for the great difficulty his readers and translators encounter searching for paraphrasable or translatable meaning in his work.

Another element of Breton's style which deserves mention is his use of recurring themes and symbolic motifs, such as the revolver as a synecdochic image for rebellion or revolt of any kind. These recurring thematic and symbolic elements in Breton's work can frequently be used as contextual clues for interpreting his most difficult works.

The poetry of André Breton expresses three key ideas—the liberating power of the imagination, the transformation of the material world into a utopian state, and the exploration of human potentiality through love between the sexes—which recur, with increasing elaboration, throughout the course of his work and constitute the essence of his Surrealist vision.

POWER OF IMAGINATION

Breton's faith in the liberating power of the human imagination, although suggested and influenced by his contact with modern psychoanalytic thought, especially that of Freud on the operations of the unconscious, goes far beyond the notion of simply releasing the bound or "repressed" energies which is the therapeutic basis of psychoanalytic practice. For Breton, the unconscious is not an enclosed inner space, or reservoir, of trapped energy; it is, rather, the way out of the everyday world of material reality into the realm of the surreal. According to the Surrealists, this realm—where human reason and imagination no longer struggle against each other but function in harmony—is the ultimate reality, and man's goal in life is to seek out continually the signs of this reality, which, when directly experienced, is capable of transforming the life of the person. Although Breton envisioned the realm of the surreal as accessible to all men who seek it, it was especially important for the artist, whose goal was to capture the fleeting traces of *le merveilleux* (the marvelous) in his writing.

The Surrealists recommended a number of different methods for attaining this experience. Two, in particular, are frequently used and referred to in Breton's work: the surrendering of the person to the *hasard objectif* (objective chance) of the universe, and the evocation of the "primary processes" of the unconscious through such procedures as automatic writing. The first of these methods is illustrated well in "Au regard des divinités" ("In the Eyes of the Gods"), one of Breton's early poems from *Clair de terre* (the light of Earth):

> Shortly before midnight near the landing-stage
> If a dishevelled woman follows you, pay no attention.
> It's the blue. You need fear nothing of the blue.
> There'll be a tall blonde vase in a tree.
> The spire of the village of melted colors
> Will be your landmark. Take it easy,
> Remember. The dark geyser that hurls fern-tips
> Towards the sky greet
> Greets you.

This poem reads like, and in fact is intended to be, a set of instructions for encountering the marvelous through the technique of objective chance.

Breton's other primary technique for evoking the marvelous—using the unfettered association of ideas in the unconscious to produce automatic writing—is illustrated by "Au beau demi-jour" ("In the Lovely Half-light"), a poem from *L'Air de l'eau* (air of the water):

In the lovely half-light of 1934
The air was a splendid rose the colour of red mullet
And the forest when I made ready to enter it
Began with a tree that had cigarette-paper leaves
For I was waiting for you. . . .

UTOPIAN IDEAL

Not only did Breton believe in the power of the creative imagination to transform the life of individual men, but also he believed in the possibility of transforming society itself into a Socialist utopia, and he came to believe that the Communist International movement was a means to that end. Breton's association with the Communist Party, which began about 1930, was an increasingly divisive force among the French Surrealists. Many who were willing to accept Surrealism's aesthetic and philosophical premises did not believe that this view of life could ever transform the material world of nations and societies. Breton saw this resistance against political involvement as an indication of insufficient commitment, while those who resisted engagement countered by emphasizing the restrictive nature of the Communist Party, its repressive disciplinary practices, and its hostility to artistic activity that did not directly further the interests of the Party itself. Regardless of the problems it created for him, Breton never gave up this utopian faith, as the choice of subject for his last major poetic work, *Ode to Charles Fourier*, makes clear.

TRANSFORMATIVE POWER OF LOVE

The third key idea that informs Breton's poetry is one which, like his belief in the liberating power of the imagination, was shared by many of the Surrealists: the belief that romantic love was the means by which man might establish an enduring link between the mundane world of material reality and the limitless, eternal world of surreality. At times, the mere presence of the beloved is enough to evoke such a response, and some of Breton's most moving poetry deals with this experience. The idea is expressed in two principal forms in Breton's love poetry. The first is the belief in woman as muse:

The beloved becomes the source of contact with the realm of surreality, where, Breton's friend Paul Éluard (the greatest of the Surrealist love poets) wrote, "all transformations are possible." This belief is clearly expressed in two of Breton's best poems: the famous "catalog-poem" *Free Union*, which celebrates the magical connection between the poet's beloved and the unspoiled world of nature, and *Fata Morgana*, which celebrates the ecstatic elation of the poet at the advent of a new love. The second form taken by this belief in the magical power of love is the equation of poetic creation itself with sexual love, as in "Sur la route de San Romano" ("On the Road to San Romano"): "Poetry is made in a bed like love/ Its rumpled sheets are the dawn of things."

It was these three ideas—together with the support of countless writers, scattered across the world, who identified themselves with the Surrealist ideal—which sustained Breton throughout a career that lasted more than fifty years. Although Breton died in 1966, the beliefs that he helped to formulate and that he expressed so brilliantly in his own poetry continue to exist.

OTHER MAJOR WORKS

LONG FICTION: *Nadja*, 1928 (English translation, 1960).

NONFICTION: *Les Champs magnétiques*, 1921 (with Philippe Soupault); *Les Pas perdus*, 1924; *Poisson soluble*, 1924; *Manifeste du surréalisme*, 1924 (*Manifesto of Surrealism*, 1969); *Légitime Défense*, 1926; *Le Surréalisme et la peinture*, 1928, 1945, 1965; *L'Immaculée Conception*, 1930 (with Paul Éluard); *Second Manifeste du surréalisme*, 1930 (*Second Manifesto of Surrealism*, 1969); *Les Vases communicants*, 1932; *Point du jour*, 1934; *Qu'est-ce que le surréalisme?*, 1934 (*What Is Surrealism?*, 1936); *L'Amour fou*, 1937; *Arcane 17*, 1944; *Situation du surréalisme entre les deux guerres*, 1945; *Les Manifestes du surréalisme*, 1955 (*Manifestoes of Surrealism*, 1969); *Perspective cavalière*, 1970; *What Is Surrealism? Selected Writings*, 1978.

BIBLIOGRAPHY

Aspley, Keith. *André Breton the Poet*. Glasgow, Scotland: University of Glasgow, 1989. Biography and criticism with a bibliography of Breton's poetry.

Balakian, Anna. *André Breton: Magus of Surrealism*, 1971. Biography by an expert in Surrealist art and literature.

_____. *Surrealism: The Road to the Absolute*. 3d ed. Chicago: University of Chicago Press, 1986. Updated with a new introduction. A critical history of Surrealist literature.

Benedikt, Michael. *The Poetry of Surrealism: An Anthology*. Boston: Little, Brown, 1975. With introduction, critical notes, and translations.

Breton, André. *Conversations: The Autobiography of Surrealism*. Translated and with an introduction by Mark Polizzotti. New York: Paragon House, 1993. Collection of interviews with Breton.

Carrouges, Michel. *André Breton and the Basic Concepts of Surrealism*. University: University of Alabama Press, 1974. Biography and an introduction to Surrealism with bibliographic references.

Polizzotti, Mark. *Revolution of the Mind: The Life of André Breton*. New York: Farrar, Straus, and Giroux, 1995. A thorough biography of the artist and poet highlighting his lifelong adherence to Surrealist principles even at the expense of personal relationships. With an extensive bibliography and index.

Steven E. Colburn;
bibliography updated by the editors

NICHOLAS BRETON

Born: London(?), England; c. 1545
Died: London, England; c. 1626

PRINCIPAL POETRY

A Smale Handfull of Fragrant Flowers, 1575
The Workes of a Yonge Wyt Trust Up with a Fardell of Pretie Fancies, 1577
A Floorish upon Fancie, 1577
The Toyes of an Idle Head, 1582
A Handfull of Holesome Hearbes, 1584
Brittons Bowre of Delights, 1591
Pilgrimage to Paradise, 1592
The Phoenix Nest, 1593

A Solemne Passion of the Soules Love, 1595
The Arbor of Amorous Devices, 1597
England's Helicon, 1600
Pasquils Mad-Cappe, Throwne at the Corruptions of These Times, 1600
Pasquils Fooles-Cappe, 1600
Pasquils Passe and Passeth Not, 1600
Pasquils Mistresse: Or, The Worthie and Unworthie Woman, 1600
Melancholike Humours, 1600
The Soules Heavenly Exercise, 1601
The Ravisht Soule, and the Blessed Weeper, 1601
No Whippinge nor Trippinge, but a Kinde Friendly Snippinge, 1601
The Longing of a Blessed Heart: Or, Breton's Longing, 1601
The Soules Harmony, 1602
The Mothers Blessing, 1602
Olde Mad-Cappes New Gally-mawfrey, 1602
A True Description of Unthankfulnesse, 1602
The Passionate Shepheard, 1604
The Soules Immortal Crowne, 1605
Honest Counsaile, 1605
The Honour of Valour, 1605
The Uncasing of Machiavels Instructions, 1613
I Would, and Would Not, 1614
The Hate of Treason, 1616
The Countess of Pembroke's Passion, 1853
Poems, 1952 (Jean Robertson, editor)

OTHER LITERARY FORMS

After 1600, Nicholas Breton's attention turned to prose essays, dialogues, and fiction, including proverb collections and character sketches. *Auspicante Jehova: Maries Exercise* (1597) and *Divine Considerations of the Soule* (1608) are devotional treatises; such works as *Wits Private Wealth* (1607) and *Crossing of Proverbs* (1616) collect proverbs and other practical advice; *Wits Trenchmour: Or, A Conference Between a Scholler and Angler* (1597) and *The Figure of Foure* (1597) discourse upon daily life, including angling and other country pleasures. Breton's dialogues of youth and age, country and city, traveler and stay-at-home include *A Dialogue Full of Pithe and Pleasure* (1603), *The Wil of Wit, Wits Will or Wils Wit* (1597), *An Olde Mans Les-*

son and a Young Mans Love (1605). The vogue for traveler's tales appears not only in the dialogues but also in prose tales such as *Wonders Worth the Hearing* (1602) and *A Mad World, My Masters* (1603), while contemporary events are addressed in *A Murmurer* (1607), on the occasion of the Gunpowder Plot. Breton's romantic fiction, *The Strange Fortune of Two Excellent Princes* (1600) and *Grimellos Fortunes* (1604) frequently contains lyrics within the narrative, including the frequently anthologized "I would thou wert not fair, or I were wise." Always highly popular in London's booming pamphlet market, Breton was particularly successful with the epistolary *A Poste with a Packet of Mad Letters*, a much-reprinted series begun around 1603. His modern reputation as a prose writer depends chiefly on his contributions to the prose character, as in his *Characters upon Essaies, Morall and Divine* (1615), *The Good and the Badde* (1616), and especially *Fantasticks* (1626), containing characterizations of love, money, the seasons, the holidays, the times of day, and the months of the year. Many of the aforementioned titles (those without dates) may be found in Alexander B. Grosart's informative volumes on *The Works in Verse and Prose of Nicholas Breton* (1879). Breton's prose works were immensely successful best-sellers, a fact often cited to account for the extreme rarity of copies today.

ACHIEVEMENTS

One of the first English authors to earn a living entirely by writing, Nicholas Breton spent fifty years producing literary works which encompass the height of the Renaissance and the beginning of the Jacobean period. A transitional figure, he provides a link between two related but highly contradictory sensibilities. Working in the major poetic categories of moral allegory in the style of Edmund Spenser, of lyric and pastoral in the Arcadian mode, of devotional meditation akin to that of Robert Southwell, and of popular verse satire, Breton bridges the gap between traditional and progressive, literary and colloquial, in a controlled and assured presentation which appears almost classical in its decorum. He treats the major topics of human and divine love, moral virtue, holiness, and spiritual experience, honor and humility, court and country, the real versus the ideal social

world, and the emotions of exultation and melancholy, integration and alienation. His settings in the Arcadian bowers of Renaissance pastoral prefigure Marvellian gardens, while his perception of the freshness and vigor of rural life, coupled with the depth and complexity of urban experience, helps to form the modern apprehension of the change in cultural values characteristic of early commercial capitalism. His conception of contemporary psychology of humors and the melancholy stance connects classical and medieval typology to the "humourous" characters of Ben Jonson and the seventeenth century dramatists, embodying the tension between traditional humanism and the new commercial ethic.

Always a popular writer with a keen sense of self-presentation and audience awareness, Breton's Renaissance poetic looks forward to Metaphysical paradox. With careful prosody, simple diction, clear thought, and accessible imagery, he writes a consistently craftsmanlike verse which, as C. S. Lewis has noted in his definitive *English Literature in the Sixteenth Century* (1944), escapes the confines of the drab, undergoing gradual "aurification" into the golden. As one of the first such poets, and one with so long and distinguished a record of successful publication, Nicholas Breton helped establish the poetics of the high Renaissance. Perhaps because of a lingering bias against the "popular" writer, or perhaps simply because of the extreme rarity of his surviving books, Breton has not always been accorded the attention he merits in literary histories and anthologies, an omission which still waits to be remedied.

BIOGRAPHY

The Breton, or Britton, family traced its roots to the company of William the Conqueror and held ancestral lands in Lincolnshire and in Layer-Breton, Essex, where Sir John LeBretoune was a knight banneret at the time of Edward I. Nicholas Breton's father, William, sought his living in London trade, establishing a respectable fortune speculating in church properties which had been confiscated during the Reformation. By the time of Nicholas's birth around 1545, the family comprised prosperous members of London's mercantile class, holding its "capitall mansion house," according to William Breton's will, in Redcrosse Street, maintaining its country seats as well.

Following their father's death, the Breton sons' financial situation underwent a significant change, one which dictated the need to pursue professional careers. The marriage of the young men's mother, Elizabeth Bacon Breton (through whom the family was remotely connected with Sir Francis Bacon's family), to the poet George Gascoigne drained William Breton's substantial legacy away from his sons in a series of complicated legal maneuvers. Nevertheless, Nicholas Breton's youth seems to have been comfortable and even advantageous, being, as he was, a part of the cultured middle class which so enjoyed the widening horizons of the English Renaissance. Although he seems to have been destined for one of the professions, Breton spent only a short while at Oriel College and never attained an academic degree. Nevertheless, he was familiar with classical and contemporary authors (Ovid, Francisco Petrarch, Dante, Torquato Tasso, Ludovico Ariosto, and Pastor Fido became his literary models) and with the courtly arts, which were to play a prominent role in his career as a poet in search of a patron. Although not much is known about his domestic life other than that he frequently adopted the literary pose of paterfamilias, it is known that he married Ann Sutton around 1592, and the births of four of their children and the deaths of two appear in the parish register of St. Giles, Cripplegate. For the apocryphal tradition that Ann was an "unquiet wife," little evidence can be found.

Of greater relevance to his literary career was Breton's close association with the Sidney circle, in the aura of which most of his lyric and divine poems were written. Mary Sidney, Countess of Pembroke, appears as the ideal lady, a paragon of wisdom; the record of Breton's largely unsuccessful pursuit of her favor appears in various of his tales.

Although his early canon is still uncertain, Breton's literary career seems to have begun around 1575; this rather late date suggests that his poems had been circulating in manuscript from some time before. In any case, *A Floorish upon Fancie* was published in 1577. In 1589, Breton was mentioned in George Puttenham's *Arte of English Poesy* (reprinted in 1970), and he had the dubious fortune to be mocked by Thomas Nashe

in 1591. The 1590's saw the publication of his first mature works, lyric and devotional poems in the Arcadian or Spenserian manner. His first aesthetically successful poem, the *Pilgrimage to Paradise*, a moral allegory in the Spenserian style with lyrics in the pastoral mode of Arcadianism, signals his break with the older tradition of Gascoigne. Many of Breton's lyrics, some still unidentified, appeared in the popular anthologies of the period. That his reputation as a lyric poet was firmly established is evidenced by the publication of *Brittons Bowre of Delights* by Richard Jones in 1591, which capitalized on the poet's name even though only about half the verses in the volume are Breton's, including his rather pedestrian elegy on the death of Sir Philip Sidney, "Amoris Lachrimae." *The Arbor of Amorous Devices* contains what is possibly Breton's best-known lyric, "Phillida and Coridon," played as a morning song by three musicians in country garb for Queen Elizabeth's entertainment at Elvetham, Hampshire, in 1591.

At the end of the century, Breton's attention turned to meditative devotional poetry with an intensity that his appreciative nineteenth century editor, Alexander B. Grosart, attributes to a conversion experience. The devotional series, from *A Solemne Passion of the Soules Love* to *The Soules Harmony*, presents a search for repentance, absolution, and spiritual union with the transcendent in the Christian Platonist and progressive English Protestant tradition. Breton's religious thought, while intensely personal and meditative, is always staunchly orthodox and accessible, avoiding the religious syncretism and esoteric influences characteristic of some of his contemporaries; it is staunchly conservative in its condemnation of what was popularly conceived of as atheism, represented as Machiavellianism or Epicureanism.

Throughout this period at the turn of the century, Breton adopted with increasing regularity the mask of the melancholy poet. This mask was a product of the contemporary psychology of humors and very conventional in the pastoral lyric; easy to see in this stance, however, is the growing alienation of the artist, divorced from both courtly influence and the common life, and always uncertain of status, conscious of the division between the pamphleteer's market and the calling of the

New Poet whose advent had been perceived by Spenser. In his immensely popular *Pasquil* series, entertaining and edifying verse satires in the colloquial vein, Breton plays upon the melancholy aspect of the satirist. After the death of Elizabeth in 1603, his energies turned away from divine poetry to conventional moralizing in the popular mode, especially in the role of a crusty old paternal type, and ultimately away from verse to prose, particularly in the form of the dialogue and the character. It is as a prose writer that he is primarily thought of in seventeenth century studies. No one is sure of the circumstances or even the date of his death which, as is perhaps fitting for one who lived so entirely by his pen, is usually assumed to be 1626, the year his last printed work, *Fantasticks*, was published.

ANALYSIS

Nicholas Breton's earliest published works introduce the theme of love and its loss, a concern which perhaps dominates all of his verse. In the role of a self-deprecating journeyman poet trying his wings in "small handfuls" of flowers or herbs, sentiments "trussed up," "floorishes," or "toyes," Breton addresses courtly—that is, fanciful—love in a landscape peppered with gardens, dream visions, and the familiar courtly personifications of desire versus disdain. Fancy, the spirit of courtly love, keeps a school and a fort manned with allegorical figures and rustic types, where the young poet-lover receives an education in the ways of the court and courtliness. Banished into rural obscurity, he must struggle for reinstatement, a trial by which he learns to distrust "fansy fonde," affected courtliness, and infatuation, and to practice the important Bretonian virtue of patience—the long suffering of undeserved slights in an atmosphere of pervasive, although vague, dissatisfaction, at the close of which he abruptly rejects all and turns his thoughts to eschatology. Although slight in themselves, and hopelessly old-fashioned in the style of Gascoigne and the older generation, these early works do establish the persona of the speaker, the themes of love and the ethical-religious life, and the pastoral mode for the mature works to come.

LYRIC POETRY

Of these mature works, surely the best-known are Breton's many lyrics, published in the popular verse an-

thologies. These lyrics are in the Petrarchan vein and the pastoral mode; to them Breton owes his reputation as a poet of "sweetness and purity," of a great sensitivity for nature and rural life. The earliest lyrics in *Brittons Bowre of Delights*, although conventional in imagery and plodding in meter, still possess a simple, musical appeal, whether celebrating ideal courtly love or complaining against love and fortune. One of Breton's favorite devices is foretelling doomsday in a series of unlikely perfections never found in the world, such as when "Words shall be deeds, and men shall be divine." In these poems and those in *The Phoenix Nest*, Breton introduces his pastoral lady, Phyllis, or Phillida, and the "silly shepherd" poet, whose vulnerable expressiveness permits the restorative working of the idyll, as well as his familiar setting of the garden with its herbal and rustic lore, such as in "A Strange Description of a Rare Garden-plot," where all the herbs are "weeds of wo," allegorical flowers.

The well-known "Phillida and Coridon," or "In the merry moneth of May," shows the naïve pastoral ideal in its dialogue, which begins in courtly coquetry ("He would loue, and she would not") but quickly moves into a pastoral world of frankness and good nature, and thus to lovers' oaths, "with kisses sweet concluded." The poem ends with a pastoral apotheosis in which Phillida becomes "Lady of the May," the queen of love, and that emotion, so long "abused" and "deluded" by courtly affection, is set right. This ideal world is darkened in "A sweete Pastorall," or "Good Muse rock me asleepe," by loss of love, the wreck of the shepherd's flock, and the silencing of the birds. In *The Arbor of Amorous Devices* the lady has become even more ideal, perhaps in keeping with the growing influence of Mary Sidney, more wise and "rich" in accomplishments, and more associated with virtue (Phillis) as opposed to the erotic Venus, whose Amor she blinds in "A Pastoral" ("On a hill there grows a flower").

Ultimately human love is rejected in favor of the divine. In Sonnet 3 of *The Passionate Shepheard*, Breton celebrates the advent of "wise" over foolish love and castigates "Lust the excremente of love." For the shepherd Bonerto, ideal love becomes the means of restoring faith and reason to a world darkened by age, death, and care; he says to his Aglaia, "I hate the world, but for they [thy] love." In this late collection of perhaps earlier verses, the shepherd and his lady live in the country of Minerva, or wisdom. In simple Marvellian couplets, they celebrate the pastoral ideal, free from dissimulation and conflict, which is the blight of the urban world. Breton's pastoral lyric attempts to re-create the Elizabethan Arcadia in a context which looks forward to Augustan gardens.

Among all of Breton's lyrics, perhaps the single most perfect is "A Sweet Lullabie," a simple, expressive treatment of the Bretonian topics of faithlessness and patience in an abandoned woman's song to her child, "Thy fathers shame, thy mothers griefe." Although it is crying, the infant is mercifully unaware of life's more sorrowful realities and the difficulties ensured by its uncertain legitimacy. The "Poor soule that thinkes no creature harme" is an eloquent contrast to an unfeeling world. As the baby is comforted by the song, the mother begins to hope that the child's charms can restore innocence and rightness to the world, securing the grace of both God and its "father false." The poem ends with the mother's wish that upon her death the child may vindicate her reputation, "Tell how by love she purchast blame," and appeal to its father's "gentle heart"—for although "His sugred words that me betrayde," he is yet of a "noble mind." This leads to a reversed ending in which the child laughs while the mother weeps, asking that it be shielded from the world's cruel inconstancy, "thy fathers qualitie."

MORAL ALLEGORY

Turning from the lyric to more serious moral allegory in the Spenserian mode, Breton's *Pilgrimage to Paradise* recounts a dream vision in which the poet-pilgrim journeys from the "vain conceits" of courtliness to heavenly delights. Passing through the wilderness of the world with its assorted mythical temptations and metamorphosed creatures, he confronts the seven-headed monster of vice, the familiar medieval specter of the deadly sins, which he overcomes with angelic assistance, after avoiding the twin pitfalls of melancholy on one hand and overweening ambition on the other. Joining medieval personification to heroic epic, Breton illustrates the virtue of patience—here, informed moral choice—by setting ethical extremes, wealth and wisdom, gold and grace, against one another. To cross a turbulent sea, the pilgrim joins forces with a stoic

fisherman, who has fled the court for a life of stalwart independence, thus uniting the active and the contemplative. The two negotiate a number of nautical perils to enter the city of the world, leading to a favorite Bretonian portrayal of a variety of human types— courtiers, merchants, churchmen, and foolish lovers— creating the city as a center of discontent, "outwarde wealth so ful of inwarde wo." Next, they encounter a more positive image of Renaissance culture, the university, and then the idealized court of Elizabeth, the "princely Queen," followed immediately by its dark mirror-image, a bloody battlefield, one of the small Brueghelesque landscapes which constitute an interesting aspect of Breton's vision. Ultimately they arrive at the church "Not built of lime or stone," a royal garden, a vision of the eternal bucolic in which is neither weed nor worm. The second part of the Pilgrimage, the "Countesse of Pembrokes love," presents the Countess as "true loves saint," the Phoenix of an earthly paradise addressing divine love in a soliloquy overheard by the poet. Rejecting all worldly pleasures and comparing herself to Mary Magdalen, she longs to be united with Christ, the true Phoenix.

This early Breton poem shows his Christian Platonist view of *caritas*, divine love, the basis of Breton's poetry in the many "passions" that followed. An undated but probably contemporary poem, addressed to Mary Sidney and, possibly for that reason, sometimes ascribed to her, is *The Countess of Pembroke's Passion*— "passion" being a Bretonian term for an extended meditation delineating the speaker's religious emotions. Repenting his early "fruitless labours and ruthless love," the poet meditates upon Christ's passion, especially the example it gives of patience. Compared to later meditative poetry in the Metaphysical tradition, Breton's poem might seem conventional, but it does contain an unaffected, calm piety, a simple conversational style, plain diction and imagery, as well as a dynamic emotional tone cast in simple yet flowing sestinas rhyming *ababcc*.

Breton's devotional poetry connects earlier religious polemic with later meditative poetry by developing the themes of the moral allegory in an interior and contemplative vein, attempting—in the style of Southwell, but without his extravagance—to cast religious experience in lyrical imagery. *A Solemne Passion of the Soules Love*, perhaps the most consistently satisfying of these attempts, celebrates the creative relationship between divine love and the human world. Standard biblical images join the more Petrarchan Phoenix and sun to create a sense of the contradiction between human weakness and divine perfection—lowly pebble and "azurde ski"—to be resolved through meditation. This exploration of spiritual transcendence, from despondency to ecstasy, appears most plainly in a two-part divine poem, *The Ravisht Soule, and the Blessed Weeper*, which first explores the experience of spiritual enlightenment (ravishment), and then offers the example of Mary Magdalen, whose lament and consolation at Christ's tomb is overheard in the poet's dream vision. *The Longing of a Blessed Heart*, an extended definition of divine-Platonic love, illustrates the relationship between the divine and the human and the transformation of the natural world by love. The poem's definition distinguishes *caritas* from other kinds of love in a discursive, conversational style anticipating the mood of seventeenth century meditative poetry: "Some thinke it [love] is a babe of Beautie's getting,/ Nurst up by Nature, and Time's onely breeding;/ A pretty work to set the wits a wheeting."

In his successful *Pasquil* series, Breton extends the quality of love or charity to the social world in an attempt to correct the vices of an increasingly complex order, applying an essentially medieval form to the matter of emerging seventeenth century policy. Prefiguring Jonsonian comedy of humors, Breton's satirist is a humorist suffering from extreme feelings motivated by anger or sorrow to which he gives vent in impassioned speech. In *Pasquils Mad-Cappe, Throwne at the Corruptions of These Times*, the satirist inveighs against the abuse of wealth and power, the ascendance of illusion over reality, folly above reason, conditions motivated by "Pride, power, and pence." His multitude of wealthy rascals is set against the good poor man "free from Fancie's vanities," who goes begging among the rich asses and dunces. "It is money makes or mars the man," Pasquil says, offering instead a pastoral ideal where "Pride shall goe down, and virtue shall encrease." *Pasquils Fooles-Cappe* addresses those too obtuse to heed the first jeremiad in order to bring about a more "honest kindness,"

without swaggerers, spendthrifts, lazy wives, wandering husbands, absentminded professors, or unscrupulous satirists. In the later installments of the *Pasquil* series, the conditions of melancholy and ambivalence render all human choice valueless. In *I Would, and Would Not*, the poet first claims and then rejects the entire gamut of human enterprise, resolving finally to preserve his own identity as a "religious servant" of common sense and a corrector of folly. It is not difficult to see in these complaints the dissatisfaction connected with the poet's uncertain status, the dangers of dwelling continually in the "fancy," concerns which appear in "An Epigraph upon Poet Spencer" in the *Melancholike Humours*, where the Spenserian characters lament that their creator has been forgotten.

PROVERBS AND APHORISMS

In a lighter, more familiar vein are the sententious proverbs and aphorisms so popular among London's common readers, sentiments for wall samplers such as the Polonius-like patter of *Honest Counsaile*: "Nor pull up Hearbes, and cherish Weedes,/ Nor tittle-tattle, more than needs," or the maternal pithiness of *The Mothers Blessing*, or a twist on the familiar in a Machiavellian father's ruthless counsel in *The Uncasing of Machiavels Instructions*, properly rejected by his pious son. In *Pasquils Mistresse* the satirist debates the opposing characters of the worthy woman, whose Platonic intellect is her glory, and her unworthy opposite, the victim of feeling and folly.

Especially after the accession of James, Breton's moral verse occupies a considerably less lofty plane. *The Soules Immortal Crowne*, a heroic encomium of the seven moral virtues dedicated to the King, is remarkable chiefly for the extent to which "vertue," a variation of Renaissance *virtú* implying will and strength, displaces patience. Other verses dwell upon gratitude and its polar opposite, ingratitude, the most virulent extreme of which Breton saw in the Gunpowder Plot of 1607. The end of *The Hate of Treason*, written for that occasion, glorifies the Jacobean court, castigating the mad aspirations of the "rebellious beastly Rablement," as *The Honour of Valour* glorifies the marital virtues of Lord Mountjoy by contrasting his stalwart traditionalism with the "drosse" of the present court in a vision of the eternal heroic rising above the "Dunghill" of contemporary policy. Although a far cry from the vision of the earlier divine poetry, these heroic ventures show Breton's concern with the ability of the human to transcend its limitations.

Whereas Breton's lyrics and moral allegory had early undergone the Elizabethan transformation from drab to golden, his later divine poetry and verse satire connect that change to the emerging seventeenth century consciousness. Always decorous in tone and diction yet iconoclastic in its perception of audience and of the self, Breton's Renaissance verse, set squarely in the mainstream of the moral and intellectual currents of his time, looks forward to the Metaphysical and the neoclassical alike.

OTHER MAJOR WORKS

LONG FICTION: *The Strange Fortune of Two Excellent Princes*, 1600; *Grimellos Fortunes*, 1604.

NONFICTION: *The Figure of Foure*, 1597; *Auspicante Jehova: Maries Exercise*, 1597; *Wits Trenchmour: Or, A Conference Between a Scholler and Angler*, 1597; *The Wil of Wit, Wits Will or Wils Wit*, 1597; *Wonders Worth the Hearing*, 1602; *A Mad World, My Masters*, 1603; *A Dialogue Full of Pithe and Pleasure*, 1603; *A Poste with a Packet of Mad Letters*, 1603; *An Olde Mans Lesson and a Young Mans Love*, 1605; *Wits Private Wealth*, 1607; *A Murmurer*, 1607; *Divine Considerations of the Soule*, 1608; *Crossing of Proverbs*, 1616; *The Court and Country*, 1618.

MISCELLANEOUS: *Characters upon Essaies, Morall and Divine*, 1615; *The Good and the Badde*, 1616; *Fantasticks*, 1626; *The Works in Verse and Prose of Nicholas Breton*, 1879 (2 volumes; Alexander B. Grosart, editor).

BIBLIOGRAPHY

Atkinson, Colin B., and Jo B. Atkinson. "Four Prayer Books Addressed to Women During the Reign of Elizabeth I." *The Huntington Library Quarterly* 60, no. 4 (1999): 407-423. Discusses the changes in the place of women in religious thought and practice throughout the sixteenth century. Examines *A Table for Gentlewomen*, *A Handfull of Holesome Hearbs*, Breton's *Auspicante Jehova*, and *The Monument of Matrones*.

Bullen, Arthur Henry. *Elizabethans*. New York: E. P. Dutton, 1924. Bullen sketches the life and work of ten English authors of the Elizabethan period. He repeats the sketchy details known about Breton's life, then shows how the prolific author fits into his historic context. Interesting reading for all students.

Garnett, Richard, and Edmund Grosse. *English Literature: An Illustrated Record*. 2d ed. 2 vols. New York: Macmillan, 1935. Garnett and Grosse include a substantial essay on Breton and place him in context of the English literary history. This is an older study, but a valuable one. Suitable for all levels.

Kunitz, Stanley, and Howard Haycraft, eds. *British Authors Before 1800: A Biographical Dictionary*. New York: Wilson, 1952. Provides a short biographical entry that seems to be based on the information provided in Sir Sidney Lee's article. Points out that Breton's literary influences come from the medieval period and not from his English Renaissance contemporaries. Breton was thought to have been a little too prolific. His only work of any distinction is his pastoral poems.

Lee, Sir Sidney. "Nicholas Breton." In *The Dictionary of National Biography*, edited by Sir Leslie Stephen and Sir Sidney Lee. Vol. 2. Reprint. London: Oxford University Press, 1921-1922. This essay is the most interesting and detailed article about the life of Breton. Lee describes why Breton's birth and death dates are in doubt and insinuates that the poet had an affair with his patroness, Mary Sidney, the Countess of Pembroke. Provides a detailed primary biography along with the whereabouts of Breton's few remaining first editions.

Tannenbaum, Samuel Aaron, and Dorothy R. Tannenbaum. *Nicholas Breton: A Concise Bibliography*. New York: S. A. Tannenbaum, 1947. Breton has been almost completely ignored by scholars over the last three centuries. The Tannenbaums have published one of the only sources of any kind available on this Elizabethan poet. It is immensely valuable for the serious Breton student.

Janet Polansky;
bibliography updated by the editors

BREYTEN BREYTENBACH

Born: Bonnievale, South Africa; September 16, 1939

PRINCIPAL POETRY

Die ysterkoei moet sweet, 1964
Die huis van die dowe, 1967
Kouevuur, 1969
Lotus, 1970
Oorblyfsels, 1970
Skryt, 1972
Met ander woorde, 1973
'N Seisoen in die Paradys, 1976 (poetry and prose;
    A Season in Paradise, 1980)
Voetskrif, 1976
Sinking Ship Blues, 1977
*And Death as White as Words: An Anthology of
    the Poetry of Breyten Breytenbach*, 1978 (A. J.
    Coetzee, editor)
*In Africa Even the Flies Are Happy: Selected Poems,
    1964-1977*, 1978 (Denis Hershon, translator)
Eklips: Die Derde bundel van die ongedanste dans,
    1983
YK, 1985
Lady One, 2000

OTHER LITERARY FORMS

In addition to his poetry, Breyten Breytenbach has written the short stories *Katastrofes* (1964; catastrophes) and *De boom achter de maan* (1974; the tree behind the moon), the biographical *A Season in Paradise* and *The True Confessions of an Albino Terrorist* (1983), a record of his prison experiences. This last, his best-known work, describes his decision to return to South Africa with the intention of establishing a revolutionary organization. The ideas are presented indirectly: Instead of the simple diary chronology, as might be anticipated, he devises a complex literary structure. A series of interrogations and confessions, made to an impersonal, elusive, but threatening figure, Mr. Interrogator, are interrupted by "inserts," which act as a kind of chorus providing lyrical speculation and philosophic debate among the evidence of the persecution he was suffering. Breytenbach

Breyten Breytenbach (© Jerry Bauer)

makes his most defiant challenge to the regime with subtle literary technique rather than blatant accusation.

ACHIEVEMENTS

Breyten Breytenbach's distinction occurs at two levels. The fact that he writes his poetry in Afrikaans has limited his audience outside South Africa. His immense reputation within that country derives from the same fact. He was part of the so-called Sestiger movement of the 1960's, which revolutionized Afrikaans literature. For the first time, Afrikaans was made to describe radical attitudes that horrified the Afrikaner establishment, whose puritanism and reactionary beliefs had until then controlled all literary expression. Understandably, conventional social attitudes made his work highly controversial. The old with anger, the young with excitement, saw Breytenbach as a literary iconoclast who broke the controls that had traditionally restricted both form and subject of Afrikaans poetry and who linked Afrikaner concerns with the dangerously experimental, outspoken, and often-censored writings being published in English, the language of those who had traditionally sought to extirpate the culture of the Afrikaner "volk."

All of his work has provoked bitter attack and equally violent counterattack. For every critic who denounced the blasphemy and radicalism of his work, others praised his originality that liberated the Afrikaans language from a narrow and bigoted orthodoxy. Internationally, his poetry is known in translation, but he is far more renowned as a political figure, as a fighter against apartheid. His prison memoirs, *The True Confessions of an Albino Terrorist*, have been accepted as an important addition to the literary condemnations of the Pretoria regime.

His literary honors are many. He was awarded the A. P. B. Literary Prize for *Die ysterkoei moet sweet*, and the Afrikaans Press Corps Prize for *Die ysterkoei moet sweet* and *Katastrofes*, both in 1964. He won the South African Central News Agency prizes in 1967 for *Die huis van die dowe*, in 1969 for *Kouevuur*, and in 1970 for *Lotus*. *Skryt* earned him the Lucie B. and C. W. Van der Hoogt prize from the Society of Netherlands Literature in 1972, while *Voetskrif* earned him a prize from the Perskor newspaper group in 1976. The Pris des Sept (an international publisher's prize to provide funding for six foreign translations of Breytenbach's work) was won in 1977, the Hertzog Prize from South African Academy of Science and Arts in 1984, and the Rapport Prize for Literature from the Afrikaans newspaper *Rapport* in 1986 for *YK*.

BIOGRAPHY

Breyten Breytenbach was born in a conservative small town, Bonnievale, on the western side of Cape Town. He entered the then-unsegregated Cape Town University to study painting. The opportunity, for him, was revolutionary. For the first time, Breytenbach met Africans as equals, mixed with left-wing student groups, and delighted in his intellectual freedom and his escape from the narrowness and racism of his upbringing. He became a member of the radical African National Congress. At twenty-one, he left for Paris, completing his liberation, or revolt, from his family and race.

He married a Vietnamese woman (illegal under his country's race acts). "It was . . . against the moral principles of the Christian Community that two human beings of different skin colour should lie together." He had no choice but to remain in Paris, where he worked as an art-

ist. He was prevented from returning with his wife even to accept the national prizes that were being awarded his work. A brief visit was arranged in 1972, during which his wife stayed across the border in independent and unsegregated Swaziland. This discrimination and rejection fostered his resentment. In 1975, he decided on active involvement and made plans almost as bizarre in practice as they were optimistic in intention. He returned on a forged French passport to set up a revolutionary organization for whites called Okhela, which would use sabotage and guerrilla action to overthrow the government.

There is still some confusion about his true motives and expectations. Given his wide fame, his attempt at disguise was ludicrous. He was arrested, and charged under the Terrorism Act. His unexpected apologies to the court allowed him to escape a potential death penalty, but he was sentenced to nine years imprisonment for terrorism. Frequent international appeals effected his release in 1982, and he returned to Paris, where he continued his writing and committed involvement with anti-apartheid movements.

Breytenbach spent the 1990's writing a number of fiction and nonfiction titles, many of which explore the politics and post-apartheid era of South Africa, as well as two memoirs. His work as a painter increased in visibility with a number of one-man exhibitions held at the South African Association of Arts in Cape Town and at the UNISA Art Gallery in Pretoria, and in France, the Netherlands, Sweden, and Germany. He also co-founded the Gorée Foundation on the Gorée Islands off the coast of Senegal, which helps promote democratic unity on the African continent. In 2000 he was appointed a visiting professor in the University of Cape Town's School of Humanities, an appointment that lasts for three years. He also dedicated part of his time to his continuing work with the University of New York, serving in the Graduate School of Creative Writing.

ANALYSIS

The poetry of Breyten Breytenbach is both highly personal and highly public. This paradox is explained by his intense emotional involvement with the society in which he was born, a society that is condemned universally for its racism and bigotry. His sensitivity to this relationship readily leads self-expression into public posture. He was constantly antagonistic to apartheid, yet he realized that he was inevitably a part of it. The consequent dilemma may begin to explain the moods of near suicidal despair and depression that are found in his more intimate poems. Brought up among cosmic cruelties, it must have seemed to him that the opportunity for any individual to find separate solace was as delusive as it was reprehensible. That admission contains within it one of the reasons for the constant emotional tension encountered in his revealing verse.

Another way in which Breytenbach's work may be considered personal is the close link it has with his actual experience. The sequence of his poems follows the events that were occurring in his life as an exile and a political prisoner. By exploring and confronting the anxieties he faces as a human being, he indicates that his responses are based upon political conviction but have a deeper psychological origin than radical activism. Breytenbach defies and rejects apartheid in his writing through introspective self-analysis, rather than through a more open and formal stand. There is an almost neurotic emotion that commands the efflorescence of extraordinarily violent language and metaphor, but it affects only the poetic surface. By implication, as much as by direct statement, there clearly remains an underlying political stance in Breytenbach's poetry. Breytenbach denounces the regime with an anger that derives some of its intensity from his own sense of personal affront as well as his predetermined and principled political beliefs. The man is the poet and the poet is a political activist. The paradox provokes a revealing duality of aims between poet as artist and poet as spokesman. This divergence has preoccupied both writers and critics in the twentieth century. The essential elements of the controversy have never been convincingly resolved. What is the proper role of a poet who exists under an oppressive regime? Does the urge toward declamatory affirmation make poetry mere propaganda? Jean-Paul Sartre's famous essay "What Is Literature?" explores this issue with typical acuity. Does moral and political commitment minimize the expression of the more universal human truths which many believe constitute the ultimate reason for poetry? Breytenbach's work both explores and exemplifies this dilemma. These are the issues that must be considered as one examines the volumes of poetry that have come from his pen. Across a period of twenty years, these ideas have confirmed his development as a writer and signaled his commitment to revolution.

DIE YSTERKOEI MOET SWEET

Breytenbach's earliest poetry, collected in *Die ysterkoei moet sweet* (the iron cow must sweat), gives immediate early evidence of his capacity for a striking vigor of imagery. His language is extravagant and unexpected. Expressions such as "blood like peaches in syrup," "people are biting at each other's gullets," and "spiky Jesus stands out on a cross," from a single poem, exhibit his evocative originality. At the center of his use of language is a vividly confident assurance remarkable in so youthful a poet. His effusive self-confidence is particularly apparent in comparison to the formality and polished moderation of the poets of the Afrikaner establishment. In spite of this verbal virility, the mood that Breytenbach's brilliant language expresses is curiously negative. There are hints of suicide. "I am not yet ready/ for I must still learn how to die." He emphasizes death often enough to suggest that some psychological imbalance, almost a neurosis, exists within the poet even in his earlier years. There is fear, also, as if he realized the conclusions of his combative attitudes. "But keep Pain far from Me o Lord/ That others may bear it/ Be taken away into custody,/ Shattered/ Stoned/ Suspended/ Lashed. . . ."

Yet all is not gloom; there is also a gentle deprecatory irony: "Ladies and gentlemen allow me to introduce you to Breyten Breytenbach," begins one poem which concludes with a comment so infinitely more poignant, given our knowledge of his future: "Look he is harmless, have mercy upon him." Perhaps he was not. Certainly, no one did.

The later poems in this volume are written from Paris after his departure from South Africa, occasioned partly by political constraints, but more by his desire to explore the cosmopolitan world beyond the margins of Cape Town. Quickly there is an awareness of disillusion, albeit he proclaimed his satisfaction. "I can't complain." "I'm happy here." Away from his country, freed from its constant social tensions that rapidly became his own, he has a new freedom of choice. It is precisely that luxury, however, that requires him to determine what he will do with such a dramatic opportunity. For a South African, the relief of exile is always attended by some guilt. The decision can be interpreted as cowardly escape or as bold defiance. In this new context of liberation, Breytenbach must ask himself those unanswerable questions: "What were your grand resolutions?/ or is your existence only a matter of compromise?/ what are you looking for here/ without the excuse of being young . . . and what are you planning to do?" South Africa refuses to be wished away. The recognition of distance more acutely induces memory. In contrast to Paris, "somewhere the aloes are shining/ somewhere some are smelling fresh guavas." (Aloes are the floral symbol of South Africa.) The mood is sad and fretful. Escape does not constitute solution "because other worlds and other possibilities exist you know."

Only in some of the later poems dedicated to his new wife does any happier note appear: "I press my nose in the bouquet of your neck/ how ripe how intoxicating its fragrance the smell of life/ you live." Even so intense an intimacy is laced with an insistent bitterness of spirit. "You are a butterfly of trembling light/ and inside you already your carcase is nibbling."

DIE HUIS VAN DIE DOWE

Similarly, the second collection, *Die huis van die dowe* (the house of the deaf), though intended to celebrate love, expresses his persistent self-doubt: "Pain bruises us all to a more intimate shade—/ . . . which can never heal, the dreams." The bitterness of the words suggests that the freedom that Breytenbach so eagerly sought by departure has proved geographic rather than spiritual. "No restful eye/ and no rest or surrender or cellars or the cool of sleep." His agitation is both personal and professional. There are insistent expressions of concern about his poetry; inspiration seems to be weakening without the violent indignation that the daily experience of South Africa provided. He realizes that there has begun to be a separation between his life and his work. He observes that "My fire has slaked/ I must stand to one side." More vulgarly, "My arsehole is full of myself," a crudely worded but significant condemnation since, unlike more circumspect poets, he deplores an introspective style. The intention to escape from the constrictions of self was to determine his decision to play a public role as an activist, rather than as a poet-spokesman.

SENSE OF ISOLATION

He soon began to achieve some international recognition, but this publicity did not fulfill him, since it seemed totally remote from his indigenous commitment to South Africa. Success only increased his sense of painful isolation. "I'm a globe-trotter . . . as thirsty as ever" and "from a lot of travelling/ the heart grows mute and waterlogged." No political condemnation of his country will drive away his exile's longing. Of his own city, Cape Town, he writes, "that's how I love you/ as I have dreamed of you . . ./ my cape, godcape, lovecape, capeheart . . . Fairest cape in all the world."

His urge toward verse remains strong, though its effect seems constantly tainted even while he uses it to sustain his personal and ardent life. "Give me a pen/ so that I can sing/ that life is not in vain." Perhaps he presents his own reflection in a poem he dedicated to Yousef Omar, and recognizes the same emotions and the same fate: "His heart is a clot of fear/ the man is not a hero/ he knows he'll have to hang/ for he is stupid/ and wanted to believe." One might hope that Breytenbach's disillusionment is not so comprehensive, but his doubts persist in his private life. He yearns for love: "Give me a love/ like the love I want to give to you," while suggesting that desire is equivocal.

KOUEVUUR

Breytenbach explores his anxieties further in his *Kouevuur* (coldfire-gangrene). Some of these poems show the beginnings of disintegration in both form and statement. Burning with an inner bitterness, he finds himself giving others the advice he should have taken to his own heart: "Above all watch out for the slimy black paw paw/ of bitterness, black child—/ he that eats of it dies on bayonets." He might well have deliberated upon this truth. In this collection, passionate lyric poems are matched by violent expressions of self-condemnation. His political work distracts him from poetry and yet at the same time its obligations tease him with the more shocking thought that writing may no longer be considered an adequate response to South African circumstances. He is increasingly aware of how separated he has become from his country. "You ask me how it is living in exile, my friend/ What can I say?/ that I'm too young for bitter protest/ and too old for wisdom and acceptance/ of my destiny."

Acceptance of destiny was gradually invading Breytenbach's thoughts, but his unexpected reversal of the anticipated attitudes of youth and age display the convolutions of his present moods. Return was legally forbidden with a "non-European" wife, and therefore his marriage required that he express his gradual recognition of the permanence of exile (which he somewhat casually chose as a young man) and its painful results: "Yes, but that I now also know the rooms of loneliness/ the desecration of dreams, the remains of memories." The "if" in the following line indicates both admission and anxiety: "I've been thinking if I ever come back." He realizes that there are the outward changes, that he will appear, "wearing a top hat/ a smart suit . . . new Italian shoes for the occasion," garb that defines his new European citizenship. He can only hope that "ma knows it's me all the same." He can still write lyrically of his love, of the happiness that it has brought. "I love you—you lead me through gardens/ through all the mansions of the sun . . ./ love is sweeter than figs." Or even more tenderly, "sleep my little love/ sleep well sleep dark/ wet as sugar in coffee/ be happy in your dreams." Love is a pleasure that provides no resolution of his confusion. Old age is seen not as a conclusion but as a period of harmony and calm. It provides comfort in allowing escape from the obligations of action that he and others had imposed, and permits abdication from oppressive responsibility: "That's the answer, to be an old man, a naked/ treedweller, too old to climb down."

LOTUS

The *Lotus* collection is specifically addressed to his wife. There are lines of unusual exhilaration and intensity. "For my love travels along with you/ my love must stay with you like an angel." Yet such elevated emotions are not entirely convincing. More typical is the ambivalent self-flagellation of the following lines: "I'm in love with my loneliness/ because I'm alone/ . . . Two things I have to say:/ I'm alone, but I love you."

OORBLYFSELS

In *Oorblyfsels*, Breytenbach's increasing emotional disgust spills over. His psychological dismay urges him toward greater political assertiveness. He describes himself with shame as "I, a white African featherless fowl." He turns upon his entire race, equating whiteness with evil, blaming whites for his own cursed Afrikaner inheritance: "whitedom." "The white man knows only the sun/ knows nothing of black or man." This judgment exacerbates his ferocious inner conflicts. It requires that he accept connection with the atrocity he perceives and condemns, but from which he cannot free himself. No matter his protestations of racial neutrality, he is one of them. His admission of this is more angry than sad, "I am German/ I am cruel/ I am white, I steal." It becomes an inverse communion with his soul. It is a kind of litany of social condemnation in which, in color terms, he must include himself.

SKRYT

By the time the even more belligerent *Skryt* (write) was written, the political accusations are more apparent than the introspective anxieties which provide their source. It is South Africa that Breytenbach has in mind when he describes, from a different coast, how "the ocean washes like blood against the land/ I stand on my knees where the hearts are laid down/ sand in my throat like grievances that cannot be stomached." His inspection is factual; his response has become pathological. He contemplates with increased awareness what Africa has suffered, comprehending that in his own country "to live black is a political crime." He also contemplates how Africa might survive. "Africa so often pillaged, purified, burnt!/ Africa stands in the sign of fire and flame." His hatred for his country intensifies. He excoriates it mercilessly as "this is hell with God." He roundly condemns its people, seeing them as villains "lugging an attache case with shares and gold in one hand/ and a sjambok [whip] in the other." It would be far simpler if such denegration could remain purely political, but inevitably he incorporates the same scathing attitudes into his more intimate analyses. The fact that the regime survives increases his sense of incompetence and inadequacy. Gloomily he reports on his present state: "You grow less agile, more compliant/ . . . yet death walks in your body . . . and by the time you want to smash the day with your fist/ and say: look my people are rising up! . . . you've forgotten the silences of the language." He expresses his failure as a poet, a lover, and as a revolutionary: "I fold the dead of that/ which we/ called love/ in chalk dark words/ bury it here/ within this paper/ that a God should fill the gaps." It is clear that only some defiant and unequivocal action will satisfy his needs, but that action would not cure his heart's malaise.

MET ANDER WOORDE

Ironically, South Africa's liberation would not affect Breytenbach's own. It is this despairing admission that permeates the 1973 collection *Met ander woorde* (in other words). Poetry can provide no adequate means of resolving the racial and social impasse of South Africa. In this book he more openly announces his intention for more explicit assaults on the system. "Now that death/ begins to seek out the eyes/ a single burning purpose remains/ to grow stronger towards the end/ you feel you are bound to yourself/ by an underground movement." Yet is he, the poet-artist, the person capable of carrying out such deliberate service? Can an intellectual become a functioning revolutionary? In a self-deprecatory way, Breytenbach offers himself some disguised advice in a wry and comic metaphor: "When the canopy of sky tears/ then all the stars fall out:/ you know you can't let a drunk man work on the roof."

In spite of this warning, his determination to transmute his art and philosophy into action drove him to the deeds that resulted in arrest, trial, and conviction. His incarceration did not free his spirit from his recognition of racial guilt. The fact that he had so demonstrably and publicly suffered in the cause of revolution did not purge him of his association from Afrikaner history. Given what he was, or more accurately, what he thought himself to be, there were no acts he could perform that would satisfy him nor assuage his inner despair. Even Afrikaans, the language which he had done so much to vivify, seems to be the vehicle in which the oppression is expressed. "We ourselves are aged./ Our language is a grey reservist a hundred years old and more." The Afrikaans language defines the racist system, "For we are Christ's executioners./ . . . We bring you the grammar of violence/ and the syntax of destruction."

A few poems survived his incarceration, though many were lost and stolen. Some are personal, for the painful imposition of extended solitary confinement necessitated an introspection which opened up vistas of self-awareness impossible during the cosmopolitan distractions of his Paris exile. Part of this discovery is expressed in purely physical terms. "I feel the apples of decay in my chest/ and in my wrists the jolt of trains./ Now—after how many months of solitary confinement?"

POEMS FROM PRISON

At the conclusion of *The True Confessions of an Albino Terrorist* are thirteen poems that record his last days in jail and his liberation. He tries to write but thinks little of his efforts: "A man has made himself a poem/ for his birthday the sixteenth of the ninth—/ o, no not a fancy affair with room and rhyme/ and rhythm and iambs and stuff. . . ." He can rejoice in the memories that fill the long hours of his confinement. They are sometimes recalled with irony: "Do you remember when we were dogs/ you and I?" Other moments are recollected more poignantly, "He will remember—/ mornings before daybreak." Memory is reinforced by the arrival of a letter, "word from outside." He tells, "I fled to your letter, to read/ that the small orange tree is a mass of white blossoms." This ordinary world becomes richer and more exotic when set against the one he inhabits where, "in the middle of the night/ the voice of those/ to be hanged within days/ rise up already sounding thin."

Finally, there is the bliss of release. "I arrive on this first day already glistening bright/ among angel choirs." Then the return to the haven of Paris, where he writes one of the few expressions of unalloyed delight to be found in his poetry: "Listen to that same wind calling/ through the old old Paris streets/ you're the one I love and I'm feeling so good." The final couplet has a fine ring, so positive in contrast to his earlier anxieties. He still speaks of death, but his attitude is now devil-may-care: "Burn, burn with me love—to hell with decay to live is to live, and while alive to die anyway."

OTHER MAJOR WORKS

LONG FICTION: *Om te vlieg*, 1971; *Mouroir: Mirrornotes of a Novel*, 1984.

SHORT FICTION: *Katastrofes*, 1964; *De Boom achter de Maan*, 1974; *Die Miernes swel op*, 1980.

NONFICTION: *The True Confessions of an Albino Terrorist*, 1983; *End Papers*, 1986; *Boek: Dryfpunt*, 1987; *Terugkeer naar het Paradijs: Een Afrikaans Dagboek*, 1993 (*Return to Paradise*, 1993); *The Memory of Birds in Times of Revolution*, 1996; *Dog Heart: A Memoir*, 1999.

PLAY: *Boklied: 'N Vermaaklikheid in drie bedrywe*, pb. 1998.

MISCELLANEOUS: *Judas Eye and Self-Portrait/ Deathwatch*, pb. 1988.

BIBLIOGRAPHY

Breytenbach, Breyten. *Dog Heart: A Memoir*. New York: Harcourt Brace, 1999. A violent yet eloquent memoir of the African National Congress activist and author which explores the fusion of violence and gentleness, turbulence and dignity.

Cope, Jack. *The Adversary Within: Dissident Writers in Afrikaans*. Atlantic Highlands, N.J.: Humanities Press, 1982. A historical and critical analysis of Afrikaans literature in the twentieth century.

Jolly, Rosemary Jane. *Colonization, Violence, and Narration in White South African Writing: André Brink, Breyten Breytenbach, and J. M. Coetzee*. Athens: Ohio University Press, 1996. Examines violence in the context of apartheid and colonialism and the representation of pain and suffering in narrative form. Includes an introduction to the critical issues of South African literature. Includes bibliographic references.

Weschler, Lawrence. *Calamities of Exile: Three Nonfiction Novellas*. Chicago: University of Chicago Press, 1998. Includes a brief biography of Breytenbach.

John Povey;
bibliography updated by the editors

ROBERT BRIDGES

Born: Walmer, Kent, England; October 23, 1844
Died: Boar's Hill, near Oxford, England; April 21, 1930

PRINCIPAL POETRY

Poems, 1873
The Growth of Love, 1876, revised 1890
Poems, Second Series, 1879
Poems, Third Series, 1880
Prometheus the Firegiver, 1884 (verse masque)
Nero Part I, 1885 (verse drama)
Eros and Psyche, 1885
The Feast of Bacchus, 1889 (verse drama)
Palicio, 1890 (verse drama)
The Return of Ulysses, 1890 (verse drama)

The Christian Captives, 1890 (verse drama)
Achilles in Scyros, 1890 (verse drama)
Shorter Poems, Books I-IV, 1890
The Humours of the Court, 1893 (verse drama)
Shorter Poems, Book V, 1893
Nero Part II, 1894 (verse drama)
Poetical Works of Robert Bridges, 1898-1905 (6 volumes)
Demeter, 1905 (verse masque)
Poems Written in MCMXIII, 1914
October and Other Poems, 1920
The Testament of Beauty, 1927-1929, revised 1930
Poems, 1931 (M. M. Bridges, editor)

OTHER LITERARY FORMS

Although Robert Bridges wrote poetry extensively, he was also a prolific scholar. His monograph on *Milton's Prosody* (1893, 1901) is a model of research. His *Collected Essays, Papers, Etc.* have been published in thirty parts by Oxford University Press (1927-1936). Bridges is probably most known in modern times for his correspondence with Gerard Manley Hopkins (1844-1889). Hopkins's letters to Bridges have been published (Oxford University Press, 1935, 1955), but Bridges destroyed his letters to Hopkins. The *Correspondence of Robert Bridges and Henry Bradley (1900-1923)* has been published (1940), as well as his *Three Friends: Memoirs of Digby Mackworth Dolben, Richard Watson Dixon, and Henry Bradley* (1932). Bridges also wrote a few poems in Latin.

ACHIEVEMENTS

Robert Bridges was poet laureate of England from 1913 until his death in 1930. In the last years of his life, he was generally thought to be the leading lyric poet of his time. His restrained, classical style was opposed to the extremes of Ezra Pound and T. S. Eliot and the rising tide of modernism in literature. Since his death, Bridges has fallen into obscurity. His six volumes of collected poems and plays are seldom read even by specialists. Even if Bridges is not rehabilitated as a poet, however, he will be remembered as a significant scholar and editor. Bridges saved the poems of his friend Gerard Manley Hopkins from obscurity by editing them in 1918, giving the world one of the major precursors of modernism. Bridges's studies of language and metrics were pioneering work and he was one of the first to carry out real literary research in the modern sense. Finally, he is an important innovator in poetic form, whose discoveries place him on a par with acknowledged revolutionaries such as T. S. Eliot, Ezra Pound, Gerard Manley Hopkins, and Walt Whitman as a creator of new forms of expression in poetic language.

BIOGRAPHY

Robert Seymour Bridges explicitly requested that no biography or biographical study should ever be made of him. He destroyed many of his personal papers and his heirs have respected his wishes. Although there is no formal biography, the outlines of his life are well-known. Robert Bridges was the next-to-last child in a family of nine, born to comfortable landed gentry. Bridges went to Eton in 1854, where he showed an inclination toward the "Oxford Movement." He matriculated at Corpus Christi College, Oxford University, in 1863, where he was athletic and popular as an undergraduate. He rowed stroke in the Corpus Christi boat in 1867, but took only a gentleman's second class degree in *literae humaniores*, the study of classical languages and the literature and philosophy of ancient Greece and Rome. At Oxford he became a close friend of the brilliant but somewhat eccentric Gerard Manley Hopkins, who became one of the most important modernist poets in English. Bridges and Hopkins carried on an extensive correspondence after their undergraduate days; although Bridges destroyed his letters to Hopkins, Hopkins's letters to Bridges have been published and provide a fascinating glimpse into the poetic workshop of these two talented men and their complicated personal relationship. Although Bridges was independently wealthy, he entered medical studies after he had completed the work for his B.A. degree at Oxford and earned his degree in medicine in 1874. He practiced for some time in various hospitals in London, sometimes under grueling conditions. In 1877 he was appointed assistant physician in the Hospital for Sick Children, Great Ormond Street. In 1881 he suffered a severe illness, apparently pneumonia with complications, and retired from his medical career at the age of thirty-seven.

In 1882 Bridges moved to Manor House, Yattendon, Berkshire. Two years later he married Monica Waterhouse, the daughter of a famous architect. There, too, he and Harry Ellis Wooldridge produced *The Yattendon Hymnal* (1895-1899). In 1907, he moved to his final residence, Chilswell House, at Boar's Hill near Oxford. After his first collection of *Poems* in 1873, Bridges had been publishing lyric poetry and closet dramas steadily. His fame as a poet and man of letters increased over the decades until he was appointed poet laureate of England to succeed Alfred Austin in 1913. That year, together with Henry Bradley, Logan Pearsall Smith, and Walter Raleigh, he founded the society for Pure English. In his final years Bridges was an enormously influential figure in the literary world, editing the poems of his long-since dead friend, Gerard Manley Hopkins, in 1918, and composing his long philosophical poem *The Testament of Beauty* (1927-1929, 1930). He was decorated with the Order of Merit in 1929 and received honorary degrees from Oxford, St. Andrews University, Harvard, and the University of Michigan. He died at Boar's Hill, near Oxford, April 21, 1930.

ANALYSIS

In the first half of the twentieth century, a literary revolution occurred. Ezra Pound, T. S. Eliot, and their associates overpowered the previous genteel Victorian style of polite verse. To the advocates of this modernist revolution, the lyric poems of Robert Bridges seemed to represent everything corrupt in art: Bridges was traditional, a craftsman, controlled, impersonal, polished, moral, and optimistic. Although he had served as poet laureate from 1913 until 1930 and was a very influential and respected writer for the last forty years of his life, the use of modernism obliterated his fame within a few years after his death, so that he is virtually unknown by readers today. This fall from favor is not justified, and probably Bridges will one day be restored to his rightful position as a counterweight to T. S. Eliot in the 1920's, a worthy opponent of the new wave.

Bridges wrote only a few significant poems as a schoolboy. His serious inspiration came rather late, so that the poems collected in his first book, *Poems*, appear to have been written mainly in the preceding year. The 1873 collection is uneven, sometimes unsophisticated, and Bridges later tried to buy and destroy all the copies printed. He rewrote, added some poems, and deleted others entirely for his second series (1879) and his third series (1880). The *Shorter Poems* in four books published in 1890 grew out of the earlier volumes and established him as one of the leading poets of his time.

POEMS, THIRD SERIES

The 1880 *Poems, Third Series*, contains the justly famous "London Snow." This poem, written in rhymed iambic pentameter, describes London under an unusually heavy snowfall. Characteristically, Bridges describes the scene with detachment and great attention to detail. He tries to be accurate and not to inject an "unreal" sentiment into the scene. He tries to avoid the "pathetic fallacy," or the projection of imagined feelings onto Nature. "When men were all asleep the snow came flying,/ In large white flakes falling on the city brown." There is nothing supernatural in Bridges's scene, nor is there any extravagant emotion. The snow falls until the city is buried under a seven-inch, bright-white coating. The citizens of London awake early because of the unaccustomed light reflected from the whiteness. The city is strangely hushed as business has come to a halt. Schoolboys taste the pure snow and throw snowballs. The trees are decked with snowy robes. Only a few carts struggle through the nearly deserted streets and the sun gleams on the dome of St. Paul's Cathedral. Then, "sombre men, past tale of number" go forth to battle against the snow, trampling dark paths as they clear the streets and break the charm of the scene.

This moving poem in the plain style contrasts with the dark life in the city and the momentary ability of nature to create a miraculous transformation in the very heart of man's urban environment. It suggests the momentary, but muted, spark of recognition of the city workers that there is some power of Nature above human control. Bridges never resorts to any word or image in his text which is not plausible, easily understood, and "realistic." Comparing his description of London to T. S. Eliot's urban scenes, the reader easily sees a contrast between the modernist vision and the calm, controlled, delicate feelings of the more traditional work of Bridges.

Another highly praised poem in the 1880 *Poems, Third Series* is "On a Dead Child." Bridges was for some years a terribly overworked young doctor in an ur-

ban hospital. He once calculated that he had less than two minutes to spend with each of his patients a day. There is no doubt that he saw much of death. Under the circumstances, it would be easy to become callous, to shut out feelings altogether. On the other hand, no topic is more likely to lead the artist into sentimentality than the death of a young child. Bridges's poem delicately employs understatement. The speaker is probably a physician whose very young patient has just died. The poem is written in seven stanzas each of four lines rhyming *abba*. The length of the lines varies, probably following in a muted way the practice of "sprung rhythm" which Hopkins and Bridges developed in some of their lyrics. In the first three stanzas, the speaker notes how beautiful the dead child is, how disappointed the hopes of its parents must be. Then as the speaker performs his last services to the corpse, it seems that the infant hand clasps and holds his fingers momentarily. He thinks then about the universality of death hanging over all people; "Little at best can all our hopes avail us/ To life this sorrow, or cheer us, when in the dark,/ Unwilling, alone we embark." Bridges typically recognizes the hardness of the human lot, born to pain and death. He states plainly and directly man's condition, then faces it without whining or screaming, but with optimistic courage. In the death of a child he sees the death of all humankind. There is no use pretending that death is not fearful; still, the manful course is to face fate with whatever assistance reason can offer.

"LOW BAROMETER"

The poem which best exemplifies Bridges's mind and art is "Low Barometer." Written in seven stanzas, each of four lines rhyming *abab*, the poem imitates the long measure of the hymnal or the four-stress ballad line. Romantic poets frequently wrote poems about storms; typically they would imagine themselves standing on a mountain peak in the middle of lightning and rain, calling for their spirits to match the wild frenzy of nature. Bridges's poem attacks such Romantic evocations. He does not want emotional storms; he prefers reason, control, understatement. A low reading on the barometer signals a coming storm, and the first stanza describes such an impending gale. On such a night, when the storm beats against the house, supernatural fears arise in man, terrors of "god or ghost." When man imagines weird presences, his "Reason kens he herits in/ A haunted house." Reason becomes aware of the feeling of guilt and fear normally suppressed in everyday life. This "Pollution and remorse of time" awakened by the storm is aroused in the depths of the mind, like some monster which with "sightless footsteps" mounts the stair and bursts open the door. Some men try to control such horrible feelings by religion, but the monstrous images roam the earth until Nature itself at dawn withdraws the storm and thrusts "the baleful phantoms underground" once more. Nature restores calm and order in the end.

THE GROWTH OF LOVE

Many poets celebrate raw emotion: love, fear, or anger at its highest pitch. Bridges did not value emotion for its own sake. He felt that feeling should be restrained by reason, although reason itself knows that it is not sufficient to meet man's ultimate crises, such as death. A wise man seeks control and balance; only the ignorant gives himself over to uncontrolled emotion. Bridges wrote a sonnet sequence, *The Growth of Love*, first published in 1876 in twenty-four sonnets, but extensively revised in later versions. This work is modeled on the sonnet sequence of William Shakespeare, although the individual poems are written more in the style of John Milton. The traditional erotic sonnet sequence takes the form of the utterances of a lover; some of the poems in the sequence are addressed to the beloved lady praising her beauty, some are poems of seduction, and some are laments at her "cruelty." Frequently the sonnet sequence has an overall plot, involving a rival for the lady's affection, who receives the lover's scorn. Other poems address a faithless beloved, in which the lover is caught in a love-hate relationship with his lady. Usually the sequence traces the progress of a love affair as the lover approaches the lady, woos her, wins her, rejoices in his victory, but sees her affections cool as another lover intrudes into his domain.

Bridges constructs *The Growth of Love* in the tradition of such a sequence, but typically he "tones down" the violence of emotion in each of the traditional postures. The reader expects the lover to be hot and passionate, but Bridges's speaker is calm and analytical as he examines his relationship. As a picture of human love, these poems are disconcertingly cool. It is frequently the case that erotic poetry is a vehicle for a religious or philosophical idea. For example, the biblical Song of Solomon appears to be spoken by a lover to his beloved, but an analogical reading of the text reveals that the song is about the love of man and God. Probably Bridges intended his erotic sonnet sequence to have a similar analogical meaning. If one understands the beloved to be, not a woman, but the ideal moral perfection in life, the overall detachment in the work is understandable. The broad argument of *The Growth of Love* is reflected in Bridges's later long philosophical poem *The Testament of Beauty*.

POETICAL WORKS

The *Poetical Works of Robert Bridges* were published between 1898 and 1905 in six volumes. More than four of these volumes are composed of poetical dramas and masques. Obviously, Bridges spent much effort in writing dramatic poetry. Equally obviously, these plays are quite unsuitable for the stage, lacking action and sharp characterization. All of the plays except *Nero Part I* were intended to be performed, but only the masques *Prometheus the Firegiver* and *Demeter* and the play *The Humours of the Court* (1893) were actually produced—and these in amateur renditions only. It is difficult to see why Bridges expended so much energy in this kind of writing. In contrast, Robert Browning began his literary career with a series of more or less failed plays, but went on to develop his dramatic monologues as a new and powerful form of poetry; one can see Browning building on his early failures. No such clear line of development, however, is discernible in Bridges. Most of his plays were written in the decade of the 1880's, and when his influential collected *Poems* of 1890 appeared, his lyric poems were seen not to represent a logical progression from the dramatic works with which he had been occupied.

His best plays are historical: *Nero Part I* and *Nero Part II*. While this study of the decline of the Roman emperor Nero into madness and violence is a reasonable topic for a play, it is one unsuited to Bridges's talents. When the author of such work writes the speeches of a mad character, he must assume the mask and speak with a certain amount of sympathy for the eccentric point of view of a madman. In Bridges's best poetry, however, unlike Browning in his dramatic poems, he never plays the devil's advocate; and it is precisely this that is required for a satisfactory dramatic treatment of Nero, one of those figures who, like the fearful men in the storm in "Low Barometer," are swept up by the "unbodied presences" and "horrors of unhoused crime." Bridges never puts himself *inside* such figures; he always stands outside them, describing them, judging them, evaluating them. While this is the strength of his poetry, it makes it nearly impossible for him to bring to life a character who is vicious or insane.

Bridges wrote four masques based on classical mythology; his model was probably Milton's *Comus* (1634). Albert Guérard in *Robert Bridges: A Study of Traditionalism in Poetry* (1942) maintains that Bridges's earliest and most impressive masque, *Prometheus the Firegiver*, "symbolizes the substitution of the God of Love of the New Testament for the Angry God of the Old Testament; or, more generally, of modern Christianity for all less 'human' religions." Many readers, however, will agree with Bridges's friend and best critic, Gerard Manley Hopkins, who warned him that he should not try to write about the Greek gods in any case, because they were frigid and remote from modern experience.

THE TESTAMENT OF BEAUTY

In his last years, Bridges wrote a long philosophical poem, *The Testament of Beauty*. The poem falls into four books: *Introduction, Selfhood, Breed, Ethick.* The overall problem is to fit modern science into a meaningful framework: the relationship of Darwinian theories of evolution to the moral purpose behind death and suffering. *The Testament of Beauty* seems to move digressively and its argument is not entirely clear. The *Introduction* discusses at length the ramifications of evolution. The second book, *Selfhood*, studies egotism, self-preservation, and selfishness in their manifestations in the lowest forms of life up to their presence in man's highest artistic accomplishments and his darkest violence. The book discusses the carnage of World War I. Can all evolution be moving toward such pointless destruction? The third book, *Breed*, treats sexual instinct. It traces the growth of love from elementary sex to spiritual love. The fourth book, *Ethick*, explores the role of "reason" in conduct. As one would expect from Bridges's other works, "reason" is the key, the difference between humane, ethical behavior and mere brutal-

ity. Reason balances the instincts and the impulses of the human organism, molding evolutionary pressures into moral refinement.

MILTON'S PROSODY

Bridges's study of the metrical form of Milton's poetry is one of the earliest examples of truly scientific observation applied to literary problems. *Milton's Prosody* was first published in 1893 and later republished in expanded form with the inclusion of a paper by his associate William Johnson Stone, "Classical Metres in English Verse," in 1901. Poetry differs from prose, Bridges contends, in that poetry maintains some controlled repetition or patterning in the language which is not found in normal, everyday speech. For Bridges, there were four types of meter in English verse: (1) accentual syllabic, (2) accentual, (3) syllabic, and (4) quantitative. Each controls a different element of language so as to create a repetitive pattern. Accent involves the relative loudness with which a syllable is pronounced. Some poems, such as traditional ballads, seem to follow a pattern only in the number of loudly pronounced syllables in each line, no matter how many unstressed syllables occur. This is purely accentual verse. Other poems seem to have the same number of syllables in corresponding lines, but varying numbers of accents. This is syllabic verse. Classical poetry in Latin and Greek appeared to have been regulated by long and short vowel sounds, and it was traditionally thought that patterns of long and short syllables could be made up into "feet," or metrical units, based on the vowel quantity of each syllable. In Milton's *Paradise Lost* (1667), however, Bridges discerned an accentual-syllabic system which forms its patterns of repetition based on both the number of syllables in each line and the position of the more loudly pronounced syllables.

What is unusual about Bridges's study is his method of basing his generalizations on close scientific observation. Critics of his work might argue that when he deals with Milton's language, there is room for much misunderstanding. Is he talking about the production of sound by the human voice apparatus or is he talking about the code of written speech, so many marks on a page? Is he perhaps talking about the way the human mind apprehends sound? Apparently he is governed by thinking of language as the production of sound. He says that language has *stress*, unwittingly referring perhaps to the stress felt when one pronounces a syllable more loudly than another by exercising the diaphragm muscles. So long as one grants that he is talking about the production of sound, his study seems well-argued.

Milton's Prosody is subtitled *An Examination of the Rules of the Blank Verse in Milton's Later Poems, with an Account of the Versification of "Samson Agonistes," and General Notes*. Typically the blank verse line has three characteristics: (1) it has ten syllables (2) it has five stresses (3) it is rising; the stresses are on the even-positioned syllables. Bridges first establishes that these characteristics occur in *Paradise Lost* and then examines cases which seem to deviate from the norm, trying for a generalization that can account for all exceptions, much as a law of physics is deemed "true" when it explains all occurrences. In separate chapters he examines exceptions to the number of syllables being ten, the number of stresses being five, and the position of stresses being rising. These discussions are too detailed for summary here, but they should be examined by any serious student of English metrics. When Bridges turns to Milton's later poems, *Paradise Regained* and *Samson Agonistes* (both 1671), he finds that there is a much less rigid patterning, and he tries to account for the wider variations found in these poems.

The final section of Bridges's 1901 volume is taken up with William Johnson Stone's "Classical Metres in English Verse: A History and Criticism of the Attempts Hitherto Made, Together with a Scheme for the Determination of the Quantity of English Syllables, Based on Their Actual Phonetic Condition." This essay is particularly important because it is the basis for Bridges's actual experiments in writing English poetry in the quantitative measures of Latin and Greek. Stone's study, however, contains many doubtful statements about the nature of classical languages. He believed that there was no difference between the classical long/short vowel quantity and modern spoken English vowels, and this assumption is improbable. Nevertheless, Stone proposes a method for determining the quantity of English vowels and for establishing in modern English a meter comparable to his understanding of Latin and Greek meters. Stone's death caused Bridges to feel obliged to justify or demonstrate Stone's theory in practice, and so Bridges

attempted the metrical experiments published in his collected poems. Bridges also made a number of translations from classical languages into English in which he tried to preserve in English the metrical quantitative structure of the original language. Some of these translations are of extremely high artistic quality, such as the translation of Homer's *Iliad*, Book XXIV.

LATER YEARS

From about 1890 to 1930 Bridges was considered one of England's leading lyric poets. His fame was eclipsed at his death, but he has become established as an important, if minor, poet, part of the background against which the great modernists rebelled. His most important contribution to literature has not as yet been fully recognized: He was a pioneering scholar and experimentalist in metrics, and his greatest achievement was not (as he thought) his dramatic poems nor his long philosophical verse but his experiments in quantitative meters.

OTHER MAJOR WORKS

PLAYS: *Prometheus the Firegiver*, pb. 1884 (verse masque); *Nero Part I*, pb. 1885 (verse drama); *The Feast of Bacchus*, pb. 1889 (verse drama); *Palicio*, pb. 1890 (verse drama); *The Return of Ulysses*, pb. 1890 (verse drama); *The Christian Captives*, pb. 1890 (verse drama); *Achilles in Scyros*, pb. 1890 (verse drama); *The Humours of the Court*, pb. 1893 (verse drama); *Nero Part II*, pb. 1894 (verse drama); *Demeter*, pb. 1905 (verse masque).

NONFICTION: *Milton's Prosody: An Examination of the Rules of the Blank Verse in Milton's Later Poems with an Account of the Versification of "Samson Agonistes," and General Notes*, 1893, revised 1901; *John Keats*, 1895; *The Necessity of Poetry*, 1918; *Collected Essays, Papers, Etc.*, 1927-1936; *Three Friends: Memoirs of Digby Mackworth Dolben, Richard Watson Dixon, and Henry Bradley*, 1932; *Correspondence of Robert Bridges and Henry Bradley, 1900-1923*, 1940.

BIBLIOGRAPHY

Guérard, Albert, Jr. *Robert Bridges: A Study of Traditionalism in Poetry*. 1942. Reprint. New York: Russell & Russell, 1965. This standard work on Bridges includes a comprehensive study of the lyric, dramatic, and philosophical poems. Guérard contends that Bridges is misunderstood if regarded only as a poet of happy emotions and that he is intensely serious and his view of life is far from completely rosy. The dramatic poems and plays form the bulk of Bridges' work, and their study has been neglected. This book, heavily influenced by the critic Yvor Winters, defends Bridges' traditionalism. Includes a conspectus of Bridges' sources and analogues.

Phillips, Catherine. *Robert Bridges.* New York: Oxford University Press, 1992. This biography discusses the ways in which Bridges reflected his Victorian background and examines his friendship with Gerard Manley Hopkins. Phillips demonstrates the ways in which Bridges, who lived until 1930, anticipated a number of modern advancements.

Ritz, Jean-Georges. *Robert Bridges and Gerard Hopkins, 1863-1889: A Literary Friendship.* London: Oxford University Press, 1960. Bridges and the late Victorian poet Gerard Manley Hopkins were close friends from the days of their college years at Oxford. Ritz discusses Bridges's academic interests and friendships and analyzes in detail his correspondence with Hopkins. (Only Hopkins's letters to Bridges have survived.) Particularly valuable is the presentation of each poet's discussion of the verse of the other. Hopkins endeavored to give Bridges's poems more drama and a personal touch. Ritz is especially informative on the way in which Bridges's poetry reflects his character.

Smith, Nowell Charles. *Notes on "The Testament of Beauty."* London: Oxford University Press, 1931. Still a standard guidebook to Bridges's most famous poem. Smith begins with a brief discussion of its theme. The poem attempts to present the place of man in the universe, principally using Charles Darwin's theory of evolution as a background. It thus aims to be a modern equivalent of Lucretius's *On the Nature of Things,* summing up science and philosophy poetically. The bulk of the book consists of detailed notes on the poem. The author explains unusual words, paraphrases Bridges's meaning, and points out references to other poets such as John Milton and William Wordsworth.

Sparrow, John. *Robert Bridges.* London: Longmans, Green, 1962. Sparrow centers his study on Bridges's doctrine that poetry should express beauty, understood as a form of goodness. Bridges had the ability to portray vividly scenes from nature, a principal source of his poetic inspiration. His diction is carefully calibrated to evoke the moods he wishes to convey. He was particularly adept at using difficult meter as an instrument of emotional presentation. Although Sparrow devotes some attention to Bridges's failures, he rates him among the foremost English poets as he was unsurpassed in the creation of beautiful poems.

Stanford, Donald E. *In the Classic Mode: The Achievement of Robert Bridges.* Newark: University of Delaware Press, 1978. This book offers a detailed analysis of Bridges's experiments in meter: accentuated verse, quantitative meter, and neo-Miltonic syllabics. The work aims to give a full portrait of Bridges's literary corpus and includes the most detailed discussions of his plays in the secondary literature. Bridges's criticism also comes in for attention, particularly his study of John Keats. The discussion of George Santayana's influence on *The Testament of Beauty* is excellent.

Todd K. Bender

JOSEPH BRODSKY

Born: Leningrad, U.S.S.R.; May 24, 1940
Died: Brooklyn, New York; January 28, 1996

PRINCIPAL POETRY

Stikhotvoreniya i poemy, 1965
Elegy to John Donne and Other Poems, 1967
Ostanovka v pustyne: Stikhotvoreniya i poemy, 1970
Debut, 1973
Selected Poems, 1973
Konets prekrasnoi epokhi: Stikhotvoreniya, 1964-1971, 1977
Chast' rechi: Stikhotvoreniya, 1972-1976, 1977
V Anglii, 1977
Verses on the Winter Campaign 1980, 1980
A Part of Speech, 1980

Rimskie elegii, 1982

Novye stansy k Avguste: Stichi k M.B., 1962-1982, 1983

Uraniia: Novaya kniga stikhov, 1987

To Urania: Selected Poems, 1965-1985, 1988

Chast' rechi: Izbrannye stikhi, 1962-1989, 1990

Bog sokhraniaet vse, 1991

Forma vremeni, 1992 (2 volumes; volume 2 includes essays and plays)

Rozhdestvenskie stikhi, 1992, 2d edition 1996 (*Nativity Poems*, 2001)

Izbrannye stikhotvoreniya, 1957-1992, 1994

So Forth, 1996

Collected Poems in English, 2000

OTHER LITERARY FORMS

Joseph Brodsky's essays and reviews, some of which have been collected in *Less than One* (1984), are valuable in their own right; brilliant, arrogant, and idiosyncratic, they establish Brodsky as one of the finest poet-essayists of the twentieth century. Among Brodsky's subjects are Osip and Nadezhda Mandelstam, Marina Tsvetayeva (unlike most of his prose, his two essays on Tsvetayeva, one brief and one extended, were written in Russian, the language Brodsky normally reserves for his poetry), W. H. Auden, Constantine Cavafy, and Eugenio Montale. The essay "Less than One" is an extraordinary meditation on the city of Leningrad, part memoir and part cultural history.

ACHIEVEMENTS

Joseph Brodsky is generally recognized as one of the most gifted poets writing in Russian in the twentieth century; for many, there is little question of his having any rivals. Perhaps Brodsky's most remarkable achievement was his ability to continue writing poems in Russian despite the hardships of political persecution within the Soviet Union and, later, the alienation from the everyday rhythms of the Russian language imposed by his exile to the United States. Brodsky matured as a poet in a Leningrad devoid of poetic "movements"; indeed, the sense of being alone as a poet pervades his work to an unusual degree. It is difficult to assess Brodsky's generation of poets. The work of contemporaries whom he has praised, poets such as Evgeni Rein and Anatol' Naiman,

is available only sporadically in the West, and then in the limited distribution of the émigré presses.

Brodsky's poems have been translated into many languages, including French, German, Italian, Swedish, Czech, and Hebrew, but it is the English translations that won him high regard and a rather wide audience in the West. Brodsky's participation in the translation process, given his own fine skills as a translator, ensured high-quality versions which sound like anything but adaptations from another language. Brodsky was accorded many honors, including Guggenheim and MacArthur Foundation Fellowships, an honorary doctorate from Yale University, membership in the American Academy of Arts and Letters, and the Nobel Prize for Literature in 1987. He was appointed the Poet Laureate Consultant in Poetry in 1991-1992.

Joseph Brodsky, Nobel laureate in literature for 1987.
(© The Nobel Foundation)

BIOGRAPHY

Joseph Aleksandrovich Brodsky was born in Leningrad on May 24, 1940. Brodsky's mother worked as a translator, an occupation her son was to take up as well; his father worked as a news photographer. During the German blockade of the city, Brodsky spent some time with his grandparents. He has recalled a somewhat later time of fear during the government-orchestrated anti-Semitic hysteria of 1953, when it seemed that his family might be "resettled" far from Leningrad. During these last years of Stalinism, Brodsky was an unenthusiastic student; he left school in 1955 to pursue independent studies in various languages and literatures. In 1956, he began learning Polish, a language which gave him access to Western literature not available in Russian; he recalled that he first read the works of Franz Kafka and William Faulkner in Polish translation, and he encountered the poetry of Czesław Miłosz, whom he called "one of the greatest poets of our time, perhaps the greatest."

The year 1956, when Brodsky was only sixteen, was crucial in establishing his sense of himself and of Russia. When Brodsky refered to himself as a member of the "generation of 1956," he had in mind the shock of recognition forced by the invasion of Hungary, a recognition of his status as a poet in a totalitarian state. If Brodsky saw Stalinism less as a political era than as a "state of mind," then the events of 1956, three years after the death of Stalin, proved the ugly endurance of a repressive regime which soon began to harass Brodsky personally.

Brodsky made several trips away from Leningrad on geological expeditions, traveling throughout the Soviet Union to the Amur River near China, Central Asia, the Caspian Sea region in the South, and the White Sea area in the North, where he was to spend nearly two years in exile a few years later. These travels exposed Brodsky to a variety of landscapes and may in part account for the powerful, if unattractive, natural descriptions in his mature verse. His travels permitted him a great deal of freedom, but his vaguely unorthodox movements and affiliations eventually drew the attention of KGB officials. Brodsky was first arrested in 1959 and twice confined to mental hospitals. These visits provided the setting for his most ambitious long poem, a dialogue between "Gorbunov i Gorchakov" ("Gorbunov and Gorcha-

kov"). Brodsky had begun writing poems as early as 1958, though he later dated his first serious work from about 1963 (the year of his elegy to John Donne).

Arrested again and tried in 1964, Brodsky was sentenced in March to five years exile and hard labor; the charge was "parasitism." In effect, Brodsky was put on trial for identifying himself as a poet without "proof" in the form of a university degree or membership in the Writers' Union. The notes from his trial, smuggled out of Leningrad and excerpted often in articles about Brodsky, make for perverse evidence for his belief that the spiritual activity of writing poetry cannot be tolerated by a state which defines writing as a political act. Many Soviet cultural figures of international renown, including Dmitri Shostakovich and Kornei Chukovskii, testified on Brodsky's behalf and agitated for his early release, often at great professional and personal risk. As a result, Brodsky served only twenty months of his term, doing agricultural work in a small "village"—actually just a few huts in the wilderness—near Arkhangel'sk. He continued reading and writing; his first acquaintance with the works of W. H. Auden came in 1965, in translation. (He had known Robert Frost's poems as early as 1962 and was astonished by Frost's "hidden, controlled terror.")

Auden's influence is apparent in Brodsky's poem written on the occasion of T. S. Eliot's death in 1965; the lament looks ahead to the mature verse that Brodsky was writing on his return to Leningrad that year. It was at this time that his friends succeeded in shortening the length of his prison term. Anna Akhmatova, whom Brodsky had first met in 1960, was chief among this group of friends. Though he did not recall initially feeling an affinity with Akhmatova, Brodsky and she became close friends. His work owes more to the style and preoccupations of Osip Mandelstam than to Akhmatova, but Brodsky found in Akhmatova a living link to Russia's great poetic tradition, a poet who had known Mandelstam well, a poet who incarnated in her life and in her verse Russia's great upheavals.

Brodsky matured a great deal as a poet between 1965 and 1972. He gave readings to small groups of students, and even managed to have four of his poems published in 1966 and 1967 in official publications of Soviet cultural organs. A first volume of his poems had appeared without his authorization in the United States in 1965; a revised version, which included new poems, came out in 1970. Brodsky supported himself in Leningrad as a translator during these years, producing Russian versions of writers ranging from Andrew Marvell and John Donne to Tom Stoppard. Brodsky did nothing, however, to become more acceptable to the Soviet regime during these seven years in Leningrad. In 1972, he was exiled from the Soviet Union; he was not even told where the plane he was boarding would take him—to Siberian exile, or to freedom in the West. The plane landed in Vienna, where Brodsky was met by an American Slavicist, Carl Proffer, with an invitation to teach in Ann Arbor, Michigan. In Vienna, Brodsky sought out W. H. Auden, who arranged for him to participate in the Poetry International in London and generally smoothed his way for his introduction to the West.

Settling in the United States, Brodsky slowly began a life of teaching, writing, giving readings, and meeting fellow poets. He has taught at the University of Michigan, Queens College, the Five Colleges (Amherst, Hampshire, Mount Holyoke, Smith, and the University of Massachusetts), New York University, and Columbia University. In 1981, he became the Five College Distinguished Professor of Literature, with tenure at Mount Holyoke College; he also spent time teaching at Columbia. Brodsky became an American citizen in 1977. He won the Nobel Prize for Literature in 1987 and served as the poet laureate of the United States in 1991. He died in Brooklyn, New York, on January 28, 1996.

ANALYSIS

In describing his poetry, Joseph Brodsky had said that his "main interest is the nature of time," a theme which also recurs with obsessive frequency in his essays. Beginning even before his exile to Arkhangel'sk in 1964 and persisting in his most recent works, there is a preoccupation with endings, with concluding moments which illuminate with sudden new depth the meaning of all that has come before. Brodsky, whose stance as a poet is that of a watcher and listener rather than that of a participant and speaker, records his sense of a period of time in a manner that is more transcendental than teleological. In a 1962 poem, "Ogon', ty slyshish' . . ." ("The Fire Is Dying Down"), Brodsky observes how the room

and objects around him absorb the shifts in time marked by the changing fire. A sense of lateness advances on the poet "from the corners"; he finds himself "suddenly at the center." Time has paused so palpably that the "clock hands have completely disappeared." The fire dies by the end of this twenty-line poem, but its brightness does not abandon the attentive watcher, who remains behind in the room's darkness. Just as it is important that the clock hands are not only invisible but also *silent*, silence being the analogue of time's halt, so it is crucial in the last line that the fire glows not in the poet's eyes, but in the room itself. The encroaching darkness of the dying fire becomes an external event that marks the inner fact of the poet's eyes growing cold, "motionless."

"SONNET"

In another short lyric of 1962, a poem of fourteen lines with only a few near-rhymes and simply titled "Sonet" ("Sonnet"), Brodsky explores a moment defined by a different kind of ending. Speaking to a loved woman, the poet envisions a new eruption of Vesuvius which will someday cover their dusty city with ash. He hopes that when the eruption begins, he will be able to set off for her house, so that future excavators will find them still embraced. The poem stops time in that final embrace, preserved by a layer of ash. The embrace and the ash are equally sustaining for the poet, who notes the passing clouds, a frequent emblem for the passing of time in Brodsky's poems. It is typical of Brodsky's poems that the very moment which destroys a city and all life in it also contains the possibility of preservation against decay.

The poem mirrors this contrast between the threat of change and the saving power of volcanic ash in its formal arrangement. As in many early Brodsky poems, the unit of division in the poem is the line. Without enjambments and virtually without rhyme (there is some sound interlocking in the first four lines), the poem's ordering principle is the sequence of its thoughts, expressed at the even pace of one clause per line. The exception is line twelve, "then I would like for them to find me," a single thought in two clauses (in Russian), the crucial turning point of the poem. The meter of the poem is iambic, mostly feminine pentameter, five-footed iambs being the commonest line length in Brodsky's repertoire in the 1960's, and the most successful. The sonnet feels experimental, though, because there are two lines of two and four metric feet, respectively, and virtually no rhyme, as if it were testing the boundaries of its own timing. Like Brodsky's many unrhymed sonnets, the poem shows how time can be controlled, slowed or hurried, within the conventions of meter and rhyme; the final picture of an unending embrace literally suspends time, so that the poem challenges, visually as well as verbally, the unspoken condition of all Brodsky's work, the effect of time on man.

The tender lyrics of early, as well as later, Brodsky, are balanced by verses of ironic distance and glittering wit. In some poems, such as the famous "Pamiatnik" ("Monument"), the serious if slightly mocking tones of the first lines ("Let's build a monument/ at the end of a long city street") turns toward a sarcastic finale—in this case prepared for by the poem's accumulation of petty details from Leningrad life: "Let's build a monument to lies." That final sentence indicts monument building as yet another hypocritical activity in a society whose public life proves inevitably false. In a longer poem, "Dva chasa v rezervuare" ("Two Hours in a Reservoir"), Brodsky mixes German and Yiddish phrases into a running monologue. The speaker pronounces his thoughts as they furiously charge past him in whatever language comes to his lips: "Enter and *exeunt* devils, thoughts./ Enter and *exeunt* guests, years." Narrative fragments about Faust and Johann Wolfgang von Goethe, Dr. Faustus and Thomas Mann, interrupt speculations about God and poetry and the fact that man is hurtling toward his death. The poem extends Brodsky's preoccupation with time, quoting Faust's famous desire to seize and hold one beautiful moment, a line Brodsky might be expected to appreciate—indeed, one he uses more than once. The poem's pace, though, is breakneck, the puns (particularly between languages) rampant, and the humor of the piece as pungent as it is inventive. Brodsky's search for ways to understand the passing of time, often defined by its endpoints, emerges in poems as varied as the witty "Odnoi poetesse" ("To a Certain Poetess"), where a relationship has outlived love, or the delicate "Aeneas i Dido" ("Aeneas and Dido"), where the moment of parting is captured poignantly by details—passing clouds, the hem of a tunic, a fish chasing after a ship at sail.

"AENEAS AND DIDO"

"Aeneas and Dido" deals with the end of a myth, and the poem concludes with a memorable picture. Dido watches Aeneas looking through a window, both of them realizing that the new gusts of wind will make it possible for Aeneas to set sail and leave Dido behind. Windows appear frequently in Brodsky's poems, often framing a landscape seen from within a room. Indeed, space becomes almost the conceptual framework through which time is explored in Brodsky's poems: His remark that literature shows what time does to a man was made in a talk titled "Language as Otherland," and the titles of his poems often locate lyrics spatially as well as temporally. Examples of this can be found in each stage of his career, including "Zimnim vecherom v Ialte" ("A Winter Evening in Yalta"), "Dekabr' vo Florentsii" ("December in Florence"), and "Osen' v Norenskoi" ("Autumn in Norenskaia").

SETTING

Brodsky's settings are occasionally interiors; small rooms become intimate settings for discovering the world outside and, always, oneself. In "Sumev otgorodit'sia . . ." ("Now that I've walled myself off from the world"), glimpses of puddles and fir trees merge with the domestic drama of a poet studying his face in a mirror. Brodsky has moments of self-description, framed by mirrors and windows, reminiscent of the later works of Akhmatova, though Brodsky always seems in search of some truth deeper than the self-image a piece of glass presents him. Self and other, interiors and landscapes interpenetrate one another in Brodsky's poems; as furiously as he seeks boundaries, walling himself off spatially, or describing endpoints in time, spaces and periods of time run into one another, and the confusions press the poet all the more in his attempt at self-definition.

Brodsky's landscapes are inseparable from the homesickness which pervades his verse. There *is* no place called "home" which is exempt. While he was in internal exile in Arkhangl'sk, Brodsky compared himself to Ovid; in the West, he has described scenes as diverse as Cape Cod and Cuernavaca, hills and lagoons and sluggish rivers, stopovers in St. Mark's Piazza or along Roman roads. Brodsky loves Venice, a city which glows through his poems like Leningrad, but there is not any landscape, any visual image of indoor or outdoor space with which the poet is not somehow at odds.

New places provide fresh scenes for seeing, new ways to show what one must see. If the goal of his poetry is, as Brodsky said in 1972, "to show man the true scale of what is happening," then landscape and cityscape finally offer a figurative vocabulary for philosophical apperceptions. The "scale" for Brodsky is never political but always personal, a fact which made him politically suspect in the Soviet Union.

PHILOSOPHY

Brodsky's philosophical preoccupations (the nature of "reality," and what it means for time to pass) and figures of expression (mythological plots, interior and exterior landscapes) are constants in his poetry, of which he continues to find new variations. There is, however, a more distinct sense of development in the prosodic features of Brodsky's poems, and these changes provide the clearest indications of his battle with Russian poetic tradition. Certain Brodskian themes resemble those of poets whom he is known to admire: the parting and exile of Mandelstam, the meditations on death of Evgeni Baratynskii, the monuments of Alexander Pushkin if not of Gavrila Derzhavin, the epistolary acts of self-definition of Dmitry Kantemir. In the case of Brodsky's verse forms, however, there are only a few poems with rather self-conscious and specific models, the most notable being his poem on the death of Eliot, written in the form and spirit of Auden's "In Memory of W. B. Yeats."

POETIC FORMS

Brodsky's early poems strive to carve their own prosodic molds, using simple, assertive sentences, and a structuring free-verse line the firm closure of which allows few enjambments. The rhymes are experimental, often only hints at sound repetitions. In the early 1960's, Brodsky experimented with the placement of the line in such poems as "Ryby zimoi" ("Fish in Winter") and "Stikhi pod èpigrafom" ("Verses with an Epigraph"). Poems such as these make the most startling break with Russian prosodic tradition, spread over a page in complex patterns of indentation like those of E. E. Cummings (whom Brodsky admired in his youth). More deeply radical, though, and more difficult to sustain, are poems with very long verse lines, such as "Proplyvaiut

oblaka" ("Clouds Swim By"). Here Brodsky repeats and interweaves similar phrases to break up long lines, while subtly binding them more tightly one to another. In later poems, Brodsky has used refrains to the same effect: The word "stifling" recurs as a one-word sentence in "Kolybel'naia Treskovogo Mysa" ("Lullaby of Cape Cod"). The long line has led Brodsky to explore ternary meters (several poems use anapest pentameter); in some cases, various kinds of ternary meters appear fleetingly with rhymes or near-rhymes structuring the poem. The impression in "Clouds Swim By" is one of fluidity which is being formidably if flexibly shaped, perhaps the most appropriate form for a poem that describes the changing shapes of clouds overhead.

Longer verse lines have come into Brodsky's work with complex sentences, as well as enjambments more abrupt than those previously found in Russian poetry. Regular meters are usually used, though they are the less common meters of iambic pentameter (not the common meter in Russian as it is in English; Russian depends far more on iambic tetrameter) and anapest pentameter. There are striking ventures in stanzaic form, the most remarkable in "Gorbunov and Gorchakov." In this long poem, Brodsky limits himself to an *abababababab* sequence in each ten-line stanza; the poem contains fourteen sections of ten such stanzas and is actually a conversation, sustaining the rhythms and dictions of colloquial speech within its very demanding form.

With these additional formal complexities, Brodsky has entered a grammatical universe adequate to the expression of his metaphysical questions. As has been noted by Richard Sylvester, Brodsky's complex sentences convey an ever-changing nexus of logical relationships, where words such as "because," "despite," "when," "where," and "if" become the all-important links in sentences dependent on several semantic fields. In such late poems as the cycle "Chast' rechi" ("A Part of Speech"), subject matter, diction, even stylistic level may change in such quick succession as to seem arbitrary: One poem in the cycle begins "A list of some observations." Yet Brodsky's poetry has become anything but inscrutable; his complex forms provide myriad vehicles perfectly suited for exploring themes of fragmentation, decay, solitary observation, and intense recollection.

A PART OF SPEECH

In Brodsky's well-received collection, *A Part of Speech*, images and underlying questions extend the issues raised in his earlier poems. The desire to focus on particular points in time finds him often retreating into memory. The orientation toward the past was felt keenly in poems from the 1960's; one of Brodsky's best-known poems is "Ostanovka v pustyne" ("A Halt in the Wilderness"), where the razing of an Orthodox church is witnessed as a gesture of senseless modernization. Time as a category has tragic dimensions for Brodsky, as he himself has said. Near the end of "A Halt in the Wilderness," he speaks acerbically of "the relay race of human history." That poem looks ahead to ask what sacrifices the new era might demand, but there is no redeeming belief in progress for Brodsky. In his essays, Brodsky has dwelt on the evils of the twentieth century; he offers his readers little consolation and certainly no respite from personal responsibility in the dogmas of ideology or religion. In "Lullaby of Cape Cod," Brodsky defines his sense of human knowledge and its limitations in lines that resonate beyond his experience of emigration: "Having sampled two/ oceans as well as continents, I feel that I know/ what the globe itself must feel: there's nowhere to go."

Akhmatova found that in Brodsky's first poems the speaking voice was extremely solitary. The sense of bearing a unique vision is undiminished in Brodsky's recent poems, ranging from the varieties of quantification in "Lullaby of Cape Cod" to the equation that acts as a fluctuating refrain in "Èkloga IV-ia (Zimniaia)" ("Winter Eclogue: IV"): "Time equals cold." The more nearly oxymoronic Brodsky's declarations, the more finely he has sharpened his sense of the metaphysical conceit into an instrument for measuring a vision which is always just evading the poet's means of expression.

There is no expectation of finding the "right" metaphor, as frequent images of echoless space imply. "A glance," wrote Brodsky in "A Part of Speech," "is accustomed to no glance back." Brodsky's poems are less a relief from solitude than a journey forth, a journey deeper and farther into the "otherland" of language. To say that the journey is "merely long" is to say nothing, and to say everything. Brodsky writes in "Lullaby of Cape Cod":

Far longer is the sea.
At times, like a wrinkled forehead, it displays
a rolling wave. And longer still than these
is the strand of matching beads of countless days;
and nights.

To observe that the break between "days" and "nights" is radical in terms of syntax and prosody is to describe Brodsky's poetics; to add that the break is unbearably long, that it expresses a discontinuity central to his metaphysical premises, is to initiate an examination of Brodsky's underlying themes at the level on which he deserves to be understood.

TO URANIA

Two collections of Brodsky's poetry contain translations of his Russian poems, by him and by others, as well as poems written in English. For this reason, there is a noticeable incongruence of themes and styles. *To Urania: Selected Poems, 1965-1985*, contains poems from his earlier collections *A Part of Speech* and *Uraniia*. They express the poet's nostalgia for his homeland and are elegies for parents and friends, mixed with his musings about historical events and European cities, in which intellectually he felt at home as much as in his homeland. Moreover, fourteen cantos in his peculiar bardic style are actually a dialogue between two patients in a Soviet psychiatric ward. Brodsky indulges in his familiar attempts to fathom the mysteries of memory of the things past and to reconcile the limits of time and space, as he has done throughout his poetic career. References to political matters, especially their seamy side, are also vintage Brodsky. Elements of a realistic and a spiritual, almost metaphysical approach to poetry are masterfully proportioned, as in many of his collections. Subdued sorrow of an exile unable or unwilling to forget the old and fully accept the new breaks through the veneer of bombastic intonations. Finally, his difficulties in mastering fully the idiom of a foreign language are manifested in sporadic rough renditions of English idioms.

SO FORTH

The collection *So Forth* offers poems written during the last decade of Brodsky's life. As in *To Urania*, they are both translations and poems written originally in English. Considered by some critics as a collection of perhaps his best poetry (while others point out his awkwardness in juggling the two languages), *So Forth* displays Brodsky's ability to conform his remarkable erudition and never fully satisfied curiosity to his unique style. Even though, as in *To Urania*, he tries his best to be a poet-citizen of the world, the deep sorrow that he was forced out of his homeland is beautifully expressed in the poem "In Memory of My Father: Australia," in which the poet sees in a dream his father sailing as a ghost to Australia, that is, being free to travel. Not all poems are somber and heavy. Some are surprisingly light, as is the poem "A Song"—dancing, as it were, like a child in play. Yet, most of Brodsky's late poems are elegiac, somber, ironic, always reminding his readers of sorrow and death.

OTHER MAJOR WORKS

NONFICTION: *Less than One: Selected Essays*, 1986; *Watermark*, 1992; *Vspominaia Akhmatova*, 1992; *On Grief and Reason: Essays*, 1995; *Homage to Robert Frost*, 1996 (with Seamus Heaney and Derek Walcott).

BIBLIOGRAPHY

Bethea, David M. *Joseph Brodsky and the Creation of Exile*. Princeton, N.J.: Princeton University Press, 1994. A critical analysis that compares and contrasts Brodsky to the poet's favorite models—Donne, Auden, Mandelstam, and Tsvetaeva—and analyzes his fundamental differences with Nabokov. Various critical paradigms are used throughout the study as foils to Brodsky's thinking. Includes a bibliography and index.

Loseff, Lev, and Valentina Polukhina, eds. *Brodsky's Poetics and Aesthetics*. New York: St. Martin's Press, 1990. In this collection of essays, various authors discuss such topics as politics and poetics, affinities between Brodsky and Osip Mandelstam, the theme of exile, and individual aspects of Brodsky's poetics and poems.

_____. *Joseph Brodsky: The Art of a Poem*. New York: St. Martin's Press, 1999. In the second collection of essays on Brodsky the editors concentrate on individual poems and on purely aesthetic aspects of his poetry. The essays, written in both Russian and English, analyze in depth the most significant of Brodsky's poems, using citations in Russian and English.

MacFadyen, David. *Joseph Brodsky and the Baroque*. Montreal: McGill-Queen's University Press, 1998. A thorough analysis of the baroque elements in Brodsky's poetry and of the affinities with, and influence of, philosophers Søren Kirkegaard and Lev Shestov and the poet John Donne. The comparison of Brodsky's poetry before and after exile is especially poignant.

_____. *Joseph Brodsky and the Soviet Muse*. Montreal: McGill-Queen's University Press, 2000. An assessment of Brodsky's significance as a shaper and remaker of Soviet poetry in his early years. The contact with, and influence of, the writings of Joyce, Dos Passos, Hemingway, Robert Frost, Boris Pasternak and Marina Tsvetayeva are chronicled, with suitable citations, in Russian and English, from Brodsky's poetry. Very useful for the understanding of Brodsky's development as a poet.

Polukhina, Valentina. *Joseph Brodsky: A Poet for Our Time*. Cambridge: Cambridge University Press, 1989. An encompassing study of essential aspects of Brodsky's poetry by a leading Russian expert. Using examples of poems in Russian and English the author follows the gradual emergence of Brodsky as a poet of his generation and his contribution to modern world poetry. The chapter on his struggle with the Soviet "empire" is of special interest.

Rigsbee, David. *Styles of Ruin: Joseph Brodsky and the Postmodernist Elegy*. Westport, Conn.: Greenwood Press, 1999. Rigsbee examines Brodsky's contribution to postmodernist poetry, particularly through his pronounced trend toward elegy. A poet himself and a translator of Brodsky, the author adds to his analyses a personal touch as well as that of an expert of the craft.

Taylor, John. "On the Ledge: Joseph Brodsky in English." *Michigan Quarterly Review* 40, no. 3 (Summer, 2001): 594. Critical analysis of some of Brodsky's poetry from *Collected Poems in English*.

Volkov, Solomon. *Conversations with Joseph Brodsky: A Poet's Journey Through the Twentieth Century*. New York: Free Press, 1998. This translation of a book of conversations with Brodsky by his New York friend offers a microscopic glimpse into his inner and aesthetic world. Wide-ranging interviews explore poetry in general and Russian culture through Brodsky's experience, as well as his relationship to poetic figures in the West.

Stephanie Sandler,
updated by Vasa D. Mihailovich

EMILY BRONTË

Born: Thornton, Yorkshire, England; July 30, 1818
Died: Haworth, Yorkshire, England; December 19, 1848

PRINCIPAL POETRY

Poems by Currer, Ellis, and Acton Bell, 1846 (with Charlotte Brontë and Anne Brontë)
The Complete Poems of Emily Jane Brontë, 1941 (C. W. Hatfield, editor)
Gondal's Queen: A Novel in Verse by Emily Jane Brontë, 1955 (Fannie E. Ratchford, editor)

OTHER LITERARY FORMS

Although Emily Brontë published only one novel, *Wuthering Heights*, it is this work for which she is best known. When the novel was published in 1847, it won some praise for its originality and power, but in general, reviewers found its violence disturbing and its dominant character, Heathcliff, excessively brutal. *Wuthering Heights* did not offer the charm and optimism that many readers wanted to find in a work of fiction. As is often the case with original work, it took time for the world to appreciate it fully; today, however, *Wuthering Heights* is given a prominent place among the significant novels of the nineteenth century, and is often discussed for its elaborate narrative structure, its intricate patterns of imagery, and its powerful themes of the soul's anguish and longing.

By the time Brontë began *Wuthering Heights*, she had long been using her imagination to create stories full of passionate intrigue and romance. First, as a young

child she participated in a series of family games called Young Men's Plays, tales of military and political adventures primarily directed and recorded by the older children, her sister Charlotte and her brother Branwell. After Charlotte left for school in 1831, Emily and her younger sister Anne began their own creation, a long saga of an island they called Gondal, placed in the north Pacific yet very much resembling their own Yorkshire environment. They peopled this island-world with strong, passionate characters. Unfortunately, nothing remains of their prose chronicle of Gondal. Two journal fragments and two of the birthday notes that she and Anne were in the habit of exchanging make mention of this land. These notes also offer some insight into the everyday world of the Brontë household and are of great interest for this reason. The only other extant prose, besides a few unrevealing letters, is a group of five essays which she wrote in French as homework assignments while a

Emily Brontë (Library of Congress)

student in Brussels. This material has since been translated by Lorine White Nagel and published under the title *Five Essays Written in French* (1948). Some similarities can be seen between the destructive and powerful descriptions of nature and human character discussed in these essays and the world of Brontë's poetry and fiction.

ACHIEVEMENTS

Emily Brontë did not at first desire public recognition for her poetry. In fact, when her sister Charlotte accidentally discovered a notebook of her poems, it took time for Emily to accept this discovery, even though Charlotte found the poems impressive and uncommon. More time was required for Charlotte to persuade this very private poet to join with her and Anne in a small publishing venture. Once persuaded, Emily did contribute twenty-one of her poems to the slim, privately printed volume *Poems by Currer, Ellis, and Acton Bell.* To disguise her sex, each sister chose a pseudonym corresponding to the first letter of her name. This disguise also protected Emily's privacy, which she very much desired to keep; she resented Charlotte's later unintentional disclosure of Ellis Bell's true identity. This disclosure occurred after the three sisters had all published novels under the name of Bell, arousing considerable curiosity in the literary world. Unfortunately, their collection of poems sold only two copies. Later, after Emily's death, Charlotte, convinced of her sister's talent, tried to keep her poetic reputation alive by including eighteen previously unpublished poems in a second edition of *Wuthering Heights* and Anne's first novel, *Agnes Grey* (1847); however, despite her efforts, it was not until the twentieth century that Emily Brontë's poems received any serious critical attention.

Interest in the poetry began as biographers sought to piece together the life of the Brontë family. It increased when the fantasyland of Gondal was discovered. Attempts were made to reconstruct the story from the poems, for it became clear that Emily had written many of her poems as part of that world of passion and guilt. Further attention was given to the poetry as *Wuthering Heights* gained in recognition, although readers were inclined to interpret the poems merely as an apprenticeship to a more masterful novel. Only since the mid-

twentieth century has criticism begun to focus on the poems for their own sake.

Because of the seeming quietness of Brontë's life and because she was never part of a literary circle beyond that of her own home, there is a temptation to see her as an example of the isolated genius, sculpturing her forms in an instinctive style. On the contrary, Brontë was a skillful poet working within the traditions of her Romantic predecessors, handling standard poetic forms with subtle and effective variations. Although the dramatic extremes she found in the works of Sir Walter Scott and George Gordon, Lord Byron led her at times to employ conventional phrases and touches of melodrama, at her best she was able to embody in controlled verse an intensity of genuine feeling which sprang from a love of nature and a worship of the imagination. In her poems of the night winds and the whirling snowstorms of the moors, she distinguishes herself as a poet of nature's starkly vital powers. In her poems of the imagination, she places herself in the visionary company of William Wordsworth and William Blake. Throughout her poetry she expresses the desire of the soul to transcend the mortal limitations of time and space in order to merge with a larger presence, the source of all energy and life. She was an artist faithful to her visions, whose poems attest the strength of the individual soul.

BIOGRAPHY

Emily Jane Brontë was the fifth of six children, five girls and a boy, born to an Anglican clergyman of Irish descent, Patrick Brontë, and his Cornish wife, Maria Branwell. When Emily was two years old, the family moved to Haworth, where her father had accepted a permanent curacy. Haworth, a place now often associated with the Brontë name, is a village on the moors of West Riding, Yorkshire in the north of England. In Emily's day, this rural spot was quite removed from the changing events of city life. The parsonage itself is an isolated building of gray stone near an old cemetery with its slanting worn tombstones. In this somber-looking house, in this quiet village, Emily spent most of her life.

The people filling this world were few in number. As parson's children, Emily and her brother and sisters were not encouraged to associate with the village children, who were regarded as lower in social status. Their father seems to have valued his privacy, often keeping to himself, even dining alone, although there is no reason to doubt his affection for his children. As a result of these social limitations, the children provided their own entertainment, which often consisted of acting out imaginative games and later writing them down. Their education was in part provided by their aunt, Elizabeth Branwell, who came to care for them after their mother died in September, 1821, shortly after their arrival in Haworth. Tutors in art and music were occasionally hired for the children, and at least two libraries were available to them: their father's, and that of the Keighley Mechanics' Institute.

Emily left Haworth few times in her life. When she did, it was usually to continue her education or to gain employment. At the age of six, she and three of her sisters—Maria, Elizabeth, and Charlotte—were sent to the Clergyman Daughters' School at Cowan Bridge. Their stay was brief, for when the two older sisters, Maria and Elizabeth, were stricken with tuberculosis, from which they later died, their father had all his daughters sent home. Several years later, in 1835, Emily attended school for a few months at Roe Head with Charlotte. Their plan was to prepare themselves better for one of the few occupations open to them, that of governess. While at Roe Head, Emily became extremely distressed with her situation. In later years, after her death, Charlotte indicated that she believed the cause to have been intense homesickness. Shortly after this rather unsuccessful venture from home, Emily did leave again, this time to take a position as a teacher at a large school near Halifax called Law Hill; but again her stay was brief. She returned home, obviously unhappy with her life as a teacher. One last trip from Haworth was taken in 1842, when she accompanied Charlotte to Brussels to attend Madame Héger's school. The sisters wanted to increase their knowledge of German and French in order to become better qualified to open their own school, a project which was to remain only in the dreaming and planning stages. While in Brussels it again became clear that Emily was not comfortable in an environment strange to her, and when the sisters returned home in November, 1842, for their aunt's funeral, Emily remained, seemingly content to do so. Thereafter, she stayed at the parsonage, helping with the household chores. Her family

accepted this choice and considered her contribution to the running of the household a valuable one. In September, 1848, Emily caught a cold while attending her brother's funeral. It developed into an inflammation of the lungs from which she never recovered. Her death was perhaps hastened by her refusal to seek medical attention until the very end.

Much consideration has been given to Brontë's inability to adjust to life away from Haworth. Emphasis has been placed on her love of the moors, which was so intense that she could not long be away from the heather and open fields. It is true that her work indicates an abiding—at times compelling—love for their somber beauty; however, some attention should also be given to the fact that all of these journeys from home required adjusting to a structured world, one perhaps hostile to the private world of her imagination. It is clear that the powers of the imagination played a dominant role in Brontë's emotional life from her childhood on. Apparently, at home in the parsonage, she found an environment which suited the needs of her imagination and its creative powers.

As the fame of the Brontë family increased, Emily Brontë herself became a figure of legend. She was described as a passionate genius of almost mythic proportions, possessing supreme will and strength. This interpretation was encouraged very early by Charlotte, whose respect for her sister increased greatly during the last months of her life: In Charlotte's eyes, her seemingly unobtrusive sister had become a solitary being, towering above others, heroically hastening to her death. So long has this view been presented that it is now inextricably woven with Emily Brontë's name and image. She herself left so few biographical clues that perhaps the actual woman must always be seen from a distance; however, in her work there is indeed evidence of a poet of original, imaginative power, who, having chosen her God of Visions, was able to give poetic expression to the essential emotions of the human soul.

ANALYSIS

When interpreting Emily Brontë's poetry, one must first confront the Gondal problem: What is the significance of that exotic world of emotional drama that so occupied her imagination? Some readers argue that this imaginary world of rebellion and punishment, death and lost love, permeated all her work; others maintain that her finer poems were composed outside its dramatic, at times melodramatic, influences. Brontë's own division of the poems into two notebooks, one titled "Gondal Poems," the other left untitled, would suggest a clear separation; yet a subjective lyrical voice can be heard in many of the Gondal poems, and echoes of the Gondal drama can be heard in non-Gondal material. Since the original prose saga has been lost, perhaps no completely satisfactory solution can be found; nevertheless, a thematic approach to Brontë's poetry does provide a unifying interpretation.

Many of her Gondal characters are isolated figures who yearn for a time of love or freedom now lost. In the non-Gondal poems, the same voice of longing can be heard: The speakers of such poems as "The Philosopher" and "To Imagination" desire a time of union and harmony, or, as in "O Thy Bright Eyes Must Answer Now," a time of freedom from the restraints of reason and earthly cares. The Gondal characters, with their exotic-sounding names (such as Augusta Geraldine Almeda and Julius Brenzaida), are not beings separate and distinct from the poet herself; they are masks through which Brontë speaks. Therefore, although Brontë often uses the dramatic forms of direct address, inquiry, and dialogue, none of her poems can be adequately analyzed as if it were a dramatic monologue prefiguring the work of Robert Browning. She does not attempt to delineate a character through the subtleties of his speech in a particular time and place. The desperate situations in which she places her dramatic figures merely provide appropriate circumstances in which to express the emotional and at times mystical experiences of her own private world. Continually, her poems emphasize the creative power of the individual spirit as it struggles to define itself in relation to the "Invisible," the unseen source of all existence. This struggle in all its intensity is the predominant theme of her poetry, whether it is set in a Gondal prison or on a Yorkshire moor.

Intensity is one of Brontë's distinguishing characteristics. Her poetry gives the impression of having been cut as close to the center of feeling as possible. The portrayal of such passionate intensity can easily lead to excessive exclamations in which meaning is scattered, if

not lost; in Brontë's case, however, her skillful handling of form provides the needed restraint. She achieves this control over her subject through such structuring devices as simple metrical patterns (she was especially fond of tetrameter and trimeter), strong monosyllabic rhymes, parallel phrasing, repetition of key words, and appropriately placed pauses. Her use of these devices allows her to shape the intensity into ordered movements appropriate to the subject, whether it be a mournful one or one of joyous celebration.

"ROSINA ALCONA TO JULIUS BRENZAIDA"

One of the best examples of Brontë's use of these structuring techniques to control feeling can be found in her best-known love poem, "Rosina Alcona to Julius Brenzaida," one of her Gondal poems often anthologized under the title "Remembrance." Rosina Alcona is addressing her lover Julius, now dead for fifteen years. She asks to be forgiven for going on with her own life after losing him. The anguish which the speaker feels is captured in the wavelike rhythms established in the first stanza through the use of pauses and parallel phrasing: "Cold in the earth, and the deep snow piled above thee!/ Far, far removed, cold in the dreary grave!" Monosyllabic rhyme and the repetition of significant words also aid in embodying the emotional quality of a yearning that is held in check.

Brontë often achieves control through repetition of a key word, one that is repeated but with varying connotations. In the beginning lines of the poem, the word "cold" presents two aspects of the literal circumstances: The lover lies cold in the grave, and the coldness of winter is upon the land. As the poem progresses, "cold" evolves in meaning to encompass the life of the speaker as well. Without her lover, the warmth and light of her life are gone. He was both the sun and stars, and without him the heavens are now dark. Her life through the fifteen years following Julius's death has been winter, continually as barren as the snow-covered land, and to endure such barrenness she herself has had to become "cold." She has had to "check the tears of useless passion" and to chill the "burning wish" to follow him to the grave. Moreover, losing him to death has taught her one of the "cold" realities of life: "existence can be cherished" even after all love and joy are gone from one's own life.

This expanded definition of the word "cold" is underscored by Brontë's use of antithesis, another technique typical of her style. In stanza three, Brontë juxtaposes the image of the lover lying cold and still in his grave and the wild movements of the weather which will ultimately lead to the warmth of spring. In the final stanza, she returns to the same pair of opposites: stillness and movement. The speaker refuses to indulge too much in "Memory's rapturous pain," her wild feelings of love and sorrow, for fear that she could not then face the "empty world again," the still frozen world of her own life. With this last description of the "empty world," Brontë returns to the image of coldness with which she began, and the tolling, elegiac poem is brought to rest, although with the phrase "rapturous pain" she points to the restless, unreconciled feelings of the speaker. These conflicting desires between the longing to remember lost love and the need to forget point in turn to the paradoxical nature of the whole poem: The speaker tells of the necessity of forgetting her lover, and yet the poem itself attests to her loving memory of him.

"THE PHILOSOPHER"

In the non-Gondal poem "The Philosopher" there is a description of "warring gods" within the "little frame" of the speaker's physical self. This image could easily serve as a metaphor for much of Brontë's poetry: Within the confines of poetic structure she attempts to hold conflicting forces and their related images. "Oh Thy Bright Eyes Must Answer Now" is a significant poem in the Brontë canon, for it clearly sets forth the dimensions of these conflicts. The first half of the poem presents the conflict between imagination and reason, between spiritual needs and earthly cares. The speaker turns to the "bright eyes" of the "radiant angel" of her vision, to summon it to speak and defend her choice to worship its power, rejecting the demands of Reason, who in "forms of gloom" with a "scornful brow" judges and mocks her "overthrow." By the world's standards, she has been overthrown, for she has failed to achieve wealth and glory. She has shunned the "common path" and chosen the "strange road."

The second half of the poem examines the inner conflict regarding her relationship to the overseeing "radiant angel" of this strange road. In stanza five, she addresses this angel as "Thee, ever present, phantom thing—/ My slave, my comrade, and my King!" The speaker controls the influence, good or ill, of this angel. Consequently, he is her slave, and yet he is a comrade, an equal who is always with her, bringing her "intimate delight," and finally—seeming to contradict completely these two roles of slave and comrade—he is her King, directing and dictating. In these lines Brontë is expressing the conflicting desires within the soul itself: a desire to remain free without being isolated, and a desire to maintain individual identity while simultaneously merging with a larger and more powerful being.

The last stanza of this poem points to the troublesome question underlying the complicated life of Brontë's visions: Is she wrong to choose a faith that allows her own soul to grant her prayers? In a very real way, her own imagination has conjured up the angel who will defeat Reason. It is characteristic of Brontë to place such emphasis on individual power and will. Although this emphasis prefigures the work of later writers in which the self creates its own reality and its own gods, the unorthodox road that Brontë chose to follow did not lead her to this extreme conclusion. The last two lines of "Oh Thy Bright Eyes Must Answer Now" return to her "God of Visions": He must "plead" for her. Her power was expressed in her choice to worship him, and now he must come to defend her.

GOD OF VISIONS AND NATURE

Throughout Brontë's work there remains an emphasis on an outside power which could and would exist whether she herself existed or not. One of the last written and most famous of her poems, "No Coward Soul Is Mine," is a ringing affirmation of her faith in her choice of visions. Her soul stands sure in its relationship to the "Being and Breath" that "can never be destroyed." When suns and universes are gone, it will still remain.

Many of Brontë's poems describing nature also concern this prevailing spirit, and occasionally they seem to present a pantheistic vision; however, although the natural world clearly had the power to stir and inspire her, nature and her God of Visions are not synonymous. Primarily, Brontë uses nature to parallel a state of mind or soul, as she does in "Remembrance," where the cold snow-covered hills objectify the restrained feelings of the speaker. Often the open moors and the movement of the winds are used to embody the wild, free feelings of the human soul. In "Aye, There It Is! It Wakes To-night," Brontë uses the powerful and violent images of the storm to describe a person being transformed into pure spirit as her soul awakens to knowledge of some supreme spiritual power. Like lightning, her "feeling's fires flash," her gaze is "kindled," a "glorious wind" sweeps all memory of this mortal world from her mind, and she becomes "the essence of the Tempest's roaring." The last stanza concludes that this visionary experience prefigures the life of the soul after death, when, free from the prison of the body, it shall rise: "The dungeon mingle with the mould—/ The captive with the skies." In these last two lines, Brontë plays upon a rather conventional simile of the body as prisonhouse of the soul to create an original effect. First, she unexpectedly and suddenly introduces the word "mould" to represent the process of the body's decay and the dust to which it returns, and second, she compares the action of the soul after death to this process of decay: The body will "mingle" with the earth; the soul with the skies. There is in this last line a sense of triumphant release, effectively represented in the long vowel sound of "skies" which sharply contrasts with the earlier mournful sounds of "cold" and "mould." Throughout the poem, Brontë has again controlled an intensely emotional subject through antithesis, simple monosyllabic rhymes, and terse metrical patterns.

"JULIAN M. TO A. G. ROCHELLE"

Perhaps the most famous of Brontë's poems depicting this visionary experience is the lengthy fragment of the Gondal poem "Julian M. to A. G. Rochelle," which Brontë published under the title "The Prisoner." The fragment consists of lines 13-44 and lines 65-92 of the original with four new lines added at the end to provide an appropriate conclusion. This slightly revised excerpt, although beginning with the voice of Julian telling of his decision to wander rather casually through the family dungeons, primarily concerns the mystical experiences of one of the prisoners. When she speaks, she displays a spirit undefeated by her imprisonment. Her body is able to endure the chains, for her soul is open to a nightly "messenger" who offers her the hope of "eternal liberty." Her response to this messenger occurs in a series of stages. First, she experiences a mingling of pain and

pleasure as visions rise before her. Then she loses all awareness of her earthly self; the world and the body are forgotten. She then is able to experience an "unuttered harmony." Her outward senses and conscious mind have become numb in order that the "inward essence" can be released. In the final stage, this inward essence—in one burst of energy, as if leaping—attempts to merge with the "Invisible," the "Unseen," which she also describes as a "home" and a "harbour." At this point, because she cannot completely escape the body and still live, she suddenly and painfully returns to a knowledge of her earthly self and its prison, the literal prison in which she finds herself and the prison of her own body. Only after death can she finally and permanently join with the "Unseen," and so she looks forward to Death as heralding the complete and lasting union with the source of these nightly divine visions.

Brontë's decision to excerpt these particular stanzas from one of her Gondal poems, and the fact that once excerpted they still function as a unified whole, again suggest that Gondal merely provided the stage and the costumes for a drama that was actually taking place in Brontë's own self. In fact, in this case the poem benefits from the cutting of the frame stanzas which are full of conventional descriptions of stone dungeons and Lord Julian's somewhat expected romantic response to the fair prisoner. Obviously, Brontë's interest and poetic talent lay in examining and capturing the visionary experience.

OTHER MAJOR WORKS

LONG FICTION: *Wuthering Heights*, 1847.

NONFICTION: *Five Essays Written in French*, 1948 (Lorine White Nagel, translator); *The Brontë Letters*, 1954 (Muriel Spark, editor).

BIBLIOGRAPHY

Barnard, Robert. *Emily Brontë*. New York: Oxford University Press, 2000. First published in 2000 by the British Library, London, this overview of Brontë's life and work has been incorporated into Oxford's British Library Writers' Lives series. Bibliography, maps, illustrations (some in color), index.

Chitham, Edward. *The Birth of "Wuthering Heights": Emily Brontë at Work*. New York: St. Martin's Press,

1998. A work of careful scholarship, incorporating and eclipsing much that has been discovered and postulated about the novel's origins, composition, and relation to Emily's and her sisters' writing. Includes an account of the novel's progress from original idea to submission.

Chitham, Edward, and Tom Winnifrith. *Brontë Facts and Brontë Problems*. Basingstoke, England: Macmillan, 1983. Contains four essays on the poetry of Emily Brontë, one of which questions the Ratchford thesis. Others look at the influence of Percy Bysshe Shelley, other sources of inspiration, and the development of vision. Includes an index.

Davies, Stevie. *Emily Brontë*. Plymouth, England: Northcote House, in association with the British Council, 1998. Part of the Writers and Their Work series for students, a basic, brief biographical introduction to the writer as well as an overview of her work. Bibliographical references, index.

Duthie, Enid L. *The Brontës and Nature*. Basingstoke, England: Macmillan, 1986. Duthie admires the terseness and Blakean quality of the poetry but is more concerned in placing it in a wider context in its response to nature. Supplemented by a select bibliography and an index.

Gerin, Winnifred. *Emily Brontë*. New York: Oxford University Press, 1971. This biography remains one of the most useful in considering Emily Brontë as a poet, since it systematically integrates poetry with biography, quoting crucial poems fully. Contains appendices, a full bibliography, and an index.

Homans, Margaret. *Women Writers and Poetic Identity: Dorothy Wordsworth, Emily Brontë, and Emily Dickinson*. Princeton, N.J.: Princeton University Press, 1980. Three major nineteenth century writers are compared in terms of difficulty in being poetesses. Includes an index.

Hughes, Glyn. *Brontë*. New York: St. Martin's Press, 1996. British novelist Hughes makes a valiant effort to turn the quietly tragic lives of the Brontë family into compelling biographical fiction. A careful, earnest, and competently written book.

Pykett, Lynn. *Emily Brontë*. Basingstoke, England: Macmillan, 1989. One of the Women Writers series, it offers in two chapters a rereading of her poetry in

terms of its issue with Romanticism as well as with Victorian stereotyping. Complemented by a bibliography and an index.

Diane D'Amico;
bibliography updated by the editors

RUPERT BROOKE

Born: Rugby, England; August 3, 1887
Died: Aboard a hospital ship on the Aegean Sea; April 23, 1915

PRINCIPAL POETRY

Poems, 1911
1914 and Other Poems, 1915
Collected Poems, 1915
Complete Poems, 1932
The Poetical Works of Rupert Brooke, 1946 (Geoffrey Keynes, editor)

OTHER LITERARY FORMS

Rupert Brooke's lasting work is to be found exclusively in his poetry, but his work in several other literary forms at least deserves mention. Brooke was attracted to the theater, and two of his works, one as a critic and one as an artist, reflect this interest. *John Webster and the Elizabethan Drama* (1916) was written as his fellowship dissertation and later published; although much criticized for its lack of scholarly decorum, it reveals a lively style and an author fascinated with the remarkable developments in Elizabethan theater. His only play, a one-act tragedy titled *Lithuania* (1935), can be read with some satisfaction despite its bizarre plot and uncertain tone. As always with Brooke, his skill with language helps to camouflage his errors and excesses. As a journalist, Brooke mixed with strong effect the lyricism of a poet with the enthusiastic observations of an excited traveler, most prominently in a series of articles which described his tour of the United States, Canada, and the South Seas, written for the *Westminster Gazette*. In these delightful pieces he adeptly and wittily penetrates such subjects as the American personality, a baseball game at

Rupert Brooke (Library of Congress)

Harvard, the grandeur of the Rocky Mountains, and others. These display British wonder, sometimes dismay, at the "new world" but always stop short of tasteless condescension. Finally, Brooke was a masterful and enthusiastic correspondent; one finds in his letters enchanting representations of matters both personal and universal as he comments on a variety of subjects.

ACHIEVEMENTS

Any attempt to measure the achievement of Rupert Brooke, poet, must also account for the impact of Brooke as a dashing public figure in life, and as a hero and martyr in death. This is not to devalue the richness of his best verse, for his canon is mostly sound, and the tragedy of his early death is amplified by the tragedy of artistic potential cut short. Still, if ever a poet has been linked with an era, his physical presence and intellectual attributes defining the sentiments of a nation and its people, then that poet is Rupert Brooke. Any evaluation of his work is at once confused and enriched by the clamor that surrounded his life, art, and death. His life as student, citizen, and soldier reflects values prized by the British as they entered the twentieth century and endured World War I.

His art is complex, but not in a metaphysical way. Rather, its mystery can be ascribed to the tension produced when the convictions of a traditionalist in matters of form and structure are linked with the passionate voice of an exuberant Romantic. Brooke's preference for sonneteering is well known. His topics and themes are more often quaint and predictable than unique and shocking (an effect he often desired to achieve). The poetry is classically graceful and romantically intense, always ultimately sustained by a gift for language. Finally, however, Brooke's death during World War I, the sometimes crude publicity which surrounded it and his memory, and the subsequent legendary status accorded him ensured for all time that critics would find it difficult to separate his life from his art, in an attempt to assess his legacy.

BIOGRAPHY

Rupert Chawner Brooke was born in Rugby, England, on August 3, 1887. His father, William Parker Brooke, was a Rugby schoolmaster, an undistinguished but competent classical scholar, a person perhaps most noticeable for his very lack of noticeable traits. Rupert's mother, Mary Ruth Cotterill, dominated the family and is often described as an organizer—energetic, efficient, strict, even domineering. One of Rupert's brothers, Dick, died after a short illness in 1907; another, Alfred, was killed in World War I three months after Rupert's death. Several commentators have made much of the death of a child who would have been Rupert's older sister, implying that somehow Rupert was always affected by the notion of being a disappointing replacement for an adored and much-lamented daughter.

Rupert realized many benefits from, but at the same time was assuredly strained by, his family's association with the British educational system. Although not unhealthy, neither was he robust, and he was heartily encouraged to develop his intellectual skills first and foremost. As a youth he exhibited a tendency to role-play, most often typified by world-weariness and grandiloquent language. His more engaging qualities included an active mind, interest if not excellence in some sports, and (to understate) a pleasing appearance which later became a significant part of his legend.

His life at Rugby was notable for the variety of his academic, social, and even athletic interests, and for his ability to develop close friendships with interesting people, a trait that stayed with Brooke always. Many of his friends were remarkable and passionately loyal to him; even mere acquaintances could not deny intense curiosity about him. As a poet, his early works show a young man enchanted with words and full of the impulse to parody the masters. He was more enthusiastic than polished, becoming increasingly so with each English poet whose secrets he discovered, digested, and imitated. Brooke adored writing contests and seemed to delight in shocking the sensibilities of his friends and family.

As a student at King's College, Cambridge, Rupert continued these activities, but now for the first time found real independence from his family in a stimulating and glamorous setting. In addition to his reading and writing, he now discovered the delights of political debate, the mysteries of such disciplines as psychology, and the pleasures of acting. He excitedly joined political discussions, joined the Cambridge Fabian Society, and worked diligently on its behalf. As an actor he exhibited no real talent, in spite of his ability to deliver poetic lines with great enthusiasm and a physical presence which, according to many, was spectacular. His career at Cambridge, undistinguished academically, was nevertheless solid. He cultivated still more fascinating friends, showed a preference for "modern" works, and matured as a poet. At the same time he confessed a weary tolerance for life, an attitude that his many activities would seem to contradict.

After his formal education and before World War I, Brooke found both peace and adventure. He spent some time reading and writing in a charming setting, Grantchester, and reveled in his surroundings and leisure, a welcome relief from his school years. For excitement, Brooke embarked in 1913 to explore America and the South Seas, an excursion financed by the *Westminster Gazette*; the newspaper had commissioned him to send back impressions of his tour. He must have enjoyed himself; the pace was hectic and he was greeted enthusiastically and with respect by his various hosts. His articles, often supremely "British" and critical of a general lack of culture in the Americas, are nevertheless important and enjoyable, suggesting increasing powers of observation and description.

His return to Britain was personally triumphant and satisfying. Brooke had confessed homesickness during his travels, but was little prepared for his outright joy at once again reaching British soil. His friends greeted him exuberantly and a series of social and artistic activities kept him busy. His future, as artist, as critic, even perhaps as politician, seemed assured.

His dreams were to be stalled, shattered, and canceled by World War I. It is a curious measure of the impact of Brooke's work and personality that he, with limited exposure to battle, eventually dying of blood poisoning, should ultimately be accorded the lavish praise of his countrymen, who saw him as the spokesman for a generation of heroes. With many of his friends, he had expressed early disgust for the very notion of war, but changed attitudes quickly, voicing the desire to find high adventure while ridding the world of the Prussian menace. He joined the Artists' Rifles, sought a commission, and eventually landed a post as a sublieutenant in the Royal Naval Division. His only significant action was to march with a brigade in relief of Antwerp, a time during which he witnessed the realities of war. The column, however, retreated quickly after a few days of occupying trenches.

Later, his division received its orders for the Aegean, and Gallipoli. En route, Brooke contracted dysentery; his condition weakened, he would fail and seem to rally from time to time; he lingered, and finally died, April 23, 1915, at the age of twenty-seven, aboard a French hospital ship, in the company of a school friend. He was buried the same day on the nearby island of Skyros, where a memorial was later raised in his honor.

Brooke's memory, however, lived on, sometimes in ways which were flattering and meaningful, other times in ways which were distorted and tasteless. The poet who wrote with conviction about fair England and the soldier's duty and privilege to serve was mourned and eulogized by many, not the least of whom was Winston Churchill, who had recognized the value of Brooke's verse. Beyond his work, there were other matters, more difficult to pinpoint, but significant nevertheless, which contributed to his fame. His background, education, and even his dashing good looks (he was called the "fairhaired Apollo," to his embarrassment) represented what was best about "the Empire," and much of the British approach to this war was intimately involved, of course, with "the Empire" and all it implied. It is too bad, in a way, that this fine poet and remarkable person has had to bear these burdens, for the excessive publicity obscures what is best about his work and life. Paul Fussell has rightly called World War I an "ironic" war; by that he means that the gestures and ideals of the participants appear almost ludicrous in the context of the brutal efficiency of the new century. There is much that is ironic about World War I's most famous poet, too, for today Brooke is often admired, often condemned; but in both cases, usually for the wrong reasons.

ANALYSIS

Anyone who wishes to be objective in his evaluation of Brooke's short poetic career must acknowledge Brooke's weaknesses as well as his strengths. There is the untempered voice of boyish spontaneity, the popularizer of mindless and almost laughable patriotic sentimentalism, the friendly versifier of late Georgian poetry which did little but describe nature redundantly. This Rupert Brooke penned such lines as "There was a damned successful Poet; There was a Woman like the Sun./ And they were dead. They did not know it." ("Dead Men's Love"); he probably deserves ridicule for having done so. On the other hand, fortunately, there is also the exuberant *and* mature voice of a craftsman, the defender of the noble sentiments of a nation in crisis, and the innovative artist who sought freshness and vitality even as he worked within traditional forms. This Brooke deserves acclaim.

The best approaches to understanding and appreciating the poetry of Rupert Brooke are to reveal the themes of place and sentiment which dominate his works, and to recognize the fascinating way in which he blends structural integrity and fluency which appears spontaneous, passionate, bordering on the experimental.

"THE OLD VICARAGE, GRANTCHESTER"

Perhaps the work which most reveals these traits is "The Old Vicarage, Grantchester." Written in Berlin in 1912, this unusual poem, sometimes flippantly comic and other times grossly nostalgic, shows Brooke's tendency to idealize the past, or the "other place," wherever and whenever he was not. Written in octosyllabic couplets, it can be praised for the clarity and tension of its best lines; it can also be condemned for the immature slackness of its worst. A homesick traveler, Brooke sits at a café table in Berlin, conscious of the activity, much of it repulsive, about him. He begins with a graceful recounting of the natural splendor of Grantchester and its environs, but these pleasant thoughts are rudely interrupted by the guttural sound of the German language spoken around him—"*Du lieber Gott!*"—which sets up an immediate and abrupt passage in which the "here" and "there" are effectively juxtaposed.

The sudden introduction of a phrase, in Greek, which means "if only I were," is a nice touch (linking classical and British civilization), followed by repetition of his desire, to be "in Grantchester, in Grantchester." There is a long catalog of reasons why one would wish to be "in Grantchester," detailing not only the natural splendor of the place, but also much more. Among the many pleasures, the most notable are the educational tradition (especially a reverence for classics), familiar and comfortable personalities, and the respect for truth and decorous behavior which may be found there.

It is true that this poem is extended far too long and becomes tediously redundant; it is just as true that some of the lines cause the reader to cringe, often because Brooke seems not to have considered the veracity of his assertions ("And men and women with straight eyes,/ Lithe children lovelier than a dream"), at other times because his slickness is *only* cute ("Ah God! to see the branches stir/ Across the moon at Grantchester!"). Still, one finds "The Old Vicarage, Grantchester" to be solid, mostly complete, if slightly flawed. First, Brooke manages to describe Grantchester fully, with sufficient detail to make the reader understand why the poet is moved to such excess and to sympathize with him. This is not only a celebration of pastoral elegance but also a characterization of the people of Grantchester verging on a statement of values tending toward thematic richness. The vocabulary of fiction employed here is no accident, as the poem has many qualities of the introductory chapters of a novel, complete with protagonist and dramatic action. Second, there is an irony in some of the passages which establishes a tone distinctly superior to juvenile "romanticizing."

In short, "The Old Vicarage, Grantchester" represents the best and worst of Brooke; not surprisingly, it is the kind of poem that leads to conflicting and confusing evaluations of his work. Those who praise him for his sensitive descriptions of his homeland, those who see in the poem evidence of wit and sparkling phrasing, and those who cringe at his excessive sentimentality will all find here numerous examples to support their contentions.

THE "1914" SONNETS

Whereas "The Old Vicarage, Grantchester" is vintage Brooke, he is best known for his sonnets, particularly those he wrote during 1914, shortly before his death, which glamorized the fate of martyred soldiers. Brooke evidently found great satisfaction in the sonnet form, and obviously the long relationship was liberating rather than inhibiting, for he showed thematic and structural flexibility while remaining true to the principles of sonneteering. In addition to his evocation of place, Brooke treated in his sonnets such diverse subjects as death, memory, time, psychic phenomena, growing up, lust, and, of course, the pain and pleasure of idealized love as found in the grand traditions of the sonnet. He wrote in the Petrarchan manner, complete with the requisite imagery of the distant and taunting enamorata; he mastered the English form and the difficult closing couplet of the Shakespearean sonnet; and he exhibited the logical strength and confidence so apparent in the Miltonic brand. When bored, he tried variations, such as introducing a sonnet with the couplet (as in "Sonnet Reversed"); his experiments are never disruptive, but suggestive of the strength of the form, and anticipatory of later twentieth century inventions (E. E. Cummings, for example, might be mentioned here).

The five "1914" sonnets reflect Brooke's facility in the sonnet form, while at the same time incorporating sentiments which touched his countrymen profoundly. All deal with the transcending reward which awaits those who make the supreme sacrifice for home and country during the Great War. Again, depending on one's perspective, the sonnets are either inspiring and gallant calls-to-arms for a generation of martyrs, or naïve and morbid musings which typify the tragic waste of the conflict. The first, "Peace," alludes, ironically, to the new life evident in those whose existence had turned stale, who now benefit from clarity of purpose. Those who must die lose little except "body" and "breath," and are glad to escape their environment. The second sonnet in this sequence, "Safety," can be linked with

"Peace," in that those who are sacrificed are referred to as "we." Again the comforting thought recurs that a soldier's death (what might be called a "good death") is to be embraced, not feared, for it presumes the existence of a condition beyond suffering and fear, beyond time, even.

The next two sonnets of 1914, "The Dead" (I) and "The Dead" (II), refer to the martyrs in the third person, but the philosophy remains much the same. In the first, the poet calls for public recognition of an honorable departure from life: "Blow out, you bugles, over the rich Dead!/ There's none of these so lonely and poor of old,/ But, dying, has made us rarer gifts than gold." Ancestral dignity is the rationale for these extreme sentiments; "holiness," "honor," and "nobleness" are evoked as those who pour out "the red sweet wine of youth" are finally able to realize their true "heritage." In the second sonnet of this pair, the celebration is of a pastoral bent, not only in the description of those youths who exist so intimately with the natural world (". . . Dawn was theirs,/ And the sunset, and the colours of the earth."), but also in the elegiac sestet, where the world of the dead is little-changed in its excellence.

In "The Soldier," Brooke writes in the first person. Perhaps it is this immediacy ("If I should die, think only this of me") which made the sonnet so touching for his countrymen. More likely it is the sentiments expressed which captured the tragedy of a proud nation losing its best young men in war, and somehow finding solace in the loss. Some might even call the poem overbearing, chauvinistic. In the opening lines, the poet asserts that mourning should be brief, for wherever he may lie, that spot becomes "for ever England," where the "rich earth" is more enriched by "a dust whom England bore, shaped, made aware." In the sestet, lest the reader think that only the physical is to be exalted, Brooke suggests that the English soul, "this heart," or "pulse in the eternal mind" will inhabit the universe, much to our advantage.

GEORGIAN INFLUENCE

Brooke's poetry, then, is by turns admirable and condemnable. Yet another way to account for this baffling but intriguing trait is to place his work in relationship to what is called "The Georgian Revolt." Brooke's role in this curious, little-understood era was a significant one:

First, he was a close friend of Edward Marsh, whose Georgian anthologies set the tone for the period and who was eventually chosen to write Brooke's official biography; second, Brooke contributed to the anthologies and worked diligently to publicize the "Georgian" productions; third, the nature of Brooke's public and artistic reputation is as debatable as the confused reputation of "Georgian" poetry.

What "Georgian" has come to mean, of course, is the overly romantic, intellectually slack, structurally contrived efforts of a few "waspish" poets who refused to accept the birth of the twentieth century. The original plan of Marsh, Brooke, and others had been to provide a forum through which a new, energetic brand of modern poetry could transcend the stifling dominance of what was being called "Edwardian" poetry. The early volumes of Georgian work reveal this kind of energy, at least in comparison to later volumes after the war, when many of the best contributors had either died (Brooke and Isaac Rosenberg, among others), lost interest (Robert Graves, Siegfried Sassoon), or gone their own ways (Ezra Pound, D. H. Lawrence). Unfortunately, the later examples of Georgian poetry are frequently used by critics to describe the whole movement; for poets and critics of the late 1920's and 1930's, who demanded rock-hard language and precise imagery, there was nothing to do but to attack the Georgians with a vengeance.

OTHER MAJOR WORKS

PLAY: *Lithuania*, pb. 1935 (one act).

NONFICTION: *John Webster and the Elizabethan Drama*, 1916; *Letters from America*, 1916; *The Prose of Rupert Brooke*, 1956; *The Letters of Rupert Brooke*, 1968.

BIBLIOGRAPHY

Brooke, Rupert, Walter de la Mare, and Maurice Browne. *Rupert Brooke*. Port Washington, N.Y.: Kennikat Press, 1968. The eulogistic lecture by de la Mare given in 1919, four years after Brooke's death, helped perpetuate the image of Brooke as a wit, closer in spirit to the young John Donne than to George Gordon, Lord Byron, and Percy Bysshe Shelley; Browne's recollections, first published in 1927, reinforce that view.

Delaney, Paul. *The Neo-Pagans: Rupert Brooke and the Ordeal of Youth*. New York: Free Press, 1987. In 1911, Virginia Woolf half-derisively gave Brooke and his carefree circle the label "neo-pagans." In this balanced appraisal, Delaney focuses on the flaws in the group's philosophies that undermined their optimism about the future, causing conflicts and fragmenting their relationships. Contains notes and references, a bibliography, and an index.

Hale, Keith, ed. *Friends and Apostles: The Correspondence of Rupert Brooke and James Strachey: 1905-1914*. New Haven, Conn.: Yale University Press, 1998. This collection of letters records the friendship and love shared by Brooke and Strachey, who first met at the age of ten. They were both eighteen and students at Cambridge University when they renewed their acquaintance, which marks the beginning of the collection.

Jones, Nigel H. *Rupert Brooke: Life, Death, and Myth*. London: Richard Cohen Books, 1999. W. B. Yeats called Rupert Brooke "the most beautiful man in England." Jones draws on Brooke's previously unpublished letters to reveal what the publisher calls the "unsentimental truth." *The Times* of London comments, "Brooke is sharply perceived, his inner corrosion convincingly described and analyzed."

Lehmann, John. *The Strange Destiny of Rupert Brooke*. New York: Holt, Rinehart and Winston, 1981. In this highly praised combination of biography and literary criticism, Lehmann explores Brooke's psychological history and explains why Brooke's friends expressed conflicting judgments about his character and abilities. Contains an index and a brief biography.

Read, Mike. *Forever England*. Edinburgh: Mainstream, 1997. This biography allows Brooke to speak for himself through the inclusion of poems and other writings. The work also provides a well-rounded picture of prewar England, providing detailed background to various persons and places alluded to in the texts.

Rogers, Timothy. *Rupert Brooke: A Reappraisal and Selection from His Writings, Some Hitherto Unpublished*. London: Routledge & Kegan Paul, 1971. Rogers says that Brooke has often been judged unfairly; the poetry has created the myth, and the myth has obscured the best in Brooke's work. Along with his collection of representative prose and verse, Rogers provides critical commentary, arguing persuasively that the charge of dullness frequently leveled at Brooke is unwarranted. A bibliography concludes this slight volume.

Robert Edward Graalman, Jr.;
bibliography updated by the editors

GWENDOLYN BROOKS

Born: Topeka, Kansas; June 7, 1917
Died: Chicago, Illinois; December 3, 2000

PRINCIPAL POETRY

A Street in Bronzeville, 1945
Annie Allen, 1949
The Bean Eaters, 1960
Selected Poems, 1963
We Real Cool, 1966
The Wall, 1967
In the Mecca, 1968
Riot, 1969
Family Pictures, 1970
Aloneness, 1971
Black Steel: Joe Frazier and Muhammad Ali, 1971
Aurora, 1972
Beckonings, 1975
Primer for Blacks, 1980
To Disembark, 1981
Black Love, 1982
The Near-Johannesburg Boy, 1986
Blacks, 1987
Gottschalk and the Grand Tarantelle, 1988
Winnie, 1988
Children Coming Home, 1991

OTHER LITERARY FORMS

In addition to the poetry on which her literary reputation rests, Gwendolyn Brooks published a novel, *Maud Martha* (1953); a book of autobiographical prose, *Re-port from Part One* (1972); and volumes of children's verse. An episodic novel, *Maud Martha* makes some use of autobiographical materials and shares many of the major concerns of Brooks's poetry, particularly concerning the attempts of the person to maintain integrity in the face of crushing environmental pressures. *Report from Part One* recounts the personal, political, and aesthetic influences which culminated in Brooks's movement to a black nationalist stance in the late 1960's. She also wrote introductions to, and edited anthologies of, the works of younger black writers. These introductions frequently provide insight into her own work. Several recordings of Brooks reading her own work are available.

ACHIEVEMENTS

Working comfortably in relation to diverse poetic traditions, Gwendolyn Brooks has been widely honored. Early in her career, she received numerous mainstream literary awards, including the Pulitzer Prize for Poetry in 1950 for *Annie Allen*. She became poet laureate of Illinois in 1969 and has received more than fifty honorary doctorates. Equally significant, numerous writers associated with the Black Arts Movement recognized her as an inspirational figure linking the older and younger generations of black poets. Brooks's ability to appeal both to poetic establishments and to a sizable popular audience, especially among young blacks, stems from her pluralistic voice which echoes a wide range of precursors while remaining unmistakably black. Her exploration of America in general and Chicago in particular links her with Walt Whitman and Carl Sandburg. Her exploration of the interior landscape of humanity in general and women in particular places her in the tradition of Emily Dickinson and Edna St. Vincent Millay. At once the technical heir of Langston Hughes in her use of the rhythms of black street life and of Robert Frost in her exploration of traditional forms such as the sonnet, Brooks nevertheless maintains her integrity of vision and voice.

This integrity assumes special significance in the context of African American writing of the 1950's and 1960's. A period of "universalism" in black literature, the 1950's brought prominence to such poets as Brooks, LeRoi Jones (Amiri Baraka), and Robert Hayden. During this period of intellectual and aesthetic integration, Brooks never abandoned her social and racial heritage to strive for the transcendent (and deracinated) universalism associated by some African American critics with T. S. Eliot. Responding to William Carlos Williams's call in *Paterson* (1946-1951) to "make a start out of particulars and make them general," Brooks demonstrated unambiguously that an African American writer need not be limited in relevance by concentrating on the black experience.

The 1960's, conversely, encouraged separatism and militancy in African American writing. Even while accepting the Black Arts Movement's call for a poetry designed to speak directly to the political condition of the black community, Brooks continued to insist on precision of form and language. While Jones changed his name to Amiri Baraka and radically altered his poetic voice, Brooks accommodated her new insights to her

previously established style. An exemplar of integrity and flexibility, she both challenges and learns from younger black poets such as Haki R. Madhubuti (Don L. Lee), Sonia Sanchez, Carolyn Rodgers, and Etheridge Knight. Like Hughes, she addresses the black community without condescension or pretense. Like Frost, she wrote technically stunning "universal" poetry combining clear surfaces and elusive depths.

A recipient of more than fifty honorary doctorates, Brooks was appointed to the Presidential Commission on the National Agenda for the Eighties; she was the first black woman elected to the National Institute of Arts and Letters. She was named Consultant in Poetry to the Library of Congress for 1985-1986; received the Shelley Memorial Award in 1975 and the Frost Medal in 1989, both awarded by the Poetry Society of America; and received the Academy of American Poets Fellowship in 1999.

BIOGRAPHY

Gwendolyn Brooks's poetry bears the strong impress of Chicago, particularly of the predominantly black South Side where she lived most of her life. Although she was born in Topeka, Kansas, Brooks was taken to Chicago before she was a year old. In many ways she devoted her career to the physical, spiritual, and, more recently, political exploration of her native city.

Brooks's life and writings are frequently separated into two phases, with her experience at the 1967 Black Writers' Conference at Fisk University in Nashville serving as a symbolic transition. Prior to the Conference, Brooks was known primarily as the first black Pulitzer Prize winner in poetry. Although not politically unaware, she held to a somewhat cautious attitude. The vitality she encountered at the Conference crystallized her sense of the insufficiency of universalist attitudes and generated close personal and artistic friendships with younger black poets such as Madhubuti, Walter Bradford, and Knight. Severing her ties with the mainstream publishing firm of Harper and Row, which had published her first five books, Brooks transferred her work and prestige to the black-owned and operated Broadside Press of Detroit, Third World Press of Chicago, and Black Position Press, also of Chicago. Her commitment to black publishing houses remained un-

Gwendolyn Brooks (© Jill Krementz)

wavering despite distribution problems which rendered her later work largely invisible to the American reading public.

Educated in the Chicago school system and at Wilson Junior College, Brooks learned her craft under Inez Cunningham Stark (Boulton), a white woman who taught poetry at the South Side Community Art Center in the late 1930's and 1940's. Brooks's mother, who had been a teacher in Topeka, had encouraged her literary interests from an early age. Her father, a janitor, provided her with ineffaceable images of the spiritual strength and dignity of "common" people. Brooks married Henry Blakely in 1939 and her family concerns continued to play a central role in shaping her career. The eleven-year hiatus between the publication of *Annie Allen* and *The Bean Eaters* resulted at least in part from her concentration on rearing her two children, born in 1940 and 1951. Her numerous poems on family relationships reflect both the rewards and the tensions of her own experiences. Her children grown, Brooks concentrated on teaching, supervising poetry workshops, and speaking publicly. These activities brought her into contact with a wide range of younger black poets, preparing her for her experience at Fisk. As poet laureate of Illinois, she encouraged the development of younger poets through personal contact and formal competitions.

The division between the two phases of Brooks's life should not be overstated. She evinced a strong interest in the Civil Rights movement during the 1950's and early 1960's; her concern with family continued in the 1980's. Above all, Brooks lived with and wrote of and for the Chicagoans whose failures and triumphs she saw as deeply personal, universally resonant, and specifically black. She died in Chicago on December 3, 2000, at the age of eighty-three.

ANALYSIS

The image of Gwendolyn Brooks as a readily accessible poet is at once accurate and deceptive. Capable of capturing the experiences and rhythms of black street life, she frequently presents translucent surfaces which give way suddenly to reveal ambiguous depths. Equally capable of manipulating traditional poetic forms such as the sonnet, rhyme royal, and heroic couplet, she employs them to mirror the uncertainties of characters or personas who embrace conventional attitudes to defend themselves against internal and external chaos. Whatever form she chooses, Brooks consistently focuses on the struggle of people to find and express love, usually associated with the family, in the midst of a hostile environment. In constructing their defenses and seeking love, these persons typically experience a disfiguring pain. Brooks devotes much of her energy to defining and responding to the elusive forces, variously psychological and social, which inflict this pain. Increasingly in her later poetry, Brooks traces the pain to political sources and expands her concept of the family to encompass all black people. Even while speaking of the social situation of blacks in a voice crafted primarily for blacks, however, Brooks maintains the complex awareness of the multiple perspectives relevant to any given experience. Her ultimate concern is to encourage every individual, black or white, to "Conduct your blooming in the noise and whip of the whirlwind" ("The Second Sermon on the Warpland").

A deep concern with the everyday circumstances of black people living within the whirlwind characterizes many of Brooks's most popular poems. From the early "Of De Witt Williams on His Way to Lincoln Cemetery" and "A Song in the Front Yard" through the later "The Life of Lincoln West" and "Sammy Chester Leaves 'Godspell' and Visits UPWARD BOUND on a Lake Forest Lawn, Bringing West Afrika," she focuses on characters whose experiences merge the idiosyncratic and the typical. She frequently draws on black musical forms to underscore the communal resonance of a character's outwardly undistinguished life. By tying the refrain of "Swing Low Sweet Chariot" to the repeated phrase "Plain black boy," Brooks transforms De Witt Williams into an Everyman figure. Brooks describes his personal search for love in the pool rooms and dance halls, but stresses the representative quality of his experience by starting and ending the poem with the musical allusion.

"WE REAL COOL"

"We Real Cool," perhaps Brooks's single best-known poem, subjects a similarly representative experience to an intricate technical and thematic scrutiny, at once loving and critical. The poem is only twenty-four words long, including eight repetitions of the word "we." It is suggestive that the subtitle of "We Real Cool" specifies the presence of only seven pool players at the "Golden Shovel." The eighth "we" suggests that poet and reader share, on some level, the desperation of the group-voice that Brooks transmits. The final sentence, "We/ die soon," restates the *carpe diem* motif in the vernacular of Chicago's South Side.

On one level, "We Real Cool" appears simply to catalog the experiences of a group of dropouts content to "sing sin" in all available forms. A surprising ambiguity enters into the poem, however, revolving around the question of how to accent the word "we" which ends every line except the last one, providing the beat for the poem's jazz rhythm. Brooks said that she intended that the "we" *not* be accented. Read in this way, the poem takes on a slightly distant and ironic tone, emphasizing the artificiality of the group identity which involves the characters in activities offering early death as the only release from pain. Conversely, the poem can be read with a strong accent on each "we," affirming the group identity. Although the experience still ends with early death, the pool players metamorphose into defiant heroes determined to resist the alienating environment. Their confrontation with experience is felt, if not articulated, as existentially pure. Pool players, poet, and reader cannot be *sure* which stress is valid.

Brooks crafts the poem, however, to hint at an underlying coherence in the defiance. The intricate internal rhyme scheme echoes the sound of nearly every word. Not only do the first seven lines end with "we," but the penultimate words of each line in each stanza also rhyme (cool/school, late/straight, sin/gin, June/soon). In addition, the alliterated consonant of the last line of each stanza is repeated in the first line of the next stanza (Left/lurk, Strike/sin, gin/June) and the first words of each line in the middle two stanzas are connected through consonance (Lurk/strike, Sing/thin). The one exception to this suggestive texture of sound is the word "Die" which introduces both a new vowel and a new consonant into the final line, breaking the rhythm and subjecting the performance to ironic revaluation. Ultimately, the power of the poem derives from the tension between the celebratory and the ironic perspectives on the lives of the plain black boys struggling for a sense of connection.

"THE MOTHER"

A similar struggle informs many of Brooks's poems in more traditional forms, including "The Mother," a powerful exploration of the impact of an abortion on the woman who has chosen to have it. Brooks states that the mother "decides that *she*, rather than her world, will kill her children." Within the poem itself, however, the motivations remain unclear. Although the poem's position in Brooks's first book, *A Street in Bronzeville*, suggests that the persona is black, the poem neither supports nor denies a racial identification. Along with the standard English syntax and diction, this suggests that "The Mother," like poems such as "The Egg Boiler," "Callie Ford," and "A Light and Diplomatic Bird," was designed to speak directly of an emotional, rather than a social, experience, and to be as accessible to whites as to blacks. Re-creating the anguished perspective of a persona unsure whether she is victim or victimizer, Brooks directs her readers' attention to the complex emotions of her potential Everywoman.

"The Mother" centers on the persona's alternating desire to take and to evade responsibility for the abortion. Resorting to ambiguous grammatical structures, the persona repeatedly qualifies her acceptance with "if" clauses ("If I sinned," "If I stole your births"). She refers to the lives of the children as matters of fate ("Your luck") and backs away from admitting that a death has taken place by claiming that the children "were never made." Her use of the second person pronoun to refer to herself in the first stanza reveals her desire to distance herself from her present pain. This attempt, however, fails. The opening line undercuts the evasion with the reality of memory: "Abortions will not let you forget." At the start of the second stanza, the pressure of memory forces the persona to shift to the more honest first person pronoun. A sequence of spondees referring to the children ("damp small pulps," "dim killed children," "dim dears") interrupts the lightly stressed anapestic-iambic meter which dominates the first stanza. The concrete images of "scurrying off ghosts" and "devouring" children with loving gazes gain power when contrasted with the dimness of the mother's life and perceptions. Similarly, the first stanza's end-stopped couplets, reflecting the persona's simplistic attempt to recapture an irrevocably lost mother-child relationship through an act of imagination, give way to the intricate enjambment and complex rhyme scheme of the second stanza, which highlight the mother's inability to find rest.

The rhyme scheme—and Brooks can rival both Robert Frost and W. B. Yeats in her ability to employ various types of rhyme for thematic impact—underscores her struggle to come to terms with her action. The rhymes in the first stanza insist on her self-doubt, contrasting images of tenderness and physical substance with those of brutality and insubstantiality (forget/get, hair/air, beat/ sweet). The internal rhyme of "never," repeated four times, and "remember," "workers," and "singers," further stresses the element of loss. In the second stanza, Brooks provides no rhymes for the end words "children" in line 11 and "deliberate" in line 21. This device draws attention to the persona's failure to answer the crucial questions of whether her children did in fact exist and of whether her own actions were in fact deliberate (and perhaps criminal). The last seven lines of the stanza end with hard "d" sounds as the persona struggles to forge her conflicting thoughts into a unified perspective. If Brooks offers coherence, though, it is emotional rather than intellectual. Fittingly, the "d" rhymes and off-rhymes focus on physical and emotional pain (dead/instead/made/afraid/said/died/cried). Brooks provides no easy answer to the anguished question: "How is the truth to be told?" The persona's concluding cry of "I loved you/ All" rings with desperation. It is futile but it is not a lie. To call "The Mother" an antiabortion poem distorts its impact. Clearly portraying the devastating effects of the persona's action, it by no means condemns her or lacks sympathy. Like many of Brooks's characters, the mother is a person whose desire to love far outstrips her ability to cope with her circumstances and serves primarily to heighten her sensitivity to pain.

Perhaps the most significant change in Brooks's poetry involves her analysis of the origins of this pervasive pain. Rather than attributing the suffering to some unavoidable psychological condition, Brooks's later poetry indicts social institutions for their role in its perpetuation. The poems in her first two volumes frequently portray characters incapable of articulating the origins of their pain. Although the absence of any father in "The Mother" suggests sociological forces leading to the abortion, such analysis amounts to little more than spec-

ulation. The only certainty is that the mother, the persona of the sonnet sequence "The Children of the Poor," and the speaker in the brilliant sonnet "My Dreams, My Works Must Wait Till After Hell" share the fear that their pain will render them insensitive to love. The final poem of *Annie Allen*, "Men of Careful Turns," intimates that the defenders of a society which refuses to admit its full humanity bear responsibility for reducing the powerless to "grotesque toys." Despite this implicit accusation, however, Brooks perceives no "magic" capable of remedying the situation. She concludes the volume on a note of irresolution typical of her early period: "We are lost, must/ Wizard a track through our own screaming weed." The track, at this stage, remains spiritual rather than political.

POLITICS

Although the early volumes include occasional poems concerning articulate political participants such as "Negro Hero," her later work frequently centers on specific black political spokespersons such as Malcolm X, Paul Robeson, John Killens, and Don L. Lee. As of the early 1960's, a growing anger informs poems as diverse as the ironic "The Chicago *Defender* Sends a Man to Little Rock," the near-baroque "The Lovers of the Poor," the imagistically intricate "Riders to the Blood-Red Wrath," and the satiric "Riot." This anger originates in Brooks's perception that the social structures of white society value material possessions and abstract ideas of prestige more highly than individual human beings. The anger culminates in Brooks's brilliant narrative poem "In the Mecca," concerning the death of a young girl in a Chicago housing project, and in her three "Sermons on the Warpland."

THE "WARPLAND" POEMS

The "Warpland" poems mark Brooks's departure from the traditions of Euro-American poetry and thought represented by T. S. Eliot's *The Waste Land* (1922). The sequence typifies her post-1967 poetry, in which she abandons traditional stanzaic forms, applying her technical expertise to a relatively colloquial free verse. This technical shift parallels her rejection of the philosophical premises of Euro-American culture. Brooks refuses to accept the inevitability of cultural decay, arguing that the "waste" of Eliot's vision exists primarily because of our "warped" perceptions. Seeing white society as the embodiment of these distortions, Brooks embraces her blackness as a potential counter-balancing force. The first "Sermon on the Warpland" opens with Ron Karenga's black nationalist credo: "The fact that we are black is our ultimate reality." Clearly, in Brooks's view, blackness is not simply a physical fact; it is primarily a metaphor for the possibility of love. As her poem "Two Dedications" indicates, Brooks sees the Euro-American tradition represented by the Chicago Picasso as inhumanly cold, mingling guilt and innocence, meaningfulness and meaninglessness, almost randomly. This contrasts sharply with her inspirational image of the Wall of Heroes on the South Side. To Brooks, true art assumes meaning from the people who interact with it. The Wall helps to redefine black reality, rendering the "dispossessions beakless." Rather than contemplating the site of destruction, the politically aware black art which Brooks embraces should inspire the black community to face its pain with renewed determination to remove its sources. The final "Sermon on the Warpland" concludes with the image of a black phoenix rising from the ashes of the Chicago riot. No longer content to accept the unresolved suffering of "The Mother," Brooks forges a black nationalist politics and poetics of love.

"THE BLACKSTONE RANGERS"

Although her political vision influences every aspect of her work, Brooks maintains a strong sense of enduring individual pain and is aware that nationalism offers no simple panacea. "The Blackstone Rangers," a poem concerning one of the most powerful Chicago street gangs, rejects as simplistic the argument, occasionally advanced by writers associated with the Black Arts Movement, that no important distinction exists between the personal and the political experience. Specifically, Brooks doubts the corollary that politically desirable activity will inevitably increase the person's ability to love. Dividing "The Blackstone Rangers" into three segments—"As Seen by Disciplines," "The Leaders," and "Gang Girls: A Rangerette"—Brooks stresses the tension between perspectives. After rejecting the sociological-penal perspective of part one, she remains suspended between the uncomprehending affirmation of the Rangers as a kind of government-in-exile in part two, and the recognition of the individual person's continuing pain in part three.

Brooks undercuts the description of the Rangers as "sores in the city/ that do not want to heal" ("As Seen by Disciplines") through the use of off-rhyme and a jazz rhythm reminiscent of "We Real Cool." The disciplines, both academic and corrective, fail to perceive any coherence in the Rangers' experience. Correct in their assumption that the Rangers do not want to "heal" themselves, the disciplines fail to perceive the gang's strong desire to "heal" the sick society. Brooks suggests an essential coherence in the Rangers' experience through the sound texture of part one. Several of the sound patterns echoing through the brief stanza point to a shared response to pain (there/thirty/ready, raw/sore/corner). Similarly, the accent cluster on "Black, raw, ready" draws attention to the pain and potential power of the Rangers. The descriptive voice of the disciplines, however, provides only relatively weak end rhymes (are/corner, ready/city), testifying to the inability of the distanced, presumably white, observers to comprehend the experiences they describe. The shifting, distinctively black, jazz rhythm further emphasizes the distance between the voices of observers and participants. Significantly, the voice of the disciplines finds no rhyme at all for its denial of the Rangers' desire to "heal."

This denial contrasts sharply with the tempered affirmation of the voice in part two which emphasizes the leaders' desire to "cancel, cure and curry." Again, internal rhymes and sound echoes suffuse the section. In the first stanza, the voice generates thematically significant rhymes, connecting Ranger leader "*Bop*" (whose name draws attention to the jazz rhythm which is even more intricate, though less obvious, in this section than in part one) and the militant black leader "*Rap*" Brown, both nationalists whose "country is a Nation on no *map*." "Bop" and "Rap," of course, do not rhyme perfectly, attesting to Brooks's awareness of the gang leader's limitations. Her image of the leaders as "Bungled trophies" further reinforces her ambivalence. The only full rhyme in the final two stanzas of the section is the repeated "night." The leaders, canceling the racist association of darkness with evil, "translate" the image of blackness into a "monstrous pearl or grace." The section affirms the Blackstone Rangers' struggle; it does not pretend to comprehend fully the emotional texture of their lives.

Certain that the leaders possess the power to cancel the disfiguring images of the disciplines, Brooks remains unsure of their ability to create an alternate environment where love can blossom. Mary Ann, the "Gang Girl" of part three, shares much of the individual pain of the characters in Brooks's early poetry despite her involvement with the Rangers. "A rose in a whiskey glass," she continues to live with the knowledge that her "laboring lover" risks the same sudden death as the pool players of "We Real Cool." Forced to suppress a part of her awareness—she knows not to ask where her lover got the diamond he gives her—she remains emotionally removed even while making love. In place of a fully realized love, she accepts "the props and niceties of nonloneliness." The final line of the poem emphasizes the ambiguity of both Mary Ann's situation and Brooks's perspective. Recommending acceptance of "the rhymes of Leaning," the line responds to the previous stanza's question concerning whether love will have a "gleaning." The full rhyme paradoxically suggests acceptance of off-rhyme, of love consummated leaning against an alley wall, without expectation of safety or resolution. Given the political tension created by the juxtaposition of the disciplines and the leaders, the "Gang Girl" can hope to find no sanctuary beyond the reach of the whirlwind. Her desperate love, the more moving for its precariousness, provides the only near-adequate response to the pain that Brooks saw as the primary fact of life.

OTHER MAJOR WORKS

LONG FICTION: *Maud Martha*, 1953.

NONFICTION: *The World of Gwendolyn Brooks*, 1971; *Report from Part One*, 1972; *Young Poet's Primer*, 1980.

CHILDREN'S LITERATURE: *Bronzeville Boys and Girls*, 1956; *The Tiger Who Wore White Gloves*, 1974; *Very Young Poets*, 1983.

EDITED TEXT: *Jump Bad: A New Chicago Anthology*, 1971.

BIBLIOGRAPHY

Baker, Houston A., Jr. *The Journey Back: Issues in Black Literature and Criticism*. Chicago: University of Chicago Press, 1980. The value of Baker's treatment of Brooks (accessible through the index) is his examination of the shift in her thinking and her art generated by her experience at the Fisk University Writers' Conference in 1967. Baker sets her in the context of the larger movement toward a "Black Aesthetic."

Bolden, B. J. *Urban Rage in Bronzeville: Social Commentary in the Poetry of Gwendolyn Brooks, 1945-1960*. Chicago: Third World Press, 1999. A critical analysis focused on the impact of Brooks's early poetry. Bolden examines *A Street in Bronzeville, Annie Allen*, and *The Bean Eaters* in clear historical, racial, political, cultural, and aesthetic terms.

"Gwendolyn's Words: A Gift to Us." *Essence* 31, no. 11 (March, 2001): A18. Discusses the career of Brooks, the first African American to win a Pulitzer Prize. Begins with an account of her early life and documents the sequence of her compositions. Also covers her professional relationship with Haki R. Madhubuti, who helped publish her works.

Kent, George E. *A Life of Gwendolyn Brooks*. Lexington: University Press of Kentucky, 1990. This biography, actually completed in 1982 just before Kent's death, is based on interviews with Brooks and her friends and family. Integrates discussions of the poetry with a chronicle of her life. Especially valuable is an extensive recounting of the events and speeches at the 1967 Fisk conference, which changed the direction of her poetry. D. L. Melhem's afterword provides an update to 1988.

Melhem, D. L. *Gwendolyn Brooks: Poetry and the Heroic Voice*. Lexington: University Press of Kentucky, 1987. Beginning with a biographical chapter, Melhem employs a generally laudatory tone as he subsequently looks closely at the earlier poetry collections (through *Aloneness*). He surveys the later works within a single chapter, and also examines *Maud Martha* and *Bronzeville Boys and Girls*. Melhem's treatment gives attention to both structures and themes. Includes notes and an index, as well as a bibliography of her works (organized by publisher, in order to show the commitment she made to small black-run presses after the late 1960's).

Miller, R. Baxter, ed. *Black American Poets Between Worlds, 1940-1960*. Tennessee Studies in Literature 30. Knoxville: University of Tennessee Press, 1986.

To this collection Harry B. Shaw contributes "Perceptions of Men in the Early Works of Gwendolyn Brooks," which looks at *A Street in Bronzeville*, *Annie Allen*, *Maud Martha*, and *The Bean Eaters* for their largely positive depictions of urban African American men. "Define . . . the Whirlwind: Gwendolyn Brooks's Epic Sign for a Generation," by R. Baxter Miller, focuses on Brooks's epic achievement "In the Mecca." Each of these essays has notes, and the book is indexed.

Mootry, Maria K., and Gary Smith, eds. *A Life Distilled: Gwendolyn Brooks, Her Poetry and Fiction*. Urbana: University of Illinois Press, 1987. An introductory overview by Mootry is followed by a look at Brooks's sense of place ("The World of Satin-Legs, Mrs. Sallie, and the Blackstone Rangers" by Kenny J. Williams), her aesthetic (essays by George E. Kent, Norris B. Clark, and R. Baxter Miller), and the militancy that emerged in her "second period" (by William H. Hansel). The middle section comprises essays on individual collections, while the book's final two essays examine *Maud Martha*. Features notes, and a selected bibliography that not only lists Brooks's works but also surveys critical sources in great detail, including book reviews and dissertations. No index is provided.

Washington, Mary Helen. "An Appreciation: A Writer Who Defined Black Power for Herself." *The Los Angeles Times*, December 8, 2000, p. E1. Discusses the young Brooks, who, when just starting her writing career, attended the 1967 Fisk University Writers' Conference, encountered the young black militants led by Amiri Baraka, and was converted. She branded her earlier writing "white writing" and resolved to change.

Wright, Stephen Caldwell, ed. *On Gwendolyn Brooks: Reliant Contemplation*. Ann Arbor: University of Michigan Press, 1996. This resource judiciously selects and assembles the most important writings to date about the works of Gwendolyn Brooks in the form of reviews and essays. Three-part organization helpfully separates the reviews from the essays and the later essays from the rest.

Craig Werner;
bibliography updated by the editors

STERLING BROWN

Born: Washington, D.C.; May 1, 1901
Died: Takoma Park, Maryland; January 13, 1989

PRINCIPAL POETRY

Southern Road, 1932
The Last Ride of Wild Bill and Eleven Narrative Poems, 1975
The Collected Poems of Sterling A. Brown, 1980

OTHER LITERARY FORMS

Sterling Brown produced several studies of African American literature: *Outline for the Study of the Poetry of American Negroes* (1931), *The Negro in American Fiction* (1937), and *Negro Poetry and Drama* (1937). With Arthur P. Davis and Ulysses Lee, he edited *The Negro Caravan* (1941). Brown also published numerous scholarly pieces in leading journals on subjects relating to African American culture and literature.

ACHIEVEMENTS

Sterling Brown is considered an important transitional figure between the Harlem Renaissance era and the period immediately following the Depression. Brown's fame is based not only on his poetry but also on his achievements as a critic, folklorist, scholar, and university teacher. As an acknowledged authority on African American culture, Brown served on many committees and boards and participated in numerous scholarly and research activities. Among these were the Carnegie Myrdal Study, the American Folklore Society, the Institute of Jazz Studies, the editorial board of *The Crisis*, the Federal Writers' Project, and the Committee on Negro Studies of the American Council of Learned Societies.

Brown's poems and critical essays have been anthologized widely, and he was a memorable reader of his own poetry, especially on such recordings as *The Anthology of Negro Poets* (Folkways) and *A Hand's on the Gate*. He cowrote an article with Rayford Logan on the American Negro for *Encyclopaedia Britannica*. Brown was a Guggenheim Fellow (1937-1938) and a Julius Rosenwald Fellow (1942). He was an eminent faculty member at Howard University in Washington, D.C.,

Sterling Brown (© Scurlock Studio)

from 1929 to 1969. In 1987, Brown won the Frost Medal, awarded by the Poetry Society of America.

BIOGRAPHY

Born into an educated, middle-class African American family, Sterling Allen Brown was the last of six children and the only son of Adelaide Allen Brown and the Reverend Sterling Nelson Brown. His father had taught in the School of Religion at Howard University since 1892, and the year Brown was born, his father also became the pastor of Lincoln Temple Congregational Church. The person who encouraged Brown's literary career and admiration for the cultural heritage of African Americans, however, was his mother, who had been born and reared in Tennessee and graduated from Fisk University. Brown also grew up listening to tales of his father's childhood in Tennessee, as well as to accounts of his father's friendships with noted leaders such as Frederick Douglass, Blanche K. Bruce, and Booker T. Washington.

Brown attended public schools in Washington, D.C., and was graduated from the well-known Dunbar High

School, noted for its distinguished teachers and alumni; among the latter were many of the nation's outstanding black professionals. Brown's teachers at Dunbar included literary artists such as Angelina Weld Grimke and Jessie Redmon Fauset. Moreover, Brown grew up on the campus of Howard University, where there were many outstanding African American scholars, such as historian Kelly Miller and critic and philosopher Alain Locke.

Brown received his A.B. in 1922 from Williams College (Phi Beta Kappa) and his M.A. in 1923 from Harvard University. Although he pursued further graduate study in English at Harvard, he never worked toward a doctorate degree; however, Howard University, the University of Massachusetts, Northwestern University, Williams College, Boston University, Brown University, Lewis and Clark College, Lincoln University (Pennsylvania), and the University of Pennsylvania eventually granted him honorary doctorates. In September, 1927, he was married to Daisy Turnbull, who shared with him an enthusiasm for people, a sense of humor, and a rejection of pretentious behavior; she was also one of her husband's sharpest critics. She inspired Brown's poems "Long Track Blues" and "Against That Day." Daisy Turnbull Brown died in 1979. The Browns had one adopted child, John L. Dennis.

In 1927, "When de Saints Go Ma'ching Home" won first prize in an *Opportunity* writing contest. From 1926 to 1929, several of the poems that Brown later published in *Southern Road* were printed in *Crisis, Opportunity, Contempo,* and *Ebony and Topaz.* His early work is often identified with the outpouring of black writers during the New Negro Movement, for he shared with those artists (Claude McKay, Countée Cullen, Jean Toomer, and Langston Hughes) a deep concern for a franker self-revelation and a respect for the folk traditions of his people; however, Brown's writings did not reflect the alien-and-exile theme so popular with the writers of the Renaissance.

Brown's teaching career took him to Virginia Seminary and College, Lincoln University (Missouri), and Fisk University. He began teaching at Howard University in 1929 and remained there until his retirement in 1969. He was also a visiting professor at Atlanta University, New York University, Vassar College, the

University of Minnesota, the New School, and the University of Illinois (Chicago Circle). Several years after coming to Howard University, Brown became an editor with the Works Progress Administration's Federal Writers Project. Along with a small editorial staff, he coordinated the Federal Writers Project studies by and about blacks. Beginning in 1932, Brown supervised an extensive collection of narratives by former slaves and initiated special projects such as *The Negro in Virginia* (1940), which became the model for other studies. His most enduring contribution to the project was an essay, "The Negro in Washington," which was published in the guidebook *Washington: City and Capital* (1937).

Brown's first fifteen years at Howard were most productive. During this period (1929-1945), he contributed poetry as well as reviews and essays on the American theater, folk expressions, oral history, social customs, music, and athletics to *The New Republic, The Journal of Negro Education, Phylon, Crisis, Opportunity*, and other journals. His most outstanding essay, "Negro Characters As Seen by White Authors," which appeared in *The Journal of Negro Education* in 1933, brought attention to the widespread misrepresentation of black characters and life in American literature. Only after Brown's retirement from Howard in 1969 did he begin reading his poems regularly there. This long neglect has been attributed to certain conservative faculty members' reluctance to appreciate a fellow professor whose interests were in blues and jazz. Brown was widely known as a raconteur. Throughout his career as a writer, he challenged fellow African American writers to choose their subject matter without regard to external pressures and to avoid the error of "timidity." He was a mentor who influenced the black poetry movement of the 1960's and 1970's, and poets such as Margaret Walker, Gwendolyn Brooks, Langston Hughes, and Arna Bontemps, along with critics such as Addison Gayle and Houston Baker, learned from him.

In the five years before his retirement, Brown began to exhibit stress caused by what he perceived to be years of critical and professional neglect as well as unfulfilled goals. Inclined toward periods of deep depression, he was occasionally hospitalized in his later years. He died in Takoma Park, Maryland, on January 13, 1989.

ANALYSIS

The poetry of Sterling Brown is imbued with the folk spirit of African American culture. For Brown there was no wide abyss between his poetry and the spirit inherent in slave poetry; indeed, his works evidence a continuity of racial spirit from the slave experience to the African American present and reflect his deep understanding of the multitudinous aspects of the African American personality and soul.

The setting for Brown's poetry is primarily the South, through which he traveled to listen to the folktales, songs, wisdom, sorrows, and frustrations of his people, and where the blues and ballads were nurtured. Brown respected traditional folk forms and employed them in the construction of his own poems; thus he may be called "the poet of the soul of his people."

SOUTHERN ROAD

Brown's first published collection of poems, *Southern Road*, was critically acclaimed by his peers and colleagues James Weldon Johnson and Alain Locke, because of its rendering of the living speech of the African American, its use of the raw material of folk poetry, and its poetic portrayal of African American folk life and thought. Later critics such as Arthur P. Davis, Jean Wagner, and Houston Baker have continued to praise his poetry for its creative and vital use of folk motifs. Some of the characters in Brown's poetry, such as Ma Rainey, Big Boy Davis, and Mrs. Bibby, are based on real people. Other characters, such as Maumee Ruth, Sporting Beasley, and Sam Smiley seem real because of Brown's dramatic and narrative talent. He is also highly skilled in the use of poetic techniques such as the refrain, alliteration, and onomatopoeia, and he employs several stanzaic forms with facility. Brown's extraordinary gift for re-creating the nuances of folk speech and idiom adds vitality and authenticity to his verse.

Brown is successful in drawing upon rich folk expressions to vitalize the speech of his characters through the cadences of Southern speech. Though his poems cannot simply be called "dialect poetry," Brown does imitate Southern African American speech, using variant spellings and apostrophes to mark dropped consonants. He uses grunts and onomatopoeic sounds to give a natural rhythm to the speech of his characters. These techniques are readily seen in a poem that dramatizes the poignant story of a "po los boy" on a chain gang. This poem follows the traditional folk form of the work song to convey the convict's personal tragedy.

Brown's work may be classed as protest poetry influenced by poets such as Carl Sandburg and Robert Frost; he is able to draw upon the entire canon of English and American poetry as well as African American folk material. Thus he is fluent in the use of the sonnet form, stanzaic forms, free-verse forms, and ballad and blues forms.

In *Southern Road*, several themes express the essence of the Southern African American's folk spirit and culture. Recurring themes and subjects in Brown's poetry include endurance, tragedy, and survival. The theme of endurance is best illustrated in one of his most anthologized poems, "Strong Men," which tells the story of the unjust treatment of black men and women from the slave ship, to the tenant farm, and finally to the black ghetto. The refrain of "Strong Men" uses rhythmic beats, relentlessly repeating an affirmation of the black people's ability and determination to keep pressing onward, toward freedom and justice. The central image comes from a line of a Carl Sandburg poem, "The strong men keep comin on." In "Strong Men," Brown praises the indomitable spirit of African Americans in the face of racist exploitation. With its assertive tone, the rhythm of this poem suggests a martial song.

Some of the endurance poems express a stoic, fatalistic acceptance of the tragic fate of the African American, as can be seen in "Old Man Buzzard," "Memphis Blues," and "Riverbank Blues." Another important aspect of the endurance theme as portrayed by Brown is the poetic characters' courage when they are confronted with tragedy and injustice. In the poem "Strange Legacies," the speaker gives thanks to the legendary Jack Johnson and John Henry for their demonstration of courage.

"THE LAST RIDE OF WILD BILL"

Brown's poems reflect his understanding of the often tragic destinies of African Americans in the United States. No poet before Brown had created such a comprehensive poetic dramatization of the lives of black men and women in America. Brown depicts black men and women as alone and powerless, struggling nevertheless to confront an environment that is hostile and un-

just. In this tragic environment, African American struggles against the schemes of racist whites are seen in "The Last Ride of Wild Bill," published in 1975 as the title poem of a collection. A black man falls victim to the hysteria of a lynch mob in "Frankie and Johnnie," a poem that takes up a familiar folktale and twists it to reflect a personal tragedy that occurs as a result of an interracial relationship. Brown emphasizes that in this story the only tragic victim is the black man. The retarded white girl, Frankie, reports her sexual experience with the black man, Johnnie, to her father and succeeds in getting her black lover killed; she laughs uproariously during the lynching. "Southern Cop" narrates the mindless killing of a black man who is the victim of the panic of a rookie police officer.

Yet Brown's poems show black people not only as victims of whites but also as victims of the whole environment that surrounds them, including natural forces of flood and fire as well as social evils such as poverty and ignorance. Rural blacks' vulnerability to natural disasters is revealed in "Old King Cotton," "New St. Louis Blues," and "Foreclosure." In these poems, if a tornado does not come, the Mississippi River rises and takes the peasant's arable land and his few animals, and even traitorously kills his children by night. These poems portray despairing people who are capable only of futile questions in the face of an implacable and pitiless nature. The central character of "Low Down" is sunk in poverty and loneliness. His wife has left and his son is in prison; he is convinced that bad luck is his fate and that in the workings of life someone has loaded the dice against him. In "Johnny Thomas," the title character is the victim of poverty, abuse by his parents and society, and ignorance. (He attempts to enroll in a one-room school, but the teacher throws him out.) Johnny ends up on a chain gang, where he is killed. The poem that most strongly expresses African American despair of the entire race is "Southern Road," a convict song marked by a rhythmic, staccato beat and by a blues line punctuated by the convict's groaning over his accursed fate:

> My ole man died—hunh—
> Cussin' me;
> Old lady rocks, bebby,
> huh misery.

SLIM GREER POEMS

The African American's ability to survive in a hostile world by mustering humor, religious faith, and the expectation of a utopian afterlife is portrayed in poems depicting the comical adventures of Slim Greer and in one of Brown's popular poems, "Sister Lou." The series of Slim Greer poems, "Slim Greer," "Slim Lands a Job," "Slim in Atlanta," and "Slim in Hell," reveal Brown's knowledge of the life of the ordinary black people and his ability to laugh at the weaknesses and foolishness of blacks and whites alike. With their rich exaggerations, these poems fall into the tall tale tradition of folk stories. They show Slim in Arkansas passing for white although he is quite dark, or Slim in Atlanta laughing in a "telefoam booth" because of a law that keeps blacks from laughing in the open. In "Slim Lands a Job," the poet mocks the ridiculous demands that Southern employers make on their black employees. Slim applies for a job in a restaurant. The owner is complaining about the laziness of his black employees when a black waiter enters the room carrying a tray on his head, trays in each hand, silver in his mouth, and soup plates in his vest, while simultaneously pulling a red wagon filled with other paraphernalia. When the owner points to this waiter as one who is lazy, Slim makes a quick exit. In "Slim in Hell," Slim discovers that Hell and the South are very much alike; when he reports this discovery to Saint Peter, the saint reprimands him, asking where he thought Hell was if not the South.

"SISTER LOU"

In "Sister Lou," one of his well-known poems, Brown depicts the simple religious faith that keeps some blacks going. After recounting all the sorrows in Sister Lou's life, the poem pictures Heaven as a place where Sister Lou will have a chance to allow others to carry her packages, to speak personally to God without fear, to rest, and most of all to take her time. In "Cabaret," however, Brown shows the everyday reality that belies the promises God made to his people: The black folk huddle, mute and forlorn, in Mississippi, unable to understand why the Good Lord treats them this way. Moreover, in poems such as "Maumee Ruth," religion is seen as an opium that feeds people's illusions. Maumee Ruth lies on her deathbed, ignorant of the depraved life led by her son and daughter in the city, and needing the religious lies preached to her in order to attain a peaceful death.

"REMEMBERING NAT TURNER"

Sterling Brown's poems embrace themes of suffering, oppression, and tragedy yet always celebrate the vision and beauty of African American people and culture. One such deeply moving piece is "Remembering Nat Turner," a poem in which the speaker visits the scene of Turner's slave rebellion, only to hear an elderly white woman's garbled recollections of the event; moreover, the marker intended to call attention to Turner's heroic exploits, a rotting signpost, has been used by black tenants for kindling. A stoic fatalism can be seen in the poem "Memphis Blues," which nevertheless praises the ability of African Americans to survive in a hostile environment because of their courage and willingness to start over when all seems lost: "Guess we'll give it one more try." In the words of Sterling Brown, "The strong men keep a-comin' on/ Gittin' stronger. . . ."

OTHER MAJOR WORKS

NONFICTION: *Outline for the Study of the Poetry of American Negroes*, 1931; *The Negro in American Fiction*, 1937; *Negro Poetry and Drama*, 1937; *The Negro Caravan*, 1941 (Arthur P. Davis and Ulysses Lee, editors).

BIBLIOGRAPHY

Davis, Arthur P. "Sterling Brown." In *From the Dark Tower: Afro-American Writers, 1900-1960*. Washington, D.C.: Howard University Press, 1982. A comprehensive study by the dean of African American critics, who knew Brown personally and taught with him at Howard on African American writers during the 1950's. The essays on individual writers are supplemented by ample introductory material, and there is also an extensive bibliography, listed by author.

Ekate, Genevieve. "Sterling Brown: A Living Legend." *New Directions: The Howard University Magazine* 1 (Winter, 1974): 5-11. A tribute to the life and works of Sterling Brown in a magazine published by the university where he taught for forty years. This article analyzes Brown's literary influence on younger poets and assesses his importance in the African American literary canon.

Redding, Saunders. *To Make a Poet Black*. Chapel Hill: University of North Carolina Press, 1939. This pioneering study gives an effective overview of the intellectual and literary influences and processes involved in the development of African American poets. Although it includes only a few pages on Brown himself, it is essential background reading in African American poetics.

Sanders, Mark A. *Afro-Modernist Aesthetics and the Poetry of Sterling A. Brown*. Athens: University of Georgia Press, 1999. Criticism and interpretation of Brown and his poetry in the context of twentieth century African American literature and intellectual life.

Thelwell, Ekwueme Michael. "The Professor and the Activists: A Memoir of Sterling Brown." *The Massachusetts Review* 40, no. 4 (Winter, 1999/2000): 617-638. A fond memoir of Brown written by one of his students at Howard University. Offers a glimpse into Brown's personality, political bent, and place as a black intellectual during the tumultuous 1960's.

Wagner, Jean. "Sterling Brown." In *Black Poets of the United States, from Paul Laurence Dunbar to Langston Hughes*. Urbana: University of Illinois Press, 1973. A comprehensive and insightful study of the poetry of Brown, covering the subjects, themes, and nuances of his poetry. Wagner's writing on Brown is warm and appreciative.

Betty Taylor-Thompson;
bibliography updated by the editors

ELIZABETH BARRETT BROWNING

Born: Coxhoe Hall, County Durham, England; March 6, 1806
Died: Florence, Italy; June 29, 1861

PRINCIPAL POETRY
The Battle of Marathon, 1820
An Essay on Mind, with Other Poems, 1826
The Seraphim and Other Poems, 1838
Poems, 1844
Poems: New Edition, 1850 (including *Sonnets from the Portuguese*)
Casa Guidi Windows, 1851
Aurora Leigh, 1856
Poems Before Congress, 1860
Last Poems, 1862

OTHER LITERARY FORMS

Elizabeth Barrett Browning was an accomplished Greek scholar, and from her translations she learned a great deal of her own prosody. In 1833, she published a weak translation of Aeschylus's *Prometheus Bound*. In 1850, she included in her collected poems an entirely new and substantially improved version of the same play. "The Daughters of Pandarus," a selection from the *Odyssey* (c. 800 B.C.E.), was translated for Anna Jameson's *Memoirs and Essays Illustrative of Art, Literature, and Social Morals* in 1846. She modernized selections from *The Canterbury Tales* (1387-1400) for R. H. Horne's edition of Geoffrey Chaucer in 1841. She submitted occasional translations to periodicals, such as

Elizabeth Barrett Browning (Library of Congress)

three hymns of Gregory Nazianzen which appeared in the *Athenaeum*, January 8, 1842. Mrs. Browning also published a modest amount of prose criticism. Four articles on Greek Christian poets appeared anonymously in the *Athenaeum* during 1842. For the same journal, she published five articles (all in 1842) reviewing an anthology of English verse titled *The Book of the Poets* (1842). Later in the same year, she reviewed a new edition of William Wordsworth. In 1843, she reviewed R. H. Horne's *Orion: An Epic Poem in Three Books* (1843) for the *Athenaeum*, and then she gave up literary criticism in order to devote more time to her poetry.

ACHIEVEMENTS

Elizabeth Barrett Browning's principal biographer, Gardner Taplin, believes that "It is the quality of her life even more than her artistic achievements which will live" (*The Life of Elizabeth Barrett Browning*, 1957). The reasons for this fact, he believes, are to be found "in her fulfillment as [a woman], in her courageous and impassioned protests against injustice to individuals and subject peoples, and in her broad, generous, idealistic, Christian point of view." Literary critics since her time have insisted upon thinking of Mrs. Browning as a great woman poet, or as the Sappho of the age, or as the first woman to write a sustained sequence of sonnets. Her husband thought of her simply as having written the finest sonnets since William Shakespeare. The headnote to "Seraphim" indicates specifically that she invited comparison with Aeschylus. "A Drama of Exile" is a continuation of the Adamic drama just beyond the events described by John Milton and clearly invites comparison with him. Her sonnets can be compared with those of Petrarch, Shakespeare, Milton, and William Wordsworth. Whether she meets the measure of these models is problematical in some cases, doubtful in others. Still, her aim is consistently high and her achievement is historically substantial. She gave a strong voice to the democratic revolution of the nineteenth century; she was a vigorous antagonist of those she thought were the enemies of children, of the world's dispossessed, and of popular government.

BIOGRAPHY

In 1861, Elizabeth Barrett Browning died in her husband's arms in a rented apartment (unfurnished for the sake of economy). She had been born in one of the twenty marbled bedrooms of her father's estate, Coxhoe Hall. Mr. Barrett, her father, had inherited a substantial fortune and the promise of remunerative properties from his family in Jamaica. When Elizabeth was three years old, the family moved to a still larger home, Hope End, in Herefordshire. This was to be her home until the abolition of slavery brought about sharp retrenchments in the Barrett family's affairs in 1832. After three years at Sidmouth, on the channel coasts, the family moved to London. Elizabeth was twenty-nine. Her family's congregational Protestantism and its strong support for the Reform Bill of 1832 had already helped to establish the intellectual landmarks of her poetry—Christian idealism and a sharp social conscience. In London, as her weak lungs became a source of chronic anxiety, the dark and reclusive habits which were to lend a fearful realism to Elizabeth Barrett's ideals became fixed in her mode of life.

Such anxiety found its consolations in a meditative piety which produced an increasingly intense inwardness in the poet. This fact partly explains why her poems are so commonly reflective, and so rarely narrative or dramatic. Eventually, she even gave up attending chapel services. In 1837, her lungs were racked by a persistent cough. In 1838, she left London for Torquay, hoping the sea air would afford her some relief. When her brother Edward ("Bro") had concluded his visit there and planned to return to London, Elizabeth pleaded with him to stay. He did so, but in the summer of 1840, as he was boating with friends, a sudden squall capsized the boat; and Bro was drowned. Elizabeth, who had been using laudanum fairly steadily since arriving in Torquay, almost lost her mind from guilt and distress. Macabre visions came to her and prompted in her a sharply balanced ambivalence between a wish to live and a wish to die.

Elizabeth returned to the family home at 50 Wimpole Street in London, more nervous and withdrawn than ever. She rarely descended the stairs, and in the darkened room came to depend ever more heavily on the morphine, "my amreeta, my elixir," which dulled her physical and spiritual pains. She called her room a "hermitage," a "convent," a "prison." The heavy curtains were always drawn. After her marriage, the images of her poems became less abstract and more concrete as she came to participate afresh in the parade of life's affairs. For readers of her poetry, the Casa Guidi windows of later years seem dramatically open as the colorful banners and the sounds of singing pass by.

In January of 1845, Robert Browning, then an obscure poet, wrote to thank Elizabeth for praising him in a poem she had recently published. She replied to the letter but was not anxious to meet him. She had already declined twice to receive calls from the venerable Wordsworth, whom she had met earlier. She did receive Browning several months later, however, and their famous courtship began. Both parties claimed that they had never been in love before, yet Elizabeth did have a history of strong attachments to men. When she had lived at Hope End, her informal tutor in Greek, H. S. Boyd, had become so confidential with her that quarrels with his wife resulted over the time spent with Elizabeth. At Sidmouth, she had formed a friendship with George Hunter, a minister, whose wife was allegedly mad. Years later, during Browning's courtship, Hunter even followed him once to Elizabeth's room, where an unseemly encounter took place. Browning, on the other hand, characteristically formed strong attachments to women—the Flowers sisters, Fanny Haworth, Julia Wedgwood. Still, for these two idealists, love was something quite particular, not a vague sentiment, and their claim seems authentic enough.

The principal obstacle to their courtship was Elizabeth's father. Strong-willed, pietistic, politically liberal, Edward Moulton Barrett saw Robert Browning as a footloose adventurer with a barely supportable claim to being a sometime-poet. Browning had no reliable means of support, and Mr. Barrett was certain that if the two were married Browning would merely live off Elizabeth's ample but not boundless fortune.

On September 12, 1846, while her family was away, Elizabeth, nearly fainting with fear, made her way to Saint Marylebone Parish Church. Robert met her there, and they were married. It was the first time he had seen her away from Wimpole Street. She returned home for one week and then slipped out of the house to begin the long journey to Italy with her husband. She never saw her father again. He wrote her a cruelly condemnatory letter, disinherited her, and sent her books out of the

house to be stored (the bills to go to Elizabeth). She was forty years old, a poet widely respected in England and America.

The Brownings' most enduring home in Italy was at Florence in the Casa Guidi, a fifteenth century palace located very near the palace of the Grand Duke of Tuscany. Although Mrs. Browning's health was a constant concern to them, it is nevertheless clear that in Italy she recovered something of the vitality of her youth. She lived quietly with her husband, but enjoyed occasional walks to the bridges of the Arno and trips to the local churches, which were filled with incomparable treasures of art. She entertained guests more readily than she had in London and was able to accept the praise which great figures of the world brought to her doorstep in recognition of her growing fame.

In 1846, Cardinal Giovanni Masoni-Ferretti was elected Pope Pius IX. He immediately freed thousands of political prisoners, provoking the anger of the Austrian government. Disturbances broke out in Florence. The grand duke granted the people of Tuscany a constitution. The ecstatic populace of Florence marched to the Ducal Palace—right beneath the Casa Guidi windows. Later, however, when it appeared that Austria would intervene, the pope refused to sanction a war between two Catholic countries, and the hopes of Italian nationalists were curtailed. Riots broke out; the liberals saw their near goals slipping away—and, in 1851, Elizabeth published *Casa Guidi Windows*, a reflection on these events.

Elizabeth's health was in fact sufficiently improved that on March 9, 1849, she was able to deliver a child—her only one—without the expected complications. Indeed, she became exhilarated and active just after the birth of her son, seeming much stronger than when she first married.

During the last ten years of her life, Mrs. Browning traveled extensively between Venice, Paris, and England. She found England, however, a somewhat alien place, more unyielding in manner than the Continent. When she was in London, she wrote seeking a reconciliation with her father, asking him at least to see her child. In reply, she received two packets containing the letters she had written home in the years since her marriage—all unread.

At the close of 1856, back in Italy, Mrs. Browning published a "novel in verse," *Aurora Leigh*. Critics gave the book a somewhat ungenerous reception, but the public bought out issue after issue. It was a genuine bestseller. She was by now a true celebrity.

One volume of poems remained to her. In many ways it was her most controversial. *Poems Before Congress* is hardly a book, more nearly a pamphlet of poems. In it she praises Louis Napoleon, who had raised the fears of England again—Napoleon *redivivus*. English friends alleged that Mrs. Browning was politically unsophisticated for supporting the French. Mrs. Browning replied, however, that this Napoleon would pry Italy loose from Austrian fingers; thus, her refrain is the same—Italian nationalism. The freedom of her adopted land would not be abandoned just because it caused fears at home. In the same spirit with which she had opposed slavery when abolition meant the loss of her family's fortune, she now opposed colonialist friends. Some in her own day said that Mrs. Browning was politically naïve; but no one has ever denied the magnanimity of her love for humankind.

As the Italian national movement gained strength, Giuseppe Mazzini, Giuseppe Garibaldi, and the Conte di Cavour all unified great territorial patches of the peninsula; but Mrs. Browning's strength waned. She could no longer keep up with her husband's vitality. She languished under the long struggle with her weak lungs. On a June night in 1861, protesting the fuss made over her, she lay down to sleep. Later she roused and, struggling to cough, relaxed into death.

ANALYSIS

Elizabeth Barrett Browning did not think it a kindness when critics praised her as a "woman poet." She would think it much closer to essentials if she were praised instead as a Christian poet. An evangelical of an old Victorian strain, she prized learning, cultivated Greek as the language of the Christian revelation, studied the work of the church fathers, and brought a fine intellectual vigor to the manifestly Christian ethos which shapes her work.

Like her husband, Mrs. Browning suffered somewhat at the close of the nineteenth century from the uncritical applause of readers who praised the religious thought in her work merely as religious thought. A century after her death—and again like her husband—Mrs. Browning began to enjoy the approbation of more vigorous critics who called attention to an element of intellectual toughness in her work which earlier critics had ignored. Now it is widely agreed that her poetry constitutes a coherent working out of evangelical principles into a set of conclusions which bear on the most pressing issues of modern times: the progress of liberal democracy, the role of militant nationalism, the ambivalences of the "woman question," and the task of the poet in a world without decisive voices.

In each case, the resolution she works toward is a further realization of the evangelical principle of the priesthood of persons. In many evangelical thinkers, a contradiction appears at this point: The antinomian doctrine of the depravity of man seems to contravene the doctrine of the high efficacy of individual thought; evangelicalism has, therefore, often encouraged a strong anti-intellectual bias among its followers. Since redemption is a matter of divine grace extended to childlike faith, there is no great need for secular learning. Mrs. Browning, however, worked out a reconciliation of the dilemma: Fallen men can govern themselves well by a system of checks and balances which allows the many (because it is in their interest to do so) to restrain the venality of the powerful few. This reconciliation of the evangelical paradox allowed Mrs. Browning not only to affirm the great egalitarian movements of her day, but also to believe that in them history was making "progress" on an enormous, though not continuous, scale. As a result, the poet is able to maintain a rather rigorous evangelicalism which is progressive, yet is not so facile and glibly optimistic as her early readers sometimes supposed. If it is her evangelicalism which endeared her to her own age, it is her wry, even grim sense of the role which personal failures must play in any realistic expectation of progress which has interested later critics.

THE SERAPHIM AND OTHER POEMS

The evolution of the ideas discussed above can be traced from Mrs. Browning's first serious volume, *The Seraphim and Other Poems*, to her *Last Poems*. The title poem of the first volume is an attempt to transform the story of Jesus's crucifixion into a classical tragedy. She had just finished translating Aeschylus's *Prometheus*

Bound and was determined to make of Christ a hero equal in tragic significance to Prometheus. Two angels descend from heaven, attending the death of Christ. The entire perspective given to the reader is through the eyes of these two angels. The poem fails because readers never see its tragic hero; they only hear from afar three among Christ's last sayings. Thus, Jesus never appears in the poem as a dramatic figure. It is possible, of course, that Mrs. Browning was reluctant to bring Christ on stage and put fictitious words in his mouth. It seems hopeless, then, to expect that the hero will evoke the tragic empathies which Prometheus does; thus, her poem is not a genuinely tragic drama.

POEMS

In her second major volume, *Poems*, Mrs. Browning makes two important advances. The first is that her leading poem, "A Drama of Exile," is no longer a mere account of events. Rather, there is more invention and conflict than in earlier poems: Outside the garden, surrounded by a sinister-seeming nature, Eve meets Lucifer for the first time since her fall. On this occasion she rejects him. Then, in a mystical vision, Adam and Eve see and hear the omnipotent Christ rebuking the taunting spirits of fallen nature and the pride of the triumphant Lucifer. Eve now forgives Lucifer and Christ forgives Eve. Here, the poet ventures a dramatic representation of her views with a series of invented situations which constitute a small episode in her effort to build a poetically Christian mythology.

The second advance of this volume over her previous one is technical. It is at this point in her career that Mrs. Browning begins to experiment with the sonnet. The volume contains twenty-eight sonnets on various subjects. All are Italian in form (divided between an octet and a sestet), and in all cases the first eight lines rhyme *abba abba*. In the last six lines, however, Mrs. Browning uses two different patterns. Some of the poems end with a *cdcdcd* pattern. Others end *cdecde*. The profit to the poet is that her attempts with the sonnet force on her a verbal economy which is more rigorous than that in her earlier volumes. Petrarch, for example, brought this Italian form to its pitch of perfection, allowing himself the five rhyme values of *abcd* and *e* (two rhyme values fewer than William Shakespeare uses); Mrs. Browning occasionally restricts herself to four rhyme values in a single sonnet—*abcd*. This practice imposes upon her vocabulary even stricter limits than those imposed by either the Petrarchan or the Shakespearean form. Furthermore, the sonnets—some about grief, tears, and work, with two about George Sand—force her to be less diffuse. They force her to find the concrete image which will quickly communicate a complex feeling, rather than simply talking the feeling out as she does earlier: "Experience, like a pale musician, holds a dulcimer of patience in his hand. . . ." Her religious sentiments also are forced into sharper images: "pale-cheeked martyrs smiling to a sword."

It is also in *Poems* that she includes the romance "Lady Geraldine's Courtship," which was to have significant repercussions for her. It is in this poem that she praises Robert Browning—eliciting his first letter to her—and it is here that she first attempts a theme which will not be fully realized until *Aurora Leigh:* that romance is plausible but handicapped in an unromantic (that is, an industrial, mercantile) age.

The last poem in the volume of 1844, though brief, is an important one in the poet's canon. "The Dead Pan" consists of thirty-nine stanzas, each containing six lines of iambic tetrameters (which do occasionally fall into an unheroic jog-trot), together with a seventh line of four syllables acting as a refrain. The poem produces just the image necessary to give Mrs. Browning's religious thought the freshness, clarity, and invention necessary if she is to avoid mere clichés of faith in the search for an authenticating power in her poems. The subject of the poem is the ancient claim made by Plutarch (in *De Oraculorum Defectu*) that at the very hour of Christ's crucifixion a supernatural cry went out across the sea, "Great Pan is dead," and that from that moment the pagan oracles lost their vision and power. In the poem, Mrs. Browning utters a long roll call of the pagan deities, and names them to witness that the prophetic power of an old world, mythopoeic and visionary, personified in the spirits of place—of forest, stream, and grotto—has been subsumed by a Christianity which is the new crown triumphant to a faded, classical past.

The poem is also a challenge to the skepticism and materialism of the poet's own age. The Christian religion has subsumed the ancient gifts of mystery and vision and has sanctified them by a revelation which marks them as being true, and by an ethic which adds to them the imperative to love. For Mrs. Browning, the oracular voice of the modern world is heard in poetry. Some nineteenth century thinkers believed that, with the death of the mythopoeic consciousness, men had entered an age of rational secularism from which there could be no historical return. Matthew Arnold was such a thinker. For him, the loss of mythopoeic sensibility implied the loss of tragic sensibility. Against this sort of plaintive skepticism Mrs. Browning raised her protest. The Christian narrative constitutes the mythos of modern times, and the oracular voice of poetry constantly reinvigorates this mythology. The creativity and the virtuoso invention of Christian poets proves the vitality of the myths from which they draw, to which they add their stories and songs. Pan is dead, but the spirit—now illuminated by science—is as quick as ever.

POEMS: NEW EDITION

Mrs. Browning's next collection appeared six years later, after her famous elopement to Italy. *Poems* is marked by the distinction of containing *Sonnets from the Portuguese*, which prior to this time had been available only in a small private edition. These forty-four sonnets had been completed in 1847. They are technically more sure-handed than the earlier ones. The same Italian octet is here *abba*, *abba*, but Mrs. Browning has decided unequivocally on a sestet which rhymes *cdcdcd*. The *e* rhyme has disappeared. She limits herself to four rhyme values in each sonnet. The effect is a tight, organically unified sequence of sonnets. This impression of technical unity is enhanced by the single-minded theme of the poems: "this very love which is my boast." The poet has nevertheless avoided sameness in the sonnets by avoiding clichés and by writing from her own varied experience of love. For her, love had been exhilarating and risky during the days of her engagement; it had cruelly forced on her the determination to defy her father; it had sorrowfully juxtaposed her frailty to Robert's vigor; it had pitted her will to live against her expectation of an early death. These experiences provide the images which keep her poems from being merely conventional and confessional. Throughout them all there is a grim sense of herself which tries to avoid melodramatic self-deprecation on the one hand, while expressing an honest sense of her own limits on the other. This ironic view of

herself gives the poems an underlying psychological realism which holds their Romanticism in check: "What can I give thee back, O liberal/ and princely giver" (Sonnet VIII); "Accuse me not, beseech thee, that I wear/ Too calm and sad a face" (Sonnet XV); "Unlike are we, unlike, O princely heart" (Sonnet III).

CASA GUIDI WINDOWS

In 1851, Mrs. Browning published her sustained political poem, *Casa Guidi Windows*. By this time she had found a clear political expression for her evangelical ethic, "Manhood's right divine . . . to elect and legislate." The poem is written in iambic pentameter, which is well suited to protracted discourse. To avoid a too-liberal capitulation to prosaic looseness, however, the poet uses a generalized rhyme scheme, *ababab cdcdcd efefef*, through verse paragraphs of various lengths. The interlocking triple rhymes serve as a restraint on the rhetoric of the poem, but it is not a heavy-handed check. The incidents in the poem are few; thus, the burden of success is thrown upon its ideas.

During 1847, the Brownings were living in apartments in the Guidi Palace overlooking the Piazza del Gran Duca, a public square in Florence. From her windows Mrs. Browning was witness to a number of enthusiastic demonstrations of popular support for an Italian nationalism aimed at severing Italy's dependence upon the Austrian hierarchy—a dependence forced upon the country in the post-Napoleonic European settlement engineered by Prince Metternich. This nationalism culminated in a revolt which failed in 1848. From her windows, Mrs. Browning saw the joyful crowds agitating for national autonomy. Part I of her poem celebrates their libertarian hopes, "*O bella libertà*." The Florence of Dante, Petrarch, and Boccaccio is a political prisoner; its poets and artists are suppressed. Still, it is not merely for the sake of its heroic past that Italy deserves to be free. "We do not serve the dead—the past is past. God lives and lifts his glorious mornings up/ Before the eyes of men awake at last. . . ." It is God who has made men free. Piety is on the side of liberty. The first part of the poem is a rhetorical appeal to the Grand Duke of Florence, and especially to Pope Pius IX, to side with the people in this great controversy. The poet's evangelical suspicion of Church authority is laid aside in the hope that "authority" will do justice against Austria.

Part II of *Casa Guidi Windows* was written in 1851 after the failure of the revolution. Mrs. Browning had seen somber faces of the defeated loitering in the square. The leaders, she believed, had failed the people. The duke had taken "the patriot's oath," but "Why swear at all," she asks, "thou false Duke Leopold." The pope has also vacillated: "Priests, priests—there's no such name," she protests. Her evangelical instinct was true; the pope has failed; "All Christians! Levi's (priestly) tribe is dispossest." Her grim disappointments at the failure of Italian nationalism in Part II are balanced against the exalted hopes of Part I and are resolved into a more subdued hopefulness for the future: "We will trust God. The blank interstices/ Men take for ruins, He will build into/ With pillared marbles. . . ." Popular sovereignty will win out.

AURORA LEIGH

Mrs. Browning's longest poem, *Aurora Leigh*, appeared at Christmas, 1856. It is a narrative poem fulfilling her earlier wish to set a romance in an unromantic age. The ironies of such a circumstance are resolved for her when it becomes manifest to the protagonists that love is not only a "romantic" experience, but also a universal ethic. It therefore disarms the meanness of spirit, the poverty of values which the poet associated with the growing skepticism of a scientific and industrial age. The poem consists of nine books of approximately (but by no means uniformly) twelve hundred lines each, all in unrhymed iambic pentameter—blank verse. The poet had by then discovered from her own experience, as so many English-language poets have, the suitability of blank verse for high eloquence upon serious subjects. Although this poem has a more detailed narrative framework than most of Mrs. Browning's poems, it still is characterized by long reflective passages in which she devotes intense thought to the important ideas that arise from the narrative events. From the beginning, critics have observed that her characters are not persuasive, the incidents seem improbable, and the diction is uniformly stilted. The themes discussed, however, are confronted with a directness and boldness almost unequaled among Victorian poets.

Aurora Leigh is born in Italy of an English father and an Italian mother. Orphaned early, she travels to England to be reared by her father's sister. She becomes a retir-ing, moderately successful poet. Her cousin Romney, who has inherited the Leigh title and fortune, is a deeply compassionate Christian socialist with a strongly activist disposition. Aurora and Romney are drawn to each other, yet they so little understand each other that there is constant friction between them. This concatenation of events and characters allows Mrs. Browning to bring together all of the ideas she most cares about and to work them out in a single crowning achievement. The state-of-England question (the poor and the privileged), the Germanic North and the Latin South (England and Italy), the condition of women, the role of the artist in a socially conscious world, the nature of progress, nationalism, and the impact of science are among the issues finally woven into the poem. After years of circling about each other, proposed marriages to third parties, and the exhaustion of Romney's fortune on an ungrateful community of the poor, Aurora and Romney recognize that their ambivalence toward each other is actually a rigorous—that is, a not very sentimental—form of love.

The issues of the poem are resolved in the most comprehensive working out of these problems which Mrs. Browning ever undertook. Romney acknowledges that his social activism has been too doctrinaire, too manipulative; it has ignored the practical realities of human experiences. Aurora acknowledges that the ferocity of her independence has masked a deep need for intimacy. Each finds that love—as both an ethic and a sentiment—gives complexity and vitality both to the social question (Romney's problem) and to individual identity (Aurora's problem). The poet believes that this kind of love is grounded in an eternal Divine and is therefore the key to resolving the antinomies in an age of conflict—nationalists against empires, poor against rich, men against women, faith against doubt.

CHRISTIANITY

According to Lionel Trilling, "Behind the [nineteenth century] struggle of romanticism and rationalism lies . . . the diminution of the power of Christianity" (*Matthew Arnold*, 1939). Mrs. Browning was keenly interested in this issue, and her poetry, when viewed as an organic whole, is a substantial and single-minded effort to infuse fresh force into Christian thought by a poetic quickening of the Christian mythos, as many of her poetic fictions show. For example, in "A Drama of Exile," Christ appears to Adam and Eve in a vision, "in the midst of the Zodiac"; he rebukes the Earth Spirits who have been taunting the people for their sins. "This regent and sublime Humanity," he tells the spirits "Though fallen, exceeds you . . . by their liberty to fall."

The poet's effort to take the ancient images of Christendom and elaborate them by sheer poetic invention into a revivified myth gives her work its unity; but it also imposes upon her poems certain inherent limitations. She never quite comes to grips with the possibility that if Pan is truly dead, then her own vision lacks oracular authenticity. In "The Seraph and the Poet," however, she presses her case that the modern visionary is the poet:

> Sing, seraph with the glory
> heaven is high;
> Sing, poet with the sorrow! earth is low: The universe's
>   inward voice cry "Amen" to either song for joy and
>   woe:
> Sing, seraph—poet,—sing on equally!

By imputing death to Pan, Mrs. Browning has imputed death to other mythologies than her own. All mythologies, however, share a common epistemology, a common access to the morning-time sense of the world and to the tragic conception of human experience. Mrs. Browning severs these ties which her mythology shares with the other great visionary images of the universe. This separation imposes upon her conception of faith a somewhat sectarian and doctrinaire limit. It means that her themes tend to be stated as issues (nationalism, poverty) rather than ideas. In her poems, there is no rigorous testing of her own first principles. Still, she is one of the great libertarians of her age, and all the disinherited of the world—children, women, slaves, poets—and all who love freedom will find in her work a brave and unequivocal voice.

OTHER MAJOR WORKS

NONFICTION: *The Letters of Elizabeth Barrett Browning*, 1897; *The Letters of Robert Browning and Elizabeth Barrett Barrett*, 1898; *Diary by E. B. B.: The Unpublished Diary of Elizabeth Barrett Browning, 1831-1832*, 1969 (Philip Kelly and Ronald Hudson, editors).

MISCELLANEOUS: *Prometheus Bound, Translated from the Greek of Aeschylus: And Miscellaneous Poems*, 1833.

BIBLIOGRAPHY

Dally, Peter. *Elizabeth Barrett Browning: A Psychological Portrait*. London: Macmillan, 1989. In a confident and matter-of-fact tone, Dally traces Browning's feelings about her fate, family, marriage, and literary life. Beginning with Browning's childhood regret that the family fortune grew from the slave trade, Dally records her emotional life through childhood, courtship, marriage, and life in Italy. Contains notes, a select bibliography, and an index.

Forster, Margaret. *Elizabeth Barrett Browning: A Biography*. London: Chatto & Windus, 1988. This full-length biography of Browning expands our understanding of her childhood years through hundreds of letters uncovered since the standard works of Dorothy Hewlett (1952) and Gardner Taplin (1957). Forster uses feminist critics in her interpretation of the long poem *Aurora Leigh*, which is now considered a major work. An essential chronological study. Supplemented by thirty-three illustrations, a chronology, notes, a bibliography, and an index.

Hewlett, Dorothy. *Elizabeth Barrett Browning: A Life*. New York: Alfred A. Knopf, 1952. Intending to return Browning to the high esteem given to her in her lifetime and by Robert Browning, Hewlett adds historical and political background to her detailed study of family letters and memorabilia. Includes interesting anecdotes, poem drafts, a playbill from early family theatricals, ten illustrations, references, and an index.

Kizer, Carolyn. "Ms. Browning's Heavy Heart: Elizabeth Barrett Browning's Last Poems." *The Paris Review* 42, no. 154 (Spring, 2000): 210-215. An insightful discussion of one of Browning's last poems, "My Heart and I." With reference to the early drafts of the poem, Kizer documents its progress line-by-line. Also discusses Robert Browning's role in the revival of these poems.

Leighton, Angela. *Elizabeth Barrett Browning*. Brighton, England: Harvester Press, 1986. Part of a series titled Key Women Writers, this valuable study uses feminist theory to revisit the most frequently anthologized poems of Browning and to explore the less well-known works. Topics include the influence of family, the male literary tradition, her sexual isolation, and political opinions. Complemented by notes, a bibliography, and an index.

Markus, Julia. *Dared and Done*. New York: Knopf, 1995. Novelist-turned-literary-historian Markus lifts the veil of misconception that has long concealed the truth about the love and marriage of Elizabeth Barrett and Robert Browning. As Markus chronicles the personal and artistic growth of this devoted couple, she insightfully analyzes their social and political milieu and how it shaped their lives and poetry.

Mermin, Dorothy. *Elizabeth Barrett Browning: The Origins of a New Poetry*. Chicago: University of Chicago Press, 1989. Part of a series titled Women in Culture and Society, this essential study brings Browning out of the sentimental arena and reveals her as a poet who negotiated her way through fierce gender and class barriers. Eight chapters arranged chronologically focus on her emotional and artistic development. Contains notes, a bibliography, and an index.

Stephenson, Glennis. *Elizabeth Barrett Browning and the Poetry of Love*. Ann Arbor: University of Michigan Research Institute, 1989. The linguistic and thematic problems of a woman poet writing about love in a male-dominated poetic tradition forced Browning to invent a feminine rhetoric. Women wrote about love from within a conventional mask. In this study, Barrett Browning is shown to have rejected the mask and dramatized new possibilities in her early ballads as well as in her sonnets and longer poetic works. Includes notes, a bibliography, and an index.

Taplin, Gardner. *The Life of Elizabeth Barrett Browning*. London: John Murray, 1957. Until Margaret Forster's 1988 biography, Taplin's was the standard work on Browning. It filled a major gap in Victorian studies with a comprehensive study of letters and other sources. It is still useful. Twenty chapters give a chronological picture of the poet's early family life of wealth and comfort, her decision to elope and live in Italy, and her literary success. Contains notes, a bibliography, an index, and ten plates.

Wallace, Jennifer. "Elizabeth Barrett Browning: Knowing Greek." *Essays in Criticism* 50, no. 4 (October, 2000): 329-353. Although Victorian women writers were expected to be emotional and sentimental rather than intellectual, Browning was one of the most scholarly woman poets of the nineteenth century. Wallace discusses the way in which Browning broke the stereotypes of women during her time, and the ways in which this affected her writing.

L. Robert Stevens;
bibliography updated by the editors

ROBERT BROWNING

Born: Camberwell, London, England; May 7, 1812
Died: Venice, Italy; December 12, 1889

PRINCIPAL POETRY
Pauline, 1833
Paracelsus, 1835
Sordello, 1840
Bells and Pomegranates, 1841-1846 (includes *Dramatic Lyrics*, 1842, and *Dramatic Romances and Lyrics*, 1845)
Christmas Eve and Easter Day, 1850
Men and Women, 1855 (2 volumes)
Dramatis Personae, 1864
The Ring and the Book, 1868-1869 (4 volumes)
Balaustion's Adventure, 1871
Prince Hohenstiel-Schwangau: Saviour of Society, 1871
Fifine at the Fair, 1872
Red Cotton Nightcap Country: Or, Turf and Towers, 1873
Aristophanes' Apology, 1875
The Inn Album, 1875
Pacchiarotto and How He Worked in Distemper, 1876
The Agamemnon of Aeschylus, 1877 (drama translation in verse)
La Saisiaz, and The Two Poets of Croisac, 1878
Dramatic Idyls, 1879-1880 (in two parts)

Jocoseria, 1883

Ferishtah's Fancies, 1884

Parleyings with Certain People of Importance in Their Day, 1887

The Poetical Works of Robert Browning, 1888-1894 (17 volumes)

Asolando, 1889

Robert Browning: The Poems, 1981 (2 volumes)

OTHER LITERARY FORMS

Robert Browning wrote letters copiously. Published volumes of his correspondence include *The Letters of Robert Browning and Elizabeth Barrett Browning, 1845-1846* (1926, 2 volumes; Robert B. Browning, editor), as well as volumes of correspondence between Browning and Alfred Domett, Isa Blagden, and George Barrett. Baylor University holds extensive manuscript and document collections concerning Browning from which *Intimate Glimpses from Browning's Letter File: Selected from Letters in the Baylor University Browning Collection* was published in 1934. An additional collection of about four hundred *New Letters of Robert Browning* has also been published (1950; W. C. DeVane and Kenneth L. Knickerbocker, editors).

For a short time, Browning also attempted to write plays. Unfortunately, the impracticality of performing his particular dramas on stage doomed them to failure. The majority of these works can be found in the *Bells and Pomegranates* series, published between 1841 and 1846.

ACHIEVEMENTS

Robert Browning is, with Alfred, Lord Tennyson, one of the two leading Victorian poets. Although Browning did not invent the dramatic monologue, he expanded its possibilities for serious psychological and philosophical expression, and he will always be considered a master of the dramatic poem. Browning's best poetry appears in three volumes: *Men and Women, Dramatis Personae*, and *The Ring and the Book*. Browning typically writes as if the poem were an utterance of a dramatic character, either a creation of his own imagination or his re-creation of some historical personage. He speaks through a mask, or dramatic persona, so that his poems must be read as little plays, or as scenes or frag-

Robert Browning (Library of Congress)

ments of larger dramas. The dramatic mask allowed him to create in his audience a conflict between sympathy and judgment: As the reader often judges the dramatic speaker to be evil, he nevertheless sympathizes with his predicament. The dramatic monologue allows the author to explore the thoughts and feelings of deviant psychology to an extent seldom practiced before. On the other hand, when the author always speaks through a character, taking on the limitations and prejudices of a dramatic figure, he conceals his own feelings and ideas from his reader. His critics charge that he evaded the writer's most important duty by failing to pass judgment on his characters, and by presenting murders, villains, and whores without a word of moral reprobation. He is accused of valuing passion for its own sake, failing to construct his own framework of values that would allow the reader to evaluate and judge the ethical position of his characters. Nevertheless, Browning deserves to be read as a serious innovator in poetic form; his conception of dramatic character influenced modern fiction as well as poetry.

BIOGRAPHY

Robert Browning was born in a London suburb, Camberwell, on May 7, 1812. His family could be characterized as comfortably middle-class, politically liberal, and dissenting in religion. His father, a prosperous employee of the Bank of England, had collected a large private library. The family was dominated to some extent by the powerful personality of Browning's mother, the former Sarah Anna Wiedemann from Dundee, who was deeply committed to the Congregational religion. At a time when Oxford and Cambridge were religious institutions, admitting only Anglican students, Browning attended the newly instituted University of London for a short time in 1828, but he did not complete a coherent course of study. Browning was largely self-taught and, like many autodidacts, he had difficulty appreciating how deeply learned he was and judging what his more conventionally educated audience would be likely to know. His poetry bristles with allusions and historical references that require a specialist's explanation.

As a boy, Browning showed remarkable enthusiasm for the work of Percy Bysshe Shelley. Such an admiration is particularly surprising in the light of their divergent beliefs. Shelley was antireligious, especially in his youth, and was in fact expelled from his university for publishing a pamphlet on the necessity of atheism, while Browning's mother was firmly committed to a fundamentalist and emotional Christian belief. In any event, throughout his life, Browning depicted churchmen in an unfavorable light in his poems—a tendency that is perhaps understandable in a follower of Shelley, but one that suggests considerable tension between the mother and her son over religious matters. Shelley glorified the romantic rebel, as in his depiction of Prometheus, for example; Browning's father, on the other hand, was employed by the Bank of England, and the family comfort depended on the stability and success of that existing order. Shelley's extremely liberal ideas about politics and personal relationships must have been difficult to fit harmoniously into the boy's comfortable, religious, suburban home life.

In 1852, when Browning was forty years old, a collection of letters supposed to have been written by Shelley was published, and Browning was engaged to write the preface. The letters were discovered later to be spurious and the volume was withdrawn from publication, but Browning's preface remains one of his most important explanations of his artistic theory. In the preface, Browning makes his famous distinction between "objective" and "subjective" writers, which can be imagined as the difference between the mirror and the lamp. An objective poet reflects or mirrors the outer world, making it clearer and easier to understand by writing about what takes place outside himself. The subjective poet, however, is like a lamp projecting from his inner flame a light by which the reader sees everything in a new way. Although the words "subjective" and "objective" seem to get hopelessly tangled as the argument proceeds, it appears that Browning views his dramatic characters as lamps, shedding their light on the world, allowing the reader to imagine the inner flame that produces such rays of fancy and imagination, shaping and distorting whatever they fall upon.

At the age of twenty, Browning published *Pauline*, which was to be the first step in a massive work projected to be the utterances of a series of characters distinct from the author himself. The work is in the tradition of Romantic confessional writing. John Stuart Mill wrote an unpublished review of *Pauline*, which eventually came to Browning's attention, in which he accused the poet of having a more intense and morbid self-consciousness than he had ever before seen in a sane man. These cutting words are particularly ironic coming from the author of Mill's *Autobiography* (1873), a totally self-conscious production. Nevertheless, Browning was stung by the criticism and in the future tried to hide his own identity, his personal self, ever more cleverly behind the mask of dramatic speakers. *Pauline* was followed by *Paracelsus* and *Sordello*. These three works all treat the predicament of an artist or seer at odds with his environment and his historical age. The phenomenon of alienation, estrangement from one's own culture and time, is one of Browning's repeated topics, as is the role of the artist and the artist's relationship to society at large. Betty B. Miller in *Robert Browning: A Portrait* (1953) argues that there is a close identification between Browning and the central characters in these three works, so that Paracelsus is Browning, his garden at Wurzburg is identical to Browning's garden at the family home in Camberwell, and so on.

For about ten years, from 1837 to 1847, Browning devoted much of his energy to writing stage plays. These must be considered practical failures, although *Strafford* (1837) ran for five performances on the professional stage with the famous tragedian William Charles Macready in the hero's role. Browning had difficulty in treating external action, which is necessary in a staged performance, and turned instead to internal conflicts which were invisible to his audience. Although the plays simply did not work on stage, they were the workshop for the great dramatic monologues in *Men and Women* and *Dramatis Personae*.

In 1845-1846 Browning courted the semi-invalid poet Elizabeth Barrett. They were married on September 12, 1846, and fled immediately to Italy. The popular imagination has clothed this romance in a gauze of sentimentality, so that Browning appears as a knight in shining armor rescuing his maiden from her ogre of a father. Even a cursory reading of the Browning-Barrett letters suggests that the romance was rather more complicated and contradictory. Miller's *Robert Browning: A Portrait* suggests that Browning had a need to be dominated by a woman. His mother supplied that role until her death in 1840, and then he found her surrogate in Elizabeth Barrett, who was a considerably more famous writer than he was at the time. Miller points to places where Elizabeth simply took the controlling hand in their relationship and points to the nine-year period of silence between *Men and Women* and *Dramatis Personae* as the consequence of Elizabeth's domination of Browning until her death, June 29, 1861. The truth is probably not so sinister as Miller thinks, nor so blissful as depicted in modern popular plays such as *Robert and Elizabeth*. There appear to have been areas of gross disagreement between Elizabeth and Robert that would have been difficult to reconcile in day-to-day life. For example, Elizabeth, like Browning's mother, believed in the spiritual world, while Browning distrusted those who made supernatural claims.

The publication of *The Ring and the Book*, along with the earlier *Men and Women* and *Dramatis Personae*, established Browning as one of the major writers of the nineteenth century. *The Ring and the Book* tells, from a number of sharply differing points of view, the story of a scandalous murder case. It resembles the plan of Browning's earliest work, *Pauline*, in that it represents the speech of "Brown, Smith, Jones, and Robinson," who are characters quite distinct from the author. It was a project of which Elizabeth had disapproved in her lifetime. Browning's later works became more and more cryptic and complex as he further pushed his ideas of dramatized poetry, but his fame grew rapidly, spurred by the formation of the Browning Society in London in 1881. Following his death in Venice, December 12, 1889, his body was moved to England and interred in Westminster Abbey.

ANALYSIS

Boyd Litzinger in *Time's Revenges: Browning's Reputation as a Thinker 1889-1962* (1964) reviews the critical reception of Browning's work during the decade after his death and finds that his immense popularity was based on three chief beliefs among his readers: Browning was a defender of Christianity, although his specific beliefs were subject to considerable doubt; he was admired for an optimistic worldview and his works were thought to urge man to higher and higher efforts to improve his condition; and he was considered to be a serious philosopher and man of ideas.

This analysis seems seriously misguided. Browning's religious teachings are contradictory at best. His frequent comic and hostile portraits of churchmen are hard to reconcile with conventional Christian belief. His alleged optimism does not account for the gray sadness of Andrea del Sarto's world or the bloody trial of Count Guido or even the dauntless but perhaps meaningless call of Childe Roland's horn in the face of the Dark Tower. As a "philosopher," Browning seems to have a taste more for questions than for answers, and although he expands certain ideas such as the conflict of social role versus private personality or the concept of magnificent failure, he does not develop a coherent system comparable to the philosophic poetry of John Milton.

From the perspective of the present, Browning claims a place of first importance as a protomodernist, a writer who anticipated some of the major developments in art and literature occurring at the beginning of the twentieth century. His use of the dramatic monologue anticipated and to a degree influenced the limited and unreliable narration of such masterpieces of modernism as Joseph Conrad's *Heart of Darkness* (1902) and Ford Madox Ford's *The Good Soldier* (1915). His conception of relativistic and fragmented worlds in which a character is not at home anticipated the vision of T. S. Eliot's *The Waste Land* (1922). His sense of character, defined by the conflict between social roles and internal impulses held in a sometimes unstable equilibrium, was confirmed by modern psychology. Browning is most interesting when seen not as a Victorian sage but as a forerunner of modernism.

"PORPHYRIA'S LOVER"

"Porphyria's Lover," published along with "Johanes Agricola" under the caption "Madhouse Cells" in *Dramatic Lyrics*, exemplifies Robert Browning's use of the dramatic monologue. Written in sixty lines of iambic quatrameter (rhymed *ababb*), the poem is spoken entirely by a dramatic character, much like the soliloquies in William Shakespeare's plays. Typically, the monologue can occur only at a moment of inaction, enabling the character to pause from whatever he has been doing and reflect for a moment. What he proceeds to say implies a larger framework of surrounding circumstances: the dramatic situation. Understanding the dramatic situation within a monologue necessitates reader participation in order to discover the circumstances that are only implied in the poem.

By looking closely at the text of "Porphyria's Lover," the reader learns that the speaker is a man who has just strangled his lover, Porphyria. The dead woman's head rests on his shoulder as he speaks, and he looks with approval upon the murder he has committed. The speaker relates the events of the dark, stormy evening: Alone in a cottage, he waited for his beloved Porphyria to enter. Evidently, her absence had been the result of her attendance at a "gay feast," one of the "vainer ties" which Porphyria presumably cultivated. Left alone, the speaker had become obsessed by the need for Porphyria's presence, and, when she finally entered the cottage, her lover could only think, "mine, mine, fair, perfectly pure and good." Strangling her in her own hair, he has propped her dead head on his shoulder, and so he sits as he speaks his monologue. Exultant that he has done the perfect thing, he ends his speech with the words, "And yet God has not said a word."

The dramatic monologue is always spoken by a dramatic character, creating a condition called limited narration. Everything that the reader hears is limited to what the speaker sees, thinks, and chooses to tell. Frequently, limited narration can be "unreliable," so that the reader has reason to believe that the speaker is mistaken or lying. In "Porphyria's Lover" the problem of unreliable narration occurs when the speaker says that the perfect thing to do in his situation was to strangle his beloved.

Some critics point to a poem such as this and assert that Browning's form of writing is vicious, that he evades his duty as a moral teacher by not passing judgment on his characters' actions. In reply, many scholars argue that Browning has indeed provided sufficient guidance for the reader to form a normative judgment, thus overriding the limited and defective judgment of the murderer. The careful reader of this poem will find much evidence to indict the speaker as a madman and criminal. His very mention of God in the closing line reveals an expectation of punishment. Such an expectation could only result from a subconscious admission of guilt. Thus, even the murderer in a deranged way has brought a moral judgment upon himself. Browning has developed a situation that produces a conflict in the reader between sympathy for the character and judgment of him. The beauty rather than the fault of this poem is Browning's mastery at creating such a conflict and involving the reader in its solution.

"MY LAST DUCHESS"

"My Last Duchess," another poem published in *Dramatic Lyrics*, exhibits many of the features discussed with reference to "Porphyria's Lover," while showing a considerable advance in artistic power and seriousness. Browning's dramatic poems fall into three categories: soliloquies, in which the persona speaks alone or *solus* on stage; monologues, in which a single speaker on stage addresses a defined dramatic audience, who must be imagined present; and epistles, monologues constructed as if they were letters written from one character to another. "My Last Duchess" is a monologue, having a speaking persona and a clearly defined dramatic audience. The dramatic situation of this poem is derived from history. The subtitle of the poem is "Ferrara," and it is likely that the persona is Browning's dramatization of

Alfonso II, the fifth Duke of Ferrara. Alfonso II married Lucrezia de' Medici, daughter of Cosimo I de' Medici, Duke of Florence. The de' Medici family were newly arrived upstarts in comparison with the more ancient house of Ferrara. The Duchess of Alfonso II, Lucrezia de' Medici, died at the age of seventeen in 1561, it being said that she was poisoned. Three years later Alfonso contracted to marry Barbara, niece of the Count of Tyrol.

The dramatic situation of "My Last Duchess" probably involves Duke Alfonso II imagined as addressing an envoy from the Count of Tyrol in order to negotiate the details of his wedding with Barbara. One of the main objectives of the Duke's speech is to "soften up" his adversary in the negotiations so as to extract from him the maximum dowry and to exact the most dutiful compliance with his wishes by his future wife and in-laws. The reader must imagine the Duke walking with his guest in the Duke's art gallery while an entertainment is going on for the other guests in the lower hall of his castle. The Duke pauses before a painting covered by a curtain, asks his guest to sit, and opens the curtain to display a striking portrait of his previous wife, who is dead. While the envoy contemplates the picture of the dead former wife, the Duke explains that he was not completely happy with his last mate. She did not appreciate the value of his "nine hundred years old name" and so the Duke "gave commands" and her annoying smiles stopped completely. She stands in the portrait as if alive, and he invites the envoy to gaze on her. Then the Duke suggests that they join the party below, mentioning in passing that he is sure that the Count will give him any dowry that he desires. As they descend the stairs, the Duke points out a statue of the pagan god Neptune taming a sea horse, which recapitulates the struggle of the Duke with the envoy. The envoy has no chance of winning a contest of will with the Duke, just as the sea horse must submit to the god of the sea. The power is all in the Duke's hands.

"THE BISHOP ORDERS HIS TOMB AT ST. PRAXED'S CHURCH"

"The Bishop Orders His Tomb at St. Praxed's Church" appeared in *Dramatic Romances*. Subtitled "Rome, 15—," it appears to refer to a real place, the church of St. Praxed near Rome, but unlike "My Last Duchess" it does not seem to refer to a particular person

or historical event. One must construct a general idea of a worldly bishop in Italy in the sixteenth century on his deathbed speaking these lines. The dying man has his "nephews" or illegitimate sons, including his favorite, Anselm, at his bedside to communicate his last wishes to them. From the details of his speech, the reader learns that the sons' mother, the Bishop's mistress, was a beautiful woman, and that the Bishop had a rival for power called old Gandolf, who is buried in St. Praxed's Church. The Bishop orders his sons to build him a tomb in the church that will put Gandolf's to shame by its richness. Such a tomb will be costly to build, but the dying bishop makes a shocking revelation to the boys: There was once a fire in the church from which the Bishop saved an enormous semiprecious stone, a lump of lapis lazuli, which he hid. He now tells the boys where to find the buried treasure, provided they will put it on his funeral statue as a decoration.

The depiction of the Bishop's character is a study in hypocrisy. One expects a churchman to be humble and honest, to deny his physical desires, to abstain from sex and the gratification of worldly lusts. As his mind wanders and he nears death, this bishop appears to be just the opposite. Rather than living celibate, he has fathered these sons who stand around him and he has loved their voluptuous mother. Rather than showing generosity to his enemies, even at the moment of death he is filled with petty jealousy of old Gandolf. He has stolen the church's jewel from the conflagration. He even confuses Christianity and paganism as he describes the frieze he wants on his tomb as a mixture of erotic pagan elements and Christian scenes. Next to the depiction of the virgin martyr St. Praxed, he wants a Bacchic orgy with "one Pan ready to twitch the Nymph's last garment off."

Works such as "The Bishop Orders His Tomb at St. Praxed's Church" were influential on the novel and the short story as well as on modern poetry, for they expanded the notion of character in fiction. Character is sometimes defined as what man habitually chooses to do. A character is said to be a liar if he usually lies. Another is a brave man if he usually refuses to run from danger. Browning writes many poems about churchmen, perhaps because their ethical character is so sharply defined. The minute one sees a character dressed as a bishop, one expects that this man will habitually act in a certain way, that his actions will be loving, self-sacrificing, humble, Christian, and that he will not put his faith in the material world, but concern himself with heavenly goals. Browning puts such a character in a moment of unusual stress in which his expected role crumbles, and one sees through his public face to an inner set of unexpected feelings. At any other time in his life, the Bishop of St. Praxed's, dressed in his robes and healthy and strong, would never have revealed that he was subject to lust, greed, pride, and all the un-Christian characteristics he reveals to his sons on his deathbed. Browning has found a moment when the Bishop's public face cracks and his inner personality is revealed. The poem explores the conflict between the public role and the private personality of a man.

"BISHOP BLOUGRAM'S APOLOGY,"

In addition to "The Bishop Orders His Tomb at St. Praxed's Church," Browning wrote a number of other poems about religious hypocrites, including "Bishop Blougram's Apology," published in *Men and Women*. The dramatic situation is a nineteenth century dinner party given by Blougram for a young newspaperman, who is an unbeliever. Blougram talks at length to the younger man and, perhaps a bit intoxicated by his own importance or an unusual amount of wine, confesses some things that he would not normally say in public because they do not fit the expected role of a bishop. The newspaperman Gigadibs despises Blougram because, while the Bishop is intelligent enough to know that miracles and the historically untrue parts of the Bible are mere superstition, he nevertheless publicly professes to believe in them. He must therefore be a hypocrite. Apparently Gigadibs has also accused the Bishop of profiting from his profession of belief and so achieving a comfortable and powerful position in life. Perhaps the poem refers to the Roman Catholic Cardinal Wiseman and Cardinal John Henry Newman, whose *Apologia pro Vita Sua* (1864) may be reflected in the title of Browning's poem.

Blougram's reply to Gigadibs's charges is important for an understanding of Browning's idea of characterization in fiction. At line 375 and following, Blougram suggests that Gigadibs thinks that a few intelligent people will always look at Blougram and "know me whether I believe in the last winking virgin, as I vow, and am a fool, or disbelieve in her and am a knave." Even so, Blougram maintains that these intelligent people will be those most fascinated with him because he maintains an impossibly contradictory balance:

> You see lads walk the street . . . what's to note in that? You see one lad o'erstride a chimney-stack; him you must watch—he's sure to fall, yet stands! Our interest's on the dangerous edge of things. The honest thief, the tender murderer, the superstitious atheist . . . we watch while these in equilibrium keep the giddy line midway: one step aside, they're classed and done with. I, then, keep the line. . . .

Browning's characters are people caught in impossible contradictions, frequently between their expected or usual pattern of behavior and some contrary inner impulse. The situations named by Blougram as fascinating are explored in Browning's poetry: The tender murderer is Porphyria's lover, for example. As in nearly all of Browning's dramatic poems, "Bishop Blougram's Apology" leaves the reader struggling to find a normative judgment. Is Blougram a hypocritical exploiter of religion for his own worldly benefit and therefore subject to scorn, or is he something else? Even though the concluding lines of the poem are spoken as if in the voice of Browning himself, it is still difficult to say whether one should approve of Blougram or despise him. In that impossible "equilibrium" the reader is fascinated.

"ANDREA DEL SARTO"

Browning took the dramatic situation of the poem "Andrea del Sarto" mainly from Giorgio Vasari's *Lives of the Painters* (1550, 1568) which includes a discussion of the painter Andrea del Sarto, called the "faultless painter" because of the technical perfection of his art. Andrea married a widow, Lucrezia del Fede, in 1512 and was subsequently summoned from Florence, Italy, to work at the court of Francis I of France at Fontainebleau. According to Vasari's story, Francis I gave Andrea money to purchase art works in Florence, but he misappropriated the funds and had to live in hiding because he allowed himself to be dominated by the artful and wicked Lucrezia. A self-portrait of Andrea and Lucrezia hung in the Pitti Palace at Florence while the Brownings were residents in Italy. Mrs. Browning's cousin, John Kenyon, asked Browning to send him a photograph of the painting and, so the story goes, Browning composed and sent him this poem instead.

The poem illustrates the idea of the "magnificent failure," one of Browning's most important concepts. In order to understand the "magnificent failure" the reader must be aware of thinking current in the 1850's concerning the relation of art to society. For example, John Ruskin in *The Stones of Venice* (1851-1853) makes a distinction between slave art and free art. Slave art, such as an Egyptian pyramid, sets up a simple design so that any slave can execute it perfectly. Free art, such as a Gothic cathedral, engages the creative impulses of every worker so that it is never completed and is marked by the luxuriant variety of every worker's creation. A perfect, finished, polished work of art signifies that the artist set his design too low, did not strive to reach beyond the limits of his power. Perfect art is the sign of moral degeneration. Andrea's painting is slave's work because it is perfect.

In the poem, Andrea del Sarto is speaking to his dramatic audience, and his wife Lucrezia, who is impatient with him, wishes to go out in the evening to join her "cousin," or lover, who is whistling for her in the street. In the opening lines, the reader learns that Lucrezia is not kind to the painter and that he must bribe her to stay with him a few minutes. Andrea is unhappy, thinking how his art is not of the highest order despite all its perfection. He never fails to make a perfect drawing because he never sets his design beyond his ability, "but a man's reach should exceed his grasp, or what's a heaven for?" He considers a painting by Raphael and shows how the drawing of an arm in it is poor, but when he corrects the draftmanship, he loses all of the "play, the insight and the stretch" of the imperfect original. He laments his lost productive times when he worked in France and regrets that he must now live in exile. He pathetically asks Lucrezia to be his companion so that he can work more and give her more money. At the conclusion of the poem, Lucrezia's "cousin" whistles for her again while Andrea, who is a faultless painter, envies the glory of less perfect artists.

Andrea paints designs that never challenge his ability and completes perfectly all his undertakings. Ironically, this perfection in art signifies his moral degeneration, for he is a slave to the beautiful but ignorant and unfeeling Lucrezia and to the profit motive, so that he must paint trivial works to earn gold, which Lucrezia simply gives to her "cousin" lover. Artists such as Raphael fail in their work because they set their sights so high that they can never finish or complete their designs perfectly. Although they fail, their works are magnificent. Andrea's perfect works are merely slavish.

"CHILDE ROLAND TO THE DARK TOWER CAME"

In the middle of the nineteenth century, there was a revival of interest in knightly romances and the "matter of Britain," the ancient stories concerning King Arthur's court, evident in Tennyson's *Idylls of the King* (1859) and many other poems of the period. Frequently, the failed quest of the courtly romance was a vehicle for the idea of magnificent failure. Arthur had tried to establish a court of perfect chivalry, but he had failed in the attempt. Nevertheless, his failure was more noble than a practical compromise would have been. Each of his knights must fail in some important way, suffer humiliation and death, even as Christ did, so that the nobility of their endeavor may show forth. Browning's "Childe Roland to the Dark Tower Came" is in this tradition of the courtly failed quest and the magnificent failure.

The subtitle of the poem refers to Shakespeare's *King Lear* (1606), specifically a song by the character Edgar in Act III, scene 4. Lear on the heath encounters Edgar disguised as a madman. Lear calls him a philosopher and takes him with his company. At the conclusion of the scene, Edgar pronounces some riddling or nonsense lines, including "Child Rowland to the dark tower came." These are apparently garbled snatches of traditional ballads. "Childe" means any untested knight, and Browning's poem constructs a nightmare quest for his untried knight, Childe Roland, who tells of his weird adventure. The poem is best considered a journey into the mind, a psychological rather than a physical quest. Childe Roland tells of his perilous journey across a wasted land in which a cripple advises him to turn into an "ominous tract" where the Dark Tower hides. As soon as he leaves the road, it vanishes. Everything in the enchanted land is sick, wounded, and in torment. Childe Roland thinks of his companions who have failed before him. He crosses a river and stumbles unaware on the "round squat turret." He imagines he sees all his dead companions ranged along the hillside overlooking the arena, yet "dauntless" he sets his horn to his lips and blows the cry, "Childe Roland to the Dark Tower Came."

Like many of Browning's poems, this work seems laden with ambiguity. There are at least three possibilities: The tower is not the true object of a knight's quest and thus Childe Roland is lost when he takes the advice of the cripple to leave the highroad, and he is punished for deviating from his proper goal; or, the tower is the true quest, but Childe Roland's discovery is that it is worthless and ugly when he finds it (therefore, his life is wasted); or, the tower is the quest and is in itself meaningless, but the dedication of Roland creates success out of failure—although the tower is "squat" and ugly, he has played his proper role and even in the face of overwhelming forces, he blows defiance, dauntless to the last.

"Childe Roland to the Dark Tower Came" invites comparison with the surrealist nightmares of Franz Kafka, and Browning's use of a wasteland as a symbol for man's alienation and his evocation of a failed courtly quest foreshadow T. S. Eliot's *The Waste Land*. "Childe Roland to the Dark Tower Came" is one of Browning's most interesting works and it foreshadows developments in the modernist revolution some fifty years after its publication.

THE RING AND THE BOOK

The Ring and the Book is Browning's most important poem. Written in blank verse, rhymed iambic pentameter, it appeared in four volumes between November, 1868, and February, 1869. In 1860, Browning came across in Florence a collection of old documents and letters telling the story of the murder trial of Guido Franceschini, who was executed in Rome in 1698. Browning called this volume *The Old Yellow Book*; it has been translated into English by Charles W. Hodell and was published in 1911.

From the lawyers' arguments and other documents emerges a particularly sordid case of "divorce Italian style." In 1693, Count Guido Franceschini, an impoverished nobleman forty years old, from the north of Italy, married a thirteen-year-old commoner, Francesca Pompilia, in Rome. She was the daughter of Pietro and Violante Comparini. Pietro had opposed the marriage,

knowing that the count was not as wealthy as he seemed. His wife, however, was attracted by the possibility of a nobleman for a son-in-law and contrived to have the marriage take place. The Comparini family gave all their possessions as dowry to Count Guido, expecting to live in comfort on his estate. The count, angry to find that the Comparini family was less wealthy than he imagined, harassed them until they were forced to flee from his house. They sued for the return of Pompilia's dowry on grounds that she was not their natural daughter, but a common prostitute's child whom they had adopted. Count Guido increased his cruelty to his child bride, even though she sought help from the local bishop and governor. Pompilia fled from Count Guido's castle with the dashing young priest Caponsacchi in 1697 but Count Guido apprehended the couple near Rome on April 28, 1697. They were charged with adultery; Caponsacchi was banished, and Pompilia was confined to a nunnery from which she was released on bond to bear her child, a son, at the house of the Comparini on December 18, 1697, almost exactly nine months after her flight from Guido's castle with Caponsacchi. Her son Gaetano stood to inherit the count's name and estate. Two weeks later, Count Guido broke into the Comparini house and murdered Pietro and Violante, and left Pompilia mortally wounded. Pompilia lived four more days, long enough to accuse Count Guido of the assault. He and his companions were arrested fleeing toward his estate.

The bulk of *The Old Yellow Book* presents the legal arguments in this dark case. The murders were admitted, but Count Guido claimed that he was justified as an injured husband to defend his honor. When he was found guilty, he appealed to the pope, who refused to intervene. Count Guido was beheaded February 22, 1698, in Rome, while his accomplices were hanged. Finally, a convent brought suit to claim the estates forfeited by Pompilia's allegedly adulterous action, but a court ruled that she was innocent and gave all property to her son Gaetano.

Browning converted the material of *The Old Yellow Book* into one of the first relativistic narrative masterpieces. Some authors tell their readers what to think about their characters; others make their readers think for themselves. Browning is one of the latter, presenting his readers with questions rather than giving them answers. In twelve books, Browning tells and retells the story of Pompilia, Count Guido, and the priest Caponsacchi, through their eyes and through the eyes of their lawyers, the eyes of the pope considering Guido's appeal, and the eyes of three factions of the vulgar population of Rome. Naturally, when Guido explains his action, he not only argues in defense of what he did, but also actually believes that he is right. In his own mind, he is blameless. Likewise, when the reader sees through the limitations and prejudices of Pompilia or of Caponsacchi, the point of view dictates what is right and what is wrong. Many readers coming to Browning's text try to penetrate the tangle of conflicting judgments and opinions presented in these twelve books, and try to say that Browning's sympathy lies with Pompilia or that the pope speaks for the author. Yet, if there is a single, clear-cut normative judgment, why did Browning feel compelled to write the contradictory monologues that argue against it? More likely, Browning intentionally created a powerful experimental literary form, rather like the limited narration novels of Henry James. Browning's text provides a complicated stimulus, but each reader constructs in his mind his own evaluation of the relative guilt or justification of Count Guido, Pompilia, Caponsacchi, the pope, and the Comparini family.

Stories are sometimes said to fall into two classes. There are stories such as mediocre mystery tales that cannot bear a second reading. Once the audience has heard the tale to its end, they know "who done it." All questions are solved, so that a second reading would be unnecessary and boring. On the other hand, there is a second kind of story that is so constructed that each reading only deepens the questions in the readers' minds. Every reader is drawn back to the text over and over and the third or fourth reading has as much interest as the first. In *The Ring and the Book* Browning converted a gruesome but mediocre mystery tale into a work of this second type which poses troubling questions about right and wrong, judging and pardoning. Every character evokes some spark of sympathy when allowed to speak for himself or herself. Every character seems subject to guilt when seen through hostile eyes.

The Ring and the Book illustrates Browning's concern with the infinite moment, the instant when a character can act decisively to break out of his characteristic pattern of expected behavior and do the unforeseen. The priest Caponsacchi's flight with the count's child-bride is an example of the dizzy equilibrium between expected social behavior and contradictory impulse. The reader asks, "How could he do it and still be a priest of God, forsaking his vows of celibacy and all his ordinary rules of conduct?" The reader can imagine what it is to be a priest and what it is to be a lover, but how can there exist such a contradictory character as a lover/priest? The same question can be posed for Pompilia, the child-like innocent yet renegade wife, who is the final winner of them all eventually when her son inherits the estate. The reader has seen many times in literature the child-like, innocent woman, and equally often has encountered the sexual sharpster, but how can these contradictory roles be balanced in a single character?

OTHER MAJOR WORKS

PLAYS: *Strafford*, pr., pb. 1837; *Pippa Passes*, pb. 1841; *King Victor and King Charles*, pb. 1842; *The Return of the Druses*, pb. 1843; *A Blot in the 'Scutcheon*, pr., pb. 1843; *Colombe's Birthday*, pb. 1844; *Luria*, pb. 1846; *A Soul's Tragedy*, pb. 1846 (the seven preceding titles were published in the *Bells and Pomegranates* series, 1841-1846).

NONFICTION: *The Letters of Robert Browning and Elizabeth Barrett Browning, 1845-1846*, 1926 (Robert B. Browning, editor); *Intimate Glimpses from Browning's Letter File: Selected from Letters in the Baylor University Browning Collection*, 1934; *Browning's Essay on Chatterton*, 1948 (Donald A. Smalley, editor); *New Letters of Robert Browning*, 1950 (W. C. DeVane and Kenneth L. Knickerbocker, editors); *The Letters of Robert Browning and Elizabeth Barrett Barrett, 1845-1846*, 1969 (Elvan Kintner, editor).

MISCELLANEOUS: *The Works of Robert Browning*, 1912 (10 volumes; F. C. Kenyon, editor); *The Complete Works of Robert Browning*, 1969-1999 (16 volumes).

BIBLIOGRAPHY

Armstrong, Isobel. *Robert Browning*. Athens: Ohio University Press, 1975. This fairly simple book provides the best general introduction to the poet, his life, his cultural context, and his work. Armstrong identifies the outstanding features of the major poems and presents sound basic readings. Supplemented by a full index and a helpful bibliography.

Chesterton, G. K. *Robert Browning*. New York: Macmillan, 1903. Although somewhat dated, this medium-length book is full of perceptive insights and is one of the best overviews of the poet. Chesterton opens up the major monologues by relating them to one another and showing how they contribute to the evolution of Browning's thought. The index is helpful for cross-referencing.

Crowell, Norman B. *A Reader's Guide to Robert Browning*. Albuquerque: University of New Mexico Press, 1972. An extremely useful volume for those interested in sampling critical approaches to Browning's major dramatic monologues. Crowell summarizes the stands taken by various previous readers, raising questions and suggesting openings for further interpretations. Can also be used as a guide to basic research, but it does not cover the longer works.

DeVane, W. C. *A Browning Handbook*. Rev. ed. New York: Appleton-Century-Crofts, 1955. For two generations of literary students, this was the first reference on Browning, and it has not been superseded. Contains entries for the major phases of Browning's life and for all of his writing. Although easy to use if the student has specific topics to pursue, the focus is old-fashioned, concentrating on a biographical and a literary-historical background. Includes a thorough index.

Hair, Donald S. *Robert Browning's Language*. Toronto: University of Toronto Press, 1999. Of all the major poets who have adopted the English language as their instrument, Browning, perhaps more than anyone, has exhibited the most sophisticated and modulated command of his medium. Hair undertakes the heroic task of uncovering Browning's theory of language. The result is a fine analysis that reestablishes the poet's importance.

Irvine, William, and Park Honan. *The Book, the Ring, and the Poet: A Biography of Robert Browning*. New York: McGraw-Hill, 1974. A standard academic biography of the poet, this study is thorough, meticulous, detailed, fully documented, and illustrated. Although rather heavy for beginning students, it collects more biographical information than any other source. Complemented by an index and a select bibliography.

Jack, Ian. *Browning's Major Poetry*. Oxford, England: Clarendon Press, 1973. One of the leading scholars of Victorian literature presents detailed analyses of Browning's primary works. Contains definitive, substantial accounts, deep and rewarding, but sophisticated. the critical apparatus is complete, with a solid index and a bibliography.

Markus, Julia. *Dared and Done*. New York: Knopf, 1995. Novelist-turned-literary-historian Markus lifts the veil of misconception that has long concealed the truth about the love and marriage of Elizabeth Barrett and Robert Browning. As Markus chronicles the personal and artistic growth of this devoted couple, she insightfully analyzes their social and political milieu and how it shaped their lives and poetry.

Todd K. Bender;
bibliography updated by the editors

WILLIAM CULLEN BRYANT

Born: Cummington, Massachusetts; November 3, 1794
Died: New York, New York; June 12, 1878

PRINCIPAL POETRY

The Embargo: Or, Sketches of the Times, a Satire, 1808
Poems, 1821, 1832, 1834, 1836, 1839
The Fountain and Other Poems, 1842
The White-Footed Deer and Other Poems, 1844
Poems, 1854
Thirty Poems, 1864
Hymns, 1864, 1869
Poems, 1871, 1875
The Poetical Works of William Cullen Bryant, 1876
The Flood of Years, 1878

OTHER LITERARY FORMS

William Cullen Bryant wrote a substantial body of prose: tales, editorials, reviews, letters, appreciations, sketches or impressions, and critical essays. In 1850, he published *Letters of a Traveller: Or, Notes of Things Seen in Europe and America*; in 1859, *Letters of a Traveller, Second Series*; and in 1869, *Letters from the East*. He reviewed the careers of a number of his contemporaries in such pieces as *A Discourse on the Life and Genius of James Fenimore Cooper* (1852) and *A Discourse on the Life and Genius of Washington Irving* (1860). In 1851, he published his *Reminiscences of the Evening Post*, and in 1873, a collection of *Orations and Addresses*. His *Lectures on Poetry*, delivered to the Athenaeum Society in 1826, was published in 1884.

ACHIEVEMENTS

William Cullen Bryant's central achievement as a man of letters was his contribution to the developing sense of a national identity. Although Bryant's verse is often indistinguishable from the eighteenth and nine-

William Cullen Bryant (Hulton Archive)

teenth century English verse of his models, he begins to draw lines of contrast, first, by his choice of subject matter—prairies, violets, gentians, Indian legends—and, second, by developing a characteristic poetic voice which can be seen in retrospect to be the early stage of the development of a nationally distinctive poetry.

Bryant's participation in the formative stages of American poetry was a natural corollary to the second of his two major achievements, his career as a journalist. As the editor and part-owner of the *Evening Post* for almost fifty years, he championed liberal social and political causes which were as much a part of the newly emerging national identity as was his poetry. His vigorous support of freedom of the press, of abolition, of the Republican Party, and of John Frémont and Abraham Lincoln, are among his most notable achievements as a journalist.

Although minor in comparison with his two major achievements, Bryant's lectures on poetic theory to the Athenaeum Society in 1826 shed light on his own poetry and on some of the cultural assumptions of his period. Bryant's emphasis on "moral uplift and spiritual refinement" as the aim of poetry is balanced by his interest in native speech and natural imagery as resources to be tapped by the poet.

BIOGRAPHY

William Cullen Bryant was born on November 3, 1794, in Cummington, Massachusetts, to Dr. Peter and Sarah Snell Bryant. The poet enjoyed a close family life and, from an early age, benefited from the positive influences of both parents, as well as from those of his maternal grandfather, Ebenezer Snell. The latter's Calvinist influence, though muted, is evident in the language of the poetry and in the recurrent image of an angry God threatening retribution for man's sins. His mother's gentler religious influence bore directly on his precocity as a reader in general, and of the Bible in particular, at the age of four. Bryant was later to remember those conducting the religious services of his very early childhood experiences as "often poets in their extemporaneous prayers."

A counter, and as time passed more prevailing, influence was that of his liberal physician father, Dr. Peter Bryant, who encouraged the poet in his early experiments with satires, lampoons, and pastorals. Under that encouraging tutelage, Bryant published his first poem of substance, "The Embargo," in 1808, at the age of thirteen; three years later he set about translating the third book of the *Aeneid*. In 1817, Dr. Bryant took copies of several of his son's poems to his friend Willard Phillips, one of the editors of the *North American Review*. "Thanatopsis" and one other poem were published immediately in the journal's September issue. "Inscription for the Entrance to a Wood" and "To a Waterfowl" appeared subsequently.

Meanwhile, Bryant had been preparing himself for a legal career and was admitted to the bar in 1815. He began practicing law in 1816 in Great Barrington, Massachusetts. In 1825, he assumed editorship of the *New York Review*, and in 1829 he began his fifty-year career as a major journalist when he became part-owner and editor-in-chief of the New York *Evening Post*. From that position he was to champion freedom of speech, abolition, the right of workmen to strike, Frémont, the Republican Party, and Lincoln and the Union cause. When he died in 1878, the *Evening Post* continued his policies under the leadership of his son-in-law, Parke Godwin.

Although Bryant was to continue writing poetry throughout his life, most of it, and particularly those poems on which his reputation rests, was written by the early 1830's. By the middle of the century, though he was still an active and vigorous journalist, he had become something of an institution to writers such as Nathaniel Hawthorne, Herman Melville, and Oliver Wendell Holmes. Ralph Waldo Emerson included Bryant among the imagined faculty of his ideal college, because, as he noted in his journal, "Bryant has learned where to hang his titles, namely by tying his mind to autumn woods, winter mornings, rain, brooks, mountains, evening winds, and wood-birds. . . . [He is] American."

Bryant married Frances Fairchild in 1821. They had two daughters, Fanny and Julia, who inherited the sizable estate left at his death on June 12, 1878, which resulted from a fall and head injury on May 29.

ANALYSIS

William Cullen Bryant wrote his poetry over a fifty-year span, but the apex of his career came in the early 1830's, very close to an exact midpoint between Wil-

liam Wordsworth's 1800 preface to the *Lyrical Ballads* (1798) and Walt Whitman's *Leaves of Grass* (1855). In retrospect, Bryant's poetry, especially his blank verse, can be seen in terms of a development moving from Wordsworth's theories and examples to the American model of Whitman's free verse, celebrating the self and the newly emerging national identity. At its best, Bryant's verse reflects the evolutionary dynamics of a national poetry in the making; at its worst, it is stale repetition of eighteenth century nature poetry, cast in static imitation of Wordsworthian models.

Bryant's affirmative resolution of his brooding preoccupation with the mutability of all things is another characteristic that places him in the early mainstream of the emerging national literature. He will continue to be read for his place in literary history, for the fuller understanding of the development of that national literature of which he contributes, even if his verse were wholly uncongenial to the contemporary reader. His celebration of the American landscape and his affirmation of a progressive spirit became overtly central themes for Ralph Waldo Emerson, Henry David Thoreau, and Whitman. Bryant's best poetry prefigures the American Renaissance in both content and form, theme and style, and thus he continues to be read, and to be readable, as one of America's literary pioneers.

"THANATOPSIS"

"Thanatopsis," one of Bryant's earliest successes and his most enduring one, survives as a poem rather than as an artifact because its rhythmic and syntactic fluidity has kept it readable for well over a century and a half. Blank verse has always offered the poet writing in English the best medium, short of free verse, for such fluidity, and that fact, along with the survival of the Romantic ideal of a natural or colloquial language, goes a long way toward explaining the poem's survival. Since, however, it is obvious that not all of Bryant's blank verse has been so successful, "Thanatopsis" invites a more detailed examination. The basis of its rhythmic character lies primarily in the relationship between the blank verse structure and the sentence structure. Since few of the lines are end-stopped, the syntactic rhythm is stronger than the theoretical rhythm of blank verse—that is, of five-stress, iambic lines. An examination of the great variety of sentence length relative to line length and of the accentual stress pattern of both will provide some illustrative detail for this aspect of the poem's character.

There are three thematic sections in the poem, the second beginning at line thirty-one, with "Yet not to thine . . . ," the third at line seventy-three, with "So live. . . ." The opening independent clause of section one, ending with a semicolon in line three, has all the rhetorical quality of a sentence. It and the opening sentence of section two are two-and-a-half lines long. The third section has only one sentence, running through the final nine lines of the poem. Two other very long sentences are those beginning at line eight, running over eight lines, and at line sixty-six, running over six. The two shortest sentences are at lines twenty-nine and sixty, respectively. The first of these, beginning with "The oak/ Shall send his roots abroad," has twelve syllables, two more than the blank verse line. the latter has only nine syllables, one short of the prescribed ten. Even this shortest sentence, however, occupies parts of two lines, thus contributing to rather than diminishing the dominance of the syntactic over the verse structure. That dominance prevails in large part simply because of the variety of sentence lengths, which constitute a variety of rhetorical subunits within the thematic and blank verse structures of the poem. the relationship between these syntactical subunits and the blank verse can be best illustrated by simple scansion of representative passages.

The poem begins with a two-and-a-half line independent clause: "To him who in the love of Nature holds/ Communion with her visible forms, she speaks/ A various language. . . ." If, for the sake of illustration, one ignores the sentence-sense of this phrase, the first two lines scan perfectly as iambic pentameter. The artificiality of the resulting illustration is so apparent, however, as to prompt a quick second scansion of the clause as a whole, which shifts the emphasis from line units to grammatical units—to, in this case, an introductory prepositional phrase, a relative clause, and a main clause. In that second scansion, "who," as the first word of the relative clause, is stressed, immediately throwing off the iambic regularity of the first reading. "In" loses its stress, becoming the first syllable of an anapest, "in the love." A second anapest occurs in line two in "visible forms." The most dramatic alteration of the blank verse line comes at the end of the grammatical unit in line

three, where the rhythm shifts momentarily from rising to falling, to the dactyl of "various," and the trochee of "language."

The opening lines of section two, lines thirty-one through thirty-three, maintain a greater iambic regularity than does the first clause, although at the end of the sentence, "couch," the first word of line thirty-three, is stressed and is followed by the anapest "more magnificent."

In the closing nine-line sentence of the poem, the syntactic counterpoint to the blank verse rhythm is of a more subtle kind. The opening anapests of line seventy-four, "The innumerable," *if* one sounds the schwa in the middle of the word, is followed immediately by the initial stress of "caravan." The rhythm of the prepositional phrase "in the silent halls," of line seventy-six, prevails over the artificiality of a strict iambic reading which calls for a stress on "in." Anapests occur in each of the final four lines. Line seventy-eight has an initial stress on "Scourged," and the final line has the interesting juxtaposition of stresses in "About him," that is probably best described as a spondee.

The language of "Thanatopsis," particularly the dominance of syntactical over blank verse rhythm, is very close to what might be called the vernacular mode. Except for its diction, the "still voice" of the poem approximates, almost as closely as does Whitman's free verse, the voice of American colloquial speech. A dramatic illustration of that characteristic can be made by reading "Thanatopsis" side by side with almost any poem of Henry Wadsworth Longfellow's. Adjustments must be made from the late twentieth century perspective to accommodate Bryant's diction and imagery to that sense of his achievement, but in "Thanatopsis" those adjustments can be made rather easily. Except for the second-person pronouns, "thee," "thou," and "thine," there is very little diction that dates the poem.

IMAGERY

If Bryant's rhythm and diction point forward in time to the emerging American voice, his imagery and his overt moral didacticism provide the ballast which holds him most securely to his own time. The general and abstract plane of much of his imagery clearly reflects eighteenth century influence. In some instances, it clogs the otherwise fluid syntax, effectively cutting off any prospects of vitality for the modern sensibility. One of his better poems, "A Forest Hymn," suffers in this way because of the density of images such as "stilly twilight," "mossy boughs," "venerable columns," "verdant roof," and "winding aisles."

Although the imagery of "Thanatopsis" is typical in this respect—that is, its imagery is more general and abstract than particular and concrete—it does not impede the syntactic flow of the poem. This is due, in part, to the fact that the subject of the poem, the meditation on death, calls for and sustains general imagery as much as any subject can. The "innumerable caravan" of the dead and the "silent halls of death" have no concrete, experiential counterparts. The "gay" and "the solemn brood of care," on the other hand, do, and they contribute to that eighteenth century ballast which counteracts Bryant's forward motion. Those countermelodies of the static and the dynamic, of the past and of the present progressive, are nowhere more evident than in the closing lines of the first section of the poem, which juxtapose the stock images of the "insensible rock" and the "sluggish clod" with the concrete imagery of one of the most memorable lines in American poetry: "The oak/ Shall send his roots abroad and pierce thy mould."

The blank verse and the theme of "Thanatopsis" together make the general imagery less obtrusive than it is in many of Bryant's poems. The same can be said of his overt moral didacticism, which is better sustained in this blank verse meditation on death than it is in poems such as "The Yellow Violet," "To the Fringed Gentian," and "To a Waterfowl," where the fragile lyricism is overburdened for twentieth century sensibility by the didactic uses to which he puts the flowers and the birds.

"A FOREST HYMN" AND "THE PRAIRIES"

Other blank verse poems which hold up well in much the same way as does "Thanatopsis" are "A Forest Hymn" and "The Prairies," although the eighteenth century stock imagery somewhat impedes the syntactic and rhythmic flow of the former. "The Prairies," on the other hand, is remarkable for the fluid sweep of its opening thirty-four lines of impressionistic description, motivated by Bryant's first visit to Illinois in 1832. The marvelously vibrant sense of life in these lines provides an excellent example of the major counterpoint in Bryant's poetry to the stoic resignation evinced in the earlier

meditation on death. The terms of that early poem are broader than those of what might be called a mortality theme; the counterpoint in Bryant is really between the two larger themes of mutability and plenitude. His prevailing preoccupation is not so much with mortality as with change, and that somber theme is countered by his affirmative sense of a natural plenitude that guarantees a continuing replenishment of all that passes.

OTHER MAJOR WORKS

POETRY TRANSLATIONS: *The Iliad of Homer*, 1870; *The Odyssey of Homer*, 1871, 1872.

NONFICTION: *Letters of a Traveller: Or, Notes of Things Seen in Europe and America*, 1850; *Reminiscences of the Evening Post*, 1851; *A Discourse on the Life and Genius of James Fenimore Cooper*, 1852; *Letters of a Traveller, Second Series*, 1859; *A Discourse on the Life and Genius of Washington Irving*, 1860; *Letters from the East*, 1869; *Orations and Addresses*, 1873; *Lectures on Poetry*, 1884; *The Letters of William Cullen Bryant*, 1975-1992 (6 volumes; William Cullen Bryant II and Thomas G. Voss, editors); *Power for Sanity: Selected Editorials of William Cullen Bryant, 1829-1861*, 1994.

EDITED TEXT: *A Library of Poetry and Song*, 1871.

BIBLIOGRAPHY

Bryant, William Cullen. *Power for Sanity: Selected Editorials of William Cullen Bryant, 1829-1861*. Bryant's own work provides insight into his intellectual life and his times.

Curtis, George William, 1824-1892. *The Life, Character and Writings of William Cullen Bryant: A Commemorative Address Delivered Before the New York Historical Society, at the Academy of Music, December 30, 1878*. New York, C. Scribner's Sons, [1879]. Of value for its contemporaneity, having been delivered in the year of Bryant's death.

Glueck, Grace. "Three Nineteenth-Century Minds, One Vision of Nature." *The New York Times*, February 16, 2001, p. E38. In the annals of male bonding, the friendship of three celebrated nineteenth century Americans—the poet and journalist Bryant and the painters Asher B. Durand and Thomas Cole—

should rank high. This article examines the nature of their close relationship.

Justice, James H. "The Fireside Poets: Hearthside Values and the Language of Care." In *Nineteenth-Century American Poetry*, edited by A. Robert Lee. New York: Barnes & Noble Books, 1985. Asserting that the "Fireside Poets" established poetry as an American treasure, Justice presents Bryant as one of the firmest to show how personal values could be merged with public service. His conversion from older verse styles to newer, Romantic ones is the focus of the discussion of his work. Complemented by notes and an index.

Krapf, Norbert. *Under Open Sky: Poets on William Cullen Bryant*. New York: Fordham University Press, 1986. This resource, which includes both prose and poetry by twenty contemporary poets, pays tribute to Bryant, America's first nature poet. The writings give both a broad and deep appraisal of Bryant's poetic legacy.

McLean, Albert F. *William Cullen Bryant*. Rev. ed. Boston: Twayne, 1989. The first four chapters survey Bryant's life, examine his poems of nature, analyze "Thanatopsis" in detail, and classify several poems of "progress." The last three chapters evaluate Bryant's prose and translations, explicate his poetic theory and style, and review his reputation. Supplemented by a chronology, notes, a select bibliography, and an index.

Peckham, Harry Houston. *Gotham Yankee: A Biography of William Cullen Bryant*. New York: Vantage Press, 1950. Reprint. Folcroft, Pa.: Folcroft Library Editions, 1970. Correcting misrepresentations of Bryant, Peckham describes him as a poet with an interesting personality and an interesting career as a journalist and poet. In eleven chapters, Bryant's life is narrated from its beginnings, when he was a delicate child, through his legal work of drudgery, to his last years of eloquence. Contains illustrations, notes, a bibliography, a chronology, and an index.

Ringe, Donald A. *The Pictorial Mode: Space and Time in the Art of Bryant, Irving, and Cooper*. Lexington: University Press of Kentucky, 1971. Bryant is given priority among writers who shared a pictorial aesthetic. Representation of space in Bryant's poetry is analyzed as a view of expansive nature, with precision of detail in the play of light and shadow. Time is examined as a force of contrast and continuity. Includes notes and an index.

Lloyd N. Dendinger;
bibliography updated by the editors

CHARLES BUKOWSKI

Born: Andernach, Germany; August 16, 1920
Died: San Pedro, California; March 9, 1994

PRINCIPAL POETRY

Flower, Fist and Bestial Wail, 1959
Poems and Drawings, 1962
Longshot Poems for Broke Players, 1962
Run with the Hunted, 1962
It Catches My Heart in Its Hand, 1963
Crucifix in a Deathhand, 1965
Cold Dogs in the Courtyard, 1965
The Genius of the Crowd, 1966
The Curtains Are Waving, 1967
At Terror Street and Agony Way, 1968
Poems Written Before Jumping out of an Eight Story Window, 1968
A Bukowski Sampler, 1969
The Days Run Away Like Wild Horses over the Hills, 1969
Fire Station, 1970
Mockingbird Wish Me Luck, 1972
Me and Your Sometimes Love Poems, 1973 (with Linda King)
While the Music Played, 1973
Burning in Water, Drowning in Flame, 1974
Africa, Paris, Greece, 1975
Scarlet, 1976
Maybe Tomorrow, 1977
Love Is a Dog from Hell, 1977
We'll Take Them, 1978
Legs, Hips, and Behind, 1978
Play the Piano Drunk Like a Percussion Instrument Until the Fingers Bleed a Bit, 1979

Charles Bukowski (© Connuzzi)

Dangling in the Tournefortia, 1981

The Last Generation, 1982

War All the Time: Poems, 1981-1984, 1984

The Roominghouse Madrigals: Early Selected Poems, 1946-1966, 1988

Last Night of the Earth Poems, 1992

Bone Palace Ballet: New Poems, 1997

What Matters Most Is How Well You Walk Through the Fire, 1999

Open All Night: New Poems, 2000

OTHER LITERARY FORMS

In addition to poetry, Charles Bukowski published both stories and novels and first achieved recognition with *Notes of a Dirty Old Man* (1969). This volume brought him to the attention of many who were previously unfamiliar with his work. In conjunction with his first novel, *Post Office* (1971), and a volume titled *Erections, Ejaculations, Exhibitions and General Tales of Ordinary Madness* (1972), about half of which was reissued in *Life and Death in the Charity Ward* (1973), *Notes of a Dirty Old Man* established his reputation as

a no-holds-barred commentator, full of rage yet capable of surrealistic farce. In addition to subsequent novels which include *Factotum* (1975), *Women* (1978), *Ham on Rye* (1982), and *Hollywood* (1989), there is *South of No North* (1973), which reprints both *Confessions of a Man Insane Enough to Live with Beasts* (1965) and *All the Assholes of the World and Mine* (1966); a picture narrative of his trip abroad, *Shakespeare Never Did This* (1979); a screenplay, *Barfly* (1987); and assorted illustrations. His sketches underscore his farcical tone, especially in *You Kissed Lilly* (1978), a satire of the comics in which his Thurberesque style complements his prose.

ACHIEVEMENTS

Charles Bukowski was awarded few honors during his lifetime. In 1974 he was given a National Endowment for the Arts grant, and he won a Loujon Press Award and the Silver Reel Award from the San Francisco Festival of the Arts for documentary film. Bukowski was always considered a maverick who was perceived by many academics and literary institutions to be hostile and antipoetic. His frank approach to life and writing is still too often considered simplistic or crude. While Bukowski's literary achievements are still widely unrecognized and critically undervalued in the United States, he is already considered a classic American author in Europe. A new era of appreciation seemed to begin in the 1990's with the publication of several laudatory collections of critical analyses of his works. Few people familiar with Charles Bukowski's work are indifferent to it. While he neither won nor curried favor among academic or mainstream poets, he has attained an international reputation and has been widely translated. From the first, he sought to create a "living poetry of clarity" which defies the proprieties and "cages" established by academics and editors. He has been compared with Henry Miller, Jack London, Louis-Ferdinand Céline, Antonin Artaud, François Villon, and Arthur Rimbaud and had an acknowledged influence on Tom Waits, his musical heir.

He carried the Beat manifesto to its logical conclusion without compromising his vision or pandering to the idolatrous public. By incorporating the vantage point of the underclass, he artistically wrought the unfashionable voices of the streets, the factories, the racetracks, and other less seemly social enclaves. He fused the rawness of life with a personal sensitivity; he conveyed the horrors as well as the pathos of poverty, blue-collar jobs, hangovers, and jail yards. He was never a media personality, as the Beats were. Once it became financially feasible, he began refusing all invitations for readings to guard his private self, convinced that it was readings which had killed Dylan Thomas. This reticence, with his exclusive reliance on small publishers, made his international reputation all the more impressive.

Perhaps his most significant achievement was his successful forging of a new American poetics characterized by its accessibility and its spontaneous narrative voice. Unlike T. S. Eliot's "vertical poetry," Bukowski's is a "horizontal poetry" which photographs the jagged surfaces of society and forces the reader to peer into the baser regions of human existence, to see humankind for what it is. His unique blend of powerful, physical imagery and sardonic wit allows the reader to grasp and yet transcend the essential absurdity of existence.

BIOGRAPHY

One cannot come to terms with the poetry of Henry Charles Bukowski, Jr., without acknowledging the fact that his is an extremely personal and autobiographical poetry; the terror and agony are not merely "felt-life" but life as Bukowski knew it. His survival was a thing of wonder. As Gerald Locklin notes, he "not only survived problems that would kill most men [but] survived with enough voice and talent left to write about it." He was a practicing alcoholic whose life revolved around the racetrack, women, and writing.

Born to a German mother and an American serviceman father on August 16, 1920, in Andernach, Germany, Bukowski came to the United States in 1922 with his family. They settled in Los Angeles, later the milieu for much of Bukowski's work. His father, a milkman, was a harsh and often violent man who struggled with his own powerlessness by wielding a razor strap. The resultant hostility and animosity, evident in many of his poems, coupled with a blood disease which left his face badly pockmarked, predisposed Bukowski to a life on the fringes of society.

At about the age of sixteen, partly to escape and partly because of a desire to become a writer, Bukowski began to haunt the public library, seeking literary models. His own self-directed reading was far more important in shaping his literary credo than the two years he spent at Los Angeles City College. He was drawn to the works of Louis-Ferdinand Céline, John Fante, Fyodor Dostoevski, Ivan Turgenev, and the early Ernest Hemingway; in later years, he was attracted by Franz Kafka and Albert Camus. Just as the creative writing class in which he had enrolled seemed fraudulent and banal, however, so too did the voices of many of the "masters."

Bukowski's career as a writer had a rather fitful start. After receiving hundreds of rejections, "Aftermath of a Lengthy Rejection Slip" was accepted by *Story* in 1944 and *Portfolio* published "20 Tanks from Kasseldown." These publications were followed by ten years of virtual silence during which only four pieces were published. Toward the end of this literary hiatus, two important changes occurred. He began working sporadically at the post office, where he stayed fourteen years (until 1970, when John Martin of Black Sparrow Press convinced him to quit). This job provided the first steady source of income Bukowski had known. More important, however, was the shock of landing in the charity ward in 1955 near death from a bleeding ulcer. After receiving eleven pints of blood, he emerged "900 years older," promptly disregarded the warnings to quit drinking, and began publishing poetry in various little magazines. It was his appearance in *Outsider* and his friendship with editors Jon and Gypsy Lou Webb, who dubbed him "outsider of the year" in 1962, that launched his career. With their assistance, he began to develop an important reputation among editors and readers of the little magazines, ultimately establishing a friendship with John and Barbara Martin, who published the bulk of his work.

The barrage of women in his work revealed Bukowski's penchant for womanizing; he seemed to fall from one affair to another, yet his work revealed several significant pairings. Toward the beginning of his ten-year silence, he met Jane, "the first person who brought me any love," and began a relationship which was to continue until she finally died of alcoholism. While their relationship, as *Factotum* demonstrates, was interrupted by intervening affairs, his cross-country meandering, and his two-and-a-half-year marriage to Barbara Fry, a Texas millionairess who edited *Harlequin*, it was a durable bond which inspired countless sensitive poems. Following Jane's death, Bukowski became involved with Frances, who bore his only child, Marina. Much later, both Linda King and Linda Lee Beighle were to play central roles in his life. The works dedicated to these women constitute a tribute of sorts and demonstrate that while his personal life was often tempestuous, he had the capacity and need for love. This is important to bear in mind to avoid misreading his oeuvre by exaggerating his sexism. Bukowski published prodigiously in his last decade and died from leukemia in 1994.

ANALYSIS

Living on the periphery of society, Charles Bukowski forged a brutally honest poetic voice. The futility and senselessness of most human endeavor conjoined with the desperation and essential solitude of the individual are constants reinforcing his "slavic nihilism." The trick, he suggested, is "carrying on when everything seems so terrible there is no use to go on. . . . You face the wall and just work it out. . . . Facing it right with yourself, alone." It is this kind of courage and stoicism which informs Bukowski's canon. He was neither a poet's poet nor a people's poet, but a personal poet who used his craft to ensure his own survival.

Bukowski's "tough guy" image was less posturing than self-protective. One senses that he was an idealist soured by the ravages of time, wearied by political betrayals and rather appalled by the vacuity of the American left and contemporary American writers who seem to be playing it safe and producing pallid prose and senselessly arcane poetry. Interestingly, in his best poems, the tough guy persona falls away and one discovers a sensitive poet who chose to adopt a savage bravado. Clearly, he knew the reality of the seamy side of life; his poetry teems with grotesque and sordid imagery; but unlike those who would write in order to reform, Bukowski was content to capture the pathos and rawness of the streets.

His first four chapbooks properly acclimate the reader to Bukowski's dual vision—his rawness and his compassion. They also reveal the risks inherent in this kind of personal, reportorial poetry. At his best, he blended seemingly incongruous elements to plunge the reader into a surreal landscape. At his worst, he succumbed to self-pity, mired in his own mundane reality.

FLOWER, FIST AND BESTIAL WAIL

Flower, Fist and Bestial Wail is the most consistently crafted of the four books and includes one of his best-known poems, "The Twins," which transforms his lingering animosity toward his father into a transcendent statement of shared humanity and mortality. The poem is replete with antithetical images: "We looked exactly alike, we could have been twins. . . . he had his bulbs on the screen ready for planting while I was laying with a whore from 3rd street." His own ambivalence is suggested by the scarecrow image he presented as he realized "I can't keep him alive no matter how much we hated each other." So, he stands, "waiting also to die." Read in conjunction with "All-Yellow Flowers," "The Twins" establishes one of the dominant motifs in Bukowski's work—the transient nature of life and the exaggerated import which human beings attach to ephemera.

These poems have the cadence of impending catastrophe. Beginning with "Ten Lions and the End of the World," Bukowski moved from the mundane to the apocalyptic without missing a beat; he forged a vantage point which is both ironic and sentimental as he pondered the cost of the pell-mell pace of modern life.

In Bukowski's world almost anything was possible. Although the potential for violence was ever present, it defied logic. His was the spirit of farce. He constantly challenged the contours of reality. He employed a farcical dialectic to conjoin the bizarre and the mundane; he used brutal undercutting, as in "Love Is a Piece of Paper Torn to Bits," in which a ship out of control and a wife being "serviced" by another are divested of significance while a worrisome cat is promoted to center stage. By focusing on the cat and the "dishes with flowers and vines painted on them," he effectively understated his angst. Similarly, in "I Cannot Stand Tears," a guard kills a wounded goose because "the bird was crying and I cannot stand tears."

Also evident in this first volume is Bukowski's justification for callous machismo as a defense against "the lie of love"; he established his argument by infusing his poems with countless oxymorons which rearranged the signposts of reality. In "Soiree," a bottle becomes a "dwarf waiting to scratch out my prayers," and in "His Wife, the Painter," a bus becomes "insanity sprung from a waving line"; he spoke of the sunlight as a lie and markets smelling of "shoes and naked boys clothed." "Soiree" also announces the impossibility of sustaining a relationship; "Did I Ever Tell You" captures the tragicomic element of love. The inescapable conclusion from this panoply is that love is futile, duplicitous, or, at best, based on mutual concessions. This explains the frequent crassness in Bukowski's work, which was already evident in "No Charge."

LONGSHOT POEMS FOR BROKE PLAYERS

Longshot Poems for Broke Players contains several poems which do justice to the existentialism and craftsmanship which Bukowski demonstrated in his first volume. "The State of World Affairs from a Third Floor Window," for example, melds an essentially voyeuristic point of view with reflections on a nuclear-infested world. Its tone is mellow and its counterpoint suggests the possibility of survival. Survival, it seems, is a matter of perspective, a point forcefully echoed in "The Tragedy of the Leaves," which embodies Bukowski's belief that what was needed was "a good comedian, ancient style, a jester with jokes upon absurd pain; pain as absurd because it exists." It concludes with an empathetic identification with his landlady "because the world had failed us both."

The surrealism of "What a Man I Was," which lampoons the legendary status of various Western heroes, is accelerated and refined in "The Best Way to Get Famous Is to Run Away," which revolves around the proverbial desire to live underground, away from the masses and the absurdity of explaining "why." Inherent in this piece, as well as in "Conversations in a Cheap Room" and "Poems for Personnel Managers," is the unattainability of resonance, the inability to comprehend the suffering of others: "Age was a crime . . . Pity picked up the marbles and . . . Hatred picked up the cash." A blend of the sensitive and ironic, an easy movement through cliché and culture dignifies these pieces. The result is a litany of sorts dedicated to those who have fallen through the cracks of the dream, unveiling a world of fraudulent promises which routinely casts aside those who do not conform to the dictates of propriety.

RUN WITH THE HUNTED AND IT CATCHES MY HEART IN ITS HAND

Run with the Hunted, the most uneven of Bukowski's early works, is more freewheeling than *Poems and Drawings*; it displays flashes of insight in "Old Man, Dead in a Room" and reaches innovative heights in "Vegas." Bukowski interwove the abstract and the concrete to capture the impossibility of communication and the essential insanity of social and artistic convention. The majority of the poems, however, seem self-indulgent and pointlessly crass.

Having gained recognition from the early chapbooks, Bukowski assumed a surer direction. *It Catches My Heart in Its Hand* culls some of the best from the early chapbooks and adds many new pieces. In this work, Bukowski mocked his own former self-pity and transforms it into a literary device with which to document the passage of time, as in "Old Poet" and "The Race." The danger of sanctifying art receives a lighter handling in "The Talkers," which is both a critique of "art for art's sake" and a renunciation of those who would hide behind abstraction and pretense.

CRUCIFIX IN A DEATHHAND AND THE GENIUS OF THE CROWD

Artistic distance is even more evident in *Crucifix in a Deathhand*, which centers around reawakened memories, senses deadened by the workaday world, and actual confrontations with death. In "Sunflower" and "Fuzz," for example, Bukowski muted his personal voice to universalize his own anguish; he often seemed, as in "Grass," to be observing himself. The workaday world, the province of "little men with luck and a headstart" emerges as deadening in "Machinegun Towers & Timeclocks" and "Something for the Touts, the Nuns, the Grocery Clerks and You. . . ." Bukowski was equally contemptuous of the bovine mentality of the masses and the group-think of the counterculture. In "This," he elevated himself above any prescriptions and became his own measuring rod. His is the stance of the loner, seeking pleasures where he finds them and deferring to no one. Survival, he suggested, demands egotism; otherwise, one can only await the fiery cleansing of the bomb contemplated in "A Report Upon the Consumption of Myself."

Bukowski's disdain for all that is average becomes more overt in a single-poem chapbook, *The Genius of the Crowd* (1966), a jeremiad cautioning the poet to avoid the profane influence of the culture. More boldly than any previous poem, it unmasks Bukowski's contempt for the masses and asserts that "There is enough treachery, hatred, violence, absurdity in the average human being to supply any given army on any given day." This is reinforced by the suggestion that most preaching is duplicitous, a game of mirrors.

Cold Dogs in the Courtyard

A very different impression is gleaned from *Cold Dogs in the Courtyard*, over which Bukowski was given editorial control. In a prefatory note, he explained that he chose those poems he felt had been unduly neglected. What emerges is a collection keynoted by an almost tender melancholia. "Imbecile Night," for example, establishes a delicate balance with which he endured the dreary cadence of darkness. Informing these poems is a sense of awe as he notes the consonance of nature's marvels and human invention, especially apparent in "It's Nothing to Laugh About." Compounding this is the poignant juxtaposition of the substantial and the ephemeral, as in "Existence," a poem built around the post office and the exaggerated importance attached to "dead letters." Like the roof in "2 Outside as Bones Break in My Kitchen," the letters maintain but fail to nurture the human spirit.

In "Layovers," the memories of lost love and the dreams of renewal serve as a reprieve from Bukowski's encounters with death. Serving a similar function are encounters with the unexpected, as in "Experience," and anarchistic protests such as the one depicted in "What Seems to Be the Trouble, Gentlemen?" These poems work, in part, because they lack the self-congratulatory tone of *The Genius of the Crowd* and the self-indulgence of *The Curtains Are Waving* (1967). *The Curtains Are Waving* again reveals the limits of Bukowski's style; in an attempt to come to terms with his angst, he is left decrying his fate.

At Terror Street and Agony Way

By the time *At Terror Street and Agony Way* appeared, Bukowski had apparently regained artistic control; the volume substitutes self-mockery for self-pity. While he continued to probe the plight of those caught under the technocratic juggernaut, he did so more emblematically and with greater levity. In "Red and Gold Paint," he conceives of luck and art as miracles against the cunning caprices of bosses, wars, and the weather. It is only playing against the odds, he repeatedly suggests, which ensures survival. Those who relinquish the good fight or never begin, he implied in "Reunion," may ingratiate themselves, but they never really live.

This volume is more thematically unified by the primacy of terror and agony in Bukowski's perspective. The lost innocence of "As I Lay Dying," the gratuitousness of "Beerbottle," and the resultant agony of blinding dreams in "K.O." quietly undergird the wanton destruction of "Sunday Before Noon" and the defeated dreams of "7th Race." Similarly, "I Wanted to Overthrow the Government" records Bukowski's suspicion of revolutionary schemes: "The weakness was not Government but Man, one at a time . . . men were never as strong as their ideas and . . . ideas were governments turned into men."

Poems Written Before Jumping out of an Eight Story Window and A Bukowski Sampler

Bukowski's next volume, *Poems Written Before Jumping out of an Eight Story Window*, constitutes a reversal. Absent are the literary allusions, the calm and urbanity of *At Terror Street and Agony Way*. The old shrillness is back as Bukowski donned the "beast" persona and vented his spleen, abandoning all finesse. Rapine, murder, and gothic elements dominate; an alcoholic fog blurs his vision. Even the best piece, "The Hairy Hairy Fist, and Love Will Die," despite its relentless "beat" and its examination of the individual turned back on himself, deafened by silence, is reduced in magnitude.

The publication of *A Bukowski Sampler* in 1969 signaled a change. In a little less than eighty pages, Doug Blazek assembled some of the best of Bukowski's work. His selection, a fairly representative one allowing the neophyte a full taste of Bukowski, also includes an editor's introduction, a letter from Bukowski, and several tributes from admirers of his work. Published about six months after *Notes of a Dirty Old Man*, the volume was directed at the growing Bukowski audience and the burgeoning counterculture.

The Days Run Away Like Wild Horses over the Hills

While *The Days Run Away Like Wild Horses over the Hills* again culls poems from the early chapbooks, the majority of the pieces are new and fresh. Since the book was dedicated to Jane, it is not surprising to find death as the leitmotiv. What is surprising is the almost sensual tone. In several poems to Jane, one can feel both the depth of Bukowski's love and the anguish which her death occasioned. While there are the obligatory accounts of womanizing, these pale before his elegies to Jane and his references to Frances and Marina. His attitude is encapsulated in "Birth," where the male dominion is muted by "small female things and jewels."

Allusions are multiplied without pretension; in "Ants Crawl My Drunken Arms," he criticized the banality of popular culture which prefers Willie Mays to Bach and the killing realities which essentially devoured Arthur Rimbaud, Ezra Pound, and Hart Crane. In "The Sharks" and "The Great One," the artist emerges as victim, and in "The Seminar" and "On a Grant" the pretense and incestuousness of the literary establishment are mocked through both the form and the content of the poems.

MOCKINGBIRD WISH ME LUCK

In *Mockingbird Wish Me Luck*, his next collection, Bukowski probed the culturally sanctioned disparities and skewed priorities which produce "shipping clerks who have read the Harvard Classics" and allow the powerful "a 15 percent take on the dream." "Hogs in the Sky" suggests that survival is a miracle, and yet, no more than a proper rehearsal for death "as old age arrives on schedule." The paraplegic who continues to play the longshots in "The World's Greatest Loser" is merely an extreme illustration of the fact that "nobody had any luck." Hence, the aspiring writer becomes a random assassin in "The Garbageman" and an ace crapshooter in "Moyamensing Prison."

Much of the humor in these poems is self-deprecatory, as in "The Last Days of the Suicide Kid," but subtler ironies emerge as well: the cost of success in "Making It" and the very real risk of becoming a noted writer in "The Poet's Muse." Bukowski recognized that often the skid row bums have more brains, more wit, and sometimes more satisfaction than those who have "won." Again it is a question of perspective—something which is a rare commodity in America, he notes in "Earthquake."

The second part of this volume is teeming with primordial images and energies. Monkey feet, lions, and mockingbirds stalk and taunt the poet and reader while the mass media relentlessly promote diversions and distractions. The gullibility of the masses, not a new theme, is used to establish Bukowski's own superiority and contempt for platitudes. Recording his experiences with the draft board in "WW2," he compared himself to the draftees, concluding: "I was not as young as they." Not as young, perhaps, because he, like Robinson Jeffers, whom he eulogizes in "He Wrote in Lonely Blood," has solitary instincts and an understanding of what is essential. Yet, in both "The Hunt" and "The Shoelace," he realized that it is the little things which tip the scale and "sometimes create unemployed drunks . . . trying to grab for grunion."

The final section of *Mockingbird Wish Me Luck* is unified by the risks of love. Love, a tenuous miracle, endures for Bukowski only with Marina, who is the subject of several poems. "The Shower" suggests that others, like Linda King, will eventually pass out of his life despite the depth of their mutual feelings. At the other extreme are the large number of women who are sought because they are, by definition, "one-week stands." The only alternative to the ebb and flow is represented by the "old fashioned whore" and the "American matador" who opt out of conscriptive relationships.

BURNING IN WATER, DROWNING IN FLAME

These conversational poems are often riddled by the banter and banality which characterize the bulk of daily interactions, yet Bukowski insisted on the need for style—"a fresh way to approach a dull or dangerous thing." Herein lies the key to Bukowski's poetic credo— he did not seek new themes, but, rather, reworked the old from a new angle of vision. This approach is especially germane to *Burning in Water, Drowning in Flame*, which reprints many poems that had gone out of print and redirected his probing of such phenomena as love's impermanence. *Burning in Water, Drowning in Flame* constitutes a fitting conclusion to the third stage of Bukowski's career. Including sections of poems from *It Catches My Heart in Its Hand*, *Crucifix in a Deathhand*, and *At Terror Street and Agony Way* (to which *The Curtains Are Waving* has been added), it was a testimony to his growing reputation, and, having been published by one of the more prestigious small presses, accomplished the aim of *A Bukowski Sampler* with considerable finesse.

In addition to making selections from earlier volumes, this one includes a section of new poems. These are not gentle poems. Beginning with "Now," which compares writing poetry with lancing boils, Bukowski moved to "Zoo," which questioned whether, in fact, humans have evolved significantly. "The Way" represents a brutal culmination, resembling the cascading cadence of Allen Ginsberg's "Howl" while managing not to fall away or to lose its sardonic tone.

The reportorial style which informs these poems is wryly explained in "Deathbed Blues" and panned in "My Friend, Andre," and while it is not always effective, at its best it gives testimony to the moral dignity which is attainable despite the depravity which threatens to consume the human spirit. "Death of an Idiot," which calls to mind "Conversations with a Lady Sipping a Straight Shot" in *The Days Run Away Like Wild Horses over the Hills*, displays compassion and achieves its impact by understatement.

LOVE IS A DOG FROM HELL

Bukowski's later poetry is more persistently autobiographical and more finely honed than his earlier work. Many of the poems, especially in *Love Is a Dog from Hell*, have fictional analogues in *Women*. A tendency already apparent in "Hell Hath no Fury . . ." in *Burning in Water, Drowning in Flame*, becomes more evident here; the poems often seem merely to have been transplanted into (or from) the novel. Similarly, several of the poems in *Dangling in the Tournefortia* correspond to *Shakespeare Never Did This*, and others clearly reveal the influence of Bukowski's move to San Pedro—a move which has not tempered his perspective.

Love Is a Dog from Hell, like the chapbook *Scarlet* which it incorporates, has loves and lusts as its primary focus. The proper context for viewing these poems is suggested by Bukowski's comment that "love is ridiculous because it can't last and sex is ridiculous because it doesn't last long enough." It was the tragicomedy which impelled him. Refusing to defer to feminist sensibilities, he related one sexual adventure after another, capturing both the eternal search and the predictable defeats which await everyone in "Another Bed."

Women are portrayed in a variety of stances; sometimes merely objects, they are at other times capable of turning the male into an object, as the black widow spi-

der in "The Escape" and the teeth mother in "A Killer" are inclined to do. The women range from aspiring artists and reformers to whores, and the latter have the edge "because they lie about nothing." While some may take offense at the sexism in these pieces, it seems to cut both ways; the men are no less demeaned than the women. This is still the world of the streets where proprieties and pretense fall away. In poems such as "One for Old Snaggle-tooth," dedicated to Frances, Bukowski's sensitivity is economically and precisely conveyed.

The second section is concerned with the tragedies and inhumanities which transform artists into madmen or panderers. "What They Want" reads like a top ten list of artistic casualties. The artist emerges as vulnerable and damned in "There Once Was a Woman Who Put Her Head in an Oven," which calls to mind Sylvia Plath. Yet, in "The Crunch," Bukowski suggested that the artist is able to utilize the isolation and failure which drive others over the edge. Both survival and creativity seem to demand solitude, as long as it is not irreversible.

PLAY THE PIANO DRUNK LIKE A PERCUSSION INSTRUMENT UNTIL THE FINGERS BEGIN TO BLEED A BIT

Primarily a reissue of several chapbooks, *Play the Piano Drunk Like a Percussion Instrument Until the Fingers Begin to Bleed a Bit* lacks the thematic unity of the preceding volume, but it does demonstrate Bukowski's iconoclasm and his ability to revive old themes. The title deadpans the conception of the typewriter as a musical instrument, a theme first introduced in "Chopin Bukowski" in *Love Is a Dog from Hell*.

Beginning with "Tough Company," which turns poems into gunslingers waiting to receive their due, Bukowski unleashed his acerbic wit against ersatz holiday gaiety, feigned idealism, parental protocol, the notion of a limited nuclear war, and the pretense of civilization, which is compared to fool's gold in "Through the Streets of Anywhere." While there is a sense of absurdity and subterfuge rampaging through these poems, there is also a sense of durability and substance. Again the losers at the racetrack bars, in the bowels of the slaughterhouses, and in the sterile rooming houses are pummeled but maintain their dignity, accepting their exclusion and their inability to affect their fates: "We are finally tricked and slapped to death like lovers' vows, bargained out of any gain." They await the arrival of the urban renewal cranes in "2347 Duane," and while they occasionally master the bravado of Bogart, as in "Maybe Tomorrow," more often they simply await death, as in "The Proud Thin Dying." If one is careful, "Horse and Fist" implies, one may yet survive despite the open-endedness of the game. In the meantime, it is best to "play the piano drunk like a percussion instrument until the fingers begin to bleed a bit."

DANGLING IN THE TOURNEFORTIA

There is an interesting movement in *Dangling in the Tournefortia*. Several of the early poems are retrospective, establishing a counterpoint against which to view his status—something which is overt in poems such as "Guava Tree." It seems that he was suspicious of his newly won success, recognizing that he "can fail in many more ways now," as he said in "Fear and Madness," knowing that there are more "suckerfish" who will insist upon intruding and fretting about the state of his soul. Yet, "Notes Upon a Hot Streak" revealed the pleasure he took in the "lovable comedy" which "they are letting me win for this moment."

While success did not temper his perspective, it did temper his rage; even his references to his father's brutality were softened, and while death continued to loom, it no longer threatened to overwhelm him or his poetry. The more balanced tone is reinforced by his use of the tournefortia, a tropical tree with delicate flowers and a fleshy fruit, as a metaphor for the interplay of love and lust, being and nothingness. Again the tempestuous love affairs are paraded, sometimes callously but often with a quick parry, as in "The Descent of the Species" and "Snap Snap." In "The Lady in Red," he explores the compensatory function served by heroes such as Dillinger during the Depression; in "Fight On" and "Blue Collar Solitude," the needed respite offered by a good street brawl and/or several drinks; and in "Nothing," seeing a supervisor besotted somehow eases the pain and agony of the job.

THE LAST GENERATION

As one of the most prolific and well-known of the underground poets, Bukowski pinned his success on the authenticity of his voice. Even a casual encounter with his work reveals the lack of pretense and the refusal to kowtow to the critics. He refused to be beaten; as he sug-

gested in *The Last Generation*, a single-poem broadside, it may be harder to be a genius with the proliferation of publishers and writers, but it is worth the attempt. There are too many unsung characters of the "unholy parade" and too many poems which demand to be written.

His bawdiness no less than his free-form style constituted a manifesto of sorts. American poetry has long been cautious and unduly arcane, thereby excluding a large part of the potential poetry audience and a wide range of subjects and sentiments. Booze, hard loving, and horse racing, while not generally seen as poetic subjects, dominate Bukowski's oeuvre. His crassness, which weakened some of his pieces, was in his best work complemented by a sensitive understanding of the fringes of society. Beneath the veneer, one senses a man who was unaccustomed to and rather afraid of love; a man who simultaneously disdained and applauded the masses because of his own ambivalent self-concept.

COLLECTIONS OF THE 1990'S

In the 1990's Bukowski softened a bit and reflectively examined his feelings about aging and death. His last book of poems published in his lifetime was *Last Night of the Earth Poems*, his longest poetry collection. Like all of his poetry, the poems here are rich in sarcasm and filled with antiauthoritarian diatribes, madness, satire, and death. Yet while death has always been a facet of Bukowski's poetry, here it is not the death that stalked Bukowski through forty years of poetry, resulting from alcohol abuse or depravity. Rather, it is the end of a long-lived life. Bukowski reveals that he is and has been involved in the great seasonal cycles of life: birth, death, and rebirth; pain, sorrow, and love. The subtle sensitivity of the volume is also present in its obvious love poems, many seemingly addressed to Linda Lee Beighle.

Bone Palace Ballet is divided into five sections that outline his life, from recollections that romanticize his drunken youth as a time when there was a "feeling of/ joy and gamble in/ the air" ("Beeting on the Muse") to the final section presenting poems that take stock of his life and square-off with death. *Open All Night*, like the collection of his poems titled *What Matters Most Is How Well You Walk Through the Fire*, is an expansive volume full of the grizzled mutterings that readers have come to expect from Bukowski: Former lovers, binge drinking, disillusioned souls, and the racetrack are well represented. Like other works of the 1990's, however, *Open All Night* reveals a more wistful Bukowski, an aging writer who was fearlessly confronting his mortality. Writing was never about praise or fame, he says, but "for myself/ to save what is left of/ myself." Bukowski is finally able to admit: "I've had a good run./ I can toss it in without regret."

OTHER MAJOR WORKS

LONG FICTION: *Post Office*, 1971; *Factotum*, 1975; *Women*, 1978; *Ham on Rye*, 1982; *You Get So Alone at Times That It Just Makes Sense*, 1986; *Hollywood*, 1989.

SHORT FICTION: *Notes of a Dirty Old Man*, 1969; *Erections, Ejaculations, Exhibitions and General Tales of Ordinary Madness*, 1972; *Life and Death in the Charity Ward*, 1973; *South of No North*, 1973; *The Most Beautiful Woman in Town and Other Stories*, 1983; *The Day It Snowed in L.A.*, 1986.

SCREENPLAY: *Barfly*, 1987.

NONFICTION: *Shakespeare Never Did This*, 1979 (photographs by Michael Montfort); *The Bukowski/ Purdy Letters: A Decade of Dialogue, 1964-1974*, 1983; *Screams from the Balcony: Selected Letters, 1960-1970*, 1993; *Reach for the Sun: Selected Letters, 1978-1994*, 1999; *Beerspit Night and Cursing: The Correspondence of Charles Bukowski and Sheri Martinelli, 1960-1967*, 2001.

MISCELLANEOUS: *You Kissed Lilly*, 1978; *Run with the Hunted: A Charles Bukowski Reader*, 1993; *Betting on the Muse: Poems and Stories*, 1996.

BIBLIOGRAPHY

Cain, Jimmie. "Bukowski's Imagist Roots." *West Georgia College Review* 19 (May, 1987): 10-17. Cain draws a parallel between Bukowski's poetry and the work of William Carlos Williams, America's premier Imagist poet. Cain claims that Bukowski's rough-and-tumble poetry shows palpable Imagist influences. For advanced students.

Cherkovski, Neeli. *Bukowski: A Life*. South Royalton, Vt.: Steerforth, 1997. This volume is "a slightly different version" of Cherkovski's *Hank: The Life of Charles Bukowski*, published by Random House in 1991. Its strength resides in the writer's close access to the subject during their early friendship and material from interviews with Bukowski. It purports to include the "wilder stories" which Bukowski regretted were previously omitted. The bibliography has been updated.

McDonough, Tom. "Down and (Far) Out." *American Film* 13 (November, 1987): 26-30. McDonough discusses how Bukowski's real-life alcoholism was portrayed in the 1987 biographical film *Barfly*. In the film, the drunken Bukowski was played by actor Mickey Rourke, while Faye Dunaway played his drinking companion. Gives an interesting popular insight to Bukowski's life.

Sounes, Howard. *Charles Bukowski: Locked in the Arms of a Crazy Life*. New York: Grove, 1999. Sounes indicates at the beginning of this book how Bukowski strived markedly to "improve upon" his life and make it even "more picaresque" than it was. Successfully conjures up the voice of this outrageous character and offers clear-eyed insight into his extraordinary life.

Wakoski, Diane. "Charles Bukowski." In *Contemporary Poets*, edited by James Vinson and D. L. Kirkpatrick. 4th ed. New York: St. Martin's Press, 1985. Wakoski traces Bukowski's rising popularity but laments the fact that though "Americans . . . honor truth," and Bukowski's poems are distinguished by their unself-pitying truthfulness, he has not received much serious criticism. Includes a list of his publications up to 1984.

C. Lynn Munro,
updated by Sarah Hilbert

BASIL BUNTING

Born: Scotswood-on-Tyne, England; March 1, 1900
Died: Hexham, England; April 17, 1985

PRINCIPAL POETRY
Redimiculum Matellarum, 1930
Poems: 1950, 1950
First Book of Odes, 1965

Loquitur, 1965

The Spoils: A Poem, 1965

Briggflatts, 1966

Two Poems, 1967

What the Chairman Told Tom, 1967

Collected Poems, 1968, new edition 1978

Descant on Rawley's Madrigal (Conversations with Jonathan Williams), 1968

Uncollected Poems, 1991

The Complete Poems, 1994

OTHER LITERARY FORMS

Basil Bunting wrote little aside from poetry. Although he claimed that he had no use for literary criticism, he did write a small amount of critical prose. With Ezra Pound, Bunting edited the *Active Anthology* (1933), which contained a number of his poems. He contributed prose to *Agenda* and *Poetry*. In an article titled "English Poetry Today" (*Poetry*, February, 1932), Bunting descants on the poetry of the time. His remarks reveal much about his own poetic practice. The poet also elaborates upon his attitudes in an interview titled "Eighty of the Best . . ." (*Paideuma*, Spring, 1980).

ACHIEVEMENTS

Basil Bunting, in his own self-deprecating estimation, was a "minor poet, not conspicuously dishonest." His poetic career, like his life, was quixotic. He began in the tradition of the 1920's, following the lead of Pound and Louis Zukofsky, but his work did not appear in print until a limited edition of 1930 was published in Milan. His adherence to the school of Pound and the relative obscurity of his work kept him from being read by a British audience who had turned to the new men of the 1930's such as W. H. Auden, Louis MacNeice, and Stephen Spender. A collection of his poems published twenty years later in Texas (the poet himself was residing in Persia) did little to widen his audience. It was not until the 1960's, especially with the publication of *Briggflatts*, that Bunting was rediscovered.

Bunting was quick to acknowledge the influence of Pound and Zukofsky. He was a close friend of Pound, who dedicated *Guide to Kulchur* (1938) jointly to Bunting and Zukofsky. Bunting's early poems exhibit the brittle precision, vigor, and social commentary of

Pound's *Cantos* (1925-1972). In these early poems one also finds, ingeniously rendered in modern idiom, showpiece passages of Horace, Lucretius, Niccolò Machiavelli, the Persian poet Firdusi, Rūdakī of Samarkand, and others (Bunting was a master of languages). Such "translations" are actually free resurrections in English of the poetry of another language. Again after the manner of Pound, Bunting skillfully captures the character of the speaker in Browningesque dramatic monologues. T S. Eliot's influence looms large in Bunting's use of literary allusion and his expression of the bleaker side of existence. Bunting frequently echoed Eliot's style, but with satiric intent. He believed Eliot's later poetry to be dishonest in its support of reactionary social and literary institutions. Nevertheless, he owed much to Eliot both in his use of allusion and in the creation of mood.

Bunting's place in letters is secured through his handling of rhythm, rhyme, meter, assonance, consonance, alliteration—in short, the sounds of poetry. He claimed Edmund Spenser as an influence. His emphasis was on everything that a poem gains by being spoken aloud. In his early Latin translations he experimented with meters

Basil Bunting

difficult to employ in a stressed language such as English. Later poems exhibit a free play of heavy stresses filled with spondees, trochees, and dactyls, against no identifiable iambic background. Rather, stress corresponds to the meaning of the words. Some critics have doubted the existence of recognizable rhythms in Bunting's mature poetry, but the presence of so many stressed syllables creates its own kind of meter. The poet himself has suggested that his dominant meter is the four-beat line of Old English oral poetry. In his most accomplished poem, *Briggflatts*, rough monosyllables force precise speech; the reader finds that he must articulate each consonant, exaggerating frequent stresses. The effect is not the contortions of Gerard Manley Hopkins's sprung rhythm, but rather the ictus of a pagan drum beat—without the monotony of Rudyard Kipling's meter. Against his line of strong stress the poet plays a counterpoint of assonance, consonance, internal rhyme, and alliteration. This play of sounds does much to achieve a music which, according to Bunting, is the being of poetry.

Bunting's poetic career blossomed late, with the publication of *Briggflatts*, an autobiographical poem in which he triumphantly reclaims the speech of his native Northumbria. The influence of William Wordsworth is clear in this poem, and one feels that more than any other modern poet Bunting was able to achieve the Romantic ideal of using the language of ordinary men. With flinty precision, this language of real men is forged into masculine, heavily stressed lines which resonate sounds and themes from one to another. This is Bunting's major poetic accomplishment.

BIOGRAPHY

Basil Bunting was born in Scotswood-on-Tyne, Northumberland, on March 1, 1900. He was reared and educated a Quaker and speaks fondly of the Briggflatts Meeting House, constructed by the Friends in 1675. When he was eighteen, Bunting refused the draft and was imprisoned in Wormwood Scrubs Prison for a year. Glimpses of the harsh prison conditions can be found in the poem "Villon" (1925). After release, he studied at the London School of Economics. At about the same time, he began to write Imagist poetry. This early work contains, in the manner of Pound, dramatic monologues and vignettes from other poets, but the influence of

Eliot, whom he met in the mid-1920's, also makes itself known. Bunting left for Paris in 1923, beginning an odyssey which kept him out of England for much of the next fifty years. From Paris he joined Pound in Rapallo, where the two became close friends. There he met and married Marian Culver, an American. The marriage lasted until 1935 and produced three children.

In the late 1920's Bunting was for a short time music critic of *The Outlook* in London. He returned to Italy where he lived until 1933. In Rapallo, Bunting and Pound edited the *Active Anthology*, which contained a number of Bunting's earliest poems. These are the most Poundian of Bunting's work. In the 1930's he lived in the United States, and from 1937 to 1939 he earned a living as captain of a private yacht which sailed the Mediterranean and crossed to the United States. The rise of Adolf Hitler overcame his pacifism and in 1939 he returned to England to join the Royal Air Force. Bunting spent most of the war in Iran, where his facility with languages was put to good use in Intelligence. After the war he stayed in Iran as Persian correspondent for *The Times*. In 1948 he married an Iranian, Sima Alladadian. Many of his Middle Eastern experiences are captured in *The Spoils*, a poem written in 1951 but not published until 1965. In 1951 he returned to England. In the mid-1960's, the Pound critic Hugh Kenner was instrumental in bringing Bunting to the University of California at Santa Barbara, where he taught until he accepted a position at the University of Durham, England. He subsequently retired to Black Fells Village, Northumberland, England. Bunting died in Hexham, England, in 1985.

ANALYSIS

Until the publication of *Briggflatts*, Basil Bunting's poetry was largely ignored, both because it had been published obscurely and because it was viewed as highly derivative—mere Poundian pastiche. In retrospect, the poems of the 1920's and 1930's show to what extent this estimation is unjustified. It is impossible to deny that—on the road to developing his own voice—Bunting wrote poems that were strongly influenced by Eliot's manner and, more particularly, Pound's. Even in his earliest work, however, Bunting can be identified by the sound of his lines, especially by the cadence of stresses which alliteration reinforces and to which assonance and internal rhyme frequently add counterpoint. This attention to sound is very characteristic of his work. In his own estimation, while music is not all there is to a poem, it is the one essential ingredient. In the *Collected Poems* he classified his short lyrics as "Odes" and his longer poems as "Sonatas." (More than one critic, of course, has denied any but a metaphorical connection between music and poetry.) By "music," Bunting seems to be making a claim for a special interplay between the sound and meaning of words in a poem; his use of the word "ode" seems to be an appeal to poetry's source in the chants and dances of the Greek chorus. While Bunting did not appropriate the strophe and antistrophe format in the manner of Pindar, his heavily stressed meter resembles those complex rhythms best expressed in dance. In fact, Bunting claimed that, aside from its use in poetry, meter is perhaps best expressed through physical movement. Bunting's heavily stressed lines can be best appreciated in a comparison with the oral chants which accompany primitive dance.

THE "OVERDRAFTS"

Perhaps the best way to approach Bunting is by way of the loose verse translations he calls "overdrafts." Here Bunting follows Pound's lead, attempting to revive in the idiom of modern English the spirit of a foreign poem. As David Gordon has shown (*Paideuma*, Spring, 1980), Bunting was able, in a 1931 translation from Horace, to create an English accentual syllabic version of *ionic a minore* meter. In this and other similar performances the poet extends the range of English metrics and prepares himself for the heavily stressed line which distinguishes his poetry. Not only is the meter of the original poem revitalized, but also the words of the poem are rendered in a modern idiom which sometimes defies the sense and historical/cultural setting of the original. Thus, the lady in the Horatian passage is deprived of "gin." She has mislaid her "workbox." Her lover is a "middle-weight pug" who wears "track-shorts." In the notes to the *Collected Poems*, the poet indicates that such "mistranslation" is intentional.

The "overdrafts" record something of the poet's interests over the years. In 1927 he translated a passage of Lucretius, and in 1931 two by Horace. In 1932, he rendered a few lines of Louis Zukofsky into Latin. He translated Catullus into English in 1933, the Persian

poet Firdusi in 1935, Rūdakī of Samarkand in 1948, Manuchehri in 1949, and Saʾdī in 1949. Perhaps the most striking translation is a passage from Machiavelli titled "How Duke Valentine Contrived" (1933). This short narrative of Italian intrigue is presented in delightfully colloquial English. Duke Valentine, the reader is told admiringly, was a "first rate humbug" who fools his enemies with "rotten promises." When the duke decides to "put an end" to his enemies, one of them is seen "blubbering" over his fate. Such unobtrusive use of colloquialism revitalizes the story for modern readers.

From the earliest odes, Bunting's style is characterized by its concentration. While these short poems owe much to Pound, they sometimes lack the clarity of visual impression native to Imagist poetry. Nevertheless, they frequently capture an emotion with sleight of hand, as when they speak of the "pangs of old rapture," the "angriness of love," and the "savour of our sadness," and they frequently exhibit tactile and auditory images not easily achieved in poetry. For Bunting, waves of the sea consist not only in their visual impression, but also in their sound, "crying a strange name." A rain storm is seen in a "mudmirrored mackintosh," but its dampness is also "wiped and smeared" in tactile experience. Grass is "silent," a lake "slinks," children are "scabby." Visual images are never really separate from sound and touch. Thus, the mosaic of the Imagist poem is felt as "stone shouldering stone." Many of the odes might be classified as love poetry, but their view of human emotion and sexuality is as stark as their rough meter suggests.

THE SONATAS

Bunting's longer poems, his "Sonatas," exhibit the same concentration as his "Odes." Some readers have objected that their "musical" qualities require too much of mind and memory for even the most avid reader. "Villon" has been accused of obscurity, lacking both a central persona and a metrical norm through which a reader might trace musical variations. In the early poetry the use of voices rather than a persona shows the influence of Eliot rather than that of Pound. Bunting's is a poetry of mood and allusion. "Villon," a meditation on life and death, salutes a kindred spirit who lives after death only in the tracings of poetry. In the poem, the poet's own experiences in prison are incorporated in an appreciation of Villon's loneliness and suffering. Bunting's close identification with Villon the man arises from his own experiences in prison. Like Villon, Bunting saw himself as a powerless outsider commenting on the characters who people social institutions. The poem is a fit beginning for a poetic career which casts a dour eye on human life.

The wit of Bunting's social commentary is reminiscent of that of George Bernard Shaw, though it contains more of the spirit of George Orwell (in prose) and of Charles Chaplin (in motion pictures). In "Chomei at Toyama" (1932) the reader is given a delightful picture of human society, painted by a man who chooses to live poor and alone rather than be the editor of "the Imperial Anthology." Bunting enjoys making fun of the petty official (see ode 23 "The Passport Officer") and the artist who sells himself to the party line. Especially biting is the portrait of the playwright (in "Aus Dem Zweiten Reich," 1931) who is known for having written more plays than William Shakespeare. This caricature of a man is able to speak about plays, politics, and poetry without saying anything at all. For Bunting, poetry requires honesty. He gives no quarter to the humbug, cheat, cheapjack, and boaster.

Bunting saw in Eliot's lighter verse and in his conversion to institutional Christianity a wandering from the honesty which true poetry requires. More important, he disliked what he considered Eliot's lack of economy. He preferred William Butler Yeats's greater concentration but denounced what he considered to be Yeats's own posturing. Bunting criticized the word "horseman" in Yeats's epitaph as a pandering to social elitism as well as an improper violation of the meter of the line. Much of Bunting's career can be seen as an effort to escape a natural inclination to write in the manner of Eliot. "Attis: Or Something Missing" (1931) is a satirical pastiche capturing Eliot's technique in ways that Bunting could never expunge from his own poetry. For Bunting, what seems to be "missing" from Eliot's work is the inner fortitude to denounce imposture in a corrupt social establishment of which Eliot so much wanted to be a part. Here the sharp meter and concentrated images which Bunting learned from Pound do much to hide Eliot's influence. In "The Well of Lycopolis" (1935) Bunting presents a wasteland more dour than Eliot's. It is Dante's *Inferno* transposed to the ordinary world, an *Inferno* without metaphysical extension, with neither *Purgatorio* nor *Paradiso*. Against the relief of Bunting's poetry, Eliot's Romanticism becomes glaringly obvious.

THE SPOILS

The lengthy sonata titled *The Spoils* is frequently read as a transition to the poetry of *Briggflatts*. In its own right *The Spoils* is a poem of great beauty, capturing the essence of Middle Eastern life and culture. In this poem Bunting follows his former practice of including his own experiences—gathered during and after the war—with the literature and history which created the spirit of the region. The images of the poem are, in fact, "the spoils" which the poet brings back in his native tongue. Bunting's feeling for the interconnectedness of poetry and dance shows in allusions to the biblical Song of Songs, which arose, so scholars conjecture, as a play or chant probably enacted at the wedding service. It is in *The Spoils* that the distinctively Anglo-Saxon meter (characteristic of *Briggflatts*) begins to predominate. By easing the line and allowing more unstressed syllables back into his verse, the poet is able to capture the rhythms of an ancient chant. In such lines the effect is heightened by the use of pure English monosyllables. The result is not a predictable iamb, but instead a line of three and four heavy stresses thrown in sharp relief.

BRIGGFLATTS

Bunting conquers the heavily stressed line in *Briggflatts*, a poem which returns to claim the poet's birthright in the language of Northumberland and the beat of Anglo-Saxon poetry. This autobiographical poem no longer merely incorporates Bunting's experience. *Briggflatts* is a return to roots, not only to the language and countryside of Northumbria, but also to the Romantic project of expressing the poet in the poetry. Here Bunting's professed debt to Wordsworth, a "Northerner," becomes apparent in the sweetly recounted spots of childhood memory, in the employment of the language of the common man, and in the identification with place by which a man can measure the unfolding of his life. *Briggflatts* records the poetic life of Bunting. Pound is there, and Eliot too. Their voices are now muted, however, against Bunting's own clear Northumbrian song. The poem is composed of simple English monosyllables which are artfully placed together with precision and condensation. To use the poet's own image, the pebbles are arranged in a mosaic. Most important is the seeming artlessness of the whole; gone are the set pieces and the satiric pastiche. In their place is the compact music of Domenico Scarlatti, with "never a boast or a see-here."

OTHER MAJOR WORKS

EDITED TEXT: *Active Anthology*, 1933 (with Ezra Pound); *Selected Poems*, 1971 (of Ford Madox Ford); *Selected Poems of Joseph Skipsey*, 1976.

BIBLIOGRAPHY

Agenda 8 (Autumn, 1966). The entire issue is devoted to Bunting's poetry and includes essays by established critics and poets. Kenneth Cox discusses Bunting's economy of language and willingness to take risks with unexpected word choice. Robert Creeley notes Bunting's deep English roots and his ear for the English language. Sir Herbert Read comments on Bunting's insistence on music in poetry, and Charles Tomlinson explores the roots of that music in the work of Ezra Pound and William Carlos Williams and examines the musical structure of *Briggflatts*.

Agenda 19 (Spring, 1978). Another special issue on Bunting and his poetry. Peter Dale sets out to attack Bunting's analogy of poetry with music and tries to find meaning instead, while Roland John discusses why the critics have neglected Bunting's work. Peter Makin wonders to what degree the sound of a poem can communicate emotion, and Anthony Suter wonders also whether Bunting neglects meaning in his pursuit of sound. Also examines Bunting's creative process in an interview with Peter Quartermain.

Alldritt, Keith. *The Poet as Spy: The Life and Wild Times of Basil Bunting*. London: Aurum Press, 1998. This biography of Bunting chronicles the poet's early and lasting struggle to attain recognition for his talents, covering his imprisonment in 1918 for his role as conscientious objector to his travails in England, Iran, and Italy. Discusses the influence of Ezra Pound on his career and work, and their eventual split.

Forde, Victoria. *The Poetry of Basil Bunting*. Newcastle upon Tyne: Bloodaxe Books, 1991. This volume is a revision of the author's 1972 Ph.D. thesis. Includes a useful biography of the poet, accompanied by more than thirty photographs of and by Bunting. Covers the marital and financial troubles faced by the Bunting family and the effect these had upon his writing. The commentary stays close to the texts, elucidating Bunting largely through his own statements.

Makin, Peter. *Bunting: The Shaping of His Verse*. Oxford: Clarendon Press, 1992. Makin's biography covers many of the same aspects of Bunting's life as Forde's, but more penetratingly. Makin's discussion of the poetry is more in-depth, and his scholarship is unassailable.

Paideuma 9 (Spring, 1980). This issue gathers essays on, and tributes to, Bunting. In the analysis of "Villon," Peter Dale considers three ways of using musical form in poetry, David Gordon charts the use of rhythm and idiom in Bunting's career, and Hugh Kenner pays tribute to Bunting's distinctive reading voice. One of the best and most enjoyable essays is Carroll Terrell's "Basil Bunting in Action," which is a mixture of criticism, memoir, biography, and documentary.

Quartermain, Peter. *Basil Bunting: Poet of the North*. Durham, N.C.: Basil Bunting Poetry Archive, 1990. This twenty-four-page pamphlet is the text of a lecture delivered on Bunting's poetry. The talk was given in the Mountjoy lecture series.

Terrell, Carroll F. *Basil Bunting: Man and Poet*. Orono, Maine: National Poetry Foundation, 1981. Contains an introduction by the editor as well as an annotated bibliography of critical works. The first three essays are biographical and are followed by essays on Bunting's "Sonatas" and the odes. A five-essay section on *Briggflatts* is followed by sections on his criticism and translations. Supplemented by a primary bibliography and an index.

Weatherhead, Andrew Kingsley. *The British Dissonance: Essays on Ten Contemporary Poets*. Columbia: University of Missouri Press, 1983. Weatherhead discusses Bunting's poetry in an essay alongside those of other British poets such as Ted Hughes, Anselm Hollo, Charles Tomlinson, and Matthew Mead. Supplemented by an index and a bibliography of works by the poets.

Wm. Dennis Horn;
bibliography updated by the editors

ROBERT BURNS

Born: Alloway, Ayrshire, Scotland; January 25, 1759
Died: Dumfries, Scotland; July 21, 1796

PRINCIPAL POETRY

Poems, Chiefly in the Scottish Dialect, 1786 (Kilmarnock edition), 1787 (Edinburgh edition), 1793 (2 volumes)

OTHER LITERARY FORMS

As a pure poet, Robert Burns had neither the time nor the desire for other literary forms. For *The Scots Musical Museum*, edited by James Johnson between 1787 and 1803, he wrote "Notes on Scottish Song," wherein he tried to collect all of the information he could about the poetic tradition of his native land. He suggested possibilities for authorship, identified the poems' native regions and the occasions of their composition, cited fragments and verses of traditional songs, and set forth critical comments and engaging anecdotes.

Following the publication and success of the 1786 edition of his *Poems*, Burns set off on a series of trips that carried him over much of Scotland. Narratives of two of those journeys, *Journal of a Tour in the Highlands Made in 1787* and *Journal of the Border Tour*, eventually found their way into print in 1834.

ACHIEVEMENTS

Robert Burns's most significant poetry was written in what may loosely be termed Scots—the northern dialect of English spoken regularly by Scottish peasants and informally by Scottish gentry. When the poet attempted to write in standard eighteenth century British English, he came forth as a different person: stiff, conventional, and genteel, seemingly trying too hard to find his place within the poetic tradition of his day. No matter what the dialect, however, literary historians have termed Burns a "pre-Romantic," a poet who anticipated William Wordsworth, gave new life to the English lyric, relied heavily upon literary forms and legends peculiar to the Scottish folk culture, and (certainly the most Wordsworthian quality of them all) wrote in the actual language of the common people. Few realize, however, that the pre-

Romantic label is based primarily on Burns's songs, while the bulk of his poetry was written in the forms favored by the majority of eighteenth century poets. He also wrote satire, verse epistles to friends and fellow poets, and even a variation on the mock-epic narrative ("Tam O'Shanter"). An argument could easily be advanced that Burns ranks as a first-rate practitioner of those forms.

Nevertheless, as a writer of satire, epistle, and mock-heroic, Burns does not belong entirely to the neoclassical mainstream which followed John Dryden, Alexander Pope, and Oliver Goldsmith. With his dialect and intricate stanza forms, his poems evinced a heartiness and exuberance, and even a certain "roughness." Burns had little use for Horace, Homer, and the other models for English neoclassicism; instead, he turned to a clearer tradition that had been established during the so-called golden age of Scottish poetry by the major Scottish Chaucerians: Robert Henryson (1430-1506), William Dunbar (1465-1530), and Gavin Douglas (1474-1522). Following the efforts of Allan Ramsay (1686-1758) and Robert Fergusson (1750-1774)—earlier Scottish poets who had collected the ancient poems and had written new ones based on

Robert Burns (Library of Congress)

the older models—Burns committed himself to the bards and songs of his native land. He refined the work of his eighteenth century predecessors, but he was also perceptive enough to learn from them and to retain characteristic subjects, forms, stanza patterns, and language.

No matter how academic, the discussion of Burns's poetry seems never to circumvent his songs. Almost to a line, those short pieces have gained wider fame and prompted more discussion than have his longer poems. Burns wrote more than three hundred songs on every subject imaginable within the context of late eighteenth century Scotland. Within the confines of those songs, Burns gave himself almost totally to the emotions of the moment; he reached out, touched the essence of rural Scotland, and brought it lyrically to life. He gave his readers the excitement and the genuineness of love, work, friendship, patriotism, and even inebriation (a point that has been greatly overemphasized). He portrayed universal character types, national heroes as well as lowly tavern revelers, and he took delight in sketching the grand parades of humanity as they passed before his vivid and lyrical imagination. Thus, Burns's poetic achievement was really very simple. He assumed the mantle of Scotland's national poet at a time when the country was struggling to preserve its cultural identity. Yet, if Burns spoke for Scotland, he stood also for all English-speaking people, who, as they prepared to undergo the political and technological traumas of the nineteenth century, needed frequent reminders of their national, political, and artistic heritage.

BIOGRAPHY

Robert Burns was born on January 25, 1759, in Alloway, some three miles south of the seaport town of Ayr. He was the first son of William Burnes (the original spelling of the family name that the poet eventually altered) and Agnes Broun. The father belonged to a lowly class of Scots agricultural society: He was a cottar, one who occupied a cottage on a farm in exchange for labor. As such, he engaged in a constant struggle to keep himself, his illiterate wife, and their seven children fed and clothed. In 1766, the elder Burnes leased seventy acres near Ayr and committed his family to farming. High rents and poor soil, however, only increased the size of the family debt.

Young Robert studied at a small village school, where, for three years, he read English literature, wrote essays, and learned mathematics. After the practicalities of elementary education had been mastered, further learning came only as time would permit. The local schoolmaster, John Murdock, managed to teach the boy some French, and in 1775, the sixteen-year-old Burns journeyed across the Doon River to Kirkoswald, where he studied the rudiments of surveying. At home, the senior Burnes assumed responsibility for the balance of his son's education: geography, history, devotional and theological literature, and more mathematics. Although chores related to the family farm assumed a high priority, young Burns managed to find time for the Bible, Presbyterian theology, and any books he could beg or borrow from friends and neighbors.

In 1777, William Burnes moved his family some twelve miles to the northwest, to Lochlie Farm, between Tarbolton and Mauchline. There, eighteen-year-old Robert emerged as a sociable, sensitive, and handsome young man. He debated in the Tarbolton Bachelors' Club, a group of serious albeit boisterous young men; he joined the Freemasons; he discovered women. In 1781, he attempted to embark upon a business career in the flax-dressing industry at Irvine, on the coast. The venture proved to be a failure, and for the most part Burns rooted himself to the family farm in central Ayrshire, where he remained until the publication of the Kilmarnock edition of his *Poems, Chiefly in the Scottish Dialect* in 1786. William Burnes died in 1784, leaving his family heavily in debt. Robert and his brother Gilbert remained on the farm, however, and the poet's early verse indicates the degree to which he involved himself in the activities, associations, and gossip of the local people.

Burns had begun to write poetry around 1773, when he was fourteen. The poems tended, primarily, to be song lyrics in the Scots vernacular, although (probably as a result of Murdock's influence) he tried his hand at some moral and sentimental pieces in standard English. The manuscripts of those poems reveal considerable roughness. Burns needed models, and not until he came upon the work of two Scots poets, Robert Fergusson and Allan Ramsay, did he learn how to write nonlyrical poetry in the Scots vernacular that would appeal to the hearts and minds of his countrymen. Three years prior to the publication of the Kilmarnock edition, he put together a commonplace book (several versions of which have been published), containing both his poems and remarks concerning his poetic development. Thus, the period 1785-1786 marked Burns's most significant literary output. It also proved to be the time when he would have to pay dearly for liaisons with various young women of the area. In May, 1785, his first daughter was born to Elizabeth Paton, a former servant; in all, he fathered nine illegitimate children, four by his future wife, Jean Armour (those were two sets of twins). He accepted responsibility for rearing and supporting all of them. Another affair with a servant girl, Mary Campbell—the "Highland Mary" of the song—ended tragically when the girl died giving birth to another Burns child.

Despite these domestic problems, the Kilmarnock edition of poems was published, bringing Burns success and some money. More important, the volume took him out of Ayrshire and into Edinburgh, where he gained the praise of the critic Henry Mackenzie (1745-1831) and the publisher William Creech (1745-1815), and where he arranged for publication and subscriptions for a new edition of his poems. From November, 1786, to mid-1788, Burns lived in Edinburgh, seeking to establish himself in its social and intellectual atmosphere. Although his congenial personality and intellectual curiosity appealed to the upper levels of Edinburgh society, they were not enough to erase the stigma of low social birth. The upper classes ultimately rejected him. Thus, the young poet drifted to the late-hour social clubs frequented by printers, booksellers, clerks, and schoolmasters. Through it all, he pondered about how to earn a living, since neither poetry nor social contacts enabled him to meet his financial obligations. Four separate tours throughout Scotland and the editorship of James Johnson's *The Scots Musical Museum* yielded no relief from financial pressures.

In March, 1788, Burns rented a tract of land for farming in Ellisland, Dumfriesshire, after which he finally married Jean Armour. He then began a struggle to support his family, a contest that was not eased even upon his securing an appointment (September, 1789) as tax collector and moving to Dumfries. His literary activities were limited to collecting and writing songs, in addition to the composition of some nonlyric pieces of moderate quality. Although "Tam O'Shanter" belongs to this period, Burns misused his talents by trying to emulate the early eighteenth century poets—composing moral epistles, general verse satires, political ballads, serious elegies, and prologues for theatrical pieces.

Burns died on July 21, 1796, the result of a heart condition that had existed since his youth. The details of his life have been much overstated, particularly the gossip about his drinking and his excessive sexual appetite. For serious students of his poetry, Burns's autobiography can be found within the sound and the sense of his writing.

ANALYSIS

To an extraordinary degree, Robert Burns is *the* poet of Scotland, a Scotland that—despite its union with England—remained for him and his readers a totally independent cultural, intellectual, social, and political entity. Undoubtedly, Burns will always be identified exclusively with Scotland, with its peculiar life and manners communicated to the outside world through its distinctive dialect and fierce national pride. He justly deserves that identification, for he not only wrote about Scottish life and manners, but he also sought his inspiration from Scotland—from his own Ayrshire neighborhood, from its land and its people.

THE INFLUENCE OF SCOTLAND

Scotland virtually drips from the lines of Burns's poetry. The scenes of the jocular "Jolly Beggars" have their source in Poosie Nansie's inn at Mauchline, while the poet and Tam O'Shanter meet the witches and the warlocks at midnight on the very real, local, and familiar Alloway Kirk. Indeed, reality obscures even the boldest attempts at erudite romanticism. Burns alludes to actual persons, to friends and acquaintances whom he knew and loved and to whom he dedicated his songs. When he tried his hand at satire, he focused upon local citizens, identifying specific personages or settling for allusions that his eighteenth century Scottish readers would easily recognize. In "The Cotter's Saturday Night"—which features a clear portrait of his own father—the poet reflects his deep attachment to and sincere pride in the village of Alloway and the rural environment of Ayrshire. He viewed the simple scenes in "The Cotter's Saturday Night" as the real essence of Scotland's heritage. Burns began with a sincere love and respect for his neighbors, and he sustained that attitude throughout his life and his work. Without the commitment to Scotland, he never would have conquered the hearts of its native readers nor risen to become the acknowledged national poet of the land north of the Tweed.

Burns's poetry gained almost immediate success among all classes of the Scottish population. He knew of what he wrote, and he grasped almost immediately the living tradition of Scottish poetry, assimilating the qualities of that tradition into his own verse forms and distinct subject matter. For example, the stanzaic forms in such poems as "To a Mouse" (and its companions) had been in existence for more than three hundred years. Burns early had become familiar with the Scottish Chaucerians (John Major, James I of Scotland, Robert Henryson, William Dunbar, Gavin Douglas, Sir David Lindsay) and the folk poets closer to his own day (Allan Ramsay, James Macpherson, Robert Fergusson); he took the best from their forms and content and made them his own. Thus, he probably could not be termed an "original" poet, although he had to work hard to set the tone and style to his readers' tastes. His countrymen embraced his poetry because they found the cadence, the music, and the dialect to be those of their own hearts and minds. The vigor and the deep love may have been peculiar to Burns, but the remaining qualities had existed longer than anyone could determine.

Still, writing in the relatively remote confines of Scotland at the end of the eighteenth century, Burns was not totally alien to the neoclassical norm of British letters. If Alexander Pope or Henry Fielding or Tobias Smollett could focus upon reality and write satires to expose the frailties of humankind, so could Burns be both realistic and satiric. In his most forceful poems—such as "Holy Willie's Prayer," "The Holy Fair," "Address to the Unco Guid"—he set out to expose the religious hypocrites of his day, but at the same time to portray, clearly and truthfully, both the beautiful and the ugly qualities of Scottish life and character. Burns's poetry may not always be even in quality or consistent in force, but it certainly always conveys an air of truthfulness.

If Burns's poetry reverberates with the remoteness of rural Scotland, it is because he found the perfect poetic environment for the universal themes of his works. In 1803, William Wordsworth stood beside his grave and contemplated "How Verse may build a princely throne/ On humble truth." The throne was carved out of Burns's understanding of the most significant theme of his time—the democratic spirit (which helps to explain Wordsworth's tribute). Throughout, the Scottish bard salutes the worth of pure man, the man viewed outside the context of station or wealth. Certainly, Burns was sensitive to the principles and causes that spawned the revolutions in America and in France; in fact, closer to home, the Jacobite rebellion sparked by the landing of the Young Pretender from France had occurred only nine years before the poet's birth. By nature, he was a political liberal, and his poems take advantage of every opportunity for man or beast to cry for freedom. Again, it was Wordsworth who identified Burns as a poet of the literary revolution—Romanticism—that later rushed through the open gates and into the nineteenth century.

POETIC QUALITIES

Few will question that, ultimately, Burns's strength as a poet is to be found in the lyrical quality of his songs. That quality simply stood far above his other virtues—his ability to observe and to penetrate until he discovered the essence of a particular subject, his skill in description and satire, and his striving to achieve personal and intellectual independence. In his songs, he developed the ability to record, with the utmost ease, the emotions of the common people of whom he wrote. Burns's reliance on native Scottish tradition was both a limitation and a strength. For example, although he genuinely enjoyed the poetry of James Thomson (1700-1748), the Edinburgh University graduate who ventured to London and successfully challenged the artificiality of English poetry, Burns could not possibly have written a Scottish sequel to *The Seasons* (1726-1730). Instead, he focused upon the simple Scottish farmer, upon the man hard at work and enjoying social relationships, not upon the prevalent eighteenth century themes of solitude and retirement. In Burns, then, the reader sees strong native feeling and spontaneous expression, the source of which was inherited, not learned.

Another quality of Burns's poetry that merits attention is his versatility, the range of human emotions that exists throughout his verse. He could function as a satirist, and he could sound the most ardent notes of patriotism. His humor was neither vulgar nor harsh, but quiet, with considerable control—as in "Address to the Deil," "To a Mouse," and "To a Mountain Daisy." As a lover, as one who obviously loved to love and be loved, he wrote lyrical pieces that could capture the essence of human passion. The lyric forms allowed for the fullest expression of his versatility, most of which came about during the last ten years of his relatively short life.

CAPTURING NATIONAL SPIRIT

From 1787 until his death in the summer of 1796, Burns committed himself to steady literary activity. He became associated with James Johnson, an uneducated engraver and enthusiastic collector and publisher of Scottish songs. From 1787 to 1804, Johnson gathered those songs into a five-volume *Scots Musical Museum*, and Burns served as his principal editor. Then the poet became associated with George Thomson, whose *Select Collection of Scottish Airs* reached six volumes between 1793 and 1811. Burns's temperament seemed suited to such a combination of scholarly activity and poetic productivity, but he never accepted money for his contributions. The writing, rewriting, and transformation of some three hundred old songs and ballads would serve as his most singular gift to his nation. In reworking those antiquated songs and popular ballads, he returned to Scotland, albeit in somewhat modified form, a large portion of its culture that had for so long remained in obscurity. Thus, an old drinking song emerged as "Auld Lang Syne," while a disreputable ballad became "John Anderson My Jo." Finally, the Johnson and Thomson collections became outlets for certain of his more famous original songs: "For A' That and A' That," "Scots, Wha Hae wi' Wallace Bled," as well as such love lyrics as "Highland Mary" and "Thou Lingering Star." Because of his love of and gift for the traditional Scots folk songs and ballads, Burns wrote and sang for Scotland. He became the voice and the symbol of the people and captured the national sentiment.

MELANCHOLY STRAINS

It would be a mistake, however, to assume that all is happily rustic, nationalistic, or patriotic with Burns. On the contrary, he has a decidedly melancholy or mournful strain. A look at such poems as "A Bard's Epitaph" and the "Epistle to a Young Friend" demonstrates that the intellect and the passion of the poet were far from being

comfortably adjusted. A conflict raged within the mind and heart of Burns as the sensibilities of an exceedingly gifted soul vied with the sordid lot that was his by birth and social position (or the lack of it). Despite the appearance and even the actuality of productivity during his last five years, the final stage of Burns's career reflects, in the soberest of terms, the degradation of genius. Nevertheless, his muse remained alive and alert, as his passions seethed within him until they found outlets in rhyme.

Burns controlled his passion so that, particularly in his songs, there is abundant evidence of sense and beauty. To his credit, he remained aware of the conflict within him and drew strength from the clash of experiences, of habits, and of emotions which, somehow, he managed to regulate and harmonize. Few will argue that certain of the songs ("Mary Morison," "My Nanie O," and "Of A' the Airts the Wind Can Blow") hang heavy with serious and extremely pathetic and passionate strains. Since such heaviness had its origin in the Scottish tradition, Burns could effectively hide his own melancholy behind the Lugar or the banks of Bonnie Doon.

THE MORAL ELEMENT

Such conclusions invariably lead to the question of a religious or moral element in Burns's poetry. Assuredly, the more religious among Burns scholars have difficulty with such poems as "The Holy Fair," "Holy Willie" and the satiric pieces in which the poet ridiculed religious and ecclesiastical ideals and personages. No doubt Burns's own moral conduct was far from perfect, but the careful reader of his poetry realizes immediately that Burns never ridiculed religion; rather, he heaped scorn only upon those religious institutions that appeared ridiculous and lacked the insight to recognize obvious weaknesses. Indeed, the poet often seems to be looking for virtue and morality, seeking to replace the sordid scenes of his own world with the piety of another time and place. He sought a world beyond and above the grotesqueness of his own debauchery, a world dominated by order, love, truth, and joy. That is about the best he could have done for himself. Even had Burns been the epitome of sobriety, morality, and social and religious conformity, religious expression would probably not have been high on his list of poetic priorities. He inherited the poetic legacy of Scotland—a national treasure found outside the limits of the Kirk, a vault not of hymns and psalm paraphrases, but of songs and ballads. Such were the constituent parts of Burns's poetic morality.

Burns's language and poetic methods seem to distract only the impatient among his readers. To begin with, he believed that the vernacular ought never to be seen as low or harsh, or even as prostituted English. Rather, Burns came to know and to understand the Scots dialect and to manipulate it for his own poetic purpose. At the outset, he claimed to have turned his back upon formal bodies of knowledge, upon books, and to have taken full advantage of what he termed "Nature's fire" as the only learning necessary for his art. Nature may have provided the attraction toward the Scots dialect, but Burns himself knew exactly what to do with it.

Close attention to his letters and to the details of his life will yield the steps of his self-education. He read Thomas Salmon's *Geographical and Historical Grammar* (1749) and a *New System of Modern Geography, History, and Modern Grammar* (1770), by William Guthrie (1708-1770), both of which provided descriptions and examples of Scotland's traditions and language, although nothing of poetic contexts. Then he turned to Jethro Tull (1680-1740), the Hungerford farmer and inventor, who wrote several volumes on the general subject of "horse-hoeing husbandry" (1731-1739), and to the Reverend Adam Dickson of Edinburgh, who wrote *A Treatise on Agriculture* (1762, 1765, 1769) and the two-volume *The Husbandry of the Ancients* (1788). Thus, Burns was well versed in the specifics of rural Scotland by the time he discovered his most helpful source, the poetry of Robert Fergusson, who had managed successfully to capture the dialect of enlightened Edinburgh. Burns had his models, and he simply shifted the sounds and the scenes from Scotland's capital to rural Ayrshire.

POEMS

To simplify matters even further, Burns himself had actually stood behind the plow. Little wonder, then, that the Kilmarnock edition of the *Poems* succeeded on the basis of such pieces as "The Twa Dogs," "The Holy Fair," "Address to the Deil," "Halloween," "The Cotter's Saturday Night," "To a Mouse," and "To a Mountain-Daisy." Burns had effectively described Scottish life as Scots themselves (as well as those south of the Tweed)

had come to know it. More important, the poems in that initial collection displayed to the world the poet's full intellectual range of wit and sentiment, although his readers received nothing that had not already been a part of their long tradition. Essentially, the Edinburgh edition of the following year gave the world more of the same, and Burns's readers discovered that the poet's move from Ayrshire to Edinburgh had not changed his sources or his purpose. The new poems—among them "Death and Dr. Hornbook," "The Brigs of Ayr," "Address to the Unco Guid," "John Barleycorn," and "Green Grow the Rushes"—still held to the pictures of Scottish life and to the vernacular, still held to the influence of Robert Fergusson's *Scots Poems* (1773).

By the time Burns had done some substantive work on James Johnson's *The Scots Musical Museum*, however, his art had assumed a new dimension, the writing and revision of the Scots song. The poet became a singer, providing his own accompaniment by the simple means of humming to himself as he wrote, and trying (as he explained) to catch the inspiration and the enthusiasm so strongly characterized in the traditional poetry. He set out to master the tune, then to compose for that particular strain. In other words, he demanded that for the song, musical expression must dictate the poetic theme. Nevertheless, Burns was the first to admit his weakness as a musician, making no claims even to musical taste. For him, as a poet, music was instinctive, supplied by nature to complement his art. Thus, he felt unable to deal with the technical aspects of music as a formal discipline. What he *could* do, however, was to react quickly to what he termed "many little melodies" and to give new and fresh poetic and musical expression to something like "Scots Wha Hae," one of the oldest of Scottish airs. Through the songs, Burns clearly preserved tradition, while, at the same time, he maintained his originality. This tradition was the genuine expression of the people who, from generation to generation, echoed the essence of their very existence; Burns gave it sufficient clarity and strength to carry it forward into the next century and beyond. The effect of those more than three hundred songs was, simply, to cede Burns the title of Scotland's national poet—a title that he earned because of his poetic rather than his political voice.

"Tam O' Shanter"

Perhaps the one poem that demonstrates Burns's ability as a serious and deliberate craftsman, a true poet, is "Tam O' Shanter" (1790, 1791). More than anything else, that piece of 224 lines transports its creator away from the "Heaven-taught plowman" image, from the label of the boy genius whose poetry is nothing more than one large manifestation of the spontaneous overflow of his native enthusiasm. Burns wrote "Tam O' Shanter" for a volume on Scottish antiquity and based it on a witch story told about Alloway Kirk, an old ruin near the poet's house in Ayr. Yet, he turned that tale into a mockheroic rendering of folk material that comes close, in genre and in poetic quality, to Geoffrey Chaucer's "The Nun's Priest's Tale." Burns specifically set out to construct his most sustained and most artistic production; in his own words, he remained aware of the "spice of roguish waggery" within the poem, but he also took considerable pains to ensure that the force of his poetic genius and "finishing polish" would not go unrecognized. Burns's manipulation of his dipsomaniacal hero and his misadventures constitutes a masterful blending of the serious and the comic. The moralists of his day objected vehemently to the ribald elements of the poem. Early in the next century, William Wordsworth, whose strongest drink was probably water, attacked the attackers of "Tam O' Shanter" (as well as those who objected to all of Burns's poetry on moral grounds) by labeling them impenetrable dunces and narrow-minded puritans. Wordsworth saw the poem as a delightful picture of the rustic adventurer's convivial exaltation; if the poem lacked clear moral purpose, maintained England's laureate, it at least provided the clearest possible moral effect.

Literary legacy

The final issue raised by Burns's poetry is his place in literary history—an issue that has always prompted spirited debate. There is no doubt that Burns shares common impulses with Wordsworth and the Romantic movement, particularly in his preoccupation with folklore and the language of the people, yet neither is there any evidence of Burns's fundamental dissatisfaction with the dominant critical criteria and principal literary assumptions of eighteenth century England. The readers of his songs will be hard put to discover lush scenery or majestic mountains, or even the sea—although all were in easy reach of his eye and his mind. If he expressed no poetic interest in such aspects of nature close at hand, however, he turned even less in the direction of the distant and the exotic.

Instead, he looked long and hard at the farmer, the mouse, the louse, and he contemplated each; the mountains, the nightingale, the skylark he also saw, but chose to leave them to the next generation of poets. In other words, Burns did not seek new directions for his poetry; instead, he took full advantage of what existed and of what had come before. He grasped literary imitation firmly and gave that form the most significance and prominence it had enjoyed since the late Restoration and the Augustan age. Burns wrote satire and he wrote songs, but he invented neither. Rather, he served as an exploiter of tradition; he gathered inherited motifs, rhetorical conventions, and familiar language and produced art. The reader of the present century should see no less or expect no more from Burns's poetical character.

Other major works

NONFICTION: *Journal of a Tour in the Highlands Made in 1787*, 1834 (Allan Cunningham, editor); *Journal of the Border Tour*, 1834 (Cunningham, editor); *The Letters of Robert Burns*, 1931 (2 volumes; John De Lancey Ferguson, editor).

Bibliography

Bentman, Raymond. *Robert Burns*. Boston: Twayne, 1987. This complete introduction to the life and works of Robert Burns describes Burns's background, analyzes his poetry and songs, then places him in the context of late eighteenth century literature. Includes an annotated secondary bibliography and is suitable for high school students and college undergraduates.

Daiches, David. *Robert Burns and His World*. New York: Viking Press, 1971. A well-illustrated book that combines Burns's biography with snippets of his writing. Daiches explains how Scottish society profoundly influenced Burns's work. A lively book that is suitable for all students.

Fitzhugh, Robert T. *Robert Burns, the Man and Poet: A Round, Unvarnished Account*. Boston: Houghton Mifflin, 1970. Fitzhugh mixes poetry with anecdote in this biography of Burns. He has even attached an appendix with Burns's health record, gleaned from his correspondence. The author analyzes Burns's poetic writing separately from his songs, for he asserts that Burns did not consider his songs to be poetry.

Jack, R. D. S., and Andrew Noble, eds. *The Art of Robert Burns*. London: Vision Press, 1982. The nine essays contained in this book place Burns in a wide social and literary context, outside his native Scotland. They seek to show Burns as a complex writer, and not merely a "cosy representative of Scottish virtues." Suitable for intermediate and advanced students.

McIntyre, Ian. *Dirt and Deity: A Life of Robert Burns*. London: HarperCollins, 1995. Written for the bicentenary of Burns's death, this biography organizes previous research into Burns's life, telling its story as much as possible through Burns's letters and the correspondence and memoirs of those who knew him.

Noble, Andrew. *Robert Burns and English Romanticism*. Brookfield, Vt.: Ashgate, 2001. Scholarly examination of Burns in the context of the great literary tradition of his time.

Skoblow, Jeffrey. *Dooble Tongue: Scots, Burns, Contradiction*. Cranbury, N.J.: Associated University Presses, 2001. Places Burns and his poetics in historical and Scottish cultural context. Bibliographical references, index.

Snyder, Franklyn Bliss. *The Life of Robert Burns*. 1932. Reprint. Hamden, Conn.: Shoestring Press, 1968. An excellent biography of Burns, although some of the writing seems dated. Snyder recounts Burns's life in a sentimental way that reduces the poet to a Scottish stereotype. Yet it is a factual account accessible to all levels of students.

Samuel J. Rogal;
bibliography updated by the editors

SAMUEL BUTLER

Born: Strensham, England; February 8, 1612
Died: London, England; September 25, 1680

PRINCIPAL POETRY
Hudibras, Parts 1-3, 1663, 1664, 1678

OTHER LITERARY FORMS

Samuel Butler wrote essays and prose in addition to verse. His best-known essay is "The Case of King Charles I Truly Stated," which argues that the execution of Charles I was unjustified. Butler's essay was published in Robert Thyer's *The Genuine Remains in Verse and Prose of Samuel Butler* (1759), and it displays his excellent understanding of English law—an understanding that plays an important role in *Hudibras*—and his ability to pick apart a point of view, a trait manifested in his carefully reasoned satire.

Of greater literary significance are his "characters," which were probably composed during 1667 to 1669, nearly two hundred of which have been uncovered since Butler's death. The most complete edition of his characters was edited by Charles W. Daves in 1970 as *Samuel Butler, 1612-1680: Characters*. As with *Hudibras*, Butler took a popular literary form of the seventeenth century and modified it to suit his satiric purposes. His "characters" feature politicians, judges, lovers, and zealots, and in each sketch, he demonstrates his abhorrence of immoderation, his contempt for hypocrisy, his disgust with irrational thought, and his willingness to expose fraud and ostentation wherever they might be found. Although some of the characters were intended for publication, others were probably intended to serve as raw material which Butler could mine for his poetry.

ACHIEVEMENTS

Samuel Butler's greatest achievement was to embody in a single work the failures, hypocrisy, and foolishness of an age. *Hudibras* captures the dark spirit of seventeenth century England, and the wit which made his contemporaries regard Butler as a great comic satirist also reveals the flaws in their philosophies. In Butler's stingingly accurate portrait of his time lies much of his literary strength and weakness. If one reads and understands *Hudibras*, one learns to understand the culture of Oliver Cromwell's England and of Restoration England. Butler's misanthropic point of view illuminates his society; even though he was a Loyalist, and the surface thrust of *Hudibras* is an attack on Cromwellian Puritans, Butler spares no one from his sharp insights. *Hudibras* is necessarily specific, and Butler's allusions to events and people were readily recognized in his time. Such particularity has made Butler's satire dependent on his readers' understanding of the 1600's. Thus, what made Butler's contemporaries laugh and wince may puzzle modern readers.

Hudibras brought Butler fame; he became known as "Hudibras Butler" or simply as "Hudibras." Such verse is still called Hudibrastic, and its imitations are called Hudibrastic satires. The poem stands out not only as one of the great achievements in satire but also as a work that inspired multitudes of imitations and helped to shape the forms of satire after its time. Its influence stretched from the seventeenth century to America after the revolution. Indeed, the poem's assault on cultural elitism appealed to antimonarchists and egalitarians, in spite of Butler's evi-

Samuel Butler (Hulton Archive)

dent Loyalist views. Butler expanded the bounds of satire, writing in verse when contemporary literary theorists said satire was best suited to prose. Critics still argue over whether *Hudibras* is satire, burlesque, heroic satire, satirical burlesque, or something else entirely. Butler showed that satire could, like *Don Quixote de la Mancha* (1605, 1615), mock a literary genre, expose the foibles of a class of people, and provide insights into the intellectual controversies of an era. Butler influenced the satirists who followed him, although few produced works that could match *Hudibras* for wit, insight, and bitterness.

BIOGRAPHY

Two distinct portraits of Samuel Butler have developed since his death—one traditional and the other historical. Most sketches of Butler's life rely on the traditional version, based primarily on the accounts of John Aubrey, who knew him, and Anthony à Wood, a contemporary of Butler who admitted that he was uncertain of his facts. One reason why most short biographies rely on the traditional accounts is that the historical ones have been uncertain and contradictory. Evidence in the form of letters, notes, and public documents has been hard to come by, and new evidence sometimes contradicts the old. Only since the mid-twentieth century has historical evidence begun to supplant the traditional version of Butler's life.

Both versions agree on the major aspects of Butler's youth. He was born in Strensham, England, on February 8, 1612, and was baptized on February 14. His father, also named Samuel, was a farmer who rented property from the local gentry and had a home and lands in Barbourne. The elder Butler was evidently learned and maintained a large and diverse library that he left to his eight children when he died. Samuel was then only fourteen years of age.

Butler probably attended King's School in Worcester, north of Strensham. Tradition claims that he also attended college—perhaps Oxford, although records show no evidence of his having continued his formal education after leaving King's School. He probably became a secretary for various gentlemen and gentlewomen. Through these people, he became acquainted with some of the leading minds of his day, possibly including John Seldon, a legal historian who knew Ben Jonson, Thomas Hobbes, and others. Butler had ample opportunity to observe the pretentiousness of England's social and intellectual elite, and he may have learned about England's laws and theology from such people as Seldon.

In 1642, King Charles I raised his standard at Nottingham. In 1649, he was executed. Tradition has it that during these tumultuous years, Butler served as a clerk to Sir Samuel Luke, a member of Parliament from Bedfordshire, and that Luke served as the model for the character Hudibras. Other models have been suggested by historians, yet Butler probably used several Puritans as inspiration for Hudibras. He might have begun *Hudibras* before 1649, and it might have been his response to having to survive by serving parliamentarians while harboring loyalist sentiments.

Some accounts indicate that fragments of *Hudibras* were copied and circulated before the Restoration. Butler had already written essays defending the monarchy and was almost certainly working on *Hudibras* when Oliver Cromwell died in 1658. Charles II entered London in 1660, at which time works by Loyalists became popular. When *Hudibras*, Part I, was published in late 1662 (it was postdated 1663), it caught the fancy of the public and of the king; Charles II was said to quote from the poem from memory. Butler probably made enough money from the sale of *Hudibras*, Part I, and later *Hudibras*, Part II, to live well.

Butler apparently invested his money unwisely; or, perhaps he spent it too rapidly. Some accounts assert that Charles II gave Butler three hundred pounds as a royal grant. Other accounts maintain that Charles II gave Butler a one hundred pound annuity. Others assert that both were given; still others mention neither. What seems likely is that Charles II was dilatory in fulfilling any promises he made to Butler. By 1673, Butler had become secretary to the Duke of Buckingham. Not until 1677, apparently, did Charles II provide Butler with any monetary support. In 1678, *Hudibras*, Part III, was published, in part to provide Butler with income beyond that which came from his secretarial work.

Tradition holds that Butler was unjustly neglected by an ungrateful king who failed to fulfill promises made to the poet. History indicates that Charles II was freer with his promises than with his money. Butler's own sharp misanthropic wit may have cost him royal and noble help; he seems to have found fault with everyone he knew—a practice that might have alienated potential patrons. Regardless of what he was promised and what he actually received, he lived in a poor part of London and died on September 25, 1680, in genuinely miserable poverty. He was buried in the graveyard of St. Paul's, in Covent Garden. A bust of him resides in the Poets' Corner of Westminster Abbey.

ANALYSIS

HUDIBRAS

Samuel Butler's stature as a poet is founded on one work: *Hudibras*. In it, he demonstrates considerable skill in prosody; yet many critics are uncertain about the work's status as poetry, describing it as doggerel. One of Butler's objectives in *Hudibras* is the debasement of heroic verse; thus, although he is undoubtedly a poet, his verse is not what is commonly thought of as poetry. This contradiction is one of many inherent in Butler's great work. He displays a broad knowledge of literature and philosophy—a knowledge which is the product of an inquisitive and thoughtful mind—yet he presents his knowledge only to portray it as foolish. Although *Hudibras* became famous as a political satire and remains best known for its portrayal of seventeenth century English politics, two of its three parts are devoted to social satire. It is above all distinguished by its verse, which spawned a school of imitations called Hudibrastic, and its wit and vigor, which make for a lively narrative. Its satire is unusually sophisticated and wide-ranging, attacking a poetic genre, a style of verse, and the politics, theology, and manners of Butler's society.

METER AND VERSIFICATION

Hudibras is written in rhyming tetrameter couplets, a verse form that in Butler's day was associated with heroic poetry. Philosophically a rationalist, Butler objected to poetry which defied probability by describing magic, fairies, enchanted castles, flying horses, and other fantastic places, creatures, and events. Thus, he took a verse form that would be familiar to his audience and subverted it by using it to describe false heroes and sordid events and by employing strange rhymes and odd plays on words. *Hudibras* abounds with such irreverent rhymes as: "And Pulpit, Drum Ecclesiastik,/ Was beat with fist, instead of a stick," from Part I; and from Part II,

Quoth *Hudibras*, You lie so ope,
That I, without a *Telescope*,
Can find your Tricks out, and descry
Where you tell truth, and where you lie

Throughout his poem, Butler's verse is exuberantly barbaric; the rhymes are wildly original, and the wordplay is rapid and clever. Instead of romantic language, Butler creates witty wordplay, thus trivializing heroic verse.

LANGUAGE

Much of Butler's brilliance as a poet is manifested in his mutilation of language. By deliberately using his couplets to present doggerel, he subverts the ideas he wishes to attack with his diction. Analytically gifted and capable of perceiving truth in the folly of others, he insists on expressing his rationalist understanding of truth by exposing the particulars of folly. His analytical character and rationalist point of view make him seem more part of the modern era than of the English Renaissance that nurtured him. His models were works such as Edmund Spenser's *The Faerie Queene* (1590-1596) and Miguel de Cervantes' *Don Quixote*, but he could not empathize with *The Faerie Queene* as he could with *Don Quixote*. Thus, he mocks Spenser's epic work and its kin with satire more harsh than that found in Cervantes' satirical romance. Butler's verse mocks not only ideas but also the very modes in which they are expressed.

SATIRIC CONTENT

Butler includes careful allusions to *The Faerie Queene*, the masterwork of English Renaissance heroic verse, to emphasize his implicit intent to satirize the Arcadian romances of his sixteenth century predecessors. Each canto of *Hudibras* begins with an "argument," as does each canto of *The Faerie Queene*. More important, the name *Hudibras* is taken from Spenser's poem: "He that made loue vnto the eldest Dame,/ Was hight Sir *Huddibras*, an hardy man;/ Yet not so good of deedes, as great of name." Butler takes this character who was "not so good of deedes" and places him in Puritan England. This act, coupled with his perverse versification, makes *Hudibras* satirical in its most fundamental elements: language and character.

The first part of *Hudibras* is organized by the elements of an epic quest. Like Cervantes' *Don Quixote*, *Hudibras* features a knight-errant who misperceives his world. Hudibras, the character, seems much like Don Quixote; he seeks to right wrongs, is afflicted by low characters whose natures he misapprehends, and is accompanied by a sort of squire. Even his fatness seems, in context, to be in deliberate contrast to Quixote's thinness. Yet, for all the seeming borrowing from *Don Quixote*, Hudibras is significantly different from his predecessor, just as Butler's misanthropic view of life is different from that of Cervantes. Given the misery inflicted on Cervantes, one might expect him to have a cold view of the world, but *Don Quixote* is a gentle satire and readers can sympathize with its unfortunate protagonist. Hudibras is an inherently unsympathetic character; he is boorish, greedy, cowardly, and self-righteous. Don Quixote seeks giants; Hudibras seeks nonconformity with Puritanical notions of virtue. One tries to combat the masters of evil; the other bullies only those who appear weak. In addition, Don Quixote's companion, Sancho Panza, is a slow but good-natured man, while Hudibras's companion, Ralph, is an angry man who despises Hudibras and rivals his master in greed, deceit, and foolishness. Butler's treatment of his characters is cold, dispassionate, and often harsh; Cervantes' compassion is a notable feature of his work.

Whatever the origins of Butler's misanthropy, his evenhanded scorn makes *Hudibras* curiously egalitarian. Butler, a royalist, leaves no character unscathed, and no idea is introduced for purposes other than to expose its emptiness. Hudibras, the Puritan, is an obvious target of Butler's antipathy, but Ralph is a religious Independent and receives the same treatment from Butler, who describes Ralph's manner of learning as one "that costs no pains/ Of Study, Industry, or Brains." Their antagonists are often cruel and usually equally self-righteous, no matter what their political leanings.

PLOT

The plot of *Hudibras* follows a traditional pattern of romance. A knight-errant, spurned by a woman, seeks to lose his sense of loss in questing. While on his quest, he encounters dangers and assorted exotic characters. Eventually, he wins the attentions of a woman. In the case of questing Hudibras, his first adventure involves an encounter with bearbaiters and a fiddler with a wooden leg. Hudibras sees a village audience dancing merrily to the fiddler Crowdero's music and watching the bear. As a good Puritan magistrate, he is offended by the frivolity of the dancers and the immorality of the bearbaiters. Further, he recognizes the public merrymaking as a threat to public order and thus to the government. As a good logician, Hudibras deduces that such a threat represents a Roman Catholic plot to overthrow the Protestant government; the merrymakers are conspirators, and Crowdero is their leader. Hudibras seeks to arrest the fiddler and a fight ensues. In the melee, the knight-errant falls from his mount onto the bear, angering the animal. It escapes its keeper and scatters the mob. Victorious, Hudibras and Ralph place Crowdero in the village stocks. Trulla, a physically powerful woman, leads the villagers in a counterattack. After much confusion, Hudibras and Ralph are defeated and replace Crowdero in the stocks. The first part of the poem ends with the Puritan and the Independent debating both the blame for their failure and the relative importance of logic and inspiration.

SOCIOPOLITICAL CONTEXT

No great imagination is required for one to understand how the tale of the follies of a Puritan would have appealed to King Charles II and the Royalists. Some of Butler's contemporaries read specific political figures into the roles of the villagers, yet Butler's satire is too general to support such identifications. Ideas are the targets of his satirical wit; thus, Hudibras's reasoning is more representative of Butler's satire than are the comic characters that people his narrative. Hudibras, the Puritan, sees a Popish plot where none could possibly be; he is so consumed by theory and prejudice that he does not understand reality. This notion is the heart of Butler's satire. In the crazy behavior of Hudibras in Part I, Butler expresses his contempt for the way the Puritans interpreted reality. If his satire is taken as a portrait of ideas, then Butler finds the ideas of the Puritans to be empty, hypocritical, and warped.

In Parts II and III, Butler's satire shifts from the political to the social. In this shift, Butler anticipates the thematic thrust of Restoration comedy, which focused on society and on the relationship between men and women. Hudibras is released from the stocks through the intercession of the Widow, who helps Hudibras on the basis of his promise to take a whipping as punishment for his misbehavior. Hudibras plans for Ralph to take his whipping for him and plots to marry the Widow, who is rich. Ralph

also wants the Widow for himself. Much of the narrative focuses on the efforts of Hudibras to evade a whipping and to woo the Widow. In the process, Butler reveals the ethical depravity not only of Hudibras but of the other characters as well, and he exposes the emptiness of the love conventions of the epic romance. Even the intended victim of Hudibras and Ralph, the Widow, is no innocent. She does not mind someone marrying her for her money if he is open about it. Her objections to Hudibras and Ralph are based on their subterfuges: the lies about the whipping, the pretense of love, and the general duplicity. The decreased contemporary popularity of Parts II and III, in comparison to Part I, was probably a tribute to the accuracy of Butler's satire rather than a reflection of any loss of inspiration. While Part I exposed the falseness of the preceding generation, Parts II and III illustrated the hypocrisies of its intended readership; Butler's audience was asked to see its own falseness, thus anticipating Alexander Pope's *The Dunciad* (1728-1743), Jonathan Swift's satires, and the more gentle comedies of William Wycherley, William Congreve, and Richard Sheridan.

OTHER MAJOR WORKS

MISCELLANEOUS: *The Genuine Remains in Verse and Prose of Samuel Butler*, 1759 (Robert Thyer, editor); *Characters, Observations, and Reflexions from the Notebooks*, 1908 (A. R. Waller, editor); *Samuel Butler, 1612-1680: Characters*, 1970 (Charles W. Daves, editor).

BIBLIOGRAPHY

Henderson, Philip. *Samuel Butler: The Incarnate Bachelor.* Bloomington: Indiana University Press, 1954. One of the best biographies of Butler and the first to deal with Butler's private life. Focuses on Butler's personality rather than his work. Readable and illuminating. Argues against such mistaken prevailing views that Butler hated his father. Contains a detailed chronology.

Holt, Lee. *Samuel Butler.* Rev. ed. Boston: Twayne, 1989. In his critical evaluation, Holt summarizes and quotes extensively from a wide range of Butler's work, much of it no longer available. Extends the reader's knowledge of Butler's varied accomplishments. Includes biographical information, a chronology, notes, references, a lengthy selected bibliography, and an index with brief annotations.

Parker, Blanford. *The Triumph of Augustan Poetics: English Literary Culture from Butler to Johnson.* New York: Cambridge University Press, 1998. Written for an audience familiar with seventeenth and eighteenth century history and thought yet accessible to the nonspecialist. Parker's study includes a chapter on Samuel Butler and his part in a vigorous, tumultuous, and original period in English culture. Includes bibliographic references.

Raby, Peter. *Samuel Butler: A Biography.* Iowa City: University of Iowa Press, 1991. This biography makes much of the suffering in Butler's youth, which was occasioned by repeated whippings by his father for the slightest infractions and his grandfather's long headmastership of a school at which Butler was enrolled. Includes a bibliography.

Richards, Edward Ames. *Hudibras in the Burlesque Tradition.* Reprint. New York: Octagon Books, 1972. Explores the burlesque elements in Butler's *Hudibras.* Bibliography.

Snider, Alvin Martin. *Origin and Authority in Seventeenth Century England: Bacon, Milton, Butler.* Toronto, Ont.: University of Toronto Press, 1994. Explores the way in which Francis Bacon, John Milton, and Butler shared thematic interest and discourse in the genesis of ideas by focusing on their signature works: *Novum Organum, Paradise Lost,* and *Hudibras.*

Swartchild, William G. *The Character of a Roundhead: Theme and Rhetoric in Anti-Puritan Verse Satire, From 1639 Through "Hudibras."* New York: Russell and Russell, 1966. Provides history and criticism of English satire and the influence of Puritan mores within the genre, using Butler's work as a focal point for the discussion.

Veldkamp, Jan. *Samuel Butler: The Author of "Hudibras."* Reprint. Folcroft, Pa.: Folcroft Library Editions, 1977. Offers analysis of the religious aspects of Butler's seminal work, *Hudibras.*

Wasserman, George W. *Samuel "Hudibras" Butler.* Boston, Mass.: Twayne, 1976. Provides criticism and interpretation of Butler's most noted work.

Kirk H. Beetz;
bibliography updated by the editors

WITTER BYNNER

Born: Brooklyn, New York; August 10, 1881
Died: Santa Fe, New Mexico; June 1, 1968

PRINCIPAL POETRY
An Ode to Harvard and Other Poems, 1907
The New World, 1915
Spectra: A Book of Poetic Experiments, 1916
Grenstone Poems, 1917
The Beloved Stranger, 1919
A Canticle of Pan, 1920
Pins for Wings, 1920
Caravan, 1925
Indian Earth, 1929
Eden Tree, 1931
Against the Cold, 1933
Guest Book, 1935
Selected Poems, 1936
Take Away the Darkness, 1947
Book of Lyrics, 1955
New Poems, 1960
Selected Poems, 1978
Light Verse and Satires, 1978

OTHER LITERARY FORMS

Witter Bynner was a man of letters, and he wrote several plays, numerous reviews, and a considerable amount of miscellaneous prose, along with some widely acclaimed literary translations. His plays include *Tiger* (1913), *The Little King* (1914), and *Cake* (1926). Most important among his prose productions are *The Persistence of Poetry* (1929) and *Journey with Genius: Recollections and Reflections Concerning the D. H. Lawrences* (1951). Bynner's translations include, from Greek, Euripides' *Iphigenia in Tauris* (1915); from French, *A Book of Love* (1923), by Charles Vildrac; and from Chinese, *The Jade Mountain: A Chinese Anthology* (with Kiang Kang-hu), which appeared in 1929, and *The Way of Life According to Laotzu: An American Version* (1944).

ACHIEVEMENTS

Although many of Witter Bynner's literary contemporaries left the United States to seek inspiration in Europe, Bynner himself, after visiting Europe, decided to remain in the country of his birth. During his long life he developed a passion for Chinese culture and for Mexico, but he remained a conspicuous part of the American community of letters from early in the century until his last days in Santa Fe. In 1910, Bynner was a charter member of the Poetry Society of America. In 1954, the Poetry Society of America awarded Bynner the Gold Medal of the Alexander Droutzkoy Memorial Award, and, in 1962, he was elected to the National Institute of Arts and Letters.

BIOGRAPHY

Harold Witter Bynner was born in Brooklyn, New York, on August 10, 1881. His early childhood was spent in New York, Norwich, Connecticut, and, after his father died in 1891, Brookline, Massachusetts, where Bynner completed high school. From 1898 to 1902, he attended Harvard University, where fellow student Wallace Stevens recruited him for the staff of the Harvard *Advocate*. Upon graduation from Harvard, Bynner secured a semieditorial position with *McClure's* magazine, where he remained for four years, during which time he associated with a number of professional writers, including O. Henry, and resolved to pursue a writing career. Eventually, Bynner left New York and *McClure's* and moved to New Hampshire to write. He also began giving lectures on literature and supporting the movement for women's suffrage.

Bynner began publishing volumes of his poetry in 1907 with *An Ode to Harvard and Other Poems*. He also experimented with drama and engaged in some translation during this early period. Being both annoyed and amused by the pretensions of trendy literary movements in this period, Bynner and his friend Arthur Davison Ficke created a bogus movement based on ludicrous aesthetic principles. This supposed movement, Spectrism, was a satirical takeoff on the 1912 London movement called Imagism, and, to Bynner's delight, it actually duped a number of writers and critics who should have known better but who could not resist associating themselves with the latest fad. In the course of developing this hoax, Bynner adopted the nom de plume of Emanuel Morgan, a name he often employed even after the hoax had been recognized for what it was.

After some publications that were part of his Spectric joke, Bynner's next publication was a volume titled *Grenstone Poems*. In the year of this book's publication, Bynner and Ficke visited Asia, and Bynner's subsequent enthusiasm for Chinese culture became a shaping force on the rest of his life. In 1918, he met Kiang Kang-hu, a Chinese scholar, and the two eventually agreed to collaborate on the English translation of some Chinese poetry. This translation project was to be the most ambitious literary effort of Bynner's career. Drawing upon Kiang Kang-hu's expertise in Chinese language and literature, Bynner applied his own fluency of phrasing and felicity of diction to the Chinese texts. The complete translation of the three hundred poems would appear as *The Jade Mountain* in 1929.

In 1922, Bynner moved to Santa Fe, New Mexico, where he was visited by D. H. Lawrence and his wife Frieda. He journeyed with them on an expedition to Mexico described decades later in *Journey with Genius*. He continued writing poetry and plays and, in 1929, published the essay "The Persistence of Poetry." Living in Santa Fe, still a small and rather sleepy community with a significant population of artists, Bynner combined his literary endeavors with his concerns for issues which were not to become fashionable until after his death (racial justice and environmentalism). He spent most of the rest of his life in Santa Fe, with frequent visits to Mexico, where he bought a house in Jalisco in 1940. In 1926, Bynner had met Robert Hunt, who moved to Santa Fe in 1930, becoming Bynner's assistant and companion for more than thirty years.

Bynner continued to write and publish poetry throughout the 1930's. In 1937, he received a substantial inheritance upon the death of his mother. In 1943, working without the assistance of his old friend Kiang Kang-hu, Bynner began a "translation"—actually a version based upon other translations—of a work he was to publish in 1944 as *The Way of Life According to Laotzu*. Another volume of poetry, *Take Away the Darkness*, appeared in 1947. In 1950, Bynner and Hunt spent several months in North Africa and Europe. In 1952, the two men again visited Europe, returning to New Mexico in the late autumn.

Despite his age, Bynner was still composing poetry, although at a diminished pace. By the mid-1950's, Bynner's health had begun to deteriorate seriously, and he had become nearly blind. Hunt, who was considerably younger, assumed responsibility for his care. Yet Bynner produced another volume of poetry, *New Poems*, in 1960 as he approached the age of eighty. It was the last collection published while he was alive. In 1962, Bynner was elected to the National Institute of Arts and Letters. Less than two years later, his companion and caretaker Robert Hunt died of a sudden heart attack. Bynner himself suffered a major stroke early in the next year. He remained under constant medical care in Santa Fe until his death on June 1, 1968.

ANALYSIS

Witter Bynner's poetry has not enjoyed popularity in the years since his death, probably because he wrote mainly for himself and was consequently his own best audience. This fact sets him apart from the more famous poets of the twentieth century, and any assessment of his work as a whole must take it into consideration. Readers tend to find him facile to the point of glibness, and his wit sometimes seems misplaced. It is also easy, perhaps excessively so, to dismiss his quasi-mystical philosophical convictions. Yet when the poetry of the first half of the twentieth century is assessed generally, Bynner emerges as an honest if garrulous voice and a poet whose response to the modernist predicament is quite possibly as creditable as anyone else's.

"AN ODE TO HARVARD"

Bynner's first significant published poem was "An Ode to Harvard." In this poem, written at the beginning of his long career, Bynner assumes an imposing poetic voice which speaks in hieratic tones that implicitly warn against the analysis of vision. The incantatory rhymes reinforce the Wordsworthian tone, and the whole passage resounds with an honest sincerity rarely, if ever, paralleled in Bynner's subsequent poetry. Yet the very uniqueness of this poem requires the reader of Bynner to examine it carefully. When Bynner sent William Butler Yeats a copy of his poem, the great Irish poet responded, "you have the control of a powerful, eloquent, vehement language and thought that rushes on impetuous to its sentient end." It is not clear what Yeats meant by "to its sentient end," but Bynner evidently soon changed his mind about continuing to write in this fashion, and he adopted

the witty, facile, sometimes even gossipy style that pervaded his work for the next half-century. However, the assertion in this passage of the oneness of life, the shared destiny of living things, remains one of Bynner's essential poetic premises throughout his long life.

POETIC FORMS AND THE UNITY OF LIFE

In "The Dead Loon" (1917), Bynner reflects upon the random killing of a wild bird by "a clever fool," an event which brings him a nightmarish vision of his own death. He concludes, "That dead loon is farther on the way than we are," but states it "is with me now and with the evening star."

As in the Harvard ode, Bynner concludes with a vision of the unity of life, here illuminated by "the evening star," Venus, the divine power of love. The poetry of Bynner increasingly foregrounds wit and the picturesque, and the playful and the clever become dominant concerns, perhaps too often, but it is only fair to point out that Bynner remains a poet of compassion who is concerned with justice in all things, except perhaps when it comes to other literary people. His poetry ranges in form from free verse to formal, structured patterns; his primary characteristic is finesse. In another poem from *Grenstone Poems*, this finesse is evident in the characteristic lines

> She has a thousand presences,
>   As surely seen and heard
> As birds that hide behind a leaf
>   Or leaves that hide a bird.

This musical quatrain makes no pretense of profundity, but its pleasing structure is momentarily enigmatic, and the birds and leaves of the final two lines form a chiasmus, which is one of Bynner's favorite poetic devices. Such a chiasmus ends his poem "D. H. Lawrence," which concludes, "Whether you are a man wishing to be an animal/ Or an animal wishing to be a man." Here the structure emphasizes the paradoxicality of life and the relativity of perspective, and surely it suggests the importance for Bynner of synthesizing colloquial language, poetic form, and the most natural modes of human thought.

"EPITHALAMIUM AND ELEGY"

One of the most direct personal statements in Bynner's poetry is made in his "Epithalamium and Elegy" (1926), which begins, "My single constancy is love of life." In this poem he celebrates life and declares that he will be content to depart from it in time. Bynner found this theme in Chinese poetry as well, as may be seen in in a passage he translated from Laotzu nearly twenty years later: "It is said, 'there's a way where there's a will';/ But let life ripen and then fall./ Will is not the way at all:/ Deny the way of life and you are dead."

The poet's passion for life is often suggested by his meditations upon death, which he frequently describes in terms of physical disintegration. In "Epithalamium and Elegy," he had asked, "Can I be tragical, in having had/ My love of life by life herself subdued?" Yet the prospect of disintegration was implicit even in the closing lines of the Harvard ode, and Bynner faces it directly in such poems as "Idols" (1929) and "Correspondent" (1935), which begins "Words, words and words! What else, when men are dead,/ Their small lives ended and their sayings said,/ Is left of them'?"

Bynner ultimately decides to defy ordinary disintegration, commanding in "Testament" (1947) that his body be burned. The lines suggest a passion for remaining whole, while later Bynner acknowledges the impossibility of doing so.

OTHER MAJOR WORKS

PLAYS: *Tiger*, pb. 1913; *The Little King*, pb. 1914; *Snickerty Nick*, pb. 1919 (with Julia Elsworth Ford); *Cake*, pb. 1926.

NONFICTION: *The Persistence of Poetry*, 1929; *Journey with Genius: Recollections and Reflections Concerning the D. H. Lawrences*, 1951.

TRANSLATIONS: *Iphigenia in Tauris*, 1915, revised 1956 (of Euripides); *A Book of Love* (of Charles Vildrac), 1923; *The Jade Mountain: A Chinese Anthology*, 1929, revised 1939 (with Kiang Kang-hu); *The Way of Life According to Laotzu: An American Version*, 1944.

EDITED TEXT: *The Sonnets of Frederick Goddard*, 1931.

BIBLIOGRAPHY

Kraft, James. *Who Is Witter Bynner? A Biography*. Albuquerque: University of New Mexico Press, 1995. A treatment of Bynner's colorful life supplemented by selections from his poems and letters, along with a number of photographs.

_____, ed. *The Selected Witter Bynner: Poems, Plays, Translations, Prose, and Letters*. Albuquerque: University of New Mexico Press, 1995. A characteristic selection of Bynner's writings, introduced by the editor and including a chronology, a bibliography, and a useful index.

_____. *The Works of Witter Bynner: Selected Poems, Light Verse and Satires, The Chinese Translations, Prose Pieces, Selected Letters*. New York: Farrar, Straus, Giroux, 1978. The main source of primary materials and an essential work for Bynner studies.

Lindsay, Robert O. *Witter Bynner: A Bibliography*. Albuquerque: University of New Mexico Press, 1967. This detailed descriptive bibliography of Bynner's publications is valuable, although the list of secondary sources is out of date.

Wilbur, Richard. "The Poetry of Witter Bynner." *The American Poetry Review* 6, no. 6 (November/December, 1977): 3-8. A perceptive commentary on some specific poems and Bynner's poetry in general, written by a distinguished poet.

Robert W. Haynes

GEORGE GORDON, LORD BYRON

Born: London, England; January 22, 1788
Died: Missolonghi, Greece; April 19, 1824

PRINCIPAL POETRY

Fugitive Pieces, 1806
Poems on Various Occasions, 1807
Hours of Idleness, 1807
Poems Original and Translated, 1808
English Bards and Scotch Reviewers, 1809
Hints from Horace, 1811
Childe Harold's Pilgrimage, Cantos I-IV, 1812-1818, 1819 (the four cantos published together)
The Curse of Minerva, 1812
Waltz: An Apostrophic Hymn, 1813

The Giaour, 1813

The Bride of Abydos, 1813

The Corsair, 1814

Ode to Napoleon Buonaparte, 1814

Lara, 1814

Hebrew Melodies Ancient and Modern, 1815

The Siege of Corinth, 1816

Parisina, 1816

Poems, 1816

The Prisoner of Chillon, and Other Poems, 1816

Monody on the Death of the Right Honourable R. B. Sheridan, 1816

The Lament of Tasso, 1817

Manfred, 1817 (verse drama)

Beppo: A Venetian Story, 1818

Mazeppa, 1819

Don Juan, Cantos I-XVI, 1819-1824, 1826 (the sixteen cantos published together)

Marino Faliero, Doge of Venice, 1821 (verse drama)

The Prophecy of Dante, 1821

Sardanapalus, 1821 (verse drama)

The Two Foscari, 1821 (verse drama)

Cain: A Mystery, 1821 (verse drama)

The Vision of Judgment, 1822

Heaven and Earth, 1822 (verse drama)

The Age of Bronze, 1823

The Island, 1823

Werner: Or, The Inheritance, 1823 (verse drama)

The Deformed Transformed, 1824 (unfinished verse drama)

The Complete Poetical Works of Byron, 1980-1986 (5 volumes)

Other literary forms

It should be noted that the titles of George Gordon, Lord Byron's principal poetic works include dramatic as well as lyrical and narrative works. Lord Byron wrote eight plays in all, most of which focused on either speculative or historical subjects and were never intended for the stage. He designated them "mental theatre," or closet drama modeled after classical principles, and clearly regarded the plays as among his most important productions. Complementing Byron's extraordinarily prolific and diverse career as a poet is his versatility as a writer of epistolary prose. During his lifetime Byron composed more than twenty-nine hundred letters, which have been scrupulously edited by Leslie A. Marchand and published between 1973 and 1982 in twelve volumes under the title *Byron's Letters and Journals*. The sheer immensity of this correspondence is matched only by the unlimited range and immediacy of Byron's voice as he speaks without reserve on a variety of topics. In addition to these private documents, along with John Keats's letters the most revealing correspondence of the British Romantic poets, Byron also published the combative *Letter to [John Murray] on the Rev. W. L. Bowles' Strictures on the Life and Writings of Pope* (1821) and, in the first number of Leigh Hunt's *The Liberal* (1822), "A Letter to the Editor of 'My Grandmother's Review.'" *The Parliamentary Speeches of Lord Byron*, comprising three addresses he made while a member of the House of Lords, was issued in 1824, well after he had grown disillusioned with what he called "Parliamentary mummeries."

Achievements

If poets can be judged by the intellectual and cultural myths which they inspire, then George Gordon, Lord Byron, must be deemed the most broadly influential of the Romantic writers. Through his creation of a brooding and defiant persona known as the "Byronic Hero"—according to Peter L. Thorslev, Jr., a composite blend of the attributes of Cain, Ahasuerus, Satan, Prometheus, Rousseau's Child of Nature, the Man of Feeling, the Gloomy Egoist, the Gothic Villain, and the Noble Outlaw—Byron exerted a profound impact on the entire nineteenth century and its conception of the archetypal Romantic sensibility. The essential trait that came to be associated with "Byronism" is what Bertrand Russell, in his *History of Western Philosophy* (1945), identifies as "Titanic cosmic self-assertion." Signifying less a specific stance than a generalized attitude, the phrase denotes a proud, often despairing, rebellion against any institutional or moral system that threatens to rob the self of its autonomy, centrality, and independence. Something of the extent to which this outlook captured the imagination of the age can be gauged from a brief list of artists and thinkers whose works reflect Byron's influence: in Germany, Johann Wolfgang von Goethe, Heinrich Heine, Ludwig van Beethoven, and Friedrich Nietz-

George Gordon, Lord Byron (Library of Congress)

believing his own fictions and always examines his experience with obsessive honesty. In conversations with his friend and confidante Lady Blessington, Byron thus confessed to being "so changeable . . . such a strange *mèlange* of good and evil, that it would be difficult to describe me," but he goes on to say: "There are but two sentiments to which I am constant—a strong love of liberty, and a detestation of cant." These last qualities undoubtedly explain why the vein of satire was so congenial to him as a poet. In both the barbed heroic couplets of *English Bards and Scotch Reviewers*, the scathing burlesque that launched his career, and the seriocomic use of ottava rima in *Don Juan*, the epic satire which he never lived to complete, Byron sought to expose the smug complacencies and absurd pretensions of his time and, if possible, to restore to it the ability to see itself objectively. The dark *Weltschmerz* of poems such as *Childe Harold's Pilgrimage* may attest his personal despair over whether that goal could ever be accomplished, but in all his variegated moods he writes with energetic conviction born of "sincerity and strength." Byron's seminal achievement, therefore, may be his capacity for embodying the strivings of a deeply restless age, for articulating those longings and doing what all great poets do—namely, to return the imagination to the world.

BIOGRAPHY

George Gordon, the sixth Lord Byron, was born with a clubbed right foot, a deformity that caused him considerable suffering throughout his life and did much to shape his later character. He was descended from two aristocratic and colorful families: His father, who died when Byron was three years old, was Captain John ("Mad Jack") Byron, a rake and fortune hunter who traced his ancestry back to the time of William the Conqueror; his mother, Catherine Gordon of Gight, was the irascible and outspoken heiress who liked to boast of her lineal connection to James I of Scotland. After her husband squandered the Gordon inheritance, Mrs. Byron moved to Aberdeen, where she reared her son under straitened financial circumstances and the Calvinistic creed of Scottish Presbyterianism. With the death of his great-uncle in 1798, the ten-year-old Byron became a titled English peer and took up residence at the patrimonial estate of Newstead Abbey in Nottingham. During

sche; in France, Honoré de Balzac, Stendhal, Hector Berlioz, and Eugène Delacroix; in Russia, Aleksandr Pushkin and Fyodor Dostoevski; and in America, Herman Melville. Even Matthew Arnold, that most Wordsworthian of Victorian critics, admitted in his 1850 poem "Memorial Verses" that the collective English soul "Had *felt* him like the thunder's roll." Thirty-one years later, Arnold's view had not changed: "The power of Byron's personality," he wrote, approvingly quoting A. C. Swinburne, "lies in . . . '*the excellence of sincerity and strength.*'"

What fascinated nineteenth century audiences about Byron was not simply the larger-than-life character of the man transmuted into art but also the flinty integrity of his mind that penetrated all deception and constantly tested the limits of skepticism. In this respect Byron seems peculiarly modern. Although often considered a Romantic paradox because of various antitheses in his nature (he led the Romantic revolution toward "expression" in poetry, for example, but was thoroughly Augustan in his literary ideals and a lifelong admirer of Alexander Pope), he rarely succumbs to the temptation of this period the precocious young lord fell in love with two cousins named Mary Duff and Margaret Parker, was initiated into premature sexual dalliance by a nurse, and began his zealous regimen of swimming, boxing, fencing, and horsemanship to compensate for his physical lameness.

While at Harrow (1801-1805) and subsequently at Cambridge (1805-1807), Byron started to develop some of the strong attachments and habits that remained with him into adulthood. Though he little relished formal schooling, he periodically immersed himself in reading, became infatuated with Mary Chaworth, and cultivated lasting friendships with his half sister Augusta Leigh as well as with John Cam Hobhouse, Scrope Davies, Francis Hodgson, and others. He also incurred sizable debts for his extravagant revelries at Newstead during college vacations, and, simultaneously, he was entering the arena of literary authorship. His first few volumes of juvenilia, *Fugitive Pieces* and *Poems on Various Occasions*, were privately printed and circulated; *Hours of Idleness*, however, his ensuing venture into the public domain, prompted caustic notice by Henry Brougham, which in turn fueled the retaliatory satire of *English Bards and Scotch Reviewers*. Shortly thereafter, tiring of his life of routine dissipation, Byron prepared to leave England.

The next seven years were momentous ones in Byron's life. Before committing himself to what he thought might eventually be a Parliamentary career, he determined to broaden his education by visiting other lands and peoples. Accordingly, in 1809 he embarked with Hobhouse on an exhilarating tour through Portugal, Spain, Malta, Albania, Greece, and Asia Minor. The vivid scenes and experiences of this two-year excursion provided Byron with the materials for Cantos I-II of his autobiographical travelogue *Childe Harold's Pilgrimage* and his several Eastern tales in verse. Eight months after his return to England in 1811, *Childe Harold's Pilgrimage* was published and Byron became an overnight celebrity: "I awoke one morning," wrote the nobleman-poet, "and found myself famous." Because Byron was readily identified with the melancholic, jaded, and quasi-erotic hero of his poem, he was besieged by ladies of fashion and lionized by the beau monde of Regency London. Foremost among those giddily vying for the attentions of the handsome and aristocratic young author

was Lady Caroline Lamb, a flamboyant, decidedly eccentric woman who to her delight discovered Byron to be "mad—bad—and dangerous to know." Perhaps as much to escape such frenzied pursuit as for any other reason, Byron in early 1815 married Annabella Milbanke, a demure and somewhat priggish "bluestocking" whom Byron dubbed "my Princess of Parallelograms." The ill-fated marriage dissolved a year later, after the birth of a daughter Augusta Ada, when Lady Byron learned of her husband's incestuous relations with his half sister. Socially ostracized by all but his close friends and beset by creditors, Byron left England on April 25, 1816, never to return.

The legendary final phase of Byron's career, which saw his full maturation as a poet, was crowded with events that ensured his lasting renown. Journeying through France to Switzerland, he spent his first summer in exile near Geneva, where he met two other expatriates, Percy Bysshe Shelley and Mary Shelley, with whom he enjoyed many evenings of intellectual conversation. While there, Byron also completed Canto III of *Childe Harold's Pilgrimage*, began *Manfred*, and tried unsuccessfully to stay uninvolved with Mary Shelley's persistent stepsister Claire Clairmont, who, in January, 1817, bore him a daughter, Allegra. By the spring of that year Byron had established himself in Venice, "the greenest isle" of his imagination, where he diverted himself with numerous affairs while periodically exploring the antiquities of Florence and Rome.

The atmosphere of Italy did much to stimulate his literary creativity in new directions. By the end of 1817 he finished *Childe Harold's Pilgrimage* IV, an elegiac canto signaling Byron's decisive break with the past, and, influenced by John Hookham Frere's *Whistlecraft* (1817), a mock-heroic satirical poem in the flexible form of ottava rima, he completed the experimental *Beppo*, which looks forward to the narrative style of *Don Juan*. The period from 1818 to 1822 brought additional changes. Wearying of his promiscuous debaucheries on the Grand Canal in Venice, Byron met the Countess Teresa Guiccioli of Ravenna, then nineteen years old, and soon became her devoted *cavalier servente*. This attachment, in turn, drew him into the revolutionary Carbonari struggle against Austrian rule in Northern Italy, an interest reflected in his political dramas (*Marino*

Faliero, The Two Foscari, and *Sardanapalus*). With the defeat of the Carbonari movement in 1821, Byron followed the Gambas, Teresa's family, to Pisa, where he again joined the Shelley circle, which now included Edward John Trelawny and Thomas Medwin, and composed his devastating satire *The Vision of Judgment.* News of Shelley's drowning in July, 1822, however, stunned and sobered Byron. Shortly thereafter, he left for Genoa with Countess Guiccioli, but found his thoughts increasingly preoccupied with the Greek War of Independence. The final chapter of his life, always dominated by the trait that Lady Blessington called "mobility," forms a fitting memorial to Byron's restless spirit. Elected a member of the London Greek Committee, a Philhellene organization, the poet felt obligated to translate his political convictions into action. Despite skepticism concerning various Greek leaders' loyalty to the cause and despite a presentiment of his own imminent death, Byron set forth to do what he could. Sailing for Missolonghi in late December, 1823, he devoted his personal fortune and energy to forming a united front against the Turks. Four months later he died of a fever; to this day he is hailed as a national hero by the Greek people.

ANALYSIS

The history of Lord Byron's poetic development intersects at every stage with the saga of his life; yet it is only one of many paradoxes that he valued the writing of poetry primarily for the opportunity it afforded him to escape what he termed "my own wretched identity." More than anything else, poetry for Byron was a means both of sublimation and, ultimately, of self-realization. In his letters he thus suggests the former function when he speaks of poetry as "the lava of the imagination whose eruption prevents an earthquake," the volcanic metaphor signifying the cathartic release that the process of writing afforded him. The precise way in which it fulfilled the second function, however, is less obvious. Through the dynamics of self-projection, of investing much of his own multifaceted character in his personae, Byron strives to transcend the narrow limits of "personality" and achieve a more comprehensive perspective on himself and his experience. The essential goal of this artistic quest, which constitutes a progressive ontology, is delineated in Canto III of *Childe Harold's Pilgrim-*

age: "'Tis to create, and in creating live/ A being more intense." To trace Byron's growth as a poet, therefore, is to witness him reaching beyond subjectivism and attempting to realize that intensity of being that comes about through the continuous act of self-creation.

HOURS OF IDLENESS

Any account of Byron's achievement must begin with the poems collected in *Hours of Idleness* and the early satires. In the preface to the 1807 miscellany, his highly self-conscious debut as a poet, the nineteen-year-old Byron calls attention to himself by posing as an unlikely author (one "accustomed, in my younger days, to rove a careless mountaineer on the Highlands of Scotland"), by minimizing the merits of his literary endeavor ("to divert the dull moments of indisposition, or the monotony of a vacant hour, urged me 'to his sin'"), and by passing preemptive judgment on his work ("little can be expected from so unpromising a muse"). Such ingenuous posturing is clearly meant to invite, under the guise of dismissing, public recognition and acclaim. Despite the transparency of the subterfuge, the poems comprising *Hours of Idleness* form a revealing self-portrait in which Byron, while paraphrasing past idioms in poetry and exploiting eighteenth century literary conventions, obliquely seeks to discover a mythologized pattern for his emerging sense of himself. The one theme sounded repeatedly is what Robert F. Gleckner designates "the ruins of paradise," or the fall from youthful innocence. As he explores the experience of spiritual loss and shattered illusions, Byron can be seen moving toward this latter belief that "the great object of life is Sensation—to feel that we exist—even though in pain."

Admittedly imitative in style, often to the point of mannerism, *Hours of Idleness* revolves around several episodes of separation and disenchantment that, for the speaker, spell the end of an idealized, prelapsarian past. The short poem "Remembrance," composed in 1806 but not published until 1832, epitomizes both the tone and outlook of the volume as a whole:

> My days of happiness are few:
> Chill'd by misfortune's wintry blast,
> My dawn of life is overcast,
> Love, Hope, and Joy, alike adieu!—
> Would I could add Remembrance too!

Although the lines verge on doggerel, the same mood of melancholic nostalgia informs such other generally more successful poems as "On Leaving Newstead Abbey," "The First Kiss of Love," "On a Distant View of the Village and School of Harrow on the Hill," and "Lachin y Gair." In all of these works Byron cannot disown the power of memory because, though denounced as a curse, it alone provides glimpses of what in "Childish Recollections" he refers to as "the progress of my youthful dream," the foundation for his concept of self. This tension gives rise in other lyrics to a plangent wish to escape the "dark'ning shades" of maturity, regaining the uncompromised or "freeborn soul." Knowing the fatuity of the desire, however, the poet resorts at last to a kind of protective cynicism. In "To Romance," for example, abandoning what he derides as the "motley court" of "Affectation" and "sickly Sensibility," he admits that "'tis hard to quit the dreams,/ Which haunt the unsuspicious soul" but abjures the past as illusory and refuses any longer to be the dupe of his romantic fancy. Embittered by his early discovery, as Byron was later to write in *Childe Harold's Pilgrimage* III, that "life's enchanted cup but sparkles near the brim," the poet in *Hours of Idleness* fluctuates between moments of elegiac regret and tenacious hope, the ambivalent response itself prefiguring the skeptical idealist of the major poems to follow.

POETIC ACRIMONY

The Popean satires, which were composed shortly after the 1807 collection, disclose Byron's reaction to his disillusionment and punctured faith. In *English Bards and Scotch Reviewers*, *Hints from Horace*, and *The Curse of Minerva*—all written during the next four years—Byron lashes out at various individuals whom he regarded as typifying the literary and moral shortcomings of his age. The motto of "these degenerate days," he announces in *English Bards and Scotch Reviewers*, is "Care not for feeling," and so in arraigning nearly all his contemporaries except Samuel Rogers and Thomas Campbell he poses as the hardened realist determined to expose error on every hand: "But now, so callous grown, so changed since youth,/ I've learned to think, and sternly speak the truth." In the diatribe Byron often vents his anger indiscriminately, but the acrimony of his attack stems from a keen sense of embarrassment

and outrage at the reception accorded *Hours of Idleness* by such critics as Henry Brougham in the *Edinburgh Review*. Thus, before indicating all those "afflicted," as his preface charges, "with the present prevalent and distressing *rabies* for rhyming," Byron debunks himself as well:

> I, too, can scrawl, and once upon a time
> I poured along the town a flood of rhyme,
> A school-boy freak, unworthy praise or blame;
> I printed—older children do the same.
> 'Tis pleasant, sure, to see one's name in print;
> A Book's a Book, altho' there's nothing in't.

The same irreverent or iconoclastic spirit pervades *Hints from Horace*, a mocking jab at contemporary literary practice from the vantage point of Horace's *Ars Poetica* (13-8 B.C.E., *The Art of Poetry*), and *The Curse of Minerva*, a Swiftian condemnation of Lord Elgin for his despoiling Greek sculpture. In these strident satires Byron alters his earlier poetic stance through two mechanisms: by adopting the voice of savage indignation and by spurning the accepted standards of his age. The detachment that he tries to win through both devices is another step toward his large aesthetic goal of self-realization.

INTERTWINED MODALITIES

A crucial phase in that ongoing process involves the composition, spanning the period from 1809 to 1817, of *Childe Harold's Pilgrimage* and, to a lesser extent, of the exotic Oriental tales that include *The Giaour*, *The Bride of Abydos*, *The Corsair*, and *Lara*. These verse narratives are significant because in them two sides of Byron's complexity as an artist are counterbalanced— the usually antithetical modes that Keats, in his letters, conceptualizes as the "egotistical sublime" and "the camelion [sic] Poet." Though Keats associated the first quality with William Wordsworth, the element of the "egotistical sublime" in Byron reveals itself in the highly developed reflexivity of his semiautobiographical poems and in his tendency to concentrate on his own immediate thoughts and emotions. At the same time, however, there emerges an equal but opposite impulse that reflects Byron's essentially centrifugal rather than centripetal habit of mind. This is his characteristic propensity for employing a gamut of masks or personae through which he endeavors to escape the restrictive confines of self-consciousness, especially as molded by memory, and to achieve the intensity of being that comes with self-transcendence. Together, these intertwined modalities, the "egotistical" and the "chameleonic," make up the unique "strength" of Byron's imagination.

Readers of the time were nevertheless inclined to recognize only the former tendency in his works and so to find him guilty of facile exhibitionism. Certainly when Byronism was rampant no one impersonated Byron better than Byron himself; yet, if one allows for this susceptibility, the earnestness with which the poet responded to his detractors is instructive. Echoing the well-known protest lodged in his 1820 "Reply to Blackwood's *Edinburgh Magazine*," he expostulated a year later to Thomas Moore that "a man's poetry is a distinct faculty, or soul, and has no more to do with the everyday individual than the Inspiration with the Pythoness when removed from her tripod." Similarly, in the privacy of his journal for 1813, while writing the very poems that incurred the charge, he remarks: "To withdraw *myself* from *myself* (oh that cursed selfishness!) has ever been my sole, my entire, my sincere motive in scribbling at all; and publishing is also the continuance of the same object, by the action it affords to the mind, which else recoils upon itself." The vehemence of these statements should not be allowed to obscure Byron's clear point regarding the psychology of composition. The vicarious world of poetry, as he views it, makes possible a release from the concentricity of the mind that otherwise, to borrow two of his favorite images in *Childe Harold's Pilgrimage*, would sting itself to death like the scorpion ringed by fire or consume its scabbard like a rusting sword.

Childe Harold's Pilgrimage

Byron first expands upon this aesthetic in *Childe Harold's Pilgrimage* III-IV, but some attention to the earlier cantos is prerequisite to understanding the later two. When he began the travelogue in 1809 while touring Europe and the Levant, Byron conceived of a work in Spenserian stanza form which would depict, in the eighteenth century tradition of topographical or "locodescriptive" poetry, his vivid impressions of the scenes and peoples he visited, intermixed with meditative reflections. "For the sake of giving some connection to the piece," which otherwise, according to the preface, "makes no pretension to regularity," Byron introduces the "fictitious character" of Harold, who serves as the nominal hero-protagonist, although this syntactical function is about all that can be claimed for him. Out of "the fulness [sic] of satiety," it is true, Harold "resolve[s]" to leave England behind, having run through "Sin's long labyrinth"; yet in his wandering pilgrimage through Spain, Portugal, Albania, and Greece he remains a curiously static, one-dimensional figure and is little more than a partial projection of Byron's darker moods (for example, misanthropy, remorse, cynicism, and forced stoicism). As such, he adumbrates the explicit theme of Cantos I-II: that is, "Consciousness awaking to her woes." Neither Harold nor Byron, however, has yet learned "what he might be, or he ought," and it is somehow fitting that Canto II should close in a Greece stripped of its ancient grandeur and heroes.

Throughout this half of the poem, Byron's protagonist bears a marked resemblance to the poet himself, but it is well not to overlook the punning assertion made in the 1812 preface that Harold is "the child of imagination." Shortly before the publication of Cantos I-II, in a letter to Robert Charles Dallas, Byron reinforces the distinction between himself and his central character: "If in parts I may be thought to have drawn from myself, believe me it is but in parts, and I shall not own even to that . . . I would not be such a fellow as I have made my hero for all the world." The disclaimer has not won wide acceptance, largely because in the holograph copy of the poem Byron initially christened his protagonist "Childe Burun"; yet the first two cantos themselves substantiate the dissociation which Byron's comment to Dallas emphasizes. On the one hand, they dramatize the alienated figure of Harold, who, like the tortured hero of *Lara*, is portrayed as "a stranger in this breathing world,/ An erring spirit from another hurled;/ A thing of dark imaginings"; on the other hand, they are mediated by a separate narrator who, distanced from the foreground objectively recognizes that "the blight of life" that overtakes men like Harold is "the demon Thought," or the canker of self-consciousness. In actuality, *both* entities are Byron, and through the dichotomy he seeks to plumb his own contradictory nature.

By the time that Byron came to write Canto III, however, life had paradoxically imitated art: Exiled from England by public vilification for his alleged cruelty toward his wife, the poet became that which before he had only imaged. This turn of events contributed to a new coalescence or ironic similarity between the author and his persona. Byron still does not identify himself completely with his titular hero, but he is now able to assimilate Harold as an exponent of himself without capitulating to the kind of Haroldian angst that suffuses Cantos I-II. He seems to register this altered orientation in the following lines: "Yet am I changed; though still enough the same/ In strength to bear what time can not abate,/ And feed on bitter fruits without accusing Fate." Implicit in the passage, with its allusion to John Milton's *Paradise Lost* (1667), is an undertone of confidence that even despair can be transformed into a source of stimulation and proof of his endurance. Byron now is speaking *in propria persona*. No longer rhapsodizing as in Canto I "a youth,/ Who ne in virtue's ways did take delight," he is instead dealing with himself as a social and moral pariah—"the wandering outlaw of his own dark mind." The full assurance that he can avoid entrapment from within remains to be found, but the seeds of spiritual recovery are before him.

The groundwork is laid at the start of Canto III when, after the framing device of an apostrophe to his daughter, Byron declares his artistic manifesto for the work: "'Tis to create, and in creating live/ A being more intense, that we endow/ With form our fancy, gaining as we give/ The life we image, even as I do now." Reflecting Shelley's influence on Byron in 1816, the passage continues and reveals that the poet now views his quotidian identity as "Nothing," as a hollow fiction, while the project of art discloses to him an ideal "other" or truer self which he will appropriate through the act of creating. The poem itself, in short, becomes the vehicle for self-discovery. Thus, although Harold continues to be much the same character as he was in Cantos I-II, what has changed greatly is Byron's positioning of himself as artist vis-à-vis the poem. He no longer depends on his protagonist as a surrogate or alter ego; even though the disease of self-consciousness has not been expunged, his faith has been restored in the imagination's ability to locate new horizons of meaning in an otherwise entropic world.

Both the third and fourth cantos of *Childe Harold's Pilgrimage* contain clear evidence of his shift in outlook. The two major scenes visited in Canto III are Waterloo and the Swiss Alps, locales which by their historical associations stand symbolically opposed. In the former, Byron finds only the tragic vanity of life and the futility of worldly ambition; in the latter, he surveys the benign sublimity and undisturbed repose of nature. Initially, it would seem that he is elevating one sphere above the other, idealizing the serenity of "throned Eternity" in contrast to the agitation of "earth-born jars." He is, to some extent, but in a unique manner. Rather than treating these landscapes as discrete alternatives, Byron exploits them as provisional constructs for raising questions and defining some of his own misgivings about the human condition. Thus, if at Waterloo he rejects the "wretched interchange of wrong for wrong" within society, in the Alps he sees nothing "to loathe in nature, save to be/ A link reluctant in a fleshly chain."

In much the same way, he responds ambivalently to the fallen figureheads of each domain—Napoleon Bonaparte and Jean Jacques Rousseau—whom he envisions as variants of himself. Both the Napoleon who was "conqueror and captive of the earth" and the "inspired" Rousseau whose oracles "set the world in flame" were men of unbounded energy, yet each was responsible for the shambles of the French Revolution and each was subverted by "a fever at the core,/ Fatal to him who bears, to all who ever bore." Byron recognizes their failure as potentially his own as well: "And *there* hath been thy bane," he proclaims. The stanza's rhetoric reverberates with his affinity for these individuals and suggests that Byron, as Jerome J. McGann observes in *Fiery Dust* (1968), is coming to the realization that "to 'know oneself' one must submit to immediate and partial acts of perception." Within *Childe Harold's Pilgrimage* III, therefore, the poet moves further toward the understanding that to be human means to be a pilgrim, but a pilgrim ever in the process of redefining himself and the world that he inherits.

Canto IV continues the archetypal pattern of the journey, in this case one extending from Venice to Rome, but broadens at the end to reveal a significantly matured Byron arriving at the genuine goal or embodiment of his questing spirit. Centered around the elegiac motif or *sic transit gloria mundi*, the last canto weighs the respective claims of both art and nature to permanence as Byron tries to decipher the enigma of man's existence. "The moral of all human tales," he postulates, is the inevitability of ruin and unfulfilled hopes, such that "History, with all her volumes vast,/ Hath but *one* page." This stark lesson occasionally moves the poet to invective, as when he declares that "Our life is a false nature—'tis not in/ The harmony of things." Nevertheless, in the poetry of Torquato Tasso, the sculpture of Venice, and the Colosseum in Rome, he discerns a grandeur and genius which transcend the melancholy attrition of time. That discovery, in turn, rekindles conviction as to the vitality of his own essential self, a realization heightened when Byron finds that he has outgrown the fictive prop of Harold:

> But where is he, the Pilgrim of my song,
> The being who upheld it through the past?
>
> .   .   .   .
>
> He is no more—these breathings are his last;
> His wanderings done, his visions ebbing fast,
> And he himself as nothing. . . .

In the poem's concluding apostrophe to the sea near Albano, conceived as a "glorious mirror" and thalassic "image of Eternity," Byron achieves the true goal toward which he has been tending all along. Awesome in its untrammeled energy, the ocean becomes the symbol of the creating self that the poet has reclaimed. "My Pilgrim's shrine is won," writes Byron, for "I am not now/ That which I have been." With that declaration, Byron enters upon the last great phase of his poetic career.

DON JUAN

The monumental epic *Don Juan* forms the inspired climax to Byron's evolution as an artist, but to understand how this is so requires brief attention to a disturbing undercurrent in *Childe Harold's Pilgrimage*. Despite the general movement toward self-apprehension in that work, there yet occur moments when the inadequacy of language to articulate "all I seek,/ Bear, know, feel" subverts the poet's faith in his enterprise. Thus, although in Canto III he would willingly believe that "there may be/ Words which are things," he has not found them; nor is he able to disguise from himself the knowledge that language is part of the disintegrated syntax of a fallen world. Along the same lines, after pondering in Canto IV the disappointed ideals of such poets as Dante and Petrarch, he ruefully admits that "what we have of feeling most intense/ Outstrips our faint expression." The intransigence of language, its inherent circularity as an instrument of meditation, was for Byron tied to the kind of Metaphysical despair dramatized in *Manfred* and *Cain*, and by way of overcoming those quandaries he adopts in *Don Juan* a more radically versatile poetics.

The chief difference between *Childe Harold's Pilgrimage* and his later "epic of negation," as Brian Wilke describes *Don Juan* in *Romantic Poets and Epic Tradition* (1965), lies in Byron's refusal any longer to be controlled by "the stubborn heart." After opening with the farce of Juan's sexual initiation, before which he pauses to berate Plato as a charlatan, Byron makes his new outlook resoundingly clear:

> No more—no more—Oh! never more, my heart,
> Canst thou be my sole world, my universe!
>
> .   .   .   .
>
> The illusion's gone for ever, and thou art
> Insensible, I trust, but none the worse,
> And in thy stead I've got a good deal of judgment,
> Though heaven knows how it ever found a lodgement.

Cognizant of the fictiveness of all experience, he plans to make his rambling medley of a poem mirror the manifold delusions and deceptions that man allows to impose upon his right of thought. In the face of such knowledge "Imagination droops her pinion," turning "what was once romantic to burlesque"—lines aptly capturing the shift from his stance in *Childe Harold's Pilgrimage*. In composing his "versified Aurora Borealis," however, Byron obviously sensed a creative exhilaration linked to his complete separation of himself from his hero. His letters written during the work's early stages reveal an exuberant confidence in the undertaking which, as he told Thomas Moore, was "meant to be a little quitely facetious upon every thing." Thus, addressing his old friend Douglas Kinnaird in 1819, he expressed a typically high-spirited opinion of his achievement: "As to 'Don Juan'—confess—confess—you dog—and be candid—that it is the sublime of *that there* sort of writing—it may be bawdy . . . but it is not *life*, is it not *the thing*?—Could any man have written it—who has not lived in the world?"

Byron's governing purpose in *Don Juan* is to "show things really as they are,/ Not as they ought to be." Toward that end he does not forbear lampooning all the assorted follies and philistine pretenses of "that microcosm on stilts,/ Yclept the Great World," for he sees its attachment to illusion as the root cause of men's inability to recognize or accept the truth about themselves. Byron's attack is all the more effective because he exempts neither himself as poet nor the function of language from his skeptical scrutiny. Overturning all conventional notions of structure and voice in poetry, he is intent upon making his "nondescript and ever-varying rhyme" demystify itself at every turn. Both serious and cynical, he consequently avers that compared to the epic myths of Vergil and Homer "this story's actually true," then later reminds his audience that his work "is only fiction,/ And that I sing of neither mine nor me." Nearly every stanza of *Don Juan* unmasks itself in similar fashion through the whimsical freedom of Byron's style. Fearless of incongruities in a world permeated by fraud, the poem's narrator defends his fluid cynicism in the name of verisimilitude (his aim is to "show things existent") while simultaneously debunking traditional concepts of authorial integrity: "If people contradict themselves, can I/ Help contradicting them, and everybody,/ Even my veracious self?" True "sincerity" in these terms is equated with inconsistency, paradox, and radical doubt, an outlook anticipated as early as 1813 when Byron, with uncanny self-knowledge and prescience, remarked in his journal that "if I am sincere with myself (but I fear one lies more to one's self than to any one else), every page should confute, refute, and utterly abjure its predecessor." By constantly deflating the artifices on which his own poem is built, Byron seeks to generate a self-critical model for exposing the larger abuses of his society.

Don Juan is, as William Hazlitt was quick to note in *The Spirit of the Age* (1825), a "poem written about itself," but foremost among the vices it satirizes are the contemporary prevalence of cant and the moral blindness or hypocrisy which it fosters. Both traits are first encountered in the character of Donna Inez, Juan's mother, in Canto I. A prodigy of memory whose brain is filled with "serious sayings darken'd to sublimity," she is walking homily—"Morality's prim personification"—who sees to it that her son is taught from only the most carefully expurgated classics. Unable to find anything to censure or amend in her own conduct, Donna Inez nevertheless carries on a clandestine affair with Don Alfonso, the husband of her close friend Julia, and later writes in fulsome praise of Catherine the Great's "maternal" attentions to Juan. Such self-deceiving and myopic piety moves Byron to wish for "a *forty-parson power* to chant/ Thy praise, Hypocrisy," the vice that he regards as endemic to his age and culture at all levels.

On a larger scale, he dramatizes the disastrous consequences of cant and its ability to obscure human realities in the Siege of Ismail episode beginning in Canto VII. Here his target is in part the gazettes and their debased glorification of war, particularly as they promote "the lust of notoriety" within modern civilization. Spurred on by the hope of being immortalized in the newspapers or war dispatches, a polyglot collection of soldiers join with the Russians in devastating the Turkish fortress. Before recounting scene after scene of the mindless butchery, in which thirty thousand are slain on both sides, Byron reflects on whether "a man's name in a *bulletin*/ May make up for a *bullet in* his body." The final irony is that the gazettes, preoccupied with trivial gossip of the beau monde at home, generally garble the names of the dead and thoroughly distort the facts of the campaign. Determined to unriddle "Glory's dream," Byron shows that it is founded on nothing more than an abject appetite for fame and conquest. His greatest ire is reserved for someone such as the Russian leader Aleksandr Suwarrow, who, in a dispatch to Catherine after the slaughter, can glibly write, "'Glory to *God* and to the Empress!' (*Powers/ Eternal! such names mingled!*) 'Ismail's our's.'" The same purblind insensitivity, he charges, makes it possible for Wordsworth to speak of carnage as "'God's daughter.'" In all these instances, Byron shows how language is a ready instrument for the perversion of thought and action.

His own aesthetic in *Don Juan* thus bases itself on an unswerving respect for truth, "the grand desideratum" in a society glutted with cant and equivocation. Early in the poem he comments that his is "the age of oddities let loose," such that "You'd best begin with truth, and when you've lost your/ Labour, there's sure market for imposture." The lines also echo his mocking dedication of the work to Robert Southey, who succeeded Henry James Pye as poet laureate in 1813, and his arraignment there of the other so-called Lake Poets. Having disowned the radical politics of their youth, they are depicted as comprising a "nest of tuneful persons" who now warble sycophantic praise for the Tory regime of King George III. Their apostasy in Byron's eyes is all the more reprehensible because they have, in effect, become the hirelings of the "intellectual eunuch Castlereagh," a master of oratorical "trash of phrase/ Ineffably—legitimately vile." To counteract this mounting Tower of Babel in his age, Byron persistently explodes the enchantment of words and their tendency to falsify reality. There is, accordingly, an underlying method to his chameleonic *mobilité* and digressiveness in the poem, for he demonstrates that only by doubting the language-based constructs, which man imposes upon experience, can he, like the poet himself, avoid the pitfall of "universal egotism." Viewed in this light, the whole of *Don Juan* becomes an open-ended experiment in linguistic improvisation, a poem that demythologizes the very act by which it comes into being.

Because Byron's mock-epic attempts to encompass no less than "life's infinite variety," any synopsis of its innumerable subjects and themes is doomed to failure. From the opening line in which the narrator declaims "I want a hero" and then seems arbitrarily to settle on "our ancient friend Don Juan," it is evident that the ensuing comedy will follow few established conventions or patterns. This impression is reinforced later in Canto XIV, when Byron points out his technique in composing *Don Juan:* "I write what's uppermost, without delay." The stated casualness in approach, however, belies the artistic integrity of the satire. Jerome J. McGann, in *Don Juan in Context* (1976), convincingly shows that the poem is "both a critique and an apotheosis of High Romanticism," primarily because it implicitly denies that any imaginative system can be an end unto itself while also endeavoring to reinsert the poetic imagination back into the context of a fallen world. If there is one crux around which the entire mosaic turns, it is that of the fundamental opposition between nature and civilization. After Juan's idyllic love affair with Haidée, "Nature's bride," is destroyed by her jealous father in Canto IV, Byron suggests that the Fall is man's permanent condi-

tion; he conducts his hero into slavery at Constantinople in Canto V, into the bloodbath of the Siege of Ismail in Cantos VII-VIII, into the lustful tyranny of the Russian Empress in Cantos IX-X, and finally into the fashionable corruptions of English society in Cantos XI-XVII. Not all, however, is moral cannibalism. By the introduction of such unspoiled figures as Haidée at the start and Aurora Raby at the end, Byron ascribes a certain redemptive value to natural innocence that offsets, even if it does not quite counterbalance, the ruling vices of society. *Don Juan* thus immerses itself in all the unflattering details of "life's infinite variety," but always with the purpose of embodying the human realities with which the artist must deal. Byron distills the complexity of the matter in a few words: "I write the world."

LEGACY

Byron has often been criticized as a poet for his many supposed failures—for not projecting a coherent metaphysic, for not developing a consistent attitude to life, for not resisting the Siren call of egotism, for not paying sufficient attention to style, and for not, in short being more like Wordsworth, Samuel Taylor Coleridge, Keats, and Shelley. Because he did not adopt the vatic stance of his contemporaries or espouse their belief in organicism, he has been labeled the leading exemplar of Negative Romanticism. Common to such estimates, however, is a reluctance to recognize or concede Byron's uniqueness as a poet. Although he did not share with others of his time an exalted conception of the imagination as being equivalent, in Keats's metaphor, to "Adam's dream," he was able ultimately to do what the other four poets generally could not—namely, to accept the mixed quality of human experience. Through his ironic detachment and comic vision he permanently enlarged the domain of poetry and made it meaningful in a fresh way. This he accomplished through his skeptical idealism and his acceptance of his own paradoxes as a man and poet. "I am quicksilver," he wrote to a friend in 1810, "and say nothing positively." Therein lies perhaps the essence of his "sincerity" and "strength," traits that continue to make him an enduring cultural force.

OTHER MAJOR WORKS

NONFICTION: *Letter to [John Murray] on the Rev. W. L. Bowles' Strictures on the Life and Writings of*

Pope, 1821; "A Letter to the Editor of 'My Grandmother's Review,'" 1822; *The Blues: A Literary Eclogue*, 1823; *The Parliamentary Speeches of Lord Byron*, 1824; *Byron's Letters and Journals*, 1973-1982 (12 vols.; Leslie A. Marchand, editor).

BIBLIOGRAPHY

Blackstone, Bernard. *Byron: A Survey.* London: Longman, 1975. Blackstone is something of a maverick among scholars, and his approach to Byron is unusual. Blackstone possesses a strong awareness of the significance of Byron's places, and his readings are full of provocative insights into the deepest levels of significance in the poems. Sometimes, he makes Byron sound more like William Blake than Byron, but open-minded readers will find this book stimulating and rewarding.

Bloom, Harold, ed. *George Gordon: Lord Byron.* New York: Chelsea House, 1986. A collection of nine critical essays. Bloom's overview of Byron's major poems, G. Wilson Knight's seminal essay on the conflict in Byron between "history and tragic insight," Northrop Frye's emphasis on the interconnections of Byron's poetry and his life, and George M. Ridenour's essay on Byron's poems of 1816 are all suitable for beginning students. The other essays are more suitable for those with some prior knowledge of Byron's poetry and criticism.

Eisler, Benita. *Byron: Child of Passion, Fool of Fame.* New York: Alfred A. Knopf, 1999. A narrative biography that does justice to the love affairs that made Byron notorious while giving ample coverage of the reasons Byron is an influential and important poet. Includes bibliographic references.

Garrett, Martin. *George Gordon, Lord Byron.* New York: Oxford University Press, 2001. This brief, well-illustrated biography, designed for students in grades nine and above, is a good introduction to Byron. Replete with choice quotations and primary source references. Includes an index.

Graham, Peter W. *Don Juan and Regency England.* Charlottesville: University Press of Virginia, 1990. Six self-contained but interrelated essays that explore Byron's comic masterpiece in the context of various aspects of the culture of Regency England.

Graham argues that in *Don Juan*, Byron continually advocated a cosmopolitan point of view, satirizing traditional English insularity. Readers should have some familiarity with *Don Juan* before tackling this volume, but Graham writes jargon-free prose and each essay is highly illuminating.

McGann, Jerome J. *Fiery Dust: Byron's Poetic Development.* Chicago: University of Chicago Press, 1968. One of the most important modern studies of Byron. McGann examines the continuity of Byron's poetic development and the "phenomenon of Byronic self-expression": how Byron used the materials of his own life to create a Byronic personality in his work. The longest section is on *Childe Harold's Pilgrimage*, partly because it reveals so much about Byron's life and thoughts at that time. Also discusses *The Giaour, The Prisoner of Chillon and Other Poems, Cain*, and other tales and plays.

Manning, Peter J. *Byron and His Fictions.* Detroit: Wayne State University Press, 1978. Emphasis is on the psychological perspectives of Byron. Manning detects recurrent psychological themes in Byron's poetry, particularly an Oedipal conflict, and he uses this insight to shed light on recurring plot patterns and the experiences of Byron's heroes. Manning's approach is not as narrow as this might suggest. He skillfully integrates psychoanalytic concepts with other, more traditional approaches, and the result is a very rewarding and illuminating study.

Marchand, Leslie A. *Byron: A Portrait.* Chicago: University of Chicago Press, 1970. The best biography for the general reader. It is based on Marchand's definitive three-volume biography published in 1957, but includes research done in the 1960's. Marchand's portrait of Byron is balanced and free of bias. Includes fifty-six illustrations, genealogical tables, and two maps showing Byron's travels from 1809 to 1811, and Byron's Greece.

Rutherford, Andrew. *Byron: A Critical Study.* Edinburgh, Scotland: Oliver & Body, 1961. An excellent introduction to Byron's poetry, suitable for the general reader. More than half the book is devoted to the later satires, which Rutherford regards as Byron's best work. He places a low value on the earlier phase of Byron's work, including *Childe Harold's Pilgrimage* and the tales, a view which has been challenged by a number of later critics, including Jerome J. McGann.

Wilson, Frances. *Byromania: Portraits of the Artist in Nineteenth- and Twentieth-Century Culture.* New York: St. Martin's Press, 1999. This volume of eleven essays sheds light on the scandalous nature of Byron's fame, including his carefully wrought self-presentation, as well as the extraordinary popularity of his work and persona. The poet is viewed through multiple, if sometimes contradictory perspectives, the essays varying in tone from academic to humorous.

Robert Lance Snyder;
bibliography updated by the editors

C

CAEDMON

Born: Northumbria, England; early seventh century
Died: Whitby Abbey, Northumbria, England; c. 680

PRINCIPAL POETRY
"Hymn," c. 670

OTHER LITERARY FORMS

The "Hymn" is the only work that has been definitely attributed to Caedmon.

ACHIEVEMENTS

The history of Caedmon, the first voice in English poetry, is passed down through the cleric and historian Saint Bede the Venerable who, in his *Ecclesiastical History of the English People* (731), tells the story of the humble layman to whom the gift of poetry was given one night in a dream. Bede lists many works composed by Caedmon; the only piece that can be identified with any certainty, however, is the nine-line "Hymn" fragment in praise of God the Creator.

Brief though it is, this poem defines and directs the course of English poetry, combining for the first time the meters of Nordic heroic poetry with the subject matter of the Scriptures, Christianizing the literary tradition and speaking for a culture. That the "Hymn" was held in great esteem is evidenced by the fact that versions of it exist in seventeen manuscripts ranging from the early eighth to the later fifteenth century; Caedmon's "Hymn" is the only piece of early poetry to have been preserved in this manner. Caedmon is a figure of shadow and legend, with a single biographical source and no written records; his hymn is a rich and appropriate beginning for the English poetic tradition.

BIOGRAPHY

The single source for the life of Caedmon, Bede's *Ecclesiastical History of the English People*, was completed in 731. Written in Latin and later translated into Old English, Bede's history describes the Abbey of Whitby in Northumbria, founded by St. Hilda and ruled by her from 658 until 680. Twin communities, one for men and one for women, flourished under the direction of the Abbess. To this abbey came the layman Caedmon, not to test a religious vocation but to seek employment in caring for the monastery animals. Caedmon was not young when he came to Whitby, Bede comments, but no mention is made of his earlier life. Humble and unassuming, Caedmon had his quarters with the farm animals and lived almost unnoticed by the other monastery residents.

Because of his extreme shyness, the story continues, Caedmon was never able to take his turn at the recitation and singing when, as was the custom, the harp was passed around after the communal evening meal. In order to avoid embarrassment, Caedmon would always find some excuse to leave the gathering and tend the animals, knowing that he would not be able to sing and entertain the others should the harp be passed to him. Bede's account, it should be remarked, is an invaluable description of this culture; the secular (not religious) music, the gathering to drink beer together, the shared responsibility for entertainment—all these facets of early English life are clarified in the *Ecclesiastical History of the English People.*

One evening, having left the gathering, Caedmon was sleeping when he had a dream. "Someone" came to him and commanded, "Caedmon, sing me something." When Caedmon protested, the visitant repeated the direction, asking that Caedmon sing of "the beginning of created things." Still in his dream, Caedmon obeyed the vision, breaking into song of the "first-shaping." The vision vanished.

When he awakened, unsure of what had happened, Caedmon found that he was able to recall the entire song. Still led by divine urgings, he went to the Abbess, sang the "Hymn" for her, and explained the occurrence of the night before. St. Hilda, realizing that the powers of God were involved, encouraged Caedmon, exhorting him to devote his life to composing music for the glory and praise of God.

Thereafter Caedmon became a monk, spending his days composing music. His gift stayed with him always, although he never learned to read or write. Others in the monastery would read the Scripture aloud; Caedmon would then make a metrical paraphrase of what he had heard. Because the gift of inspiration was to serve God's glory, Bede explains, Caedmon was able to compose only religious verse. Bede lists many of Caedmon's compositions, all of them biblical; poems of similar subject matter appeared in a 1655 Junius Manuscript by François Dujon. Dujon believed that the four scriptural poems were originals from Caedmon; modern scholarship, however, rejects any such claim. It may be that other members of the monastery imitated Caedmon's gift, or, more likely, that later writers were moved to continue the tradition. The remarkable care taken to preserve the hymn suggests that it was widely regarded as the first piece of English alliterative poetry.

According to Bede, Caedmon died in the monastery at Whitby after receiving the Eucharist and falling into a peaceful slumber. Given his story, it would be surprising if Bede were to record any other sort of death, for he clearly intends to shape the Caedmon narrative to an argument for the religious inspiration of poetry.

ANALYSIS

Although Bede's *Ecclesiastical History of the English People* details the composition of Caedmon's "Hymn" it does not reproduce it, giving instead a prose paraphrase. Bede, himself a fine stylist, remarks quite accurately that his Latin prose cannot reproduce a vernacular hymn; poetry, he points out, does not translate well. In most of the early manuscripts of the *Ecclesiastical History of the English People*, however, the poem itself is included, often as a marginal gloss but occasionally in the body of the manuscript itself. There are seventeen of these manuscripts, both in Caedmon's own Northumbrian and in West Saxon, with the majority in the latter.

In his *Anglo-Saxon Poetry* (1980), Jeff Opland terms Bede's story of Caedmon "a source of unparalleled importance in any attempt to reconstruct the history of oral poetry in Anglo-Saxon times." The claim is not extravagant. Caedmon's fragment reaches back into the heroic tradition for meter and form, blends it with Christian myths for inspiration and story, and originates English poetry as it is now known. Histories of English literature rightly devote major sections to such great figures as Geoffrey Chaucer, William Shakespeare, and John Mil-

ton. Nearly eight hundred years before Chaucer burst into joyous couplets, Caedmon, the precursor, burst into praise.

"HYMN"

The nine lines of the "Hymn" are given here in a modern English translation:

Now let us herald	heaven-kingdom's guardian,
Maker of might	and his mind-thoughts,

The work of the wonder-
  Father
	When he of wonders, each
	  one

Eternal Lord	established in the beginning.
He first shaped	for the sons of men
Heaven as a roof	the holy Creator;
And then the middle-earth	for mankind, the Protector
Eternal Lord,	afterwards made
For men, this firmament,	Our Father almighty.

The "Hymn" is a kind of early English psalm; it sings the praises of God, invites the hearers to join in, details the specifics of creation, and moves to a realization that all life has been created not only for God's glory but also for the "sons of man," those who revere and love God. Although Caedmon had been instructed to sing of the "making of things," he chooses—or is inspired to choose—lyric rather than narrative, praise rather than instruction.

It is not surprising to the contemporary reader that Caedmon would sing a song in praise of God in response to a dream vision, but it is significant in the history of English poetry that formal Christianity had been introduced in England less than a century before. The Romans who had occupied the island had been Christians, but without formal practice of the religion, Christianity had nearly died out, preserved only in small pockets. Not until Pope Gregory sent St. Augustine to the island in 597 did a formal mission begin; by Caedmon's time, England had reverted to Christianity, and the great monastic tradition which was to stimulate learning was beginning to flower.

INSPIRATION

Critical debate flourishes over the nature of Caedmon's inspiration. Was he inspired to "remember" songs and rhythms he had already heard? Was he moved to sing a hymn whose words he may not even have understood? Was he simply an instrument for God's power? Was he indeed a deliberate composer? It is of course tempting to align Caedmon with both the biblical tradition of the unknowing prophet who speaks the words God puts in his mouth and the "seer" who sees and describes but does not always understand. Bede clearly identifies Caedmon as the one selected by God not only for divine glory but also to begin a tradition; because Bede was writing almost fifty years after Caedmon lived, he had an interesting perspective. Whatever one's theories of critical inspiration, the Caedmon "Hymn" holds irresistible appeal for the scholar who finds the Christian tradition and metrical artistry in such a rich blend.

GOD AS KING

Caedmon's words describe God as king and father, powerful and provident, clearly reflecting the concept of king as the one responsible for his people's welfare and who, in return for praise and veneration, will reward his subjects with care for their needs. The creation references suggest a sort of giant mead hall, with heaven as a roof; the sons of men are all enclosed, safe from enemies, and singing their gratitude. This same anthropomorphism runs throughout most early English poetry; God is like his people in the most literal sense. At the same time, there is a strong suggestion of transcendence or otherness. Twice God is described as eternal and the focus of the poem is clearly on the marvels and wonders of this incomprehensible but splendid "wonder-Father." The poem is charged with energy; there is something peculiarly English about the emphasis on God's actions, deeds: God establishes, shapes, makes—words suggesting concrete and deliberate actions. The deeds, however, are more than mere activities; they are "mind-thoughts," concepts put into reality by the creativity of God. The creative outburst of the poet hymns the creative energy of the first Shaper. The poet, both as an inspired mystic and as a worker dependent on the lord of the monastery for sustenance, shines through these lines.

This first voice in English poetry, therefore, is essentially religious in its themes. Like the voice in the psalms, the speaker views the array of creation and claims it "for the sons of men," echoing the Genesis story as well. It is not surprising that the scriptural stories which appear in early poetry are elemental tales of creation, providence, and power; they are also, however, dramatic narratives which eventually were incorporated into the saints' legends and traditions. Although Bede explains that all of Caedmon's poetry was religious and rooted in Scripture, the nine-line fragment which begins the tradition is an especially appropriate inauguration.

"HYMN" COMPOSITION

The Caedmon "Hymn" has far greater significance for the student of literature as the first example of the poetic form which would influence English poetry through the fifteenth century, recurring from time to time in later writers even into the twentieth. The four-stress, alliterative line, here less precise and sophisticated than in *Beowulf* and in much later works of writers such as William Langland and the Pearl-Poet, gives to English poetry a grace and strength which bring the ancient Nordic heroic literature into the developing English language.

Essentially, the poetry works in this way: Each line has four stresses, two on each side of the pause or caesura. Unstressed syllables are not significant and may occur in any quantity or, occasionally, not at all. Of the four stresses, two or more will alliterate with one another, the stress directly after the pause serving as the "rhyme-giver" or alliterative key. Vowels assonate with other vowels. The first four lines of Caedmon's hymn, then, move as follows, with stresses underlined:

Nu sculon herigan	heofonrices weard
Metodes meahte	and his modgepanc,
Weorc wuldorfaeder,	swa he wundra gehwaes,
Ece drihten,	or onstealde.

The pace is majestic, deliberate; the unstressed syllables, falling as they do in two's and three's, give an almost chantlike tone to the poetry. The alliteration serves the singer, who would be using a small harp like instrument for accompaniment, and unifies the poem, setting up expectations and satisfying them in more than one way. Although the poem does not formally play with rhyme, it does make use of several sound devices; some later verse in this tradition uses internal and occasionally external rhyme as well. The alliterative rhythms, however, give the poem its most definitive structure.

The poem also shows the first use of kennings, rich figures of speech which make tiny metaphors, usually hyphenated, for common terms. Here the kennings are relatively simple; later, in *Beowulf*, for example, they become more graphic. The more complex the notion, the more apt the kennings are: Heaven, for example, becomes "heaven-kingdom"; God is "wonder-Father"; earth becomes "middle-yard." God's creative word-become-act is "mind-thought," the most complex of the kennings.

BIBLIOGRAPHY

Fry, Donald K. "Caedmon as a Formulaic Poet." In *Oral Literature: Seven Essays*, edited by Joseph J. Duggan. New York: Barnes & Noble Books, 1975. Drawing on Bede's *Ecclesiastical History*, Fry presents Caedmon's "Hymn" as an oral composition and Caedmon as the founder of "Old English Christian vernacular poetry." Fry accomplishes this by examining the Latin and Old English versions of the "Hymn" to determine the genesis of diction.

_____. "The Memory of Caedmon." In *Oral Traditional Literature: A Festschrift for Albert Bates Lord*, edited by John Miles Foley. Columbus, Ohio: Slavica, 1981. Fry proposes that Caedmon's *Hymn* was written on a formulaic basis. He defines "formulaic" as the "typical traditionally expressed" and states that this type of poetry is easy to memorize and, therefore, is more easily disseminated to the nonliterate public.

Greenfield, Stanley B., and Daniel G. Calder. *A New Critical History of Old English Literature*. New York: New York University Press, 1986. Although only devoting thirteen pages of text to Caedmon, this book provides excellent insight into Caedmon's *Hymn* and problems that have confronted scholars for centuries. Useful for a broad overview of Old English literature.

Gurteen, Stephen Humphreys. *The Epic Fall of Man: A Comparative Study of Caedmon, Dante, and Milton*. 1896. Reprint. New York: Haskell House, 1964. Temecula, Calif.: Reprint Services Corporation, 1992. Gurteen is primarily concerned with a particular aspect of Christian poetic literature of England but has included in this study Dante's *Inferno* in contrast with the strong and weak points in Caedmon's and John Milton's treatments of the subject. Thirty-eight illustrations.

Hieatt, Constance B. "Caedmon in Context: Transforming the Formula." *Journal of English and Germanic Philology* 84 (October, 1985): 485-497. Supplies evidence that Caedmon's "Hymn" may draw not only from traditional pagan themes as background for its Christian base but also from inherited oral tradition, therefore echoing the established "type-scene."

Ireland, Colin. "An Irish Precursor of Caedmon." *Notes and Queries* 44, no. 1 (March, 1997): 2-4. Ireland discusses Colman mac Leneni and Caedmon and the traits they shared.

Kennedy, Charles W., trans. *The Caedmon Poems*. New York: E. P. Dutton, 1916. This older translation offers a host of supporting materials, including the translator's introduction, other major Anglo-Saxon poems, reproductions of the drawings of the Junius Manuscript, and a bibliography.

O'Keeffe, Katherine O'Brien. "Orality and the Developing Text of Caedmon's 'Hymn.'" *Speculum: A Journal of Medieval Studies* 62 (January, 1987): 1-20. Approaches Caedmon's "Hymn" from an oral and literate background and from the consequential reception as opposed to a more traditional study of the composition. Stresses the gradual shift from the oral tradition to the written one and analyzes the ramifications of this shift.

Zimmermann, Gunhild. *The Four Old English Poetic Manuscripts: Texts, Context, and Historical Background*. Heidelberg, Germany: C. Winter, 1995. In addition to the Caedmon manuscript, includes and comments upon the Exeter book the Vercelli book, the Nowell codex, and Old English poetry in general.

Katherine Hanley;
bibliography updated by the editors

PEDRO CALDERÓN DE LA BARCA

Born: Madrid, Spain; January 17, 1600
Died: Madrid, Spain; May 25, 1681

PRINCIPAL POETRY
Psalle et sile, 1741
Poesías, 1845
Obra lírica, 1943

Sus mejores poesías, 1954

Poesías líricas en las obras dramáticas de Calderón, 1964

Los sonetos de Calderón en sus obras dramáticas, 1974

OTHER LITERARY FORMS

Pedro Calderón de la Barca is known primarily as a verse dramatist, an occupation to which he was dedicated during his entire life. He wrote more than one hundred plays, most of which were published during his life or soon after his death. Some of the better known include *Amor, honor, y poder* (1623; love, honor, and power); *El sitio de Breda* (pr. 1625; the siege of Breda); *El príncipe constante* (wr. 1629; *The Constant Prince*, 1853); *La dama duende* (wr. 1629, pr., pb. 1936; *The Phantom Lady*, 1664); *Casa con dos puertas, mala es de guardar* (wr. 1629, pr., pb. 1936; *A House with Two Doors Is Difficult to Guard*, 1737); *La devoción de la cruz* (1634; *Devotion to the Cross*, 1832); *Los cabellos de Absalón* (wr. c. 1634, pb. 1684; the hair of Absalom); *La vida es sueño* (pr. 1635; *Life Is a Dream*, 1830); *El mayor encanto, amor* (pr. 1635; *Love, the Greatest Enchantment*, 1870); *A secreto agravio, secreta venganza* (pb. 1637; *Secret Vengeance for Secret Insult*, 1961); *El mágico prodigioso* (pr. 1637; *The Wonder-Working Magician*, 1959); *El alcalde de Zalamea* (pr. 1643; *The Mayor of Zalamea*, 1885); *El médico de su honra* (pb. 1637; *The Surgeon of His Honor*, 1853); *El pintor de su deshonra* (wr. 1640-1642. pb. 1650; *The Painter of His Dishonor*, 1853); *La hija del aire, Parte I* (pr. 1653; *The Daughter of the Air, Part I*, 1831); and *La hija del aire, Parte II*, pr. 1653 (*The Daughter of the Air, Part II*, 1831).

ACHIEVEMENTS

Pedro Calderón de la Barca lived during Spain's Golden Age, his death marking the end of that most productive period of Spanish letters. He was known as a poet and dramatist in his teens, and in his early twenties he took several poems to the poetic jousts held in 1620 and 1622 to commemorate the beatification and canonization of Saint Isidro. He was awarded a prize in the second contest, and Lope de Vega, who was the organizer of the two events, praised the young poet highly on

Pedro Calderón de la Barca (Hulton Archive)

both occasions. Indeed, throughout his life, Calderón continued to write lyric poetry, the great bulk of which, however, is incorporated into his plays. His first dated play, *Amor, honor, y poder* is from 1623, and subsequently he established himself so well in the theatrical scene that, when Lope de Vega died in 1635, Calderón became the official court dramatist, a position he held until his death. Calderón proved a worthy successor of Lope de Vega, for he wrote more than two hundred dramatic pieces, a total second only to that of Lope de Vega. Calderón produced several masterpieces, including *Life Is a Dream*, one of the great works of Spain's Golden Age. In addition, he was the supreme master of the *auto*, or Eucharist play, a dramatic form which he refined and improved progressively and to which he was dedicated almost exclusively during the last years of his life.

BIOGRAPHY

Pedro Calderón de la Barca was born in Madrid into a family of some nobility. His father, Diego Calderón de la Barca, came from the valley of Carriedo, in the mountains of Santander, and was a secretary to the treasury board under Philip II and Philip III. Calderón's mother, Ana María de Henao, was from a noble family of the Low Countries that had moved to Spain long before. Calderón was their third child.

Soon after Calderón was born, his family moved to Valladolid, following the transfer of the court, and there the boy learned his first letters. When the court returned permanently to Madrid, and with it his family, Calderón, then nine years old, was placed in the Colegio Imperial of the Jesuits, where he studied Latin and the humanities for five years.

Calderón's mother died in 1610, and his father married Juana Freyre four years later, only to die himself the following year. His death was followed by a bitter and costly lawsuit between Juana and the Calderón children, ending favorably for Juana. Calderón had entered the University of Alcalá de Henares in 1614, but, after his father's death, he transferred to the University of Salamanca to be under the supervision of his uncle. In Salamanca, he studied canon law and theology, planning to become a priest and take charge of a chaplaincy endowed by his maternal grandfather. Calderón abandoned his studies in 1620, however, and returned to Madrid, where for some time he led a turbulent life. He and his brothers, Diego and José, were engaged in a fight which resulted in the murder of Diego de Velasco. The father of Velasco demanded retribution, and the Calderón brothers settled the case by paying six hundred ducats (a substantial sum in those days).

While in Salamanca, Calderón had started writing poetry and drama; in Madrid, he entered the poetic competitions of 1620 and 1622, organized to celebrate the beatification and canonization of Saint Isidro. Calderón's entries won the praise of Lope de Vega, judge of the contests and editor of its proceedings. The works that Calderón presented to these jousts are of interest not only because they are his earliest extant poems but also because they are among his few surviving nondramatic poems.

The next few years took Calderón away from Spain. He enlisted in the Spanish army and went to Northern Italy and to Flanders, where he probably witnessed the defeat that the Spaniards inflicted on the Flemish, an event that he dramatized so well in *El sitio de Breda*. The poet returned to Madrid around 1625, and soon afterward he entered the service of Duke Frías. From that

time on, Calderón fully committed himself to the theater, constantly writing new plays and staging them with all the available machinery and scenery. According to Pérez de Montalbán, Calderón had written many dramas by 1632—all of which had been performed successfully—as well as a substantial body of lyric verse. Consequently, he was enjoying an enviable reputation as a poet.

About that time, the dramatist was involved in another unhappy event. Pedro de Villegas wounded one of Calderón's brothers very seriously, and in pursuit of Villegas, Calderón, accompanied by some police officers, violated the sanctity of the Trinitarians' convent. The entire court reacted negatively to this event, including Lope de Vega, who protested violently because his daughter Marcela was in the convent. Calderón was reprimanded for his actions, but nothing more, and he even made fun of the affair in *The Constant Prince*. His popularity was already larger than the gravity of his actions, and, therefore, he came out of it unscathed.

In 1635, the Retiro Gardens and Palaces were opened with great festivities, and Calderón's play, *El mayor encanto, amor*, was staged for the occasion. Lope de Vega died that same year, and Calderón became officially attached to the court, furnishing dramas for the exclusive entertainment of the Royal Palace. In recognition of his services, King Philip IV made Calderón a knight of the Order of Santiago in 1637. As such, he participated in the liberation of Fuenterrabía that same year, and with the army of Count Duke Olivares, he took part in the pacification of Catalonia, serving loyally and courageously until 1642, in recognition of which he was awarded a monthly pension of thirty gold crowns.

The war of Catalonia made an impact on Calderón, aggravated by the fact that his brother José lost his life in the conflict. Nevertheless, he went back to Madrid and continued his occupation as court dramatist, increasingly enjoying the favor of the king, who put in his hands the arrangement of the festivities for the arrival of the new Queen, Mariana de Austria, in 1649.

During these years, Calderón, about whose intimate life little is known, fathered a son out of wedlock. This son, born around 1647, died before reaching adulthood, while his mother died soon after his birth. Calderón, who had been contemplating the idea for some time, determined to become a priest. He was ordained in 1651, and two years later Philip IV appointed him to the chaplaincy of the New Kings in the Cathedral of Toledo. Calderón moved to that city, but he kept in contact with Madrid, supplying the court with new plays and *autos* on a regular basis. While in Toledo, and inspired by the inscription of the cathedral's choir, he wrote the poem *Psalle et sile* (sing and be silent), an unusually self-revealing work.

Calderón returned to Madrid in 1663 as the chaplain of honor to Philip IV, who had created that position to ensure Calderón's presence in the court. Later that year, Calderón joined the Natural Priests of Madrid, and he became head of the congregation afterward, remaining in that position until his death. He led a quiet life during that time, dedicated to his priestly duties and restricting his literary activity to the writing of Eucharist plays and an occasional drama for the court. He still enjoyed an immense popularity, and his plays were staged frequently. Three volumes of his *Partes* (1636-1684; collected plays) appeared during this period (two had been published in 1636 and 1637), although he disowned four dramas of the last volume and one of the Eucharist plays. Preparation was under way to publish his entire dramatic production, a task that was undertaken by Juan de Vera Tassis after Calderón's death.

Calderón died on May 25, 1681; his death marked the end of the Golden Age of Spanish literature. Following his desires, the dramatist was buried during a simple ceremony, but a gorgeous one took place a few days later to satisfy the many admirers who wanted to pay homage to the playwright for the last time.

ANALYSIS

There are extant only about thirty nondramatic poems by Pedro Calderón de la Barca. Most of them are short poems, composed for a particular occasion, usually in praise of someone in whose collection they would appear.

USE OF SONNETS

As he did in his plays, Calderón employed a variety of verse forms in his nondramatic poems, but the sonnet is the prevalent form. The sonnet had been an important part of Spanish poetry since Juan Boscán and Garcilaso de la Vega assimilated the Italian poetic form into Castilian verse, but it was losing popularity during Calderón's time, as he observes in one of his plays, *Antes que todo es mi dama* (wr. c. 1636, pb. 1662; my lady comes before everything else). Fifteen of Calderón's nondramatic poems are sonnets; added to the sonnets that he included in his dramatic works and the one inserted in the longer poem *Psalle et sile*, they make a total of eighty-six sonnets, collected in a single volume by Rafael Osuna in 1974.

Calderón's sonnets reflect the main poetic currents of his times; Gongorism and *conceptismo* are both present, with a preference for the latter. In general, Calderón's sonnets reveal the poet's desire for a poetry of geometric perfection, evident in the parallel constructions, the *enumeratio* of concepts and *recopilación* or recapitulation of them in the final line, and other rhetorical techniques. They are also filled with the rich imagery that the poet uses in all of his literary production. The nondramatic sonnets are, in general, less convincing than those found in the plays, given their occasional character, but some of them are well constructed and worthy of praise. Among these are the sonnet dedicated to Saint Isidro, beautiful in its simplicity; the one written in honor of Saint Teresa de Ávila, which shows a fervent respect for the reformer of the Carmelitans; the one inserted in *Psalle et sile*, which hails the Cathedral of Toledo as a symbol of faith; and the one praising King Philip IV's hunting skills, the best of all, according to Osuna.

USE OF ROMANCE VERSE

Another poetic form that Calderón used with great skill is the romance. He gives a particular lightness to this traditional verse form, making the poem flow with ease, always adapting it appropriately to the theme he is poeticizing. In this meter, Calderón wrote his only two extant love poems, an ascetic composition, and a self-portrait in verse that reveals his comic genius. This last is, unfortunately, incomplete, yet the 173 lines of the fragment are rich in wit. Calderón first describes his physical appearance—not forgetting any part of his body—in a very unflattering manner. He proceeds to tell the reader about his studies in Salamanca, referring to his mother's desire that he become a priest, his dedication to the theater, and his days as a soldier, adding jokingly that none of these occupations enabled him to find a decent woman who would marry him. The poet, however, does not let this situation affect him, for he has learned that, "as a philosopher says, it makes good sense to adapt to the times." Based on this thinking, he involves himself with two women because he prefers two ugly maids to a beautiful lady. The poem ends abruptly in an argument against Plato's concept of love. The sarcastic tone of the opening lines informs the entire composition; for example, when referring to his lack of responsibility, the poet observes that his peccadilloes are excused by everyone because he is a Salamanca graduate. The tone of the poem is far from Calderón's characteristic sobriety, although it is possible that he wrote other poems of this nature which have not survived. Because of the reference to the time he spent in the army, the poem must have been written sometime between 1625 and 1637, for he became very disappointed with the reality of war during the Catalonian uprising.

"DECIMA"

It is in his serious compositions that Calderón shows his best abilities as a poet. In them, as in some of his philosophical plays, Calderón is preoccupied with the reality of death. The best poem of this type is "Décimas a la muerte" ("Decima"), the tone of which is reminiscent of Jorge Manrique's *Coplas por la muerte de su padre* (1492; *Ode*, 1823), although it is less impressive than that fifteenth century masterpiece. Its themes include the brevity of life; the justice of death, which ends every man's life equally; and the *ubi sunt* topos. Absent from it is the theme of fame, so strong in Manrique and present elsewhere in Calderón's works. Here, the poet is deeply pessimistic: "Everything resolves to nothingness,/ all comes from dirt, and dirt becomes,/ and thus it ends where it began." This sense of pessimism is heightened by the fact that there is only a vague reference to eternal life at the end of the poem. The emphasis is placed on the "end" of everything and the absurdity of life, on a pervasive lack of meaning.

A similar attitude is expressed in another poem, "Lágrimas que vierte un alma arrepentida" (1672; tears of a repentant soul). Written in Calderón's old age, "Lágrimas que vierte un alma arrepentida" reveals his strong religious sentiments. The poet presents himself with humility, declaring that he is a sinner, full of vices, and asks God to forgive him. The poem is an expression of love for Christ; it recalls Saint Teresa of Ávila and the anonymous "Soneto a Cristo crucificado" ("Sonnet to Christ Crucified").

PSALLE ET SILE

Calderón's longest poem is *Psalle et sile*, written in Toledo while the poet was in charge of the chaplaincy of the New Kings (1653-1663). The 525-line poem was inspired by the words inscribed at the entrance of the cathedral's choir. Calderón tries to explain the meaning of the inscription, which, because of its location, implies a request or command to those who enter the choir. How is it possible to sing and be silent at the same time? The poet praises silence as the greatest moderation and as the language of God, with whom one can communicate only in the silence of one's soul. Calderón adds, however, that "he who speaks with propriety does not break silence." To speak with propriety, one has to concentrate on the subject of the conversation. In the same manner, one needs to concentrate when conversing with God, which can be done only by meditating. If one is immersed in meditation, then one is speaking the language of God—that is, one is truly silent. At the same time, one could sing songs without interrupting the mental conversation with God. Following this reasoning, it is possible to sing and to be silent simultaneously, utterly absorbed in spiritual communication with God.

OTHER MAJOR WORKS

PLAYS: *Amor, honor, y poder*, pr. 1623; *El sitio de Breda*, pr. 1625; *El príncipe constante*, pr. 1629 (*The Constant Prince*, 1853); *La dama duende*, wr. 1629, pr., pb. 1936 (*The Phantom Lady*, 1664); *Casa con dos puertas, mala es de guardar*, wr. 1629, pr., pb. 1636 (*A House with Two Doors Is Difficult to Guard*, 1737); *Los cabellos de Absalón*, wr. c. 1634, pb. 1684; *La devoción de la cruz*, pb. 1634 (*Devotion to the Cross*, 1832); *El gran teatro del mundo*, wr. 1635, pr. 1649 (*The Great Theater of the World*, 1856); *El mayor encanto, amor*, pr. 1635 (*Love, the Greatest Enchantment*, 1870); *La vida es sueño*, pr. 1635 (*Life Is a Dream*, 1830); *Antes que todo es mi dama*, wr. c. 1636, pb. 1662; *Partes*, pb. 1636-1684; *El médico de su honra*, pb. 1637 (*The Surgeon of His Honor*, 1853); *A secreto agravio, secreta venganza*, pb. 1637 (*Secret Vengeance for Secret Insult*, 1961); *El mágico prodigioso*, pr. 1637 (*The Wonder-Working Magician*, 1959); *El pintor de su deshonra*, wr. 1640-1642, pb. 1650 (*The Painter of His Dishonor*, 1853); *El alcalde de Zalamea*, pr. 1643 (*The Mayor of Zalamea*, 1853); *La hija del aire, Parte I*, pr. 1653 (*The Daughter of the Air, Part I*, 1831); *La hija del aire, Parte II*, pr. 1653 (*The Daughter of the Air, Part II*, 1831); *El laurel de Apolo*, pr. 1659; *La púrpura de la rosa*, pr. 1660; *Hado y divisa de Leonido y Marfisa*, pr. 1680.

BIBLIOGRAPHY

Acker, Thomas S. *The Baroque Vortex: Velázquez, Calderón, and Gracián Under Philip IV*. New York: P. Lang, 2000. A volume in the Currents in Comparative Romance Languages and Literatures series, this comparative study places Calderón in both a literary and historical context. Bibliographical references.

Fitzgerald, Edward. *Eight Dramas of Calderón*. Chicago: University of Illinois Press, 2000. Fitzgerald adheres to the lyrical quality of the original text in this English version. Includes the latest editions of the classic translations of *The Mayor of Zalamea* and *Life Is a Dream*. Incorporates the latest of Fitzgerald's versions or textual alterations.

Kurtz, Barbara E. *The Play of Allegory in the Autos Sacramentales of Pedro Calderón de la Barca*. Washington, D.C.: Catholic University of America Press, 1991. This analysis of the allegorical elements is interesting for its consideration of historical and social contexts as well as literary structure. This study is one of the most comprehensive investigations into the genre of *autos sacramentales* and Golden Age literature. Kurtz supports her thorough analysis with ample textual examples from Calderón's plays and from works by other playwrights.

Muir, Kenneth, and Ann L. Mackenzie. *Three Comedies by Pedro Calderón de la Barca*. Lexington: The University Press of Kentucky, 1985. The translators present English versions of the lesser-known works *A House with Two Doors Is Difficult to Guard*, *Mornings of April and May*, and *No Trifling with Love*. Their translations are well documented and readable. Each play is prefaced with explanatory background notes. Extensive bibliographical material.

Suscavage, Charlene E. *Calderón: The Imagery of Tragedy*. New York: Peter Lang, 1991. Although concerned with the plays, focuses on Calderón's language and figures of speech. Bibliographical references.

Juan Fernández Jiménez;
bibliography updated by Carole A. Champagne
and the editors

CALLIMACHUS

Born: Cyrene, a Greek colony in North Africa; c. 305 B.C.E.
Died: Alexandria, Egypt; c. 240 B.C.E.

PRINCIPAL POETRY

Callimachus is said to have written eight hundred books, an astonishing output even if one takes into account the generally shorter length of the ancient scroll. Of his poetry, only the six *Hymni* (*Hymns*, 1755)—ranging from one hundred to three hundred lines, all but one in dactylic hexameter—and the *Epigrammata* (*Epigrams*, 1793)—sixty-four short poems, most of them in elegiac couplets—survived from antiquity more or less intact in the manuscript tradition. The *Aitiōn* (*Aetia*, 1958), originally seven thousand lines in four books; the *Iamboi* (*Iambi*, 1958); the *epyllion* or "little epic" *Ekalē* (*Hecale*, 1958); the *Lock of Berenice*, 1755; and a handful of lyric poems are extant only in fragmentary form, as they were discovered on papyri found in Egypt or were partially quoted by later ancient authors.

In addition, nearly four hundred fragments, ranging from one line to fifty, which cannot be placed for certain in any larger context, attest the wide range and varied content of Callimachus's otherwise unknown verse. Only the titles of these other compositions survive to tantalize modern scholars. For Callimachus's *Hymns* and *Epigrams*, the numerical systems of A. W. Mair in his book *Callimachus: Hymns and Epigrams* (1955) are used. For Callimachus's *Iambi*, the numerical system of C. A. Trypanis in *Callimachus: Aetia, Iambi, Hecale,*

Minor Epic and Elegiac Poems, and Other Fragments (1958, 1975) is used.

OTHER LITERARY FORMS

Callimachus himself was a scholar and literary critic as well as a poet and wrote prose monographs on subjects as diverse as the names of tribes, rare words, barbarian customs, and marvelous occurrences throughout the world. Unfortunately, none of the prose is extant.

ACHIEVEMENTS

Callimachus is the preeminent "Alexandrian" poet, the most daring, technically skilled, and prolific among the writers practicing their art in that Hellenized Egyptian city during the third century B.C.E. Like his contemporaries Theocritus and Apollonius Rhodius, Callimachus wrote allusive, learned, yet dramatic poetry; unlike these two fellow Alexandrians, however, he seems to have mined deliberately the widest variety of genres. Moreover, he alone among the poets whose work survives from this period crafted and refined throughout his career a poetic dogma, a highly developed notion of what a poem should be. In this, one could compare him with Ezra Pound among modern poets, continually urging his colleagues to "make it new" and exerting a powerful influence on subsequent generations of poets. Callimachus, who was also like Pound in being a scholar of poetry, renewed the Greek poetic tradition in two ways: He cultivated forms that had fallen into disuse (such as the hymnic), and he infused traditionally nonpersonal poetry with allusions to his own time and condition. A hymn, for example, could become a vehicle for praise of the patron monarch Ptolemy and for pronouncements on style, while purporting to praise Zeus or Apollo; a funerary epigram might be turned in the poet's hands to serve as a sophisticated joke.

It was Callimachus's achievement to compose poetry that satisfied a discerning, restricted audience—the royal court at Alexandria and other scholar-poets—without becoming hopelessly obscure or dated. Instead, his poetry in all genres usually attains the ideal he set: Lightness of tone is wedded to brevity, urbane manner, erudite content, and exclusive allusions. That these qualities were prized in poetry is evidenced by the many papyrus fragments later discovered to contain works by Callimachus—far more than those of any other author, including the very popular Euripides. Ironically, this "exclusive" poet obtained a far-from-exclusive audience, perhaps because his verse challenged the reader as it simultaneously offered rare pleasures. His influence extended even beyond the Greek-speaking lands; the verse of the Roman poets Ennius, Catullus, Horace, Vergil, and Propertius, and the poetic stance which each assumes, would be unthinkable without the example of Callimachus.

In turn, from the poets writing during the reign of the Emperor Augustus, the English "Augustans" inherited the Callimachean poetic ideal; Alexander Pope's *The Rape of the Lock* (1712, 1714) echoes the Alexandrian poet's *Lock of Berenice*, although Pope added the mock-epic tone. Indeed, Callimachean aesthetic principles are so much a part of the European literary tradition that they may be taken for granted. Yet, whenever a new poetic movement (Imagism, for example) challenges outworn canons of taste, jettisons tedious narrative, and turns instead to highly crafted "small" verse forms, the creators of the new poetry are treading the path first cleared by the Alexandrian poet.

BIOGRAPHY

Callimachus was not a native Alexandrian; he grew up and seems to have begun composing poetry in Cyrene, a Greek city of North Africa. From a commentary on a lost portion of his long poem, the *Aetia*, it appears that Callimachus represented himself as once dreaming that he was transported from his boyhood home in Libya to Mt. Helicon, the place on the mainland of Greece which was considered the traditional home of the Muses. He thus alludes to an early initiation into his art.

Neither his date of birth nor his parentage is known, but Callimachus's family apparently prided itself on being descended from Battus, the legendary eighth century B.C.E. founder of Cyrene. From this assumption it may be deduced that his education was that of an aristocrat. On moving to Alexandria, however, which was one of the main cultural centers of Hellenistic Greek civilization, Callimachus was initially a marginal figure; family connections did not help. He held the position of schoolmaster in the suburb of Eleusis, which was not a lucrative job. Several of his epigrams that mention his poverty have been thought to date from this period (c. 280-270 B.C.E.); nevertheless, it should be remembered that the topic of poverty (*penia*) was a convention in Greek literature as early as Hesiod (fl. 700 B.C.E.), a poet whom Callimachus admired and imitated. When, therefore, the poet addresses a lover in Epigram 34 M., "You know that my hands are empty of wealth . . . ," and proceeds to beg affection, the words are most likely those of a persona rather than of the poet himself.

At some later point, Callimachus received an appointment to the great library at Alexandria, perhaps after an introduction to Ptolemy II Philadelphus, the library's royal patron (who ruled from 285 to 246 B.C.E.). Callimachus's ground breaking compilation of the 120-volume *Pinakes* (tablets), a catalog of the library's hundred thousand or so papyrus scrolls of Greek literature, entailed far more than merely listing titles, involving him in decisions about genre, authorship, authors' biographies, and the arrangement of sections within each work. This extensive piece of literary history provided the poet with a wealth of material—often obscure—from which to fashion learned verse.

Despite his important contributions there, Callimachus was never appointed head of the library. Some controversy may have been involved, as literary infighting was surely a part of his life, but the details of his arguments with various contemporaries remain vague. Ancient commentators mention a feud between Callimachus and Apollonius, the author of the epic *Argonautica* (third century B.C.E.). Callimachus's preference for brevity and disdain for pseudo-Homeric epic apparently prevailed for a time: Apollonius is said to have left, humbled, to live on the island of Rhodes. Callimachus's *Ibis*, now lost, a piece of darkly worded invective which Ovid later imitated, may have hastened its victim's departure from Alexandria. Other personal enemies apparently were attacked through allusions in the revised prologue of the *Aetia*.

While much of his poetry continues such artistic debates, several of Callimachus's poems might best be understood in a different light—as responses to occasions at the royal court which demanded expression on the part of an "attached" poet. The *Lock of Berenice*, for example, commemorates an actual event, the dedication of a wife's lock of hair to petition the gods for the safe return of her husband, Ptolemy III, as he departed for war in 247 B.C.E. (This is the only datable poem extant.) Again, court happenings might be alluded to in that portion of the *Hymn to Zeus* that mentions Zeus's rule over his older brothers; the entire composition may be an elaborate, half-veiled praise of Callimachus's patron. It is surely not a real hymn meant for ritual recitation. Unfortunately, nothing is known of the poet's relation with the royal family other than that their patronage extended until his death at an advanced age. This social situation in its broader implications must be kept in mind: What appears to be Callimachean allusive indirection often might have resulted from politic discretion.

ANALYSIS

Since the legacy of Callimachus lies so much in his theory of style, it is best, first, to examine several of his extended metaphors describing the ideal style; then his major works can be evaluated according to his own aesthetic standards.

EPIGRAM 30 M.

In most cases, Callimachus's pronouncements about poetry are blended skillfully with other topics. Epigram 30 M. is a good example. The seven-line poem builds on the poet's exclusive tastes:

> I hate a cyclical poem, take no delight in the road
> That carries many to and fro. I detest
> A lover that wanders, nor do I drink from a well;
> All held in common I abhor. . . .

Then the poet dramatically changes tack. What began as a literary manifesto ends abruptly as a bitter personal love poem:

> Lysaniē, you are beautiful, beautiful . . .
> But before Echo speaks this, someone says
> "Another possesses him."

The reader is left in suspense, yet he could eventually conclude that the poet, true to his lonely principle in life as in art, is here abandoning the one thing he does *not* hate.

The long, undistinguished epic poems, called "cyclic" because they complete the Trojan War myth cycle, represent for Callimachus all that one should avoid in verse. Even though his *Hymn to Apollo* uses the centuries-old Homeric meter and epic diction, the poem in praise of the god is startlingly fresh and compresses details of geography, ritual, history, and myth, into a dramatic framework. The final lines, which express Callimachus's aversion for the epic form, are spoken by the god of poetry himself, using the images of Epigram 30 M. again—wide thoroughfares and water. To "Envy" (Callimachus's unnamed detractors), whispering in Apollo's ear like a court sycophant about the hateful poet "who does not sing as many things as the sea" (that is, vast epics), the god replies with a kick. He cites the filthiness of the "great stream" Euphrates; in an oracular tone, he says that Demeter's shrine is watered by "bees" (priestesses of the goddess) that carry water only from pure, undefiled streams. Envy is thus defeated.

Purity of water, insectlike artisanship—these are metaphors for Callimachus's light, unencumbered verse. The two images are combined once more in the combative prologue to the "collected poems" edition of the *Aetia*. After acknowledging the objection that he has not written "one long poem," Callimachus again uses the dramatic mask of Apollo to defend his own application of *techne* (skill) rather than bulk and big noises: As a youth, he saw the god, who instructed the poet to "nourish a slender Muse," to imitate the cicada. Callimachus's final prayer to become "the light one, the winged," living on dew, takes on a more personal note, for now he desires the insect's levity in order to shake off burdensome old age.

AETIA

How does Callimachus in his verse attain this cicada-like freedom of expression? The *Aetia* itself can show. Although nearly half the length of the *Iliad* (c. 800 B.C.E.) when extant in full, this was certainly not "one long poem" but rather an episodic meandering through every sort of Greek ritual lore, a poem that explained (like the poet's prose works) curious customs—why the Parians, for example, sacrifice without flute music, or why the Lindians honor Heracles with blasphemy. A scholar's poem, the *Aetia* has the dramatist's voice behind its narrative, choosing exact details and often breaking into direct speech. Here Callimachus's novel narrative technique appears to be built on deliberate random changes of topic, like the flitting of an industrious insect.

The story of Acontius and Cydippe, one of the longer, completely separable stories within the *Aetia*, illuminates the Callimachean method very well. An introduction, sprinkled allusively with obscure proper names, relates the legendary beauty of this pair of lovers and tells how Acontius by means of an inscribed apple contrived to bind Cydippe on oath to love him, so that her attempts to marry others are all divinely thwarted. Then the poet focuses on one such attempt at marriage with another. Seeming to lose the narrative thread, however, he begins to describe the history of the ritual prenuptial sleep which Cydippe and her husband-to-be must take; but the poet breaks off: "Hold back, shameless soul, you dog!" Such rituals are too holy to tell; "having much knowledge is bad for one who does not control the tongue," he says. Clearly, the aposiopesis (falling silent) technique is employed only to show off, in elegant manner, a vast erudition, and at the same time it is a technique that prevents the reader from being bored with the extraneous details of the digression. Finally, the poet makes his transition to another topic by a surprising bibliographical reference, an unheard-of device in serious epic poems: "Cean, your clan, the Acontiadae, dwell in honored numbers at Iulis still. This love-match we heard from old Xenomedes, who set down once the entire island in a mythological history." At one stroke, the scholar-poet gives the *aetion* (cause) which he set out to tell—the origin of this clan—and turns his narrative to other Cean myths with a librarian's remark.

The levity of Callimachus can be appreciated in other ways; it is not merely narrative flightiness. Indeed, he sometimes employs old conventions for the sake of elaborate jokes. A few of his epigrams have their origin in this technique. There were generic social precedents for these short poems: the inscription-verses on tombs and on dedicated shrine offerings. The poet subverts both. A four-line poem poses as a tombstone epitaph to commemorate a youth who allegedly was putting garlands on his stepmother's tomb ("thinking now that she had changed life and her nature as well") when the woman's *stēlē* toppled and killed him. The last line is both traditional in its address to passersby, and humorous: "O step-sons, shun even a step-mother's grave." In imitation of a dedicatory object, Callimachus wrote another poem which plays on the similarity in Greek between the word for sea and the word for salt. Like a shipwrecked sailor who traditionally offered an oar or clothing to the gods who saved him from drowning, the speaker, Eudemus, in Epigram 48 M. dedicates his salt-cellar: Now he has become rich and no longer eats frugally and so is "saved from the salt."

EPIGRAM 2 M.

Lest it be thought that the poet only plays, one other epigram might be mentioned to acknowledge the elegiac strain and the ability to evoke intense feeling also to be found in Callimachus. Perhaps his most famous short poem, Epigram 2 M., is that addressed to Heraclitus:

> Someone told me of your death, Heraclitus, and put me
> In tears; I remembered the many times we both
> By conversing put the sun to sleep. . . .

Although his friend has been "ashes long since now," Callimachus in recalling him affirms the love of the art of poetry which the two friends shared:

> But your nightingales are still alive;
> Hades, who snatches all, will not put hand on them.

The light touch—of tone, as in many epigrams, of allusiveness and narrative pace, as in the *Aetia*—characterizes Callimachus's approach to other genres as well. Never satisfied with remaining at work in any single verse form, he seems to have intended to appropriate all, even writing tragedy and comedy (now lost). Doubtless this approach was criticized by his contemporaries as evidence of a lack of staying power; it was scorned as *polyeideia* (writing in many forms). Today, one sees this method as the prime virtue of Callimachean art. Three other works—*Iambi, Hymns*, and *Hecale*—show the advantages Callimachus derived from this stylistic tenet.

IAMBI

The thirteen poems of the *Iambi* present a much modulated form of the invective traditionally associated with the genre of poetry written in this meter as practiced by Archilochus and Hipponax in archaic Greece. Attacks on personal enemies are replaced in these compositions by a mild correction of received opinion: The true story of a well-known proverb occupies Iambus 11 T., and similar antiquarian interests take up the description of statues, the origin of a footrace on Aegina, the reason that sows are slaughtered in a certain Aphrodite

cult. These *Iambi* show Callimachus, as in the *Aetia*, crossing prose genres of historiography and mythology with disused poetic forms to create something new. In the few *Iambi* which mention contemporaries, the names in question are tangential to the poem. Thus, Iambus 2 T. relates one of Aesop's fables about the way in which animals lost their voices to men; only at the end does the poet intrude: "Eudemus, therefore, has a dog's voice, Philton a donkey's. . . ." Such a technique, distancing the original purpose of the iambic form, allows Callimachus to expand its range. He adapts it thereby to the changed social conditions of the third century B.C.E., in which the cosmopolitan court, rather than the tightly knit city-state, is the intended audience.

HYMNS AND HECALE

The *Hymns* and *Hecale*, finally, allow Callimachus's light handling to be traced through two interrelated effects. First, there is once again generic innovation; second, the innovation is tied to narrative methods of compressing, arranging, and ordering point of view, all of which are new.

The hymn, since the time of Homer, was a narrative commemorating the deeds of a particular divinity; it was framed by praises of the god. Callimachus, however, in the *Hymn to Apollo* and other hymns re-creates dramatically the god's epiphany at his shrine. The poem adopts a second-person narrator, rather than the more distant, epic-sounding, third-person narration. Immediately noticeable, too, is the way in which Callimachus allies poetry with secret and holy ritual: to hear the poem, one must be an initiate, like the worshipers of Apollo. It is not far from such poetry to the Roman lyricist Horace's claim to be "priest of the Muses."

The *Hecale*, on the other hand, rather than being a reworking of a very old genre, is a completely new form, the *epyllion*, which arose in the Alexandrian period of Greek literature. Who its exact inventor was is not known with certainty. Theocritus wrote several; Callimachus may simply have perfected the use of this form. The purpose of the "little epic" is not to tell all the deeds of a hero, for that ambition would require the scope of the detested "cyclic" poem. Instead, only one, often little-known episode in the life of a hero, one with plenty of local-color possibilities, is selected. In the case of the *Hecale*, it is Theseus's capture of a destructive bull which has been ravaging Marathon, near Athens. The scale of the narrative is further reduced by the poet's intense focus on the events of the night before the heroic feat, rather than on the deed itself. Theseus's visit to the rustic hut of an old woman named Hecale, the simple supper she prepares for him, their conversation—all are described in painstakingly realistic detail. There is pathos (the hero returns later to find the woman has died), erudition (the origin of the Hecale-feasts is explained), and a good deal of stylistic tour de force (into the "heroic" hexameter the poet fits the words "bread-box," "baking oven," and other commonplace terms). Although most of the poem survives in fragments, it was intact and widely imitated from Vergil's time to the thirteenth century. Fragmentary as the *Hecale* remains, it is nevertheless a fitting testament to its author's lifelong urge to distill, renew, and perpetuate essential and lively poetry.

BIBLIOGRAPHY

Calame, Claude. "Legendary Narratives and Poetic Procedure in Callimachus's 'Hymn to Apollo.'" In *Hellenistica Gronigana: Proceedings of the Gröningen Workshops on Hellenistic Poetry*, edited by Annette Harder. Gröningen: Egbert Forster, 1993. An examination of how Callimachus weaves both Greek and Roman mythology and the classical poetic tradition into his verse. Sheds new light on a subject which is central to Callimachus's achievements. Very helpful in understanding how Callimachus used existing material from earlier periods.

Cameron, Alan. *Callimachus and His Critics*. Princeton, N.J.: Princeton University Press, 1995. A wide-ranging survey of Callimachus's literary reputation over the centuries, noting that his elaborate verbal precision has become his hallmark. Cameron shows how, and to some extent why, Callimachus worked so diligently to achieve that literary effect.

Ferguson, John. *Callimachus*. Boston: Twayne, 1980. This volume provides the essential background to a study of Callimachus. Much of the information here remains remarkably fresh and useful. As with many ancient authors, the essential "facts" about Callimachus and his works have remained relatively unchanged, making this still an excellent starting point for any exploration of Callimachus, his times and his works.

Gutzwiller, Kathryn. *Poetic Garlands: Hellenistic Epigrams in Context*. Berkeley: University of California Press, 1998. Although it concentrates most of its attention on Callimachus's *Epigrammata*, this work goes beyond that to look at the poetic convention of the epigram in the larger realm of classical literature. Because this genre was of major importance to ancient literature (as well as having an enduring impact on the Western tradition), this is an important work to consult.

Hollis, A. S. Introduction to *Callimachus' "Hecale."* Oxford: Clarendon Press, 1990. The *Hecale*, Callimachus's retelling of the story of how the Athenian hero Theseus tamed the bull of Marathon, was the poet's effort to show that he too was capable of crafting epic verse. Hollis places this key work of Callimachus into both the poet's canon and the Western poetic tradition, helping to explain its importance and enduring achievements.

Thomas, Richard F. "Callimachus Back in Rome." In *Hellenistica Gronigana: Proceedings of the Gröningen Workshops on Hellenistic Poetry*, edited by Annette Harder. Gröningen: Egbert Forster, 1993. A useful survey of Callimachus's reputation outside the eastern Mediterranean.

Williams, Frederick. "Callimachus and the Supranormal." In *Hellenistica Gronigana: Proceedings of the Gröningen Workshops on Hellenistic Poetry*, edited by Annette Harder. Gröningen: Egbert Forster, 1993. Since Callimachus can be as much noted for his works based on myths and legends as for his lyric poetry, this study provides an interesting and useful review of how the poet deploys the supranormal world and events in his works.

Richard Peter Martin;
bibliography updated by Michael Witkoski

LUÍS DE CAMÕES

Born: Lisbon, Portugal; c. 1524
Died: Lisbon, Portugal; June 10, 1580

PRINCIPAL POETRY

Os Lusíadas, 1572 (*The Lusiads*, 1655)
Cancioneiro, 1580
Rimas, 1595 (*The Lyrides*, 1803, 1884)

OTHER LITERARY FORMS

Although Luís de Camões does not seem to have tried to compete with his great compatriot, the dramatist Gil Vicente, Camões did write three short *autos* (short plays). *Enfatriões* (pr. 1540; amphytrions), an adaptation of Plautus's comedy, was probably staged in 1540 as a scholar's exercise or for an academic celebration at Coimbra University. The *El-Rei Seleuco* (pr. c.1542; the play of King Seleuco), based on Plutarch, was performed in the home of Estácio da Fonseca, one of the king's officials, perhaps on the occasion of a wedding, very likely in 1542 during the poet's sojourn in Lisbon and at court. Finally, *Filodemo*, the longest, most classical, and most mature of Camões's plays, was presented in Goa in 1555 to honor the newly appointed governor of India, Francisco Barreto.

Luís de Camões (Library of Congress)

ACHIEVEMENTS

No Iberian lyric poet has been more successful than Luís de Camões in the expression of feeling. Indeed, he represents all of Peninsular poetry at its peak. Lord Byron, whose inspiration introduced new emotion into literature, admired the authenticity of Camões's lyricism and understood the human truth in his verse. In all his work, Camões was able to combine native Portuguese traditions with the classical influences and with the vital spirit of the Renaissance.

Camões is probably best known for his epic poem, *The Lusiads*. The focal point in this work is not Vasco da Gama, realistically characterized as the uncultivated captain that he was, but the Portuguese conquistadores as a whole—who, in the tradition of their ancestors, set out to create the vast Portuguese Empire for themselves and posterity. Although Camões wrote his propaganda to glorify the nation at its peak, he recognized the weakness of the imperial structure for the future. Such objectivity regarding the empire—and the honesty to express his views to the king, to whom he dedicated his poem—bespeak Camões's faith in the best principles of the Renaissance and his confidence in himself as the poet most representative of his time.

BIOGRAPHY

Although he has had many biographers, little is known for certain of the adventuresome life of Luís de Camões, who represented so well in his life and works the Renaissance man and the Portuguese conquistador. The son of Simão Vas de Camões and Ana de Macedo or Sá, Camões was possibly related, through his paternal grandmother, to Vasco da Gama, as well as to other Portuguese notables dating as far back as 1370. Camões was a gentleman, then, although always of scant financial resources. It is clear, too, that he possessed a vast erudition. Because of the quantity and quality of Camões's learning, it is likely that he studied at Coimbra University and therefore that he was born in Coimbra, as he probably would have been too poor to move there from Lisbon.

With some reputation as well as noble birth, Camões went to Lisbon between 1542 and 1545, to frequent the court and enjoy the greater activity of the capital. His enjoyment was short-lived, unfortunately, for in 1546 or 1547 he was banished to Ribatejo because of his passion for a lady of the court whose parents did not approve. It is known that during the years from 1547 to 1549, Camões was in Ceuta, Morocco, winning his spurs as a proper young nobleman but losing an eye, probably in combat with the Moors. In 1549, he was back in Lisbon, where he led a Bohemian existence until 1553, when, in a brawl, he injured his adversary so seriously that he was jailed.

Camões was released only on the condition that he depart for India, which he did on March 7, 1553, after having been enlisted as a soldier for three years. His ship, the splendid *São Bento*, commanded by Fernão Alvares Cabral, capsized at the Cape of Good Hope but arrived at Goa in September, 1554. Despite his constant involvement in numerous military expeditions, Camões wrote regularly, presenting his short play *Filodemo* to the governor of India, Francisco Barreto, on the occasion of his installation in 1555. In 1556, the poet was in Macao, perhaps in the capacity of the governor's "officer for deceased and absentees," perhaps in prison for embezzlement, perhaps composing portions of *The Lusiads*. Internal evidence does reveal that, shipwrecked near the mouth of the Mecon River on his return to Goa, Camões swam to safety with his epic poem, albeit his Chinese sweetheart, Dinamene, drowned. Back in Goa in 1559 or 1560, he was imprisoned for debt.

After sixteen difficult years in the Orient, the weary poet decided in 1568 to return to Portugal with Pero Barreto Rolim, who, for an unknown reason, left Camões, without resources, in Mozambique. There Camões remained until 1569, when the well-known chronicler Diogo do Couto rescued him and took him back to Lisbon on the *Santa Fé* in 1569 or 1570. Camões had all but completed his great epic as his country was about to engage in the bloody Battle of Alcácer-Quibir (1578). The Inquisition's approval to publish *The Lusiads* was signed by King Sebastian on September 24, 1571, and two editions, one authentic, the other plagiarized, appeared in 1572. Pensioned by the king, the greatest of Portuguese poets struggled to survive—but probably without the rumored need to beg—until his death in 1580.

ANALYSIS

During his lifetime, Luís de Camões never published his complete works. Many of his lyric poems were circulated as *separata* from admirer to admirer; many others were printed in the collective *cancioneiros* (songbooks), both during his day and posthumously. Those that the poet had collected in his personal *Parnaso* (Parnassus) were stolen from him. The first complete collection of Camões's lyrics appeared under the editorship of Fernão Rodrigues Lobo Soropita in Lisbon in 1595; the first critical edition, prepared by José Maria Rodriques and Alfonso Lopes Vieira, did not appear until 1932.

Camões's life was a continual *via dolorosa*, filled with love but also with sorrow and disaster. It was a life that taught him the entire gamut of tragic emotions, which his destiny called him to express in his lyrics. With very rare exceptions, Camões's songs, odes, elegies, *redondilhas*, and sonnets are composed of the passion and anguish caused him by his misadventures throughout a considerable part of the then vast Portuguese Empire and transmitted by him directly and sincerely to his sensitive readers of all times. It is not surprising that such an unfortunate lyric poet should so ably and faithfully interpret the human heart. He does not move the reader with sensuous images or brilliant technique alone. Constantly transformed and vibrant in his pain, Camões pours the wealth of his own varied experiences and tormented soul into each well-constructed stanza. Seldom capable of stirring the reader with their cold, almost inert poetics, Sá de Miranda, António Ferreira, and other contemporary poets pale before Camões, whose language is clear, grave, profound, dramatic, moving, and always harmonious.

Many were the women loved by Camões. Chief among them were Isabel Tavares, or "Belisa," the cousin whom he won in his youth in Coimbra; Catarina de Ataíde, or "Natércia," a lady of the court on whose account he was banished; Dinamene, the Chinese slave girl lost at sea; and Barbara, another slave woman about whom little is known. Although he treats other themes, often combining those of Portuguese tradition and those of the Renaissance, Camões's lyrics center on love—as do those of the great Petrarch, whom he emulated, cited, and sometimes paraphrased. Indeed, the Italian poet's influence was keenly felt by virtually all European lyric poets in the fifteenth and sixteenth centuries—in the Platonic transformation of erotic love, beyond the grave as well as in life, and in the quality of his imagery and mellifluous rhythms. Not only does Camões represent the apotheosis of the angelic beloved—framing her in all the attributes of incorruptible grace and revering her with feelings of purest chastity—but also all nature shares in the poet's joy or anguish. Further, Camões uses metric forms—sonnets, songs, tercets, sestinas, and decasyllables—identical to those of Petrarch. The latter, however, was conscious of having made Laura's name famous through his work, whereas Camões's convulsive passion and pain seem more genuinely felt, more dramatic, and more human.

Platonism transformed Camões's emotion, tenderly sublimating it. Apart from Petrarch, Camões knew something of Plato's idealism, as may be seen in the *redondilhas maiores* beginning "Sobolos os rios que vão" ("Over the Rivers That Flow"). Written in despair when the poet was still in Goa or Mozambique, this long poem quivers with his painful longing for home and inner peace: Suffering the evils of Babylon, Camões weeps and moans nostalgically for the joys of Zion and glimpses the Promised Land. It may be said that Camões was more comprehensive than Petrarch in the matter of form, for he excelled in the traditional *redondilha* of the *cancioneiros* and in the inventions of the Renaissance alike. Doubtless first influenced by the graceful verse of Sá de Miranda, as were all the contemporary practitioners of the Italian style in Portugal, Camões learned as well, not only directly from Petrarch and Jacopo Sannazzaro (not to mention Vergil) but also from the Spanish Italianate poets Juan de Boscán and Garcilaso de la Vega. Ultimately, Camões rivaled Dante and Petrarch in the sonnet and song of Sicilian origin. Moreover, no lyric poet in Portuguese before or since has achieved Camões's transparency, plasticity, harmony, and taste in language, whether in the expression of abstract thought, concrete nature, or personal feeling.

THE LUSIADS

Although it is Camões's lyric poetry that holds the greater interest for today's reader, it is *The Lusiads* that made its author universally famous. The idea of creating an epic poem concerning Portuguese expansion had existed from the fifteenth century, both in and out of Portugal. The Italian Humanist Poliziano, whose work later inspired Camões to a degree, had offered his services to João II to sing of his deeds in Latin verse. In the prologue to the *Cancioneiro general* (1516; general songbook), Garcia de Resende laments that the accomplishments of the Portuguese have not been properly glorified. Despite his repeated aversion to the military life on land and sea, António Ferreira encouraged his colleagues to write such an epic, and he himself attempted the epic style in several odes. This aspiration on the part of the Humanists was related to their ambition to revive the classical genres, including the epic; the voyages of the Portuguese could easily be compared to those of Ulysses and Aeneas.

Camões, too, sought to meet the challenge of the Homeric model that so engaged other Humanists. The maritime setting of the *Odyssey* (c. 800 B.C.E.) and other ancient poems was indeed appropriate for the central theme of a Portuguese epic, as was the nationalism of the *Aeneid* (29-19 B.C.E.) for the official ideology of the Portuguese expansion, according to which the nation was fulfilling a divine mandate by extending both the empire and the faith. In the midst of wars between Protestants and Catholics—not to mention between rulers of the same religion, such as Charles V and Francis I—and above all in the face of the Turkish onslaught in the Mediterranean, the Lusitanians accepted their sacred mission as had the Crusaders before them.

It is unknown precisely when the young Camões set about writing *The Lusiads*, although it was probably composed between 1545 and 1570, but there is evidence in his collection of lyric poetry of early intentions to glorify the great deeds of his people. Camões's title, signifying "the Portuguese" (descended, according to legend, from Luso, a companion of Bacchus), incorporated a term created and used in several works by André de Resende, a scholar famous throughout Europe and a consummate Humanist. *The Lusiads*, first published in 1572, comprises ten cantos of ottava rima; the lengths of the cantos vary, ranging from eighty-seven stanzas (canto 7) to 156 stanzas (canto 10).

The poet begins by explaining the subject, invoking the Muses of the Tagus to grant him the proper sublime tone and flowing, grandiloquent style, and dedicating the poem to King Sebastian. The remainder of the work is divided between two main story lines, the first relating the history of Portugal prior to King Manuel (cantos 3,

4, and 8) and the second, the voyage of Vasco da Gama to India (cantos 1, 2, 5, 7, 9, and 10). Imitating Vergil, who has Aeneas narrate the history of his people and his own nautical adventures to Dido, Camões imagines Vasco and Paul da Gama telling different parts of their story to other characters. With this device, it was possible for Camões to introduce the historical narratives of the Lusos, ancient and modern, derived from the nationalistic works of João de Barros, into the description of the extraordinary voyage of Vasco da Gama, based on several written accounts as well as oral tradition, and at the same time maintain the structural balance of the poem. Thus, the history of past heroes seems related to that of current ones, with no interruption in the logical sequence of the action. The poem concludes with a sorrowful, poignant censure of the nation's decadence and with the poet's firm exhortation to the king to conquer Morocco.

Da Gama's voyage was insufficient to give artistic unity to the poem, however, for a work of art requires unity of action—that is, the convergence of the events in a dramatic situation and its denouement. Camões found no plot in the voyage, only a chronological sequence of events. Moreover, human characters and passions are indispensable in motivating the action of a narrative poem. Camões, however, failed to find these qualities in his historical figures—so much so that his characters more often resemble statues in a procession than human beings. It is perhaps for these reasons that, in keeping with the rules of the genre and, once more, with Vergil as his chief model, Camões invented a mythological plot of impassioned gods. The psychological interest, then, does not reside in the difficulties and complications of da Gama's voyage but in the rivalry between Venus, patron of the Portuguese, and Bacchus, who is their enemy. This rivalry accounts for the obstacles that the fleet encounters on the eastern coast of Africa (the fictitious storm occurring at the end rather than the beginning of the trip) and for the intrigues that create enemies for the Portuguese. Disguised, Bacchus makes trouble for the protagonists, provokes mistrust of the newcomers, and stirs up the gods of the sea to unleash the storm against them. On the other hand, Venus intercedes on their behalf with Jupiter, who enlists the nymphs to weaken the efforts of the sea gods.

In general, the gods are more human than the humans, and the action depends on and revolves about them. The poet, however, strives for a realistic interpretation, at least within the realm of Christian miracle. The contacts between the gods and humans take place in dreams or through incarnations. Furthermore, the gods could be interpreted as angelic, demonic, or astrological forces—all very acceptable to the poet's contemporaries. At the end of the poem, the mythological fiction dissipates, and on the Isle of Love, the sea nymphs grant the returning sailors every favor, even immortality. Da Gama replaces Adamastor and Neptune as the lover of Thetis, who herself declares the use of mythology allegorical.

As a Humanist, Camões combined a reverence for the classical world with the passionate exploratory spirit characteristic of the Renaissance. Thus, his epic is a compendium of lore—geographical, nautical, and otherwise—much of which he acquired at first hand on his far-flung travels.

Indeed, the vigor of the Renaissance is consistently reflected in Camões's brilliant verse. Certain episodes reveal his genius in the dramatic description of the concrete. His accounts of the Battle of Aljubarroto (canto 4) and of the tourney of the Twelve English Peers (canto 6) are extraordinarily vivid portrayals of war. The poignant assassination of Inês de Castro (canto 3) is a scene worthy of Euripides, while the Old Man of Restelo, weeping and cursing at da Gama's departure (canto 6), and Adamastor, threatening the Lusitanian heroes and sobbing at the disappearance of the beautiful nymph (canto 5), are pathetic figures drawn with the realistic power of Dante. The furious waves and ominous winds (canto 6) and the "bloodsucking" waterspout (canto 5) are remarkable in their exact representational qualities, rivaling the naturalism of Albrecht Dürer or Michelangelo. Finally, the Isle of Love (canto 9) is a typical scene of pagan sensuality that depicts most vividly the voluptuousness to which the men of the Renaissance were so susceptible.

At the same time, Camões excelled in making his form follow his function. Many of his concise formulas have become engraved in the collective memory of the Portuguese people. Despite transpositions and other syntactical liberties modeled on Latin and despite an excess of mythological allusions, Camões's phrases are usually clear and precise. The prodigious sense of rhythm characteristic of his verse is sometimes adapted to the movement and sounds of battle, with much onomatopoeia, sometimes to the tedious calm of the doldrums on the equator, sometimes to the aroused ardor of desire, sometimes to the crystalline lyricism of Venus's island paradise. Coupled with a capacity for picturesque imagery, these devices make Camões the foremost exponent of the sensuous Renaissance.

The explicit ideological content of *The Lusiads* is of much less interest today than its artistic realization. The notion of Portugal as a model for the disunited Christian nations of Europe, already expressed by Gil Vicente and others, was perhaps advanced more eloquently and strikingly by Camões. That Portugal represented Western culture as opposed to the barbarism of the rest of the world, however, is not borne out by the bloodthirsty tale of Portuguese history as told by the poet. The noble warriors of *The Lusiads* faithfully reflect the ideology of the class to which Camões himself belonged. His sword in one hand and his pen in the other, he expressed a way of life—aristocratic, warlike, and highly individualistic.

Camões's influence on the Baroque period, which in some respects he foreshadowed, was substantial. The term "poet" was said to be synonymous with his name. Editions of his lyric poetry began to appear immediately following his death, and new editions of the lyrics and *The Lusiads* were published throughout the seventeenth century—so enthusiastically that many works were incorrectly attributed to Camões. Biographies, commentaries, and criticism soon followed. Camões's first editors, André de Resende and Soropita, were his first disciples in the lyric as well, and because of Camões's prestige at court, Francisco de Portugal, more an imitator than a genuine poet, enjoyed considerable favor. As for narrative or didactic epics in Portuguese, more than thirty were composed between 1572 and 1656 alone, each exploiting different aspects of Camões's work and attempting to resolve the problems of the genre; as the Portuguese ideology of expansion deteriorated, the epic became a historical novel in verse. Although the importance of *The Lusiads* remains great, Camões's influence as a lyric poet has been more fruitful.

OTHER MAJOR WORKS

PLAYS: *Enfatriões*, pr. 1540; *El-Rei Seleuco*, pr. c. 1542; *Filodemo*, pr. 1555.

BIBLIOGRAPHY

Monteiro, George. *The Presence of Camões: Influences on the Literature of England, America, and Southern Africa.* Lexington: University Press of Kentucky, 1996. An introduction to Camões and an investigation of his influence on a number of writers. Includes bibliographic references and an index.

Nicolopulos, James. *The Poetics of Empire in the Indies: Prophecy and Imitation in "La araucana" and "Os lusíadas."* University Park: Pennsylvania State University Press, 2000. An Investigation of literary representations of sixteenth century Iberian colonialism and imperialism. Camões' poem *Os lusíadas*, an epic celebration of early Portuguese maritime expansion in the Indian Ocean, is interpreted.

Richard A. Mazzara;
bibliography updated by the editors

THOMAS CAMPION

Born: London, England; February 12, 1567
Died: London, England; March 1, 1620

PRINCIPAL POETRY

Poemata, 1595
A Booke of Ayres, 1601 (with Philip Rosseter)
Two Bookes of Ayres, 1613
Songs of Mourning, 1613
The Third and Fourth Booke of Ayres, 1617
The Ayres That Were Sung and Played at Brougham Castle, 1618
Thomae Campiani Epigrammatum Libri II, 1619

OTHER LITERARY FORMS

Thomas Campion wrote a critical essay of poetics, *Observations in the Art of English Poesie* (1602), and a book of music theory, *A New Way of Making Fowre*

Parts in Counter-point (c. 1617), the one work of his that remained in print throughout the seventeenth century.

ACHIEVEMENTS

England has always had a strong claim to one of the finest literatures in the West. Most critics agree, moreover, that the literature of the late English Renaissance—stretching from Edmund Spenser through William Shakespeare to John Milton—was the true golden age. With music, however, it is a different story; usually England imported rather than exported musical ideas. The Germans, George Frideric Handel (later naturalized as a British subject) in the eighteenth century and Felix Mendelssohn in the nineteenth, dominated English music. For two brief periods, however, England was Europe's musical innovator—the mid-fifteenth century, when John Dunstable's music taught continental composers the new style, and the decades spanning the sixteenth and seventeenth centuries, when William Byrd, Thomas Morley, Thomas Wheelkes, and especially John Dowland ushered in England's musical golden age. Baldassare Castiglione's *The Courtier* (1528) advises the Renaissance gentleman to be adept at both poetry and music, and most educated persons had some level of expertise in both, but only one man in that twin golden age deserves to be called both a first-rate poet and a first-rate composer: Thomas Campion. Most composers would either set words by others as John Dowland did—often producing truly moving music to inferior words, as in his famous "Come heavy sleep"—or they would write their own words with even worse literary results, as Campion's friend Philip Rosseter did in his half of *A Booke of Ayres*, which he jointly produced with Campion. Most poets would entitle a work, hopefully, "Song" and wait for a composer to do his share—as John Donne did, for example, in "Song: Goe and Catch a Falling Star." Campion, however, wrote both words and music and thus is the distillation of the English Renaissance.

BIOGRAPHY

Thomas Campion was born into a circle of lawyers. His father, John Campion, was a legal clerk in the Chancery Court, with social ambitions left unrealized at his death in 1576, when his son was nine years old. Campion's mother, Lucy, was a middle-class woman with some property inherited from her family. She had earlier married another lawyer, Roger Trigg, and borne him a daughter, Mary. Trigg died in 1563, and a year later she married John Campion, bearing Thomas and his sister Rose. After John's death, she again waited a year and married yet another lawyer, Augustine Steward. When she died and Steward married a woman named Anne Sisley, Campion was left orphaned at the age of fourteen, living with foster parents, who immediately (1581) sent him with Thomas Sisley, Anne's child from a previous marriage, to Peterhouse, Cambridge.

While at Cambridge, Campion was a friend of Thomas Nashe and may have met other literary figures there also—fellow students Christopher Marlowe, Thomas Kyd, and Robert Greene, as well as Edmund Spenser's friend, the don Gabriel Harvey, who theorized about quantitative meter. Cambridge, the nurturing ground of early Puritanism, left Campion uninterested in religion—a fact that may have contributed to his decision to leave in 1584 without the usual clerical degree—but it was there that he first developed an interest in literature and music.

After a hiatus of nearly two years, Campion resumed his education by entering Gray's Inn, London, to study law—a move that his family connections made nearly inevitable. At Gray's Inn, however, Campion preferred literature and music to his legal studies, earning no degree in his eight years there and seemingly being interested mostly in the periodic revels, especially student dramatic productions. He contributed some songs to masques—good preparation for his later career as masque writer to the Jacobean nobility. It is possible that Campion met William Shakespeare at this time, for *The Comedy of Errors* was performed at Gray's Inn in 1594, shortly before Campion left. Like his younger contemporary and fellow law student, John Donne, Campion was circulating his poetry privately and gaining a solid reputation as a poet before he appeared in print; it is also probable that Campion was singing his songs to his own lute accompaniment at this time. Five of these songs appeared pseudonymously at the end of the 1591 edition of Sir Philip Sidney's *Astrophel and Stella*.

During his years at Gray's Inn, Campion accompanied the military expedition led by the Earl of Essex to

Brittany to help the French fend off a Spanish invasion (1591). His poetic achievements there were more notable than his military ones: No record of his activities survives aside from two Latin poems he composed about his experiences, the epigrams "De Se" and "In Obitum Gual. Devoreux fratris clariss. Comitis Essexiae." Latin, indeed, was Campion's favored language at this time; his first published volume of poetry, *Poemata*, is a lengthy volume of Latin poems, mostly epigrams.

Soon after he abandoned law and Gray's Inn, he met the lutenist Philip Rosseter, who remained Campion's closest friend for the rest of his life. It was Rosseter who changed the direction of Campion's career. Latin was a fashionable language in the English Renaissance for those with literary ambitions; even as late as Milton, poets were expected to produce in Latin as well as English. Its accessibility to the general public, however, was limited. At this time Campion began serious production of poetry whose main intent was to entertain—first his lute songs and then his masques. In 1601 he published jointly with Rosseter *A Booke of Ayres*, containing forty-two songs, the first twenty-one by Campion and the last twenty-one by Rosseter.

The following year Campion published a work in prose that gained him some fame–*Observations in the Art of English Poesie*. Possibly a reflection of the literary interests of his Cambridge days, the treatise is the last—and best—defense of quantitative meter in English verse. In the 1580's a group of men led by Gabriel Harvey, Edmund Spenser, and Sir Philip Sidney began an attempt to rescue English poetry from the dreary fourteeners and poulter's measures that everyone seemed to be writing. Influenced by French theorists, they tried to write poetry based on duration (quantity) of syllables rather than stress (accent). Such an attempt was, perhaps, inevitable in the English Renaissance, for, like so much else, it was based upon Greek and Latin models. The failure of the attempt, however, was inevitable because English inherited the strong Germanic accent from the Anglo-Saxon language and thus could not be forced to do what Greek and Latin, without the strong Germanic accent, could do naturally. Some of Spenser's and Sidney's more unreadable pieces are quantitative; then they abandoned the attempt and became great poets. Campion's *Observations in the Art of English*

Poesie is actually a resurrection of this dead theory, and as a resurrected body should be, his theory was considerably stronger than the dead one. Instead of calling for an exacting measurement of long and short vowels and count of neighboring consonants, Campion appealed to variety: Use of the eight basic feet of quantitative meter would rescue English poetry from the monotony of the unending alternation of stresses and non-stresses. Campion made two mistakes in his treatise, however: First, he overlooked the fact that varying stressed instead of quantitative feet would do the job better and, second, he called the drab accentual verse that he was arguing against "rhyme." Samuel Daniel thus responded with his eloquent *The Defence of Ryme* (1603) and finally put to rest the English quantitative theory without a reply from Campion.

Campion, however, had left the field. Late in 1602 or thereabouts he went to France and enrolled in the University of Caen to study medicine. One might expect that Campion's stay at Caen would be similar to those at Cambridge and Gray's Inn, especially considering Caen's reputation for revels and entertainments of all sorts. This time, however, Campion persevered and received his degree, returning to London in 1605 to establish a medical practice. His reputation as a poet and musician was still strong, and this perhaps attracted sufficient patients among the nobility to keep his practice going on a secure if not lucrative level. His later verse reveals an occasional medical metaphor.

Campion wrote little during the next few years while he was establishing himself in his profession, publishing nothing between his *Observations in the Art of English Poesie* in 1602 and his five major works in his most productive year of 1613, except for *Lord Hay's Masque* in 1607. With the accession of James I to the English throne in 1603, the masque moved from the universities and inns of court to the homes of the fashionable nobility. Prospero's masque celebrating the engagement of Miranda and Ferdinand in Act IV of Shakespeare's *The Tempest* (1611) gives a good indication of the nature and function of the masque to the Jacobeans: A noble family would celebrate an important occasion, especially a wedding, with an entertainment combining music, drama, and visual spectacle, based on classical myth and employing allegory. Campion, Ben Jonson, and a number of other poets became popular as masque writers in the early seventeenth century, Campion producing five masques or masquelike entertainments, three of them in 1613.

One of the three, *The Somerset Masque* (1613), involved Campion in one of Jacobean England's worst scandals. In 1611, Robert Carr, King James's favorite and later earl of Somerset, began a liaison with Frances Howard, the Countess of Essex. The relationship was partly a political one, since it was part of an attempt by the powerful Howard family to gain more power. The Countess's marriage to Essex was annulled, and Somerset, against the advice of his close friend, Sir Thomas Overbury, married her in late 1613. Campion's *The Somerset Masque* provided part of the nuptial entertainment. Out of spite, Somerset and his wife maneuvered Overbury into insulting the king and thus landed him in the Tower of London, where their agents slowly poisoned him to death. Part of the money paid by Somerset to the agents was conveyed by two unwitting accomplices, Sir Thomas Munson and Thomas Campion. At the subsequent trial, Campion was questioned, but no charges were brought against him, while Munson was wrongly sentenced to imprisonment in the Tower. He was imprisoned until 1617, when he was exonerated, but by that time his health had broken. Campion was the physician who attended him.

In addition to his courtly entertainments, Campion published four books of *ayres* to add to his earlier one: *Two Bookes of Ayres* published jointly in 1613 and *The Third and Fourth Booke of Ayres*, also published jointly, in 1617. The third book was dedicated to the recently released Munson and the fourth book to Munson's son, indications of Campion's loyalty to his friends. In 1618 he published *The Ayres That Were Sung and Played at Brougham Castle*—in honor of the king's visit there— a hybrid work sharing characteristics with his other books of airs and also his masques. His last work, generating a symmetry of closure, was similar to his first: *Thomae. Campiani Epigrammatum Libre II*, a long collection of Latin poems, mostly epigrams, some of which appeared in his earlier volume.

One other publishing event in Campion's life, however, needs to be mentioned. The date of *A New Way of Making Fowre Parts in Counter-point* has not yet been determined by scholars, some preferring 1618-1619 and others, more persuasively, 1613-1614. The work is a short treatise on music theory and thus is a complement to his *Observations in the Art of English Poesie*. Before Campion, music was largely polyphonic, with each voice contributing its own melody to a rather complex whole. Campion's system minimized the melodic independence of the three lower voices. It seemed to work well enough, for it produced pleasant music, and his treatise was included in John Playford's popular *Introduction to the Skill of Music* (1660) and appeared in subsequent editions of that book until 1694, when a treatise by Henry Purcell replaced it.

Campion died on March 1, 1620. He was fifty-three years old, a lifelong bachelor. He left his very modest estate, valued at twenty-two pounds, to his friend and collaborator, Philip Rosseter.

ANALYSIS

In one sense, Thomas Campion was typically Elizabethan: Classical mythology, amorous encounters with either distant courtly ladies or willing country maids, and superficial religious emotions provided his subjects and themes. Although much of his verse lacks the substance of William Shakespeare's, Ben Jonson's, and John Donne's, it is highly musical poetry, in which the careful modulation of sounds produces the illusion of music even when divorced from a musical setting. Campion's poetry depends, in short, on the ear more than most; if one is not fortunate enough to have a recording of "Never Weather-Beaten Sail" or "I Care Not for These Ladies," one should at least read these poems aloud to gain some idea of their music. This is the quality that draws Campion out of the ranks of mediocre Renaissance poets who wrote on similar conventional themes.

Campion was most successful in the writing of short poems. His airs, upon which his reputation rests, include some of the best art songs written in English. Even his longer masques are appealing because they are essentially a succession of short pieces linked together; their mythological/allegorical plots contribute little to their success, for the frequent beautiful songs and the occasional interesting speech generate the ceremonious pageantry necessary to the masque. Critics have called Campion a miniaturist, and that description is apt.

Campion learned quantitative meter at first hand by studying and writing Latin poetry. His two volumes of Latin verse, which stand at opposite ends of his creative life, largely consist of epigrams and occasional poems. Epigrams poking fun at his friend, the inept poet Barnabe Barnes, praising famous people such as Francis Drake, Prince Henry, Sir Philip Sidney, William Camden, and Francis Bacon, consoling his friend Thomas Munson, extolling imaginary ladies with Roman names, and celebrating ordinary objects such as portable clocks, remind one of Ben Jonson's similar works in English. One rather long epigram, "In Obitum Gual. Devoreux fratris clariss. Comitis Essexiae," is an elegy for Walter Devoreux, brother of Essex, who died at the siege of Rouen (1591); Campion was there and wrote the poem while the battle was still in progress. One particularly short epigram, interesting for its subject, provides a good example:

> About the Epigram
> Similar to biting pepper, the acid epigram
> Is not gracious to each taste: no one denies its use.

Among these short, useful, and sometimes acrid poems, Campion included several longer, more ambitious works, including a somewhat epic poem of 283 lines, "Ad Thamesin," celebrating the English victory over the Spanish Armada, and the 404-line Ovidian *Umbra* (1619), recounting the story of Iole, who conceived a child by the god Phoebus while she was asleep—an erotic situation which recurs in Campion's airs. These longer pieces lack the pungency of the short epigrams and are by no means first-rate poems. They do, however, contain some of the music of Campion's English airs and represent his longest productions of purely quantitative meter. The relative lack of success of these longer poems, together with the appeal of many of the shorter ones, is an indication that Campion was a miniaturist in both languages.

The famous argument between Jonson and his stage designer Inigo Jones about which element of the masque was the more important—the plot or the mechanical contrivances generating the masque's spectacle—could easily have had Campion as a third participant. Campion's masques are distinguished neither for their elaborate stage design, even though the ingenious Jones was his frequent collaborator, nor for their drama, but for their music. In contrast to Jonson's masques, Campion's appear dramatically thin: There is never a plot, only a situation, and characters are little more than mouths to deliver speeches and sing songs. It is arguable, however, that the success of a masque depends only on those qualities generating pageantry, and dramatic energy is not necessarily one of them.

LORD HAY'S MASQUE

Campion's *Lord Hay's Masque* was presented in 1607 to celebrate the marriage of King James's favorite, the Scotsman James Hay, and the English lady Honora Denney. The political situation of a recently crowned Scottish king on the English throne attempting to consolidate his two realms provides the background for this, Campion's most successful masque. There are thus three levels of meaning in the masque: the marriage of Hay and Denney, the union of Scotland and England, and the mythological reconciliation between Diana (allegorically Queen Elizabeth), who wished to keep her maids of honor virgins, and Apollo (allegorically King James), who wished to marry them to his knights. In anger Diana has changed Apollo's knights into trees, and in the course of the masque they regain their rightful shapes. Campion's song "Now hath Flora rob'd her bowers" is a moving poem in praise of marriage; its music is best described as majestic.

THE LORD'S MASQUE

The Lord's Masque, presented as part of the ceremonies attending Princess Elizabeth's wedding to Frederick, Elector of Palantine (February 14, 1613), and *The Caversham Entertainment*, presented the following April to entertain Queen Anne on her way to Bath to recover from her depression brought on by the wedding, are related pieces, this circumstantial link being strengthened by their joint publication. *The Lord's Masque* is a stately allegory in which Orpheus, representing music, frees Entheus, representing "poetic fury," from the control of Mania, or madness. The result of that liberation is a Latin poem recited by a Sybil praising the marriage of the young couple. *The Caversham Entertainment*, in contrast, is lighthearted and totally lacking in plot. A Cynic, a Traveller, and a Gardener appear severally and together before the queen, sing some rural songs, and debate issues such as the necessity of human companionship and the value of music.

THE SOMERSET MASQUE

The Somerset Masque is unintentionally ironic, given the outcome of the sorry marriage it celebrates. Delegates from the four corners of the globe are attacked by the allegorical figures Error, Rumour, Curiosity, and Credulity as they sail toward England to attend the marriage. The allegorical characters cause confusion and chaos until the Fates, Eternity and Harmony, appear to restore order. The irony is that the rumors circulating about Robert Carr and his bride Frances Howard and the murder of Sir Thomas Overbury were true. A further irony is that with this masque Campion's career as entertainer to the Jacobean nobility came to an end; it is unprovable but likely that his connection with Lord Somerset was the reason.

A BOOKE OF AYRES, TWO BOOKES OF AYRES, AND THE THIRD AND FOURTH BOOKE OF AYRES

Campion's five books of airs are somewhat misleadingly titled because the first, published jointly in 1601 with Rosseter, stands apart from the numbering, which starts with his second. All five are fairly homogeneous, containing a mixture of amorous and religious verse, between twenty-one and twenty-nine airs per book. The Rosseter collection contains, perhaps, the highest proportion of truly first-rate airs. The later books contain slightly more religious airs than the earlier (except for the first book, which is solely religious, and the second book, which is solely amorous), but this is counterbalanced by the increased earthiness of the later amorous airs, as for example in "Beauty, since you so much desire," from the fourth book, which is an almost word-for-word rendition of "Mistress, since you so much desire" from the Rosseter collection except for the important fact that the seat of "Cupid's fire" is no longer in the lady's eyes but in her genitals. Campion is even called upon to apologize for some of these lyrics, telling the reader that he may turn the page if he wishes and that Chaucer was guilty of greater breaches of taste than he is.

Campion's airs are his most important contribution to literature. They are short poems, usually two or three stanzas, on conventional Renaissance subjects characterized by sensitive modulations of sound, especially vowels. They are, moreover, set to music exceptional for both melodic skill and aptness to the words. The technique of mirroring in music what is stated in words is called "word painting," and Campion was a master of it. For example, in "Fire, fire, fire" from the third book, the refrain contains the repeated words, "O drown both me, O drown both me," and the music descends from a higher to a lower pitch. Similarly, in "Mistress, since you so much desire" from the Rosseter collection and its revision "Beauty, since you so much desire" from the fourth book, the refrain repeats the words "But a little higher" four times, each time ascending the scale. Again, in "When to her Lute Corinna Sings" from the Rosseter collection, the line "the strings do break" is set with a quick sixteenth note musical phrase; in order to maintain the tempo a lutenist would play this measure percussively.

This type of word painting, clever as it is, is not without dangers, as Campion himself admits in his prologue to the Rosseter collection, likening the excessive word painting of some of his contemporaries to an unskilled actor who, whenever he mentions his eyes, points to them with his finger. Much of Campion's word painting is subtle, as in "Though you are young," from the Rosseter collection, where the air's main theme, the strength of age as compared to the ephemerality of youth, is mirrored in the lute accompaniment which repeats a chord in an inverted position, that is, a lower string sounding a note higher than its next highest neighbor. Subtle in a different way is Campion's famous and much anthologized "There is a Garden in Her Face" from the fourth book. Part of the refrain, "Till cherry ripe," is repeated several times to a London street-seller's cry, with the indication that the lady celebrated in this air may be had for a price—an irony lost to the reader innocent of the music. "Never weather-beaten sail" from the first book is, perhaps, Campion's most subtle and most successful attempt at word painting. The subject of the air is the world-weariness of the singer and his desire to die and thus, like a storm-tossed ship, reach a safe harbor. A lesser composer would have set the words to music mirroring the distress and weariness of the words, but Campion writes a melody which can only be described as confident and joyous—a tension creating two perspectives, the earthly and the heavenly, and forcing the listener to see earthly troubles from a divine point of view.

OTHER MAJOR WORKS

PLAYS: *Lord Hay's Masque*, pr., pb. 1607; *The Lord's Masque*, pr., pb. 1613; *The Caversham Entertainment*, 1613 (masque); *The Somerset Masque*, pr. 1613.

NONFICTION: *Observations in the Art of English Poesie*, 1602; *A New Way of Making Fowre Parts in Counter-point*, c. 1617.

BIBLIOGRAPHY

Booth, Mark W. *The Experience of Songs*. New Haven, Conn.: Yale University Press, 1981. Booth's chapter "Art Song" is an exhaustive reading of the musical and lyrical aspects of Campion's "I Care Not for These Ladies," an "anticourtly" pastoral song. While he devotes some attention to the music of the poem, Booth focuses on the lyrics, finding them more complex than earlier critics had believed.

Coren, Pamela. "In the Person of Womankind: Female Persona Poems by Campion, Donne, Jonson." *Studies in Philology* 98, no. 2 (Spring, 2001): 225-250. Analysis of the use of the female persona in Campion's "A Secret Love or Two, I Must Confesse."

Davis, Walter R. *Thomas Campion*. Boston: Twayne, 1987. Devotes separate chapters to Campion's biography, poetry, music, theory, masques (the Renaissance "multimedia show"), and reputation. Contains a two-page chronology, extensive notes, a selected bibliography with brief annotations, and an index. Essential for Campion scholars.

Lindley, David. *Thomas Campion*. Leiden, Netherlands: E. J. Brill, 1986. Discusses Campion's poetry, his music, the relationship between his music and poetry, and his masques. Provides some literary, musical, and political contexts but focuses on the works. Contains extensive analyses of individual masques and poems, and a select bibliography.

Lowbury, Edward, Timothy Salter, and Alison Young. *Thomas Campion: Poet, Composer, Physician*. New York: Barnes & Noble Books, 1970. Despite its title, the book stresses music. Reviews Campion's critical reputation, provides a biographical chapter, discusses the relationship between music and poetry, and examines his masques, his poem/songs, and his literary and music criticism. Six pages are devoted to "interactions." Select bibliography.

Ryding, Erik S. *In Harmony Framed: Musical Humanism, Thomas Campion, and the Two Daniels*. Kirksville, Mo.: Sixteenth Century Publishers, 1993. Contrasts the poetic and musical work of the Daniel brothers, John and Samuel, with Thomas Campion. The author categorizes Campion with the Renaissance humanists. Includes a bibliography.

Wilson, Christopher. *Words and Notes Coupled Lovingly Together: Thomas Campion, a Critical Study*. New York: Garland, 1989. Contains a biographical outline, a review of Campion's scholarship, an examination of the Campion canon, brief discussions of the poetry and the music, and thorough treatments of *Observations in the Art of English Poesie* and his musical theories. Includes an extensive commentary on the masques and a comprehensive bibliography.

Robert E. Boenig;
bibliography updated by the editors

ERNESTO CARDENAL

Born: Granada, Nicaragua; 1925

PRINCIPAL POETRY

Gethsemani, Ky., 1960

La hora O, 1960

Epigramas: Poemas, 1961 (*Epigramas*, 1978)

Oración por Marilyn Monroe y otros poemas, 1965 (*Marilyn Monroe and Other Poems*, 1975)

El estrecho dudoso, 1966 (*The Doubtful Strait*, 1995)

Antología de Ernesto Cardenal, 1967

Salmos, 1967 (*The Psalms of Struggle and Liberation*, 1971)

Mayapán, 1968

Poemas reunidos, 1949-1969, 1969

Homenaje a los indios americanos, 1969 (*Homage to the American Indians*, 1973)

La hora cero y otros poemas, 1971 (*Zero Hour and Other Documentary Poems*, 1980)

Antología, 1971

Poemas, 1971

Canto nacional, 1973

Oráculo sobre Managua, 1973

Poesía escogida, 1975

El Evangelio en Solentiname, 1975 (*The Gospel in Solentiname*, 1976)

Apocalypse and Other Poems, 1977

Antología, 1978

Canto a un país que nace, 1978

Poesía de uso: Antología, 1949-1978, 1979

Poesía, 1979

Nueva antología poética, 1979

Tocar el cielo, 1981

Wasala: Poems, 1983

Antología: Ernesto Cardenal, 1983

Poesía de la nueva Nicaragua, 1983

Vuelos de Victoria, 1984 (*Flights of Victory*, 1985)

Quetzalcóatal, 1985

With Walker in Nicaragua and Other Early Poems, 1949-1954, 1985

From Nicaragua with Love: Poems, 1976-1986, 1986

Cántico cósmico, 1989 (*The Music of the Spheres*, 1990; *Cosmic Canticle*, 1993)

Los ornis de oro, 1991

Golden UFOs: The Indian Poems, 1992

Telescopio en la noche oscura, 1993

El Río San Juan: Estrecho dudoso en el centro de América, 1993

Antología nueva, 1996

Ernesto Cardenal

OTHER LITERARY FORMS

Part 1 of Ernesto Cardenal's autobiography, *Vida perdida* (lost life), was published in 1999 by the publishing firm Seix Barral in Barcelona, Spain. The English translation was initiated in 2000. During 2001 the author was editing the second volume of his autobiography, which continues his journey back to Nicaragua during the post-Somoza era. It is an excellent biographical resource and starting place for exploring the poet's fascinating life and thought. The chapters devoted to his years as a Trappist monk in Gethsemani, Kentucky, and correspondence with the Catholic mystic, theologian, and writer Thomas Merton enlighten the reader attempting to comprehend the corpus of Cardenal's poetry.

Cardenal wrote essays and other prose works as he served as minister of culture in Nicaragua and as a director of Casa de los Tres Mundos, a literary and cultural organization in Granada, Nicaragua. *Vida en el amor* (1970; *To Live Is to Love*, 1972; *Abide in Love*, 1995) is a collection of meditations written after his novitiate years at Gethsemani.

ACHIEVEMENTS

Ernesto Cardenal was instrumental in the rebirth of Nicaragua's identity as "a nation of poets," as it became known after Rubén Darío immortalized the poet-nation at the beginning of the twentieth century. Cardenal's life is as fascinating as his poetry. Controversy over the literary and political value of his work resulted from his attempts to reconcile the many roles he had played, from monk to priest to governmental official to promoter of literacy and the arts. His political ideology seemed inconsistent as he switched public roles. From a bourgeois family background, he espoused Marxism and militancy, then Christianity and nonviolent resistance. This dichotomy is evident in his work, but these ideological conflicts enhance rather than detract from his poetic corpus.

Consistent in his belief that art is linked to politics, his poetry actively supported the revolution that in 1979 overthrew the regime begun by dictator Anastasio Somoza García. After a functional social democracy was established in Cardenal's homeland, he served as an unofficial yet visible cultural ambassador. He was instrumental in the organization of community-based literacy and poetry workshops that have earned national as well as international success.

The poet has also been praised as an artist. His sculpture won recognition in the United States as well as in Central America and Mexico. A stone sculpture of Christ dominates the courtyard of the Trappist monastery in Gethsemani, Kentucky, where he served as a novitiate from 1957 to 1959.

Cardenal was honored with several awards for his literary achievements as well as for public service. In 1972 he received the Christopher Book Award for *The Psalms of Struggle and Liberation*. In 1980 he received the Premio de La Paz grant, sponsored by Libreros de la República Federal de Alemania. He received state-sponsored honors and honorary doctorates from several European nations.

BIOGRAPHY

Ernesto Cardenal was born in 1925 in Granada, Nicaragua. He studied at the Universidad Nacional Autónoma de México. After graduating in 1947, he moved to the United States in order to study North American literature at Columbia University in New York from 1948 to 1949.

After traveling for a year throughout Europe, he returned to Nicaragua. He translated and published North American poetry and anonymously wrote political poems against the dictatorship of Anastasio Somoza García. The Chilean poet Pablo Neruda published works by the unknown Cardenal in *La Gaceta de Chile*. While in Nicaragua, Cardenal managed a bookstore that promoted national writers and published *El hilo azul*, a poetry journal.

In 1954 Cardenal participated in an armed assault against the Somoza regime, known as the April Rebellion, and continued to write anonymous political poems. Three years later, he drastically changed directions by entering the Monastery of Our Lady of Gethsemani in Kentucky, where he met Thomas Merton, his spiritual mentor and lifelong friend. Poor health forced Cardenal to transfer to the Benedictine Monastery in Cuernavaca, Mexico. There, he wrote his poetry collection *Gethsemani, Ky.* and the meditations *Abide in Love*. He continued his theological studies in the Seminary of la Ceja in Colombia. While at la Ceja, he wrote poems later collected and translated as *Homage to the American Indians*. He was ordained a Roman Catholic priest in 1965.

With the guidance of Merton, Cardenal planned to establish the spiritual community of Solentiname on Lake Nicaragua. He created a school for the native folk arts, poetry workshops, and the political movement of Liberation Theology. He visited Cuba in order to study its revolutionary process. In 1976 Cardenal represented Solentiname in the Russell Tribunal for human rights violations in Latin America. In 1977, after Sandinista leaders had ordered Cardenal on a diplomatic mission, Somoza's army destroyed Solentiname. Cardenal was exiled from Nicaragua until the government of reconstruction appointed him minister of culture in 1979. He served internationally in the cause of peace and disarmament. After earning the Rubén Darío Prize, the highest Nicaraguan honor, he was honored by the governments of France and Germany, among those of other nations. Several international universities bestowed honorary doctorates upon Cardenal.

Cardenal's autobiography *Vida perdida* is an excellent source for biographical information, though not necessarily more accurate than objective sources. References to literary influences and Cardenal's creative contemporaries permeate the text. His complex values and belief system shines through his personal history as he reminisces about his literary production as spiritual experiences, with an unaffected style laced with self-effacing humor.

In *Vida perdida*, Cardenal defines himself as a Christian Marxist whose first calling is to serve God. His service is politically committed, focusing on the Central American peasants. His poems not only spoke for the voiceless; they enabled Cardenal to promote and publish poetry collections by "ordinary people," allowing them a personal as well as collective poetic voice.

ANALYSIS

Revolutionary political ideology is blended with Roman Catholic theology in Cardenal's poetry. Like Pablo Neruda, he hopes to motivate readers to change social injustices. His overt messages do not overshadow their poetic forms, and technical mastery is not compromised by theme. Cardenal's poetry is not just his second calling. Rather, it serves and as integral part of his first calling, operating as a tool of his spiritual mission to convert and enlighten. His poems reveal hard and ugly truths about Nicaragua and contemporary societies as they evangelize.

He developed the concept of *exteriorismo* with his poet friend José Coronel Utrecho. Through this technique, words present the world directly through its object rather than by abstraction. Cardenal referred to impure poetry as that seeming closer to prose for its prosaic references. *Interiorista* poetry is composed of abstract or symbolic words that have traditionally poetic connotations. Utrecho and Cardenal believed that the only poetry that could express the Latin American reality and reach the people in a revolutionary way was *exteriorista*. Cardenal's presentation of prosaic elements is innovative, and he connects images through techniques of montage, interpolation, and intertextuality.

"HORA 0"

Among the most militant political poems that serve as a call to action, "Hora 0" epitomizes Cardenal's *exteriorista* mission of words: "I did it," dijo después Somoza./ "I did it for the good of Nicaragua./ . . . de armas;/ todos marcados U.S.A., MADE IN U.S.A. . . ." The vivid reality of the United States supplying arms to the Nicaraguan dictatorship is juxtaposed with William Walker's invasion and scenes of exploitation, oppression, and glimpses of truth filtered through sound bites, news clips, and elements from the mass media.

"MARILYN MONROE"

"Marilyn Monroe" exemplifies *exteriorismo* as it is applied to themes beyond the Nicaraguan experience. This prayer reveals how a woman was destroyed by Hollywood. Cardenal relates the cultural icon to the degradation and exploitation of women. This poem connects Monroe to the Virgin Mary and demonstrates how both images of the ideal woman have been desecrated and violated by a godless, hedonistic society. He begins his prayer:

Father
Receive this girl known throughout the world as Marilyn
    Monroe
though that was not her real name
(but You know her real name, that of the orphan raped at
    nine
and the shopgirl who had tried to kill herself at just 16.)
and who now appears before You without makeup
without her Press Agent
without photographs or signing autographs
lonely as an astronaut facing the darkness of outer
    space . . .

THE MUSIC OF THE SPHERES

Cardenal developed the genre of the canto in the way that Ezra Pound and Pablo Neruda created their own cantos. Cardenal credited Pound as a major influence on his poetic style. Disparate images are juxtaposed, lyrical and prosaic lines are mingled, and spiritual elements are combined with images of materialism and consumerism, in which commercialization replaces emotional and spiritual spontaneity. Technical skill is balanced by immediate and relevant messages.

The Music of the Spheres encapsulates the canto form. More than forty cantos create a vision of cosmic development that refers to astronomy, biology, physics, history, mythology, philosophy, politics, and theology. Science blends with spirituality to form a harmonic whole.

The organization of interconnected canticles resembles Pound's subdivisions of a long poem into thematic units. As a whole, the canticles' lyric quality predominates. They sing their praises to creation as they reach out to the cosmos to grasp its elemental clues to origins. These cantos chronicle political and economic realities, harmoniously combined with spiritual transcendence.

Cardenal's original masterwork follows the tradition of epic poems from Homer to Dante to Pound.

OTHER MAJOR WORKS

NONFICTION: *Vida en el amor*, 1970 (*To Live Is to Love*, 1972; *Abide in Love*, 1995); *En Cuba*, 1972 (*In Cuba*, 1974); *Cardenal en Valencia*, 1974; *La santidad de la revolución*, 1976; *La paz mundial y la revolución de Nicaragua*, 1981; *Vida perdida*, 1999.

TRANSLATIONS: *Catulo-Marcial en versión de Ernesto Cardenal*, 1978 (of Gaius Valerius Catullus; *Tu paz es mi paz*, 1982 (of Ursula Schulz's *Dein Friede sei mein Friede*).

EDITED TEXTS: *Antología de la poesía norte-americana*, 1963 (with Coronel Urtecho); *Literatura indígena americana: Antología*, 1966 (with Jorge Montoya Toro); *Poesía nicaragüense*, 1973; *Poesía nueva de Nicaragua*, 1974; *Poesía cubana de la revolución*, 1976; *Antología de poesía primitiva*, 1979; *Poemas de un joven*, 1983 (by Joaquín Pasos); *Antología: Azarias H. Pallais*, 1986.

BIBLIOGRAPHY

Cardenal, Ernesto. *Abide in Love*. Translated by Thomas Merton and Mev Puleo. Maryknoll, N.Y.: Orbis Books, 1995. Merton provides a detailed introduction and Puleo's meticulous translations enhance this new edition of the collection *Vida en el amor*.

_____. *Apocalypse and Other Poems*. Edited by Robert Pring-Mill and Donald D. Walsh. New York: New Directions, 1977. Both editors, Cardenal experts, provide insightful introductions to the collection. The translators include the editors, along with Thomas Merton, Kenneth Rexroth, and Mireya Jaimes-Freyre.

_____. *The Doubtful Strait = El estrecho dudoso*. Translated by John Lyons. Bloomington: University of Indiana Press, 1995. Tamara Williams provides a substantial introduction to this collection. It is a detailed critical study of its genesis, technical, thematic, and stylistic elements, and historical and literary influences. Demonstrates how an epic quality is developed through the continuous thread of the quest throughout this collection.

_____. *Flights of Victory*. Translated by Marc Zimmerman. Maryknoll, N.Y.: Orbis Books, 1985. Presents the collection with a critical study of the historical context as well as technical and thematic elements that distinguish it from other works. Zimmerman examines the elements of *exteriorismo*, which was influenced by the Central American vanguards of revolutionary poets. This study demonstrates how Cardenal utilized *exteriorismo* in order to create poetry of national resistance to Anastacio Somoza García in the name of Sandino.

Dawes, Greg. *Aesthetics and Revolution: Nicaraguan Poetry, 1979-1990*. Minneapolis: University of Minnesota Press, 1993. The chapter "Poetry and Spiritual Materialism: Ernesto Cardenal" discusses how Cardenal's Marxism, seen through a Christian lens, affected his poetry. Dawes believes that Cardenal's work reinterprets theology itself. Through the practice of Liberation Theology, religious states such as faith and salvation are returned to the social sphere. Cardenal's impact on Nicaraguan politics as well as literature is demonstrated throughout the book.

Rowe, William. *Poets of Contemporary Latin America: History and the Inner Life*. New York: Oxford University Press, 2000. In the chapter "Ernesto Cardenal: Eros and Belief Under Epic Necessity," Rowe explores the poems as differing proposals of attention for each collection. He avoids making critical artistic decisions from political, religious, or erotic perspectives. Rowe believes that these preconceptions make the poems' words serve as a vehicle for a higher cause, rather than enable them to be appreciated for their intrinsic artistic value.

Sarabia, Rosa. *Poetas de la palabra hablada*. London: Tamesis, 1997. This study examines the oral nature of several Latin American writers. The chapter "La historia como musa en la poesía de Ernesto Cardenal" focuses on historical influences, including Native American mythology. The contemporary reality also influences the politically conscious poet as spokesman for the voiceless who are suffering injustices. This study demonstrates how past and contemporary realities, along with an oral tradition, find their voices in Cardenal's poetry. Available only in Spanish.

Carole A. Champagne

3-15-04

3-15-04